DRUGS AND SOCIETY

THIRTEENTH EDITION

GLEN R. HANSON, PhD, DDS

Associate Dean
Director, Utah Addiction Center
Professor
School of Dentistry
University of Utah
Salt Lake City, Utah

PETER J. VENTURELLI, PhD

Professor Emeritus
Department of Sociology and
    Criminology
Valparaiso University
Valparaiso, Indiana

ANNETTE E. FLECKENSTEIN, PhD

Professor
School of Dentistry
University of Utah
Salt Lake City, Utah

JONES & BARTLETT
LEARNING

World Headquarters
Jones & Bartlett Learning
5 Wall Street
Burlington, MA 01803
978-443-5000
info@jblearning.com
www.jblearning.com

Jones & Bartlett Learning books and products are available through most bookstores and online booksellers. To contact Jones & Bartlett Learning directly, call 800-832-0034, fax 978-443-8000, or visit our website, www.jblearning.com.

Substantial discounts on bulk quantities of Jones & Bartlett Learning publications are available to corporations, professional associations, and other qualified organizations. For details and specific discount information, contact the special sales department at Jones & Bartlett Learning via the above contact information or send an email to specialsales@jblearning.com.

Copyright © 2018 by Jones & Bartlett Learning, LLC, an Ascend Learning Company

All rights reserved. No part of the material protected by this copyright may be reproduced or utilized in any form, electronic or mechanical, including photocopying, recording, or by any information storage and retrieval system, without written permission from the copyright owner.

The content, statements, views, and opinions herein are the sole expression of the respective authors and not that of Jones & Bartlett Learning, LLC. Reference herein to any specific commercial product, process, or service by trade name, trademark, manufacturer, or otherwise does not constitute or imply its endorsement or recommendation by Jones & Bartlett Learning, LLC and such reference shall not be used for advertising or product endorsement purposes. All trademarks displayed are the trademarks of the parties noted herein. *Drugs and Society, Thirteenth Edition* is an independent publication and has not been authorized, sponsored, or otherwise approved by the owners of the trademarks or service marks referenced in this product.

There may be images in this book that feature models; these models do not necessarily endorse, represent, or participate in the activities represented in the images. Any screenshots in this product are for educational and instructive purposes only. Any individuals and scenarios featured in the case studies throughout this product may be real or fictitious, but are used for instructional purposes only.

11098-2

Production Credits

VP, Executive Publisher: David D. Cella
Publisher: Cathy L. Esperti
Editorial Assistant: Carter McAlister
Director of Production: Jenny L. Corriveau
Production Editor: Kristen Rogers
Director of Marketing: Andrea DeFronzo
VP, Manufacturing and Inventory Control: Therese Connell
Composition: Cenveo® Publisher Services
Cover Design: Michael O'Donnell
Director of Rights & Media: Joanna Gallant
Rights & Media Specialist: Jamey O'Quinn
Media Development Editor: Troy Liston

Cover and Title Page Images: A rocks glass, © Yeko Photo Studio/ShutterStock, Inc.; Three pills, © Maksud/ShutterStock, Inc.; An iced coffee, © Yeko Photo Studio/ShutterStock, Inc.; Rolling a joint, © Nikita Starichenko/ShutterStock, Inc.; Steroids used by an athlete, © Jupiterimages/liquidlibrary/Thinkstock; An aisle of pills, © Jupiterimages/Photos.com/Thinkstock; A spray can, © Mikael Damkier/ShutterStock, Inc.; A cigarette, © Mariusz Szachowski/ShutterStock, Inc.; A drug user, © iStockphoto/Thinkstock
Printing and Binding: LSC Communications
Cover Printing: LSC Communications

Library of Congress Cataloging-in-Publication Data
Names: Hanson, Glen (Glen R.), author. | Venturelli, Peter J., author.
  | Fleckenstein, Annette E., author.
Title: Drugs and society / Dr. Glen R. Hanson, Peter J. Venturelli, Annette
  E. Fleckenstein.
Description: 13e. | Burlington, MA : Jones & Bartlett Learning, [2018]
  | Includes bibliographical references and index.
Identifiers: LCCN 2016043260 | ISBN 9781284110876 (pbk.: alk. paper)
Subjects: | MESH: Substance-Related Disorders
Classification: LCC RM301 | NLM WM 270 | DDC 362.29—dc23
LC record available at https://lccn.loc.gov/2016043260

6048

Printed in the United States of America
21 20 19 18 17   10 9 8 7 6 5 4 3 2

BRIEF CONTENTS

CONTENTS

CHAPTER 4
Homeostatic Systems and Drugs   135

CHAPTER 5
How and Why Drugs Work   157

CHAPTER 6
CNS Depressants:
Sedative-Hypnotics   184

CHAPTER 7
Alcohol: Pharmacological Effects 206

CHAPTER 8
Alcohol: Behavioral Effects 233

FEATURES

HOLDING THE LINE

POINT/COUNTERPOINT

PRESCRIPTION FOR ABUSE

FAMILY MATTERS

DO GENES MATTER?

PREFACE

This thirteenth edition further enhances the reputation of *Drugs and Society* as one of the leading texts on drug use and/or abuse. This text communicates to students how drug use and/or abuse can lead to emotional, psychological, social, and medical disorders of ordinary people. The authors have integrated their expertise in the fields of drug abuse, pharmacology, and sociology by using their expertise and knowledge of teaching, research experiences, and drug prevention and treatment to create an edition that reflects the most important and current information relative to drug abuse issues available in a textbook. For example, this edition includes new information on important topics such as the following: (1) the relentless escalation of prescription abuse and related overdose deaths by opioid analgesics; (2) street products known as marijuana wax, Spice, and Ivory Wave and the persistent appearance and attempted management of related synthetic substances in these illicit products; (3) tobacco regulation by the Food and Drug Administration (FDA) and the continued increase in the popularity of e-cigarettes; (4) the use of the fifth edition of the American Psychiatric Association's (2013) *Diagnostic and Statistical Manual of Mental Disorders* (*DSM*-5) for diagnosing drug abuse or substance use disorders and psychiatric mental disorders; as well as many other important drug use and abuse topics.

Drugs and Society is an exceptionally comprehensive text on drug use and abuse and drug-related problems, with current and updated references to substantiate and support the latest findings about drug use and abuse information. This text is also written on a personal level and directly addresses the drug information college and university students need from the sociological, psychological, and pharmacological perspectives, addressing both micro- and macrolevel drug use and abuse information. Many chapters include excerpts from personal experiences with recreational drug users, habitual (often addicted) drug users, and former drug users. Students will find these personal accounts both interesting and insightful. This particular approach has been inspired by instructors, students, and reviewers, resulting in a truly unique text that combines comprehensive presentation of the latest drug information with personal accounts.

Drugs and Society is a multiperspective text offering university students from a range of disciplines the opportunity to gain a realistic and comprehensive understanding of drug use and abuse and drug-related problems in our society. Students in nursing, physical education or kinesiology, and other social sciences, such as psychology, social work, sociology, and criminology, will find that our text provides useful and timely perspectives and information to help them understand the following:

* Social, psychological, pharmacological, and biological explanations why drug use and abuse occur
* The outcomes of drug use and abuse
* How to prevent and treat drug use and abuse
* How drugs/medications can be effectively used for therapeutic purposes

To achieve these goals, we have presented the most current, objective, and authoritative views on drug abuse in an easily understood manner. The thirteenth edition of *Drugs and Society* continues to teach students from different disciplines how to understand the complexity of drug use and abuse from pharmacological, neurobiological, psychological, and sociological perspectives.

What Is New and Improved?

Drugs and Society, Thirteenth Edition, includes updated statistics and current examples of the key principles being taught in this text and frequently uses the new *DSM*-5 as a source for updated information. The new topical coverage includes discussion of the following:

* The most recent information on developments in states that have or intend to legalize recreational and medical marijuana use, as well as coverage of the differences between the two major types of marijuana (*Cannabis sativa* and *Cannabis indica*)
* The current status of prescription abuse, including opiate painkillers, stimulants (e.g., performance enhancers), and the central nervous system (CNS) sedative/hypnotics
* Details on public advertising of prescription products and resulting consumer controversies
* The most recent information on the personal and social consequences of use of methamphetamine and narcotic analgesics
* The latest status of over-the-counter (OTC) stimulants and decongestants as well as abuse of OTC products and the efforts to switch more prescription drugs to OTC status
* Updated data and major drug use findings of drug abuse by middle schoolers, adolescents, young adults, middle-aged adults, and senior citizens

- Coverage of current topics such as steroid abuse in baseball, OxyContin abuse, restrictions on pain pills, marijuana legalization, heroin potency, designer drugs, synthetic drugs (Spice and K2), and marijuana wax
- The latest details and information on injection-drug abusers and HIV/AIDS globally and in the United States
- How risk and protective factors directly affect drug abuse
- The most recent information on alcohol and other drug use problems in preadolescent, adolescent, college, and noncollege populations
- The most recent survey data from the National Household Survey on Drug Use and Health (NHSDUH), Monitoring the Future, the Centers for Disease Control and Prevention (CDC), the Center for Behavioral Health Statistics and Quality (CBHSQ), the Substance Abuse and Mental Health Services Administration (SAMHSA), the U.S. Department of Justice (USDOJ), the National Council on Alcoholism and Drug Dependence (NCADD), the Bureau of Justice Statistics (BJS), the National Institute on Drug Abuse (NIDA), and the World Health Organization (WHO)

Chapter Breakdown

The multidisciplinary material in the text encompasses pharmacological, biomedical, sociological, and social-psychological perspectives.

Chapter 1 provides a thorough overview: the historical and current dimensions of drug use (statistics and trends) and the most common currently abused licit (such as OTC and prescription drugs) and illicit types of drugs. Included are the latest findings regarding the abuse of stimulants (including Ritalin and Adderall), bath salts, prescription and performance-enhancing drugs, hallucinogens/psychedelics and other similar drugs, depressants, alcohol, nicotine, cannabis (marijuana and hashish), synthetic cannabinoids, designer drugs/synthetic drugs or synthetic opioids, anabolic steroids, inhalants/organic solvents, and narcotics/opiates.

Chapter 2 comprehensively explains drug use/abuse and addiction from multidisciplinary theoretical standpoints, including the latest theoretical biological, psychological, social-psychological, and sociological perspectives.

Chapter 3 discusses new drug development (both OTC and prescription) and how the law deals with drugs of abuse and individuals who abuse them.

Chapter 4 helps students understand the basic biochemical operations of the nervous and endocrine systems and explains how psychoactive drugs and anabolic steroids alter such functions.

Chapter 5 instructs students about the factors that determine how drugs affect the body. This chapter also details the physiological and psychological variables that determine how and why people respond to drugs used for therapeutic and recreational purposes.

Chapters 6 through 14 focus on specific drug groups that are commonly abused in the United States. Those drugs that depress brain activity are discussed in the following chapters:

- **Chapter 6** Sedative-hypnotic agents
- **Chapters 7** Alcohol use from a pharmacological perspective
- **Chapter 8** Alcohol use from a social scientific and behavioral perspective
- **Chapter 9** Opioid narcotics

Drugs that stimulate brain activity are covered in the following chapters:

- **Chapter 10** Amphetamines, bath salts
- **Chapter 11** Nicotine

The last major category of substances of abuse is hallucinogens, also known as psychedelics, which can alter the senses and create hallucinatory and/or distorted experiences. These substances are discussed in the following chapters:

- **Chapter 12** Hallucinogens, such as LSD, mescaline, Ecstasy, and PCP
- **Chapter 13** Marijuana, marijuana wax, and synthetic cannabinoids (Spice-related types of drugs)
- **Chapter 14** Inhalants

Although most drugs that are abused cause more than one effect (e.g., cocaine can be a stimulant and have some hallucinatory properties), the classification we have chosen for this text is frequently used by experts and pharmacologists in the drug abuse field and is based on the most likely drug effect. All of the chapters in this section are similarly organized. They discuss the following:

- The historical origins and evolution of the agents so students can better understand society's attitudes toward, and regulation of, these drugs

- Previous and current clinical uses of these drugs to help students appreciate distinctions between therapeutic use and abuse
- Patterns of abuse and distinctive features that contribute to each drug's abuse potential
- Nonmedicinal and medicinal therapies for drug-related dependence, withdrawal, and abstinence

Chapter 15 explores the topic of drugs and drug therapy. Like illicit drugs, nonprescription, prescription, and herbal drugs can be misused if not understood. This chapter helps students to appreciate the benefits of proper drug use as well as to recognize that licit (legalized) drugs also can be problematic, and a problem that has been declared by many experts, politicians, and news media to be the greatest drug abuse issue in the United States. This chapter also discusses the recent surge in abuse of prescription drugs such as opioid painkillers, stimulants, and CNS depressants; the dramatic increase in overdose deaths caused by these substances; and how to mitigate these problems.

Chapter 16 explores drug use in several major subcultures of special populations: athletes/those involved in sports, women, adolescents, college students, HIV/AIDS populations, the drug-using subculture of participants in the popular entertainment community, and Internet users seeking information and purchasing illicit drugs.

Chapter 17 acquaints students with drug abuse prevention. This chapter focuses on the following topics: (1) the most prominent factors affecting an individual's use of drugs, (2) major types of drug prevention programs, (3) major types of drug users that must be recognized before creating a prevention program, (4) the four levels of comprehensive drug prevention programs for drug use and abuse, (5) major family factors that can affect the use of drugs, (6) primary prevention programs in higher education, (7) four recent large-scale prevention programs, and (8) two additional prevention measures that may substitute for the attraction to drug use.

Chapter 18 focuses on assessing addiction, the issue of comorbidity, and principles and forms of drug dependence treatment.

HOW TO USE THIS BOOK

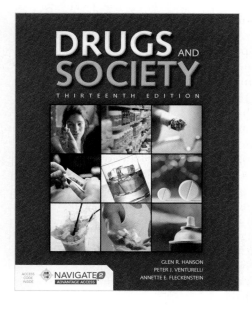

Besides including the most current information concerning drug use and abuse topics, each chapter includes updated and helpful learning aids for both students and instructors. Utilizing these feature boxes for classroom and/or blog discussions and debates or as individual reflective writing assignments can help to drive stronger comprehension and retention of core concepts while reinforcing critical-thinking skills.

HOLDING THE LINE
Cold Restrictions

Starting on September 30, 2006, it became somewhat more difficult for a person with a cold, and a lot more difficult for persons desiring to make methamphetamine from decongestant ingredients, to readily obtain adequate OTC cold medicine for their needs. This is due to a federal law to stop the manufacture of methamphetamine in illegal meth labs found in homes, garages, or basements. To achieve this objective, the restrictions require customers to show a picture ID to purchase cold medicine such as NyQuil Cold & Flu, Actifed Cold & Allergy, and Claritin-D. These and similar decongestant products that contain drugs that can be converted into methamphetamine must be kept behind the store counters in most states. Customers must sign a logbook identifying what they purchased and where they live. The logbook remains on file for 2 years.

This law restricts purchase to 3 to 6 grams of product per day and 9 grams per month. In Oregon and Mississippi these medicines are only available by prescription.

Data from Food and Drug Administration (FDA). "Legal Requirements for the Sale and Purchase of Drug Products Containing Pseudoephedrine, Ephedrine, and Phenylpropanolamine." 2014. Available http://www.fda.gov/drugs/drugsafety/informationbydrugclass/ucm072423.htm; Health & Wellness. "Why Cold Medicines Have Moved Behind the Counter." Women's Health. 2013. Available www.sheknows.com/health-and-wellness/articles/7629/why-some-cold-medicines-have-moved-behind-the-counter;

• **Holding the Line:** Vignettes that help readers assess governmental efforts to deal with drug-related problems.

▶ CASE IN POINT
The Newborn Victims

"*G*uilty, that's how I feel," Nicole said as she waited in a hospital conference room. No one could blame Nicole for her anguish and feelings of culpability as she watched her 5-pound, 5-day-old son intensely squirming in his white blanket; after all, it was her history of abusing opioid narcotics that caused her son's suffering. Although his discomfort and pain were obvious, Nicole could imagine how much worse her son would feel if he had not been given a dose of morphine to suppress his opiate cravings, high-pitched cry, and intense withdrawal symptoms. Without this morphine dose to mitigate his narcotic physical dependence, the newborn's body would have been writhing in agony, shaking, overcome with severe diarrhea, unable to eat, and completely miserable. Nicole knew that her son's body had become dependent on the methadone she was taking while he was in the womb. She remembered back 10 years when she was first prescribed a potent opioid painkiller to relieve pain associated with surgery to treat her obesity. In the years following, she gradually increased her dependence on these analgesics until she was downing up to a dozen of these pills at a time. Although she avoided turning to heroin, she

did spend all the money she could get her hands on to illegally obtain medications such as Vicodin and OxyContin to satisfy her narcotic habit. After several years she finally sought professional help and began to receive legal daily doses of the potent narcotic methadone to replace her body's need for the narcotics. While methadone treatments made it possible for her to avoid the illegally obtained prescription painkillers, to avoid severe withdrawal during her pregnancy Nicole used methadone daily while her son was in utero. The consequence was that while Nicole's opioid-dependent body did not experience withdrawal, her son's developing body, much like his mother's, was physically dependent on these drugs by the time he was born. Also like his mother, now that he was born, he required daily narcotic treatment to prevent withdrawal from his mother's methadone.

In recent years many hospitals claim there has been a flood of babies born dependent on drugs the mothers have been using during their pregnancies. One doctor compared this trend to the spread of Ebola: "Nobody had it, and then all of a sudden everybody had it."

Data from Tully, M. "Meet Heroin's Tiniest Victims: Newborns." *USA Today*. (1 June 2015). Available http://www.USAtoday.com/story/news/nation-now/2015/06/01/heroin-babies-morphine-opiate-drugs/28299459/

• **Case in Point:** Examples of relevant clinical and/or social issues that arise from the use of each major group of drugs.

HERE AND NOW
The Truth About Light Cigarettes

Many smokers choose low-tar, mild, or light cigarettes because they believe that these cigarettes may be less harmful to their health than regular or full-flavor cigarettes. Unfortunately, light cigarettes do not reduce the health risks of smoking. The only way to reduce risk to oneself and others is to stop smoking completely. Common questions concerning light cigarettes include the following:

Q. Are light cigarettes less hazardous than regular cigarettes?

A. No. Light cigarettes are no safer than regular cigarettes. According to the National Cancer Institute, tar exposure from a light cigarette can be just as high as that from a regular cigarette if the smoker takes deeper, longer, or more frequent puffs.

Q. Why would someone smoking a light cigarette take bigger puffs than with a regular cigarette?

A. Features of cigarettes that reduce the yield of machine-measured tar also reduce the yield of nicotine. Thus, smokers may take larger and more frequent puffs, inhale more deeply, or smoke extra cigarettes each day to get enough nicotine to satisfy their craving.

Q. Are machine-measured tar yields misleading?

A. Yes. The ratings cannot be used to predict how much tar a smoker will actually take in because the way the machine smokes a cigarette is not necessarily the same as how an individual smokes. Taking deeper, longer, and more frequent puffs will lead to greater tar exposure.

Q. Do light cigarettes cause cancer?

A. Yes. People who smoke any kind of cigarette are at much greater risk of lung cancer than people who do not smoke.

Data from National Cancer Institute (NCI). "'Light' Cigarettes and Cancer Risk." 2010. Available http://www.cancer.gov/about-cancer/causes-prevention/risk/tobacco/light-cigarettes-fact-sheet

- **Here and Now:** Current events that illustrate the personal and social consequences of drug abuse.

FAMILY MATTERS

Family Addictions and Genetics

Substance abuse, alcoholism, and associated trauma seem to have both genetic and environmental components, the interaction of which can have serious consequences. For example, alcoholism tends to run in families. Thus, children of alcoholics are at high risk to become alcohol users themselves because of their genetic vulnerability as well as because of the traumatic environments to which they are often exposed. Levels of conflict in families characterized by alcoholism are much higher than in families with no alcoholism. The environment to which children with alcoholic parents are exposed may include a lack of communication, emotional and physical violence, isolation, and financial problems. At least half of all cases of child maltreatment are linked to a prevalence of substance abuse and alcoholism in the home. It has also been reported that children who receive prenatal exposure to drugs are two to three times more likely to be neglected or abused.

Data from Learn.Genetics. "Drugs of Abuse." University of Utah Genetics (2015) Available http://learn.genetics.utah.edu/content/addiction/abuse/

- **Family Matters:** Examples of how genetics and heredity contribute to drug abuse and its issues.

PRESCRIPTION FOR ABUSE

Benzodiazepines: The Good and the Bad

Jenn is a freelance book editor who has been using the benzodiazepine drug known as Valium for years. She describes this drug as essential for quickly managing her problems associated with extreme anxiety. She claims that Valium is the only thing that effectively relaxes her when she gets into the seat of a car, after nearly dying in two car accidents as a teenager. She admits that when she takes Valium she "feels so much better—and can finally relax. Sometimes that makes all the difference in the world." She claims that benzodiazepines work almost immediately, in contrast to antidepressant drugs, which are also prescribed to relieve anxiety, but require several weeks of treatment to achieve full efficacy. Benzodiazepines have also been shown to be effective in the treatment for insomnia, seizures, and alcohol withdrawal. However, these sedative hypnotic drugs are not without controversy. For example, most physicians will not prescribe benzodiazepines for more than a few weeks. With long-term treatment, the benzodiazepines cause the body to develop physical dependence, resulting in withdrawal if the drugs are discontinued "cold-turkey." Long-term use also can result in abuse and addiction. Short-term use can also adversely affect the user by interfering with cognition and decision-making, as well as impairing reflexes and motor functions. Consequently, it is recommended that doctors manage their benzodiazepine-using patients carefully and avoid prescribing these drugs for long periods of time, especially in adults.

Fawcett, K. "Benzodiazepine: Helpful or Harmful?" *U.S. News & World Report* (19 February 2015). Available http://health.usnews.com/health-news/patient-advice/articles/2015/02/19/benzodiazepines-helpful-or-harmful

- **Prescription for Abuse:** Current stories that illustrate the problems of prescription abuse and its consequences.

▶POINT/COUNTERPOINT

How the "Juice" Was and Is Flowing in Baseball

We embrace instant gratification in the United States. We are a society that embraces "bigger, faster, stronger" and winning at all costs (Dvorchak 2005). This concept now applies to professional sports. A sampling from news sources reveals the following:

- "Jose Canseco, a Major League Baseball player for the Oakland Athletics and Texas Rangers (among other teams), wrote a tell-all book titled *Juiced*, in which he exposed not only the rampant use of performance-enhancing substances in baseball.... A steroid devotee since the age of 20, Conseco goes beyond admitting his own usage ... [to claiming that] he often injected [Mark] McGwire while they were teammates.... According to Canseco, steroids and human growth hormone gave McGwire and Sammy Sosa (whose own usage was 'so obvious, it was a joke') the strength, stamina, regenerative ability, and confidence they needed for [the] record setting home run duels often credited with restoring baseball's popularity after the 1994 strike" (Amazon.com 2005).

- "[S]everal star athletes, including New York Yankees slugger Jason Giambi, have reportedly

- **Point/Counterpoint:** Features that expose students to different perspectives on drug-related issues and encourage them to draw their own conclusions.

KEY TERMS

primary prevention
prevention of using any drug use

secondary prevention
preventing casual and/or recreational drug use from advancing to drug dependence

- **Key Terms:** Highlighted definitions of new terminology that is conveniently located on the same page as their discussion in the text.

Learning Objectives

On completing this chapter, you should be able to:

> Know which drugs are most likely to be abused by athletes and why.
> Describe the use of drug testing in athletic competitions.
> Identify where users obtain anabolic steroids.
> Describe the purpose and goals of the Adolescents Training and Learning to Avoid Steroids (ATLAS) prevention program.
> Explain two major ways the history of drug abuse among women differs from that of men.
> Explain the major reasons why adolescents use substances of abuse.
> Explain which types of parents are more likely to raise drug-abusing adolescents.
> List the types of drugs adolescents are most likely to abuse.
> List two major findings from research regarding drug use by college students.
> Know what "club drugs" are and how they are used.
> Explain how drug abuse contributes to the spread of HIV/AIDS.
> Know the key statistics regarding HIV/AIDS.
> List the major strategies to prevent HIV infection.
> Know how the use of alcohol and other drugs is presented in popular movies and songs.
> Understand how users can access the Internet to purchase licit and illicit types of drugs.

- **Learning Objectives:** Goals for learning are listed at the beginning of each chapter to help students identify the principal concepts being taught.

LEARNING PORTFOLIO

Key Terms

amnesiac	187
anesthesia	187
antihistamines	187
anxiolytic	187
barbiturates	186
benzodiazepines	186
club drug	192
detoxification	200
hypnotic	187
paradoxical effects	190
REM sleep	190
sedatives	187

Discussion Questions

1. Why did benzodiazepine drugs replace barbiturates as the sedative-hypnotic drugs most prescribed by physicians?
2. Which features of CNS depressants give them abuse potential?
3. Why is long-term use of the benzodiazepines more likely than short-term use to cause dependence?
4. Why are some physicians careless when prescribing benzodiazepines for patients suffering from severe anxiety?
5. Currently, sleep aid products are available OTC. Should the FDA also allow sedatives to be sold without a prescription? Support your answer.
6. Are there any real advantages to using barbiturates as sedatives or hypnotics? Should the FDA remove them completely from the market?
7. What types of people are most likely to abuse CNS depressants? Suggest ways to help these people avoid abusing these drugs.
8. Should propofol be scheduled, and if so, as what category?
9. What is the appeal of using GHB? Why is it used to commit sexual assaults?
10. What dangers are associated with treating individuals who are severely dependent on CNS depressants?
11. Why are CNS depressants often combined with alcohol, and what is the consequence?
12. Why is detoxification by itself usually insufficient to achieve long-term therapeutic success when dealing with severe CNS depressant dependence?

Summary

1. Several unrelated drug groups cause CNS depression, but only a few are actually used clinically for their depressant properties. The most frequently prescribed CNS depressants are benzodiazepines, which include drugs such as Valium, Ambien, and Xanax. Barbiturates once were popular, but, because of their severe side effects, they are no longer prescribed by most clinicians except to treat some seizures. Much like barbiturates, drugs such as chloral hydrate and methaqualone are little used today. Finally, some OTC and prescription antihistamines, such as diphenhydramine, hydroxyzine, and promethazine, are used for their CNS depressant effects.
2. The clinical value of CNS depressants is dose dependent. When used at low doses, these drugs relieve anxiety and promote relaxation (sedatives). When prescribed at higher doses, they can cause drowsiness and promote sleep (hypnotics). When administered at even higher doses, some of the depressants cause anesthesia and are used for patient management during surgery.

- **Discussion Questions:** Provocative and engaging questions at the end of each chapter encourage students to discuss, ponder, and critically analyze their own feelings and biases about the information presented in the book.

- **Summary:** Concise summaries found at the end of each chapter correlate with the learning objectives.

Because of these updated features, we believe that this edition of *Drugs and Society* is particularly "user friendly," has the most current and accurate information available in a textbook, and will encourage student motivation and learning.

Resources to Accompany *Drugs and Society, Thirteenth Edition*

Navigate 2 Advantage Access for Drugs and Society, Thirteenth Edition is a complete, interactive online courseware solution combining authoritative content with interactive tools, assessments, and grading functionality.

This online course combines a host of interactive activities to facilitate learning and allow students to check their progress using quizzes and assessments. Course setup is easy with the preplanned lessons and lecture outlines found within the platform. *Navigate 2* is flexible and allows instructors to customize content. Automatic grading saves time and provides on-demand analysis of how students are progressing in the course, allowing the instructor to tailor the teaching based on student needs. Other tools such as a built-in calendar, system email, and a robust grade book are also available within *Navigate 2*.

With *Navigate 2 Advantage Access*, students can immediately evaluate their understanding of important concepts and objectives by easy toggling between textbook narrative, activities, and assessments, enabling them to process, synthesize, and retain course concepts in less time through rich media content.

Navigate 2 Advantage Access for Drugs and Society, Thirteenth Edition includes the following:

- An interactive, animated eBook with personalization tools such as highlighting, bookmarking, and notes

- Student resources, including a full study guide separated by chapter, a course glossary, PowerPoint presentations, discussion questions, assignments, chapter readings, and more!

ACKNOWLEDGMENTS

The many improvements that make this the best edition of the *Drugs and Society* series could not have occurred without the hard work and dedication of numerous people.

We are indebted to the many reviewers who evaluated the manuscript at different stages of development. Much of the manuscript was reviewed and greatly improved by comments and suggestions from the following:

- R. Todd Coy, PhD, Colby-Sawyer College
- Maureen P. Edwards, PhD, CHES, Montgomery College
- Ethel Elkins, MHA, MA, LCSW, LMFT, LMHC, University of Southern Indiana
- Amanda S. Eymard, MSN, RN, Nicholls State University
- Donna E. Fletcher, PhD, LCAS, CSI, Lenoir-Rhyne University
- Susan A. Lyman, PhD, CHES, University of Louisiana at Lafayette
- Dr. Susan Milstein, CHES, CSE, Montgomery College
- William J. Schoen Jr., MA, University of Colorado Denver
- Caren L. Steinmiller, PhD, The University of Toledo
- John Stogner, MS, University of Florida

The authors would like to express, once again, their gratitude for the comments and suggestions of users and reviewers of previous editions of *Drugs and Society*. They would also like to acknowledge Peter Myers for his substantial contributions to a previous edition of this text.

At their respective institutions, each of the authors would like to thank a multitude of people too numerous to list individually but who have given them invaluable assistance.

Dr. Fleckenstein gratefully acknowledges the support of her family in her participation in the preparation of this revised text. Also appreciated is the support of her colleagues at the University of Utah School of Dentistry.

At Valparaiso University, Professor Venturelli is grateful to Jason Kresich, the department's former student aide, who has recently completed his master's degree and is now gainfully employed in Boston, Massachusetts. Jason continues to assist me on developmental phases of this book and assisted me in revising a number of the ancillary materials for this new edition, including proofreading chapter drafts. I am also grateful for Shaun Patterson and his expertise in creating most of the tables and figures, which provide the latest information contained in these chapters. Professor Venturelli would also like to gratefully acknowledge all of the other interviewees (students and working people) who were interviewed for hours on end regarding their information, opinions, and personal use and/or experiences (past and present) with drugs. Even though the final copy of revised chapters remains the author's responsibility, this edition has been substantially enhanced by all their efforts, loyalties, and the dedicated assistance of others, which at Jones & Bartlett Learning includes Cathy Esperti and Carter McAlister. Working with these and other professionals and dedicated staff members at Jones & Bartlett Learning has been instructive, productive, and very rewarding.

Dr. Hanson is particularly indebted to his wife, Margaret, for her loving encouragement. Without her patience and support this endeavor would not have been possible. She reminds him that what is truly important in this world is service to our family and to each other. Also appreciated is the support of his children and his colleagues at the University of Utah School of Dentistry, School of Medicine, and College of Pharmacy.

Dr. Glen R. Hanson is the associate dean of the School of Dentistry, and a professor in the School of Dentistry and Department of Pharmacology and Toxicology at the University of Utah. He is also the director of the Utah Addiction Center at the University of Utah. During his approximately 30 years in academics he has received more than $30 million from the National Institute on Drug Abuse (NIDA), affiliated with the National Institutes of Health (NIH), to research the neurobiology of drug abuse and has authored more than 230 scientific papers and 50 book chapters on the subject. Dr. Hanson has lectured on drug abuse topics throughout the world. He served as the director of the Division of Neuroscience and Behavioral Research at NIDA, after which he became NIDA's acting director from 2001 to 2003. Dr. Hanson works with scientists, public officials, policy makers, and the general public to more effectively deal with problems of drug abuse addiction.

Dr. Peter J. Venturelli has been the coauthor of this text since the second edition of *Drugs and Society* in 1988. In addition to revising this text every 2 years, Dr. Venturelli's experiences and qualifications in academia and professional life include publishing research in drug and ethnic anthologies and scholarly journals, authoring more than 58 conference papers at national professional sociological meetings, serving in elected and administrative positions in professional sociological and drug research, associations, receiving research grants involving drug use and ethnicity, authoring the latest drug research, serving as a board member at the Baldwin Research Institute (alcohol and drug retreats), and teaching undergraduate and graduate students for the past 30 years.

Dr. Annette E. Fleckenstein has been a coauthor of *Drugs and Society* since its seventh edition and is a professor in the School of Dentistry at the University of Utah. She has researched the neurobiology of substance abuse for over 20 years, lectured on substance abuse-related topics throughout the United States and abroad, and authored more than 110 scientific papers and book chapters on this and related subjects. Dr. Fleckenstein has been a NIDA-funded researcher for 20 years and has a long history of lecturing to undergraduate, graduate, and professional students.

© Christian Mueller/Shutterstock, Inc.

Did You Know?

▶ The popular use of legal drugs, particularly alcohol and tobacco, has caused far more deaths, sickness, violent crimes, economic loss, and other social problems than the use of all illegal drugs combined.

▶ The effect a drug has depends on multiple factors: (1) the ingredients of the drug and its effect on the body, (2) the traditional use of the drug, (3) individual motivation, and (4) the social and physical surroundings in which the drug is taken.

▶ The first attempts to regulate drugs were made as long ago as 2240 BC.

▶ After marijuana, illicit prescription drugs are now the second leading drug of abuse.

▶ Drug abuse is an "equal-opportunity affliction." This means that drug consumption is found across all income levels, social classes, genders, races, ethnicities, lifestyles, and age groups.

▶ Among racial/ethnic groups in the United States, past-month illicit drug use is highest among African Americans and whites and lowest among Asians.

▶ Approximately 70% of drug users in the United States are employed (18 years or older) either full time or part time, and 76% of full- or part-time employees are heavy drinkers.

▶ In major industry categories, past-month illicit drug use was highest in accommodations and food services; arts, entertainment, and recreation; and management; the highest amount of heavy alcohol use was found in the mining, construction, and accommodations and food services industries.

▶ Approximately 60% of individuals arrested for most types of crimes test positive for illegal drugs at the time of their arrest.

Learning Objectives

On completing this chapter you should be able to:

❯ Explain how drug use is affected by biological, genetic, and pharmacological factors, as well as cultural, social, and contextual factors.

❯ Develop a basic understanding of drug use and abuse.

❯ Explain when drugs were first used and under what circumstances.

❯ Indicate how widespread drug use is and who the potential drug abusers are.

❯ List four reasons why drugs are used.

❯ Rank in descending order, from most common to least, the most commonly used licit and illicit drugs.

❯ Name three types of drug users, and explain how they differ.

❯ Describe how the mass media promote drug use.

❯ Explain when drug use leads to abuse.

❯ List and explain the stages of drug dependence.

❯ List the major findings regarding drugs and crime.

❯ Describe employee assistance programs, and explain their role in resolving productivity problems.

❯ Explain the holistic self-awareness approach.

Introduction

Each year, at an accelerating rate, social change driven by technology not only affects us individually, but also affects our family, community, city, nation, and the world. It can be said that technology is one of the primary forces driving social change at an unprecedented and relentless speed, affecting our everyday lives.

As an example of technological change, let us look at the transformation of the telephone into cellular phone technology. In all likelihood, your great-grandparents had a single black stationary rotary type of landline phone at home to use for communicating with friends and family living at a distance. Your grandparents experienced newer and more stylized versions of the same telephone, with perhaps one or two other telephones installed in another part of their home. While growing up, your parents had the same landline type of telephone, but it came in an array of colors and was more stylized, and there were multiple extensions of this phone throughout their home in bedrooms, hallways, and/or kitchens. Today, your available technology may still include a landline phone[1] with additional features such as voice mail, call waiting, call forwarding, and call blocking, to name a few of many other standard feature options available with landline phones.

An outgrowth of the landline phone and the radio-phone, which was used in the military, is a gadget that most of us carry today without any sense of technological awe. The cell phone, with over 7 billion worldwide subscribers (Nair 2015), and its recent cousin, the smartphone, named as such because it includes additional software functions resembling a computer, are portable warehouses of technological services that connect to a cellular network. Current cell phones can include an array of accessories and services beyond making phone calls, including caller identification; voice messaging; voice memos; an alarm clock; a stopwatch; calendars; appointment scheduling; current times and temperatures in different cities around the world; a calculator; video games; text messaging (or SMS); a camera with photo albums; Internet service; email; infrared; Bluetooth; an MP3 player; storage for downloaded music, movies, and/or podcasts; geographic positioning system (GPS) features; radio broadcasts; maps; stock market quotes; weather; reminders; Skype or FaceTime; and iTunes, to name a few "basic" applications. Literally hundreds of thousands of applications ("apps") offer an array of information, accessories, and services. The completely portable cell phone with its keypad or touchscreen did not exist for the general public 38 years ago. Further, newer generations of cell phones will include unimaginable new applications, accessories, and services.

Consider another example. More than likely, your great-grandparents wrote letters on manual typewriters (or by hand). Your grandparents wrote letters on electric typewriters, whereas your parents started writing letters on electric typewriters and then had to change to computers. Today, you often communicate with family members and friends by email, text messaging, Facebook, Twitter, Google+, Skype, and Pinterest. Although you may perceive many of the electronic devices surrounding your life as normal, a visit to a science and technology museum can offer many surprises and, more than likely, an appreciation for how things were and how much they have changed.

These examples illustrate how technology is in a continuous state of development and how it affects our day-to-day lives. In a sense, the technology we use today will be replaced tomorrow as newer and more advanced forms of innovation give birth to new technology and software.

What does this have to do with drug use and/or abuse? Just as electronics continually evolve, drugs follow similar paths of evolution. Today, there are thousands of new drugs available that are used either legally or illegally. These drugs are used for medicinal purposes, recreational purposes, or to achieve effects that do not include maintaining health. Some people in society use drugs to cope with pressures emanating from social change. Others use and eventually abuse drugs to cope with, delay, or postpone reality. For some, illicit drug use becomes a primary method for instant recreation, a way to avoid anxieties, or a substitute to fulfill human desires and pleasures.

Despite the extensive amount of available information regarding the dangers of drug use and an increasing number of laws prohibiting nonmedical drug use, many people today continue to abuse legal and illegal types of drugs.

---

[1]Landline phones continue to disappear from U.S. households; approximately 41% of American homes do not have a landline phone or do not use the ones they have (Luckerson 2014; Stobbe 2014).

Drug Use

Anyone can become dependent on and addicted to a drug. The desire to use a drug before drug dependence and addiction occur is both seductive and indiscriminate of its users. Most people do not realize that drug use causes at least three major simultaneous changes:

1. The social and psychological basis of the attraction to a particular drug can be explained as feeling rewarded or satisfied because social pressures can appear to have become postponed, momentarily rectified, or neutralized and perceived as nonproblematic.
2. Pharmacologically, the nonmedical use of most drugs alters body chemistry largely by interfering with its proper (homeostatic) functioning. Drugs enhance, slow down, accelerate, or distort the reception and transmission of reality.
3. The desire may satisfy an inborn or genetically programmed need or desire.

Many argue that our "reality" would become perilous and unpredictable if people were legally free to dabble in their drugs of choice. Many do not realize, however, that, if abused, even legal drugs can alter our perception of reality, become severely addicting, and destroy our social relationships with loved ones. Before delving into more specific information, we begin by posing some key questions related to drug use that will be discussed in this chapter:

- What constitutes a drug? *is alcohol a drug?*
- What are the most commonly abused drugs? *in the US?*
- What are designer drugs?
- How widespread is drug abuse?
- What are the extent and frequency of drug use in our society?
- What are the current statistics on and trends in drug use?
- What types of drug users exist?
- How do the media influence drug use?
- What attracts people to drug use
- When does drug use lead to drug dependence?
- When does drug addiction occur?
- What are the costs of drug addiction to society?
- What can be gained by learning about the complexity of drug use and abuse?

Dimensions of Drug Use

To determine the perception of drug use in our country, we asked several of the many people we interviewed for this text, "What do you think of the extent and the amount of drug use in our society?" The following are four of the more typical responses:

I think it is a huge problem, especially when you think about the fact that there are so many people doing drugs. Even in my own family, my sister's kids have had drug problems. My niece became addicted to cocaine, nearly died one night from overdosing, had to leave college for a year and go into rehab. I cannot emphasize enough how this was one of the most beautiful (physically and mentally sharp) and polite nieces I ever had. The rest of the family had no idea why she left school last year. Then, just last week, my sister tearfully announced during a Christmas gathering that Cindee was heavily into drugs while attending her second year of college. We were all shocked by this information. Now, just think how many other kids are addicted to such junk while the people who really care and love them do not have a clue. If the kids are having to deal with this, just stop and think how many other people in other jobs and professions are battling or have caved into their drugs of choice.

How many workers are there on a daily basis doing jobs that require safety and are "high" on drugs? This is a scary thought. Just think of a surgeon on drugs, or an airline pilot. Yes, we have big monster problems with controlling drug use. *(From Venturelli's research files, female dietician in Chicago, age 43, February 9, 2003)*

A second response to the same question:

I use drugs, mainly weed and alcohol, and at least once a month I have a night of enjoying coke with several friends. As long as I am not a burden on my family, I think drug use is a personal choice. Locking up people for their drug use is a violation of my rights as a human being. For many years now, our government has not been able to stop recreational drug use, this is despite the millions that have been arrested, and countless numbers of other drug users incarcerated. What's the point of all this? If after so many years of trying to enforce drug laws has met with failure, we need to take a long hard look at the small percentage of people like me who are fully employed, have families, pay our taxes regularly and outside of drug use, are fully functioning adults. The funny thing is that the two drugs [referring to alcohol and tobacco] that are legalized are far worse or at least as debilitating as the drugs that are legally prohibitive [sic]. Drug use is a personal choice and unless you are causing problems for other people, it should remain a personal choice. If I am using drugs on a particular night at home either by myself or with friends and we are not outside causing problems, we should not be in violation of any drug law or laws. Substances to get high have been around for hundreds and probably thousands of years, these substances that some of us like should not be any concern to others. Even my pet cat loves his catnip and appears to get a high from it; should I prohibit this little pleasure? I let him occasionally have it even if, for example, my neighbor thinks catnip is affecting the normal nature of my cat. How about if I get a rise from snorting or smoking one of the herbs in my kitchen cabinet? Whose business is it if I like to use herbs in this manner? Maybe we should also outlaw catnip and herbs? Again, drug use for whatever purpose is a personal decision and all the laws against the use of drugs are not going to stop me from using drugs. *(From Venturelli's research files, male residing in a Midwestern town, age 27, May 6, 2010)*

A third response to the same question:

My drug use? Whose business is it anyway? As long as I don't affect your life when I do drugs, what business is it but my own? We come into the world alone and leave this world alone. I don't bother anyone else about whether or not so and so uses drugs, unless of course, their drug use puts me in jeopardy (like a bus driver or pilot high on drugs). On certain days when things are slow, I even get a little high on cocaine while trading stocks. These are the same clients who I have had for years and who really trust my advice. Ask my clients whether they are happy with my investment advice. I handle accounts with millions of dollars for corporations and even the board of education! Never was my judgment impaired or adversely affected because of too much coke. In fact, I know that I work even better under a little buzz. Now, I know this stuff has the potential to

become addictive, but I don't let it. I know how to use it and when to lay off for a few weeks. *(From Venturelli's research files, male investment broker working in a major metropolitan city in California, age 48, June 2, 2000)*

A fourth response, to the same question, from an interviewee who recently moved from Indiana to Colorado:

Well, things are changing regarding drug use purely for recreational purposes. I am referring to marijuana of course. In Colorado, marijuana is now legalized. I also think this is the way it should be not only in Colorado but also throughout the country. I can now actually see how state after state will eventually legalize marijuana. There will be holdout states, like usually deep southern states, but it's just a matter of time. I think it was Oakland, California, where by taxing the sale of marijuana, the city was collecting a nice amount of tax revenues from marijuana sales. If I am not in error, it was reported as millions of dollars they were collecting. Now, don't you think this alone will attract other cities and states to legalize and tax this drug in order to gain tax revenues, especially when state and city tax revenues are in dire need to increase revenue coming in? It won't be the spread of liberalism that will legalize marijuana; it will be common business sense that will get rid of the ridiculous laws outlawing marijuana use and sales. I have always smoked pot and nothing has ever stopped me. On top of this add the millions who feel the same way. If you don't want to use this drug to relax like others may use alcohol that is fine but leave the users alone and stop making law violators! It is still illegal and you [referring to this interviewer] and I know that all these laws and the millions upon millions spent on trying to stop marijuana drug users have not worked, so why keep this up? Again, why prohibit something that given its history cannot be stopped? *(From Venturelli's research files, male attorney, currently practicing law and residing in the state of Colorado, age 33, January 2, 2013)*

These four interviews reflect vastly contrasting views and attitudes about drug use. The first interview shows the most contrast from the second, third, and fourth interviews. The second, third, and fourth interviews show a similarity of views about drug use, largely from an insider's (the user's) perspective, indicative of a strong determination and belief that drug use should not be legally controlled and should be left to the discretion of users. Although much about these viewpoints can certainly be debated, an interesting finding is that such vastly different views about drug use are not only evident, but, more important, often divide drug users and nonusers. From a more social psychological standpoint, drug users and/or sympathizers of drug use are often considered **insiders** with regard to their drug use, whereas nonusers and/or those who are against drug use are **outsiders**. These two classifications result in very different sets of values and attitudes about drug usage. Such great differences of opinion and views about drugs and drug use often result from the following sources: (1) prior socialization experiences, such as family upbringing, relations with siblings, and types of peer group associations; (2) the amount of exposure to drug use and drug users; (3) the age of initial exposure to drug use; and (4) whether an attitude change has occurred regarding the acceptance or rejection of using drugs. Keep in mind that this text views the following four principal factors as affecting how a drug user experiences a drug:

- *Biological, genetic, and pharmacological factors*: Substance abuse and addiction involve biological and genetic factors. The pharmacology of drug use focuses on how the ingredients of a particular drug affect the body and the nervous system and, in turn, a person's experience with a particular drug.
- *Cultural factors*: Society's views of drug use, as determined by custom and tradition, affect our initial approach to and use of a particular drug.
- *Social factors*: The motivation for taking a particular drug is affected by needs such as diminishing physical pain; curing an illness; providing relaxation; relieving stress or anxiety; trying to escape reality; self-medicating; heightening awareness; wanting to distort and change visual, auditory, or sensory inputs; or strengthening confidence. Included in the category of social factors is the belief that attitudes about drug use develop from the values and attitudes of other drug users; the norms in their communities, subcultures, peer groups, and families; and the drug user's personal experiences with using drugs. (These are also known as influencing social factors.)
- *Contextual factors*: Specific contexts define and determine personal dispositions toward drug

use, as demonstrated by moods and attitudes about such activity. Specifically, these factors encompass the drug-taking social behavior that develops from the physical surroundings where the drug is used. For example, drug use may be perceived as more acceptable at fraternity parties, while socializing with drug-using friends, outdoors in a secluded area with other drug users, in private homes, secretly at work, or at music concerts.

Paying attention to the cultural, social, and contextual factors of drug use leads us to explore the sociology and psychology of drug use. Equally important are the biological, genetic, and pharmacological factors and consequences that directly focus on why and how drugs may be appealing and how they affect the body—primarily the central nervous system and brain functions.

Although substances that affect both mind and body functioning are commonly called *drugs*, researchers in the field of drug or substance abuse use a more precise term: **psychoactive drugs (substances)**. Why the preference for using this term as opposed to *drugs*? Because the term *psychoactive drugs* is more precise regarding *how* drugs affect the body. This term focuses on how drugs affect the **central nervous system (CNS)**, the part of the nervous system composed of the spinal cord and brain that is responsible for integrating sensory information and responding accordingly. In particular, the term encompasses how psychoactive drugs alter mood, consciousness, thought processes, perception, and/or behavior. Psychoactive drugs can be used to treat physical, psychological, or mental illness. In addition, with continued use,

KEY TERMS

insiders
people on the inside; those who approve of and/or use drugs

outsiders
people on the outside; those who do not approve of and/or use drugs

psychoactive drugs (substances)
drug compounds (substances) that affect the central nervous system and alter consciousness and/or perceptions

central nervous system (CNS)
part of the nervous system composed of the spinal cord and brain that is responsible for integrating sensory information and responding accordingly

our bodies can tolerate increasingly larger doses of drugs, often resulting in the need for progressively greater amounts to achieve the same level of effect. For many substances, a user is at risk of moving from occasional to regular use or from moderate to heavy use, ultimately culminating in chronic use. A chronic user may then risk **addiction** (a mostly psychological attachment) and experience **withdrawal symptoms** that are physical and/or psychological in nature whenever the drug is not supplied.

Generally speaking, any substance that modifies the nervous system and state of consciousness is a **drug**. Such modification includes one or more of the following: enhancement, inhibition, or distortion of the body, affecting patterns of behavior and social functioning. Psychoactive drugs are classified as either **licit** (legal) or **illicit** (illegal). (See **Table 1.1** for a list of slang terms used by drug users.) For example, coffee, tea, cocoa, alcohol, tobacco, and **over-the-counter (OTC)** drugs are licit. When licit drugs are used in moderation, they often go unnoticed and are often socially acceptable. Marijuana, cocaine, crack, and all of the hallucinogenic types of drugs are examples of illicit drugs. With the exception of marijuana— which some states allow for medical use and small

Examples of illicit drugs that can become costly once drug dependence occurs.

amounts for personal use—federal law continues to prohibit the possession and use of all of these drugs.

Researchers have made some interesting findings about legal and illegal drug use:

- The use of legal substances such as alcohol and tobacco is much more common than the use of illegal drugs such as marijuana, cocaine, heroin, and hallucinogens (psychedelics). Other legal drugs, such as depressants and stimulants, although less popular than alcohol and tobacco, are still more widely used than heroin and LSD.
- The popular use of licit drugs, particularly alcohol and tobacco, has caused far more deaths, sickness, violent crimes, economic loss, and other social problems than the combined use of all illicit drugs. (See **Figure 1.1** for an illustrated comparison.)
- Societal reaction to various drugs changes with time and place. Today, opium is an illegal drug and widely condemned as a pan-pathogen (a cause of all ills). In the 18th and 19th centuries, however, it was a legal drug and was popularly praised as a panacea (a cure for all ills). Alcohol use was widespread in the United States in the early 1800s, became illegal during the 1920s, and then was legalized a second time and has been widely used since the 1930s. Cigarette smoking is legal in all countries today. In the 17th century, it was illegal in most countries, and smokers were sometimes harshly punished. For example, in Russia, smokers could lose their noses; in Hindustan (India), they could lose their lips; and in China, they could lose their heads (Thio 1983, 1995, 2000). Today, new emphasis in the United States

KEY TERMS

addiction
generally refers to the psychological attachment to a drug(s); addiction to "harder" drugs such as heroin results in both psychological and physical attachment to the chemical properties of the drug, with the resulting satisfaction (reward) derived from using the drug in question

withdrawal symptoms
psychological and physical symptoms that result when a drug is absent from the body; physical symptoms are generally present in cases of drug dependence to more addictive drugs such as heroin; physical and psychological symptoms of withdrawal include perspiration, nausea, boredom, anxiety, and muscle spasms

drug(s)
any substances that modify (either by enhancing, inhibiting, or distorting) mind and/or body functioning

licit drugs
legalized drugs such as coffee, alcohol, and tobacco

illicit drugs
illegal drugs such as marijuana, cocaine, and LSD

over-the-counter (OTC)
legalized drugs sold without a prescription

TABLE 1.1 A Sampling of 73,300 Slang Terms Relating to Drugs, Drug Use, and the Drug Trade

Slang Term	What It Means	Slang Term	What It Means
24-7	Crack cocaine	Blunt	Marijuana and/or cocaine inside a cigar
80	OxyContin pill	Boost and shoot	Steal to support a drug habit
714s	Methaqualone	Brain ticklers	Amphetamines
3750	Marijuana and crack rolled in a joint	Brown bombers	LSD
Abolic	Veterinary steroids	Brown sugar	Heroin
A-bomb	Marijuana cigarette with heroin or opium	Buddha	Potent marijuana spiked with opium
AC/DC	Codeine cough syrup	Bull dog	Heroin
Acid, acid cube	LSD, sugar cube with LSD	Bundle	Heroin
Acid freak	Heavy user of LSD	Ditch weed	Inferior quality marijuana
Adam	Methylenedioxymethamphetamine (MDMA)	Dr. Feelgood	Heroin
Air blast	Inhalants	Easy lay	Gamma hydroxybutyrate (GHB)
All star	User of multiple drugs	Fantasy	GHB
Amped	High on amphetamines	Flower flipping	Ecstasy (MDMA) mixed with mushrooms
Angel dust	PCP	Forget-me-drug	Rohypnol
Author	Doctor who writes illegal prescriptions	Fries	Crack cocaine
Baby habit	Occasional use of drugs	Garbage rock	Crack cocaine
Balloon	Heroin supplier; a penny balloon that contains narcotics	Hit the hay	Smoke weed
Bam	Amphetamine; depressants	Hippie crack	Inhalants
Barbies	Depressants	Hot ice	Smokable methamphetamine
Battery acid	LSD	Huff, huffing	Inhalants, to sniff an inhalant
Batu	Smokable methamphetamine	Ice cream habit	Occasional use of a drug
Beam me up, Scottie	Crack dipped in PCP	Idiot pills	Depressants
Beannies	Methamphetamine	Kiddie dope	Prescription drugs
Beast	Heroin, LSD	Lemonade	Heroin; poor quality drugs
Belladonna	PCP	Lunch money drug	Rohypnol
Bender	Drug party	Magic mushroom	Psilocybin/psilocin
Biker's coffee	Methamphetamine and coffee	Monkey dust	PCP
Bin Laden	Heroin (after 9/11)	Moon gas	Inhalants
Black beauties	Amphetamines, depressants	Mother's little helper	Depressants
Blasted	Under the influence of drugs	Nose candy	Cocaine
Blow your mind	Getting high on hallucinogens	Paper boy	Heroin peddler

(continues)

TABLE 1.1 A Sampling of 73,300 Slang Terms Relating to Drugs, Drug Use, and the Drug Trade (*continued*)

Slang Term	What It Means	Slang Term	What It Means
Pepsi habit	Occasional use of drugs	Tornado	Crack cocaine
Pony	Crack cocaine	Totally spent	Hangover after MDMA
Ringer	Good hit of crack, to hear bells	Water-water	Marijuana cigarettes dipped in embalming fluid or laced with PCP
Shot	To inject a drug, an amount of coke	West Coast	Ritalin (ADHD drug)
Soda	Injectable cocaine	Working man's cocaine	Methamphetamine
Special "K"	Ketamine	Zig Zag man	Marijuana rolling papers
Strawberry	LSD; female who trades sex for crack or money to buy crack	Zombie	PCP; heavy user of drugs
The devil	Crack cocaine	Zoom	Marijuana laced with PCP

Reproduced from Office of National Drug Control Policy (ONDCP). *Street Terms: Drugs and the Drug Trade.* Washington, DC: Office of National Drug Control Policy, 2016. Available http://www.streetlightpublications.net/misc/ondcp.htm

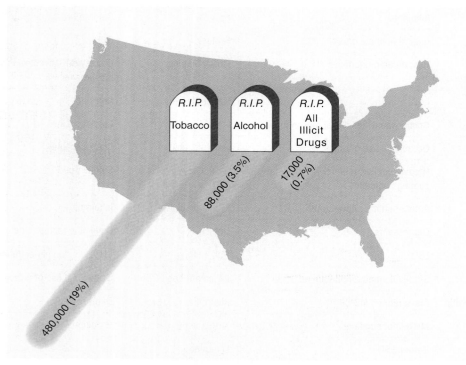

FIGURE 1.1 Cigarette smoking and exposure to tobacco smoke cause approximately 480,000 premature deaths annually in the United States (includes deaths from secondhand smoke; 278,544 deaths annually among men and 201,773 deaths annually among women). In the United States, more than 88,000 deaths each year are caused by excessive alcohol consumption (direct and indirect causes of death include drunk driving, cirrhosis of the liver, falls, cancer, and stroke). The 17,000 yearly death rate due to illicit drug use is significantly lower in comparison to yearly alcohol and tobacco death rates. Moreover, the average American is 25 times more likely to die from tobacco-related illnesses (cardiovascular diseases, respiratory diseases, and cancer) than from illicit drug-related illnesses. More deaths are caused each year by tobacco use than by all deaths from human immunodeficiency virus (HIV), illegal drug use, alcohol use, motor vehicle injuries, suicides, and murders combined. Americans are five times more likely to die from alcohol-related illnesses than from illicit drug use.

Data from Mokdad, A. H., J. S. Marks, D. F. Stroup, and J. L. Gerberding. "Actual Causes of Death in the United States, 2000." *Journal of the American Medical Association (JAMA)*, 291 (10 March 2004):1238–1245; Centers for Disease Control and Prevention (CDC). "Smoking and Tobacco Use: Tobacco-Related Mortality." 2015a. Available http://www.cdc.gov/tobacco/data_statistics/fact_sheets/health_effects/tobacco_related_mortality/; Centers for Disease Control and Prevention (CDC). "Fact Sheets—Alcohol Use and Your Health." 2015b. Available http://www.cdc.gov/alcohol/fact-sheets/alcohol-use.htm; Centers for Disease Control and Prevention (CDC). "2013 Mortality Multiple Cause Micro-Data Files." Atlanta, GA: Centers for Disease Control and Prevention, 2014.

on the public health hazards from cigarettes again is leading some people to consider new measures to restrict or even outlaw tobacco smoking.

Table 1.2 introduces some of the terminology that you will encounter throughout this text. It is important that you understand how the definitions vary.

TABLE 1.2 Commonly Used Terms

Term	Description
Gateway drugs	The word *gateway* suggests a path or entryway leading to an entrance. Gateway is a theory that the early use of alcohol, tobacco products, and marijuana (the most heavily used illicit type of drug) leads to the use of more powerfully addictive drugs such as cocaine, heroin, and highly addictive prescription medicines.
Medicines	Compounds generally prescribed by a physician that treat, prevent, or alleviate the symptoms of disease. (These can also include over-the-counter [OTC] drugs purchased at pharmacies.)
Prescription medicines	Drugs that are prescribed by a physician. Common examples include antibiotics, antidepressants, and drugs prescribed to relieve pain, induce stimulation, or induce relaxation. These drugs are taken under a physician's recommendation because they are more potent than OTC drugs. In the United States, on a yearly basis, physicians write approximately 4.0 billion prescriptions (The Henry J. Kaiser Family Foundation 2015), with sales totaling $374 billion in 2015 (Chicago Tribune 2015).
Over-the-counter (OTC)	OTC drugs can be purchased at will without seeking medical advice or a prescription. Examples include aspirin, laxatives, diet pills, cough suppressants, and sore throat medicines. Approximately 1000 active ingredients are used in the more than 100,000 OTC products available in the marketplace today (Consumer Healthcare Products Association [CHPA] 2012), and it is estimated that there are more than 300,000 marketed OTC drug products (U.S. Food and Drug Administration 2015). In 2010, $23 billion was spent in the United States on OTC medicines* (CHPA 2012).
Drug misuse	The unintentional or inappropriate use of prescribed or OTC drugs. Misuse includes, but is not limited to, (I) taking more drugs than prescribed; (2) using OTC or psychoactive drugs in excess without medical supervision; (3) mixing drugs with alcohol or other drugs, often to accentuate euphoric effects or simply not caring about the effects of mixing drugs; (4) using old medicines to self-treat new symptoms of an illness or ailment; (5) discontinuing certain prescribed drugs at will or against a physician's recommendation; and (6) administering prescription drugs to family members or friends without medical approval and supervision.
Drug abuse	Also known as *chemical or substance abuse*. The willful misuse of either licit or illicit drugs for recreation, perceived necessity, or convenience. Drug abuse differs from drug use in that drug use is taking or using drugs, whereas drug abuse is a more intense and often willful misuse of drugs, often to the point of becoming addicted.
Drug addiction	Drug addiction involves noncasual or nonrecreational drug use. A frequent symptom is intense psychological preoccupation with obtaining and consuming drugs. Most often psychological and—in some cases, depending on the drug—physiological symptoms of withdrawal are manifested when the craving for the drug is not satisfied. Today, more emphasis is placed on the psychological craving (mental attachment) to the drug than on the more physiologically based withdrawal symptoms of addiction.

*This amount excludes OTC sales by Walmart and does not include vitamins, minerals, and nutritional supplements.
Data from The Henry J. Kaiser Family Foundation. "Total Number of Retail Prescription Drugs Filled at Pharmacies." Kaiser Family Foundations, 2016. Available http://kff.org/other/state-indicator/total-retail-rx-drugs/?currentTimeframe=0&sortModel=%7B"colId": "Location","sort":"asc"%7D;Tribune Wire Reports. "U.S. Prescription Drug Spending Jumps to Record $374 Billion." *Chicago Tribune*, 14 April 2015. Available http://www.chicagotribune.com/business/ct-drug-spending-0415-biz-20150414-story.html; U.S. Food and Drug Administration. "Drug Applications for Over-the-Counter (OTC) Drugs." 2015. Available http://www.fda.gov/drugs /developmentapprovalprocess/howdrugsaredevelopedandapproved/approvalapplications/over-the-counterdrugs/default.htm; Consumer Healthcare Products Association (CHPA). "The Value of OTC Medicine to the United States." Washington, DC: Booz&Co and Consumer Healthcare Productions Association, 2012. Available http://www.yourhealthathand.org/images/uploads/The_Value_of_OTC_Medicine _to_the_United_States_BoozCo.pdf

Major Types of Commonly Abused Drugs

The six types of major drugs in use are (1) prescription drugs, (2) over-the-counter drugs, (3) recreational drugs (e.g., coffee, tea, alcohol, tobacco, and chocolate), (4) illicit drugs, (5) herbal preparations (generally derived from plants), and (6) commercial drugs (paints, glues, pesticides, and household cleaning products).

To begin, we now briefly examine the major drugs of use and often abuse. The drugs examined next are prescription drugs, performance-enhancing drugs, stimulants, bath salts, hallucinogens (psychedelics) and other similar compounds, depressants, alcohol, nicotine, cannabis (marijuana and hashish), synthetic cannabis (Spice and K2), anabolic steroids, inhalants/organic solvents, narcotics/opiates, and designer drugs/synthetic drugs and synthetic opioids. A brief overview of each is provided.

▌ Prescription and Performance-Enhancing Drugs

In the United States, young people frequently abuse prescription drugs; the only illicit drug that is abused more frequently is marijuana (Center for Behavioral Health Statistics and Quality [CBHSQ] 2015). In 2015, 2.5% of illicit drug users, more than 6.5 million people aged 12 or older, used prescription-type psychotherapeutic drugs nonmedically.

> *Misuse and abuse of prescription medicine continues to be the third most prevalent drug abuse behavior measured among teens, following use of marijuana and alcohol. In addition, Hispanic and African American teens are more likely to report misusing or abusing prescription drugs compared to their Caucasian counterparts, with 27% of Hispanics, 29% of African Americans, and 20% of Caucasians reporting use (Partnership for Drug-Free Kids and MetLife Foundation 2013).*

An estimated 655,000 adolescents aged 12 to 17 were current nonmedical users of

prescription-type psychotherapeutic drugs in 2014. This number corresponds to 2.6% of adolescents. Similarly, with regard to nonmedical use of prescription-type psychotherapeutic drugs among young adults aged 18 to 25, in 2014 an estimated 1.6 million were current users, which corresponds to 4.4% of young adults (CBHSQ 2015). By comparison, 8.4% of the population aged 12 or older were current users of marijuana.

A number of national studies and published reports indicate that the intentional abuse of prescription drugs such as pain relievers, tranquilizers, stimulants, and sedatives to get high is a growing concern—particularly among teens—in the United States. Psychotherapeutic drugs warrant special attention, given that they now make up a significantly larger part of the overall U.S. drug problem than was true 10 to 15 years ago. This is, in part, because use increased for many prescription drugs over that period and because use of a number of street drugs has declined substantially since the middle to late 1990s. It seems likely that young people are less concerned about the dangers of using these prescription drugs outside of a medical regimen because they are widely used for legitimate purposes. (Indeed, the low levels of perceived risk for sedatives and amphetamines observed among 12th graders illustrate this point.) Also, prescription psychotherapeutic drugs are now being advertised directly to the consumer, which implies that they are both widely used and safe to use (Johnston et al. 2016).

In fact, among young people ages 12 to 17 prescription drugs have become the second most abused illegal drug, behind marijuana (CBHSQ 2015). The National Institute on Drug Abuse (NIDA 2014a and CBHSQ 2015) reported that its national survey found that 20% of high school students said they had taken a drug such as Ritalin, Xanax, or OxyContin without having a doctor's prescription, and, according to the Centers for Disease Control and Prevention (CDC 2010), one in five U.S. high school students have taken a prescription drug without a doctor's prescription. In 2014, Adderall and Vicodin were the two prescription drugs abused most often by adolescents (NIDA 2014a).

Three categories of prescription drugs that are currently abused are narcotics, depressants, and stimulants. Narcotics (e.g., OxyContin, Vicodin, Percocet) include analgesics or **opioids** that are generally prescribed for physical pain. Abuse occurs when they are used nonmedically because

KEY TERM

opioids
drugs derived from opium

of their euphoric and numbing effects. Depressants (e.g., Xanax, Valium, Librium) are generally used to treat anxiety and sleep disorders. These drugs are abused because of their sedating properties. Stimulants (e.g., Ritalin, Dexedrine, Meridia) are used to treat attention deficit disorder (ADD), attention deficit hyperactivity disorder (ADHD), and asthma. These drugs are abused because of their euphoric effects and energizing potential.

The two drugs in the stimulants category that are most often abused are Ritalin (methylphenidate hydrochloride) and Adderall (amphetamine). These prescription drugs are legitimately prescribed for ADHD, ADD, and narcolepsy (a sleep disorder) (Center for Substance Abuse Research [CESAR] 2003). When used nonmedically, they are taken orally as tablets or the tablets are crushed into a powder and snorted (a far more popular method). Students often illegally purchase these tablets for $5 each from other students who have a legal prescription for the medication.

> I feel like Dr. Pill. All these brothers [fraternity brothers] are always looking for me at parties so that I can sell them a few tabs. What the heck, I make extra money selling Ritalin, enough to buy essentials like beer and cigarettes. *(From Venturelli's research files, male undergraduate student at a Midwestern university, age 20, December 9, 2004)*

And,

> Funny how when I go back to the frat house during homecoming there are other undergrads who have taken over my business and continue to sell their prescribed Ritalin mostly for partying. *(A second interview with the same former student, age 26, now employed in real estate, October 2, 2010)*

These drugs often are used in conjunction with alcohol or marijuana to enhance the high or for staying awake to increase comprehension and remain focused while reading or studying for an exam (CESAR 2003). Both prescription drugs (Ritalin and Adderall) are readily available and can be easily obtained by teenagers, who may abuse these drugs to experience a variety of desired effects. Increasingly, younger adolescents are obtaining prescription drugs from classmates, friends, and family members or are stealing the drugs from school medicine dispensaries and from other people for whom the drug has been legitimately prescribed.

Ritalin, Adderall, and other stimulant abusers tend to be late middle school, high school, and college students. Other findings regarding teen abuse of stimulants Ritalin and Adderall include the following (Partnership for Drug-Free Kids 2016):

- One in eight teens (about 2.7 million) report having misused or abused Ritalin or Adderall at least once in their lifetime.
- 9% of teens (about 1.9 million) report having misused or abused Ritalin or Adderall in the past year.
- One in four teens (26%) believe that prescription drugs can be used as a study aid.
- Almost one-third of parents (29%) say they believe that ADHD medication can improve a child's academic or testing performance, even if the teen does not have ADHD.
- One in six parents (16%) believe that using prescription drugs to get high is safer than using street drugs.
- More than half of teens (56%) indicate that it is easy to get prescription drugs from their parents' medicine cabinet. In fact, about half of parents (49%) say anyone can access their medicine cabinet.

In addition, the Partnership for Drug-Free Kids and MetLife Foundation (2013) note that Hispanic and African American teens are more likely to report misusing or abusing prescription drugs compared to their white counterparts, with 27% of Hispanics, 29% of African Americans, and 20% of Caucasians reporting use.

With regard to college students using Adderall, the findings include the following (Muir Wood 2016):

- Full-time college students were twice as likely as non–full-time college students to abuse Adderall.
- About 6.4% of college students admitted to unauthorized Adderall use in 2006–2007.
- College students who abused Adderall were three times as likely to abuse marijuana, eight times as likely to abuse prescription tranquilizers, and five times as likely to abuse prescription painkillers.
- Cocaine use is more common among college students who use Adderall, and students who use both drugs face an increased risk of heart attack, heart problems, and stroke.

■ Stimulants

Some stimulants can be considered to be **gateway drugs** (see definition in Table 1.2); these substances act on the CNS by increasing alertness, excitation, euphoria, pulse rate, and blood pressure. Insomnia and loss of appetite are common outcomes. The user initially experiences pleasant effects, such as a sense of increased energy and a state of euphoria, or "high." In addition, users feel restless and talkative and have trouble sleeping. High doses used over the long term can produce personality changes. Some of the psychological risks associated with chronic stimulant use include violent, erratic, or paranoid behavior. Other effects can include confusion, anxiety, and depression and loss of interest in sex or food. *Major stimulants* include amphetamines, cocaine and crack, methamphetamine (meth), and methylphenidate (Ritalin). *Minor stimulants* include, cocoa, theophylline, theobromine, sugar, caffeine, and nicotine (the most addictive minor stimulant).

■ Bath Salts

Bath salts are a designer drug that contains substituted cathinones; they produce similar effects as amphetamines and cocaine (Coppola and Mondola 2012; Spiller et al. 2011). The usual method of taking this drug is sniffing or snorting, but it can also be taken orally, smoked, or mixed with a solution and then injected into a vein. According to Dr. Mark Ryan, director of the Louisiana Poison Center, bath salts are "the worst drug" he has seen in his 20 years there, noting that "with LSD, you might see pink elephants, but with this drug, you see demons, aliens, extreme paranoia, heart attacks, and superhuman strength like Superman. . . . If you had a reaction, it was a bad reaction" (Vargas-Cooper 2012, p. 60). Other reactions include "very severe paranoia, suicidal thoughts, agitation, combative/violent behavior, confusion, hallucination/psychosis, increased heart rate, hypertension, chest pain, death or serious injury. The speed of onset is 15 minutes, while the length of the high from these drugs is 4–6 hours" (Partnership at DrugFree.Org 2013). In October 2011, these synthetic stimulants were listed as Schedule I substances under the Controlled Substances Act. The Drug Enforcement Administration (DEA) classifies illicit drugs under Schedules I through V, largely depending on their abuse potential. Synthetic stimulants are classified as Schedule I drugs, meaning that they have a high potential for abuse.

■ Hallucinogens/Psychedelics and Other Similar Drugs

Whether synthetic or grown naturally, hallucinogens and psychedelic drugs produce a very intense alteration of perceptions, thoughts, and feelings. They most certainly influence the complex inner workings of the human mind, causing users to refer to these drugs as psychedelics (because they cause hallucinations or distortion of reality and thinking). In addition to amplifying states of mind, hallucinogens induce a reality that is

Courtesy of DEA.

Packets of bath salts sold in head shops.

Courtesy of DEA.

reported to be qualitatively different from that of ordinary consciousness. For example, while the user is under their influence, these drugs can affect the senses of taste, smell, hearing, and vision. Tolerance to hallucinogens builds very rapidly, which means that increasing amounts of this drug are needed for similar effects. Hallucinogens

KEY TERM

gateway drugs
alcohol, tobacco, and marijuana—types of drugs that when used excessively may lead to using other and more addictive drugs such as cocaine, heroin, or "crack"

include LSD, mescaline, **MDMA** (Ecstasy), phency-clidine (PCP), psilocybin or "magic mushrooms," ketamine, and the more potent (hybrid) varieties of marijuana, hashish, and opium that are smoked.

■ Depressants

These drugs depress the CNS. If taken in a high enough quantity, they produce insensibility or stupor. Depressants are also taken for some of the same reasons as hallucinogens, such as to relieve boredom, stress, or anxiety. In addition, the effects of both opioids (drugs that are derived from opium) and morphine derivatives appeal to many people who are struggling with emotional problems and looking for physical and emotional relief, and in some cases to induce sleep. Depressants include alcohol (ethanol), barbiturates, benzodiazepines (such as diazepam [Valium]), and methaqualone (Quaalude).

■ Alcohol

Known as a gateway drug, **ethanol** is a colorless, volatile, and pungent liquid produced through the fermentation of grains, berries, or other fruits and vegetables. Alcohol is a depressant that mainly affects the CNS. Excessive amounts of alcohol often cause a progressive loss of inhibitions, flushing and dizziness, loss of coordination, impaired motor skills, blurred vision, slurred speech, sudden mood swings, vomiting, irregular pulse, and memory impairment. Chronic heavy use may lead to high blood pressure, arrhythmia (irregular heartbeat), and cirrhosis (severe liver deterioration).

■ Nicotine

Nicotine is also considered a gateway drug. It is a very addictive, colorless, highly volatile liquid alkaloid found in all tobacco products, including cigarettes, chewing tobacco, pipe tobacco, and cigars. Because nicotine is highly addictive and tobacco use is still socially acceptable under certain circumstances, smokers often start young and have a very difficult time quitting. Long-term use of tobacco products can lead to several different chronic respiratory ailments and cancers.

■ Cannabis (Marijuana and Hashish)

Cannabis is the most widely used illicit drug* in the United States. Marijuana consists of the dried and crushed leaves, flowers, and seeds of the

---

*Federal law specifies that Cannabis is an illicit drug while state laws in 25+ states have currently legalized this drug.

Cannabis sativa plant, which readily grows in many parts of the world. Delta-9-tetrahydrocannabinol (THC) is the primary psychoactive, mind-altering ingredient in marijuana that produces euphoria (often referred to as a "high"). Plant parts (mainly the leaves and buds of the plant) are usually dried, crushed, and smoked much like tobacco products. Other ways of ingesting marijuana include finely crushing the leaves and mixing them into the butter or oil that goes into cookie or brownie batter and baking the batter. Another current derivative is **marijuana wax**, also known as wax or ear wax, butter, honey oil, shatter, BHO (which stands for "butane honey oil" or "butane hash oil"), and dabs. To date, this is one of the most powerful and the most potent (80% pure THC) types of marijuana on both the illegal and legal drug markets (in states where marijuana has either been decriminalized or medically sanctioned), with smoking or vaporizing this type of marijuana leading to a "quicker, stronger high" (Kimble 2013). Finally, hashish is a cannabis derivative that contains the purest form of resin and also has very high amounts of THC.

■ Designer Drugs/Synthetic Drugs or Synthetic Opioids

In addition to the most commonly abused illicit drug categories just described, innovations in technology have produced new categories known as **designer drugs/synthetic drugs or synthetic opioids**. These relatively new types of drugs are developed by people who seek to circumvent the

KEY TERMS

MDMA
a type of illicit drug known as Ecstasy or Adam and having stimulant and hallucinogenic properties

ethanol
the pharmacological term for alcohol; a consumable type of alcohol that is the psychoactive ingredient in alcoholic beverages; often called grain alcohol

marijuana wax
a more recent, extremely potent cannabis product with approximately 80% THC levels made by using butane to extract the THC, producing a "waxy" residue that is smoked or vaporized that is highly hallucinogenic, often resulting in high levels of physical and mental impairment

designer drugs/synthetic drugs or synthetic opioids
new drugs that are developed by people intending to circumvent the illegality of a drug by modifying a drug into a new compound; Ecstasy is an example

Designer pills made from the illicit drug Ecstasy. This drug has some stimulant properties like amphetamines as well as hallucinogenic properties like LSD.

illegality of a drug by modifying the drug into a new compound. Ecstasy is an example of a designer drug/synthetic drug or synthetic opioid. Such drugs are created as **structural analogs** of substances already scheduled and legally prohibited under the Controlled Substances Act. Structural analogs are the drugs that result from altered chemical structures of already existing illicit drugs. Generally, these drugs are created by an underground chemist whose goal is to make a profit by creating compounds that mimic, change, or intensify the psychoactive effects of controlled substances. The number of designer drugs that are created and sold illegally is very large.

Anyone with knowledge of college-level chemistry can alter the chemical ingredients and produce new designer drugs, although it may be nearly impossible to predict their properties or effects except by trial and error. Currently, three major types of synthetic analog drugs are available through the illicit drug market: analogs of PCP; analogs of fentanyl and meperidine (both synthetic narcotic analgesics), such as Demerol or MPPP (also called MPTP or PEPAP); and analogs of amphetamine and methamphetamine (which have stimulant and hallucinogenic properties), such as MDMA, known as Ecstasy or Adam, which is widely used on college campuses as a euphoriant.

The production of these high-technology psychoactive substances is a sign of the new levels of

KEY TERM

structural analogs
a new molecular species created by modifying the basic molecular skeleton of a compound; structural analogs are structurally related to the parent compound

risk and additional challenge to the criminal justice system. As the production and risk associated with the use of such substances increase, the need for a broader, better-informed view of drug use becomes even more important than in the past.

SYNTHETIC CANNABIS: SPICE AND K2

Synthetic marijuana is made by mixing a raw Schedule I drug and analogue powder chemicals with surfactants, acetone, and glue and then spraying it with *damiana*, a dried vegetable matter, to create a product that can be smoked. To manufacture bath salts, Schedule I drugs and analogues are mixed and cut with adulterants and then packaged for snorting or ingesting (U.S. Department of Justice 2016).

Synthetic cannabinoids are substances that are designed to affect the body in a manner similar to marijuana but that are not derived from the marijuana plant (Office of National Drug Control Policy [ONDCP] 2013b). They are most often smoked like marijuana. Street names for synthetic cannabis include Spice, K2, Mr. Smiley, Red X Dawn, and Blaze. "A package of K2, a synthetic marijuana, is a concoction of dried herbs sprayed with chemicals, used in the herbal blends that are sold in head shops on the Internet to a growing number of teens and young adults" (Caldwell 2010, p. 30). Many of the contents are listed as inactive on the product packaging (DEA 2012). A retired organic chemistry researcher from Clemson University reports such medical problems from synthetic cannabis use as "overdoses, cases of addiction, and even suicide" (Caldwell 2010, p. 30).

K2 contains synthetic cannabinoids that affect the body in similar fashion as marijuana.

K2 and Spice are generic trademarks that first went on sale in 2000, initially as legal herbs. Several years later, it was discovered that they contained synthetic cannabinoids that affected the body in a similar fashion as marijuana (cannabis). In July 2012, federal law placed this drug under Schedule I, making it an illegal drug with the highest abuse potential. The illegality of this drug removed it from retail sales.

As mentioned, prior to 2012, Spice was sold as a legal herb-based alternative to cannabis. The ingredients list contained only herbs, with no cannabinoid constituents; however, the listed ingredients seemed suspiciously unlikely to produce the drug's reported effects. Herbs listed on packages of Spice included *Nymphaea caerulea, Leonotis leonurus, Zornia latifolia, Canavalia maritima, Scutellaria nana, Pedicularis densiflora, Nelumbo nucifera*, and *Leonurus sibiricus*. A lab in Germany tested for the presence of these ingredients, and they were not found. Numerous other organizations have now tested the material, and three chemicals have been identified in various Spice products, including JWH-018, HU-210, and a homologue of CP-47,497 (Erowid Center 2013). In addition to these three chemicals, which were recently outlawed under the jurisdiction of the Emergency Controlled Substances Act, the following have also been added as controlled substances: AM678, JWH-019, JWH-200, JWH-250, JWH-081, JWH-122, JWH-398, AM2201, AM694, SR-19 and RCS-4, SR-18 and RCS-8, and JWH-203 (Erowid Center 2013).

Another study indicated that the following have been found in samples of Spice (U.S. Department of Justice 2011):

- *CP-47,497*: A synthetic cannabinoid agonist without the classical cannabinoid chemical

structure. Although CP-47,497 is likely to have similar effects in humans as delta-9-tetrahydrocannabinol (Δ9-THC), the main active ingredient of marijuana, CP-47,497 and its homologues are now a controlled substance classified as a Schedule I drug in the United States.

- *HU-210 and HU-211*: First synthesized around 1988, these are structurally and pharmacologically similar to Δ9-THC. HU-210 was recently purported to be found in the herbal mixture Spice, sold in European countries mainly via Internet shops. HU-210 is a Schedule I controlled substance in the United States; HU-211 is not a controlled substance in the United States, although it may fall under the federal Analogue Act of outlawed drugs because it is categorized as a THC substance and is similar to those THC substances that occur naturally in marijuana.

- *JWH-018, JWH-073, and JWH-074*: These are synthetic cannabinoid agonists without the classic cannabinoid chemical structure. The substances have been identified in herbal products such as Spice, K2, and others sold via the Internet and head shops. Although JWH-018, JWH-073, and JWH-074 are likely to have the same effects in humans as Δ9-THC, they are not controlled in the United States.

The U.S. Army, U.S. Marines, U.S. Air Force, and U.S. Navy have also outlawed this drug, and violators risk immediate expulsion from service and incarceration. (For information regarding the extent of Spice use, see "Here and Now: Spice/K2: Past and Current Usage Rates.")

HERE AND NOW
Spice/K2: Past and Current Usage Rates

Spice, also known as herbal incense, is dried, shredded plant material treated with a cannabinoid analog. Although labels on spice products will list the ingredients as "natural" psychoactive plant products, chemical analyses show that their active ingredients are primarily synthetic cannabinoids added to the plant material. These synthetic analogs function similarly to the active ingredient in marijuana, delta-9-tetrahydrocannabinol (Δ9-THC) (Substance Abuse and Mental Health Services Administration [SAMHSA] 2014).

K2 and Spice are two names for a more recently created psychoactive designer drug whose dried, leafy, natural herbs are sprayed with a psychoactive

chemical; it is then smoked so the user can experience euphoric effects. In 2011, prior to the Synthetic Drug Abuse Prevention Act being signed into law, one in nine U.S. high school seniors reported having used synthetic marijuana. A large sample survey found that annual prevalence was 11.4%, ranking synthetic marijuana as the second most widely used class of illicit drug after marijuana among 12th graders (Johnston et al. 2013). In 2012, use among 12th graders remained virtually unchanged at 11.3%. Eighth, 10th, and 12th graders were asked if they associated a great risk with trying synthetic marijuana once or twice; the results showed that there was quite a low level of perceived

(continues)

HERE AND NOW

Spice/K2: Past and Current Usage Rates (*continued*)

risk (only 23% and 25%, respectively, thought there was great risk in using once or twice).

Another study at a large public university in the state of Georgia between November 2011 and March 2012 found that 14% of undergraduate students reported synthetic cannabinoid use, with the highest level of use among male students largely identifying with the lesbian, gay, bisexual, or transgender (LGBT) community (CESAR 2013). This was the first known study to obtain a detailed profile of users of any type of synthetic cannabinoid. Findings indicated the following:

1. The average age of first use was 18 years.

2. The percentage ever using synthetic cannabinoids was twice as high for males as for females (19% vs. 9%).

3. Heavier users were more likely to identify themselves as LGBT; significantly less usage was found in students identifying themselves as heterosexual (27% vs. 14%).

More current findings are that "[e]fforts at the federal and state levels to close down the sale of these substances appear to be having an effect" (Johnston et al. 2015). Use fell by a statistically significant amount in 2015 for the three grades combined (8th, 10th, and 12th graders). The percentages of students saying they used any synthetic marijuana in the past 12 months now stand at 3%, 4%, and 5% in grades 8, 10, and 12, respectively—down considerably from the 4%, 9%, and 11% observed in those same grades in 2012. According to the authors of the study, "While there has been some increase in the proportion of students seeing use of this drug as dangerous, it hardly seems enough to account for the considerable declines in use, which leads us to conclude that efforts to reduce availability have been successful to some degree" (Johnston et al. 2015).

Data from Johnston, L. D., P. M. O'Malley, J. G. Bachman, and J. E. Schulenberg. *Monitoring the Future National Results on Drug Use: 2012 Overview, Key Findings on Adolescent Drug Use.* Ann Arbor, MI: Institute for Social Research, The University of Michigan, 2013; Center for Substance Abuse Research (CESAR). "Study Finds that 14% of Undergraduate Students at a Southeastern University Report Synthetic Cannabinoid Use; Users More Likely to Be Male and Identify as LGBT." *CESAR FAX* (20 May 2013). Available http://www.cesar.umd.edu; Johnston, L. D., P. M. O'Malley, R. A. Miech, J. G. Bachman, and J. E. Schulenberg. *Monitoring the Future National Survey Results on Drug Use, 1975–2015: Overview, Key Findings on Adolescent Drug Use.* Ann Arbor, MI: Institute for Social Research, The University of Michigan, February 2016.

Inhalants. These volatile chemicals, which include many common household substances, are often the most dangerous drug, per dose, a person can take. In addition, inhalants are most often used by young children.

■ Anabolic Steroids

Steroids are a synthetic form of the male hormone testosterone. They are often used to increase muscle size and strength. Medically, steroids are used to increase body tissue, treat allergies, or reduce swelling. Steroids are available in either liquid or pill form. Athletes have a tendency to use and abuse these drugs because dramatic results can occur with regard to increased body mass and muscle tissue. Some side effects include heart disease, liver cancer, high blood pressure, septic shock, impotence, genital atrophy, manic episodes, depression, violence, and mood swings.

■ Inhalants/Organic Solvents

Inhalants and organic solvents also are often considered gateway drugs and are very attractive to and popular among preteens and younger teenagers. Products used include gasoline, model airplane glue, and paint thinner. When inhaled, the vapors from these solvents can produce euphoric effects. Organic solvents can also refer to certain foods, herbs, and vitamins, such as "herbal Ecstasy."

© Michael Newman/PhotoEdit, Inc.

■ Narcotics/Opiates

These drugs depress the CNS and, if taken in a high enough quantity, produce insensibility or stupor. Narcotics or opiates are highly addictive. Narcotics include heroin, opium, morphine, codeine, meperidine (often a substitute for morphine, also known as Demerol), Darvon, and Percodan.

An Overview of Drugs in Society

Many people think that problems with drugs are unique to this era. In reality, drug use and abuse have always been part of nearly all—past and present—human societies. For example, the Grecian oracles of Delphi used drugs, Homer's Cup of Helen induced sleep and provided freedom from care, and the mandrake root mentioned in the first book of the Bible, Genesis, produced a hallucinogenic effect. In Genesis 30:14–16, the mandrake is mentioned in association with bartering for lovemaking:

> In the time of wheat harvest Reuben went out, found some mandrakes in the open country, and brought them to his mother Leah. Then Rachel asked Leah for some of her son's mandrakes, but Leah said, "Is it so small a thing to have taken away my husband, that you should take my son's mandrakes as well?" However, Rachel said, "Very well, let him sleep with you tonight in exchange for your son's mandrakes." So when Jacob came in from the country in the evening, Leah went out to meet him and said, "You are to sleep with me tonight; I have hired you with my son's mandrakes." That night he slept with her.

Ancient literature is filled with references to the use of mushrooms, datura, hemp, marijuana, opium poppies, and so on. Under the influence of some of these drugs, many people experienced extreme ecstasy or sheer terror. Some old pictures of demons and devils look very much like those described by modern drug users during so-called bummers, or bad trips. The belief that witches could fly may also have been drug induced because many natural preparations used in so-called witches' brews induced the sensation of disassociation from the body, as in flying or floating.

As far back as 2240 BC, attempts were made to regulate drug use. For instance, in that year, problem drinking was addressed in the Code of Hammurabi, where it was described as "a problem of men with too much leisure time and lazy dispositions." Nearly every culture has experienced drug abuse, and as found in the historical record, laws were enacted to control the use of certain types of drugs.

■ How Widespread Is Drug Abuse?

As mentioned earlier, drug abuse today is more acute and widespread than in any previous age (see "Here and Now: Numbers of Past Month: Illicit Drug Users and Illicit Drug Use Among People Aged 12 or Older by Age Group"). The evidence for this development is how often large quantities of illicit drugs are seized in the United States as well as throughout the world (see "Here and Now: *The World Factbook*: Current Global Status of Illicit Drugs and Drug Use"). Media exposure about illicit drug use is more likely to occur today than in the past. On any given day, you can scan most major national and international newspapers and run across stories about illegal drug manufacture, storage and distribution, use and/or abuse, and convictions. Drug use is an "**equal-opportunity affliction**." This means that no one is immune from the use and/or abuse of both licit and illicit drugs. Research shows that drug consumption is found across the many different

Amanda Geiger never saw the drunk driver.

Friends Don't Let Friends Drive Drunk.

Photo by Michael Mazzeo

U.S. Department of Transportation

Courtesy of the Advertising Council.

Although the media is often credited with glamorizing dangerous drug use, many successful prevention campaigns have used TV, radio, and print media as outlets. Since the Advertising Council began their "Friends Don't Let Friends Drive Drunk" campaign, 79% of Americans have stopped an intoxicated friend from getting behind the wheel.

KEY TERM

equal-opportunity affliction
refers to the use of drugs, stressing that drug use cuts across all members of society regardless of income, education, occupation, social class, or age

income, education, social class, occupation, race and ethnic, lifestyle, and age groups. To date, no one has proved to be immune from drug use and/or abuse.

Many of us, for example, are dismayed or surprised when we discover that certain individuals we admire—our family members (a mother, father, aunt, uncle, cousin, grandparent), close friends, workmates, celebrities, politicians, athletes, clergy, law enforcement personnel, physicians, academics,

and even the seemingly upstanding man or woman next door—either admit to, are accused of, need treatment for, or are arrested for licit and/or illicit drug use. We are also taken aback when we hear that cigarettes, alcohol, and marijuana abuse are commonplace in many public and private middle schools. Furthermore, most of us know of at least one (and many times more than one) close friend or family member who appears to secretly or not so secretly use drugs.

HERE AND NOW

Numbers of Past-Month Illicit Drug Users and Age Groups by People Aged 12 and Older, 2014

In 2014, an estimated 27 million Americans aged 12 or older were current (past-month) illicit drug users, meaning that they had used an illicit drug during the month prior to the survey interview (**Figure A**). The most commonly used illicit drug in the past month was marijuana, which was used by 22.2 million people aged 12 or older. An estimated 6.5 million people

reported nonmedical use of psychotherapeutic drugs in the past month, including 4.3 million nonmedical users of prescription pain relievers. Thus, the number of current nonmedical users of pain relievers was second to marijuana among specific illicit drugs. Smaller numbers of people in 2014 were current users of the other illicit drugs shown in Figure A.

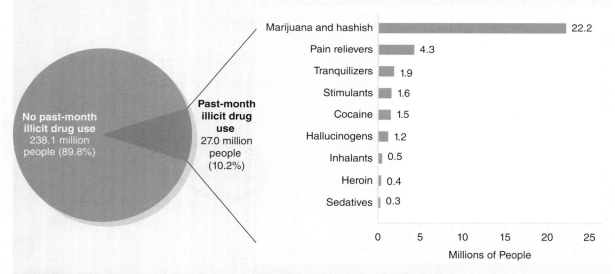

FIGURE A   Number of past-month illicit drug users among persons aged 12 or older: 2014.

Data from Center for Behavioral Health Statistics and Quality (CBHSQ). Behavioral health trends in the United States: Results from the 2014 National Survey on Drug Use and Health. Rockville, MD: Substance Abuse and Mental Health Services (SAMHSA), HHS Publication No. SMA 15-4927, NSDUH Series H-50, 2015. Available http://www.samhsa.gov/ data/

The estimated 27 million people aged 12 or older who were current illicit drug users in 2014 (Figure A) represent 10.2% of the population aged 12 or older (**Figure B**). Stated another way, 1 in 10 individuals aged 12 or older in the United States used illicit drugs in the past month. The percentage of people aged 12 or older who were current illicit drug users

in 2014 was higher than the percentages from 2002 to 2013. The rise in illicit drug use among those aged 12 or older since 2002 may reflect an increase in illicit drug use by adults aged 26 or older and, to a lesser extent, increases in illicit drug use among young adults aged 18 to 25 relative to the years before 2009.

HERE AND NOW

Numbers of Past-Month Illicit Drug Users and Age Groups by People Aged 12 and Older, 2014 (*continued*)

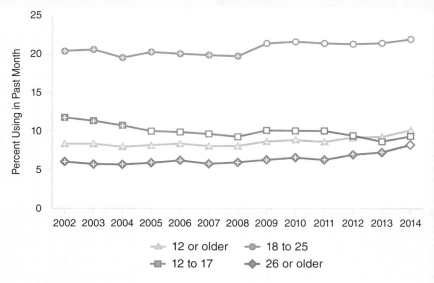

+ Difference between this estimate and the 2014 estimate is statistically significant at the .05 level.

FIGURE B   Past-month illicit drug use among persons aged 12 or older by age group: 2001–2014.

Data from Center for Behavioral Health Statistics and Quality (CBHSQ). Behavioral health trends in the United States: Results from the 2014 National Survey on Drug Use and Health. Rockville, MD: Substance Abuse and Mental Health Services (SAMHSA), HHS Publication No. SMA 15-4927, NSDUH Series H-50, 2015. Available http://www.samhsa.gov/ data/

....

Data from Center for Behavioral Health Statistics and Quality (CBHSQ). *Behavioral Health Trends in the United States: Results from the 2014 National Survey on Drug Use and Health.* NSDUH Series H-50, HHS Publication No. (SMA) 15-4927, Rockville, MD: Substance Abuse and Mental Health Services, 2015. Available http://www.samhsa.gov/data/

■ Extent and Frequency of Drug Use in Society

Erich Goode (2012), a much-respected sociologist, lists four types of drug use:

- *Legal instrumental use.* Taking prescribed drugs and OTC drugs to relieve or treat mental or physical symptoms.
- *Legal recreational use.* Using such licit drugs as tobacco, alcohol, and caffeine to achieve a certain mental or psychic state.
- *Illegal instrumental use.* Taking drugs without a prescription to accomplish a task or goal, such as taking nonprescription amphetamines to drive through the night or relying excessively on barbiturates to get through the day.
- *Illegal recreational use.* Taking illicit drugs for fun or pleasure to experience euphoria, such as abusing prescribed methylphenidate (Ritalin) as a substitute for cocaine.

Why has the prevalence of licit and illicit drug use remained consistent since 1988? Why has this trend occurred, when federal, state, and local government expenditures for fighting the drug war have been increasing at the same time? There are several possible answers, none of which, by itself, offers a satisfactory response. One perspective notes that practically all of us use drugs in some form, with what constitutes "drug use" being merely a matter of degree. A second explanation is that more varieties of both licit and illicit drugs are available today. One source estimated that approximately 80% of all currently marketed drugs were either unknown or unavailable 30 years ago (Critser 1996). Regarding prescriptions, "the average number of prescriptions per person, annually, in 1993 was seven, and in 2005 it was 12 (Critser 2005, p. 23) and in 2011, 13 prescriptions per person in the U.S." Another source stated, "The retail sales of all OTC drugs that includes approximately 27 categories of drugs totaled over $32.1 billion in 2015" (CHPA 2016). In

HERE AND NOW

The World FactBook: Current Global Status of Illicit Drugs and Drug Use in Selected Countries

Afghanistan

Afghanistan is world's largest producer of opium; poppy cultivation increased 7%, to a record 211,000 hectares* in 2014 from 198,000 hectares in 2013, while eradication dropped sharply. However, Afghanistan has had relatively low opium yields due to poor weather that has kept potential opium production—6,300 metric tons—below the record set in 2007. The Taliban and other antigovernment groups participate in and profit from the opiate trade, which is a key source of revenue for the Taliban inside Afghanistan. Widespread corruption and instability in Afghanistan impede counterdrug efforts. Most of the heroin consumed in Europe and Eurasia is derived from Afghan opium. Afghanistan is also struggling to respond to a burgeoning domestic opiate addiction problem and is vulnerable to the laundering of drug money through informal financial networks. Afghanistan also has extensive illicit cultivation of cannabis and is a regional source of hashish.

Argentina

Argentina is a transshipment country for cocaine headed for Europe, heroin headed for the United States, and ephedrine and pseudoephedrine headed for Mexico. Some money laundering occurs, especially in the Tri-Border Area. Law enforcement corruption is also a problem. Argentina is a source for precursor chemicals, and there is increasing domestic consumption of drugs in urban centers, especially cocaine base and synthetic drugs (2008 data).

Aruba

This is a transit point for U.S.- and Europe-bound narcotics, with some accompanying money-laundering activity. A relatively high percentage of its population consumes cocaine.

Australia

Tasmania is one of the world's major suppliers of licit opiate products. The government maintains strict controls over areas of opium poppy cultivation and the output of poppy straw concentrate. It is a major consumer of cocaine and amphetamines.

Bahamas

The Bahamas is a transshipment point for cocaine and marijuana bound for the United States and Europe; it is also an offshore financial center.

Belgium

Belgium is a growing producer of synthetic drugs and cannabis. It is a transit point for U.S.-bound Ecstasy and a source of precursor chemicals for South American cocaine processors. It is a transshipment point for cocaine, heroin, hashish, and marijuana entering Western Europe. Despite a strengthening of legislation, the country remains vulnerable to money laundering related to narcotics, automobiles, alcohol, and tobacco. Significant domestic consumption of Ecstasy is also a problem.

Bolivia

Bolivia is the world's third-largest cultivator of coca (after Colombia and Peru), with an estimated 30,000 hectares under cultivation in 2011, a decrease of 13% over 2010. It is also the third-largest producer of cocaine, estimated at 265 metric tons of potential pure cocaine in 2011, a 29% increase over 2010. Bolivia is a transit country for Peruvian and Colombian cocaine destined for Brazil, Argentina, Chile, Paraguay, and Europe, due to its weak border controls. Money-laundering activity related to the narcotics trade is a problem, as is domestic cocaine consumption (2013).

Brazil

The second-largest consumer of cocaine in the world, Brazil is an important market for Colombian, Bolivian, and Peruvian cocaine. It is an illicit producer of cannabis and trace amounts of coca cultivation in the Amazon region, used for domestic consumption. The government has a large-scale eradication program to control cannabis. It is an important transshipment country for Bolivian, Colombian, and Peruvian cocaine headed for Europe and is also used by traffickers as a way station for narcotics air transshipments between Peru and Colombia. It has experienced an upsurge in drug-related violence and weapons smuggling. Illicit narcotics proceeds are often laundered through the financial system, with significant illicit financial activity in the Tri-Border Area (2008).

Burma

Burma is the world's third-largest producer of illicit opium, with estimated production in 2012 of 690 metric tons, an increase of 13% over 2011. Poppy cultivation in 2012 totaled 51,000 hectares, a 17% increase over 2011. Shan state is the source of 94.5% of

HERE AND NOW

The World FactBook: Current Global Status of Illicit Drugs and Drug Use in Selected Countries (continued)

Burma's poppy cultivation; lack of government will to take on major narco-trafficking groups and lack of serious commitment against money laundering continues to hinder the overall antidrug effort. It is a major source of methamphetamine and heroin for regional consumption (2013).

Canada

Canada is a producer of cannabis for the domestic drug market and export to United States. The use of hydroponics technology permits growers to plant large quantities of high-quality marijuana indoors, some of which is destined for the United States. Production of Ecstasy has also increased. Canada is vulnerable to narcotics money laundering because of its mature financial services sector.

China

China is a major transshipment point for heroin produced in the Golden Triangle region of Southeast Asia. Domestic consumption of synthetic drugs and heroin from Southeast and Southwest Asia is increasing. It is a source country for methamphetamine and heroin chemical precursors, despite new regulations on its large chemical industry. Nongovernmental organizations (NGOs) claim that more people have been convicted and executed for drug offences in China than anywhere else in the world (2008 data).

Colombia

Columbia is an illicit producer of coca, opium poppy, and cannabis. It is the world's leading coca cultivator, with 83,000 hectares in coca cultivation in 2011, a 17% decrease over 2010, producing the potential for 195 metric tons of pure cocaine. It is also is the world's largest producer of coca derivatives, and supplies cocaine to nearly all of the U.S. market and the great majority of other international drug markets. Columbia is an important supplier of heroin to the U.S. market, although opium poppy cultivation is estimated to have fallen to 1100 hectares in 2009, and pure heroin production to 2.1 metric tons. In 2012, aerial eradication efforts sprayed herbicide over 100,549 hectares, in addition to manual eradication of 30,486 hectares. A significant portion of narcotics proceeds are either laundered or invested in Colombia through the black market peso exchange.

Germany

Germany is a source of precursor chemicals for South American cocaine processors. It is a transshipment point for and consumer of Southwest Asian heroin, Latin American cocaine, and European-produced synthetic drugs. It is also a major financial center.

Guatemala

Guatemala is a major transit country for cocaine and heroin. In 2005, it cultivated 100 hectares of opium poppy after reemerging as a potential source of opium in 2004, with potential production of less than 1 metric ton of pure heroin. Marijuana cultivation is mostly for domestic consumption. Its proximity to Mexico makes Guatemala a major staging area for drug trafficking (particularly for cocaine). Money laundering and corruption are serious problems in Guatemala.

Haiti

Haiti is a Caribbean transshipment point for cocaine en route to the United States and Europe; there is also substantial bulk cash smuggling activity. Colombian narcotics traffickers favor Haiti for illicit financial transactions. Corruption is pervasive, and the country is a significant consumer of cannabis.

Iran

Despite substantial interdiction efforts and considerable control measures along the border with Afghanistan, Iran remains one of the primary transshipment routes for Southwest Asian heroin to Europe. Iran has reached out to neighboring countries to share counterdrug intelligence. It also suffers one of the highest opiate addiction rates in the world and has an increasing problem with synthetic drugs. Iran regularly enforces the death penalty for drug offences, but lacks anti-money-laundering laws.

Ireland

Ireland is a transshipment point for and consumer of hashish from North Africa en route to the United Kingdom and the Netherlands. It is also a minor transshipment point for heroin and cocaine destined for Western Europe. Ireland is also a consumer of European-produced synthetic drugs and South American cocaine. Despite recent legislation, narcotics-related money laundering that relies on currency exchanges,

(continues)

HERE AND NOW

The World FactBook: Current Global Status of Illicit Drugs and Drug Use in Selected Countries (*continued*)

trusts, and shell companies involving the offshore financial community remains a concern.

Israel

Israel is increasingly concerned about Ecstasy, cocaine, and heroin abuse. These drugs arrive in country from Lebanon and, increasingly, from Jordan. Israel is also a money-laundering center.

Italy

Italy is an important gateway for and consumer of Latin American cocaine and Southwest Asian heroin entering the European market. Organized crime is involved in money laundering and smuggling.

Mexico

A major drug-producing and transit nation, Mexico is the world's second-largest opium poppy cultivator. Opium poppy cultivation in 2009 rose 31% over 2008 to 19,500 hectares, yielding a potential production of 50 metric tons of pure heroin, or 125 metric tons of "black tar" heroin, the dominant form of Mexican heroin in the western United States. Marijuana cultivation increased 45% to 17,500 hectares in 2009. The Mexican government conducts the largest independent illicit-crop eradication program in the world. Mexico continues to be the primary transshipment country for U.S.-bound cocaine from South America, with an estimated 95% of annual cocaine movements toward the United States stopping in Mexico. Major drug syndicates control the majority of drug trafficking throughout the country. It is a producer and distributor of Ecstasy, a significant money-laundering center, a major supplier of heroin, and the largest foreign supplier of marijuana and methamphetamine to the U.S. market (2007 data).

Morocco

Morocco is one of the world's largest producers of illicit hashish. Shipments of hashish are mostly directed to Western Europe. It is also a transit point for cocaine from South America destined for Western Europe. Morocco is a significant consumer of cannabis.

Netherlands

The Netherlands is a major European producer of synthetic drugs, including Ecstasy, and a cannabis cultivator. It is an important gateway for cocaine, heroin, and hashish entering Europe and a major source of U.S.-bound Ecstasy. Its large financial sector is vulnerable to money laundering. The Netherlands is also a significant consumer of Ecstasy.

Nigeria

Nigeria is a transit point for heroin and cocaine intended for European, East Asian, and North American markets. It is a consumer of amphetamines, a safe haven for Nigerian narco-traffickers operating worldwide, and a major money-laundering center. Nigeria also faces massive corruption and criminal activity. Nigeria has improved some of its anti-money-laundering controls, resulting in its removal from the Financial Action Task Force's (FATF) Noncooperative Countries and Territories List in June 2006. However, Nigeria's anti-money-laundering efforts continue to be monitored by the FATF.

Pakistan

Pakistan is a significant transit area for Afghan drugs, including heroin, opium, morphine, and hashish, bound for Iran, Western markets, the Gulf States, Africa, and Asia. Financial crimes related to drug trafficking, terrorism, corruption, and smuggling remain problems. Opium poppy cultivation was estimated at 2,300 hectares in 2007, with 600 of those hectares eradicated. Federal and provincial authorities continue to conduct antipoppy campaigns that utilize forced eradication, fines, and arrests.

Panama

Panama is a major cocaine transshipment point. It is a primary money-laundering center for narcotics revenue because of its status as an offshore financial center. Money-laundering activity is especially heavy in the Colón Free Zone. Although monitoring of financial transactions is improving, official corruption remains a major problem. There are negligible signs of coca cultivation.

Peru

Until 1996, Peru was the world's largest coca leaf producer. Today, Peru is the world's second-largest producer of coca leaf, lagging far behind Colombia. Cultivation of coca in Peru was estimated at 40,000 hectares in 2009, a slight decrease over 2008. It is the second-largest producer of cocaine, estimated at 225 metric tons of potential pure cocaine in 2009. Finished cocaine is shipped out from Pacific ports to the international drug market; increasing amounts of base and finished cocaine, however, are being moved to Brazil, Chile, Argentina, and Bolivia for use in the Southern Cone (the region of South America comprising the countries of

HERE AND NOW

The World FactBook: Current Global Status of Illicit Drugs and Drug Use in Selected Countries (*continued*)

Brazil, Paraguay, Uruguay, Argentina, and Chile) or are being transshipped to Europe and Africa. Peru is experiencing increasing domestic drug consumption.

Poland

Despite diligent counternarcotics measures and international information sharing on cross-border crime, Poland is a major illicit producer of synthetic drugs for the international market as well as a minor transshipment point for Southwest Asian heroin and Latin American cocaine to Western Europe.

South Africa

South Africa is a transshipment center for heroin, hashish, and cocaine and a major cultivator of marijuana in its own right. Cocaine and heroin consumption in South Africa is on the rise. It is the world's largest market for illicit methaqualone, usually imported illegally from India through various East African countries, but it is increasingly producing its own synthetic drugs for domestic consumption. It is an attractive venue for money launderers given the increasing level of organized criminal and narcotics activity in the region and the size of the South African economy.

United States

The United States is the world's largest consumer of cocaine (shipped from Colombia through Mexico and the Caribbean), Colombian heroin, and Mexican heroin and marijuana. It is also a major consumer of Ecstasy and Mexican methamphetamine and a minor consumer of high-quality Southeast Asian heroin. An illicit producer of cannabis, depressants, stimulants, hallucinogens, and methamphetamine, the United States is also a money-laundering center.

Worldwide Facts: Illicit Drugs

Cocaine

Worldwide coca leaf cultivation in 2013 likely amounted to 165,000 hectares, assuming a stable crop in Bolivia. Colombia produced slightly less than half of the worldwide crop, followed by Peru and Bolivia. Potential pure cocaine production increased 7% to 640 metric tons in 2013. Colombia conducts an aggressive coca eradication campaign. Peru has increased its eradication efforts, but remains hesitant to eradicate coca in key growing areas.

Opiates

Worldwide illicit opium poppy cultivation increased in 2013, with potential opium production reaching 6,800 metric tons. Afghanistan is world's primary opium producer, accounting for 82% of the global supply. Southeast Asia is responsible for 12% of global opium, with Pakistan producing 3% of global opium. Latin America produced 4% of global opium, most being was refined into heroin destined for the U.S. market.

---

* A hectare is a metric measurement used throughout the world. One hectare is equivalent to 2.47 acres.

Courtesy of Central Intelligence Agency. *The World Factbook 2013–14*. Washington, DC: Central Intelligence Agency, 2014. Available https://www.cia.gov/library/publications/the-world-factbook/fields/2086.html. Accessed March 27, 2016.

---

the United States alone, the rate of yearly prescription growth from 2012 to 2013 was up 1% (IMS Health 2013). In 2013, the total global prescription pharmaceutical market had sales of $950 billion; in 2016, sales were expected to reach $1.2 trillion (Herper 2012). Similarly, Reuters reports that "[G]lobal pharmaceutical sales are expected to reach $1.1 trillion in 2014" (Berkrot 2010, p. 1). Further, CBS News reported "that 40% of Americans are on at least one prescription drug, and more than half receive at least two prescriptions" (Fearnow 2013).

Other findings reflecting problems with prescription drug use are as follows (NIDA 2014b):

- Fifty-two million people in the United States older than age of 12 have used prescription drugs nonmedically in their lifetime.

- Approximately 6.1 million Americans have used prescription drugs nonmedically in the past month.
- Although the United States is just 5% of the world's population, it consumes 75% of the world's prescription drugs.
- With regards to obtaining prescription drugs, 54.2% reported obtaining them for free from a friend or relative, 18.1% from one doctor, and 16.6% buying or taking them from a friend or relative.

Such figures indicate that it may be more difficult to find people who do not use psychoactive drugs compared to individuals who do.

Further, a third category of drug sales has joined OTC and prescription drugs: herbal medicines, vitamins, minerals, enzymes, and other natural potions. According to Boyles (2009), "Out-of-pocket spending on herbal supplements, chiropractic visits, meditation, and other forms of complementary and alternative medicines (CAM) was estimated at $34 billion in a single year" and "Americans spend almost a third as much money out-of-pocket on herbal supplements and other alternative medicines as they do on prescription drugs." A more recent study found that "Americans will spend $21 billion on vitamins and herbal supplements in 2015. If protein powders are included, supplements are as big a market as all organic foods combined" (Scott 2015). This is even though the U.S. Preventive Services Task Force does not recommend regular use of any multivitamins or herbs.

Other findings regarding these types of drugs include (Scott 2015):

- 50% of Americans take multivitamins.
- One in five U.S. adults take herbal supplements.
- Americans will spend $21 billion on supplements in 2015.
- The FDA only spot tests 1% of the 65,000 dietary supplements on the market.

Drug use is so common that the average household in the United States owns about five drugs, of which two are prescription drugs and the other three are OTC drugs. Of the many prescriptions written by physicians, approximately one-third modify moods and behaviors in one way or another. A 2010 National Institute on Drug Abuse (NIDA 2010) study and other research indicate that more than 60% of adults in the United States have, at some time in their lives, taken a psychoactive drug (one that affects mood or consciousness). More than one-third of adults have used or are using depressants or sedatives.

A third explanation is that "in the modern age, increased sophistication has brought with it techniques of drug production and distribution that have resulted in a worldwide epidemic of drug use" (Kusinitz 1988, p. 149). In the 1980s and 1990s, for example, illicit drug cartels proliferated, and varieties of marijuana with ever-increasing potency infiltrated all urban and rural areas in the United States, as well as the world. Many of these varieties are crossbred with ultra-sophisticated techniques and equipment available everywhere.

Finally, even coffee has undergone a technological revolution. Higher levels of caffeine content have become available worldwide. This trend has led to the phenomenal growth of the following: (1) franchise duplication of gourmet coffee bars in the United States (e.g., Starbucks, Peet's, Three Brothers Coffee); (2) sales of espresso and cappuccino coffeemakers for home use, with accompanying coffee grinders or coffee pods and capsules; and (3) sales of specialized coffees and teas through a multitude of email coffee/tea clubs.

Approximately 25 years ago, it was difficult to purchase a cup of espresso or cappuccino in a typical restaurant; today, availability of such types of coffees is commonplace. Even at university unions and libraries, airports, shopping malls, and inner-city coffee shops, it is not unusual to see people lined up waiting to order and purchase their specially made and specially flavored coffee or tea. This is just one example of how caffeine (often seen as a benign drug) has evolved, with many new varieties of coffee beans from exotic islands and countries coming together with more sophisticated electronic equipment, with the result that the idea of simple brewing has been relegated to the past. The standard American "cup of coffee in the morning" has spilled into including coffee during the afternoon and evening. This is a small example of a much-tolerated drug maintaining its own impressive history of development, increased use, complexity in developing many more varieties, and added sophistication.

▌ Drug Use: Statistics, Trends, and Demographics

An incredible amount of money is spent each year for licit (legal) and illicit (illegal) chemicals that alter consciousness, awareness, or mood. The following are six categories of widely used licit and illicit types of psychoactive drugs:

1. *Social drugs:* Approximately $90 billion is spent on alcohol each year. Another $51.9 billion goes toward tobacco products, of which 90% comes from cigarette sales. The other 5% accounts for the $2 billion or so spent on cigars, chewing tobacco, pipe tobacco, roll-your-own tobacco, and snuff tobacco. During 2014, nearly 264 billion cigarettes were sold in the United States, a decrease from approximately 273 billion sold in 2013. About 13 billion cigars, including 12.4 billion large cigars and cigarillos and 0.6 billion little cigars, were sold in the United States in 2014 (CDC 2015a). Smokeless tobacco sales totaled approximately 124.6 million pounds in the United States in 2011, an increase from

122.6 million pounds sold in 2010 (CDC 2015a). E-cigarette sales in 2012 were approximately $500 million and in 2013 were projected to increase by $1 million per year (ECIG Review Central 2014). E-cigarettes account for 5% of the tobacco market, and 47.6% of current smokers have tried e-cigarettes and 55.4% of smokers who have quit used e-cigarettes (*The Motley Fool* 2015). In addition, $5.7 billion is spent on coffee, tea, and cocoa.

2. *Prescription drugs*: As mentioned earlier, the prescription pharmaceutical market racked up $950 billion in worldwide sales in 2012. The United States is the world's largest pharmaceutical market. In 2012, $237.5 to $240.5 billion of pharmaceutical prescription drugs were sold (IMS Health 2012, 2013). According to the *Pharmacy Times* (2007), total purchases of outpatient prescription medicines increased from approximately 2 billion to nearly 3 billion from 1997 to 2004.

3. *Over-the-counter (patent) drugs*: These products, including cough and cold items, external and internal analgesics, antacids, laxatives, antidiarrheal products, sleep aids, sedatives, and so on, had $30.8 billion in sales in 2014, with U.S. households spending, on average, about $338 per year on OTC products. Eighty-one percent of adults use OTC medicines as a first response to minor ailment (CHPA 2016).

4. *Illicit drugs*. A report prepared by the Rand Corporation for the White House estimated that over a 10-year period, from 2000 to 2010, an astonishing $1 trillion were spent on illicit drugs (Ferner 2014). Pinpointing specific types of drugs, another source indicated that "[d]rug users in the United States spend on the order of $100 billion annually on cocaine, heroin, marijuana, and meth. While this total figure has been stable over the decade, there have been important compositional shifts. In 2000, much more money was spent on cocaine than marijuana; in 2010 the opposite was true" (Rand Corporation 2014).

5. *Nonmedical use of prescription-type drugs:* Misuse of prescription drugs is second only to marijuana as the nation's most prevalent illicit drug problem and is a major public health concern, with approximately 22 million persons initiating nonmedical pain reliever use since 2002 (CBHSQ 2013). Combined 2010 and 2011 data indicate that about 1 in 22 (4.6%) persons aged 12 or older nationwide reported having used pain relievers nonmedically in the past year, which was lower than the rate using combined 2009 and 2010 data (4.9%) (CBHSQ 2013). Finally, as mentioned above, in 2015, 2.5% of illicit drug users, over 6.5 million persons age 12 or older, used prescription-type psychotherapeutic drugs nonmedically. Even the very young are not immune to significant nonmedical use of prescription-type drugs. For example, 2.8% of 8th graders, 7.2% of 10th graders, 10.5% of 12th graders, 7.5% of college students, and 8.6% of young adults had used narcotics, specifically OxyContin and Vicodin (Johnston et al. 2012) (see "Here and Now: Sources of Prescription Drugs Misused by Youths").

6. *Miscellaneous*: Finally, the amount spent on inhalants and other miscellaneous drugs, such as nutmeg and morning glory seeds, cannot be estimated.

Regarding nationwide trends in the use of illicit drug use in 2013, the following findings are noteworthy (NIDA 2015):

- Illicit drug use in the United States has been increasing. In 2013, an estimated 24.6 million Americans aged 12 or older—9.4% of the population—had used an illicit drug in the past month. This number is up from 8.3% in 2002. The increase mostly reflects a recent rise in use of marijuana, the most commonly used illicit drug.
- Marijuana use has increased since 2007. In 2013, there were 19.8 million current users—about 7.5% of people aged 12 or older—up from 14.5 million (5.8%) in 2007.
- Use of most drugs other than marijuana has stabilized over the past decade or has declined. In 2013, 6.5 million Americans aged 12 or older (or 2.5%) had used prescription drugs nonmedically in the past month. Prescription drugs include pain relievers, tranquilizers, stimulants, and sedatives. And 1.3 million Americans (0.5%) had used hallucinogens (a category that includes ecstasy and LSD) in the past month (NIDA 2015).
- Most people use drugs for the first time when they are teenagers. There were just over 2.8 million new users of illicit drugs in 2013, or about 7,800 new users per day. Over half (54.1%) were under 18 years of age.
- More than half of new illicit drug users begin with marijuana. Next most common are prescription pain relievers, followed by inhalants (which is most common among younger teens).

- Drug continues to increase among people in their fifties and early sixties. This increase is, in part, due to the aging of the baby boomers, whose rates of illicit drug use have historically been higher than those of previous generations.
- Binge and heavy drinking are more widespread among men than women. In 2013, 30.2% of men and 16.0% of women 12 and older reported binge drinking in the past month. And 9.5% of men and 3.3% of women reported heavy alcohol use.
- After alcohol, marijuana has the highest rate of dependence or abuse among all drugs. In 2013, 4.2 million Americans met clinical criteria for dependence or abuse of marijuana in the past year—more than twice the number for dependence/abuse of prescription pain relievers (1.9 million) and nearly five times the number for dependence/abuse of cocaine (855,000).
- Drug use is highest among people in their late teens and twenties. In 2013, 22.6% of 18- to 20-year-olds reported using an illicit drug in the past month. **Table 1.3** shows that in regard to age groups, 18- to 25-year-olds are by far the heaviest users and experimenters in terms of past-month and past-year usage.

TABLE 1.3 Trend Data on the Prevalence of Illicit Drug Use: 2009–2014

	2009	2010	2011	2012	2013	2014
Used in Past Month						
All ages 12+	8.7	8.9	8.7	9.2	9.4	10.2
12–17	9.8	10	9.9	9.4	8.7	9.2
18–25	21.3	21.5	21.3	21.3	21.5	21.9
26–34	12.5	13.9	13	13.9	15.3	15.3
35+	5.3	5.3	5.4	6.1	6.2	7.5
Used in Past Year						
All ages 12+	15.1	15.3	14.9	16	15.9	16.7
12–17	19	19.2	18.6	17.7	17.1	17.2
18–25	35.8	35	35	36.2	35.7	36.1
26–34	21.9	22.7	21.6	23.9	25.6	25.3
35+	9.1	9.6	9.3	10.6	10.2	11.8
Used in Lifetime (Ever Used)						
All ages 12+	47.1	47.3	47	48	48.6	49.2
12–17	26.1	25.4	25.1	24	23.1	22.9
18–25	58.4	57.6	57.2	57.8	57.1	56.7
26–34	59.4	60	60	60.8	61.7	61.2
35+	48.4	49	49	50.5	51.3	52.2

Data from Substance Abuse and Mental Health Services Administration (SAMHSA). *Results from the 2007 National Survey on Drug Use and Health: National Findings.* Office of Applied Studies, NSDUH Series H-36, HHS Publication No. (SMA) 09-4435. Rockville, MD: Substance Abuse and Mental Health Services Administration, 2008; Substance Abuse and Mental Health Services Administration (SAMHSA). *Results from the 2009 National Survey on Drug Use and Health: Volume II. Technical Appendices and Selected Prevalence Tables.* Office of Applied Studies, NSDUH Series H-38B, HHS Publication No. (SMA) 10-4586 Appendices. Rockville, MD: Substance Abuse and Mental Health Services Administration, 2010; Substance Abuse and Mental Health Services Administration (SAMHSA). *Results from the 2011 National Survey on Drug Use and Health: Summary of National Findings.* NSDUH Series H-44, HHS Publication No. (SMA) 12-4713. Rockville, MD: Substance Abuse and Mental Health Services Administration, 2012. *Results from the 2013 National Survey on Drug Use and Health: Summary of National Findings.* NSDUH Series H-48, HHS Publication No. (SMA) 14-4863. Rockville, MD: Substance Abuse and Mental Health Services Administration, 2014; Center for Behavioral Health Statistics and Quality (CBHSQ). *Behavioral Health Trends in the United States: Results from the 2014 National Survey on Drug Use and Health.* NSDUH Series H-50, HHS Publication No. (SMA) 15-4927. Rockville, MD: Substance Abuse and Mental Health Services Administration, 2015.

HERE AND NOW
Sources of Prescription Drugs Misused by Youths

Friends and family are the most common source of prescription drugs misused* by youths in the United States, according to an analysis of data from the National Survey on Drug Use and Health (NSDUH). Around one-half of youths who reported misusing prescription stimulants (50%), tranquilizers (47%), or sedatives (47%) in the past year said that they most recently obtained the medication for free from friends or family, as did one-third of those who reported the misuse of prescription opioids. The second most common source for obtaining stimulants, tranquilizers, and sedatives was purchasing from a friend/relative, drug dealer/stranger, or the Internet, and the second most common source for obtaining prescription opioids was acquiring them from a physician.

Another source (Read 2012) reported that teens get their prescription drugs from the following locations:

- In the medicine cabinet
- At a neighbor's house
- Online
- A friend of a friend

- At schools
- At parties

According to a University of Florida study, "[u]sing someone else's medication is the most common form of prescription stimulant misuse among adolescents," with researchers finding that 88% of teens who used the drugs nonmedically in the past 30 days said "they had obtained the medications from someone else" (ScienceDaily 2016). Friends and family are the most common source of prescription drugs misused* by youths in the U.S., according to an analysis of data from the National Survey on Drug Use and Health (NSDUH). Around one-half of youths who reported misusing prescription stimulants (50%), tranquilizers (47%), or sedatives (47%) in the past year said that they most recently obtained the medication for free from friends or family, as did one-third of those who reported the misuse of prescription opioids. The second most common source for obtaining stimulants, tranquilizers, and sedatives was purchasing from a friend/relative, drug dealer/stranger, or the Internet, while the second most common source for obtaining prescription opioids was acquiring it from a physician (CESAR FAX 2009 and Schepis and Krishnan-Sarin 2009).

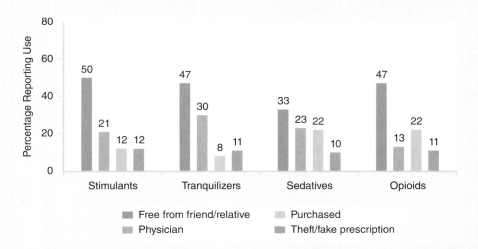

Most recent source of prescription medicines misused in the past year among youths aged 12 to 17: 2005 and 2006.

(*continues*)

HERE AND NOW

Sources of Prescription Drugs Misused by Youths (*continued*)

* *Misuse* was defined as "any intentional use of a medication with intoxicating properties outside of a physician's prescription for a bona fide medical condition, excluding accidental misuse."

Note: Respondents also reported that prescription medicines were obtained "some other way" (stimulants, 5%; tranquilizers, 4%; sedatives, 12%; opioids, 7%). Data are from 36,992 adolescents aged 12 to 17 participating in the 2005 and/or 2006 National Survey on Drug Use and Health. Of these youths, 8.3% reported any prescription drug misuse in the past year, 7% reported opioid misuse, 2% reported tranquilizer misuse, 2% reported stimulant misuse, and 0.4% reported sedative misuse.

Reproduced from University of Maryland, Center for Substance Abuse Research (CESAR). "Friends and Family Are Most Common Source of Prescription Drugs Misused by Youths." *CESAR FAX* 18(32) (2009) using data from Schepis, T.S., and S. Krishnan-Sarin. "Sources of Prescriptions for Misuse by Adolescents: Differences in Sex, Ethnicity, and Severity of Misuse in a Population-Based Study." *Journal of the American Academy of Child and Adolescent Psychiatry* 48(8) (2009): 828–836.

Table 1.4 shows a more recent percentage of population and estimated number of alcohol, tobacco, and illicit drug users in the United States among persons aged 12 or older. In looking at past-month usage, an estimated 13.9 million Americans, or 52.7% of the total U.S. population age 12 or older, were drinkers. Statistics also reveal that with regard to past-month usage of cigarettes, approximately 55.2 million Americans (20.8%) smoked cigarettes and 22.1 million 8.4% used marijuana/hashish in 2014 (see Table 1.4).

TABLE 1.4 National Household Survey on Drug Abuse: 2014

Percentage of population and estimated number of alcohol, tobacco, and illicit drug users in the United States among persons aged 12 or older.

	LIFETIME*		PAST MONTH	
	Percentage	**Number of Users (in thousands)**	**Percentage**	**Number of Users (in thousands)**
Alcohol	82.1	217,765	52.7	139,677
Cigarettes	61.0	161,789	20.8	55,241
Marijuana/hashish	44.2	117,213	8.4	22,188
Nonmedical use of any psychotherapeutics†	20.5	54,395	2.5	6537
Smokeless tobacco	17.1	45,290	3.3	8662
Cocaine	14.8	39,200	0.6	1530
Crack	3.6	9424	0.1	354
Hallucinogens	15.0	39,647	0.4	1173
LSD	9.4	25,035	0.1	287
Ecstasy	6.6	17,548	0.2	609
PCP	2.4	6388	0.0	33
Pain Relievers	13.6	36,064	1.6	4325
OxyContin	2.7	7031	0.1	356
Tranquilizers	9.4	24,851	0.7	1875
Inhalants	8.0	21,293	0.2	546

(*continues*)

TABLE 1.4 National Household Survey on Drug Abuse: 2014 (*continued*)

Percentage of population and estimated number of alcohol, tobacco, and illicit drug users in the United States among persons aged 12 or older.

	LIFETIME*		PAST MONTH	
	Percentage	Number of Users (in thousands)	Percentage	Number of Users (in thousands)
Stimulants	8.5	22,530	0.6	1595
Methamphetamine	4.9	12,943	0.2	569
Sedatives	3.0	7,826	0.1	330
Heroin	1.8	4,813	0.2	435
Any illicit drug§	49.2	130,332	10.2	26,983
Illicit Drugs Other Than Marijuana§	30.2	80,119	3.3	8,719

Note: The results obtained from this national survey were completed at 142,938 addresses, and 68,736 completed interviews were obtained. The survey was conducted from January 2014 through December 2014. Weighted response rates for household screening and for interviewing were 89.0% and 74.4%, respectively.

* Lifetime refers to ever used. This column shows the use of drugs from highest to lowest percentages as well as the number of persons using.

† Nonmedical use of prescription-type psychotherapeutics includes the nonmedical use of pain relievers, tranquilizers, stimulants, or sedatives but does not include over-the-counter drugs.

§ Illicit drugs include marijuana/hashish, cocaine (including crack), heroin, hallucinogens, inhalants, or prescription-type psychotherapeutics used nonmedically. Illicit drugs other than marijuana include cocaine (including crack), heroin, hallucinogens, inhalants, or prescription-type psychotherapeutics used nonmedically.

Data from Center for Behavioral Health Statistics and Quality (CBHSQ). *Behavioral Health Trends in the United States: Results from the 2014 National Survey on Drug Use and Health.* NSDUH Series H-50, HHS Publication No. (SMA) 15-4927. Rockville, MD: Substance Abuse and Mental Health Services Administration, 2015.

▪ Current Patterns of Licit and Illicit Drug Use

Table 1.4 shows that illicit drug use remains an alarming problem. In looking at lifetime use of illicit types of drugs, it is estimated that approximately 27 million Americans aged 12 years or older were current illicit drug users in 2014. This number represents 10.2% of the population aged 12 years or older (CBHSQ 2015). The leading types of lifetime use of drugs (see **Figure 1.2**) were alcohol (82.1%), cigarettes (61.0%), use of any illicit drug (49.2%), marijuana (44.2%), cocaine (14.8%), hallucinogens (15.0%; mainly LSD and Ecstasy), pain relievers (13.6%; not including OTC drugs), inhalants (8%), stimulants (8.5%; not including OTC drugs), and heroin (1.8%).

Figure 1.3 shows the number of past-month illicit drug users among persons age 12 or older in 2011. The category "illicit drugs" shows the highest use (22.5 million), followed by use of marijuana (18.1 million), psychotherapeutics (6.1 million), cocaine (1.4 million), hallucinogens (1 million), inhalants (0.6 million), and heroin (0.3 million).

NONMEDICAL USE OF PSYCHOTHERAPEUTICS (PAIN RELIEVERS)

Figure 1.4 shows the four categories of prescription-type drugs (pain relievers, tranquilizers, stimulants, and sedatives) that currently are or have been available by prescription; see the Case in Point highlighting the number of painkiller prescriptions in each of the 50 states, plus the District of Columbia in 2012 (CDC 2014). These groupings also include drugs that may be available as prescription medications but currently are much more likely to be manufactured and distributed illegally; one such drug is methamphetamine, which is included under stimulants. Major findings regarding the age groups are the following:

● *Aged 12 to 17*: An estimated 655,000 adolescents aged 12 to 17 were current nonmedical users of psychotherapeutic drugs in 2014. This number corresponds to 2.6% of adolescents. The 2014 estimate for current nonmedical use of psychotherapeutic drugs among adolescents was lower than the estimates in most years from 2002 to 2009.

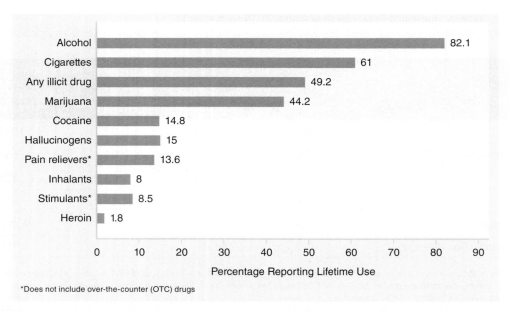

FIGURE 1.2 Percentage of U.S. residents aged 12 or older reporting lifetime use of alcohol, tobacco, and illicit drugs: 2014.

Data from Center for Behavioral Health Statistics and Quality (CBHSQ). *Behavioral Health Trends in the United States: Results from the 2014 National Survey on Drug Use and Health.* NSDUH Series H-50, HHS Publication No. (SMA) 15-4927. Rockville, MD: Substance Abuse and Mental Health Services Administration, 2015.

• *Aged 18 to 25*: In 2014, an estimated 1.6 million young adults aged 18 to 25 were current nonmedical users of psychotherapeutic drugs, which corresponds to 4.4% of young adults. The 2014 estimate for current nonmedical use of psychotherapeutic drugs among young adults was lower than the estimates from 2002 to 2010.

• *Aged 26 or Older*: In 2014, 4.3 million adults aged 26 or older were current nonmedical users of psychotherapeutic drugs. This number corresponds to 2.1% of adults aged 26 or older. The 2014 estimate for current nonmedical use of psychotherapeutic drugs among those aged 26 or older was similar to the estimates for most years between 2002 and 2013.

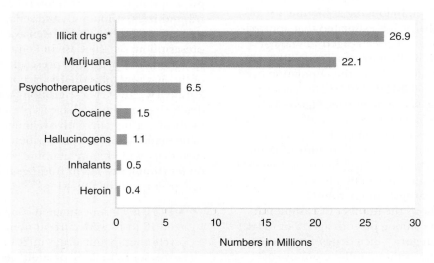

FIGURE 1.3 Past-month use of selected illicit drugs among persons aged 12 or older: 2014.
[1] Illicit drugs include marijuana/hashish, cocaine (including crack), heroin, hallucinogens, inhalants, or prescription-type psychotherapeutics used nonmedically.

Data from Center for Behavioral Health Statistics and Quality (CBHSQ). *Behavioral Health Trends in the United States: Results from the 2014 National Survey on Drug Use and Health.* NSDUH Series H-50, HHS Publication No. (SMA) 15-4927. Rockville, MD: Substance Abuse and Mental Health Services Administration, 2015.

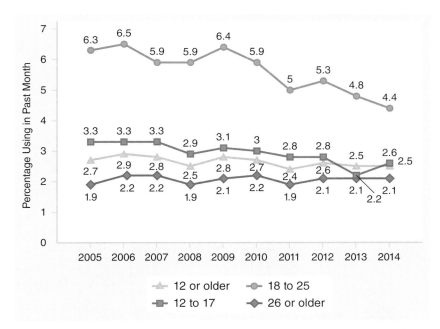

FIGURE 1.4 Past-month nonmedical use of types of psychotherapeutic drugs (pain relievers, tranquilizers, stimulants, and sedatives) among persons aged 12 or older: 2005–2014

Reproduced from Center for Behavioral Health Statistics and Quality (CBHSQ). *Behavioral Health Trends in the United States: Results from the 2014 National Survey on Drug Use and Health.* NSDUH Series H-50, HHS Publication No. (SMA) 15-4927. Rockville, MD: Substance Abuse and Mental Health Services Administration, 2015.

▶ CASE IN POINT

Figures A and B: State Differences in the Number of Painkiller Prescriptions per 100 People

The color-coded U.S. map (**Figure A**) shows the number of painkiller prescriptions per 100 people in each of the 50 states, plus the District of Columbia in 2012 (CDC 2014). The major findings from this map are as follows:

- Some states have significantly more painkiller prescription per person than other states (CDC 2014).
- Healthcare providers show significant state differences in prescribing pain killers.

Some states (**Figure B**) have more painkiller prescriptions per person than others.

The illustration below shows health care providers in different states prescribe at different levels resulting in significant variances with some states having more painkiller prescriptions per person than others.

- "Ten of the highest prescribing states for narcotic painkillers are in the South, with Alabama, Tennessee and West Virginia leading the nation" (Thompson 2014).
- "The Northeast, especially Maine and New Hampshire, had the most prescriptions per person for long-acting/extended-release painkillers and for high-dose painkillers" (Thompson 2014).
- States with the lowest pain prescription per 100 people are New Jersey, New York, Hawaii, Minnesota, and California.
- "Prescriptions for oxymorphone varied the most between states, out of all narcotic medications. Nearly 22 times as many prescriptions were written for oxymorphone in Tennessee as were written in Minnesota" (Thompson 2014).

Data from Centers for Disease Control and Prevention (CDC). "Vital Signs: Opioid Painkiller Prescribing Infographic." 2014. Available http://www.cdc.gov /vitalsigns/opioid-prescribing/infographic.html; Thompson, D. "The States with the Worst Prescription Painkiller Problem." New York: CBS Interactive, Inc., 1 July 2014. Available http://www.cbsnews.com/news/the-states-with-the-worst-prescription-painkiller-problem/

(continues)

▶ CASE IN POINT

Figures A and B: State Differences in the Number of Painkiller Prescriptions per 100 People (*continued*)

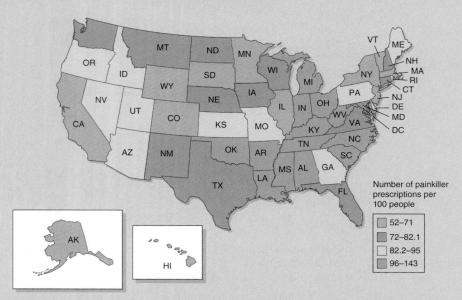

Number of painkiller prescriptions per 100 people

- 52–71
- 72–82.1
- 82.2–95
- 96–143

FIGURE A   This color-coded U.S. map shows the number of painkiller prescriptions per 100 people in each of the 50 states, plus the District of Columbia in 2012.

Data from IMS, National Prescription Audit (NPATM), 2012.

Health care providers in different states prescribe at different levels.

Number of painkiller prescriptions per 100 people

Lowest   Average   Highest

	AZ 82			
	NE 79 MT 82			
	WA 77 VA 78			
	ND 75 WI 76	SC 102		
	TX 74 MD 74	NC 97 OH 100		
	IA 73 NM 74	NV 94 MO 95		
	CT 72 FL 73	DE 91 KS 94		
	CO 71 NH 72	RI 90 GA 91		
NJ 63	WY 70 MA 71	PA 88 OR 89	MS 120	AL 143
NY 60 MN 62	VT 67 IL 68	DC 86 UT 86	AR 116 LA 118	WV 138 TN 143
HI 52 CA 57	AK 65 SD 66	ME 85 ID 86	MI 107 IN 109	OK 128 KY 128

State Abbreviation — GA 91 — Number of painkiller prescriptions per 100 people

SOURCE: IMS, National Prescription Audit (NPA™), 2012.

FIGURE B   Figures A and B: State Differences in the Number of Painkiller Prescriptions per 100 People Some states (Figure B) have more painkiller prescriptions per Person than others. The illustration below shows health care providers in different states prescribe at different levels resulting in significant variances with some states having more painkiller prescriptions per person than others.

Reproduced from Centers for Disease Control and Prevention (CDC). "Vital Signs: Opioid Painkiller Prescribing infographic." Atlanta, GA: National Center for Injury Prevention and Control, 2014. Available http://www.cdc.gov/vitalsigns/opioid -prescribing/infographic.html

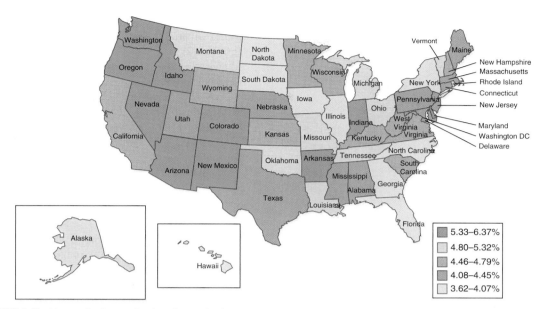

FIGURE 1.5   Nonmedical use of pain relievers in the past year among persons aged 12 or older, by state: Percentages, annual averages based on 2013 and 2014.

Reproduced from Center for Behavioral Health Statistics and Quality (CBHSQ). *Behavioral Health Trends in the United States: Results from the 2014 National Survey on Drug Use and Health*. NSDUH Series H-50, HHS Publication No. (SMA) 15-4927. Rockville, MD: Substance Abuse and Mental Health Services Administration, 2015.

Figure 1.5 shows the nonmedical use of pain relievers in past year among person's aged 12 or older, by state.

Figure 1.6 shows past-month use of illicit drugs among persons aged 12 or older, by age group, in 2013–2014. With regard to age patterns, the following trends are apparent:

- Rates of drug use shows substantial variation by age group.
- In comparing 2013 with 2014, past-month illicit drug use was similar across age groups.
- In comparing 2013 with 2014 across all age groups, past-month illicit drug use increased slightly in 2014.
- The highest percentage of illicit drug use was among 18- to 25-year-olds (21.5% in 2013; 22% in 2014).
- Of the four age groups (12 or older, 12 to 17, 18 to 25, and 25 older), those 25 or older had the lowest percentage of past-month illicit drug use.

RACIAL AND ETHNIC DIFFERENCES

Figure 1.7 shows average past-month illicit drug use among persons age 12 or older by race and ethnicity (black or African American, white, Hispanic or Latino, and Asian) for 2014. The figures in this chart reveal the following trends:

- In 2014, from highest to lowest, racial/ethnic groups had the following rates of illicit drug use: black or African American (12.4%), whites

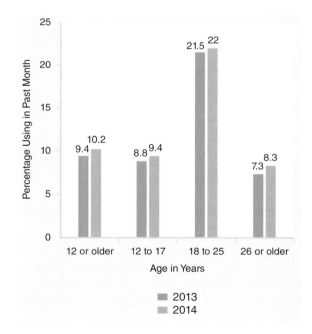

FIGURE 1.6   Percentage of past-month illicit drug use among persons aged 12 or older, by age: 2013 and 2014.

Reproduced from the Center for Behavioral Health Statistics and Quality (CBHSQ). *Behavioral Health Trends in the United States: Results from the 2014 National Survey on Drug Use and Health*. NSDUH Series H-50, HHS Publication No. (SMA) 15-4927. Rockville, MD: Substance Abuse and Mental Health Services Administration, 2015.

(10.4%), Hispanic or Latino (8.9%), and Asian (4.1%). (Note: Two or more races [13.5%] and American Indians or Alaska Natives [13.4%] are not shown in Figure 1.7 because the sample sizes for these two groups were too small for reliable trend presentation.)

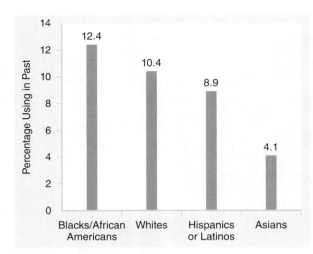

FIGURE 1.7   Past-month illicit drug use among persons age 12 or older, by race/ethnicity: 2014

Reproduced from Center for Behavioral Health Statistics and Quality, Substance Abuse and Mental Health Services Administration. *Behavioral Health Trends in the United States: Results from the 2014 National Survey on Drug Use and Health.* NSDUH Series H-50, HHS Publication No. (SMA) 15-4927. Rockville, MD: Substance Abuse and Mental Health Services Administration, 2015.

- As in past years when this research was conducted, Asians continue to have the lowest percentage of current illicit drug use, just as many other racial and ethnic group studies on drug use have found previously.
- The current illicit drug use rate for blacks or African Americans, whites, Hispanics or Latinos, and Asians increased from 2011 to 2014.* (Latest published findings in the breakdown of illicit drugs among Hispanic groups, indicates that Puerto Ricans were the heaviest users of illicit drugs, followed by Mexican Americans, and Cuban Americans. Central and South Americans had the lowest amount of current illicit drug use [SAMHSA 2012].)

In 2014, the following were the major findings regarding illicit drug use by gender, pregnant women, education, college students, and criminal justice populations/arrestees (SAMHSA 2014b):

GENDER

- In 2013, as in prior years, the rate of current illicit drug use among persons aged 12 or older was higher for males (11.5%) than for females (7.3%). Males were more likely than females to be current users of several different illicit drugs, including marijuana (9.7 vs. 5.6%), cocaine (0.8 vs. 0.4%), and hallucinogens (0.7 vs. 0.3%).

- In 2013, the rate of current illicit drug use was higher for males than females aged 12 to 17 (9.6 vs. 8.0%).
- Likewise, in 2013, the rate of current marijuana use was higher for males than females aged 12 to 17 (7.9 vs. 6.2%), which is a change from 2012 when the rates of current marijuana use for males and females were similar (7.5 and 7.0%).
- Among females aged 12 to 17, the rate of current marijuana use decreased from 7.2% in 2002 and 2003 to 6.2% in 2013.

PREGNANT WOMEN

- Among pregnant women aged 15 to 44, 5.4% were current illicit drug users based on data averaged across 2012 and 2013. This was lower than the rate among women in this age group who were not pregnant (11.4%). Among pregnant women aged 15 to 44, the average rate of current illicit drug use in 2012–2013 (5.4%) was not significantly different from the rate averaged across 2010–2011 (5.0%)
- The rate of current illicit drug use in the combined 2012–2013 data was 14.6% among pregnant women aged 15 to 17, 8.6% among women aged 18 to 25, and 3.2% among women aged 26 to 44.

EDUCATION

Illicit drug use rates in 2013 were correlated with educational status of adults aged 18 or older. The rate of current illicit drug use was lower among college graduates (6.7%) than those with some college education but no degree (10.8%), high school graduates with no further education (9.9%), and those who had not graduated from high school (11.8%) (SAMHSA 2014b).

COLLEGE STUDENTS

In the college-age population (persons ages 18 to 22 years), the most significant findings regarding college students and illicit drug use are as follows:

- In 2013, the rate of current illicit drug use was 22.3% among full-time college students aged 18 to 22. This was similar to the rate among other persons aged 18 to 22 (23.0%), which included part-time college students, students in other grades or types of institutions, and nonstudents.

In 2013, about one-quarter of male full-time college students aged 18 to 22 were current illicit drug users (26.0%). This rate was higher than the rate of current illicit drug use among female full-time college students aged 18 to 22 (19.2%). Similarly, 23.6% of male full-time college students aged 18 to 22 were current marijuana users compared with 16.6% of female full-time college students aged 18 to 22.

Among full-time college students aged 18 to 22 in 2013, the rate of current illicit drug use was 9.4% for Asians, 19.7% for blacks, 21.5% for Hispanics, and 25.1% for whites.

CRIMINAL JUSTICE POPULATIONS/ARRESTEES

Certain significant findings and correlations are unique to criminal justice populations:

In 2013, an estimated 1.7 million adults aged 18 or older were on parole or other supervised release from prison at some time during the past year. About one-quarter (27.4%) were current illicit drug users, with 20.4% reporting current use of marijuana and 12.1% reporting current nonmedical use of psychotherapeutic drugs. These rates were higher than those reported by adults aged 18 or older who were not on parole or other supervised release during the past year (9.3% for current illicit drug use, 7.5% for current marijuana use, and 2.4% for current nonmedical use of psychotherapeutic drugs) (SAMHSA 2014b).

In 2013, an estimated 4.5 million adults aged 18 or older were on probation at some time during the past year. More than one-quarter (31.4%) were current illicit drug users, with 23.5% reporting current use of marijuana and 12.3% reporting current nonmedical use of psychotherapeutic drugs. These rates were higher than those reported by adults who were not on probation during the past year (9.0% for current illicit drug use, 7.3% for current marijuana use, and 2.3% for current nonmedical use of psychotherapeutic drugs) (SAMHSA 2014b).

"An estimated 56% of state prisoners, 45% of federal prisoners, and 64% of jail inmates have a mental health problem ... at the time of the survey ... conducted by the Urban Institute, ... 49% of state prisoners, 40% of federal prisoners, and 60% of jail inmates had a symptom of a mental disorder, such as developmental and personality disorders, as well as clinical symptoms as specified in the *Diagnostic and Statistical Manual of Mental Disorders*, Fourth Edition (DSM-IV)" (KiDeuk, Becker-Cohen, and Serakos, 2015).

In 2011, 197,050 sentenced prisoners were under federal jurisdiction. Of these, 94,600 were serving time for drug offenses (Carson and Sabol 2012).

In 2010, Home Health Testing (2010) reported that drugs were involved in a wide range of crimes, including violent crimes (78%), property crimes (83%), weapons offenses (77%), and parole violations (77%).

Arrestee Drug Abuse Monitoring (ADAM) reports that at the time of arrest 40% of arrestees tested positive for the presence of multiple drugs. Approximately 40% tested positive for marijuana, 30% tested positive for cocaine, and 20% tested positive for crack (National Institute of Justice [NIJ] 2009). These three drugs are the most prevalent drugs that arrestees test positive for at the time of arrest. (The 2013 ADAM II report provides a comparison of the results over the years [ONDCP 2013a].)

■ Types of Drug Users

Just as a diverse set of personality traits exists (e.g., introverts, extroverts, type A, obsessive-compulsive, and so on), drug users also vary according to their general approach or orientation, frequency of use, and types and amounts of the drugs they consume. Some are occasional or moderate users, whereas others display a much stronger attachment to drug use. In fact, some display such obsessive-compulsive behavior that they cannot let a morning, afternoon, or evening pass without using drugs. Some researchers have classified such variability in the frequency and extent of usage as fitting into three basic patterns: experimenters, compulsive users, and "floaters" or "chippers" (members of the last category drift between experimentation and compulsive use).

Experimenters begin using drugs largely because of peer pressure and curiosity, and they confine their use to recreational settings. Generally, they more often enjoy being with peers who

KEY TERM

experimenters
first category of drug users, typified as being in the initial stages of drug use; these people often use drugs for recreational purposes

also use drugs recreationally. Alcohol, tobacco, marijuana, prescription drugs, hallucinogens, and many of the major stimulants are the drugs they are most likely to use. They are usually able to set limits on when these drugs are taken (often preferred in social settings), and they are more likely to know the difference between light, moderate, and chronic use.

Compulsive users, in contrast, "devote considerable time and energy to getting high, talk incessantly (sometimes exclusively) about drug use … [and 'funny' or 'weird' experiences] … and become connoisseurs of street drugs" (Beschner 1986, p. 7). For compulsive users, recreational fun is impossible without getting high. Other characteristics of these users include the need to escape or postpone personal problems, to avoid stress and anxiety, and to enjoy the sensation of the drug's euphoric effects. Often, they have difficulty assuming personal responsibility and suffer from low self-esteem. Many compulsive users are from dysfunctional families, have persistent problems with the law, and/or have serious psychological problems underlying their drug-taking behavior. Problems with personal and public identity, excessive confusion about their sexual identity and at times sexual orientation, boredom, family discord, childhood sexual and/or mental abuse, academic pressure, and chronic depression all contribute to the inability to cope with issues without drugs.

Floaters or chippers initially focus more on using other people's drugs without maintaining a steady supply of drugs. Nonetheless, floaters or chippers, like experimenters, are generally light to moderate drug users. Floaters or chippers feel a largely unconscious need to seek pleasure from using drugs and the desire to relieve moderate to serious psychological problems. Even though most are on a path to drug dependence, at this stage they may generally drift between or simultaneously intermix with other experimental drug-taking peers and chronic drug-using peers. In a sense, these types of drug users feel marginally attached to conventional society and often appear to conventional members of society as norm abiding, while masking their secret drug use. At this stage, floaters or chippers are not yet firmly attached to compulsive users often because they have not made the commitment to continually do drugs. (See "Signs and Symptoms: Who Is More Likely to Use Licit and Illicit Drugs?")

SIGNS & SYMPTOMS

Who Is More Likely to Use Licit and Illicit Drugs?

Many factors influence whether an adolescent tries drugs, including the availability of drugs within the neighborhood, community, and school and whether the adolescent's friends are using them. The family environment is also important: violence, physical or emotional abuse, mental illness, or drug use in the household increase the likelihood an adolescent will use drugs. Finally, an adolescent's inherited genetic vulnerability; personality traits such as poor impulse control or a high need for excitement; mental health conditions such as depression, anxiety, or ADHD; and beliefs such as that drugs are "cool" or harmless make it more likely that an adolescent will use drugs (NIDA 2014).

According to the National Institute of Drug Abuse (2014), adolescents experiment with drugs or continue taking them for several reasons, including:

- *To fit in*: Many teens use drugs "because others are doing it"—or they think others are doing it—and they fear not being accepted in a social circle that includes drug-using peers.

- *To feel good*: Abused drugs interact with the neurochemistry of the brain to produce feelings of pleasure. The intensity of this euphoria differs by the type of drug and how it is used.

- *To feel better*: Some adolescents suffer from depression, social anxiety, stress-related disorders, and physical pain. Using drugs may be an attempt to lessen these feelings of distress. Stress especially plays a significant role in starting and continuing drug use as well as returning to drug use (relapsing) for those recovering from an addiction.

- *To do better*: Ours is a very competitive society, in which the pressure to perform athletically and academically can be intense. Some adolescents may turn to certain drugs like illegal or prescription stimulants because they think those substances will enhance or improve their performance.

- *To experiment*: Adolescents are often motivated to seek new experiences, particularly those they perceive as thrilling or daring.

(continues)

SIGNS & SYMPTOMS

Who Is More Likely to Use Licit and Illicit Drugs? *(continued)*

Finally, when attempting to determine who among drug users has a greater likelihood of becoming addicted, one research finding reports that "As with many other conditions and diseases, vulnerability to addiction differs from person to person. Your genes, mental health, family and social environment all play a role in addiction" (Helpguide.org n.d.). The following risk factors increase a person's vulnerability to addiction (Helpguide.org n.d.):

- Family history of addiction
- Abuse, neglect, or other traumatic experiences
- Mental disorders such as depression and anxiety
- Early use of drugs
- Method of administration (smoking or injecting a drug may increase its addictive potential)

Data from National Institute of Drug Abuse (NIDA). *Principles of Adolescent Substance Use Disorder Treatment: A Research-Based Guide.* Bethesda, MD: National Institute on Drug Abuse, January 2014. Available https://www.drugabuse.gov/sites/default/files/podata_1_17_14.pdf; Helpguide.org. "Drug Abuse and Addiction." n.d. Available http://www.helpguide.org/articles/addiction/drug-abuse-and-addiction.htm

■ Drug Use: Mass and Electronic Media and Family Influences

Studies continually show that the majority of young drug users come from homes in which drugs are liberally used (Goode 1999; National Association for Children of Alcoholics 2005; SAMHSA, Office of Applied Studies 1996). Children from these homes constantly witness drug use at home, often on a daily basis. For instance, parents may consume large quantities of coffee to wake up in the morning and other forms of medication throughout the day: cigarettes with the morning coffee, pills for either treating or relieving an upset stomach, vitamins for added nutrition, or aspirin for a headache. Finally, before going to bed, the grown-ups may take a few "nightcaps" or a sleeping pill to relax. The following is an interview related to the overuse of drugs:

Yeah, I always saw my mom smoking early in the morning while reading the newspaper and slowly sipping nearly a full pot of coffee. She took prescription drugs for asthma, used an inhaler, and took aspirin for headaches. When she accused me of using drugs at concerts, I would pick up her pack of cigarettes and several prescription bottles and while she was raging on me, I would quietly wave all her drugs close up in front of her face. She would stop nagging within seconds and actually one time I think she wanted to laugh but turned away toward the sink and just started washing cups and saucers. The way I figure it, she has her drugs, and I have mine. She may not agree with my use of my drugs but then she is not better either. It's great to have a drug-using family ain't it? *(From Venturelli's research files, male college student, age 20, June 12, 2000)*

This next interview is an example of how "pill-pilfering" can easily occur:

Yes, I came from a home with dozens of pharmacy prescriptions and with medicine cabinets crammed with over-the-counter drugs. In fact, my mom noticed that certain friends of mine were helping themselves to our medicine cabinet. At first, she told my dad that I was taking the pills. Finally, she had to remove most of the prescription medicines from the guest bathroom and hide them in her bedroom bathroom. This was about four years ago when I was in high

KEY TERMS

compulsive users
second category of drug users, typified by an insatiable attraction followed by a psychological dependence on drugs

floaters or chippers
third category of drug users; these users vacillate between the need for pleasure-seeking and the desire to relieve moderate to serious psychological problems; this category of drug user has two major characteristics: (1) a general focus mostly on using other people's drugs (often without maintaining a personal supply of the drug) and (2) vacillation between the characteristics of chronic drug users and experimenter types

school. She was right, several of my friends had a knack of lifting tabs from other homes when visiting friends. I know that one of my friends was into this when he told another friend of mine that our home had a nice variety of great drugs in the bathroom. Now, I know why my friends always had to go to the bathroom whenever they would stop by to see me. *(From Venturelli's research files, male attending a mid-size university in the Midwest, age 20, June 6, 2010)*

Some social scientists believe that everyday consumption of legal drugs—caffeine, prescription and OTC drugs, and alcohol—is fueled by the pace of modern lifestyles and greatly accelerated by the influence of today's increasingly sophisticated mass media.

If you look around your classroom building, the dormitories at your college, your college library, or your own home, evidence of mass media and electronic equipment can be found everywhere. Cultural knowledge and information are transmitted via media through electronic gadgets we simply "can't live without," to the point that they help us define and shape our everyday reality. One recent survey reports that "digital peer pressure appears to have played a significant role in getting teens started on drugs and booze—something that was not the case before the era of social networking sites. Seventy-five percent of respondents said that seeing Facebook pictures of their peers partying with alcohol and marijuana encourages other teens to imitate them" (Huffington Post 2012, p. 1). In addition, "[c]ompared to teens who have not seen pictures on Facebook or other social networking sites of kids getting drunk, passed out, or using drugs, teens who have seen such pictures are: [f]our times likelier to have used marijuana, [m]ore than three times likelier to have used alcohol; and [a]lmost three times likelier to have used tobacco" (CASA Columbia 2012, p. 3).

With regards to drug advertising, television remains the most influential medium. Today, most homes (82%) have more than one television (Nielson 2016). Nielsen (2016) also reports that "in 2009 the average American home had 2.86 TV sets, which is roughly 18% higher than in 2000 (2.43 sets per home)." Just as the number of televisions in the average home has been increasing over the last 30 years, "Drug firms … [have been increasing] … their spending on television advertising to consumers seven-fold from 1996 to 2000" (CBS News 2002). "Drug makers in 2014 spent $4.5 billion marketing prescription drugs, up

from $3.5 billion in 2012. That's also up from the $2.5 billion drug makers spent in 2000, or $3.39 billion in 2015 dollars when adjusted for inflation" (Millman 2015).

As an example, "[i]n 2014, two widely recognized erectile dysfunction drugs that have been on the market for more than a decade—Pfizer's Viagra and Eli Lilly's Cialis—ranked among the top five, …. Pfizer's advertising budget for its 'little blue pill' has more than doubled in the past five years to $232 million, and the company notably started marketing directly to women" (Millman 2015).

As another example, "Each year, the top 14 major alcohol marketers spent more than a $3.45 billion dollars on 'measured media' advertising, that is television, radio, print, online, direct mail and outdoor ads" (Federal Trade Commission [FTC] 2015). "The advertising budget for one beer—Budweiser—is more than the entire budget for research on alcoholism and alcohol abusers" (Kilbourne 1989, p. 13). Other findings indicate that "Alcohol companies spent $4.9 billion on television advertising between 2001 and 2005. They spent 2.1% of this amount ($104 million) on 'responsibility advertisements'" (Center on Alcohol Marketing and Youth [CAMY] 2007). "For the entire period from 2001 to 2003, Anheuser-Busch spent 20 times more on product ads than on 'responsibility' ads, and placed 30 times as many product ads as 'responsibility' ads" (CAMY 2005).

Radio, newspapers, and magazines are also saturated with advertisements for OTC drugs that constantly offer relief from whatever illness you may have. There are pills for inducing sleep and those for staying awake, as well as others for treating indigestion, headache, backache, tension, constipation, and the like. Using these medicinal compounds can significantly alter mood, level of consciousness, and physical discomfort. Experts warn that such drug advertising is likely to increase.

In the early 1990s, the Food and Drug Administration (FDA) lifted a 2-year ban on consumer advertising of prescription drugs; since then, there has been an onslaught of new sales pitches. In their attempts to sell drugs, product advertisers use the authority of a physician or health expert or the seemingly sincere testimony of a product user. Viewers, or listeners are strongly affected by testimonial advertising because these drug commercials can appear authentic and convincing.

The constant barrage of commercials, including many for OTC drugs, relays the message that, if

HERE AND NOW

Abuse of Licit and Illicit Drugs by the Elderly

SAMHSA (2012) reports the following regarding drug misuse and abuse by the elderly:

Older adults are among those most vulnerable to medication misuse and abuse because they use more prescription and over-the-counter (OTC) medications than other age groups. They are likely to experience more problems with relatively small amounts of medications because of increased medication sensitivity as well as slower metabolism and elimination. Older adults are at high risk for medication misuse due to conditions like pain, sleep disorders/insomnia, and anxiety that commonly occur in this population. They are, therefore, more likely to receive prescriptions for psychoactive medications with misuse and abuse potential, such as opioid analgesics for pain and central nervous system depressants like benzodiazepines for sleep disorders and anxiety. Approximately 25% of older adults use prescription psychoactive medications that have a potential to be misused and abused. Older adults are more likely to use psychoactive medications for longer periods than younger adults. Longer periods of use increases the risk of misuse and abuse. In addition to concerns regarding misuse of medications alone, the combination of alcohol and medication misuse has been estimated to affect up to 19% of older Americans.

Scope of the Problem: Drug Use and Abuse Among Older Adults

- "An estimated 4.8 million adults aged 50 and older have used an illicit drug in the past year....The prevalence of illicit drug use was higher among adults aged 50 to 59 than those aged 60 and older) (Reardon 2012).

- "Overall, alcohol was the most frequently reported primary substance of abuse for persons aged 50 or older. Opiates were the second most commonly reported primary substance of abuse, reported most frequently by individuals aged 50 to 59. These individuals also had the highest proportions of inpatient admissions for cocaine, marijuana, and stimulant abuse" (Bogunovic 2012).

- Marijuana use was more common than nonmedical use of prescription-type drugs for adults aged 50 to 54 and those aged 55 to 59 (6.1% vs. 3.4%

and 4.1% vs. 3.2%, respectively), but among those aged 65 or older nonmedical use of prescription-type drugs was more common than marijuana use (0.8% vs. 0.4%) (NSDUH Report 2009).

- Marijuana use was more common than nonmedical use of prescription-type drugs among males aged 50 or older (4.2% vs. 2.3%), but among females the rates of marijuana use and nonmedical use of prescription-type drugs were similar (1.7% and 1.9%) (*The NSDUH Report* 2009).

- "Among adults aged 50 or older, the prevalence rates of any illicit drug use and marijuana use in the past year were higher among males than females" (Crabb 2014).

- "Among adults aged 50 or older who used illicit drugs in the past year, 45.2% used only marijuana, 31.5% used only prescription-type drugs nonmedically, and 5.6% used only other illicit drugs (including cocaine, heroin, hallucinogens, or inhalants) with the remainder using other combinations of illicit drugs" (Crabb 2014).

- "The number of Americans aged 50+ years is increasing as large numbers of baby boomers reach age 50 years or older, and this cohort uses more psychoactive drugs than older cohorts" (Li-Tzy and Blazer 2011).

- Many Americans who are now young or middle-aged will carry their use and abuse of alcohol and other drugs with them into old age—and they will also live longer (SAMHSA 2013).

- Older adults are more likely to take prescribed psychoactive medications for longer periods of time than younger adults and run an additional risk of becoming addicted to their prescribed medications (SAMHSA 2013).

An example of elderly drug abuse includes the following:

Oh, I started with cigarettes when I was fourteen. Then came the alcohol when I was sixteen, and now I am now 62 years old and still playing around with drugs. I have several friends who still smoke weed, but not too many around who continue like I do. I generally smoke cigarettes, weed (as they call it today), sometimes buy a little bag of coke and smoke that, too, and drink alcohol. I don't do the coke much because I like

(continues)

HERE AND NOW

Abuse of Licit and Illicit Drugs by the Elderly (*continued*)

to smoke it, and it is tough on the heart. My drug using friends who are around my age don't really know about the coke use; they think I stopped this years ago. I still have days when I long for it, but I have enough of a hard time with the weed and the drinking. My children do not know how much I drink since I live alone, and they even think I have nothing to do with weed. So, I guess I am a closet user. At times I am sorry to continue with these unnecessary drugs, and it's even darn right embarrassing if anyone finds out. Even the cigarettes are a pain in the butt. I just need to get high every now and then, and I don't know why. I think it is something genetic since I want to quit all these drugs but simply do not do it. You asked if I think a lot of the elderly use drugs unnecessarily [drugs used without medical purposes]. Yes, there are many of us, especially the baby boomers who still smoke weed, but we kind of keep it secret. So, if the numbers of users my age are increasing, I would double the real number of users. As I said, many of us just keep it secret because we still work, have good jobs with a lot of responsibilities, and our kids would look down on us if they knew. You asked if I feel addicted to these drugs. Yes, I am addicted since I really don't want to quit everything, yet it is not good for my health and still keep using these drugs. Isn't this a classic example of addiction, which is to keep using drugs even though you know they are not good for you? If it's not addiction, what else would it be? *(From Venturelli's research files, male, age 62, April 22, 2011)*

Data from Reardon, C. "The Changing Face of Older Adult Substance Abuse." *Social Work Today* 12 (January/February 2012):8; Bogunovic, O. "Substance Abuse in Aging and Elderly Adults." Psychiatric Times, 27 July 2012. Available http://www.psychiatrictimes.com/geriatric-psychiatry/substance-abuse-aging-and-elderly-adults; Substance Abuse and Mental Health Service Administration (SAMHSA). "Older Americans Behavioral Health, Issue Brief 5: Prescription Medication Misuse and Abuse Among Older Adults." Rockville, MD: Older Americans: Behavioral Health Technical Assistance Center, 2012. Available http://www.aoa.acl.gov/AoA_Programs/HPW/Behavioral/docs2/Issue%20Brief%205%20Prescription%20Med%20Misuse%20Abuse.pdf; The NSDUH (National Survey on Drug Use and Health) *Report.* "Illicit Drug Use Among Older Adults." Rockville, MD: U.S. Department of Health and Human Services (USDHHS), Office of Applied Studies (OAS), 2012; Crabb, G. "Illicit Drug Use Among Older Adults." Naples, FL: Dr. George Crabb, Physician and Addiction Expert, 7 March 2014. Available http://drgeorgecrabb.com/uncategorized/illicit-drug-use-among-older-adults.html; Li-Tzy, W., and D. G. Blazer. "Illicit and Nonmedical Drug Use Among Older Adults: A Review." *Journal of Aging Health* 23 (2011):481–504; Substance Abuse and Mental Health Services Administration (SAMHSA). *Substance Abuse Among Older Adults.* Rockville, MD: National Center for Biotechnology Information, 2013.

you are experiencing restlessness or uncomfortable symptoms, taking drugs is an acceptable and normal response. As a result, television viewers, newspaper and magazine readers, and radio listeners are led to believe or unconsciously select the particular brand advertised when confronted with dozens upon dozens of drug choices for a particular ailment. In effect, this advertising reaffirms the belief that drugs are necessary when taken for a real or an imagined symptom.

Drug Use and Drug Dependence

Why are so many people attracted to drugs and the effects of recreational drug use? Like the ancient Assyrians, who sucked on opium lozenges, and the Romans, who ate hashish sweets some 2000 years ago, many users claim to be bored, in pain, frustrated, unable to enjoy life, or alienated. Such people turn to drugs in the hope of finding oblivion, peace, inner connections, outer connections (togetherness), or euphoria. The fact that many OTC drugs never really cure the ailment, especially if taken for social and psychological reasons, and the fact that frequent use of most drugs increases the risk of addiction, do not seem to be deterrents. People continue to take drugs for many reasons, including the following:

- Searching for pleasure and using drugs to heighten good feelings.
- Taking drugs to temporarily relieve stress or tension or provide a temporary escape for people with anxiety.
- Taking drugs to temporarily forget one's problems and avoid or postpone worries.
- Viewing certain drugs (such as alcohol, marijuana, and tobacco) as necessary to relax after a tension-filled day at work.
- Taking drugs to fit in with peers, especially when peer pressure is strong during early and late adolescence; seeing drugs as a rite of passage.

- Taking drugs to enhance religious or mystical experiences. (Very few cultures teach children how to use specific drugs for this purpose.)
- Taking drugs to relieve pain and some symptoms of illness.
- Resuming drug use from teenage and young adult period(s) of life, for example, elderly baby boomers who may have used drugs in their youth.

It is important to understand why, historically, many people have been unsuccessful in eliminating the fascination with drugs. To reach such an understanding, we must address questions dealing with (1) why people are attracted to drugs, (2) how experiences with the different types of drugs vary (here, many attitudes are conveyed from the "inside"—the users themselves), (3) how each of the major drugs affects the body and the mind, (4) how patterns of use vary among different groups, and (5) what forms of treatment are available for the addicted.

■ When Does Use Lead to Abuse?

Views about the use of drugs depend on one's perspective. For example, from a pharmacological perspective, if a patient is suffering severe pain because of injuries sustained from an automobile accident, high doses of a narcotic such as morphine or Demerol should be given to control discomfort. While someone is in pain, no reason exists not to take the drug. From a medical standpoint, once healing has occurred and pain has been relieved, drug use should cease. If the patient continues using the narcotic because it provides a sense of well-being or he or she has become dependent to the point of addiction, the pattern of drug intake is then considered abuse. Thus, the amount of drug(s) taken or the frequency of dosing does not necessarily determine abuse (even though individuals who abuse drugs usually consume increasingly higher doses). Most important is the motive for taking the drug, which is the principal factor in determining the presence of abuse.

Initial drug abuse symptoms include (1) excessive use, (2) constant preoccupation about the availability and supply of the drug, (3) denial in admitting the excessive use, and (4) reliance on the drug. All of these four factors frequently result in producing the initial symptoms of withdrawal whenever the user attempts to stop taking the drug. As a result, the user often begins to neglect other responsibilities or ambitions in favor of using the drug.

Even the legitimate use of a drug can be controversial. Often, physicians cannot decide even among themselves what constitutes legitimate use of a drug. For example, MDMA (Ecstasy) is currently prohibited for therapeutic use, but in 1985, when the **Drug Enforcement Administration (DEA)** was deciding MDMA's status, some 35 to 200 physicians (mostly psychiatrists) were using the drug in their practice. These clinicians claimed that MDMA relaxed inhibitions and enhanced communication and was useful as a psychotherapeutic adjunct to assist in dealing with psychiatric patients (Leventhal 1996; Schecter 1989). From the perspective of these physicians, Ecstasy was a useful medicinal tool. However, the DEA did not agree and made Ecstasy a Schedule I drug. Schedule I excludes any legitimate, legal use of the drug in therapeutics; consequently, according to this ruling, anyone taking Ecstasy is guilty of drug abuse (Goode 2012) and is violating drug laws.

If the problem of drug abuse is to be understood and solutions are to be found, identifying the causes of the abuse is most important. When a drug is being abused, it is not legitimately therapeutic; that is, it does not improve the user's physical or mental health. When drug use is not used for therapeutic purposes, what is the motive for taking the drug?

There are many possible answers to this question. Initially, most drug abusers perceive some psychological advantage when using these compounds. For many, the psychological lift is significant enough that they are willing to risk social exclusion, health problems, and dramatic changes in personality, arrest, incarceration, and fines to have their drug. The psychological effects that these drugs cause may entail an array of diverse feelings. Different types of drugs have different psychological effects. The type of drug an individual selects to abuse may ultimately reflect his or her own mental state.

For example, people who experience chronic depression, feel intense job pressures, are unable to focus on accomplishing goals, or have a sense of inferiority may find that a stimulant such as cocaine or an amphetamine-type of drug appears to provide immediate relief—a solution to a set

KEY TERM

Drug Enforcement Administration (DEA)
the principal federal agency responsible for enforcing U.S. drug laws

of psychological frustrations. These drugs cause a spurt of energy, a feeling of euphoria, a sense of superiority, and imagined self-confidence. In contrast, people who experience nervousness and anxiety and want instant relief from the pressures of life may choose a depressant such as alcohol or barbiturates. These agents sedate, relax, provide relief, and even have some amnesiac properties, allowing users to suspend or forget their immediate pressing concerns or problems. People who perceive themselves as creative or who have artistic talents may select hallucinogenic types of drugs to "expand" their minds, heighten their senses, and distort what appears to be a confining and sometimes monotonous nature of reality. As individuals come to rely more on drugs to inhibit, deny, accelerate, or distort their realities, they run the risk of becoming psychologically dependent on drugs.

Some have argued that taking a particular drug to meet a psychological need, especially if a person is over 21 years of age, is not very different from taking a drug to cure an ailment. The belief here is that physical needs and psychological needs are really indistinguishable. In fact, several drug researchers and writers, including Szasz (1992) and Lenson (1995), believe that drug taking is a citizen's right and a personal matter involving individual decision making. They see drug taking as simply a personal choice to depart from or alter consciousness. Lenson states that taking drugs for recreational purposes is simply an additional form of diversity, a type of mental diversity that should exist with many other acceptable forms of diversity, such as cultural, racial, religious, gender, and sexual orientation diversity. (For additional elaboration on these views, see Venturelli 2000.) Obviously, this is a very different and often extremely controversial point of view that can easily cause polemic and very debatable perspectives!

▌ Drug Dependence

This section introduces some underlying factors that lead to drug dependence. Our discussion emphasizes drug dependence instead of addiction because the term *addiction* is both controversial and relative, as evidenced with celebrities and rock and movie stars and their drug dependence, including some who have died from drug dependence. Stars such as Charlie Sheen, Mel Gibson, and Ben Affleck (alcoholism); John Belushi, Lindsay Lohan, and Robin Williams (alcoholism and cocaine); Robert Downey, Jr. (cocaine and heroin); Michael Jackson (prescription drugs); Philip Seymour Hoffman (illegal drug); Cory Monteith (illegal drug and alcohol); Chris Kelly (illegal drug); Whitney Houston (illegal drug); Amy Winehouse (alcohol); and Eminem (analgesic prescription drugs) are just a few examples.

Even when drug dependence becomes fullfledged, addiction remains debatable, with many experts unable to agree on one set of characteristics that constitutes addiction. Furthermore, the term *addiction* is viewed by some as a pejorative that adds to the labeling process.

The main characteristics necessary for drug dependence are as follows:

- Both physical and psychological factors precipitate drug dependence. Recently, closer attention has been focused on the mental (psychological) attachments than on the physical addiction to drug use as principally indicative of addiction—mostly, the craving aspect of wanting the drug for consumption.
- More specifically, psychological dependence refers to the need that a user may feel for continued use of a drug to experience its effects. Physical dependence refers to the need to continue taking the drug to avoid withdrawal symptoms that often include feelings of discomfort and illness.
- With repeated use there is a tendency to become dependent on and addicted to most psychoactive drugs.
- Addiction to a drug sets in when the drug user has advanced within the dependence phase. (Having an addiction to a drug is simply an advanced stage of dependence.)
- Generally, the addiction process involves mental (psychological) and physical (physiological/ biophysiological) dependence.

Figure 1.8 shows that the process of addiction involves five separate phases: relief, increased use, preoccupation, dependency, and withdrawal. Initially, the **relief phase** refers to the relief experienced by using a drug, which allows a potential addict to escape one or more of the following feelings: boredom, loneliness, tension, fatigue, anger, or anxiety. The **increased use phase**

KEY TERMS

relief phase
satisfaction derived from escaping negative feelings by using the drug

increased use phase
taking increasing quantities of the drug

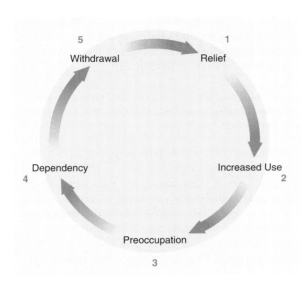

FIGURE 1.8 Stages of drug dependence.

involves taking greater quantities of the drug. The **preoccupation phase** consists of a continuous interest with and concern for the substance—that is, always having a supply of the drug and taking the drug is perceived as "normal" behavior. The **dependency phase** is synonymous with addiction. In this phase, more of the drug is sought without regard for the presence of negative physical symptoms, such as congested coughing and/or shortness of breath in cases of cigarette and marijuana addiction, blackouts from advanced alcohol abuse, and moderate to acute soreness and inflammation of nasal passages from snorting cocaine. The **withdrawal phase** involves such symptoms as itching, chills, tension, stomach pain, or depression from the nonuse of the addictive drug and/or an entire set of psychological concerns mainly involving an insatiable craving for the drug (Monroe 1996).

The Costs of Drug Use to Society

Many of the costs of drug addiction go beyond the user. Society pays a high price for drug addiction. Consider, for example, the loss of an addicted person's connection with reality and the loss of responsible dedication to careers and professions, illnesses experienced by the addicted individual, marital strife, shortened lives, and so on. Additionally, the dollar costs of addiction are also enormous.

The **National Institute on Drug Abuse (NIDA)** has estimated that the typical narcotic habit costs the user approximately $150 a day to support his or her addiction. The precise dollar amount spent to support a narcotic addiction largely depends on the geographic location where the drug is procured and used, availability of the drug affecting the price, and numerous other factors. For example, a heroin addict, will spend "$150–200 per day in order to support his or her habit" (Heroin.net 2016), which adds up to $54,750 to $73,000 per year just to maintain the drug supply. It is impossible for most addicts to get this amount of money legally; therefore, many support their habits by resorting to criminal activity or by working as or for drug dealers.

Most crimes related to drugs involve theft of personal property—primarily burglary and shoplifting—and, less commonly, assault and robbery (often mugging). Estimates are that a heroin addict must steal three to five times the actual cost of the drugs to maintain the habit, which becomes an astronomical and impractical amount per year. Further, it is not unusual with crack and heroin use that a high proportion of hardcore addicts resort to pimping and prostitution (with no accurate figures available regarding the cost of drug-related prostitution), although some law enforcement officials have estimated that prostitutes take in a total of $10 billion to $20 billion per year. It has also been estimated that nearly three out of every four prostitutes in major cities have a serious drug dependency.

In looking at the history of past-month methamphetamine (meth) users in the United States, we find that according to the yearly National Survey on Drug Use and Health (NSDUH) there were 569,000 (0.2%) users in 2014 (CBHSQ 2015). There were 440,000 (0.2%) users in 2011; 353,000 (0.1%) in 2010; 502,000 (0.2%) in 2009; 314,000 (0.1%) in 2008; 731,000 (0.3%) in 2006; and 530,000 (0.2%) in 2007 (SAMHSA 2012). In 2012, there were 133,000 new users of

KEY TERMS

preoccupation phase
constant concern with the supply of the drug

dependency phase
synonym for addiction

withdrawal phase
physical and/or psychological effects derived from not using the drug

National Institute on Drug Abuse (NIDA)
the principal federal agency responsible for directing research related to drug use and abuse

methamphetamine aged 12 or older, with the same number the previous year but a continuing a general downward trend across the past decade (SAMHSA 2012).

In the late 1990s there was a significant concern regarding the nationwide increase in clandestine laboratories involved in synthesizing or processing this type of illicit drug. Such laboratories produced amphetamine-type drugs, heroin-type drugs, designer drugs, and LSD and processed other drugs of abuse such as cocaine and crack. The DEA reported that 390 laboratories were seized in 1993, a figure that increased to 967 in 1995. Another example of the phenomenal growth of methamphetamine laboratories was found in Missouri. From 1995 to 1997, seizures of such labs in Missouri increased by 535% (Steward and Sitarmiah 1997). "In Dawson County in western Nebraska … 'The percentage of meth-related crimes is through the roof' … as reiterated by an investigator with the county sheriff's office…. In the state as a whole, officials discovered 38 methamphetamine laboratories in 1999; last year [2001] they discovered 179" (Butterfield 2002, p. A23). In 2012, the total number of meth clandestine laboratory incidents was 11,210, and included lab, dumpsite, and Chem/Glass/Equipment incidents (USDOJ 2013). Regarding seizures of this drug, one report states that "36,572 pounds: That's the amount of methamphetamine seized near the U.S.–Mexico border at U.S. Border Patrol stations and Customs and Border Protection ports of entry near the border from 2005 to 2011" (Chen 2013). In 2015, the state of Indiana had the highest amount of clandestine methamphetamine lab incidents, resulting in 1530 site seizures (Meth. IN.gov 2015). The reasons for such dramatic increases and usage are related to the enormous profits and relatively low risk associated with these operations. As a rule, clandestine laboratories are fairly mobile and relatively crude (often operating in a kitchen, basement, or garage) and are run by individuals with only elementary chemical skills.

Another interesting discovery was that these laboratories were not always stationary in locations such as garages, barns, homes, apartments, and so on. Although these stationary labs predominated, especially in the production of methamphetamine, mobile labs also made an appearance:

Cooking in cars and trucks helped producers in two ways: It eludes identification by law enforcement and motion helps the chemical reaction [of methamphetamine production]. Motels are a new production setting … [though fewer in number today]. Clandestine labs are also set up in federal parklands, where toxic byproducts pose a danger to hikers and campers. (ONDCP 2002, p. 58)

To demonstrate how a drug such as methamphetamine affects society, in 2003, the following was reported:

With portable meth labs popping up everywhere from motel bathrooms to the back seat of a Chevy, it was only a matter of time before they made their way onto campus. Last November, a custodian notified campus police at [University in Texas] about what appeared to be a lab set up in a music practice room in the [university's] Fine Arts Center. "We found beakers of red liquid, papers and other residue, and the room had this horrible odor…."

Students were on vacation, so the practice room, which had its windows blackened out, would have afforded the occupant a few days to cook. [One campus police official] … speculates that this is just the beginning: "Labs are popping up on campuses all over the country. It's just too easy now. You can get the recipe on the Internet. Still, how could someone be so brazen as to set up an operation next to the French horn section?" (Jellinek 2003, p. 54)

Because of a lack of training, inexperience, and the danger of experiencing the effects of methamphetamine while making the drug, the chemical "cooking" procedures are performed crudely, sometimes resulting in adulterants and impure products. Such contaminants can be very toxic, causing severe harm or even death to the unsuspecting user as well as a greater likelihood of sudden explosion (Drug Strategies 1995). Fortunately, when looking at all the illicit drugs produced by such underground laboratories, such outbreaks of physically harmful drugs do not occur very often. Partial proof of this is found in the small number of news stories of deaths or poisonings from illicit drugs. Nevertheless, because profit drives these clandestine labs, which obviously have no government supervision, impurities or "cheap fillers" are always possible so that greater profits can be made. Here, caution is very advisable in that drug purchasers do not have any guarantees when purchasing powerful illicit drugs.

Society continues paying a large sum even after users, addicts, and drug dealers are caught and sentenced because it takes from $75 to $1500 per day to keep one person incarcerated. A recent post by the Federal Register (2015) reports that "The fee to cover the average cost of incarceration for Federal inmates in Fiscal Year 2014 was $30,619.85 ($83.89 per day). (Please note: There were 365 days in FY 2014.) The average annual cost to confine an inmate in a Residential Reentry Center for Fiscal Year 2014 was $28,999.25 ($79.45 per day)."

Supporting programs such as methadone maintenance costs much less. New York officials estimate that methadone maintenance costs about $3000 per year per patient. For nonhospital residential treatment, methadone costs average around $76.13 per day. With outpatient methadone programs, daily costs average around $17.78 per day (Methadone Centers 2016), which is much less than the cost of incarceration.

A more long-term effect of drug abuse that has substantial impact on society is the medical and psychological care often required by addicts due to disease resulting from their drug habit. Particularly noteworthy are the communicable diseases spread because of needle sharing within the drug-abusing population, such as hepatitis and HIV.

In the United States, the Centers for Disease Control and Prevention (CDC) estimates that 1,218,400 persons aged 13 years and older are living with HIV infection, including 156,300 (12.8%) who are unaware of their infection. Over the past decade, the number of people living with HIV has increased, while the annual number of new HIV infections has remained relatively stable. Still, the pace of new infections continues at far too high a level—particularly among certain groups (CDC 2015b). (Acquired immune deficiency syndrome [AIDS] has a tendency to develop within 5 to 10 years of the onset of HIV.) Worldwide, approximately 35 million people are living with HIV/AIDS (CDC 2016). This number includes people living in sub-Saharan Africa, Asia, Latin America and the Caribbean, Eastern Europe, Central Asia, North America, Western and Central Europe, North Africa and the Middle East, and Oceania (Clinton 2006).

In the United States, HIV is spread primarily through unprotected sexual intercourse and sharing of previously used needles to inject drugs. HIV in the injecting–drug-user subpopulation is transmitted in the small (minuscule) amount of contaminated blood remaining in the used needles. The likelihood of a member of the drug-abusing population contracting HIV directly correlates with the frequency of injections and the extent of needle sharing. Care for AIDS patients lasts a lifetime, and many of these medical expenses come from federal- and state-funded programs. Many cities throughout the United States have publicly funded programs that distribute new, uncontaminated needles to drug addicts. The needles are free of charge in exchange for used injection needles in order to prevent the spread of HIV and hepatitis B and C from contaminated needles. These programs are often referred to as **needle-exchange programs**.

Also of great concern is drug abuse by women during pregnancy. Some psychoactive drugs can have profound, permanent effects on a developing fetus. The best documented is fetal alcohol syndrome (FAS), which can affect the offspring of alcoholic mothers. Cocaine and amphetamine-related drugs can also cause irreversible congenital changes when used during pregnancy. All too often, the affected offspring of addicted mothers become the responsibility of welfare organizations. In addition to the costs to society just mentioned, other costs of drug abuse include drug-related deaths, emergency room visits and hospital stays, and automobile fatalities.

■ Drugs, Crime, and Violence

There is a long-established close association between drug abuse and criminality. The beliefs (hypotheses) for this association range along a continuum between two opposing views: (1) criminal behavior develops as a means to support addiction, and (2) criminality is inherently linked to the user's personality and occurs independently of drug use (Bureau of Justice Statistics [BJS] 2006; Drug Strategies 1995; McBride and McCoy 2003). In other words, does drug addiction cause a person to engage in criminal behavior such as burglary, theft, and larceny to pay for the drug habit? Or, does criminal behavior stem from an already existing criminal personality such that drugs are used as an adjunct to commit such acts? In other words, are drugs used in conjunction with crime to sedate and give the added confidence needed to commit daring law violations?

KEY TERM

needle-exchange programs
publicly funded programs that distribute new, uncontaminated needles to drug addicts in exchange for used injection needles in order to prevent the spread of HIV and hepatitis B and C

The answers to these questions have never been clear because findings that contradict one view in favor of the other continue to mount on both sides. Part of the reason for the controversy about the relationship between criminal activity and drug abuse is that studies have been conducted in different settings and cultures, employing different research methods, and focusing on different addictive drugs. As a result, too many factors are involved to allow us to distinguish the cause from the result. We know that each type of drug has unique addictive potential and that interpretation of exactly when a deviant act is an offense (violation of law) varies. Furthermore, we know that people think differently while under the influence of drugs. Whether criminalistic behavior is *directly* caused by the drug use or whether prior socialization and peer influence work in concert to cause criminal behavior remains unclear. Certainly, we think it would be safe to believe that prior socialization, law-violating peers, and drugs are strong contributing factors for criminal behavior.

Although this controversy about the connection between drugs and crime continues to challenge our thinking, the following findings are also noteworthy:

- The United States ranks first the world in the number of people incarcerated in federal and state correctional facilities. In 2014, 1,561,500 prisoners were under the jurisdiction of state and federal correctional authorities (BJS 2015a). Almost half (48%) of the federal inmates were serving time for drug offenses (Carson and Sabol 2012).
- The United States incarcerates more people for drug offenses than any other country (Natarajan et al. 2008; Sentencing Project 2013).
- With an estimated 24.6 million Americans struggling with current (within 30 days of use) drug use and/or dependence (SAMHSA 2014b), the growth of the prison population continues to be driven largely by incarceration for drug offenses.
- In 2006, "17% of State and 18% of Federal prisoners committed their crime to obtain money for drugs" (Mumola and Karberg 2007, p. 1). Approximately one out of every six major crimes is committed because of the offender's need to obtain money for drugs.
- An estimated 516,900 black males were in state or federal prison on December 31, 2014,

on sentences of more than 1 year, which was 37% of the sentenced male prison population. White males made up an additional 32% of the male population (453,500 inmates), followed by Hispanic males (308,700 inmates, or 22%). White females in state or federal prison at yearend 2014 (53,100 prisoners) outnumbered black (22,600) and Hispanic females (17,800) combined (BJS 2015b).

- 80% of offenders abuse drugs or alcohol (National Council on Alcoholism and Drug Dependence [NCADD] 2015).
- Nearly 50% of jail and prison inmates are clinically addicted (NCADD 2015).
- Approximately 60% of individuals arrested for most types of crimes test positive for illegal drugs at arrest (NCADD 2015).
- In 2011, 45% of arrestees tested positive for marijuana during their arrest, 41% for cocaine, 61% for opiates, and 61% for methamphetamine (ONDCP 2012).
- The Arrestee Drug Abuse Monitoring Program (ADAM) reports that arrestees are tested for the presence of 10 drugs. The proportion of arrestees testing positive for any of the 10 drugs ranged from 63% in Atlanta to 83% in Chicago and Sacramento. Arrestees testing positive for multiple drugs in their system ranged from 12% in Atlanta to 50% in Sacramento (ONDCP 2014).
- Marijuana remained the most commonly detected drug in urine testing, from 34% of ADAM II arrestees testing positive in Atlanta to 59% in Sacramento. Those who obtained marijuana in the prior 30 days reported little difficulty obtaining the drug, indicating an overall high availability of the drug in all sites (ONDCP 2014).
- In federal prisons in 2015, the Bureau of Justice Statistics (2015b) reports that almost all (99.5%) drug offenders in federal prison were serving sentences for drug trafficking.
- Cocaine (powder or crack) was the primary drug type for more than half (54%) of drug offenders in federal prison.
- Race of drug offenders varied greatly by drug type. Blacks were 88% of crack cocaine offenders, Hispanics or Latinos were 54% of powder cocaine offenders, and whites were 48% of methamphetamine offenders (BJS 2015b).
- More than one-third (35%) of drug offenders in federal prison at sentencing had either no or minimal criminal history (BJS 2015b).

- 52% of female jail inmates were found to be dependent on alcohol or drugs, compared to 44% of male inmates (BJS 2015b).
- Jail inmates between the ages of 25 and 44 had the highest rate of substance dependence or abuse (7 in 10 inmates). Those age 55 or older had the lowest rate (nearly 5 in 10 inmates) (Karberg and James 2002).
- More than 50% of drug or property offenders were dependent on or had abused a substance, compared to over 60% of violent and public-order offenders (Karberg and James 2002).
- Women and white inmates were more likely to have used drugs at the time of their offense (Karberg and James 2002).
- Thirty-two percent of state and 26.4% of federal prison inmates reported being under the influence of drugs at the time of their offense in 2004 (see **Table 1.5**). Approximately 44% were incarcerated for drug offenses in state prisons and 32% were incarcerated in federal prisons. Of these, 46% in state prisons and 21% in federal prisons were arrested for possession. Forty-two percent were serving time in state prisons and 34% were serving time in federal prisons for trafficking in drugs. One outcome of these findings is that one out of every four major crimes committed—violent, property, and drug offenses—involves an offender who is under the influence of drugs (Mumola and Karberg 2007).
- Of the 1,561,231 arrests for drug law violations in 2014, 83.1% (1,297,384) were for possession of a controlled substance. Only 16.9% (263,848) were for the sale or manufacturing of a drug (DrugWarFacts.org 2016).

In regard to the connection between drug use and crime, the following findings can be summarized: (1) drug users in comparison to nondrug users are more likely to commit crimes, (2) a high percentage of arrestees are often under the influence of a drug while committing crimes, and (3) a high percentage of drug users arrested for drug use and violence are more likely to be under the influence of alcohol and/or stimulant types of drugs such as cocaine, crack, and methamphetamines.

Drug-related crimes are undoubtedly overwhelming the U.S. judicial system. Table 1.5 shows the percentage of state and federal inmates reporting being under the influence of drugs at the time of their offenses in 2004. Approximately 29%

TABLE 1.5 Percentage of State and Federal Inmates Reporting Being Under the Influence of Drugs at the Time of Their Offense: 2004

	State (%)	Federal (%)
Total[a]	32.1	26.4
Violent offenses	27.7	24.0
Homicide	27.3	16.8
Sexual assault[b]	17.4	13.8
Robbery	40.7	29.4
Assault	24.1	20.1
Property offenses	38.5	13.6
Burglary	41.1	:
Larceny/theft	40.1	:
Motor vehicle theft	38.7	:
Fraud	34.1	9.3
Drug offenses	43.6	32.3
Possession	46.0	20.9
Trafficking	42.3	33.8
Public order offenses[c]	25.4	18.7
Weapons	27.6	27.8
Other public order	24.6	8.0

[a] Includes offenses not shown.

[b] Includes rape and other sexual assault.

[c] Excluding DWI/DUI.

: Not calculated; too few cases to permit calculation.

Data from Mumola, C. J., and J. C. Karberg. *Drug Use and Dependence, State and Federal Prisoners*. Washington, DC: U.S. Dept. of Justice (USDOJ), Office of Justice Programs (OJP), 19 January 2007: 1–12.

of state and federal prisoners were under the influence of drugs for violent offenses (e.g., homicide, sexual assault, robbery, assault), 26% for property offenses (e.g., burglary, larceny/theft, motor vehicle theft, fraud), 38% for drug offenses (possession, trafficking), and 22% for public order offenses (e.g., weapons, other public order offenses) (Mumola and Karberg 2007). Furthermore, nearly 40% of the young people (often younger than 21 years of age) in adult correctional facilities reported drinking before committing a crime.

DRUG CARTELS

Drug cartels are defined as large, highly sophisticated organizations composed of multiple drug-trafficking organizations (DTOs) and **drug cells** with specific assignments, such as drug transportation, security/enforcement, or money laundering. (A drug cell is similar to a terrorist cell, consisting of only three to five members to ensure operational security. Members of adjacent drug cells usually do not know each other or the identity of their leadership.) Drug cartel command-and-control structures are based outside the United States; however, they produce, transport, and distribute illicit drugs domestically with the assistance of DTOs that are either a part of or in an alliance with the cartel. Here are some reports of incidents in the world of drugs, violence, and crime:

> As a political analyst living and working in Mexico for the last three decades, I have watched with horror how the United States–Mexico drug war strategy has led to the explosion of violence and criminal activity here. The deep-rooted complicity between government officials and security forces on the one hand and cartels on the other means that the training, equipment and firepower given in aid and sold to the Mexican government fuel violence on both sides.
>
> The lines blur. The cartels are not fighting the state for political power; they are seeking to protect a $40 billion drug-trafficking business that has been converted into a war for control of territory, a war against the people. (Carlsen 2016)
>
> In recent years, ... (notorious drug lord "El Chapo") ... Guzman extended the operations of his Sinaloa cartel to an estimated 50 countries across Latin America, Africa, and Europe, even hooking up with one of the most notorious Italian mafias, the 'Ndrangheta. (Fausset and Wilkinson 2014)
>
> In Mexico, [former] President Felipe Calderon may [have been] the constitutionally elected leader of the nation [in 2007], but in reality, drug cartels and warlords exercise de facto authority over much of the area.... Drug trafficking overwhelmingly is the prevailing social malady throughout the country, particularly along the border with the United States. In spite of lengthy declarations by government officials in Mexico City and Washington, and their insistence that important battles are being won against drug trafficking, criminal organizations like the Tijuana cartel continue to thrive, ruling over whole sections of the Mexican countryside like sectoral feudal lords.... The governor of the state of Nuevo Leon (bordering the United States), Natividad Gonzalez Paras, has declared that: "Unfortunately, the drug problem has escalated significantly in the past six to seven years. It is a national problem affecting most of the country's states. It is a dispute between cartels or organizations to control locations, cities, and routes." (Birns and Sánchez 2007)

In another news report:

> Once known merely as "mules" for Colombia's powerful cocaine cartels, today Mexico's narcotics traffickers are the kingpins of this hemisphere's drug trade, and the front line of the war on drugs has shifted from Colombia to America's back door.
>
> In August 2005, the *Christian Science Monitor* reported that according to senior U.S. officials, in the biggest reorganization since the 1980s, Mexican cartels had leveraged the profits from their delivery routes to wrest control from the Colombian producers. As a result, Mexican drug lords are in control of what the U.N. estimates is a $142 billion a year business in cocaine, heroin, marijuana, methamphetamine, and other illicit drugs.
>
> The new dominance of Mexican cartels has caused a spike in violence along the 2000-mile U.S.–Mexico border where rival cartels are warring against Mexican and U.S. authorities. Drugs are either flown from Colombia to Mexico in small planes, or, in the case of marijuana and methamphetamine, produced locally.

KEY TERMS

drug cartels
large, highly sophisticated organizations composed of multiple drug-trafficking organizations (DTOs) and cells with specific assignments, such as drug transportation, security/enforcement, or money laundering

drug cells
are similar to terrorist cells, consisting of only three to five members to ensure operational security; members of adjacent drug cells usually do not know each other or the identity of their leadership

Then, they're shipped into the U.S. by boat, private vehicles, or in commercial trucks crossing the border....

The Sept. 26 edition of the *San Antonio Express-News* reported that a new method of intimidation is being utilized by Mexican drug cartels—beheadings. So far this year, at least 26 people have been decapitated in Mexico, with heads stuck on fences, dumped in trash piles, and even tossed onto a nightclub dance floor. In the latter act of violence, which took place in early morning hours of Wednesday, Sept. 6, five heads were scattered on the dance floor of a bar in the state of Michoacan, notorious for drug trafficking. No arrests for the killings have been announced. (Worldpress.org 2006)

And, in another news report:

The dead policeman is found propped against a tree off a dirt road on the outskirts of the city. He is dressed like a cartoon version of a Mexican cowboy wearing a blanket. The murder and symbolic mutilation of *policìa* has become almost routine in Caliacán, capital of the Mexican state of Sinaloa: Pablo Aispuro Ramìrez is one of 90 cops to be killed here this year. There is a note pinned to the body, a warning to anyone who dares to oppose the powerful drug lord who ordered the execution "I'm a copycowboy!" the note reads. "Ahoo-ya! There are going to be more soon." (Lawson 2008, p. 76)

In addition,

The Tijuana-based Felix drug cartel and the Juarez-based Fuentes cartel began buying legitimate businesses in small towns in Los Angeles County in the early 1990s.... They purchased restaurants, used-car lots, auto-body shops and other small businesses. One of their purposes was to use these businesses for money-laundering operations. Once established in their community, these cartel-financed business owners ran for city council and other local offices. (Farah 2006, quoting an excerpt from *In Mortal Danger* by Tom Tancredo, a former U.S. Congressman, Colorado)

These news briefs are just a very small sampling of the types of crimes and violence perpetrated by drug dealers. It is clear that production, merchandising, and distribution of illicit drugs have developed into a worldwide operation worth hundreds of billions of dollars (Goldstein 2001); one publication states that the United Nations (UN) estimates that the global world drug trade is worth $320 billion annually (Stopthedrugwar. org 2005). These enormous profits have attracted organized crime, both in the United States and abroad, and all too frequently even corrupt law enforcement agencies (McShane 1994). For the participants in such operations, drugs can mean incredible wealth and power. For example, dating back to 1992, Pablo Escobar was recognized as a drug kingpin and leader of the cocaine cartel in Colombia, and he was acknowledged as one of the world's richest men and Colombia's most powerful man (Wire Services 1992). With his drug-related wealth, Escobar financed a private army to conduct a personal war against the government of Colombia (Associated Press 1992); until his death in 1993, he was a serious threat to his country's stability.

In December 1999, the notorious Juarez drug cartel was believed to be responsible for burying more than 100 bodies (including 22 Americans) in a mass grave at a ranch in Mexico. All of the deaths were believed to be drug related. According to a news story on this gruesome discovery, the alleged perpetrator, Vincente Carrillo Fuentes, is one among dozens of drug lords and lieutenants wanted by U.S. law enforcement agents (Associated Press 1999). A more current drug lord, Ismael "el Mayo" Zambada, age 62, is "one of Mexico's most wanted drug lords, who has never been arrested despite a $5 million reward offered in the United States" (Campbell 2010, p. 1). This same news release indicated that the drug trade would not end until drug cartels are eliminated. Such occurrences, which are often reported by the mass media, indicate the existence of powerful and dangerous drug cartels that are responsible for the availability of illicit drugs around the world.

And finally, more recent information involves another drug kingpin, "El Chapo" Guzman:

Born in Badiraguato, Mexico, Joaquín Guzmán Loera entered the drug trade as a teenager. Nicknamed "El Chapo," he founded the Sinaloa cartel in 1989, over time building it into an immensely profitable global drug-trafficking operation. Known for his violent actions and powerful influence, Guzmán has successfully orchestrated daring escapes from maximum-security prisons in his home country. One such escape came in July 2015, although he was recaptured the following January in the Mexican city of Los Mochis....

Guzmán coupled that success with serious muscle. He established gangs with names such as "Los Chachos," "Los Texas," "Los Lobos," and "Los Negros" to protect his empire. Over the years, Guzmán's men have been accused of committing more than 1000 murders throughout Mexico, the casualties including both incompetent henchmen and rival bosses....

On January 8, 2016, Mexican President Enrique Peña Nieto announced on Twitter that Mexican authorities had recaptured Guzmán after a shootout earlier that morning in the city of Los Mochis.

"Mission Accomplished," the President wrote. "We have him." (Bio. 2016)

Drug-related violence takes its toll at all levels, as rival gangs fight to control their "turf" and associated drug operations. Innocent bystanders often become unsuspecting victims of the indiscriminate violence. For example, a Roman Catholic cardinal was killed on May 24, 1993, when a car he was a passenger in was inadvertently driven into the middle of a drug-related shootout between traffickers at the international airport in Guadalajara, Mexico. Five other innocent bystanders were killed in the incident (Associated Press 1993). Finally, it was recently reported that, when spotted, the Mexican army engages in shooting at cartel members and likewise armed cartel members shoot back. When this occurs, mostly in border towns and cities in Mexico, innocent bystanders, many of them children, are often caught in the crossfire and are routinely killed (Del Bosque 2010). On April 13, 2010, one report cites just such an incident. In Acapulco, Mexico, 24 people died, half of whom were innocent bystanders: "[T]he shootout broke out in the middle of the day in the center of the town as it was full of bystanders" (Associated Press 2010, p. 38). In many other incidents, unsuspecting people have been injured or killed by drug users who, while under the influence of drugs, commit violent criminal acts.

▌ Drugs in the Workplace: A Persistent Affliction

"He was a good, solid worker, always on the job—until he suddenly backed his truck over a 4-inch gas line." If the line had ruptured, there would have been a serious explosion, according to the driver's employer. The accident raised a red flag: "under the company's standard policy, the employee was tested for drugs and alcohol. He was positive for both" (Edelson 2000, p. 3).

Another tragic incident involving drug use occurred in Alvin, Texas, in December 2012, when "a 20-year-old man ran over two young boys, ages 11 and 12, in front of their father after having too much drink. Later, the driver was killed by gunshot, and the boys' father was charged" (Project Know 2016).

Generally, once drug use becomes habitual, drug use is brought into the workplace, because, second to the home and social environments, the work environment for full-time employees is the place where they spend the most time. The National Household Surveys, for example, found evidence of significant drug use among full-time workers, with approximately 7% to 9% drinking while working. In the surveys, 64.3% of full-time workers reported alcohol use within the past month (SAMHSA 2012). Some 6.4% of full-time workers reported marijuana use within the past month. Part-time employees were slightly more likely to be past-month illicit drug users in comparison to full-time workers in 2010 (11.2 % vs. 8.4%) (SAMHSA 2012).

WORKER SUBSTANCE ABUSE IN DIFFERENT INDUSTRIES

Substance use in the workplace negatively affects U.S. industry through lost productivity, workplace accidents and injuries, employee absenteeism, low morale, and increased illness. The loss to U.S. companies due to employees' alcohol and drug use and related problems is estimated at billions of dollars a year. Research shows that the rate of substance use varies by occupation and industry (Larson et al. 2007). Studies also have indicated that employers vary in their treatment of substance use issues and that workplace-based employee assistance programs (EAPs) can be a valuable resource for obtaining help for substance-using workers (Delaney, Grube, and Ames 1998; Reynolds and Lehman 2003).

Regarding employment, highlights from SAMHSA (2014b) indicate the following:

ILLICIT DRUG USE

- Current illicit drug use differed by employment status in 2013 and 2014. Among adults age 18 or older, the numbers and percentage of illicit drug use was higher for unemployed persons (2.1 million users, or 18.2%, in 2013 and 2 million, or 18.7%, in 2014) than for those who were employed full time (10.8 million, or 9.1%,

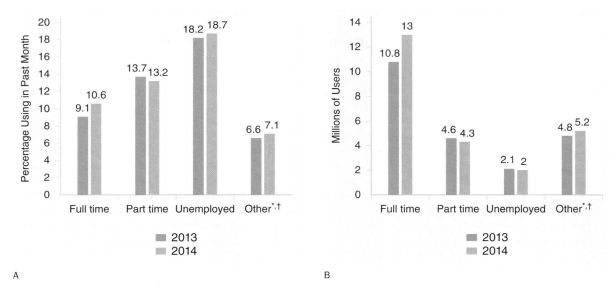

FIGURE 1.9 Panel A shows the percentages of past-month illicit drug use among persons aged 18 or older by employment status in 2013 and 2014. Panel B shows the numbers in millions of past-month illicit drug users based on employment status.

* Difference between this estimate and the 2014 estimate is statistically significant at the .05 level.

† The Other employment category includes retired persons, disabled persons, homemakers, students, or other persons not in the labor force.

Reproduced from Center for Behavioral Health Statistics and Quality (CBHSQ). *Behavioral Health Trends in the United States: Results from the 2014 National Survey on Drug Use and Health.* NSDUH Series H-50, HHS Publication No. (SMA) 15-4927. Rockville, MD: Substance Abuse and Mental Health Services Administration, 2015.

in 2013 and 13 million, or 10.6%, in 2014) or part time (4.6 million, or 13.7%, in 2013 and 4.3 million, or 13.2%, in 2014). The rate of other employment, which includes retired and disabled person, homemakers, students, or other persons not in the labor force, was 4.8 million (6.6%) in 2013 and 5.2 million (7.1%) in 2014. These rates were all similar to the corresponding rates in 2012 (see **Figure 1.9**).

- Of the 22.4 million current illicit drug users aged 18 or older in 2013, 15.4 million (68.9%) were employed either full or part time.

ALCOHOL USE

- The rate of current alcohol usage in 2013 was 65.8% for full-time employed adults aged 18 or older, which was higher than the rate for unemployed adults (53.8%). The rates of binge drinking were similar for adults who were employed full time and those who were unemployed (30.5% and 31.3%, respectively).
- Among adults in 2013, most binge and heavy alcohol users were employed. Among the 58.5 million adults who were binge drinkers, 44.5 million (76.1%) were employed either full or part time. Among the 16.2 million adults who were heavy drinkers, 12.4 million (76.0%) were employed.

TOBACCO USE

- In 2013, current cigarette smoking was more common among unemployed adults aged 18 or older (40.1%) than among adults who were working full time or part time (22.8% and 23.4%, respectively).
- Current use of smokeless tobacco in 2013 was higher among adults aged 18 or older who were employed full time (4.8%) and those who were unemployed (4.9%) than among those who were employed part time (2.2%) and those in the "other" employment category, which includes persons not in the labor force (1.9%).

SUBSTANCE DEPENDENCE

- Rates of substance dependence or abuse were associated with current employment status in 2013. A higher percentage of unemployed adults aged 18 or older were classified with dependence or abuse (15.2%) than were full-time employed adults (9.5%) or part-time employed adults (9.3%).
- Over half of the adults aged 18 or older with substance dependence or abuse were employed full time in 2013. Of the 20.3 million adults who were classified with dependence or abuse, 11.3 million (55.7%) were employed full time.

Highlights from SAMHSA, Office of Applied Studies (2007), indicate the following (see **Figure 1.10**):

- Among the 19 major industry categories, the highest rates of past-month illicit drug use among full-time workers ages 18 to 64 were found in accommodations and food services (19.1%) and arts, entertainment, and recreation (13.7%).
- The industry categories with the lowest rates of past-month illicit drug use were found in mining (5.0%), educational services (4.8%), and public administration (4.3%).
- The overall rate of past-month illicit drug use among full-time workers aged 18 to 64

was 8.6%. Rates of past-month illicit drug use ranged from 19.1% among workers in the accommodations and food services industry to 4.3% among workers in the public administration industry. These findings remained true even when controlling for gender and age differences across industries.

- The overall rate of past-year substance use disorder among full-time workers aged 18 to 64 was 9.5%. Rates of past-year substance use disorder ranged from 16.9% among workers in the accommodations and food services industry to 5.5% among workers in the educational services industry.
- Although the accommodations and food services industry group had the highest rate of past-year

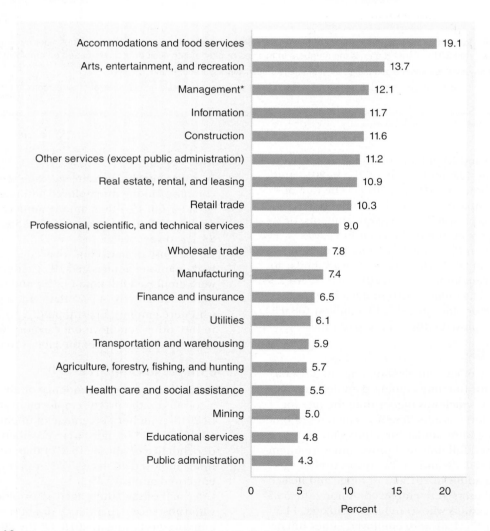

FIGURE 1.10   Illicit drug use by industry category: Past-month illicit drug use among full-time workers aged 18 to 64: 2011–2012, combined.

* The full title of this category is "Management of companies and enterprises, administration, support, waste management, and remediation services."

Reproduced from Substance Abuse and Mental Health Services Administration (SAMHSA). *The National Survey on Drug Use and Health (NSDUH) Report. Worker Substance Use, by Industry Category.* Rockville, MD: Office of Applied Studies, 24 March 2012.

substance use disorder, this finding did not remain true after controlling for age and gender distributions. *This indicates that the high rate can be attributed to the demographic composition of the accommodation and food services industry.*

Although not shown in Figure 1.10, the following findings have also been reported (CBHSQ 2012 unless otherwise noted):

- The overall rate of past-month heavy alcohol use among full-time workers aged 18 to 64 was 8.7%. Rates of past-month heavy alcohol use ranged from 17.5% among workers in the mining industry to 4.4% among workers in the healthcare and social assistance industry.
- Workers in the mining (17.5%) and construction (16.5%) industries had the highest rates of past-month heavy alcohol use. For the workers in the construction industry, this finding remained true even when controlling for gender and age differences across industries. This indicates that there is something unique about past-month heavy alcohol use for the construction industry that would remain even if the construction industry had the same gender and age distribution of any other industry. However, for the mining industry, this higher rate did not remain when controlling for age or gender differences. *This indicates that the high heavy alcohol use rate in the mining industry can be attributed to the demographic composition of the mining industry.*
- Approximately 80% of large companies test for drug use, and approximately 60% of medium companies and 26% of small companies perform such testing. Of those companies that drug test, more than 90% use urine analysis, less than 20% use blood analysis, and less than 6% use hair analysis.
- Most companies that administer drug tests test for marijuana, cocaine, opiates, amphetamines, and PCP.
- Age is the most significant predictor of marijuana and cocaine use. Younger employees (18 to 24 years) are more likely to report drug use than older employees are (25 years or older).
- In general, unmarried workers report roughly twice as much illicit drug and heavy alcohol use as married workers. Among food preparation workers, transportation drivers, and mechanics, and in industries such as construction and machinery (not electrical), the discrepancy between married and unmarried workers is especially notable.

- Workers who report having three or more jobs in the previous 5 years are twice as likely to be current or past-year illicit drug users as those who held two or fewer jobs over the same period (NCADD 2016).
- 70% of the estimated 14.8 million Americans who use illegal drugs are employed (NCADD 2016).
- Marijuana is the most commonly used and abused illegal drug by employees, followed by cocaine, with prescription drug use steadily increasing (NCADD 2016).
- Workers in occupations that affect public safety, including truck drivers, firefighters, and police officers, report the highest rate of participation in drug testing.
- "Among full-time workers, heavy drinkers and illicit drug users are more likely than those who do not drink heavily or use illicit drugs to have skipped work in the past month or have worked for three or more employers in the past year" (Robert Wood Johnson Foundation 2001, p. 45).
- Most youths do not cease drug use when they begin working.

In summarizing this research on employees who abuse alcohol or other drugs, five major findings emerge: (1) these workers are three times more likely than the average employee to be late to work, (2) they are three times more likely to receive sickness benefits, (3) they are 16 times more likely to be absent from work, (4) they are five times more likely to be involved in on-the-job accidents (note that many of these hurt others, not themselves), and (5) they are five times more likely to file compensation claims.

Employee Assistance Programs

Many industries have responded to drugs in the workplace by creating **drug testing** and **employee assistance programs (EAPs)**. Most often, drug testing generally involves urine screening, blood screening, and/or hair follicle analysis that is undertaken to identify which employees are using

KEY TERMS

drug testing
urine, blood screening, or hair analysis used to identify those who may be using drugs

employee assistance programs (EAPs)
drug assistance programs for drug-dependent employees

drugs and which employees may have current or potential drug problems. EAPs are employer-financed programs administered by a company or through an outside contractor. More than 400,000 EAPs have been established in the United States.

The following are some important findings regarding workplace substance use policies and programs among full-time workers:

- Full-time workers aged 18 to 64 who used illicit drugs in the past month were generally less likely than those who did not use illicit drugs in the past month to work for an employer with a written policy about employee use of alcohol and drugs. Similarly, full-time workers who drank heavily in the past month were less likely than those who did not drink heavily to have an employer that provided these workplace policies and programs (SAMHSA 2014c).
- Of employees ages 18 to 64 who had used an illicit drug in the past month, 32.1% worked for an employer who offered educational information about alcohol and drug use, 71% were aware of a written policy about drug and alcohol use in the workplace, and 45.4% worked for an employer who maintained an EAP or other type of counseling program for employees who have an alcohol- or drug-related problem (SAMHSA, OAS 2007).
- Among full-time workers who used alcohol heavily in the past month, 37.2% worked for an employer who provided educational information about drug and alcohol use, 73.7% were aware of written policies about drug and alcohol use, and 51.1% had access to an EAP at their workplace (SAMHSA, OAS 2007)
- The most common EAP service that companies utilize is for job stress (87.9%), followed by substance abuse (84.1%), bereavement (83.4%), work–life balance (82.8%), and relationship counseling (82.2%), with slightly lower percentages mainly involving elder care/child care/parenting issues (78.3%), family violence (75.2%), harassment (73.2%), and financial or legal services (72.6%) (Pyrillis 2014).
- Approximately three-quarters of companies have an EAP (Pyrillis 2014).
- "U.S. enrollment in EAPs has increased by 285% since 2002, according to a 2011 survey

by Open Minds, a market research firm based in Gettysburg, Pennsylvania. More than 97% of companies with more than 5000 employees have an EAP and continued growth is expected, according to the Employee Assistance Research Foundation" (Pyrillis 2014).

EAP programs are designed to aid in identifying and resolving productivity problems associated with employees' emotional or physical concerns, such as those related to health, marital problems, family relationships, financial issues, and substance abuse. EAPs have also expanded their focus to combat employee abuse of OTC and prescription drugs in addition to illicit psychoactive substances. Overall, the programs attempt to formally reduce problems associated with impaired job performance.

Regarding drug testing today, the Society for Human Resource Management (SHRM) conducted an online survey taken by 454 randomly selected human resource managers from diverse organizations (U.S. Department of Labor 2009). The following drug testing practices were in effect:

- 84% of employers required new hires to pass drug screenings.
- 74% used drug screening when reasonable suspicion of drug use was determined.
- 58% of organizations used post-accident drug screening.
- 39% used random drug screening.
- 14% used scheduled drug testing.

Further, 70% of those responding to this survey indicated that their organization has a written policy that addresses drug testing. From these survey results, we can see that the future for employee drug testing is very bright. In all probability, if you have not already experienced such a screening, you will experience one at some point in your working life.

Today, drug testing can include the following (U.S. Department of Labor 2016):

- *Urine*: Testing for drug metabolites in a person's urine.
- *Breath*: The breath-alcohol test is the most common test for finding out how much alcohol is currently in the blood.
- *Hair*: Analysis of hair provides a much longer "testing window," giving a more complete drug-use history going back as far as 90 days.
- *Oral fluids*: *S*aliva, or oral fluids, collected from the mouth also can be used to detect traces of drugs and alcohol. Oral fluids are

KEY TERMS

oral fluids
oral fluid testing analyses a saliva sample for drugs of abuse and their metabolites

easy to collect (a swab of the inner cheek is the most common collection method), harder to adulterate or substitute, and may be better at detecting specific substances, including marijuana, cocaine, and amphetamines/methamphetamines.

* **Sweat**: Another type of drug test consists of a skin patch that measures drugs in sweat. The patch, which looks like a large adhesive bandage, is applied to the skin and worn for some length of time. A gas-permeable membrane on the patch protects the tested area from dirt and other contaminants. Although relatively easy to administer, this method has not been widely used in workplaces and is more often used to maintain compliance with probation and parole.

The following drugs that are detectable differ in the length of time they are detectable (U.S. Department of Labor 2016):

* Alcohol: 1 oz. for 1.5 hours
* Amphetamines: 48 hours
* Barbiturates: 2 to 10 days
* Benzodiazepines: 2 to 3 weeks
* Cocaine: 2 to 10 days
* Heroin metabolites: Less than 1 day
* Morphine: 2 to 3 days
* LSD: 8 hours
* Marijuana: Casual use, 3 to 4 days; chronic use, several weeks
* Methamphetamine: 2 to 3 days
* Methadone: 2 to 3 days
* PCP: 1 week

Venturing to a Higher Form of Consciousness: The Holistic Self-Awareness Approach to Drug Use

Whenever drug use leads to abuse, it rarely results from a single, isolated cause. Instead, it is often caused or preceded by multiple factors, which may include combinations of the following:

* Hereditary (genetic) factors
* Psychological conditioning
* Peer group pressures
* Inability to cope with the stress and anxiety of daily living
* Quality of role models
* Degree of attachment to a family structure
* Level of security with gender identity and sexual orientation
* Personality traits
* Perceived ethnic and racial compatibility with society as a whole and socioeconomic status (social class)

As authors, we strongly endorse and advocate a **holistic self-awareness approach** that emphasizes a healthy balance among mind, body, and spirit. Health and wellness can be achieved only when these three domains of existence are free from any unnecessary use of psychoactive substances. The holistic philosophy is based on the idea that the mind has a powerful influence on maintaining health. All three—mind, body, and spirit—work as a unified whole to promote health and wellness. Similarly, we are in agreement with holistic health advocates who emphasize the following viewpoint:

Holistic Health is based on the law of nature that a whole is made up of interdependent parts. The earth is made up of systems, such as air, land, water, plants and animals. If life is to be sustained, they cannot be separated, for what is happening to one is also felt by all the other systems. In the same way, an individual is a whole made up of interdependent parts, which are the physical, mental, emotional, and spiritual. While one part is not working at its best, it impacts all the other parts of that person.... A common explanation is to view wellness as a continuum along a line. The line represents all possible degrees of health. The far left end of the line represents premature death. On the far right end is the highest possible level of wellness or maximum well-being. The center point of the line represents a lack of apparent disease. This places all levels of illness on the left half of the wellness continuum. The right half shows that even when no illness seems to be present, there is still a lot of room for improvement.... Holistic Health is an ongoing process. As a lifestyle, it includes a personal commitment to be moving toward

KEY TERMS

sweat
sweat is used for drug testing; a skin patch is used to absorb sweat that is analyzed for the presence of cocaine, marijuana, opiates, amphetamine, methamphetamine, and PCP.

holistic self-awareness approach
emphasizes that nonmedical and often recreational drug use interferes with the healthy balance among the mind, the body, and the spirit

the right end of the wellness continuum. No matter what their current status of health, people can improve their level of well-being. Even when there are temporary setbacks, movement is always headed toward wellness. (Walter 1999, pp. 1–2)[2]

This passage embodies the essence of achieving a holistic self-awareness perspective by presenting a unified blend of different perspectives that can add to our awareness of what is at stake when the goal of drug use is for nonmedical purposes, such as using drugs for the sole purpose of achieving a high. Knowing about the holistic self-awareness perspective should expand people's often limited and narrow values and attitudes about drug use so that the information about and the use of drugs are viewed and understood from pharmacological, psychological, and sociological perspectives.

As mentioned earlier, understanding drug use is important not only for comprehending our own health, but also for understanding the following:

- Why and how others can become attracted to drugs
- How to detect drug use and abuse in others

---

[2]Reproduced from Walter, S. *The Illustrated Encyclopedia of Body-Mind Disciplines.* New York: Rosen Publishing Group, 1999. Used with permission.

- What to do (remedies and solutions) when family members and/or friends abuse drugs
- How to help and advise drug abusers about the pitfalls of substance use
- What the best available educational, preventive, and treatment options are for victims of drug abuse
- What danger signals can arise when others you care about exceed normal and/or necessary drug usage

Awareness and knowledge about drug use and/or abuse coupled with holistic health awareness can result in self-awareness, and self-awareness leads to self-understanding and self-assurance. Maintaining at least some belief in holistic self-awareness, either as a humanistic philosophy or adding this philosophy into a religious orientation you may already have, should increase an understanding of your own drug use practices as well as those of family members and close friends. By including at least some aspect of holistic self-awareness regarding the use of psychoactive substances, you will be better equipped to understand not only yourself but also others who may be in need of advice and role modeling.

LEARNING PORTFOLIO

Discussion Questions

1. Give an example of a drug-using friend and describe how he or she may be affected by biological, genetic, pharmacological, cultural, social, and contextual factors.

2. Discuss and debate whether the often considered "benign" drug known as marijuana is or is not addictive. In your discussion/debate, consider the finding in Table 1.4 by the Center for Behavioral Health Statistics and Quality that in 2014 for persons aged 12 or older, 44.2% of illicit drug users (117.2 million) had used marijuana during their lifetime and past-month users of this drug accounted for 8.4% of all illicit drug users (22.1 million). Do you think this often-perceived "less addictive" drug is harmless to society?

3. What is the future of prescription drug abuse? For example, how much will it increase in the years to come? Do you think prescription drugs will ever become *the* drugs of choice for recreational and/or abusive use? Will prescription drug abuse ever surpass the use of marijuana? Should parents be prosecuted for not guarding their legally prescribed drugs if their children are caught using them?

4. In reviewing the ancient historical uses of drugs, how do you think drug use today is different from than in the past? Explain your answer.

5. Why do Americans use so many legal drugs (e.g., alcohol, tobacco, and OTC drugs)? What do you think is primarily responsible for such extensive nonmedical and recreational drug use?

6. Table 1.3 shows that the amount of drug use remained stable from 2009 to 2014 (showing little change in usage rates for past-month usage for persons aged 18 to 25 years). Cite two reasons why you think this high stable trend has occurred despite the media campaigns promoted by private organizations, state governments, the federal government, and efforts by law enforcement organizations against recreational drug use.

7. Because most casual and experimental drug users do not gravitate toward excessive drug use, should these two groups be left alone or perhaps be given legal warnings or fines? Overall, how do you think recreational drug users be punished by society?

8. Do the mass media promote drug use, or do they merely reflect our extensive use of drugs? Provide some evidence for your position.

9. At what point do you think drug use leads to abuse? When do you think drug use does not lead to abuse?

10. What do you believe is the relationship between drug use and crime? Does drug use cause crime or is crime simply a manifestation of personality?

11. What principal factors are involved in the relationship between drugs and crime?

Key Terms

addiction	6
central nervous system (CNS)	5
compulsive users	36
dependency phase	43
designer drugs/synthetic drugs or synthetic opioids	13
drug cartels	48
drug cells	48
Drug Enforcement Administration (DEA)	41
drug(s)	6
drug testing	53
employee assistance programs (EAPs)	53
equal-opportunity affliction	17
ethanol	13
experimenters	35
floaters or chippers	36
gateway drugs	12
holistic self-awareness approach	55
illicit drugs	6
increased use phase	42
insiders	5
licit drugs	6
marijuana wax	13
MDMA	13
National Institute on Drug Abuse (NIDA)	43
needle-exchange programs	45
opioids	10
oral fluids	54
outsiders	5
over-the-counter (OTC)	6
preoccupation phase	43
psychoactive drugs (substances)	5
relief phase	42
structural analogs	14
sweat	55
withdrawal phase	43
withdrawal symptoms	6

12. Should all employees be randomly tested for drug use? If not, which types of employees or occupations should randomly drug test?

13. List and rank order at least three things you found very interesting regarding drug use in this chapter.

14. Should all students and faculty be randomly drug tested at their schools and universities? Why or why not?

15. Do you think that the holistic self-awareness approach advocated by the authors regarding drug use is a viable one that can be used successfully for stopping drug use? Why or why not? What, if any, additional improvements can be made to strengthen this approach?

Summary

1. Biological issues; genetic issues; pharmacological issues; and cultural, social, and contextual issues are the four principal factors responsible for determining how a drug user experiences drug use. Biological, genetic, and pharmacological factors take into account how a particular drug effects and affects the body. Cultural factors examine how society's views, determined by custom and tradition, effect and affect the use of a particular drug. Social factors include the specific reasons why a drug is taken and how drug use develops from factors such as family upbringing, peer group alliances, subcultures, and communities. Contextual factors account for how drug use behavior develops from the physical surroundings in which the drug is taken.

2. Initial understanding of drug use includes the following key terms: drug, gateway drugs, medicines and prescription medicines, over-the-counter (OTC), drug misuse, drug abuse, and drug addiction.

3. Mentions of drug use date back to biblical times and ancient literature that goes back to 2240 BC. Under the influence of drugs, many people experienced feelings ranging from extreme ecstasy to sheer terror. At times, drugs were used to induce sleep and provide freedom from care.

4. Drug users are found in all occupations and professions, at all income and social class levels, and in all age groups. No one is immune to drug use. Thus, drug use is an equal-opportunity affliction.

5. According to sociologist Erich Goode (2012), drugs are used for four reasons: (a) legal instrumental use, (b) legal recreational use, (c) illegal instrumental use, and (d) illegal recreational use.

6. The most commonly used licit and illicit lifetime drugs (rated from highest to lowest in the percentages [frequency] of use) are alcohol, cigarettes, marijuana/hashish, nonmedical use of any psychotherapeutics, smokeless tobacco, cocaine, hallucinogens, pain relievers, tranquilizers, inhalants, stimulants, sedatives, and heroin.

7. The three types of drug users are experimenters, compulsive users, and floaters or chippers. Experimenters try drugs because of curiosity and peer pressure. Compulsive users use drugs on a full-time basis and continually desire to escape from or alter reality. Floaters or chippers vacillate between experimental drug use and chronic drug use.

8. The mass media tend to promote drug use through advertising. The constant barrage of OTC drug commercials relays the message that if you are experiencing some symptom, taking drugs is an acceptable option.

9. Drug use leads to abuse when the following occurs: (a) excessive use, (b) constant concern and preoccupation about the availability and supply of the drug, (c) refusal to admit excessive use, and (d) reliance on the drug.

10. The stages of drug dependence are *relief* from using the drug, *increased use* of the drug, *preoccupation* with the supply of the drug, *dependency* or addiction to the drug, and experiencing (either or both) physical and/or psychological *withdrawal* effects from not using the drug.

11. The following are the major findings of the connection between drugs and crime: (a) drug users are more likely to commit crimes, (b) arrestees are often under the influence of drugs while committing their crimes, and (c) drugs and violence often go hand in hand, especially when alcohol, cocaine, crack, methamphetamine, or other stimulant types of drugs are used.

12. Employee assistance programs (EAPs) are employer-financed programs administered by a company or through an outside contractor. More than 400,000 EAPs have been established in the United States They are designed to aid in identifying and resolving productivity problems associated with employees' emotional or physical concerns, such as those related to health, marriage, family, bereavement, finances, and substance abuse. Recently, EAPs have expanded their focus to combat employee abuse of OTC and prescription drugs as well as illicit psychoactive substances.

13. The holistic self-awareness philosophy is based on the idea that the mind, body, and spirit have a powerful influence on maintaining health. These three domains—mind, body, and spirit—work best when unobstructed by unnecessary drug use, and when all three domains work in a unified manner to promote health and wellness.

References

Associated Press. "Program to Fight Drug Smuggling Costs U.S. a Lot, Produces Little." *Salt Lake Tribune* 244 (17 August 1992): A-1.

Associated Press. "Mexican Cardinal, Six Others Killed in Cross-Fire as Drug Battles Erupt in Guadalajara." *Salt Lake Tribune* 246 (25 May 1993): A-1.

Associated Press. "Discovery of Mexican Graves Unlikely to Slow Flow of Drugs." *The Times* (Munster, Indiana) (5 December 1999): A-13.

Associated Press. "Mexico: Drug War Death Toll Worsens, 11 Die in One Shootout, 24 in a Day in Small-Town Gun Battles." *Post Tribune* (Northwest Indiana) 100 (14 March 2010): 38.

Berkrot, B. "Global Drug Sales to Top $1 Trillion." Thomson Reuters (20 April 2010). Available http://www.-reuters.com/article/idUKTRE63J0Y520100420

Beschner, G. "Understanding Teenage Drug Use." In *Teen Drug Use*, edited by G. Beschner and A. Friedman, 1–18. Lexington, MA: D.C. Heath, 1986.

Bio. "Joaquin 'El Chapo' Guzman Loera." n.d. Available http://www.biography.com/people/el-chapo-joaquin-guzman-loera

Birns, L., and A. Sánchez. "The Government and the Drug Lords: Who Rules Mexico?" Worldpress.org. 23 April 2007. Available http://www.worldpress.org/Americas/2763.cfm

Boyles, S. "Americans Spend $34 Billion on Alternative Medicines." WebMD. 2009. Available http://www.rxlist.com/script/main/art.asp?articlekey=104255#

Bureau of Justice Statistics (BJS). *Drugs and Crime Facts: Drug Law Violations.* Washington, DC: U.S. Department of Justice, Office of Justice Programs, 2006.

Bureau of Justice Statistics (BJS). "U.S. Prison Population Declined One Percent in 2014." Washington, DC: U.S. Department of Justice, Office of Justice Programs, 17 September 2015a.

Bureau of Justice Statistics (BJS). "Drug Offenders in Federal Prison: Estimates of Characteristics Based on Linked Data." Washington, DC: U.S. Department of Justice, Office of Justice Programs, 27 October 2015b.

Butterfield, F. "As Drug Use Drops in Big Cities, Small Towns Confront Upsurge." *New York Times* (11 February 2002): A23. Available http://www.nytimes.com/2002/02/11/us/as-drug-use-drops-in-big-cities-small-towns-confront-upsurge.html?scp=1&sq=As%20Drug%20Use%20Drops%20in%20Big%20Cities,%20Amall%20Towns%20Con front%20Upsurge,%20Butterfield,%20Fox&st=cse

Caldwell, A. A. "U.S. Cracks Down on Fake Pot." *Post-Tribune* (Merrillville, IN) 101 (December 2010): 30.

Campbell, R. "Mexican Cartels Cannot Be Defeated, Drug Lord Says." Thomson Reuters (4 April 2010). Available http://www.reuters.com/article/idUSTRE6331DZ20100404

Carlsen, L. "The Opinion Pages/Letter: The Drug War and Mexico." *New York Times* (25 January 2016). Available http://www.nytimes.com/2016/01/26/opinion/the-drug-war-and-mexico.html?rref=collection%2Ftimestopic%2FMexican%20Drug%20Trafficking&action=click&contentCollection=world&region=stream&module=stream_unit&version=latest&contentPlacement=7&pgtype=collection

Carson, E. A., and W. J. Sabol. *Prisoners in 2011.* NCJ239808. Washington, DC: U.S. Department of Justice, Bureau of Justice Statistics, December 2012. Available http://bjs.ojp.usdoj.gov/content/pub/pdf/p11.pdf

CASA Columbia. *National Survey of American Attitudes on Substance Abuse XVII: Teens.* New York: QEV Analytics, August 2012. Available http://www.casacolumbia.org/upload/2012/20120822teensurvey.pdf

CBS News. "Drug Advertising Skyrockets." CBS Worldwide. 13 February 2002. Available http://www.cbsnews.com/2100-204_162-329293.html

Center for Behavioral Health Statistics and Quality (CBHSQ). "The NSDUH Report: State Estimates of Nonmedical Use of Prescription Pain Relievers." Rockville, MD Substance Abuse and Mental Health Services Administration, 8 January 2013.

Center for Behavioral Health Statistics and Quality (CBHSQ). *Behavioral Health Trends in the United States: Results from the 2014 National Survey on Drug Use and Health.* NSDUH Series H-50, HHS Publication No. (SMA) 15-4927. Rockville, MD: Substance Abuse and Mental Health Services Administration, 2015.

Center for Substance Abuse Research (CESAR). "Ritalin and Adderall Abused by Students as Party Drugs and Study Aids." *CESAR FAX* (1 December 2003). Available http://www.cesar.umd.edu

Center on Alcohol Marketing and Youth (CAMY). "Alcohol Industry 'Responsibility' Advertising on Television, 2001 to 2003." Washington, DC: Center on Alcohol Marketing and Youth, 20 July 2005. Available http://www.camy.org/_docs/resources/reports/archived-reports/alcohol-industry-responsibility-advertising-tv-01-03-full-report.pdf

Center on Alcohol Marketing and Youth (CAMY). *Drowned Out: Alcohol Industry's Responsibility: Advertising on Television, 2001–2005.* Washington, DC: Center on Alcohol Marketing and Youth, 2007: 1–4.

Centers for Disease Control and Prevention (CDC). *CDC Survey Finds that 1 in 5 U.S. High School Students Have Abused Prescription Drugs.* Atlanta, GA: U.S. Department of Health and Human Services, 3 June 2010. Available http://www.cdc.gov/HealthyYouth/yrbs/pdf/press_release_yrbs.pdf

Centers for Disease Control and Prevention (CDC). "Vital Signs: Opioid Painkiller Prescribing infographic." 2014. Available http://www.cdc.gov/vitalsigns/opioid-prescribing/infographic.html

Centers for Disease Control and Prevention (CDC). "Economic Facts About U.S. Tobacco Production and Use." 2015a. Available http://www.cdc.gov/tobacco/data_statistics/fact_sheets/economics/econ_facts/index.htm#sales

Centers for Disease Control and Prevention (CDC). "HIV in the United States: At A Glance." 2015b. Available http://www.cdc.gov/hiv/statistics/overview/ataglance.html

Centers for Disease Control and Prevention (CDC). "Global HIV/AIDS." 2016. Available http://www.cdc.gov/globalaids/

Chen, K. "Meth Seizures at U.S. Ports of Entry on the Rise." Center for Investigative Reporting, 20 June 2013. Available http://cironline.org/blog/post/meth-seizures-us-ports-entry-rise-4739

Clinton, Bill. "My Quest to Improve Care." *Newsweek* CXLVII (15 May 2006): 50–53.

Consumer Healthcare Products Association (CHPA). "The Value of OTC Medicine to the United States." Washington, DC: Booz&Co and Consumer Healthcare Products Association, 2012. Available http://www.yourhealthathand.org/images/uploads/The_Value_of_OTC_Medicine_to_the_United_States_BoozCo.pdf

Consumer Healthcare Products Association (CHPA). "Statistics on OTC Use." 2016. Available http://www.chpa.org/marketstats.aspx

Consumer Healthcare Products Association (CHPA). "OTC Retail Sales 1964-2015." 2016. Available http://www.chpa.org/OTCRetailSales.aspx

Coppola, M., and R. Mondola. "Synthetic Cathinones: Chemistry, Pharmacology and Toxicology of a New Class of Designer Drugs of Abuse Marketed as 'Bath Salts' or 'Plant Food.'" *Toxicology Letters* 211(2) (2012): 144–149.

Critser, G. "Oh, How Happy We Will Be: Pills, Paradise, and the Profits of the Drug Companies." *Harper's Magazine* (June 1996): 39–48.

Critser, G. *Generation RX: How Prescription Drugs Are Altering American Lives, Minds and Bodies.* Boston, MA: Houghton-Mifflin, 2005.

Delaney, W., J. W. Grube, and G. M. Ames. "Predicting Likelihood of Seeking Help Through the Employee-Assistance Program Among Salaried and Union Hourly Employees." *Addiction* 93 (1998): 399–410.

Del Bosque, M. "Mexico's Future in 2010, Calderon's Failed Drug War." *Texas Observer* (5 January 2010): 1–2. Available http://www.texasobserver.org/lalinea/calderons-war-on-drugs-is-a-failure

Drug Enforcement Administration (DEA). *Drug Fact Sheet: K2 or Spice.* Washington, DC: U.S. Department of Justice (DOJ), 2012. Available http://www.justice.gov/dea/pr/multimedia-library/publications/drug_of_abuse.pdf#page=62

Drug Strategies. *Keeping Score: What We Are Getting for Our Federal Drug Control Dollars 1995.* Washington, DC: Drug Strategies, 1995.

DrugWarFacts.org. "Crime, Arrests, and US Law Enforcement." 2016. Available http://www.drugwarfacts.org/cms/Crime#sthash.Hlaogs9z.fqvRrxej.dpbs

Edelson, E. "Drug Use in the Workplace Plummets." *Cannabis News* (February 2000). Available http://cannabisnews.com/news/4/thread4627.shtml

ECIG Review Central. "E-Cig Sales to Hit 100 Billion or More in Next Decade?" ECigReviewCentral.com. 2 January 2014. Available http://ecigreviewcentral.com/e-cig-sales-to-hit-100-billion-or-more-in-next-decade/

Erowid Center. "Spice Product: Legal Status." Erowid.org. 2013. Available http://www.erowid.org/chemicals/spice_product/spice_product_law.shtml

Farah, J. "Invasion USA: Mexican Drug Cartels Take Over U.S. Cities." WorldNet Daily, 18 June 2006. Available http://www.worldnetdaily.com/news/article.asp?article_id=50518

Fausset, R., and T. Wilkinson. "'El Chapo' Guzman: Life of the Cartel King of Sinaloa." *Los Angeles Times* (22 February 2014). Available http://www.latimes.com/world /worldnow/la-fg-wn-guzman-arrest-20140222-story.html

Fearnow, B. "Study: 70 Percent of Americans on Prescription Drugs." CBS Atlanta, 19 June 2013. Available http://atlanta.cbslocal.com/2013/06/19/study-70 -percent-of-americans-on-prescription-drugs-one-fifth -take-5-or-more/

Federal Register. "Annual Determination of Average Cost of Incarceration." Washington, DC: Office of the Federal Register (OFR), 9 March 2015. Available https://www .federalregister.gov/articles/2015/03/09/2015-05437 /annual-determination-of-average-cost-of-incarceration

Federal Trade Commission (FTC). *Self-Regulation in the Alcohol Industry: Report of the Federal Trade Commission.* Washington, DC, March 2015. Available https://www.ftc .gov/system/files/documents/reports/self-regulation -alcohol-industry-report-federal-trade-commission /140320alcoholreport.pdf

Ferner, M. "Americans Spent About a Trillion Dollar on Illegal Drugs in the Last Decade." Huffington Post (13 March 2014). Available http://www.huffingtonpost .com/2014/03/13/americans-trillion-dollars-drugs_n _4943601.html

Goldstein, A. *Addiction: From Biology to Drug Policy.* New York: Oxford University Press, 2001.

Goode, E. *Drugs in American Society,* 5th ed. Boston, MA: McGraw-Hill, 1999.

Goode, E. *Drugs in American Society,* 8th ed. New York: McGraw-Hill, 2012.

Heroin.net. "How Much Does Heroin Cost?" 2016. Available http://heroin.net/about/how-much-does-heroin -cost/#the-street-cost-of-heroin

Herper, M. "Why Big Pharma Won't Get Its Piece of the $1.2 Trillion Global Drug Market." *Forbes* (12 July 2012). Available http://www.forbes.com/sites/matthew herper/2012/07/12/the-global-drug-market-will-swell -to-1-2-trillion-while-big-pharma-treads-water/

HomeHealthTesting. "FactsAboutPrisonandDrugUse." 2010. Available http://www.homehealthtesting.com/blog /2010/06/facts-about-prison-and-drug-use/

Huffington Post. "School Drug Use: Survey Finds 17 Percent of High School Students Drink, Smoke, Use Drugs During the School Day." 23 August 2012. Available http://www.huffingtonpost.com/2012/08/23/annual -survey-finds-17-pe_n_1824966.html

IMS Health. *IMS Retail Drug Monitor.* London, UK: IMS Health, 2012.

IMS Health. "World Pharma Market Summary: Analytics and Insights from IMS Health." London, UK: IMS Health, 2013.

Jellinek, J. "Musical Meth Lab Uncovered." *Rolling Stone* (20 February 2003): 54.

Johnston, L. D., P. M. O'Malley, J. G. Bachman, and J. E. Schulenberg. *Monitoring the Future: National Survey Results on Drug Use, 1975–2011, Volume I: Secondary School Students.* Bethesda, MD: National Institute on Drug Abuse, 2012.

Johnston, L. D., P. M. O'Malley, R. A. Miech, J. G. Bachman, and J. E. Schulenberg. *Monitoring the Future National Survey Results on Drug Use, 1975–2015: Overview, Key Findings on Adolescent Drug Use.* Ann Arbor, MI: Institute for Social Research, University of Michigan, February 2016.

Karberg, J. C., and D. J. James. *Special Report, Substance Dependence, Abuse, and Treatment of Jail Inmates, 2002.* Bureau of Justice Statistics (BJS). Washington, DC: U.S. Department of Justice, Office of Justice Programs, 2002.

KiDeuk K., M. Becker-Cohen, and M. Serakos. *Research Report: The Procession and Treatment of Mentally Ill Persons in the Criminal Justice System.* Washington, DC: Urban Institute, March 2015.

Kilbourne, J. "Advertising Addiction: The Alcohol Industry's Hard Sell." *Multinational Monitor* (June 1989): 13–16.

Kimble, J. "Everything You Need to Know About Marijuana Wax." Atlanta, GA: Complex Media Inc., 22 October 2013. Available http://www.complex.com/pop-culture /2013/10/marijuana-wax-facts-info/

Kusinitz, M. "Drug Use Around the World." In *Encyclopedia of Psychoactive Drugs,* edited by S. Snyder. Series 2. New York: Chelsea House, 1988.

Larson, S. L., J. Eyeman, M. S. Foster, and J. C. Gfroerer. *Worker Substance Use and Workplace Policies and Programs.* DHHS Publication No. SMA 07-4273, Analytic Series A-29. Rockville, MD: Substance Abuse and Mental Health Services Administration, Office of Applied Studies, 2007.

Lawson, G. "The War Next Door: As Drug Cartels Battle the Government, Mexico Descends into Chaos." *Rolling Stone* 1065 (13 November 2008): 74–81, 108–111.

Lenson, D. *On Drugs.* Minneapolis, MN: University of Minnesota Press, 1995.

Levinthal, C. F. *Drugs, Behavior, and Modern Society.* Boston, MA: Allyn and Bacon, 1996.

Luckerson, V. "Landline Phones Are Getting Closer to Extinction." *Time* (8 July 2014). Available http://time .com/2966515/landline-phones-cell-phones/

McBride, D. C., and C. B. McCoy. "The Drugs–Crime Relationship: An Analytical Framework." In *Drugs, Crime, and Justice,* edited by L. K. Gaines and B. Kraska, 100–119. Prospect Heights, IL: Waveland Press, 2003.

McShane, L. "Cops Are Crooks in N.Y.'s 30th Precinct." *Salt Lake Tribune* 238 (18 April 1994): A-5.

Meth.IN.gov. "Statistics." 2015. Available http://www.in.gov/meth/2330.htm

Methadone Centers. "What Is the Typical Methadone Clinic Cost?" 31 March 2016. Available http://www.methadonecenters.com/typical-methadone-clinic-cost/

Millman, J. "It's True: Drug Companies Are Bombarding Your TV with More Ads Than Ever." *The Washington Post* (23 March 2015). Available https://www.washingtonpost.com/news/wonk/wp/2015/03/23/yes-drug-companies-are-bombarding-your-tv-with-more-ads-than-ever/

Monroe, J. "What Is Addiction?" *Current Health* 2 (January 1996): 16–19.

The Motley Fool. "Did the CDC Just Save the Electronic Cigarette Industry?" 21 November 2015. Available http://www.fool.com/investing/general/2015/11/21/did-the-cdc-just-save-the-electronic-cigarette-ind.aspx

Muir Wood. "Teen Adderall Abuse." Muir Wood Teen Boys & Girls Outpatient Program, 2016. Available http://www.muirwoodteen.com/adderall-abuse/

Mumola, C. J., and J. C. Karberg. *Drug Use and Dependence, State and Federal Prisoners, 2004.* Washington, DC: U.S. Department of Justice, 19 January 2007: 1. Available http://bjs.ojp.usdoj.gov/content/pub/pdf/dudsfp04.pdf

Nair, R. "Internet & Mobile Phone Users Worldwide 2015: 50% Populations on Internet [Report]." Dazeinfo, 27 May 2015. Available http://dazeinfo.com/2015/05/27/internet-mobile-phone-users-worldwide-2000-2015-report/

Natarajan, N., A. Petteruti, N. Walsh, and J. Ziedenberg. "Substance Abuse Treatment and Public Safety (A Policy Brief)." Justice Policy Institute. January 2008. Available http://www.justicepolicy.org/images/upload/08_01_REP_DrugTx_AC-PS.pdf

National Association for Children of Alcoholics. *Children of Addicted Parents: Important Facts.* Rockville, MD: HopeNetworks, 2005. Available http://www.hopenetworks.org/addiction/Children%20of%20Addicts.htm

National Council on Alcoholism and Drug Dependence, Inc. (NCADD). "Alcohol, Drugs and Crime." New York: National Council on Alcoholism and Drug Dependence, 27 June 2015.

National Council on Alcoholism and Drug Dependence, Inc. (NCADD). "Drugs and Alcohol in the Workplace." New York: National Council on Alcoholism and Drug Dependence, Inc. 2016.

National Institute of Justice (NIJ). *ADAM II, 2008 Annual Report.* Arrestee Drug Abuse Monitoring Program II (ADAM). U.S. Department of Justice (DOJ), Office of National Drug Control Policy. Washington, DC: U.S. Government Printing Office, 2009.

National Institute on Drug Abuse (NIDA). *Prescription Medications.* Bethesda, MD: U.S. Government Printing Office, 2010.

National Institute on Drug Abuse (NIDA). "Drug Facts: High School and Youth Trends." December 2014a. Available https://www.drugabuse.gov/publications/drugfacts/high-school-youth-trends

National Institute on Drug Abuse (NIDA). "Popping Pills: Prescription Drug Abuse in America." 2014b. Available https://www.drugabuse.gov/related-topics/trends-statistics/infographics/popping-pills-prescription-drug-abuse-in-america

National Institute on Drug Abuse (NIDA). "Drug Facts: Nationwide Trends." Bethesda, MD: National Institutes of Health, 2015.

Nielsen. "More Than Half the Homes in the U.S. Have Three or More TVS." New York: The Nielsen Company, 2016. Available http://www.nielsen.com/us/en/insights/news/2009/more-than-half-the-homes-in-us-have-three-or-more-tvs.html

Office of National Drug Control Policy (ONDCP). *Pulse Check: Trends in Drug Abuse.* Washington, DC: Executive Office of the President, Office of National Drug Control Policy, 2002.

Office of National Drug Control Policy (ONDCP). *What America's Users Spend on Illegal Drugs, 2000–2006.* Washington, DC: Executive Office of the President, 2012.

Office of National Drug Control Policy (ONDCP). *ADAM (Arrestee Drug Abuse Monitoring Program) II, 2012 Annual Report.* Washington, DC: Office of National Drug Control Policy, May 2013a. Available http://www.whitehouse.gov/sites/default/files/ondcp/policy-and-research/adam_ii_2012_annual_rpt_final_final.pdf

Office of National Drug Control Policy (ONDCP). "Synthetic Drug (a.k.a. K2, Spice, Bath Salts, etc.)." 2013b. Available http://www.whitehouse.gov/ondcp/ondcp-fact-sheets/synthetic-drugs-k2-spice-bath-salts

Office of National Drug Control Policy (ONDCP). *ADAM II: 2013 Annual Report Arrestee Drug Abuse Monitoring Program II.* Washington, DC: Executive Office of the President, January 2014. Available https://www.whitehouse.gov/sites/default/files/ondcp/policy-and-research/adam_ii_2013_annual_report.pdf

Partnership at Drugfree.org. "Drug Guide: Bath Salts." 2013. Available http://www.drugfree.org/drug-guide/bath-salts

Partnership for Drug-Free Kids. "National Study: Teen Misuse and Abuse of Prescription Drugs Up 33 Percent

Since 2008." New York: Partnership for Drug Free Kids, 2016.

Partnership for Drug-Free Kids and MetLife Foundation. *The Partnership Attitude Tracking Study.* New York: Partnership for Drug-Free Kids, 2013. Available http://www.drugfree.org/wp-content/uploads/2014/07/PATS-2013-FULL-REPORT.pdf

Pharmacy Times. "Drug Spending Increases Dramatically in 8 Years." 73 (July 2007): 2.

Project Know. "15 of the Most Horrific Drinking and Driving Accidents." 2016. Available http://www.projectknow.com/15-of-the-most-horrific-drinking-and-driving-accidents/

Pyrillis, R. "Special Report: EAPs: Devoid of Data." 5 June 2014. Available http://www.workforce.com/articles/20497-eaps-devoid-of-data

Reynolds, G. S., and W. E. Lehman. "Levels of Substance Use and Willingness to Use the Employee Assistance Program." *Journal of Behavioral Health Services and -Research* 30 (2003): 238–248.

Robert Wood Johnson Foundation. *Substance Abuse: The Nation's Number One Health Problem.* Prepared by the Schneider Institute for Health Policy for the Robert Wood Johnson Foundation, Brandeis University. Princeton, NJ: Robert Wood Johnson Foundation, February 2001.

Schecter, M. "Serotonergic-Dopaminergic Mediation of 3,4-Methylenedioxy-Methamphetamine (MDMA, Ecstasy)." *Pharmacology, Biochemistry and Behavior* 31 (1989): 817–824.

Scott, C. "Americans Spend Billions on Vitamins and Herbs That Don't Work." Healthline News, 9 March 2015. Available http://www.healthline.com/health-news/americans-spend-billions-on-vitamins-and-herbs-that-dont-work-031915

Sentencing Project. "Drug Policy News." 5 February 2013. Available http://www.sentencingproject.org/template/page.cfm?id=128

Spiller, H. A., M. L. Ryan, R. G. Weston, and J. Jansen. "Clinical Experience with and Analytical Confirmation of 'Bath Salts' and 'Legal Highs' (Synthetic Cathinones) in the United States." *Clinical Toxicology* 49 (2011): 499–505.

Steward, P., and G. Sitarmiah. "America's Heartland Grapples with Rise of Dangerous Drug." *Christian Science Monitor* (13 November 1997): 1, 18.

Stobbe, M. "More U.S. Households Hanging Up Their Landline Phones." Associated Press (8 July 2014). Available http://www.dailyfinance.com/2014/07/08/more-us-households-dump-landline-telephones/

Stopthedrugwar.org. "Global: World Drug Trade Worth $320 Billion Annually, UN Says." 1 July 2005: 1–2. Available http://stopthedrugwar.org/chronicle-old/393/320billion.shtml

Substance Abuse and Mental Health Services Administration (SAMHSA). *Results from the 2006 National Survey on Drug Use and Health: National Findings.* Rockville, MD: Substance Abuse and Mental Health Services Administration, 2007.

Substance Abuse and Mental Health Services Administration (SAMHSA). *Results from the 2011 National Survey on Drug Use and Health: Summary of National Findings.* NSDUH Series H-44, HHS Publication No. SMA 12-4713. Rockville, MD: Substance Abuse and Mental Health Services Administration, 2012.

Substance Abuse and Mental Health Services Administration (SAMHSA). "Spice, Bath Salts, and Behavioral Health." *Advisory* 13 (2014a). Available http://store.samhsa.gov/shin/content/SMA14-4858/SMA14-4858.pdf

Substance Abuse and Mental Health Services Administration (SAMHSA). *Results from the 2013 National Survey on Drug Use and Health: Summary of National Findings.* NSDUH Series H-48, HHS Publication No. (SMA) 14-4863. Rockville, MD: Substance Abuse and Mental Health Services Administration, 2014b.

Substance Abuse and Mental Health Services Administration (SAMHSA). *The NSDUH Report: Workplace Policies and Programs Concerning Alcohol and Drug Use.* National Survey on Drug Use and Health, Rockville, MD, 7 August 2014c.

Substance Abuse and Mental Health Services Administration (SAMHSA), Office of Applied Studies (OAS). *The Relationship Between Family Structure and Adolescent Substance Use.* Rockville, MD: U.S. Department of Health and Human Services, July 1996.

Substance Abuse and Mental Health Services Administration (SAMHSA), Office of Applied Studies (OAS). *The National Survey on Drug Use and Health (NSDUH) Report. Worker Substance Use, by Industry Category.* Rockville, MD: Substance Abuse and Mental Health Services Administration, 2007.

Substance Abuse and Mental Health Services Administration (SAMHSA), Office of Applied Studies (OAS). *Results from the 2008 National Survey on Drug Use and Health: National Findings.* NSDUH Series H-36, DHHS Publication No. SMA 09-4435. Rockville, MD: Office of Applied Studies, 2009.

Szasz, T. *Our Right to Drugs: The Case for a Free Market.* Westport, CT: Praeger, 1992.

Thio, A. *Deviant Behavior,* 2nd ed. Boston: Houghton Mifflin, 1983: 332–333.

Thio, A. *Deviant Behavior,* 4th ed. New York: Harper Collins College, 1995.

Thio, A. *Deviant Behavior,* 6th ed. New York: Pearson Education, 2000.

U.S. Department of Justice (USDOJ). "Total of All Meth Clandestine Laboratory Incidents Including Labs, Dumpsites, Chem/Glass/Equipment." 27 January 2013. Available http://www.justice.gov/dea/resource-center/meth_lab_maps/2012.jpg

U.S. Department of Justice (USDOJ). "Multiple Defendants in synthetic Marijuana, Bath Salts Distribution Ring Sentenced." Western District of Tennessee: U.S. Attorney's Office, 29 January 2016. Available https://www.justice.gov/usao-wdtn/pr/multiple-defendants-synthetic-marijuana-bath-salts-distribution-ring-sentenced

U.S. Department of Labor. *SHRM Survey Reveals Majority of HR Professionals' Organizations Drug Test.* Washington, DC: U.S. Government Printing Office, Department of Labor, 2009.

U. S. Department of Labor. "Drug-Free Workplace Advisor: Workplace Testing." Washington, DC: U.S. Department of Labor, 2016.

Vargas-Cooper, N. "Bathlands." *Spin* (July/August 2012): 58–64, 94.

Venturelli, P. J. "Drugs in Schools: Myths and Reality." In *Annals of the American Academy of Political and Social Science*, edited by W. Hinkle and S. Henry, 567. Thousand Oaks, CA: Sage, 2000.

Walter, S. "Holistic Health." In *Illustrated Encyclopedia of Body–Mind Disciplines*, edited by N. Alison, 1–2. New York: Rosen Publishing Group, 1999. Available http://ahha.org/rosen.htm

Wire Services. "Cocaine Kingpin Escapes After Bloody Shootout." *Salt Lake Tribune* 244 (23 July 1992): A-1.

Worldpress.org. "Mexico: Drug Cartels a Growing Threat." 2 November 2006. Available http://www.worldpress.org/Americas/2549.cfm#down

© Huntstock/Thinkstock.

CHAPTER 2
Explaining Drug Use and Abuse

Did You Know?

▶ Contrary to public perception, addiction is a complex disease.

▶ Most drugs of abuse include both physical and psychological addictions.

▶ Every culture has experienced problems with drug use or abuse. As far back as 2240 BC, Hammurabi, the Babylonian king and lawgiver, addressed the problems associated with excessive use of alcohol.

▶ Today, there are many more varieties of drugs, and many of these drugs are more potent than they were years ago.

▶ According to biological theories, drug abuse has an innate physical beginning stemming from physical characteristics that cause certain individuals either to experiment with or to crave drugs to the point of abuse.

▶ Abuse of drugs by some people may represent an attempt to relieve underlying psychiatric disorders.

▶ No single theory can explain why most people use drugs.

▶ People who perceive themselves as drug users are more likely to develop serious drug abuse problems.

Learning Objectives

On completing this chapter you should be able to:

❯ List three to five major contributing factors responsible for addiction.

❯ List and briefly explain three models used to describe addiction.

❯ List six reasons why drug use or abuse is a more serious problem today than it was in the past.

❯ List and briefly describe the genetic and biophysiological theories that explain how drug use often leads to abuse.

❯ Explain how drugs of abuse act as positive reinforcers.

❯ Explain the major differences between substance use disorders and substance-induced disorders (addictive disorders).

❯ Understand how drug addiction can co-occur with various types of mental disorders.

❯ Briefly define and explain reinforcement or learning theory and some of its applications to drug use and abuse.

❯ Briefly explain sensation-seeking individuals and drug use.

❯ List and briefly describe the four sociological theories broadly known as social influence theories.

❯ Explain the link between drug use and other types of devious behaviors.

❯ List and describe three factors in the learning process that Howard Becker believes first-time users go through before they become attached to using illicit psychoactive drugs.

❯ Define the following concepts as they relate to drug use: *primary deviance, secondary deviance, master status,* and *retrospective interpretation*.

❯ Explain how Reckless's containment theory accounts for the roles of both internal and external controls regarding the attraction to drug use.

❯ Understand how making low-risk and high-risk drug choices directly affects drug use.

Introduction

In this chapter, we focus on the major explanations of drug use and/or abuse. The questions we explore are: Why would anyone voluntarily consume drugs that are not medically needed or required? Why are some people particularly attracted to altering their minds with drugs? Why are others uneasy and uncomfortable with the euphoric effects of recreational drug use? Why do some people repeatedly subject their bodies and minds to the harmful effects of recreational and nonprescribed drug use and eventual addiction, stop their drug use, and then repeatedly relapse to drug use? What logical reasons could explain such irrational behavior?

Following are four perspectives regarding drug use:

First perspective:

I have had a long relationship with drug use. With the exception of one drug that I will never do again, I usually end up having a "romance" with drug use. I have tried and still like the use of weed, booze, and coke.... [referring to cocaine] Let's face it, I like the high feeling whenever I have time to myself and when I am off work. Weekends are best at least one night during my weekends off. When I was younger I was worse and did a lot of drugs no matter what day of the week it was. How many times I would go to school high on weed! Many of my school friends knew I was high in school and only one teacher was ever suspicious about my drug use and he was a younger teacher who had heard from a friend of mine who was in the same English class. This guy had a blabbermouth even though he was a good friend. Today, I am 24 and still enjoy smoking weed every now and then. It has tapered off now that I am older, but whether it is alcohol or marijuana it is something I still like. My dad had problems with alcohol all his life and this is probably where my attraction and use of these two drugs comes from. I think a lot of it is inborn like it's genetic or something because I am the type that immediately likes the buzzed feeling. I don't try other drugs because I thoroughly enjoy what I do use and know that there are other drugs out there I could easily like and want to continue using. I even like the buzz I get from some prescribed medicines whenever I am sick and they change my conscious state of mind. Yes, drugs and I get along well—always did. *(From Venturelli's research files, graduate student and part-time waiter in northwest Indiana, age 24, October 9, 2015)*

Second perspective:

I grew up in a home with no alcohol present. I never saw my mom or dad drink alcohol. I think when they got married both of them had alcoholic parents. I never knew my grandparents since they died before I was born. My older brother remembers my grandfather since he lived until my brother was 7. He remembers that my grandfather would come over to visit and he was usually acting "weird." Later in life, he realized that my grandfather was probably drinking a lot and was probably under the influence. Anyway, before I was born my grandfather died of a stroke and my mom tells me that it was from drinking too much. He also had liver problems and my dad just recently told me his liver was shot from too much drinking. I tried bringing home a bottle of wine once and my mom and dad just watched me sip a glass without saying a word. They refused to have a drink with me and I recall how odd I felt doing this that when I look back on it, I was probably hurting their feelings. Anyway, I went away to college and during my first year, I started drinking a lot, got into all kinds of trouble with my college friends, law enforcement, my RA in a dorm I was living in, and the Dean of Students, and nearly flunked out of college that first year. After experiencing all these newfound problems, I decided that drinking alcohol was not for me. Besides, I was hurting my parents real bad when I was having these problems. Today at 31, I probably have a few drinks several times a year, but I am not really a drinker. One drink and I feel it right away. I can drink a sweet drink like a margarita, but many of my real close friends do not drink alcohol. I am just not around people who drink and actually, except for some college friends when I was attending Ball State who drank, I hardly ever had friends who drank. I had a girlfriend a few years ago but our relationship ended when I got tired of watching her drink while I waited to leave the bars at the end of the night. How drinkers want to keep drinking is very noticeable to a nondrinker. I also had an acquaintance at work who [sic] would call me several nights a week, and I had to listen to his incoherent conversations while he was drinking at home. I got tired of this, and one night I said that I prefer not to talk to him when he was drinking at home. Shortly after that conversation, he and his girlfriend moved away and I never heard from him again. What attracts people to drinking baffles me, and why they continue drinking when they have had plenty already is even more puzzling. I don't think they realize how stupid they act when intoxicated. Fuzzy thinking, uncoordinated, and [how] loud they become are other things I notice. Today, I am dealing with a stepson who is not only drinking at 16 but has also used other types of drugs and I can say that from dealing with his drug use, I am very much against the use of any drugs that are not necessary. *(From Venturelli's research files, male, age 31, May 18, 2010)*

Third perspective:

When you ask about drug use, I literally draw a blank. This topic is really unknown to me. In my family, my grandparents on my dad's side were big-time drinkers. I think . . . my dad's experiences and especially . . . the car crash that killed my grandparents when they were in their 50s while coming home from a wedding after drinking heavily affected my dad very much. My mom comes from a Mormon family, so obviously she also does not drink any alcohol. My parents raised me and my three brothers without any examples or experiences regarding drug use. In my family, my wife and I hardly ever use any types of drugs—not even much of over-the-counter drugs. Occasionally, I will have a half a glass of wine several times a year, but I have to admit, I would rather be drinking water or freshly squeezed fruit juice. I just do not like the taste and the mild effect that such a small amount of alcohol has on me. As you can imagine, I am very much against the use of any types of drugs, especially the illicit types of drugs. Drugs are addictive and people should not be doing or taking drugs. Taking drugs for fun does not have any real positive outcomes, and in the end, causes a lot of misery to families, and medical problems. I am quite certain that all of our family friends are nondrinkers and I know for certain that our best friends do not use any of the recreational types of drugs. You could say our lives are really drug free. Everything we do as a family is in the absence of drug use. *(From Venturelli's research files, male graduate university student, age 36, May 19, 2007)*

Fourth perspective:

I am very much a party hog. I really like to party with my friends. I did get some friends in trouble a couple of times by supplying the alcohol and we had a raid by the police in La Porte at my house and got into a lot of trouble with my mom and dad. I just live for weekends when we get together getting high and laughing about all kinds of stupid stuff in the straight world. Last week I overdid it again but this time had to go to the hospital for overdosing. I did Seconal, Xanax, Valium, and Librium, kept passing out and my friends took me to the emergency room where they had to pump my stomach. Will I do that again? Hopefully not because about a half hour later I would probably have been dead as the emergency doctor told me. My mom and dad found out and they warned me that the next time they will call the police. My dad is now convincing me to get help and will pay for it. I will try it but I am not giving up on the parties no matter what the rehab people say. I am only happy when I am buzzed and I think someday that will wear off when I am older. My older brother was the same way but not as bad as me and today he hardly drinks anymore is married and will soon have his first kid, so he had to give it up. I know I will do the same but for now this is my only time to have fun but I will do it more responsibly I guess. *(From Venturelli's research files, male, age 16, high school student, September 23, 2015)*

The preceding excerpts show extensive differences in values and attitudes regarding drug use. The perspective of the first interviewee represents a type of drug user who is not only strongly attracted to drug use but also markedly enjoys the drug experience of altering his consciousness. He includes the rationalized belief that his attraction to drugs has a biological basis. He also mentions that at a young age he was convincingly affected by his drug-using peers. The second interview shows how the emphasis on not using drugs in the interviewee's family was intergenerationally transmitted and persisted across two generations. After having some preliminary experiences with drug use, the interviewee in this second interview matures into a person shunning any recreational chemical alteration of his reality. The perspective of the third interviewee shows that if a person's early environment is drug free, then drug use is not an option. Finally, the perspective of the fourth interviewee represents a type of drug user who is largely unaware of the pitfalls of drug addiction and is recklessly involved with substance abuse. These four views represent a diverse range of motivations and reasons that influence people to either use or not use drugs.

Why such differences in drug use? In this chapter, we offer plausible substantive explanations why people use drugs recreationally and examine the underlying motivations regarding drug use. We will draw from major theoretical explanations in order to determine and explain probable causes *why* people use recreational drugs, over-the-counter drugs, and prescription drugs that more often than not leads to drug abuse and addiction.

To accomplish these goals, this chapter will explain the use and abuse of drugs from literally dozens of other perspectives within the major biological, psychological, and sociological perspectives. Moreover, as we attempt to offer major theoretical and scientific explanations for drug use, you should develop an advanced understanding of the following:

- How and why drugs are so seductive
- The process of becoming drug addicted
- How attachment and/or addiction to drugs results in self-selected physical and psychological damage on the drug users and others as they become "hijacked" by drug use
- Why so many people succumb to nonmedical and recreational drug use

Finally, the problem of drug use is not only alarmingly widespread in the United States, but also extensive throughout the world.

Drug Use: A Timeless Affliction

Historical records document drug use as far back as 2240 BC, when Hammurabi, the Babylonian king and lawgiver, addressed the problems associated with drinking alcohol. Even before then, the Sumerian people of Asia Minor, who created the cuneiform (wedge-shaped) alphabet, included references to a "joy plant" that dates from about 5000 BC. Experts indicate that the plant was an opium poppy used as a sedative (International Network of People Who Use Drugs [INPUD] n.d.; O'Brien et al. 1992).

Virtually every culture has experienced problems with drug use or abuse. Today's drug use problems are part of a very long and rich tradition:

> These [intoxicating] substances have formed a bond of union between men of opposite hemispheres, the uncivilized and the civilized; they have forced passages which, once open, proved of use for other purposes; they produced in ancient races characteristics which have endured to the present day, evidencing the marvelous degree of intercourse that existed between different peoples just as certainly and exactly as a chemist can judge the relations of two substances by their reactions. (Louis Lewin, *Phantasica*, in Rudgley 1993, p. 3)

The quest for explaining drug use is more important than ever as the problem continues to evolve. There are many reasons why drug use and abuse are even more serious issues now than they were in the past:

- From 1960 to the present, drug use has become a widespread phenomenon.
- Today, drugs are much more potent than they were years ago. "For comparison, the national average of marijuana's THC [tetrahydrocannabinol] content in 1978 was 1.37%, in 1988 it was 3.59%, in 1998 4.43%, and in 2008 8.49%. . . ." (ProCon.org 2012).
  THC, or tetrahydrocannabinol—marijuana's main psychoactive ingredient—in the marijuana samples rose from about 4%in 1995 to about 12 percent in 2014" (Blaszczak-Boxe 2016, p. 1)
- The highest tested sample ever tested between 1975 and 2009 had 33.12% THC (domestic) and 37.20% THC (nondomestic). Another recent study indicated that the most potent strains of marijuana contain 25% THC (Hellerman 2013).
- Whether they are legal or not, drugs are extremely popular. Their sale is a multibillion-dollar-a-year business, with a major influence on many national economies.
- More so today than years ago, both licit and illicit drugs are introduced and experimented with by youths at a younger age. Older siblings, friends, and acquaintances often supply these drugs.
- Through the media, people in today's society are more affected by direct television and radio advertising, especially by drug companies that are "pushing" their newest drugs. Similarly, advertisements and sales promotions

(coupons) for alcohol, coffee, tea, and vitamins are targeted to receptive consumer audiences, as identified through sophisticated market research.

- Today, there is greater availability and wider dissemination of drug information. Literally thousands of websites provide information on drug usage, chat rooms devoted to drug enthusiasts, and instructions on how to make drugs (mainly for recreational purposes) or purchase them on the Internet. On a daily basis, hundreds of thousands of spam emails are automatically sent regarding information on purchasing over-the-counter (OTC) drugs and prescription drugs without medical authorization (medical prescription). "The percentage of spam in email traffic averaged 85.2% in 2009" (Bondarenko et al. 2010).
- Approximately 18.9% of spam mail consists of medications and health-related goods and services (Bondarenko et al. 2010).
- Crack and other manufactured drugs offer potent effects at low cost, vastly multiplying the damage potential of drug abuse (Clatts et al. 2008; Inciardi, Lockwood, and Pottieger 1993; Office of National Drug Control Policy [ONDCP] 2003).
- Drug use endangers the future of a society by harming its youth and potentially destroying the lives of many young men and women. When gateway drugs, such as alcohol and tobacco, are used at an early age, a strong probability exists that the use will progress to other drugs, such as marijuana, cocaine, and amphetamines. Early drug use will likely lead to a lifelong habit, which usually has serious implications for the future.
- Drug use and especially drug dealing are becoming major factors in the growth of crime rates among the young. Membership in violent delinquent gangs is growing at an alarming rate. Violent shootings, drive-by killings, carjacking, and "wilding" occur frequently in cities (and increasingly in small towns).
- Seven in 10 drug users work full time (*Capitol Times* 1999). More recent findings indicate that of 2.9 million adults ages 18 to 64 employed full time who had co-occurring **substance use disorder** and serious psychological distress, nearly 60% were not treated for either problem, and less than 5% were treated for both problems (Substance Abuse and Mental Health Services Administration [SAMHSA] 2008b). Further, most binge and heavy alcohol users

were employed in 2011. Among 56.5 million adult binge drinkers, 42.1 million (74.4%) were employed either full or part time. Among 15.5 million heavy drinkers, 11.6 million (74.9%) were employed (SAMHSA 2012). Such startling findings regarding employment and drug use suggest not only decreased productivity, absenteeism, job turnover, and medical costs but also near or serious accidents and mistakes caused by workers.

- Another related problem is that drug use is especially serious today because we have become highly dependent on the expertise of others and highly dependent on technology. For example, the operation of sophisticated machines and electronic equipment requires that workers and professionals be free of the intoxicating effects of mind-altering drugs. Imagine the chilling fact that on a daily basis a certain percentage of pilots, surgeons, and heavy-equipment operators are under the influence of mind-altering drugs while working or that a certain percentage of school-bus drivers are under the effects of, say, marijuana and/or cocaine.

With remarkable and unsurpassed excellence in scientific, technological, and electronic accomplishments, one might think that in the United States drug use and abuse would be considered irrational behavior. One might also think that the allure of drugs would diminish on the basis of the statistically high proportions of accidents, crimes, domestic violence and other relationship problems, and early deaths that result from the use and abuse of both licit and illicit drugs. Yet, as the latest drug use figures show, knowledge of these effects does not deter drug use.

Considering these costs, what explains the continuing use and abuse of drugs? What could possibly sustain and feed the attraction to use mind-altering drugs? Why are drugs used when the consequences are so well documented and predictable?

KEY TERM

substance use disorder
the American Psychiatric Association's *Diagnostic and Statistical Manual of Mental Disorders*, fifth edition (*DSM-5*; 2013), used by clinicians and psychiatrists for diagnosing mental disorders, combines substance abuse and substance dependence into a single condition called *substance use disorder*

In answering these questions, we need to list some basic reasons why people take drugs:

- People may be searching for pleasure.
- Drugs may relieve stress or tension or provide a temporary escape for people with excessive anxieties or severe depression.
- Peer pressure is a strong influence, especially for young people.
- In some cases, drugs may enhance religious or mystical experiences.
- Drugs are used to enhance recreational pursuits, such as the popular use of Ecstasy at raves and music festivals.
- Some believe that illicit use of drugs can enhance work performance, such as the use of cocaine by stockbrokers, office workers, and lawyers.
- Drugs (primarily performance-enhancing drugs) can be used to improve athletic performance.
- Drugs can relieve pain and the symptoms of an illness.

Although these reasons may indicate some underlying causes of excessive or abusive drug use, they also suggest that the variety and complexity of explanations and motivations are almost infinite. For any one individual, it is seldom clear when the drug use shifts from nondestructive use to abuse and addiction. When we consider the wide use of such licit drugs as alcohol, nicotine, and caffeine, we make the following discoveries: (1) more than 88% of the U.S. population use different types of drugs on a daily basis (SAMHSA 2012), (2) nearly half (49%) have tried an illicit drug by the time they finish high school (Johnston et al. 2013), and (3) three out of four students (75%) have consumed alcohol (more than just a few sips) by the end of high school, and nearly half (47%) have done so by 8th grade (Johnston et al. 2013).

Further, some drugs can mimic many of the hundreds of moods people can experience. We can, therefore, begin to understand why the explanations for drug use and abuse are multiple and depend on both socialization experiences and biological differences. As a result of these two factors, which imply hundreds of variations, explanations for drug use cannot be forced into one or two theories.

Researchers have tackled the drug use and abuse question from three major theoretical positions: biological, psychological, and sociological perspectives. Although the remainder of this chapter discusses these three major types of theoretical explanations, before delving into them we begin with a discussion of the motivation or "engine" responsible for the consistent attraction to recreational and/or nonmedical use of drugs—namely, addiction.

The Origin and Nature of Addiction

Humans can develop a very intense relationship with chemicals. Most people have chemically altered their mood at some point in their lives, if only by consuming a cup of coffee or a glass of white wine, and a majority do so occasionally. Yet for some individuals chemicals become the center of their lives, driving their behavior and determining their priorities, even to the point at which catastrophic consequences to their health and social well-being ensue. Although the word *addiction* is an agreed-upon term referring to such behavior, little agreement exists as to the origin, nature, or boundaries of the concept of addiction. It has been classified as a very bad habit, a failure of will or morality, a symptom of other problems, or a chronic disease in its own right.

Although public perception of drug abuse and addiction as a major social problem has waxed and waned over the past 20 years, the social costs of addiction have not: the total criminal justice, health, insurance, and other costs in the United States are roughly estimated at $90 billion to $185 billion annually, depending on the source. Despite numerous prevention efforts, the "War on Drugs," and a decline in the heavy drug use of the 1960s and 1970s, lessons learned in one decade seem to quickly pass out of awareness.

For example, the rate of annual use of marijuana among 12th graders in 1992 was approximately 22%; in 2014, it had increased to approximately 35% (Johnston et al. 2015). Alcohol and cigarettes also create problems when used by the very young:

Alcohol and cigarettes are the two major licit drugs included in the Monitoring the Future Studies (MTF) surveys, though even these are legally prohibited for purchase by those the age of most of our respondents. Alcohol use is more widespread than use of *illicit drugs*. About seven out of ten 12th-grade students (69%) have at least tried alcohol, and approximately four out of ten (42%) are current drinkers—that is, they reported consuming some alcohol in the 30 days prior to the survey. Even among 8th graders, the proportion of students reporting any alcohol use in their lifetime is nearly one third (30%), and about one ninth (11%) are current (past 30-day) drinkers.

Of greater concern than just any use of alcohol is "binge" drinking—having five or more drinking a row at least once in the prior two weeks.

"Among 12th graders, binge drinking peaked in 1979 along with overall illicit drug use. The prevalence of binge drinking then declined substantially from 41% in 1983 to 28% in 1992, a drop of almost one third (also the low point of any illicit drug use). Although illicit drug use rose sharply in the 1990s, binge drinking rose by only a small fraction, and that rise was followed by some decline at all three grades. By 2014, proportional declines since the recent peaks reached in the 1990s were 69%, 48%, and 38% for grades 8, 10, and 12, respectively" (Johnston et al. 2015, p. 38).

Further, the very large numbers of 8th graders who have already begun using the so-called gateway drugs (tobacco, alcohol, inhalants, and marijuana) suggest that a substantial number are also at risk of proceeding further to such drugs as LSD, cocaine, amphetamines, and heroin. Government officials and researchers believe that *decreases* in perceived and believed harmfulness of using a drug are often leading indicators of future increases in actual use of that drug. "The authors of this study suggest that these trends may reflect 'generational forgetting' of the dangers of these drugs, leaving the newer cohorts vulnerable to a resurgence of use" (Center for Substance Abuse Research [CESAR] 2007, p. 7). From these major studies, it is apparent that both licit and illicit types of drugs continue to penetrate into increasingly younger age groups.

■ Defining Addiction

Addiction is described as a complex disease. In 1964, the World Health Organization (WHO) of the United Nations defined it as "a state of periodic or chronic intoxication detrimental to the individual and society, which is characterized by an overwhelming desire to continue taking the drug and to obtain it by any means" (pp. 9–10). Accordingly, addiction is characterized as compulsive, at times uncontrollable, drug craving, seeking, and use that persist even in the face of extremely negative consequences (National Institute on Drug Abuse [NIDA] 1999). This relentless

pursuit of a drug of choice occurs despite the fact that the drug is usually harmful and injurious to bodily and mental functions.

The word *addiction*, derived from the Latin verb *addicere*, refers to the process of binding to things. Today, the word largely refers to a chronic adherence to drugs. This can include both physical and psychological dependence. *Physical dependence* is the body's need to constantly have the drug or drugs; *psychological dependence* is the mental inability to stop using the drug or drugs.

The *Diagnostic and Statistical Manual of Mental Disorders*, fifth edition (*DSM-5*), published by the American Psychiatric Association (APA 2013), differentiates between substance use disorders and **substance-induced disorders (addictive disorders)**. Substance-related and addictive disorders largely stem from activation of the reward pathways in the brain (which provide the pleasurable feeling from the high that a drug produces); also, those with

> lower levels of self control, which may reflect impairments of the brain inhibitory mechanisms, may be particularly predisposed to develop substance use disorders.... The following conditions may be classified as substance-induced: intoxication, withdrawal, and other substance/medication-induced mental disorder (psychotic disorder, bipolar and related disorder, depressive disorders, anxiety disorders, obsessive-compulsive and related disorders, sleep disorder, sexual dysfunctions, delirium, and neurocognitive disorders). (APA 2013, p. 481)

The diagnosis of substance use disorder[1] includes the following:

- *Pharmacological*: The diagnosed individual may take the substance in larger amounts or over a longer period of time than was originally intended.

---

[1]In the *DSM-5*, substance abuse and substance dependence have been combined into a single condition called *substance use disorder*.

KEY TERM

substance-induced disorders (addictive disorders)
a type of substance-related disorder that involves problems caused by the direct effects of a substance such as intoxication, withdrawal, and other substance/medication-induced mental disorders

- *Excessive time spent obtaining the substance.* The individual may spend an excessive amount of time obtaining and/or recovering from the drug(s) and its effects; in severe cases, nearly all of the individual's daily activities revolve around the substance.
- *Craving.* The user has an intense desire or urge for the drug (cannot think of anything other than securing and using the drug).
- *Social impairment.* The individual fails to fulfill major role obligations at work, school, or home despite having persistent or recurrent social or interpersonal problems caused by the effects of the substance; this includes withdrawal from personal and/or family obligations and/or hobbies and interests.
- *Risky use of the substance.* The individual may continue substance use despite knowledge of having a persistent or recurrent physical or psychological problem. He or she is unable to abstain from using the substance despite difficulties in using.
- *Tolerance.* The individual needs increased amounts or else experiences a diminished effect when using the same amount of the substance.
- *Withdrawal.* "Withdrawal . . . is a syndrome that occurs when blood or tissue concentrations of a substance decline in an individual who had maintained prolonged heavy use of substance" (APA 2013, p. 484). (Often after developing withdrawal symptoms, "the individual is likely to [resume consuming] the substance to relieve the symptoms . . . of withdrawal" [APA 2013, p. 484].)

KEY TERMS

moral model
the belief that people abuse alcohol because they choose to do so

disease model
the belief that people abuse alcohol because of some biologically caused condition

characterological or personality predisposition model
the view of chemical dependency as a symptom of problems in the development or operation of the system of needs, motives, and attitudes within the individual

personality disorders
a broad category of psychiatric disorders, formerly called "character disorders," that includes the antisocial personality disorder, borderline personality disorder, schizoid personality disorder, and others; these serious, ongoing impairments are difficult to treat

Finally, an additional definition of addiction is also noteworthy. The National Institute on Drug Abuse (NIDA) defines addiction as

a chronic, relapsing brain disease that is characterized by compulsive drug-seeking and use, despite harmful consequences. It is considered a brain disease because drugs change the brain—they change its structure and how it works. These brain changes can be long lasting and can lead to the harmful behaviors seen in people who abuse drugs. (NIDA 2008a, p. 5)

▌ Models of Addiction

Various models attempt to describe the essential nature of drug addiction. Newspaper accounts of "inebriety" in the 19th and early 20th centuries contain an editorializing undertone that looks askance at the poor morals and lifestyle choices followed by the inebriate. This view has been termed the **moral model**, and although it may seem outdated from a modern scientific standpoint, it still characterizes an attitude among many traditional North Americans and members of many ethnic groups.

The prevailing concept or model of addiction in the United States is the **disease model**. Most proponents of this concept specify addiction to be a chronic and progressive disease, over which the sufferer has no control. This model originated in part from research among members of Alcoholics Anonymous (AA) performed by Jellinek (1960), one of the founders of addiction studies. He observed a seemingly inevitable progression in his subjects, during which they made many failed attempts to stop drinking. This philosophy is currently espoused by the recovery fellowships of AA and Narcotics Anonymous (NA) and, to a large extent, the treatment field in general. It has even permeated the psychiatric and medical establishments' standard definitions of addiction. There are many variations within the broad rubric of the disease model. This model has been bitterly debated: viewpoints range from fierce adherence to equally fierce opposition, with intermediate views casting the disease concept as a convenient myth (Smith, Milkman, and Sunderworth 1985).

Those who view addiction as another manifestation of something gone awry with the personality system adhere to the **characterological or personality predisposition model**. Every school of psychoanalytic, neopsychoanalytic, and psychodynamic psychotherapy has its specific "take" on the subject of addiction (Frosch 1985). Tangentially, many addicts are also diagnosed with **personality disorders** (formerly known as "character disorders"), such as impulse control disorders and sociopathy. Although few addicts are treated by **psychoanalysis** or psychoanalytic psychotherapy, a characterological type of model was a formative influence on the drug-free, addict-run "therapeutic community" model, which uses harsh confrontation and time-extended, sleep-depriving group encounters. People who follow the therapeutic community model conclude that addicts must have withdrawn behind a **"double wall" of encapsulation**, where they failed to grow, making such techniques necessary.

Others view addiction as a "career," a series of steps or phases with distinguishable characteristics. One career pattern of addiction includes six phases (Clinard and Meier 2011; Waldorf 1983):

1. Experimentation or initiation
2. Escalation (increasing use)
3. Maintenance or "taking care of business" (optimistic use of drugs coupled with successful job performance)
4. Dysfunction or "going through changes" (problems with constant use and unsuccessful attempts to quit)
5. Recovery or "getting out of the life" (arriving at a successful view about quitting and receiving drug treatment)
6. Ex-addict (having successfully quit)

Finally, after examining countless theories that attempt to list and/or predict the stages of addiction to alcohol, tobacco, and/or illicit drug use, the following set of stages appears to be the most salient regarding addiction to drug use: (1) initial initiation and use of the drug, (2) patterned continuation into using the drug, (3) transition to drug abuse, (4) attempts at cessation (stopping the use), and (5) relapse (a return to abusive usage).

■ Factors Contributing to Addiction

Many, perhaps millions, of individuals use or even occasionally abuse drugs without compromising their basic health, legal, and occupational status and social relationships. Why do a significant minority become caught up in abuse and addictive behavior? The answer stems from the fact that many factors (not a single one) generally contribute to an individual becoming addicted (Syvertsen 2008). **Table 2.1** represents a compilation of factors identified as complicit in the origin or etiology of addiction, taken from the fields of psychology, sociology, and addiction studies.

In addition to the social and cultural factors listed in Table 2.1, other "cultural" risk factors for development of alcohol abuse include the following:

- Drinking at times other than at meals
- Drinking alone
- Drinking perceived as a reliever of stress and/or anxiety
- Patterns of solitary drinking (immediately drinking, smoking marijuana, or using other drugs after work; weekend drinking; late night drinking)
- Drinking defined as a rite of passage into an adult role
- Recent introduction of a chemical into a social group with insufficient time to develop informal social control over its use (Marshall 1979)

It is important to recall that the mix of risk factors differs for each person. It varies according to individual, peer, family, age, social, and cultural idiosyncrasies. Most addiction treatment professionals believe that it is difficult, if not impossible, to tease out these factors before treatment, when the user is still "talking to a chemical," or during early treatment, when the brain and body are still recuperating from the effects of long-term abuse. Once a stable sobriety is established, one can begin to address any underlying problems. An exception is the mentally ill chemical abuser, whose treatment requires special considerations from the outset.

In addition to the factors just listed, a number of age-dependent stressors and conflicts sometimes promote drug misuse. Risk factors that apply especially to adolescents include the following:

- Peer norms favoring use
- Misperception of peer norms (users set the tone)
- Power of age group (peer norms vs. other social influences)
- Conflicts that generate anxiety or guilt, such as dependence versus independence, adult maturational tasks versus fear, new types of roles versus familiar safe roles

KEY TERMS

psychoanalysis
a theory of personality and method of psychotherapy originated by Sigmund Freud, focused on unconscious forces and conflicts and a series of psychosexual stages

"double wall" of encapsulation
an adaptation to pain and avoidance of reality, in which the individual withdraws emotionally and further anesthetizes himself or herself by chemical means

TABLE 2.1 Risk Factors for Addiction

Risk Factor	Leading to This Effect
Biologically Based Factors (genetic, neurological, biochemical, and so on)	
A less subjective feeling of intoxication	More use to achieve intoxication (warning signs of abuse absent)
Easier development of tolerance; liver enzymes adapt to increased use	Easier to reach the addictive level
Lack of resilience or fragility of higher (cerebral) brain functions	Easy deterioration of cerebral functioning, impaired judgment, and social deterioration
Difficulty in screening out unwanted or bothersome outside stimuli (low stimulus barrier)	Feeling overwhelmed or stressed
Tendency to amplify outside or internal stimuli (stimulus augmentation)	Feeling attacked or panicked; need to avoid emotion
Attention deficit hyperactivity disorder and other learning disabilities	Failure, low self-esteem, or isolation
Biologically based mood disorders (depression and bipolar disorders)	Need to self-medicate against loss of control or pain of depression; inability to calm down when manic or to sleep when agitated
Psychosocial/Developmental "Personality" Factors	
Low self-esteem	Need to block out pain; gravitation to outsider groups
Depression rooted in learned helplessness and passivity	Use of a stimulant as an antidepressant
Conflicts	Anxiety and guilt
Repressed and unresolved grief and rage	Chronic depression, anxiety, or pain
Posttraumatic stress syndrome (as in veterans and abuse victims)	Nightmares or panic attacks
Social and Cultural Environment	
Availability of drugs	Easy frequent use
Chemical-abusing parental model	Sanction; no conflict over use
Abusive, neglectful parents; other dysfunctional family patterns	Pervasive sense of abandonment, distrust, and pain; difficulty in maintaining attachments
Group norms favoring heavy use and abuse	Reinforced, hidden abusive behavior that can progress without interference
Misperception of peer norms	Belief that most people use or favor use or think it's cool to use
Severe or chronic stressors, as from noise, poverty, racism, or occupational stress	Need to alleviate or escape from stress via chemical means
Alienation factors: isolation, emptiness	Painful sense of aloneness, normlessness, rootlessness, boredom, monotony, or hopelessness
Difficult migration/acculturation with social disorganization, gender/generation gaps, or loss of role	Stress without buffering support system

- Teenage risk taking, sense of omnipotence or invulnerability
- Use defined as a rite of passage into adulthood
- Use perceived as cool, glamorous, sexy, facilitating intimacy, fun, and so on

Risk factors that apply especially to middle-aged individuals include the following:

- Loss of meaningful role or occupational identity due to retirement
- Loss, grief, or isolation due to loss of parents, divorce, or departure of children ("empty nest syndrome")
- Loss of positive body image
- Dealing with a newly diagnosed illness (e.g., diabetes, heart problems, cancer)
- Disappointment when life's expectations are not met

Even in each of these age groups a combination of factors is at play. The adolescent abuser might have risk factors that were primarily neurological vulnerabilities, such as undiagnosed attention deficit hyperactivity disorder (ADHD). Alternatively, he or she may experience failure and rejection at school, disappoint his or her parents, or be labeled odd, lazy, or unintelligent (Kelly and Ramundo 2006).

In response to the information presented in Table 2.1, a student who was a recovering alcoholic commented, "You're an alcoholic because you drink!" He had a good point: the mere presence of one, two, or more risk factors does not create addiction. Drugs must be available, they must be used, and they must become a pattern of adaptation to any of the many painful, threatening, uncomfortable, or unwanted sensations or stimuli that occur in the presence of genetic, psychosocial, or environmental risk factors. Prevention workers often note the presence of multiple messages encouraging use: the medical use of minor tranquilizers to offset any type of psychic discomfort; the marketing of alcohol as sexy, glamorous, adult, and facilitative of social interaction; and so forth.

The Vicious Cycle of Drug Addiction

First, the man takes a drink, then the drink takes a drink, then the drink takes the man.

—*Traditional Chinese proverb*

Drug addiction develops as a process; it is not a sudden occurrence. The body makes a series of physiological adaptations to the presence of alcohol and other drugs. For instance, brain cell tolerance and increased metabolic efficiency of the liver can develop, necessitating consumption of more of the chemical to achieve the desired effect. Physical dependence can also develop, in which cell adaptations cause withdrawal syndromes to occur in the absence of the chemical.

Other factors can promote the cycle of addiction. For instance, drug abuse impairs cerebral functioning, including memory, judgment, behavioral organization, ability to plan, ability to solve problems, and motor coordination. Thus, poor decision making, impaired and deviant behavior, and overall dysfunction result in adverse social consequences, such as accidents, loss of earning power and relationships, and impaired health. Such adverse social and health consequences cause pain, depression, and lowered self-esteem, which may result in further use of the drug as an emotional and physical anesthetic. The addict often adapts to this chronically painful situation by erecting a defense system of denial, minimization, and rationalization; the chemical blunting of reality may exacerbate this denial of reality. It is unlikely, at this point, that the addict or developing addict will feel compelled to cease or cut back on drug use on his or her own (Tarter, Alterman, and Edwards 1983).

Family, friends, and colleagues often unwittingly "enable" the maintenance and progression of addiction. Examples include making excuses for addicts, literally and figuratively bailing them out, taking up the slack, denying and minimizing their problems, and otherwise making it possible for addicts to avoid facing the reality and consequences of what they are doing to themselves and others. Although these friends and family members may be motivated by simple naïveté, embarrassment, or misguided protectiveness, there are often hidden gains in taking up this role, known popularly as *codependency* (Beattie 1987; Mental Health America [MHA] 2010). Varieties of cultural and organizational factors also operate in the workplace or school that allow denial of the existence or severity of abuse or dependency. This triad of personal denial, peer and kin denial and codependency, and institutional denial represents a formidable impediment to successful intervention and recovery (Miller 1995; Myers 1990).

■ Other Nondrug Addictions

The addictive disease model and the 12-step recovery model followed by AA and NA have appeared

Like drug use, gambling can become addictive.

so successful for many addicts and their families and friends that other unwanted syndromes have been added to the list of "addictions." The degree to which the concept of addiction fits these syndromes varies. Gambling, for example, shows progressive worsening, loss of control, relief of tension from the activity, and continuance despite negative (often disastrous) consequences experienced by the addicted gambler. Recovering gamblers claim to experience a form of withdrawal. Gamblers Anonymous is a fellowship that has formed to assist its members. Clearly, gambling as an activity has much in common with chemical addictions, but it was debated as to whether it belonged in the category of addiction. However, for the first time in its publishing history, the most recent edition of the *Diagnostic and Statistical Manual of Mental Disorders* (*DSM-5*) includes dependence on gambling as a mental disorder.

Many other groups have followed in the footsteps of Gamblers Anonymous, including those related to eating (Overeaters Anonymous) and sexual relationships (The Augustine Fellowship, Sex and Love Addicts Anonymous). In recent years, any excessive or unwanted behaviors,

KEY TERM

genetic and biophysiological theories
explanations of addiction in terms of genetic brain dysfunction and biochemical patterns

including excess shopping, hoarding, chocolate consumption, and even Internet use, have been labeled "addictions," which has led to satirical reporting in the press. Addiction professionals lament the overdefinition, which they believe trivializes the seriousness and suffering of rigorously defined addictions.

Major Theoretical Explanations: Biological

Biological explanations have tended to use genetic theories and the disease model to explain drug addiction. The view that alcoholism is a sickness dates back approximately 200 years (Conrad and Schneider 1980; Heitzeg 1996). The disease perspective is upheld by Jellinek's (1960) view that alcoholism largely involves a loss of control over drinking and that the drinker experiences clearly distinguishable phases in his or her drinking patterns. For example, concerning alcoholism, the illness affects the abuser to the point of loss of control. Thus, the disease model views drug abuse as an illness in need of treatment or therapy.

According to biological theories, drug abuse has a beginning stemming from physical characteristics that cause certain individuals either to experiment with or to crave drugs to the point of abusive use. **Genetic and biophysiological theories** explain addiction in terms of genetics, brain dysfunction, and biochemical patterns.

Biological explanations emphasize that the central nervous system (CNS) reward sensors in some people are more sensitive to drugs, making the drug experience more pleasant and more rewarding for these individuals (Khantzian 1998; Mathias 1995; NIDA 2014). In contrast, others find the effects of drugs of abuse very unpleasant; such people are not likely to be attracted to these drugs (Farrar and Kearns 1989; Grant 2013; National Health Service [NHS] 2015).

Most experts acknowledge that biological factors play an essential role in drug abuse. These factors likely determine how the brain responds to these drugs and why such substances are addictive. It is thought that by identifying the nature of the biological systems that contribute to drug abuse problems, improved prevention and treatment methods can be developed (Koob 2000; Kuehn 2010; NIDA 2008b).

All the major biological explanations related to drug abuse assume that these substances exert their **psychoactive effects** by altering brain chemistry or neuronal activity (in the basic functional cells of the brain). Specifically, the drugs of abuse interfere with the functioning of **neurotransmitters**—chemical messengers used for communication between brain regions.

The following sections detail three principal biological theories that help explain why some drugs are abused and why certain people are more likely to become addicted when using these substances.

■ Abused Drugs as Positive Reinforcers

Biological research has shown that stimulating some brain regions with an electrode causes very pleasurable sensations. In fact, laboratory animals would rather self-administer stimulation to these brain areas than eat or engage in sex. It has been demonstrated that drugs of abuse also activate these same pleasure centers of the brain (NIDA 2008b; Weiss 1999).

It is generally believed that most drugs with abuse potential enhance pleasure centers by causing the release of specific brain neurotransmitters such as **dopamine** (Bespalov et al. 1999; NIDA 2008b). How do drugs work in the brain?

> All drugs of abuse directly or indirectly target the brain's reward system by flooding the circuit with dopamine. Dopamine is a neurotransmitter present in regions of the brain that regulates movement, emotion, cognition, motivation, and feelings of pleasure. The overstimulation of this system, which rewards our natural behavior, produces the euphoric effects sought by people who abuse drugs and teaches them to repeat the behavior. (NIDA 2008b, p. 17)

Brain cells become accustomed to the presence of these neurotransmitters and crave them when they are absent, leading the person to seek more drugs (NIDA 2008b; Spanagel and Weiss 1999). In addition, it has been proposed that overstimulation of these brain regions by continual drug use "exhausts" these dopamine systems and leads to depression and an inability to experience normal pleasure (Volkow 1999).

■ Drug Abuse and Psychiatric Disorders

Biological explanations are thought to be responsible for the substantial overlap that exists between drug addiction and mental illness (NIDA 2007) (see "Do Genes Matter? What Is the Relationship Between Addiction and Levels of Mental Disorders?").

■ Genetic Explanations

Why does one person become dependent on drugs while another, exposed to the same environment and experiences, does not?

—*Schaffer Library of Drug Policy (1994, p. 1)*

One biological theory receiving scrutiny suggests that inherited traits can predispose some individuals to drug addiction (Lemonick with Park 2007; MacPherson 2010). Such theories have been supported by the observation that increased frequency of alcoholism and drug abuse exists among children of alcoholics and drug abusers (APA 2000; Uhl et al. 1993, 2002). Using adoption records of some 3000 individuals from Sweden, researchers Cloninger, Gohman, and Sigvardsson conducted one of the most extensive research studies examining genetics and alcoholism. They found that "children of alcoholic parents were likely to grow up to be alcoholics themselves, even in cases where the children were reared by nonalcoholic adoptive parents almost from birth" (Doweiko 2015, p. 37). Such studies estimate that drug vulnerability due to genetic influences accounts for approximately 38% of all cases, whereas environmental and social factors account for the balance (Uhl et al. 1993).

Other studies attempting to identify the specific genes that may predispose the carrier to drug abuse problems have suggested that a brain target site (called a receptor) for dopamine is altered in a manner that increases the drug abuse vulnerability (Genetic Science Learning Center 2015; Radowitz 2003; Wyman 1997). Studies that test for genetic factors in complex behaviors such as drug abuse are very difficult to conduct and interpret. It is sometimes impossible to design experiments that distinguish among genetic, social, environmental, and psychological influences in human populations. For example, inherited traits are

KEY TERMS

psychoactive effects
how drug substances alter and affect the brain's mental functions

neurotransmitters
the chemical messengers released by nervous (nerve) cells for communication with other cells

dopamine
a neurotransmitter present in regions of the brain that regulate movement, emotion, cognition, motivation, and feelings of pleasure; it mediates the rewarding aspects of most drugs of abuse

DO GENES MATTER?

What Is the Relationship Between Addiction and Other Mental Disorders?

There is some good evidence that a comorbid relationship exists between addiction and other mental disorders (Center for Behavioral Health Statistics and Quality [CBHSQ] 2015; NIDA 2008a, 2010).

What Is Comorbidity?

Comorbidity is a term used to describe two or more disorders or illnesses occurring in the same person. They can occur at the same time or one after the other. Comorbidity also implies interactions between the illnesses that can worsen the course of both.

Is Drug Addiction a Mental Illness?

Yes, addiction changes the brain in fundamental ways, disturbing a person's normal hierarchy of needs and desires and substituting new priorities connected with procuring and using the drug. The resulting compulsive behaviors that weaken the ability to control impulses, despite the consequences, are similar to hallmarks of other mental illnesses.

How Common Are Comorbid Drug Addiction and Other Mental Illnesses?

Many people who are addicted to drugs are also diagnosed with other mental disorders, and vice versa. For example, compared with the general population, people addicted to drugs are roughly twice as likely to suffer from mood and anxiety disorders, with the reverse also true.*

Why Do These Disorders Often Co-occur?

Although drug use disorders commonly occur with other mental illnesses, this does not mean that one caused the other, even if one appeared first. In fact, establishing causality or even directionality (i.e., which came first) can be difficult. However, research suggests the following possibilities for their co-occurrence:

- Drug abuse may bring about symptoms of another mental illness. Increased risk of psychosis in some marijuana users suggests this possibility.
- Mental disorders can lead to drug abuse, possibly as a means of **self-medication**. Patients suffering from anxiety or depression may rely on alcohol, tobacco, and other drugs to temporarily alleviate their symptoms.

These disorders could also be caused by common risk factors, such as

- *Overlapping genetic vulnerabilities*: Common genetic factors may make a person susceptible to both addiction and other mental disorders or to having a greater risk of a second disorder once the first appears.
- *Overlapping environmental triggers*: Stress, trauma (such as physical or sexual abuse), and early exposure to drugs are common factors that can lead to addiction and other mental illnesses.
- *Involvement of similar brain regions*: Brain systems that respond to reward and stress, for example, are affected by drugs of abuse and may show abnormalities in patients who have certain mental disorders.
- *Drug use disorders and other mental illnesses are developmental disorders*: This means they often begin in the teen years or even younger—periods when the brain experiences dramatic developmental changes. Early exposure to drugs of abuse may change the brain in ways that increase the risk for mental disorders. Also, early symptoms of a mental disorder may indicate an increased risk for later drug use.

How Are These Comorbid Conditions Diagnosed and Treated?

The rate of comorbidity between drug use disorders and other mental illnesses calls for a comprehensive

KEY TERMS

comorbidity
two or more disorders or illnesses occurring in the same person; they can occur either simultaneously or one after the other; also implies interactions between the illnesses that can worsen the course of both

self-medication
a method of self-care in which an individual uses nonprescribed drugs to treat untreated and often undiagnosed medical ailments involving his or her psychological condition; self-prescribed drugs can include recreational drugs, psychoactive drugs, alcohol, and/or herbal products in order to alleviate or diminish mental distress, stress and anxiety, mental illnesses, and/or psychological trauma

(continues)

DO GENES MATTER?

What Is the Relationship Between Addiction and Other Mental Disorders? (continued)

approach that identifies and evaluates both. Accordingly, anyone seeking help for either drug abuse/addiction or another mental disorder should be checked for both and treated accordingly.

Several behavioral therapies have shown promise for treating comorbid conditions. These approaches can be designed to target patients according to specific factors such as age or marital status. Some therapies have proved more effective for adolescents, whereas others have shown greater effectiveness for adults; some therapies are designed for families and groups, others for individuals.

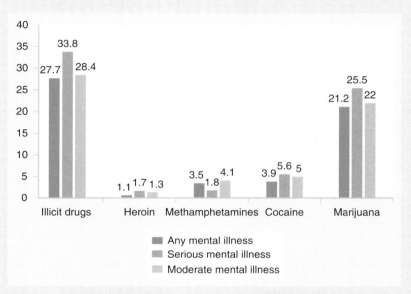

Past-year percentage of specific drug usage and levels of mental illness ages 18 and older.

Reproduced from Center for Behavioral Health Statistics and Quality (CBHSQ). *Behavioral Health Trends in the United States: Results from the 2014 National Survey on Drug Use and Health.* Rockville, MD: Health and Human Services (HHS) and National Survey on Drug Use and Health (NSDUH), 2015.

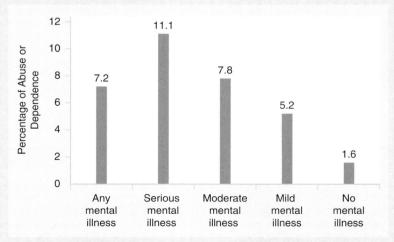

Past-year percentage of drug abuse or dependence and levels of mental illness ages 18 and older.

Reproduced from Center for Behavioral Health Statistics and Quality (CBHSQ). *Behavioral Health Trends in the United States: Results from the 2014 National Survey on Drug Use and Health.* Rockville, MD: Health and Human Services (HHS) and National Survey on Drug Use and Health (NSDUH), 2015.

(continues)

DO GENES MATTER?

What Is the Relationship Between Addiction and Other Mental Disorders? *(continued)*

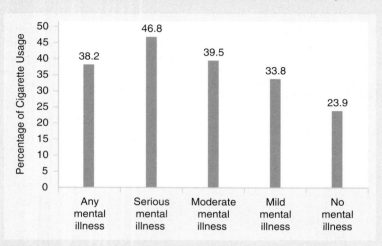

Past-year percentage of cigarette usage and levels of mental illness ages 18 and older.

Reproduced from Center for Behavioral Health Statistics and Quality (CBHSQ). *Behavioral Health Trends in the United States: Results from the 2014 National Survey on Drug Use and Health.* Rockville, MD: Health and Human Services (HHS) and National Survey on Drug Use and Health (NSDUH), 2015.

Although several medications exist for treating addiction and other mental illnesses, most have not been studied in patients with comorbidities. For example, individuals addicted to heroin, prescription pain medications, cigarettes, or alcohol can be treated with appropriate medications to ease withdrawal symptoms and drug craving; similarly, separate medications are available to help improve the symptoms of depression and anxiety. More research is needed, however, to better understand how such medications act when combined in individuals with comorbidities, or whether such medications can be dually effective for treating comorbid conditions.

....

* Substance abuse and substance dependence are considered *substance use disorders*—a category under mental disorders—when they meet the diagnostic criteria delineated in the *Diagnostic and Statistical Manual of Mental Disorders*, fifth edition (*DSM-5*). Drug dependence, as *DSM-5* defines it, is synonymous with the term *addiction* (even though *DSM-5* does not use the term *addiction*). Criteria for drug abuse hinge on the harmful consequences of repeated use but do not include compulsive use, tolerance, or withdrawal. Because the focus of this chapter is on comorbid drug use disorders and other mental illnesses, the terms *mental illness/mental disorders* will refer here to disorders other than drug use, such as depression, schizophrenia, anxiety, and mania. The terms *dual diagnosis, mentally ill chemical abuser,* and *co-occurrence* are also used to refer to drug use disorders that are comorbid with other mental illnesses.

Adapted from National Institute on Drug Abuse (NIDA). "Comorbidity: Addiction and Other Mental Disorders." *NIDA InfoFacts.* Bethesda, MD: U.S. Department of Health and Human Services, 2011: 1–2 and Center for Behavioral Health Statistics and Quality [CBHSQ] 2015

known to be major contributors to psychiatric disorders, such as schizophrenia and depression. Many people with one of these illnesses also have a substance abuse disorder (APA 2013; SAMHSA 2015). A high incidence of an abnormal gene in a cocaine-abusing population, for example, not only may be linked to drug abuse behavior but also may be associated with depression or another psychiatric disorder (Uhl, Persico, and Smith 1992; Uhl et al. 2002).

Theoretically, genetic factors can directly or indirectly contribute to drug abuse vulnerability in several ways:

- Taking drugs of abuse, thus encouraging their use, may relieve psychiatric disorders that are genetically determined.
- In some people, reward centers of the brain may be genetically determined to be especially sensitive to addictive drugs; thus, the use of

drugs by these people would be particularly pleasurable and would lead to a high rate of addiction.

- Volkow states that "drug addiction is a disease of the human brain" (Volkow 2016) and that ". . . [i]n the brains of addicts, there is reduced activity in the prefrontal cortex where rational thought can override impulsive behavior" (Kuehn 2010, p. 1905; Lemonick with Park 2007, p. 43).

- Character traits, such as insecurity and vulnerability, that often lead to drug abuse behavior may be genetically determined, causing a high rate of addiction in people with those traits (Kuehn 2010).

- Factors that determine how difficult it is to break away from drug addiction may be genetically determined, causing severe craving or very unpleasant withdrawal effects in some individuals. People with this predisposition are less likely to abandon their drug of abuse.

The genetic theories for explaining drug abuse may help us to understand the reasons that drug addiction occurs in some individuals but not in others. In addition, if genetic factors play a major role in drug abuse, it might be possible to use genetic screening to identify those people who are especially vulnerable to drug abuse problems and to help such individuals avoid exposure to these substances.

Major Theoretical Explanations: Psychological

Psychological theories mostly deal with mental or emotional states, which are often associated with or exacerbated by social and environmental factors. Psychological explanations of addiction include one or more of the following: escape from reality, boredom (Burns 1997), inability to cope with anxiety, destructive self-indulgence to the point of constantly desiring intoxicants, blind compliance with drug-abusing peers, self-destructiveness, and conscious and unconscious ignorance regarding the harmful effects of abusing drugs. Other authors write the following:

[P]sychological theory explains that drug use and abuse begins because of the unconscious motivations within all of us. We are not aware of these motivations, not even when they manifest themselves. So, there are unconscious conflicts and motivations that reside within us as well as our reactions to early events in our lives that move a person toward drug use and abuse. The motivations for drug use are within us, and we are not aware of them, nor are we aware that those are the reasons we have chosen to turn to drugs. In this case, the person may be weak or without self-esteem or even see themselves in the opposite manner, as all-important. Drug use then becomes a sort of crutch to make up for all that is wrong with their lives and wrong with their selves. (Moore 2008, p. 1)

Psychologists propose several possible causes of addiction. First, people may engage in harmful behaviors because of an abnormality, or "psychopathology," that manifests itself as mental illness. Second, people may learn unhealthy behavior in response to their environment. Third, people's thoughts and beliefs create their feelings. This, in turn, determines their behavior (Horvath et al. 2015).

Freud established early psychological theories. He linked "primal addictions" with masturbation and postulated that all later addictions, including those involving alcohol and other drugs, were caused by ego impairments. Freud said that drugs compensate for insecurities that stem from parental inadequacies, which themselves may cause difficulty in adequately forming bonds of friendships. He claimed that alcoholism is an expression of the death instinct, as are self-destruction, narcissism, and oral fixations. Although Freud's views represent interesting intuitive insights often not depicted in other theories, his theoretical concerns are difficult to observe and test, and they do not generate enough concrete data for quantitative testing and verification.

■ Distinguishing Between Substance Abuse and Mental Disorders

The APA has established widely accepted categories of diagnosis for behavioral disorders, including substance use disorder (which includes substance abuse and substance dependence). As standardized diagnostic categories, the characteristics of mental disorders have been analyzed by professional committees over many years and today are summarized in the latest version of the *Diagnostic and Statistical Manual of Mental Disorders* (*DSM-5*). In addition to categories for severe psychotic disorders and other more common mental disorders, experts in the field of psychiatry have established specific diagnostic criteria for various forms of substance abuse. All patterns of drug abuse that are described in this text have a counterpart description and classification in the *DSM-5* for medical professionals. For example, the *DSM-5* discusses the mental disorders resulting from the use or abuse of sedatives, hypnotics, or antianxiety drugs; alcohol; narcotics; amphetamine-like drugs; cocaine; caffeine; nicotine (tobacco); hallucinogens; phencyclidine (PCP); inhalants; and cannabis (marijuana). This manual of psychiatric diagnoses discusses in detail the mental disorders related to the drug use, the side effects of medications, and the consequences of toxic exposure to these substances (APA 2013).

Because of the similarities between, and the coexistence of, substance-related mental disorders and primary psychiatric disorders, it is sometimes difficult to distinguish between the two. However, for proper treatment to be rendered, the designation and characteristics of a mental disorder and a psychiatric disorder should be differentiated. According to *DSM-5* criteria, both substance abuse and substance dependence, together known as substance use disorder, can be identified by the occurrence and consequences of pharmacological factors, the amount of time spent obtaining the substance, craving, social impairment, risky use of the substance, and tolerance and withdrawal. (These categories were defined earlier in this chapter.)

According to the National Alliance on Mental Illness (NAMI), the relationship between substance abuse or dependency and mental illness is often termed **dual diagnosis**. Dual diagnosis is a very broad diagnosis because it often assumes multiple causes. It can range from someone developing mild depression because of binge drinking to someone's symptoms of bipolar disorder becoming more severe when that person abuses heroin during periods of mania (NAMI 2015).

The following relationships are possible when mental illness and substance use occur simultaneously (NAMI 2015):

- Drugs and alcohol can be a form of self-medication.
- Drugs and alcohol can worsen underlying mental illnesses.

KEY TERM

dual diagnosis
an individual who is simultaneously manifesting a mental health disorder(s) and addiction to drug use at the same time (e.g., a drug addict experiencing depression or anxiety)

- Drugs and alcohol can cause a person without mental illness to experience the onset of symptoms for the first time.
- Men are more likely than women to develop a co-occurring disorder.
- Individuals who are lower in socioeconomic status, military veterans, and people with more general medical illnesses are more like to develop a co-occurring disorder.

According to the *DSM-5*, the following information can also help distinguish between substance use disorder and primary mental disorders: (1) personal and family medical, psychiatric, and drug histories; (2) physical examinations; and (3) laboratory tests to assess physiological functions and determine the presence or absence of drugs. However, the possibility of a primary mental disorder should not be excluded just because the patient is using drugs—remember, many drug users use drugs to self-medicate their primary psychiatric problems (alcoholrehab.com 2015a; NIDA 2008a). Self-medicating is a method of self-care in which an individual uses nonprescribed drugs to treat untreated and often undiagnosed medical ailments involving their psychological condition.

The coexistence of underlying psychiatric problems in a drug user is suggested by the following circumstances: (1) the psychiatric problems do not match the usual drug effects (e.g., use of marijuana usually does not cause severe psychotic behavior), (2) the psychiatric disorder was present before the patient began abusing substances, and (3) the mental disorder persists for more than 4 weeks after substance use ends. The *Diagnostic and Statistical Manual of Mental Disorders*, five edition, text revision (*DSM-5*), makes it clear that clarifying the relationship between mental disorders and substances of abuse is important for proper diagnosis, treatment, and understanding (APA 2013; NIDA 2007, 2008a).

■ The Relationship Between Personality and Drug Use

Since medieval times, personality theories of increasing sophistication have been used to classify long-term behavioral tendencies or traits that appear in individuals; these traits have long been considered to be influenced by biological or chemical factors. Although such classification systems have varied widely, nearly all have shared two commonly observed dimensions of personality: introversion and extroversion. Individuals who show a predominant tendency to turn their thoughts and feelings inward rather than to direct attention outward have been considered to show the trait of *introversion*. At the opposite extreme, a tendency to seek outward activity and share feelings with others has been called *extroversion*. Of course, every individual shows a mix of such traits in varying degrees and circumstances.

In some earlier research studies, introversion and extroversion patterns have been associated with levels of neural arousal in brainstem circuits (alcoholrehab.com 2015b; Apostolides 1996; Carlson 1990; Gray 1987), and these forms of arousal are closely associated with effects caused by drug stimulants or depressants.

Drugs like cocaine, alcohol, or Prozac all affect these processes and an individual's degree of extroversion. They can artificially correct an ineffective dopamine system and make someone feel more sociable or motivated to pursue a goal. Low levels of serotonin, correlated with depression, may make people more responsive to dopamine and more susceptible to dopamine-stimulating drug use such as the use of cocaine, alcohol, amphetamine, opiates, and nicotine (Lang 1996).

Such research hypothesizes that people whose systems produce high levels of sensitivity to neural arousal may find high-intensity external stimuli to be painful and may react by turning inward. With these extremely high levels of sensitivity, such people may experience neurotic levels of anxiety or panic disorders. At the other extreme, individuals whose systems provide them with very low levels of sensitivity to neural arousal may find that moderate stimuli are inadequate to produce responses. To reach moderate levels of arousal, they may turn outward to seek high-intensity external sources of stimulation (Eysenck and Eysenck 1985; Gray 1987; Rousar et al. 1995).

Because high- and low-arousal symptoms are easy to create by using stimulants, depressants, or hallucinogens, it is possible that these personality patterns of introversion or extroversion affect how a person reacts to substances. For people whose experience is predominantly introverted or extroverted, extremes of high or low sensitivity may lead them to seek counteracting substances that become important methods of bringing experience to a level that seems bearable.

■ Theories Based on Learning Processes

How are drug use patterns learned? Regarding learning, operant conditioning explains how human beings acquire new patterns of behavior by the close association or pairing of one

significant reinforcing stimulus with another less significant or neutral stimulus. Also known as **social learning theory** (Bandura 1977; explained more fully in the "Social Learning Theory" section later in this chapter), this theory emphasizes that learned associations occur in the presence of other people using drugs coupled with other, often preconceived associations with the attitudes of society and friends about drug use (Gray and Bjorklund 2014). In this method of learning, people form expectations and become used to certain behavior patterns. This specific process of learning is known as conditioning, and it explains why pleasurable activities may become intimately connected with other activities that are also pleasurable, neutral, or even unpleasant. In addition, people can turn any new behavior into a recurrent and permanent one by the process of **habituation**—repeating certain patterns of behavior until they become established or habitual.

The basic process by which learning mechanisms can lead a person into drug use is also described in Bejerot's **addiction to pleasure theory** (Bejerot 1965, 1972, 1975; Dixon 2015; NIDA 1980). This theory assumes that it is biologically normal to continue a pleasure stimulus once started. Several research findings support this theory, indicating that "a strong, biologically based need for stimulation appears to make sensation-seeking young adults more vulnerable to drug abuse" (Mathias 1995, p. 1). Dixon (2015) and Khantzian (1998) also support this view. Another research finding complementing this theory states, "Certain areas of the brain, when stimulated, produce pleasurable feelings. Psychoactive substances are capable of acting on these brain mechanisms to produce these sensations. These pleasurable feelings become reinforcers that drive the continued use of the substances" (Gardner 1992, p. 43). People at highest risk for drug use and addiction are those who maintain

KEY TERMS

social learning theory
a theory that places emphasis on how an individual learns patterns of behavior from the attitudes of others, society, and peers

habituation
repeating certain patterns of behavior until they become established or habitual

addiction to pleasure theory
a theory assuming that it is biologically normal to continue a pleasure stimulus once begun

a constant preoccupation with getting high, seek new or novel thrills in their experiences, and are known to have a relentless desire to pursue physical stimulation or dangerous behaviors; these are classified as **sensation-seeking individuals** (Zuckerman 2000, 2007).

Drug use may also be reinforced when it is associated with receiving affection or approval in a social setting, such as within a peer group relationship. Initially, the use of drugs may not be very important or pleasurable to the individual; however, eventually the affection and social rewards experienced when drugs are used become associated with the drug. Drug use and intimacy may then become perceived as very worthwhile.

I don't know how to explain why but an attractive part of cocaine use is the instant feeling of intimacy with others who are also snorting this drug. You just don't want to leave the scene when the lines are cut on the glass surface and people are taking turns snorting coke. Even after I have had four or five lines and the conversation is very friendly and engaging, leaving the scene because someone is waiting for you at home or even if you have to meet with someone that night does not matter. Usually, everyone is feeling high, a lot of feelings of togetherness, and open to intimate conversation. I never saw anyone getting violent or anything like that, but I hear that it can happen especially if you have a grudge against someone before doing the coke. I think that coke just makes you more open and if you are an angry person then it will just bring it out in you. My experiences have been that everyone is just so friendly and everyone just pretends not to be overly anxious to do the next line. Actually, everyone is kind of pretending, because what they really want is more powder up their nose and an unending amount of time for talking the night away. *(From Venturelli's research files, male graduate student, residing in Chicago, age 26, May 18, 2000)*

Ten years later at age 36, the author was able to interview the same interviewee:

Back then I was a graduate student the last time you interviewed me. After I completed my master's degree I worked as a financial advisor and though I gave up regular use, on rare occasions I still have a hook up for cocaine and use it. It's a small amount on nearly a year basis. Why do I still dabble in it? The pleasures I had as a graduate student are still with me is my honest answer and it's still good but back then it was so often with so many memories of the good times. The last time I did snort cocaine was over a year ago and it's only when I visit a certain friend who also intermittently uses this drug. We just briefly revisit the past and it's all-good and everything but being 10 years older, I cannot get overinvolved with this drug as I used to 10 years ago. I have a lot more at stake regarding the clientele I have built up in addition to family responsibilities. My kids growing up would not be too happy if they knew their father uses drugs and my wife would be shocked that I still dabble in this. My wife is a school-teacher and is fully engaged with teaching her students. For me it is like revisiting something in my past but when I meet up with my friend we do it and then leave it there for about a year or so. I think it's those prior experiences and good times that bring me to spend one or two nights a year to reuse this drug. *(From Venturelli's research files, financial advisor, age 36, July 2010)*

It is important to keep in mind that the amount of a drug taken can affect the extent of sociability, as the following interview indicates:

Yes, I did read that quote [referring to the preceding quote] about how friendly everyone is while snorting lines. Well, I bet that person does not do too much coke—maybe it is like a weekend thing. What I am trying to say is that everyone is friendly at the beginning when snorting lines, but after doing a lot of snorting, people get real quiet—they sort of geek out. You see, too much of it at any one time makes you feel overloaded. It's like an amphetamine bombardment. In the beginning, it is like a "dusting" and people can become real friendly and talkative, but after doing it for an hour or so, it gets to you. Whenever I overdo it, and it is easy to do so, I become real quiet and several times even when I tried to change my mood by having sex, I could not even "get it up" so to speak. I usually do very well when I just have a little, but too much certainly can cause the sexual desire to peak, but the follow through is an entirely different matter. Too much just geeks you out after a while. *(From Venturelli's research files, male construction worker in Indiana, age 28, June 9, 2007)*

KEY TERM

sensation-seeking individuals
types of people who characteristically are continually seeking new or novel thrills in their experiences

Through the conditioning process, a pleasurable experience such as drug taking may become associated with a comforting or soothing environment. When this happens, two different outcomes may result. First, the user may feel uncomfortable taking the drug in any other environment. Second, the user may become very accustomed or habituated to the familiar environment as part of the drug experience. The user may not experience the same level of rush or high in this environment and in response may take more drugs or seek a different environment.

Finally, through this process of conditioning and habituation, a drug user becomes accustomed to unpleasant effects of drug use such as withdrawal symptoms. Such unpleasant effects and experiences may become habituated—neutralized or less severe in their impact—so that the user can continue taking drugs without feeling or experiencing the negative effects of the drug.

■ Social Psychological Learning Theories

Other aspects of reinforcement or learning theory focus on how positive social influences by drug-using peers reinforce the attraction to drugs. Social interaction, peer camaraderie, social approval, and drug use work together as positive reinforcers to sustain drug use (Akers 1992). Thus, if the effects of drug use become personally rewarding "or become reinforcing through conditioning, the chances of continuing to use are greater than for stopping" (Akers 1992, p. 86; Everyday Psychology 2012). It is through learned expectations or association with others who reinforce drug use that individuals learn the pleasures of drug taking (Becker 1963, 1967). Similarly, if drug use leads to poor and disruptive social interactions, drug use may cease.

Note that positive reinforcers, such as peers, other friends and acquaintances, family members, and drug advertisements, do not act alone in inciting and sustaining drug use. Learning theory, as defined here, also relies on some variable amounts of imitation and trial-and-error learning methods.

Finally, **differential reinforcement**—defined as the ratio between favorable and unfavorable reinforcers for sustaining drug use behavior—must be considered. The use and eventual abuse of drugs can vary with certain favorable or unfavorable reinforcing experiences. The primary determining conditions are listed here:

- The amount of exposure to drug-using peers versus non–drug-using peers

- The general preference for drug use in a particular neighborhood or community
- The age of initial use (younger adolescents are more greatly affected than are older adolescents)
- The frequency of drug use among peers

Major Theoretical Explanations: Sociological

Sociological explanations for drug use share important commonalities with psychological explanations under social learning theories. The main features distinguishing psychological and sociological explanations are that psychological explanations focus more on how the internal states of the drug user are affected by social relationships within families, peers, and other close and more distant relationships, whereas sociological explanations focus on how factors external to the drug user affect drug use. Such outside forces include the types of families, adopted lifestyles of peer groups, and neighborhoods and communities in which avid drug users reside. The sociological perspective views the motivation for drug use as largely determined by the types and quality of bonds (attachment vs. detachment) that the drug user or potential drug user has with significant others and with the social environment in general. The degree of influence and involvement with external factors affecting the individual compared with the influence exerted by internal states distinguishes sociological from psychological analyses.

As previously stated, no one biological or psychological theory can adequately explain why most people use drugs. People differ from one another in terms of personality, motivational factors, upbringing, learned priority of values and attitudes, and problems faced. Because of these differences, many responses and reasons exist why people take drugs, which results in a plurality of theoretical explanations. Furthermore, the diverse perspectives of biology, psychology, and sociology offer their own explanations for drug use and abuse.

KEY TERM

differential reinforcement
ratio between reinforcers, both favorable and disfavorable, for sustaining drug use behavior

There are two sets of sociological theories: social influence and social structural. **Social influence theories** focus on microscopic explanations that concentrate on the roles played by significant others and their impact on an individual. **Structural influence theories** focus on macroscopic explanations of drug use and the assumption that the organizational structure of society has a major independent impact on an individual's use of drugs. The next sections examine these theories.

▪ Social Influence Theories

The theories presented in this section are (1) social learning, (2) role of significant others in socialization, (3) labeling, and (4) subculture theories. These theories share a common theme: An individual's motivation to seek drugs is caused by social influences or social pressures.

SOCIAL LEARNING THEORY

Social learning theory explains drug use as learned behavior. Conventional learning occurs through imitation, trial and error, improvisation, rewarded behavior, and cognitive mental associations and processes (Akers and Sellers 2008; Liska and Messner 1999; Ritzer and Goodman 2010). Social learning theory focuses directly on how drug use and abuse are learned through interaction with other drug users. "[The] . . . motivations to use drugs are learned through associations with significant others in small, informal groups such as peer groups and families. It is in these intimate settings that individuals acquire attitudes regarding drugs and their use and observe the behavior of others" (Bahr and Hoffmann 2016, p. 200).

This theory emphasizes the pervasive influence of *primary groups*—that is, groups that share a high amount of intimacy and spontaneity and whose members are emotionally entwined. Families and long-term friends are examples of primary groups. In contrast, secondary groups share segmented relationships in which interaction is based on prescribed roles. An example of a secondary group is the relationship between a customer and a salesclerk in a grocery store or relationships between employees scattered throughout a corporation. Social learning theory addresses a type of interaction that is highly specific. This type of interaction involves learning specific motives, techniques, and appropriate meanings that are commonly attached to a particular type of drug.

The following are examples of first-time users learning drug-using techniques from their social circles:

The first time I tried smoking weed, nothing much happened. I always thought it was like smoking a cigarette. When the joint came around the first time, I refused it. The next time it came around, I noticed everyone was looking at me. So, I took the joint and started to inhale, then exhale. My friend sitting next to me said something to the effect, "Dude, hold it in; don't waste it. This is good weed and we don't have that much between us." Right after that, we did some "shotguns." This is where someone exhales directly into your mouth— lips to lips. My friend filled my lungs with his exhaled weed breath. After the first comment about holding it in, I started to watch how everyone was inhaling and realized that you really don't smoke weed like an ordinary cigarette; you have to hold in the smoke. *(From Venturelli's research files, male high school student in a small Midwestern town, age 16, February 15, 1997)*

I first started using drugs, mostly alcohol and pot, because my best friend in high school was using drugs. My best friend Tim [a pseudonym] learned from his older sister. Before I actually tried pot, Tim kept telling me how great it was to be high on dope; he said it was much better than beer. I was really nervous the first time I tried pot with Tim and another friend, even though I heard so much detail about it from Tim. The first time I tried it, it was a complete letdown. The second time (the next day, I think it was), I remember I was talking about a teacher we had and in the middle of the conversation, I remember how everything appeared different. I started feeling happy and while listening to Tim as he poked jokes about the teacher, I started to hear the background music more clearly than ever before. By the time the music ended and a new CD started, I knew I was high. *(From Venturelli's research files, male student at a private liberal arts college in the Midwest, age 22, February 15, 1997)*

KEY TERMS

social influence theories
sociological theories that view a person's day-to-day social relations as a primary cause for drug use

structural influence theories
theories that view the structural organization of a society, peer group, or subculture as directly responsible for drug use

First time I tried acid [LSD], I didn't know what to expect. Schwa [a pseudonym] told me it was a very different high from grass [marijuana]. After munching on one "square" [one dose of LSD]—after about 20 minutes—I looked at Schwa and he started laughing and said, "Feelin' the effects, Ki-ki?" I said, "Is this it? Is this what it feels like? I feel weird." With a devious grin . . . Schwa said, "Yep. We are now on the runway, ready to take off. Just wait a little while longer, it's going to get better and better. Fasten your seat belts!" *(From Venturelli's research files, male, age 33, May 6, 1996)*

Learning to perceive the effects of the drug is the second major outcome in the process of becoming a regular user. Here, the ability to feel the authentic effects of the drug is being learned. The more experienced drug users in the group impart their knowledge to naïve first-time users. The coaching information they provide describes how to recognize the euphoric effects of the drug.

I was just curious after watching my roommate with his friends frequently passing around a joint and remember always saying "I'll pass on that" many times. One night I just tried it with my roommate late at night. I really did not know how to even smoke it, but my roommate made more coaching comments as I was taking hits. The first few puffs nothing happened, but after I took in two huge hits, and coughing as it nearly choked me, I started to feel different. I had kind of a mellow feeling. I was talking about something and in the middle of the conversation I started to focus on everything around me like I was in some kind of trance, not heavy, but my mind was in several places as I spoke. After a few moments, I said, "I feel different not like I drank alcohol but just feel different." My roommate smiled and said, "You like the feeling?" I said I did not know but there was nothing bad in my feelings about what I had just done. It was like a change in the way I was processing input coming in. I remember saying that I felt kind of like light-headed and relaxed. My roommate said something like "Welcome to the world of marijuana, Mr. Schaffer [pseudonym]!" We just both laughed. *(From Venturelli's research files, male attending a small, private liberal arts college in the Midwest, age 18, May 21, 2010)*

Another example of learning to perceive the effects:

One night several of us wanted to try weed so at my college dorm we went to see a friend of mine who always had plenty of week so we could try some. Ron was a new friend who the day before agreed to let me and two of my guys on my dorm floor smoke some up. Two out of three of us had never smoked weed and it wasn't long before he lit up his little pipe and all four of us took in hits. We were passing it around and during the first few hits I did not feel anything at all and being a nonsmoker I watched my other friend who smokes cigarettes inhale the marijuana so I could also smoke it up. After two hits nothing was happening. However, after Ron got up to turn up the music playing on his computer and at that moment I was thinking that maybe nothing is going to happen. As I was thinking that maybe I was not inhaling it properly I suddenly started to feel different and within seconds the feelings were more intense. Definitely reality had gone through a change! At the same time I also felt a little freaked out because I did not know if others were having similar experiences. A few minutes later I finally blurted out "Hey, I am high on marijuana!" Suddenly everyone was amused and one friend of mine roared with laughter. As soon as I made this comment everyone became very animated and acted much sociable. I remember feeling like I was thinking on multiple levels—at times my mind was racing with many different thoughts. It was so different from an alcohol high. It definitely was more of a mental high than a body high. I started out being skeptical of the high and was hoping that the effect would weaken, but as everyone was enjoying themselves I changed my mind that the effects were positive and feeling this different was a new experience. I think other people experiencing the high helped knowing I was not alone and my other friends were in the same state of mind. In answering your question (asked by the interviewer) whether I used this drug in the days and weeks ahead I would have to say yes I did but I would only do it on weekends late at night with my roommate hours before going to sleep. No, I did not become attached to it because I am pretty busy with school and work and keep a busy schedule. I tried doing some homework one night while feeling the effects of weed but I ended up not competing much because getting high distracts me from any work I have to do and usually ended up doing nothing and just chilling out. With my heavy schedule of classes during this last semester and work schedule, I don't have any time during the week to waste away. Did I develop any kind of attachment to the pleasant feelings from a marijuana high? Not really, maybe a very weak attachment because throughout the week I knew I would fall behind in not doing my homework. I came to the conclusion that although getting high was a lot of fun, I planned ahead when I would do the drug so that it did not interfere with other things that had to be completed. A good thing was that my roommate was a lot more hesitant in using this drug for fear of drug testing at his part-time job. In fact, most times I did this drug with another dorm student who was an avid user. I also think that if my roommate liked the drug more was not so preoccupied with completing his degree in 3 instead of 4 years I would have used it much more often. *(From Venturelli's research files, male attending a private liberal arts college in the Midwest, age 22, November 2015)*

Once drug use has begun, continuing the behavior involves learning the following sequence: (1) identifying where and from whom the drug can be purchased, (2) maintaining steady contact with suppliers of the drug (i.e., drug dealers), (3) maintaining the secrecy of use from authority figures and casual non–drug-using acquaintances, (4) evaluating your experiences with the drug as pleasurable, (5) using with more frequency, and (6) replacing non–drug-using friends with drug-using friends.

ROLE OF SIGNIFICANT OTHERS

After a pattern of drug use has been established, the learning process plays a role in sustaining drug-taking behavior. Edwin Sutherland (1947; Akers 2009; Inderbitzin, Bates, and Gainey 2013; Liska and Messner 1999), a pioneering criminologist in sociology, believed that the mastery of criminal behavior depended on the frequency, duration, priority, and intensity of contact with others who are involved in similar behavior (Heitzeg 1996). This theory can also be applied to drug-taking behavior.

In applying Sutherland's principles of social learning, which he called differential association theory, to drug use, the focus is on how other members of social groups reward criminal behavior and under what conditions this deviance is perceived as important and pleasurable.

Becker and Sutherland's theories explain why adolescents may use psychoactive drugs. Essentially, both theories say that the use of drugs is learned during intimate interaction with others who serve as a primary group. (See "Here and

This child is role-playing largely by imitating the habits of a significant other.

Now: Symptoms of Drug and Alcohol Abuse" for information on how the role of significant others can determine a child's disposition toward or away from illicit drug uses and "Here and Now: How Not to Encourage Your Teen to Use Drugs.")

Learning theory also explains how adults and the elderly are taught the motivation for using a particular type of drug. This learning occurs through influences such as drug advertising, with its emphasis on testimonials by avid users, by medical experts, and by actors and actresses portraying physicians or nurses. Listeners, viewers, and readers who experience such commercials promoting a particular brand name of OTC drugs are flooded with the necessary motives, preferred techniques, and appropriate attitudes for consuming drugs. When drug advertisements and medical experts recommend a particular drug for specific ailments, in effect they are authoritatively persuading viewers, listeners, or readers that taking a drug will soothe or cure the medical problem presented.

ARE DRUG USERS MORE LIKELY TO BE DEVIOUS?

Social scientists—primarily sociologists and social psychologists—believe that many social development patterns are closely linked to drug use. Based on the age when an adolescent begins to consume alcohol and other drugs, predictions can be made about his or her sexual behavior, academic performance, and other behaviors, such as lying, cheating, fighting, and using marijuana. Similar predictions can be made when the adolescent begins using marijuana. More recent studies (CBHSQ 2015; CESAR 2011) show that there is a strong relationship between adolescent behavior problems and alcohol use.

Figure 2.1 shows the percentages of adolescents (aged 12 to 17) using alcohol, cigarettes,

HERE AND NOW
How Not to Encourage Your Teen to Use Drugs

Parents may unwittingly encourage their teens to recreationally experiment with alcohol and other drugs. The following are four things that may encourage teens to recreationally experiment with alcohol and other drugs of abuse:

- *Being unclear or not voicing your opinion about drug use*: Before your child becomes affected by peer pressure, you should take a stance on drug use. Clearly indicate that experimentation with recreational drug use is not acceptable (Sack 2013). Be certain to create an open atmosphere about your teen's opinions about drug use. If there is a family history of drug or alcohol problems, more concentrated discussions should be a primary goal without being overbearing.

- *Not practicing what you preach*: Be a positive model for your child. "Children pay closer attention to what you do than what you say. Even fiercely independent teens are adversely affected by their parents, so if you drink excessively or use drugs, don't be surprised if your teen follows suit. Having a parent who uses drugs is a strong predictor of adolescent substance abuse" (Sack 2013). Similarly, never provide alcohol or any other drugs to your teen and his or her friends in your home.

- *Denying suspicions about your teen's probable drug use*: Often, bringing up these suspicions and discussing your suspicions with your teen can be unpleasant. These suspicions often result from changes in your teen, such as "moodiness, new friends, much less or much more energy, weight loss or gain, or inattention to personal hygiene" (Sack 2013). Although at times adolescence is difficult to understand, remaining actively involved with your teen allows the parent to witness first-hand beginnings in the use of drugs. At this time, denial may be more comfortable than voicing your suspicions, but denial can become deadly, in that if drug use is occurring, more than likely it will advance to more dangerous levels.

- *Waiting to get help*: The period of adolescence can be filled with challenges. "From moment to moment it can be difficult to know the right thing to do or say, but there are a few ways you can't go wrong. Spend lots of quality time with your teen and if something seems amiss, talk about it. For those occasions when talking doesn't get you anywhere, get help. Your teen's drug use isn't your fault, but you are a critical part of the solution" (Sack 2013).

Data from Sack, D. "5 Things Parents Do That May Encourage Teen Substance Abuse." Huffington Post: Parents (4 March 2013). Available http://www.huffingtonpost.com/david-sack-md/teen-substance-abuse_b_2792838.html

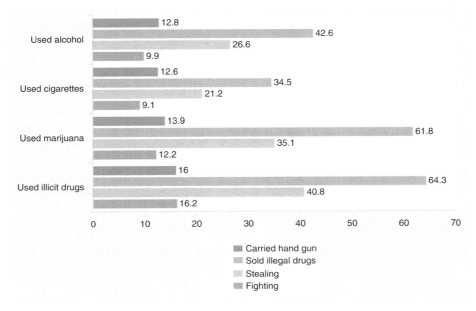

FIGURE 2.1 Percentages of adolescents (Aged 12 to 17) engaging in drug use and various types of deviant behavior

Center for Behavioral Health Statistics and Quality (CBHSQ). *2014 National Survey on Drug Use and Health: Detailed Tables.* Rockville, MD: Substance Abuse and Mental Health Services Administration, 2015.

HERE AND NOW

Symptoms of Drug and Alcohol Abuse

Following are profiles of children who are less likely and more likely, respectively, to use and abuse drugs.

Less Likely to Use Drugs

- Child comes from a strong family.
- Family has a clearly stated policy against drug use.
- Child has strong religious convictions.
- Child is an independent thinker, not easily swayed by peer pressure.
- Parents know the child's friends and the friends' parents.
- Child often invites friends into the house and their behavior is open, not secretive.
- Child is busy and productive and pursues many interests.
- Child has a good, secure feeling of self.
- Parents are comfortable with their own use of alcohol, drugs, and pills; set a good example in using these substances; and are comfortable in discussing their use.
- Parents set a good example in handling crises.
- Child maintains at least average grades and good working relationships with teachers.

More Likely to Use Drugs

Note: A child will usually display more than one of the symptoms that follow when experimenting with drugs. Please remember that any number of the symptoms could also be the result of a physical impairment or disorder.

- Red, watery eyes; pupils larger or smaller than usual; blank stare.
- Abrupt change in behavior (e.g., from very active to passive, loss of interest in previously pursued activities such as sports or hobbies).
- Diminished drive and ambition.
- Moodiness.
- Shortened attention span.
- Impaired communication such as slurred speech or jumbled thinking.
- Significant change in quality of schoolwork.
- Deteriorating judgment and loss of short-term memory.
- Distinct lessening of family closeness and warmth.
- Suddenly popular with new friends who are older and unknown to family members.
- Isolation from family members (hiding in bedroom or locking bedroom door).
- Sneaking out of the house.
- Secretive or suspicious behavior.
- Sudden carelessness regarding appearance.
- Inappropriate overreaction to even mild criticism.
- Secretiveness about whereabouts and missing personal possessions.
- Use of words that are odd and unfamiliar.
- Secretiveness or desperation for money.
- Rapid weight loss or appetite loss.
- "Drifting off" beyond normal daydreaming.
- Extreme behavioral changes such as hallucinations, violence, and unconsciousness that could indicate a dangerous situation close at hand and needing fast medical attention.
- Nonprescribed or unidentifiable pills.
- Unfamiliar looking devices (e.g., smoking paraphernalia, pills, smaller plastic baggies or pipes, or other hidden paraphernalia in a child's or adolescent's bedroom).
- Articles missing from the house. (Child could be stealing money or household articles in order to sell or trade in order to pay for drugs.)
- Sudden appearance and possession of new items in the teen's bedroom—often electronic items—from money spent, bartered, or exchanged from drug dealing.
- Unexplained need for money or contradictory explanations regarding the need for money.

Data from L.A.W. Publications. *Let's All Work to Fight Drug Abuse.* Addison, TX: C&L Printing Company, 1985: 38; Drug Strategies. *Santa Barbara Profile: Alcohol, Tobacco, and Other Drugs.* Washington, DC: Drug Strategies, 1999; Liddle, H. *AAMFT Consumer Update: Adolescent Substance Abuse. American Association for Marriage and Family Therapy (AAMFT).* Alexandria, VA: American Association for Marriage and Family Therapy, 2001; Witmer, D. "Teen Drug Use Warning Signs." About.com. 2013.

marijuana, and use of other illicit drugs and engaging in various types of deviant behavior, namely, carrying a handgun, selling illegal drugs, stealing, and fighting. Highest to lowest percentages indicate the following (CBHSQ 2015):

- 64.3% of adolescents using illicit drugs, 61.8% using marijuana, 42.6% using alcohol, and 34.5% using cigarettes sold illegal drugs.
- 40.8% of adolescents using illicit drugs, 35.1% using marijuana, 26.6% using alcohol, and 21.2% using cigarettes were involved in stealing.
- 16% of adolescents using illicit drugs, 13.9% using marijuana, 12.8% using alcohol, and 12.6% using cigarettes carried a handgun.
- 16.2% of adolescents using illicit drugs, 12.2% using marijuana, 9.9% using alcohol, and 9.1% using cigarettes engaged in physical fighting.

Figure 2.2 shows early alcohol use among Washington, DC, public high school students (aged 16 and older) and the onset of other risky behaviors, such as past-month underage alcohol use, carrying a weapon, binge drinking, past-year consideration of suicide, use of a nonprescribed prescription drug, and driving after drinking alcoholic beverages. A key factor that predominates is the significantly higher percentages in each of

the risky behaviors examined when adolescents first tried alcohol *before* age 13 versus significantly lower percentages with adolescents who first tried alcohol *after* age 13 or never used alcohol (CESAR 2011):

- Nearly one-quarter (21%) of Washington, DC, public high school students were early drinkers, having first tried alcohol before age 13.
- Early drinkers, defined as adolescents trying alcohol before age 13, were more than twice as likely than nonearly drinkers (adolescents who first tried alcohol after age 13 or never used alcohol) to have used alcohol, carried a weapon, binged on alcohol, considered suicide, used a nonprescribed prescription drug, and driven after drinking.
- Although not shown in Figure 2.1, this study also found that early drinkers were also more likely (but less than twice as likely) to have done the following:
  - Used marijuana in the past month (40% vs. 23%)
  - Ridden in a car with a drinking driver (32% vs. 20%)
  - Physically fought in the past year (52% vs. 34%)
  - Been in a gang/crew in the past year 24% vs. 18%)
  - Had sex in the past 3 months (50% vs. 41%)

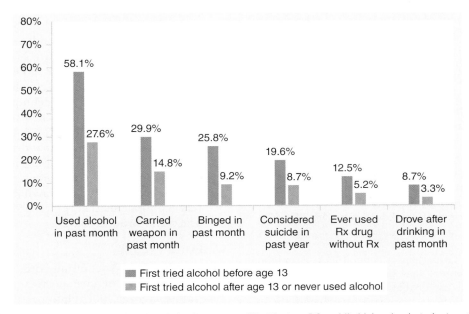

FIGURE 2.2   Early alcohol use and other risky behaviors among Washington, DC, public high school students aged 16 or older.

Data from the 2011 DC The Youth Risk Behavior Survey (YRBS), Office of the State Superintendent of Education (OSSE), District of Columbia.

Data from the Center for Substance Abuse Research (CESAR). "District Youth in Brief: Early Alcohol Use: Is Early Alcohol Among DC Public High School Students Associated with Other Risky Behaviors?" University of Maryland, College Park, MD: Center for Substance Abuse Research (CESAR), (Volume 3, Issue 8), September 2011. Available http://www.cesar.umd.edu/cesar/pubs/20110901%20DC%20YinB%203-8.pdf

Other studies show that early intense use of alcohol or marijuana represents a move toward less conventional behavior, greater susceptibility to peer influence, increased delinquency, and lower achievement in school. In general, drug abusers have 14 characteristics in common:

1. Their drug use usually follows clear-cut developmental steps and sequences. Use of legal drugs, such as alcohol and cigarettes, almost always precedes use of illegal drugs.
2. Use of certain drugs, particularly habitual use of marijuana, is linked to amotivational syndrome, which some researchers believe is a general change in personality.[2] This change is characterized by apathy, lack of interest, and inability to accomplish or difficulty accomplishing goals. Past research also clearly shows that marijuana use is often responsible for attention and short-term memory impairment and confusion (NIDA 1996).
3. Immaturity, maladjustment, or insecurity usually precede the use of marijuana and other illicit drugs.
4. Those more likely to try illicit drugs, especially before age 12, usually have a history of poor school performance and classroom disobedience.
5. Delinquent or repetitive deviant types of behavior usually precede involvement with illicit drugs.
6. A set of values and attitudes that facilitates the development of deviant behavior exists before the person tries illicit drugs.
7. A social setting in which drug use is common, such as communities and neighborhoods in which peers use drugs indiscriminately, is likely to reinforce and increase the predisposition to drug use.
8. Drug-induced behaviors and drug-related attitudes of peers are usually among the strongest predictors of subsequent drug involvement.
9. Children who feel their parents are distant from their emotional needs are more likely to become drug addicted (see "Here and Now: Does Divorce Affect Adolescent Drug Use?").

10. The younger people are when they begin using drugs, the higher the probability of continued and accelerated drug use. Likewise, the older people are when they start using drugs, the lower the probability of accelerated use and addiction. The period of greatest risk of initiation and habitual use of illicit drugs is usually over by the early 20s.
11. The family structure has changed, with substantially more than half (58.6%) of all women (72 million) in the United States now working outside the home (U.S. Department of Labor 2011). A higher divorce rate has led to many children being raised in single-parent households. How the lack of a stay-at-home parent or how membership in a single-family household affects the quality of childcare and nurturing is difficult to assess.
12. Mobility obstructs a sense of permanency, and it contributes to a lack of self-esteem. Often, when children are repeatedly moved from one location to another, their community becomes nothing more than a group of strangers. They may have little pride in their home or community and have no commitment to society.
13. Among minority members, a major factor involved in drug dependence is a feeling of powerlessness due to discrimination based on race, social standing, or other attributes. Groups subject to discrimination have a disproportionately high rate of unemployment and below-average incomes. In the United States, approximately 15.6 million children (21%) are reared in poverty (Landau 2010). The adults they have as role models may be unemployed and experience feelings of powerlessness. Higher rates of delinquency and drug addiction occur in such settings.
14. Abusers who become highly involved in selling drugs begin by witnessing that drug trafficking is a lucrative business, especially in rundown neighborhoods. In some communities, selling drugs seems to be the only available route to real economic success (Jones 1996; Shelden, Tracy, and Brown 2001).

LABELING THEORY

Although controversy continues over whether labeling is a theory or a perspective (Akers 1968, 1992; Heitzeg 1996; Plummer 1979), this text takes the position that labeling is a theory (Cheron 2001; Hewitt and Shulman 2010; Liska and Messner 1999), primarily because it explains something very important with respect to drug

---

[2]Some argue that perhaps a general lack of ambition (lethargic behavior) may precede rather than result from marijuana use or that amotivational syndrome is present in some heavy marijuana users before the initial use of this drug, and when the drug is used, the syndrome becomes more pronounced. In any case, some drug researchers believe that when used steadily, marijuana and the amotivational syndrome occur together.

HERE AND NOW
Does Divorce Affect Adolescent Drug Use?

"When parents make a decision to divorce . . ., children are expected to cope with the decision. Except in cases involving abuse, it is rare that children will thrive during a divorce. The impact of divorce is that children will have problems and experience symptoms" (Conner 2011; Heritage Foundation 2016). One of the major symptoms listed by Conner (see also Doherty and Needle 1991; Kelly 2000), a clinical psychologist, is drug or alcohol abuse. Further, as an example of how drug users may be affected by socialization, a study conducted by Needle (Conner 2011; Needle, Su, and Doherty 1990; NIDA 1990; Siegel and Senna 1994) found higher drug use among adolescents whose parents divorced (also see Heritage Foundation 2016). According to the study, children who are adolescents when their parents divorce exhibit more extensive drug use and experience more drug-related health, legal, and other problems than their peers (Heritage Foundation 2016). This study linked the extent of teens' drug use to their age at the time of their parents' divorce. Teenagers whose parents divorce were found to use more drugs and experience more drug-related problems than two other groups of adolescents: those who were age 10 or younger when their parents divorced, and those whose parents remained married.

This study has important implications for drug abuse prevention efforts. Basically, it says not everyone is at the same risk for drug use. People at greater risk can be identified, and programs should be developed to meet their special needs.

In this research project, drug use among all adolescents increased over time. However, drug use was higher among adolescents whose parents had divorced when their children were either preteens or teenagers. Drug use was highest for those teens whose parents divorced during their children's adolescent years. Such families also reported more physical problems, family disputes, and arrests.

The research results showed that distinct gender differences existed in the way that divorce affected adolescent drug use, whether the divorce occurred during the offspring's childhood or adolescent years. Males whose parents divorced reported more drug use and drug-related problems than females. Females whose caretaking parents remarried experienced increased drug use after the remarriage. By contrast, males whose caretaking parents remarried reported a decrease in drug-related problems following the remarriage.

The researchers caution that these findings may have limited applicability because most of the families studied were white and had middle- to high-income levels. Needle also notes that the results should not be interpreted as an argument in favor of the nuclear family. Overall, divorce affects adolescents in complex ways and remarriage can influence drug-using behavior; particularly when disruptions occur during adolescence, such turmoil can "trigger" a desire for extensive recreational licit and illicit drug use, often leading to drug abuse.

Data from Conner, M. G. "Children During Divorce." *Michael G. Conner*, 24 August 2011. Heritage Foundation. "Family and Adolescent Well-being." Washington, DC: The Heritage Foundation, 2016. Available http://www.familyfacts.org/briefs/34/family-and-adolescent-well-being; Needle, R. H., S. S. Su, and W. J. Doherty. "Divorce, Remarriage, and Adolescent Substance Use: A Prospective Longitudinal Study." *Journal of Marriage and the Family* 52 (1990): 157–159; National Institute on Drug Abuse (NIDA). "Study Finds Higher Use Among Adolescents Whose Parents Divorce." *NIDA Notes* 5 (Summer 1990): 10; Siegel, L .J., and J. J. Senna. *Juvenile Delinquency: Theory, Practice and Law*. St. Paul, MN: West, 1994.

use. Although **labeling theory** does not fully explain why initial drug use occurs, it does detail the processes by which many people come to view themselves as socially deviant from others. Note that the terms *deviant* (in cases of individuals) and *deviance* (in cases of behavior) are sociologically defined as involving the violation of significant social norms held by conventional society. The terms are not used in a judgmental manner, nor are the individuals judged to be immoral or "sick"; instead, the terms refer to an absence of the patterns of behavior expected by conventional society.

Labeling theory says that other people whose opinions we value have a determining influence

KEY TERM

labeling theory
the theory emphasizing that other people's perceptions directly influence one's self-image

over our self-image (Best and Luckenbill 1994; Goode 2010; Liska and Messner 1999). (For an example of how labeling theory applies to real-life situations, see "Case in Point: Specific Signs of Marijuana Use.")

Implied in this theory is the idea that we exert only a small amount of control over the image we portray. In contrast, members of society, especially those we consider to be significant others, have much greater influence and power in defining or redefining our self-image. The image we have of ourselves is vested in the people we admire and look to for guidance and advice. If these people come to define our actions as deviant, then their definition becomes incorporated as a "fact" of our reality.

We can summarize labeling theory by saying that the labels we use to describe people have a profound influence on their self-perceptions. For example, imagine a fictitious individual named Billy. Initially, Billy does not see himself as a compulsive drug user but as an occasional recreational drug user. Let us also assume that Billy is very humorous, unpretentious, and very outspoken about his drug use and likes to exaggerate the amount of marijuana he smokes on a daily basis. Slowly, Billy's friends begin to perceive him as a "real stoner." According to labeling theory, what happens to Billy? Because of being noticed when "high," his self-presentation, and the comments he makes about the pleasures of drug use, his friends may begin to reinforce the exaggerated drug use image. At first, Billy may enjoy the reflected image of a "big-time" drug user, but after nearly all of his peers maintain a constant exaggerated image, his projected image may turn negative, especially when his friends show disrespect for his opinions. In this example, labeling theory predicts that Billy's perception of himself will begin to mirror the consistent perception expressed by his accusers. If

he is unsuccessful in eradicating the addict image or, in this example, the "stoner" image, Billy will reluctantly concur with the label that has been thrust on him. Or, to strive for a self-image as an occasional marijuana user, Billy may abandon his peers so that he can become acceptable once more in the eyes of other people.

An important originator of labeling theory is Edwin Lemert (Lemert 1951; Liska and Messner 1999; Williams and McShane 1999), who distinguished between two types of deviance: primary and secondary. **Primary deviance** is inconsequential deviance, which occurs without having a lasting impression on the perpetrator. Generally, most first-time violations of law, for example, are primary deviations. Whether the suspected or accused individual has committed the deviant act does not matter. What matters is whether the individual identifies with the deviant behavior.

Secondary deviance develops when the individual begins to identify and perceive himself or herself as deviant. The moment this transition occurs, deviance shifts from being primary to secondary. Many adolescents casually experiment with drugs. If, however, they begin to perceive themselves as drug users, then this behavior is virtually impossible to eradicate. The same holds true with OTC drug abuse. The moment an individual believes that he or she feels better after using a particular drug, the greater the likelihood that he or she will consistently use the drug.

Howard Becker (1963) believed that certain negative status positions (such as alcoholic, mental patient, ex-felon, criminal, drug addict, and so on) are so powerful that they dominate others (Pontell 1996; Williams and McShane 1999). In the earlier example, if people who are important to Billy call him a "druggie," this name becomes a powerful label that takes precedence over any other status positions Billy may occupy. This label becomes Billy's **master status**—that he is a mindless "stoner." Even if Billy is also an above-average biology major, an excellent musician, and a dependable and caring person, such factors become secondary because his primary status has been recast as a "druggie." Furthermore, once a powerful label is attached, it becomes much easier for the individual to uphold the image dictated by members of society and simply to act out the role expected by significant others. Master status labels distort an individual's public image because other people expect consistency in role performance.

Once a negative master status has been attached to an individual's public image, labeling

KEY TERMS

primary deviance
any type of initial deviant behavior in which the perpetrator does not identify with the deviance

secondary deviance
any type of deviant behavior in which the perpetrator identifies with the deviance

master status
major status position in the eyes of others that clearly identifies an individual, for example, doctor, professor, alcoholic, heroin addict

▶ ## CASE IN POINT

Specific Signs of Marijuana Use

This excerpt, from the author's files, illustrates labeling theory:

After my mom found out, she never brought it up again. I thought the incident was over—dead, gone, and buried. Well . . . it wasn't over at all. My mom and dad must have agreed that I couldn't be trusted anymore. I'm sure she was regularly going through my stuff in my room to see if I was still smoking dope. Even my grandparents acted strangely whenever the news on television would report about the latest drug bust in Chicago. Several times that I can't ever forget were when we were together and I could hear the news broadcast on TV from my room about some drug bust. There they all were whispering about me. My grandma asking if I "quitta the dope." One night, I overheard my mother reassure my dad and grandmother that I no longer was using dope. You can't believe how embarrassed I was that my own family was still thinking that I was a dope fiend. They thought I was addicted to pot like a junkie is addicted to heroin! I can tell you that I would never lay such a guilt trip on my kids if I ever have kids. I remember that for 2 years after the time I was honest enough to tell my mom that I had tried pot, they would always whisper about me, give me the third degree whenever I returned late from a date, and go through my room looking for dope. They acted as if I was hooked on drugs. I remember that for a while back then I would always think that if they think of me as a drug addict, I might as well get high whenever my friends "toke up." They should have taken me at my word instead of sneaking around my personal belongings. I should have left syringes lying around my room!

Approximately 17 years after this interview was conducted, this author was able to revisit the same interviewee, who at the time of this second interview was 37 years of age. After showing him the same excerpt I had written, he commented,

You know, Professor, while today marijuana use is no longer such a big deal, I can still tell you that it took years to finally convince my family that I was not a "big time drug user." Though my grandma is now dead, I can still remember how she would look at me when I would tell her that I just smoke it once in a while. I knew she never believed that I was just an occasional user by the look on her face, when she would ask ". . . and last night when you went out, did you smoke the dope again?" My mom, who is now living with her sister, still mentions how I went wild those days when I was drugging it up! Yes, I have to say it had a big impact on me when my own family believed I was a drug addict back then. I will never forget those looks from my family every time I would walk into the house on weekends when I would return from a night out with my friends.

Interview with a 20-year-old male college student at a private university in the Midwest, conducted by Peter Venturelli on November 19, 1993. Second interview with same interviewee, 37 years of age, June 2010.

theorist Edwin Schur asserted that retrospective interpretation occurs. **Retrospective interpretation** is a form of "reconstitution of individual character or identity" (Schur 1971, p. 52). It largely involves redefining a person's image within a particular social stereotype, category, or group (see cartoon as an illustration). In the eyes of his peers, Billy is now an emotional, intelligent, yet weird or "freaky" stoner.

Finally, William I. Thomas's (1923) contribution to labeling theory can be summarized in the following theorem: "If men define situations as real, they are real in their consequences" (p. 19). Thus, in applying this dictum by Thomas to drug use, when someone is perceived as a drug user, the perception becomes the reality of that

KEY TERM

retrospective interpretation
social psychological process of redefining a person in light of a major status position, for example, homosexual, physician, professor, alcoholic, convicted felon, or mental patient

person's character and, in turn, shapes his or her self-perception.

SUBCULTURE THEORY

Subculture theory speaks to the role of peer pressure and the behavior resulting from peer group influences. In all groups, there are certain members who are more popular and respected and, as a result, exert more social influence than other peer members. Often, these more socially endowed members are group leaders, task leaders, or emotional leaders who possess greater ability to influence others. Drug use that results from peer pressure demonstrates the extent to which these more popular and respected leaders can influence and pressure others to initially use or abuse drugs. These four excerpts from interviews illustrate subculture theory:

> I started using drugs at a young age. I was 8 years old when my friend Linda and I would smoke cigarettes while my mom and dad were running the bar business. I would take a pack of cigarettes from my dad's tavern and we would go into a little clubhouse we built out of plywood and we would smoke one cigarette after another hidden in that little clubhouse my older brother built for me. It was not long before I would also sneak in some liquor along with cigarettes and Linda and I would get buzzed on the alcohol and cigarettes and we would giggle and laugh while we were sitting in this little hutlike place and we thought we were having so much fun. My mom and dad never checked on us while we were in the hut and if I was wanted by my mom or dad they would call out my name from the back entrance door of the back kitchen and I either yelled back I am here or at times I would stroll in—really check-in quickly—and they would be busy with the business never suspecting anything was wrong. We did this a few times a week and it was like a secret we both kept away from our parents. I always saw everyone was drinking and smoking in my dad's bar so why not do the same with my friend Linda? A few years later, I did the same thing with my two male friends when I would stop by their parents' apartments during

This cartoon illustrates the reflective process in retrospective interpretation that often occurs in daily conversations when we think that our unspoken thoughts are undetectable and hidden. In reality, however, these innermost thoughts are clearly conveyed through body language and nonverbal gestures.

the weekdays when their parents were at work. I was always the kid who had the cigarettes and we would go for walks down a nearby alley and I would supply the smokes. Now that I think about this we were lucky we never got caught with our secret behavior. *(From Venturelli's research files, male office worker, residing in Chicago, age 47, July 12, 2015)*

A second account:

> I first started messing around with alcohol in high school. In order to be part of the crowd, we would sneak out during lunchtime at school and get "high." About 6 months after we started drinking, we moved on to other drugs. . . . Everyone in high school belongs to a clique, and my clique was heavy into drugs. We had a lot of fun being high throughout the day. We would party constantly. Basically, in college, it's the same thing. *(From Venturelli's research files, male student at a small, religiously affiliated private liberal arts college in the Southeast, age 19, February 9, 1985)*

A third account:

> I remember Henri was from Holland, and he never tried coke. One night all three of us were at Joe's apartment and Joe had a hefty amount of coke that he brought out from his bedroom. We started snorting it and when it was Henri's

KEY TERM

subculture theory
explains drug use as a peer-generated activity

turn he said, "I never did this and maybe I shouldn't do it now." Paul, who was also a good friend of Henri, said "Come on Henri, it won't do that much to you." Henri looked at each of us and shot back with "Okay, I will try it once." Well, that night Henri had about as much coke as the two of us had. It was all okay until Henri suddenly got sick and vomited a good number of times. We spent a good part of the night taking care of Henri making sure he did not pass out and made sure to get him back to his apartment and call it a night. Henri was just not used to the coke and we probably let him have too much being his first time. *(From Venturelli's research files, all three mentioned were seniors at a liberal arts college in Chicago, August 18, 2009)*

The fourth interview illustrates how friendship, coupled with subtle and not-so-subtle peer pressure, influences the novice drug enthusiast:

There I was on the couch with three of my friends, and as the joint was being passed around, everyone was staring at me. I felt they were saying, "Are you going to smoke with us or will you be a holdout again?" *(From Venturelli's research files, male university student, age 20, April 10, 1996)*

In sociology, charismatic leaders, defined as leaders with distinction in the eyes of others, are viewed as possessing status and power. In drug-using peer groups, such experienced drug users have power over inexperienced drug users. Members of peer groups are often persuaded to experiment with drugs if the more popular members say, "Come on, try some, it's great" or "Trust me, you'll really get off on this, come on, just try it." In groups where drugs are consumed, the extent of peer influence coupled with the art of persuasion and *camaraderie* or friendship are powerfully persuasive and cause the spread of drug use.

A further extension of subculture theory is the *social and cultural support perspective*. This perspective explains drug use and abuse in peer groups as resulting from an attempt by peers to solve problems collectively. In the neoclassic book *Delinquent Boys: The Culture of the Gang* (1955), Cohen pioneered a study that for the first time showed that delinquent behavior is a collective attempt to gain social status and prestige within the peer group (Liska and Messner 1999; Siegel and Senna 1994; Williams and McShane 1999). Members of certain peer groups are unable to achieve respect within the larger society. Such status-conscious youths

find that being able to commit delinquent acts and yet evade law enforcement officials is admirable in the eyes of their delinquent peers. In effect, Cohen believed, delinquent behavior is a subcultural solution for overcoming feelings of status frustration and low self-esteem largely determined by lower class status.

Although Cohen's emphasis is on explaining juvenile delinquency, his notion that delinquent behavior is a subcultural solution can easily be applied to drug use and abuse primarily in members of lower-class peer groups. Underlying drug use and abuse in delinquent gangs, for example, results from sharing common feelings of alienation and low self-esteem and a collective feeling of escaping from a society that appears uncaring, noninclusive, distant, and hostile.

Consider the current upsurge in violent gang memberships. In such groups, not only is drug dealing a profitable venture, but drug use also serves as a collective response to alienation and estrangement from conventional middle-class society. The hope of sudden monetary gain from drug dealing is perceived as a quick ticket into the middle class. In cases of violent minority gang members, the alienation results from racism, poverty, effects of migration and acculturation, and effects of minority status in a white, male-dominated society such as the United States (Glick and Moore 1990; Moore 1978, 1993; Sanders 1994; Thornberry 2001).

■ Structural Influence Theories

Structural influence theories focus on how elements in the *organization* of a society, group, or subculture affect the motivation and resulting drug use behavior that is for nonmedical—most often recreational—use. The belief is that no single factor in the society, the group, or the subculture produces the attraction to drug use but rather that the organization itself or the lack of organization largely causes this behavior to occur.

Social disorganization and social strain theories (Bahr and Hoffmann 2016; Liska and Messner 1999; Werner and Henry 1995) identify the different types of social change that are disruptive and explain how, in a general sense, people are adversely affected by rapid social change. Social disorganization theory asks, "What in the larger structure and organization of the social order causes people to deviate?" Social strain theory offers an explanation regarding what causes some people to break away from social conformity. For example, this theory suggests that an inability to achieve sought-after goals, such as earnestly working hard yet being unable to meet financial obligations, compels some people out of shear frustration to deviate in achieving financial stability. One outcome viewed as a solution can result in drug dealing in order to achieve economic sustainability.

Overall, social disorganization theory describes a situation in which, because of rapid social change, previously conformity committed and affiliated individuals no longer find themselves integrated into a community's social, commercial, religious, and economic institutions. When this type of alienation occurs, community members may, despite the fact that their parents served as role models of social conformity, find themselves increasingly disconnected from conventional living, resulting in a lack of effective attachment to the social order. As a result, these disconnected or "disaffiliated" people may, for example, be led to deviant behavior, such as drug dealing or drug use, as an attractive quick-fix solution to their financial problems.

An essential factor for effective and sustainable socialization is trusting, longer-term relationships within a relatively stable environment. As will be discussed later in this chapter, when major identity development and personality transformations occur during the teen years, some stability and trusting relationships in the immediate environment are crucial. Today, however, most

An example of feeling stressed and experiencing strain from an overly demanding society.

Westernized societies (including the United States) are experiencing rapid social and technological development and social changes that result in more destabilizing and disorienting factors that affect us (Gergen 2000; Ritzer 1999, 2011).

Even though on the surface most people in society adapt to continually evolving social and technological social changes, on a cognitive level many people find themselves overwhelmed with the continual frantic pressure to keep up on a daily basis. The drive to keep up with social and technological innovation is more demanding today than ever before (Gergen 2000). The constant need to keep pace with change and the increasing multiplicity of realities and ever more contradictory realities produced by such change often appear barely controllable and increasingly chaotic. People who are less skillful in coping with the rapid pace caused by social and technological changes have difficulty in successfully maintaining a stable self-identity. For example, consider the large number of people who need psychological counseling and therapy because they find themselves unable to cope with personal, family, and work-related problems and conflicts. In one study, "an estimated 26.2% of Americans ages 18 and older—about one in four adults—suffer from a diagnosable mental disorder in a given year" (Kessler et al. 2005, p. 617). The following interview shows how such confusion and lack of control can easily lead to drug use:

Interviewee: The world is really much more complicated today than it was when I was growing up. Everything has a tendency to be in a perpetual state of flux.

Interviewer: Can you explain what you mean by the continual state of flux?

Interviewee: No one agrees with anything anymore. There are all these very divergent opinions. Just look at gay marriage for example. If my parents were alive today, I keep thinking what would my parents say about all this disagreement regarding marriage between two people? You know there was a time when marriage was always between a man and woman—not today. I know my parents never had to mentally deal with all these contrasting opinions. Even in their days I am sure they had contradictory ways of doing things but those other ways were never mainstream. I just think we are always on the cusp of total disagreements about things and ways of doing things.

Interviewer: How do you think people today cope with all this change?

Interviewee: Good and interesting question. Everything that was considered normal in the past is now up for grabs! People who never had a voice have a voice today. This is both good and bad.

Interviewer: Can you explain what you mean by good and bad?

Interviewee: Well, it's good for individuals to be liberated but I think it's bad for social agreement and social organization. It's like everything is being deconstructed. Sometimes I think about all these contradictory perspectives and honestly I resolve my uncertainty by taking time out breaks by altering my reality. I do this by getting together with friends and we drink at least one night per week so we can get high laugh, sit back, and relax. In reality, I really think we cope with all this perceived mental turmoil by drinking in order to forget (really anesthetizing) or to suspend all the tension and turmoil in our daily lives. I also think with a good number of drug users the good feelings associated with their drug use is the ability to have time in order to cast out mental tension and conflict. I think as we "progress" as a society, drug use will only get worse because it becomes a great alternative coping mechanism for increasing numbers of people. *(From Venturelli's research files, male, Ph.D. graduate student attending a prominent university in Chicago, age 29, January 7, 2016)*

Similarly, an interview illustrates how a work environment can affect drug use:

I had one summer job once where it was so busy and crazy that a group of us workers would go out on breaks just to get high. We worked the night shift and our "high breaks" were between 2:00 and 5:00 in the morning. *(From Venturelli's research files, female first-year college student, age 20, July 28, 1996)*

CURRENT SOCIAL CHANGE IN MOST SOCIETIES

Does social change per se cause people to use and abuse drugs? In response to this question, social change—defined as any measurable change caused by technological advancement that disrupts cultural values and attitudes about everyday life—does not by itself cause widespread drug use. In most cases, social change materialistically advances a culture by profoundly affecting the manner in which things are accomplished. At the same time, rapid social change disrupts day-to-day behavior anchored by tradition, which has a tendency to fragment such conventional social groups as families, neighborhoods, and communities. By **conventional behavior**, we mean behavior that is largely dictated by custom and tradition that is evaporating away or goes into a state of flux because of the accelerating speed of social change.

Examples of social change include the number of youth subcultures that proliferated during the 1960s (e.g., beatniks, mods, bikers, hippies) (Yinger 1982) and other more recent lifestyles and subcultures, such as rappers, punk rockers, potheads, Goths, street artists, skinheads, Satanists, gangstas, hipsters, and rave enthusiasts (Wooden 1995). Furthermore, two other subcultures, teenagers and the elderly, have become increasingly independent and, in some subgroups, alienated from other age groups in society (see **Figure 2.3**).

Simply stated, today's social, religious, and political institutions no longer effectively dictate, embrace, influence, and lead people as they did in the past. Consequently, people are free to explore different means of expression and a vast array of recreational pursuits. For many, this liberating experience leads to attractive and novel outcomes; for others, this freedom from conventional societal norms and attitudes creates a type of alienation that can lead to drug use and abuse as self-medication.

The following two excerpts, gathered from interviews, illustrate social disorganization and strain theories:

Honest to God, I know things occur much faster than they did 20 years ago. Change is happening faster and occurs more often. What helps is doing some drugs at night at home. I either drink alcohol or do lines of coke. Two different highs but I like them both. This is about the only recreation I have except for the TV at night, after working all darn day nonstop writing letters, answering phone calls, attending meetings, having to go on-site for inspections, and many other things I do each day. *(From Venturelli's research files, male home security systems manager, age 29, Chicago, Illinois, June 23, 2000)*

KEY TERM

conventional behavior
behavior largely dictated by custom and tradition, which is often disrupted by the forces of rapid technological change

FIGURE 2.3 Levels of technological development and resulting subcultures.

*Represents a newly developed and separate stage of identification and expression from the prior era.

Second interview:

> Just as CNN flashes one news item after another at rapid speed, my life is similar. Most work days are so crammed with trying to constantly keep up, maintain my house and all that property upkeep demands, take care of the kids when my wife works nights, help clean the house, cook meals for all of us (since I am better at cooking than my wife), and dozens of other demands, that when the kids are finally asleep my wife and I try to relax with some combination of alcohol and weed. (We had to give up the coke because the kids are getting older and we don't mind if they find out we drink and smoke dope but the other stuff is out of the question. We don't want them to ever know we did coke.) Plus, those nights of staying up late when doing coke is too much for me now at this age. Really, the only time we can relax is when the kids are asleep and we can have a few drinks before going to bed. I keep hoping things will slow down, but it seems to either remain at the same frenzied pace or even get worse each year.
> *(From Venturelli's research files, male residing in a Midwestern town, age 31, February 10, 2010)*

Currently, there is a lack of reliable quantitative (statistical) evidence clearly proving that unprecedented rapid social change *per se* directly causes drug use. However, in looking at the impact of rapid social change and how it causes disaffiliation with established traditional social order, social disorganization theory may provide a better explanation for the formation and development of subcultural groups that use and often abuse illicit

drugs as a response to the chaos created by rapid social change. Examples include the increasing use of methamphetamines in blue-collar subcultures, cocaine use in professional middle- and upper-middle-class occupational groups, crack use by disenfranchised and poor minority groups, opiates by Hispanic/Latina women (SAMHSA 2009), and heroin use by middle- and upper-middle-class youth subcultures.

Figure 2.3 illustrates how the number of life-cycle stages increases depending on a society's level of technological development. Overall, it implies that, as societies advance from preindustrial to industrial to our current postindustrial type of society, new subcultures emerge at an increasing rate of development (see Fischer 1976 for similar thinking). In contrast to industrial and postindustrial societies, preindustrial societies do not have as many separate and distinct periods and cycles of social development. What is shown in Figure 2.3 and implied here is that the greater the number of distinct life cycles, the greater the fragmentation between the members of different stages of development. Generation gaps (conflicting sets of values and attitudes between age cohorts) cause much ignorance and lack of insight between age-group subcultures. This often leads to separation and fragmentation across age groups who develop and live within distinct lifestyle patterns, increasing the likelihood of conflict.

CONTROL THEORY

The final major structural influence theory, **control theory**, emphasizes influences outside the self as the primary cause for deviating to drug use and/or abuse. Control theory places importance on positive socialization. **Socialization** is the process by which individuals learn and internalize the attitudes, values, and behaviors needed to participate in conventional society. Generally, control theorists believe that human beings can easily become deviant if left without the social controls imposed by family, social groups, and organizations. Thus, control theory theorists emphasize the necessity of maintaining bonds to family, school, peer groups, and other social, political, and religious organizations (Liska and Messner 1999; Thio 2010). In the 1950s and 1960s, criminologist Walter C. Reckless (1961; Liska and Messner 1999; Siegel and Senna 1994) developed the containment theory. According to this theory, the socialization process results in the creation of strong or weak internal and external control systems. The degree of self-control, high or low frustration tolerance, positive or negative self-perception, successful or unsuccessful goal achievement, and either resistance or adherence to deviant behavior determine internal control. Environmental pressures, such as social conditions, may limit the accomplishment of goal-striving behavior; such conditions include poverty, minority group status, inferior education, and lack of employment.

The external, or outer, control system consists of effective or ineffective supervision and discipline; consistent or inconsistent moral training; and positive or negative acceptance, identity, and self-worth. Many believe that latchkey or unsupervised children have a higher risk of becoming delinquent due to nonexistent and/or inconsistent supervision and a lack of moral guidance experienced by latchkey or unsupervised children. Oftentimes, drug-addicted parents socialize children who develop delinquent tendencies because such parents are more likely to be inconsistent with discipline and adherence to disciplinary rules as a result of their drug addiction(s).

In applying control theory to the use or abuse of drugs, if an individual has a weak external social control system largely composed of a social environment lacking conformity to conventional and lawful behavior, then the internal control system, largely composed of coherent internal values and attitudes prohibiting drug use, must compensate for the external acceptance of drug use. Similarly, if an individual's external social control system prohibits drug use, his or her internal control system will not be seriously challenged. If, however, either the internal or the external

TABLE 2.2 Likelihood of Drug Use

Individual Internal Control	External Social Control	
	Strong	**Weak or Nonexistent**
Strong	Least likely (almost never)	Less likely (probably never)
Weak	More likely (probably will)	Most likely (almost certain)

control system is contradictory (weak internal vs. strong external), or the worst-case scenario in which both internal and external controls are weak, drug abuse is more likely to become an outcome.

Table 2.2 shows the likelihood of drug use resulting from either strong or weak internal and external control systems. It indicates that if both internal and external controls are strong, the use and abuse of drugs are less likely to occur. Travis Hirschi (1971), a much-respected sociologist and social control theorist, believes that delinquent behavior tends to occur when people lack (1) attachment to others, (2) commitment to goals, (3) involvement in conventional activity, and (4) belief in a common value system (Liska and Messner 1999; Thio 2010). If a child or an adolescent is not bonded or circumscribed into a family setting or school curriculum and is not in alliance with nondelinquent peers, then the drift into delinquent behavior is inevitable.

We can apply Hirschi's theories to drug use as follows:

- Drug users are less likely than nonusers to be closely attached to conventional parents.
- Scholastically successful students are less likely to use drugs.
- Drug users are less likely to participate in social clubs and organizations and engage in team sport activities.

KEY TERMS

control theory
theory that emphasizes that when people are left without bonds to other groups (peers, family, social groups) they generally have a tendency to deviate from upheld values and attitudes

socialization
the growth and development process responsible for learning how to become a responsible, functioning human being

• Drug users are very likely to have friends whose activities are congruent with their own attitudes. Drug users tend to associate with other drug users (similar to delinquents associating with other delinquents). Likewise, non–drug-using adolescents often associate with non–drug-using adolescents.

The following excerpt illustrates how control theory works:

I was 15 when my mother confronted me with drug use. I nearly died. We have always been very close and she really cried when she found my "dugout" [paraphernalia that holds a quantity of marijuana] and a "one hitter" [a tubular device for smoking very small quantities of this drug] in her car. My fear was that she would inquire about my drug use with our next-door neighbors, whose children were my best friends. The neighbor residing on the left of our house was one of my high school teachers who knew me from the day I was born. The neighbor on the right side of our house was our church pastor. For a while after she confronted me, I just sneaked around more whenever I wanted to get high. After a few months, I became so paranoid of how my mother kept looking at me when I would come in at night that I eventually stopped smoking weed. Our family is very close and the town I live in (at that time the population was 400) was filled with gossip. I could not handle the pressure, so I quit. *(From Venturelli's research files, female postal worker residing in a small Midwestern town, age 22, February 9, 1997)*

In conclusion, control theory depicts how conformity with supportive groups may prevent deviance. It suggests that social control is both formerly and informally prescribed by family, school, and peer group expectations. In addition, individuals who are not equipped with an internal system of self-control reflecting the values and beliefs of conventional society or who feel personally alienated from major social institutions are more likely to deviate without feeling guilty for their actions, often because parental or peer pressure results in a suspension or modification of internal beliefs.

Danger Signals of Drug Abuse

How does one know when the use of drugs moves beyond normal use? Many people are prescribed drugs that affect their moods. Using these drugs

as prescribed can be important for both physical and emotional health. Sometimes, however, it may be difficult to decide when use of drugs to handle stress or anxiety becomes inappropriate. It is important that your use of drugs does not result in either dependency or addiction. The following are some danger signals that can help you evaluate your drug use behavior:

1. Do people who are close to you often ask about your drug use? Have they noticed any changes in your moods or behavior?
2. Do you become defensive when a friend or relative mentions your drug or alcohol use?
3. Do you believe you cannot have fun without alcohol or other drugs?
4. Do you frequently get into trouble with the law, school officials, family, friends, or significant others because of your alcohol or other drug use?
5. Are you sometimes embarrassed or frightened by your behavior under the influence of drugs or alcohol?
6. Have you ever switched to a new doctor because your regular physician would not prescribe the drug you wanted?
7. When you are under pressure or feel anxious, do you automatically take a sedative, a drink, or both?
8. Do you turn to drugs after becoming upset, after confrontations or arguments, or to relieve uncomfortable feelings?
9. Do you take drugs more often than prescribed or for purposes other than those recommended by your doctor?
10. Do you take prescription drugs that have not been prescribed by a physician?
11. Do you often combine drugs and alcohol to heighten the effects?
12. Do you drink or take drugs regularly to help you sleep or even to relax?
13. Do you take an illicit or nonprescribed drug to get going in the morning?
14. Do you find it necessary or nearly impossible to not use alcohol and/or other drugs to have sex?
15. Do you find yourself not wanting to be around friends who do not use drugs or drink on a regular basis?
16. Have you ever seriously confronted the thought that you may have a drug addiction problem?
17. Do you make promises to yourself or others that you will stop getting drunk or using drugs?
18. Do drink and/or use drugs alone?

A higher number of "yes" answers indicate a greater likelihood that you are abusing alcohol and/or drugs. Many places offer help at the local level, such as programs in your community listed in the phone book or online under "Drug Abuse Help" or "Drug Counseling," including SMART Recovery at www.smartrecovery.org, Saint Jude Retreats at www.soberforever.net, or the National Council on Alcoholism and Drug Dependence (NCADD) at www.alcoholalcoholism.org/?gclid =CJPXhvvwzrkCFdFDMgodoBwAEg. Other resources include community crisis centers, telephone hotlines, and the National Mental Health Association.

■ Low-Risk and High-Risk Drug Choices

Some very real risks are associated with recreational drug use. Low-risk and high-risk drug choices refer to two major levels of alcohol and other drug use. **Low-risk drug choices** refer to values and attitudes that keep the use of alcohol and other drugs in control. **High-risk drug choices** refer to values and attitudes that lead to using drugs habitually and addictively, resulting in emotional, psychological, and physical health problems. Low-risk choices include abstinence from all drugs or remaining in true control of the quantity and frequency of drugs taken.

Low-risk choices require self-monitoring your consumption of alcohol and other drugs to reduce your risk of an alcohol and other drug-related problem. Both "low-risk" and "high-risk" are appropriate descriptive concepts that allow us to focus on the health and safety issues involved in drug use and refer to developing and maintaining completely different values and attitudes in your approach to alcohol and other drugs.

This chapter described numerous factors influencing drug use, theoretical explanations, and reasons why people start using or abusing drugs. A good number of theories were covered that attempt to explain initial and habitual use. Some people can easily become addicted to alcohol and other drugs because of inherited characteristics, personality, mental instability or illness, and vulnerability to present situations. Others who have more resistance to alcohol and drug addiction may have stronger convictions and abilities to cope with different situations.

MAINTAINING A LOW-RISK APPROACH

To minimize the risk of alcohol and drug-related problems, we suggest you remain aware of the following:

- Investigate your family drug history. Does anyone in your family have a history of alcohol or drug abuse? How many members of your family who have alcohol or drug problems are blood relatives? In other words, are you more likely to become dependent on alcohol or drugs because of the possibility of inherited genes or because of the values and attitudes to which you are exposed?
- Do you particularly enjoy the effects of alcohol and other drugs? Do you spend a lot of time thinking about how "good" it feels to be high?
- Does it seem as if the only time you really have fun is when you are using alcohol and other drugs?
- Keep in mind the following accepted findings:
  - *Body size:* A small person typically becomes more impaired by drug use than a larger person does.
  - *Gender:* Women typically become more impaired than men of the same size, especially with regard to alcohol use but with other types of drugs as well.
  - *Other drugs:* Taking a combination of drugs generally increases the risk of impairment and, in some combinations, accidental death.
  - *Fatigue or illness:* Fatigue and illness increase the risk for alcohol and drug impairment.
  - *Mindset:* As you set out to drink or use other drugs, are you expecting heavy use of alcohol or heavy involvement with drugs to the point of inebriation or severe distortion of reality as the evening's outcome? More important, what view do you have regarding moderate versus heavy use of drugs?
  - *Empty stomach:* Taking drugs on an empty stomach increases drug effects.

Also keep in mind that most excessive drug use comes with the following risks:

- It is against all school policies.
- It is unlawful behavior (risky with the law).
- Excessive alcohol and other drug use usually leads not only to public attention but also

KEY TERMS

low-risk drug choices
developing values and attitudes that lead to controlling the use of alcohol and drugs

high-risk drug choices
developing values and attitudes that lead to using drugs both habitually and addictively

to criminal justice attention (police and the courts). Jail time or prison, fines, costly forced rehabilitation programs, and community service work are possible outcomes.

- The defense costs involved in even simple drug possession charges are often $3000 to $8000 (often beyond an individual's ability to pay for such legal services).
- A criminal record is a public record and can be acquired or suddenly come to the attention of school officials (especially loan officers and/or government loan personnel), credit bureaus, as well as any other community members.

We leave you with this question: *Are excessive drug use and the resulting drug dependence still worth such risks?* This question is critical, especially when we know that the more often drugs are consumed, the greater the potential not only for drug dependence and addiction but also for damage to health, personal well-being, family and interpersonal relationships, and community respect.

LEARNING PORTFOLIO

Discussion Questions

1. Define the terms *addiction, tolerance, dependence,* and *withdrawal.*
2. Describe and contrast the disease and characterological (personality predisposition) models of addiction.
3. List and briefly discuss several major biological, social, and cultural factors that may be responsible for addiction to drugs.
4. In addition to better cultivation techniques, cite several other possible reasons why the potency (THC levels) of the average marijuana joint has substantially increased since the 1960s.
5. Given that more than approximately 88% of the U.S. population are daily drug users in some form, do you think we need to reexamine our strict drug laws, which may be punishing a sizable number of drug users in our society who stubbornly want to use their drugs of choice?
6. Is there any way to combine the biological and sociological explanations for why people use drugs so that the two perspectives do not conflict? (Sketch out a synthesis between these two sets of theoretical explanations.)
7. Describe the relationship between mental illness and drug abuse.
8. Is the relationship between drug abuse and mental illness important? Why or why not?
9. Do you accept the behavioristic view that one school of psychology offers for explaining why people come to abuse drugs? (In a general sense, this view primarily states that when behavior is rewarded, people repeat behaviors that are rewarded.) Explain your answer in terms of how this occurs with drug users and drug abusers.
10. In reviewing psychological and sociological theories, which theory do you think best explains drug use? Defend your answer.
11. Does differential association theory take into account non–drug-using individuals whose socialization environment was drug infested? Explain your answer.
12. Are drug users socialized differently? Defend your answer. If you think this is true, *how* are they socialized differently?
13. Can divorce be blamed for adolescent drug use? Why or why not? If so, to what extent?
14. To what extent do you think rapid social change is a major cause of drug use and abuse? Cite three examples of how the speed of change in today's society may explain current drug use.
15. Is making low-risk choices regarding drug use a more effective approach for eliminating or moderating drug use rather than advocating "Just say no"?

Key Terms

addiction to pleasure theory 83

characterological or personality predisposition model 72

comorbidity 78

control theory 100

conventional behavior 99

differential reinforcement 85

disease model 72

dopamine 77

"double wall" of encapsulation 73

dual diagnosis 82

genetic and biophysiological theories 76

habituation 83

high-risk drug choices 103

labeling theory 93

low-risk drug choices 103

master status 94

moral model 72

neurotransmitters 77

personality disorders 72

primary deviance 94

psychoactive effects 77

psychoanalysis 73

retrospective interpretation 95

secondary deviance 94

self-medication 78

sensation-seeking individuals 84

social influence theories 86

socialization 101

social learning theory 83

structural influence theories 86

subculture theory 96

substance use disorder 69

substance-induced disorders (addictive disorders) 71

Summary

1. Chemical dependence has been a major social problem throughout U.S. history.

2. People define chemical addiction in many ways. The essential feature is a chronic attachment to drug use despite significant negative outcomes and consequences.

3. The major models of addiction are the moral model, the disease model, and the characterological or personality predisposition model.

4. Transitional periods, such as adolescence and middle age, are associated with unique sets of risk factors.

5. Drug dependence that advances to addiction generally occurs in stages affecting a minority of drug users who become caught up in vicious cycles that worsen their situation, causing psychological and biological abnormalities as they increase their drug usage. Although not inevitable, drug use has a general tendency to advance to severe drug dependence, also known as addiction.

6. Drug use is more serious today than in the past because (a) it has increased dramatically since 1960, (b) today's illicit drugs are more potent than in the past, (c) the media present drug use as rewarding, (d) drug use physically harms members of society, and (e) drug use and drug dealing by violent gangs continues to increase at alarming rates.

7. Genetic and biophysiological theories explain addiction in terms of genes, psychiatric disorders, reward centers in the brain, character traits, brain dysfunction, and biochemical patterns.

8. Drugs of abuse interfere with the functioning of neurotransmitters, chemical messengers used for communication between brain regions. Drugs with abuse potential enhance the pleasure centers by causing the release of a specific brain neurotransmitter, such as dopamine, which acts as a positive reinforcer.

9. The American Psychiatric Association classifies severe drug dependence as substance use disorder. Drug abuse can cause mental conditions that mimic major psychiatric illnesses, such as schizophrenia, severe anxiety disorders, and suicidal depression.

10. Four genetic factors can contribute to drug abuse: (a) many genetically determined psychiatric disorders are relieved by drugs of abuse, which, in turn, encourages their use; (b) high rates of addiction result from people who are genetically sensitive to addictive drugs; (c) such character traits as insecurity and vulnerability, which often have a biological basis, can lead to drug abuse behavior; and (d) the inability to break away from a particular type of drug addiction may in part be genetically determined, especially when severe craving or very unpleasant withdrawal effects dominate.

11. Introversion and extroversion patterns have been associated with levels of neural arousal in brainstem circuits. These forms of arousal are closely associated with effects caused by drug stimulants or depressants.

12. Reinforcement or learning theory says that the motivation to use or abuse drugs stems from how the "highs" from alcohol and other drugs reduce anxiety, tension, and stress. Positive social rewards and influences by drug-using peers also promote drug use.

13. Social influence theories include social learning, the role of significant others, labeling, and subculture theories. Social learning theory explains drug use as a form of learned behavior. Significant others play a role in the learning process involved in drug use and/or abuse. Labeling theory says that other people we consider important can influence whether drug use becomes an option for us. If key people we admire or fear come to define our actions as deviant, then the definition becomes a "fact" in our reality. Subculture theories trace original drug experimentation, use, and/or abuse to peer pressure and influence.

14. A number of consistencies in socialization patterns are found among drug abusers, ranging from immaturity, maladjustment, and insecurity to exposure and belief that a life with drug use is appealing and that selling drugs is a very lucrative business.

15. Sociologist Howard Becker believes that first-time drug users become attached to drugs because of three factors: (a) they learn the

techniques of how to use the drug, (b) they learn to perceive the pleasurable effects of drugs, and (c) they learn to enjoy the drug experience.

16. Primary deviance is when deviant behavior is initially tried, yet the perpetrator does not identify with the deviant behavior; hence, it is inconsequential deviant behavior. Secondary deviance is when the perpetrator begins to identify with the deviant behavior (i.e., "Yes, I am a drug user, so what if I am?").

17. Both internal and external social control should prevail concerning drug use. Internal control deals with internal psychic and internalized social attitudes. External social control is exemplified by living in a neighborhood and community in which drug use and abuse are severely criticized or not tolerated as a means to seek pleasure or avoid stress and anxiety.

18. Low-risk and high-risk drug use choices refer to the process of developing values and attitudes toward alcohol and other drugs. Low-risk drug choices encompass values and attitudes leading to a controlled use of alcohol and drugs—from total abstinence to very moderate use. High-risk choices encompass values and attitudes leading to using drugs both habitually and addictively.

References

Akers, R. L. "Problems in the Sociology of Deviance: Social Definition and Behavior." *Social Forces* 6 (June 1968): 455–465.

Akers, R. L. *Drugs, Alcohol, and Society: Social Structure, Process, and Policy.* Belmont, CA: Wadsworth, 1992.

Akers, R. L. *Social Learning and Social Structure: A General Theory of Crime and Deviance.* New Brunswick, NJ: Transaction, 2009.

Akers, R. L., and C. S. Sellers. *Criminological Theories: Introduction, Evaluation, and Application.* New York: Oxford University Press, 2008.

alcoholrehab.com. "Introversion and Addiction." Drug and Alcohol Rehab Asia (DARA Thailand). 2015a. Available http://alcoholrehab.com/addiction-articles/introversion-and-addiction/

alcoholrehab.com. "Self-Medication and Substance Abuse." Drug and Alcohol Rehab Asia (DARA Thailand). 2015b. Available http://alcoholrehab.com/drug-addiction/self-medication-substance-abuse/

American Psychiatric Association (APA). "Substance-Related Disorders." In *Diagnostic and Statistical Manual of Mental Disorders (DSM-IV-TR)*, 4th ed. revised, 191–295. Washington, DC: American Psychiatric Association, 2000.

American Psychiatric Association (APA). "Substance-Related and Addictive Disorders." In *Diagnostic and Statistical Manual of Mental Disorders (DSM-5)*, 5th ed., 481–589. Washington, DC: American Psychiatric Association, 2013.

Apostolides, M. "Special Report: The Addiction Revolution: Old Habits Get New Choices." *Psychology Today* 29 (1996): 33–43, 75–76.

Bahr, S. J., and J. P. Hoffmann. "Social Scientific Theories of Drug Use, Abuse, and Addiction." In *The Handbook of Drugs and Society*, edited by Henry H. Brownstein, 197–217. West Sussex, UK: John Wiley and Sons, 2016.

Bandura, A. *Social Learning Theory.* Englewood Cliffs, NJ: Prentice Hall, 1977.

Beattie, M. *Codependent No More.* San Francisco: Harper, 1987.

Becker, H. S. *Outsiders: Studies in the Sociology of Deviance.* New York: Free Press, 1963.

Becker, H. S. "History, Culture, and Subjective Experience: An Exploration of the Social Basis of Drug-Induced Experiences." *Journal of Health and Social Behavior* 8 (1967): 163–176.

Bejerot, N. "Current Problems of Drug Addiction." *Lakartidingen* (Sweden) 62(50) (1965): 4231–4238.

Bejerot, N. *Addiction: An Artificially Induced Drive.* Springfield, IL: Thomas, 1972.

Bejerot, N. "The Biological and Social Character of Drug Dependence." In *Psychiatrie der Gegenwart, Forschung und Praxis*, 2nd ed., edited by K. P. Kisker, J. E. Meyer, C. Muller, and E. Stromogrew, Vol. 3, 488–518. Berlin: Springer-Verlag, 1975.

Bespalov, A., A. Lebedev, G. Panchenko, and E. Zvartau. "Effects of Abused Drugs on Thresholds and Breaking Points of Intracranial Self-Stimulation in Rats." *European Neuropsychopharmacology: The Journal of the European College of Neuropharmacology* 9 (1999): 377–383.

Best, J., and D. F. Luckenbill. *Organizing Deviance*, 2nd ed. Englewood Cliffs, NJ: Prentice Hall, 1994.

Blaszczak-Boxe, A. "Potent Pot: Marijuana Is Stronger Now Than It Was 20 Years Ago." *Livescience*, 8 February 2016. Available http://www.livescience.com/53644-marijuana-is-stronger-now-than-20-years-ago.html

Bondarenko E., D. Gudkova, M. Namestnikova. "Kaspersky Security Bulletin: Spam Evolution 2009." Kaspersky Lab, 17 February 2010. Available https://securelist.com/analysis/kaspersky-security-bulletin/36285/kaspersky-security-bulletin-spam-evolution-2009/

Burns, D. B. "The Web of Caring: An Approach to Accountability in Alcohol Policy." In *Designing Alcohol and Other*

Drug Prevention Programs in Higher Education. Newton, MA: Higher Education Center for Alcohol and Other Drug Prevention, 1997.

Capitol Times. "Seven in 10 Drug Users Work Full-Time." 1999. Available http://www.mapinc.org/drugnews /v99/n983/a01.html

Carlson, N. *Psychology: The Science of Behavior,* 3rd ed. Boston: Allyn and Bacon, 1990.

Center for Behavioral Health Statistics and Quality (CBHSQ). *2014 National Survey on Drug Use and Health: Detailed Tables.* Rockville, MD: Substance Abuse and Mental Health Services Administration, 2015.

Center for Substance Abuse Research (CESAR). "Early Alcohol Users More Likely to Report Substance Use and Criminal Activity as Young Adults." September 2003. Available http://www.cesar.umd.edu/cesar/cesarfax /vol12/12-36.PDF

Center for Substance Abuse Research (CESAR). "Eighth Graders' Perceived Harmfulness of Ecstasy, LSD, and Inhalant Use Continues to Decrease; Suggests Vulnerability to Resurgence of Use." 23 April 2007. Available http://www.cesar.umd.edu/cesar/cesarfax/vol16/16 -16.pdf

Center for Substance Abuse Research (CESAR) [Adopted by]. "District Youth in Brief: Early Alcohol Use. Is Early Alcohol Among DC Public High School Students Associated with Other Risky Behaviors?" September 2011. Available http://www.cesar.umd.edu/cesar /pubs/20110901%20DC%20YinB%203-8.pdf

Cheron, J. M. *Symbolic Interactionism: An Introduction, an Interpretation, an Integration,* 7th ed. Upper Saddle River, NJ: Prentice Hall, 2001.

Clatts, M., D. L. Welle, L. A. Goldsamt, and S. E. Lankenau. "An Ethno-Epidemiological Model for the Study of Trends in Illicit Drug Use." In *The American Drug Scene: An Anthology,* edited by J. A. Inciardi and K. McElrath, 225–249. New York: Oxford University Press, 2008.

Clinard, M. B., and R. F. Meier. *Sociology of Deviant Behavior,* 14th ed. Belmont, CA: Wadsworth Cengage Learning, 2011.

Cohen, A. K. *Delinquent Boys: The Culture of the Gang.* Glencoe, IL: Free Press, 1955.

Conner, M. G. "Children During Divorce." 24 August 2011. Available http://crisiscounseling.com/TraumaLoss /DivorceChildren.htm

Conrad, P., and J. W. Schneider. *Deviance and Medicalization.* St. Louis, MO: Mosby, 1980.

Dixon, P. *Addicted to Pleasure: Nature of Drug Addiction.* London: Global Change, Ltd., 2015. Available http://www .globalchange.com/truth-about-drugs-chapter-3.htm

Doherty, W. J., and R. H. Needle. "Psychological Adjustment and Substance Use Among Adolescent Before and After a Parental Divorce." *Child Development* 62 (1991): 328–337.

Doweiko, H. E. *Concepts of Chemical Dependency,* 9th ed. Belmont, CA: Brooks/Cole Cengage Learning, 2015.

Drug Strategies. "Santa Barbara Profile: Alcohol, Tobacco, and Other Drugs." Washington, DC: Drug Strategies, 1999.

Everyday Psychology. "Two Theories of Drug Addiction, Positive Reinforcement and Negative Reinforcement." 2012. Available http://www.psychpost.org/2012/08 /two-theories-of-drug-addiction-positive.html

Eysenck, H. J., and M. W. Eysenck. *Personality and Individual Differences: A Natural Science Approach.* New York: Plenum Press, 1985.

Farrar, H., and G. Kearns. "Cocaine: Clinical Pharmacology and Toxicology." *Journal of Pediatrics* 115 (1989): 665–675.

Fischer, C. S. *The Urban Experience.* New York: Harcourt Brace Jovanovich, 1976.

Frosch, W. A. "An Analytic Overview of the Addictions." In *The Addictions: Multidisciplinary Perspectives and Treatments,* edited by H. Milman and H. Shaffer, 160–173. Lexington, MA: Lexington Books/D.C. Heath, 1985.

Gardner, E. L. "Brain Reward Mechanisms." In *Substance Abuse: A Comprehensive Textbook,* 2nd ed., edited by J. H. Lowinson, P. Ruiz, R. B. Millman, and J. G. Langrod, 60–69. Baltimore: Lippincott Williams & Wilkins, 1992.

Genetic Science Learning Center. "Contact Us." *Learn Genetics,* 1 December 2015. Available http://learn .genetics.utah.edu/content/addiction/genes/

Gergen, K. *The Saturated Self: Dilemmas of Identity in Contemporary Life.* New York: Basic Books, 2000.

Glick, R., and J. Moore, eds. *Drugs in Hispanic Communities.* New Brunswick, NJ: Rutgers University Press, 1990.

Goode, E. *Deviant Behavior,* 9th ed. Upper Saddle River, NJ: Prentice Hall, 2010.

Grant, Kara-Leah. "9 Things Nobody Tells You About Recreational Drug Use in Your Youth." *Elephant Journal,* 26 February 2013. Available http://www.elephantjournal .com/2013/02/9-things-nobody-tells-you-about -recreational-drug-use-in-your-youth/

Gray, J. A. *The Psychology of Fear and Stress,* 2nd ed. Cambridge, UK: Cambridge University Press, 1987.

Gray, P., and D. F. Bjorklund. *Psychology,* 7th ed. London: Worth Publishers, 2014.

Heitzeg, N. A. *Deviance: Rulemakers and Rulebreakers.* Minneapolis, MN: West, 1996.

Hellerman, C. "Is Super Weed, Super Bad?" CNN.com. 9 August 2013. Available http://www.cnn .com/2013/08/09/health/weed-potency-levels/

Heritage Foundation. "Family and Adolescent Well-Being." FamilyFacts. 2016. Available http://www.familyfacts .org/briefs/34/family-and-adolescent-well-being

Hewitt, J. P., and D. Shulman. *Self and Society: A Symbolic Interactionist Social Psychology,* 11th ed. Boston: Allyn and Bacon, 2010.

Hirschi, T. *Causes of Delinquency*, 2nd ed. Los Angeles: University of California Press, 1971.

Horvath A. T, K. Misra, A. K. Epner, G. M. Cooper. 2015. "Psychological Causes of Addiction." Available http://www.amhc.org/1408-addictions/article/48345-psychological-causes-of-addiction

Inciardi, J. A., D. Lockwood, and A. E. Pottieger. *Women and Crack Cocaine*. New York: Macmillan, 1993.

Inderbitzin, M., K. Bates, and R. Gainey. *Deviance and Social Control: A Sociological Perspective*. Thousand Oaks, CA: Sage Publications, 2013.

International Network of People Who Use Drugs (INPUD). "INPUD's International Diaries: Timeline of Events in the History of Drugs." n.d. Available https://inpud.wordpress.com/timeline-of-events-in-the-history-of-drugs/

Jellinek, E. M. *The Disease Concept of Alcoholism*. Highland Park, NJ: Hillhouse Press, 1960.

Johnston, L. D., P. M. O'Malley, J. G. Bachman, and J. E. Schulenberg. *Monitoring the Future: National Survey Results on Drug Use: 2012 Overview, Key Findings on Adolescent Drug Use*. Ann Arbor: Institute for Social Research, University of Michigan, 2013.

Johnston, L. D., P. M. O'Malley, R. A. Miech, J. G. Bachman, and J. E. Schulenberg. *Monitoring the Future: National Survey Results on Drug Use: 2014 Overview, Key Findings on Adolescent Drug Use*. Ann Arbor: Institute for Social Research, University of Michigan, 2015.

Jones, J. *Hep-Cats, Narcs, and Pipe Dreams: A History of America's Romance with Illegal Drugs*. Baltimore, MD: Johns Hopkins University Press, 1996.

Kelley, K. B. "Children's Adjustment in Conflicted Marriage and Divorce: A Decade Review of Research." *Journal of the American Academy of Child and Adolescent Psychiatry* 39 (August 2000): 963–973.

Kelly, K., and P. Ramundo. *You Mean I'm Not Lazy, Stupid, and Crazy?!* New York: Scribner, 2006.

Kessler, R. C., W. T. Chiu, O. Demler, and E. E. Walters. "Prevalence, Severity, and Comorbidity of Twelve-Month DSM-IV Disorders in the National Comorbidity Survey Replication (NCS-R)." *Archives of General Psychiatry* 62 (2005): 617–627.

Khantzian, E. J. "Addiction as a Brain Disease." *American Journal of Psychiatry* 155 (June 1998): 711–713.

Koob, G. "Drug Addiction." *Neurobiology of Disease* 7(5) (October 2000): 543–545.

Kuehn, B. M. "Integrated Care Key for Patients with Both Addiction and Mental Illness." *Journal of the American Medical Association* 303 (19 May 2010): 1905–1907.

Landau, E. "Children's Quality of Life Declining, Says Report." CNN.com. 2010. Available http://www.cnn.com/2010/HEALTH/06/08/children.wellbeing/index.html

Lang, S. "Cornell Psychologist Finds Chemical Evidence for a Personality Trait and Happiness." *Cornell University Science News* (11 October 1996). Available http://news.cornell.edu/stories/1996/10/dopamine-linked-personality-trait-and-happiness

L.A.W. Publications. *Let's All Work to Fight Drug Abuse*. Addison, TX: C&L Printing, 1985.

Lemert, E. M. *Social Psychology: A Systematic Approach to the Theory of Sociopathic Behavior*. New York: McGraw-Hill, 1951.

Lemonick, M. D., with A. Park. "The Science of Addiction." *Time* (14 July 2007): 42–48.

Liddle, H. "AAMFT Consumer Update: Adolescent Substance Abuse." American Association for Marriage and Family Therapy (AAMFT), 2001. Available http://www.aamft.org/familytherapyresources/searchproc.asp?kw=&st=&at=&ad=&pr=&yp=&sort=Author&pg=155&sd=desc

Liska, A. E., and S. F. Messner. *Perspectives on Crime and Deviance*. Upper Saddle River, NJ: Prentice Hall, 1999.

MacPherson, K. "It Takes a Rat to Show How Drugs Alter Brains." *The Star Ledger* (28 August 2010): 1–2. Available http://www.nj.com/specialprojects/index.ssf?/specialprojects/addicts/addicts0826.html

Marshall, M. "Conclusions." In *Beliefs, Behavior, and Alcoholic Beverages: A Cross-Cultural Survey*, edited by M. Marshall, 451–457. Ann Arbor: University of Michigan Press, 1979.

Mathias, R. "Novelty Seekers and Drug Abusers Tap Same Brain Reward System, Animal Studies Show." *NIDA Notes* 10(4) (July/August 1995): 1–5.

Mental Health America (MHA). "Co-dependency." 2010. Available http://www.nmha.org/go/codependency

Miller, N. S. *Addiction Psychiatry: Current Diagnosis and Treatment*. New York: Wiley, 1995.

Moore, J. *Homeboys: Gangs, Drugs and Prison in the Barrios of Los Angeles*. Philadelphia: Temple University Press, 1978.

Moore, J. "Gangs, Drugs, and Violence." In *Gangs: The Origins and Impact of Contemporary Youth Gangs in the United States*, edited by S. Cummings and D. J. Monti, 27–46. Albany: State University of New York Press, 1993.

Moore, J. "Psychological Theory of Drug Abuse." Yahoo Health. 22 October 2008: 1–2. Available http://www.associatedcontent.com/article/1117664/psychological_theory_of_drug_abuse.html?cat=5

Myers, P. L. "Sources and Configurations of Institutional Denial." *Employee Assistance Quarterly* 5(B) (1990): 43–54.

National Alliance on Mental Illness (NAMI). "Dual Diagnosis." 2015. Available https://www.nami.org/Learn-More/Mental-Health-Conditions/Related-Conditions/Dual-Diagnosis

National Health Service (NHS). "Drugs and the Brain." n.d. Available at http://www.nhs.uk/Livewell/drugs/Pages/Dodrugsdamagebrain.aspx

National Institute on Drug Abuse (NIDA). *Theories on Drug Abuse: Selected Contemporary Perspectives*. NIDA Research Monograph Series. U.S. Department of Health and Human Services. Rockville, MD: U.S. Government Printing Office, 1980.

National Institute on Drug Abuse (NIDA). "Study Finds Higher Use Among Adolescents Whose Parents Divorce." *NIDA Notes* 5 (Summer 1990): 10.

National Institute on Drug Abuse (NIDA). "Attention and Memory Impaired in Heavy Users of Marijuana." Rockville, MD: Office of the National Institute on Drug Abuse, 20 February 1996.

National Institute on Drug Abuse (NIDA). *Principles of Drug Addiction Treatment.* National Institutes of Health Publication No. 99-4180, October 1999.

National Institute on Drug Abuse (NIDA). "Addiction and Co-Occurring Mental Disorders." *NIDA Notes* 21 (February 2007): 3.

National Institute on Drug Abuse (NIDA). *Comorbidity: Addiction and Other Mental Illnesses.* Research Report Series. Bethesda, MD: U.S. Department of Health and Human Services, 2008a.

National Institute on Drug Abuse (NIDA). *Drugs, Brains, and Behavior: The Science of Addiction.* Bethesda, MD: National Institutes of Health, U.S. Department of Health and Human Services, 2008b.

National Institute on Drug Abuse (NIDA). "Comorbidity: Addiction and Other Mental Disorders." Bethesda, MD: U.S. Department of Health and Human Services, 2009: 1–2.

National Institute on Drug Abuse (NIDA). "Comorbidity: Addiction and Other Mental Disorders." 2010. Available https://www.drugabuse.gov/sites/default/files/rrcomorbidity.pdf

National Institute on Drug Abuse (NIDA). "Drugs, Brains, and Behavior: The Science of Addiction." Bethesda, MD: National Institutes of Health (NIH) and National Institute on Drug Abuse, July 2014. Available https://www.drugabuse.gov/publications/drugs-brains-behavior-science-addiction/drugs-brain

Needle, R. H., S. S. Su, and W. J. Doherty. "Divorce, Remarriage, and Adolescent Substance Use: A Prospective Longitudinal Study." *Journal of Marriage and the Family* 52 (1990): 157–159.

O'Brien, R., S. Cohen, G. Evans, and J. Fine. *The Encyclopedia of Drug Abuse,* 2nd ed. New York: Facts on File, 1992.

Office of National Drug Control Policy (ONDCP). *Drug Facts: Cocaine.* Rockville, MD: White House Drug Policy Clearing House, November 2003.

Plummer, K. "Misunderstanding Labeling Perspectives." In *Deviant Interpretations,* edited by D. Downes and P. Rock, 85–121. London: Robertson, 1979.

Pontell, H. N. *Social Deviance,* 2nd ed. Upper Saddle River, NJ: Prentice Hall, 1996.

ProCon.org. "Medical Marijuana: Is Marijuana Significantly More Potent Now Than in the Past?" 7 February 2012. Available http://medicalmarijuana.procon.org/view.answers.php?questionID=000336

Radowitz, J. V. "Smoking and Drug Abuse Traits Linked to Genes." *The Independent,* 18 June 2003, Independent Digital (UK) Ltd.

Reckless, W. C. "A New Theory of Delinquency." *Federal Probation* 25 (1961): 42–46.

Ritzer, G. *Enchanting a Disenchanted World: Revolutionizing the Means of Consumption.* Thousand Oaks, CA: Pine Forge Press, 1999.

Ritzer, G. *The McDonaldization of Society,* 6th ed. Thousand Oaks, CA: Pine Forge Press, 2011.

Ritzer, G., and D. Goodman. *Sociological Theory,* 8th ed. New York: McGraw-Hill Higher Education, 2010.

Rousar, E., K. Brooner, M. W. Regier, and G. E. Bigelow. "Psychiatric Distress in Antisocial Drug Abusers: Relation to Other Personality Disorders." *Drug and Alcohol Dependence* 34 (1995): 149–154.

Rudgley, R. *Essential Substances: A Cultural History of Intoxicants in Society.* New York: Kodansha International, 1993.

Sack, D. "5 Things Parents Do That May Encourage Teen Substance Abuse." Huffington Post: Parents (4 March 2013). Available http://www.huffingtonpost.com/david-sack-md/teen-substance-abuse_b_2792838.html

Sanders, W. B. *Gangbangs and Drive-bys: Grounded Culture and Juvenile Gang Violence.* New York: Aldine De Gruyter, 1994.

Schaffer Library of Drug Policy. *Technologies for Understanding and Preventing Substance Abuse and Addiction. Chapter 3: Biology and Pharmacology.* 18 October 1994. Available http://www.druglibrary.org/schaffer/library/studies/ota/ch3.htm

Schur, E. M. *Labeling Deviant Behavior.* New York: Harper & Row, 1971.

Shelden, R. G., S. K. Tracy, and W. B. Brown. *Youth Gangs in American Society,* 2nd ed. Belmont, CA: Wadsworth/Thomson Learning, 2001.

Siegel, L .J., and J. J. Senna. *Juvenile Delinquency: Theory, Practice and Law.* St. Paul, MN: West, 1994.

Smith, D., E. Milkman, and S. Sunderworth. "Addictive Disease: Concept and Controversy." In *Addictions: Multidisciplinary Perspectives and Treatments,* edited by H. Milkman and H. J. Shaffer, 145–159. Lexington, MA: Lexington Books/D.C. Heath, 1985.

Spanagel, R., and F. Weiss. "The Dopamine Hypothesis of Reward: Past and Current Status." *Trends in Neuroscience* 22 (1999): 521–527.

Substance Abuse and Mental Health Services Administration (SAMHSA). *Study Shows Strong Relationship Between Adolescent Behavior Problems and Alcohol Use.* Press Release. Rockville, MD: U.S. Department of Health and Human Services, 1 March 2000.

Substance Abuse and Mental Health Services Administration (SAMHSA). *National Survey on Drug Use and Health (NSDUH) Report. Marijuana Use and Delinquent Behaviors*

Among Youths. Research Triangle Park, NC: Substance Abuse and Mental Health Services Administration, Office of Applied Studies, 16 May 2008a: 1–5.

Substance Abuse and Mental Health Services Administration (SAMHSA). *National Survey on Drug Use and Health (NSDUH) Report. Substance Use Disorder and Serious Psychological Distress by Employment Status.* Rockville, MD: Substance Abuse and Mental Health Services Administration, Office of Applied Studies, 2008b.

Substance Abuse and Mental Health Services Administration (SAMHSA). "Substance Abuse Treatment: Addressing the Specific Needs of Women." Rockville, MD: U.S. Department of Health and Human Services, 2009.

Substance Abuse and Mental Health Services Administration (SAMHSA). *Results from the 2011 National Survey on Drug Use and Health: Summary of National Findings.* NSDUH Series H-44, HHS Publication No. (SMA) 12-4713. Rockville, MD: Substance Abuse and Mental Health Services Administration, 2012.

Substance Abuse and Mental Health Services Administration (SAMHSA). *Substance Abuse Disorders.* Rockville, MD: U.S. Department of Health and Human Services, 27 October, 2015. Available http://www.samhsa.gov /disorders/substance-use

Sutherland, E. *Principles of Criminology,* 4th ed. Philadelphia: Lippincott, 1947.

Syvertsen, J. L. "Some Considerations on the Disease Concept of Addiction." In *The American Drug Scene: An Anthology,* edited by J. Inciardi and K. McElrath, 16–26. New York: Oxford University Press, 2008.

Tarter, R. E., A. Alterman, and K. L. Edwards. "Alcoholic Denial: A Biopsychosociological Interpretation." *Journal of Studies on Alcohol* 45 (1983): 214–218.

Thio, A. *Deviant Behavior,* 10th ed. Boston: Allyn and Bacon, 2010.

Thomas, W. I., with D. S. Thomas. *The Child in America.* New York: Knopf, 1923.

Thornberry, T. P. "Risk Factors for Gang Membership." In *The Modern Gang Reader,* 2nd ed., edited by J. Miller, C. L. Maxson, and M. W. Klein, 32–42. Los Angeles: Roxbury, 2001.

Uhl, G., K. Blum, E. Noble, and S. Smith. "Substance Abuse Vulnerability and D-2 Receptor Genes." *Trends in Neurological Sciences* 16 (1993): 83–88.

Uhl, G., G. I. Elmer, M. C. LaBuda, and R. W. Pickens. "Genetic Influences in Drug Abuse: Human Substance Abuse Vulnerability and Genetic Influences." In *Neuropsychopharmacology—5th Generation of Progress,* edited by K. Davis, D. Charney, J. T. Coyle, and C. Nemeroff. Philadelphia, PA: Lippincott Williams & Wilkins, 2002. Available http://www.acnp.org/g4/GN401000174/CH270.html

Uhl, G., A. Persico, and S. Smith. "Current Excitement with D-2 Dopamine Receptor Gene Alleles in Substance Abuse." *Archives of General Psychiatry* 49 (February 1992): 157–160.

U.S. Department of Labor. "Quick Stats on Women Workers, 2010." Washington, DC: U.S. Department of Labor, 2011. Available http://www.dol.gov/wb/factsheets/QS -womenwork2010.htm

Volkow, N. "Cocaine and the Changing Brain: Changes in Human Brain Systems After Longterm Cocaine Use." 1 February 1999. Available http://archives.drugabuse .gov/meetings/CCB/Volkow.html

Volkow, N. D. "Biography of Dr. Nora Volkow." Rockville, MD: National Institute on Drug Abuse (NIDA), February 2016. Available https://www.drugabuse.gov /about-nida/directors-page/biography-dr-nora-volkow

Waldorf, D. "Natural Recovery from Opiate Addiction: Some Social Psychological Processes of Untreated Recovery." *Journal of Drug Issues* 13 (1983): 237–280.

Weiss, F. "Cocaine Dependence and Withdrawal— Neuroadaptive Changes in Brain Reward and Stress Systems." 1999. Available http://archives.drugabuse.gov /meetings/CCB/Weiss.html

Werner, E., and S. Henry. *Criminological Theory: An Analysis of Its Underlying Assumptions.* Fort Worth, TX: Harcourt Brace College, 1995.

Williams, F. P., III, and M. D. McShane. *Criminological Theory,* 3rd ed. Upper Saddle River, NJ: Prentice Hall, 1999.

Witmer, D. "Teen Drug Use Warning Signs." About.com. 2013. Available http://parentingteens.about.com/cs /drugsofabuse/a/driug_abuse20.htm

Wooden, W. S. *Renegade Kids, Suburban Outlaws: From Youth Culture to Delinquency.* Belmont, CA: Wadsworth/ Thomson Learning, 1995.

World Health Organization Expert Committee on Addiction-Producing Drugs. *World Health Organization Technical Report* 273 (1964): 9–10.

Wyman, J. "Promising Advances Toward Understanding the Genetic Roots of Addiction." *NIDA Notes* 12 (July/ August 1997): 1–5.

Yinger, M. J. *Countercultures: The Promise and the Peril of a World Turned Upside Down.* New York: Free Press, 1982.

Zuckerman, M. "Are You a Risk Taker? What Causes People to Take Risks? It's Not Just a Behavior. It's a Personality." *Psychology Today* (1 November 2000). Available http://www.psychologytoday.com/articles/200011/are -you-risk-taker

Zuckerman, M. *Sensation Seeking and Risky Behavior.* Washington, DC: American Psychological Association, 2007.

CHAPTER 3

Drug Use, Regulation, and the Law

Photo by John B. Snyder. Courtesy of U.S. Army.

Did You Know?

▶ Some patent medicines sold at the turn of the 20th century contained opium and cocaine and were highly addictive.

▶ For fiscal year 2015, the U.S. federal budget request for interdiction efforts, which includes intercepting and ultimately disrupting shipments of illegal drugs and their precursors, as well as the proceeds, totaled approximately $3.9 billion.

Learning Objectives

On completing this chapter you should be able to:

> Identify the major criteria that determine how society regulates drugs.

> Explain the significance of the Pure Food and Drug Act of 1906 and why it was important in regulating drugs of abuse.

> Describe the changes in drug regulation that occurred because of the Kefauver–Harris Amendment of 1962.

> Identify and explain the stages of testing for an investigational new drug.

> Discuss the special provisions (exceptions) made by the Food and Drug Administration (FDA) for drug marketing.

> Outline the procedures used by the FDA to regulate nonprescription drugs.

> Outline the major approaches used to reduce substance abuse.

> Explain the main arguments for and against legalizing drugs.

> List the most common types of drug testing.

Introduction

Society mandates that it maintains control over which drugs are permissible and which drugs are prohibited. Through legislation, we decide which drugs are licit or illicit. We decide which licit drugs are readily available "over-the-counter" (OTC) and which can be obtained by prescription only. Thus, drug laws prohibit indiscriminate use of what society defines as a drug. In this chapter, you will come to better understand how society attempts to control drug use and abuse. In particular, this chapter examines the development of drug regulations in the United States that apply to both the manufacture of drugs and the control of their use. Although many think that the regulation of drug manufacturing and drug abuse lie at opposite ends of the spectrum, regulation of drug manufacturing and abuse actually evolved from similar processes.

Cultural Attitudes About Drug Use

Currently, cultural attitudes in the United States regarding the use of drugs blend beliefs in individuals' right to live their lives as they desire with society's obligation to protect its members from the burdens imposed by uncontrolled behavior. The history of drug regulation consists of regulatory swings in response to attempts by government to balance these two factors while responding to public pressures and perceived public needs. For example, more than 100 years ago, most people expected the government to protect citizens' rights to produce and market new foods and substances; they did not expect or desire the government to regulate product quality or claims. Instead, the public relied on private morals and common sense to obtain quality and protection in an era of simple technology. Unfortunately, U.S. society had to learn by tragic experience that its trust was not well placed; many unscrupulous entrepreneurs were willing to risk the safety and welfare of the public in an effort to maximize profits and acquire wealth. In fact, many medicines of these earlier times were not merely ineffective but often dangerous.

Because of the advent of high technology and the rapid advancements society has made, we now rely on highly trained experts and government watchdog agencies for consumer information and protection. Out of this changing environment have evolved two major guidelines for controlling drug development and marketing:

1. Society has the right to protect itself from the damaging effects of drug use. This concept not only is closely aligned with the emotional and highly visible issues of drug abuse but also includes protection from other drug side effects. Thus, although we expect the government to protect society from drugs that can cause addiction, we also expect it to protect us from drugs that cause cancer, cardiovascular disease, or other threatening medical conditions.

2. Society has the right to demand that drugs approved for marketing be safe and effective to the general public. If drug manufacturers promise that their products will relieve pain, those drugs should be analgesics; if they promise that their products will relieve depression, those drugs should be antidepressants; if they promise that their products will relieve stuffy noses, those drugs should be decongestants.

The public, through the activities of regulatory agencies and statutory enactments, has attempted to require that drug manufacturers produce safe and effective pharmaceutical products. Closely linked to these efforts is the fact that society uses similar strategies to protect itself from the problems associated with the specific drug side effect of dependence or addiction, which is associated with drug abuse.

The Road to Regulation and the FDA

In the late 1800s and early 1900s, sales of uncontrolled medicines flourished and became widespread. Many of these products were called *patent medicines*, which signified that the ingredients were secret, not that they were patented. The decline of patent medicines began, in part, as a consequence of the 1906 Pure Food and Drug Act. This legislation required manufacturers to indicate the amounts of 11 dangerous products, including alcohol, cocaine, heroin, and morphine, on the label of each product (FDA 2012c). It became obvious at this time that many medicinal products on the market labeled "nonaddictive" were, in fact, potent drugs "in sheep's labeling" and could cause severe dependence. However, most government interest at the time centered on regulation of the food industry, not drugs.

The shortcomings in the Pure Food and Drug Act quickly became obvious. In particular, the law did not allow the government to stop the distribution of dangerous preparations. As one example, an extract of horsetail weed, Banbar, was marketed by a shirt salesman as an injection-free cure for diabetes. Although the FDA established in court that diabetics were dying while on this preparation even though insulin was available, the government lost its case because it could not meet the standard of establishing fraud (FDA 2009a, 2012c). As another example, no federal statute prevented the sale of a dangerous diet preparation containing dinitrophenol, a product that accelerated metabolism and created serious side effects, including cataracts (FDA 2012c). Further, in 1911, the U.S. Supreme Court ruled that this act did not prohibit false therapeutic claims, but only misleading and false statements about the identity or ingredients of a drug (FDA 2009b).

The Pure Food and Drug Act was modified, albeit not in a consumer-protective manner, by the Sherley Amendment in 1912. The distributor of a cancer "remedy" was indicted for falsely claiming on the label that the contents were effective. The case was decided in the U.S. Supreme Court in 1911. Justice Holmes, writing for the majority opinion, said that, based on the 1906 act, the company had not violated any law because legally all it was required to do was accurately state the contents and their strength and quality. The accuracy of the therapeutic claims made by drug manufacturers was not controlled. Congress took the hint and passed the Sherley Amendment to add to the existing law the requirement that labels should not contain "any statement . . . regarding the curative or therapeutic effect . . . which is false and fraudulent." However, the law required that the government prove fraud, which turned out to be difficult (and is still problematic). This amendment did not improve drug products but merely encouraged pharmaceutical companies to be more vague in their advertisements (Temin 1980).

It was not until a drug company unwittingly produced a toxic product that killed over 100 people, many of whom were children, that the FDA was given control over drug safety in the 1938 federal Food, Drug, and Cosmetic Act (FDA 2012b; Hunter, Rosen, and DeChristoforo 1993). The bill had been debated for several years in Congress and showed no promise of passage. Then, a pharmaceutical company decided to sell a liquid form of a sulfa drug (one of the first antibiotics)

and found that the drug would dissolve well in a chemical solvent (diethylene glycol) that was comparable to antifreeze. The company marketed the antibiotic as Elixir Sulfanilamide without testing the solvent for toxicity. Under the 1906 Pure Food and Drug Act, the company could not be prosecuted for the toxicity of this form of drug or for not testing the formulation of the drug on animals first. It could only be prosecuted for mislabeling the product on the technicality that the term *elixir* refers to a solution in alcohol, not a solution in diethylene glycol. Again, it was apparent that the laws in place provided woefully inadequate protection for the public.

The 1938 act differed from the 1906 law in several ways. Companies had to file applications with the government for all new drugs showing that they were safe (not effective—just safe) for use as described. The drug label had to provide instructions regarding safe use of the drug. The act demanded that safe tolerances be set for unavoidable poisonous substances and authorized the establishment of standards of identity, quality, and fill-of-container for foods. In addition, the act eliminated a Sherley Amendment requirement to prove intent to defraud in drug misbranding cases (FDA 2014g).

Before passage of the 1938 act, an individual could go to a doctor and obtain a prescription for any nonnarcotic drug or go to the pharmacy directly if this person had already decided what was needed. The labeling requirement in the 1938 act allowed drug companies to create a class of drugs that could not be sold legally without a prescription. It has been suggested that the FDA's actions were motivated by the frequent public misuse of two classes of drugs developed before passage of the 1938 law: sulfa antibiotics and barbiturates. People often took too little of the antibiotics to cure an infection and too much of the barbiturates and became addicted.

The 1938 Food, Drug, and Cosmetic Act allowed the manufacturer to determine whether a drug was to be labeled prescription or nonprescription. The same product could be sold as prescription by one company and as OTC by another. After the Durham–Humphrey Amendment was passed in 1951, almost all new drugs were placed in the prescription-only class. The drugs that were patented and marketed after World War II included potent new antibiotics and phenothiazine tranquilizers such as Thorazine. Both the FDA and the drug firms thought these products were potentially too dangerous to sell OTC. The Durham–Humphrey Amendment established the criteria, which are still used today, for determining whether a drug should be classified as prescription or nonprescription (FDA 2014g). Basically, if a drug does not fall into one of the following three categories, it is considered nonprescription:

- The drug is habit-forming.
- The drug is not safe for self-medication because of its toxicity.
- The drug is a new compound that has not been shown to be completely safe.

In addition, the Durham–Humphrey Amendment required any drug that is potentially harmful or habit-forming to be dispensed under the supervision of a healthcare practitioner as a prescription drug and must carry the statement, "Caution: Federal law prohibits dispensing without prescription" (FDA 2009c).

In 1959, Senator Estes Kefauver initiated hearings concerned with the enormous profit margins earned by drug companies due to the lack of competition in the market for new, patented drugs. Testimony by physicians revealed that an average doctor in clinical practice often was not able to evaluate accurately the efficacy of the drugs he or she prescribed. The 1938 law did not give the FDA authority to supervise clinical testing of drugs; consequently, the effectiveness of drugs being sold to the public was not being determined. Both the Kefauver and Harris Amendments put forth in Congress were intended to deal with this problem but showed no likely signs of becoming law until the thalidomide tragedy occurred.

During the Kefauver hearings, the FDA received an approval request for Kevadon, a brand of thalidomide that was to be marketed in the United States. **Thalidomide** had been used in Europe, Canada, and Africa to treat morning sickness in pregnant women. Despite ongoing pressure, medical officer Frances Kelsey refused to allow the request to be approved because of insufficient safety data (FDA 2012a). By 1962, the horrifying effects of thalidomide on developing fetuses became known. There are two approximately 24-hour intervals early in pregnancy when thalidomide can alter the development of the arms and legs of an embryo. If a woman takes thalidomide on one or both of these days, the infant could be born with abnormally developed arms and/or legs (called **phocomelia**, from the Greek words for "flippers," or "seal-shaped limbs"). Even though Kevadon was never approved for marketing in the United States, the manufacturers had distributed more than 2 million tablets in the United States for investigational use—a type of use that the regulations

© Time & Life Pictures/Getty Images

Characteristic limb deformities caused by thalidomide.

of that period left largely unchecked. Once the damaging effects of thalidomide became known, the FDA attempted quickly to recover the drug from patients and providers. For her efforts, Kelsey received the President's Award for Distinguished Federal Civilian Service in 1962, the highest civilian honor available to a government employee (FDA 2014a; National Library of Medicine [NLM] 2015).

Although standard testing probably would not have detected the congenital effect of thalidomide and the tragedy would likely have occurred anyway, these debilitated infants prompted passage of the 1962 Kefauver and Harris Amendments. They strengthened the government's regulation of both the introduction of new drugs and the production and sale of existing drugs. The amendments required, for the first time, that drug manufacturers demonstrate the efficacy as well as the safety of their drug products. The FDA was empowered to retract approval of a drug that was already being marketed. In addition, the agency was permitted to regulate and evaluate drug testing by pharmaceutical companies and mandate standards of good drug-manufacturing policy.

KEY TERMS

thalidomide
a sedative drug that, when used during pregnancy, can cause severe developmental damage to a fetus

phocomelia
a birth defect; impaired development of the arms, legs, or both

▪ The Rising Demand for Effectiveness in Medicinal Drugs

To evaluate the effectiveness of the more than 4000 drug products that were introduced between 1938 and 1962, the FDA contracted with the National Research Council to perform the Drug Efficacy Study. This investigation started in 1966 and ran for 3 years. The council was asked to rate drugs as either effective or ineffective. Although the study was supposed to be based on scientific evidence, this information often was not available, which meant that conclusions sometimes relied on the clinical experience of the physicians on each panel; these judgments were not always based on reliable information.

A legal challenge resulted when the FDA took an "ineffective" drug off the market and the manufacturer sued. This action finally forced the FDA to define what constituted an adequate and well-controlled investigation. Adequate, documented clinical experience was no longer satisfactory proof that a drug was safe and effective. Each new drug application now had to include information about the drug's performance in patients compared with the experiences of a carefully defined control group. The drug could be compared with (1) a placebo, (2) another drug known to be active based on previous studies, (3) the established results of no treatment, or (4) historical data about the course of the illness without the use of the drug in question. In addition, a drug marketed before 1962 could no longer be grandfathered in. If the company could not prove the drug had the qualifications to pass the post-1962 tests for a new drug, it was considered a new, unapproved drug and could not legally be sold.

▪ Regulating the Development of New Drugs

The amended federal Food, Drug, and Cosmetic Act in force today requires that all new drugs be registered with and approved by the FDA. The FDA is mandated by Congress to (1) ensure the rights and safety of human subjects during clinical testing of experimental drugs, (2) evaluate the safety and efficacy of new treatments based on test results and information from the sponsors (often health-related companies), and (3) compare potential benefits and risks to determine whether a new drug should be approved and marketed. Because of FDA regulations, all pharmaceutical companies must follow a series of steps when seeking permission to market a new drug (see **Figure 3.1**).

REGULATORY STEPS FOR NEW PRESCRIPTION DRUGS

STEP 1: PRECLINICAL RESEARCH AND DEVELOPMENT
A chemical must be identified as having potential value in the treatment of a particular condition or disease. The company interested in marketing the chemical as a drug must run a series of tests on at least two or more animal species. Careful records must be kept of side effects, absorption, distribution, metabolism, excretion, and the dosages of the drug necessary to produce the various effects. Carcinogenic, mutagenic, and teratogenic variables are tested. The dose–response curve must be

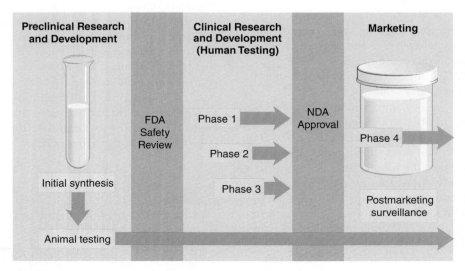

FIGURE 3.1 Steps required by the FDA for reviewing a new drug.

determined along with potency, and then the risk and benefit of the substance must be calculated. If the company still believes there is a market for the substance, it forwards the data to the FDA to obtain an investigational new drug (IND) number for further tests.

STEP 2: CLINICAL RESEARCH AND DEVELOPMENT

Animal tests provide some information, but ultimately tests must be done on the species for which the potential drug is intended—that is, humans. These tests usually follow three phases.

Phase 1 is called the *initial clinical stage*. Small numbers of volunteers (usually 20 to 100), typically healthy people but sometimes patients, are recruited to establish drug safety and dosage ranges for effective treatment and to examine side effects. Medical students, paid college student volunteers, and other volunteers are often studied after obtaining informed consent. The data from Phase 1 clinical trials are collected, analyzed, and sent to the FDA for approval before beginning the next phase of human subject testing.

Phase 2 testing is called the *clinical pharmacological evaluation stage*. The effects of the drug are tested to eliminate investigator bias and to determine side effects and the effectiveness of the treatment. Because the safety of the new drug has not been thoroughly established, a few patients (perhaps 100 to 300 volunteers) with the medical problem the drug is intended to treat participate in these studies. Statistical evaluation of this information is carried out before proceeding with Phase 3 testing.

Phase 3 is the *extended clinical evaluation stage*. By this time, the pharmaceutical company has a good idea of both drug effectiveness and dangers. The drug can be offered safely to a wider group of participating clinics and physicians, who cooperate in the administration of the potential drug—when medically appropriate—to as many as thousands of volunteer patients who have given informed consent.

This stage makes the drug available on a wide experimental basis. Sometimes, by this point, the new drug has received some publicity, and people with the particular disease for which the drug was developed may actively seek out physicians licensed to experiment with it.

During Phase 3 testing, safety checks are made and any side effects that might show up as more people are exposed to the drug are noted. After the testing program concludes, careful analysis is made of the effectiveness, side effects, and recommended dosage. If there are sufficient data to demonstrate that the drug is safe and effective, the company submits a new drug application (NDA) as a formal request that the FDA consider approving the drug for marketing. The application usually comprises many thousands of pages of data and analysis, and the FDA must sift through it and decide whether the risks of using the drug justify its potential benefits. The FDA usually calls for additional tests before the drug is determined to be safe and effective and before granting permission to market it.

STEP 3: PERMISSION TO MARKET

At this point, the FDA can allow the drug to be marketed under its patented name. In 2014, the average cost of developing a new drug was $2.6 billion (Tufts Center for Drug Development 2014; see "Here and Now: The Cost of Prescription Drug Development").

Once the drug is marketed, it continues to be closely scrutinized for adverse effects. This postmarketing surveillance is often referred to as Phase 4, and it is important because, in some cases, negative effects may not show up for a long time. For example, it was determined in 1970 that diethylstilbestrol (DES), when given to pregnant women to prevent miscarriage, causes an increased risk of a rare type of vaginal cancer in their daughters when these children enter their teens and young adult years. The FDA subsequently removed from the market the form of DES that had been used to treat pregnant women.

HERE AND NOW
The Cost of Prescription Drug Development

According to a 2014 study by the Tufts Center for the Study of Drug Development, the development of a new prescription medicine that successfully obtains marketing approval is estimated to cost $2.6 billion. This figure is based on an estimated average

"out-of-pocket cost" of approximately $1.4 billion and expected returns that investors forgo while a drug is in development of approximately $1.2 billion.

According to the study, the estimated average cost of post–FDA-approval studies to test new indications,

(continues)

HERE AND NOW

The Cost of Prescription Drug Development (*continued*)

dosage strengths, dosing regimens, and new formulations, as well as to monitor safety and long-term side effects as an FDA condition of approval, is an additional $312 million, with all figures expressed in 2013 dollars.

These newest figures are substantially higher than in past years. According to the study's principal author, Joseph A. DiMasi, these increases have been driven largely by both increases in out-of-pocket costs for individual drugs and higher failure rates for drugs in human trials.

Data from Tufts Center for Drug Development. "Cost to Develop and Win Marketing Approval for a New Drug Is $2.6 Billion." 18 November 2014. Available: http://csdd.tufts.edu/news/complete_story/pr_tufts_csdd_2014_cost_study

EXCEPTIONS: SPECIAL DRUG-MARKETING LAWS

Concerns have been raised that the process used by the FDA to evaluate prospective drugs is laborious and excessively lengthy. Hence, an amendment was passed to accelerate the evaluation of urgently needed drugs. The so-called *fast-track rule* has been applied to the testing of certain drugs used for the treatment of rare cancers, acquired immunodeficiency syndrome (AIDS), and some other diseases. Fast tracking is a process designed to expedite the review of drugs to treat serious diseases and fill an unmet medical need. Filling an unmet medical need is defined as providing a therapy where none exists or providing one that may be potentially better than therapy available currently (FDA 2014e).

According to the FDA,

Determining whether a condition is serious is a matter of judgment, but generally is based on whether the drug will have an impact on such factors as survival, day-to-day functioning, or the likelihood that the condition, if left untreated, will progress from a less severe condition to a more serious one. AIDS, Alzheimer's, failure and cancer are obvious examples of serious conditions. However, diseases such as epilepsy, depression and diabetes are also considered to be serious conditions. (FDA 2014e)

Many drugs that qualify for fast tracking also qualify for *priority review* by the FDA. A priority review designation "will direct overall attention and resources to the evaluation of applications for drugs that, if approved, would be significant improvements in the safety or effectiveness of the treatment, diagnosis, or prevention of serious conditions when compared to standard applications" (FDA 2014f). Its goal is to reduce the time it takes for the FDA to review a new drug application, with a goal of completion in 6 months (compared to 10 months under standard review). Significant improvement may include (1) enhanced effectiveness in treatment, diagnosis, or prevention, (2) increased patient compliance that is predicted to lead to fewer serious adverse outcomes, (3) evidence of safety and effectiveness in a new subpopulation, or (4) substantial reduction or elimination of treatment-limiting drug reactions (FDA 2014f).

The *breakthrough therapy designation* is designed to accelerate the review and development of agents that are intended to treat a serious condition. It requires clinical evidence indicating that the drug may provide significant improvement over existing therapy on a clinically significant endpoint(s). For purposes of breakthrough therapy designation, a "clinically significant endpoint generally refers to an endpoint that measures an effect on irreversible morbidity or mortality (IMM) or on symptoms that represent serious consequences of the disease" (FDA 2014c). The designation has several benefits, including eligibility for all fast-track designation features (FDA 2014c, 2015b).

Of note, it is possible that drugs for serious conditions that fill an unmet medical can be approved based on a **surrogate** or **intermediate clinical endpoint**. This process is referred to as *accelerated approval* (FDA 2014b).

KEY TERMS

surrogate endpoint
a physical sign, laboratory measurement, radiographic image, or other measure that is expected to predict clinical benefit, but is not itself a measure of clinical benefit

intermediate clinical endpoint
a measure of a therapeutic effect that is considered reasonably likely to predict the clinical benefit of a drug, such as an effect on irreversible morbidity and mortality

Processes such as fast tracking, breakthrough designations, accelerated approval, and/or priority review have shortened review periods for drugs that treat very serious conditions. As one example, the FDA reviewed Gleevec, a treatment for chronic myeloid leukemia, in 2.5 months (Motl, Miller, and Burns 2003). According to the FDA (2014d), 46% of the 41 novel new drugs approved in 2014 were designated as fast track, breakthrough, or both; 61% were designated for priority review; and 20% were approved under the FDA's accelerated approval program.

Another special marketing law that has had considerable impact is the Orphan Drug Law. It allows drug companies to receive tax advantages if they develop drugs that are not very profitable because they are useful in treating only small numbers of patients, such as those who suffer from rare diseases. A *rare disease* is defined as one that affects fewer than 200,000 people in the United States. Fewer than 10 products supported by industry for rare diseases came to market between 1973 and 1983. The Orphan Drug Act provided the first significant incentives to drug developers to support needed medical products for approximately 25 million Americans with rare diseases. Since its passage in 1984, over 400 products for rare diseases have received approval for marketing (FDA 2015a).

One additional attempt to accelerate the drug review is exemplified by the Prescription Drug User Fee Act of 1992. This law required drug manufacturers to pay fees to the FDA for the evaluation of NDAs. Congress required the FDA to use these fees to hire more reviewers so as to facilitate the review processes (FDA 2014g).

REGULATION OF NONPRESCRIPTION DRUGS

The Durham–Humphrey Amendment to the Food, Drug, and Cosmetic Act made a distinction between prescription and nonprescription (OTC) drugs and required the FDA to regulate OTC drug marketing. In 1972, the FDA initiated a program to evaluate the effectiveness and safety of the nonprescription drugs on the market and to ensure that they included appropriate labeling. Panels of drug experts that included physicians, pharmacologists, and pharmacists reviewed the so-called active ingredients in the OTC medications. Based on the recommendations of these panels, the active ingredients were placed in one of the following three categories:

I. Generally recognized as safe and effective for the claimed therapeutic indication

II. Not generally recognized as safe and effective or unacceptable indications

III. Insufficient data available to permit final classification

By 1981, the panels had made initial determinations about over 700 ingredients in more than 300,000 OTC drug products and submitted more than 60 reports to the FDA.

In the second phase of the OTC drug review, the FDA evaluated the panels' findings and submitted a tentative adoption of the panels' recommendations (after revision, if necessary), following public comment and scrutiny. After some time and careful consideration of new information, the agency issued a final ruling and classification of the ingredients under consideration.

■ The Effects of the OTC Review on Today's Medications

The review process for OTC ingredients has had a significant impact on the public's attitude about OTC products and their use (both good and bad) in self-medication. It was apparent from the review process that many OTC drug ingredients did not satisfy the requirements for safety and effectiveness. Consequently, it is almost certain that, in the future, OTC medicines will contain fewer active ingredients but that these drugs will be safer and more effective than ever before.

In addition, with heightened public awareness, greater demand has been brought to bear on the FDA to make better drugs available to the public for self-medication. In response to these pressures, the FDA has adopted a **switching policy**, which allows the agency to review prescription drugs and evaluate their suitability as OTC products. According to the Consumer Healthcare Products Association, 700 drugs that would have required a prescription only 20 years ago have been switched to OTC status (FDA 2011). The following criteria must be satisfied if a drug is to be switched to OTC status:

- The drug must have been marketed by prescription for at least 3 years.
- Use of the drug must have been relatively high during the time it was available as a prescription drug.
- Adverse drug reactions must not be alarming, and the frequency of side effects must not have

KEY TERM

switching policy
an FDA policy allowing the change of suitable prescription drugs to over-the-counter status

increased during the time the drug was available to the public.

In general, this switching policy has been well received by the public. The medical community and the FDA are generally positive about OTC switches as well. Some concerns remain, however, that the wider access to more effective drug products will lead to increased abuse or misuse of OTC products. Hence, emphasis is placed on adequate labeling and education to ensure that consumers have sufficient information to use OTC products safely and effectively.

The Regulation of Drug Advertising

Much of the public's knowledge and impressions about drugs come from advertisements. It is difficult to ascertain the amount of money currently spent by the pharmaceutical industry to promote its products. However, according to data cited by The Pew Charitable Trusts (2013), the pharmaceutical industry spent over $27 billion on drug promotion in 2012. This included over $3 billion on advertising to consumers (primarily through television commercials) and $24 billion on marketing to physicians.

The economics of prescription drugs are unique because a second party, the health professional, dictates what the consumer, the patient, will purchase. As a general rule, the FDA oversees most issues related to advertising of prescription drugs. In contrast, the Federal Trade Commission (FTC) regulates OTC advertising (FDA 2015c).

According to the FDA (2015d), physicians indicate that, for the most part, the advertisements for prescription drugs on television and radio have had both positive and negative effects on their patients and practices. The FDA has conducted surveys directed toward physicians to better understand how direct-to-consumer (DTC) prescription drug promotion affects the patient–doctor relationship, with the intent of informing the agency if advertising rules need to be changed in order to ensure better consumer understanding of the risks and benefits of prescription drugs. Highlights of the surveys include the following:

- Most physicians surveyed agreed that because their patient saw a DTC advertisement, he or she asked thoughtful questions. Approximately the same percentage of physicians thought the advertisements made their patients more aware of potential therapies.

- The physicians surveyed indicated that the advertisements did not convey information about risks and benefits equally well. In fact, 78% of physicians responded that their patients understand the possible *benefits* of the drug very well or somewhat. In contrast, 40% of physicians indicated that their patients understand the possible *risks*. In addition, 65% responded that DTC advertisements confused patients.
- Approximately 75% of physicians surveyed indicated that DTC advertisements cause patients to think that the drug is more efficacious than it is, and many physicians felt some pressure to prescribe something when patients mentioned DTC advertisements.
- The physicians surveyed reported that patients understand that they need to consult a health-care provider concerning appropriate treatments. Eighty-two percent responded either "very well" or "somewhat" when asked if they believe that their patients understand that only a physician can decide if a drug is appropriate for them.

A significant amount of prescription drug promotion is directed at health professionals. The approaches employed by manufacturers to encourage health professionals to prescribe their products include advertising in prestigious medical journals, direct mail advertising, and some radio and television advertising. Government advertising regulations control all printed and audio materials distributed by drug salespeople. Perhaps the most effective sales approach is for drug representatives to personally visit health professionals; this tactic is harder to regulate.

Many people in and out of the medical community have questioned the ethics of drug advertising and marketing in the United States and are concerned about the negative impact that deceptive promotion has on target populations. One of the biggest problems in dealing with misleading or false advertising is defining such deception. Probably the best guideline for such a definition is summarized in the Wheeler–Lea Amendment to the FTC Act:

The term *false advertisement* means an advertisement, other than labeling, which is misleading in a material respect; and in determining whether any advertisement is misleading, there shall be taken into account not only representations . . . but the extent to which the advertisement fails to reveal facts.

Tough questions are being asked as to how much control should be exerted over the pharmaceutical industry to protect the public without excessively infringing on the rights of these companies to promote their products. The solutions to these problems will not be simple. Nevertheless, efforts to keep drug advertisements accurate, and informative are worthwhile and are necessary if the public is expected to make rational decisions about drug use (see "Here and Now: Drug Advertising: What's in an Ad?").

■ Federal Regulation and Quality Assurance

No matter what policy is adopted by the FDA and other drug-regulating agencies, there will always be those who criticize their efforts and complain that they do not do enough or that they do too much. On the one hand, the FDA has been blamed for being excessively careful and requiring too much testing before new drugs are approved for marketing. On the other hand, when new drugs are released and cause serious side effects, the FDA is condemned for being ineffective in its control of drug marketing.

Importantly, federal regulations do not ensure drug safety or effectiveness for everyone. Too many individual variables alter the way individuals respond to drugs, making such universal assurances impossible. Federal agencies can only deal with general policies and make general decisions. For example, what if the FDA determines that a given drug is reasonably safe in 95% of the population and effective in 70%? Are these acceptable figures, or should a drug be safe in 99% and effective in 90% before it is deemed suitable for general marketing? What of the 5% or 1% of the population who will be adversely affected by this drug? What rights do they have to be protected?

There are no simple answers to these questions. Federal policies are inevitably compromises that assume that the clinician who prescribes the drug and/or the patient who buys and consumes it will be able to identify when use of that drug is inappropriate or threatening. Unfortunately, sometimes drug prescribing and drug consuming are done carelessly and unnecessary side effects occur or the drug is ineffective.

It is always difficult to predict the future. Nevertheless, with the dramatic increase in new and better drugs becoming available to the public, it is not likely that federal or state agencies will diminish their role in regulating drug use. Now more than ever, the public demands safer and more effective drugs. This public attitude will likely translate into even greater involvement by regulatory agencies in issues of drug development, assessment, and marketing.

Drug Abuse and the Law

The negative experiences described earlier in this chapter that Americans had at the turn of the 20th century with addicting substances such as opium led to the *Harrison Act of 1914*. It marked the first legitimate effort by the federal government to regulate and control the production, importation, sale, purchase, and

HERE AND NOW

Drug Advertising: What's in an Ad?

The FDA regulates the advertising of prescription drugs. Federal law does not bar drug companies from advertising any kind of prescription drug, even ones with the potential for severe injury, addiction, or withdrawal. The FDA cannot limit the amount of resources spent on prescription advertisements. It encourages pharmaceutical companies to use language that is clear and understandable to the general public.

According to the FDA, requirements of product claim advertisements include the following, but are not limited to:

- The generic and brand name of the drug
- An FDA-approved use for the drug
- A statement that a product is available by prescription only
- "Fair balance" description of the benefits and risks of the product

Data from Food and Drug Administration (FDA). "Product Claim Ad (Correct)." 2016. Available http://www.fda.gov/Drugs/ResourcesForYou/Consumers /PrescriptionDrugAdvertising/ucm082284.htm distribution of addicting substances. The Harrison Act served as the foundation and reference for subsequent laws directed at regulating drug abuse issues.

Today, the Comprehensive Drug Abuse Prevention and Control Act of 1970 largely determines the ways in which law enforcement agencies deal with substance abuse. This act divided substances with abuse potential into categories based on the degree of their abuse potential and their clinical usefulness. The classifications, which are referred to as *schedules*, range from I to V. *Schedule I* substances have, in general, high abuse potential and no currently approved medicinal use; health professionals cannot prescribe them. *Schedule II*

drugs also have high abuse potential but are approved for medical purposes and can be prescribed with restrictions. The distinctions among *Schedule II through V* substances reflect the likelihood of abuse occurring and the degree to which the drugs are controlled by governmental agencies. The least addictive and least regulated of the substances of abuse are classified as Schedule V drugs (see "Here and Now: Controlled Substance Schedules").

In determining into which schedule a drug or other substance should be placed or whether a substance should be decontrolled or rescheduled, several factors are considered (U.S. Department of Justice [USDOJ] 2011). Specific findings are not

HERE AND NOW

Controlled Substance Schedules

Controlled substances classified as Schedule I, II, III, IV, or V drugs are described here.

Schedule I

- The drug or other substance has a high potential for abuse.
- The drug or other substance has no currently accepted medical use in treatment in the United States.
- There is a lack of accepted safety for use of the drug or other substance under medical supervision.

Schedule II

- The drug or other substance has a high potential for abuse.
- The drug or other substance has a currently accepted medical use in treatment in the United States or a currently accepted medical use with severe restrictions.
- Abuse of the drug or other substance may lead to severe psychological or physical dependence.

Schedule III

- The drug or other substance has less potential for abuse than the drugs or other substances in Schedules I and II.
- The drug or other substance has a currently accepted medical use in treatment in the United States.

- Abuse of the drug or other substance may lead to moderate or low physical dependence or high psychological dependence.

Schedule IV

- The drug or other substance has a low potential for abuse relative to the drugs or other substances in Schedule III.
- The drug or other substance has a currently accepted medical use in treatment in the United States.
- Abuse of the drug or other substance may lead to limited physical dependence or psychological dependence relative to the drugs or other substances in Schedule III.

Schedule V

- The drug or other substance has a low potential for abuse relative to the drugs or other substances in Schedule IV.
- The drug or other substance has a currently accepted medical use in treatment in the United States.
- Abuse of the drug or other substance may lead to limited physical dependence or psychological dependence relative to the drugs or other substances in Schedule IV.

Reproduced from U.S. Department of Justice, U.S. Drug Enforcement Administration (DEA). "Drugs of Abuse." 2011. Available http://www.justice.gov/dea/docs/drugs_of_abuse_2011.pdf. Accessed December 29, 2015.

required for each factor. The factors include the following:

- The actual or relative abuse potential of the drug.
- Scientific evidence of the pharmacological effects of the drug.
- The state of current scientific knowledge regarding the substance. (This factor and the one above are closely related. However, the above factor is primarily concerned with pharmacological effects, whereas this factor deals with all scientific knowledge with respect to the drug.)
- Its history and current pattern of abuse.
- What, if any, risk there is to the public health.
- The psychological or physiological dependence liability of the drug.
- The scope, duration, and significance of abuse.
- Whether the substance is an immediate precursor of a substance already controlled. The Controlled Substance Act allows inclusion of immediate precursors on this basis alone into the appropriate schedule and thus safeguards against possibilities of clandestine manufacture.

Penalties for illegal use and/or trafficking of these agents vary according to the agent's schedule, amount possessed, and number of previous drug-associated offenses (see **Table 3.1**).

Noteworthy, the Controlled Substance Act made no provision for disposal of unwanted or unused prescription medications, except to relinquish these to law enforcement. This lead to the accumulation of unused drugs in homes, and increased the likelihood of misuse and abuse. The Secure and Responsible Drug Disposal Act was enacted to address this problem (see "Here and Now: Secure and Responsible Drug Disposal Act").

TABLE 3.1 Federal Drug-Trafficking Penalties

Drug/Schedule	Quantity	Penalties	Quantity	Penalties
Cocaine (Schedule II)	500–4999 g mixture	**First Offense:** Not less than 5 years and not more than 40 years. If death or serious bodily injury, not less than 20 years or more than life. Fine of not more than $5 million if an individual, $25 million if not an individual. **Second Offense:** Not less than 10 years and not more than life. If death or serious bodily injury, life imprisonment. Fine of not more than $8 million if an individual, $50 million if not an individual.	5 kg or more mixture	**First Offense:** Not less than 10 years and not more than life. If death or serious bodily injury, not less than 20 years or more than life. Fine of not more than $10 million if an individual, $50 million if not an individual. **Second Offense:** Not less than 20 years, and not more than life. If death or serious bodily injury, life imprisonment. Fine of not more than $20 million if an individual, $75 million if not an individual. **2 or More Prior Offenses:** Life imprisonment. Fine of not more than $20 million if an individual, $75 million if not an individual.
Cocaine base (Schedule II)	28–279 g mixture		280 g or more mixture	
Fentanyl (Schedule II)	40–399 g mixture		400 g or more mixture	
Fentanyl analogue (Schedule I)	10–99 g mixture		100 g or more mixture	
Heroin (Schedule I)	100–999 g mixture		1 kg or more mixture	
LSD (Schedule I)	1–9 g mixture		10 g or more mixture	
Methamphetamine (Schedule II)	5–49 g pure or 50–499 g mixture		50 g or more pure or 500 g or more mixture	
PCP (Schedule II)	10–99 g pure or 100–999 g mixture		100 g or more pure or 1 kg or more mixture	

Drug/Schedule	Quantity	Penalties
Other Schedule I and II drugs (and any drug product containing gamma hydroxybutyric acid)	Any amount	**First Offense:** Not more than 20 years. If death or serious bodily injury, not less than 20 years or more than life. Fine $1 million if an individual, $5 million if not an individual. **Second Offense:** Not more than 30 years. If death or serious bodily injury, life imprisonment. Fine $2 million if an individual, $10 million if not an individual.
Flunitrazepam (Schedule IV)	Less than 1 g	

(continues)

TABLE 3.1 Federal Drug-Trafficking Penalties (*continued*)

Drug/Schedule	Quantity	Penalties
Other Schedule III drugs	Any amount	**First Offense:** Not more than 10 years. If death or serious bodily injury, not more than 15 years. Fine not more than $500,000 if an individual, $2.5 million if not an individual. **Second Offense:** Not more than 20 years. If death or serious injury, not more than 30 years. Fine not more than $1 million if an individual, $5 million if not an individual.
All other Schedule IV drugs (other than 1 g or more of Flunitrazepam)	Any amount	**First Offense:** Not more than 5 years. Fine not more than $250,000 if an individual, $1 million if not an individual. **Second Offense:** Not more than 10 years. Fine not more than $500,000 if an individual, $2 million if other than an individual.
All Schedule V drugs	Any amount	**First Offense:** Not more than 1 year. Fine not more than $100,000 if an individual, $250,000 if not an individual. **Second Offense:** Not more than 4 years. Fine not more than $200,000 if an individual, $500,000 if not an individual.

Drug	Quantity	First Offense	Second Offense
Marijuana (Schedule I)	1000 kg or more mixture or 1000 or more marijuana plants	Not less than 10 years or more than life. If death or serious bodily injury, not less than 20 years, or more than life. Fine not more than $10 million if an individual, $50 million if other than an individual.	Not less than 20 years or more than life. If death or serious bodily injury, life imprisonment. Fine not more than $20 million if an individual, $75 million if other than an individual.
Marijuana (Schedule I)	100–999 kg mixture or 100–999 marijuana plants	Not less than 5 years or more than 40 years. If death or serious bodily injury, not less than 20 years or more than life. Fine not more than $5 million if an individual, $25 million if other than an individual.	Not less than 10 years or more than life. If death or serious bodily injury, life imprisonment. Fine not more than $8 million if an individual, $50 million if other than an individual.
Marijuana (Schedule I)	50–99 kg mixture or 50–99 marijuana plants	Not more than 20 years. If death or serious bodily injury, not less than 20 years or more than life. Fine $1 million if an individual, $5 million if other than an individual.	Not more than 30 years. If death or serious bodily injury, life imprisonment. Fine $2 million if an individual, $10 million if other than an individual.
Hashish (Schedule I)	More than 10 kg		
Hashish oil (Schedule I)	More than 1 kg		
Marijuana (Schedule I)	1–49 marijuana plants; less than 50 kg mixture	Not more than 5 years. Fine not more than $250,000, $1 million if other than an individual.	Not more than 10 years. Fine $500,000 if an individual, $2 million if other than individual.
Hashish (Schedule I)	10 kg or less		
Hashish oil (Schedule I)	1 kg or less		

Data from U.S. Drug Enforcement Administration (DEA). "Federal Trafficking Penalties." n.d. Available: https://www.dea.gov/druginfo/ftp3.shtml. Accessed April 22, 2016.

HERE AND NOW

Secure and Responsible Drug Disposal Act

Prescription drug abuse is a major problem. According to the 2014 Substance Abuse and Mental Health Services Administration (SAMHSA) National Survey on Drug Use and Health, 2.5% of Americans aged 12 or older had abused prescription drugs in the past month prior to the survey. In 2013, approximately 2 million persons aged 12 or older used psychotherapeutics nonmedically for the first time within the past year, which averages to about 5500 initiates per day. Rates averaged across 2012 and 2013 indicated that more than 50% of nonmedical users of tranquilizers, pain relievers, stimulants, and sedatives aged 12 or older got the prescription drugs they had most recently used "from a friend or relative for free."

The Controlled Substances Act made no legal provisions for patients to rid themselves of unwanted pharmaceutical controlled substances except to give them to law enforcement. Pharmacies, physician offices, and hospitals were not permitted to accept the drugs. To combat this problem, President Barack Obama signed into law the 2010 Secure and Responsible Drug Disposal Act. This act authorized the Drug Enforcement Administration (DEA) to develop and implement regulations that outline methods to transfer unused or unwanted pharmaceutical controlled substances to authorized collectors for the purpose of disposal. The act also permitted long-term-care facilities to do the same on behalf of residents or former residents.

In 2014, the DEA implemented its final rule for the disposal of controlled substances. It authorizes certain DEA registrants (distributors, reverse distributors, manufacturers, retail pharmacies, narcotic treatment programs, and hospitals/clinics with an on-site pharmacy) to amend their DEA registration to become authorized collectors. Law enforcement continues to have autonomy with respect to how these agencies collect pharmaceutical controlled substances, including holding take-back events.

Drug Enforcement Administration (DEA). *DEA Releases New Rules That Create Convenient but Safe and Secure Prescription Drug Disposal Options.* 8 September 2014. Available: http://www.dea.gov/divisions/hq/2014/hq090814.shtml; Substance Abuse and Mental Health Services Administration (SAMHSA). *Results from the 2013 National Survey on Drug Use and Health: Summary of National Findings.* NSDUH Series H-48, HHS Publication No. SMA 14-4863. Rockville, MD: Substance Abuse and Mental Health Services Administration, 2014.

Center for Behavioral Health Statistics and Quality. *Behavioral Trends in the United States: Results from the 2014 National Survey on Drug Use and Health.* NSDUH Series H-50 HHS Publication No. SMA 15-4927. Rockville, Md. Substance Abuse and Mental Health Services Administration, 2015.

■ Drug Laws and Deterrence

As previously indicated, drug laws often do not serve as a satisfactory deterrent against the use of illicit drugs. People have used and abused drugs for thousands of years despite governmental restrictions. It is very likely they will continue to do so, even with stricter laws and greater support for law enforcement.

Nationwide, law enforcement made an estimated 12,196,959 arrests in 2012. Of these arrests, an estimated at 1,552,432 arrests were for drug abuse violations. An estimated 1,282,957 were for driving under the influence (Federal Bureau of Investigation [FBI] 2013). This problem represents a tremendous cost to society in terms of damaged lives and family relationships; being arrested for a drug-related crime seriously jeopardizes a person's opportunity to pursue a normal life. Drug taking is closely tied to societal problems, and it will remain a problem unless society provides more meaningful experiences to those who are most susceptible to drug abuse. Improved education and increased support should be given to preteens because that is the age when deviant behavior starts. In cases in which drug education programs have been successful in involving students, the amount of drug taking and illegal activity seems to have decreased.

■ Factors in Controlling Drug Abuse

Three principal issues influence laws regarding drug abuse:

1. If a person abuses a drug, should he or she be treated as a criminal or as a sick person afflicted with a disease?
2. How is the user distinguished from the distributor of an illicit drug, and who should be

more harshly punished—the person who creates the demand for the drug or the person who satisfies the demand?

3. Are the laws and associated penalties effective deterrents against drug use or abuse, and how is effectiveness determined?

In regard to the first issue, drug abuse may be considered both an illness and a crime. It can be a psychiatric disorder, an abnormal functional state in which a person is compelled (either physically or psychologically) to continue using the drug. It becomes a crime when the law, reflecting social opinion, makes abuse of the drug illegal. Health issues are clearly involved because uncontrolled abuse of almost any drug can lead to physical and psychological damage. Because the public must pay for healthcare costs or societal damage, laws are created and penalties are implemented to prevent or correct drug abuse problems (see Table 3.1 on federal trafficking penalties).

Concerning the second issue, drug laws have always been more lenient on the user than the seller of a drug of abuse. Actually, it is often hard to separate user from pusher because many drug abusers engage in both activities. Because huge profits are often involved, some people may not use the drugs they peddle and are only pushers; the law tries to deter use of drugs by concentrating on these persons but has questionable success. Organized crime is involved in major drug sales, and these "drug rings" have proved difficult to eliminate.

KEY TERMS

supply reduction
a drug reduction policy aimed at reducing the supply of illegal drugs and controlling other therapeutic drugs

demand reduction
attempts to decrease individuals' tendencies to use drugs, often aimed at youth, with emphasis on reformulating values and behaviors

inoculation
a method of abuse prevention that protects drug users by teaching them responsibility

drug courts
a process that integrates substance abuse treatment, incentives, and sanctions and places nonviolent, drug-involved defendants in judicially supervised rehabilitation programs

interdiction
a policy of cutting off or destroying supplies of illicit drugs

In regard to the third issue, considerable evidence indicates that, in the United States, criminal law has only limited success in deterring drug abuse. During 2014, approximately 38.7% of 12th graders used an illicit drug during the prior 12 months; marijuana/hashish was used by 35.1% and cocaine by 2.6% (Johnston et al. 2015). It is clear that the drug abuse problem is far from being resolved, and many feel that some changes should be made in how we deal with this problem.

Strategies for Preventing Drug Abuse

The U.S. government and the public became concerned about the increasing prevalence of drug use during the 1960s, when demonstrations and nationwide protests against the Vietnam War proliferated as youth (mostly college students) rebelled against what they viewed as an unnecessary and unjust war. During the 1960s and early 1970s, for the first time, large numbers of middle- and upper–middle-class youth began using licit and illicit gateway drugs on a massive scale. In response, the government developed strategies for combating drug use and abuse. Important strategies it employed were **supply reduction**, **demand reduction**, and **inoculation**. More recently, the use of **drug courts** has become a major strategy.

▌ Supply Reduction Strategy

Early attempts at drug abuse prevention included both the Harrison Narcotic Act of 1914 and the 18th Amendment (Prohibition) to the U.S. Constitution. Both laws were intended to control the manufacture and distribution of classified drugs, with legislators anticipating that these restrictions would compel people to stop using drugs. The laws enforced supply reduction, which involves a lessening, restriction, or elimination of available drugs.

Supply reduction drug prevention policy attempts to curtail the supply of illegal drugs or their precursors and exert greater control over other, more therapeutic drugs. Part of the supply reduction policy includes **interdiction**, which includes decreasing the amounts of these agents that are carried across U.S. borders by using foreign crop eradication measures and agreements, by imposing stiff penalties for drug trafficking, and by controlling alcoholic beverages through licensing.

The United States dedicates enormous resources to interdiction programs. For fiscal year 2015, the U.S. federal budget request for interdiction efforts, which includes intercepting and ultimately disrupting shipments of illegal drugs and their precursors, as well as the proceeds, totaled approximately $3.9 billion (Office of National Drug Control Policy [ONDCP] 2014). Although seizures of large caches of illicit drugs are reported routinely in the national press, the evidence is mixed as to whether the availability of drugs has diminished substantially. One can argue that as long as a strong demand for these psychoactive agents exists, demand will be satisfied if the price is right. Even if interdiction successfully reduces the supply of one drug of abuse, if demand persists, that drug is usually replaced by another drug with similar abuse potential.

■ Demand Reduction Strategy

The demand reduction approach attempts to minimize the actual demand for drugs. Through programs and activities often aimed at youth, emphasis is placed on reformulating values, attitudes, skills, and behaviors conducive to resisting drug use. As part of this strategy, support for medical and group drug treatment programs for abusers is encouraged. Although this approach does not address the drug supply, it does attempt to curb and eventually eliminate the need to purchase drugs by reducing the buyer's demand.

Drug abuse is a complex and very individual problem, with many causes and aggravating factors. Even so, experience has shown that prevention and treatment are better strategies and, in the long run, less costly than interdiction or incarceration (Kreit 2009). The following are some suggestions and strategies for how to reduce demand for drugs:

- The top priority of any prevention program, if it is to provide a long-term solution, must be reduction of drug demand by youth. Children must be the primary focus in any substance abuse program. Achieving success requires stabilizing defective family structures, implementing school programs that create an antidrug attitude, establishing a drug-free environment, and promoting resistance training to help youth avoid drug involvement. In addition, children should be encouraged to become involved in alternative activities that can substitute for drug-abusing activity. Potential drug abusers need to be convinced that substance abuse is personally and socially damaging and unacceptable.

- Education about drug abuse must be carefully designed and customized for the target population or group. For example, education based on scare tactics is not likely to dissuade adolescents from experimenting with drugs. Adolescents are at a stage of development when they feel invincible, and graphically depicting the potential health consequences of drug and alcohol abuse has little impact. A discussion about the nature of addiction and the addiction process is more likely to influence their attitudes. Adolescents need to understand why people use drugs to appreciate the behavior patterns in themselves. Other important topics that should be discussed are how drug abuse works and why it leads to dependence. To complement drug education, adolescents also should be taught coping strategies that include effective decision-making and problem-solving skills.

- Attitudes toward drug abuse and its consequence must be changed. The drug use patterns of many people, both young and old, are strongly influenced by their peers. If individuals believe that drug abuse is glamorous and contributes to acceptance by friends and associates, the incidence of drug abuse will remain high. In contrast, if the prevailing message in society is that drug abuse is unhealthy and not socially acceptable, the incidence will be much lower.

- Replacement therapy has been shown to be a useful approach to weaning the individual off of drugs of abuse. A common example of this strategy is the use of the narcotic methadone to treat the heroin addict. Use of methadone prevents the cravings and severe effects of withdrawal routinely associated with breaking the heroin habit. Unfortunately, many heroin addicts must be maintained on methadone indefinitely. Even though methadone is easier to control and is less disruptive than heroin, one drug addiction has been substituted for another, which draws criticism. Replacement therapy certainly is not the entire answer to all drug abuse problems, but it often can provide a window of opportunity for behavioral modification so that a long-term solution to the abuse problem is possible.

■ Inoculation Strategy

The inoculation method of abuse prevention aims to protect drug users by teaching them responsibility. The emphasis is on being accountable, rational, and responsible about drug use, and informing users about the effects of drugs on both mind and bodily function. Nonalcohol parties and responsible drinkers who use designated drivers are outcomes of applying inoculation strategy.

■ Drug Courts

Drug courts are designed to deal with nonviolent, drug-abusing offenders. As of June 2014, more than 3400 drug courts were in place in the United States. More than half target adults, including DWI (driving while intoxicated) offenders and a growing number of military veterans; others address juvenile, child welfare, and different case types (National Institute of Justice [NIJ] 2015). Drug courts integrate mandatory drug testing, substance abuse treatment, sanctions, and incentives in a judicially supervised setting. These courts hold offenders accountable for their actions and provide them with the support and tools necessary to rebuild their lives and become productive members of the community.

Recent statistics indicate that drug courts are effective. For example, the National Institute of Justice's Multisite Adult Drug Court Evaluation (National Criminal Justice Referral Service [NCJRS] 2015) found that:

- Participants reported less drug use (56% vs. 76%) and were less likely to test positive (29% vs. 46%) than comparable offenders.
- Participants reported less criminal activity (40% vs. 53%) and had fewer rearrests (52% vs. 62%) than comparable offenders.
- Treatment investment costs were higher for participants, but because there was less recidivism, drug courts saved an average of $5680 to $6208 per offender overall.

An example of the many public awareness advertisements that caution against drinking and driving.

Current and Future Drug Use

During the administrations of former Presidents Ronald Reagan and George H. W. Bush (1980–1992), the official policy of the U.S. federal government included a "get tough" attitude about drug abuse. Slogans such as "Just Say No" and "War on Drugs" reflected the frustration of a public that had been victimized by escalating crime (many incidents were drug related); personally touched by drug tragedies in families, at work, or with associates and friends; and economically strained by dealing with the cost of the problem.

Much remains to be accomplished in the fight against substance abuse. For example:

- National Survey on Drug Use and Health (NSDUH) data indicate that, in 2013, 9.4% of individuals 12 years or older had used illicit drugs during the month prior to the survey (SAMHSA 2014).
- In 2011, the overall rate of current illicit drug use among persons aged 12 or older (9.4%) was similar to the rates in 2010 (8.9%) and 2012 (9.2%), but it was higher than the rates in 2002–2009 and 2011 (SAMHSA 2014).

Fighting the War on Drugs is clearly difficult and complex. Despite substantial efforts, significant problems still exist and require the attention of politicians, clinicians, law enforcement agencies, families, counselors, and all concerned citizens.

■ Drug Legalization Debate

The persistence of the drug abuse problem and the high cost in dollars and frustration of waging the War on Drugs have energized the ongoing debate regarding legalizing the use of drugs of abuse. Proponents of legalization are no longer limited to libertarians and so-called academic intellectuals. Increasingly, this group includes representatives of a distressed law enforcement system. For example, some discontented judges whose courts are swamped with drug cases and police officers who spend much of their on-duty time dealing with and arresting abusers have asserted that many of the drug laws are wasteful and/or ineffective.

Individuals and groups promoting the legalization of all substances of abuse commonly cite several arguments. For instance, proponents often contend that if drugs were legalized violence and crime would become less frequent. These individuals point out that users often commit crimes to pay for illicit drugs. If these drugs were legal, then the tremendous profits associated with drugs because of their illegal status would disappear and, once gone, the black market and criminal activity associated with drugs would be eliminated. Furthermore, legalization would decrease law enforcement costs by eliminating the backlog of drug-related court cases and reduce populations in overcrowded prisons.

Conversely, opponents of drug legalization believe that legalization would lead to increased availability of drugs, which would, in turn, lead to increased use. They point out that the use of drugs, especially methamphetamine, phencyclidine (PCP), and cocaine, is often associated with violent criminal behavior. Numerous studies demonstrate the links among drugs, violence, and crime; the link between alcohol, a legal substance, and crime is also well documented. According to legalization opponents, drug use would merely increase the incidence of crime, even if the drugs were legally purchased. Accordingly, the economic (as well as social) cost to society would increase.

Legalization proponents claim that making illicit drugs licit would not cause more of these substances to be consumed, nor would addiction increase. They note correctly that many individuals use drugs in moderation. Furthermore, many would choose not to use drugs, just as many abstain currently from tobacco and alcohol. Opponents contend that if drugs were made licit and more widely available, usage and addiction rates would increase. These individuals contend that legalizing drugs sends a message that drug use (like tobacco and alcohol) is acceptable and encourages drug use among individuals who currently do not use drugs.

Proponents claim that drug legalization would allow users the right to practice a diversity of consciousness. Just as diversity of race, ethnicity, sexual orientation, religion, and other varied lifestyles is allowed, legalization of drugs would permit individuals to alter their consciousness without legal repercussions as long as they do not harm or threaten the safety and security of others. Moreover, proponents argue that education, health care, road building, and a wide array of other worthwhile causes would benefit from the taxes that could be raised by legalizing and then taxing drugs. They argue that the United States has spent billions of dollars to control drug production, trafficking, and use with few, if any,

positive results. They contend that the money spent on drug control should be shifted to other, more productive endeavors.

Opponents believe that health and societal costs would increase with drug legalization. It has been predicted that drug treatment costs; hospitalization for long-term, drug-related diseases; and treatment of the consequences of drug-associated family violence would further burden our already strapped healthcare system. Such a policy would increase costs to society due to greater medical and social problems resulting from greater availability and increased use of drugs. Two of the most frequently abused substances, alcohol and tobacco, are both legal and readily available today. These two substances cause more medical, social, and personal problems than all the illicit drugs of abuse combined.

Although arguments for both sides warrant consideration, extreme policies are not likely to be implemented; instead, a compromise will most probably be adopted. For example, areas potentially ripe for compromise include the following (Kalant 1992):

- *Selective legalization*: Eliminate harsh penalties for those drugs of abuse that are the safest and least likely to cause addiction, such as marijuana.
- *Control of substances of abuse by prescription or through specially approved outlets*: Have the availability of the illegal drugs controlled by physicians and trained clinicians rather than by law enforcement agencies.
- *Discretionary enforcement of drug laws*: Allow greater discretion by judicial systems for prosecution and sentencing of those who violate drug laws. Such decisions would be based on perceived criminal intent.

In conclusion, drug legalization remains a highly divisive issue in the United States. Although legalization would lessen the number of drug violators involved in the criminal justice system, the problems associated with legalizing current illicit drugs cause many members in our society to view this idea with disfavor. As stated earlier, opponents of legalization argue that we already have substantial problems with licit drugs such as tobacco and alcohol. According to them, legalizing additional types of drugs would produce a substantial increase in the rate of addiction and in the social and psychological problems associated with drug use. Proponents favoring legalization assert that,

Substance abuse can lead to serious legal problems.

despite the current drug laws and severe penalties for drug use, people continue to use illicit drugs.

▌ Drug Testing

In response to the demand by society to stop the spread of drug abuse and its adverse consequences, drug testing has been implemented in some situations to detect drug users. The most common types of drug testing use breathalyzers and laboratory studies of urine, blood, and hair specimens. Urine and blood testing are preferred for detecting drug use. Hair specimen testing must overcome technical problems, including complications from hair treatment (e.g., hair coloring) and environmental absorption, before hair can be used as a definitive proof of drug use.

The drugs of abuse most frequently tested for are marijuana, cocaine, amphetamines, narcotics, sedatives, and anabolic steroids. Drug testing is often mandatory in some professions in which public safety is a concern (such as airline pilots, railroad workers, law enforcement employees, and medical personnel) and for employees of some organizations and companies as part of general policy (such as the military, many federal agencies, and some private companies). Drug testing also often is mandatory for participants in sports at all levels—whether in high school, college, international, or professional competition—to prevent unfair advantages that might result from the pharmacological effects of these drugs and to discourage the spread of drug abuse among

athletes. Likewise, drug testing is used routinely by law enforcement agencies to assist in the prosecution of those believed to violate drug abuse laws. Finally, drug testing is used by health professionals to assess the success of drug abuse treatment—that is, to determine whether a dependent patient is diminishing his or her drug use or has experienced a relapse in drug abuse habits.

Drug testing to identify drug offenders is usually accomplished by analyzing body fluids (in particular urine), although other approaches (such as analysis of expired air for alcohol) are also used. To understand the accuracy of these tests, several factors should be considered:

- *Testing must be standardized and conducted efficiently.* To interpret testing results reliably, it is essential that fluid samples be collected, processed, and tested using standard procedures. Guidelines for proper testing procedures have been established by federal regulatory agencies as well as scientific organizations. Deviations from established protocols can result in false positives (tests that indicate a drug is present when none was used), false negatives (tests that are unable to detect a drug that is present), or inaccurate assessments of drug levels.
- *Sample collection and processing must be done accurately.* In many cases, drug testing can have punitive consequences (e.g., athletes cannot compete or employees are fired if results are positive). Consequently, drug users often attempt to outsmart the system. Some individuals have attempted to avoid submitting their own drug-containing urine for testing by filling specimen bottles with "clean" urine from artificial bladders hidden under clothing or in the vagina or by introducing "clean" urine into their own bladders just before collection. To confirm the legitimacy of the specimen, it often is necessary to have the urine collection witnessed directly by a trustworthy observer. To ensure that the fluid specimens are not tampered with, samples should be immediately coded and movement of each sample from site to site during analysis should be documented and confirmed.
- *Just as it is important that testing identify individuals who are using drugs, it is also important that those who have not used drugs not be wrongfully accused.* To avoid false positives, all samples that test positive in screening (usually via fast and inexpensive procedures) should be analyzed again using more

accurate, sensitive, and sophisticated analytical procedures to confirm the results.

• *Confounding factors that interfere with the accuracy of the testing can be inadvertently or deliberately present.* For example, excessive intake of fluid or use of diuretics increases the volume of urine formed and decreases the concentration of drugs, making them more difficult to detect.

The dramatic increase in drug testing since 1985 has caused some experts to question its value in dealing with drug abuse problems. Drug testing often is linked exclusively to punitive consequences, such as disqualification from athletic competition, loss of job, or even fines and imprisonment. Use of drug testing in such negative ways often does little to diminish the number of drug abusers or deal with their personal problems. However, drug-testing programs can have positive consequences by identifying drug users who require professional care. After being referred for drug rehabilitation, the offender can be monitored using drug testing to confirm the desired response to therapy. In addition, tests can identify individuals who put others in jeopardy because of their drug abuse habits when they perform tasks that are dangerously impaired by the effects of these drugs (e.g., airline pilots, train engineers, and truck drivers).

■ Pragmatic Drug Policies

Several principles for a pragmatic drug policy emerge from a review of past drug policies and an understanding of the drug-related frustrations of today. To create drug policies that work, the following suggestions are offered:

• Given the difficulties and high cost of efforts to prevent illicit drugs from reaching the market, it is logical to deemphasize interdiction and instead stress programs that reduce demand. To reduce demand, drug education and drug treatment must be top priorities.

• Government and society need to better understand the role played by law in their efforts to reduce drug addiction. Antidrug laws by themselves do not eliminate drug problems; indeed, they may even create significant social difficulties (e.g., as did the Prohibition laws banning all alcohol use). Used properly and selectively, however, laws can reinforce and communicate expected social behavior and values (e.g., laws against public drunkenness or against driving a vehicle under the influence of alcohol).

• Programs that employ public consensus should be implemented more effectively to campaign against drug abuse. For example, antismoking campaigns demonstrate the potential success that could be achieved by programs that alter drug abuse behavior. Similar approaches can be used to change public attitudes about drugs through education without making moral judgments and employing crusading tactics. Society needs to engage in more collaborative programs in which drug-using individuals and their families, communities, and helping agencies work together.

LEARNING PORTFOLIO

Key Terms

Discussion Questions

1. Describe the FDA approval process for assessing the safety and efficacy of a newly developed drug. What are advantages and disadvantages of this process?
2. Identify the principal legislative initiatives that mandate that drugs be proven safe or effective.
3. What are the principal advantages and disadvantages of switching products from prescription to OTC status?
4. What could account for the vast differences in attitudes and opinions regarding drug use and the law voiced by drug users/abusers and nonusers of drugs?
5. Would decriminalization of illicit drug use increase or decrease drug-related social problems? Justify your answer.
6. Compare and contrast supply reduction, demand reduction, and inoculation strategies for dealing with drug abuse.
7. List the principal arguments for and against legalizing drugs of abuse such as marijuana and cocaine.

Summary

1. Societies have evolved to believe that they have the right to protect themselves from the damaging impact of drug use and abuse. Consequently, governments, including that of the United States, have passed laws and implemented programs to prevent social damage from inappropriate drug use. In addition, such societies have come to expect that drugs are effective.
2. The 1906 Pure Food and Drug Act was not a strong law, but it required manufacturers to include on labels the amounts of alcohol, morphine, opium, cocaine, heroin, and marijuana extract in each product. It represented the first real attempt to make consumers aware of the active contents in the drug products they were consuming.
3. The 1938 Federal Food, Drug, and Cosmetic Act gave the FDA control over drug safety.
4. The 1951 Durham–Humphrey Amendment to the Food, Drug, and Cosmetic Act made a formal distinction between prescription and nonprescription drugs.
5. The Kefauver–Harris Amendment of 1962 required manufacturers to demonstrate both the efficacy and the safety of their products.
6. Drugs to be considered for marketing must first be tested for safety in animals. Following these initial tests, if the FDA favorably reviews the drug, it is given IND status. It then generally undergoes three phases of human clinical testing before receiving final FDA approval.

7. In 1972, the FDA initiated a program to ensure that all OTC drugs were safe and effective. Panels were selected to evaluate the safety and effectiveness of OTC drug ingredients. Each of the ingredients was classified into a particular category: I, II, or III.

8. The switching policy of the FDA allows the agency to review prescription drugs and evaluate their suitability as OTC products.

9. Controversy exists as to how best to reduce substance abuse. A principal strategy used by governmental agencies to achieve this objective is interdiction; the majority of money used to fight drug abuse is spent on trying to stop and confiscate drug supplies. Experience has proved that interdiction is often ineffective. To reduce drug abuse, demand for these substances must be diminished. Youth must be a top priority in any substance abuse program. Finally, education should be used to change attitudes toward drug abuse and its consequences. Potential drug abusers need to be convinced that substance abuse is personally and socially damaging and is unacceptable.

10. Major strategies for combating drug use and abuse are supply reduction, demand reduction, and inoculation. Supply reduction involves using drug laws to control the manufacture and distribution of classified drugs. Demand reduction aims to reduce the actual demand for drugs by working mainly with youth and teaching them to resist drugs. Inoculation aims to protect potential drug users by teaching them responsibility and explaining the effects of drugs on bodily and mental functioning.

11. Drug courts are designed to deal with nonviolent, drug-abusing offenders. They require substance abuse treatment and implement sanctions in a judicially supervised program. This emerging strategy has had positive social and economic impacts.

12. In response to the demand by society to stop the spread of drug abuse and its adverse consequences, drug testing has been implemented in some situations to detect drug users. Common drug testing uses breathalyzers and analysis of urine, blood, and hair specimens. Urine and blood testing are the preferred methods of testing for drug use. Hair specimen testing must overcome a number of technical problems, including complications caused by hair treatment and environmental absorption, before it can be used as a definitive proof of drug use.

References

Federal Bureau of Investigation (FBI). "Crime in the United States 2012." 2013. Available https://www.fbi.gov/about-us/cjis/ucr/crime-in-the-u.s/2012/crime-in-the-u.s.-2012/persons-arrested/persons-arrested

Food and Drug Administration (FDA). "Promoting Safe and Effective Drugs for 100 Years." 2009a. Available http://www.fda.gov/AboutFDA/WhatWeDo/History/ProductRegulation/PromotingSafeandEffectiveDrugsfor100Years/default.htm

Food and Drug Administration (FDA). "This Week in FDA History—May 29, 1911." 2009b. Available http://www.fda.gov/AboutFDA/WhatWeDo/History/ThisWeek/ucm117875.htm

Food and Drug Administration (FDA). "This Week in FDA History—Oct. 26, 1951." 2009c. Available http://www.fda.gov/AboutFDA/WhatWeDo/History/ThisWeek/ucm117875.htm

Food and Drug Administration (FDA). "Now Available Without a Prescription." 2011. Available http://www.fda.gov/Drugs/ResourcesForYou/Consumers/ucm143547.htm

Food and Drug Administration (FDA). "50 Years: The Kefauver-Harris Amendments." 2012a. Available http://www.fda.gov/Drugs/NewsEvents/ucm320924.htm

Food and Drug Administration (FDA). "FDA History—Part II." 2012b. Available http://www.fda.gov/AboutFDA/WhatWeDo/History/Origin/ucm054826.htm

Food and Drug Administration (FDA). "How Chemists Pushed for Consumer Protection—The Food and Drugs Act of 1906." 2012c. Available http://www.fda.gov/AboutFDA/WhatWeDo/History/CentennialofFDA/Chemistsandthe1906Act/ucm126648.htm

Food and Drug Administration (FDA). "About the Office of Scientific Investigations." 2014a. Available http://www.fda.gov/AboutFDA/CentersOffices/OfficeofMedicalProductsandTobacco/CDER/ucm091393.htm

Food and Drug Administration (FDA). "Accelerated Approval." 2014b. Available http://www.fda.gov/ForPatients/Approvals/Fast/ucm405447.htm

Food and Drug Administration (FDA). "Breakthrough Therapy." 2014c. Available http://www.fda.gov/ForPatients/Approvals/Fast/ucm405397.htm

Food and Drug Administration (FDA). "CDER Approved Many Innovative Drugs in 2014." 2014d. Available http://blogs.fda.gov/fdavoice/index.php/tag/fast-track/

Food and Drug Administration (FDA). "Fast Track." 2014e. Available http://www.fda.gov/ForPatients/Approvals/Fast/ucm405399.htm

Food and Drug Administration (FDA). "Priority Review." 2014f. Available http://www.fda.gov/ForPatients/Approvals/Fast/ucm405405.htm

Food and Drug Administration (FDA). "Significant Dates in U.S. Food and Drug Law History." 2014g. Available http://www.fda.gov/AboutFDA/WhatWeDo/History/Milestones/ucm128305.htm

Food and Drug Administration (FDA). "FDA Marks Orphan Drug Law Milestone." 2015a. Available http://www.fda.gov/ForIndustry/DevelopingProductsforRareDiseasesConditions/OOPDNewsArchive/ucm333527.htm

Food and Drug Administration (FDA). "Frequently Asked Questions: Breakthrough Therapies." 2015b. Available http://www.fda.gov/RegulatoryInformation/Legislation/SignificantAmendmentstotheFDCA

Food and Drug Administration (FDA). "Prescription Drug Advertising: Questions and Answers." 2015c. Available http://www.fda.gov/Drugs/ResourcesForYou/Consumers/PrescriptionDrugAdvertising/UCM076768.htm

Food and Drug Administration (FDA). "The Impact of Direct to Consumer Advertising." 2015d. Available http://www.fda.gov/Drugs/ResourcesForYou/Consumers/ucm143562.htm

Hunter, J. R., D. L. Rosen, and R. DeChristoforo. "How FDA Expedites Evaluation of Drugs." *Welcome Trends in Pharmacy* (January 1993): 2–9.

Johnston, L. D., P. M. O'Malley, J. G. Bachman, and J. E. Schulenberg. *Monitoring the Future: National Survey Results on Drug Use, 1975–2014. Volume 2, College Students and Adults ages 19–55.* Ann Arbor, MI: Institute for Social Research, University of Michigan, Ann Arbor, 2015.

Kalant, H. "Formulating Policies on the Non-medical Use of Cocaine." In *Cocaine: Scientific and Social Dimensions.*

Ciba Foundation Symposium 166, 261–276. New York: Wiley, 1992.

Kreit, A. *Toward a Public Health Approach to Drug Policy.* Washington, DC: American Constitutional Society for Law and Policy, March 2009.

Motl, S., S. J. Miller, and P. Burns. "Established by FDA to Expedite Patient Access to Medications." *American Journal of Health-System Pharmacy* (February 2003): 339–345.

National Criminal Justice Referral Service (NCJRS). "Drug Courts—Facts and Figures." Available http://www.ncjrs.gov/spotlight/drug_courts/facts.html

National Institutes of Justice (NIJ). "Drug Courts." 2015. Available http://www.nij.gov/topics/courts/drug-courts/Pages/welcome.aspx

National Library of Medicine (NLM). "Dr. Francis Kathleen Oldham Kesley." 2015. Available https://www.nlm.nih.gov/changingthefaceofmedicine/physicians/biography_182.html

Office of National Drug Control Policy (ONDCP). "National Drug Control Budget FY 2015 Funding Highlights." 2014. Available https://www.whitehouse.gov/sites/default/files/ondcp/about-content/fy_2015_budget_highlights_-_final.pdf

Substance Abuse and Mental Health Services Administration (SAMHSA). *Results from the 2013 National Survey on Drug Use and Health: Summary of National Findings.* NSDUH Series H-48, HHS Publication No. (SMA) 14-4863. Rockville, MD: Substance Abuse and Mental Health Services Administration, 2014.

Temin, P. *Taking Your Medicine: Drug Regulation in the United States.* Cambridge, MA: Harvard University Press, 1980.

The Pew Charitable Trusts. "Persuading the Prescribers: Pharmaceutical Industry Marketing Its Influence on Physicians and Patients." 2012. Available http://www.pewtrusts.org/en/research-and-analysis/fact-sheets/2013/11/11/persuading-the-prescribers-pharmaceutical-industry-marketing-and-its-influence-on-physicians-and-patients

Tufts Center for Drug Development. "Cost to Develop and Win Marketing Approval for a New Drug Is $2.6 Billion." 18 November 2014. Available http://csdd.tufts.edu/news/complete_story/pr_tufts_csdd_2014_cost_study

U.S. Department of Justice (USDOJ). *Drugs of Abuse: A DEA Resource Guide.* 2011. Available http://www.justice.gov/dea/docs/drugs_of_abuse_2011.pdf

© Daisy Daisy/Shutterstock, Inc.

Did You Know?

▶ The brain is composed of approximately 100 billion neurons that communicate with one another by releasing chemical messengers called neurotransmitters.

▶ Many drugs exert their effects by interacting with specialized protein regions in cell membranes called receptors.

▶ Some natural chemicals produced by the body have the same effect as narcotic drugs; these chemicals are called endorphins.

▶ The body produces a natural substance called anandamide that has effects similar to those produced by marijuana and drugs that are related to THC (tetrahydrocannabinol).

▶ The illegal drug products known as "Spice" have ingredients that alter the cannabinoid systems of the brain.

▶ Drugs that affect the neurotransmitter dopamine usually alter perception of pleasure, mental state, and motor activity and can cause addiction behavior.

▶ The hypothalamus is the principal brain region for control of the endocrine system.

Learning Objectives

On completing this chapter you should be able to:

❭ Explain the similarities and differences between the nervous and endocrine systems.

❭ Describe how a neuron functions.

❭ Describe the role of receptors in mediating the effects of hormones, neurotransmitters, and drugs.

❭ Distinguish between receptor agonists and antagonists, and describe how their effects relate to those of neurotransmitters.

❭ Describe the different features of the principal neurotransmitters associated with drug addiction.

❭ Outline the principal components of the central nervous system, and explain their general functions.

❭ Identify which brain areas are most likely to be affected by drugs of abuse and how these effects contribute to drug dependence.

❭ Be familiar with the endorphin and cannabinoid nervous systems and their role in substance abuse and recent drug abuse problems (e.g., Spice).

❭ Distinguish between the sympathetic and parasympathetic nervous systems.

❭ Identify the principal components of the endocrine system.

❭ Explain how and why anabolic steroids are abused and the health impact attributed to abuse.

Introduction

Why is your body susceptible to the influence of drugs, some natural products (e.g., herbs), and other substances? Part of the answer is that your body is constantly adjusting and responding to its environment in an effort to maintain internal stability and balance. This delicate process of dynamic adjustments—**homeostasis**—is necessary to optimize bodily functions and is essential for survival. These continual adjustments help to maintain physiological and psychological balances and are mediated by the release of endogenous regulatory chemicals (such as neurotransmitters from neurons and **hormones** from glands). Many drugs, including substances that are abused, exert intended or unexpected effects by altering the activity of these regulatory substances, which changes the status and function of the **nervous system** and/or **endocrine system** and associated organs. For example, all drugs of abuse, including new "synthetic designer" psychoactive substances, profoundly influence mental states by altering the chemical messages of the neurotransmitters in the brain, and some alter endocrine function by affecting the release and activity of hormones. By understanding the mechanisms of how drugs alter these body processes, we are able to distinguish drug benefits and risks and devise therapeutic strategies to deal with related biomedical problems.

This chapter is divided into two sections. The first section is a brief overview that introduces the basic concept of how the body is controlled by nervous systems and explains why drugs influence the elements of these systems. The second section is intended for readers who desire a more in-depth understanding of the anatomical, physiological, and biochemical basis of homeostatic functions. In this second section, the elements of the nervous system are discussed in greater detail, followed by an examination of its major divisions: the central, peripheral, and autonomic nervous systems (CNS, PNS, and ANS, respectively). The components and operation of the endocrine system also are discussed in specific relation to drugs. The use of anabolic steroids is presented as an example of drugs of abuse that have powerful effects on the endocrine system.

Overview of Homeostasis and Drug Actions

The body continuously adjusts to both internal and external changes in the environment. To cope with these adjustments, the body systems include elaborate self-regulating mechanisms. The name given to this compensatory action is *homeostasis*, which refers to the maintenance of internal stability or equilibrium of the body and its functions. For example, homeostatic mechanisms control the response of the brain to changes in the physical, social, and psychological environments, as well as regulate physiological factors such as body temperature, metabolism, nutrient utilization, and organ functions. The two principal systems that help human beings maintain homeostasis are the nervous system (discussed in Section 1) and the endocrine system (described in Section 2). They are independent yet work together in a coordinated manner, and often both are influenced by common factors, such as drugs.

Section 1: Introduction to Nervous Systems

All nervous systems consist of specialized cells called **neurons** and **glia** (or non-neuronal cells). The glia are supporting cells and are critical for protecting and providing sustenance to the neurons. Although the glia are necessary for survival of the neurons and proper functioning of the nervous systems, because they do not appear to be direct targets of the drugs of abuse this cell population will not be discussed in detail. Neurons are

KEY TERMS

homeostasis
maintenance of internal stability; often biochemical in nature

hormones
chemical messengers released into the blood by glands

nervous system
relating to the brain, spinal cord, neurons, and their associated elements

endocrine system
relating to hormones, their functions, and sources

neurons
specialized nerve cells that make up the nervous system and release neurotransmitters

glia
supporting cells that are critical for protecting and providing sustenance to the neurons

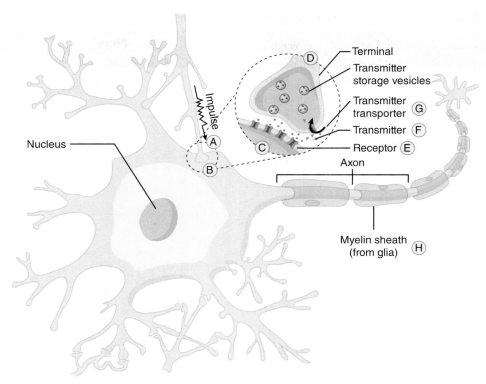

FIGURE 4.1   The process of sending messages by neurons. The receiving region (B) of the neuron is activated by an incoming message (A) near the neuronal cell body. The neuron sends an electricity-like chemical impulse (C) down the axon to its terminal (D). The impulse causes the release of neurotransmitters (F) from their storage vesicles out of the terminal to transmit the message to the target. This is done when the neurotransmitter molecules activate the receptors on the membranes of the target cell (E). The activated receptors then cause a change to occur in intracellular functions of the target cell. The transmitters often are taken back up into the terminal by a transmitter transporter (G). Glial cells (glia) surround the neurons and their axons as a myelin sheath (H) providing insulation to enhance their abilities to send impulses and to support their other cellular functions.

responsible for conducting the homeostatic functions of the brain and other parts of the nervous system by receiving and sending information. The transfer of messages by neurons includes electrochemical processes that involve the following elements (see **Figure 4.1**):

- Glia surround the neuron and its processes to support its ability to send chemical messages by insulating with myelin sheaths (H); they also provide nutrients for the neuron.
- The receiving region of the neuron (B) is affected by an electrochemical message (A) that either excites it (causing the neuron to send its own message) or inhibits it (preventing the neuron from sending a message).
- If the message is excitatory, a chemical impulse (A) (much like electricity) moves from the receiving region of the neuron, down its wirelike processes (called **axons**), to the sending region (called the terminal) (D). When the electrochemical impulse reaches

the terminal, chemical messengers called neurotransmitters (F) are released (for examples see **Table 4.1**).
- The neurotransmitters travel very short distances and bind to specialized and specific receiving proteins called **receptors** on the outer membranes of their target cells (E).
- Activation of receptors by their associated neurotransmitters causes a change in the activity of the target cell. The target cells can be other neurons or cells that make up organs (such as the heart, lungs, kidneys, and so on), muscles, or glands.

KEY TERMS

axon
an extension of the neuronal cell body along which electrochemical signals travel

receptors
special proteins in a membrane that are activated by natural substances or drugs to alter cell function

TABLE 4.1 Common Neurotransmitters of the Brain Affected by Drugs of Abuse

Neurotransmitter	Type of Effect	Major Central Nervous System Changes	Drugs of Abuse That Influence the Neurotransmitter (Drug Action)
Dopamine	Inhibitory–excitatory	Euphoria Agitation Paranoia	Amphetamines (e.g., methamphetamine), cocaine (activate), "bath salt" active ingredients
GABA (gamma-aminobutyric acid)	Inhibitory	Sedation Relaxation Drowsiness Depression	Alcohol, diazepam-type, barbiturates (activate)
Serotonin	Inhibitory	Sleep Relaxation Sedation	LSD (activate), Ecstasy/MDMA
Acetylcholine	Excitatory–inhibitory	Mild euphoria Excitation Insomnia	Tobacco, nicotine (stimulate)
Endorphins	Inhibitory	Mild euphoria Blockage of pain Slow respiration	Narcotics (activate)
Anandamide	Inhibitory	Relaxation Increased sense of well-being	Tetrahydrocannabinol/marijuana (stimulate), Spice active ingredients

Neurons are highly versatile and, depending on their functions, can send discrete excitatory or inhibitory messages to their target cells or organs. Neurons are distinguished by the types of chemical substances they release as neurotransmitters to send their messages. The neurotransmitters represent a wide variety of molecules that are classified according to their functional association as well as their ability to stimulate or inhibit the activity of target neurons, organs, muscles, and glands. They are discussed in greater detail in Section 2.

An example of a common neurotransmitter used by neurons in the brain to send messages is the substance dopamine. When released from neurons associated with the pleasure center in the brain, dopamine causes substantial euphoria by activating its receptor on target neurons (Berridge and Kringlebach 2015). This effect is relevant to drugs of abuse because the addictive properties of these substances (e.g., amphetamine or cocaine) relate to their ability to stimulate dopamine release from these neurons, and thus cause pleasant euphoric effects in the user (Kishi et al. 2014).

It is important to understand that many of the desired and undesired effects of psychoactive drugs (which alter the mental functions of the brain), such as the drugs of abuse, are due to their ability to alter the neurotransmitters associated with neurons. Some of the transmitter messenger systems most likely to be affected by drugs of abuse are listed in Table 4.1 and are discussed in greater detail in Section 2.

Section 2: Comprehensive Explanation of Homeostatic Systems

For those desiring a more complete understanding of the consequences of drug effects on the homeostatic systems of the body, this section provides an in-depth discussion of the anatomical and physiological nature and biological arrangements of the nervous and endocrine systems. Because drugs of abuse are most likely to exert their psychoactive effects on neurons and their receptor targets, the nervous system is presented

FAMILY MATTERS

What About Genes?

Research strongly suggests that at least 50% of our susceptibility to experiencing drug addiction (and maybe more for nicotine and alcohol) is determined by genes we receive from our parents. In other words, addiction vulnerabilities are often inherited, and genes at least partially explain why problems with drug abuse are much more abundant in some families. Although this is an evolving science, approximately 100 genes have already been linked to issues related to drug dependence (Drgon et al. 2010).

Although these genetic findings are very exciting to scientists and have helped us understand why drug addiction occurs, the clinical value of such discoveries is controversial. For example, the public is often skeptical about testing for, and using, genetic information in the clinical management of diseases, especially those with negative overtones such as drug addiction. In addition, physicians and other clinicians are not sure how they can use genetic information in their everyday practices. However, despite the reluctance by both patients and practitioners, genetics is likely to play a critical role in the future development of more effective management of drug abuse problems. For example, once the genetic factors that cause addiction vulnerabilities are identified and mapped it will be possible to do genetic screening to identify individuals

who are at greatest risk for developing drug abuse disorders. Such genetic screens will not only identify a high-risk person, but also provide information as to what the vulnerability is and how to best prevent or treat the problems. It is likely that such analysis will be part of a more comprehensive and integrated genetic screen that tests for vulnerability to hundreds of common psychiatric and physical diseases and will provide a general readout of a person's potential for physical and emotional health (Learn.Genetics 2013).

Courtesy of Lisa G. Shaffer, Signature Genomic Laboratories.

Data from Drgon, T., P. Zhang, C. Johnson, D. Walther, J. Hess, M. Nino, and G. R. Url. "Genome Wide Association for Addiction: Replicated Results and Comparisons of Two Analytic Approaches." *PLoS One* 5 (2010): e8832; Learn.Genetics. "Genes and Addiction." University of Utah, Genetic Science Learning Center. 2015. Available http://learn.genetics.utah.edu/content/addiction/genes/

first and in greater depth, followed by a briefer description of endocrine function.

■ The Building Blocks of the Nervous System

The nervous system is composed of the brain, spinal cord, and all the neurons that connect to other organs and tissues of the body. Nervous systems enable an organism to receive information about the internal and external environment and to make the appropriate responses essential to survival. Considerable money and scientific effort are currently being dedicated to exploring the mechanisms whereby the nervous system functions and processes information, resulting in frequent exciting discoveries. Much of the exciting new knowledge about this system comes from the

study of **genetics** (i.e., the study of cellular DNA and its functions) and **molecular biology** (i.e., the study of cellular functions and their regulation). These disciplines include research tools that help us to understand how genes regulate factors such as inheritability and the role of gene expression in determining risk factors for drug addiction that are passed from parents to offspring (Jones and Comer 2015; Learn.Genetics 2015; see "Family Matters: What About Genes?").

KEY TERMS

genetics
study of cellular DNA and its functions

molecular biology
study of cellular functions and their regulation

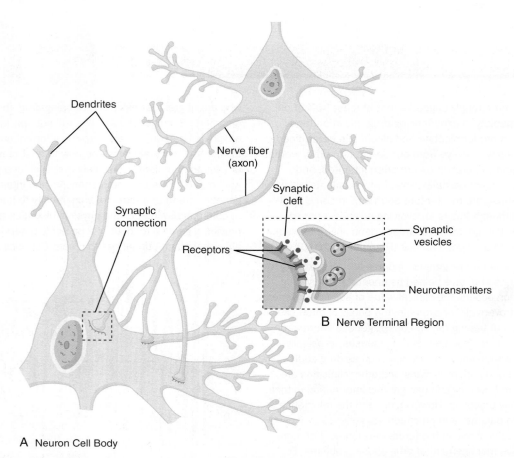

FIGURE 4.2 (A) Each neuron may have many synaptic connections. They are designed to deliver short bursts of a chemical transmitter substance into the synaptic cleft, where the substance can act on the surface receptors of the receiving nerve cell membrane. Before release, molecules of the chemical neurotransmitter are stored in numerous vesicles, or sacs. (B) A close-up of the synaptic terminals, showing the synaptic vesicles. The gap between the synaptic terminal and the target membrane is the synaptic cleft.

THE NEURON: THE BASIC STRUCTURAL UNIT OF THE NERVOUS SYSTEM

The fundamental building block of the nervous system is the nerve cell, or neuron. Each neuron in the CNS (brain and spinal cord) is in close proximity with other neurons, forming a complex network. The human brain contains about 100 billion neurons, each of which is composed of similar components but with different shapes, sizes, and distinguishing neurochemistry. Neurons do not form a continuous cellular network. They always remain separate, never actually touching. The typical point of communication between one neuron and another is called a **synapse**. On average, each neuron in the brain makes about 2000 synaptic connections with neurons nearby and sometimes with those located many millimeters away in other brain regions. The gap (called the **synaptic cleft**) between neurons at a synapse may be only 0.00002 millimeters wide, but it is essential for proper functioning of the nervous system (see **Figure 4.2**).

The neuron has a cell body with a nucleus and receiving regions called **dendrites**, which are short, treelike branches that are influenced by information from the environment and surrounding neurons, such as released neurotransmitters.

The axon of a neuron is a threadlike extension that receives information from the dendrites near the cell body, in the form of an electrochemical

KEY TERMS

synapse
site of communication between a message-sending neuron and its message-receiving target cell

synaptic cleft
a minute gap between the neuron and target cell, across which neurotransmitters travel

dendrites
short branches of neurons that receive transmitter signals

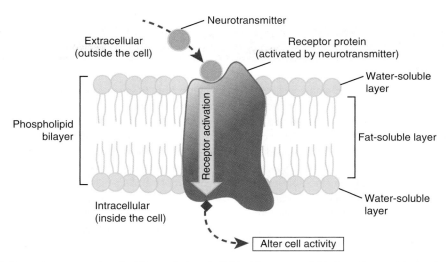

FIGURE 4.3 Cell membranes consist of a bilayer of phospholipids. The water-soluble layers are pointed outward and the fat-soluble layers are pointed toward each other. Large proteins, including receptors, float in the membrane. Some of these receptors are activated by neurotransmitters to alter the activity of the cell.

impulse; then, like an electrical wire, it transmits the impulse to the cell's terminal. Although most axons are less than 30 millimeters in length (i.e., about 1 inch), some may be quite long; for example, some axons extend from the spinal cord to the toes.

At the synapse, information is transmitted chemically to the next neuron, as shown in Figure 4.1. A similar synaptic arrangement also exists at sites of communication between neurons and target cells in organs, muscles, and glands; that is, neurotransmitters are released from the message-sending neurons and activate receptors located in the membranes of message-receiving target cells.

There are two types of synapses: excitatory and inhibitory. The *excitatory synapse* initiates an impulse in the receiving neuron when stimulated, thereby causing release of neurotransmitters or increasing activity in the target cell. The *inhibitory synapse* diminishes the likelihood of an impulse in the receiving neuron or reduces the activity in other target cells. A receiving neuron or target cell may have thousands of synapses connecting it to other neurons and their excitatory or inhibitory information (see Figure 4.2A). The final cellular activity is a summation of these many excitatory and inhibitory synaptic signals and underscores the connectivity and complexity of these systems.

THE NATURE OF DRUG RECEPTORS

Receptors are special proteins located in the membranes of receiving neurons and other target cells (see **Figure 4.3**). They help regulate the activity of cells in the nervous system and throughout the body. These selective protein sites on specific cells act as transducers to communicate the messages

caused by endogenous messenger substances (chemicals produced and released within the body), such as neurotransmitters and hormones. The receptors process the complex information each cell receives as it attempts to maintain metabolic stability, or homeostasis, and fulfill its functional role (Putney and Askari 2013). Many drugs used therapeutically and almost all drugs of abuse exert their effects on the body by directly or indirectly interacting (either to activate or antagonize) with these receptors.

Understanding how receptors interact with specific drugs has led to some interesting results. For example, **opiate receptors** (sites of action by narcotic drugs such as heroin and morphine) are naturally present in animal and human brains (Befort 2015). Why would human and animal brains have receptors for opiate narcotics, which are plant chemicals? Discovery of the opiate receptors suggested the existence of internal (endogenous) neurotransmitter substances in the body that normally act at these receptor sites and have effects like narcotic drugs, such as codeine and morphine. This finding led to the identification of the body's own opiates, the **endorphins** (Sabatowski et al. 2004). Another endogenous system that has been discovered

KEY TERMS

opiate receptors
receptors activated by opioid narcotic drugs such as heroin and morphine

endorphins
neurotransmitters that have narcotic-like effects

PRESCRIPTION FOR ABUSE

The "Spice" of Life

"Of course, banning it will make criminals out of all the teens that use it. That's what we want, right?" This is a quote from a teenager who has used a relatively recent drug phenomenon called *Spice* or *K2* and is concerned that Spice will be outlawed by the government, making it harder, and illegal, to obtain. Its popularity is causing considerable concern among healthcare professionals and law enforcement agencies. Spice consists of products marketed as herbal incense; however, these herbs are sprayed with a variety of synthetic chemicals (more than 50 varieties) that mimic THC and, when smoked, cause adverse effects, including a marijuana-like experience. Spice products are often available in smoke shops and head shops in the United States. Little is known about their adverse effects, but their similarity to THC suggests that the pharmacological actions are likely to resemble those of marijuana. Therein lies the dilemma: because of the lack of knowledge concerning these cannabinoid-like ingredients, it is difficult for government agencies to effectively regulate Spice products. These products have enjoyed dramatic popularity with teen and young adult consumers who have come to refer to them as "legal marijuana highs." Needless to say, agencies such

as the Drug Enforcement Administration (DEA) and other federal and local law enforcement groups are concerned about the adverse effects of Spice and its likelihood to cause dependence. Despite regulatory problems, they recommend its tight control or even elimination when possible. In contrast, many young consumers and so-called personal freedom advocates believe that until there is reliable proof that Spice causes serious adverse and addicting effects they should not be deprived of using and "enjoying" these products and their diverse ingredients.

Courtesy of DEA.

Data from Aarthun, S. "Synthetic Marijuana a Growing Trend Among Teens, Authorities Say." CNN Health. 2010. Available http://www.cnn.com/2010 /HEALTH/03/23/synthetic.marijuana/index.html; Bowman, N. "No Sugar Just Spice: It's Still Not Very Nice." *Toxicology Today*. Utah Poison Control Center 17 (2015): 4; Lisi, D. "Patients May Be Using Synthetic Cannabinoids More Than You Think." *Journal of Emergency Medical Services* 39 (2014): 56–59.

because of specific receptor targets in the brain is the **cannabinoid system**. This is an example of novel CNS pathways identified and characterized because of our ability to study and understand genetics (Matsuda 1997). These include pathways that are characterized by proteins activated by THC (tetrahydrocannabinol), the active ingredient in marijuana. These cannabinoid receptors are linked to functions associated with mood, reward, motivation, pain perception,

decision making, and appetite (Befort 2015). Because of their involvement in such critical CNS functions, the cannabinoid receptors are more than just targets for marijuana. These cannabinoid receptors are activated by "designer" drugs, such as Spice, that can cause a marijuana-like effect. These drugs have been referred to as false pot, legal weed, or new marijuana (Lisi 2014; see "Prescription for Abuse: The 'Spice' of Life"), and likely can also be manipulated medically for legitimate therapeutic purposes. As with the endorphins, natural neurotransmitter substances have been discovered in the brain that selectively activate the cannabinoid receptors. These substances have a fatty-acid nature and include the substance **anandamide** (Shim 2010).

Specific receptors have also been found for the CNS depressant diazepam (Valium), which activates benzodiazepine receptors (Skolnick 2012).

KEY TERMS

cannabinoid system
biological target of tetrahydrocannabinol in marijuana

anandamide
a naturally occurring fatty-acid neurotransmitter that selectively activates cannabinoid receptors

FIGURE 4.4 Interaction of agonist and antagonist with membrane receptor. When this receptor is occupied and activated by an agonist, it can cause cellular changes. When blocked by an antagonist, the receptor cannot be activated.

Although less is known about the natural benzodiazepine system, it is likely that natural substances are also produced in the brain that mimic the effects of Valium and cause natural sedation and relaxation; however, as of yet, the identity of these Valium-like natural transmitters remains a mystery.

Much remains unknown about how receptors respond to or interact with drugs. Through the use of molecular biology techniques, many of these receptors have been found to initiate a cascade of linked chemical reactions that can change intracellular environments to produce either activation or inactivation of cellular functions and metabolism (Ferguson 2007).

Receptors that have been isolated and identified are protein molecules; it is believed that the shape of the protein is essential in regulating a drug's interaction with a cell. If the drug is the proper shape and size and has a compatible electrical charge, it may substitute for the endogenous messenger substance and activate the receptor protein by causing it to change its shape, or conform. These molecular events have given us insight into why drug abuse occurs and how to prevent and treat addiction (Koob and Volkow 2010).

AGONISTIC AND ANTAGONISTIC EFFECTS ON DRUG RECEPTORS

A drug may have two different effects on a receptor when interaction occurs: **agonistic** or **antagonistic**. As shown in **Figure 4.4**, an agonistic drug interacts with the receptor and produces some type of cellular response, whereas an antagonistic drug interacts with the receptor but prevents that response.

An agonistic drug mimics the effect of a messenger substance (such as a neurotransmitter) that is naturally produced by the body and interacts with the receptor to cause some cellular change. For example, narcotic drugs are agonists that mimic the naturally occurring endorphins and activate opiate receptors; the THC in marijuana is an agonist that activates cannabinoid receptors. An antagonist has the opposite effect: it inhibits the sequence of metabolic events that a natural substance or an agonist drug can stimulate, usually without initiating an effect itself. Thus, the drug naloxone (created to treat heroin overdoses) is an antagonist at the opiate receptors and blocks the effects of narcotic drugs, such as heroin, as well as the effects of the naturally occurring endorphins. In contrast, as of yet in the United States, there is no Food and Drug Administration (FDA)–approved antagonist for the cannabinoid receptors. The drug Rimonabant (which was developed to suppress appetite) blocks the cannabinoid receptors; however, due to significant psychiatric side effects this drug is not available in most countries for clinical use (Drugs.com 2015).

KEY TERMS

agonistic
a type of substance that activates a receptor

antagonistic
a type of substance that blocks a receptor

Other cannabinoid antagonists are being developed with the hope that they can be used clinically without serious side effects (MarketResearch.com 2015).

NEUROTRANSMITTERS: THE MESSENGERS

Many drugs affect the activity of neurotransmitters by altering their synthesis, storage, release, or deactivation (e.g., metabolism). By changing these processes, a drug may modify or block information transmitted by these neurochemical messengers. Thus, by altering the amount of neurotransmitters, such drugs can act indirectly, like agonists and antagonists, even though they do not directly change neurotransmitter receptors. They do influence the activity of these receptors by altering the amount of neurotransmitters available to naturally influence receptor function.

Experimental evidence shows that many different neurotransmitters exist, although much remains to be learned about their specific functions. These biochemical messengers are selectively released from specific neurons. Transmitters frequently altered by drugs of abuse include acetylcholine (ACh), norepinephrine, epinephrine, dopamine, serotonin, gamma-aminobutyric acid (GABA), the endorphins (peptides), and cannabinoids such as anandamide (fatty acids) (Gray and Nicoll 2015). Because of the unique shapes and chemical features, each neurotransmitter affects only its specific receptors (Boundless 2016). Drugs can also affect these receptors if they are sufficiently similar in shape to the neurotransmitters. **Figure 4.5** summarizes some of the important features of the common neurotransmitters. Neurotransmitters are inactivated after they have done their job by diffusion away from their receptor target or by metabolism (by enzymes), or they are taken back up into the neuron by selective transporter proteins. If a deactivating enzyme or the reuptake is blocked by a drug, the effect of the transmitter may be prolonged or intensified.

ACETYLCHOLINE

Large quantities of acetylcholine (ACh) are found in the brain. ACh is one of the major neurotransmitters in the autonomic portion of the peripheral nervous system (PNS), which is discussed later in the chapter.

Neurons that respond to ACh are distributed throughout the brain. Depending on the region, ACh can have either excitatory or inhibitory effects. The receptors activated by ACh have

---

Acetylcholine
Chemical type: Choline product
Location: CNS—Basal ganglia, cortex, reticular activating system
PNS—Neuromuscular junction, parasympathetic system
Action: Excitatory (nicotine receptor) and inhibitory (muscarinic receptor)

Anandamide
Chemical type: Fatty acid
Location: CNS—Cortex, cerebellum, limbic system
Other—Immune system, pain regions, reproductive system
Action: Relaxation, analgesia, hunger

Dopamine
Chemical type: Catecholamine
Location: CNS—Basal ganglia, limbic system, hypothalamus
Action: Usually inhibitory

Endorphins
Chemical type: Peptide (small protein)
Location: CNS—Basal ganglia, hypothalamus, brain stem, spinal cord
Other—Gut, cardiovascular system
Action: Inhibitory (narcotic-like effects)

Epinephrine
Chemical type: Catecholamine
Location: CNS—Minor
PNS—Adrenal glands
Action: Usually excitatory

GABA
Chemical type: Amino acid
Location: CNS—Basal ganglia, limbic system, cortex
Action: Usually inhibitory

Norepinephrine
Chemical type: Catecholamine
Location: CNS—Limbic system, cortex, hypothalamus, reticular activating system, brain stem, spinal cord
PNS—Sympathetic nervous system
Action: Usually inhibitory; some excitation

Serotonin (5HT)
Chemical type: Tryptophan-derivative
Location: CNS—Basal ganglia, limbic system, brain stem, spinal cord, cortex
Other—Gut, platelets, cardiovascular
Action: Usually inhibitory

FIGURE 4.5 Features of common neurotransmitters.

been divided into two main subtypes based on the response to two drugs derived from plants: muscarine and nicotine. Muscarine (a substance in mushrooms that causes mushroom poisoning) and similarly acting drugs activate **muscarinic** receptors.

Nicotine, whether experimentally administered or inhaled by smoking tobacco, stimulates **nicotinic** receptors.

CATECHOLAMINES

Catecholamines include the neurotransmitter compounds norepinephrine, epinephrine, and dopamine, all of which have similar chemical structures. Neurons that synthesize catecholamines convert the amino acids (building blocks of proteins) phenylalanine or tyrosine to dopamine. In some neurons, dopamine is further converted to norepinephrine and finally to epinephrine (see **Figure 4.6**).

After release, most of the catecholamines are taken back up into the neurons that released them, to be used over again; this process is called *reuptake*. An enzymatic breakdown system also metabolizes the catecholamines to inactive compounds. The reuptake process and the activity of metabolizing enzymes, especially monoamine oxidase (MAO), can be greatly affected by some of the drugs of abuse. If these deactivating enzymes or reuptake systems are blocked, the concentration of norepinephrine and dopamine may build up in the brain, significantly increasing the effect. Cocaine, for example, prevents the reuptake of norepinephrine and dopamine in the brain, resulting in continual stimulation of neuron catecholamine receptors.

NOREPINEPHRINE AND EPINEPHRINE

Although norepinephrine and epinephrine are structurally very similar, their receptors are selective and do not respond with the same intensity to either transmitter or to **sympathomimetic** drugs. Just as the receptors to ACh can be separated into muscarinic and nicotinic types, the norepinephrine and epinephrine receptors are classified into alpha and beta categories. Receiving cells may have alpha- or beta-type receptors, or both. Norepinephrine acts predominantly on alpha receptors and with less action on beta receptors.

The antagonistic (blocking) action of many drugs that act on these catecholamine receptors can be selective for alpha receptors, whereas others block only beta receptors. This distinction can be therapeutically useful. For example, beta receptors tend to stimulate the heart, whereas alpha receptors constrict blood vessels; thus, a

FIGURE 4.6 Synthetic pathway for catecholamine neurotransmitters. The starting material is the amino acid tyrosine. By enzymatic action the tyrosine becomes L-DOPA and is then converted to dopamine, followed by norepinephrine and finally epinephrine.

drug that selectively affects beta receptors can be used to treat heart ailments without directly altering the state of the blood vessels (Robertson and Biaggioni 2012).

DOPAMINE

Dopamine is a catecholamine transmitter that is particularly influenced by drugs of abuse

KEY TERMS

muscarinic
a receptor type activated by acetylcholine (ACh); usually inhibitory

nicotinic
a receptor type activated by acetylcholine (ACh); usually excitatory

catecholamines
a class of biochemical compounds including the transmitters norepinephrine, epinephrine, and dopamine

sympathomimetic
agents that mimic the effects of norepinephrine or epinephrine

FIGURE 4.7 Functional components of the central nervous system. The caudate nucleus is part of the basal ganglia and important for behavior selection and motor activity. Limbic structures include the hypothalamus, thalamus, medial forebrain bundle, and frontal lobe of the cerebrum; they are important for controlling emotions and other mental states. The insula has been identified as important for motivation.

(Deadwyler 2010; O'Brien 2006). Most, if not all, drugs that elevate mood have abuse potential or cause psychotic behaviors and alter the activity of dopamine in some way, particularly in brain regions associated with regulating mental states and reward systems. In addition, dopamine is an important transmitter in controlling movement and fine muscle activity as well as endocrine functions. Thus, because many drugs of abuse affect dopamine neurons, they can also alter all of these functions.

SEROTONIN

Serotonin (5-hydroxytryptamine, or 5HT) is synthesized in neurons and elsewhere (e.g., in the gastrointestinal tract and platelet-type blood cells) from the dietary source of tryptophan. Tryptophan is an essential amino acid, meaning that human beings do not have the ability to synthesize it and must obtain it through their diet. Like the catecholamines, serotonin is degraded by the enzyme MAO; thus, drugs that alter this enzyme affect levels of not only catecholamines, but also serotonin.

Serotonin is also found in the upper brain stem, which connects the brain and the spinal cord (see **Figure 4.7**). Axons from serotonergic neurons are distributed throughout the entire CNS. Serotonin generally inhibits action of its target neurons. One important role of the serotonergic neurons is to prevent overreaction to various stimuli. Consequently, a change in serotonergic systems can cause aggressiveness, excessive motor activity, exaggerated mood swings, insomnia, and abnormal sexual behavior. Serotonergic neurons also help regulate the release of hormones from the hypothalamus. Because many drugs of abuse affect serotonin systems, use of these drugs can interfere with these systems.

Alterations in serotonergic neurons, serotonin synthesis, and serotonin degradation have been proposed to be factors in mental illness and to contribute to the side effects of many drugs of abuse. In support of this hypothesis is the fact that drugs such as psilocybin and lysergic acid diethylamide (LSD), which have serotonin-like chemical structures, are frequently abused because of their hallucinogenic properties and can cause psychotic effects.

■ Major Divisions of the Nervous System

The nervous system can be divided into two major components: the **central nervous system (CNS)** and the **peripheral nervous system (PNS)**. The CNS consists of the brain and spinal cord (see Figure 4.7), which receive information through the input nerves of the PNS. This sensory information allows the CNS to evaluate the specific status of all organs and the general status of the body. After receiving and processing this information, the CNS reacts by regulating muscle and organ activity through the output nerves of the PNS (eMedicineHealth 2015).

The PNS is composed of neurons whose cell bodies or axons are located outside the brain or spinal cord. It consists of input and output nerves to the CNS. The PNS input to the brain and spinal cord conveys sensory information such as pain, pressure, and temperature, whereas its output activities are separated into somatic types (control of voluntary muscles) and autonomic types (control of unconscious functions, such as essential organ [e.g., heart] and gland [e.g., adrenal gland] activity).

THE CENTRAL NERVOUS SYSTEM

The human brain is an integrating (information processing) and storage device with abilities unequaled by the most complex computers. It not only can handle a great deal of information simultaneously from the senses but also can evaluate and modify the response to the information rapidly. Although the brain weighs only 3 pounds, its 100 billion neurons give it the potential to perform a multitude of functions, often simultaneously.

The following are some important brain regions particularly influenced by drugs of abuse.

THE RETICULAR ACTIVATING SYSTEM

The reticular activating system (RAS) is an area of the brain that receives input from all of the sensory systems as well as from the cerebral cortex. The RAS is found at the junction of the spinal cord and the brain (see Figure 4.7). One of its major functions is to control the brain's state of arousal (sleep vs. awake).

Because of its complex, diffuse network structure, the RAS is very susceptible to the effects of drugs. It is sensitive to the effects of LSD, potent stimulants such as cocaine and amphetamines, and CNS depressants such as alcohol and benzodiazepines (e.g., Valium). Norepinephrine and ACh are important neurotransmitters in the RAS. High levels of epinephrine, norepinephrine, or stimulant drugs, such as amphetamines, activate the RAS. In contrast, drugs that block the actions of another transmitter, ACh, called **anticholinergic** drugs (e.g., antihistamines), suppress RAS activity, causing sleepiness.

THE BASAL GANGLIA

The basal ganglia include the caudate nucleus and are the primary centers for involuntary and finely tuned motor functions involving, for example, posture and muscle tone. In addition, these structures are involved in establishing and maintaining behaviors. Two important neurotransmitters in the basal ganglia are dopamine and ACh. Damage to neurons in this area may cause Parkinson's disease, the progressive yet selective degeneration of the main dopaminergic neurons in the basal ganglia. The structures of the basal ganglia are especially important for developing addictions and affecting decision making.

A close association exists between control of motor abilities and control of mental states. Both functions rely heavily on the activity of dopamine-releasing neurons. Consequently, drugs that affect dopamine activity usually alter both systems, resulting in undesired side effects. For example,

KEY TERMS

central nervous system (CNS)
one of the major divisions of the nervous system, composed of the brain and spinal cord

peripheral nervous system (PNS)
includes the neurons outside the CNS

anticholinergic
agents that antagonize the effects of acetylcholine

heavy use of tranquilizers (drugs that block dopamine receptors such as chlorpromazine [Thorazine]) in the treatment of psychotic patients can produce Parkinson-like symptoms. If such drugs are administered daily over several years, problems with motor functioning may become permanent. Drugs of abuse, such as stimulants, increase dopamine activity, causing enhanced motor activity as well as psychotic behavior.

THE LIMBIC SYSTEM

The limbic system includes an assortment of linked brain regions located near to and including the hypothalamus (see Figure 4.7). Besides the hypothalamus, the limbic structures include the thalamus, medial forebrain bundle, **nucleus accumbens**, and front portion of the cerebral cortex. Functions of the limbic and basal ganglia structures are inseparably linked; drugs that affect one system often affect the other as well.

The primary roles of limbic brain regions include regulating emotional activities (such as fear, rage, and anxiety), memory, modulation of basic hypothalamic functions (such as endocrine activity), and activities such as mating, procreation, and caring for the young. In addition, reward centers are also believed to be associated with limbic structures, particularly in the nucleus accumbens. For this reason, it is almost certain that the mood-elevating effects of drugs of abuse are mediated by these limbic systems of the brain.

For example, studies have shown that, when given the option, laboratory animals will self-administer most stimulant drugs of abuse (such as amphetamines and cocaine) through a cannula surgically placed into limbic structures (such as the medial forebrain bundle, nucleus accumbens, or frontal cerebral cortex). This self-administration is achieved by linking injection of the drug into the cannula with a lever press or other activity by the animal (Hanson et al. 2012). It is thought that the euphoria or intense "highs" associated with these drugs result from their effects on these brain regions. Some of the limbic system's principal transmitters include dopamine,

norepinephrine, and serotonin; dopamine activation in the caudate nucleus and nucleus accumbens especially appears to be the primary reinforcement that accounts for the abuse liability of most drugs (Frankel et al. 2011; Hanson et al. 2012).

THE CEREBRAL CORTEX

The unique features of the human cerebral cortex give human beings a special place among animals. The cortex is a layer of gray matter made up of nerves and supporting cells that almost completely surrounds the rest of the brain and lies immediately under the skull (see Figure 4.7). It is responsible for receiving sensory input, interpreting incoming information, and initiating voluntary motor behavior. Many psychoactive drugs, such as psychedelics, dramatically alter the perception of sensory information by the cortex and cause hallucinations that result in strange behavior.

A particularly critical part of the cortex is called the **frontal cortex**. This and associated cortical areas store memories, control complex behaviors, help process information, and play a role in decision making. Some psychoactive drugs disrupt the normal functioning of these areas, thereby interfering with an individual's ability to deal effectively and rationally with complex issues. Consequently, the behavior of persons addicted to drugs often appears bizarre and inappropriate, and in extreme cases can even lead to violence and criminal behavior (Anderson and Bokor 2012).

THE INSULA

The insula is a structure recently implicated in drug addiction. It is located deep in the brain, connected with the pleasure pathways, and appears to be important for motivation. A recent finding determined that smokers who sustain an injury to their insula lose interest in using tobacco. This region has been associated with other addiction behaviors as well (Droutman, Read, and Bechara 2015).

THE HYPOTHALAMUS

The hypothalamus (see **Figure 4.8**) is located near the base of the brain. It integrates information from many sources and serves as the CNS control center for the ANS and many vital support functions such as cardiovascular activity, hormone release, and temperature and appetite regulation (Kyrou and Tsigos 2009). It also serves as the primary point of contact between the nervous and endocrine systems. Because the hypothalamus helps control the ANS, it is responsible for

KEY TERMS

nucleus accumbens
part of the CNS limbic system and a critical brain region for reward systems

frontal cortex
cortical region essential for information processing and decision making

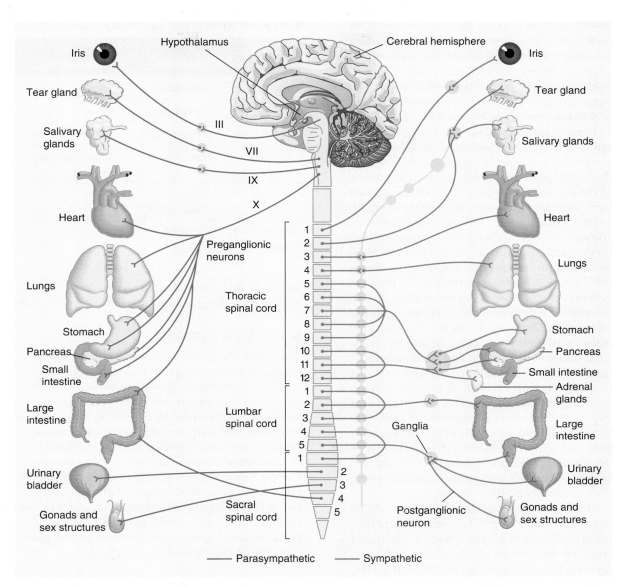

FIGURE 4.8 Autonomic pathways of the parasympathetic and sympathetic nervous systems and the organs affected.

maintaining homeostasis in the body; thus, drugs that alter its function can have a major impact on systems that control homeostasis. The catechol-amine transmitters are particularly important in regulating the function of the hypothalamus, and most drugs of abuse that alter the activity of nor-epinephrine and dopamine are likely to alter the activity of this brain structure as well.

project outside of the CNS to involuntary muscles, organs, and glands; thus, the ANS is considered part of the PNS. The ANS is an integrative, or regulatory, system that does not require conscious control (i.e., you do not have to think about it to make it function). It is usually considered pri-marily a motor or output system. A number of drugs that cannot enter the CNS because of the

■ The Autonomic Nervous System

Although the cell bodies of the neurons of the **autonomic nervous system (ANS)** are located within the brain or spinal cord, their axons

KEY TERM

autonomic nervous system (ANS)
controls the unconscious functions of the body

blood–brain barrier are able to affect the ANS only. The ANS is divided into two functional components: the sympathetic and the parasympathetic nervous systems (Westfall and Westfall 2006). Both systems include neurons that project to most visceral organs and to smooth muscles, glands, and blood vessels (see Figure 4.8).

The two components of the ANS generally have opposite effects on an organ or its function. The working of the heart is a good example of sympathetic and parasympathetic control. Stimulation of the parasympathetic nervous system slows the heart rate, whereas stimulation of the sympathetic nerves accelerates it. These actions constitute a constant biological check and balance, or regulatory system. Because the two parts of the ANS work in opposite ways much of the time, they are considered physiological antagonists. These two systems control most of the internal organs, the circulatory system, and the secretory (glandular) system. The sympathetic system is normally active at all times; the degree of activity varies from moment to moment and from organ to organ. The parasympathetic nervous system is organized mainly for limited, focused activity and usually conserves and restores energy rather than expends it. For example, it slows the heart rate, lowers blood pressure, aids in absorption of nutrients, and is involved in emptying the urinary bladder. **Table 4.2** lists the structures and/or functions of the sympathetic and parasympathetic nervous systems and their effects on one another.

The two branches of the ANS use two different neurotransmitters. The parasympathetic branch releases ACh at its synapses, whereas the sympathetic neurons release norepinephrine. An increase in epinephrine in the blood released from the adrenal glands (see the next section) or the administration of drugs that enhance norepinephrine activity causes the body to respond as if the sympathetic nervous system had been activated. As previously mentioned, such drugs are referred to as *sympathomimetics*. Thus, taking amphetamines (which enhance the sympathetic nervous system by releasing norepinephrine and epinephrine) raises blood pressure, speeds up heart rate, reduces motility of the stomach walls, and may cause the pupils of the eyes to enlarge; other so-called uppers, such as cocaine, have similar effects.

Drugs that affect ACh release, metabolism, or interaction with its respective receptor are referred to as *cholinergic* drugs. They can either

TABLE 4.2 Sympathetic and Parasympathetic Control

Structure or Function	Sympathetic	Parasympathetic
Heart rate	Accelerates	Slows
Breathing rate	Accelerates	Slows
Stomach wall	Reduces motility	Increases motility
Skin blood vessels	Constricts	Dilates (vasomotor function)
Iris of eye	Constricts (pupil enlarges)	Dilates
Vomiting center	Stimulates	—

mimic or antagonize the parasympathetic nervous system, according to their pharmacological action.

▮ The Endocrine System

The endocrine system consists of glands, which are ductless (meaning that they secrete their chemical messengers, called hormones, directly into the bloodstream) (see **Figure 4.9**). These hormones are essential in regulating many vital functions, including metabolism, growth, tissue repair, and sexual behavior, to mention just a few. In contrast to neurotransmitters, hormones tend to have a slower onset, a longer duration of action, and a more generalized target. Although a number of tissues are capable of producing and releasing hormones, three of the principal sources of these chemical messengers are the pituitary gland, the adrenal glands, and the sex glands.

ENDOCRINE GLANDS AND REGULATION

The pituitary gland is often referred to as the *master gland*. It controls many of the other glands that make up the endocrine system by releasing regulating factors and growth hormone. Besides controlling the brain functions already mentioned, the hypothalamus helps control the activity of the pituitary gland and thereby has a very prominent effect on the endocrine system.

The adrenal glands are located near the kidneys and are divided into two parts: the outer surface, called the *cortex*, and the inner part, called the *medulla*. The adrenal medulla is actually a component of the sympathetic nervous system and releases adrenaline (another name for *epinephrine*) during sympathetic stimulation. Other important

FIGURE 4.9 Examples of some glands and their respective hormones in the endocrine system.

hormones released by the adrenal cortex are called *corticosteroids*, or just **steroids**. Steroids help the body respond appropriately to crises and stress. In addition, small amounts of male sex hormones (chemically related to the steroids), called **androgens**, are released by the adrenal cortex. The androgens produce anabolic effects that increase the retention and synthesis of proteins, causing growth in the mass of tissues such as muscles and bones (Chrousos 2015).

Sex glands are responsible for the secretion of male and female sex hormones that help regulate the development and activity of the respective reproductive systems. The organs known as gonads include the female ovaries and the male testes. The activity of the gonads is regulated by hormones released from the pituitary gland (see Figure 4.9) and, for the most part, remains suppressed until puberty. After activation, estrogens and progesterones are released from the ovaries, and androgens (principally testosterone) are released from the testes. These hormones are responsible for the development and maintenance of the secondary sex characteristics. They influence not only sex-related body features but also emotional states, suggesting that these sex hormones enter the brain and significantly affect the functioning of the limbic systems.

For the most part, drugs prescribed to treat endocrine problems are intended as replacement therapy. For example, diabetic patients suffer from a shortage of insulin produced by the pancreas, so therapy consists of insulin injections. Patients who suffer from dwarfism receive insufficient growth hormone from the pituitary gland; thus, growth hormone is administered to stimulate normal growth. Because some hormones can affect growth, muscle development, and behavior, they are sometimes abused to enhance athletic performance or bodybuilding and may be referred to as *performance enhancers*.

THE ABUSE OF HORMONES: ANABOLIC STEROIDS

Androgens are the hormones most likely to be abused in the United States. In 2015, these drugs were self-administered by 1.7% of high school

KEY TERMS

steroids
hormones related to the corticosteroids released from the adrenal cortex

androgens
male sex hormones

► CASE IN POINT

Winning ... But at What Cost?

The ability of drugs such as steroids and other "performance-enhancing" substances to make athletes run faster, be stronger, and endure longer is no longer disputed. What is disputed is the question of "At what cost?" The message being sent by today's star athletes all too often is unsettling. For example, the winner of the 2006 Tour de France, Floyd Landis, was heralded to be just what cycling needed in order to move beyond the multiple scandals related to cyclists' drug use. His apparent squeaky clean image was based on a Mennonite background and charismatic personality. But this façade was quickly stripped away when arbitrators ruled two to one to remove his 2006 Tour de France title because of lab tests that identified synthetic testosterone in his urine. Despite being banned from the sport and losing all credibility, as well as $2 million, Landis continued to claim his innocence for several years. However, in May 2010 he finally confessed to a long history of "doping" that began in 2002 and included the use of performance-enhancing drugs such as the blood-booster erythropoietin (EPO) and blood transfusions to increase endurance, as well as testosterone and human growth hormone (HGH) to elevate strength. He admitted to spending as much as $90,000 a year for his doping regimens. Landis's desire to win at all costs resulted in his winning nothing but rather becoming the very first cyclist to lose his Tour de France title because of drugs.

More recently, another world-famous cyclist, and a multiple Tour de France champion, Lance Armstrong, was convicted of using performance-enhancing drugs such as steroids to win his Tour de France competitions from 1998 to 2004. As a result, Armstrong was stripped of his victories and banned from further Tour de France competition.

In a bizarre turn of events, Landis became a whistleblower for the federal government, who joined with him in 2013 on behalf of the U.S. Postal Service (former sponsors of Armstrong), in a lawsuit filed against Armstrong for breaches of the Sponsorship Agreements. If the government wins its case, it could cost Armstrong up to $100 million in damages, with Landis potentially getting a cut of the money as the whistleblower.

Times Topics. "Floyd Landis." *New York Times* (May 2010). Available http://topics.nytimes.com/top/reference/timestopics/people/l/floyd_landis/index .htm; Schrotenboer, B. "Feud Escalates Between Lance Armstrong, Floyd Landis." *USA Today* (4 September 2015). Available www.usatoday.com/story/sports /cycline/2015/09/04/lance-armstrong-nike-trek-witness-lawsuit/71672710/

seniors in this country (Johnston et al. 2015). Testosterone, the primary natural androgen, is produced by the testes. Naturally produced androgens are essential for normal growth and development of male sex organs as well as secondary sex characteristics such as male hair patterns, voice changes, muscular development, and fat distribution. The androgens are also necessary for appropriate growth spurts during adolescence (Snyder 2006). Accepted therapeutic use of the androgens is usually for replacement in males with abnormally functioning testes.

Androgens clearly have an impressive effect on development of tissue (Chrousos 2015). In particular, they cause pronounced growth of muscle mass and a substantial increase in body weight in young men with deficient testes function. Because of these effects, androgens are classified as **anabolic** (able to stimulate the conversion of nutrients into tissue mass) **steroids** (they are chemically similar to the steroids).

KEY TERM

anabolic steroids
compounds chemically similar to steroids that stimulate production of tissue mass

In addition, many athletes and trainers know that, when taken in very high doses, androgens can enhance muscle growth and increase strength above that achieved by normal testicular function, thereby improving athletic performance (Chrousos 2015). Because of this effect, male and female athletes, as well as nonathletes who are into body-building and sports, have been attracted to these drugs in hopes of enlarging muscle size, improving their athletic performances, and enhancing their physiques despite their risks to both body and careers (see "Case in Point: Winning ... But at What Cost?").

Several studies have suggested that anabolic hormones can have especially substantial negative effects. Athletic trainers and managers claim to see increases in severe injuries such as tears of muscles and ligaments due to aggravated trauma in overmuscled bodies exposed to these steroids (Druginfo 2015). These drugs can also affect the limbic structures of the brain. Consequently, they may cause excitation and a sense of superior strength and performance in some users. These effects, coupled with increased aggressiveness, could encourage continual use of these drugs. Other CNS effects, however, may be disturbing to the user. Symptoms that may occur with very high doses include uncontrolled rage ("roid rage"), headaches, anxiety, insomnia, and perhaps paranoia (Chrousos 2015). Because of concern about the abuse potential and side-effect profile of anabolic steroids, these drugs are controlled as Schedule III substances.

DESIGNER STEROIDS

In an attempt to circumvent the restriction on steroid use, some athletes have used the "designer" steroid known as tetrahydrogestrinone (THG). The FDA banned THG in products classified as nutritional supplements. Because of concerns that

Anabolic steroids can cause pronounced growth of muscle mass.

athletes were using THG to enhance performance, professional athletic organizations and the International Olympic Committee test athletes for this drug and disqualify them from competition if it is detected (Carmody 2013).

Conclusion

All psychoactive drugs affect brain activity by altering the ability of neurons to send and receive chemical messages. Consequently, drugs of abuse exert their addicting effects by stimulating or blocking the activity of CNS neurotransmitters or their receptors. Thus, to appreciate why these drugs are abused and the nature of their dependence, how neurons and their neurotransmitter systems function must be understood. In addition, many scientists believe that elucidating how substances of abuse affect nervous systems will help identify why some persons are at greater risk for abuse problems and will lead to new and more effective methods for preventing and treating drug addiction.

LEARNING PORTFOLIO

Key Terms

Discussion Questions

1. What are the similarities and differences between neurotransmitters and hormones?
2. Why is it important for the body to have chemical messengers (such as neurotransmitters) that can be quickly released and rapidly inactivated?
3. Why are receptors so important in understanding the effects of drugs of abuse?
4. What role do the opioid and cannabinoid systems play in drug abuse, and how can these neurosystems be used therapeutically?
5. What is the importance of the cannabinoid system with regard to recent "illegal" products known as Spice?
6. Why is it not surprising that drugs that affect the catecholamine transmitters also affect the endocrine system?
7. What are some mechanisms whereby a drug of abuse can increase the activity of dopamine transmitter systems in the brain?
8. How can knowing that the nucleus accumbens of the brain is important for motivation be used to treat drug addiction?
9. Why might a drug of abuse that damages the cerebral cortex make the user especially vulnerable to addiction?

Summary

1. The nervous and endocrine systems help mediate internal and external responses to the body's surroundings. Both systems release chemical messengers to achieve their homeostatic functions. These messenger substances are called neurotransmitters and hormones, and they carry out their functions by binding to specific receptors throughout the CNS and other systems of the body. Many drugs exert their actions by influencing these chemical messengers either to mimic (agonists) or block (antagonists) their effects.
2. The neuron is the principal cell type in the nervous system. This specialized cell consists of dendrites, a cell body, and an axon. It communicates with other neurons and organs by releasing neurotransmitters, which can either excite or inhibit at their target sites.
3. The chemical messengers from glands and neurons exert their effects by interacting with special protein regions in membranes called receptors. Because of their unique construction, receptors interact only with molecules that have specific shapes. Activation of receptors can alter the functions of the target system.

4. Endorphin (opioid) and cannabinoid systems were discovered due to drugs of abuse such as the opioid narcotics and marijuana, respectively. Besides being the target of drugs of abuse, these systems also have the potential to be pharmacologically manipulated to achieve therapeutic outcomes.

5. Agonists are substances or drugs that stimulate receptors. Antagonists are substances or drugs that bind to receptors and prevent them from being activated.

6. A variety of substances is used as neurotransmitters by neurons in the body. The classes of transmitters include the catecholamines, serotonin, acetylcholine, GABA, peptides, and cannabinoids. These transmitters are excitatory, inhibitory, or sometimes both, depending on which receptor is being activated. Many drugs selectively act to either enhance or antagonize these neurotransmitters and their activities.

7. The central nervous system consists of the brain and spinal cord. Regions within the brain help to regulate specific functions. The hypothalamus controls endocrine and basic body functions. The basal ganglia include the caudate nucleus and are primarily responsible for controlling motor activity and learned behaviors. The limbic system regulates mood and mental states and establishing behaviors and helps mediate the rewarding properties of drugs of abuse. The cerebral cortex helps interpret and process information, plays a role in decision making, and responds to input information.

8. The limbic system and its associated transmitters, especially dopamine and serotonin, are major sites of action for the drugs of abuse. Substances that increase the activity of dopamine cause a sense of well-being and euphoria, which encourages psychological dependence.

9. The autonomic nervous system is composed of the sympathetic and parasympathetic systems; neurons associated with these systems release noradrenaline and acetylcholine as their transmitters, respectively. These systems work in an antagonistic fashion to control unconscious, visceral functions such as breathing and cardiovascular activity. The parasympathetic nervous system usually helps conserve and restore energy in the body, whereas the sympathetic nervous system is continually active.

10. The endocrine system consists of glands that synthesize and release hormones into the blood. Distribution via blood circulation carries these chemical messengers throughout the body, where they act on specific receptors. Some of the principal structures include the pituitary, adrenals, and gonads (testes and ovaries).

11. Anabolic steroids are structurally related to the male hormone testosterone. They are often abused by both male and female athletes trying to build muscle mass and are referred to as *performance enhancers*. The continual use of high doses of anabolic steroids can cause annoying and dangerous side effects. The long-term effects of low, intermittent doses of these drugs have not been determined. Because of concerns voiced by most medical authorities, anabolic steroids have been classified as Schedule III substances.

References

Anderson, P., and G. Bokor. "Forensic Aspects of Drug-Induced Violence." *Journal of Pharmacy Practice* 25 (2012): 41–49.

Befort, K. "Interactions of the Opioid and Cannabinoid Systems in Rewards: Insights from Knockout Studies." *Frontiers in Pharmacology.* 6 (2015). Available www.ncbi.nlm.nih.gov/pmc/articles/PMC438341

Berridge, K., and M. L. Kringelbech. "Pleasure Systems in the Brain." *Neuron* 86 (2015): 646–664.

Boundless. "Types of Neurotransmitters by Function." 15 June 2016. Available https://www.boundless.com/physiology/textbooks/boundless-anatomy-and-physiology-textbook/nervous-tissue-11/neurophysiology-113/types-of-neurotransmitters-by-function-619-3349/

Carmody, T. "Hacking Your Body: Lance Armstrong and the Science of Doping." The Verge. 17 January 2013. Available http://www.theverge.com/2013/1/17/3886424/programming-your-body-lance-armstrong-and-doping-technology

Chrousos, G. "The Gonadal Hormones and Inhibitors." In *Basic and Clinical Pharmacology*, 13th ed., edited by B. Katzung, S. Masters, and A. Trevor, 696–722. New York: McGraw-Hill, 2015.

Deadwyler, S. "Electrophysiological Correlates of Abused Drugs: Relation to Natural Rewards." *Annals of the New York Academy of Science* 1187 (2010): 140–147.

Droutman, V., S. Read, and A. Bechara. "Revisiting the Role of the Insula in Addiction." *Trends in Cognitive Sciences* 19 (2015): 414–420.

Drugs.com. "Acomplia." 2015. Available http://www.drugs.com/acomplia.html

Druginfo. "Steroids." 2015. Available www.druginfo.adf.org.au/fact-sheets/steroids

eMedicineHealth. "Anatomy of the Central Nervous System." 2015. Available www.emedicinehealth.com/anatomy_of_the_central_nervous_system/article_em.htm

Ferguson, S. "Phosphorylation-Independent Attenuation of GPCR Signaling." *Trends in Pharmacological Science* 28 (2007): 173–179.

Frankel, P. S., A. J. Hoonakker, M. E. Alburges, J. W. McDougall, L. M. McFadden, A. E. Fleckenstein, and G. R. Hanson. "Effect of Methamphetamine Self-Administration on Neurotensin Systems of the Basal Ganglia." *Journal of Pharmacology and Experimental Therapeutics* 336 (2011): 809–815.

Gray, J., and R. Nicoll. "Introduction to the Pharmacology of CNS Drugs." In *Basic and Clinical Pharmacology*, 13th ed., edited by B. Katzung and A. Trevor. 362–368. New York: McGraw-Hill, 2015.

Hanson, G. R., A. J. Hoonakker, M. E. Alburges, L. M. McFadden, C. M. Robson, and P. S. Frankel. "Response of Limbic Neurotensin Systems to Methamphetamine Self-Administration." *Neuroscience* 203 (2012): 99–107.

Johnston, L. D., R. A. Miech, P. O'Malley, J. G. Bachman, and J. E. Schulenberg. "Use of Ecstasy, Heroin, Synthetic Marijuana, Alcohol, Cigarettes Declined Among US Teens in 2015." University of Michigan News Service: Ann Arbor, MI, 2015. Available at http://www.monitoringthefuture.org/data/15data.html

Jones, J., and S. Comer. "A Review of Pharmacogenetic Studies of Substance-Related Disorders." *Drug and Alcohol Dependence* 152 (2015): 1–14.

Kishi, T., Y. Matsuda, N. Iwata, and C. Correll. "Antipsychotics for Cocaine or Psychostimulant Dependence: Systematic Review and Meta-analysis of Randomized, Placebo-Controlled Trials." *Journal of Clinical Psychiatry* 74 (2014): 1169–1180.

Koob, G. F., and N. Volkow. "Neurocircuitry of Addiction." *Neuropsychopharmacology* 35 (2010): 217–238.

Kyrou, I., and C. Tsigos. "Stress Hormones: Physiological Stress and Regulation of Metabolism." *Current Opinions in Pharmacology* 9 (2009): 787–793.

Learn.Genetics. "Genes and Addiction." University of Utah, Genetic Science Learning Center. 2015. Available http://learn.genetics.utah.edu/content/addiction/genes/

Lisi, D. "Patients May Be Using Synthetic Cannabinoids More Than You Think." *Journal of Emergency Medical Services* 39 (2014): 56–59.

MarketResearch.com. "Cannabinoid Receptor Type 1 (CB1) Antagonists—Pipeline Insights, 2015." DelveInsight (18 May 2015). Available: http://www.marketresearch.com/DelveInsight-v4028/Cannabinoid-Receptor-Type-CB1-Antagonists-9604068/

Matsuda, L. "Molecular Aspects of Cannabinoid Receptors." *Critical Reviews in Neurobiology* 11 (1997): 143–166.

O'Brien, C. "Drug Addiction and Drug Abuse." In *The Pharmacological Basis of Therapeutics*, 11th ed., edited by L. Brunton, J. Lazo, and K. Parker, 607–627. New York: McGraw-Hill, 2006.

Putney, J., and A. Askari, "Modification of Membrane Function by Drugs." In *Membrane Physiology*, edited by T. Anreoli, J. Hoffman, and D. Fanestil, 417–443. New York: Plenum, 2013.

Robertson, D., and I. Biaggioni. "Adrenoceptor Antagonist Drugs." In *Basic and Clinical Pharmacology*, 12th ed., edited by B. Katzung, S. Masters, and A. Trevor, 151–168. New York: McGraw-Hill, 2012.

Sabatowski, R., D. Shafer, S. Kasper, H. Brunsch, and L. Radbruh. "Pain Treatment: A Historical Overview." *Current Pharmaceutical Design* 10 (2004): 701–716.

Shim, J. Y. "Understanding Functional Residuals of the Cannabinoid CB1 Receptor for Drug Discovery." *Current Topics in Medicinal Chemistry* (6 April 2010): 779–798.

Skolnick, P. "Anxioselective Anxiolytics: On a Quest for the Holy Grail." *Trends in Pharmacological Sciences* 33 (2012): 611–620.

Snyder, P. "Androgens." In *The Pharmacological Basis of Therapeutics*, 11th ed., edited by L. Brunton, J. Lazo, and K. Parker, 1573–1585. New York: McGraw-Hill, 2006.

Westfall, T., and D. Westfall. "Neurotransmission. The Autonomic and Somatic Motor Nervous Systems." In *The Pharmacological Basis of Therapeutics*, 11th ed., edited by L. Brunton, J. Lazo, and K. Parker, 137–181. New York: McGraw-Hill, 2006.

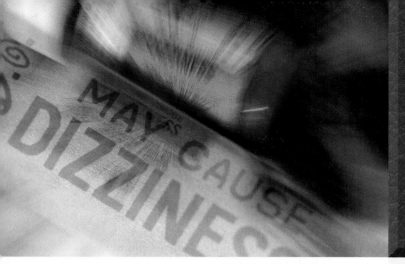

© Jennifer Okamoto/FogStock/Thinkstock.

Did You Know?

▶ In the United States, 20% of total hospital costs are due to medical care for health damage caused by substances of abuse.

▶ The same dose of a drug does not have the same effect on everyone.

▶ In excessive doses, almost any drug or substance can be toxic.

▶ Of strokes among young Americans, 65% are related to cigarette, cocaine, or amphetamine use.

▶ Many people who abuse cocaine also abuse alcohol to counter unpleasant side effects.

▶ Many of the overdose deaths caused by prescription drugs are due to unanticipated drug interactions.

▶ Many drugs are unable to pass from the blood into the brain due to the blood–brain barrier.

▶ Gender affects responses to alcohol and tobacco.

▶ Hereditary factors may predispose some individuals to becoming psychologically dependent on drugs with abuse potential.

Learning Objectives

On completing this chapter you should be able to:

❭ Describe some of the common unintended drug effects.

❭ Explain why the same dose of a drug may affect individuals differently.

❭ Explain the difference between potency and toxicity.

❭ Describe the concept of a drug's margin of safety.

❭ Identify and give examples of additive, antagonistic, and potentiative (synergistic) drug interactions.

❭ Identify the pharmacokinetic factors that can influence the effects caused by drugs.

❭ Cite the physiological and pathological factors that influence drug effects.

❭ Explain the significance of the blood–brain barrier to psychoactive drugs.

❭ Define *threshold dose*, *plateau effect*, and *cumulative effect*.

❭ Discuss the role of the liver in drug metabolism and the consequences of this process.

❭ Define *biotransformation*.

❭ Describe the relationships among drug tolerance, withdrawal, rebound, physical dependence, and psychological dependence and how they can affect drug abuse patterns.

❭ Discuss the significance of placebos in drug therapy and drug abuse.

❭ Describe drug craving, and explain its relationship to drug addiction and relapse.

Introduction

A common belief is that drugs can solve most of life's serious physical, emotional, and medical problems. Although medications are essential to treatment for many diseases, excessive reliance on drugs causes unrealistic expectations that may lead to dangerous—even fatal—consequences. For example, drug addiction (frequently referred to as *substance or drug use disorder*) (American Psychiatric Association [APA] 2013) and dependence often follow from such unrealistic drug expectations. Obviously, not every person who uses drugs inappropriately becomes a drug addict, nor are patients who use drugs as prescribed by their doctor immune from becoming physically and mentally dependent on their prescribed medications. In fact, because of individual variability, it is difficult to predict accurately which drug users will or will not have drug problems such as addiction and dependence, although identifying persons with risk factors may make prevention strategies for drug abuse more effective.

In this chapter, we consider the factors that account for the variability of drug responses—that is, what determines how the body responds to drugs and why some drugs work but others do not. First, we review the general effects of drugs, both intended and unintended. The correlation between the dose and response to a drug is addressed next, followed by a discussion of how drugs interact with one another. The section on pharmacokinetic factors considers how drugs are introduced into, distributed throughout, and eliminated from the body, along with physiological and pathological variables that modify how drugs affect the body. The final sections in the chapter consider concepts important to understanding drug abuse, such as tolerance, physical versus psychological dependence, and addiction.

The Intended and Unintended Effects of Drugs

When physicians prescribe drugs, their objective is usually to cure or relieve symptoms of a disease. Frequently, however, drugs cause unintended

KEY TERMS

side effects
unintended drug responses

withdrawal
unpleasant effects that occur when use of a drug is stopped

effects that neither the physician nor the patient expected. These are called **side effects**.

A response that is considered a side effect in one situation may, in fact, be the therapeutic objective in another. For example, the antihistamines found in many over-the-counter (OTC) drugs have an intended main effect of relieving allergy symptoms, but they often cause annoying drowsiness as a side effect; in fact, for this reason their labels include warnings that they should not be used while driving a car. These antihistamines are also included in OTC sleep aids, in which their sedating action is the desired main effect.

Side effects can influence many body functions and occur in any organ (see **Figure 5.1**). The following are basic kinds of side effects that can result from drug use:

- Nausea or vomiting
- Changes in mental alertness, such as sedation or anxiety
- Dependence, which compels people to continue using a drug because they want to achieve a desired effect or because they fear unpleasant reactions, called **withdrawal**, that occur when use of the drug is discontinued
- Allergic reactions (hypersensitive reactions or sensitization), often experienced as rashes or breathing difficulty
- Changes in cardiovascular activity altering the activity of the heart or blood pressure

This short list of side effects demonstrates the types of risks involved whenever any drug (prescription, nonprescription, illicit, and even some herbal products) is used. Consequently, before taking a drug, whether for therapeutic or recreational use, you should understand its potential problems and determine whether the benefits justify the risks. For example, it is important to know that morphine is effective for relieving severe pain, but it also depresses breathing and retards intestinal activity, causing constipation. Likewise, amphetamines can be used to suppress appetite for losing weight or to manage ADHD (attention deficit hyperactivity disorder), but they also increase blood pressure and stimulate the heart and may interfere with sleep. Cocaine is a good local anesthetic, but it can be extremely addicting and can cause tremors or even seizures. The greater the danger associated with using a drug, the less likely that the benefits will warrant its use.

Adverse effects of drugs of abuse are particularly troublesome in the United States. Studies have suggested that hundreds of billions of dollars are spent each year in the United States because

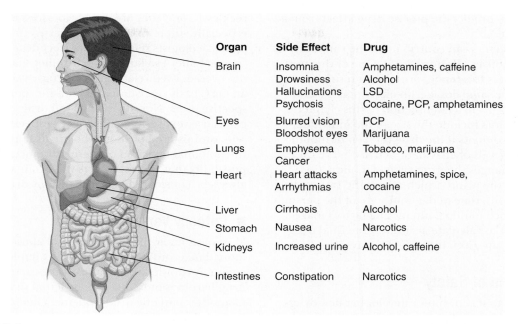

Organ	Side Effect	Drug
Brain	Insomnia	Amphetamines, caffeine
	Drowsiness	Alcohol
	Hallucinations	LSD
	Psychosis	Cocaine, PCP, amphetamines
Eyes	Blurred vision	PCP
	Bloodshot eyes	Marijuana
Lungs	Emphysema	Tobacco, marijuana
	Cancer	
Heart	Heart attacks	Amphetamines, spice,
	Arrhythmias	cocaine
Liver	Cirrhosis	Alcohol
Stomach	Nausea	Narcotics
Kidneys	Increased urine	Alcohol, caffeine
Intestines	Constipation	Narcotics

FIGURE 5.1 Common side effects with drugs of abuse. Almost every organ or system in the body can be negatively affected by the substances of abuse.

of medical care and premature deaths related to the use of addicting substances (National Institute on Drug Abuse [NIDA] 2015b).

The Dose–Response Relationship of Therapeutics and Toxicity

All effects—both desired and unwanted—are related to the amount of drug administered. A small concentration of drug may have one effect, whereas a larger dose may create a greater effect or a different effect entirely. Because some correlation exists between the response to a drug and the quantity of the drug dose, it is possible to calculate **dose–response** curves (see **Figure 5.2**).

Once a dose–response curve for a drug has been determined in an individual, it can be used to predict how that person will respond to different doses of the drug. For example, the dose–response curve for user B in Figure 5.2 shows that 400 milligrams of ibuprofen will relieve only 50% of the user's headache. It is important to understand that not everyone responds the same way to a given dose of drug. Thus, in Figure 5.2, although 400 milligrams of ibuprofen gives 50% relief from a headache for user B, it relieves 100% of the headache for user A and none of the headache for user C. This variability in response can make it

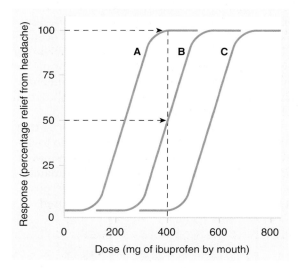

FIGURE 5.2 Dose–response curve for relieving a headache with ibuprofen in three users. User A is the most sensitive and has 100% headache relief at a dose of 400 milligrams. User B is the next most sensitive and experiences 50% headache relief with a 400-milligram dose. The least sensitive is user C: with a 400-milligram dose, user C has no relief from a headache.

KEY TERM

dose–response
correlation between the amount of a drug given and its effects

difficult to predict the precise drug effect from a given dose.

Many factors can contribute to the variability in drug responses (Holford 2015). One of the most important is **tolerance**, or reduced response over time to the same dosage, an effect that is examined carefully in a later section of this chapter. Other factors include the size of the individual, stomach contents if the drug is taken by mouth, different levels of enzymatic activity in the liver (which changes the drug via metabolic action), acidity of the urine (which affects the rate of drug elimination), time of day, and state of the person's health. Such multiple interacting factors make it difficult to calculate accurately the final drug effect for any given individual at any given time.

■ Margin of Safety

An important concept for developing new drugs for therapy, as well as for assessing the probability of serious side effects for drugs of abuse, is the **margin of safety**. The margin of safety is determined by the difference between the doses necessary to cause the intended (therapeutic or recreational) effects and the toxic unintended effects. The larger the margin of safety, the less likely that serious adverse side effects will occur when using the drug to treat medical problems or even when abusing it. Drugs with relatively narrow margins of safety, such as heroin or cocaine, have a very high rate of serious reactions in populations who abuse these substances.

There is no such thing as the perfect drug that goes right to the target in the body, has no toxicity, produces no side effects, and can be removed or neutralized when not needed. Unfortunately, most effective drugs are potentially dangerous if the doses are high enough, if they are used

KEY TERMS

tolerance
changes in the body that decrease response to a drug even though the dose remains the same

margin of safety
range in dose between the amount of drug necessary to cause a therapeutic effect and that needed to create a toxic effect

potency
amount of drug necessary to cause an effect

toxicity
capacity of one drug to damage or cause adverse effects in the body

recklessly, or if they are used by persons who are especially vulnerable to their adverse effects. Pharmacologists refer to the perfect drug as a "magic bullet"; so far, no magic bullets have been discovered. Even relatively safe drugs available on an OTC basis can cause problems for some prospective users. Not surprisingly, all drugs of abuse can cause very serious side effects, especially when self-administered by users who are unfamiliar with the potential toxicities of these substances. The possibility that adverse effects will occur should always be considered before using any drug.

■ Potency Versus Toxicity

Most of us know that some drugs of abuse are more dangerous than others. For example, it is common knowledge that abuse of the narcotic drug heroin is more likely to be lethal than abuse of another narcotic drug, codeine. One important feature that makes heroin more dangerous than codeine is its high potency. **Potency** is a way of expressing how much of a drug is necessary to cause an effect, whether it be desired or toxic. The smaller the dose required to achieve a drug action, the greater the drug potency.

The concept of potency can also be used to describe a drug's ability to create a therapeutic effect. More potent medications require lower doses to be effective. Knowledge of a drug's potency is essential if it is to be used properly and safely.

Toxicity is the capacity of a drug to upset or even destroy normal body functions. Toxic compounds are often called *poisons*, although almost any compound—including sugar, table salt, aspirin, and vitamin A—can be toxic at sufficiently high doses. If a foreign chemical is introduced into the body, it may disrupt the body's normal functions. In many instances, the body can compensate for this disruption, perhaps by metabolizing and rapidly eliminating the chemical, and little effect is noted. Sometimes, however, the delicate balance is altered and the person becomes sick or even dies. If the body's functional balance is already under stress from disease, the introduction of a drug may have a much more serious effect than its use in a healthy person who can adjust to its toxicity.

A drug with high potency often is toxic even at low doses; therefore, the amount given must be carefully measured and the user closely monitored. If caution is not taken, serious damage to the body or death can occur. Very potent drugs that are abused, such as heroin-related drugs, are particularly dangerous because they are often consumed by unsuspecting users who are ignorant of the drug's extreme toxicity. Potency depends on many factors, such as the drug's absorption, its distribution in the body, individual metabolism, the form of excretion, the rate of elimination, and its activity at the site of action (Lange 2015).

Drug Interaction

A drug's effects can be dramatically altered when other drugs are also present in the body; this effect is known as **drug interaction** (Lange 2015). A typical example of multiple drug use occurs when you treat your common cold. Because of your many cold-related symptoms, you may consume an assortment of pain relievers, antihistamines, decongestants, and anticough medications all at the same time.

Multiple drug use can create a serious medical problem because many drugs influence the actions of other drugs (Lange 2015). Even physicians may be baffled by unusual effects when multiple drugs are consumed. Frequently, drug interactions are misdiagnosed as symptoms of a disease. Such errors in diagnosis can lead to inappropriate treatment and serious health consequences. Complications can arise that are dangerous, even fatal. The interacting substance may be another drug, or it may be some substance in the diet or in the environment, such as a pesticide. Because approximately 20% of Americans take some type of herbal supplement, herbs are commonly interacting with both prescription and nonprescription drugs. For example, the herb Echinacea, which is often used to treat colds, can slow the metabolism of caffeine, leading to side effects such as jitters, headaches, and insomnia (Drugs.com 2014). These interactions are not surprising given that some of the herbs contain drugs that occur naturally. Consequently, an herb that causes sedation, such as melatonin, almost certainly will enhance the depressing effects of either prescription or nonprescription sleep aids. Drug interaction is an area in which more research and public education are required (Drugs.com 2014).

Depending on the effect on the body, drug interaction may be categorized into three types: additive, antagonistic (inhibitory), and potentiative (synergistic) (Lange 2015).

■ Additive Effects

Additive interactions are the summation of effects of drugs taken concurrently. An example of an additive interaction results from using aspirin and acetaminophen (Tylenol) at the same time. The pain relief provided is equal to the sum of the two analgesics, which could be achieved by a comparable dose of either drug alone. Thus, if a 300-milligram tablet of Bayer aspirin were taken with a 300-milligram tablet of Tylenol, the relief would be the same as if two tablets of either Bayer aspirin or Tylenol were taken instead.

■ Antagonistic (Inhibitory) Effects

Antagonistic interactions occur when one drug cancels or blocks the effect of another drug. For example, if you take antihistamines to reduce nasal congestion, you may be able to antagonize some of the drowsiness often caused by these drugs by using a central nervous system (CNS) stimulant such as caffeine.

Often, drug abusers who use two drugs at the same time are trying to antagonize the unpleasant side effects of the first drug by administering the second. It has been reported that approximately 34% of the 500,000 emergency visits caused by cocaine consumption also involve the use of alcohol (DrugWise n.d.; Fettiplace et al. 2015). The combined use of these two drugs may be a major factor in drug-related cardiovascular problems and death in emergency rooms (DrugWise n.d.; Fettiplace et al. 2015). Nevertheless, it appears that some users may coadminister these drugs in an attempt to antagonize the disruptive effects of alcohol with the stimulant action of the cocaine.

■ Potentiative (Synergistic) Effects

The third type of drug interaction is known as *potentiation*, or **synergism**. Synergism occurs when the effect of a drug is enhanced by the presence of another drug or substance, whether synthetic or naturally occurring (Lange 2015). A common

KEY TERMS

drug interaction
presence of one drug alters the action of another drug

additive interactions
effects created when drugs are similar and actions are added together

antagonistic interactions
effects created when drugs cancel one another

synergism
ability of one drug to enhance the effect of another; also called potentiation

example is the combination of alcohol and opioid analgesics such as oxycodone (e.g., OxyContin). It has been estimated that many of the people who die each year from prescription overdosing have alcohol and a prescribed CNS depressant in their system (Jones, Paulozzi, and Mack 2014). When such depressants are taken together, CNS functions become impaired and the person becomes groggy. A person in this state may forget that he or she has taken the pills and repeat the dose. The combination of these two depressants (or other depressants, such as antihistamines) can interfere with the CNS to the point where vital functions such as breathing and heartbeat are severely impaired.

Although the mechanisms of interaction among CNS depressants are not entirely clear, these drugs likely enhance one another's direct effects on inhibitory chemical messengers in the brain. In addition, interference by alcohol with liver-metabolizing enzymes contributes to the synergism that arises with the combination of alcohol and some depressants, such as barbiturates (Walker 2015).

▮ Dealing with Drug Interactions

Although many drug effects and interactions are not very well understood, it is important to be aware of them. A growing body of evidence indicates that many of the drugs and substances we deliberately consume will interact and produce unexpected and sometimes dangerous effects (see **Table 5.1**). It is alarming to know that many of the foods we eat and some chemical pollutants also interfere with and modify drug actions. Pesticides, traces of hormones in meat and poultry, traces of metals in fish, nitrites and nitrates from fertilizers, and a wide range of chemicals—some of which are used as food additives—have been shown, under certain conditions, to interact with some drugs (Mazur, Marchitti, and Zastre 2015; Shapiro 2015).

It is essential that the public be educated about the interactions most likely to occur with drugs that are prescribed, self-administered legitimately (e.g., OTC drugs and herbal products), or taken recreationally (e.g., drugs of abuse) and that women are particularly vulnerable (see "Prescription for Abuse: Problems with Prescription Abuse in Women") (CDC 2013). People need to be aware that OTC and herbal drugs are as likely to cause interaction problems as prescription drugs. For example, an OTC or herbal decongestant that contains mild CNS stimulants (e.g., pseudoephedrine) taken with potent CNS stimulants, such as cocaine and amphetamines, can cause interactions that

TABLE 5.1 Common Interactions with Substances of Abuse

Drug	Combined with	Consequence of Interaction
Sedatives		
Diazepam (Valium), triazolam (Halcion)	Alcohol, barbiturates	Increase sedation
Stimulants		
Amphetamines, Ritalin	Insulin	Decrease insulin effect
	Antidepressants	Cause hypertension
Narcotics		
Heroin, morphine	Valium	Increase sedation
	Anticoagulant	Increase bleeding
	Antidepressants	Cause sedation
	Amphetamines	Increase euphoria
Tobacco		
Nicotine	Blood pressure medication	Elevate blood pressure
	Amphetamines, cocaine	Increase cardiovascular effects
Alcohol		
	Cocaine	Produces cocaethylene, which enhances euphoria and toxicity

fatally affect the heart and brain. If any question arises concerning the possibility of drug interaction, individuals should talk to their physician, pharmacist, or other healthcare providers.

Many drug abusers are multiple drug (*polydrug*) users with little concern for the dangerous interactions that might occur. It is common, for example, for drug abusers to combine multiple CNS depressants to enhance their effects, to combine a depressant with a stimulant to titrate a CNS effect (to determine the smallest amount that can be taken to achieve the desired "high"), or to experiment with a combination of stimulants, depressants, and hallucinogens just to see what happens. The effects of such haphazard drug mixing are impossible to predict, difficult to treat in

PRESCRIPTION FOR ABUSE

© Michal Kowalski/Shutterstock

Prescription Abuse Problems with Prescription Abuse In Women

After her father died prematurely, Tina Orr felt she was also destined to die early. At the age of 35, Tina, like her father, went to an early grave due to a prescription overdose. Tina's sister described her as the the most amazing mother I'd ever met, incredibly kind and patient Her daughter was her whole world...she was so happy." However, as she struggled with worsening medical conditions, including obesity, problems with a growing prescription dependence became evident. Even though at one time she was receiving five different prescriptions, none seem to solve her

medical and emotional difficulties. Her sister says that just before her death she seemed to be upbeat planning to go back to school.

Problems with prescription overdoses are a particular problem for women and usually involve painkillers and drugs for mental illnesses. Some explanations for this problem is that women tend to have more chronic pain and emotional disorders for which they receive prescription painkiller drugs, as well as antidepressants and antianxiety medications. They also tend to develop dependence to these medications faster than men, resulting in escalating use and major withdrawal symptoms when trying to discontinue their drug use.

Because of these disturbing patterns of prescription overdoses in women, it is important that those who prescribe these medications discuss all the medications being used by their female patients (including OTC drug products). These women need to understand they should only use the prescription drugs as directed by a healthcare provider, store them in a secure place, not share their prescriptions with anyone else, and dispose of medications properly as soon as treatment is completed.

Centers for Disease Control and Prevention (CDC). "Prescription Painkiller Overdoses: A Growing Epidemic, Especially Among Women." July 2013. Available http://www.cdc.gov/vitalsigns/PrescriptionPainkillerOverdoses/index.html

emergency situations, and all too frequently fatal (see "Prescription for Abuse: Deadly Drug Mix").

Pharmacokinetic Factors That Influence Drug Effects

Although it is difficult to predict precisely how any single individual will be affected by drug use, the following major factors represent different aspects of the body's response that should be considered when attempting to anticipate a drug's effects (Holford 2015):

- How does the drug enter the body? (administration)
- How does the drug move from the site of administration into the body's system? (absorption)

- How does the drug move to various areas in the body? (distribution)
- How and where does the drug produce its effects? (activation)
- How is the drug inactivated, metabolized, and/or excreted from the body? (biotransformation and elimination)

These issues relate to the **pharmacokinetics** of a drug and are important considerations when predicting the body's response. They can impact the drug levels that are detected in the body when a drug test is conducted.

KEY TERM

pharmacokinetics
the study of factors that influence the distribution and concentration of drugs in the body

Method of Administration	Onset	Duration	Effect
Smoking			
Cocaine	Fast (~15 seconds)	Brief (10–15 minutes)	Potent and strong
Heroin	Fast (~20 seconds)	Short (1–2 hours)	Potent and strong
Intravenous			
Cocaine	Fast (20 seconds)	Short (30 minutes)	Potent and strong
Heroin	Fast (1–2 minutes)	Short (1–2 hours)	Potent and strong
Snorting			
Cocaine	Moderate (~10 minutes)	Short (45 minutes)	Less potent
Heroin	Moderate (~15 minutes)	Short (1–2 hours)	Less potent
Oral			
Cocaine (coca leaf)	Slow (30 minutes)	Moderate (~2–4 hours)	Minor
Methadone	Slow (30–60 minutes)	Long (24 hours)	Less euphoria/ used for treatment

FIGURE 5.3 Relationship between the method of drug administration and drug effects.

▮ Forms and Methods of Taking Drugs

Drugs come in many forms. How a drug is formulated—solution, powder, capsule, or pill—influences the rate of passage into the bloodstream, and consequently its efficacy. The means of introducing the drug into the body will also affect how quickly the drug enters the bloodstream and how it is distributed to the site of action, as well as how much will ultimately reach its target and exert an effect (Holford 2015) (see **Figure 5.3**). The principal forms of drug administration are *oral ingestion, inhalation, injection*, and *topical application*.

ORAL INGESTION

One of the most common and convenient ways of taking a drug is orally. This type of administration usually introduces the drug into the body by way of the stomach or intestines. Following oral administration, it is difficult to control the amount of drug that reaches the site of action, for three reasons:

1. The drug must enter the bloodstream after passing through the wall of the stomach or intestines without being destroyed or changed to an inactive form. From the blood, the drug must diffuse to the target area and remain there in sufficient concentration to have an effect.

2. Materials in the stomach or intestines, such as food, may interfere with the passage of some drugs through the gut lining and thus prevent drug action. For example, food in your stomach will diminish the effects of alcohol by altering its absorption.

3. The liver might metabolize orally ingested drugs too rapidly, before they are able to exert an effect. The liver is the major detoxifying organ in the body, which means it removes chemicals and toxins from the blood and usually changes them into an inactive form that is easy for the body to excrete. This function is essential to survival, but it creates a problem for the pharmacologist in developing effective drugs or the physician prescribing the correct dose of a drug to treat a serious disease. The liver is especially problematic to oral administration because the substances absorbed from the digestive tract usually go to the liver before being distributed to other parts of the body and their site of action. For this reason, cocaine taken orally is not very effective.

INHALATION

Some drugs are administered by inhalation into the lungs through the mouth or nose. The lungs include large beds of capillaries, so chemicals

PRESCRIPTION FOR ABUSE

Deadly Drug Mix

The death of another celebrity because of mixing drugs, including illicit and prescription drugs, as well as alcohol, has become an all too common occurrence. Usually there are many questions: Why did this happen? Could it have been avoided? How do we stop it from happening in the future? It seems almost incomprehensible that people who seem to have everything lose it all due to a drug overdose, leaving their loved ones, as well as an adoring public, not understanding how it could happen. **Table A** lists some of the celebrities who lost their lives from 2009–2014 due to an intentional or accidental overdose of drug combinations. This list does not include those overdosing on a single drug or those who overdosed but did not die.

TABLE A Celebrity Deaths Due to Intentional or Accidental Overdose of Drug Combinations: 2009–2014

Name	Fame	Cause of Death	Drug Category	Year	Age at Death
Joan Rivers	Actress	Therapeutic complication with propofol sedation	Prescription drugs	2014	81
Cory Monteith	Actor	Toxic mix of heroin and alcohol	Illegal drugs and alcohol	2013	31
Lisa Robin Kelly	Actress	Multiple-drug intoxication	Illegal drugs	2013	43
Chris Kelly	Rapper	Fatal overdose	Illegal drugs	2013	34
Whitney Houston	Singer	Prescription drugs and cocaine	Illegal and prescription drugs	2012	48
Michael Baze	Horse jockey	Cocaine and oxymorphone	Illegal and prescription drugs	2011	28
Derek Boogaard	Ice hockey player	Alcohol and oxycodone	Alcohol and prescription	2011	28
Erica Blasberg	Golfer	Multiple prescriptions	Prescription	2010	25
Andy Irons	Surfer	Multiple prescriptions	Prescription	2010	32
Edward Fatu	Wrestler	Multiple prescriptions	Prescription	2009	36
Michael Jackson	Singer and pop icon	Propofol and prescriptions	Prescriptions	2009	50

Data from Drugs.com. "Drug-Related Deaths-Notable Celebrities." n.d. Available http://www.drugs.com/celebrity_deaths.html

capable of crossing membranes can enter the blood as rapidly as they can via intravenous (IV) injection and can be equally as dangerous (Halford 2015). Ether, chloroform, and nitrous oxide anesthetics are examples of drugs that are therapeutically administered by inhalation. Nicotine, cocaine, methamphetamine, tetrahydrocannabinol (THC; active ingredient in marijuana), heroin, and products known as Spice are drugs of abuse that can be inhaled as smoke (de Havenon et al. 2011; Lisi 2014; Mathias 1997). One serious problem with inhalation is the potential for irritation to the mucous membrane lining of the lungs; another is that the drug may have to be continually inhaled to maintain the concentration necessary for an effect. Inhalation of illicit drugs of abuse is common to prevent contracting the human immunodeficiency virus (HIV), which can be transmitted by IV injection with contaminated needles (NIDA 2015a).

Drugs can be introduced into the body using various methods, such as pills, capsules, oral liquids, topicals, or injections.

INJECTION

Some drugs are given by **intravenous (IV)**, **intramuscular (IM)**, or **subcutaneous (SC)** injection. A major advantage of administering drugs by IV is the speed of action; the dosage is delivered rapidly and directly, and often less drug is needed because it reaches the site of action quickly. This method can be very dangerous if the dosage is calculated incorrectly, the drug effects are unknown, or the user is especially sensitive to the drug's adverse effects.

In addition, impurities in injected materials may irritate the vein; this issue is a particular problem in the drug-abusing population, in which needle sharing frequently occurs. The injection itself injures the vein by leaving a tiny point of scar tissue where the vein is punctured. If repeated injections are administered into the same area, the elasticity of the vein is gradually reduced, causing the vessel to collapse.

Intramuscular injection can damage the muscle directly if the drug preparation irritates the tissue or indirectly if the nerve controlling the muscle is damaged. If the nerve is destroyed, the muscle will degenerate (atrophy). A subcutaneous injection may damage the skin at the point of injection if a particularly irritating drug is administered. Another danger of drug injections arises when

KEY TERMS

intravenous (IV)
drug injection into a vein

intramuscular (IM)
drug injection into a muscle

subcutaneous (SC)
drug injection beneath the skin

contaminated needles are shared by drug users. This danger has become a serious problem in the spread of infectious diseases, such as acquired immunodeficiency syndrome (AIDS), which is caused by HIV, and hepatitis. For example, in 2013, ~10% of the 47,000 diagnoses of HIV infection in the United States were due to intravenous drug use (CDC 2015).

TOPICAL APPLICATION

Those drugs that readily pass through surface tissue such as the skin, the lining of the nose, and under the tongue can be applied topically for systemic (whole-body) effects. Although many drugs do not appreciably diffuse across these tissue barriers into the circulation, there are notable exceptions. For example, a product to help quit smoking, a nicotine transdermal patch (Nicoderm), is placed on the skin; the drug passes through the skin and enters the body to prevent tobacco craving and withdrawal. In addition, several drugs of abuse, such as heroin and cocaine, can be "snorted" into the nose and rapidly absorbed into the body through the nasal lining (Dixon n.d.).

■ Distribution of Drugs in the Body and Time–Response Relationships

Following administration (regardless of the mode), most drugs are distributed throughout the body in the blood. The circulatory system consists of many miles of arteries, veins, and capillaries and includes 5 to 6 liters of blood. Once a drug enters the bloodstream by passing through thin capillary walls, it is rapidly diluted and carried to organs and other body structures. It requires approximately 1 minute for the blood, and consequently the drugs it contains, to circulate completely throughout the body.

Transdermal nicotine patches are popular smoking cessation aids.

FACTORS AFFECTING DISTRIBUTION

Drugs have different patterns of distribution depending on the following chemical properties (Byron 2015):

- Their ability to pass across membranes and through tissues
- Their molecular size (large versus small molecules)
- Their solubility properties (do they dissolve in water or in fatty [oily] solutions?)
- Their tendency to attach to proteins and tissues throughout the body

These distribution-related factors are very important because they determine whether a drug can pass across tissue barriers in the body and reach its site of action. By preventing the movement of drugs into organs or across tissues, these barriers may interfere with drug activity and limit the therapeutic usefulness of a drug if they do not allow it to reach its site of action. Such barriers may also offer protection by preventing entry of a drug into a body structure where it can cause problems.

Blood is carried to the nerve cells of the brain in a vast network of thin-walled capillaries. Drugs that are soluble in fatty (oily) solutions are most likely to pass across these capillary membranes (known as the **blood–brain barrier**) into the brain tissue. Most psychoactive drugs, such as the drugs of abuse, are able to pass across the blood–brain barrier with little difficulty. However, many water-soluble drugs cannot pass through the fatty capillary wall; such drugs are not likely to cross this biological barrier and affect the brain. An interesting practical application of this pharmacokinetic principle is the use of "vaccines" to treat nicotine (Glatter 2013), methamphetamine, or cocaine (Kosten et al. 2014) dependence. Like other vaccines, this approach stimulates the body to produce antibodies against a chemical target that is introduced into the body (often injected under the skin). Consequently, when specially formulated nicotine or cocaine (a chemical form that causes an immunoreaction) is injected into the body, it stimulates the production of reactive antibodies in the patient. These antibodies will then bind to nicotine or cocaine that is later consumed and has entered into the bloodstream. With the attached antibody, the drug is too large to get across biological barriers such as the blood–brain barrier and often becomes pharmacologically inactive. This means that the antibodies prevent nicotine or cocaine from being rewarding or from having effects on the brain in general and help the addict to stop using the substance (Kosten et al. 2014).

A second biological barrier, the placenta, prevents the transfer of certain molecules from the mother to the fetus. A principal factor that determines passage of substances across the placental barrier is molecule size. Large molecules do not usually cross the placental barrier, whereas small molecules do. Because most drugs are relatively small molecules, they usually cross from the maternal circulation into the fetal circulation; thus, most drugs (including drugs of abuse) taken by a woman during pregnancy enter and affect the fetus. This can cause a baby of a narcotic-using mother, for example, to experience severe withdrawal symptoms after birth (Tully 2015; see "Case in Point: The Newborn Victims").

REQUIRED DOSES FOR EFFECTS

Most drugs do not take effect until a certain amount has been administered and a crucial concentration has reached the site of action in the body. The smallest amount of a drug needed to elicit a response is called its **threshold dose**.

The effectiveness of some drugs may be calculated in a *linear* (straight-line) fashion—that is, the more drug that is taken, the more drug that is distributed throughout the body, and the greater the effect. However, many drugs have a maximum possible effect, regardless of dose; this is called the **plateau effect**. OTC medications, in particular, have a limit on their effects. For example, use of the nonprescription analgesic aspirin can effectively relieve your mild to moderate pain, but aspirin will not effectively treat your severe pains, regardless of the dose taken. Other drugs may cause distinct or opposite effects, depending on the dose. For example, low doses of alcohol may appear to act like a stimulant, causing the drinker to be talkative and social, whereas high doses usually cause sedation, resulting in drowsiness and eventually sleep or, in extreme cases, even coma.

KEY TERMS

blood–brain barrier
selective filtering between the cerebral blood vessels and the brain

threshold dose
minimum drug dose necessary to cause an effect

plateau effect
maximum drug effect, regardless of dose

► **CASE IN POINT**

The Newborn Victims

"*G*uilty, that's how I feel," Nicole said as she waited in a hospital conference room. No one could blame Nicole for her anguish and feelings of culpability as she watched her 5-pound, 5-day-old son intensely squirming in his white blanket; after all, it was her history of abusing opioid narcotics that caused her son's suffering. Although his discomfort and pain were obvious, Nicole could imagine how much worse her son would feel if he had not been given a dose of morphine to suppress his opiate cravings, high-pitched cry, and intense withdrawal symptoms. Without this morphine dose to mitigate his narcotic physical dependence, the newborn's body would have been writhing in agony, shaking, overcome with severe diarrhea, unable to eat, and completely miserable. Nicole knew that her son's body had become dependent on the methadone she was taking while he was in the womb. She remembered back 10 years when she was first prescribed a potent opioid painkiller to relieve pain associated with surgery to treat her obesity. In the years following, she gradually increased her dependence on these analgesics until she was downing up to a dozen of these pills at a time. Although she avoided turning to heroin, she did spend all the money she could get her hands on to illegally obtain medications such as Vicodin and OxyContin to satisfy her narcotic habit. After several years she finally sought professional help and began to receive legal daily doses of the potent narcotic methadone to replace her body's need for the narcotics. While methadone treatments made it possible for her to avoid the illegally obtained prescription painkillers, to avoid severe withdrawal during her pregnancy Nicole used methadone daily while her son was in utero. The consequence was that while Nicole's opioid-dependent body did not experience withdrawal, her son's developing body, much like his mother's, was physically dependent on these drugs by the time he was born. Also like his mother, now that he was born, he required daily narcotic treatment to prevent withdrawal from his mother's methadone.

In recent years many hospitals claim there has been a flood of babies born dependent on drugs the mothers have been using during their pregnancies. One doctor compared this trend to the spread of Ebola: "Nobody had it, and then all of a sudden everybody had it."

Data from Tully, M. "Meet Heroin's Tiniest Victims: Newborns." *USA Today*. (1 June 2015). Available http://www.USAtoday.com/story/news/nation-now /2015/06/01/heroin-babies-morphine-opiate-drugs/28299459/

TIME–RESPONSE FACTORS

An important factor that determines responses is the time that has elapsed between when a drug was administered and the onset of its effects. The delay in effect after administering a drug often relates to the time required for the drug to disseminate from the site of administration to the site of action. Consequently, the closer a drug is placed to the target area, the faster the onset of action.

The drug response is often classified as immediate, short term, or **acute**, referring to the response after a single dose. The response can also be **chronic**, or long term—a characteristic usually associated with repeated doses. The intensity and quality of a drug's acute effect may change considerably within a short period of time. For example, the main intoxicating effects of a large dose of alcohol generally peak in less than 1 hour and then gradually taper off. In addition, an initial stimulating effect by alcohol may later change to sedation and depression.

The effects of long-term, or chronic, use of some drugs can differ dramatically from the effects noted with their short-term, or acute, use. The administration of small doses may not produce any immediately apparent detrimental effect, but chronic use of the same drug (frequent use over a long time) may yield prolonged effects that do not become apparent until years later. Although for most people there are minimal effects caused by short-term use of small doses of

KEY TERMS

acute
immediate or short-term effects after taking a single drug dose

chronic
long-term effects, usually after taking multiple drug doses

tobacco, its chronic use has damaging effects on heart and lung functions (Jorenby 2015). Because of these long-term consequences, research on tobacco and its effects often continues for years, making it difficult to unequivocally prove a correlation between specific diseases or health problems and use of this substance. Thus, the results of tobacco research are often disputed by tobacco manufacturers with vested financial interests in the substance and its public acceptance.

Another important time factor that influences drug responses is the interval between multiple administrations. If sufficient time for drug metabolism and elimination does not separate doses, a drug can accumulate within the body. This drug buildup due to relatively short dosing intervals is referred to as a **cumulative effect**. Because of the resulting high concentrations of drug in the body, unexpected prolonged drug effects or toxicity can occur when multiple doses are given within short intervals. This situation occurs with cocaine or methamphetamine addicts who repeatedly administer these stimulants during "binges" or "runs," increasing the likelihood of dangerous effects.

❚ Inactivation and Elimination of Drugs from the Body

Immediately after drug administration, the body begins to eliminate the substance in various ways. The time required to remove half of the original amount of drug administered is called the **half-life** of the drug. The body eliminates the drug either directly without altering it chemically or (in most instances) after it has been metabolized (chemically altered) or modified. The process of changing the chemical or pharmacological properties of a drug by metabolism is called **biotransformation**. **Metabolism** usually makes it possible for the body to inactivate, detoxify, and excrete drugs and other chemicals, although metabolism can sometimes actually cause a drug such as heroin to become *more* active.

The liver is the primary organ that metabolizes drugs in the body. This complex biochemical laboratory contains hundreds of enzymes that continuously synthesize, modify, and deactivate biochemical substances such as drugs. The healthy liver is also capable of metabolizing many of the chemicals that occur naturally in the body (such as hormones). These metabolizing enzymes are highly regulatable. Genetic variations in their structures can account for a wide

variation in their activity, influencing onset, duration, and potency of drug effects, thereby affecting vulnerability to developing dependence and addiction (see "Family Matters: Genetics of Metabolic Enzymes and Alcoholism"). After the liver enzymes metabolize a drug (the resulting chemicals are called **metabolites**), the products usually pass into the urine or feces for final elimination. Drugs and their metabolites can appear in other places as well, such as sweat, saliva, or expired air.

The kidneys are probably the next most important organs for drug elimination because they remove metabolites and foreign substances from the body. The kidneys constantly eliminate substances from the blood. The rate of excretion of some drugs by the kidneys can be altered by making the urine more acidic or more alkaline. For example, nicotine and amphetamines can be cleared faster from the body by making the urine slightly more acidic, and salicylates and barbiturates can be cleared more rapidly by making it more alkaline. Such techniques are used in emergency rooms and can be useful in the treatment of drug overdosing. Changing urine acidity is also a technique used by drug abusers to accelerate elimination of substances from their body that would be identified by drug tests and result in disqualification from sports competition, loss of a job, or even termination of parole and a return to incarceration (Get the Facts 2016).

The body may eliminate small portions of drugs through perspiration and exhalation. Approximately 1% of consumed alcohol is eliminated in the breath and thus may be measured with a breathalyzer; this apparatus is used by police

KEY TERMS

cumulative effect
buildup of a drug in the body after multiple doses taken at short intervals

half-life
time required for the body to eliminate and/or metabolize half of a drug dose

biotransformation
process of changing the chemical properties of a drug, usually by metabolism

metabolism
chemical alteration of drugs by body processes

metabolites
chemical products of metabolism

FAMILY MATTERS

Genetics of Metabolic Enzymes and Alcoholism

It has been known for a long time that alcoholism frequently clusters in some families, and even to some extent in some races, suggesting that its expression is strongly influenced by heritability and gene expression. However, only lately, because of sophisticated molecular biology techniques, have we finally been able to identify some of the specific genes involved and how their expression influences the development of alcoholism. A particularly compelling discovery is the finding that liver enzymes known as alcohol dehydrogenases exist in several variant forms that are determined by a person's genetics. One variant of this enzyme, known as ADH2, appears to be associated with decreased incidences of alcoholic liver cirrhosis. The protective properties of this gene expression likely relates to its ability to rapidly metabolize alcohol into acetaldehyde, which, in turn, causes facial flushing, nausea, headache, and drowsiness. It is thought that these adverse effects reduce alcohol consumption and the associated damage to the liver, especially in some Asian populations.

Data from He, L., T. Deng, and H. Luo. "Genetic Polymorphism in Alcohol Dehydrogenase 2 (ADH2) Gene and Alcoholic Liver Cirrhosis Risk." *International Journal of Clinical and Experimental Medicine* 8 (2015): 7786–7793.

officers in evaluating suspected drunk drivers. Most people are aware that consumption of garlic will change body odor because garlic is excreted through perspiration. Some drugs are handled in the same way. The mammary glands are modified sweat glands, so it is not surprising that many drugs are concentrated and excreted in milk during lactation, including antibiotics, nicotine, barbiturates, caffeine, and alcohol. Excretion of drugs in a mother's milk can pose a particular concern during nursing because the excreted drugs can be consumed by and affect the infant (March of Dimes 2015).

The breathalyzer takes advantage of the fact that alcohol is partially eliminated from the body in the breath.

■ Physiological Variables That Modify Drug Effects

As previously mentioned, individuals' responses to drugs vary greatly, even when the same doses are administered in the same manner. This variability can be especially troublesome when dealing with drugs that have a narrow margin of safety. Many of these variables reflect differences in the pharmacokinetic factors just discussed and are associated with diversity in body size, composition, or functions. They include the following factors (Hussar 2015):

- *Age*: Changes in body size and makeup occur throughout the aging process, from infancy to old age. Changes in the rates of drug absorption, biotransformation, and elimination also arise as a consequence of aging. As a general rule, young children and elderly people should be administered smaller drug doses (calculated as drug quantity per unit of body weight) due to their immature or compromised body processes.
- *Gender*: Variations in drug responses due to gender usually relate to differences in body size, composition, or hormones (male vs. female types, e.g., androgens vs. estrogens). Most clinicians find many more similarities than differences between males and females relative to their responses to drugs, although there are

clinically relevant differences in the effects of alcohol and tobacco on males and females.

- *Pregnancy:* During the course of pregnancy, unique factors must be considered when administering drugs. For example, the physiology of the mother changes as the fetus develops and puts additional stress on organ systems, such as the heart, liver, and kidneys. This increased demand can make the woman more susceptible to the toxicity of some drugs. In addition, as the fetus develops, it can be very vulnerable to drugs with **teratogenic** properties (which cause abnormal development). Consequently, it is usually advisable to avoid taking any drugs during pregnancy, if possible.

■ Pathological Variables That Modify Drug Effects

Individuals with diseases or compromised organ systems need to be particularly careful when taking drugs. Some diseases can damage or impair organs that are vital for appropriate and safe responses to drugs. For example, hepatitis (inflammation of and damage to the liver caused by a viral infection) interferes with the metabolism and disposal of many drugs, resulting in a longer duration of drug action and increased likelihood of side effects. Similar concerns are associated with kidney disease, which compromises renal activity and diminishes excretion capacity. Because many drugs affect the cardiovascular system (especially drugs of abuse, such as stimulants, tobacco, and alcohol), patients with a history of cardiovascular disease (heart attack, stroke, hypertension, or abnormal heart rhythm) should be particularly cautious when using drugs. They should be aware of medicines that stimulate the cardiovascular system, especially those that are self-administered, such as OTC decongestants and diet aids. These drugs should be either avoided or used only under the supervision of a physician.

■ Pharmacokinetics and Drug Testing

Drug testing has become an important part of the prevention, detection, and treatment of drug abuse. Many of the pharmacokinetic elements discussed in this section have important implications on drug testing and its ability to reliably determine which, how much, and when drugs have been abused. For example, how rapidly a drug gets into the blood or the urine after it is consumed, how long it stays in the body, and what its metabolites are can all profoundly influence drug testing outcomes. However, even though we have come to rely a great deal on drug testing to evaluate employees, discourage athletes from cheating, and determine compliance in persons with a history of drug abuse problems, we should appreciate that this technology has significant drawbacks that should be considered if we are to accurately interpret its outcomes. To illustrate this point, see "Here and Now: Drug Test Results Can Be Flawed."

Adaptive Processes and Drug Abuse

Your body systems are constantly changing so they can establish and maintain balance in their physiological and mental functions; such balance is necessary for optimal functioning of all organ systems, including the brain, heart, lungs, gastrointestinal tract, liver, and kidneys. Sometimes, drugs interfere with the activity of the body's systems and compromise their normal workings. These drug-induced disruptions can be so severe that they can even cause death. For example, stimulants can dangerously increase the heart rate and blood pressure and cause heart attacks, whereas CNS depressants can diminish brain activity, resulting in unconsciousness and a loss of breathing reflexes.

To protect against potential harm, the organ systems of the body can adjust to disruption. Of particular relevance to drugs of abuse are the adaptive processes known as *tolerance* and **dependence** (both psychological and physical types) and the related phenomenon of *withdrawal* (see **Figure 5.4**).

Tolerance and dependence are closely linked, most likely resulting from multiple drug exposures, and thought to be caused by similar mechanisms. Tolerance occurs when the response to the same dose of a drug decreases with repeated use

KEY TERMS

teratogenic
something that causes physical defects in a fetus

dependence
physiological and psychological changes or adaptations that occur in response to the frequent administration of a drug

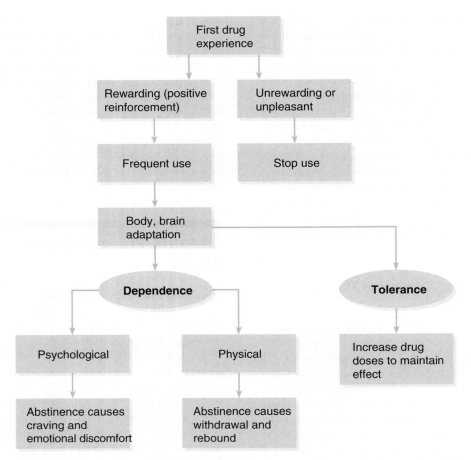

FIGURE 5.4 The relationship and consequences of adaptive processes to drug abuse. The processes discussed in the text are highlighted in the figure.

(Luscher 2015). Increasing the dose can sometimes compensate for tolerance to a drug of abuse. For the most part, the adaptations that cause the tolerance phenomenon are also associated with altered physical and psychological states that lead to dependence. The user develops dependence in the sense that if the drug is no longer taken, the systems of the body become overcompensated and unbalanced, causing withdrawal. In general, withdrawal symptoms are opposite in nature to the direct effects of the drug that caused the dependence (Luscher 2015).

Although tolerance, dependence, and withdrawal are all consequences of adaptation by the body and its systems, they are not inseparable processes. It is possible to become tolerant to a drug without developing dependence, and vice versa (see **Table 5.2**). The following sections provide greater detail about these adaptive drug responses, which are very important for many therapeutic drugs and almost all drugs of abuse (Luscher 2015).

■ Tolerance to Drugs

The extent of tolerance and the rate at which it is acquired depend on the drug, the person using the drug, the dosage, and the frequency of administration. Some drug effects may be reduced more rapidly than others when drugs are used frequently. Tolerance to effects that are rewarding or reinforcing often causes users to increase the dosage. Sometimes abstinence from a drug can reduce tolerance, but with renewed use the tolerance can return quickly. It is important to remember that the body does not necessarily develop tolerance to all effects of a drug equally.

TABLE 5.2 Tolerance, Dependence, and Withdrawal Properties of Common Drugs of Abuse

Drug	Tolerance	Psychological Dependence	Physical Dependence	Withdrawal Symptoms (Include Rebound Effects)
Barbiturates	■■	■■	■■■	Restlessness, anxiety, vomiting, tremors, seizures
Alcohol	■■	■■	■■■	Cramps, delirium, vomiting, sweating, hallucinations, seizures
Benzodiazepines	■	■■	■■	Insomnia, restlessness, nausea, fatigue, twitching, seizures (rare)
Narcotics (heroin)	■■■	■■	■■■	Vomiting, sweating, cramps, diarrhea, depression, irritability, gooseflesh
Cocaine, amphetamines	■*	■■■	■■	Depression, anxiety, drug craving, need for sleep ("crash"), anhedonia
Nicotine	■	■■	■■	Highly variable; craving, irritability, headache, increased appetite, abnormal sleep
Caffeine	■	■	■	Anxiety, lethargy, headache, fatigue
Marijuana	■	■	■	Irritability, restlessness, decreased appetite, weight loss, abnormal sleep
LSD (lysergic acid diethylamide)	■■	■	—	Minimal
PCP (phencyclidine)	■	■	■	Fear, tremors, some craving, problems with short-term memory

■■■ Intense ■■ Moderate ■ Some — Not significant
*Can sensitize.

HERE AND NOW
Drug Test Results Can Be Flawed

We often rely on the outcomes of drug testing to make critical decisions about whom we should hire or fire, who has violated conditions of their parole and should go back to jail, which athlete has cheated and should be disqualified from competition, or how well a patient is responding to drug treatment. However, although results from drug testing can be an important tool, drug testing is far from perfect, and its flaws should be considered when basing important decisions upon its outcomes. The following are facts and myths about this technology that should be remembered:

- *Fact*: The poppy seeds on a single bagel are sufficient to test positive for opioid narcotics such as Lortab or Vicodin.

- *Fiction*: Most standard drug tests screen for the opioid drug oxycodone (active ingredient in Oxy-Contin), methadone, and the very potent opioid drug fentanyl. (Explanation: This is false because if these are drugs of interest, they must be specially requested to be included in the screening.)

- *Fact*: In 2009, about 150 million drug tests were conducted in the United States.

- *Fact*: Most physicians do not know what drugs are included in a "standard" drug test.

- *Fact*: About 5% to 10% of tested patients will have inaccurate results.

- *Fiction*: Passive inhalation of marijuana or cocaine accounts for 20% of the positives when testing

(continues)

HERE AND NOW

Drug Test Results Can Be Flawed (*continued*)

for these substances. (Explanation: This is false because casual breathing of cocaine or marijuana smoke is insufficient to cause a positive outcome on standard drug tests.)

- Fiction: Methods to mask or falsify a drug test never work. (Explanation: Actually, efforts to mask a positive drug test appear to work about 50% of the time. Strategies such as adding bleach or household cleaner such as Drano to urine samples can mask drug detection.)

Data from Fiore, K. "APA: Drug Test Results Often Flawed." MedPage Today. 23 May 2010. Available http://www.medpagetoday.com/MeetingCoverage?APA/20253

The exact mechanisms by which the body becomes tolerant to different drug effects are not completely understood but may be related to those mechanisms that cause dependence (Hussar 2014). Several processes have been suggested as candidates. Potent depressants such as barbiturates stimulate the body's production of metabolic enzymes, primarily in the liver, and cause drugs to be inactivated and eliminated faster. In addition, evidence suggests that a considerable degree of CNS tolerance to some drugs develops independent of changes in the rate of metabolism or excretion. This process reflects the adaptation of drug target sites in nervous tissue, such as neurotransmitter receptors, so that the effect produced by the same concentration of drug decreases over time.

Another type of drug response that can appear to be tolerance but is actually a learned adjustment is called behavioral compensation. Drug effects that are troubling may be compensated for or hidden by the drug user. Thus, alcoholics learn to speak and walk slowly to compensate for the slurred speech and stumbling gait that alcohol consumption usually causes. To an observer, it might appear as though the pharmacological effects of the drug are diminished,

but they are actually unchanged. Consequently, this type of adaptation is not a true form of tolerance.

OTHER TOLERANCE-RELATED FACTORS

The tolerance process can affect drug responses in several ways. We have discussed the effect of tolerance that diminishes the action of drugs and causes the user to compensate by increasing the dose. The following are examples of two other ways that processes related to tolerance can influence drug responses.

REVERSE TOLERANCE (SENSITIZATION)

Under some conditions, a response to a drug is elicited that is the opposite of tolerance. This effect is known as **reverse tolerance**, or sensitization. If you were sensitized, you would have the same response to a lower dose of a drug as you initially did to the original, higher dose. This condition seems to occur in users of morphine as well as amphetamines and cocaine (Addiction Blog 2014).

Although the causes of reverse tolerance are still unclear, some researchers believe that its development depends on how often, how much, and in which setting the drug is consumed. It has been speculated that this heightened response to drugs of abuse may reflect adaptive changes in the nervous tissues (target site of these drugs). The reverse tolerance that occurs with cocaine use may be responsible for the psychotic effects or the seizures caused by its chronic use (Addiction Blog 2014).

KEY TERM

reverse tolerance
enhanced response to a given drug dose; opposite of tolerance

CROSS-TOLERANCE

Development of tolerance to a drug sometimes can produce tolerance to other similar drugs. This phenomenon, known as **cross-tolerance**, may be due to altered metabolism resulting from chronic drug use. For example, a heavy drinker will usually exhibit tolerance to barbiturates, other depressants, and anesthetics because the alcohol has induced (stimulated) his or her liver metabolic enzymes to inactivate these other drugs more rapidly. Cross-tolerance might also occur among drugs that cause similar pharmacological actions. For example, if adaptations have occurred in nervous tissue that cause tolerance to one drug, such changes might produce tolerance to other similar drugs that exert their effects by interacting with that same nervous tissue site. This is common with all of the opioid narcotics, including both prescription (e.g., morphine) and illegal (e.g., heroin) drugs (Alcohorehab.com 2015).

∎ Drug Dependence

Drug dependence can be associated with either physiological or psychological adaptations. Physical dependence reflects changes in the way organs and systems in the body respond to a drug, whereas psychological dependence is caused by changes in attitudes and expectations. In both types of dependence, the individual experiences a need (either physical or emotional) for the drug to be present for the body or the mind to function normally.

PHYSICAL DEPENDENCE

In general, the drugs that cause physical dependence also are associated with a drug withdrawal phenomenon called the **rebound effect**. This condition is also sometimes referred to as the *paradoxical effect* because the symptoms included in rebound phenomena are nearly opposite to the direct effects of the drug. For example, a person regularly consuming alcohol or benzodiazepines will be depressed physically while the drug is in the brain but during withdrawal may become irritable, hyperexcited, and nervous and generally show symptoms of extreme stimulation of the nervous system and perhaps even life-threatening seizures. These reactions constitute the rebound effect.

Physical dependence may develop with high-intensity use of such common drugs as alcohol, Xanax, narcotics, and other CNS depressants. However, with moderate, intermittent use of these drugs, most people do not become significantly physically dependent. Those who do become physically dependent often experience damaged social and personal skills and relationships and impaired brain and motor functions.

Withdrawal symptoms resulting from physical dependency can be mitigated by administering a sufficient quantity of the original drug or one with similar pharmacological activity. The latter case, in which different drugs can be used interchangeably to prevent withdrawal symptoms, is called **cross-dependence**. For example, benzodiazepines and other CNS depressants can be used to treat the abstinence syndrome experienced by the chronic alcoholic. Another example is the use of methadone, a long-acting narcotic, to treat withdrawal from heroin (Alcoholrehab.com 2015). Such therapeutic strategies allow the substitution of safer and more easily managed drugs for dangerous drugs of abuse and play a major role in treatment of drug dependency.

PSYCHOLOGICAL DEPENDENCE

Psychological dependence has been described as an intense desire to consume a drug that is linked to craving when the drug is not being used (NewDay Counseling 2015). This sense of dependence usually causes repeated self-administration of the drug in a fashion described as abuse and can lead to substance use disorder. Such dependence may be found either independent of or associated with physical dependence. Psychological dependence does not produce the physical discomfort, rebound effects, or life-threatening consequences that can be associated with physical dependence. Even so, it does produce intense cravings and strong urges that frequently draw former drug abusers back to their habits of drug self-administration. In many instances, psychological

KEY TERMS

cross-tolerance
development of tolerance to one drug causes tolerance to related drugs

rebound effect
form of withdrawal; paradoxical effects that occur when a drug has been eliminated from the body

cross-dependence
dependence on a drug can be relieved by other similar drugs

psychological dependence
dependence that results because a drug produces pleasant mental effects

aspects may be more significant than physical dependence in maintaining chronic drug use. Thus, the major problem with cocaine or nicotine dependence is not so much the physical aspect, because withdrawal can be successfully achieved in a few weeks; rather, strong urges often cause a return to chronic use of these substances because of psychological dependence.

How does psychological dependence develop? If the first drug trial is rewarding, a few more rewarding trials will follow until drug use becomes a conditioned pattern of behavior. Continued positive psychological reinforcement with the drug leads, in time, to primary psychological dependence. Primary psychological dependence, in turn, may produce uncontrollable compulsive abuse of any psychoactive drug in certain susceptible people, leading to physical dependence. The degree of drug dependence is contingent on the nature of the psychoactive substance, the quantity used, the duration of use, and the characteristics of the person and his or her environment.

Even strong psychological dependence on some psychoactive substances does not necessarily result in injury or social harm. For example, typical dosages of mild stimulants such as coffee usually do not induce serious physical, social, or emotional harm. Even though the effects on the CNS are barely detectable by a casual observer, strong psychological dependence on stimulants like tobacco and caffeine-containing beverages may develop; however, the fact that their dependence does not typically induce antisocial and destructive behavior distinguishes them from most forms of dependence-producing drugs.

Psychological Factors

The general effect of most drugs is greatly influenced by a variety of psychological and environmental factors. Unique qualities of an individual's personality, his or her past history of drug and social experience, attitudes toward the drug, expectations of its effects, and motivation for use are extremely influential. These factors are often referred to collectively as the person's **mental set**. The setting, or total environment, in which a drug is taken may profoundly modify its effect.

The mental set and setting are particularly important in influencing the responses to psychoactive drugs (drugs that alter the functions of the brain). For example, ingestion of LSD, a commonly abused hallucinogen, can cause pleasant, even spiritual-like experiences in comfortable, congenial surroundings. In contrast, when the same amount of LSD is consumed in hostile, threatening surroundings, the effect can be frightening, taking on a nightmarish quality.

■ The Placebo Effect

The psychological factors that influence responses to drugs, independent of their pharmacological properties, are known as **placebo effects**. The word *placebo* is derived from Latin and means "I shall please." The placebo effect is most likely to occur when an individual's mental set is susceptible to suggestion. A placebo drug is a pharmacologically inactive compound that the user thinks causes some therapeutic or physiological change. In some persons or in particular settings, a placebo substance may have surprisingly powerful consequences (Feinberg 2013). For example, a substantial component of most pain is perception. Consequently, placebos administered as pain relievers and promoted properly can provide dramatic relief. Therefore, in spite of what appears to be a drug effect, the placebo is not considered a pharmacological agent because it does not directly alter any body functions by its chemical nature.

The bulk of medical history may actually be a history of confidence in the cure—a history of placebo medicine—because many effective cures of the past have been shown to be without relevant pharmacological action, suggesting that their effects were psychologically mediated. In fact, even today, some people argue that placebo effects are a significant component of most drug therapy, particularly when using OTC medications or herbal products. It is important when testing new drugs for effectiveness that drug experiments be conducted in a manner that allows a distinction to be drawn between pharmacological and placebo effects. Such studies can usually be done by treating one group with the real drug and another group with a placebo that looks like the drug and then comparing the responses to both treatments.

KEY TERMS

mental set
the collection of psychological and environmental factors that influence an individual's response to drugs

placebo effects
effects caused by suggestion and psychological factors independent of the pharmacological activity of a drug

Addiction (Substance Use Disorder) and Abuse: The Significance of Dependence

The term *addiction* has many meanings. It often is used interchangeably with *dependence, drug abuse,* or *substance use disorder* (APA 2013). The traditional model of the addiction-producing drug is based on opiate narcotics and requires the individual to develop tolerance and both physical and psychological dependence. This model often is not satisfactory because only a few commonly abused drugs fit all of these parameters. It is clearly inadequate for many drugs that can cause serious dependency problems but that produce little tolerance, even with extended use (see Table 5.2).

Because it is difficult to assess the contribution of physical and psychological factors to drug dependency, determining whether all psychoactive drugs truly cause drug addiction poses a challenge. To alleviate confusion, it has been suggested that the term *dependence* (either physical or psychological) or *substance use disorder* be used instead of *addiction.* However, because of its acceptance by the public, the term *addiction* is not likely to disappear from general use. In addition, addiction often implies compulsive behavior (i.e., a need to have and use a drug despite negative consequences), which can be independent of physical dependence. This confusion is likely to continue until some consensus can be reached regarding how to best define this concept.

Some have speculated that the only means by which drug dependence/addiction can be eliminated from society is to prevent exposure to those drugs that have the potential to be abused. Because some drugs are such powerful, immediate reinforcers (i.e., they cause a rapid reward), it is feared that rapid dependence (psychological) will occur when anyone uses them. Although it may be true that most people, under certain conditions, could become dependent on some drug with abuse potential, in reality most people who have used psychoactive drugs do not develop significant psychological or physical dependence or addiction. For example, approximately 87% of those who use alcohol experience minimal personal injury and few negative social consequences. Of those who have used stimulants, depressants, or hallucinogens for illicit recreational purposes, only 10% to 20% become significantly dependent

(O'Brien 2006). The following sections discuss some possible reasons for this variability.

■ Hereditary Factors

The reasons why some people readily develop dependence on psychoactive drugs and others do not are not well understood. Of importance may be heredity, which predisposes some people to drug abuse (Learn.Genetics 2015), and the interaction of genetic vulnerability with high-risk environments (see "Family Matters: Family Addictions and Genetics"). For example, studies of identical and fraternal twins have revealed a greater similarity in the rate of alcoholism for identical twins than for fraternal twins if alcohol abuse begins before the age of 20 years (Adamec 2015). Because identical twins have 100% of their genes in common whereas fraternal twins share significantly fewer of their genes, these results suggest that genetic factors can be important in determining the likelihood of alcohol dependence (O'Brien 2006; Scott and Taylor 2007). It is possible that similar genetic factors contribute to other types of drug dependence as well.

■ Drug Craving

Frequently, a person who becomes dependent develops a powerful, uncontrollable desire for drugs during or after withdrawal from heroin, cocaine, alcohol, nicotine, or other addicting substance. This desire for drugs is known as *craving.* Because researchers do not agree as to the nature of craving, there does not exist a universally recognized scientific definition or an accepted method to measure this psychological phenomenon; however, it is thought to be distinct from the phenomenon of withdrawal. Some drug abuse experts claim that craving is the principal cause of drug abuse and relapse after treatment; others believe that it is not a cause but a side effect of drugs that produce dependence. One definition is that drug cravings are to addicts what obsessions and compulsions are to obsessive compulsive disorder (OCD) (Waters Edge Recovery 2014). Craving is often assessed by (1) questioning patients about the intensity of their drug urges; (2) measuring physiological changes, such as increases in heart and breathing rates, sweating, and subtle changes in the tension of facial muscles; and (3) determining patients' tendency to relapse into drug-taking behavior (Sayette 2016).

Evidence indicates that at least two levels of craving can exist. For example, cocaine users experience an acute craving when using the drug itself, but the ex-cocaine abuser can have chronic cravings that are triggered by familiar environmental cues that elicit positive memories of cocaine's reinforcing effects.

Although it is not likely that craving itself causes drug addiction, it is generally believed that if pharmacological or psychological therapies could be devised that reduced or eliminated drug craving treatment of drug dependence would be more successful. Thus, many researchers are attempting to identify medications or psychological strategies that interfere with the development and expression of the craving phenomenon.

▮ Other Factors

If a drug causes a positive effect in the user's view, it is much more likely to be abused than if it causes an aversive experience (see Figure 5.4). Perhaps genetic factors influence the brain or personality so that some people find taking drugs an enjoyable experience (at least initially), whereas others find the effects very unpleasant and uncomfortable (**dysphoric**) (Vergne and Anton 2010). Other factors that could contribute significantly to drug use patterns include (1) peer pressure (especially in the initial drug experimentation); (2) home, school, and work environments; (3) feeling lonely or bullied; and (4) media influence (Bellum 2013). It is estimated that 30% to 60% of drug abusers have some underlying psychiatric illness, such as personality disorder, major depression, bipolar disorder, or schizophrenia (Dual Diagnosis n.d.). In some cases, the drug user may be attempting to relieve symptoms associated with the mental disorder by self-medicating with the

KEY TERM

dysphoric
characterized by unpleasant mental effects; the opposite of euphoric

FAMILY MATTERS

Family Addictions and Genetics

Substance abuse, alcoholism, and associated trauma seem to have both genetic and environmental components, the interaction of which can have serious consequences. For example, alcoholism tends to run in families. Thus, children of alcoholics are at high risk to become alcohol users themselves because of their genetic vulnerability as well as because of the traumatic environments to which they are often exposed. Levels of conflict in families characterized by alcoholism are much higher than in families with no alcoholism. The environment to which children with alcoholic parents are exposed may include a lack of communication, emotional and physical violence, isolation, and financial problems. At least half of all cases of child maltreatment are linked to a prevalence of substance abuse and alcoholism in the home. It has also been reported that children who receive prenatal exposure to drugs are two to three times more likely to be neglected or abused.

Data from Learn.Genetics. "Drugs of Abuse." University of Utah Genetics (2015) Available http://learn.genetics.utah.edu/content/addiction/abuse/

substance of abuse (Buckley and Brown 2006; Purse 2013).

It is difficult to identify all of the specific factors that influence the risk of drug abuse for each individual. If such factors could be identified, treatment would be improved, and those at greatest risk for drug abuse could be identified and informed of their vulnerability. **Table 5.3** lists the prevalence, demographics, and clinical profiles of those who have been diagnosed with drug use disorder.

TABLE 5.3 Epidemiology of Drug Use Disorder

In order to appreciate the magnitude and implications of drug use disorder (i.e., addiction or drug dependence), it is necessary to understand the prevalence, demographics, and clinical profiles of those diagnosed with this condition according to the American Psychiatric Association's (2013) *Diagnostic and Statistical Manual of Mental Disorders*, fifth edition (DSM-5). This table presents an epidemiological overview of drug use disorders to help the reader appreciate their overwhelming implications.

Category	Incidence (%)	Category	Incidence (%)
TOTAL		**Ubanicity, lifetime**	
12 month	3.9%	Urban	10.1%
Lifetime	9.9%	Rural	9.3%
Male lifetime	12.3%	**Region, lifetime**	
Female lifetime	7.7%	Northeast	10.8%
Race/ethnicity, lifetime		Midwest	10.0%
White	10.8%	South	8.4%
Black	9.9%	West	11.5%
Native American	17.2%	**Psychiatric disorder, lifetime**	**Risk of Co-occurrence (normal risk = 1)**
Asian/Pacific Islander	4.2%		
Hispanic	7.2%	Alcohol use disorder	4.0
Age (years), lifetime		Nicotine use disorder	3.6
18–29	14.2%	Any mood disorder	1.5
30–44	12.0%	Bipolar	1.4
45–64	9.7%	Anxiety disorder	1.3
≥65	2.0%	Posttraumatic stress disorder	1.5
Education, lifetime		Antisocial personality disorder	2.0
< High school	10.2%		
High school	11.6%	**% Who receive treatment, lifetime**	**Incidence**
Some college or higher	9.1%	Total	24.6%
Family income ($), lifetime		Detoxification	9.5%
0–19,999	13.5%	Rehabilitation program	12.5%
20,000–34,999	10.5%	Physician or other healthcare professional provides	11.4%
35,000–69,999	9.6%		
>70,000	7.2%		

Data from Grant, B., T. Saha, W. Ruan, R., Goldstein, Chou, S. P., Jung, J., Zhang, H., Smith, S. M., Pickering, R. P., Huang, B., and Hasin, D. S. "Epidemiology of DSM-5 Drug Use Disorder." *JAMA Psychiatry* 73 (2016): 39–47.

LEARNING PORTFOLIO

Key Terms

Discussion Questions

1. How does the concept of drug "potency" apply to the therapeutic use and the abuse of drugs?
2. How can drug interactions be both detrimental and beneficial? Give examples of each.
3. Why would a drug with a relatively narrow margin of safety be approved by the Food and Drug Administration for clinical use? Give an example.
4. What are possible explanations for the fact that you (for example) may require twice as much of a drug to get an effect as does your friend?
5. Why might the blood–brain barrier prevent a drug from having abuse potential?
6. Why would the consumption of a drug of abuse by a nursing mother be a problem for the infant? Give an example.
7. Contrary to your advice, a friend is going to spend $20 on methamphetamine. What significance will the pharmacokinetic concepts of threshold, half-life, cumulative effect, and biotransformation have on your friend's drug experience?
8. How would the factors of tolerance, physical dependence, rebound, and psychological dependence affect a chronic heroin user?
9. Why would the lack of physical dependence on LSD for some drug abusers make it less likely to cause addiction than cocaine, which does cause physical dependence?

Summary

1. All drugs have intended and unintended effects. The unintended actions of drugs can include effects such as nausea, altered mental states, dependence, a variety of allergic responses, and changes in the cardiovascular system.
2. Many factors can affect the way an individual responds to a drug: dose, inherent toxicity, potency, and pharmacokinetic properties such as the rate of absorption into the body, the way it is distributed throughout the body, and the manner in which and rate at which it is metabolized and eliminated. The form of the drug as well as the manner in which it is administered can also affect the response to a drug.
3. Potency is determined by the amount of a drug necessary to cause a given effect. Toxicity is the ability of the drug to affect the body adversely. A drug that is very toxic is very potent in terms of causing a harmful effect.
4. A drug's margin of safety relates to the difference in the drug doses that cause a therapeutic or a toxic effect. The bigger the difference, the greater the margin of safety.

5. Additive interactions occur when the effects of two drugs are combined; for example, the analgesic effects of aspirin plus acetaminophen are additive. Antagonistic effects occur when the effects of two drugs cancel; for example, the stimulant effects of caffeine tend to antagonize the drowsiness caused by antihistamines. Synergism (potentiation) occurs when one drug enhances the effect of another; for example, alcohol enhances the CNS depression caused by Valium.

6. Pharmacokinetic factors include absorption, distribution, biotransformation, and elimination of drugs. These factors can vary substantially between persons and have a significant impact on the outcome and interpretation of drug testing outcomes.

7. Many physiological and pathological factors can alter the response to drugs. For example, age, gender, and pregnancy are all factors that should be considered when making drug-related decisions. In addition, some diseases can alter the way in which the body responds to drugs. Medical conditions associated with the liver, kidneys, and cardiovascular system are of particular concern.

8. For psychoactive drugs to influence the brain and its actions, they must pass through the blood–brain barrier. Many of these drugs are fat soluble and able to pass through capillary walls from the blood into the brain.

9. The threshold dose is the minimum amount of a drug necessary to have an effect. The plateau effect is the maximum effect a drug can have, regardless of dose. The cumulative effect is the buildup of the drug in the body due to multiple doses being taken within short intervals.

10. The liver is the primary organ for the metabolizing of drugs and many naturally occurring substances in the body, such as hormones. By altering the molecular structure of drugs, the metabolism usually inactivates drugs and makes them easier to eliminate through the kidneys.

11. Biotransformation is the process that alters the molecular structure of a drug. Metabolism contributes to biotransformation.

12. Drug tolerance causes a decreased response to a given dose of a drug. It can be caused by increasing metabolism and elimination of the drug by the body or by a change in the systems or targets that are affected by the drug.

13. Physical dependence is characterized by the adaptive changes that occur in the body due to the continual presence of a drug. These changes, which are often chemical in nature, reduce the response to the drugs and cause tolerance. If drug use is halted after physical dependence has occurred, the body is overcompensated, causing a rebound response. Rebound effects are similar to the withdrawal that occurs because drug use is stopped for an extended period. Psychological dependence occurs because drug use is rewarding, causing euphoria, increased energy, and relaxation, or because stopping drug use produces craving.

14. Suggestion can have a profound influence on a person's drug response. Health problems with significant psychological aspects are particularly susceptible to the effects of placebos. For example, because the intensity of pain is related to its perception, a placebo can substantially relieve pain discomfort. Other placebo responses may likewise be due to the release of endogenous factors in the body.

15. A powerful, uncontrollable desire (craving) for drugs can occur with chronic use of some drugs of abuse. Although craving by itself may not be the principal cause of drug addiction, if it can be eliminated, treatment of substance abuse is more likely to be successful.

References

Adamec, C. "Genetics in Alcoholism." Lifestrong. com. 2015. Available http://www.livestrong.com /article/97065-genetics-alcoholism/

Addiction Blog. "Tolerance to Cocaine." 2014. Available http://drug.addictionblog.org/tolerance-to-cocaine/

Alcoholrehab.com "Cross Dependency and Cross Tolerance." 2015. Available http://alcoholrehab.com /drug-addiction/cross-dependency-cross-tolerance/

American Psychiatric Association (APA). *Diagnostic and Statistical Manual of Mental Disorders,* 5th ed. Washington, DC: American Psychiatric Association, 2013.

Bellum, S. "Your Environment May Influence Drug Use." NIDA for Teens. 17 October 2013. Available https://teens.drugabuse.gov/blog/post/your-environment-may-influence-drug-use

Buckley, P., and E. Brown. "Prevalence and Consequences of Dual Diagnosis." *Journal of Clinical Psychiatry* 67 (2006): e01.

Byron, K. "Pharmacokinetics I: Absorption and Distribution." Loyola University Chicago. *Medical Therapeutics* (5 August 2015): 28–42. Available http://www.meddean.luc.edu/lumen/meded/therapy/homepage/PharmI_Block1_15.pdf

Centers for Disease Control and Prevention (CDC). "Prescription Painkiller Overdoses: A Growing Epidemic, Especially Among Women." 2013. Available http://www.cdc.gov/vitalsigns/prescriptionpainkilleroverdoses/index.html

CDC. "HIV and Injection Drug Use in the United States." Centers for Disease Control and Prevention (2015). Available http://www.cdc.gov/hiv/risk/idu.html

de Havenon, A., B. Chin, K. Thomas, and P. Afra. "The Secret Spice: An Undetectable Cause of Seizure." *Neurohospitalist* 1 (2011): 182–186.

Dixon, P. "Truth About Cocaine, Crack and Heroin Addiction." n.d. Available http://www.globalchange.com/truth-about-drugs-chapter-6.htm

Drugs.com. "18 Herbal Supplements with Risky Drug Interactions." 19 December 2014. Available https://www.drugs.com/slideshow/herb-drug-interactions-1069

DrugWise. "Drug Interactions." n.d. Available http://www.drugwise.org.uk/drug-interactions/

Dual Diagnosis. "The Connection Between Mental Illness and Substance Abuse." n.d. Available www.dualdiagnosis.org/mental-health-and-addiction/the-connection/

Feinberg, C. "The Placebo Phenomenon." *Harvard Magazine* (May–June 2013). Available http://harvardmagazine.com/2013/01/the-placebo-phenomenon

Fettiplace, M., A. Pickurk, R. Ripper, B. Kin, K. Kowal, K. Lis, D. Schwartz, D. Feinstein, I. Rubinstein, and G. Weinberg. "Cardiac Depression Induced by Cocaine or Cocaethylene in Alleviated by Lipid Emulsion More Effectively Than by Sulfobutylether-B-Cyclodextrin." *Academic Emergency Medicine* 22 (2015): 508–517.

Get the Facts. "Drug Testing." 2016. Available http://www.drugwarfacts.org/cms/Drug_Testing#sthash.YDvgTUSi.dpbs

Glatter, R. "Nicotine Vaccine May Help You Quit Smoking." *Forbes.* 26 February 2013. Available http://www.forbes.com/sites/robertglatter/2013/02/26/nicotine-vaccine-may-help-you-quit-smoking

Holford, N. "Pharmacokinetics & Pharmacodynamics: Rational Dosing and the Time Course of Drug Action." In *Basic and Clinical Pharmacology*, 13th ed., edited by B. Katzung and A. Trevor, 41–73. New York: McGraw-Hill, 2015.

Horn, J. "Important Drug Interactions and Their Mechanisms." In *Basic and Clinical Pharmacology*, 13th ed., edited by B. Katzung and A. Trevor, 1118-1131. New York: McGraw-Hill, 2015.

Hussar, D. "Tolerance and Resistance." *Merck Manual Professional Edition* (2014). Available http://www.merckmanuals.com/professional/clinical-pharmacology/factors-affecting-response-to-drugs/tolerance-and-resistance

Hussar, D. "Overview of Response to Drugs." *Merck Manuals Consumer Version* (2015). Available http://www.merckmanuals.com/home/drugs/factors-affecting-response-to-drugs/overview-of-response-to-drugs

Jones, C., L. Paulozzi, and K. Mack. "Alcohol Involvement in Opioid Pain Reliever and Benzodiazepine Drug Abuse-Related Emergency Department Visits and Drug-Related Deaths—United States, 2010." *Morbidity and Mortality Weekly Report* 63 (2014): 881–885.

Jorenby, D. "Tobacco." *Merck Manual Professional Version.* 2015. Available http://www.merckmanuals.com/professional/SearchResults?query=tobacco

Kosten, T., C. Domingo, F. Orson, and B. Kinsey, B. "Vaccines Against Stimulants, Cocaine, and Methamphetamine." *British Journal of Clinical Pharmacology* 77 (2014) 368–374.

Learn.Genetics. "Genes and Addiction." Genetic Science Learning Center, University of Utah (2015). Available http://learn.genetics.utah.edu/content/addiction/genes/

Learn.Genetics. "Drugs of Abuse." University of Utah Genetics (2015). Available http://learn.genetics.utah.edu/content/addiction/abuse/

Lisi, D. "Designer Drugs. Patients May be Using Synthetic Cannabinoids More Than you Think." JEMS 39 (2014) 56–59.

Luscher, C. "Drugs of Abuse." In *Basic and Clinical Pharmacology*, 13th ed., edited by B. Katzung and A. Trevor, 552–566. New York: McGraw-Hill, 2015.

March of Dimes. "Keeping Breast Milk Safe and Healthy." January 2015. Available http://www.marchofdimes.org/baby/keeping-breast-milk-safe-and-healthy.aspx

Mathias, R. "Rate and Duration of Drug Activity Play Major Roles in Drug Abuse, Addiction and Treatment." *NIDA Notes* 12 (March/April 1997): 8–11.

Mazur, C., S. Marchitti, and J. Zastre. "P-glycoprotein Inhibition by the Agricultural Pesticide Propiconazole and Its Hydroxylated Metabolites: Implications for Pesticide-Drug Interactions." *Toxicology Letters* 232 (2015): 34–46.

National Institute on Drug Abuse (NIDA). "Drug Facts: Inhalants." 2015a. Available http://www.drugabuse.gov/publications/drugfacts/inhalants

National Institute on Drug Abuse (NIDA). "Trends and Statistics." 2015b. Available https://www.drugabuse.gov/related-topics/trends-statistics

New Day Counseling. "Psychological Addiction." NewDay Counseling-Addiction Treatment (2015). Available https://www.savannahoutpatient.org/psychological-addiction/

O'Brien, C. "Drug Addiction and Drug Abuse." In *The Pharmacological Basis of Therapeutics*, 11th ed., edited by L. Brunton, J. Lazo, and K. Parker, 607–627. New York: McGraw-Hill, 2006.

Purse, M. "Self-Medicating: When the Cure Is the Disease." 2013. Available http://bipolar.about.com/cs/dualdiag/a/0008_dual_diag.htm

Sayette, M. "The Role of Craving in Substance Use Disorder: Theoretical and Methodological Issues." *Annual Review of Clinical Psychology* 12 (2016): 407–433

Scott, M., and R. Taylor. "Health-Related Effects of Genetic Variations of Alcohol-Metabolizing Enzymes in African Americans." *Alcohol Research and Health* 30 (2007): 18–21.

Shapiro, M. "8 Scary Food-Drug Interactions." AARP, Health Drugs and Supplements. 20 June 2015. Available http://www.aarp.org/health/drugs-supplements/info-2015/food-drug-interactions-photo.html#slide1

Tully, M. "Meet Heroin's Tiniest Victims: Newborns." *USA Today* (1 June 2015). Available http://www.USAtoday.com/story/news/nation-now/2015/06/01/heroin-babies-morphine-opiate-drugs/28299459/

Vergne, D. E., and F. Anton. "Aripiprazole: A Drug with a Novel Mechanism of Action and Possible Efficacy for Alcohol Dependence." *CNS and Neurological Disorders—Drug Targets* 9 (2010): 50–54.

Walker, T. "Americans at Risk for Alcohol-Drug Interactions." Modern Medicine Network. (2015). Available http://formularyjournal.modernmedicine.com/formulary-journal/news/americans-risk-alcohol-drug-interactions?page=full

Waters Edge Recovery. "Drug Craving: The Difference Between Want & Need." 12 September 2014. Available https://www.watersedgerecovery.com/drug-craving-the-difference-between-want-and-need/

CHAPTER 6

CNS Depressants: Sedative-Hypnotics

© tab1962/iStockphoto.com.

Did You Know?

▶ Alcohol temporarily relieves anxiety and stress because of its effects as a central nervous system (CNS) depressant.

▶ Benzodiazepines are by far the most frequently prescribed CNS depressants.

▶ Most people who are dependent on benzodiazepines obtain their drugs legally by prescription.

▶ Long-term users of Xanax can experience severe withdrawal symptoms if drug use is stopped abruptly.

▶ Our bodies probably produce a natural antianxiety substance that functions like drugs such as diazepam (Valium), triazolam (Halcion), and alprazolam (Xanax).

▶ The short-acting CNS depressants are the most likely to be abused.

▶ Gamma-hydroxybutyrate (GHB) is a Schedule I "club drug" that occurs naturally in the body and can be easily synthesized by using information available on the Internet.

Learning Objectives

On completing this chapter you should be able to:

〉 Identify the primary drug groups used for CNS depressant effects.

〉 Explain the principal therapeutic uses of the CNS depressants and their relationship to drug dose.

〉 Explain why CNS depressant drugs are commonly abused.

〉 Identify the unique features of benzodiazepines.

〉 Relate how benzodiazepine dependence usually develops.

〉 Describe the differences in effects produced by short- versus long-acting CNS depressants.

〉 Describe the CNS depressant properties of antihistamines, and compare their therapeutic usefulness to that of benzodiazepines.

〉 List the four principal types of people who abuse CNS depressants.

〉 Identify the basic principles in treating dependence on CNS depressants.

〉 Explain the unique properties of propofol as a potential drug of abuse.

〉 Explain why GHB is abused and how it relates to its analog compounds.

〉 Explain the role of detoxification in the treatment of dependency on CNS depressants.

Introduction

Central nervous system (CNS) depressants are some of the most widely used and abused drugs in the United States. Why? When taken at low doses, they all produce a qualitatively similar "high" by their disinhibitory effects on the brain. In addition, they relieve stress and anxiety and even induce sleep—effects that appeal to many people, particularly those who are struggling with emotional problems and looking for a break, physically and mentally. CNS depressants also can cause a host of serious side effects, including problems with tolerance and dependence. Ironically, many individuals who become dependent on depressants obtain them through legitimate means: a prescription given by a physician or other licensed healthcare provider. In fact, these drugs are second only to the narcotic medications as the most frequently abused group of prescription medications (National Institute on Drug Abuse [NIDA] 2015). Depressants also are available on the street, although this illicit source does not account for the bulk of the problem.

In this chapter, we briefly review the history of CNS depressants, in terms of both development and use, and then discuss the positive and negative effects these drugs can produce. Each major type of depressant drug is then reviewed in detail: benzodiazepines (Xanax- or Valium-like drugs), barbiturates, and other minor categories. We move on to an examination of abuse patterns related to depressant drugs and discuss how drug dependence and withdrawal are treated. Finally, we conclude with a discussion of natural depressants.

An Introduction to CNS Depressants

Why are CNS depressants problematic? First, in contrast to most other substances of abuse, CNS depressants are usually not obtained illicitly and self-administered but rather are prescribed under the direction of a physician. Second, use of CNS depressants can cause very alarming—even dangerous—behavior if not monitored closely; most problems associated with these drugs occur due to inadequate professional supervision and chronic use. Third, several seemingly unrelated drug groups have some ability to cause CNS depression and all too frequently are the cause of death by drug overdoses (see "Case in Point: Foster Teen Dies from Overdose and Neglect"). When these drugs are combined, bizarre and dangerous interactions can result. Particularly problematic is the combination of alcohol with other CNS depressants. Finally, CNS depressants can cause disruptive personality changes that are unpredictable and sometimes very threatening.

▶ CASE IN POINT

Foster Teen Dies from Overdose and Neglect

Steven, a 16-year-old male, was found dead in his bed on December 20, 2015, after ingesting an assortment of prescription and over-the-counter medications. Because only one of the drugs found in his body was actually prescribed for him (Zoloft), officials wondered where he had obtained the other deadly drugs, such as antianxiety and painkiller medications, that were also identified in his system. Investigators also wondered how the overdose happened in the first place. The coroner's report concluded that Steven, who was living in a foster home, was not trying to commit suicide but had accidentally overdosed on a combination of drugs with sedative properties. For some unknown reason, no one intervened when he demonstrated signs of being dangerously sedated. No one took Steven to the doctor or an emergency room even though the day before his death he could hardly walk, was unable to keep food in his mouth, had words that were slurred when he tried to talk, and could barely keep his eyes open. His grandmother claimed that Steven was ignored by his foster parent and those who should have been looking out for his welfare. While in foster care, Steven had been treated with psychiatric drugs for anxiety, depression, and suicidal thoughts. He was reported to have been using Xanax and pain drugs weeks before his death, and 80 pills plus a large sum of money were found in his room after his death, suggesting that Steven may have been dealing pills to others to earn money for his drug habit. Steven was a tragic victim not only of an inappropriate combination of sedating drugs, but also an apparent victim of social neglect.

Data from De Sa, K. "East Bay Foster Teen Overdosed on Combination of Pain Killers, Antidepressants, Alcohol." *The Mercury News* (California). (16 April 2015). Available http://www.mercurynews.com/california/ci_27929601/antioch-foster-teen-overdosed-combination-painkillers-anti-depressants

▮ The History of CNS Depressants

Before the era of modern drugs, the most common depressant used to ease tension, cause relaxation, and help forget problems was alcohol. These effects undoubtedly accounted for the immense popularity of alcohol and help explain why this traditional depressant is the most commonly abused drug of all time.

Attempts to find CNS depressants other than alcohol that could be used to treat nervousness and anxiety began in the 1800s with the introduction of bromides. These drugs were very popular until their toxicities became known. In the early 1900s, bromides were replaced by **barbiturates**. Like bromides, barbiturates were initially heralded as safe and effective depressants; however, problems with tolerance, dependence, and lethal overdoses soon became evident. It was learned that the doses of barbiturates required to treat anxiety also could cause CNS depression, affecting respiration and impairing mental functions (Charney, Mihic, and Harris 2006; Mandal 2013). The margin of safety for barbiturates was too narrow, so research for safer CNS depressants began again.

It was not until the 1950s that the first **benzodiazepines** were marketed as substitutes for the dangerous barbiturates. Benzodiazepines were originally viewed as extremely safe and free from the problems of tolerance, dependence, and withdrawal that occurred with the other drugs in this category. Unfortunately, benzodiazepines have since been found to be less than ideal antianxiety drugs. Although relatively safe when used for short periods, long-term use can cause dependence and withdrawal problems much like those associated with their depressant predecessors (Fawcett 2015). These problems have become a major concern of the medical community, as is discussed in greater detail later in the chapter.

Many of the people who become dependent on CNS depressants such as benzodiazepines began using the drugs under the supervision of a physician. Some clinicians routinely prescribe CNS depressants for patients with stress, anxiety, or apprehension without trying nonpharmacological approaches, such as psychotherapy or counseling. This practice sends an undesirable and often detrimental message to patients—that is, CNS depressants are a simple solution to their complex, stressful problems. The following quote illustrates the danger of this practice:

> I am still, unfortunately, lost in "'script addiction." ... I have gone on-line asking for pills. I could really identify with the one posting about doctors who continue to write the 'scripts to increase/continue the patient "flow." This is exactly what is happening with me and my doctor. *(From America Online Alcohol and Drug Dependency and Recovery message board.)*

During the 1970s and 1980s, there was an epidemic of prescriptions written for CNS depressants. For example, in 1973, 100 million prescriptions were written for benzodiazepines alone. Approximately twice as many women as men were taking these drugs at this time; a similar gender pattern continues today. During this period, many homemakers made CNS depressants a part of their household routine, as described in the lyrics of the song "Mother's Little Helper" on the Rolling Stones' album *Flowers*:

> "Kids are different today"
>
> I hear ev'ry mother say
>
> Mother needs something today to calm her down
>
> And though she's not really ill,
>
> There's a little yellow pill.
>
> She goes running for the shelter of a mother's little helper
>
> And it helps her on her way, gets her through her busy day.

As the medical community became more aware of the problem, the use of depressants declined. Today, efforts are being made by pharmaceutical companies and scientists to find new classes of CNS depressants that can be used to relieve stress and anxiety without causing serious side effects such as dependence and withdrawal (Olfson, King, and Schoenbaum 2015).

▮ The Effects of CNS Depressants: Benefits and Risks

The CNS depressants are a diverse group of drugs that share an ability to reduce CNS activity and diminish the brain's level of awareness. Besides the benzodiazepines, barbiturate-like drugs, and

KEY TERMS

barbiturates
potent CNS depressants, usually not preferred because of their narrow margin of safety

benzodiazepines
the most popular and safest CNS depressants in use today

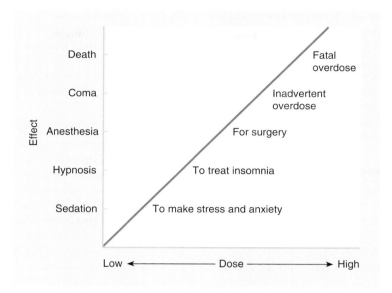

FIGURE 6.1 Dose-dependent effects of CNS depressants. The therapeutic outcome may change according to the dose administered (e.g., a low dose of a CNS depressant can be effective to relieve the anxiety associated with stress, while a higher dose may cause drowsiness and be effective in the treatment of insomnia).

alcohol, depressant drugs include **antihistamines** and opioid narcotics such as heroin.

Depressants are usually classified according to the degree of their medical effects on the body. For instance, **sedatives** cause mild depression of the CNS and relaxation. This drug effect is used to treat extreme anxiety and often is referred to as **anxiolytic**. Many sedatives also have muscle-relaxing properties that enhance their relaxing effects.

Depressants also are used to promote sleep and are frequently prescribed. Up to 70 million Americans have sleeping problems, many of whom use drugs like the benzodiazepines to help get a "good night's rest" (Szalavitz 2013). **Hypnotics** (from the Greek god of sleep, Hypnos) are CNS depressants that encourage sleep by inducing drowsiness. Often when depressants are used as hypnotics, they produce **amnesiac** effects as well. As already mentioned, the effects produced by depressants can be very enticing and encourage inappropriate use.

The effects of the CNS depressants tend to be dose dependent (see **Figure 6.1**). Thus, if you were to take a larger dose of a sedative, it might have a hypnotic effect. Often, the only difference between a sedative and a hypnotic effect is the dosage; consequently, the same drug may be used for both purposes by varying the dose. By increasing the dose still further, an anesthetic state can be reached. **Anesthesia**, a deep depression of the CNS, is used to achieve a controlled state of

unconsciousness so that a patient can be treated, usually by surgery, in relative comfort and without memory of a traumatic experience. With the exception of benzodiazepines, if the dose of most of the depressants is increased much more, coma or death will ensue because the CNS becomes so depressed that vital centers controlling breathing and heart activity cease to function properly (Trevor 2015).

As a group, CNS depressant drugs used in a persistent fashion cause tolerance. Because of the diminished effect due to the tolerance, users of

KEY TERMS

antihistamines
drugs that often cause CNS depression are used to treat allergies and are often included in over-the-counter (OTC) sleep aids

sedatives
CNS depressants used to relieve anxiety, fear, and apprehension

anxiolytic
drug that relieves anxiety

hypnotic
CNS depressant used to induce drowsiness and encourage sleep

amnesiac
causing the loss of memory

anesthesia
a state characterized by loss of sensation or consciousness

these drugs continually escalate their doses. Under such conditions, the depressants alter physical and psychological states, resulting in dependence. The dependence can be so severe that abrupt drug abstinence results in severe withdrawal that occasionally includes life-threatening seizures. Because of these dangerous pharmacological features, treatment of dependence on CNS depressants must proceed very carefully (Trevor 2015).

Types of CNS Depressants

All CNS depressants are not created equal. Some have wider margins of safety; others have a greater potential for nonmedicinal abuse. These differences are important when considering the therapeutic advantages of each type of CNS depressant. In addition, unique features of the different types of depressants make them useful for treatment of other medical problems. For example, some barbiturates and benzodiazepines are used to treat forms of epilepsy or acute seizure activity, whereas opioid narcotics are used to treat many types of pain. Some of these unique features will be dealt with in greater detail when the individual drug groups are discussed. The benzodiazepines, barbiturate-like drugs, antihistamines, and the naturally occurring gamma-hydroxybutyrate (GHB) are discussed in this chapter.

The unique features of the CNS depressants help determine the likelihood of their abuse. For example, abuse is more likely to occur with

CNS depressants can be used as hypnotics to initiate sleep.

the fast-acting depressant agents than with those agents that have long-lasting effects. Currently, nonmedicinal use of these sedatives occurs in approximately 2% to 4% of the U.S. population. This abuse is most likely to due to benzodiazepines such as Xanax and Valium (Olfson et al. 2015).

■ Benzodiazepines: Valium-Type Drugs

Benzodiazepines are widely used CNS depressants for anxiety and sleep (Olfson et al. 2015). Because of their wide margin of safety (death from overdose is rare), benzodiazepines have replaced barbiturate-like drugs for use as sedatives and hypnotics (Balestra 2009). Benzodiazepines were originally referred to as *minor tranquilizers*, but this terminology erroneously implied that they had pharmacological properties similar to those of antipsychotic drugs (*major tranquilizers*) when they are actually very different. Consequently, the term *minor tranquilizer* is usually avoided by clinicians.

The first true benzodiazepine, chlordiazepoxide (Librium), was developed for medical use and marketed around 1960. The very popular drug Valium came on the market about the same time. In fact, Valium was so well received that from 1972 to 1978 it was the top-selling prescription drug in the United States. Its popularity has since declined considerably, and it has been replaced by benzodiazepines such as alprazolam (Xanax) and lorazepam (Ativan) (Guthrie and Bostwick 2013).

Because of dependence problems, the benzodiazepines are now classified as Schedule IV drugs. In recent years, considerable concern has arisen that benzodiazepines are overprescribed. Clinicians are concerned about this overconfident attitude toward benzodiazepines and their potential for dependence and other serious side effects (Trevor 2015) and warn patients against prolonged and unsupervised administration of these drugs (Charney et al. 2006, *Physicians' Desk Reference* [*PDR*] 2013) (see "Prescription for Abuse: Benzodiazepines: The Good and the Bad").

MEDICAL USES

Benzodiazepines are used for an array of therapeutic objectives, including the relief of anxiety, treatment of neurosis, relaxation of muscles, alleviation of lower back pain, treatment of some convulsive disorders, induction of sleep (hypnotic), relief from withdrawal symptoms associated with narcotic and alcohol dependence, and induction of amnesia, usually for preoperative administration (administered just before or during surgery or very uncomfortable medical procedures) (*PDR* 2013).

MECHANISMS OF ACTION

In contrast to barbiturate-type drugs, which cause general depression of most neuronal activity, benzodiazepines selectively affect those neurons that have receptors for the neurotransmitter gamma-aminobutyric acid (GABA) (Trevor 2015). GABA is a very important inhibitory transmitter in several regions of the brain, including the limbic system, the reticular activating system, and the motor cortex. In the presence of benzodiazepines, the inhibitory effects of GABA are increased. Depression of activity in these brain regions likely accounts for the ability of benzodiazepines to alter mood (a limbic function), cause drowsiness (a reticular activating system function), and relax muscles (a cortical function). The specific GABA-enhancing effect of these drugs explains the selective CNS depression caused by benzodiazepines.

Of considerable interest is the observation that these Valium-like drugs act on specific receptor sites that are linked to the GABA receptors in the CNS. As yet, no endogenous substance has been identified that naturally interacts with this so-called benzodiazepine site. It is very likely, however, that natural molecules do exist that activate this same benzodiazepine receptor population and serve to reduce stress and anxiety by natural means (Trevor 2015). Because benzodiazepines have specific target receptors, it has been possible to develop a highly selective antagonist drug, flumazenil (Romazicon). This drug is used to treat benzodiazepine overdoses but must be used carefully because its administration can precipitate withdrawal in people taking benzodiazepines (Trevor 2015).

TYPES OF BENZODIAZEPINES

Because benzodiazepines are so popular and thus profitable, several of these drugs are available by prescription. Currently, approximately 15 benzodiazepine compounds are available in the United States, and some 20 additional benzodiazepines are marketed in other countries (Drugs.com 2015).

PRESCRIPTION FOR ABUSE

Benzodiazepines: The Good and the Bad

Jenn is a freelance book editor who has been using the benzodiazepine drug known as Valium for years. She describes this drug as essential for quickly managing her problems associated with extreme anxiety. She claims that Valium is the only thing that effectively relaxes her when she gets into the seat of a car, after nearly dying in two car accidents as a teenager. She admits that when she takes Valium she "feels so much better—and can finally relax. Sometimes that makes all the difference in the world." She claims that benzodiazepines work almost immediately, in contrast to antidepressant drugs, which are also prescribed to relieve anxiety, but require several weeks of treatment to achieve full efficacy. Benzodiazepines have also been shown to be effective in the treatment for insomnia, seizures, and alcohol withdrawal. However, these sedative hypnotic drugs are not without controversy. For example, most physicians will not prescribe benzodiazepines for more than a few weeks. With long-term treatment, the benzodiazepines cause the body to develop physical dependence, resulting in withdrawal if the drugs are discontinued "cold-turkey." Long-term use also can result in abuse and addiction. Short-term use can also adversely affect the user by interfering with cognition and decision-making, as well as impairing reflexes and motor functions. Consequently, it is recommended that doctors manage their benzodiazepine-using patients carefully and avoid prescribing these drugs for long periods of time, especially in adults.

Fawcett, K. "Benzodiazepine: Helpful or Harmful?" *U.S. News & World Report* (19 February 2015). Available http://health.usnews.com/health-news/patient-advice/articles/2015/02/19/benzodiazepines-helpful-or-harmful

TABLE 6.1 Half-Lives of Some Benzodiazepines

Drug	Half-Life (Hours)
Alprazolam (Xanax)	12–15
Chlordiazepoxide (Librium)	>100
Clonazepam (Klonopin)	20–50
Diazepam (Valium)	>100
Estazolam (ProSom)	24
Lorazepam (Ativan)	10–20
Midazolam (Versed)	1–4
Oxazepam (Serax)	5–14
Quazepam (Doral)	47–100
Temazepam (Restoril)	10–20
Triazolam (Halcion)	1.5–5.5
Zolpidem (Ambien; not a true benzodiazepine)	2–5

Data from Guthrie, S., and Bostwick, J. "Anxiety Disorders." In *Applied Therapeutics, The Clinical Use of Drugs*, 10th ed., edited by B. Alldredge, 1863–1899. Philadelphia, PA: Wolters Kluwer, 2013.

Benzodiazepines are distinguished primarily by their duration of action (see **Table 6.1**). As a general rule, the short-acting drugs are used as hypnotics to treat insomnia, thus allowing the user to awake in the morning with few aftereffects (such as a hangover). The long-acting benzodiazepines tend to be prescribed as sedatives, giving prolonged relaxation and relief from persistent anxiety. Some of the long-acting drugs can exert a relaxing effect for as long as 2 to 3 days. One reason for the long action in some benzodiazepines is that they are converted by the liver into metabolites that are as active as the original drug (Guthrie and Bostwick 2013). For example, Valium has been reported to have an approximate half-life of more than 100 hours and is converted by the liver into several active metabolites, including oxazepam (which itself is marketed as a therapeutic benzodiazepine).

KEY TERMS

REM sleep
the restive phase of sleep associated with dreaming

paradoxical effects
unexpected effects

SIDE EFFECTS

Reported side effects of benzodiazepines include drowsiness, lightheadedness, lethargy, impairment of mental and physical activities, skin rashes, nausea, diminished libido, irregularities in the menstrual cycle, blood cell abnormalities, and increased sensitivity to alcohol and other CNS depressants (Guthrie and Bostwick 2013; Trevor 2015). In contrast to barbiturate-type drugs, only very high doses of benzodiazepines have a significant impact on respiration. There are few verified instances of death resulting from overdose of benzodiazepines alone (Guthrie and Bostwick 2013). Serious suppression of vital functions can occur, however, when these drugs are combined with other depressants, most often alcohol (Guthrie and Bostwick 2013).

Although their long-term effectiveness has been challenged, benzodiazepines are used 40% to 50% of the time to treat persistent disorders such as chronic insomnia (Mercola 2014). Benzodiazepines have less effect on **REM sleep** (rapid eye movement, the restive phase) than do barbiturates. Consequently, sleep under the influence of benzodiazepines is more likely to be restful and satisfying. However, prolonged use of hypnotic doses of benzodiazepines may cause rebound increases in REM sleep and insomnia when the drug is stopped, especially if used for long periods of time (Balestra 2009; Guthrie and Bostwick 2013).

On rare occasions, benzodiazepines can have **paradoxical effects**, producing unusual responses such as nightmares, anxiety, irritability, sweating, and restlessness (Bruining 2015). Bizarre, uninhibited behavior—extreme agitation with hostility, paranoia, and rage—may occur as well.

Critics' complaints that Halcion causes unacceptable "amnesia, confusion, paranoia, hostility and seizures" (Associated Press 1994, p. D-3) prompted the Food and Drug Administration (FDA) to closely evaluate this benzodiazepine. Despite the fact that several other countries have banned Halcion, the FDA concluded that its benefits outweigh the reported risks; however, the FDA also concluded, "In no way should this [the FDA's conclusion] suggest that Halcion is free of side effects. It has long been recognized and emphasized in Halcion's labeling that it is a potent drug that produces the same type of adverse effects as other CNS sedative hypnotic drugs" (*Drug Facts and Comparisons* 2010, pp. 739–740). Although the FDA did not require that Halcion be withdrawn, it did negotiate changes in the labeling and package inserts with Halcion's manufacturer, Upjohn Pharmaceuticals. Halcion is currently only used to treat very severe short-term insomnia due to its fast action and short half-life; however, many clinicians refuse to use it at all due to its controversy (Insomnia.net n.d.).

There is no obvious explanation for the strange benzodiazepine-induced behaviors. It is possible that, in some people, the drugs mask inhibitory centers of the brain and allow expression of antisocial behavior that is normally suppressed and controlled. Related concerns have also been made public about another very popular benzodiazepine, alprazolam (Xanax). In 1990, Xanax became the first drug approved for the treatment of panic disorder—repeated, intense attacks of anxiety that can make life unbearable (McEvoy 2003). Reports that long-term use of Xanax can cause severe withdrawal effects and a stubborn dependency on the drug raised public concerns about use of benzodiazepines in general. For example, how many people are severely dependent on these CNS depressants? What is the frequency of side effects such as memory impairment, serious mood swings, and cognitive problems? And how many patients using the benzodiazepines would be better served with nondrug psychotherapy (European Monitoring Centre for Drugs and Drug Addiction 2015)? Clearly, use of the benzodiazepines to relieve acute stress or insomnia can be beneficial, but these drugs should be prescribed at the lowest dose possible and for the shortest time possible or withdrawal problems can result, as illustrated in the following quote:

> I was put on alprazolam (Xanax) two and a half years ago by [my] doctor. Now told by another doctor that it is for short-term use only and I am trying to get off slowly, but having difficulty. [I] have never used other drugs and do not have any information on the withdrawal process. *(From America Online Alcohol and Drug Dependency and Recovery message board.)*

Two relatively new benzodiazepine-like CNS depressants approved for short-term treatment of insomnia are zolpidem (Ambien) and zalephon (Sonata). Both are classified as Schedule IV drugs. They have abuse potential, especially when used chronically and when they interact with other CNS depressants, such as alcohol and narcotic analgesics (AddictionCenter 2015a).

TOLERANCE, DEPENDENCE, WITHDRAWAL, AND ABUSE

As with most CNS depressants, frequent, chronic use of benzodiazepines can cause tolerance, dependence (both physical and psychological),

and withdrawal (Guthrie and Bostwick 2013). Such side effects are usually not as severe as those of most other depressants, and they occur only after using the drugs for prolonged periods (Guthrie and Bostwick 2013).

Withdrawal can mimic the condition for which the benzodiazepine is given; for example, withdrawal symptoms can include anxiety or insomnia (Drugs.com 2015a). In such cases, a clinician may be fooled into thinking that the underlying emotional disorder is still present and may resume drug therapy without realizing that the patient has become drug dependent. This can happen after as little as 1 month of treatment. In situations in which users have consumed high doses of benzodiazepine over the long term, more severe, even life-threatening withdrawal symptoms may occur (*Drug Facts and Comparisons* 2010); depression, panic, paranoia, and convulsions (Drugs.com 2015b) have been reported (see **Table 6.2**). Severe withdrawal can often be avoided by gradually weaning the patient from the benzodiazepine (Guthrie and Bostwick 2013). Long-term use of benzodiazepines (periods

TABLE 6.2 Abstinence Symptoms of Benzodiazepines

Taking benzodiazepines more frequently, in higher doses, with higher potency for longer periods of time or if shorter acting, all increase the duration and intensity of benzodiazepine withdrawal.

Withdrawal Timeline After Abruptly Stopping Benzodiazepine Use

Duration of Abstinence	Symptoms
1–4 days	Rebound anxiety, insomnia, sweating and nausea. These symptoms tend to start sooner with shorter-acting drugs
10–14 days	Withdrawal symptoms for short-acting drugs typically persist for 10–14 days before disappearing; in contrast, withdrawal symptoms for long-acting drugs peak at this time period and eventually disappear by 3–4 weeks.
>15 days	Persons severely dependent (i.e., used high doses for many months or even years) may experience recurring random episodes of protracted withdrawal symptoms, known as PAWS, months after quitting.

Data from AddictionCenter. "What Is Benzodiazepine Withdrawal?" 2015. Available https://www.addictioncenter.com/benzodiazepines/withdrawal-and-detox/

exceeding 3 to 4 months) to treat anxiety or sleep disorders has not been shown to be therapeutically useful for most patients (Guthrie and Bostwick 2013). Even so, this approach is a common indiscriminate practice. As one user explains,

> I went through a trauma 4 years ago, and the doctor prescribed a very high dose of Ativan. Well, I soon became addicted, both emotionally and physically. . . . How do I get off? . . . This stuff is very addicting and my body can't really function without it. *(From America Online Alcohol and Drug Dependency and Recovery message board)*

It is very unusual to find nontherapeutic drug-seeking behavior in a patient who has been properly removed from benzodiazepines, unless that individual already has a history of drug abuse (Guthrie and Bostwick 2013). Research has shown that when benzodiazepines are the primary drug of abuse, these CNS depressants are usually self-administered to prevent unpleasant withdrawal symptoms in dependent users. If benzodiazepine-dependent users are properly weaned from the drugs and withdrawal has dissipated, there is no evidence that craving for the benzodiazepines occurs because people usually do not consider the benzodiazepines particularly reinforcing. An exception to this conclusion appears to be former alcoholics. Many people with a history of alcoholism find the effects of benzodiazepines rewarding; consequently, more than 25% of prior alcoholics use benzodiazepines chronically (AddictionCenter 2015b).

Benzodiazepines are commonly used as a secondary drug of abuse and combined with illicit drugs. For example, it is very common to find heroin users who are dependent on benzodiazepines as well (Jones and Holmgren 2013).

Another frequent combination is the use of benzodiazepines with stimulants such as cocaine (Gorelick 2015). Some addicts claim that this combination enhances the pleasant effects of the stimulant and reduces the "crashing" that occurs after using high doses. (More is said about benzodiazepine abuse later in this chapter.)

It should also be mentioned that benzodiazepines are occasionally used to make people vulnerable to sexual assaults referred to as *date rapes* (Dryden-Edwards 2013). The use of CNS

Courtesy of Orange County Sheriff's Office, Florida.

Rohypnol is a benzodiazepine outlawed in the United States.

depressants to commit these acts of violence is discussed in greater detail later in the chapter, but such assaults have sometimes involved the use of the **club drug** Rohypnol. Rohypnol (sometimes called Rophie, Roche, or Forget Me) is the proprietary name for flunitrazepam, a benzodiazepine. Rohypnol, which has been outlawed in the United States, comes as a tablet that can be dissolved in beverages without leaving an odor or taste and impairs short-term memory, making victims unable to recall details of the assault (NIDA 2000; Publishers Group 2002). In 2014, 0.7% of high school seniors claimed to have used this drug (Johnston 2015).

■ Barbiturates

Barbiturates are barbituric acid derivatives that are used in medicine as sedatives and hypnotics. Barbituric acid was first synthesized by A. Bayer (of aspirin fame) in Germany in 1864. The reason that he chose the name *barbituric acid* is not known. Some have speculated that the compound was named after a girl named Barbara whom Bayer knew. Others think that Bayer celebrated his discovery on the Day of St. Barbara in a tavern that artillery officers frequented. (St. Barbara is the patron saint of artillery soldiers.)

The first barbiturate, barbital (Veronal), was used medically in 1903. Since then, more than 2500 barbiturates have been synthesized; of these, about 50 were actually approved for human use. However, due to serious side effects, only a few are still prescribed for medical purposes. The names of the barbiturates traditionally end in *-al*, indicating a chemical relationship to barbital, the first one synthesized. Historically, barbiturates have played an important role in therapeutics because of their effectiveness as sedative-hypnotic agents,

KEY TERM

club drug
drug used at all-night raves, parties, dance clubs, and bars to enhance sensory experiences

which allowed them to be routinely used in the treatment of anxiety, agitation, and insomnia. However, because of their narrow margin of safety and their abuse liability, barbiturates have been largely replaced by safer drugs, such as benzodiazepines. Despite the reduced therapeutic use of the barbiturates, in 2014, 4.3% of high school seniors claimed to have recreationally used a barbiturate (Johnston 2015).

Uncontrolled use of barbiturates can cause a state of acute or chronic intoxication. Initially, there may be some loss of inhibition, euphoria, and behavioral stimulation—a pattern often seen with moderate consumption of alcohol. When taken to relieve extreme agitation or mental stress, barbiturates may cause delirium and produce other side effects that can include nausea, nervousness, rash, and diarrhea. The person intoxicated with barbiturates may have difficulty thinking and making judgments, may be emotionally unstable, may be uncoordinated and unsteady when walking, and may slur speech (not unlike the drunken state caused by alcohol).

When used for their hypnotic properties, barbiturates cause an unnatural sleep. The user awakens feeling tired, edgy, and quite unsatisfied, most likely because barbiturates markedly suppress the REM phase of sleep. (REM sleep is necessary for the refreshing renewal that usually accompanies a good sleep experience.) Because benzodiazepines suppress REM sleep (as do all CNS depressants) less severely than barbiturates, use of these agents as sleep aids is generally better tolerated.

Continued misuse of barbiturate drugs has a cumulative toxic effect on the CNS that is more life-threatening than misuse of opiates. When taken in large doses or in combination with other CNS depressants, barbiturates may cause death from respiratory or cardiovascular depression. Because of this toxicity, barbiturates have been involved in many drug-related deaths, both accidental and suicidal. Repeated misuse induces severe tolerance of and physical dependence on these drugs. Discontinuing use of short-acting barbiturates in people who are using large doses can cause dangerous withdrawal effects such as life-threatening seizures. "Signs & Symptoms: Effects of Barbiturates and Other Depressants on the Body and Mind" summarizes the range of effects of barbiturates and other depressants on the mind and body.

Concern about the abuse potential of barbiturates caused the federal government to include some of these depressants in the Controlled Substances Act. Consequently, the short-acting barbiturates, such as pentobarbital and secobarbital, are classified as Schedule II drugs, whereas the long-acting barbiturates, such as phenobarbital, are less rigidly controlled as Schedule IV drugs (DEA 2016).

EFFECTS AND MEDICAL USES

Barbiturates have many pharmacological actions. They depress the activity of nerves and skeletal, smooth, and cardiac muscles and affect the CNS in several ways, ranging from mild sedation to coma, depending on the dose. At sedative or hypnotic dosage levels, only the CNS is significantly affected. Higher anesthetic doses cause slight decreases in blood pressure, heart rate, and flow of urine. The metabolizing enzyme systems in the liver are important in inactivating barbiturates; thus, liver damage may result in exaggerated responses to barbiturate use (Trevor 2015).

Low doses of barbiturates relieve tension and anxiety, effects that give several barbiturates substantial abuse potential. The drawbacks of barbiturates are extensive and severe:

- They lack selectivity and safety.
- They have a substantial tendency to create tolerance, dependence, withdrawal, and abuse.
- They cause problems with drug interaction.

As a result, barbiturates have been replaced by benzodiazepines in most treatments, and only a few are still in medical use (Trevor 2015). Because of this decreased use, these drugs tend not to be readily available and are becoming less frequently abused in this country (Johnston 2015). The long-acting phenobarbital is still frequently used for its CNS depressant activity to alleviate or prevent convulsions in some epileptic patients and seizures caused by strychnine, cocaine, and other stimulant drugs. Thiopental (Pentothal) and other ultrashort- and short-acting barbiturates are used as anesthesia for minor surgery and as preoperative anesthetics in preparation for major surgery (Trevor 2015).

MECHANISM OF ACTION AND ELIMINATION

The precise mechanism of action for barbiturates is unclear. Like benzodiazepines, they likely interfere with activity in the reticular activating system, the limbic system, and the motor cortex. However, in contrast to benzodiazepines, barbiturates do not seem to act at a specific receptor site; they probably have a general effect that enhances the activity of the inhibitory transmitter GABA (Trevor 2015). Because benzodiazepines also

SIGNS & SYMPTOMS

Effects of Barbiturates and Other Depressants on the Body and Mind

	Body	Mind
Low dose	Drowsiness	Decreased anxiety, relaxation
	Trouble with coordination	Decreased ability to reason and solve problems
	Slurred speech	
	Dizziness	Difficulty in judging distance and time
	Staggering	
	Double vision	Amnesia
	Sleep	
	Depressed breathing	Brain damage
	Coma (unconscious and cannot be awakened)	
	Depressed blood pressure	
High dose	Death	

increase GABA activity (albeit in a more selective manner), these two types of drugs have overlapping effects. Because the mechanisms whereby they exert their effects differ, it is not surprising that these two types of depressants also have different pharmacological features.

The fat solubility of barbiturates is another important factor in the duration of their effects (Trevor 2015). Barbiturates that are the most fat soluble move in and out of body tissues (such as the brain) rapidly and are likely to be shorter acting. Fat-soluble barbiturates also are more likely to be stored in fatty tissue; consequently, the fat content of the body can influence the effects on the user. Because women have a higher body-fat ratio than men, their reaction to barbiturates may be slightly different.

Withdrawal from barbiturates after dependence has developed causes hyperexcitability because of the rebound of depressed neural systems. Qualitatively (but not quantitatively), the withdrawal symptoms are similar for all sedative-hypnotics, although they may vary in intensity and duration (Trevor 2015).

■ Other CNS Depressants

Although benzodiazepines and barbiturates are the most frequently used substances for the specific purpose of producing CNS depressant effects, many other agents, representing an array of distinct chemical groups, can similarly reduce brain activity. Although the mechanisms of action might be different for some of these drugs, if any CNS depressants (including alcohol) are combined, they will interact synergistically and can suppress respiration in a life-threatening manner. Thus, it is important to avoid such mixtures if possible. Even some OTC products, such as cold and allergy medications, contain drugs with CNS depressant actions.

Some of these drugs have significant abuse potential, so they are restricted much like other CNS depressants. In this group of depressants, methaqualone is a Schedule II drug and chloral hydrate is a Schedule IV drug. Each classification is based on the drug's relative potential for physical and psychological dependence. Abuse of Schedule II drugs may lead to severe or moderate physical dependence or high psychological dependence. Schedule IV drugs are considered much less likely to cause either type of dependence (DEA 2016).

CHLORAL HYDRATE

Chloral hydrate (Noctec), or "knock-out drops," has the unsavory reputation of being a drug that is slipped into a person's drink to cause unconsciousness. In the late 1800s, the combination of chloral hydrate and alcohol was given the name Mickey

Finn on the waterfront of the Barbary Coast of San Francisco when sailors were in short supply. An unsuspecting man would have a friendly drink and wake up as a crew member on an outbound freighter to China (Narconon n.d.).

Chloral hydrate is a good hypnotic, but it has a narrow margin of safety. This compound is a stomach irritant, especially if given repeatedly and in fairly large doses. Addicts may take enormous doses of the drug; as with most CNS depressants, chronic, long-term use of high doses will cause tolerance and physical dependence (Medline-Plus 2009).

METHAQUALONE

Few drugs have become so popular so quickly as methaqualone. This barbiturate-like sedative-hypnotic was introduced in India in the 1950s as an antimalarial agent. Its sedative properties, however, were soon discovered. It became available in the United States as Quaalude, Mequin, and Parest.

After several years of street abuse, methaqualone was classified as a Schedule II drug, and in 1984 it was reclassified to Schedule I (Drugs.com 2015c). Since 1985, methaqualone has not been manufactured in the United States because of adverse publicity, although 0.4% of high school seniors in the United States claimed to have used it in 2014 (Johnston 2015).

Common side effects of methaqualone include fatigue, dizziness, anorexia, nausea, vomiting, diarrhea, sweating, dryness of the mouth,

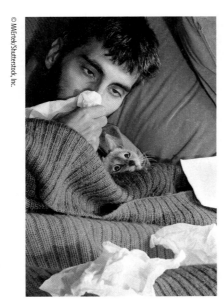

© MAErek/Shutterstock, Inc.

Antihistamines are found in OTC medicines used to relieve cold and allergy symptoms.

depersonalization, headache, and paresthesia of the extremities (a pins-and-needles feeling in the fingers and toes). Hangover is frequently reported.

ANTIHISTAMINES

Antihistamines are drugs used in both nonprescription and prescription medicinal products. The most common uses for antihistamines are to relieve the symptoms associated with the common cold, allergies, and motion sickness. Although frequently overlooked, many antihistamines cause significant CNS depression and are used as both sedatives and hypnotics (Encyclopedia.com 2006). For example, the agents hydroxyzine (Vistaril) and promethazine (Phenergan) are prescribed for their sedative effects, whereas diphenhydramine is commonly used as an OTC sleep aid (e.g., Unisom) (Krinsky 2012).

The exact mechanism of CNS depression caused by these agents is not totally known but appears to relate to their blockage of acetylcholine receptors in the brain (they antagonize the muscarinic receptor types). This anticholinergic activity helps cause relaxation and sedation and can be viewed as a very annoying side effect when these drugs are being used to treat allergies or other problems.

THERAPEUTIC USEFULNESS AND SIDE EFFECTS

Antihistamines are viewed as relatively safe agents. Compared with other more powerful CNS depressants, antihistamines do not appear to cause significant physical or psychological dependence or addiction problems, although drugs with anticholinergic activity, such as the antihistamines, are sometimes abused, especially by children and teenagers (Reeves et al. 2015). However, tolerance to antihistamine-induced sedation occurs quite rapidly. Reports of significant cases of withdrawal problems when use of antihistamines is stopped are rare. This situation may reflect the fact that these agents are used as antianxiety drugs for only minor problems and for short periods of time (often only for a single dose).

One significant problem with antihistamines is the variability of responses they produce. Different antihistamines work differently on different people. Usually, therapeutic doses cause decreased alertness, relaxation, slowed reaction time, and drowsiness. But it is not uncommon for some individuals to be affected in the opposite manner—that is, an antihistamine sometimes causes restlessness, agitation, and insomnia. There are even cases of seizures caused by toxic doses of antihistamine, particularly in children (Katzung 2012; Scharman et al. 2006). Side effects of antihistamines related to their anticholinergic effects include dry mouth, constipation, and inability to urinate. These factors probably help to discourage high-dose abuse of these drugs. However, OTC antihistamines are still sometimes taken for recreational purposes despite their unpleasant side effects (Reeves et al. 2015).

Even though antihistamines are relatively safe in therapeutic doses, they can contribute to serious problems if combined with other CNS depressants. Many OTC cold, allergy, anti-motion-sickness, and sleep aid products contain antihistamines and should be avoided by patients using the potent CNS depressants or alcohol.

NEW GENERATION OF SLEEP AIDS

In the past decade, several prescription products have been marketed for treating insomnia with the claim that they are less sedating and less likely to cause dependence than the traditional benzodiazepines and barbiturates. These heavily marketed medications include brand names such as Ambien, Lunesta, Rozerem, and Sonata. It is clear that although less sedating than the older sedative/hypnotics, this new generation of sleep aids can cause next-day sedation and have resulted in some dependency, especially when used with other CNS depressants, such as alcohol (Trevor 2015).

PROPOFOL, AN ABUSED GENERAL ANESTHETIC

Propofol (Diprivan) was initially made available in 1986 and used intravenously for rapid sedation, analgesia, and general anesthesia in hospital or outpatient clinics. Its use for these purposes continues today. It has also been used off-label (i.e., not officially approved by the FDA) to relieve severe chronic or migraine headaches in pain clinics or for sleep induction in patients suffering from insomnia. Initially, propofol was thought to be free of abuse liability. However, although physical dependence is rare, because use of this drug can cause amnesia (sometimes referred to as the "Milk of Amnesia") and euphoria and relieve stress and pain, it has been abused and even involved in suicides or accidental deaths (Elements Behavioral Health 2015), as was found to be the case in the highly publicized death of pop singer Michael Jackson (see "Case in Point: Misuse of Propofol Causes Jackson's Death").

Recent abuse problems have particularly involved medical professionals such as doctors and nurses who have access to this anesthetic. Some doctors claim it has unique features and have referred to their experience with propofol as "dancing with the white rabbit." Part of its attraction is that it is not a scheduled substance, it is easy to obtain, and its effects wear off in a matter of minutes (Elements Behavioral Health 2015).

►CASE IN POINT

Misuse of Propofol Causes Jackson's Death

Pop singer Michael Jackson died from an overdose of the potent general anesthetic propofol in June 2009. Because this drug is administered intravenously, it is only available to medical personnel in a clinical setting and should never be sent home with patients. In the case of Jackson, his personal physician had been making the drug available to help Jackson sleep and to deal with his anxiety prior to performances. A member of Jackson's staff called for help when Jackson appeared to have a severe adverse reaction to propofol that caused abnormal hot and cold sensations throughout his body. By the time help arrived, it was too late, and Jackson was deceased. The inappropriate manner in which propofol was given to Jackson reminds us how deadly this drug can be when administered inappropriately, even by a physician.

© Danny Moloshok/AP Images

Data from Wedro, B. "Michael Jackson's Death: Propofol (Diprivan) FAQ." 2011. Available http://www.medicinenet.com/script/main/art.asp?articlekey=105040

GHB (GAMMA-HYDROXYBUTYRATE): THE NATURAL DEPRESSANT

GHB is a colorless, tasteless, and odorless substance found naturally in the body resulting from the metabolism of the inhibitory neurotransmitter GABA. It was first synthesized nearly 30 years ago by a French researcher who intended to study the CNS effects of GABA (Bosch et al. 2012). It was initially believed that GHB exerted its effects by enhancing CNS GABA systems, although this mechanism has been questioned (Schep et al. 2012). Some evidence indicates that GHB is itself a neuromodulator, with its own receptor targets in the brain (Schep et al. 2012). Because of its CNS depressant effects, GHB has been used in Europe as an adjunct for general anesthesia, as a treatment for insomnia and narcolepsy (a daytime sleep disorder), and as a treatment for alcoholism and alcohol withdrawal and narcotic dependence (Townsend 2015). During the 1980s, GHB became available without a prescription in health food stores and was used principally by body builders to stimulate the release of growth hormone with the intent to reduce fat and build muscle (Townsend 2015). More recently, this substance became popular for recreational use due to what was described as a pleasant, alcohol-like, hangover-free high with aphrodisiac properties (Townsend 2015). Because of its potential for abuse, access to GHB was restricted by the DEA in 2000 (DEA 2013). In 2014, 1.0% of high school seniors were reported to have used GHB (Johnston 2015). Because of its frequent use by young people at nightclubs and bars, GHB became known as a club drug (Sumnall et al. 2008). Some of its common street names include Easy Lay, G, Goop, Liquid Ecstasy, Liquid X, and Scoop (Townsend 2015).

GHB is generally taken orally after being mixed with a liquid or beverage. It has a rapid onset and, when large doses are consumed, can cause unconsciousness and coma in 15 to 40 minutes. These dangerous effects typically require emergency room treatment. Often, the recovery is also rapid, with persons regaining consciousness in 2 to 4 hours:

> I was first offered a vial of "LiquidX" when I was 14. I was told the drug burns fat and won't give you a hangover. When drinking a beer I took an extra capful of GHB. Four hours later, I woke up in a puddle of my own vomit and my friends standing over me trying to find a heartbeat. GHB can inhibit the gag reflex causing users to choke when throwing up. That night, I discovered the razor-thin margin between

GHB is often stored as a clear, colorless, odorless liquid.

Courtesy of Orange County Sheriff's Office, Florida.

being the life of the party on GHB and being dead. (Townsend 2015)

Due to concerns about GHB abuse and side effects, an advisory warning that this substance is unsafe was first issued by the FDA in 1990. In 1997, the FDA released another warning that GHB was not approved for clinical use in the United States and was a potentially dangerous substance. Finally, due to the rising illicit use of GHB and resultant problems, this drug was made a Schedule I controlled substance by the DEA in March 2000.

Despite claims about its benign nature, statistical evidence suggests that in high doses GHB can be dangerous and even deadly (Townsend 2015). A number of documented deaths have been attributed to GHB overdoses. It has been reported that GHB use can cause significant side effects, such as hormonal problems, sleep abnormalities, drowsiness, nausea, vomiting, and changes in blood pressure (Townsend 2015). Both users and clinicians seem to agree that GHB is most dangerous when combined with other drugs, especially other CNS depressants, such as alcohol (Bosch et al. 2012).

Because GHB is illegal in the United States, it is currently available only through the underground "gray market" as a "bootleg" product manufactured by kitchen chemists and with suspicious quality and purity. The lack of reliability of these GHB-containing products and the highly variable responses of different people to this substance increase the likelihood of problems when using this depressant.

Instructions on how to make GHB are readily available on multiple Internet sites. It is typically portrayed as a relatively benign substance but one for which proper dosing is critical for "safe" use (Vendel 2009).

There is some debate as to whether the use of GHB can cause dependence and withdrawal. Some evidence suggests that chronic high-dose use of GHB may lead to prolonged abuse and a withdrawal syndrome consisting of insomnia, anxiety, and tremors that typically resolves in 3 to 12 days (Townsend 2015). Another major concern with this substance is its use in cases of date rape. Because GHB can be stored as a clear, colorless, odorless liquid, it is easily added undetected to a beverage such as an alcoholic drink (NIDA 2015; Townsend 2015). Its amnesiac and sedative properties disable users and make them vulnerable to sexual assault (NIDA 2015). Despite attempts to vigorously prosecute these cases, because the victims frequently are unable to recall details of the attack and the drug disappears so quickly from the bloodstream (its half-life is 2 to 3 hours), rape under the influence of GHB can be difficult to prove.

Other GHB-related drugs have become readily available as substitutes, although they are only legal if they are included in products technically not intended for human use. These products are supposedly promoted as chemical solvents and typically make a disclaimer that the products are not for human consumption, even though the label often implies that the product may be ingested. For example, the label on one industrial solvent stated, "Warning! Accidental ingestion … will produce GHB in your body. If you ingest some by mistake, don't take alcohol or any other drug" (U.S. Department of Justice [USDOJ] 2002). The most commonly used of these GHB analogs are gamma-butyrolactone (GBL) and 1,4-butanediol (BD) (USDOJ 2003; Vendel 2009). Because these compounds are converted into GHB in the body, they can cause serious side effects (Brunt, van Amsterdam, van den Brink 2015).

Patterns of Abuse with CNS Depressants

The American Psychiatric Association (APA) considers dependence on CNS depressants to be a psychiatric disorder. According to its widely used *Diagnostic and Statistical Manual of Mental Disorders*, 5th edition (*DSM-5*; 2013), a substance dependence disorder can be diagnosed when symptoms such as the following occur within a 12-month period:

1. The drugs are often taken in larger amounts or over a longer period of time than was intended.
2. There is a persistent desire or unsuccessful efforts to cut down or control sedative, hypnotic, or anxiolytic use.
3. A great deal of time is spent in activities necessary to obtain the sedative/hypnotics or recovering from their effects.
4. Important social, occupational, or recreational activities are given up or reduced because of sedative/hypnotic drug use.
5. Recurrent sedative/hypnotic drug use in situations in which it is physically hazardous (e.g., driving an automobile or operating machinery).
6. Tolerance and withdrawal symptoms frequently occur.
7. The person continues use of the substance despite recognizing that it causes social, occupational, legal, or medical problems (see "Case in Point: Representative Patrick Kennedy Pleads for Help").

A review of the previous discussion about the properties of CNS depressants reveals that severe dependence on these drugs can satisfy all of these *DSM-5* criteria; thus, according to the American Psychiatric Association, dependence on CNS depressants is classified as a form of mental illness.

The principal types of people who are most inclined to abuse CNS depressants include the following:

• Those who seek sedative effects to deal with emotional stress, to try to escape from problems they are unable to face. Sometimes, these individuals are able to persuade clinicians to administer depressants for their problems; at other times, they self-medicate with depressants that are obtained illegally.
• Those who seek the excitation that occurs, especially after some tolerance has developed. Instead of depression, they feel exhilaration and euphoria.
• Those who try to counteract the unpleasant effect or withdrawal associated with other drugs of abuse, such as some stimulants, lysergic acid diethylamide (LSD), and other hallucinogens.
• Those who use sedatives in combination with other depressant drugs such as alcohol and heroin. Alcohol plus a sedative gives a faster high but can be dangerous because of the multiple

▶ CASE IN POINT

Representative Patrick Kennedy Pleads for Help

On May 4, 2006, U.S. Representative Patrick Kennedy crashed his car into a Capitol barricade late at night. Fortunately, no one was seriously injured, but Kennedy agreed to plead guilty on a charge of driving under the influence of prescription drugs. The congressman had had a history of problems with CNS depressants such as sedative-hypnotics and alcohol. Since leaving Congress, Kennedy has worked to change the perception of mental illness and addiction and has lobbied for the passage of congressional bills that require group health plans to offer benefits for mental health and drug dependence at the same level as for other medical conditions. Kennedy says these conditions are not moral issues or character flaws and should be treated with the same urgency with which we treat cancer and heart disease.

Data from Bonin, R. "Patrick Kennedy Breaks the Silence." *60 Minutes* (4 October 2015). Available www.cbsnews.com/news/patrick-kennedy-on-alcoholism-mentla-health-60-min

depressant effects and synergistic interaction. Heroin users often resort to barbiturates if their heroin supply is compromised.

As mentioned earlier, depressants are commonly abused in combination with other drugs (Guthrie and Bostwick 2013). In particular, opioid narcotic users take barbiturates, benzodiazepines, and other depressants to augment the effects of a weak batch of heroin or to counteract a rapidly shrinking supply. Chronic narcotic users also claim that depressants help to offset tolerance to opioids, thereby requiring less narcotic to achieve a satisfactory response by the user. It is not uncommon to see joint dependence on both narcotics and depressants.

Another common use of depressants is by alcoholics to soften the withdrawal from ethanol or to help create a state of intoxication without the telltale odor of alcohol. Interestingly, similar strategies are also used therapeutically to help detoxify the alcoholic. For example, long-acting barbiturates or benzodiazepines are often used to wean an alcohol-dependent person away from ethanol. Treatment with these depressants helps to reduce the severity of withdrawal symptoms, making it easier and safer for alcoholics to eliminate their drug dependence.

Finally, as already mentioned, CNS depressants are used in conjunction with alcohol to commit sexual assaults. Because these drugs are sedating,

remove inhibitions, and can induce a temporary state of amnesia, they are sometimes secretly added to an alcoholic beverage to incapacitate the intended victim of a date rape.

In general, those who chronically abuse the CNS depressants prefer (1) the short-acting barbiturates, such as pentobarbital and secobarbital; (2) the barbiturate-like depressants, such as glutethimide, methyprylon, and methaqualone; or (3) the faster-acting benzodiazepines, such as diazepam (Valium), alprazolam (Xanax), or lorazepam (Ativan). Dependence on sedative-hypnotic agents can develop insidiously. Often, a long-term patient is treated for persistent insomnia or anxiety with daily exposures to a CNS depressant. When an attempt to withdraw the drug is made, the patient becomes agitated, unable to sleep, and severely anxious; a state of panic may be experienced when deprived of the drug. These signs are frequently mistaken for a resurgence of the medical condition being treated and are not recognized as part of a withdrawal syndrome of the CNS depressant. Consequently, the patient commonly resumes use of the CNS depressant, and the symptoms of withdrawal subside. Such conditions generally lead to a gradual increase in dosage as tolerance to the sedative-hypnotic develops. The patient becomes severely dependent on the depressant, both physically and psychologically, and the drug habit becomes an essential feature in

TABLE 6.3 Annual Prevalence of Abuse of CNS Depressants for 12th Graders

	1995	1998	2001	2004	2007	2009	2012	2014
Any illicit drug	39.0%	41.4%	41.4%	38.8%	35.8%	36.5%	39.7%	38.7%
All sedatives (including benzodiazepines)	4.7%	5.5%	5.7%	6.5%	6.2%	5.2%	4.5%	4.3%

Data from Johnston, L. D., P. M. O'Malley, R. A. Miech, J. G. Bachman, and J. E. Schulenberg. *Monitoring the Future: 2014 Overview, Key Findings in Adolescent Drug Use.* Ann Arbor, MI: University of Michigan, 2015. Available http://www.monitoringthefuture.org

the user's daily routines. Only after severe dependence has developed does the clinician often realize what has taken place. The next stage is the unpleasant task of trying to wean the patient from the drug (**detoxification**) with as little discomfort as possible.

The prevalence of abuse of illicit CNS depressants appeared to peak in the early 1980s for 12th graders. Illegal use of these drugs then decreased dramatically; however, abuse of these drugs has rebounded recently (see **Table 6.3**).

Treatment for Withdrawal

All sedative-hypnotics, including alcohol and benzodiazepines, can produce physical dependence and a barbiturate-like withdrawal syndrome if taken in sufficient dosage over a long period. Withdrawal symptoms include anxiety, tremors, nightmares, insomnia, anorexia, nausea, vomiting, seizures, delirium, and maniacal activity.

The duration and severity of withdrawal depend on the particular drug taken. With short-acting depressants, such as pentobarbital, secobarbital, and methaqualone, withdrawal symptoms tend to have a faster onset of action and be more severe. They begin 12 to 24 hours after the last dose and peak in intensity between 24 and 72 hours later. Withdrawal from longer-acting depressants, such as phenobarbital and diazepam, develops more slowly and is less intense; symptoms peak on the 5th to 8th day (Guthrie and Boswick 2013). Not surprisingly, the approach to detoxifying a person who is

dependent on a sedative-hypnotic depends on the nature of the drug itself (i.e., to which category of depressants it belongs), the severity of the dependence, and the duration of action of the drug. The general objectives of detoxification are to eliminate drug dependence (both physical and psychological) in a safe manner while minimizing discomfort. Having achieved these objectives, it is hoped that the patient will be able to remain free of dependence on all CNS depressants. However, in reality detoxification is rarely sufficient by itself to assure long-term abstinence from the drug.

Often, the basic approach for treating severe dependence on sedative-hypnotics is substitution with either pentobarbital or the longer-acting phenobarbital for the offending, usually shorter-acting, CNS depressant. Once substitution has occurred, the long-acting barbiturate dose is gradually reduced. Using a substitute is necessary because abrupt withdrawal for a person who is physically dependent can be dangerous, causing life-threatening seizures. This substitution treatment uses the same rationale as the treatment of heroin withdrawal by methadone replacement. Detoxification also includes supportive nutritional measures such as vitamins, restoration of electrolyte balance, and prevention of dehydration. The patient must be watched closely during this time because he or she will be apprehensive, confused, and unable to make logical decisions (Guthrie and Bostwick 2013).

If the person is addicted to both alcohol and barbiturates, the phenobarbital dosage must be increased to compensate for the double withdrawal. Many benzodiazepine addicts who enter a hospital to be treated for withdrawal are also dependent on heroin, and vice versa. In such cases, the sedative-hypnotic dependence should be addressed first because the associated withdrawal can be life-threatening. Detoxification from any sedative-hypnotic should take place under close medical supervision, typically in a hospital (O'Brien 2006).

KEY TERM

detoxification
elimination of a toxic substance, such as a drug, and its effects from the body

Detoxification of patients is often done in groups to help provide support during this difficult time.

It is important to remember that elimination of physical dependence is not a cure. The problem of psychological dependence can be much more difficult to handle. If an individual is abusing a CNS depressant because of emotional instability, personal problems, or a very stressful environment, eliminating physical dependence alone will not solve the problem, and drug dependence is likely to recur. These types of patients require intense psychological counseling and must be trained to deal with their difficulties in a more constructive and positive fashion. Without such psychological support, benefits from detoxification will only be temporary, and therapy will ultimately fail.

Natural Depressants

Some plants that contain naturally occurring CNS depressants are included in herbal products or made into herbal teas for relaxation or as treatment for sleep problems (Mestrovic 2015). Probably the best known of this group is the kava kava plant (*Piper methysticum*). This plant belongs to the pepper family and grows on South Pacific islands (Wallace 2012). Drinks and bars containing extracts from kava kava root are legally available in many health food stores, are especially popular in Polynesian populations, and are sometimes used in religious ceremonies. The extract is prepared from the part of the kava kava plant that grows beneath the surface of the ground. Small amounts of kava kava can produce euphoria and increased sociability, whereas larger doses cause substantial relaxation, lethargy, relaxed lower limbs, and eventually sleep (Livertox n.d.). Some users may experience visual and auditory hallucinations that can last 1 to 2 hours. Some users report that kava kava drinks can make the mouth numb, much like topical local anesthetics used by dentists. Rare cases have been reported of liver damage in frequent users (Livertox n.d.).

A second type of common herb that contains CNS depressants is the *Datura* family of plants. Although these botanicals are typically associated with hallucinogenic effects, in smaller amounts they sometimes can cause sedation and even induce sleep. Examples of these plants include *Datura inoxia* (devil's trumpet) and *Datura stramonium* (jimson weed or thornapple). The active ingredients in these plants are typically anticholinergic drugs such as atropine or scopolamine. In lower doses, these herbs, especially if they contain scopolamine, have been used to encourage sleep. In fact, the actions of the herbs are somewhat similar to the OTC antihistamine-containing sleep aids, which also work due to their anticholinergic actions. In higher doses, both atropine and scopolamine can cause hallucinogenic effects. The anticholinergic actions of these herbs can be quite annoying and include constipation, dry mouth, and blurred vision, just to mention a few (Encyclopedia.com 2016).

LEARNING PORTFOLIO

Key Terms

Discussion Questions

1. Why did benzodiazepine drugs replace barbiturates as the sedative-hypnotic drugs most prescribed by physicians?
2. Which features of CNS depressants give them abuse potential?
3. Why is long-term use of the benzodiazepines more likely than short-term use to cause dependence?
4. Why are some physicians careless when prescribing benzodiazepines for patients suffering from severe anxiety?
5. Currently, sleep aid products are available OTC. Should the FDA also allow sedatives to be sold without a prescription? Support your answer.
6. Are there any real advantages to using barbiturates as sedatives or hypnotics? Should the FDA remove them completely from the market?
7. What types of people are most likely to abuse CNS depressants? Suggest ways to help these people avoid abusing these drugs.
8. Should propofol be scheduled, and if so, as what category?
9. What is the appeal of using GHB? Why is it used to commit sexual assaults?
10. What dangers are associated with treating individuals who are severely dependent on CNS depressants?
11. Why are CNS depressants often combined with alcohol, and what is the consequence?
12. Why is detoxification by itself usually insufficient to achieve long-term therapeutic success when dealing with severe CNS depressant dependence?

Summary

1. Several unrelated drug groups cause CNS depression, but only a few are actually used clinically for their depressant properties. The most frequently prescribed CNS depressants are benzodiazepines, which include drugs such as Valium, Ambien, and Xanax. Barbiturates once were popular, but, because of their severe side effects, they are no longer prescribed by most clinicians except to treat some seizures. Much like barbiturates, drugs such as chloral hydrate and methaqualone are little used today. Finally, some OTC and prescription antihistamines, such as diphenhydramine, hydroxyzine, and promethazine, are used for their CNS depressant effects.

2. The clinical value of CNS depressants is dose dependent. When used at low doses, these drugs relieve anxiety and promote relaxation (sedatives). When prescribed at higher doses, they can cause drowsiness and promote sleep (hypnotics). When administered at even higher doses, some of the depressants cause anesthesia and are used for patient management during surgery.

3. The rapidly acting general anesthetic propofol has become well known because of its role in the accidental death of pop singer Michael Jackson. Although not currently scheduled, its abuse is becoming a problem with physicians and nurses who have access to it at work. Sometimes propofol is also used to relieve pain or help someone sleep.

4. Because CNS depressants can relieve anxiety and reduce stress, they are viewed as desirable by many people. If used frequently over long periods, however, they can cause tolerance that leads to dependence.

5. The principal reason that benzodiazepines have replaced barbiturates in the treatment of stress and insomnia is that benzodiazepines have a greater margin of safety and are less likely to alter sleep patterns. Benzodiazepines enhance the GABA transmitter system in the brain through a specific receptor, whereas the effects of barbiturates are less selective. Even though benzodiazepines are safer than barbiturates, dependence and significant withdrawal problems can result if the former drugs are used indiscriminately.

6. Often, benzodiazepine dependence occurs in patients who suffer stress or anxiety disorders and are under a physician's care. If the physician is not careful and the cause of the stress is not resolved, drug treatment can drag on for weeks or months. After prolonged benzodiazepine therapy, tolerance to the drug develops; when benzodiazepine use is stopped, withdrawal occurs, which itself causes agitation. A rebound response to the drug might resemble the effects of emotional stress (agitation), so use of benzodiazepine is continued. In this way, the patient becomes severely dependent.

7. The short-acting CNS depressants are preferred for treatment of insomnia. These drugs help the patient get to sleep and then are inactivated by the body; when the user awakens the next day, he or she is less likely to experience residual effects than with long-acting drugs. The short-acting depressants are also more likely to be abused because of their relatively rapid onset and intense effects. In contrast, the long-acting depressants are better suited to treating persistent problems such

as anxiety and stress. The long-acting depressants are also used to help wean dependent people from their use of short-acting compounds such as alcohol.

8. Many antihistamines cause sedation and drowsiness due to their anticholinergic effects. Several of these agents are useful for short-term relief of anxiety and are available in OTC sleep aids. The effectiveness of these CNS depressants is usually less than that of benzodiazepines. Because of their anticholinergic actions, antihistamines can cause some annoying side effects. These agents are not likely to be used for long periods; thus, dependence or serious abuse usually does not develop.

9. The people most likely to abuse CNS depressants include individuals who (a) use drugs to relieve continual stress; (b) paradoxically feel euphoria and stimulation from depressants; (c) use depressants to counteract the unpleasant effects of other drugs of abuse, such as stimulants; and (d) combine depressants with alcohol and heroin to potentiate the effects.

10. The basic approach for treating dependence on CNS depressants is to detoxify the individual in a safe manner while minimizing his or her discomfort. This state is achieved by substituting a long-acting barbiturate or benzodiazepine, such as phenobarbital or Valium, for the offending CNS depressant. The long-acting drug causes less severe withdrawal symptoms over a longer period of time. The dependent person is gradually weaned from the substitute drug until he or she is depressant-free.

11. GHB is a naturally occurring substance related to the neurotransmitter GABA that has been used for its sedating, euphorigenic, and muscle-building properties. It also has been used to debilitate victims of date rape during sexual assaults. Because of concerns that this substance is frequently abused, GHB was classified as a Schedule I drug in 2000.

12. Some plants such as kava kava that contain naturally occurring CNS depressants are included in herbal teas for relaxation or treatment of insomnia.

References

AddictionCenter. "Sleeping Pill Addiction and Abuse." 2015a. Available https://www.addictioncenter.com /sleeping-pills/#

AddictionCenter. "Xanax Addiction and Abuse." 2015b. Available https://addictioncenter.com/benzodiazepines /xanax/

American Psychiatric Association (APA). *Diagnostic and Statistical Manual of Mental Disorders*, fifth edition. Washington, DC: American Psychiatric Association, 2013.

Associated Press. "Woman Who Used Halcion Defense Hangs Self." *Salt Lake Tribune* 248 (27 July 1994): D-3.

Balestra, K. "Critics Cite Serious Side Effects of Benzodiazepine Antidepressants." *The Washington Post* (30 June 2009). Available http://www.washingtonpost.com/wp-dyn /content/article/2009/06/29/AR2009062903105.html

Bartholow, M. "Top 200 Drugs of 2011." *Pharmacy Times* (10 July 2012). Available http://www.pharmacytimes .com/publications/issue/2012/July2012/top-200-Drugs -of-2011

Bosch, O., B. Quednow, E. Seifritz, and T. Wetter. "Reconsidering GHB: Orphan Drug or New Model Antidepressant." *Journal of Psychopharmacology* 26 (2012): 618–628.

Bruining, H., L. Passtoor, N. Goriounova, F. Jansen, B. Hakvoort, M. de Jonge, and S. S. Poil. "Paradoxical Benzodiazepine Response: A Rationale for Bumetanie in Neurodevelopmental Disorder." *Pediatrics* 136 (2015): e539–e543.

Brunt, T. M., J. G. van Amsterdam, and W. van den Brink. "GHB, GBL and 1,4-BD Addiction." *Current Pharmaceutical Design* 20 (2014): 4176–4085.

Charney, D., S. Mihic, and R. Harris. "Hypnotics and Sedatives." In *The Pharmacological Basis of Therapeutics*, 11th ed., edited by L. Brunton, J. Lazo, and K. Parker, 401–427. New York: McGraw-Hill, 2006.

Drug Enforcement Administration (DEA). "Controlled Substances." 29 August 2016. http://www.deadiversion .usdoj.gov/schedules/orangebook/c_cs_alpha.pdf

Drug Enforcement Administration (DEA). "Gamma Hydroxybutyric Acid." Drug Enforcement Administration (2013). Available http://www.deadiversion .usdoj.gov/drug_chem_info/ghb.pdf

Drug Facts and Comparisons. "Sedatives/Hypnotics/Nonbarbiturate." Pocket Version, 14th ed., 732–748. St. Louis, MO: Wolters Kluwer Health, 2010.

Drugs.com. "Benzodiazepines." 2015a. Available http:// www.drugs.com/drug-class/benzodiazepines.html

Drugs.com. "Sedative, Hypnotic or Anxiolytic Drug Use Disorder." Harvard Health Publications. 2015b. Available http://www.drugs.com/health-guide/substance-abuse-depressants-or-sedative-hypnotic-drugs.html

Drugs.com. "History of Quaaludes." 2015c. Available http://www.drugs.com/quaaludes.html

Dryden-Edwards, R. "Benzodiazepine Abuse." eMedicineHealth. 2013. Available http://www.emedicinehealth. com/benzodiazepine_abuse/article_em.htm

Elements Behavioral Health. "Why You Should Never Abuse Propofol." 30 January 2015. Available http://www.drugaddictiontreatment.com/types-of -addiction/prescription-drug-addiction/why-you-should -never-abuse-propofol

Encyclopedia.com. "Antihistamine." 2006. Available http:// www.encyclopedia.com/topic/antihistamine.aspx

Encyclopedia.com. *"Datura stramonium."* 2016. Available http://www.encyclopedia.com/topic/Jimson_weed.aspx

European Monitoring Centre for Drugs and Drug Addiction Perspective on Drugs. "The Misuse of Benzodiazepines Among High-Risk Opioid Users in Europe." 2015. Available http://www.drugsandalcohol.ie/24052/

Fawcett, K. "Benzodiazepine: Helpful or Harmful?" *U.S. News & World Report Health* (19 February 2015). Available http://health.usnews.com/health-news/patient-advice /articles/2015/02/19/benzodiazepines-helpful-or-harmful

Gorelick, D. "Cocaine Use Disorder in Adults." UpToDate. (2015). Available http://www.uptodate.com/contents /cocaine-use-disorder-in-adults-epidemiology-pharma cology-clinical-manifestations-medical-consequences -and-diagnosis

Guthrie, S., and J. Bostwick. "Anxiety Disorders." In *Applied Therapeutics, The Clinical Use of Drugs*, 10th ed., edited by B. Alldredge, 1863–1869. Philadelphia: Wolters Kluwer, 2013.

Insomnia.net. "What's the Story with Triazolam and Insomnia?" n.d. Available http://www.insomnia.net /medications/triazolam/

Johnston, L. "Monitoring the Future 2014." Available http://www.monitoringthefuture.org

Jones, A., and A. Holmgren. "Concentrations of Alprazolam in Blood from Impaired Drivers and Forensic Autopsies Were Not Much Different but Showed a High Prevalence of Co-ingested Illicit Drugs." *Journal of Psychopharmacology* 27 (2013): 276–281.

Katzung, B. "Histamine Serotonin, and Ergot Alkaloids." In *Basic and Clinical Pharmacology*, 12th ed., edited by B. Katzung, 273–293. New York: McGraw-Hill Medical, 2012.

Krinsky, B. "Insomnia, Drowsiness, and Fatigue." In *Handbook of Nonprescription Drugs*, 867–883. Washington, DC: American Pharmacist Association, 2012.

Livertox. "Kava Kava." National Library of Medicine. n.d. Available http://livertox.nih.gov/KavaKava.htm

Mandal, A. "Barbiturate History." News Medical. 26 May 2013. Available http://www.news-medical.net/health /barbiturate-history.aspx

McEvoy, G., ed. *American Hospital Formulary Service Drug Information*. Bethesda, MD: American Society of Hospital Pharmacists, 2003.

MedlinePlus. "Chloral Hydrate." U.S. National Library of Medicine. 1 February 2009. Available https://www.nlm.nih.gov/medlineplus/druginfo/meds/a682201.html

Mercola. "Long-Term Use of Pills for Anxiety and Sleep Linked to Dementia." 2014. Available http://www.news-medical.net/health/List-of-Sedatives.aspx

Mestrovic, T. "List of Sedatives." News Medical. 23 November 2015. Available http://www.news-medical.net/health/list-of-sedative.aspx

Narconon. "History of Barbiturates." n.d. Available http://www.narconon.org/drug-information/barbiturates-history.html

National Institute on Drug Abuse (NIDA). "What Are Some of the Commonly Abused Prescription Drugs?" November 2014. Available https://www.drugabuse.gov/publications/research-reports/prescription-drugs/what-are-some-commonly-abused-prescription-drugs

National Institute on Drug Abuse (NIDA). "Commonly Abused Drugs Chart." 1 December 2015. Available https://www.drugabuse.gov/drugs-abuse/commonly-abused-drugs-charts

O'Brien, C. "Drug Addiction and Drug Abuse." In *The Pharmacological Basis of Therapeutics*, 11th ed., edited by L. Brunton, J. Lazo, and K. Parker, 607–627. New York: McGraw-Hill, 2006.

Olfson, M., M. King, and M. Schoenbaum. "Benzodiazepine Use in the United States." *JAMA Psychiatry* 72 (2015): 136–142.

Physicians' Desk Reference (PDR), 67th ed. Montvale, NJ: PDR Network, 2013.

Publishers Group. "Street Drugs." 2002. Available http://www.Streetdrugs.org

Reeves, R., M. Ladner, C. Perry, R. Burke, and J. Lazier. "Abuse of Medications That Theoretically Are Without Abuse Potential." *Southern Medical Journal* 108 (2015): 151–157.

Scharman, E., A. Erdman, P. Wax, P. Chyka, E. Caravati, et al. "Diphenhydramine and Dimenhydrinate Poisoning: An Evidence-Based Consensus Guideline for Out-of-Hospital Management." *Clinical Toxicology* (Philadelphia) 44 (2006): 205–233.

Schep, L., K. Knudsen, R. Slaughter, J. Vale, and B. Megarbane. "The Clinical Toxicology of Gamma Hydroxybutyrate, Gamma Butyrolactone and 1,4-Butanediol." *Clinical Toxicology* (Philadelphia) 50 (2012): 458–470.

Sumnall, H., K. Woolfall, S. Edwards, J. Cole, and C. Beynon. "Use, Function, and Subjective Experiences of Gamma-Hydroxybutyrate (GHB)." *Drugs and Alcohol Dependency* 92 (2008): 286–290.

Szalavitz, M. "A Sleeping Pill Without the Sleepy Head." *Time*. (5 April 2013). Available http://healthland.time.com/2013/04/05/a-sleeping-pill-without-the-sleepy-head/

Townsend, C. "The Scary Reason GHB Is Making a Comeback." The Daily Beast (19 October 2015). Available http://www.thedailybeast.com/articles/2015/10/19/the-scary-reason-ghb-is-making-a-comeback.html

Trevor, A., and W. Way. "Sedative-Hypnotic Drugs." In *Basic and Clinical Pharmacology*, 13th ed., edited by B. Katzung, 369-383. New York: McGraw-Hill Medical, 2015.

U.S. Department of Justice (USDOJ). "Information Bulletin. GHB Analogs." Product No. 2002-L0424-0034 (2002).

U.S. Department of Justice (USDOJ). "National Drug Threat Assessment 2003." National Drug Intelligence Center, Product No. 2003-Q0317-001 (January 2003).

Vendel, C. "The Drug GHB Is Deceptive, Deadly and Often Overlooked." LakeExpo.com. 23 August 2009. Available http://lakeexpo.com/news/top_stories/article_cdf11f3e-241a-515e-b457-a2c2815cbde7.html

Wallace, K. "Kava Kava as a Sleep Remedy." eHow Health. 24 December 2012. Available http://www.Ehow.com/way_5849534.kava.kava-sleep-remedy.html

CHAPTER 7

Alcohol: Pharmacological Effects

© PhotoDisc.

Did You Know?

▶ Alcohol is the most consumed drug in the world.

▶ Ethanol leads all other substances of abuse in treatment admissions.

▶ Ethanol is the only alcohol used for human consumption; most of the other common alcohols are poisonous.

▶ Some wild animals and insects become drunk after seeking out and consuming alcohol-containing fermented fruit.

▶ Alcohol-related deaths outnumber deaths related to other drugs of abuse (except tobacco) by a margin of four to one.

▶ Women who abuse alcohol are more likely to suffer depression than male abusers.

▶ The lethal level of alcohol is between 0.4% and 0.6% by volume in the blood; the blood level most states consider to be illegal in someone driving is 0.08%.

▶ Consumption of alcohol by adolescents can cause persistent damage to their brain development.

▶ Among alcoholics, liver disorders account for approximately 10% to 15% of deaths.

▶ The Food and Drug Administration (FDA) has approved a number of medications for the treatment of alcohol dependence, although they are not universally effective.

▶ Fetal alcohol syndrome (FAS) is caused by alcohol consumption during pregnancy and is characterized by facial deformities, growth deficiencies, and mental retardation in the offspring.

▶ Addictions such as alcoholism are among the most inherited of the mental illnesses.

Learning Objectives

On completing this chapter you should be able to:

❯ Explain how common alcohol (ethanol) is a drug.

❯ Explain the pharmacokinetic properties of alcohol, and describe how they influence the effects of the drug.

❯ Explain the role of alcohol in polydrug abuse.

❯ Identify the possible physical effects of prolonged heavy ethanol consumption.

❯ Explain what alcohol dependence is and how it is treated.

❯ Explain the potential cardiovascular benefits and problems of moderate alcohol use and the dose-dependent nature of these effects.

❯ Describe fetal alcohol syndrome (FAS), its cause, and its effects.

❯ Explain how prolonged consumption of alcohol affects the brain and nervous system, liver, digestive system, blood, cardiovascular system, sexual organs, endocrine system, and kidneys and how it leads to mental disorders and damage to fetuses.

❯ Describe why use of alcohol by adolescents is particularly problematic and how this should influence the discussion about underage drinking.

❯ Explain why there is concern about how college students use alcohol, and discuss how to address this problem.

❯ Explain why malnutrition is so common among alcoholics.

Introduction

This chapter focuses on how alcohol affects the body from a pharmacological perspective. Alcohol is the most widely consumed drug in the world, and for many it is as much a part of daily life as eating. Even so, most of those who use it do not understand how it works or why it can change their personalities and behavior in bizarre and unpredictable ways, causing respectable and dependable people to engage in foolish and even dangerous behaviors (Gowin 2010). In 2015, sales of alcoholic beverages in the United States totaled $266 billion (Statista 2016). As a licit drug, alcohol is extensively promoted socially through advertising, exposing underage youth to 3.9 billion noncompliant alcohol promotional impressions from 2013 to 2015 (Johns Hopkins 2015). More important, drinking is perceived as acceptable and even desirable. The popularity of this drug is clear; in 2015, 38% of high school seniors said they had been drunk (National Institute on Drug Abuse [NIDA] 2015a). Binge drinking among teens is thought to be at epidemic levels, with about 38% of the high school seniors participating in episodes of very heavy alcohol use (NIDA 2015a). Although drinking by persons younger than 21 years is illegal, adolescents aged 12 to 20 years drink 11% of all alcohol consumed in the United States, of which 90% is in the form of binge drinks (Centers for Disease Control and Prevention [CDC] 2015).

This chapter focuses on the many adverse effects of alcohol on the human body. Overall, it provides you with a foundation to understand the pharmacological nature of alcohol. Alcohol is widely consumed and leads all other addicting substances as a reason for treatment admissions (Grant et al. 2015) (see **Table 7.1**). Each year approximately 2 million people are admitted for treatment of substance dependence, and more than half of these receive treatment for alcoholism (Substance Abuse and Mental Health Services Administration [SAMHSA] 2009). We hope that such an understanding of how this drug affects the various organ systems of the body will lead to more responsible use and less abuse of alcohol.

The Nature and History of Alcohol

Alcohol has been part of human culture since the beginning of recorded history. The technology for alcohol production is ancient. Several basic ingredients and conditions are needed to produce

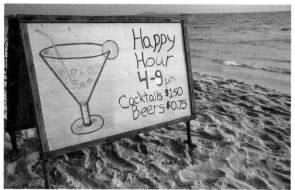

Because of frequent advertising, use of alcohol is perceived as normal and acceptable.

this substance: sugar, water, yeast, and warm temperatures.

The process of making alcohol, called **fermentation**, is a natural one. It occurs in ripe fruit and berries and even in honey that bees leave in trees. These substances contain sugar and water and are found in warm climates, where yeast spores are transported through the air. Animals such as elephants, baboons, birds, wild pigs, and bees will seek out and eat fermented fruit. Elephants under the influence of alcohol have been observed bumping into one another and stumbling around. Intoxicated bees fly an unsteady beeline toward their hives. Birds eating fermented fruit become so uncoordinated that they cannot fly or, if they do, crash into windows or branches. In fact, fermented honey, called **mead**, may have been the first alcoholic beverage.

The Egyptians had breweries 6000 years ago; they credited the god Osiris with introducing wine to humans. The ancient Greeks used large quantities of wine and credited a god, Bacchus (Dionysus), with introducing the drink. Today, we use the words *bacchanalia* and *dionysian* to refer to revelry and drunken events. The Hebrews were also heavy users of wine. The Bible mentions that Noah, just nine generations removed from Adam, made wine and became drunk.

Alcohol is produced by a single-celled microscopic organism, one of the yeasts, that breaks down sugar by a metabolic form of combustion,

KEY TERMS

fermentation
biochemical process through which yeast converts sugar to alcohol

mead
fermented honey often made into an alcoholic beverage

TABLE 7.1 Epidemiology of Alcohol Use Disorders (AUD)

Alcohol use disorder (AUD) ranks among the most prevalent mental disorders in the United States and throughout the world. The devastation caused by AUD on productivity, social, and personal functioning and financial and medical institutions is staggering. This table presents an epidemiological overview of AUD to help the reader appreciate its diversity and overwhelming implications.

Category (lifetime, unless otherwise indicated)	Percent Incidence (of total unless otherwise indicated)	Category (lifetime, unless otherwise indicated)	Percent Incidence (of total unless otherwise indicated)
12-month prevalence	13.9%	*Ubanicity*	
		Urban	29.2%
Lifetime prevalence		Rural	28.6%
Total	29.1%		
Mild	8.6%	*Region*	
Severe	13.9%	Northeast	28.8%
Lifetime prevalence for men	36%	Midwest	33.6%
Lifetime prevalence for women	22.7%	South	25.3%
		West	31.3%
Lifetime prevalence by race/ ethnicity			
White	32.6%	*Who Receive Treatment*	
Native American	43.4%	**Total AUD**	19.8%
Black	22.0%	Mild AUD	4.4%
Asian	15.0%	Moderate AUD	8.7%
Hispanic	22.9%	Severe	34.7%
Lifetime prevalence by age (years)		*Co-incidence (lifetime category in total AUD patients)*	*Significant AOR (adjusted odds ratio-risk compared to normal [1])*
18–29	37%		
30–44	34.4%	Other drug use disorder	4.1
45–64	28.2%	Nicotine use disorder	3.1
≥65	13.4%	Bipolar disorder	2.0
Education		Generalized anxiety disorder	1.2
<High school	22.3%	Panic disorder	1.3
High school	28.4%	Persistent depression	1.3
Some college or higher	30.8%	Antisocial personality disorder	1.9
Family Income ($)		Posttraumatic stress disorder	1.3
0–19,999	28.9%		
20,000–34,999	27.9%		
35,000–69,999	29.0%		
>70,000	30.0%		

Data from Grant, B., R. Goldstein, T. Saha, S. P. Chou, J. Jung, H. Zhang, R. P. Pickering, W. J. Ruan, S. M. Smith, B. Huang, and D. S. Hasin. "Epidemiology of DSM-5 Alcohol Use Disorder." *JAMA Psychiatry* 72 (2015): 757–766.

thereby releasing carbon dioxide and forming water and ethyl alcohol as waste products. Carbon dioxide creates the foam on a glass of beer and the fizz in champagne. Fermentation continues until the sugar supply is exhausted or the concentration of alcohol reaches the point at which it kills the yeast (12% to 14%). Thus, 12% to 14% is the natural limit of alcohol found in fermented wines or beers.

The **distillation** device, or still, was developed by the Arabs around AD 800 and was introduced into medieval Europe around AD 1250. By boiling the fermented drink and gathering the condensed vapor in a pipe, a still increases the concentration of alcohol, potentially to 50% or higher. Because distillation made it easier for people to get drunk, it greatly intensified the problem of alcohol abuse.

HERE AND NOW
A Century of Alcohol

An overwhelming need to consume alcohol (known today as alcoholism) was first described in the literature by Benjamin Rush in 1784, but the concept that excessive use of alcohol is a disease did not really evolve until the past 100 or so years. This perspective was encouraged by the temperance movement of the late 19th century. Because of the ill effects of alcohol, temperance legally became Prohibition in 1919. Prohibition (which made alcohol illegal) was initially successful in reducing consumption, but consumption began to rebound in the late 1920s. However, it has been suggested that Prohibition was repealed in 1933 not because it failed to reduce alcohol use, but because of shifting policy during the Great Depression that argued liquor manufacturing would create jobs and provide taxes on alcoholic beverages that could fund government programs.

The second half of the 20th century saw the emergence of the belief that genetics plays a major role in alcoholism. This concept suggests that because of inherited traits some families and individuals are more vulnerable to alcohol addiction than others. Researchers today are energetically moving forward to identify which genes might contribute to the development and expression of the addiction in an effort to improve prevention and treatment for alcoholism.

Data from Dual Diagnosis. "Disease Theory of Alcoholism." 2016. Available www.dualdiagnosis.org/alcohol-addiction/disease-theory-alcoholism/; Szalavitz, M. "Genetics: No More Addictive Personality." *Nature* 522 (2015): 548–549.

However, even before the invention of the still, alcoholic beverages had been known to cause problems in heavy users that resulted in severe physical and psychological dependence. Toward the end of the 19th century, drug addicts (including those dependent on alcohol) were shunned as immoral and undesirable. It was in the 1930s when alcoholism started to be considered a medical condition requiring treatment (Dual Diagnosis 2016). More recently, alcoholism has been officially termed as alcohol use disorder (AUD) by the American Psychiatric Association (APA 2013) (see "Here and Now: A Century of Alcohol").

Alcohol as a Drug

Alcohol (more precisely designated as ethanol) is a natural product of fermentation and considered by many to be the number one abused drug (Alcohol Abuse Essentials 2010). Its impact on college students has been particularly disturbing, with reports stating that binge drinking among such individuals is commonplace (Bishop 2012). This psychoactive substance depresses the central nervous system (CNS) while influencing almost all major organ systems of the body (Kenna 2013). Alcohol is also an addictive drug in that it may produce a physical and behavioral dependence (Kenna 2013). Although tradition and attitude are important factors in determining the use patterns of this substance, the typical consumer rarely appreciates the diversity of pharmacological effects caused by alcohol, the drug. The pharmacological action of alcohol accounts for both its pleasurable and CNS effects as well as its hazards to health and public safety.

∎ Alcohol as a Social Drug

Why is alcohol often perceived as an acceptable adjunct to such celebrations as parties, birthdays, weddings, and anniversaries, and as a way of relieving stress and anxiety? Social psychologists refer to the perception of alcohol as a **social lubricant**. This term implies that drinking is misconceived as safely promoting conviviality and social interaction and as an activity that bolsters confidence by repressing inhibitions and strengthening extroversion. Why do many people have to be reminded that alcohol is a drug like marijuana or cocaine and may have serious consequences

KEY TERMS

distillation
heating fermented mixtures of cereal grains or fruits in a still to evaporate and be trapped as purified alcohol

social lubricant
belief that drinking (misconceived as safe) represses inhibitions, strengthens extroversion, and leads to increased sociability

for some people? Four reasons explain this misconception:

1. The use of alcohol is legal.
2. Through widespread advertising, the media promote the notion that alcohol consumption is as normal and safe as drinking fruit juices and soft drinks.
3. The distribution, advertisement, and sale of alcoholic beverages are widely practiced.
4. Alcohol use has a long tradition, dating back to 4000 BC (Bachelor 2010).

■ Impact of Alcohol

Although many consider the effects of alcohol enjoyable and reassuring, the adverse pharmacological impacts of this drug are extensive. Its use causes approximately 14 million cases of alcoholism (severe alcohol dependence) at any one time; its effects are associated with more than 100,000 deaths each year in the United States (Fleming, Mihic, and Harris 2006); and it costs our society about $250 billion annually (Szalavitz 2011). It is estimated that over 2% of nighttime drivers have a blood-alcohol content that exceeds legal amounts (0.08%) (Kerlikowske 2010).

The pharmacological effects of alcohol abuse cause severe dependence, which is classified as a psychiatric disorder according to the criteria provided by the American Psychiatric Association in its *Diagnostic and Statistical Manual of Mental Disorders*, 5th edition (*DSM-5*; APA 2013). These effects also disrupt personal, family, social, and professional functioning and frequently result in multiple illnesses and accidents, violence, and crime (Hanson and Li 2003). Alcohol consumed during pregnancy can lead to devastating damage to offspring and is a principal cause of mental retardation in newborns (Hanson and Li 2003). After tobacco, alcohol is the leading cause of premature death in America. In the United States, approximately $176 billion is spent annually dealing with the social and health problems resulting from the pharmacological effects of alcohol. Of course, such estimates fall short in assessing the emotional upheaval and human suffering caused by this drug.

Despite all of the problems that alcohol causes, our free society has demanded access to this drug. At the same time, it is unthinkable to ignore its tremendous negative social impact. There are no simple answers to this dichotomy, yet clearly governmental and educational institutions could do more to protect members of society from the dangers associated with alcohol. The best weapons we have against the problems caused by alcohol are education, prevention, and treatment.

■ Alcohol and Crime

Although alcohol is considered to be a legal substance and can be consumed in public places by people 21 years of age or older without fear of being arrested, it is strongly associated with crime and other social problems. For example, the use of alcohol contributes to 40% of all violent crimes (e.g., murders, rapes, assaults, child and sexual abuse), and 37% of the approximately 2 million imprisoned offenders in the United States report that when arrested, they were under the influence of alcohol. In fact, offenders of violent crimes are far more likely to have been using alcohol than any other drug. Alcohol is particularly implicated

The use of alcoholic beverages is often associated with criminal behavior leading to incarceration.

Almost all violent crimes on college campuses involve the use of alcohol.

in violent acts when the attacker and victim are acquainted, accounting for two-thirds of such cases. In contrast, when the attacker and victim are strangers, alcohol is associated with only one-third of the cases (NCADD 2016).

More than 1 million people in the United States are arrested each year for driving under the influence (DUI) of alcohol. Because use of alcohol impairs motor functions and diminishes decision making, nearly 40% of all traffic deaths are alcohol-related (NCADD 2016).

Use of alcohol is also prevalent in incidents of violence between college students. Each year more than 600,000 college students are assaulted by another student under alcohol's influence. In fact, almost 95% of all violent crimes on college campuses involve the use of alcohol by either the victim or attacker, or both (NCADD 2016).

Despite the fact that our prisons and jails are filled with inmates who are diagnosed as positive for drug or alcohol use dependency, fewer than 20% of these prisoners receive adequate treatment. This lack of treatment available to inmates accounts for the finding that around 95% of these former prisoners return to using alcohol or drugs after release from prison, with 70% going on to commit new crimes. It has been found time and again that treatment is the most effective strategy for breaking the criminal justice cycle for persons with alcohol problems. In the long run, effective treatment could save society considerable money and suffering (National Council on Alcoholism and Drug Dependence [NCADD] 2016).

■ Alcohol and Cancer

Although the impact of alcohol consumption on cancer has been somewhat controversial, there has been little dispute that heavy long-term regular use can contribute to cancers of the mouth, gastrointestinal tract, liver, and breast (American Institute for Cancer Research [AICR] 2013). However, the opinions on the effects of moderate drinking on cancer expression have been more equivocal. It is possible that this is about to change. A major study by several public health institutions found that the daily average consumption of 1.5 drinks accounted for 30% of the approximate 20,000 alcohol-linked cancers each year. Overall, 15% of breast cancers are caused by alcohol consumption (Ward 2013). It is not known exactly how alcohol use leads to cancer expression, but it is now evident that alcohol is one of the principal causes of preventable

cancers; consequently, no health authority should recommend that if you do not drink you should start (Ward 2013).

■ Alcopops

Alcopops are sugary, fruity malt-based drinks merchandized in brightly colored packages that are attractive to adolescents. Some claim that as many as 50% of drinkers aged 20 and younger have consumed alcopops, thus confirming their great appeal to teenagers. As many as 30% of those under the age of 18 claim alcopops as their favorite alcoholic drink. Their popularity reflects teenagers' beliefs that these products are safer than most other alcoholic drinks even though many of these drinks have approximately the same alcohol content as many beers (Rasch 2012). In fact, a recent study suggests that alcopops consumption causes disproportionate harm to its teenage users in that teenagers consuming alcopops (Alcohol Justice 2015) do the following:

- Drink more alcohol per day on more days each month
- Engage in binge drinking four times more often
- Are more likely to be involved in physical fights and receive alcohol-related injuries requiring medical attention

The sweet taste and exotic flavors of these products mask their alcohol content, making them attractive to young people. Some alcopops have a higher alcohol content than beers and a lower price and are readily available (Alcohol Justice 2015). Preferred brands include Smirnoff (Diageo) and Bacardi Malt Beverages (Bacardi). Despite concern about the consumption of alcopops by underage drinkers, the marketing of these products remains relatively uncontrolled, and the Federal Trade Commission (FTC) has decided to allow the alcohol industry to regulate itself with little interference from the federal government (Alcohol Justice 2015).

■ Drinking and College Students

Alcohol consumption by college students and its negative consequences are arguably on the rise, leading to almost 2000 drinking-related deaths per year. About 45% of students have binged on alcohol in the previous month, and about 29% of students have even driven under the influence of alcohol. In addition, many sexual assaults have been linked to college drinking (see Case in Point: Drinking and College Culture: Tragic Mix). These troubling statistics regarding alcohol-related problems occurring on college campuses have been interpreted by some observers to be evidence that attempts by college presidents and chancellors to lower the minimum legal drinking age from 21 to 18 should not be encouraged. However, there is a confusing observation that the higher legal age of 21 years reduced binge drinking in noncollege 18- to 20-year-olds but had little effect on college students of the same age. One possible explanation is that most of the noncollege participants in the study were still living at home and somewhat under parental supervision, whereas most of the college students lived away from home, on their own, and often had older friends who could legally buy alcoholic products for the underage students (*New York Times* 2009). Although there is some controversy as to the severity of college drinking, everyone agrees that greater efforts should be made by colleges, government, and

businesses to prevent alcohol-related deaths, injuries, and crimes (Bishop 2012; Epstein 2010).

■ Underage Drinking

Most alcohol use starts during the teen years. Youth who start drinking alcohol at an early age

Alcopops are colorful alcohol products promoted as an alternative to beer with considerable appeal to the underage drinkers.

▶ CASE IN POINT

Drinking and College Culture: A Tragic Mix

Heavy drinking is frequently assumed to be an integral part of the college experience, but it has also been found to be a very reliable predictor of sexual assault in college. It has been shown that women who admit that they sometimes or often "overdrink" are twice as likely to be victims of attempted or completed sexual assaults as those who rarely or never drink. A county prosecutor in Michigan who has a large university under his jurisdiction tells people that alcohol is the "real date-rape drug."

Although the legal drinking age is 21, many students claim that alcohol is "liquid courage," and it "lubricates university social life" throughout the college experience, making it easier to meet and get sexually involved with other students. However, this combination can be explosive, especially for young college students exploring their sexuality in an environment floating in abundant access to beer and other alcoholic drinks. One of the many stories that can be told to illustrate this dangerous combination

is that of a freshman at Boston University who attended a fraternity party. After consuming a debilitating amount of alcohol, she vaguely remembers going upstairs with one of the fraternity members. She recalls waking up the next morning undressed and alone in a tiny room, confident that she had been raped. She also explains that she took a morning-after pill to prevent pregnancy and was tested for sexually transmitted disease; however, she was too frightened to report the incident. She recalls bumping into the man she was convinced raped her and how making eye contact resulted in a panic attack.

Nearly 80% of college students claim that drinking less would effectively prevent sexual assaults. This claim is supported by another student who was sexually assaulted while under the influence. After expressing her regret for allowing herself to get into this situation, she stated, "I was too drunk to say no. But if I wasn't drunk, I wouldn't have gone upstairs [to the bedroom] at all. Nothing that happened that night would have happened if I'd been sober."

Data from Brown, E., S. Hendrix, and S. Svriuga. "Drinking Is Central to College Culture and to Sexual Assault." *Washington Post.* (14 June 2015). Available https://www.washingtonpost.com/local/education/beer-pong-body-shots-keg-stands-alcohol-central-to-college-and-assault/2015/06/14/7430e13c-04bb-11e5-a428-c984eb077d4e_story.html

HERE AND NOW
The Epidemic of Underage Drinking

As with most things, the way teenagers consume alcohol is very different from the alcohol-consuming habits of adults. Teenagers are not inclined to sit around a table and slowly sip one or two glasses of wine with their meals or during a social gathering, but rather they drink quickly, cheaply, and completely in order to get drunk and drown their anxieties and frustrations with the sedative effects of ethanol. There are ever-increasing options to achieve this objective, including malt beverages, mixtures of alcohol plus super-caffeinated energy drinks, very sweet and fruity alcohol products merchandized in brightly colored packages, and even straight liquors. The alarming extent to which this occurs is underscored by the CDC report that 90% of all teen alcohol consumption is in the form of binge drinking and that about 200,000 adolescents end up in emergency rooms each year because of drinking problems. Even though we still have approximately 9 million underage drinkers in the United States, the good news is that from 2002 to 2013 underage drinking decreased by 26%.

Data from Listfield, E. "The Underage Drinking Epidemic." *Parade Special Report* (12 June 2011): 6–8; Pager, T. "Underaged Drinking, Binge Boozing by Minors Is on the Decline." *USA Today.* (11 June 2015). Available http://www.usatoday.com/story/news/2015/06/11/underage-binge-drinking/71021464/

have a much greater likelihood of developing alcohol dependence when they become adults (Reuters 2012). Possible explanations for this effect include (1) an altered expression of genes, which affects vulnerability to alcoholism (Dryden 2009), and (2) interference with normal development of critical brain systems important for learning, memory, attention, information processing, and proper decision making (Reinberg 2009; Trudeau 2010). In addition, early drinkers are at increased vulnerability to the effects of other drugs as an adult, such as nicotine in tobacco (American Public University 2010). Findings such as these are especially disturbing in light of the facts that nearly 40% of students consume alcohol and 22% of them have been drunk before they graduate from high school (Johnston 2016) and teenagers tend to consume alcohol in a binging fashion (Pager 2015) (see "Here and Now: The Epidemic of Underage Drinking"). It is becoming apparent that heavy exposure to the toxic effects of alcohol during adolescence may have long-lasting and profound effects on young people, leading to mental health problems throughout their lives (Ringenberg et al. 2013). For this reason, the American Academy of Pediatrics (2010) recommends that physicians discourage underage drinking by (1) screening their adolescent patients for alcohol use, (2) discussing the hazards of alcohol use with their teenage patients, (3) encouraging parents to be good role models for their children, and (4) supporting the continuation of 21 as the minimum legal drinking age. Many experts believe that parents are key to preventing alcohol use by their children. They suggest that parents who send ambiguous messages to their kids about drinking or through their words and actions encourage teen alcohol consumption are enabling this toxic behavior (Dvorak 2015) (see "Case in Point: Parents Must Say No").

The Properties of Alcohol

Technically, alcohol is a chemical structure that has a hydroxyl group (-OH; one oxygen and one hydrogen atom) attached to a carbon atom. Of the many types of alcohol, several are important for our purposes. The first is **methyl alcohol** (*methanol* or *wood alcohol*), which is made from wood products. Its metabolites are poisonous. Small amounts (4 milliliters) cause blindness by affecting the retina, and larger amounts (80 to 150 milliliters) are usually fatal. Methyl alcohol is added to ethyl alcohol (*ethanol* or *grain alcohol*, the drinking type) that is intended for industrial use so people will not drink it. A similar mixture also is sometimes added to illegally manufactured ("bootleg") liquor.

KEY TERM

methyl alcohol
wood alcohol

► CASE IN POINT

Parents Must Say No

Mike and Molly threw a graduation summer beer bash for their 18-year-old son and invited other varsity football players. Although all the young men were expected to check their car keys at the door, the beer flowed freely as the teens socialized, shouted over the loud music, and gave hugs and high-fives to the "cool parents." If you were to ask the young party participants, they likely would have nominated Mike and Molly for the "Parents of the Year" award. The parents were eager to be part of their son's life and wanted to be viewed as young-at-heart and progressive. In fact, they likely would have argued that they were wiser and better parents than those who prohibited alcohol use by their children because they "related to their son and his friends." Mike and Molly are part of the 20% to 25% of parents who supply alcohol to their teens, claiming that their teenagers are going to drink anyway, so they might as well drink at home under parental supervision. Other parents claim that drinking by adolescents is part of growing up and becoming an adult. "After all," they often say, "I drank when I was a teenager and it didn't hurt me any." Research has overwhelmingly demonstrated that underage drinking actually is a very dangerous rite of passage for many teens, and most authorities say that no amount of underage drinking is acceptable. Taking the car keys away provides minimal protection to a drunk adolescent. Consider the drunken kid who falls down the stairs, wanders into the backyard and falls into the pool and drowns, walks home after the party but staggers into the street and is hit by a car, vomits and chokes to death, and, of course, the teen who finds his or her keys and drives the car anyway. Such tragic alcohol-related accidents result in about 5,000 deaths in people under the age of 21 each year. These types of circumstances are why experts say the solution to underage drinking is not for parents to be indulgent and enable the practice, but rather for parents to never provide alcohol or condone drinking. Parents must send a clear "don't use" message because being a "cool parent" doesn't substitute for being a good parent.

© Anita Patterson Peppers/Shutterstock, Inc.

Data from Cooke, B. "Parents, Teens, and Alcohol: A Dangerous Mix." FamilyEducation.com. 1 July 2010. Available http://life.familyeducation.com/teen/drugs -and-alcohol/29591.html; English, B. "On Drinking, Parents Need to Just Say No." *Boston Globe* (16 May 2010). Available http://www.boston.com/yourtown /milton/articles/2010/05/16/on_drinking_parents_need_to_just_say_no_to_kids

Another type of poisonous alcohol, **ethylene glycol**, is used in antifreeze. A third type, **isopropyl alcohol**, is commonly used as rubbing alcohol and as an antiseptic (a solution for preventing the growth of microorganisms). These two types of alcohol are also poisonous if consumed.

Pure ethyl alcohol (ethanol) is recognized as an official drug in the U.S. Pharmacopoeia, although the various alcoholic beverages are not listed for medical use. Alcohol can be used as a solvent for other drugs or as a preservative. It is used to cleanse, disinfect, and harden the skin and to reduce sweating. A 70% alcohol solution is an effective bactericide. However, it should not be used on open wounds because it will dehydrate the injured tissue and worsen the damage. Alcohol may be deliberately injected in or near nerves to treat severe pain; it causes local anesthesia and deterioration of the nerve. In all alcoholic beverages—beer, wine, liqueurs or cordials, and distilled spirits—the psychoactive agent is the same, but the amount of ethanol varies (see **Table 7.2**). The amount of alcohol is expressed either as a

KEY TERMS

ethylene glycol
alcohol used as antifreeze

isopropyl alcohol
rubbing alcohol, sometimes used as an antiseptic

TABLE 7.2 The Concentration of Ethanol in Common Alcoholic Beverages

Type of Beverage	Concentration of Ethanol
U.S. beers	4–6%
Wine coolers	4–10%
Cocktails and dessert wines	17–20%
Liqueurs	22–50%
Distilled spirits	40% and higher

Different alcoholic beverages have a wide range of alcohol content.

percentage by volume or, in the older proof system, as a measurement based on the military assay method. To make certain that they were getting a high alcohol content in the liquor, the British military would place a sample on gunpowder and touch a spark to it. If the alcohol content exceeded 50%, it would burn and ignite the gunpowder. This test was "proof" that the sample was at least 50% alcohol. If the distilled spirits were "under proof," the water content would prevent the gunpowder from igniting. The percentage of alcohol volume is one-half the proof number. For example, 100-proof whiskey has a 50% alcohol content.

The Physical Effects of Alcohol

How does alcohol affect the body? **Figure 7.1** illustrates how alcohol is absorbed into the body. After a drink, alcohol has direct contact with the mouth, esophagus, stomach, and intestines, acting as an irritant and an **anesthetic** (blocking sensitivity to pain). In addition, alcohol influences almost every organ system in the body after entering the bloodstream. Alcohol diffuses into the blood rapidly after consumption by passing through gastric and intestinal walls (the absorption process). Once the alcohol is in the small intestine, its absorption is largely independent of the presence of food, unlike in the stomach, where food retards absorption.

The effects of alcohol on the human body depend on the amount of alcohol in the blood, known as the **blood alcohol concentration (BAC)**. This concentration largely determines behavioral and physical responses to alcoholic beverages. Relative to behavior, the circumstances in which the drinking occurs, the drinker's mood, and his or her attitude and previous experience with alcohol all contribute to the reaction to drinking. People demonstrate individual patterns of psychological functioning that may affect their reactions to alcohol as well. For instance, the time it takes to empty the stomach may be either reduced or accelerated as a result of anger, fear, stress, nausea, and the condition of the stomach tissues.

The blood alcohol level produced depends on the presence of food in the stomach, the rate of alcohol consumption, the concentration of the alcohol, and the drinker's body composition. Fatty foods, meat, and milk slow the absorption of alcohol, allowing more time for its metabolism and reducing the peak concentration in the blood. When alcoholic beverages are taken with a substantial meal, peak BACs may be as much as 50% lower than they would have been had the alcohol been consumed by itself. When large amounts of alcohol are consumed in a short period, the brain and other organs are exposed to higher peak concentrations. Generally, the more alcohol in the stomach, the greater the absorption rate. There is, however, a modifying effect of very strong drinks on the absorption rate. The absorption of drinks stronger than 100 proof is inhibited. This effect may be due to blocked passage into the small

KEY TERMS

anesthetic
a drug that blocks sensitivity to pain

blood alcohol concentration (BAC)
concentration of alcohol found in the blood, often expressed as a percentage

1. **Mouth**—Alcohol is consumed orally.

2. **Stomach**—Alcohol goes right into the stomach. A little of the alcohol passes through the wall of the stomach and into the bloodstream. Most of the alcohol continues down into the small intestine.

3. **Small intestine**—Alcohol goes from the stomach into the small intestine. Most of the alcohol is absorbed through the walls of the intestine and into the bloodstream.

4. **Bloodstream**—The bloodstream carries the alcohol to all parts of the body, such as the brain, heart, and liver.

5. **Liver**—As the bloodstream carries the alcohol around the body, it passes through the liver. The liver changes the alcohol to water, carbon dioxide, and energy. The process is called *oxidation*. The liver can oxidize only about one-half ounce of alcohol per hour. Thus, until the liver has time to oxidize all of the alcohol, the alcohol continues passing through all parts of the body, including the brain.

6. **Brain**—Alcohol goes to the brain almost as soon as it is consumed. It continues passing through the brain until the liver oxidizes all the alcohol into carbon dioxide, water, and energy.

FIGURE 7.1   How alcohol is absorbed in the body.

Data from Masters, S., and A. Trevor "The Alcohols." In *Basic and Clinical Pharmacology*, 13th ed., edited by B. Katzung, 384–395. New York: McGraw-Hill, 2015.

intestine or irritation of the lining of the stomach, causing mucus secretion, or both. (See "Here and Now: Half-Truths About Alcohol.")

Diluting an alcoholic beverage with water helps to slow absorption, but mixing with carbonated beverages increases the absorption rate. The carbonation causes the stomach to empty its contents into the small intestine more rapidly, causing a more rapid "high." The carbonation in champagne has the same effect.

Once in the blood, distribution occurs as the alcohol uniformly diffuses throughout all tissues and fluids, including fetal circulation in pregnant women or the milk of a nursing mother (BabyCenter 2010). Because the brain has a large blood supply, its activity is quickly affected by a high alcohol concentration in the blood. Body composition—the amount of water available for the alcohol to be dissolved in—is a key factor in BAC and distribution. The greater the muscle mass, the lower the BAC that will result from a given amount of alcohol. This relationship arises because muscle has more fluid volume than does fat. For example, if two men each weigh 180 pounds but one man has substantially more lean mass than the other, the former will have a lower blood alcohol level after consuming 4 ounces of whiskey. The leaner man will show fewer effects. A woman of a weight equivalent to a man generally will have a higher blood alcohol level because women generally have a higher percentage of fat. Thus, they are affected more by identical drinks.

Alcoholic beverages contain almost no vitamins, minerals, protein, or fat—just large amounts of carbohydrates (Kovacs 2010). Alcohol cannot be used by most cells; it must be metabolized by an enzyme, **alcohol dehydrogenase**, which is found almost exclusively in the liver. Alcohol provides more calories per gram than does carbohydrate or protein and only slightly less than does pure

KEY TERM

alcohol dehydrogenase
principal enzyme that metabolizes ethanol

HERE AND NOW
Half-Truths About Alcohol

Much is known about alcohol, but much more needs to be learned to effectively and safely manage its use. There are several half-truths that are commonly believed by the general public that should be clarified:

- *Belief*: Alcohol, if used in moderation, is healthy for everyone.

- *Fact*: Moderate drinking benefits only men older than 50 years of age and women who are post-menopausal. Even for these populations, the benefits appear to be minimal in persons who already have healthy lifestyles.

- *Belief*: Pound for pound, women hold their liquor as well as men.

- *Fact*: Because women have proportionally less body water and tend to metabolize alcohol more slowly than men, women become more intoxicated with comparable dose consumption per body weight.

- *Belief*: A drink before bed induces sleep.

- *Fact*: After moderate drinking, onset of sleep may be faster, but the sleep itself becomes restless, marked by frequent wakings and inability to get back to sleep.

- *Belief*: If you don't feel drunk, it is okay to drive.

- *Fact*: People are typically unable to determine accurately how much alcohol is in their system. For most states in the United States, 0.08% to 0.1% alcohol in the blood is the legal threshold for driving (i.e., it is against the law to drive with this blood alcohol content or higher), but studies have shown that driving performance is significantly impaired at half this concentration.

- *Belief*: You can sober up by taking a shower or drinking caffeine.

- *Fact*: Time is the only thing that truly sobers you up after consuming alcohol. Caffeine is a stimulant that does not neutralize the alcohol effects, but can interfere with sleeping.

Data from "Your Health: Alcohol: The Whole Truth, Seven Half-Truths About Drinking, Exposed." *Consumer Reports* 64 (December 1999): 60–61; National Institute on Alcohol Abuse and Alcoholism (NIAAA). "FAQs for the General Public." 2007. Available http://www.niaaa.nih.gov/FAQs/General-English; Greenfield, S. "Women and Alcohol Use Disorders." *Harvard Review Psychiatry* 10 (2002): 76–85; Beck, M. "Testing the Limits of Tipsy." *The Wall Street Journal* (August 2, 2011); A Forever Recovery. "5 Myths About Alcohol Abuse vs. the Facts." 5 April 2015. Available aforeverrecovery.com/blog /information/5-myths-about-alcohol-abuse-vs-the-facts

fat. Because it can provide many calories, the drinker's appetite may be satisfied; as a result, he or she may not eat properly, causing malnutrition (Kovacs 2010). The tolerance that develops to alcohol is comparable to that observed with barbiturates. Some people have a higher tolerance for alcohol and can more easily disguise intoxication.

■ Alcohol and Tolerance

Repeated use of alcohol results in tolerance and reduces many of alcohol's pharmacological effects. As with other psychoactive drugs, tolerance to alcohol encourages increased consumption to regain its effects and can lead to severe physical and psychological dependence (Fleming et al. 2006). Tolerance to alcohol is similar to that seen with CNS depressants, such as the benzodiazepines. It consists of both an increase in the rate of alcohol metabolism (due to stimulation of metabolizing enzymes in the liver) and a reduced response by neurons and transmitter systems (particularly by increasing the activity of the inhibitory neurotransmitter, gamma-aminobutyric acid [GABA]) to this drug. Development of tolerance to alcohol is extremely variable; some users can consume large quantities of this drug with minor pharmacological effects. The tolerance-inducing changes caused by alcohol can also alter the body's response to other drugs (referred to as *cross-tolerance*) and can specifically reduce the effects of some other CNS depressants (Kenna 2013).

Many chronic alcohol users learn to compensate for the motor impairments of this drug by modifying their patterns of behavior. These adjustments are referred to as **behavioral tolerance**. Examples of this adjustment include individuals altering and slowing their speech, walking more deliberately, or

KEY TERM

behavioral tolerance
compensation for motor impairments through behavioral pattern modification by chronic alcohol users

moving more cautiously to hide the fact that they have consumed debilitating quantities of alcohol.

▮ Alcohol Metabolism

Alcohol is principally inactivated by liver metabolism (Masters and Trevor 2015). The liver metabolizes alcohol at a slow and constant rate and is unaffected by the amount ingested. Thus, if one can of beer is consumed each hour, the BAC will remain constant without resulting in intoxication. If more alcohol is consumed per hour, the BAC will rise proportionately because large amounts of alcohol that cannot be metabolized spill over into the bloodstream.

▮ Polydrug Use

It is a common practice to take alcohol with other drugs, such as tobacco (Kelly et al. 2015), prescription drugs (Kenna 2013), and even illegal substances (Hedden et al. 2010); this mode of consumption is known as **polydrug use** (Kenna 2013), and it occurs in about 64% of alcoholics (Hedden et al. 2010). Mixing alcohol with other types of drugs can intensify intoxication. This probably helps explain why marijuana users are more likely to combine their marijuana use with alcohol than with other drugs (Liquori, Gatto, and Jarrett 2002; Peters and Hughes 2010). In a recent report, approximately 64% of those seeking treatment for alcoholism also were diagnosed with another drug dependence (Hedden et al. 2010).

The reasons why individuals combine alcohol with other drugs of abuse are not always apparent. The following explanations have been proposed:

- Alcohol enhances the reinforcing properties of other CNS depressants.
- It decreases the amount of an expensive and difficult-to-get drug required to achieve the desired effect.
- It helps to diminish unpleasant side effects of other drugs of abuse, such as the withdrawal caused by CNS stimulants.
- There is a common predisposition to use alcohol and other substances of abuse.

KEY TERMS

polydrug use
the concurrent use of multiple drugs

disinhibition
loss of conditioned reflexes due to depression of inhibitory centers of the brain

Clearly, coadministration of alcohol with other substances of abuse is a common practice that can be very problematic and result in dangerous interactions (AddictionCenter 2016).

▮ Short-Term Effects

The impact of alcohol on the CNS is most similar to that of sedative-hypnotic agents such as barbiturates. Alcohol depresses CNS activity at all doses (Masters and Trevor 2015), producing definable results.

At low to moderate doses, **disinhibition** occurs; this loss of conditioned reflexes reflects a depression of inhibitory centers of the brain. The effects on behavior are variable and somewhat unpredictable. To a large extent, the social setting and mental state determine the individual's response to such alcohol consumption. For example, alcohol can cause one person to become euphoric, friendly, and talkative but can prompt another to become aggressive and hostile. Low to moderate doses also interfere with motor activity, reflexes, and coordination. Often this impairment is not apparent to the affected person (CDC 2008; "Your Health" 1999).

In moderate quantities, alcohol slightly increases the heart rate; slightly dilates blood vessels in the arms, legs, and skin; and moderately lowers blood pressure. It stimulates appetite, increases production of gastric secretions, and markedly stimulates urine output. At higher doses, the social setting has little influence on the expression of depressive actions of the alcohol. The CNS depression incapacitates the individual, causing difficulty in walking, talking, and thinking. These doses tend to induce drowsiness and cause sleep. If large amounts of alcohol are consumed rapidly, severe depression of the brain system and motor control area of the brain occurs, producing incoordination, confusion, disorientation, stupor, anesthesia, coma, and even death (CDC 2008).

The lethal level of alcohol is between 0.4% and 0.6% by volume in the blood (Masters and Trevor 2015). Death is caused by severe depression of the respiration center in the brain stem, although the person usually passes out before drinking an amount capable of producing this effect. Although an alcoholic may metabolize the drug more rapidly than a light drinker, the toxicity level of alcohol stays about the same. In other words, it takes approximately the same concentration of alcohol in the body to kill a nondrinker as it does to kill someone who drinks on a regular basis.

The amount of alcohol required for anesthesia is very close to the toxic level, which is why it would not be a useful anesthetic. See "Signs & Symptoms: Psychological and Physical Effects of Various Blood Alcohol Concentration Levels" for a summary of the effects of various BAC levels.

As a general rule, it takes as many hours as the number of drinks consumed to sober up completely. Despite widely held beliefs, drinking black coffee, taking a cold shower, breathing pure oxygen, and so forth will not hasten the sobering process. Stimulants such as coffee may help keep the drunk person awake but will not improve judgment or motor reflexes to any significant extent.

THE HANGOVER

A familiar consequence of overindulgence is fatigue combined with nausea, upset stomach, headache, sensitivity to sounds, and ill temper— the hangover. These symptoms are usually most severe many hours after drinking, when little or no alcohol remains in the body. No simple explanation exists for what causes the hangover. Theories include accumulation of acetaldehyde (a metabolite of ethanol), dehydration of the tissues, poisoning due to tissue deterioration, depletion of important enzyme systems needed to maintain routine functioning, an acute withdrawal (or rebound) response, and metabolism of the impurities in alcoholic beverages (Compound Interest 2016).

SIGNS & SYMPTOMS

Psychological and Physical Effects of Various Blood Alcohol Concentration Levels

Number of Drinks*	Blood Alcohol Concentration	Psychological and Physical Effects
1	0.02–0.03%	No overt effects, slight mood elevation.
2	0.05–0.06%	Impairment begins. Feeling of relaxation, warmth; slight decrease in reaction time and in fine muscle coordination.
3	0.08–0.09%	Balance, speech, vision, hearing slightly impaired; feelings of euphoria, increased confidence; loss of motor coordination.
3-4	0.08%	Legal intoxication.
4	0.11–0.12%	Coordination and balance becoming difficult; distinct impairment of mental faculties, judgment.
5	0.14–0.15%	Major impairment of mental and physical control; slurred speech, blurred vision, lack of motor skills.
7	0.20%	Loss of motor control—must have assistance in moving about; mental confusion.
10	0.30%	Severe intoxication; minimum conscious control of mind and body.
14	0.40%	Unconsciousness, threshold of coma.
17	0.50%	Deep coma.
20	0.60%	Death from respiratory failure.

Note: For each hour elapsed since the last drink, subtract 0.015% blood alcohol concentration, or approximately one drink.

* One drink = one beer (4% alcohol, 12 oz.) or one highball (1 oz. whiskey).

Data from Ohio State Police Driver Information Seminars and the National Clearinghouse for Alcohol and Alcoholism Information, 5600 Fishers Lane, Rockville, MD 85206; Evans, W. "NTSB Wants Lower Legal Limit for Blood Alcohol." *Deseret News* 163 (15 May 2013): A1.

The body loses fluid in two ways through alcohol's **diuretic** action, which sometimes results in dehydration: (1) the water content, such as in beer, increases the volume of urine and (2) the alcohol depresses the center in the hypothalamus of the brain that controls release of a water conservation hormone (antidiuretic hormone). With less of this hormone, urine volume is further increased. Thus, after drinking heavily, especially the highly concentrated forms of alcohol, the person is thirsty. However, this effect by itself does not explain the symptoms of a hangover.

The type of alcoholic beverage one drinks may influence the hangover that results. Some people are more sensitive to particular alcohol impurities than others. For example, some drinkers have no problem with white wine but an equal amount of some red wines gives them a hangover. Whiskey, scotch, and rum may cause worse hangovers than vodka or gin, given equal amounts of alcohol, because vodka and gin have fewer impurities. There is little evidence that mixing different types of drinks per se produces a more severe hangover. It is more likely that more than the usual amount of alcohol is consumed when various drinks are sampled.

A common treatment for a hangover is to take a drink of the same alcoholic beverage that caused the hangover. This practice is called "taking the hair of the dog that bit you" (from the old notion that the burnt hair of a dog is an antidote to its bite). This treatment might help the person who is physically dependent, in the same way that giving heroin to a heroin addict eases the withdrawal symptoms. The "hair of the dog" method may work by depressing the centers of the brain that interpret pain or by relieving a withdrawal response. In addition, it may affect the psychological factors involved in having a hangover; distraction or focusing attention on something else may ease the effects.

Another remedy is to take an analgesic compound such as an aspirin–caffeine combination after drinking. This treatment is based on the belief that aspirin helps control headache, and the caffeine may help counteract the depressant effect of the alcohol. In reality, these ingredients have no effect on the actual sobering-up process. In fact, products such as aspirin, caffeine, and

Alka-Seltzer can irritate the stomach lining to the point where the person feels worse.

∎ Dependence

According to the World Health Organization, approximately 3.3 million deaths related to alcohol consumption occur each year around the world (WHO 2016). It is estimated that in the United States 12.5 million men and women suffer from alcoholism. In this group, men are three times more likely than women to develop significant dependence on this drug (Alcohol Abuse Essentials 2010).

In 2015, 37.7% of high school seniors drank enough alcohol to get drunk (Johnston 2016. Unfortunately, many people become so dependent on the psychological influences of alcohol that they become compulsive, continually consuming it. These individuals can be severely handicapped because of their alcohol dependence and often become unable to function normally in society. People who have become addicted to this drug are called alcoholics and likely include many of the 6.1% of high school seniors in 2015who would regularly drink heavily (Johnston 2016). Because of the disinhibition, relaxation, and sense of well-being mediated by alcohol, some degree of psychological dependence often develops even in routine users, and the availability of alcoholic beverages at social gatherings becomes required.

Because of the physiological effects, physical dependence also results from the regular consumption of large quantities of alcohol. This consequence becomes apparent when ethanol use is abruptly interrupted and withdrawal symptoms result. The severity of the withdrawal can vary according to the length and intensity of the alcohol habit. The prototypic withdrawal patterns are as follows (Fleming et al. 2006):

* *Stage 1 (minor)*: Restlessness, anxiousness, sleeping problems, agitation, tremors, and rapid heartbeat
* *Stage 2 (major)*: "Minor" symptoms plus hallucinations, whole-body tremors, increased blood pressure, and vomiting
* *Stage 3 (delirium tremens)*: Fever, disorientation, confusion, seizures, and fatality in 3% to 5% of cases

Recovery from alcohol dependence is a long-term process. Because of the severe withdrawal and the need for behavioral adjustments, most people relapse several times before long-term abstinence is achieved. Even people who have

KEY TERM

diuretic
a drug or substance that increases the production of urine

not used alcohol for years may relapse under very stressful circumstances, such as apparently was the case for the well-known actor Phillip Seymour Hoffman, who died from a drug overdose in 2014 after 2 decades of sobriety. Despite the occasional tragic examples of relapse after long-term sobriety, for those who achieve 5 years of sobriety relapse is not all that common and is typically less than 15%, compared to 30% relapse rate for those who are abstinent for less than a year (Manejwala 2014).

MEDICATIONS FOR DEPENDENCE

Although alcohol dependence afflicts about 4% of the adult population, only 10% to 15% of these patients receive appropriate treatment. This is partially due to the misconception that alcoholism is best dealt with by "willpower" and medicine has no role. However, as we have discussed in this chapter, chronic alcohol use has numerous neurobiological consequences, and thus it makes sense that biological strategies based on medications can be helpful in treating persons severely dependent on alcohol. The following three medications currently are approved by the FDA for adjunctive intervention (i.e., they should be used in combination with behavioral therapy) (Kenna 2013; Masters and Trevor 2015):

- The oldest drug approved for alcoholism treatment, disulfiram (Antabuse), has become less popular with many doctors because it makes users very sick and nauseous when they consume alcohol. It works by interfering with the metabolism of alcohol. It is easily avoided if the patient is anticipating drinking and is typically only helpful in the treatment of highly motivated alcoholics.
- Naltrexone (an opiate antagonist) relieves alcohol craving and helps to reduce relapse rates in alcohol-dependent patients. Although about 20% of this population have a positive response to naltrexone treatment, the other 80% are for the most part nonresponsive. One possible explanation for this finding is the existence of an opioid receptor variant in the responsive group that makes people vulnerable to the addicting effects of alcohol, which can be suppressed by naltrexone treatment. Thus, the lack of such a variant opioid gene in the majority of alcoholics could explain their lack of response to naltrexone (Falloon 2010).
- The third drug, acamprosate (Campral), blocks the release of the exciting neurotransmitter glutamate, which reduces withdrawal in abstinent alcoholics.

Although these FDA-approved medications have significantly influenced strategies used to treat alcoholism, they are far from being universally effective. There continues to be considerable research as we try to discover even more effective medications for treating the problem of alcoholism. For optimal benefit, alcoholics need to be carefully subtyped (including features such as age, gender, duration of dependence, mental status, and even genetic makeup) and matched to the appropriate medication and behavioral therapy (Johnson 2010).

■ Alcohol and Genetics

Large-scale studies of twins suggest that addictions such as alcoholism are among the most inherited types of mental illnesses. Consequently, because of our unique gene patterns some of us get hooked on alcohol whereas others can party hard but afterwards walk away without any need or desire to consume more alcohol (Wallis 2009). Research has demonstrated that the specific genes that contribute to these inherited vulnerabilities can influence elements of alcohol intake, such as excessive consumption, dampening of neuronal feedback that warns a person that he or she has consumed too much alcohol, or an enhanced sense of pleasure after drinking alcohol (Wallis 2009).

Differences in the intensity of a hangover or the negative effects of drinking such as nausea or dizziness can also be influenced by genetics (see "Family Matters: Asian Glow") and are likely to affect frequency of use and the development of addiction to alcohol. Despite the prominent role of heritability in the expression of alcohol dependence, the environment is equally as important; if it is supportive and healthy, it can diminish the genetic influence and reduce the likelihood that alcoholism will be expressed even when a person's genetics increase the risk (Wallis 2009).

The Effects of Alcohol on Organ Systems and Bodily Functions

As mentioned earlier, BAC depends on the size of the person, presence of food in the stomach, rate of drinking, amount of carbonation, and ratio of muscle mass to body fat. Furthermore, alcohol has

FAMILY MATTERS

Asian Glow

The way people are affected by drinking has a significant influence on the likelihood of addiction. For example, if drinking causes nausea, vomiting, and a very unpleasant reaction, then repeated heavy use is not likely and alcoholism probably won't occur. Two variant genes found in about 36% of Asian populations, such as Chinese, Japanese, and Koreans, cause the build up of a very annoying and unpleasant metabolite of alcohol known as acetaldehyde, which, in turn, causes side effects such as nausea, vomiting, sweating, chest pains, and flushing of the face known as the *Asian glow*. Such reactions are typically unpleasant enough to encourage those with these genes to avoid alcohol, thus protecting them against becoming alcoholics. Interestingly, the accumulation of acetaldehyde and its effects also can be promoted

independent of genetics by using the medication Antabuse. Because of its ability to block the elimination of acetaldehyde after drinking, Antabuse is given to discourage alcohol-dependent people from abusing this drug.

Data from Buddy, T. "Antabuse Treatment for Alcoholism." VeryWell. July 2015. Available http://alcoholism.about.com/od/meds/a/antabuse.htm; Wallis, C. "The Genetics of Addiction: Research Shows How Genes and the Childhood Experience Pave the Road to Substance Abuse." CNNMoney.com. 16 October 2009. Available http://money.cnn.com/2009/10/16/news/genes_addiction.fortune/index.htm

pervasive effects on the major organs and fluids of the body (NIAAA 2010). In fact, the effects of this substance on body functions potentially can be so profound and destructive that alcoholism (severe addiction) is now considered a disease (NIAAA 2010). The pervasive effects of alcohol on bodily organs are discussed in greater detail in the following sections and summarized in **Figure 7.2**.

▌ Brain and Nervous System

Every part of the brain and nervous system is affected—and in extreme cases can be damaged—by alcohol (see Figure 7.2). An important finding demonstrates that even moderate consumption of alcohol can cause shrinkage of brain volume. People who routinely drink more than 14 drinks per week lose approximately 1.6% of brain size compared to nondrinkers. The greatest effect was observed in female heavy drinkers older than 70 years of age (Reinberg 2007). In low to moderate doses, alcohol suppresses subcortical inhibitions of the cortical control centers, resulting in disinhibition. It also increases the release of endorphins, which likely contributes to the rewarding properties of alcohol; helps explain

why naltrexone, an opioid receptor antagonist, is an effective treatment for some alcoholics; and may explain why some people have a higher risk of becoming an alcoholic. In higher doses, it depresses the cerebellum, causing slurred speech and staggering gait. These doses also impair a person's ability to do tasks that require vigilance and rapid decision making. Often these people are unaware that their performance is impaired, making them potentially dangerous when engaging in activities such as driving a car (Masters and Trevor 2015).

Very high doses depress the respiratory centers of the medulla, resulting in death. Furthermore, alcohol alters the production and functioning of transmitters such as dopamine, serotonin, GABA, and brain endorphins (Ratsma, van der Stelt, and Gunning 2002). Recent findings suggest that even cannabinoid receptors—the targets of the active ingredients in marijuana—are affected by alcohol (Kenna 2013). These neurochemical effects contribute to the fact that alcohol consumption can aggravate underlying psychiatric disorders such as depression and schizophrenia (Bertolote et al. 2004) and may suggest novel ways to develop more effective therapies (Basavarajappa 2007).

FIGURE 7.2 The principal control centers of the brain affected by alcohol consumption. Note that all areas of the brain are interconnected.

Heavy drinking over many years may result in serious mental disorders and irreversible damage to the brain and peripheral nervous system, leading to permanently compromised mental function and memory and alterations in other brain systems (Baxamusa 2010). In addition, abrupt cessation of alcohol consumption in the alcoholic can result in serious withdrawal effects, such as life-threatening seizures, and require intensive emergency care (Phys.org 2009).

■ Liver

Among alcoholics, liver disorders are responsible for 10% to 15% of deaths (Fairbanks 2009). Alcohol-induced liver disease progresses in three stages (Kenna 2013). In the first stage, known as *alcoholic fatty liver*, liver cells increase the production of fat, resulting in an enlarged liver. This direct toxic effect on liver tissue is known as the **hepatotoxic effect**. This effect is reversible and can disappear if alcohol use is stopped. Several

days of drinking five or six alcoholic beverages each day produces fatty liver in males. For females, as few as two drinks of hard liquor per day several days in a row can produce the same condition. After several days of abstaining from alcohol, the liver returns to normal.

The second stage develops as the fat cells continue to multiply. Generally, irritation and swelling that result from continued alcohol intake cause **alcoholic hepatitis**. At this stage, chronic inflammation sets in and can be fatal. This second

KEY TERMS

hepatotoxic effect
a situation in which liver cells increase the production of fat, resulting in an enlarged liver

alcoholic hepatitis
the second stage of alcohol-induced liver disease in which chronic inflammation occurs; reversible if alcoholic consumption ceases

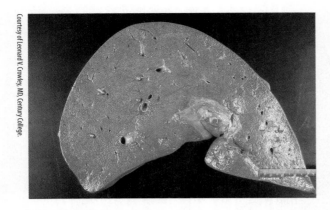

Courtesy of Leonard V. Crowley, MD, Century College.

Courtesy of CDC/Dr. Edwin P. Ewing, Jr.

A normal liver (top) as it would be found in a healthy human body. An abnormal liver (bottom) that exhibits the effects of moderate to heavy alcohol consumption.

stage also is reversible if the intake of alcohol ceases.

Unlike stages 1 and 2, stage 3 is not reversible. Scars begin to form on the liver tissue during this stage. These scars are fibrous, and they cause hardening of the liver as functional tissue shrinks and deteriorates. This condition of the liver is known as **cirrhosis** and often is fatal.

The liver damage caused by heavy alcohol consumption can cause problems when taking drugs that affect liver function. For example, the over-the-counter analgesic acetaminophen (Tylenol) can have a deleterious effect on the liver, especially when the function of this organ has already been compromised by alcohol (Masters and Trevor 2015).

KEY TERM

cirrhosis
scarring of the liver and formation of fibrous tissues; results from alcohol abuse; irreversible

▪ Digestive System

The digestive system consists of gastrointestinal structures involved in processing and digesting foods and liquids; it includes the mouth, pharynx, esophagus, stomach, and small and large intestines. As alcohol travels through the digestive system, it irritates tissue and can even damage the tissue lining as it causes acid imbalances, inflammation, and acute gastric distress. Often, the result is gastritis (an inflamed stomach) and heartburn. The more frequently consumption takes place, the greater the irritation. One out of three heavy drinkers suffers from chronic gastritis. Furthermore, the heavy drinker has double the probability of developing cancer of the mouth and esophagus because alcohol passes these two organs on the way to the stomach.

Prolonged heavy use of alcohol may cause ulcers, hiatal hernia, and cancers throughout the digestive tract. The likelihood of cancers in the mouth, throat, and stomach dramatically increases (15 times) if the person is also a heavy smoker (Lee et al. 2005). The pancreas is another organ associated with the digestive system that can be damaged by heavy alcohol consumption. Alcohol can cause pancreatitis, pancreatic cirrhosis, and alcoholic diabetes (Federico et al. 2015).

▪ Blood

High concentrations of alcohol diminish the effective functioning of the hematopoietic (blood-building) system, decreasing production of red blood cells, white blood cells, and platelets. Problems with clotting and immunity to infection are not uncommon among alcohol abusers. Often, the result is lowered resistance to disease. Heavy drinking appears to affect the bone marrow, where various blood cells are formed. The suppression of the bone marrow can contribute to anemia, in which red blood cell production cannot keep pace with the need for those cells. Heavy drinkers are also likely to develop alcoholic bleeding disorders because they have too few platelets to form clots (Fleming et al. 2006; Masters and Trevor 2015).

▪ Cardiovascular System

The effects of ethanol on the cardiovascular system have been extensively studied, but much remains unknown. Ethanol causes dilation of blood vessels, especially in the skin. This effect accounts for the flushing and sensation of warmth associated with alcohol consumption.

The long-term effects of alcohol on the cardio-vascular system are dose dependent. Some studies have suggested that regular light to moderate drinking (two or fewer glasses of wine per day) actually reduces the incidence of heart diseases such as heart attacks, strokes, and high blood pressure by 20% to 40% in some populations (Masters and Trevor 2015), although the benefits have been challenged (Hartney 2012). The type of alcoholic beverage consumed does not appear to be important as long as the quantity of alcohol consumed is moderate (1 to 2.5 ounces per day). Although the precise explanation for this coronary benefit is not known, it has been suggested to be related to the effects of moderate alcohol doses in relieving stress and increasing the blood concentration of high-density lipoproteins (HDL) (Masters and Trevor 2015). HDL is a molecular complex used to transport fat through the bloodstream, and its levels are negatively correlated with cardio-vascular disease. In addition, moderate levels of alcohol decrease the formation of blood clots that can plug arteries and deprive tissues of essential oxygen and nutrients. The populations most likely to benefit from the protective properties of moderate levels of alcohol appear to be men older than 50 years of age and postmenopausal women. Moderate drinking on a daily average is approximately one drink (e.g., a glass of wine) for women and two drinks for men. However, it should be noted that some scientists argue that it is not the alcohol itself that protects against cardiovascular disease but the fact that moderate drinkers tend to live healthier lifestyles such as not smoking, eating good diets, and engaging in regular exercise (Rabin 2009). These confounds need further study to determine if moderate consumption of alcohol is as healthy as suggested by earlier studies. Regardless of whether moderate drinking is healthy, it is clear that drinking more than moderate amounts of alcohol can result in increased health risks that more than offset the benefits (Ward 2013).

Some of the confusion about alcohol's health influences may be due to the fact that the cardio-vascular protective effect of moderate drinking is at least partially race specific. A report suggests that alcohol use that prevents cardiovascular disease in white men may actually increase heart disease in black men (Fuchs 2004).

Because of the potential for developing addiction to alcohol and the increased health risk with heavy drinking, most health providers and researchers would not encourage a nondrinker to start to consume alcohol in an attempt to gain a health benefit. In addition, even in those populations most likely to benefit from moderate alcohol consumption, the benefit is likely to disappear in persons who already have healthy lifestyles that include low-fat diets, stress and weight management techniques, and regular exercise. In general, most clinicians believe that alcohol use kills more people (approximately 100,000 per year) than it saves, and those it kills tend to be younger (Hanson and Li 2003; "Special Report" 1997; Ward 2013).

Chronic intense use of alcohol changes the composition of heart muscle by replacing it with fat and fiber, resulting in a heart muscle that becomes enlarged and flabby. Congestive heart failure from **alcoholic cardiomyopathy** often occurs when heart muscle is replaced by fat and fiber. Other results of alcohol abuse that affect the heart are irregular heartbeat or arrhythmia, high blood pressure, and stroke. A common example of damage is "holiday heart," so called because people drinking heavily over a weekend turn up in the emergency room with a dangerously irregular heartbeat. Chronic excessive use of alcohol by people with arrhythmia causes congestive heart failure. Malnutrition and vitamin deficiencies associated with prolonged heavy drinking also contribute to cardiac abnormalities (Fairfield and Fletcher 2002).

■ Sexual Organs

Although alcohol lowers social inhibition, its use interferes with sexual functioning. As Shakespeare said in *Macbeth*, alcohol "provokes desire, but it takes away the performance." Continued alcohol use causes prostatitis, which is an inflammation of the prostate gland. This condition directly interferes with a man's ability to maintain an adequate erection during sexual stimulation. Another frequent symptom of alcohol abuse is atrophy of the testicles, which results in lowered sperm count and diminished hormones in the blood (Dhawan and Sharma 2002; Emanuele and Emanuele 2010).

■ Endocrine System

Endocrine glands release hormones into the bloodstream. These hormones function as

KEY TERM

alcoholic cardiomyopathy
congestive heart failure due to the replacement of heart muscle with fat and fiber

messengers that directly affect cell and tissue function throughout the body. Alcohol abuse alters endocrine functions by influencing the production and release of hormones and affects endocrine regulating systems in the hypothalamus, pituitary, and gonads. Because of alcohol abuse, levels of testosterone (the male sex hormone) may decline, resulting in sexual impotence, breast enlargement, and loss of body hair in men. Women experience menstrual delays, ovarian abnormalities, and infertility (Masters and Trevor 2015).

▌ Kidneys

Frequent abuse of alcohol can severely damage the kidneys. The resulting decrease in kidney function diminishes this organ's ability to process blood and properly form urine and can result in serious metabolic problems. Another consequence of impaired kidney function in alcoholics is that they tend to experience more urinary tract infections than do nondrinkers or moderate drinkers (National Kidney Foundation 2015).

▌ Mental Disorders and Damage to the Brain

Persons with mental disorders are significantly more likely to have an alcohol problem. This may be in part because heavy alcohol consumption compromises the functions of those parts of the brain that control emotions and social behavior (Healy 2009). For example, long-term heavy drinking can severely affect memory, judgment, and learning ability (Fleming et al. 2006). **Wernicke-Korsakoff's syndrome** is a characteristic psychotic condition caused by alcohol use and the associated nutritional and vitamin deficiencies. Patients who are brain-damaged cannot remember recent events, and compensate for their memory loss with confabulation (making up fictitious events that even the patient accepts as fact) (Masters and Trevor 2015).

Fetal alcohol syndrome is characterized by facial deformities, as well as growth deficiency and mental retardation.

▌ The Fetus

In pregnant women, alcohol easily crosses the placenta, and often damages the fetus in cases of moderate to excessive drinking. It can also cause spontaneous abortion due to its toxic actions. Another tragic consequence of high alcohol consumption during pregnancy is **fetal alcohol syndrome (FAS)**, which is characterized by facial deformities, growth deficiency, mental retardation, and joint and limb abnormalities (Masters and Trevor 2015). The growth deficiency occurs in embryonic development, and the child usually does not catch up after birth. The mild to moderate mental retardation does not appear to lessen with time, apparently because the growth impairment affects the functional development of the brain as well.

The severity of FAS appears to be dose related: The more the mother drinks, the more severe the fetal damage. A safe lower level of alcohol consumption has not been established for pregnant women (Masters and Trevor 2015). Birthweight decrements have been found at levels corresponding to about two drinks per day, on average. Clinical studies have established that alcohol itself clearly causes the syndrome; it is not related to the effects of smoking, maternal age, parity (number of children a woman has borne), social class, or poor nutrition. Chronic maternal alcohol consumption is the leading cause of mental retardation and congenital defects in children (Masters

© Rick's Photography/Shutterstock, Inc.

KEY TERMS

Wernicke-Korsakoff's syndrome
psychotic condition connected with heavy alcohol use and associated vitamin deficiencies

fetal alcohol syndrome (FAS)
a condition affecting children born to alcohol-consuming mothers that is characterized by facial deformities, growth deficiency, and mental retardation

and Trevor 2015). Another study demonstrated that just a few episodes of heavy drinking by a pregnant woman increases the likelihood that the offspring will also abuse alcohol later in life (Psychology Today 2007).

■ Gender Differences

Research has demonstrated that there are important pharmacological differences in how males and females respond to the consumption of alcohol. For example, in women heavy alcohol use will cause accelerated damage to the brain, liver, heart, and muscles compared to male users. These differences persist even after adjusting for the quantity of alcohol according to the differences in gender size. It is thought that at least part of the greater sensitivity of women to the effects of this drug is due to their tendency to metabolize alcohol more slowly than their male counterparts (NIDA 2015b), or it may be due to a higher percentage of body fat in females, leading to greater retention of the drug (Kenna 2013; Leigh 2007). In addition, problems associated with alcohol abuse might express differently in men and women, with females more likely to experience depression, whereas men are more likely to binge drink and engage in fighting (Norton 2007). Other differences relate to their response to treatment. Gender differences in treatment outcomes likely reflect factors such as women's tendency to have a later onset of alcohol use and associated problems, a more positive family history, more marital disruption (Gomberg 2003), and more associated psychiatric disorders, such as depression, anxiety, and stress (Kenny, Jones, and Barnett 2015; *Women's Health Weekly* 2003). Although the reasons for these differences are unclear, they must be considered as researchers and clinicians try to elucidate the causes, consequences, and most effective treatments for alcoholism.

■ Malnutrition

As previously mentioned, malnutrition is a frequent and extremely serious consequence of severe alcoholism that tends to occur most often in less affluent alcoholics. It has been suggested that malnutrition exaggerates the damage that alcohol causes to the body's organs, especially the liver. Malnutrition apparently expresses so frequently in this population because many alcoholics find it difficult to eat a balanced diet with adequate caloric intake. For example, heavy alcohol consumption often is associated with diets low in fruits and vegetables and high in calories from alcoholic beverages, added sugars, and unhealthy fats. Many alcoholics consume between 300 and 1000 kilocalories per day (2000 kilocalories per day is considered normal for an average man). In addition, most of the calories consumed by alcoholics come from alcohol, which contains 7 kilocalories/gram (less than fat, which contains 9 kilocalories/gram). The malnutrition problem is aggravated because alcohol's calories are empty; that is, alcohol does not contain other nutrients such as vitamins, minerals, protein, or fat. Because alcoholics may be deriving 50% or more of their usual caloric intake from alcoholic beverages, profound deficiencies in important nutrients result, leading to serious degeneration of health. In addition, the malnutrition problems may be further aggravated because of the damage done to the gastrointestinal tract by chronic exposure to the irritating effects of high doses of alcohol. This can damage the linings of both the stomach and intestines, thereby interfering with the proper absorption of essential nutrients from food (Thorley et al. 2015).

LEARNING PORTFOLIO

Key Terms

Discussion Questions

1. What evidence indicates that alcohol is a drug like marijuana, cocaine, or heroin?
2. Explain how alcohol is manufactured.
3. In the Western world, alcohol use has a long history. List and discuss some of these historical events, and describe how they affect present attitudes.
4. Explain how the effect of alcohol on brain function compares to that caused by other CNS depressants.
5. Explain how alcohol affects the mouth, stomach, small intestine, brain, liver, and bloodstream.
6. List at least five factors that affect the absorption rate of alcohol in the bloodstream.
7. Explain why alcohol is commonly consumed together with other drugs.
8. List three short-term effects of alcohol abuse.
9. Explain why moderate use of ethanol may prevent heart attacks.
10. Describe the symptoms and causes of a hangover.
11. What characterizes FAS?
12. How does gender affect responses to alcohol?
13. Why is malnutrition a common occurrence in alcoholics, and what are its consequences?

Summary

1. Alcohol is considered a drug because it is a CNS depressant, and it affects both mental and physiological functioning.
2. Three types of poisonous alcohols are methyl alcohol, made from wood products; ethylene glycol, used as antifreeze; and isopropyl alcohol, used as an antiseptic. A fourth type, ethanol, is the alcohol used for drinking purposes.
3. The blood alcohol level produced depends on the presence of food in the stomach, the rate of alcohol consumption, the concentration of alcohol, and the drinker's body composition.
4. Alcohol depresses CNS activity at all doses. Low to moderate doses of alcohol interfere with motor activities, reflexes, and coordination. In moderate quantities, alcohol slightly increases heart rate; slightly dilates blood vessels in the arms, legs, and skin; and moderately lowers blood pressure. It stimulates appetite, increases production of gastric secretions, and at higher doses markedly stimulates urine output. The CNS depression incapacitates the individual, causing difficulty in walking, talking, and thinking.
5. Alcohol is commonly used in combination with other drugs (a) to enhance reinforcing properties, (b) to reduce the amount of expensive or hard-to-get drug required for an effect, (c) to

reduce unpleasant side effects, or (d) because a predisposition for use of alcohol and other drugs exists.

6. According to the World Health Organization, approximately 140 million people around the world are afflicted with alcohol-related disorders. It is estimated that in the United States 12.5 million men and women suffer from alcoholism. These persons can be so severely handicapped that they are unable to function normally in society. In the United States only 10% to 12% of alcoholics receive appropriate treatment. In addition to important behavioral therapy, three medications have been approved by the FDA for adjunctive intervention for alcoholism: (a) disulfiram (Antabuse), which interferes with alcohol metabolism; (b) naltrexone (an opiate antagonist); and (c) acamprosate (Campral), which blocks the release of glutamate. Although these medications are very useful in managing alcoholics, they are not universally effective.

7. Moderate daily alcohol use can reduce cardiovascular diseases in men older than 50 years of age and in postmenopausal women.

8. Long-term heavy alcohol use directly causes serious damage to nearly every organ and function of the body.

9. Prolonged heavy drinking causes various types of muscle disease and tremors. Heavy alcohol consumption causes irregular heartbeat. Heavy drinking over many years results in serious mental disorders and permanent, irreversible damage to the brain and peripheral nervous system. Memory, judgment, and learning ability can deteriorate severely.

10. Women who are alcoholics or who drink heavily during pregnancy have a higher rate of spontaneous abortions. Infants born to drinking mothers have a high probability of suffering congenital defects such as FAS. These children have characteristic patterns of facial deformities, growth deficiency, joint and limb irregularities, and mental retardation.

11. Alcohol has pervasive effects on the major organs and fluids of the body. Every part of the brain and nervous system is affected and can be damaged by alcohol. Among alcoholics, liver disorders include alcoholic fatty liver, alcoholic hepatitis, and cirrhosis. Alcohol also irritates tissue and damages the digestive system. Heavy use of alcohol seriously affects the blood, heart, sexual organs, endocrine system, and kidneys.

12. Malnutrition is a common occurrence in severe alcoholism. It is the result of decreased caloric intake by alcoholics and the diminished consumption of essential nutrients due to the nutritional deficiency of alcoholic beverages.

References

AddictionCenter. "Polydrug Use." 21 January 2016. Available http://www.addictioncenter.com/addiction/polydrug-use/

Alcohol Abuse Essentials. "What Is Alcohol Abuse?" 2010. Available http://www.alcohol-abuse-essentials.com

Alcohol Justice. "Alcopops: Sweet, Cheap, and Dangerous to Youth." December 2015. Available http://alcoholjustice.org/images/reports/AlcopopsReportFinalWeb.pdf

American Academy of Pediatrics. "Policy Statement— Alcohol Use by Youth and Adolescents: A Pediatric Concern." 1 July 2010. Available http://pediatrics.aappublications.org/cgi/reprint/peds.2010-0438v1

American Institute for Cancer Research (AICR). "The Facts About Alcohol." 2013. Available http://www.aicr.org/reduce-your-cancer-risk/diet/elements_alcohol.html

American Psychiatric Association (APA). *Diagnostic and Statistical Manual of Mental Disorders*, 5th ed. Washington, DC: American Psychiatric Association, 2013.

American Public University. "Teenage Smoking 'Leads to Increased Susceptibility to Alcohol Withdrawal in Adulthood.'" 7 March 2010. Available http://www.thaindian.com/newsportal/health/teenage-smoking-leads-to-increased-susceptibility-to-alcohol-withdrawal-in-adulthood_100330972.html

BabyCenter. "Alcohol and Nursing Moms." BabyCenter Medical Advisory Board. April 2010. Available http://www.babycenter.com/0_alcohol-and-nursing-moms_3547.bc

Bachelor, R. "Historic Relationship Between Religion and Alcohol." Suite101.com. 30 January 2010. Available https://suite.io/rosemary-e-bachelor/2zqc25d

Basavarajappa, B. "The Endocannabinoid Signaling System: A Potential Target for Next Generation Therapeutics for Alcoholism." *Minireview of Medicinal Chemistry* 7 (2007): 769–779.

Baxamusa, B. "Alcohol Dementia Prognosis." Buzzle
.com. 2010. Available http://www.buzzle.com/articles
/alcohol-dementia-prognosis.html

Bertolote, J., A. Fleishmann, D. DeLeo, and D. Wasserman.
"Psychiatric Diagnoses and Suicide: Revisiting the
Evidence." *Crisis* 25 (2004): 147–155.

Bishop, T. "Huguely Trial Highlights Alcohol Abuse at
Colleges, Universities." *Baltimore Sun.* (18 February 2012).
Available http://articles.baltimoresun.com/2012-02
-18/health/bs-md-student-drinking-20120216_1_binge
-drinking-huguely-college-students

Centers for Disease Control and Prevention (CDC). "Frequently Asked Questions. Introduction to Alcohol."
2008. Available http://www.cdc.gov/alcohol/faqs.htm

Centers for Disease Control and Prevention (CDC). "Facts
Sheet: Underaged Drinking." 2015. Available http://
www.cdc.gov/alcohol/fact-sheets/underage-drinking
.htm

Compound Interest. "The Chemistry of a Hangover."
2016. Available www.compoundchem.com/2016/01/01
/hangover/

Dhawan, K., and A. Sharma. "Prevention of Chronic Alcohol and Nicotine-Induced Azospermia, Sterility and
Decreased Libido, by a Novel Tri-substituted Benzofla-
vone Moiety." *Life Science* 71 (2002): 3059–3069.

Dryden, J. "Young Age at First Drink May Affect Genes and
Risk for Alcoholism." Newsroom, Washington University in St. Louis. (September 2009). Available http://
news.wustl.edu/news/Pages/14669.aspx

DualDiagnosis. "Disease Theory of Alcoholism." 2016. Available
http://www.dualdiagnosis.org/alcohol-addiction
/disease-theory-alcoholism/

Dvorak, P. "Parents Who Host Teen Drinking Parties:
Not Cool, Not Smart, but They Do It Anyway." *The
Washington Post* (12 November 2015). Available
https://www.washingtonpost.com/local/parents
-who-host-teen-drinking-parties-not-cool-not-smart-but
-they-do-it-anyway/2015/11/12/a4a5a05e-8937-11e5
-9a07-453018f9a0ec_story.html

Emanuele, M., and N. Emanuele. "Alcohol and the Male
Reproductive System." National Institute on Alcohol
Abuse and Alcoholism. 2010. Available http://pubs
.niaaa.nih.gov/publications/arh25-4/282-287.htm

Epstein, J. "Students Aren't the Only Boozers." Inside
Higher Ed. 4 June 2010. Available http://www.inside-
highered.com/news/2010/06/04/acha

Evans, W. "NTSB Wants Lower Legal Limit for Blood
Alcohol." *Deseret News* 163 (15 May 2013): A1.

Fairbanks, K. "Alcoholic Liver Disease." Cleveland Clinic,
Center for Continuing Education. 2009. Available
http://www.clevelandclinicmeded.com/medicalpubs
/diseasemanagement/hepatology/alcoholic-liver-disease

Fairfield, K., and R. Fletcher. "Vitamins for Chronic Disease Prevention in Adults: Scientific Review." *Journal of
the American Medical Association* 288 (2002): 1720.

Falloon, K. "Naltrexone Has Mixed Effects in Alcoholics."
Post-Gazette.com. 30 June 2010. Available http://post
-gazette.com/pg/10181/1069113-114.stm

Federico, A., G. Cotticelli, D. Festi, R. Schiumerini, G.
Addolorato, A. Ferrulli, M. Merli, C. Lucidi, S. Milani, C.
Panella, M. Domenico, I. Vantini, L. Benini, E. Ubaldi,
M. Romano, and C. Loguercio. "The Effects of Alcohol
on Gastrointestinal Tract, Liver and Pancreas; Evidence-
Based Suggestions for Clinical Management." *European
Review for Medical and Pharmacological Sciences* 19 (2015):
1922–1940.

Fleming, M., S. Mihic, and R. Harris. "Ethanol." In *The
Pharmacological Basis of Therapeutics,* 11th ed., edited by
L. Brunton, J. Lazo, and K. Parker, 591–606. New York:
McGraw-Hill, 2006.

Fuchs, F. "Association Between Alcoholic Beverage Consumption and Incidence of Coronary Heart Disease in
Whites and Blacks—The Atherosclerosis Risk in Communities Studies." *American Journal of Epidemiology* 160
(2004): 466–474.

Gomberg, E. "Treatment for Alcohol-Related Problems:
Special Populations: Research Opportunities." *Recent
Developments in Alcoholism* 16 (2003): 313–333.

Gowin, J. "Your Brain on Alcohol: Is the Conventional Wis-
dom Wrong About Booze?" Psychology Today. 10 June
2010. Available http://www.psychologytoday.com/blog
/you-illuminated/201006/your-brain-alcohol

Grant, B., R. Goldstein, T. Saha, S. P. Chou, J. Jung,
H. Zhang, R. P. Pickering, W. J. Ruan, S. M. Smith,
B. Huang, and D. S. Hasin. "Epidemiology of DSM-5
Alcohol Use Disorder." *JAMA Psychiatry* 72 (2015):
757–766.

Hanson, G. R., and T. K. Li. "Public Health Implications of
Excessive Alcohol Consumption." *Journal of the American
Medical Association* 289 (2003): 1031, 1032.

Hartney, E. "Claims Regarding the Benefits of Red Wine
Called into Question." About.com: Addiction. 27 February
2012. Available http://addictions.about.com/b/2012
/02/27/claims-regarding-the-benefits-of-red-wine
-called-into-question.htm

Healy, M. "Alcoholism Disrupts Ability to Read Emotions, Conduct Relationships." *Los Angeles Times.* 12 August 2009. Available http://latimesblogs.latimes.com/booster_shots
/2009/08/alcoholism-disrupts-ability-to-read-emotions
-conduct-relationships-heres-how.html

Hedden, S. L., S. S. Martins, R. J. Malcolm, L. Floyd, C.
E. Cavanaugh, and W. W. Latimer. "Patterns of Illegal
Drug Use Among an Adult Alcohol Dependent Popu-
lation: Results from the National Survey on Drug Use

and Health." *Drug and Alcohol Dependence* 106 (2010): 119–125.

Johnson, B. "Medication Treatment of Different Types of Alcoholism." *American Journal of Psychiatry* 167 (2010): 630–639.

Johns Hopkins. "Center on Alcohol Marketing and Youth." Johns Hopkins Bloomberg School of Public Health. 2015. Available http://camy.org/

Johnston, L. "Monitoring the Future 1975–2015." 2016. Available http://monitoringthefuture.org/pubs/monographs/mtf-overview2015.pdf

Kelly, A., T. Evens-Whipp, G. Chan, J. Tobourou, and G. Patton. "A Longitudinal Study of the Association of Adolescent Polydrug Use, Alcohol Use, and High School Non-completion." *Addiction* 110 (2015): 627–635.

Kenna, G. "Alcohol Use Disorders." In *Applied Therapeutics, Clinical Use of Drugs*, 10th ed., edited by B. Aldredge, 2033–2054. Philadelphia, PA: Wolters Kluwer, 2013.

Kenny, S., R. Jones, N. Barnett. "Gender Differences in the Effect of Depressive Symptoms on Prospective Alcohol Expectancies Coping Motives and Alcohol Outcomes in the First Year of College." *Journal of Youth and Adolescence* 44 (2015): 1884–1897. Available http://link.springer.com/article/10.1007/s10964-015-0311-3#/page-2link.springer.com/article/10.1007%2Fs/0964-015-0311-3#/page-1

Kerlikowske, G. "Drug Czar Says More People Drive Under Influence of Drugs Than Alcohol." PolitiFact. 5 April 2010. Available http://www.politifact.com/truth-o-meter/statements/2010/apr/05/gil-kerlikowske/drug-czar-says-more-people-drive-under-influence-d/

Kovacs, B. "Alcohol and Nutrition." MedicineNet.com. 2010. Available http://www.medicinenet.com/alcohol_and_ nutrition/article.htm

Lee, C., J. Lee, D. Wu, H. Hsu, E. Kao, H. Huang, T. N. Wang, M. C. Huang, and M. T. Wu. "Independent and Combined Effects of Alcohol Intake, Tobacco Smoking and Betel Quid Chewing on the Risk of Esophageal Cancer in Taiwan." *International Journal of Cancer* 113 (2005): 475–482.

Leigh, S. "A Woman's Brain Hit Harder by Alcohol Abuse; Damage Occurs Faster and with Fewer Drinks, Study Finds." Health Day. 27 April 2007. Available http://abcnews.go.com/Health/Healthday/story?id=4506743&page=1

Liquori, A., C. Gatto, and D. Jarrett. "Separate and Combined Effects of Marijuana and Alcohol on Mood, Equilibrium and Simulated Driving." *Psychopharmacology* 163 (2002): 399–405.

Manejwala, O. "How Often Do Long-term Sober Alcoholics and Addicts Relapse." Psychology Today. 13 February 2014. Available https://www.psychologytoday.com/blog/craving/201402/how-often-do-long-term-sober-alcoholics-and-addicts-relapse

Masters, S., and A. Trevor. "The Alcohols." In *Basic and Clinical Pharmacology*, 13th ed., edited by B. Katzung, 384–395. New York: McGraw-Hill, 2015.

National Council on Alcoholism and Drug Dependence (NCADD). "Alcohol, Drugs and Crime." 2016. Available ncadd.org/about-addiction/alcohol-drugs-and-crime

National Institute on Alcohol Abuse and Alcoholism (NIAAA). "Rethinking Drinking: Alcohol and Your Health." 2010. Available http://pubs.niaaa.nih.gov/publications/RethinkingDrinking/Rethinking_Drinking.pdf

National Institute on Drug Abuse (NIDA). "Drug Use Trends Remain Stable or Decline Among Teens." 16 December 2015a. Available https://www.drugabuse.gov/news-events/news-releases/2015/12/drug-use-trends-remain-stable-or-decline-among-teens

National Institute on Drug Abuse (NIDA). "Sex and Gender Differences in Substance Use." July 2015b. Available https://www.drugabuse.gov/publications/research-reports/substance-use-in-women/sex-gender-differences-in-substance-use

NCADD. "Alcohol, Drugs and Crime." National Council on Alcoholism and Drug Dependence (2016). Available ncadd.org/about-addiction/alcohol-drugs-and-crime

National Kidney Foundation. "Alcohol and Your Kidneys." 2015. Available www.kidney.org/atoz/content/alcohol

New York Times. "Binge Drinking on Campus." 30 June 2009. Available http://www.nytimes.com/2009/07/01/opinion/01wed3.html

Norton, A. "Men and Women Show Alcohol Problems Differently." Reuters Health. 24 April 2007. Available http://www.reuters.com/article/healthNews/idUSLAU376770 20070423

Pager, T. "Underaged Drinking, Binge Boozing by Minors Is on the Decline." *USA Today* (11 June 2015). Available http://www.usatoday.com/story/news/2015/06/11/underage-binge-drinking/71021464/

Peters, E., and J. Hughes. "Daily Marijuana Users with Past Alcohol Problems Increase Alcohol Consumption During Marijuana Abstinence." *Drug and Alcohol Dependence* 106 (2010): 111–118.

Phys.org. "A New Understanding of Why Seizures Occur with Alcohol Withdrawal." 17 October 2009. Available http://www.physorg.com/news175017259.html

Psychology Today. "Pregnant and Under the Influence." 1 May 2007. Available https://www.psychologytoday.com/articles/200304/pregnant-and-under-the-influence

Rabin, R. "Alcohol's Good for You? Some Scientists Doubt It." *New York Times* (16 June 2009). Available http://www.nytimes.com/2009/06/16/health/16alco.html

Rasch, H. "Cute Packaging, Fun Flavors Make 'Alcopops' Attractive To Minors." AAP News. 27 March 2012. Available http://aapnews.aappublications.org/content /33/4/33.8.full

Ratsma, J., O. van der Stelt, and W. Gunning. "Neurochemical Markers of Alcoholism Vulnerability." *Alcohol and Alcoholism* 37 (2002): 522–533.

Reinberg, S. "Drinking Shrinks the Brain." ABC News. 2007. Available http://abcnews.go.com/Health/Healthday /story?id=4506808&page=1

Reinberg, S. "Binge Drinking May Damage Teens' Brains." ABC News. 22 April 2009. Available http://abcnews .go.com/Health/Healthday/story?id=7406188&page=1

Reuters. "Most Alcohol, Drug Abuse Starts in Teen Years—Study." 2 April 2012. Available http://www.reuters.com /article/2012/04/02/health-alcohol-teens -idUSL3E8F28OQ20120402

Ringenberg, T., J. Kalabalik, and K. Robinson. "Binge Drinking and Alcohol Poisoning in the Adolescent Population." *U.S. Pharmacist* 38 (2013): HS3–HS6.

"Special Report: Alcohol: Weighing the Benefits and Risks for You." *UC Berkeley Wellness Letter* 13 (August 1997): 4–5.

Statista. "Facts on the Alcoholic Beverage Industry." 20 January 2016. Available www.statista.com/topics /1709/alcoholic-beverages

Substance Abuse and Mental Health Services Administration (SAMHSA). "Treatment Episode Data Set (TEDS)." 2009. Available http://wwwdasis.samhsa.gov/teds08 /teds2k8natweb.pdf

Szalavitz, M. "Heavy Drinking Costs the U.S. $223.5 Billion Annually: CDC." *Time* (18 October 2011). Available http://healthland.time.com/2011/10/18/heavy -drinking-costs-the-u-s-223-5-billion-annually-cdc/

Szalavitz, M. "Genetics: No More Addictive Personality." *Nature* 522 (2015): 548–549.

Thorley, H., K. Porter, C. Fleming, T. Jones, J. Kesten, E. Marques, A. Richards, and J. Savović. "Interventions for Preventing or Treating Malnutrition in Problem Drinkers. Who Are Homeless or Vulnerably Housed: Protocol for a Systematic Review." *Systematic Reviews* 4 (2015): 131–140.

Trudeau, M. "Teen Drinking May Cause Irreversible Brain Damage." NPR. 30 June 2010. Available http://www .npr.org/templates/story/story.php?storyId=122765890

Wallis, C. "The Genetics of Addiction: Research Shows How Genes and the Childhood Experience Pave the Road to Substance Abuse." CNNMoney.com, Fortune. 16 October 2009.Availablehttp://money.cnn.com/2009/10/16/news /genes_addiction.fortune/index.htm

Ward, D. "Even Moderate Drinking Can Boost Risk of Cancer." *Deseret News*, 163 (24 February 2013): A3

WHO. "Alcohol". Media Center (2015). Available http:// www.who.int/mediacentre/factsheets/fs349/en/

Women's Health Weekly. "Female Drinkers and Drug Users Tend to Have More Depressive Disorders." 20 March 2003: 1.

"Your Health: Alcohol: The Whole Truth, Seven Half-Truths About Drinking, Exposed." *Consumer Reports* 64 (December 1999): 60–61.

© Digital Vision/Thinkstock.

Did You Know?

▶ Seventy-seven percent of the U.S. population believes that, compared to all other drugs, alcohol creates the most family problems in our society.

▶ Sixty-six percent of the adult population report that they are current alcohol drinkers, and 26% have reported excessive alcohol consumption.

▶ Americans consumed twice as much alcohol in 1830 as they do now.

▶ Of all U.S. adult minority groups, Asian Americans have the highest rate of abstinence, the lowest rate of heavy drinking, and the lowest level of drinking-related problems.

▶ People have complained about fraternity drinking since 1840.

▶ Most of the economic costs of alcohol and drug problems fall on taxpayers who do not abuse alcohol and drugs.

▶ In 2014, approximately 11% of 8th graders, 30% of 10th graders, and 50% of 12th graders drank alcohol to the point of inebriation.

▶ On weekend nights throughout the United States, 70% of all fatal single-vehicle crashes involve a driver who is legally intoxicated.

▶ Less affluent people drink less than more affluent individuals.

Learning Objectives

On completing this chapter, you should be able to:

❯ Cite some of the latest statistics on the use of alcohol.

❯ Cite the countries with the highest and lowest rates of alcohol consumption.

❯ Discuss the major ways that alcohol is costly to our society.

❯ Discuss the main events of the temperance movement and the Prohibition era.

❯ Define alcoholism, and identify the general characteristics of an alcoholic.

❯ Cite some of the cultural differences for defining problem drinkers.

❯ Explain how culture influences views about alcohol.

❯ List four cultural factors that affect our views about alcohol consumption.

❯ List four findings about alcohol consumption and college students.

❯ Provide at least three reasons why the effects of alcohol consumption differ between women and men.

❯ Understand the differences between codependency and enabling behaviors.

❯ List two major factors that alcohol treatment must consider.

Introduction

First interview:

I am the owner of this liquor store and most customers buy what they need and do not leave me with any negative impressions. However, there are a number of customers, maybe 10% who make impressions on me as well as Cindy [referring to a hired store clerk working at this liquor store]. With this small percentage of customers, you can tell by the look on their faces—often serious-looking faces—that they have a problem with the alcohol they are buying. It's a certain look that tells you they are more than likely to be seriously addicted to alcohol. Such people, both men and women, hand you the bottle they are buying and when they are paying their hand is shaking—like their hands are trembling. You can tell they want to buy the alcohol and go somewhere and gobble it up. These people are short on words, often crabby, expecting a quick purchase, and quickly head out the door. Some are dressed shabbily while others dress normally. Some look poor and with this small percentage many also look like my other working customers. These people [referring to the alleged problem drinkers] . . . usually purchase lower-end beer or hard liquor. Then there are the ones who appear to have worked a steady shift, and they are the ones with that "thirsty look." They are in a hurry to go home or wherever they go and drink it all down. This is what we think about these people. I have to say most of these problem drinkers pick out vodka then when they come up to the counter to get checked out they pull money out of their pockets and the dollars and change are dropped on the counter for a quick getaway. Others have credit cards, and most of the rejected cards come from these types of drinkers I would label down and out. If the credit card is rejected they have other ones or quickly leave, go back to their cars, and some passenger in the car hands over money so he or she can make the purchase. Then there are the talkative and lively problem drinkers in this group who often give me the feeling they are covering up a drinking problem. The joke around or mention something just so kill time while I ring up the sale. Funny how these types are quick to get away and drive off to what I think to go back home and drink. I am often left with the impression that all that friendliness is just a cover up, but then my sales associate sometimes disagrees with me after we exchange impressions. Cindy has a female's impression and mine is different at times. We do find it interesting how the majority of times we agree what we think we see in these customers after they have left the store. It's kind of sad at times to know so much and I think sometimes we are supporting their bad habits. *(From Venturelli's research files, male owner of a liquor store a smaller Midwestern town, age 56, November 5, 2015)*

Second interview:

I even knew a professor who would buy pints of whiskey as soon as we would open in the morning. He would drive off and go to your university [referring to the author's university] to teach. He was a heck of a nice fella, always ready with a joke and very pleasant to talk to, but I knew he had a problem with this stuff. *(From Venturelli's research files, female liquor store clerk in a small Midwestern town, age 50, August 9, 1999. Update: The professor with the alleged drinking problem has changed jobs and is no longer at this university.)*

Third interview:

I vividly recall at age 10 seeing at least three or four middle-aged men arrive at my father's tavern as soon as the doors were opened at 8:00 a.m. on most mornings, desperately looking for the morning's first drink of alcohol. I recall my dad would crack a raw egg into an 8-ounce glass. Draft beer and the raw egg filled the glass half full. The reason for the raw egg was to get some breakfast protein and the reason for the half-full glass of beer was because their hands were very shaky and they had to steady the drink to their mouths. Immediately following what my dad referred to as a "full" breakfast were at least several double shots of Jim Beam whiskey. These alcoholic customers had to have the drinks so that they could feel "normal" for the rest of the day. Some would even be dressed in formal attire ready to go off to their office jobs. *(Venturelli's personal observation)*

Fourth interview:

I have this friend who works as a restaurant manager and has a big drinking problem. On most evenings, he calls as soon as he reaches home from work late at night. Each time, and as he is talking to me on the phone, I can hear the jingling of the ice cubes in his glass. Sometimes he already had a few cocktails before he calls so as soon as he starts talking I can immediately distinguish by the way he speaks that he is already half-drunk. As he continues drinking and contradicting himself, in mostly a one-way conversation—him talking to me—I have to listen to a lot of nonsensical talk that makes me feel like he is using me as someone to call so he can unload all the problems that went on with his job for the day. After 10 to 15 minutes of listening, I often try to end the conversation by saying, "I have to get up real early tomorrow morning so I need to get to bed." This usually ends the conversation. I realize he is lonely (living by himself), but why do I have to endure this nearly every night? I guess I feel sorry for him, but it is unfair to be used this way. He often claims he is an alcoholic and says at least he is a functioning alcoholic. I know he puts in many hours at work, and probably because he sees so many of his customers drinking all day long maybe he develops some kind of thirst for alcohol when he is off work. How many times he asks me to take him to the liquor store to buy vodka, and the funny thing is that I hardly drink anymore. Each time I take him to buy liquor on days when he is off work he always comes out with a half-gallon bottle of vodka that is usually consumed within a week. He cannot drive since his driving record is abominable with four DUIs to date. He says in 10 years he will be able to drive again—God help us when he does! At a very young age when he received his first DUI he went off the road completely drunk and hit a barn, actually went through a barn, and killed a steer with his car! I sometimes laugh about this when I picture the accident but it is not funny. Just imagine if it was a pedestrian or another car? I know he has a big alcohol problem but it appears he also knows it without either desiring or seeking help for his alcoholism. I keep imagining what hell it must be if I had to live with him as his roommate. *(From Venturelli's research files, male high school teacher in a small Midwestern town, age 53, July 4, 2010)*

Alcohol Consumption in the United States

Similar to nearly all societies, past and present, alcohol has always been a part of American society. The preceding quotes illustrate how an individual can consume an excessive amount of a psychoactive and addictive substance without necessarily coming to the attention of anyone except perhaps a neighbor or friend, a lone liquor store owner or employee, or even a bar owner and his young son's observation. Furthermore, this same depressant chemical is often not perceived as a drug by many Americans. It is considered more of a social lubricant, something that is "always" consumed at social gatherings and perceived as normal at social gatherings.

Consider these findings from the National Household Survey on Drug Abuse in 2014 (Center for Behavioral Health Statistics and Quality [CBHSQ] 2015):

- There were 139.7 million **current drinkers** (past month) of alcohol aged 12 or older in 2014, including 60.9 million who were **binge alcohol users** and 16.3 million who were **heavy alcohol users**.
- In 2014, the percentage of people aged 12 or older that were past-month alcohol users (48%) was similar to the percentages in 2009 through 2013.
- The percentage of people aged 12 or older in 2014 who were past-month heavy alcohol users (6%) was similar to the percentages in 2011 through 2013. Estimates of binge drinking among people aged 12 or older did not change over the period from 2002 to 2014 (22.2% in 2014).

Figure 8.1 shows that the 21 to 25 age group has the highest consumption of alcohol, with 69% using alcohol, 43% binging, and 13% engaging in heavy use. The group with the second highest consumption, those aged 26 to 29 years, shows 68% using alcohol, 38% binging, and 9% engaging in heavy use (CBHSQ 2015). Additional statistics on

KEY TERMS

current drinkers
at least one drink in the past 30 days; can include binge and heavy use

binge alcohol users (binge drinking)
a pattern of drinking five or more drinks for men and four or more drinks for women on a single occasion, such as at the same time or within 2 hours of each other, on at least 1 day in the past 30 days; includes heavy use

heavy alcohol users (heavy drinking)
five or more drinks on the same occasion on each of 5 or more days in the past 30 days or consuming an average of more than one alcoholic beverage per day for women and an average of more than two alcoholic beverages per day for men and any drinking by pregnant women or underage youth

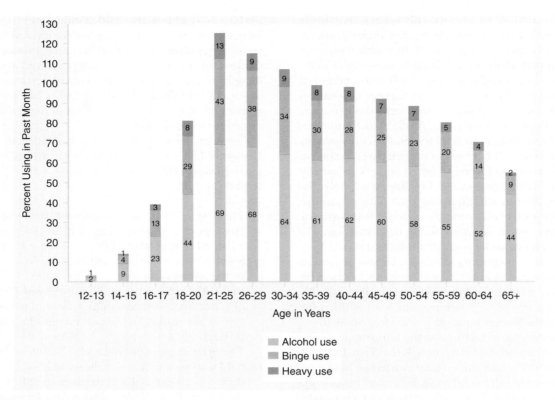

FIGURE 8.1 Current, binge, and heavy alcohol use among persons aged 12 or older, by age: 2014.

Data from Center for Behavioral Health Statistics and Quality (CBHSQ). *Behavioral Health Trends in the United States: Results from the 2014 National Survey on Drug Use and Health* (HHS Publication No. SMA 15-4927, NSDUH Series H-50). Rockville, MD, 2015. http://www.samhsa.gov/data/sites/default/files/NSDUH-DetTabs2014/NSDUH-DetTabs2014.pdf, Table 216B.

age and alcohol consumption are as follows (summarized largely from CBHSQ 2015, unless otherwise designated):

- Although alcohol use peaks at ages 21 to 25, a steady decline begins at 26 to 29 years of age through age 65 in using alcohol, binging, and engaging in heavy use.
- The 17.0 million people aged 12 or older who had an alcohol use disorder in 2014 represent 6.4% of all people aged 12 or older.
- Approximately 4.3 million young adults aged 18 to 25 in 2014 had an alcohol use disorder in the past year. This number represents 12.3% of young adults, or about one in eight young adults.
- In 2014, approximately 12.0 million adults aged 26 or older had an alcohol use disorder in the past year, representing 5.9% of the adults in this age group.
- In 2013, 52% of current underage drinkers reported that their last use of alcohol occurred in someone else's home, and 34% reported that it had occurred in their own home. Most

current drinkers aged 12 to 20 (78%) were with two or more other people the last time they drank alcohol. The rate of drinking alone the last time that underage persons drank alcohol was highest among youths aged 12 to 14 (approximately 15%) (SAMHSA 2014).
- Among current underage drinkers, 28% paid for the alcohol the last time they drank, including 8% who purchased the alcohol themselves and 21% who gave money to someone else to purchase it. Among those who did not pay for the alcohol they last drank, 37% got it from an unrelated person aged 21 or older; 25% got it from a parent, guardian, or other adult family member; and 16% got it from another person younger than 21 years old.
- In 2013, underage current drinkers were more likely than current alcohol users aged 21 or older to use illicit drugs within 2 hours of alcohol use on their last reported drinking occasion (20% vs. 6%, respectively). The most commonly reported illicit drug used by underage drinkers in combination with alcohol was marijuana (SAMHSA 2014).

- Most (84%) of the 4.6 million past year alcohol initiates in 2013 were younger than age 21 at the time of initiation (SAMHSA 2014).
- In 2013, 39% of youths aged 12 to 17 perceived great risk in having five or more drinks once or twice a week. Similarly, 39% of youths perceived great risk in smoking marijuana once or twice a week (SAMHSA 2014).
- In 2013, adults aged 21 or older who had first used alcohol at age 14 or younger were more likely to be classified with alcohol dependence or abuse than adults who had their first drink at age 21 or older (15% vs. 2.3%) (SAMHSA 2014).
- For persons aged 65 or older, 44% drank alcohol, 9% binged, and 2% reported heavy alcohol use (see Figure 8.1) (SAMHSA 2014).

An encouraging finding is that the rate of current alcohol use among youth aged 12 to 17 declined from 14.6% in 2008 to 11.6% in 2013. Youth binge and heavy drinking rates in 2013 were also lower than in 2008. Further, the 2013 rates for current and binge youth alcohol use were lower than those in 2012 (12.9% and 7.2%, respectively). More recent findings from the 2014 national Monitoring the Future Survey reveals that alcohol use by middle and high school students has been steadily declining to record low percentages. Past-month alcohol use by 12th graders decreased from highs above 70% in the late 1970s to 37% in 2014, the lowest rate since data collection began in 1975. Similarly alcohol use by 8th and 10th graders declined (Center for Substance Abuse Research [CESAR] 2015). These trends may indicate that perhaps the enforcement of alcohol drug laws (especially motor vehicle alcohol violations), campaigns and advertisements against heavy alcohol use, and increasing enforcement expenditures in the recent past have had an impact on decreasing the number of underage drinkers.

Current Statistics and Trends in Alcohol Consumption

In a 2013 Gallup poll, 64% of the adult population reported drinking alcohol, with 26% reporting excessive alcohol consumption patterns. In an earlier Gallup poll, 29% of the population reported that drinking alcohol had caused family problems, and 77% of those questioned indicated that, in comparison to all other drug problems, alcohol creates the most family problems in our society (Jones 2007; Newport 2000).

In looking at more detailed figures about consumption patterns, we find the following (summarized largely from Newport 2000, unless otherwise designated):

- Gallup polls indicate that drinking patterns have not changed much over time. As of July 9, 2012, 66% of people reported themselves as being current drinkers. In 1976 and 1977, the average was 71%. Gallup reports that the average amount drunk in the past week was 4.2 alcoholic beverages. In 1996, the average was below three drinks (Gallup 2013).
- "Nearly half of male drinkers, 48%, say they most often drink beer, followed by liquor at 26%, while 51% of female drinkers prefer wine. This pattern is consistent with prior years, although the preference for beer is down slightly between both groups compared with 2010" (Saad 2012).
- "For only the second time in two decades, wine ties beer as the top choice when U.S. drinkers are asked whether they most often drink liquor, wine, or beer. Gallup now finds nearly as many U.S. drinkers naming wine (35%) as beer (36%), while liquor still registers a distant third at 23%" (Saad 2012).
- "Gallup has consistently found a wide gender difference in preferred alcoholic beverage, going back to the initial asking of the question in 1992. Currently, 53% of men name beer as their favorite drink, while 22% say liquor and 20% wine. Among women, 52% say they drink wine most often, while 24% say liquor and 20% beer" (Jones 2013).
- In 2012, 66% of men drinking alcohol reported an average of 6.2 alcoholic beverages per week, whereas women reported 2.2 alcoholic beverages per week (Saad 2012).
- As men age, their preference for beer steadily decreases (Newport 2000).
- Overall, as both men and women age, they say wine is their favorite alcoholic beverage (Newport 2000).
- Lower-income drinkers prefer beer, whereas higher-income drinkers prefer wine (Newport 2000).
- The highest rate of family drinking problems is among 18- to 29-year-olds (Newport 2000).
- Currently, 42% of the population report family disputes caused by excessive drinking; 17% reported this problem in 2013 (Jones 2013).
- Sixty-four percent claim they drink and 36% report that they abstain. In 1999, 61% drank and 39% abstained (Newport 2000).

- "Americans who drink alcohol are about equally likely to say they drink beer (36%) or wine (35%) most often. Another 23% say liquor is their beverage of choice. That continues the trend in which beer has declined as the preferred beverage of U.S. drinkers, shrinking its advantage over wine from 20 percentage points in 1992 to one point today" (Jones 2013).

- "Twenty-one percent of drinkers say they sometimes drink more than they should. This percentage has been fairly consistent over time, ranging between 17% and 25% over the past decade. The historically high point was 35% in 1989" (Jones 2013).

- Worldwide, adults (age 21 or older) consume on average 5 liters[1] of pure alcohol from beer, wine, and spirits per year. The average alcohol consumption is highest in Europe, followed by the Americas and Africa. Alcohol consumption tends to increase with economic development; however, consumption remains low in some regions where the majority of the population is Muslim (GreenFacts 2009).

- Throughout the world, the highest per capita consumptions of alcohol from 1970 to 2006 were in Romania (10.5 liters), Austria (10.5 liters), Hungary (10.4 liters), and Russia (10.3 liters). Consumption was lowest in Norway (4.9 liters). The United Kingdom (8.3 liters) was mid-range in European consumption. Alcohol consumption in most European countries was stable from 1970 through 2006; however, in some European countries, consumption fell substantially. For example, France fell from 17.2 liters in 1970 to 10.0 liters in 2006, and Italy fell from 16.0 liters in 1970 to 8.1 liters in 2006 (Coghill, Miller, and Plant 2009).

- Illicit drug use in 2013 varied by the educational status of adults aged 18 or older. The rate of current illicit drug use was lower among college graduates (6.7%) than those with some college education but no degree (10.8%), high school graduates with no further education (9.9%), and those who had not graduated from high school (11.8%) (SAMHSA 2014).

KEY TERM

teetotalers
individuals who drink no alcoholic beverages whatsoever; a term in common usage in decades past; today, teetotalers are referred to as *abstainers*

[1] One liter is equivalent to 1.26 gallons.

- Drinking is commonly believed to be associated with poverty, yet according to a Gallup poll, the people most likely to drink have higher incomes, are younger than age 65, do not attend church, live in regions of the United States other than the South, and are more likely to identify themselves as liberals (Newport 2000).

- Prior research shows that much of the economic burden of alcohol and drug problems falls on the population of taxpayers who do not abuse alcohol and drugs. Government, private insurance, and other members of households bear most of these costs (Office of Applied Studies [OAS] 2001).

▮ Percentages of the Drinking Population: A Pyramid Model

What percentage of our society drinks alcohol? A pyramid can be constructed based on the amount of alcohol consumed, the pattern of drinking, or the "problem" or "illness" dimension (e.g., by attempting to calculate what proportion of Americans are "abusers" or "dependent"). For example, at the beginning of this chapter, several interviews discussed people who bought and consumed liquor and are prime examples of alcohol drinkers who probably imbibe approximately 1 quart per day. This, by most definitions, is a clear diagnostic criterion for a diagnosis of alcoholism. Interestingly, all four of the chapter's opening examples indicate that the alcohol drinkers are apparently functional, or at least they manage to create this impression.

The pyramid shown in **Figure 8.2** has a base of 35% who are **teetotalers**, then a layer of about 13% who occasionally drink, and a top 52% who

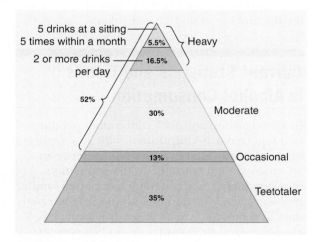

FIGURE 8.2   Broad distribution of drinking behaviors.

drink regularly. In 2013, 24.6% (58.5 million) of those aged 18 or older reported that they engaged in binge drinking in the past month; 6.8% (16,248) reported that they engaged in heavy drinking in the past month (SAMHSA 2014). Different definitions of what constitutes heavy drinking exist. Thus, if we define heavy drinking differently—for example, as more than two drinks per day—we come up with a much larger slice of the pyramid—three times as large.

In a study based on data from the National Health Interview Survey (NHIS), nearly two-thirds (65%) of U.S. adults are current drinkers (CESAR 2013). The majority of these current drinkers were infrequent (11 drinks or less in the past year) or light (3 drinks or less per week) drinkers. Around one-fourth were moderate drinkers and 8% were heavier drinkers. Men were more likely than women to be not only current drinkers (71% vs. 60%) but also moderate or heavier current drinkers (29% vs. 13%).

■ Dual Problems: Underage and Adult Drinking

As we saw in Figure 8.1, alcohol consumption does not have any age boundaries. Although all states have had a legal drinking age of 21 since 1988, a high percentage of the underage population drinks alcohol. Overall, in looking at a larger and more detailed picture of the percentages and types of groups reporting alcohol use in 2013, the following findings have been reported:

UNDERAGE ALCOHOL USE

- In 2013, about 8.7 million persons aged 12 to 20 (22.7% of this age group) reported drinking alcohol in the past month. Approximately 5.4 million (14.2%) were binge drinkers, and 1.4 million (3.7%) were heavy drinkers. All three of these rates were lower than those reported in 2012 (24.3%, 15.3%, and 4.3% percent, respectively) (SAMHSA 2014).
- Rates of current, binge, and heavy alcohol use among underage persons declined between 2002 and 2013. The rate of current alcohol use among 12- to 20-year-olds decreased from 28.8% in 2002 to 22.7% in 2013. From 2002 to 2013, the binge drinking rate declined from 19.3% to 14.2% and the rate of heavy drinking declined from 6.2% to 3.7% (SAMHSA 2014).
- Rates of current alcohol use increased with age among underage persons. In 2013, 2.1% of persons aged 12 or 13, 9.5% of persons aged 14 or

15, 22.7% of persons aged 16 or 17, and 43.8% of persons aged 18 to 20 drank alcohol during the 30 days before they were surveyed. This pattern by age has been observed since 2002. The rates in 2013 for youths aged 14 or 15, and those aged 16 or 17 were lower than the rates in 2012 (11.1% and 24.8%, respectively) (SAMHSA 2014).

- Males and females aged 12 to 20 in 2013 had similar rates of current alcohol use (23% and 22.5%, respectively). However, underage males were more likely than underage females to report binge (15.8% vs. 12.4%) or heavy alcohol use (4.6% vs. 2.7%) (SAMHSA 2013).
- Students may be more likely to drink and drive on prom and graduation nights, according to a survey of 11th- and 12th-grade students across the country. Nearly all of the students surveyed (90%) said that their peers are more likely to drink and drive on prom night, and 79% report the same for graduation night. Despite this belief, students do not seem to think that driving on these nights is dangerous. Less than one third (29%) reported that they believe that driving on prom night comes with a high degree of danger, and 25% said the same for graduation night. These findings suggest that there is a need to provide high school students with prevention messages that paint an accurate picture of the risks and consequences for drinking and driving during prom and graduation season (CESAR 2010).

ALCOHOL USE: AGE 12 OR OLDER BY ETHNICITY AND RACE

- **Figure 8.3A** shows that, among persons aged 12 or older in 2014, whites were more likely than other racial/ethnic groups to report current use of alcohol (57.7%). The rates were 49.5% for persons reporting two or more races, 44.4% for Hispanics or Latinos, 42.3% for American Indians or Alaska Natives, 44.2% for blacks, and 38.7% for Asians (CBHSQ 2015).
- In 2014, among youth aged 12 to 17, Asians had the lowest overall rates of current alcohol use as well as the lowest current use and binge drinking rates across all age groups (CBHSQ 2015).

DRIVING UNDER THE INFLUENCE OF ALCOHOL

Figure 8.3B shows that in 2013, an estimated 10.9% of persons aged 12 or older drove under the influence of alcohol at least once in the past year.

This percentage has dropped since 2004, when it was 13.5%. The 2013 estimate corresponds to 27.8 million persons (SAMHSA 2014).

Although not shown in Figure 8.3, among persons aged 12 or older, males were more likely than females (14.4% vs. 7.7%) to drive under the influence of alcohol in the past year (SAMHSA 2014).

Figure 8.3C shows that in 2013 driving under the influence of alcohol differed by age group. An estimated 3.8% of those aged 16 or 17, 10.8% of those aged 18 to 20, and 19.7% of those aged 21 to 25 reported driving under the influence of alcohol in the past year. Note that the 26- to 29-year age group had the highest percentage (20.7%) of

A

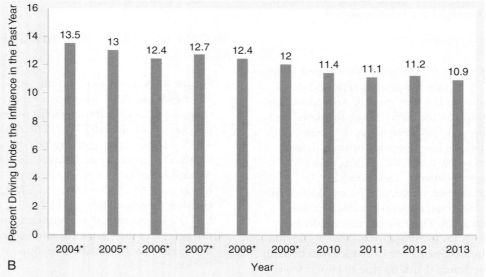

B

FIGURE 8.3 (A) Current, binge, and heavy alcohol use among persons aged 12 or older, by race/ethnicity: 2014. (B) Driving under the influence of alcohol in the past year among persons aged 12 or older: 2004–2013. (*continues*)

*Difference between this estimate and the 2013 estimate is stylistically significant at the .05 level.

Data from Center for Behavioral Health Statistics and Quality (CBHSQ). *Behavioral Health Trends in the United States: Results from the 2014 National Survey on Drug Use and Health.* HHS Publication No. SMA 15-4927, NSDUH Series H-50. Rockville, MD: Substance Abuse and Mental Health Services Administration, 2015; Substance Abuse and Mental Health Services Administration (SAMHSA). *Results from the 2013 National Survey on Drug Use and Health: Summary of National Findings.*

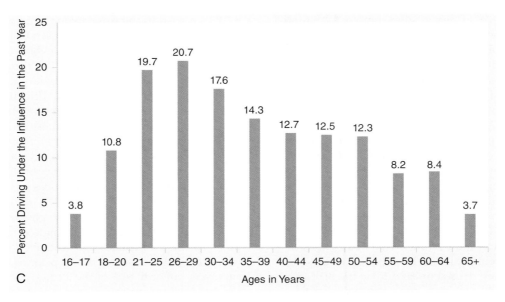

FIGURE 8.3 (*continued*) (C) Driving under the influence of alcohol in the past year among persons aged 16 or older: 2014.

Data from NSDUH Series H-48, HHS Publication No. SMA 14-4863. Rockville, MD: Substance Abuse and Mental Health Services Administration, 2014.

driving under the influence of alcohol in the past year. Beyond age 29, these rates show a general steady decline in driving under the influence with increasing age (SAMHSA 2014).

EDUCATION AND ALCOHOL USE

- Among adults aged 18 or older, the rate of past-month alcohol use increased with increasing levels of education. Among adults in 2013 with less than a high school education, 36.5% were current drinkers. In comparison, 69.2% of college graduates were current drinkers (SAMHSA 2014).
- Among adults aged 18 or older, rates of binge and heavy alcohol use varied by level of education. Among adults in 2013, those who had graduated from college were less likely than those with some college education but no degree to be binge drinkers (23.1% vs. 26.4%) or heavy drinkers (6.0% vs. 7.6%) (SAMHSA 2014).

COLLEGE STUDENTS AND ALCOHOL USE

- Young adults aged 18 to 22 who were enrolled full time in college were more likely than their peers who were not enrolled full time (i.e., part-time college students and persons not currently enrolled in college) to report current, binge, or heavy drinking. Among full-time college students in 2013, 59.4% were current drinkers, 39.0% were binge drinkers, and 12.7% were heavy drinkers. Among those not enrolled full time in college, these rates were 50.6%, 33.4%, and 9.3%, respectively.
- The pattern of higher rates of current alcohol use, binge alcohol use, and heavy alcohol use among full-time college students compared with rates for others aged 18 to 22 has remained consistent since 2002.

EMPLOYMENT STATUS AND ALCOHOL USE

- The rate of current alcohol use in 2013 was 65.8% for full-time employed adults aged 18 or older, which was higher than the rate for unemployed adults (53.8%). Rates of binge drinking were similar for adults who were employed full time and those who were unemployed (30.5% and 31.3%, respectively).
- Among adults in 2013, most binge and heavy alcohol users were employed. Among the 58.5 million adults who were binge drinkers, 44.5 million (76.1%) were employed either full or part time. Among the 16.2 million adults who were heavy drinkers, 12.4 million (76.0%) were employed.

ALCOHOL AND THE VERY YOUNG

Use of either of the two major licit drugs, alcohol and cigarettes, remains more widespread than use of any of the illicit drugs. In 2015, 27%, of 8th graders, 49% of 10th graders, 66% of 12th graders, and 79% of college students reported lifetime use of alcohol; active use was also widespread. Most important was the prevalence of occasions of heavy drinking—five or more drinks in a row at least once in the prior 2-week period—which was reported by 4.6% of 8th graders, 10.9% of 10th graders, 17.2% of 12th graders, and 35% of college students (Johnston et al. 2016). A noteworthy finding is that on a daily basis for 8th, 10th, and 12th graders combined, marijuana usage now exceeds alcohol usage.

Of greater concern than just any use of alcohol is its use to the point of inebriation. In 2014, 11% of 8th graders, 30% of 10th graders, and 50% of 12th graders said they had been drunk at least once in their lifetime. The prevalence rates of self-reported drunkenness during the 30 days immediately preceding the survey were strikingly high—3%, 11%, and 24%, respectively, for grades 8, 10, and 12 (Miech et al. 2015; see "Point/Counterpoint: Lower the Legal Drinking Age?").

With regard to the three major types of alcohol (beer, wine coolers, and liquor) used by junior high and high school students, alcohol consumption increases dramatically from 9th through 12th grades (Miech et al. 2015). In looking at 12th graders' consumption of alcohol, white underage students are much more likely to binge drink (24%) compared with African American students (11%) and Hispanic students (20%). Finally, boys in 12th grade are more likely to drink alcohol on a daily basis compared with girls of the same grade and age; daily use among boys was reported at 3%, whereas the rate among girls was reported at 0.8%. Boys are more likely than girls to drink large quantities of alcohol in a single sitting: 26% of 12th-grade males reported drinking five or more drinks in a row 2 weeks prior to being surveyed, but only 16% of the 12th-grade females reported drinking the same amount (Miech et al. 2015). When reviewing the statistics, keep in mind that females differ from males in terms of their alcohol drinking capacities.

►POINT/COUNTERPOINT

Lower the Legal Drinking Age?

Only seven countries throughout the world—the United States, Indonesia, Kazakhstan, Oman, Pakistan, Palau, and Sri Lanka are the only seven countries throughout the world that —set the minimum legal drinking age at 21. **Table 8.1** and the following figure show the exceptions to the minimum age of 21 for the consumption of alcohol as of 2015.

A clear majority of countries throughout the world, 101 of them, specify the age of 18 as the minimum age to drink alcohol (see Table 8.1). Fifteen other countries, Austria (age 18 in some areas), Belgium,* Bosnia and Herzegovina, Germany,* Georgia, Haiti, Italy, Liechtenstein, Luxembourg, Macao, Malaysia, Netherlands,* Sudan, Switzerland,* and Tokelau, set the legal drinking age to 16. Two countries, Cyprus and Malta, set the minimum at 17 years of age. Nineteen countries—Albania, Angola, Armenia, Cambodia, Comoros, Cuba, Equatorial Guinea, Ghana, Guinea-Bissau, Jamaica, Macedonia, Montenegro, Morocco, Norway, Romania, Swaziland, Togo, Uruguay, and Vietnam—do not specify any specific legal age for alcohol consumption (Hanson 2015). The majority of countries have set the minimum drinking age at 18 years, but the global average minimum

age for legal drinking is 15.9 years (Hanson 2015). Internationally, the average age at which drinking alcohol first occurs is 12 years, and about 80% of young people begin drinking alcoholic beverages regularly at age 15 or younger according to the World Health Organization (WHO) (Hanson 2015).

Arguments *against* lowering the legal limit for consuming alcohol are as follows:

- A higher minimum legal drinking age (MLDA) is effective in preventing alcohol-related deaths and injuries among youth. When the MLDA is lowered, injury and death rates increase; when the MLDA is increased, death and injury rates decline (McCartt and Kirley 2006; Wagenaar 1993).

- A higher MLDA results in fewer alcohol-related problems among youth, and an MLDA of 21 years saves the lives of more than 1000 youth each year. Conversely, when the MLDA is lowered, motor vehicle crashes and deaths among youth increase. At least 50 studies have evaluated this correlation (McCartt and Kirley 2006; Wagenaar 1993).

- Research shows that when the MLDA is 21, people younger than age 21 drink less overall and continue to do so through their early 20s (O'Malley and Wagenaar 1991).

▶POINT/COUNTERPOINT

Lower the Legal Drinking Age? (*continued*)

- Higher MLDAs reduce traffic fatalities involving drivers 18 to 20 years old by saving approximately 1000 lives each year (American Medical Association 2011).

- Although younger drivers are less likely than adults to drink and drive, their risk of crashing is substantially higher when they do drink and drive. (McCartt and Kirley 2006).

- The evidence is clear that a MLDA can deter underage drinking and driving and reduce alcohol-related crashes among young drivers (McCartt and Kirley 2006).

Arguments *for* lowering the legal limit for consuming alcohol are as follows:

- The United States has the strictest youth drinking laws in Western civilization and yet has the most drinking-related problems among its young, and there seems to be a connection between these two facts (Hanson 2009).

- A study of a large sample of young people between the ages of 16 and 19 in Massachusetts and New York after Massachusetts raised its drinking age revealed that average self-reported daily alcohol consumption in Massachusetts did not decline in comparison with New York (Hanson 2013b).

- Comparison of college students attending schools in states that had maintained, for at least 10 years, a minimum drinking age of 21 with those in states that had similarly maintained minimum drinking ages below 21 revealed few differences in drinking problems (Hanson 2013b).

- A study of all 50 states and the District of Columbia found "a positive relationship between the purchase age and single-vehicle fatalities." Thus, single-vehicle fatalities were found to be more frequent in those states with high purchase ages (Hanson 2013b).

- Comparison of drinking before and after the passage of raised minimum age legislation has generally revealed little impact on behavior. For example, a study that examined college students' drinking behavior before and after an increase in the minimum legal drinking age from 18 to 19 in New York found the law had no impact on underage students' consumption rates, intoxication rates, drinking attitudes, or drinking problems. These studies were corroborated by other researchers at a different college in the same state (Hanson 2013b).

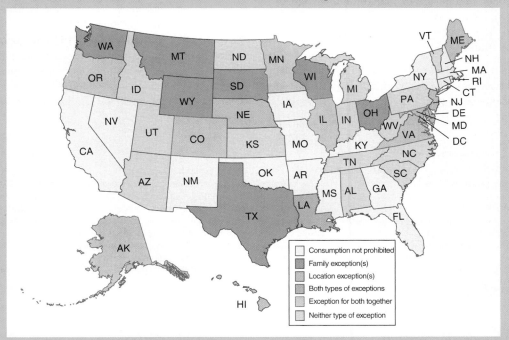

Acceptability and exceptions to the minimum age of 21 for consuming alcohol in the United States as of January 1, 2011.

Reproduced from Hanson, D. J. "Minimum Legal Drinking Ages Around the World." Alcohol Problems and Solutions. 2015. Available http://www.alcoholproblemsandsolutions.org/LegalDrinkingAge.html

(*continues*)

►POINT/COUNTERPOINT

Lower the Legal Drinking Age? (*continued*)

• An examination of East Carolina University students' intentions regarding their behavior after the increase of the MLDA to age 21 revealed that only 6% intended to stop drinking, 70% planned to change their drinking location, 21% expected to use a false or borrowed identification to obtain alcohol, and 22% intended to use other drugs. Anecdotal statements by students indicated the belief by some that it "might be easier to hide a little pot in my room than a six pack of beer" (Hanson 2013b).

Research and the information from sources in this chapter indicate that with regard to under-21 alcohol violations, the United States continues to have serious problems. Thus, we are not any better than most countries regarding the percentage of minors consuming alcohol, despite our unique MLDA of age 21 for alcohol consumption. Instead of prohibiting alcohol consumption to those younger than age 21 (which, to date, continues to be ineffective), perhaps we need to teach moderation at an early age so that the percentage of youth who decide to consume alcohol can learn to do so responsibly. Given that the MLDA of 21 years has not deterred our nation's youth from consuming alcohol, and in light of younger and younger age groups consuming alcohol, do you think it is time to reconsider lowering the age limit of alcohol consumption so that:

1. We are more in alignment with the majority of countries. At present, 82 countries allow alcohol consumption at 18 years of age and older.

2. We can eliminate costly, burdensome, and unnecessary underage drinking violations. These infractions with the law include fines, legal costs, imprisonment, court time, legal expenses, and introducing our nation's youth into the criminal justice system (which many believe should remain "lean and mean" so it can effectively prohibit and prosecute serious law violators).

3. We can teach responsible drinking and drinking in moderation, and alcohol consumption can be promoted and taught to be a "normal" part of behavior when eating or socializing with friends (like consuming coffee or fruit juice). Such prevention measures can clearly emphasize that excessive alcohol consumption is a sign of immaturity and lack of self-respect.

How successful do you think a campaign calling for lowering the legal drinking age would be with (1) family members, (2) your school, (3) your community, (4) your city/town, and (5) U.S. society in general? Would it be successful? If yes, why? If no, why not? Have you had any experiences in foreign countries where alcohol consumption was not severely restricted? If so, what did you observe?

In essence, do you think we should try to change the current drinking laws, in light of the fact that the current laws continue to be violated by youths under 21 years of age? Should the United States become like other progressive nations regarding age limits on the use of alcohol? What are the pros and cons of lowering the drinking rates in the United States? At what specific age should the consumption of alcohol be legal?

....

* 16 to 18 depending on the beverage.

Data from American Medical Association (AMA). "Facts About Youth and Alcohol." Chicago, IL: AMA Newsletter, 2011; Hanson, D. J. "Binge Drinking." Potsdam, NY: Sociology Department, State University of New York, 2009. Available http://www2.potsdam.edu/hansondj/BingeDrinking.html; Hanson, D. J. "Minimum Legal Drinking Ages Around the World." Alcohol Problems and Solutions. 2013a. Available http://www2.potsdam.edu/hansondj/LegalDrinkingAge.htm; Hanson, D. J. "Binge Drinking." Alcohol Problems and Solutions. 2013b. Available http://www2.potsdam.edu/hansondj/BingeDrinking.html; McCartt, A. T., and B. B. Kirley. "Minimum Purchase Age Laws: How Effective Are They in Reducing Alcohol-Impaired Driving?" Arlington, VA: Insurance Institute for Highway Safety, 2006. Available http://onlinepubs.trb.org/onlinepubs/circulars/ec123.pdf; O'Malley, P. M., and A. C. Wagenaar. "Effects of Minimum Drinking Age Laws on Alcohol Use, Related Behaviors and Traffic Crash Involvement Among American Youth: 1976–1987." *Journal of Studies on Alcohol* 52 (1991): 478–491; and Wagenaar, A. C. "Minimum Drinking Age and Alcohol Availability to Youth: Issues and Research Needs." In *Economics and the Prevention of Alcohol-Related Problems,* edited by M. E. Hilton and B. Bloss, 175–200. National Institute on Alcohol Abuse and Alcoholism (NIAAA) Research Monograph No. 25, NIH Pub. No. 93-3513. Bethesda, MD: National Institute on Alcohol Abuse and Alcoholism, 1993.

TABLE 8.1 World Minimum Drinking Ages

None	16	17	18	19	20	21
Albania	Austria (18 in some areas)	Cyprus	Algeria	Nicaragua	Iceland	Indonesia
Angola		Malta	Argentina	South Korea	Japan	Kazakhstan
Armenia	Belgium*		Australia		Paraguay	Oman
Cambodia	Bosnia and Herzegovina		Azerbaijan			Pakistan
Comoros	Germany*		Bahamas			Palau
Cuba	Georgia		Belarus			Sri Lanka
Equatorial Guinea	Haiti		Belize			United States (with many exceptions [see figure])
Ghana	Italy		Bermuda			
Guinea-Bissau	Liechtenstein*		Bolivia			
Jamaica	Luxembourg		Botswana			
Macedonia	Macau		Brazil (19 in some provinces)			
Montenegro	Malaysia		Burundi (none with parents)			
Morocco	Netherlands*		Cameroon			
Norway	Sudan		Canada (19 in some provinces)			
Romania	Switzerland*		Cape Verde			
Swaziland	Tokelau		Central African Republic			
Togo			Chile			
Uruguay			China			
Vietnam			Colombia			
			Costa Rica			
			Croatia			
			Czech Republic			
			Denmark			
			Dominican Republic			
			Ecuador			
			Egypt			
			El Salvador			
			Eritrea			
			Estonia			
			Ethiopia			
			Fiji (lowered from 21 in 2009)			
			Finland			
			France (no minimum age in private)			
			Gabon			

(continues)

TABLE 8.1 World Minimum Drinking Ages (*continued*)

None	16	17	18	19	20	21
			Gambia			
			Gibraltar			
			Greece			
			Guatemala			
			Guyana			
			Honduras			
			Hong Kong			
			Hungary			
			India (varies by state)			
			Iraq			
			Ireland			
			Israel			
			Jordan			
			Kenya			
			Kyrgyzstan			
			Lebanon			
			Lesotho			
			Lithuania			
			Malawi			
			Maldives			
			Mauritius			
			Mexico			
			Moldova			
			Mongolia			
			Mozambique			
			Namibia			
			Nepal			
			New Zealand			
			Niger			
			Nigeria			
			North Korea			
			Panama			
			Papua New Guinea			
			Peru			
			Philippines			
			Poland			
			Portugal			
			Puerto Rico			
			Republic of China			

TABLE 8.1 World Minimum Drinking Ages *(continued)*

None	16	17	18	19	20	21
			Republic of Congo			
			Russia			
			Rwanda			
			Samoa			
			Serbia			
			Seychelles			
			Singapore			
			Slovakia			
			Slovenia			
			South Africa			
			Spain			
			Sweden (none for low-proof beverage)			
			Syria			
			Tanzania			
			Thailand			
			Tonga			
			Trinidad and Tobago			
			Tunisia			
			Turkey			
			Turkmenistan			
			Uganda			
			Ukraine			
			United Kingdom			
			U.S. Virgin Islands			
			Vanuatu			
			Venezuela			
			Zambia			
			Zimbabwe			

*16 to 18 depending on beverage.

Reproduced from Hanson, D. J. "Minimum Legal Drinking Ages Around the World." Alcohol Problems and Solutions. 2015. Available http://www.alcoholproblemsandsolutions.org/LegalDrinkingAge.html

■ Economic Costs of Alcohol Abuse

It important to realize that "[m]ost of the costs of alcohol abuse result from the adverse effects of alcohol consumption on health" (Buddy T. 2016c). In estimating the costs of alcohol abuse as it relates to illnesses, three major categories that have to be included are: "(1) expenditures on medical treatment (a large proportion of which is for the many medical consequences of alcohol consumption; the remainder is for treatment of alcohol abuse and dependence themselves), (2) the lost productivity that results from workers' abuse of alcohol, and (3) the losses to society from premature deaths that are due to alcohol problems" (Buddy T. 2016c).

In a 2013 National Institute on Alcohol Abuse and Alcoholism (NIAAA) press release, the gravity of the economic costs was stated as follows:

- Alcohol is the most widely used drug in the United States, and alcohol problems cost the nation nearly $249 billion each year (NIAAA 2016).

- Lost productivity due to alcohol-related illness (45.7%) or premature death (21.2%) accounts for two-thirds of the costs of alcohol abuse (NIAAA 1998).
- The remaining costs of alcohol abuse include "healthcare expenditures to treat alcohol use disorders and the medical consequences of alcohol consumption (12.7%), property and administrative costs of alcohol-related motor vehicle crashes (9.2%), and various additional costs of alcohol-related crime (8.6%)" (NIAAA 1998).
- 76% of people with drug or alcohol problems are employed.
- About 19.2 million U.S. workers (15%) reported using or being impaired by alcohol at work at least once in the past year.
- On a per capita basis, the economic impact of excessive alcohol consumption in the United States is approximately $746 per person, most of which is attributable to binge drinking (Centers for Disease Control and Prevention [CDC] 2011).
- According to a study in the journal *Addiction*, in the United States approximately 2.8 million older adults (older than age 50) meet the criteria for alcohol abuse, and this number is expected to reach 5.7 million by 2020 (Yip 2014).
- Alcohol remained the most common primary substance of abuse among older adults admitted for treatment, but the proportion of admissions reporting alcohol as the primary substance of abuse dropped from 84.6% in 1992 to 59.9% in 2008 (Reardon 2012).

Problems with reduced productivity of alcohol-abusing employees include the following:

- Employees who use drugs, consume alcohol at work, or drink heavily away from work are more likely than other employees to exhibit job-withdrawal behaviors, such as spending work time on non-work-related activities, taking long lunch breaks, leaving early, or sleeping on the job (CBIA 2016).
- Employees who drink heavily off the job are more likely to experience hangovers that cause them to be absent from work, show up late or leave early, feel sick at work, perform poorly, or argue with their coworkers. People with drug or alcohol problems were more likely than others to report having worked for three or more employers in the previous year (CBIA 2016).

- Younger workers who abuse alcohol contribute to the following problems (CBIA 2016):
- *Increased healthcare costs*: Healthcare costs for employees with alcohol problems are twice those for other employees.
- *Higher risk*: People who abuse drugs or alcohol are three and a half times more likely to be involved in workplace accidents.
- *Reduced productivity*: Lost work productivity (including absenteeism and poor job performance) associated with substance abuse costs the nation an estimated $161.286 billion a year accounting for 72% of the total cost of excessive alcohol consumption (Bouchery et al. 2011; CDC 2011). (Categories included in lost productivity are impaired productivity at work, mortality, incarceration of perpetrators, impaired productivity at home, absenteeism, crime victims, fetal alcohol syndrome, impaired productivity–institution.)

Older workers who abuse alcohol cause additional problems (SAMHSA 2008c):

- Substance use disorders can exacerbate already costly medical conditions, such as heart disease and diabetes, which are more common among older adults.
- Older people who consume alcohol are highly susceptible to the damaging effects of drug–alcohol interactions—not only because they are more likely to be taking multiple medications but also because they metabolize both medications and alcohol more slowly than do younger people.
- Older adults with alcohol problems also are more likely than people without drinking problems to manage their physical pain with alcohol.
- Because overconsumption of alcohol suppresses the immune system, it puts drinkers at increased risk of infection. It also impairs the balance and judgment of older adults, increasing the likelihood of falls and other accidents.

Misuse of alcohol by employees contributes to the following (SAMHSA 2008d):

- *Higher healthcare spending*: Healthcare costs for employees with alcohol problems are twice those for other employees. Almost half of all trauma and injury visits to hospital emergency rooms are alcohol related, which helps to drive up employers' health insurance expenditures.
- *Decreased productivity*: Alcohol problems in the workplace are associated with increased

absenteeism, disability, and job turnover. Furthermore, in one survey, 14% of workers said they had to redo work within the last year because of a coworker's drinking.

- *Increased safety risks*: Up to 40% of industrial fatalities and 47% of industrial injuries can be linked to alcohol consumption and alcoholism. Alcohol-related accidents contribute to more workers' compensation claims, and more claims mean higher insurance premiums.

As mentioned previously, the economic costs of alcohol abuse to society are staggering. A statement by Ting-Kai Li, MD, director of the NIAAA, highlighted the following:

> According to the Centers for Disease Control and Prevention, alcohol is the third leading cause of preventable death in the U.S. Even more importantly from a public health perspective, alcohol misuse negatively affects the quality of life for millions of Americans. The World Health Organization ranks alcohol as one of the top ten causes of Disability Adjusted Life Years (DALYs) in the United States. Alcohol also contributes to a number of the other leading causes of DALYs, e.g., motor vehicle accidents, brain and liver disease, and cancer. Alcohol problems cost the U.S. an estimated $185 billion annually, with almost half the cost resulting from lost productivity due to alcohol-related disabilities. According to NIAAA's National Epidemiologic Survey on Alcohol and Related Conditions, over 18 million people ages 18 and older suffer from alcohol abuse or dependence and only 7 percent of them receive any form of treatment. Furthermore, heavy drinkers who do not have dependence but are nevertheless at risk for adverse health and psychosocial outcomes are seldom identified. The consequences of alcohol misuse can affect both drinkers and those around them at all stages of life, from damage due to alcohol exposure of the developing embryo, to injuries, to tissue and organ damage resulting from chronic, heavy alcohol use. Therefore, for NIAAA to achieve its goal of reducing the heavy burden of illness from alcohol misuse, the Institute's research focus must be broader than simply reducing alcohol-related mortality; it must encompass reducing the risk for all of the aforementioned negative alcohol-related outcomes at all stages of life. (Li 2008, p. 1)

In the United States, alcohol abuse and addiction are a major burden to society. Estimates of the total overall costs of alcohol abuse in the United States—including health- and crime-related costs as well as losses in productivity—exceed $235 billion (National Institute on Drug Abuse [NIDA] 2011).

Regarding how the burden of the costs of alcohol abuse is distributed across various segments of society, **Figure 8.4** shows the cost of alcohol abuse with the percentages and categories of $223.5 billion (total cost) due to excessive alcohol consumption in the United States in 2006. The following are major factors that comprise Figure 8.4; see figure (Bouchery et al. 2011 unless otherwise noted):

- The cost of excessive alcohol consumption in the United States reached $223.5 billion in 2006. The costs largely resulted from losses in workplace productivity (72.2% of the total cost), healthcare expenses for problems caused by excessive drinking (11.0% of total), law enforcement and other criminal justice expenses related to excessive alcohol consumption (9.4% of total), and motor vehicle crash costs from impaired driving (7.4% of the total) (Bouchery et al. 2011; CDC 2014); see Figure 8.4.

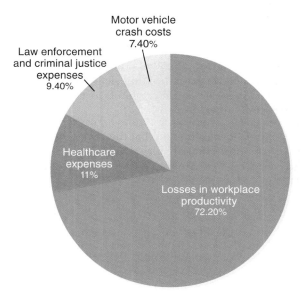

FIGURE 8.4 Cost of alcohol abuse: Percentages and categories of $223.5 billion (total cost) due to excessive alcohol consumption in the United States: 2006.

Data from Bouchery E. E, H. J. Harwood, J. J. Sacks, C. J. Simon, and R. D. Brewer. "*Economic Costs of Excessive Alcohol Consumption in the U.S., 2006.*" American Journal of Preventive Medicine 41 (November 2011): 516-524. Available http://www.ajpmonline.org/article/S0749-3797(11)00538-1/fulltext

- Overall, $94.2 billion (42.1%) of the total economic cost of excessive alcohol use was borne by government, including federal, state, and local government agencies, while almost as much $92.9 billion (41.5%) was borne by excessive drinkers and their family members.
- By cost category, excessive drinkers and their households bore 10.3% of the $24.6 billion in total healthcare expenditures related to excessive alcohol consumption. In contrast, government entities bore most (60.9%) of these costs, which is more than the proportion of total healthcare spending that is covered by government (46.1%).
- In contrast, slightly more than half (54.6%) of productivity losses were borne by excessive drinkers and their households, 35.1% by government, and the remainder by others in society.
- Nearly three-fourths of the costs borne by the federal government take the form of reduced tax revenues resulting from alcohol-related productivity losses; most of the remaining federal burden relates to healthcare costs. The burden on state and local governments (reductions in tax revenue) resulting from such productivity losses accounts for just over half, while 38% is for criminal justice and motor vehicle–related costs. Private insurance arrangements (including life, health, auto, fire, and other kinds of insurance) shoulder the burden for 10% of the total estimated cost, primarily in the area of healthcare costs and motor vehicle crashes.
- Victims of alcohol-related crimes (including homicide) and nondrinking victims of alcohol-related motor vehicle crashes bear 6% to 9% of the total costs.

Other findings include that the percentage of traffic fatalities that are alcohol related remains at around 40%, according to data from the National Highway Transportation Safety Administration's Fatality Analysis Reporting System (FARS) (CESAR 2005). In addition, the NIAAA has reported the following:

- Nearly 88,000 people (approximately 62,000 men and 26,000 women) die from alcohol-related causes annually, making it the third leading preventable cause of death in the United States (NIAAA 2015a).
- In 2013, alcohol-impaired driving fatalities accounted for 10,076 deaths (30.8% of overall driving fatalities) (NIAAA 2015a).

Current advertisement stressing the need to have a designated non-alcohol-consuming driver if others are consuming alcohol.

- Almost three quarters of the total cost of alcohol misuse is related to binge drinking (NIAAA 2015a).
- Total costs attributed to alcohol-related motor vehicle crashes were estimated to be $24.7 billion (NIAAA 2000).
- Expenditures for alcohol-related crime totaled $6.2 billion and for illicit drugs $17.4 billion (NIAAA 2000).
- Alcohol abuse is estimated to have contributed to 25% to 30% of violent crime (NIAAA 2000).
- Alcohol is officially linked to at least half of all highway fatalities, and that figure includes only legal intoxication. In all states, the cutoff for the blood alcohol level is 0.08%. In as many as 70% of all single-vehicle fatal crashes on weekend nights, the driver was legally intoxicated, and this proportion holds during most weekends throughout the United States. Interestingly, this single issue has been the only alcohol problem that has inspired very vocal and effective groups to lobby for stricter enforcement of laws against alcohol-impaired automobile driving. Groups such as MADD (Mothers Against Drunk Driving) and SADD (Students Against Drunk Driving) are the largest prevention organizations in the nation (NIAAA 2000).

History of Alcohol in America

▮ Drinking Patterns

From a peak in 1830, when the amount of alcohol ingested by the average American was 7.1 gallons per year, use declined continuously until 1871–1880, when the average was 1.72 gallons. Numbers then rose to a high in 1906–1910 of

2.6 gallons, and then fell to 1.96 gallons just before Prohibition, 1916–1919. Under Prohibition, less than a gallon of absolute alcohol per person was consumed annually, on average. During the last half of the 20th century, alcohol consumption stayed constant, within the 2- to 3-gallon range. Wine and beer gained in popularity, whereas the popularity of "spirits" (hard liquor) declined (Hanson 2009; Lender and Martin 1987).

■ Historical Considerations

Alcoholic beverages have played an important role in the history of the United States as well as in most countries throughout the world. Most likely, fermentation was the first method for making alcohol, dating to around 4200 BC. As early as AD 100, it appears that brandy was the first distilled beverage. In Ireland and Scotland, whiskey was first distilled in the 1400s, and gin began appearing in the 1600s, after being initially distilled by a Flemish physician. Other types of liquor also have distinct origins. For example, rum was first invented in Barbados in the 1650s. Bourbon was first made near Georgetown, Kentucky, in the late 1700s. In the United States, the first distillery was established in the 1600s in the area that is now New York City.

In colonial America, alcohol was viewed very favorably. From an economic standpoint, the manufacturing of rum, "which is the residue left after sugar has been made from sugar cane . . . was introduced to the world, and presumably invented, by the first European settlers in the West Indies (no one knows when it was first produced or by what individual)" (Hanson 2009). Rum became New England's largest and most profitable industry in the so-called triangle trade. It acquired this name because Yankee traders would sail with a cargo of rum to the West Coast of Africa, where they bargained the "demon" for slaves. From there, they sailed to the West Indies, where they bartered the slaves for molasses. Finally, they took the molasses back to New England, where it was made into rum, thus completing the triangle. For many years, New England distilleries flourished and the slave trade proved highly lucrative (see **Figure 8.5**). "[In] . . . 1657, a rum distillery was operating in Boston. It was highly successful and within a generation the manufacture of rum would become colonial New England's largest and most prosperous industry" (Roueche 1963, p. 178). This slave trade triangle continued until 1807, when an act of Congress prohibited the importation of slaves.

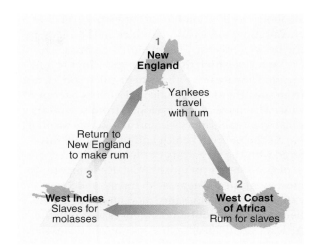

FIGURE 8.5 Slave trade triangle.

From a social standpoint, the consumption of alcohol was seen as a part of life. The colonial tavern "was a key institution, the center of social and political life" (Levine 1983, p. 66). In the 17th and 18th centuries, alcohol flowed freely at weddings, baptisms, and funerals. Especially in the 18th century, people drank at home, at work, and while traveling. In the 19th century, largely because of the temperance movement, taverns became stigmatized and were viewed as dens where the lower classes, immigrants, and mostly men would congregate. "Any drinking, [Lyman Beecher] argued, was a step toward 'irreclaimable' slavery to liquor" (Lender and Martin 1987). People in the 19th century began to report that they were addicted to alcohol. This is when the temperance movement had its effect in bringing about a change in attitudes regarding drinking.

FROM THE TEMPERANCE MOVEMENT (1830–1850) TO THE PROHIBITION ERA (1920–1933)

The time from the temperance movement to the Prohibition era was a very turbulent period in the history of alcohol in the United States. The period of heaviest drinking in the United States began during President Jefferson's term of office (1801–1809). The nation was going through uneasy times, trying to stay out of the war between Napoleon and the British allies. The transient population had increased, especially in the seaport cities, and the migration westward had begun. Heavy drinking had become a major form of recreation and a "social lubricant" at elections and public gatherings. The temperance movement never began with the intention of stopping alcohol consumption but rather with the goal of encouraging moderation. In fact, in the 1830s, at the peak of this early campaign, temperance leaders (many of whom drank beer and wine) recommended abstinence only from distilled spirits, not from the other forms of alcohol such as beer or wine. This movement developed from several very vocal spiritual leaders who preached that alcohol harms the nation's health and that alcohol interfered with the spreading of the gospel. Later, as is explained shortly in more detail, the temperance movement turned against all forms of alcohol.

Because the temperance movement was closely tied to the abolitionist movement as well as to the African American church, African Americans were preeminent promoters of temperance. Leaders such as Frederick Douglass stated, "[I]t was as well to be a slave to master, as to whisky and rum. When a slave was drunk, the slaveholder had no fear that he would plan an insurrection; no fear that he would escape to the north. It was the sober, thinking slave who was dangerous, and needed the vigilance of his master to keep him a slave" (Douglass 1892, p. 133).

Over the next decades, partly in connection with religious revivals, the meaning of temperance was gradually altered from "moderation" to "total abstinence." All alcoholic beverages were attacked as being unnecessary, harmful to health, and inherently poisonous. Over the course of the 19th century, the demand gradually arose for total prohibition (Austin 1978).

By the late 19th and early 20th centuries, a number of countries either passed legislation or created alcohol restrictions. Most of these laws and restrictions eventually failed. In the United States, attempts to control, restrict, or abolish alcohol were made, but they all met with abysmal failure. From 1907 to 1919, 34 states passed prohibition laws. Finally, on a national scale, the

18th Amendment to the Constitution was ratified in 1919 in an attempt to stop the rapid spread of alcohol addiction. In January 1920, alcohol was outlawed. As soon as such a widely used substance became illegal, criminal activity to satisfy the huge demand for alcohol flourished. Illegal outlets developed for purchasing liquor. Numerous not-so-secret **speakeasies** developed as illegal establishments where people could buy and consume alcoholic beverages despite the laws of Prohibition. **Bootlegging** was a widely accepted activity. In effect, such involvement in "dens of sin" filled the vacuum for many drinkers during Prohibition.

During the temperance movement and Prohibition period, doctors and druggists prescribed whiskey and other alcohol products known as **patent medicines** (see "Case in Point: The Great American Fraud: Patent Medicines"). By 1928, doctors made an estimated $40 million per year writing prescriptions for whiskey. Patent medicines flourished, with alcohol contents as high as 50%. Whisko, a "nonintoxicating stimulant," was 55 proof (or 27.5% alcohol). Another, Kaufman's Sulfur Bitters, was labeled "contains no alcohol" but was 40 proof (20% alcohol) and did not contain sulfur. There were dozens of others, many of which contained other types of drugs, such as opium.

Both Prohibitionists and critics of the law were shocked by the violent gang wars that broke out between rivals seeking to control the lucrative black market in liquor. More important, a general disregard for the law developed. Corruption among law enforcement agents was widespread, and organized crime began and grew to be an enormous illegitimate business. In reaction to these developments, political support rallied against Prohibition, resulting in its repeal in 1933 by the 21st Amendment. Early in the 20th century, women suffragettes had been prominent temperance organizers; paradoxically, flappers organized against Prohibition and were vital in gathering the signatures for its repeal.

Three main developments occurred because of Prohibition. First, alcohol use continued to diminish for the first 2 or 3 years after Prohibition was in effect. This trend had begun several years before the law was passed. More important, after 3 years of steady decline, the use of distilled liquors rose every year afterward. Further, even minors were becoming addicted to alcohol during this period.

Second, enforcement of laws against alcohol use was thwarted by corrupt law enforcement officials, enforcement was uneven (in some areas of the United States enforcement was lax, whereas in other areas it was very strict), and law enforcement

KEY TERM

speakeasies
small, often backroom bars where alcoholic beverages were illegally consumed and sold during the Prohibition era from 1920 to 1933 (in some states, Prohibition was longer than this period of time)

bootlegging
making, distributing, and selling alcoholic beverages during the Prohibition era

patent medicines
the ingredients in these uncontrolled "medicines" were secret, often consisting of large amounts of colored water, alcohol, cocaine, or opiates

experienced more than 50% turnover in its ranks. Corruption of law enforcement officials stands out as a paramount concern. Reportedly, 10% of law enforcement was "on the take" and had to be continually discharged.

Third, among the Western Europeans who immigrated to the United States en masse during this period, the consumption of alcohol was culturally prescribed. Prohibition against alcohol usage to the Italian, German, French, Polish, Irish, and other European-based immigrants was perceived as unnecessary and an infringement of the right to common existence. One 93-year-old Italian American émigré to Chicago exemplified some of these attitudes:

> Well, when we were not allowed to drink because of the government, I thought it was a stupid law. Many of us here in the neighborhood [a fading Italian American community on Chicago's West Side and the original home of Venturelli] made lots of money as "alki cookers."
>
> We would make the alcohol in our bathtubs and sell to other people or even to those mafia types. Oh, it was horrible cheap and crappy alcohol; if you drank too much the night before, it gave you headaches sometimes for days. On Sunday afternoons, if you walked through this neighborhood in the hot summer days, you could smell the alcohol oozing from people's windows. Nearly everyone

Al Capone ("Scarface") (center), the undisputed leader of Chicago's gang scene during Prohibition, made millions of dollars in his bootlegging operations until he was convicted of tax evasion in 1931 and eventually imprisoned in Alcatraz.

> my mother's and father's age and older at the time made extra money as alki cookers. It was actually a good law [referring to Prohibition] for making a few bucks to help out the family expenses. No one around here gave a damn about the law, because too many were "on the take" so-to-say . . . and it was not just us [referring to the local Italian Americans]. At least for us when we meet together and eat for fun, alcohol is like the air we breathe. Who the hell is going to change that, especially something so deep? *(From Venturelli's research files, male neighborhood resident, age 93, May 26, 2000)*

▶ **CASE IN POINT**

The Great American Fraud: Patent Medicines

In the late 1800s and early 1900s, before the days of U.S. Food and Drug Administration (FDA) legislation, the sale of uncontrolled medicines flourished and became widespread. Many of these products were called *patent medicines*, which signified that the ingredients were secret, not that they were patented. The law of the day seemed to be more concerned with someone's recipe being stolen than with preventing harm to the naive consumer. Some of these patent medicines included toxic ingredients such as acetanilide in Bromo-Seltzer and Orangeine and prussic (hydrocyanic) acid in Shiloh's Consumption Cure.

Most patent medicines appear to have been composed largely of either colored water or alcohol, with an occasional added ingredient such as opium or cocaine. Hostetter's Stomach Bitters with 44% alcohol could easily have been classified as liquor. Sale of Peruna (28% alcohol) was prohibited to Native Americans because of its high alcohol content. Birney's Catarrh Cure contained 4% cocaine. Wistar's Balsam of Wild Cherry, Dr. King's Discovery for Consumption, Mrs. Winslow's Soothing Syrup, and several others contained opiates as well as alcohol.

The medical profession of the middle and late 19th century was ill prepared to do battle with the ever-present manufacturers and distributors of patent medicines. Qualified physicians during this time were rare. Much more common were medical practitioners with poor training and little scientific understanding. In fact, many of these early physicians practiced a

(continues)

► **CASE IN POINT**

The Great American Fraud: Patent Medicines (*continued*)

brand of medicine that was generally useless and frequently more life-threatening than the patent medicines themselves.

In 1905, *Collier's Magazine* ran a series of articles called the "Great American Fraud," which warned of the abuse of patent medicines. This brought the problem to the public's attention (Adams 1906). *Collier's* coined the phrase "dope fiend" from *dope*, an African word meaning "intoxicating substance." The American Medical Association (AMA) joined in and widely distributed reprints of the *Collier's* story to inform the public about the dangers of these medicines, even though the AMA itself accepted advertisements for patent medicines that physicians knew were addicting. The publicity created mounting pressure on Congress and President Theodore Roosevelt to do something about these fraudulent products. In 1905, Roosevelt proposed that a law be enacted to regulate interstate commerce of misbranded and adulterated foods, drinks, and drugs. This movement received further impetus when Upton Sinclair's book *The Jungle* was published in 1906—this nauseatingly realistic exposé detailed how immigrant laborers worked under appalling conditions of filth, disease, putrefaction, and other extreme exploitations at Chicago's stockyards.

Two substances used in patent medicines helped shape attitudes that would form the basis of regulatory policies for years to come: the opium derivatives

(narcotic drugs, such as heroin and morphine) and cocaine.

This poster advertises one of the patent medicines that contained liberal doses of opium and a high concentration of alcohol. This medicine was widely used to treat tuberculosis ("consumption") around the turn of the 20th century, when more than 25% of all adult deaths were attributable to this disease. The U.S government finally forced the remedy off the market by 1920.

Data from Adams, S. H. "The Great American Fraud." *Collier's* 36(5) (1905): 17–18; (10) (1905): 16–18; (16) (1906): 18–20.

Defining Alcoholics

As discussed at the beginning of this chapter, creating absolute definitions or categories of behavior that represent an alcoholic type is very difficult because behaviors vary enormously from one person to the next; thus, most behaviors range along a continuum. Adding to this confusion is the fact that some disagreement exists among experts on what the exact criteria should be regarding the definition of an alcoholic. In other words, when can a person be defined as an alcoholic? Is it the daily drinker or the inebriated weekend drinker? What if the excessive drinking involves only one type of liquor, such as beer, which is often considered less potent than hard liquor? What if the

person is able to maintain a job and provide for his or her family? How does this type of alcoholic compare with an unemployed resident of skid row? In the minds of many Americans, an alcoholic is a derelict who frequents skid rows, train stations, and bus terminals; panders for money; and sleeps on a park bench at night. Yet, this stereotypical image of an alcoholic represents only a very small percentage of the millions of Americans who qualify as alcoholic by any of the accepted medical definitions. The more typical alcoholic, in fact, is similar to the example of the professor or businessman purchasing alcohol at a liquor store described at the opening of this chapter. In effect, most functioning alcoholics are secret or closeted drinkers who look very much like everyday working people.

■ Cultural Differences

Although more will be presented later in this chapter about the pervasive role that culture plays in drinking behavior, we begin with a quote highlighting cultural differences in interpreting alcohol consumption:

> Even definitions of a "problem drinker" differ from one culture to the next. In Poland, loss of productivity tends to demonstrate a drinking problem, while Californians emphasize drunk driving as an important and sometimes key indicator.... [Among Italian Americans, an inability to provide for one's family because of heavy drinking qualifies a person as an alcoholic.] Some methods of assessing problem drinking look to behavior that leads to a brush with the law. However, drunkenness may or may not lead to disruptive behavior.
>
> In the Netherlands, alcoholic beverage consumption is similar to that in Finland and Poland, but there is much less disruptive or public drinking. In these nations, the actual amount of alcohol consumed is not indicated by the arrest figures, the actual amount consumed (as a separate category), and the number of physical ailments caused by excessive alcohol consumption. Secondly, the social response to drunkenness may not be arrest and conviction. Ireland, for example, has traditionally used psychiatric institutions to control drunkenness. (Osterberg 1986, p. 83)

Estimates vary, but it is believed that approximately three-fourths of problem drinkers are men and one-fourth are women. The proportion of women has risen in recent years. This increase has occurred for two reasons: (1) women as problem drinkers are more visible and numerous because they now make up about half of the workforce, and (2) women are more likely to acknowledge the problem and seek treatment, especially if they are in white-collar occupations. Thus, female problem drinkers may now be more visible and more self-assured as well as more numerous.

Next, in attempting to define alcoholism, we turn to models that speak of the state of addiction. **Alcoholism** is a state of physical and psychological addiction to ethanol, a psychoactive substance. It was once viewed as a vice and dismissed as sinful, but over the years there has been a shift from this perspective to one that views alcoholism as a disease. The sinfulness perspective failed to focus on the fact that alcoholism is an addiction—an illness—and not the result of a lack of personal discipline and morality.

Attempts to expand the basic definition of alcoholism to include symptoms of the condition and psychological and sociological factors have been difficult; no one definition satisfies everyone. In 1980, the World Health Organization defined alcohol dependence syndrome as a syndrome characterized by a state, mental and usually also physical, resulting from drinking alcohol. This state is characterized by behavioral and other responses that include a compulsion to drink alcohol (like an unquenchable thirst) on a continuous or periodic basis to experience its psychic effects and sometimes to avoid the discomfort of its absence; tolerance may or may not be present (NIAAA 1980).

Another more classic explanation of alcoholism that remains popular is that "[a]lcoholism is a chronic behavioral disorder manifested by repeated drinking of alcoholic beverages in excess of the dietary and social uses of the community, to an extent that interferes with the drinker's health or his [or her] social or economic functioning" (Keller 1958, p. 78). Another definition emphasizes that "[a]lcoholism is a chronic, primary, hereditary disease that progresses from an early, physiological susceptibility into an addiction characterized by tolerance changes, physiological dependence, and loss of control over drinking. [In this definition], [p]sychological symptoms are secondary to the physiological disease and not relevant to its onset" (Gold 1991, p. 99).

A final definition, from Royce and Scratchley (2007), defines "alcoholism as a chronic primary illness or disorder characterized by some loss of control over drinking, with habituation or addiction to the drug alcohol, or causing interference in any major life function, for example: health, job, family, friends, legal or spiritual" (p. 203). In their working definition of alcoholism, Royce and Scratchley list three major factors: "(1) Some loss of control, but it need not be total . . . (2) Dependence or need can be psychological or physiological . . . and (3) Interference with normal functioning" (p. 203).

KEY TERM

alcoholism
a medical condition consisting of a physical and psychological addiction to ethanol (alcohol), a psychoactive substance

In summary, the preceding definitions either list or hint at the following major components of alcoholism (NIAAA 2007a):

- *Craving*: An overwhelming compulsion to drink even when not feasible, such as at work, while driving a car, while mowing a lawn, and so on.
- *Very impaired or loss of control*: An inability to limit one's drinking once drinking has begun; for example, one drink only before going to bed is impossible to control.
- *Physical dependence*: The presence of withdrawal symptoms when attempting to abstain from usage. Such symptoms as nausea, sweating, shakiness, and anxiety about the availability of alcohol are common.
- *Tolerance*: A need to continually increase the amount of alcohol consumed to maintain its effects (or to maintain the "buzz").

▎ Alcohol Abuse and Alcoholism Disorders

When attempting to understand the meaning of chronic drinking, one additional clarification that should be made is to distinguish between **alcohol abuse** and alcoholism. The two explanations of drinking behavior differ as a matter of degree. When speaking of alcohol abuse, the craving, loss of control, and physical dependence just listed as primary manifestations are less prominent and not as pronounced as in alcoholism. There is diminished ability to fulfill obligations and goals; more occasions of drinking at the wrong time, such as while driving; legal problems, such as driving under the influence; and relationship problems. Note that many of these problems that result from alcohol abuse are also experienced by alcoholics, but not all manifestations of alcoholics are experienced by alcohol abusers. For example, an alcoholic may repeatedly argue with family members two or three times per week, whereas an alcohol abuser may have fewer occurrences of the same type of alcohol-inspired arguments with a family member. Thus, even though the alcohol abuser has fewer occasions of uncontrollable

KEY TERM

alcohol abuse
uncontrollable drinking that leads to alcohol craving, loss of control, and physical dependence but with less prominent characteristics than found in alcoholism

drinking than the alcoholic, the drinking remains largely uncontrollable when it occurs. For many years, people with drinking problems were lumped together under the label *alcoholic*, and alcohol abusers were assumed to be suffering from the same illness. Today, because of greater understanding about addiction and addictive behaviors, the distinction between the two terms leads to a more precise understanding of excessive alcohol abuse (see "Here and Now: Do You Have an Alcohol Use Disorder?").

▎ Types of Alcoholics

Although written more than five decades ago, Jellinek's (1960) original personality typology (characterizations) differentiating the types of alcoholics remains historically interesting but dated.[2] Jellinek is credited with adding descriptive content in classifying alcohol abuse and its outcomes. Jellinek's categories are as follows:

- *Alpha alcoholism*: Mostly a psychological dependence on alcohol to bolster an inability to cope with life. The alpha type constantly needs alcohol and becomes irritable and anxious when it is not available.
- *Beta alcoholism*: Mostly a social dependence on alcohol. Often, although not exclusively, this type is a heavy beer drinker who continues to meet social and economic obligations. Some nutritional deficiencies can occur, including organic damage such as gastritis and cirrhosis.
- *Gamma alcoholism*: The most severe form of alcoholism. This type of alcoholic suffers from emotional and psychological impairment. Jellinek believed this type of alcoholic suffers from a true disease that progresses from a psychological dependence to physical dependence. Loss of control over when alcohol is consumed and how much is taken characterizes the latter phase of this type of alcoholism.

---

[2] Prior to and during the late 1950s and 1960s when Jellinek created his personality typology, the field of psychology was in a disease-centered era regarding alcoholics and alcoholism. Today, with increasing emphasis on using a more person-centered approach, people with alcohol problems in the *Diagnostic and Statistical Manual of Mental Disorders (DSM-5)* (published by the American Psychiatric Association; APA 2013) are referred to as having substance use disorders. We also have to realize that the *DSM-5* is used primarily by therapists and psychologists as a diagnostic resource for diagnosing and categorizing mental disorders.

HERE AND NOW
Do You Have an Alcohol Use Disorder?

When problem drinking becomes severe, the medical diagnosis is *alcohol use disorder*, or AUD. A diagnosis of AUD must meet certain criteria outlined in the *Diagnostic and Statistical Manual of Mental Disorders* (*DSM*). In the current edition of the *DSM*, the *DSM-5*, anyone meeting any 2 of the following 11 criteria during the same 12-month period meet the requirements for a diagnosis of AUD. The severity of an AUD diagnosis ranges from mild, moderate, to severe, based on the number of criteria met (NIAAA n.d.).

To assess whether you or a loved one may have an AUD, here are some critical questions to ask. In the past year have you:

- Had times when you ended up drinking more, or longer, than you intended?

- More than once wanted to cut down or stop drinking, or tried to, but couldn't?

- Spent a lot of time drinking? Or being sick or getting over the aftereffects?

- Experienced craving—a strong need, or urge, to drink?

- Found that drinking—or being sick from drinking—often interfered with taking care of your home or family? Or caused job troubles? Or school problems?

- Continued to drink even though it was causing trouble with your family or friends?

- Given up or cut back on activities that were important or interesting to you, or gave you pleasure, in order to drink?

- More than once gotten into situations while or after drinking that increased your chances of getting hurt (such as driving, swimming, using machinery, walking in a dangerous area, or having unsafe sex)?

- Continued to drink even though it was making you feel depressed or anxious or adding to another health problem? Or after having had a memory blackout?

- Had to drink much more than you once did to get the effect you want? Or found that your usual number of drinks had much less effect than before?

- Found that when the effects of alcohol were wearing off, you had withdrawal symptoms, such as trouble sleeping, shakiness, irritability, anxiety, depression, restlessness, nausea, or sweating? Or sensed things that were not there?

If you have any of these symptoms, your drinking may already be a cause for concern. The more symptoms you have, the more urgent the need for change. A health professional can conduct a formal assessment of your symptoms to see if an alcohol use disorder is present.

Ultimately, receiving treatment can improve an individual's chances of success in overcoming an AUD. Talk with your doctor to determine the best course of action for you and see *Rethinking Drinking* (at http://rethinkingdrinking.niaaa.nih.gov) and Treatment for Alcohol Problems: Finding and Getting Help (at http://pubs.niaaa.nih.gov/publications /Treatment/treatment.htm) for more information.

Data from National Institute on Alcohol Abuse and Alcoholism (NIAAA). "Alcohol Use Disorder." n.d. Available http://www.niaaa.nih.gov/alcohol-health/overview-alcohol-consumption/alcohol-use-disorders and the American Psychiatric Association (APA). "Substance Related and Addictive Disorders." In *Diagnostic and Statistical Manual of Mental Disorders (DSM-5)*, 5th ed., 481–589. Washington, DC: American Psychiatric Association, 2013.

- *Delta alcoholic*: Also called the "maintenance drinker" (Royce 1989), this type of alcoholic loses control over drinking and cannot abstain for even a day or two. Many wine-drinking countries, such as France and Italy, contain delta-type alcoholics who sip wine throughout most of their waking hours. Being "tipsy" but never completely inebriated is typical of the delta alcoholic.
- *Epsilon alcoholic*: This type of alcoholic is characterized as a binge drinker. The epsilon-type drinker drinks excessively for a certain period (for days and sometimes weeks) but then abstains completely from alcohol until the next binge period. The dependence on alcohol is both physical and psychological. Loss of control over the amount consumed is another characteristic of this type of alcoholic.
- *Zeta alcoholic*: This category was added to Jellinek's types to describe the moderate drinker who becomes abusive and violent. Although this type also is referred to as a "pathological drinker" or "mad drunk," zeta types may not be addicted to alcohol.

Another, much more recent classification of alcoholism subtypes includes five alcohol-dependent subtypes created by Dr. Moss and colleagues (NIAAA 2007b). Quoted extensively, the five types are the following:

- *Young adult subtype*: 31.5% of U.S. alcoholics. Young adult drinkers, with relatively low rates of co-occurring substance abuse and other mental disorders and a low rate of family alcoholism and who rarely seek any kind of help for their drinking.
- *Young antisocial subtype*: 21% of U.S. alcoholics. Tend to be in their mid-20s and had early onset of regular drinking and alcohol problems. More than half come from families with alcoholism, and about half have a psychiatric diagnosis of antisocial personality disorder. Many have major depression, bipolar disorder, and anxiety problems. More than 75% smoke cigarettes and marijuana, and many have cocaine and opiate addictions. More than one third of these alcoholics seek help for their drinking.
- *Functional subtype*: 19.5% of U.S. alcoholics. Typically, middle-aged, well-educated, with stable jobs and families. About one third have a multigenerational family history of alcoholism, about one quarter have major depressive illness sometime in their lives, and nearly 50% are smokers.
- *Intermediate familial subtype*: 19% of U.S. alcoholics. Middle-aged, with about 50% from families with multigenerational alcoholism. Almost half have had clinical depression, and 20% have had bipolar disorder. Most of these individuals smoke cigarettes, and nearly one in five have had problems with cocaine and marijuana use. Only 25% ever seek treatment for their problem drinking.

- *Chronic severe subtype*: 9% of U.S. alcoholics. Composed mostly of middle-aged individuals who had early onset of drinking and alcohol problems, with high rates of antisocial personality disorder and criminality. Almost 80% come from families with multigenerational alcoholism. They have the highest rates of other psychiatric disorders, including depression, bipolar disorder, and anxiety disorders, as well as high rates of smoking and marijuana, cocaine, and opiate dependence. Two-thirds of these alcoholics seek help for their drinking problems, making them the most prevalent type of alcoholic in treatment.

Other classifications differentiate alcoholics by their reaction to the drug as quiet, sullen, friendly, or angry types. Another method is to classify alcoholics according to their drinking patterns: occupational, social, escape, and emotional.

■ Major Traditional Distinctions Between "Wet" and "Dry" Cultures

Before delving into the next section regarding how culture defines and views the use of alcohol, it is interesting to note that alcohol researchers traditionally distinguished countries as either wet or dry. In **wet cultures**, alcohol is integrated into daily life and activities (e.g., is consumed with meals) and is widely available and accessible. In these cultures, abstinence rates are low, and wine is largely the beverage of preference. European countries bordering the Mediterranean have traditionally exemplified wet cultures.

In **dry cultures**, alcohol consumption is not as common during everyday activities (e.g., it is less frequently a part of meals), and access to alcohol is more restricted. Abstinence is more common, but when drinking occurs, it is more likely to result in

KEY TERMS

wet cultures
alcohol *is integrated* into daily life and activities (e.g., is consumed with meals) and is widely available and accessible (e.g., European countries bordering the Mediterranean have traditionally exemplified wet cultures)

dry cultures
alcohol consumption is *not* as common during everyday activities (e.g., it is less frequently a part of meals) and access to alcohol is more restricted; abstinence is more common (e.g., Scandinavian countries, the United States, and Canada)

Many cultural social interactions demand drinking together.

intoxication; moreover, wine consumption is less common. Examples of traditionally dry cultures include the Scandinavian countries, the United States, and Canada (Bloomfield et al. 2003). Recent comparative research, however, has found that, especially in Europe, the wet/dry distinction seems to be disappearing and a homogenization of consumption rates and beverage preferences is increasingly evident. Room and Mäkelä (2000) have reconsidered the simple wet/dry dichotomy and have instead proposed a new typology that considers a variety of drinking behaviors, such as the regularity of drinking and the extent of drunkenness. Such a typology may better fit the distinctions in drinking cultures that are emerging today. Nevertheless, the wet/dry dichotomy has represented a scale of extremes on which to measure drinking cultures and around which a fair amount of past research literature has been organized (Bloomfield et al. 2003).

Cultural Influences

This section explains how views of alcohol are culturally determined—that is, how culture encodes the thoughts, attitudes, values, and beliefs about alcohol, and how it influences our behavior regarding the use and abuse of alcohol.

> I started drinking heavily at college after I joined a fraternity. We had many nights of drinking and good times. When I turned 21, I got a part time job at a pizzeria waiting on tables. It was a fun job in that the owners were pretty big drug users and did not care if the student workers drank especially after hours into the early mornings sitting around the bar area after we closed for the night. I kept drinking after graduation and never paid attention to how often and how much drank. I knew it was a lot of drinking I was doing but I never thought of myself as having an alcohol problem. About 15 years later, I got married and wouldn't you know it, I married a woman who also had a drinking problem. Right now, I am in counseling for alcoholism and though I am trying to slow down on the drinking with the end goal to quit, I get mixed results. On the days I abstain after 2 days of not drinking, I find my car after work automatically drives to liquor stores. I say automatic because on the days I am not drinking I know each and every liquor store I pass while driving home with a tempting desire to stop in and buy liquor for

the night before I get home and have dinner. After a few days I just end up in the parking lot of a liquor store and give up, walk in and buy my hard liquor for another night of drinking. Nearly all of the liquor stores know me by first name and here I am close to 40 years of age and I have a pretty bad alcohol problem. My wife and I make all these promises to quit but we never do it. My wife and I are so bad that we always end up hearing the bartender making the last call for the night. We just never leave until closing time. I am on special types of drugs now that lessen the desire but it's a very hard to stop drinking for more than 2 to 3 days before we break down and resume our alcohol addiction. We are both talking about going to a rehab center to try and get a grip on stopping the alcohol. Waking up with a hangover is normal at our house, so we are still pretty bad with the drinking. *(From Venturelli's research files, male working as a mortgage loan officer, residing in northwest Indiana, age 37, January 21, 2016)*

Or,

Q: Do you consider yourself a heavy drinker?
A: No, I only drink beer.
Q: But, you are often drunk at night?
A: Yeah, but it's only beer—it certainly is a lot better than drinking the hard stuff.

These two interviews illustrate a belief shared by many Americans, which is that the milder alcohols such as beer, wine, and wine coolers are outside the domain of potentially addictive types of beverages. Some may even believe that the distilled spirits such as vodka, gin, and whiskey are the only types of addictive alcoholic beverages. Finally, the comment that "I don't use and never would use drugs; I only drink" can easily be heard being espoused by a large portion of Americans (probably a majority), who place alcohol in a completely separate category from drugs. However, each 12-ounce bottle of beer is equal to 1 ounce of liquor. Thus, two beers equal a double shot of bourbon or vodka.

■ Culture and Drinking Behavior

Another way of looking at how culture influences us is to stand outside of our culture and see how people behave when intoxicated in our culture and in a variety of other cultures in an effort to understand the real relationship among culture, alcohol, and human beings. A major contribution to our knowledge of intoxicated behavior from an outside perspective comes from the field of cultural anthropology.

As we saw earlier in the distinction between wet and dry cultures, how alcohol is used varies culturally. Does culture also affect how or in what way we view alcohol? Why would our culture differ from other cultures in the use and abuse of alcoholic beverages? We focus on these two questions in this section.

Throughout the world, cultures create a climate for the development of attitudes toward most behaviors. Like other behaviors, the use of alcohol is embedded within our culture. Culture does more than contain the attitudes and feelings that people have toward alcohol use—it dictates the variety, the attachment, and the intensity of attitudes that are held toward other people's behavior. For example, in the 1930s, American college students acquired a "reverence for strong drink" (Room 1984, p. 8). Although for decades many people believed that college students "majored in drinking," during the 1930s, students grew to consider heavy use as romantic and adult, resonating with the romantic, heavy-drinking expatriate community of writers in Paris, such as Ernest Hemingway.

American culture in general views ethanol-containing beverages as being sexy, mature, and sophisticated, facilitating socializing and enhancing status. Today, many of these beliefs are communicated through the mass media, and advertising is a key medium of communication. Advertising uses positive images to persuade observers to purchase a particular brand of alcohol. For example, what messages are found in newspapers and especially magazines about drinking certain types of wine, bourbon, gin, scotch, and the numerous types of domestic and imported beers? What attitudes are generally conveyed when a sexy, glamorous woman is dressed in formal evening attire standing next to her man in front of a perfectly glowing fireplace, smiling confidently as he stares into her eyes and sips his special-label cognac?

■ Culture and Disinhibited Behavior

The concept of **drunken comportment** was first formulated by MacAndrew and Edgerton (1969). Drunken comportment refers to the behavior demonstrated while under the influence of alcohol within the norms and expectations of a particular culture. Instead of simply labeling drinking behavior as "drunken behavior," this concept sensitizes us to how drinking behavior is influenced by cultural norms and expectations. For example, in the United States, drinking is comported to mean time out away from duties and obligations. "The symbolism of alcohol in American culture contains this motif of release and remission, as in the emergence of TGIF [Thank God It's Friday]" (Gusfield 1986, p. 203). Another example is that in some cultures, drinking occurs during celebrations and festivities, and as part of religious ceremony. In France and Italy, drinking alcohol occurs while eating with family members.

Alcohol is a **disinhibitor**, which refers to depression of the cerebral cortex functions. When this occurs, it results in a suspension of rational or thoughtful constraints on impulsive behavior. Inhibitions (inner raw feelings and attitudes) are normally controlled through rationality and logical thought processes. The popular image of office Christmas parties at which too much alcohol is consumed and parties that get out of control because of overconsumption of alcohol are examples. People at such events can easily become uncontrollable, loud, impulsive, and just plain irrational. In such situations, outbreaks of arguing and physical and verbal abuse are more likely to occur. Such behavior is disinhibited behavior.

Although all of us know that the alcohol content that is usually measured in terms of alcohol proof has an independent effect on the user, two additional factors contribute to the effects of alcohol: **set and setting** (Goode 1999; Zinberg 1984; Zinberg and Robertson 1972). *Set* is the individual's expectation of what a drug will do to his or her personality. *Setting* is both the physical environment and the social environment in which the drug is consumed. How important are these two distinctions? Some psychologists contend that both set and setting can overshadow the pharmacological effects of most drugs. In fact, set and setting are far more influential in determining a

---

KEY TERMS

drunken comportment
behavior exhibited while under the direct influence of alcohol; determined by the norms and expectations of a particular culture

disinhibitor
a psychoactive chemical that depresses thought and judgment functions in the cerebral cortex, which has the effect of allowing relatively unrestrained behavior (as in alcohol inebriation)

set and setting
set refers to the individual's expectation of what a drug will do to his or her personality; setting is the physical and social environments where the drug is consumed

drug user's experience even when less addictive drugs, such as alcohol and marijuana, are used, in contrast to more potent addictive drugs, such as cocaine and heroin. Good examples of this are when people who drink alcohol say "I felt that drink right away" or "I drank a lot last night but I had something on my mind and, dude, I was just not in the partying mood."

A review of various ethnographic studies (Marshall 1983) reveals **pseudointoxicated** behavior (i.e., people acting drunk before or seconds after the bottle is opened or as the drink is consumed) among Tahitians, Rarotongans, Chippewas, Dakotas, Pine Ridge and Teton Sioux, Aleuts, Baffin Island Inuits, and Potawatomi. The frequency of use or the amount consumed has less effect on how drinkers comport themselves; instead, the cultural values, beliefs, mental maps, and norms cause a particular behavioral outcome. Using the terminology of psychology, we would say that it is not the biochemical effects on the brain alone that account for disinhibitory behavior but rather the belief that one has been drinking a substance that has a disinhibitory effect; that is, the mental (cognitive) appraisal of the physiological state allows disinhibited behavior. In using the terminology of sociology and revising a famous sociological axiom, we could say, "What we believe to be (or personally define as true) is true in its consequences or in the obtained results." Thus, if you believe you are drunk and you act drunk, then you are drunk.

Cultures vary in how they evaluate alcohol consumption. Some religions in the United States view drinking as evil, whereas others view alcohol as a gift from God and use it in religious ceremonies. In some subcultures, excessive use of alcohol is an indication of manhood, strength, and virility; in other subcultures, excessive alcohol use in public is disgusting and embarrassing. Even drug education has different perspectives. Do we emphasize total abstinence or teach people how to drink in moderation? Why such vastly different approaches? Because our culture includes contradictory practices on this front.

Similarly, the views we maintain about alcohol abuse and addiction vary. For example, is alcoholism a disease? Is it prescribed by certain customs within ethnic groups? Does it result from some type of personality flaw? The three concepts discussed in this section—drunken comportment, set and setting, and pseudointoxication—demonstrate that social and cultural contexts exert their influences independently of the effects of alcohol consumption.

■ Culture Provides Rules for Drinking Behavior

Many cultures, such as traditional Italian and Jewish cultures, permit moderate drinking within the family, especially at meals, but disapprove of drunken behaviors. Note that many differences separate these groups. For example, Italians use wine as a food item, whereas it has only ritual value among Orthodox Jews. In one study of Scandinavian nations, by contrast, drinking was considered separated from work. Where drinking at work was permitted, however, it was allowed to go on to the point of intoxication (Makela 1986). Finnish, Polish, and Russian cultures are associated with binge drinking, whereas French culture is linked with sipping. In the United States, we encounter a vast variety of subgroups; some heavy drinkers may live in a community in which it is not considered excessive to drink with friends out of paper bags on the street in the morning. In other communities, all outdoor drinking is done in either parks, restaurants, bars, or outdoor cafés. Some people may belong to a "workplace culture of drinking" at a particular country club, construction site, or law firm, where "three-martini lunches" are not unheard of. Perhaps this type of drinking is not much different from the habits of teenage peer groups. To be "treated" for this behavior might seem as strange as going into rehab for acting "normal."

■ Culture Provides Ceremonial Meaning for Alcohol Use

The first notable work on ceremonial use and ethnic drinking practices was undertaken by Bales (1946), who attempted to explain the different rates of drinking between Jews (low) and Irish (high) in terms of symbolic and ceremonial meanings. For Jews, drinking had familial and sacramental significance, whereas for the Irish it represented male convivial bonding.

A high rate of heavy drinking was observed among the Irish in the 1800s. It was said that these individuals drank because they were Irish. Today, some descendants of the Irish continue to live the stereotype; for them, it represents

KEY TERM

pseudointoxicated
acting drunk even before alcohol has had a chance to cause its effects

"Irishness"—they drink because they are Irish. A button displayed on St. Patrick's Day proclaimed, "Today I'm Irish, Tomorrow I'm Hung Over," and a *New York Post* supplement declared this event to be "Three Days of Drinking and Revelry." With regard to Hasidic Jews, the belief is that they can "drink alcohol, [and] it is considered a 'mitzvah' (good deed) when done so on the Sabbath and on holidays" (Answers.com 2011). Further, Rabbi Daniel Siegel writes,

> [O]verall, the approach of the Jewish rabbinic tradition is to encourage the moderate use of alcohol, particularly wine, within the frameworks provided by existing commandments which require one to be happy in their fulfillment. Wine is an important part of Sabbath and holiday observances, life cycle celebrations, and the holiday of Purim. In the Hassidic world, a small amount of vodka is a legitimate preparation for listening to the teachings of the rabbi and, in oral traditions, a measured amount of alcohol on a regular basis is considered good for one's health. (Dartmouth Center on Addiction, Recovery and Education 2003, p. 3)

▐ Culture Provides Models of Alcoholism

U.S. citizens define alcoholism as a disease far more often than French Canadians or French people, for example (Babor et al. 1986). Some South Bronx Hispanics have ascribed alcoholism to "spells," spirits (Garrison and Podell 1981), the evil eye (*mal ojo*), or witchcraft (*brujeria*). The entire addiction also may be ignored or bypassed; ulcers, divorce, or car accidents that an alcohol counselor may recognize as alcoholism based may instead be traced directly to supernatural influence. One way or another, if it is attributed to a supernatural cause, a supernatural solution may be called upon to cure this problem. Thus, many seek the help of a folk curer (e.g., *espiritista, santero*). Some African Americans interpret their problems as a punishment from God, and they may subscribe to a moral model that conflicts with a disease or other psychiatric or addictive model.

▐ Cultural Stereotypes of Drinking May Be Misleading

African American drinking patterns run the gamut from middle-class cocktail lounges (as seen in liquor ads in *Ebony*), to blue-collar wakes and birthday parties, to the "bottle gang" of homeless poor. By class, middle-class African American

women drinkers are not dramatically different from middle-class white women drinkers; they are typically moderate drinkers, with few nondrinkers and heavy drinkers. Poorer African American female groups have a larger proportion of nondrinkers; among those who do drink, more are heavy drinkers. Breaking it down further, being married, older, and church affiliated has been associated with nonacceptance of heavy drinking (Gary and Gary 1985; Kinney 2000). At historically black colleges and universities, blacks have lower levels of alcohol and other types of drug consumption than are observed at colleges and universities with a majority of white students. At all colleges and universities, white students drink significantly more than do African American students (Kinney 2000).

Gordon, who studied a Connecticut city in 1981, examined three Hispanic groups, all new to the United States and all blue collar. In this group, Dominicans drank less after migration. They emphasized suave or sophisticated drinking, and they saw drunkenness as indecent (without respect). Alcoholics were seen as "sick," perhaps from some tragic experience. Guatemalans drank substantially more after migration: one-third of males were often drunk and binged most weekends. Being drunk was considered glamorous and sentimentalized—like Humphrey Bogart under the hanging lightbulb, alone in a hotel room. These individuals boasted of hangovers, even when they did not have one. The Guatemalan Alcoholics Anonymous (AA) group was alien to Puerto Ricans. Puerto Ricans broke down into middle-class American-style moderate drinkers, depressed and wife-abusing alcoholic welfare recipients, and various sorts of polydrug abusers, including those who entered into the mainland "druggie" youth culture (Gordon 1981). Among Hispanics in general, men were twice as likely to be involved in heavy drinking as both white and African American males (Kinney 2000). In fact, African American students have the lowest lifetime, annual, and 30-day prevalence rates for alcohol use; they also tend to have the lowest rates for daily drinking (NIDA 1999). Finally, a number of conclusive studies that examine the relationship between ethnic identity and the extent of illicit drug use and abuse indicate that illicit drug abuse is more likely to occur in second-generation ethnics (children of parents who immigrated to the United States) with less illicit drug use in successive ethnic generations beyond the second generation (Cheung 1993; Hjern 2016; Svensson and Hagquist 2009). Similar patterns of illicit drug use and abuse are also found in minority groups that are socially and economically disadvantaged in the United States (Gans 1992; Vaillant 1966).

Even when looking at physiological responses to alcohol, ethnicity appears to matter. The long-term effects of alcohol dependence are reported to cause more damage to the immune systems of African Americans than other ethnic groups. The greater sensitivity to alcohol and its damaging effects puts this group at an increased risk for infection and, in many cases, at a greater likelihood of death (Research Group News Release 2016).

■ Culture Provides Attitudes Regarding Alcohol Consumption

Although cultures often maintain generalized (normative) attitudes regarding alcohol use and abuse, significant differences in attitudes also exist within cultures (Arkin and Funkhouser 1992; Inciardi 1992). The United States is characterized as culturally ambivalent regarding alcohol use (Kinney 2000); that is, alcohol consumption varies enormously across our culture. Different geographic regions, diverse religious beliefs, and racial and ethnic differences result in confusing attitudes about drinking alcohol. Other factors that contribute to diversity in attitudes include social upbringing, peer group dynamics, social class, income, education, and occupational differences.

What specific impact do such attitudes have on drinking? As just mentioned, attitudes are responsible for making alcohol consumption acceptable or unacceptable—or even relished as a form of behavior. For example, in one segment of impoverished African American groups, alcohol use and abuse are so common that they have become accepted behavior. The following excerpt describes an accepted pattern of alcohol consumption:

A party without liquor or a street rap without a bottle is often perceived as unimaginable. These attitudes about drinking are shaped as youth grow up seeing liquor stores in their communities next to schools, churches, and homes. Liquor stores and bootleg dealers frequently permeate the black residential community, where in traditionally white communities they are generally restricted to commercial or business zones. With liquor stores throughout the fabric of black residential life, black youth grow up seeing men drinking in the streets and relatives drinking at home. (Harper 1986)

Contrast this attitude with orthodox religious and fundamentalist communities in which the use of alcohol and other drugs is strictly prohibited:

I was raised in a very religious, Seventh-Day Adventist family. My father was a pretty strong figure in our little church of 18 members. My mother stayed home most of the time, living in a way like an Old Testament kind of biblical life, so-to-speak. We were strict vegetarians, and all of us in the family had to be very involved with church life. The first time I ever saw alcohol outside of always hearing how corrupting it was to the mind and the body, was when I was 7. One day the father of a friend of mine—the only non-Adventist family friend I was allowed to play with—was drinking a beer in the kitchen when we walked in. I asked, "What's that?" The father's reply was "This is beer, dear John." I looked strangely at him and pretended to be amused at the father's answer. Actually, inside I remember being very surprised and scared at the same time for I was always told that people who drink alcohol were not doing what God wanted them to do in life. *(From Venturelli's research files, male university student, age 18, May 21, 1993)*

From these contrasting examples, we can see that the values expressed through group and family attitudes regarding drug use are very significant in determining the extent of alcohol consumption.

■ Culture Determines What Is Considered Acceptable Amounts of Drinking

In looking at countries with the heaviest drinking rates, it has been reported that "[n]early all of the countries with the highest levels of alcohol consumption are located in Eastern Europe. They include Russia and other former Soviet Union nations such as Belarus, Lithuania, Moldova, and Ukraine. The only top-consuming nation not located in Eastern Europe is Andorra, a principality located between France and Spain in the Pyrenees" (Hess et al. 2014). Specifically, the heaviest-drinking countries in the world, with consumption reported in liters of alcohol per capita (1 gallon equals 3.7854 liters), are, from highest to lowest, the following:

1. Belarus: 17.5 liters
2. Republic of Moldova: 16.8 liters
3. Lithuania: 15.4 liters

4. Russian Federation: 15.1 liters
5. Romania: 14.4 liters
6. Ukraine: 13.9 liters
7. Andorra: 13.8 liters
8. Hungary: 13.3 liters
9. Czech Republic: 13.0 liters
10. Slovakia: 13.0 liters (tied, 9th highest with Czech Republic)

Residents in these countries were also often among the most likely to suffer from alcohol use disorders. Five of the heaviest-drinking countries were also among the 10 highest in prevalence for alcohol use disorders, which include alcoholism and other forms of health-damaging use of alcohol. Alcohol use disorders often lead to physical problems such as liver cirrhosis and mental illnesses such as depression. The three nations with the highest rates of alcohol use disorders—Hungary, Russia, and Belarus—were also among the 10 heaviest-drinking nations (Hess et al. 2014). Note that life expectancies are shorter in nations with heavy alcohol use. According to Hess (2014), "[A]verage life expectancy at birth in high-income nations was 79.3 years as of 2012, far higher than in almost all of the heaviest drinking nations. In Romania, the average life expectancy was just 68.7 years. In Russia and Ukraine the average life expectancy was below 72 years as well."

In looking at the 10 countries with exceptionally higher amounts of alcohol consumed, we can begin to understand how cultures vary with regard to alcohol consumption and how each country's culture determines what is considered normative (acceptable) alcohol consumption. Pointing out these top 10 alcohol-consuming countries shows how, as a group, these countries vary widely when compared to other countries where alcohol consumption is much lower.

College and University Students and Alcohol Use

Over the years, alcohol use and consumption rates among college students have remained largely stable, although rates for other drugs show a lot more variance. For example, marijuana use has dramatically risen, fallen, and then risen again. In looking at alcohol consumption and college students, some interesting findings exist. The following statistics provided by Hingston and colleagues (2009) and described in *College Drinking—Changing the*

Culture (NIAAA 2010) are especially noteworthy. Each year:

- *Death*: 1825 college students between the ages of 18 and 24 die from alcohol-related unintentional injuries, including motor vehicle crashes.
- *Injury*: 599,000 students between the ages of 18 and 24 are unintentionally injured under the influence of alcohol.
- *Assault*: 696,000 students between the ages of 18 and 24 are assaulted by another student who has been drinking.
- *Sexual abuse*: 97,000 students between the ages of 18 and 24 are victims of alcohol-related sexual assault or date rape.
- *Unsafe sex*: 400,000 students between the ages of 18 and 24 have unprotected sex and more than 100,000 students between the ages of 18 and 24 report having been too intoxicated to know if they consented to having sex.
- *Academic problems*: About 25% of college students report academic consequences of their drinking including missing class, falling behind, doing poorly on exams or papers, and receiving lower grades overall.
- *Health problems/suicide attempts*: More than 150,000 students develop an alcohol-related health problem and between 1.2% and 1.5% of students indicate that they tried to commit suicide within the past year due to drinking or drug use.
- *Drunk driving*: 3,360,000 students between the ages of 18 and 24 drive under the influence of alcohol.
- *Vandalism*: About 11% of college student drinkers report that they have damaged property while under the influence of alcohol.
- *Property damage*: More than 25% of administrators from schools with relatively low drinking levels and over 50% from schools with high drinking levels say their campuses have a "moderate" or "major" problem with alcohol-related property damage.
- *Police involvement*: About 5% of 4-year college students are involved with the police or campus security as a result of their drinking, and 110,000 students between the ages of 18 and 24 are arrested for an alcohol-related violation such as public drunkenness or driving under the influence.
- *Alcohol abuse and dependence*: 31% of college students met criteria for a diagnosis of alcohol abuse and 6% for a diagnosis of alcohol dependence in the past 12 months, according

to questionnaire-based self-reports about their drinking.

Additional findings are as follows (NIAAA 2009, unless otherwise noted):

- College students drink an estimated 4 billion cans of beer annually.
- The total amount of alcohol consumed by college students each year is 430 million gallons, enough for every college and university in the United States to fill an Olympic-size swimming pool.
- As many as 360,000 of the nation's 12 million undergraduates will die from alcohol-related causes while in school. This is more than the number who will receive master's and doctoral degrees.
- Nearly 40% of all college students are binge drinkers.
- The number of college women who drink to get drunk has more than tripled in the past 10 years, rising from 10% to 35%.
- On America's college campuses, alcohol is often responsible for 28% of all students who drop out of college before completing their bachelor's degree.
- 75% of male students and 55% of female students involved in acquaintance rape had been drinking or using drugs at the time.
- For college men, alcohol consumption is inversely related to the size of the institution; that is, male students at smaller institutions consume far more than those at larger institutions. (Lack of social activities could be a precipitating factor.)
- Nearly one-quarter of student's report failing a test or project because of the aftereffects of drinking or doing drugs.
- Although only 2 in 20 college students are arrested for driving under the influence, "27% of students said they drove while under the influence of alcohol . . . [and this] . . . translates to 2.1 million students" (Boyd, McCabe, and d'Arcy 2003).
- A related consequence of alcohol abuse is motor vehicle accidents. For young people under the age of 25, motor vehicle accidents rate as the number one cause of death (Presley, Meilman, and Lyerla 1996).
- Each year an estimated 1,825 college students between the ages of 18 and 24 die from alcohol-related unintentional injuries, including motor vehicle crashes (NIAAA 2013).
- Although the average cost for book purchases for classes is about $1000 per year (Weisbaum

2014), the average student spends about $500 on alcohol each year and 10% of all college loans are actually used to finance alcohol consumption (Bissonnette 2010).

On a positive note, there is a small but very significant downward trend in alcohol use on America's campuses. In 1985, the percentage of college students who had consumed alcohol in the previous 30 days was approximately 80%. By 1990, that number had declined to 74.5%, and it continues to decline each year. However, counterbalancing this positive trend, the use of other illegitimate-type drugs continues to increase. Further, past and more current studies show that although overall alcohol consumption is slowly decreasing, binge drinking remains high on most campuses throughout the United States (English, Shutt, and Oswalt 2009; NIAAA 2015a; Wechsler et al. 2000a).

Other recent findings (NIAAA 2016) indicate the following with regard to alcohol use by college students as of 2014:

- *Prevalence of drinking:* 59.8% of full-time college students aged 18 to 22 drank alcohol in the past month, compared with 51.5% of other persons of the same age.
- *Prevalence of binge drinking:* 37.9% of college students aged 18 to 22 engaged in binge drinking (five or more drinks on an occasion) in the past month, compared with 33.5% of other persons of the same age.
- *Prevalence of heavy drinking:* 12.2% of college students aged 18 to 22 engaged in heavy drinking (five or more drinks on an occasion on five or more occasions per month) in the past month, compared with 9.5% of other persons of the same age.

The Core Institute survey is a validated survey instrument that has been administered to more than 1 million students—by far the largest sample of college students surveyed. The available figures from this survey (Core Institute 2014) indicate that, on average, approximately 81.3% of college students consumed alcohol within the year this survey was given and 68.6% consumed alcohol within the 30 days prior to when the survey was administered. The average number of drinks that students consumed was 4.4 per week. Approximately 42.8% engaged in binge drinking within 30 days before the Core Institute survey was administered. Of all the drugs reported as being used within a year of when survey was completed (annual prevalence), alcohol was the most heavily abused on college campuses, followed by tobacco (33%) and marijuana (32.5%) (Core Institute 2014).

▎ Binge Drinking

A recent Swedish study defines a binge as the consumption of half a bottle of spirits or two bottles of wine on the same occasion. Similarly, a study in Italy found that consuming an average of eight drinks a day was considered normal drinking—clearly not bingeing. In the United Kingdom, bingeing is commonly defined as consuming 11 or more drinks on an occasion. However, in the United States, some researchers have defined bingeing as consuming five or more drinks on an occasion (an "occasion" can refer to an entire day). Recently, in the United States, what constitutes binge drinking for women and men differs "[f]or women 4 or more drinks during a single occasion..." [and] "[f]or men, 5 or more drinks during a single occasion" (CDC 2016, p. 1).

The widely reported study by Wechsler and Wuethrich (2002) brought the issue of binge drinking to the public's attention. One finding by Wechsler and Wuetrich (2002) that surveyed 18,000 students involving approximately 140 campuses, revealed that 44% engaged in binge drinking, which impacted on many areas of students' lives—both their own and those of others whose lives were disrupted by this behavior (giving rise to the term *secondhand drinking*). Major findings from this study included the following:

- Of those surveyed, 84% drank alcohol during the school year, with almost half (44%) categorized as binge drinkers and 19% as frequent binge drinkers.
- One-third (33%) of schools surveyed qualified as high-binge drinking campuses. To be

Alcohol consumption is routine at many social activities for college students.

qualified for a high-binge drinking campus, more than half of the students responding to the survey had to indicate that they were binge drinkers.
- The strongest predictor for binge drinking was living in a sorority or fraternity house. Eighty percent (80%) of sorority women and 86% of fraternity men living in Greek housing qualified as binge drinkers.

Wechsler (1996, p. 36) concludes the following:

- The "typical characteristics of binge drinkers include: male, fraternity and sorority members, white, under 24 years of age, involved in athletics, and students who socialize a great deal."
- "Students involved in community service, the arts, or studying a great deal were less likely to binge drink."
- "Less than half of binge drinkers considered religion an important part of their lives."

As mentioned in the previous section, approximately 37% to 42% of all college students binge drink on a frequent basis. This type of alcohol consumption is very worrisome to anyone supporting, nurturing, protecting, caring for, or responsible for the behavior of young people in this subculture. In addition, health professionals see this as a serious form of alcohol abuse.

One may question whether all five-drink episodes qualify as binge drinking, a term that calls to mind a weekend of drinking, or Jellinek's epsilon alcoholism. However, 11.1% of males and 7.4% of females reported three or more episodes of memory loss during the past year due to drug or alcohol use, of which the overwhelming majority were alcohol related, both because alcohol is the major drug consumed by students and because it produces amnesiac episodes. Amnesiac episodes are accepted as symptoms of problem drinking behavior.

In another national survey of 17,600 students at 140 four-year colleges and universities (and one that is regularly conducted by the Harvard School of Public Health) the findings were as follows (Wechsler et al. 2000a, p. 1):

- "Overall, 44% of the students were binge drinkers. Among men, 50% were binge drinkers; among women, the figure was 39%."
- "The main reason given for binge drinking was 'to get drunk.'"
- "White students were over twice as likely to be binge drinkers compared to other racial/ethnic groups."

- "Students who said that religious participation is not very important to them were more than twice as likely to be binge drinkers compared to other students."
- "Students who said that athletic participation was very important or important to them were also one-and-a-half times more likely to be binge drinkers."
- "Residents of fraternities or sororities were four times as likely to be binge drinkers compared to other students."

Other alcohol research studies revealed the following:

- Community college students were less likely to engage in binge drinking; 29.9% had binged in the previous 2 weeks compared with 40.4% of their peers at 4-year schools.
- Approximately one-fourth of all males enrolled at 4-year colleges reported three or more binge episodes during the previous 2 weeks (NIAAA 2008).
- According to a national survey, almost 60 percent of college students ages 18 to 22 drank alcohol in the past month, and almost 2 out of 3 of them engaged in binge drinking during that same timeframe (NIH 2015c).
- Students who lived on campus were more likely to binge drink than were those who lived off campus. Furthermore, older, working, off-campus students were less likely to engage in such behavior, lowering their scores in this regard relative to the standard college student (NIAAA 2008).
- American Indian/Alaska Native students had the highest frequency of drinking episodes, binge drinking, and memory loss, followed (in order) by white, Hispanic, African American, and Asian students (NIAAA 2008, 2013).

It is not unusual for college students to over consume alcohol when they are partying.

© Yuri Arcurs/Dreamstime.com

■ Gender and Collegiate Alcohol Use

Among college students and young adults generally, there are substantial gender differences in alcohol use, with college males drinking the most. In 2014, for example, approximately 50% of all college males reported having five or more drinks in a row over the previous 2 weeks versus one-third (34%) of college females. Given that the physiological impacts of five drinks are considerably greater for the typical young female versus the typical young male, it is not surprising that we find substantial gender differences in the prevalence of having five or more drinks in a row. Throughout the years, this gender difference has narrowed gradually, with the rate declining somewhat for males and increasing somewhat for females.

The findings from the Core Institute (2014) survey consistently indicate greater frequency of male drinking, frequency of male binge drinking, and consequences of drinking. In a review of the literature addressing gender and student drinking patterns, Berkowitz and Perkins (1987) and Hensel et al. (2014) found a historical pattern of male-dominated college drinking patterns. The transition into college is associated with a doubling of the percentages of those who drink for both genders. Both men and women drink to enhance sociability or social interaction, to escape negative emotions or release otherwise unacceptable ones, and to simply get drunk. "Drinking to get drunk" is generally considered more of a male pursuit. Indeed, males are more frequently associated with binge drinking and negative public consequences than are female drinkers. Severe drunkenness and a customary rowdiness or drunken comportment are normative for male drinkers who binge, with the results including fighting, property damage, and troubles with authorities. The latter were twice as likely to be male problems.

Unsurprisingly, drinking is inversely related to academic achievement. With heavier drinkers, grades suffered for both male and female students. According to the studies cited by Berkowitz and Perkins (1987) for binge drinkers, the impact on impaired academic performance is just as great for women drinkers. More recent information (Core Institute 2014; De Jong 1995; Presley et al. 1996; Wechsler 2000a, 2000b) corroborates this finding and shows similar consequences among male and female binge drinkers in terms of health problems, personal injury, and unplanned sexual activity. Over the past few decades, drinking behaviors (amount and percentage of drinking) have been becoming more similar between males and females.

Alcohol Consumption Patterns of Women

Women are affected by alcohol differently than are men. Women possess greater sensitivity to alcohol, have a greater likelihood of addiction, and develop alcohol-related health problems sooner than men. Why do women respond differently than men to alcohol? Three reasons are (1) women have a smaller body size (men are generally larger than women); (2) women absorb alcohol sooner than men because on average they possess more body fat, and body fat does not dilute alcohol as well as water (male bodies contain more water); and (3) women possess less of a metabolizing enzyme that functions to get rid of (process out) alcohol.

In Great Britain, the proportion of women drinking has risen steadily since 1984. This increase in drinking still holds true for all age groups with the exception of women older than 65 (Alcohol Concern 2008). Other notable facts regarding women and drinking can be summarized as follows (Buddy T. 2016a, 2016d; NIAAA 2000):

- Although men begin drinking earlier in life, women are more likely than men to start drinking heavily later in life.
- Women are more easily affected by alcohol consumption, both its effects and diseases related to alcoholism—cirrhosis of the liver, stomach cancer, and so on.
- Women become intoxicated faster than men.
- Women's blood-alcohol content increases more quickly than in men.
- Women become dependent or addicted to alcohol more quickly than do men.
- Women develop alcohol liver disease after drinking less than men.
- Women develop alcohol-related brain damage sooner than men.
- Women experience more extensive alcohol-related brain damage than men.
- Women are at higher risk for getting alcohol-related cancers than men.
- Women are more likely to have a fatal alcohol-related auto crash than men.
- Women's alcohol consumption is often similar to that of people they are close to, such as a lover or husband.
- Full-time working, professionally oriented women drink at the end of their working day, whereas women who stay at home drink alcohol throughout the day.
- More women in alcohol treatment come from sexually abusive homes (70%), in comparison to men (12%).
- Today, women are more visible and their behavior, especially alcohol consumption, is more observable (e.g., drinking in bars, purchasing alcohol).

Figure 8.6 shows the prevalence estimate of alcohol use (percentage of any use and binge drinking) among women aged 18 to 44 in 2013 (CDC 2014). The U.S. median of all the states and territories for any use of alcohol by women is approximately 53.2%, and median binge drinking is 17.5% for all childbearing-age women. When looking at binge drinking rates among women, the state of Wisconsin has the highest percentage (26.1%), and Alabama has the lowest percentage (10.1%).

Figure 8.6 also shows the following:

- The following states have the *highest* percentages (20.2% to 26.1%) of childbearing women who binge on alcohol (listed from high to low): Alaska, Colorado, District of Columbia, Illinois, Iowa, Maine, Massachusetts, Michigan, Minnesota, Montana, Nebraska, North Dakota, South Dakota, and Wisconsin.
- The following states have the *second highest* percentages (16.1% to 19.9%) of childbearing women who binge on alcohol (listed from high to low): California, Connecticut, Delaware, Hawaii, Idaho, Indiana, Louisiana, Maryland, Missouri, New Hampshire, New Jersey, New York, Ohio, Oregon, Pennsylvania, Rhode Island, Virginia, Washington, and Wyoming.
- The following states have the *third highest* percentages (12.0% to 14.8%) of childbearing women who binge on alcohol (listed from high to low): Arkansas, Arizona, Florida, Georgia, Kansas, Kentucky, Maryland, Mississippi, New Mexico, North Carolina, Puerto Rico (U.S. territory), South Carolina, Texas, and West Virginia.
- The following states have the *fourth highest* percentages (*representing the lowest* percentages) (10.1% to 11.9%) of childbearing women who binge on alcohol (listed from high to low): Alabama, Guam (U.S. territory), Nevada, Oklahoma, Tennessee, Utah, and Vermont.

As a group, alcohol-abusing women are more likely to drink alone at home. A high incidence of

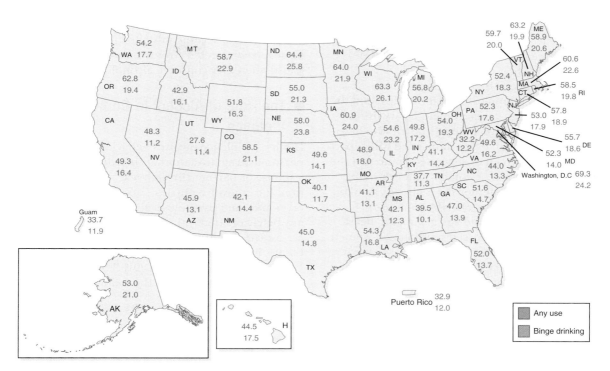

FIGURE 8.6 State-specific weighted prevalence estimates of alcohol use (percentage of any use/binge drinking) among women aged 18 to 44 years, Behavioral Risk Factor Surveillance System (BRFSS): 2013.

Data from Centers for Disease Control and Prevention (CDC). "Fetal Alcohol Spectrum Disorders (FASDs)—State-Specific Weighted Prevalence Estimates of Alcohol Use (Percentage of Any Use/Binge Drinking) Among Women Aged 18–44 Years—BRFSS, 2012." Atlanta, GA: Centers for Disease Control and Prevention. Last updated 20 May 2014. Available http://www.cdc.gov/ncbddd/fasd/data.html

alcohol abuse is found in women who are unemployed and looking for work, whereas less alcohol abuse is likely in women who are employed part time. Divorced or separated women, women who never marry, and those who are unmarried and living with a partner are more likely to use and abuse alcohol than are married women. Other high-risk groups are women in their 20s and early 30s and women with heavy-drinking husbands or partners. Other researchers (Williams et al. 1997; Wilsnack, Wilsnack, and Klassen 1986) found that women who experience depression or encounter problems with fertility or menopausal changes also demonstrate heavier drinking behavior.

Looking at specific age groups, the following conclusions have been drawn:

- The course of alcohol addiction progresses at a faster rate among women than among men. Recent research shows that "female alcoholics are generally younger than males" (Medical News Today 2007, p. 1).
- For many women, heavy drinking came after a health problem such as depression or reproductive difficulties (Register et al. 2002).
- Women in the 21- to 34-year-old age group were least likely to report alcohol-related problems

if they had stable marriages and were working full time. In other words, young mothers with full-time occupations reported less reliance on alcohol in comparison to childless women without full-time work (Register et al. 2002).

- Among nonpregnant binge drinkers, binge drinking prevalence, frequency, and intensity were highest among those aged 18 to 24 years (CDC 2010).
- Women tend to marry men whose drinking habits match their own (NIAAA 2015b).
- Young women in their 20s and early 30s are more likely to drink than older women. No one factor predicts whether a woman will have problems with alcohol, or at what age she is most at risk. However, there are some life experiences that seem to make it more likely that women will have drinking problems (NIAAA 2015b).
- Heavy drinking and drinking problems among white women are most common in younger age groups. Among African American women, however, drinking problems are more common in middle age than youth. A woman's ethnic origins—and the extent to which she adopts the attitudes of mainstream versus her native culture—influence how and when she will drink. Hispanic women who are more

"mainstream" are more likely to drink and to drink heavily (i.e., to drink at least once a week and to have five or more drinks at one time) (NIAAA 2015b).

- Research suggests that women who have trouble with their closest relationships tend to drink more than other women. Heavy drinking is more common among women who have never married, are living unmarried with a partner, or are divorced or separated (note that the effect of divorce on a woman's later drinking may depend on whether she is already drinking heavily in her marriage) (NIAAA 2015b).
- In the 35- to 49-year-old age group, the heaviest drinkers were divorced or separated women without children in the home.
- In the 50- to 64-year-old age group, the heaviest drinkers were women whose husbands or partners drank heavily.
- Women 65 years or older constitute less than 10% of drinkers with drinking problems.

Alcohol consumption has been found to be higher in women who closely work in traditionally so-called masculine occupations and levels of management, such as executives and traditional blue-collar occupations. In April 1995, former First Lady Betty Ford made the following statement:

> Today, we know that when a woman abuses alcohol or other drugs, the risk to her health is much greater than it is for a man. Yet there is not enough prevention, intervention, and treatment targeting women. It is still much harder for women to get help. That needs to change. (SAMHSA 1995, p. 14)

In fact, women risk serious health consequences when they choose to use alcohol and other drugs. Alcohol, in particular, can often be devastating to women's health.

Not only does alcohol have a greater immediate effect on women, but its long-term risks are also more dangerous. Some surveys now show that more alcohol consumption occurs among girls 12 to 17 years old than among boys of the same age. This places young women at risk of delaying the onset of puberty, a condition that can wreak havoc in terms of adolescent maturation. In regard to "[d]rinking over the long term is more likely to damage a women's health than a man's, even if the woman as been drinking less alcohol or for a shorter length of time than a man (NIAAA 2015b).

Finally, women are more likely than men to combine alcohol with prescription drugs. When the use of other drugs enters into the equation, ovulation may become inhibited and fertility may be adversely affected. Women also risk early menopause when they consume alcohol.

▋ The Role of Alcohol in Domestic Violence

Domestic violence involves behavior that one person uses against another in order to control a spouse or partner through fear and intimidation. It can involve physical, sexual, emotional, economic, and psychological abuse; it "includes any behaviors that intimidate, manipulate, humiliate, isolate, frighten, terrorize, coerce, threaten, blame, hurt, injure, or wound someone" (U.S. Department of Justice [USDOJ] 2013).

Abuse can show itself in the following ways:

- *Physical battering*: The attacks can range from bruising to punching to life-threatening choking or use of weapons.
- *Sexual abuse*: A person is forced to have sexual intercourse with the abuser or take part in unwanted sexual activity.
- *Psychological battering*: Psychological violence can include constant verbal abuse, harassment, excessive possessiveness, isolating the victim from friends and family, withholding money, and destruction of personal property (FOE 2005, p. 3).

Much attention was focused on domestic violence in the mid-1990s due to high-profile criminal cases such as those involving the Menendez brothers and O. J. Simpson. The increased emphasis on decreasing domestic violence has inspired much research into its causes and effects, as well as identifying the common traits of abusers. Studies have found a significant relationship between the incidence of battering and the abuse of alcohol; furthermore, the abuse of alcohol overwhelmingly emerges as a primary predictor of marital violence (Buddy T. 2016e; De Jong 1995; Drug Strategies 1999). A study of 2000 American couples conducted in 1993 showed that rates of domestic violence were as much as 15 times higher in households in which the husband was described as "often" being drunk as opposed to "never" drunk (Buddy T. 2016e; Collins and Messerschmidt 1993). Messerschmidt (1993) found that alcohol was present in more than half of all reported incidences of domestic abuse. Further, "[a]nother study . . . [showed] . . . that the percentage of batterers who are under the influence of alcohol when they assault their partners ranges from 48% to 87%, with most research indicating a 60% to 70% rate of alcohol abuse and a 13% to 20% rate of drug abuse" (Buddy T. 2016e).

Domestic violence also creates significant problems for its victims later in life. A study of 472 women by the Research Institute on Addictions found that 87% of female alcoholics had been physically or sexually abused as children (Drug Strategies 1999; Miller and Downs 1993; NIAAA 2015b). Research also shows the following:

On the surface it seems hard to argue with the numbers reported in domestic violence research studies. Ninety-two percent of the domestic abuse assailants reported use of alcohol or other drugs on the day of the assault, according to a recent *JAMA* [*Journal of the American Medical Association*] (Wechsler et al. 1994).

The insidiousness of domestic violence may exist because of the consistent abuse of alcohol that is associated with both abusers and victims. Given these disturbing statistics, more research and counseling programs focused on the prevention of alcoholism and subsequent domestic violence are necessary before the very foundations of identity, security, and happiness are forever destroyed. As one reformed alcoholic explains,

It was really terrible. I would drink by myself in the living room and fight with my wife in other parts of the house. I knew I needed help when I shoved her around on the night of her birthday and threw a wet kitchen washcloth and hit her in the face. Before that night, I never would have done this, but her nagging about my drinking that night got to me more than on other nights and it caused me to lose control. (*From Venturelli's research files, male, age 48, July 2010*)

■ Alcohol and Sex

Alcohol use is linked to an overwhelming proportion of unwanted sexual behaviors, including **acquaintance and date rape**, unplanned pregnancies, and sexually transmitted infections, including HIV infections (Abbey 1990; World Health Organization [WHO] 1996). Factors that immediately come to mind include disinhibition concerning restraints on sexuality, poor judgment, and unconsciousness or helplessness on the part of victims. The links between unwanted sex and substance abuse are subtler than many

imagine, however. Although disinhibition, impulsivity, and helplessness are certainly major considerations, other elements come into play, as illustrated in the following paragraphs.

A study conducted at an unnamed university in upstate New York and published in the *Journal of Adolescent Health* reports "that 19% of women, nearly one in five, said they had been a victim of attempted or completed rape, either by force or while they were incapacitated due to alcohol or drugs, during their freshman year" (Wallace 2015). Other dating violence includes physical, psychological, and sexual violence. One in 10 high school students have experienced physical violence from a dating partner in the past year (Adamo and Advocates for Youth 2014).

The following are additional data that have been reported on sexual and dating violence among young people (Adamo and Advocates for Youth 2014):

* According to data from the 2011 Youth Risk Behavior Surveillance (YRBS), nationwide, 8% of students reported that they had been physically forced to have sexual intercourse when they did not want to. Overall, the prevalence of having been forced to have sexual intercourse was higher among female (11.8%) than male (4.5%) students. For 28% of young women who were raped or sexually assaulted, the perpetrator was a former or current intimate partner.
* Young women between the ages of 16 and 24 experience the highest rate of intimate partner violence. According to one national study, 29% of the young women surveyed who had ever been in a relationship said they had been pressured to have sex or to engage in sexual activity they did not want.
* Most female victims of intimate partner violence were previously victimized by the same offender, including 77% of female victims aged 18 to 24.
* Psychological violence includes uneven power dynamics, control, jealousy, and threats regarding the relationship. In one study, 21% of teens said that they had been in a relationship with someone who wanted to keep them from seeing friends and family. The same study found

KEY TERM

acquaintance and date rape
unplanned and unwanted forced sexual attack from a friend or a date partner

that 64% of those surveyed had a partner who acted jealous and demanded to know their whereabouts at all times.

• A 2013 study of dating violence among lesbian, gay, bisexual, and transgender (LGBT) youth found that LGBT youth showed significantly higher rates of all types of dating violence victimization and perpetration experiences, compared to heterosexual youth.

Recall the drunken comportment thesis that was introduced in the section on culture and drinking behavior. Some nonreligious ceremonial drinking settings incorporate expectations of disinhibited behaviors, such as at holiday office parties. Drinking is a signal or cue that it is acceptable to be amorous, even sexually aggressive, and that the intoxicated object of one's affections will not object and is disinhibited.

Intoxicated people are not as capable of attending to multiple cues. When cues are ambiguous, drunken men are more likely to miss the ambiguity and to interpret cues as meaning that sex will occur and should be initiated. (Men are generally more likely to interpret friendly cues as sexual signals, but intoxication makes this misunderstanding more likely.) In addition, possible dangers implicit in a private setting, on a date, with a drunken male will not be picked up as often or as easily by the intoxicated and potentially victimized female (Abbey 1990).

Alcohol and the Family: Destructive Types of Social Support and Organizations for Victims of Alcoholics

■ Codependency and Enabling

Codependency and enabling generally occur together. **Codependency** (which some call

KEY TERMS

codependency
behavior displayed by either addicted or nonaddicted family members (codependents) who identify with the alcohol addict and cover up the excessive drinking behavior, allowing it to continue and letting it affect the codependent's life

enablers
those close to the alcohol addict who deny or make excuses for enabling his or her excessive drinking

co-alcoholism) refers to a relationship pattern, and enabling refers to a set of specific behaviors (Doweiko 2015). Codependency is defined as the behavior displayed by either addicted or nonaddicted family members (codependents) who identify with the alcohol addict and cover up the excessive drinking behavior. An example of codependency is when a family member remains silent when empty bottles of vodka, for example, are discovered under a bed or in the garage.

Enablers are those close to the alcohol addict who deny or make excuses for enabling the excessive drinking. Often, both codependency and enabling are done by the same person. An example is the husband who calmly conspires and phones his wife's place of employment and reports that his wife has the stomach flu when the reality is that she is too drunk or hung over to realize it is time to go to work.

Such a husband is both codependent and an enabler. He lies to cover up his wife's addiction and enables her not to face her irresponsible drinking behavior. In this example, the husband is responsible for perpetuating the spouse's addiction. Even quiet toleration of the alcoholic's addiction enables the drinker to continue the drinking behavior.

■ Children of Alcoholics (COAs) and Adult Children of Alcoholics (ACOAs)

Alcoholism is a disease of the family. Not only is there a significant genetic component that is passed from generation to generation, but the drinking problems of a single family member affect all other family members. The family environment and genetics can perpetuate a vicious and destructive cycle. "Alcoholism is also known as a family disease. Alcoholics may have young, teenage, or grown-up children; they have wives or husbands; they have brothers or sisters; they have parents or other relatives. An alcoholic can totally disrupt family life and cause harmful effects that can last a lifetime" (Parsons 2003). Children living with a nonrecovering alcoholic score lower on measures of family cohesion, intellectual-cultural orientation, active-recreational orientation, and independence. They also usually experience higher levels of conflict within the family.

Research findings indicate the following:

There are 18 million alcoholics in the U.S. according to the National Council on Alcoholism and Drug Dependence. As a result, an estimated 26.8 million children are exposed, at varying degrees, to alcoholism in the family.

These children are at higher risk for alcoholism and other drug abuse than are children of non-alcoholics, and are more likely to marry an alcoholic as well. Children of alcoholics or addicts are commonly referred to as "COA." (American Association for Marriage and Family Therapy [AAMFT] 2015)

Approximately 9.7 million children age 17 or younger were living in households with one or more adults who were classified as having a diagnosis of alcohol abuse or dependence within the previous year, according to data from the National Longitudinal Alcohol Epidemiologic Survey (NLAES). Approximately 70% of these children were biological, foster, adopted, or stepchildren. Therefore, 6.8 million children, or about 15% of children age 17 or younger, meet the formal definition of children of alcoholics (COAs) (Zucker et al. 2009).

Children of alcoholics are at high risk of developing the same attachment to alcohol as their parents. Alcoholics are more likely than nonalcoholics to have an alcoholic parent, sibling, or other relative.

Within the last decade, both COAs and adult children of alcoholics (ACOAs) have been studied extensively. Here are some major findings concerning these two groups by Zucker et al (2009, p. 24):

- COAs have an increased risk of alcohol involvement because "[g]enetically transmitted differences in response to alcohol . . . make drinking more pleasurable and/or less aversive (p. 24)."
- "Higher transmission of risky temperamental and behavioral traits . . . lead the COAs into greater contact with earlier and heavier drinking peers (p. 24)."
- COAs are two to four times more likely to develop alcoholism. In addition, both COAs and ACOAs are more likely to marry into families in which alcoholism is prevalent.
- Approximately one-third of alcoholics come from families in which one parent was or is an alcoholic.
- Both physiological and environmental factors appear to place COAs and ACOAs at greater risk of becoming alcoholics.
- COAs and ACOAs exhibit more symptoms of depression and anxiety than do children of nonalcoholic parents.
- Young children of alcoholics exhibit an excessive amount of crying, bed-wetting, and sleep problems, such as nightmares.
- Teenagers display excessive perfectionism, hoarding, staying by themselves (loners), and excessive self-consciousness.

- Phobias develop, and difficulty with school performance is not uncommon.

ACOAs have been found to share a number of characteristics. The following set of characteristics of ACOAs was developed by Dr. Janel G. Woititz in 1983 (Buddy T. 2015):

- Become isolated
- Fear people and authority figures
- Become approval seekers Be frightened of angry people
- Be terrified of personal criticism
- Become alcoholics, marry them or both
- View life as a victim
- Have an overwhelming exaggerated sense of responsibility
- Be concerned more with others than themselves
- Feel guilty when they stand up for themselves
- Become addicted to excitement
- Confuse love and pity
- "Love" people who need rescuing
- Stuff their feelings
- Lose the ability to feel
- Have low self-esteem
- Judge themselves harshly
- Become terrified of abandonment
- Do anything to hold on to a relationship
- Become "para-alcoholics" without drinking
- Become reactors instead of actors

Treatment of Alcoholism

Although treatment of alcoholism and treatment of other addictions have somewhat separate historical roots and consequently gave rise to separate therapy systems, governmental authorities, and counselor certifications, they have now merged in most states in the United States. In addition to recognizing that alcohol is a drug addiction, epidemiologically few "pure" alcoholics and drug addicts exist anymore. Most addicts drink in addition to their other drug addictions (making them poly-drug users); many alcoholics abuse other drugs; and some move through stages of heroin, methadone, and alcohol use, in that order. Alcoholism and its treatment have a few special features:

- While addicts remain in denial, the socially acceptable nature of drinking, or even of heavy drinking, makes it easier to maintain denial as a psychological defense. In contrast, it is more difficult to remain in denial of crack addiction.

- Although all addictions could result in **relapsing syndrome**, and most addicts have a tendency to relapse, the social environment that permits or even encourages drinking and the ready availability of alcohol makes it easy to relapse without a radical shift in lifestyle. Again, the alcoholic is buffered within a subcultural (social and cultural) cloud of use. Alcoholics Anonymous remains particularly vigilant in looking for signs of relapse, advising the alcoholic to "keep the memory regarding the misery of addiction green," to HALT (which stands for do not get too *hungry, angry, lonely,* or *thirsty/tired* because these are possible relapse triggers) and not to become isolated from others but to stay in the support system, making phone calls and attending "90 meetings in 90 days."
- Alcohol rehabilitation differs from other addiction treatments mainly in its medical ramifications. Alcoholism is devastating to the liver, muscles, nutritional system, gastrointestinal system, and brain. Alcoholics who have become "dry" only recently may still suffer from pancreatitis, weakness, impaired cognitive capacities, and so forth. The fact that treatment is so structured, simplified, and made into a slogan ("Don't drink and go to meetings," "Keep coming: It works") makes it possible for the bleary and confused, recently dried-out alcoholic to follow. (An AA term for this condition is *mokus.*) Although the cognitive impairment tends to clear up somewhat over a period of 6 months (unless clear cortical wasting has occurred, a condition known as "wet brain"), the alcoholic is often physically ravaged to an extent that requires years to mend the damage, if it is ever possible.
- The alcoholic is typically more emotionally fragile than other addicts in treatment.

KEY TERMS

relapsing syndrome
returning to the use of alcohol after quitting

acute alcohol withdrawal syndrome
symptoms that occur when an individual who is addicted to alcohol does not maintain his or her usual blood alcohol level

delirium tremens (DTs)
the most severe, even life-threatening, form of alcohol withdrawal, involving hallucinations, delirium, and fever

- The other major medical ramification is withdrawal. Withdrawal from alcohol and withdrawal from barbiturates are the two most severe withdrawal syndromes. Before modern medical management techniques, many individuals succumbed to **acute alcohol withdrawal syndrome**.

▌ Getting Through Withdrawal

An alcoholic who is well nourished and in good physical condition can go through withdrawal as an outpatient with reasonable safety. However, an acutely ill alcoholic needs medically supervised care. A general hospital ward is best for preliminary treatment. The alcohol withdrawal syndrome is quite similar to that for barbiturates and other sedative hypnotics. Symptoms typically appear within 12 to 72 hours after total cessation of drinking but can appear whenever the blood alcohol level drops below a certain point. The alcoholic experiences severe muscle tremors, nausea, and anxiety. In extremely acute alcohol syndromes, a condition known as **delirium tremens (DTs)** occurs, in which the individual hallucinates, is delirious, and suffers from a high fever and rapid heartbeat. Delirium tremens, commonly called *DTs*, is an uncommon but life-threatening condition.

Alcohol withdrawal syndrome reaches its peak intensity within 24 to 48 hours. About 5% of the alcoholics in hospitals and perhaps 20% to 25% who suffer the DTs without treatment die. Phenobarbital, chlordiazepoxide (Librium), and diazepam (Valium) are commonly prescribed to prevent withdrawal symptoms. Simultaneously, the alcoholic may need treatment for malnutrition and vitamin deficiencies (especially the B vitamins). Pneumonia is also a frequent complication. After the alcoholic patient is over the acute stages of intoxication and withdrawal, administration of CNS depressants may be continued for a few weeks, with care taken not to transfer dependence on alcohol to dependence on the depressants. Long-term treatment with sedatives (such as Librium or Valium) does not prevent a relapse of drinking or assist with behavioral adaptation. A prescription of disulfiram (Antabuse) may be offered to encourage patients to abstain from alcohol; it blocks metabolism of acetaldehyde so that drinking any alcohol will result in a pounding headache, flushing, nausea, and other unpleasant symptoms. The patient must decide about 2 days in advance to stop taking Antabuse before he or she can drink. Antabuse is an aid to other supportive treatments, not the sole method of therapy.

A current medical approach for treating alcohol-dependent patients includes Naltrexone (Naltrexone hydrochloride), which is an opioid antagonist prescription pharmaceutical drug: in the clinical studies, treatment with Naltrexone supported abstinence, prevented relapse and decreased alcohol consumption" (Drugs.com 2016).

■ Helping the Alcoholic Family Recover

Alcoholism is a pervasive disease that affects the entire family. The family is a system and should be viewed not as disconnected people living together, but rather as people who affect one another and play certain roles, all working to keep the system in balance. In treating alcoholism, family therapy has a very strong and bright future. Often family therapists place emphasis on the emotional patterns within alcoholic families, expecting that entire families attend counseling sessions. It is not unusual to have sessions with different generations of alcohol abusers within families. The goal is to break the cycle of alcohol abuse within families:

> family therapy in substance abuse treatment can help by using the family's strengths and resources to find ways for the person who abuses alcohol or drugs to live without substances of abuse and to ameliorate the impact of chemical dependency on both the patient and the family. Family therapy . . . can help families become aware of their own needs and aid in the goal of keeping substance abuse from moving from one generation to another. (SAMHSA 2004)

We are all familiar with the stereotype of families in which the oldest child is the "hero," the middle child is "forgotten," and the youngest is the "baby." Whatever the roles of the individuals, when the family includes an alcoholic, it means that a member of the system is ill. The system adapts to dysfunction by rearranging itself around the problem. The family is like a mobile, a sculpture with interdependent parts that revolve around one another. We are not talking about adjusting to a person with a broken leg or diabetes, but someone who is in denial—manipulative, lying, and blaming other family members. By adjusting around the addiction, the family members enable the addict to progress further along the disease path. Roles become exaggerated and

distorted. Persons may be blamed, scapegoated, or lost and forgotten. One major adaptation is related to the person who "takes up the slack" by assuming extra responsibilities and taking on the role of a parent or even spouse.

Early family therapy systems research described how the family often acts as a unit. It focused on the disturbed communication patterns within families and the process by which the family throws up a scapegoat, often in the form of a child who is presented as the "identified patient" (Kolevzon and Green 1985; SAMHSA 2004). The concept of the "super-responsible one" was first described by Virginia Satir in 1964. In modern, popular writing on addiction in the family and codependent roles of children that are carried into adulthood, all of these roles are depicted as especially characteristic of addicted families (SAMHSA 2004; Wegscheider 1991). Because such roles are so common, many individuals may identify with them and ascribe a variety of ills to their being the offspring of an addict. Many individuals do suffer tremendously from the legacy of family addiction, and some have indeed been cast in one of these roles as a by-product of addiction in the family. However, acting as if only one kind of family or one kind of addicted family exists, which transcends cultural backgrounds, is not much better than saying that all languages or religions are the same. For example, "executive authority" over younger children can be the normal role of the eldest female child in African American families as part of a broader pattern of role flexibility (Brisbane 1985, 1985/1986). When an older child plays a parental part in the family, it may represent culturally routine behavior or it may be indicative of a response to addiction in the family.

There is some gain or perceived benefit to the person playing a role, and to the system as a

Even after the alcoholic is ready for rehabilitation, the other family members will also need treatment and support.

whole, in the individual's actions, although this gain may seem very indirect and, in fact, be injurious in the long run. Although the super-responsible person may be overburdened and resentful, he or she also feels important, heroic, and capable. Over a period, this role solidifies. Perhaps the hero becomes unable to remember or imagine it any other way. If the alcoholic enters or promises to enter into recovery, it may threaten the benefits to the family member. One of many examples is a wife in a subservient role who relishes, at some level, the power, control, and authority she enjoys with an alcoholic husband or the recognition she receives in martyrdom—perhaps her only recognition in life. Another example is the child who is given executive authority, prematurely, in the family. Without knowing it, the family members may resist change, not only for what they may have to give up, but also because change is always feared. Thus, they may undermine recovery.

The role systems found in alcoholic families can be enmeshed so that everyone is hyper-responsive to and dependent on one another—disorganized, chaotic, or exploded into nothingness. The old-fashioned, middle-class alcoholic family is commonly enmeshed. This situation is more likely to arise if religion represents a barrier to divorce, and hence removal of the alcoholic.

A family counselor can help the family members understand the roles they are playing and start a process of change. This recognition allows family members to develop their own identities separate from the roles they have been playing. Two of the techniques used in understanding roles and relationships are **psychodrama** (or **role-playing**) and the **genogram**, a kind of family tree in which behavioral relationships as well as biological relationships are explored (Davis n.d.).

The family counselor can help the family members figure out their patterns of thinking, which involves certain modes of information processing. In the alcoholic family, these patterns typically involve denial, minimization, rationalization, shame, blame, and projection. Counselors also rely on certain self-statements (see "Here and Now: The 'Top Tens' of Helping Alcoholics and Their Families").

In addition, the family counselor can help the family members understand their patterns of communication. Alcoholic family communication is almost certainly a type of abnormal communication, characterized by either simple absence of communication (chaotic, destructive, manipulative, and blaming) or a combination of communication methods. What the family does in the public view, visible to the outside world ("front stage"), differs from what goes on when the family is alone ("back stage"). Some individuals may be cut off from communication or embroiled in endless argument and acrimony. Teaching people how to communicate their feelings and opinions in a direct, honest, and nonhurtful way begins the healing process.

The alcoholic family is injured, traumatized, often in debt, and collectively suffering from **posttraumatic stress disorder (PTSD)**. Grief, loss, pain, and rage are present. Healing will not take place overnight and will not occur just because the alcoholic stops drinking. The child, in particular, may have been wounded by violence, neglect, and inconsistent parenting and may have been witness to sex, violence, or depression.

KEY TERMS

psychodrama
a family therapy system developed by Jacques Moreno in which significant interpersonal and intrapersonal issues are enacted in a focused setting using dramatic techniques

role-playing
a therapeutic technique in which group members play assigned parts to elicit emotional reactions

genogram
a family therapy technique that records information about behavior and relationships on a type of family tree to elucidate persistent patterns of dysfunctional behavior

posttraumatic stress disorder (PTSD)
a psychiatric syndrome in which an individual who has been exposed to a traumatic event or situation experiences persistent psychological stress that may manifest itself in a wide range of symptoms, including re-experiencing the trauma, numbing of general responsiveness, and hyperarousal

HERE AND NOW

The "Top Tens" of Helping Alcoholics and Their Families

10 "Don'ts"

Don't "persecute" the addict. Confront lovingly.

Don't have the goal of "saving the family."

Don't start sentences with "you never" or "you always."

Don't live in the past or in the future.

Don't make excuses for the alcoholic.

Don't let the alcoholic be the center of your life.

Don't clean up after the alcoholic (literally or figuratively).

Don't protect the alcoholic from the consequences of his or her behavior.

Don't blame, excuse, justify, or rationalize.

Don't join in drinking.

10 "Dos"

Set limits, using "I" words (I need to stop).

Set limits empathetically (I know you want me to, but I can't).

Detach, lovingly, from the addict's problems.

Teach parenting skills.

Concentrate on the here and now.

Talk about violence and abuse.

Remember that you didn't cause it, you can't cure it, and you can't control it.

Take life a day at a time.

Give "self" assignments, taking care of yourself.

Accept the right to have your feelings and for others to have their feelings.

10 Alcoholic Family Self-Statements

. . . in an Actively Alcoholic Family

"Don't talk" (about how you feel, about what's going on).

"Don't trust."

"Don't feel."

"Alcoholism isn't the cause of our problems."

"Keep the status quo at all costs."

. . . in a Family Having a Hard Time Becoming Used to Sobriety

"We liked you better drunk."

"You're always away at AA meetings."

"Who are these people you're always having coffee with?"

"I felt important feeding my brothers and sisters, Mom."

"I felt important going to the school on Open School Night, Dad."

10 Roles for Spouses of Alcoholics

Rescuer

Long-suffering martyr

Blamer, conscience

Fellow drinker

Placater

Overextended, super-responsible one

Composed computer

Sick hypochondriac

Scapegoat ("it's your entire fault")

Avoider

10 Roles for Children of Alcoholics

Family hero*

Scapegoat*

Lost child*

Mascot*

Placater

Sick role

Parental child or pseudo parent to younger children

Pseudo parent to alcoholic parent

Pseudo spouse to sober parent

Place of refuge (for younger children)

*Reproduced from Wegscheider, S. *Another Chance*. Palo Alto, CA: Science and Behavior Books, 1991.

As seen in In-service Training Program, Essex County, New Jersey, Professional Advisory Committee on Alcohol and Drug Abuse. November 1993. Prepared by Peter L. Myers, PhD.

LEARNING PORTFOLIO

Key Terms

Discussion Questions

1. Why do you think alcohol has always been part of human existence?
2. Cite three positive and three negative outcomes of alcohol use in our society. Do you think the negatives outweigh the positives? If so, why? If not, why not?
3. Look at the pyramid of drinkers shown in Figure 8.2. How do you think the percentages will change 10 years, 20 years, and 30 years from now? Support your projections.
4. What are three positive and three negative outcomes regarding lowering the legal drinking age to 18?
5. Do you personally believe in the strong independent effects of set and setting and pseudointoxication? Can these psychological processes have more effects on the alcohol user than the alcohol itself? Wherever possible, give personal examples.
6. Why do you think the temperance movement and Prohibition failed? Cite three main reasons that also support the text material.
7. Research reports that LGBT and homeless people tend to abuse alcohol more than the straight (heterosexual) and nonhomeless populations. What are three reasons members of each of these subcultures have a tendency to overconsume alcohol?
8. Why do you think children and younger teens desire to consume alcohol with their peers?
9. After reviewing the different definitions of what is an alcoholic, what definition do you think is the most accurate? Write a clear definition of what you think is a "real" alcoholic.
10. What specific criteria would you include when teaching college students to drink in moderation during freshman orientation?
11. Should alcohol be available on college campuses for those 21 years of age or over? Why or why not?
12. Recall and discuss the question of how you may have unknowingly acted as an enabler for a family member or a friend. Can you cite the reason why you acted like this?

Summary

1. Slightly less than half of Americans aged 12 or older reported being current drinkers of alcohol in 2014 (48%). This translates to an estimated 139.7 million people. Approximately 22.2% participated in binge drinking at least once in the 30 days before the 2014 National Survey on Drug Use and Health. This translates to about 60.9 million binge drinkers in 2014.
2. Worldwide, adults aged 21 years or older consume on average 5 liters of pure alcohol from beer, wine, and spirits per year.

Average alcohol consumption is highest in Europe, followed by the Americas and Africa. It tends to increase with economic development. However, consumption remains low in some regions where the majority of the population is Muslim (GreenFacts 2009).

3. Among persons aged 12 years or older, whites in 2014 were more likely than other racial/ethnic groups to report current use of alcohol (57.7%). The rates were 49.5% for persons reporting two or more races, 42.3% for American Indians or Alaska Natives, 44.4% for Hispanics, 44.2% for blacks, and 38.7% for Asians (SAMHSA 2015).

4. Alcohol is the most widely used drug in the United States, and alcohol problems cost the nation nearly $249.0 billion each year (NIAAA 2016). "Two-thirds of the costs of alcohol abuse related to lost productivity, either due to alcohol-related illness (45.7%) or premature death (21.2%)" (NIAAA 1998). "Most of the remaining costs of alcohol abuse were in the form of healthcare expenditures to treat alcohol use disorders and the medical consequences of alcohol consumption (12.7%), property and administrative costs of alcohol-related motor vehicle crashes (9.2%), and various additional costs of alcohol-related crime (8.6%)" (NIAAA 1998). Seventy-six percent of people with drug or alcohol problems are employed, and approximately 19.2 million U.S. workers (15%) reported using or being impaired by alcohol at work at least once in the past year. On a per capita basis, the economic impact of excessive alcohol consumption in the United States is approximately $746 per person, most of which is attributable to binge drinking (CDC 2011).

5. Alcohol is officially linked to at least half of all highway fatalities, and that figure includes only legal intoxication. In all states, the cutoff for the blood alcohol level is 0.08%. In as many as 70% of all single-vehicle fatal crashes on weekend nights, the driver was legally intoxicated, and this proportion holds during most weekends throughout the United States. Interestingly, this single issue has been the only alcohol problem that has inspired

very vocal and effective groups to lobby for stricter enforcement of laws against alcohol-impaired automobile driving. Groups such as MADD (Mothers Against Drunk Driving) and SADD (Students Against Drunk Driving) are the largest prevention organizations in the nation.

6. In 2000, total costs attributed to alcohol-related motor vehicle crashes were estimated to be $24.7 billion. Expenditures for alcohol-related crime totaled $6.2 billion, and $17.4 billion for crime related to illicit drugs. Alcohol abuse is estimated to have contributed to 25% to 30% of violent crime.

7. The temperance movement was a response to the heaviest drinking period in the United States during President Thomas Jefferson's term in office (1801–1809). The original goal of this movement was to promote moderate use of alcohol. Largely because it was unsuccessful, the temperance movement began advocating total abstinence. Over the course of the 19th century, reformers sought to have complete prohibition enacted into law. Shortly after Prohibition laws were created, making alcohol use illegal, organized crime monopolized the production and sale of alcohol as an illicit drug.

8. There are several accepted definitions of alcoholism. Alcohol addiction involves both a physical and psychological dependence on ethanol. Most definitions include chronic behavioral disorders, repeated drinking to the point of loss of control, health disorders, and difficulty functioning socially and economically.

9. The definition of who is a problem drinker varies from one culture to the next. In Poland, a person becomes a problem drinker when there is a loss of productivity. Californians find that drunken driving violations are a key indication. For Italian Americans, an inability to provide for one's family because of heavy drinking qualifies a person as a problem drinker.

10. Culture influences our view of alcohol and alcohol consumption. Culture dictates the self-definition, attachment, and intensity of

our behavior. For example, with regard to drinking, much of how we feel after ingesting alcohol is determined by social and psychological experiences. In addition to the amount consumed, drunken comportment refers to society's expectations regarding drinking behavior. Set and setting are two important factors affecting alcohol consumption. Set refers to the individual's expectation of what a drug will do and setting refers to both the physical environment and the social environment in which the drug is consumed. Pseudointoxication refers to the psychological belief regarding how one feels under the effects of alcohol; that is, how inebriated the drinker imagines he or she is due to the effect of the consumed alcohol.

11. The broader ways in which culture influences the consumption of alcohol are the following: (a) culture provides rules for drinking behavior, (b) culture provides ceremonial meaning for alcohol use, (c) culture provides models of alcoholism, (d) cultural stereotypes of drinking may be misleading, (e) culture provides attitudes regarding alcohol consumption, and (f) culture determines what is considered acceptable amounts of drinking.

12. Use of alcohol by college students results in a significant increase in the number of incidences of death, injury, assault, sexual abuse, unsafe sex, academic problems, health problems, suicide attempts, drunk driving, vandalism, property damage, police involvement, and alcohol abuse and dependence. Additional noteworthy findings include the following: (a) college students consume an estimated 4 billion cans of beer annually, (b) nearly 40% of all college students are binge drinkers, (c) one consequence of alcohol abuse is motor vehicle accidents (the number one cause of death in people younger than age 25 is motor vehicle accidents), and (d) 75% of male students and 55% of female students involved in acquaintance rape had been drinking or using drugs at the time.

13. In comparison to men, women possess greater sensitivity to alcohol, are more likely to become addicted, and are more likely to develop health problems earlier in life than men. Three main reasons why women are more sensitive and are more easily affected by alcohol use are (a) men, in general, have larger bodies than women; (b) women absorb alcohol sooner than men because women generally have more body fat (fat does not dilute alcohol) and men's bodies contain more water; and (c) women possess less of a metabolizing enzyme that functions to get rid of (process out) alcohol.

14. Codependency and enabling generally occur together. Codependency is the behavior that a family member or close friend displays to cover up the excessive drinking. Enabling refers to anyone who helps the excessive drinker deny or makes excuses for the excessive drinking.

15. Alcoholism treatment must take into consideration physical withdrawal and denial.

References

Abbey, A. "Sex and Substance Abuse: What Are the Links?" *Eta Sigma Gamman* 22 (Fall 1990): 16–18.

Adamo, C., and Advocates for Youth. "Young People and Dating Violence: Teaching Healthy Relationship Skills to Protect Health and Well-Being." Washington, DC: Advocates for Youth, March 2014. Available http://www.advocatesforyouth.org/datingviolence

Adams, S. H. "The Great American Fraud." *Collier's* 36(5) (1905): 17–18; (10) (1905): 16–18; (16) (1906): 18–20.

Alcohol Concern. "Fact Sheet: Women and Alcohol—A Cause for Concern?" London, England. December 2008. Available http://www.alcoholconcern.org.uk/publications/factsheets/women-factsheet

American Association for Marriage and Family Therapy (AAMFT). "Children of Alcoholics." Alexandra, VA: American Association for Marriage and Family Therapy. Available https://www.aamft.org/imis15/AAMFT/Content/Consumer_Updates/Children_of_Alcoholics.aspx

Answers.com. "Can Hasidic Jews Drink Alcohol?" 2011. Available http://wiki.answers.com/Q/Can_Hasidic_Jews_drink_alcohol

Arkin, E. B., and J. E. Funkhouser, eds. *Communicating About Alcohol and Other Drugs: Strategies for Reaching Populations at Risk.* OSAP Prevention Monograph No. 5. Rockville, MD: Office of Substance Abuse Prevention, U.S. Department of Health and Human Services, 1992.

Austin, G. A. "Perspectives on the History of Psychoactive Substance Use." *National Institute on Drug Abuse Research Issues* 23. Washington, DC: U.S. Department of Health, Education, and Welfare, 1978.

Babor, T. F., M. Hesselbrock, S. Radouce-Thomas, L. Feguer, J. P. Ferrant, and K. Choquette. "Concepts of Alcoholism Among American, French-Canadian, and French Alcoholics." In *Alcohol and Culture: Comparative Perspectives from Europe and America*, edited by T. F. Babor, 98–109. New York: Academy of Sciences, 1986.

Bales, R. F. "Cultural Differences in Rates of Alcoholism." *Quarterly Journal of Studies on Alcohol* 6 (1946): 489–499.

Berkowitz, A. D., and H. W. Perkins. "Recent Research on Gender Differences in Collegiate Alcohol Use." *Journal of American College Health* 36 (September 1987): 12–15.

Bissonnette, Z. "Alcohol and College: How Much Money Are Students Really Drinking?" *Daily Finance*, AOL Inc. (5 September 2010). Available http://www.dailyfinance.com/2010/09/05/alcohol-college-money-cost-students-drinking/

Bloomfield, K., T. Stockwell, G. Gmel, and N. Rehn. *International Comparisons of Alcohol Consumption*. Bethesda, MD: National Institute on Alcohol Abuse and Alcoholism, National Institutes of Health, 2003.

Bouchery E. E, H. J. Harwood, J. J. Sacks, C. J. Simon, and R. D. Brewer. "Economic Costs of Excessive Alcohol Consumption in the U.S., 2006." *American Journal of Preventive Medicine* 41 (November 2011): 516-524. Available http://www.ajpmonline.org/article/S0749-3797(11)00538-1/fulltext

Boyd, C. J., S. E. McCabe, and H. d'Arcy. "A Modified Version of the Cage as an Indicator of Alcohol Abuse and Its Consequences Among Undergraduate Drinkers." *Substance Abuse* 24 (December 2003): 221–232.

Brisbane, F. L. "Understanding the Female Child Role of Family Hero in Black Alcoholic Families." *Bulletin of the New York State Chapter of the National Black Alcoholism Council* 4 (April 1985).

Brisbane, F. L. "A Self-Help Model for Working with Black Women of Alcoholic Parents." *Alcoholism Treatment Quarterly* 2 (Fall 1985/Winter 1986): 47–53.

Buddy T. "Women and the Effects of Alcohol: Women at Higher Risks for Serious Medical Consequences." 11 February 2016a. Available: https://www.verywell.com/women-and-the-effects-of-alcohol-63794

Buddy T. "The Combination of Domestic Abuse and Alcohol." 01 August 2016b. Available https://www.verywell.com/domestic-abuse-and-alcohol-62643

Buddy T. "The Cost of Excessive Alcohol Use in the U.S." 10 February 2016c. Available https://www.verywell.com/the-cost-of-excessive-alcohol-use-in-the-u-s-67482

Buddy T. "Alcohol Health Risks for Women." 13 July 2016d. Available https://www.verywell.com/alcohol-health-risks-for-women-63799

Buddy T. "The Combination of Domestic Abuse and Alcohol." 01 August 2016e. Available https://www.verywell.com/domestic-abuse-and-alcohol-62643

Buddy T. "Common Traits of Adult Children of Alcoholics." 01 November 2015. Available https://www.verywell.com/common-traits-of-adult-children-of-alcoholics-66557

Center for Behavioral Health Statistics and Quality (CBHSQ). *Behavioral Health Trends in the United States: Results from the 2014 National Survey on Drug Use and Health*. HHS Publication No. SMA 15-4927, NSDUH Series H-50. Rockville, MD: Substance Abuse and Mental Health Services Administration, 2015.

Center for Substance Abuse Research (CESAR). "Alcohol-Related Traffic Fatalities Remain Steady at Around 40%." 10 October 2005. Available http://www.cesar.umd.edu/cesar/cesarfax/vol14/14-41.pdf

Center for Substance Abuse Research (CESAR). "Nearly All 11th and 12th Graders Believe Their Peers Are More Likely to Drink and Drive on Prom and Graduation Nights; Less Than One-Third Think Driving on These Nights Is Dangerous." 26 April 2010. Available http://www.cesar.umd.edu

Center for Substance Abuse Research (CESAR). "Nearly Two-Thirds of U.S. Adults Are Current Drinkers; Majority Are Infrequent or Light Drinkers." 27 May 2013. Available http://www.cesar.umd.edu

Center for Substance Abuse Research (CESAR). "Past Month Alcohol Use Among U.S. 8th, 10th, and 12th Graders Continues to Decline; Approaching Levels of Marijuana Use." 27 July 2015. Available http://www.cesar.umd.edu/cesar/cesarfax/vol24/24-06.pdf

Centers for Disease Control and Prevention (CDC). "Fetal Alcohol Spectrum Disorders (FASDs)—State-Specific Weighted Prevalence Estimates of Alcohol Use (Percentage of Any Use/Binge Drinking) Among Women Aged 18–44 Years—BRFSS, 2008." 19 May 2010. Available http://www.cdc.gov/ncbddd/fasd/data.html

Centers for Disease Control and Prevention (CDC). "CDC Reports Excessive Alcohol Consumption Cost the U.S. $224 Billion in 2006." 2011. Available http://www.cdc.gov/media/releases/2011/p1017_alcohol_consumption.html

Centers for Disease Control and Prevention (CDC). "Excessive Drinking Costs U.S. $223.5 Billion." 2014. Available http://www.cdc.gov/features/alcoholconsumption/

Centers for Disease Control and Prevention (CDC). "Fact Sheets—Alcohol Use and Your Health." Atlanta, GA: Centers for Disease Control and Prevention, 25 July

2016. Available http://www.cdc.gov/alcohol/fact-sheets/alcohol-use.htm

Cheung, Y. W. "Approaches to Ethnicity: Clearing Roadblocks in the Study of Ethnicity and Substance Use." *International Journal of Addictions* 28 (July 2009): 1209-1226.

Coghill, N., P. Miller, and M. Plant. *Future Proof: Can We Afford the Cost of Drinking Too Much?* London, England: Alcohol Concern, October 2009.

Collins, J. J., and M. A. Messerschmidt. "Epidemiology of Alcohol-Related Violence." *Alcohol, Health, and Research World* 17 (1993): 93–100.

Connecticut Business and Industry Association (CBIA). "CBIA Healthy Connections." Hartford, CT: Connecticut Business and Industry Association, 23 September 2016.

Core Institute. "2013 Annual Data: Core Alcohol and Drug Survey Long Form—Form 194 Executive Summary. Carbondale, IL: Core Institute, Southern Illinois University, 25 August 2014. Available http://core.siu.edu/_common/documents/2013.pdf

Dartmouth Center on Addiction, Recovery and Education (DCARE). "Jewish Tradition: Alcohol and Judaism: One View." 18 August 2003. Available at http://www.dartmouth.edu/~dcare/topics/jewish.html

Davis, L. "Acting Out Your Issues Through Psychodrama." Sierra Tucson. n.d. Available http://sierratucson.crchealth.com/articles/psychodrama/

De Jong, J. "Scope of the Problem: Gender and Drinking." *Catalyst (Higher Education Center for Alcohol and Other Drug Prevention)* 1 (Spring 1995): 1.

Douglass, F. *Life and Times of Frederick Douglass.* New York: Collier Books, 1892 (1967): 147–148.

Doweiko, H. E. *Concepts of Chemical Dependency*, 9th ed. Belmont, CA: Brooks/Cole, Cengage Learning, 2015.

Drug Strategies. "Alcohol and Crime." *Millennium Hangover: Keeping Score on Alcohol.* 1999. Available http://www.drugstrategies.com/pdf/Score99.pdf

Drugs.com. "Naltrexone." Drugs.com., 2016. Available https://www.drugs.com/pro/naltrexone.html

English, E. M., M. D. Shutt, and S. B. Oswalt. "Decreasing Use of Alcohol, Tobacco, and Other Drugs on a College Campus: Exploring Potential Factors Related to Change." *Journal of Student Affairs Research and Practice* 46 (2009). Available http://journals.naspa.org/jsarp/vol46/iss2/art3

Federal Occupational Health (FOH). "Let's Talk." U.S. Public Health Service Program Support Center, Department of Health and Human Services. Fall 2005. Available https://foh.hhs.gov/Library/letstalk/fall2005.pdf

Gallup. "Alcohol and Drinking." 2013. Available http://www.gallup.com/poll/1582/alcohol-drinking.aspx

Gans, H. J. "Second-Generation Decline: Scenarios for the Economic and Ethnic Futures of the Post-1965 American Immigrants." *Ethnic and Racial Studies* 15 (April 1992): 173–192.

Garrison, V., and J. Podell. "Community Support Systems Assessment for Use in Clinical Interviews." *Schizophrenia Bulletin* 7 (1981): 1.

Gary, L. E., and R. B. Gary. "Treatment Needs of Black Alcoholic Women." *Alcoholism Treatment Quarterly* 2 (1985): 97–113.

Gold, M. S. *The Good News About Drugs and Alcohol.* New York: Villard Books, 1991.

Goode, E. *Drugs in American Society.* Boston: McGraw-Hill, 1999.

Gordon, A. J. "The Cultural Context of Drinking and Indigenous Therapy for Alcohol Problems in Three Migrant Hispanic Cultures." *Journal of Studies on Alcohol* (supplement 9) (1981): 217–240.

Grant, B. F., T. C. Harford, P. Chou, R. Pickering, D. A. Dawson, E. S. Stinson, and J. Noble. "Prevalence of DSM-IV Alcohol Abuse and Dependence: United States." *Alcohol Health Research World* 18 (1997): 243–248.

GreenFacts. "Scientific Facts on Alcohol." GreenFacts Scientific Board. 10 May 2009. Available http://www.greenfacts.org/en/alcohol/index.htm

Gusfield, J. R. *Symbolic Crusade: Status Politics and the American Temperance Movement*, 2nd ed. Chicago: University of Illinois, 1986.

Hanson, D. J. "History of Alcohol and Drinking Around the World." Sociology Department, State University of New York, Potsdam. 2009. Available http://www2.potsdam.edu/hansondj/Controversies/1114796842.html

Hanson, D. J. "Binge Drinking." Sociology Department, State University of New York, Potsdam. 2013b. Available http://www2.potsdam.edu/han-sondj/BingeDrinking.html

Hanson, D. J. "Minimum Legal Drinking Ages Around the World." Alcohol Problems and Solutions. 2015. Available http://www.alcoholproblemsandsolutions.org/LegalDrinkingAge.html

Harper, F. D. *The Black Family and Substance Abuse.* Detroit, MI: Detroit Urban League, 1986.

Hensel, D., T. Katherine, and R. Engs. "College Student's Health, Drinking and Smoking Patterns: What has Changed in 20 Years?" *College Student Journal* 3 (Fall 2014):378-385.

Hess, A. E. M, T. C. Frohlich, and V. Callo. "The Heaviest-Drinking Countries in the World." 24/7 Wall Street. 17 May 2014. Available http://247wallst.com/special-report/2014/05/15/the-heaviest-drinking-countries-in-the-world/

Hingston, R. W., W. Zha, and E. R. Weitzman. "Magnitude of and Trends in Alcohol-Related Mortality and Morbidity Among U.S. College Students Ages 18–24, 1998–2005." *Journal of Studies on Alcohol and Drugs* 16 (July 2009): 12–20.

Hjern, A. "Illicit Drug Abuse in Second-Generation immigrants: A Register Study in a National Cohort of Swedish Residents." Stockholm, Sweden: Centre for Epidemiology, National Board of Health and Welfare, 2016. Available http://sjp.sagepub.com/content/32/1/40.short

Inciardi, J. A. *The War on Drugs II.* Mountain View, CA: Mayfield, 1992.

Jellinek, E. M. *The Disease Concept of Alcoholism.* New Haven, CT: College and University Press, 1960.

Johnston, L. D., P. M. O'Malley, J. G. Bachman, and J. E. Schulenberg. *Monitoring the Future: National Survey Results on Drug Use, 1975–2011, Volume I: Secondary School Students.* Bethesda, MD: National Institute on Drug Abuse, 2012.

Johnston, L. D., P. M. O'Malley, R. A. Miech, J. G. Bachman, and J. E. Schulenberg. *Monitoring the Future National Survey Results on Drug Use, 1975–2015: Overview Key Findings on Adolescent Drug Use.* Ann Arbor: Institute for Social Research, University of Michigan, 2016.

Jones, J. M. "Beer Again Edges Out Wine as Americans' Drink of Choice." Gallup Poll. 12 July 2007. Available http://www.gallup.com/poll/28234/Beer-Again_Edges_Wine-Americans_Drink_Choice.aspx

Jones, J. M. "U.S. Drinkers Divide Between Beer and Wine as Favorite. Gallup/Well Being. 1 August 2013. Available http://www.gallup.com/poll/163787/drinkers-divide-beer-wine-favorite.aspx

Keller, M. "Alcoholism: Nature and Extent of the Problem: Understanding Alcoholism." *Annals of the American Academy of Political and Social Science* 315 (1958): 1–11.

Kellog, K. "Binge Drinking on College Campuses." Washington, DC: ERIC (The Educational Resources Information Center) Resource Center, 1999. Available http://files.eric.ed.gov/fulltext/ED436110.pdf

Kinney, J. *Loosening the Grip*, 6th ed. Boston: McGraw-Hill, 2000.

Kolevzon, M. S., and R. G. Green. *Family Therapy Models.* New York: Springer, 1985.

Lender, M. E., and J. K. Martin. *Drinking in America,* rev. ed. New York: Free Press, 1987.

Levine, H. G. "The Good Creature of God and the Demon Rum." In *Research Monograph No. 12: Alcohol and Disinhibition: Nature and Meaning of the Link,* 111–161. Rockville, MD: National Institute on Alcohol Abuse and Alcoholism, 1983.

Li, T.-K. *FY 2009 President's Budget Request for NIAAA—Director's Statement Before the House Subcommittee on Labor-HHS Appropriations.* Bethesda, MD: National Institute on Alcohol Abuse and Alcoholism, 5 March 2008: 1.

MacAndrew, C., and R. B. Edgerton. *Drunken Comportment: A Social Explanation.* Chicago, IL: Aldine, 1969.

Makela, K. "Attitudes Towards Drinking and Drunkenness in Four Scandinavian Countries." In *Alcohol and Culture: Comparative Perspectives from Europe and America. Annals of the New York Academy of Science* 472, edited by T. F. Babor. New York: New York Academy of Sciences, 1986.

Marshall, M. "Four Hundred Rabbits: An Anthropological View of Ethanol as a Disinhibitor." In *Alcohol and Disinhibition: Nature and Meaning of the Link.* NIAAA Research Monograph No. 12. Washington, DC: U.S. Department of Health and Human Services, 1983.

Medical News Today. "Alcohol Consumption More Detrimental to Women." RTI International. 7 May 2007.

Miech, R. A., L. D. Johnston, P. M. O'Malley, J. G. Bachman, and J. E. Schulenberg. *Monitoring the Future National Survey Results on Drug Use, 1975–2014: Volume I, Secondary School Students.* Ann Arbor, MI: Institute for Social Research, University of Michigan, 2015.

Miller, B. A., and W. R. Downs, "The Impact of Family Violence on the Use of Alcohol by Women." *Alcohol, Health, and Research World* 17 (1993): 137–143.

National Institute on Alcohol Abuse and Alcoholism (NIAAA). *Facts About Alcohol and Alcoholism.* Washington, DC: U.S. Government Printing Office, 1980.

National Institute on Alcohol Abuse and Alcoholism (NIAAA). "Economic Costs of Alcohol and Drug Abuse Estimated at $246 Billion in the United States." Rockville, MD: National Institute on Alcohol Abuse and Alcoholism, 13 May 1998. Available https://www.niaaa.nih.gov/news-events/news-releases/economic-costs-alcohol-and-drug-abuse-estimated-246-billion-united-states

National Institute on Alcohol Abuse and Alcoholism (NIAAA). *Are Women More Vulnerable to Alcohol's Effects?"* Washington, DC: U.S. Department of Health and Human Services, October 2000.

National Institute on Alcohol Abuse and Alcoholism (NIAAA). *10th Special Report to the U.S. Congress on Alcohol and Health: Highlights from Current Research.* Washington, DC: U.S. Government Printing Office, June 2000.

National Institute on Alcohol Abuse and Alcoholism (NIAAA). "Frequently Asked Questions on Alcohol Abuse and Alcoholism." 2007a. Available http://www.niaaa.nih.gov/faqs/general-english

National Institute on Alcohol Abuse and Alcoholism (NIAAA). *Researchers Identify Alcoholism Subtypes.* Bethesda, MD: Government Printing Office, 2007b. Available http://www.nih.gov/news/pr/jun2007/niaaa -28.htm

National Institute on Alcohol Abuse and Alcoholism (NIAAA). *Alcohol Research—A Lifespan Perspective.* Alcohol Alert 74. Rockville, MD: National Institute on Alcohol Abuse and Alcoholism Publication Distribution Center, January 2008.

National Institute on Alcohol Abuse and Alcoholism (NIAAA). "College Drinking Fact Sheet." Rockville, MD: National Institute on Alcohol Abuse and Alcoholism, 2009.

National Institute on Alcohol Abuse and Alcoholism (NIAAA). "College Drinking—Changing the Culture. A Snapshot of Annual High-Risk College Drinking Consequences." 21 July 2010. Available http://www .collegedrinkingprevention.gov/StatsSummaries/snap shot.aspx

National Institute on Alcohol Abuse and Alcoholism (NIAAA). "College Drinking." Rockville, MD: National Institute on Alcohol Abuse and Alcoholism, 2013.

National Institute on Alcohol Abuse and Alcoholism (NIAAA). "Alcohol Facts and Statistics." Rockville, MD: National Institute on Alcohol Abuse and Alcoholism, March 2015a.

National Institute on Alcohol Abuse and Alcoholism (NIAAA). *Alcohol: A Woman's Health Issue.* Rockville, MD: National Institute on Alcohol Abuse and Alcoholism, 2015b.

National Institute on Alcohol Abuse and Alcoholism (NIAAA). *College Drinking.* Rockville, MD: National Institute on Alcohol Abuse and Alcoholism, December 2015c.

National Institute on Alcohol Abuse and Alcoholism (NIAAA). "Alcohol Facts and Statistics." Rockville, MD: National Institute on Alcohol Abuse and Alcoholism, January 2016.

National Institute on Alcohol Abuse and Alcoholism (NIAAA). "Alcohol Use Disorder." Rockville, MD. National Institute on Alcohol Abuse and Alcoholism, n.d. Available http://www.niaaa.nih.gov/alcohol -health/overview-alcohol-consumption/alcohol-use -disorders

National Institute on Drug Abuse (NIDA). *National Survey Results on Drug Use from the Monitoring the Future Study, 1975–1998. Volume 1: Secondary School Students.* Washington, DC: U.S. Government Printing Office, 1999.

National Institute on Drug Abuse (NIDA). "NIDA Info Facts: Understanding Drug Abuse and Addiction." National Institutes of Health, U.S. Department of Health and Human Services. February 2011. Available http://www.drugabuse.gov/infofacts/understand.html

Newport, F. "Alcohol and Drinking." Gallup Organization. 13–15 November 2000. Available http://www.gallup .com/poll/1582/alcohol-drinking.aspx

Office of Applied Studies (OAS), Substance Abuse and Mental Health Services Administration (SAMHSA). *The NHSDA Report: Alcohol Use.* Rockville, MD: SAMHSA, 2001.

Osterberg, E. "Alcohol-Related Problems in Cross-National Perspective. Alcohol and Culture: Comparative Perspectives from Europe and America." *Annals of the New York Academy of Sciences* 472 (1986): 10–21.

Parsons, T. "Alcoholism and Its Effect on the Family." AllPsych and Heffner (14 December 2003). Available http://allpsych.com/journal/alcoholism.html

Presley, C., P. Meilman, and R. Lyerla. *Recent Statistics on Alcohol and Other Drug Use on American College Campuses: 1995–1996.* Carbondale, IL: Core Institute, Southern Illinois University at Carbondale, 1996.

Reardon, C. "The Changing Face of Older Adult Substance Abuse." *Social Work Today* 12 (2012): 8–18.

Register, T. C., J. M. Cline, and C. A. Shively. "Minority Women and Alcohol Use." *Alcohol Research and Health* (2002): 243–244.

Research Group News Release. "African-American Drinking Patterns More Deadly," 5 July 2016. Available https://www.verywell.com/african-american-drinking -patterns-more-deadly-63193

Room, R. "A Reverence for Strong Drink: The Lost Generation and the Elevation of Alcohol in American Culture." *Journal of Studies on Alcohol* 43 (1984): 540–545.

Room, R., and K. Mäkelä. "Typologies of the Cultural Position of Drinking." *Journal of Studies on Alcohol* 61 (2000): 475–483.

Roueche, B. "Alcohol in Human Culture." In *Alcohol and Civilization,* edited by L. P. Salvatore, 167–182. New York: McGraw-Hill, 1963.

Royce, J. E. *Alcohol Problems and Alcoholism,* rev. ed. New York: Free Press, 1989.

Royce, J. E., and D. Scratchley. *Alcoholism and Other Drug Problems.* New York: Free Press, 2007.

Saad, L. "Majority in U.S. Drink Alcohol, Averaging Four Drinks a Week." Gallup Wellbeing. 17 August 2012. Available http://www.gallup.com/poll/156770/Majority -Drink-Alcohol-Averaging-Four-Drinks-Week.aspx

Satir, V. *Conjoint Family Therapy.* Palo Alto, CA: Science and Behavior Books, 1964.

Substance Abuse and Mental Health Services Administration (SAMHSA). *Making the Link: Alcohol, Tobacco, and Other Drugs and Women's Health.* Pub. No. ML011.

Rockville, MD: U.S. Department of Health and Human Services, Spring 1995.

Substance Abuse and Mental Health Services Administration (SAMHSA). *National Household Survey on Drug Abuse: Main Findings, 1997.* Rockville, MD: Office of Applied Studies, U.S. Department of Health and Human Services, August 1999.

Substance Abuse and Mental Health Services Administration (SAMHSA). "SAMHSA Unveils Guide to Introduce Substance Abuse Treatment Providers to Family Therapy." 2004. Available http://www.samhsa.gov/news/newsreleases/040929nr_tip39.htm

Substance Abuse and Mental Health Services Administration (SAMHSA). "Issue Brief #1 for Employers: Save Your Company Money by Assuring Access to Substance Abuse Treatment." 2008a. Available http://store.samhsa.gov/shin/content/SMA08-4350/SMA08-4350.pdf

Substance Abuse and Mental Health Services Administration (SAMHSA). "Issue Brief #2 for Employers: What You Need to Know About Older Workers and Substance Abuse." 2008b. Available http://store.samhsa.gov/shin/content/SMA08-4350/SMA08-4350.pdf

Substance Abuse and Mental Health Services Administration (SAMHSA). "Issue Brief #3 for Employers: About Younger Workers and Substance Abuse." 2008c. Available http://store.samhsa.gov/shin/content/SMA08-4350/SMA08-4350.pdf

Substance Abuse and Mental Health Services Administration (SAMHSA). "Issue Brief #5 for Employers: Save Money by Addressing Employee Alcohol Problems." 2008d. Available http://store.samhsa.gov/shin/content/SMA08-4350/SMA08-4350.pdf

Substance Abuse and Mental Health Services Administration (SAMHSA). *Results from the 2011. National Survey on Drug Use and Health: Summary of National Findings.* NSDUH Series H-44, HHS Pub. No. (SMA) 12-4713. Rockville, MD: SAMHSA, 2012.

Substance Abuse and Mental Health Services Administration (SAMHSA). *National Survey on Drug Use and Health* NSDUH. Table 2.46B—Alcohol Use, Binge Alcohol Use, and Heavy Alcohol Use in the Past Month Among Persons Aged 18 or Older, by Demographic Characteristics: Percentages, 2012 and 2013. Rockville, MD: Substance Abuse and Mental Health Services Administration. Available http://www.samhsa.gov/data/sites/default/files/NSDUH-DetTabsPDFWHTML2013/Web/HTML/NSDUH-DetTabsSect2peTabs43to84-2013.htm#tab2.46b

Substance Abuse and Mental Health Services Administration (SAMHSA). *Results from the 2013. National Survey on Drug Use and Health: Summary of National Findings.* NSDUH Series H-48, HHS Pub. No. (SMA) 14-4863. Rockville, MD: Substance Abuse and Mental Health Services Administration, 2014.

Svensson, M. and C. Hagquist. "Adolescent Alcohol and Illicit Drug Use Among First- and Second-Generation Immigrants in Sweden." *Scandinavian Journal of Public Health* 38 (November 2009): 184–191. Available https://www.researchgate.net/publication/40026582_Adolescent_alcohol_and_illicit_drug_use_among_first-_and_second-generation_immigrants_in_Sweden

U.S. Department of Justice (USDOJ). "Domestic Violence." Washington, DC: U.S. Department of Justice, Office on Violence Against Women, March 2013. Available http://www.ovw.usdoj.gov/domviolence.htm

Vaillant, G. E. "Parent–Child Cultural Disparity and Drug Addiction." *Journal of Nervous and Mental Disease* 142 (June 1966): 534–539. Available http://journals.lww.com/jonmd/Citation/1966/06000/PARENT_CHILD_CULTURAL_DISPARITY_AND_DRUG.4.aspx

Wallace K. "Study Has More Disturbing Findings About Campus Rape of Freshmen Women." CNN. 20 May 2015. Available http://www.cnn.com/2015/05/20/living/feat-rape-freshmen-women-new-study/

Wechsler, H., A. Davenport, G. Dowdall, B. Moeykens, and S. Castillo. "Health and Behavioral Consequences of Binge Drinking in College. A National Survey of Students at 140 Campuses." *Journal of the American Medical Association* 272 (7 December 1994): 1672–1677.

Wechsler, H, G. W. Dowdall, A. Davenport, and W. DeJong. *Binge Drinking on Campus: Results of a National Study.* Harvard School of Public Health, Higher Education Center for Alcohol and Other Drug Prevention. Washington, DC: U.S. Department of Education, 2000a.

Wechsler, H., J. Eun Lee, M. Kuo, and H. Lee. *College Binge Drinking in the 1990s: A Continuing Problem: Results of the Harvard School of Public Health 1999 College Alcohol Study.* 1999 College Alcohol Study (CAS) Binge Drinking Survey. Boston, MA: Harvard School of Public Health, 2000b.

Wechsler, H. and B. Wuethrich. *Dying to Drink: Confronting Binge Drinking on College Campuses.* Emmaus, PA: Rodale Books, 2002.

Wegscheider, S. *Another Chance.* Palo Alto, CA: Science and Behavior Books, 1991.

Weisbaum H. "College Textbook Costs More Outrageous Than Ever." CNBC. 28 January 2014. Available http://www.cnbc.com/2014/01/28/college-textbook-costs-more-outrageous-than-ever.html

Williams, G. D., F. S. Stinson, D. A. Parker, T. C. Harford, and V. Noble. "Demographic Trends, Alcohol Abuse and Alcoholism, 1985–1995." Epidemiologic Bulletin

No. 15. *Alcohol, Health, and Research World* 11 (1997): 80–83.

Wilsnack, S. C., R. W. Wilsnack, and A. D. Klassen. "Epidemiological Research on Women's Drinking, 1978–1984." In *Women and Alcohol: Health-Related Issues.* Research Monograph No. 16. Washington, DC: U.S. Government Printing Office, 1986.

World Health Organization (WHO). "Trends in Substance Use and Associated Health Problems." *Trends in Substance Use.* Fact Sheet No. 127 (1996). Available http://www.dronet.org/lineeguida/ligu_pdf/trendsub.pdf

Yip, P. "More Senior Struggling with Substance and Alcohol Abuse." *Dallas Morning News.* (9 December 2014).

Available http://www.dallasnews.com/business/health-care/20141219-substance-and-alcohol-abuse-rising-among-elderly.ece

Zinberg, N. E. *Drug, Set, and Setting: The Basis for Controlled Intoxicant Use.* New Haven, CT: Yale University Press, 1984.

Zinberg, N. E., and J. A. Robertson. *Drugs and the Public.* New York: Simon & Schuster, 1972.

Zucker, R. A., J. E. Donovan, A. S. Masten, M. E. Mattson, and H. B. Moss. "Developmental Processes and Mechanisms—Ages 0–10." *Alcohol Research and Health* 32 (2009): 16–29.

© ermingut/iStockphoto.com.

Did You Know?

▶ The release of natural substances called endorphins activate opioid receptors and can mimic the effects of narcotics such as heroin or morphine.

▶ By the end of the 19th century, almost 300,000 Americans were addicted to opiates, primarily due to the use of patent medicines that contained opium products.

▶ Narcotics are among the most potent analgesics available today.

▶ In the past decade, treatment for nonmedical use of prescription pain relievers has increased more than fourfold and currently accounts for two-thirds of prescription abuse in the United States.

▶ Because of concerns about abuse of prescription narcotic analgesics, many clinicians are hesitant to prescribe sufficient quantities of these drugs to adequately manage severe long-term pain.

▶ Addiction to prescription narcotic analgesics rarely happens when these medications are used properly to treat pain.

▶ Evidence suggests that acupuncture reduces pain by activating a natural opioid system.

▶ Many heroin addicts have been exposed to the human immunodeficiency virus (HIV).

▶ Heroin supplies today are more potent, cheaper, and more readily available than a decade ago.

▶ One designer drug, made from the narcotic fentanyl, is 6000 times more potent than heroin.

▶ Some heroin addicts have to be treated with the narcotics methadone or buprenorphine for the rest of their lives to keep them from abusing heroin.

▶ Dextromethorphan (a common over-the-counter cough medicine chemically related to codeine), when taken in high doses, can cause phencyclidine (PCP)-like hallucinations.

Learning Objectives

On completing this chapter you should be able to:

❭ Describe the principal pharmacological effects of narcotics, their biological targets, and their main therapeutic uses.

❭ Identify the major side effects of narcotics, in particular their abuse potential.

❭ Distinguish between narcotic physical dependence and addiction.

❭ Identify the abuse patterns for heroin.

❭ Outline the stages of heroin dependence.

❭ List the withdrawal symptoms that result from narcotic dependence, list potential treatments, and discuss the significance of tolerance.

❭ Describe and compare the use of methadone and buprenorphine in treating narcotic addiction.

❭ Explain the connection between abuse of prescription opioid narcotic drugs and heroin.

❭ Identify the unique features of fentanyl that make it appealing to illicit drug dealers but dangerous to narcotic addicts.

❭ Describe how "designer" drugs have been associated with narcotics and Parkinson's disease.

❭ Describe why dextromethorphan in cough medicines is abused.

❭ Identify the opioid features of tramadol and its potential for abuse.

Introduction

In 2014, it was estimated that approximately 2 million people in the United States had an opioid drug use disorder associated with prescription painkillers, and another 600,000 were abusing heroin (Substance Abuse and Mental Health Services Administration [SAMSHA] 2015a). These facts illustrate that our society is having major problems dealing with nonmedical use of drugs known as opioid narcotics. Additional findings that further confirm the extent of the so-called opioid drug epidemic include the following (American Society of Addiction Medicine [ASAM] 2016):

* Approximately 10% of the total number of Americans with a substance use disorder abuse prescription pain relievers.
* It is estimated that almost one-quarter of those who use heroin will become addicted to opioid drugs.
* Of the approximately 47,000 persons in the United States who died from a lethal drug overdose in 2014, 40% of the deaths were related to prescription opioid pain relievers.
* The treatment admission rate for opioid drug use disorder has increased almost 10-fold in the past decade.
* 80% of new heroin users were first exposed to the opioid drugs by misusing prescription painkillers.
* In 2014, approximately 500,000 adolescents were nonmedical users of opioid analgesics.
* Most adolescents who have prescription opioid drug use disorder get their drugs for free from a friend or relative.
* Women are more likely to experience chronic pain, use prescribed opioid analgesics, receive higher doses, and use these drugs for longer time periods than men.

KEY TERMS

analgesics
drugs that relieve pain without affecting consciousness

antitussives
drugs that block the coughing reflex

opioid
relating to the drugs that are derived from opium

The term *narcotic* in general means a central nervous system (CNS) depressant that produces insensibility or stupor. The term has also come to designate those drugs and substances with pharmacological properties related to opium ingredients and their drug derivatives. All opioid narcotics activate opioid receptors and have abuse potential. Narcotics are frequently prescribed for pain relief (**analgesics**), to reduce coughing (**antitussives**), and to reduce diarrhea.

In this chapter, we introduce the opioid narcotics with a brief historical account. The pharmacological properties and therapeutic uses of these drugs are discussed, followed by a description of, and distinction between, their side effects and problems with tolerance, withdrawal, dependence, and addiction. Narcotic abuse, its risks and outcomes, is presented in detail, with special emphasis on heroin. In addition, treatment approaches for narcotic addiction, dependence, and withdrawal are included. This chapter concludes with descriptions of other commonly used opioid narcotics and related drugs.

What Are Narcotics?

The word *narcotic* has been used to label many substances, from opium to marijuana to cocaine. The translation of the Greek word *narkoticos* is "benumbing" or "deadening." The term *narcotic* is sometimes used to refer to a CNS depressant, producing insensibility or stupor, and at other times to refer to an addicting drug. Most people would not consider marijuana among the narcotics today, although for many years it was included in this category. Although pharmacologically cocaine is not a narcotic either, it is still legally classified as such. Perhaps part of this confusion is due to the fact that cocaine, as a local anesthetic, can cause a numbing effect (Addiction Blog 2014a).

For purposes of the present discussion, the term *narcotic* is used to refer to those naturally occurring substances derived from the opium poppy and their synthetic substitutes. These drugs are referred to as the **opioid** (or opiate) narcotics because of their association with opium. They have similar pharmacological features, including abuse potential, pain-relieving effects; cough suppression; and reduction of intestinal movement, often causing constipation, but useful in reducing severe diarrhea. Some of the most commonly used opioid narcotics are listed in **Table 9.1**.

TABLE 9.1 Commonly Used Opioid Narcotic Drugs and Products

Narcotic Drug	Common or Trade Names	Most Common Uses
Heroin	Horse, smack, junk (street names)	Abuse
Morphine	Several	Analgesia
Methadone	Dolophine	Treat narcotic dependence
Meperidine	Demerol	Analgesia
Oxycodone	Percodan, OxyContin	Analgesia
Propoxyphene	Darvon	Analgesia
Codeine	Several	Analgesia, antitussive
Loperamide	Imodium A-D	Antidiarrheal
Diphenoxylate	Lomotil	Antidiarrheal
Opium tincture	Paregoric	Antidiarrheal
Buprenorphine	Suboxone	Treat narcotic dependence
Tramadol	Ultram	Analgesia (considered to have weak, but significant, opioid properties)

The History of Narcotics

The opium poppy, *Papaver somniferum*, from which opium and its naturally occurring narcotic derivatives are obtained, has been cultivated for millennia. A 6000-year-old Sumerian tablet has an ideograph for the poppy shown as "joy" plus "plant," suggesting that the addicting properties of this substance have been appreciated for millennia. The Egyptians listed opium along with approximately 700 other medicinal compounds in the famous Ebers Papyrus (circa 1500 BC).

The Greek god of sleep, Hypnos, and the Roman god of sleep, Somnus, were portrayed as carrying containers of opium pods, and the Minoan goddess of sleep wore a crown of opium pods. During the so-called Dark Ages that followed the collapse of the Roman Empire, Arab traders actively engaged in traveling the overland caravan routes to China and to India, where they introduced opium. Eventually, both China and India grew their own poppies.

■ Opium in China

The opium poppy had a dramatic impact in China, causing widespread addiction (PBS n.d.). Initially, the seeds were used medically, as was opium later. However, by the late 1690s opium was being smoked and used for diversion. The Chinese government, fearful of the weakening of national vitality by the potent opiate narcotic, outlawed the sale of opium in 1729. The penalty for disobedience was death by strangulation or decapitation. Despite these laws and threats, the habit of opium smoking became so widespread that the Chinese government went a step further and forbade its importation from India, where most of the opium poppy was grown. In contrast, the British East India Company (and later the British government in India) encouraged cultivation of opium. British companies were the principal shippers to the Chinese port of Canton, which was the only port open to Western merchants. During the next 120 years, a complex network of opium smuggling routes developed in China with the help of local merchants, who received substantial profits, and local officials, who pocketed bribes to ignore the smugglers.

Everyone involved in the opium trade, but particularly the British, continued to profit until the Chinese government ordered the strict enforcement of the edict against importation. Such actions by the Chinese caused conflict with the British government and helped trigger the Opium War of 1839 to 1842. Great Britain sent in an army, and by 1842, 10,000 British soldiers had won a victory over 350 million Chinese. Because of the war, the island of Hong Kong was ceded to the British,

Opium poppies such as these are used as a source for natural opioid narcotic drugs such as heroin, morphine, and codeine.

With the development of the hypodermic needle and its use during the Civil War, heroin addiction became more likely and more severe.

and an indemnity of $6 million was imposed on China to cover the value of the destroyed opium and the cost of the war. In 1856, a second Opium War broke out. Peking was occupied by British and French troops, and China was compelled to make further concessions to Britain. The importation of opium continued to increase until 1908, when Britain and China made an agreement to limit the importation of opium from India (PBS n.d.).

▌ American Opium Use

Meanwhile, in 1803, a young German named Frederick Serturner extracted and partially purified the active ingredients in opium. The result was 10 times more potent than opium itself and was named *morphine*, after Morpheus, the Greek god

A famous cartoon, showing a British sailor shoving opium down the throat of a Chinese man, which dates back to the Opium War of 1839–1842.

of dreams. This discovery increased worldwide interest in opium. By 1832, a second compound had been purified and named *codeine*, after the Greek word for "poppy capsule" (Medical Discoveries n.d.).

The opium problem was aggravated further in 1853, when Alexander Wood perfected the hypodermic syringe and introduced it first in Europe and then in America. Christopher Wren and others had worked with the idea of injecting drugs directly into the body by means of hollow quills and straws, but the approach was never successful or well received. Wood perfected the syringe technique with the intent of preventing morphine addiction by injecting the drug directly into the veins rather than using oral administration (Golding 1993). Unfortunately, just the opposite happened; injection of morphine increased the potency and the likelihood of dependence (Maurer and Vogel 1967).

The hypodermic syringe was used extensively during the Civil War to administer morphine to treat pain, dysentery, and fatigue (Kosten and Hollister 1998). A large percentage of the soldiers who returned home from the war were addicted to morphine (National Institute on Drug Abuse [NIDA] 2013). Opiate addiction became known as the "soldier's disease" or "army disease."

By 1900, an estimated 300,000 Americans were dependent on opiates (NIDA 2013). The drug problem then became worse because of (1) Chinese laborers, who brought opium with them to the United States to smoke (it was legal to smoke

Chinese laborers often smoked heroin at the turn of the 20th century.

© National Library of Medicine.

opium in the United States at that time); (2) the availability of purified morphine and the hypodermic syringe; and (3) the lack of controls on the large number of patent medicines that contained opium derivatives (Karch 1996). Until 1914, when the Harrison Narcotic Act was passed (regulating opium, coca leaves, and their products), the average opiate addict was a middle-aged Southern white woman who functioned well and was adjusted to her role as a wife and mother. She bought opium or morphine legally by mail order from Sears and Roebuck or at the local store, used it orally, and caused very few problems. A number of physicians were addicted as well. One of the best-known morphine addicts was William Holsted, a founder of Johns Hopkins Medical School. Holsted was a very productive surgeon and innovator, although secretly an addict for most of his career. He became dependent on morphine as a substitute for his cocaine dependence (Brecher 1972).

Heroin use by soldiers fighting in Afghanistan is a great concern.

© Baris Atayman/Reuters/Landov.

Looking for better medicines, chemists found that modification of the morphine molecule resulted in a more potent compound. In 1898, diacetylmorphine was placed on the market as a cough suppressant by Bayer. It was to be a "heroic" drug, without the addictive potential of morphine—it thus received the name *heroin*.

Heroin was first used in the United States as a cough suppressant and to combat addiction to other substances (Hubbard 1998). However, its inherent abuse potential was quickly discovered. When injected, heroin is more addictive than most of the other narcotics because of its ability to enter the brain rapidly and cause a euphoric surge (DiChiara and North 1992). Heroin was banned from U.S. medical practice in 1924, although it is still prescribed legally as an analgesic or for treatment of narcotic dependence (like methadone) in other countries (Drug War Facts 2012).

The Vietnam War was an important landmark for heroin use in the United States (Hubbard 1998). It has been estimated that as many as 40% of the U.S. soldiers serving in Southeast Asia at this time used heroin to combat the frustrations and stress associated with this unpopular military action. Although only 7% of the soldiers continued to use heroin after returning home, those who were addicted to this potent narcotic became a major component of the heroin-abusing population in this country (Golding 1993).

Smoking of heroin became popular in the mid-1980s in response to the acquired immune deficiency syndrome (AIDS) epidemic. This was due to a fear of HIV infection when using infected needles to administer the drug intravenously (Hubbard 1998). The effect resulting from inhalation is as intense as that caused by injection, although a very pure drug is required for smoking. Smoking continues to be a favorite form of heroin administration today.

As experience has shown, problems with the opiate drugs such as heroin are closely linked with war and its associated miseries and pains. As our country again finds itself in the middle of an extended and increasingly less popular military engagement in the Middle East, particularly Afghanistan, problems with heroin are becoming more and more apparent (RT 2013). As during previous wars, soldiers turn to drugs like heroin to cope and even to survive emotionally in a war zone. This is reflected in comments such as "Life is unbearable. You don't know whether you're going to be alive in 10 minutes' time or not." "Life has few pleasures; you're uncomfortable . . .

the food is pretty awful, the ever-present smell of death and you see some of your closest buddies die before your very eyes." "So life is really unbearable and heroin is cheap" (Edwards 2010).

Pharmacological Effects

Even though opioid narcotics have a history of being abused, they continue to be important therapeutic agents.

■ Narcotic Analgesics

The most common clinical use of the opioid narcotics is as analgesics to relieve pain. These drugs are effective against most varieties of pain, including *visceral* (associated with internal organs of the body) and *somatic* (associated with skeletal muscles, bones, skin, and teeth) types. Used in sufficiently high doses, narcotics can even relieve the intense pain associated with some types of cancer (Gutstein and Akil 2006).

The opioid narcotics relieve pain by activating the same group of receptors that are controlled by the endogenous substances called *endorphins* (Schumacher, Basbaum, and Naidu 2015). The endorphins are a family of peptides (small proteins) that are released in the brain, in the spinal cord, and from the adrenal glands in response to stress and painful experiences. When released, the endorphins serve as transmitters and stimulate receptors designated as opioid types. Activation of opioid receptors by either the naturally released endorphins or administration of the narcotic analgesic drugs blocks the transmission of pain through the spinal cord or brain stem and alters the perception of pain in the "pain center" of the brain. Because the narcotics work at multiple levels of pain transmission, they are potent analgesics against almost all types of pain.

Interestingly, the endorphin system appears to be influenced by psychological factors as well. Thus, natural activation of opioid receptors also contributes to the regulation of emotional behaviors such as stress, learning, and memory, as well as the regulation of the brain's reward circuits (Schumacher et al. 2015). It is possible that pain relief caused by administration of placebos or nonmedicinal manipulation such as acupuncture is due in part to the natural release of endorphins (Eshkevari and Heath 2005). This relationship suggests that physiological, psychological, and

pharmacological factors are intertwined in pain management through the opioid system, which makes it impossible to deal with one without considering the others.

Although the narcotics are very effective analgesics, they do cause some side effects that are particularly alarming; thus, their clinical use usually is limited to the treatment of moderate to severe pain (Schumacher et al. 2015). Other, safer drugs, such as the aspirin-type analgesics, are preferred for pain management when possible. Often, the amount of narcotic required for pain relief can be reduced by combining a narcotic, such as codeine, with aspirin or acetaminophen (the active ingredient in Tylenol). Such combinations reduce the chance of significant narcotic side effects while providing adequate pain relief (Schumacher et al. 2015).

Morphine is a particularly potent pain reliever and often is used as the analgesic standard to which other narcotics are compared (Gutstein and Akil 2006). With continual use, tolerance develops to the analgesic effects of morphine and other narcotics, sometimes requiring a dramatic escalation of doses to maintain adequate pain control (Schumacher et al. 2015).

Because pain is expressed in different forms with many different diseases, narcotic treatment can vary considerably. Usually, the convenience of oral narcotic therapy is preferred but often is inadequate for severe pain. For short-term relief from intense pain, narcotics are effective when injected subcutaneously or intramuscularly. Narcotics can also be given intravenously for persistent and potent analgesia or administered by transdermal patches for sustained chronic pain (*Drug Facts and Comparisons* 2010). Despite the fact that most pain can be relieved if enough narcotic analgesic is properly administered, physicians frequently underprescribe narcotics or are not well trained in proper pain management or how to use the opioid narcotics responsibly (Young and Hobson 2016). Because of fear of causing narcotic addiction or creating legal problems with federal agencies such as the Drug Enforcement Administration (DEA) (see "Here and Now: A War on Doctors? Are Restrictions on Pain Pills Too Painful?"), many patients in the United States are often inadequately treated for their pain (Alford 2016). An important rule of narcotic use is that adequate pain relief should not be denied because of concern about the abuse potential of these drugs (Schumacher et al. 2015). Indeed, addiction to narcotics is rare in patients receiving these drugs for therapy unless they have a history of drug

HERE AND NOW
A War on Doctors? Are Restrictions on Pain Pills Too Painful?

Many people, especially those patients suffering from pain who are not able to convince their doctors to prescribe sufficient opioid painkillers for adequate relief, believe that the federal government, and the Drug Enforcement Administration (DEA) in particular, is scaring health providers from prescribing sufficient pain medications to relieve their suffering. The start of these problems can be traced back to the 1980s when doctors began to embrace the philosophy that relieving pain actually helped to promote healing. Over the next couple of decades prescriptions for opioid painkillers escalated dramatically, led by a drug called OxyContin, which reached sales of $1.6 billion in 2003. Related to this escalation of narcotic analgesic prescriptions was the emergence of an illegal market that sold diverted opioid painkillers in the streets, feeding a robust drug trade headed by drug dealers and drug lords. In response to this growing problem, it has been perceived that the DEA has particularly targeted prescribing health professionals and discouraged their use of these drugs to treat pain. Some feel that this strategy is somewhat misplaced based on findings that 95% of all illegal prescription drugs sold on the streets are related to thefts from pharmacies, warehouses, and trucks and that only 5% are due to illegally diverted prescriptions from health providers. Of course, there are examples of prescribers running "pill mills" in exchange for money, sex, or other drugs, but in reality these are few and far between. It is argued by some that the emphasis on investigating legitimate medical practices is an excessive incursion by law enforcement into medical practice. Thus, there are those who claim that while DEA investigations have done little to curb the access to illegal drug products, they have caused many clinicians to either underprescribe for pain management in their patients or have caused them to refuse altogether to prescribe the opioid painkillers for the control of pain.

Data from funtony47. "The War on Doctors: How the DEA Is Scaring Doctors from Prescribing Pain Medications." Daily Kos. 15 April 2015. Available http://www.dailykos.com/story/2015/4/15/1375189/-The-War-On-Doctors-How-The-DEA-is-Scaring-Doctors-from-Prescribing-Pain-Medications

abuse or have an underlying psychiatric disorder (Gutstein and Akil 2006).

Occasionally, there are outbreaks of abuse of commonly prescribed narcotic products such as OxyContin (Food and Drug Administration [FDA] 2010; "'Oxy' Kids Crisis" 2007). This product includes the opiate oxycodone, which has the approximate narcotic potency of morphine and can be obtained with relative ease. Authorities claim that the illegal pills come from doctors' offices, from dealers who fake illness to get legal prescriptions or who are writing phony orders, and from others who steal the supplies from pharmacies. OxyContin has been called *oxys*, *O.C.*, and *killers* on the street and is popular with narcotic abusers because of its rapid and potent effect. However, many, if not most, of those who use prescriptions drugs for nonmedical purposes obtain their painkillers from the medicine cabinets of a family member or a friend (Volkow 2014a). On the street, the drug can cost 10 times its prescription price. Because of its potent ability to suppress respiration, OxyContin appears to have been involved in overdose deaths throughout the country, although there is some evidence that other drugs were also involved in many of these cases. Critics claim that part of the abuse problem with OxyContin stems from overuse in situations that should be managed by a less potent and less addicting opioid analgesic.

■ Other Therapeutic Uses

Opioid narcotics are also used to treat conditions not related to pain. For example, these drugs suppress the coughing center of the brain, so they are effective antitussives. Codeine, a natural opioid narcotic, is commonly included in cough medicine. In addition, opioid narcotics slow the movement of materials through the intestines, a property that can be used to relieve diarrhea or can cause the side effect of constipation (Schumacher et al. 2015). Paregoric contains an opioid narcotic substance and is commonly used to treat severe diarrhea.

When used carefully by the clinician, opioid narcotics are very effective therapeutic tools. Guidelines for avoiding unnecessary problems with these drugs include the following (Rolfs 2008; Volkow 2014a):

- Opioid pain relievers should only be used for pain when severity warrants and after consideration of other nonopioid pain medications such as aspirin, ibuprofen, or acetaminophen (e.g., Tylenol).
- Doses and duration of use should be limited as much as possible while permitting adequate therapeutic care.
- The patient should be counseled to store the medications securely, not share with others, and dispose of drugs properly when the pain has subsided and the medication is no longer needed.
- Long-duration opioid drugs should not be used to treat acute pain, except in situations where adequate monitoring can be conducted.
- The use of opioids should be reevaluated if pain persists beyond the anticipated time period for acute pain management.
- A comprehensive evaluation should be conducted before initiating opioid treatment.
- The provider should consider conducting a screen for risk of abuse or addiction before initiating opioid treatment.
- A treatment plan should be established between the doctor and patient that includes measurable goals for reduction of pain and improvement of function.
- The patient, and if appropriate, family members, should be informed of the risks and benefits of the opioid treatment. Sometimes a written contract identifying these elements should be prepared and signed.
- Opioid treatment should be discontinued if the terms of the contract are not being met by the patient.
- If significant abuse is suspected, the clinician should discuss the concerns with the patient and help the patient find appropriate treatment.

■ Abuse of Prescription Opioid Painkillers

As already mentioned, the rapid increase in the abuse of prescription opioid painkillers has become a major problem in the United States (Volkow 2014a, 2014b). An example of what has become all too common is the tragic narcotic overdose death of Leslie Cooper near Portsmouth, Ohio. She was never known to wander the streets or dark alleys to get her opioid narcotics. She received her drugs "legally" from multiple doctors and "pain management clinics." Her problem with these prescription analgesics started when doctors prescribed potent painkillers to deal with

severe discomfort after a difficult surgery. More surgeries were necessary, which meant continual demand for, and access to, the opioid pain relievers. Something went terribly wrong, and Leslie paid the price with her life. In her system was found a deadly combination of depressant drugs prescribed for muscle relaxation and depression, and two very potent narcotic analgesics. Leslie fell asleep and did not wake up. This is an example of why the misuse of these painkillers has more than doubled emergency room visits in the past decade (Compton, Jones, and Baldwin 2016) and also has caused some critics to question whether many doctors who prescribe such drugs are sufficiently trained in proper pain or substance abuse management (Young and Hobson 2016).

PRESCRIPTION FOR ABUSE

What Makes People Vulnerable?

For most patients, the responsible use of prescription opioid analgesics is very helpful in the management of moderate to severe pain; however, a relatively small population has factors that can increase the danger of becoming addicted to these drugs as much as 25-fold. The risks that lead to this vulnerability include:

- Family history of substance abuse problems, which suggests the likelihood of genetic vulnerability
- Dependence on nicotine, alcohol, or sleeping pills
- Depression
- Use of psychiatric medications
- Age younger than 65 years

The value of identifying these risks is they may help warn clinicians about which patients require special consideration and caution when prescribing narcotics to treat their pain.

Data from American Academy of Pain Medicine. "Psychiatric Factors Linked to Increased Risk for Misuse of Opioid Medications." 23rd Annual Meeting. Abstract 151. 7 February 2007; Levran, O., D. Londono, K. O'Hara, M. Randesi, J. Rotrosen, P. Casasonte, S. Linzy, J. Ott, M. Adelson, and M. J. Kreek. "Heroin Addiction in African Americans: A Hypothesis-Driven Association Study." *Genes Brain and Behavior* 8 (2009): 531–540; Medical News Today. "Study Identifies Risk Factors for Painkiller Addiction and Links the Addiction to Genetics." 28 August 2010. Available http://www.medicalnewstoday.com/articles/199263.php; Sify News. "Risk Factors for Painkiller Addiction Identified." 28 August 2010. Available http://sify.com/news/risk-factors-for-painkiller-addiction-identified-news-scitech-ki3pEjahbic.html

Abuse problems with these drugs are partially due to the facts that these narcotic analgesics are very popular and account for over 207 million prescriptions in the United States each year (Volkow 2014a, 2014b). This means that these drugs are more readily available and their use more widely accepted than ever before. However, it is important to appreciate that when used properly (i.e., as prescribed), the likelihood of becoming addicted to these narcotics for most people is very small (likely less than 1%). But there are risk factors that make some patients more likely to have problems with these drugs; for those with these risk factors the rate of addiction jumps to 25% (Sify News 2010; see "Prescription for Abuse: What Makes People Vulnerable?").

Abuse of prescription opioid narcotics such as OxyContin and illicit narcotics such as heroin might seem to some people very different because one comes from a doctor and the other from drug dealers in the street. But in reality, because both types of drugs are opiates, they both can cause similar addictions, overdoses, and even death. In fact, a surprising rise in heroin abuse is occurring across the United States, which is likely, in part, the result of people who become addicted to the prescription opioid painkillers and switch to heroin because it is more accessible and easier to obtain.

Heroin also can cost as little as one-fifth the price of prescription medications. All too often heroin overdose deaths appear to have their origins in victims first being exposed to the opioid narcotics during a chronic treatment for pain often associated with sports-related injuries (Valenzuela 2010; Willis 2008).

■ Mechanisms of Action

As mentioned earlier, the opioid receptors are the site of action of the naturally occurring endorphin

peptide transmitters and are found throughout the nervous system, intestines, and other internal organs. Because narcotic drugs such as morphine and heroin enhance the endorphin system by directly stimulating opioid receptors, these drugs have widespread influences throughout the body.

For example, the opioid receptors are present in high concentration within the limbic structures of the brain. Stimulation of these receptors by narcotics causes release of the transmitter dopamine in the limbic regions of the brain. This effect contributes to the rewarding actions of these drugs and leads to dependence and abuse (Trigo et al. 2010; Zocchi et al. 2003; see "Signs & Symptoms: Narcotics").

■ Side Effects

One of the most common side effects of opioid narcotics is constipation. Other side effects include drowsiness, mental clouding, respiratory depression (suppressed breathing is usually the cause of death from overdose), nausea and vomiting, itching, inability to urinate, a drop in blood pressure, and constricted pupils (Kral and Ghafoor 2013; Schumacher et al. 2015). This array of seemingly unrelated side effects is due to widespread distribution of the opioid receptors throughout the body and their involvement in many physiological functions (Gourlay 2004; Trigo et al. 2010). With continual use, tolerance usually develops to some of these undesirable narcotic responses.

Drugs that selectively antagonize the opioid receptors can block the effects of natural opioid systems in the body and reverse the effects of narcotic opiate drugs (Schumacher et al. 2015). When an opioid antagonist such as the drug naloxone is administered alone, it has little noticeable effect. The antiopioid actions of naloxone become more apparent when the antagonist is injected into someone who has taken a narcotic opioid drug. For example, naloxone will cause (1) a recurrence of pain in the patient using a narcotic for pain relief, (2) the restoration of consciousness and normal breathing in the addict who has overdosed on heroin, and (3) severe withdrawal effects in the opioid abuser who has become dependent on narcotics (Schumacher et al. 2015). Because of the ability of these antagonists to block the effects of opioid drugs, they are also used as treatment for some opioid-dependent patients (Schumacher et al. 2015).

An interesting recent use of opioid antagonists is in the treatment of alcohol dependence. The FDA has approved the use of naltrexone

SIGNS & SYMPTOMS

Narcotics

Possible Signs of Use	Possible Signs of Overdose
Euphoria	Low and shallow breathing
Drowsiness	Clammy skin
Respiratory depression	Convulsions
Constricted pupils	Coma
Nausea	Death

(a narcotic antagonist) in a regular and extended-release formulation to relieve the craving of alcoholics for excessive alcohol consumption (Schumacher et al. 2015).

Abuse, Tolerance, Dependence, and Withdrawal

All the opioid narcotic agents that activate opioid receptors have abuse potential and are classified as scheduled drugs (see **Table 9.2**). Their patterns of abuse are determined by the ability of these drugs to cause tolerance, dependence, withdrawal effects, and eventually addiction. However, it is important to recognize that even though a patient treated by these drugs for pain develops physical dependence and experiences significant withdrawal when the drug is abruptly removed, they are not necessarily addicted (Hitti 2010). In fact, relatively few patients properly receiving the opioid narcotics for pain relief will go on to become truly addicted, even though they may develop physical dependence and are temporarily uncomfortable when the narcotic treatment is discontinued. This distinction between physical dependence and the compulsive need to use the opioid narcotics despite very negative consequences (i.e., addiction) is very important and needs to be appreciated in order to provide proper pain management, especially for severe long-term pain conditions (NAABT.org 2014).

The process of tolerance literally begins with the first dose of a narcotic, but tolerance does not become clinically evident until after 2 to 3 weeks of frequent use (either therapeutic or abuse related). Tolerance occurs most rapidly with high doses given in short intervals and is a common result of the extended clinical use of prescription opioid painkillers. It also is caused by abuse of these narcotics in addicted persons. The result of tolerance is that doses of these drugs must be increased (sometimes several-fold) to retain or regain the therapeutic or nonmedicinal narcotic effects. Physical dependence invariably accompanies severe tolerance (Schumacher et al. 2015). Psychological dependence can also develop with continual narcotic use because these drugs can cause euphoria and relieve stress. Such psychological dependence leads to compulsive use (Luscher 2012). Because all narcotics affect the same opioid systems in the body, developing tolerance to one narcotic drug means the person has cross-tolerance to all drugs in this group.

The development of psychological and physical dependence makes stopping the drug uncomfortable due to resulting unpleasant withdrawal effects. Someone who has used potent narcotics for a long time, such as a long-term addict, will experience severe withdrawal effects such as exaggerated pain responses, agitation, anxiety, stomach cramps and vomiting, joint and muscle aches, runny nose, and an overall flulike feeling. Although these withdrawal symptoms are not fatal, they are extremely aversive and encourage continuation of the narcotic habit (Schumacher et al. 2015).

Overall, the narcotic opioids have similar actions; there are differences, however, in their potencies, severity of side effects, likelihood of being abused, and clinical usefulness.

TABLE 9.2 Schedule Classification of Some Common Narcotics

Narcotic	Schedule
Heroin	I
Morphine	II, III
Methadone	II
Fentanyl	II
Hydromorphone	II
Hydrocodone	II
Meperidine	II
Codeine	II, III, V
Buprenorphine	III
Pentazocine	IV
Tramadol	Unscheduled
Narcotics combined with nonsteroidal anti-inflammatory drugs	III

Data from Drug Enforcement Administration, Office of Diversion Control, U.S. Department of Justice. "Controlled Substance Schedules." 2016. Available http://www.deadiversion.usdoj.gov/schedules/#list

▌ Heroin Abuse

"He loved heroin more than it loved him. I was shocked beyond imagining: he was the first of my friends to fall."

—Corey Feldman, "How to Kick Heroin" (2015)

Use of heroin and heroin-related deaths have been on the rise in the United States (Cook 2015). The likely explanations for this recent rise in popularity include the facts that high-grade heroin has become very cheap and readily available (Centers for Disease Control and Prevention [CDC] 2015). In addition, it appears that the rise in heroin use is an indirect consequence of the increase in the abuse of prescription opioid painkillers (Compton et al. 2016). For example, four out of five new heroin users start out by misusing prescription pain relievers (ASAM 2016). People who abuse prescribed opioid narcotics often increase their consumption of these drugs because they develop tolerance. This makes their habit more expensive and makes it more difficult to obtain enough of the prescription drugs to satisfy their nonmedical (addiction) needs. Consequently, these people frequently switch to street heroin, which is a fraction of the cost while still being reasonably pure and potent. Of course, this switch to heroin increases the risk of getting a bad batch of drug that is much more potent than expected or that contains other drugs that are more dangerous. The unintended outcomes can be, at the least, very dangerous and result in a trip to the emergency room or, in the extreme, an accidental overdose fatality (Gorner 2015).

Heroin is currently classified as a Schedule I drug by the DEA (see Table 9.2). It is not approved for any clinical use in the United States and is one of the most widely abused illegal drugs in the world (United Nations Office on Drugs and Crime [UNODC] 2015). It is also thought to be associated with some of the highest mortality rates and most emergency room visits of any of the illegal drugs of abuse in the United States (CDC 2015). Heroin was illicitly used more than any other drug of abuse in the United States (except for marijuana) until 20 years ago, when it was unseated by cocaine (DiChiara and North 1992). In 2015, 0.5% of high school seniors reported using heroin, and 0.8% indicated that they had used this drug sometime during their life (Johnston 2016).

From 1970 through 1976, most of the heroin reaching the United States originated from the Golden Triangle region of Southeast Asia, which includes parts of Burma, Thailand, and Laos. During that period, the United States and other nations purchased much of the legal opium crop from Turkey in an effort to stop opium from being converted into heroin. From 1975 until 1980, the major heroin supply came from opium poppies grown in Mexico. The U.S. government furnished the Mexican government with helicopters,

herbicide sprays, and financial assistance to destroy the poppy crop. Changes in political climates shifted the source of supply back to the Golden Triangle and Latin American countries and then to Afghanistan, where 92% of the world's heroin was produced in 2010 (Office of National Drug Control Policy [ONDCP] 2015).

Heroin produced in Afghanistan has taken a heavy toll on the Afghan people (Christenson 2010) (see "Here and Now: Afghans' Drug War"). It has been speculated that heroin trafficked from Afghanistan has killed more than a million people worldwide (Agence France-Presse 2010). In addition, it was a substantial problem for U.S. and NATO soldiers fighting in the Afghan War (Edwards 2010). Even today, heroin-related corruption in the Afghanistan government has made it difficult to effectively control the lucrative heroin trade from this country (ONDCP 2015). Today, the cultivation of the opium poppy remains high in Mexico, making this country the primary supplier of heroin to the United States (ONDCP 2015).

HEROIN COMBINATIONS

Heroin is typically smuggled into the United States from one of four foreign sources: Mexico, South America, Southeast Asia (e.g., Burma), or Southwest Asia (e.g., Afghanistan). It is carried into the United States hidden in commercial and private vehicles driven from Mexico or Canada or carried by couriers traveling on commercial flights. Pure heroin is a white powder. Other colors, such as brown Mexican heroin, result from unsatisfactory processing of morphine or from adulterants. Heroin is usually "cut" (diluted) with lactose (milk sugar) to give it bulk and thus increase profits. When heroin first enters the United States, it can be up to 95% pure; by the time it is sold to users, its purity can be as low as 3% or (recently) as high as 70% (ONDCP 2015; UNODC 2015). If users are unaware of the variance in purity and do not adjust doses accordingly, the results can be extremely dangerous and occasionally fatal (Gorner 2015).

Heroin has a bitter taste, so sometimes it is cut with quinine, a bitter substance, to disguise the fact that the heroin content has been reduced. Quinine can be a deadly adulterant. Part of the "flash," or immediate rush, from direct injection of heroin may be caused by this contaminant. Quinine is an irritant, and it causes vascular damage, acute and potentially lethal disturbances in heartbeat, depressed respiration, coma, and death from respiratory arrest. Opiate poisoning causes acute

HERE AND NOW

Afghans' Drug War

How goes the "war" in Afghanistan? The answer may be quite different depending on whether you are referring to the military war being fought against the Taliban with guns, explosives, and military maneuvers or the drug war being fought against poor opium farmers trying to survive on meager earnings that come from the few acres they are able to cultivate. Opium crops are particularly well suited to this land and historically brought good prices. Consequently, it is difficult to convince the poor farmers that crops that allow them to feed their families are evil and should be stopped. Despite the fact that efforts by both the Afghan and U.S. governments to educate opium farmers and help them develop profitable alternative crops reduced poppy cultivation by 22% in 2009, production of Afghan opium has risen dramatically during the Afghan War and currently is thought to provide 92% of the world's heroin. Just because they produce the opium, the Afghan people are not immune to its

problems. It is speculated that 1 in 25 Afghans is an addict, and very few resources are available to provide adequate treatment or initiate effective prevention programs. Statistics such as these are powerful evidence that the Afghans' drug war goes very badly indeed.

Data from Aljazeera. "Afghanistan's Billion Dollar Drug War." 6 May 2015. Available http://www.aljazeera.com/programmes/101east/2015/05/afghanistan-billion-dollar-drug-war-150505073109849.html; Christenson, S. "Heroin Addiction Takes Brutal Toll on Afghanistan." *San Antonio Express-News.* (24 May 2010). Available http://www.mysanantonio.com/news/military/article/Heroin-addiction-takes-brutal-toll-on-Afghanistan-787499.php

---

pulmonary edema as well as respiratory depression. To counteract the constipation caused by heroin, sometimes mannitol is added for its laxative effect.

Another potentially lethal combination emerges when heroin is laced with the much more potent artificial narcotic fentanyl. This adulterated heroin can be extremely dangerous due to its unexpected potency (Gorner 2015).

Frequently, heroin is deliberately combined with other drugs when self-administered by addicts (CDC 2015). Heroin is most frequently used with alcohol, but it is often combined with CNS stimulants, such as cocaine (Bebinger 2015). Some crack cocaine smokers turn to heroin to ease the jitters caused by the CNS stimulant. It also has been reported that heroin addicts use cocaine to withdraw or detoxify themselves from heroin by gradually decreasing amounts of heroin while

increasing amounts of cocaine. This drug combination is called **speedballing**, and addicts claim the cocaine provides relief from the unpleasant withdrawal effects that accompany heroin abstinence in a dependent user (Bebinger 2015).

Crude heroin is dark, whereas purified heroin is a white powder.

KEY TERM

speedballing
combining heroin and cocaine

PROFILE OF HEROIN ADDICTS

An estimated 600,000 to 1 million active heroin addicts live in the United States, a figure that has remained relatively stable despite changes in the number of infrequent and moderate users. Heroin addicts often search for a better and purer drug; however, if they do find an unusually potent batch of heroin, there is a good chance they will get more than they bargained for. Addicts are sometimes found dead with the needle still in the vein after injecting a particularly potent batch of heroin (ASAM 2016). More than 10,000 deaths occur annually in the United States from heroin overdoses (ASAM 2016). Death associated with heroin injection is usually due to concurrent use of alcohol or barbiturates—not the heroin alone—and frequently occur after an addict has gone weeks or months without the drug and injects the same amount of heroin he or she used before, not realizing that tolerance has worn off (Bebinger 2015).

Hard-core addicts often share a common place where they can stash supplies and equipment for their heroin encounters. These locations, called *shooting galleries*, serve as gathering places for addicts (*The Economist* 2015). Shooting galleries can be set up in homes but are usually located in less established locations such as abandoned cars, cardboard lean-tos, and weed-infested vacant lots. An entrance charge often is required of the patrons. Conditions in shooting galleries are notoriously filthy, and these places are frequented by

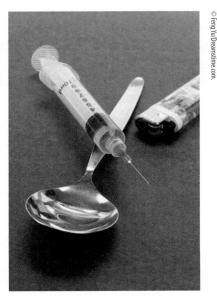

Heroin paraphernalia is usually simple and crude but effective: a spoon on which to dissolve the narcotic and a makeshift syringe with which to inject it.

intravenous heroin users with bloodborne infections that can cause AIDS or hepatitis. Because of needle sharing and other unsanitary practices, shooting galleries have become a place where serious communicative diseases are spread to a wide range of people of different ages, races, genders, and socioeconomic statuses (Nakamura 2008). In some countries, such as the United Kingdom, controversial efforts are under way to develop government-regulated shooting galleries in order to ensure sanitary conditions and the availability of clean needles for the heroin addicts to prevent their exposure to the dangers of contracting devastating and potentially deadly diseases (Leach 2009).

The heroin in shooting galleries is typically prepared by adding several drops of water to the white powder in an improvised container (such as a metal bottle cap) and lightly shaking the container while heating it over a small flame to dissolve the powder. The fluid is then drawn through a tiny wad of cotton to filter out the gross contaminants into an all-too-often used syringe where it is ready for injection.

Some addicts become fixated on the drug's paraphernalia, especially the needle. They can get a psychological high from playing with the needle and syringe. The injection process and syringe plunger action appear to have sexual overtones for them. As one reformed user explained, "I think what I miss more than heroin sometimes is just the ritual of shooting up." A heavy user concurred, explaining, "You get addicted to the needle.... Just the process of sticking something into your vein, having such a direct involvement with your body" ("Mary" 1996, p. 42; Winkler et al. 2011).

HEROIN AND CRIME

In 1971, the Select Committee on Crime in the United States released a report on methods used to combat the heroin crisis that arose in the 1950s and 1960s. This report was a turning point in setting up treatment programs for narcotic addicts. The report stated that drug arrests for heroin use had increased 700% since 1961 and that the cost of heroin-related crimes to U.S. society was estimated to exceed $3 billion per year. Other reports since that time have linked heroin addiction with crime (Fisher 2015).

Currently, many young heroin addicts come from affluent or middle-class white families (Seelye 2015; see "Here and Now: Heroin's New Terrain"). However, research shows that heavy users (usually addicts who inject their heroin) are frequently poorly educated with minimal social integration and live in neighborhoods surrounded by poverty (Nandi et al. 2010). Because of these disadvantages, these heroin addicts often have a low level of employment, exist in unstable living conditions, and socialize with other illicit drug users. Clearly, such undesirable living conditions encourage criminal activity. However, the pharmacological effects of heroin itself are not directly responsible for criminal behavior (Dalrymple 2015). Thus, there are three other factors that likely contribute to the association between heroin use and crime:

1. The use of heroin encourages antisocial behavior that is crime related. Depressants such as heroin diminish inhibition and cause people to engage in activities they normally would not. The effects of heroin and its withdrawal make addicts self-centered, demanding, impulsive, and governed by their "need" for the drug.
2. Because heroin addiction is expensive, the user is forced to resort to crime to support the drug habit (McMurran 2007).
3. A similar personality is driven to engage in both criminal behavior and heroin use. Often, heroin addicts start heroin use about the same time they begin to become actively involved in criminal activity. In most cases, the heroin user has been taking other illicit drugs, especially marijuana or prescription painkillers, years before trying heroin (Reid, Elifson, and Sterk 2007; Seelye 2015).

These findings suggest that for many heroin addicts, the antisocial behavior causes the criminal behavior rather than the criminal behavior resulting from the heroin use. Thus, the more a drug such as heroin is perceived as being illegal, desirable, and addictive, the more likely it will be used by deviant criminal populations. However, typically heroin users are not violent, although they may participate in criminal activity to fund their drug habit. Violence is more likely associated with heroin trafficking and distribution because of the criminal groups involved in this activity.

PATTERNS OF HEROIN ABUSE

It has become apparent that problems with narcotics are no longer confined to the inner cities, but have infiltrated suburban areas and small towns and afflict both rich and poor. The following are recent heroin trends (see **Table 9.3**):

- Heroin use among adolescents and young adults, after holding steady through much of the first decade in 2000, is thought to be rising due to a decrease in cost and increases in purity and availability (Ramde 2014).
- Heroin has become purer (60% to 70% purity) and cheaper ($10/bag [around 100 milligrams]) (Ramde 2014).
- Thanks to the greater purity, new users are able to administer heroin in less efficient ways, such as smoking and snorting, avoiding the dangers of intravenous use (Gray 2014). Many youths believe that heroin can be used safely if it is not injected.

TABLE 9.3 Prevalence of Heroin and Other Opioid Abuse Among High School Seniors

| Year | Annual Use | | Lifetime Use | |
	Heroin	Other Opioids	Heroin	Other Opioids
1995	1.1%	4.7%	1.6%	7.2%
1999	1.1%	6.7%	2.0%	10.2%
2002	1.0%	9.4%*	1.7%	13.5%*
2007	0.9%	9.2%	1.5%	13.1%
2009	0.7%	9.2%	1.2%	13.2%
2012	0.6%	7.9%	1.1%	12.2%
2015	0.4%	5.4%	0.8%	8.4%

* In 2002, the question text was changed in half of the questionnaire forms. The list of examples of narcotics other than heroin was updated: Talwin, laudanum, and paregoric—all of which had negligible rates of use by 2001—were replaced with Vicodin, OxyContin, and Percocet. The 2002 data presented here are based on the changed forms only; N is one-half of N indicated. In 2003, the remaining forms were changed to the new wording. Data based on all forms beginning in 2003.

Data from Johnston, L. D., P. M. O'Malley, J. G. Bachman, and J. E. Schulenberg. "Monitoring the Future." 2016. Available http://www.monitoringthefuture.org/

HERE AND NOW
Heroin's New Terrain

Courtney Griffin came from a comfortable home in southeastern New Hampshire—hardly the place where one would expect a hard-core heroin "junkie" to live. And yet Courtney's father explained at her funeral that his daughter's death was a consequence of her heroin addiction. He acknowledged her addiction secret and revealed that Courtney had lied, frequently disappeared, and stolen money from her parents to sustain a $400-a-day heroin habit. Her parents tried to "protect" their daughter by never reporting her thefts to the police and by paying her drug-related debts. Despite all of their efforts, Courtney was kicked out of the Marines because of her drug habit and was found dead from a heroin overdose at the home of her boyfriend's grandmother. Courtney was one of many victims of the recent heroin epidemic spreading into suburbs and small towns linked to a recent wave of addictions to prescription painkillers. This heroin epidemic differs demographically from that seen earlier with crack cocaine, which occurred primarily in poor and predominantly black urban areas. Another difference between the two drug epidemics is the public response. For the cocaine scourge, people demanded "zero tolerance" and severe prison terms. However, because the current heroin epidemic is predominantly found in white populations (90%), many of whom are from middle-class homes, families of the heroin "victims" are using their voice and political power to demand a more forgiving approach from government officials and law enforcement agencies: punishment is out and treatment is in.

Data from Seelye, K. "In Heroin Crisis, White Families Seek Gentler War on Drugs." *New York Times* (30 October 2015). Available http://www.nytimes .com/2015/10/31/us/heroin-war-on-drugs-parents.html

---

- Because of its association with popular fashions and entertainment, heroin has been viewed as glamorous and chic, especially by many young people, despite its highly publicized lethal consequences. The look of being "wasted" and unkempt has been referred to as "heroin chic" (Carbone 2014). However, to some extent this "druggy look" and malnourished appearance has fallen out of fashion within the glamour business because of its very negative implications and health consequences.

- Approximately 250,000 emergency room visits each year are due to heroin overdoses (Polidoro 2014).

STAGES OF DEPENDENCE

Initially, the early effects of heroin are often unpleasant, especially after the first injection (Gutstein and Akil 2006). It is not uncommon to experience nausea and vomiting after administration; gradually, however, the euphoria overwhelms the aversive effects (Powell 2015). The development of a psychological dependence on heroin or other opioid narcotics has two major stages:

1. In the rewarding stage, euphoria and positive effects occur in at least 50% of users. These positive feelings and sensations increase with continued administration and encourage use.

2. Eventually, the heroin or narcotic user must take the drug to avoid withdrawal symptoms that start about 6 to 12 hours after the last dose. At this stage, it is said that "the monkey is on his back." This stage is psychological dependence. If 1 grain of heroin (about 65 milligrams) is taken over a 2-week period on a daily basis, the user becomes physically dependent on the drug.

METHODS OF ADMINISTRATION

Many heroin users start by sniffing the powder or injecting it into a muscle (intramuscular) or under the skin ("skin popping"). Because of the increased purity and decreased cost, many of today's heroin users are administering their drug by smoking and snorting (Gray 2014).

Most established heroin addicts still prefer to **mainline** the drug (intravenous injection) (Kritz 2015). The injection device can be made from an eyedropper bulb, part of a syringe, and a hypodermic needle. Mainlining drugs causes the thin-walled veins to become scarred, and, if done

KEY TERM

mainline
to inject a drug of abuse intravenously

frequently, the veins will collapse. Once a vein is collapsed, it can no longer be used to introduce the drug into the blood. Addicts become expert in locating new veins to use: in the feet, the legs, the neck, even the temples. When addicts do not want "needle tracks" (scars) to show, they inject under the tongue or in the groin (Rehab International n.d.).

HEROIN ADDICTS, AIDS, AND HEPATITIS

Intravenous drug use, particularly heroin, substantially increases the likelihood of contracting viral infections associated with HIV/AIDS and viral hepatitis due to contact with infected blood or other body fluids because of sharing syringes and other injection paraphernalia. Although substituting snorting or smoking for intravenous drug administration reduces the likelihood of contracting these infectious diseases, it is not eliminated, as people under the influence of heroin are more likely to be exposed to these diseases because of their participation in risky sexual behaviors. Injection drug users are among the highest groups for being infected with these body fluid–born microorganisms and, in turn, are likely to infect many others as they transmit the pathogens to those with whom they associate (NIDA 2014a).

HEROIN AND PREGNANCY

> Devin acts like any normal 2-year-old. He particularly enjoys the fast-food Chick-fil-A restaurant and playing with the barbecue sauce containers. Looking at Devin gives no clue that his mother had become addicted to prescription painkillers when she discovered her pregnancy. She was urged by her sister to seek professional help immediately. Devin was born on time and was undersized at 5 pounds and 5 ounces. Devin was able to avoid the worst withdrawal symptoms after birth because he was immediately placed on methadone and gradually weaned to allow his small body to adjust to not having the painkillers that his mother had been using throughout her pregnancy. Devin was lucky: other babies under similar circumstances who do not receive proper medical care suffer through serious feeding problems, vomiting, diarrhea, muscle stiffness, and severe tremors. These babies cry constantly as they experience dangerous narcotic withdrawal, and in extreme cases they may even suffer seizures. (Colon 2011)

Many women use heroin during their pregnancy. In the United States, as many as 7000 infants are

A heroin addict "mainlining" his drug.

born each year to women who chronically used either heroin or other opioid drugs during their pregnancies (Bhuvaneswar et al. 2008). There is no evidence that prenatal exposure to opioid drugs causes overt structural damage, although incidents of lower birthweights or even reduced head size have been reported in infants born to mothers using opioid drugs (Wang 2010). The most devastating consequence of heroin or opioid use during pregnancy appears to be physical dependence in the newborn, resulting in withdrawal symptoms, usually immediately after birth. These symptoms are referred to as *neonatal abstinence syndrome*, or NAS, and are characterized by high-pitched crying, inconsolability, tightened muscle tone, tremors, vomiting, seizures, and even death. Elements of this withdrawal persist for weeks and usually require hospitalization (NIDA 2014b). Treatment for such withdrawal problems generally includes low doses of a long-lasting opioid narcotic to reduce the intensity of the symptoms and then a gradual tapering of the dose to eventually wean the infant from the drug. For heroin, this typically takes up to 2 weeks (NIDA 2014b). In addition, some evidence suggests that use of heroin during pregnancy increases the likelihood of sudden infant death syndrome (SIDS) in offspring (March of Dimes 2015).

WITHDRAWAL SYMPTOMS

After the effects of heroin wear off, the addict usually has only a few hours in which to find the next dose before severe withdrawal symptoms begin.

A single "shot" of heroin lasts only 4 to 6 hours. It is enough to help addicts "get straight," or relieve the severe withdrawal symptoms called dope sickness, but is not enough to give a desired high (Bersett and Lee 2015). Withdrawal symptoms start with a runny nose, tears, and minor stomach cramps. The addict may feel as if he or she is coming down with a bad cold (Bersett and Lee 2015). Between 12 and 48 hours after the last dose, the addict loses all of his or her appetite, vomits, has diarrhea and abdominal cramps, feels alternating chills and fever, and develops goose pimples all over (going "cold turkey"). Between 2 and 4 days later, the addict continues to experience some of the symptoms just described, as well as aching bones and muscles and powerful muscle spasms that cause violent kicking motions ("kicking the habit"). After 4 to 5 days, symptoms start to subside, and the person may get his or her appetite back. However, attempts to move on in life will be challenging because compulsion to keep using the drug remains strong.

The severity of the withdrawal varies according to the purity and strength of the drug used and the personality of the user. The symptoms of withdrawal from heroin, morphine, and methadone are summarized in **Table 9.4**. Withdrawal symptoms from opioids such as morphine, codeine, meperidine, and others are similar, although the time frame and intensity vary (Schumacher et al. 2015).

■ Treatment of Heroin and Other Narcotic Dependence

The ideal result of treatment for dependency on heroin or other narcotics is to help the addict live a normal, productive, and satisfying life without drugs (Volkow 2014a). Unfortunately, only

FIGURE 9.1 Treatment of heroin addiction. The principal aspects of treating heroin addiction include minimizing the very aversive withdrawal effect (usually with drug adjuncts); preventing relapse (usually with behavioral modification); and, if necessary, providing maintenance support with other opioid-like drugs that have longer action than heroin.

a minority of heroin addicts receive adequate treatment for their addiction. Of those who are treated, relatively few become absolutely "clean" from drug use; thus, therapeutic compromise often is necessary (see **Figure 9.1**). In the real world, treatment of heroin dependency is considered successful if the addict does the following:

- Stops using heroin
- No longer associates with dealers or users of heroin
- Avoids dangerous activities often associated with heroin use (such as needle sharing, injecting unknown drugs, and frequenting shooting galleries) (Tur 2010)
- Improves employment status

TABLE 9.4 Symptoms of Withdrawal from Heroin, Morphine, and Methadone

Symptoms	Time in Hours		
	Heroin	Morphine	Methadone
Craving for drugs, anxiety	4	6	24–48
Yawning, perspiration, runny nose, tears	8	14	34–48
Pupil dilation, goose bumps, muscle twitches, aching bones and muscles, hot and cold flashes, loss of appetite	12	16	48–72
Increased intensity of preceding symptoms, insomnia, raised blood pressure, fever, faster pulse, nausea	18–24	24–36	≥ 72
Increased intensity of preceding symptoms, curled-up position, vomiting, diarrhea, increased blood sugar, foot kicking ("kicking the habit")	26–36	36–48	–

• Refrains from criminal activity
• Is able to enjoy normal family and social relationships

For more than 30 years, many heroin addicts have achieved these goals by substituting a long-lasting synthetic narcotic, such as methadone, for the short-acting heroin (ASAM 2015). The maintenance ("substitute") narcotic is made available to heroin-dependent people through drug treatment centers under the direction of trained medical personnel. The dispensing of the substitute narcotic is tightly regulated by governmental agencies. The rationale for the substitution is that a long-acting drug such as methadone can conveniently be taken once a day to prevent the unpleasant withdrawal symptoms that occur within 4 hours after each heroin use (ASAM 2015) (see Table 9.4). Although the substitute narcotic may also have abuse potential and be scheduled by the DEA (see Table 9.2), it is given to the addict in its oral form; thus, its onset of action is too slow to cause a rush like that associated with heroin use, which means that its abuse potential is substantially less. In addition, the cost to society is dramatically reduced. According to one study, an untreated heroin addict costs the community $21,000 for 6 months, but the cost of methadone maintenance for a person dependent on heroin is only about $3000 for the same period (Palm Partners 2013; SAMHSA 2008).

Currently, methadone is approved by the FDA for "opiate maintenance therapy" in the treatment of heroin (or other narcotic) dependency (Volkow 2014a). It has been used in heroin treatment for more than 30 years. Although it is not the best treatment for every person dependent on an opiate drug, it is an effective tool for managing many heroin addicts (Simon 2016). Proper use of methadone has been shown to effectively decrease illicit use of narcotics and other undesirable behavior related to drug dependence. Although methadone does not tend to make users high, it helps heroin addicts by reducing their drug craving (Simon 2016). Often methadone-assisted therapy will be long term, perhaps for the rest of the addict's life. The methadone is typically well tolerated, although if misused it can be problematic and has been associated with a startling number of overdose deaths across the country (Rudd 2016 et al.).

A second narcotic, buprenorphine, which is used as an analgesic, also has been approved for treatment of narcotic dependence (Volkow 2014a). Because buprenorphine is both an opioid agonist and an antagonist, it has minimal potential

for dependence and is easy to manage, which makes this drug a desirable substitute for heroin (Schumacher et al. 2015). Efforts are being made to provide education and training to primary care physicians so they will be able to use buprenorphine to treat patients addicted to narcotics in their own offices (SAMHSA 2010). This novel strategy opens the door to physicians heretofore not involved in the treatment of drug addiction to become familiar with substance abuse management, which will hopefully increase opportunities to diagnose and treat these patients. There is considerable discussion as to how buprenorphine products compare to methadone in treatment of dependence on, and addiction to, opioids in general and heroin in particular. Although these issues clearly require further study, some evidence suggests that buprenorphine is usually the better and safer strategy for detoxification (i.e., treatment of withdrawal) and treatment of infants of opiate-addicted mothers. However, such claims are disputed by some experts in the field (Mental Health Daily 2015).

A third, and very different, drug approved in 2010 by the FDA to treat heroin and other opioid addictions is Vivitrol, an extended-release form of naltrexone, an opioid antagonist (National Center for Biotechnology Information [NCBI] n.d.; Tabachnick 2015). In 2006, Vivitrol was originally approved as a treatment for alcoholism because of its ability to reduce alcohol craving and its consumption (Tabachnick 2015). Vivitrol has been found to also reduce craving for narcotic drugs such as heroin. Its administration consists of a monthly deep muscle injection. Some of the potential side effects of using Vivitrol include (1) interference with thinking or reactions, (2) wheezing, (3) enhanced pain, and (4) mood changes (Drugs.com 2015b).

Table 9.5 compares the opioids that have been used for maintenance therapy. Other drugs used less frequently for similar maintenance therapy of heroin addicts include slow-release oral morphine and even heroin itself for addicts who do not respond to the other maintenance opioid drugs.

Some people, including some professionals involved in drug abuse therapy, view heroin or narcotic addiction as a "failure of the will" and see methadone treatment as substituting one addiction for another. However, evidence has demonstrated that this approach is very effective in preventing the spread of infectious diseases such as AIDS and hepatitis and helps the heroin addict to return to a normal productive life

TABLE 9.5 Comparison of Narcotic-related Drugs Used in Opiate Maintenance Therapy

Properties	Methadone (agonist)	Buprenorphine (partial agonist)	Vivitrol (antagonist)
Administration	Oral	Oral or sublingual	Injection
Frequency of doses	Daily	Daily	Monthly
Other uses	Analgesic	Analgesic	Alcohol dependence
Physical dependence	Yes	Little	No
Causes positive subjective effects	Yes	Yes	No
Abuse potential	Yes	Limited	No

Data from Capital Blue Cross. "Treatment of Opiate Addiction." 1 May 2015. Available https://www.capbluecross.com/wps/wcm/connect/b70a0ef6-d72e-49f5-a4b8-9328ec23f01e/Treatment_of_Opiate_and_Alcohol_Addiction_5-1-15.pdf?MOD=AJPERES

(McClure 2009). Unrealistic treatment expectations are sometimes imposed on heroin addicts, leading to high failure rates. For example, some methadone treatment programs distribute inadequate methadone doses to maintain heroin or narcotic abstinence (Recovery Helpdesk 2010); alternatively, narcotic-dependent patients may be told their methadone will be terminated within 6 months regardless of their progress in the program. Such ill-advised policies often drive clients back to their heroin habits and demonstrate that many professionals who treat heroin and narcotic dependency do not understand that methadone is not a cure for heroin addiction but rather a means to achieve a healthier, more normal lifestyle (McClure 2009).

It also is essential to understand that even proper treatment does not guarantee resolution of heroin or narcotic addiction (see "Case in Point: Heroin Addiction: Not a Joke"). To maximize the possibility of successful treatment, clients often must also participate in regular counseling sessions in combination with medication to help modify the drug-seeking behavior and receive on-site care from professionals, including job training, career development, education, general medical care, and family counseling. This combination of strategies is referred to as *medication-assisted treatment*, or MAT, and it provides a whole-patient approach for treating these patients, dramatically improving the success rate of narcotic dependence treatment (SAMHSA 2015a). Although only a small minority of heroin addicts become completely drug abstinent for the rest of their lives, many of them do have long periods of sustained abstinence after proper treatment (Darke et al. 2015).

Other Narcotics

A large number of nonheroin narcotics are used for medical purposes. However, many are also distributed in the streets, such as morphine, methadone, codeine, hydromorphone (Dilaudid), meperidine (Demerol), and other synthetics (hydrocodone [Vicodin] and oxycodone [OxyContin]). A few of the most commonly abused opioids are discussed briefly in the following sections. Except where noted, they are all Schedule II or III drugs (Schumacher et al. 2015).

■ Morphine

As noted earlier, morphine is the standard by which other narcotic analgesic agents are measured (Medi-Cal 2015). It has been used to relieve pain since it was first isolated in 1803. Morphine has about half the analgesic potency of heroin but 12 times the potency of codeine. It is commonly used to relieve moderate to intense pain that cannot be controlled by less potent and less dangerous narcotics. Because of its potential for serious side effects, morphine is generally used in a hospital setting where emergency care can be rendered, if necessary. Most pain can be relieved by morphine if high enough doses are used (Schumacher et al. 2015); however, morphine is most effective against continuous dull pain.

► **CASE IN POINT**

Heroin Addiction: Not a Joke

Artie Lange, who used to be a "funnyman" on *The Howard Stern Show*, was discovered by his mother bleeding on his Hoboken apartment floor. According to paramedics, Lange had been stabbed nine times with a kitchen knife. Police investigators concluded the wounds were self-inflicted and called it a suicide attempt, although Lange claims he was not trying to commit suicide, but the knife wounds were related to his heroin addiction. It was concluded that despite treatment, Lange was manifesting self-destructive tendencies that apparently led to this attempt to take his own life. His behavior has been compared to other self-destructive comics, such as Chris Farley and John Belushi, who both experienced untimely deaths apparently by accidental causes linked to their drug/heroin use.

© Aaron Settipane/Dreamstime.com.

Data from Staff. "Artie Lange Says Self-Inflicted Stab Wounds Were Due to Heroin Addiction." Rehabs.com. 6 September 2012. Available http://luxury.rehabs .com/blog/artie-lange-says-self-inflicted-stab-wounds-were-due-to-heroin-addiction/

The side effects that occur when using therapeutic doses of morphine include drowsiness, changes in mood, and inability to think straight. In addition, therapeutic doses depress respiratory activity; thus, morphine decreases the rate and depth of breathing and produces irregular breathing patterns. Like the other narcotics, it can create an array of seemingly unrelated effects throughout the body, including nausea and vomiting, constipation, blurred vision, constricted pupils, and flushed skin (Bennington-Castro 2014).

The initial response to morphine is varied. In normal people who are not suffering pain, the first exposure can be unpleasant, with nausea and vomiting being the prominent reactions. However, continual use often leads to a euphoric response and encourages dependence. When injected subcutaneously, the effects of heroin and morphine are almost identical; this situation occurs because heroin is rapidly metabolized in the body into morphine. After intravenous administration, the onset of heroin's effects is more rapid and more intense than that of morphine because heroin is more lipid soluble and enters the brain faster. Because heroin is easier to manufacture and is more potent, it is more popular in illicit trade than morphine. Even so, morphine also has substantial abuse potential and is classified as a Schedule II substance (DEA, Office of Diversion Control, U.S. Department of Justice 2016).

Tolerance to the effects of morphine can develop very quickly if the drug is used continuously. For example, an addict who is repeatedly administering the morphine to get a "kick" or maintain a high must constantly increase the dose. Such users can build up to incredible doses. Some addicts report using 200 milligrams of morphine daily; the normal analgesic dose of morphine is 50 to 80 milligrams per day (Addiction Blog 2014b). Such high doses are lethal in a person without tolerance to narcotics.

■ Methadone

Methadone was first synthesized in Germany in 1943, when natural opiate analgesics were not available because opium could not be obtained from the Far East during World War II. Methadone was first called *Dolophine*, after Adolf Hitler; one company still uses that trade name. (On the street, methadone pills have been called *dollies*.) As previously described, methadone is often substituted for heroin in the treatment of narcotic-dependent people (*Drug Facts and Comparisons* 2010). It is an effective analgesic, equal to morphine if injected and more potent if taken orally (*Drug Facts and Comparisons* 2010).

The physiological effects of methadone are the same as those of morphine and heroin. As a narcotic, methadone produces psychological dependence, tolerance, and then physical dependence and addiction if repeated doses are taken (Schumacher et al. 2015). It is effective for about 24 to 36 hours; therefore, the addict must take methadone daily to avoid narcotic withdrawal. It is often considered as addictive as heroin if injected; consequently, because methadone is soluble in water, it is formulated with insoluble, inert ingredients to prevent it from being injected by narcotic addicts.

Among methadone's most useful properties are cross-tolerance with other narcotic drugs and a less intense withdrawal response (Preda 2015). If it reaches a sufficiently high level in the blood, methadone blocks heroin euphoria. In addition, withdrawal symptoms of patients physically dependent on heroin or morphine and the postaddiction craving can be suppressed by oral administration of methadone (Meader 2010). The effective dose for methadone maintenance is 50 to 100 milligrams per day to treat severe withdrawal symptoms (Preda 2015).

The value of substituting methadone for heroin lies in its longer action. Because addicts no longer need heroin to prevent withdrawal, they often can be persuaded to leave their undesirable associates, drug sources, and dangerous lifestyles. The potential side effects from methadone are the same as those from morphine and heroin, including constipation and sedation; yet if properly used, methadone is usually a safe drug (*Drug Facts and Comparisons* 2010).

When injecting methadone, some people feel the same kind of euphoria that can be obtained from heroin. Methadone addicts receiving maintenance treatment sometimes become euphoric if the dose is increased too rapidly. There are cases of people who injected crushed methadone pills and developed serious lung conditions from particles that lodged in the tissue, creating a condition somewhat like emphysema. The number of deaths from methadone overdose have increased substantially in recent years. Data from the CDC indicate that methadone-related deaths in the United States increased more than fivefold in the past decade. The reasons for this startling increase include the following (Zielinski 2010):

- Large quantities of methadone are being stolen from legitimate businesses, such as hospitals and pharmacies, for personal use or to sell.
- Excessive amounts of methadone are being accumulated and abused by doctor-shopping, prescription fraud, or illegal Internet pharmacy websites.

- It is being misused by patients who received their methadone by legitimate prescriptions for pain.
- Because of increases in pain management clinics, it has become easier to obtain methadone.

Like heroin, methadone overdoses can be reversed by the antagonist naloxone if the person is treated in time.

■ Fentanyls

The following is a personal account of a young user of one of the most potent opioid narcotics, fentanyl:

> Each patch of fentanyl is designed to provide 72 hours of steady analgesic relief for people suffering from intense, chronic pain—every day. These fentanyl patches can be chewed, have the gel scraped out them and smoked or injected. One young abuser of these fentanyl products claims to have come close to overdosing on many occasions, and frequently passed out, as the drug slowed his breathing and pulse. He explains that these patches have made his pulse drop to 30 beats a minute while giving him the feeling of invincibility. It took the heroin-related deaths of four of his friends and fellow abusers—two of them still in their teens—to convince him to seek help. (Gatehouse and Macdonald 2015)

The fentanyls belong to a family of very potent narcotic analgesics (more than 200 times the potency of morphine) that are often administered intravenously for general anesthesia. These synthetic opioid narcotics include drugs such as sufentanil and alfentanil (Gutstein and Akil 2006). Fentanyls are also used in transdermal systems (patches on the skin) and as lollipops in the treatment of chronic pain (Adams 2010). Occasionally, reports surface of individuals abusing a fentanyl patch by licking, swallowing, or even smoking it (Gatehouse and Macdonald 2015).

It is estimated that some 100 different active forms of fentanyl could be synthesized; up to now, about 10 derivatives have appeared on the street. They are considered to be "designer" drugs. Because of their great potency, ease of production, and low cost, the fentanyls have sometimes been used to replace heroin (Fodale 2006). Fentanyl-type drugs can appear in the same forms and colors as heroin, so there is nothing to alert users that they have been sold a heroin substitute or a heroin combination (Lubran 2015). Due to their powerful effects, these drugs are especially dangerous, and incredibly small doses can cause fatal respiratory depression in an unsuspecting heroin user (Lubran 2015). It is likely that hundreds have died from overdosing with heroin laced with fentanyl. Because of the enhanced high, addicts are tempted to use these lethal combinations (Lubran 2015). Because these drugs are sometimes very difficult to detect in the blood owing to the small quantities used, there is no reliable information regarding the extent of fentanyl abuse. Fentanyl is so potent that abusing the patch has caused overdoses and even death (Gatehouse and Macdonald 2015).

∎ Hydromorphone

Hydromorphone (Dilaudid) is prepared from morphine and used as an analgesic and cough suppressant. It is a stronger analgesic than morphine and is used to treat moderate to severe pain. Nausea, vomiting, constipation, and euphoria may be less marked with hydromorphone than with morphine (Karch 1996; Way, Fields, and Way 1998). It is becoming more popular with opiate addicts due to its potency; however, combination with other CNS depressants can be fatal. On the street, it is taken in tablet form or injected (Gulur et al. 2015).

∎ Oxycodone

Oxycodone (OxyContin) is a moderate narcotic analgesic that in the past decade has been increasingly abused as the proprietary product OxyContin, creating considerable controversy. OxyContin is a long-lasting version of oxycodone and is considered to be an important and effective therapy for the treatment of severe pain from cancer or other lingering diseases (Addiction Blog 2014c). Abuse of OxyContin has been a considerable cause for alarm by officials. Street names for OxyContin include *OC, kicker, OxyCotton,* and *Rushbo* (Rehabs. com n.d.). This drug can be easily abused by simply crushing the tablet, and then ingesting, injecting, inhaling, or placing it rectally. However, recent modifications have made the drug in OxyContin less available by this process, thereby reducing its appeal to those who intend to abuse it (Diep 2013).

The problems with OxyContin are underscored by a report that, in 2015, 3.7% of high school students had abused this drug (Johnston 2016). Interestingly, the abuse rate by this population for the less potent Vicodin (hydrocodone plus acetaminophen) was almost double that for OxyContin, likely due to easier access (Johnston 2016). Deaths and trips to the emergency room caused by OxyContin have been common and are of concern to both medical and law enforcement organizations

(Bryan 2015). As a result, the FDA and DEA control OxyContin at the same level as morphine.

∎ Meperidine

Meperidine (Demerol) is a synthetic drug that frequently is used as an analgesic for treatment of moderate pain; it can be taken in tablet form or injected. This drug is sometimes given too freely by some physicians. Meperidine is about one-tenth as powerful as morphine. Tolerance develops with continued use of the drug, requiring larger doses to maintain its therapeutic action. With continual use, it causes physical dependence. Meperidine addicts may use large daily doses (3 to 4 grams per day) (Addiction Center n.d.).

∎ Hydrocodone

Hydrocodone is a synthetic opioid analgesic typically used to treat moderate to moderately severe pain. It is also used on occasions to help suppress severe coughing often associated with colds and flu. Hydrocodone is available as both immediate- and delayed-release forms and is frequently combined with acetaminophen or ibuprofen for pain relief. It is available in liquid preparations in combination with other drugs such as antihistamines and decongestants, usually to treat colds. Hydrocodone's common side effects are very similar to other opioid analgesics and include dizziness, drowsiness, constipation, and nausea and vomiting. Products containing hydrocodone, such as Vicodin and Lortab, have become extremely popular for both legitimate and illegitimate uses. Consequently, 4.4% of high school seniors reported abusing Vicodin in 2015 (Johnston 2016). The alarming abuse rate of hydrocodone led to the changing of the hydrocodone schedule classification from Schedule IV to II in 2014, making it more difficult to prescribe (Pietrangelo 2015).

∎ Buprenorphine

Buprenorphine, a mild-to-moderate narcotic analgesic, was available as a Schedule V pain reliever for years. As discussed earlier, after extensive research, this drug was approved in 2002 as an effective medication for the treatment of narcotic abuse and dependence (Schumacher et al. 2015). Buprenorphine has been shown to be effective in relieving the cravings for narcotic pain relievers with minimal tendency to cause addiction itself (Preda 2015). Although buprenorphine has been reported to have a minimal high when used properly (Preda 2015), there have been isolated reports of occasional deaths, especially when combined with other CNS depressant drugs (Sansone and Sansone 2015). Despite buprenorphine's significant safety record and its minimal propensity for abuse, its new FDA-approved indication would cause it to be dispensed to patients with drug abuse histories, so the DEA revised its classification, changing buprenorphine to a Schedule III drug.

Of particular importance is the fact that buprenorphine (in the form of Subutex and Suboxone, a combination of buprenorphine and the opioid antagonist, naloxone) has been approved for the treatment of opiate dependence in an office setting. Trained physicians are allowed to treat up to 100 narcotic-dependent patients with buprenorphine in their medical offices. This means that opioid addictions and dependence can now be treated with a prescribed medication by trained primary care physicians, in the offices of private doctors. This is an important step in what may become a revolution in addiction treatment, allowing patients to discreetly receive help from a family doctor for their substance abuse problem (Sansone and Sansone 2015). Although most physicians are not licensed to prescribe Suboxone, many are; consequently, three times more opioid addicts are being treated with Suboxone than methadone, despite the fact that this opioid drug is much more expensive (Svrluga 2015).

■ MPTP: A "Designer" Tragedy

Attempts to synthesize illicit designer versions of meperidine by street chemists have proved tragic for some unsuspecting drug addicts. In 1976, a young drug addict with elementary laboratory skills attempted to make a meperidine-like drug by using shortcuts in the chemical synthesis. Three days after self-administering his untested drug product, the drug user developed a severe case of tremors and motor problems identical to Parkinson's disease, a neurological disorder generally occurring in the elderly. Even more surprising to attending neurologists was that this young drug addict improved dramatically after treatment with levodopa, a drug that is very effective in treating the symptoms of traditional Parkinson's disease. After 18 months of treatment, the despondent addict committed suicide. An autopsy revealed he had severe brain damage that was almost identical to that occurring in classical Parkinson's patients. It was concluded that a by-product resulting from the sloppy synthesis of the meperidine-like designer narcotic was responsible for the irreversible brain damage.

This hypothesis was confirmed by a separate and independent event on the West Coast in 1981, when a cluster of relatively young heroin addicts (ages 22 to 42) in the San Francisco area also developed symptoms of Parkinson's disease. All of these patients had consumed a new "synthetic heroin" obtained on the streets, which was produced by attempting to synthesize meperidine-like drugs (Aminoff 1998; Langston et al. 1983). Common to both incidents was the presence of the compound MPTP, which was a contaminant resulting from the careless synthesis. MPTP is metabolized to a very reactive molecule in the brain that selectively destroys neurons containing the transmitter dopamine in the motor regions of the basal ganglia. Similar neuronal damage occurs in classical Parkinson's disease over the course of 50 to 70 years, whereas ingestion of MPTP dramatically accelerates the degeneration to a matter of days (Goldstein 1994). As tragic as the MPTP incident was, it was heralded as an important scientific breakthrough—MPTP is now used by researchers as a tool to study why Parkinson's disease occurs and how to treat it effectively (Munoz-Manchado et al. 2015).

■ Codeine

Codeine is a naturally occurring constituent of opium and the most frequently prescribed of the narcotic analgesics. It is used principally as a treatment for minor to moderate pain and as a cough suppressant. Maximum pain relief from codeine occurs with 30 to 50 milligrams. Usually, when prescribed for pain, codeine is combined with either a salicylate (such as aspirin) or acetaminophen (Tylenol). Aspirin-like drugs and opioid narcotics interact in a synergistic fashion to give an analgesic equivalence greater than what can be achieved by aspirin or codeine alone.

Although not especially powerful, codeine may still be abused. Codeine-containing cough syrup is currently classified as a Schedule V drug. Because the abuse potential is considered minor, the FDA has ruled that codeine cough products can be sold without a prescription; however, the pharmacist is required to keep them behind the counter and must be asked in order to provide codeine-containing cough medications. Despite the FDA ruling, many states have more restrictive regulations and require that codeine-containing cough products be available only by prescription.

Although codeine dependence is possible, it is not very common; most people who abuse codeine developed narcotic dependence previously with one of the more potent opioids. In general, because of its lower potency, large quantities of codeine are needed to satisfy a narcotic addiction; therefore, it is not commonly marketed on the street (Pietrangelo 2015).

▪ Pentazocine

Pentazocine (Talwin) was first developed in the 1960s in an effort to create an effective analgesic with low abuse potential. When taken orally, its analgesic effect is slightly greater than that of codeine. Its effects on respiration and sedation are similar to those of the other opioids, but it does not prevent withdrawal symptoms in a narcotic addict. In fact, pentazocine will precipitate withdrawal symptoms if given to a person on methadone maintenance (Pain Community Centre n.d.). Pentazocine is not commonly abused because its effects can be unpleasant, resulting in dysphoria. It is classified as a Schedule IV drug.

▪ Tramadol

Tramadol (Ultram) was first introduced into the U.S. market in 1995 as a synthetic, moderately effective analgesic sometimes used as a substitute for opioid painkillers (Drugs.com 2015a). Although tramadol itself causes some activation of opioid receptors in the brain, it appears that its analgesic properties are related to more than just its opioid actions. For example, tramadol alters GABA, noradrenaline, and serotonin transmitter systems as well, in a manner that might contribute to its atypical analgesic properties. For this reason, tramadol may have some antidepressant effects that augment its analgesic abilities (DEA 2013).

Tramadol is frequently prescribed for patients who either do not respond well or have difficulty with the opioid painkillers. Despite the fact that opioid action likely is not the sole basis of its analgesia, it is significant enough to cause some dependence issues. For example, there is an illegal street market for this substance, where it is known by names such as *chill pills* or *ultra*. There are clinicians who claim that for some patients tramadol can cause a serious opioid-like dependence (DEA 2013). Such conclusions are based on findings such as the following: (1) from 1998 to 2006 there was a sixfold increase in admissions for treatment of tramadol-related dependence; (2) for teens, tramadol is easier to get than alcohol and easy to sell on the streets; (3) emergency room visits nationwide that included tramadol as a significant component went from about 5000 in 2004 to about 20,000 in 2011; and (4) there is evidence that regular daily use of tramadol can cause physical dependence and withdrawals when discontinued abruptly (Drugs.com 2015a). These increases in tramadol-related problems correspond to an explosion in its popularity, resulting in about 26 million prescriptions being dispensed by retailers in 2008 (Smith 2010). Tramadol is available as both regular and extended-release tablets (Drugs.com 2015a).

Even though tramadol is marketed as an opioid drug with low risk of dependence and some health authorities consider it to have a relatively low dependence liability, it is clear that many patients can become addicted to this analgesic (DEA 2013). Thus, in 2014 the DEA made it a Schedule IV drug (Drugs.com 2015a). Tramadol has been associated with a wide array of side effects, including diarrhea, constipation, drowsiness, and, in rare instances, even seizures (Drugs.com 2015a).

Narcotic-Related Drugs

Although not classified as narcotics, the following drugs are either structurally similar to narcotics (dextromethorphan) or are used to treat narcotic withdrawal (clonidine) or overdose (naloxone).

▪ Dextromethorphan

Dextromethorphan is a safe and effective synthetic used in cough remedies since the 1960s and can be purchased without prescription. Although its molecular structure resembles that of codeine, this drug does not have analgesic action nor does it cause typical narcotic dependence (Consumer Healthcare Products Association [CHPA] n.d.).

Although dextromethorphan is not traditionally considered a major drug abuse problem, recent studies are cause for concern, with 3% of teens admitting to abusing products containing dextromethorphan in 2015. Because of these abuse problems, several states prohibit sales of dextromethorphan-containing products to minors (CHPA n.d.). Overdose of dextromethorphan-containing cough medicines has been reported in the United States and other countries, sometimes resulting in deadly consequences (Logan 2015 et al.; see "Here and Now: Dextromethorphan: Nothing to Cough At"). The principal symptoms of abuse include altered perceptions, sense of floating, hallucinations, visual distortions, and even paranoia and psychotic reactions. Its effects have been described to be similar to those of phencyclidine (PCP) and the general anesthetic ketamine (Ekern 2016; Morgan, Porritt, and Poling 2006). Street names for abused dextromethorphan are

DXM, triple C, Skittles, robo, and *poor man's PCP* (DEA 2014). Some suggest that both physical and psychological dependence can occur with dextromethorphan, resulting in withdrawal when its use is discontinued (Mutschler et al. 2010). Dextromethorphan is sometimes mixed with drugs such as alcohol, amphetamines, and cocaine to give unusual psychoactive interactions.

As of 2015, the DEA had taken no steps to restrict the use of dextromethorphan in over-the-counter (OTC) products; in fact, advisers to the FDA voted against placing this drug in a schedule of controlled substances, which likely will preclude the DEA from making a change in its category (DEA 2014).

Young people are becoming aware of dextromethorphan's abuse potential from websites on the Internet. A growing number of these sites have promoted dextromethorphan as a powerful OTC mind-altering drug. Included on these sites are personal experiences of users as well as directions on how to use the drug, predictions about what to expect, warning signs of adverse reactions, and instructions on how to extract dextromethorphan from OTC cough medicines (Vaults of Erowid n.d.).

■ Clonidine

Clonidine (Catapres) was created in the late 1970s. It is not a narcotic analgesic and has no direct effect on the opioid receptors; instead, it stimulates receptors for noradrenaline. Its principal use is as an oral antihypertensive (Robertson

and Biaggioni 2015). Clonidine is mentioned here because it is a nonaddictive, noneuphorigenic prescription medication with demonstrated efficacy in relieving some of the physical effects of opiate withdrawal (such as vomiting and diarrhea). However, clonidine does not alter narcotic craving or the generalized aches associated with withdrawal (Elements Behavioral Health 2013). The dosing regimen is typically a 7- to 14-day inpatient treatment for opiate withdrawal. Length of treatment can be reduced to 7 days for withdrawal from heroin and short-acting opiates; the 14-day treatment is needed for the longer-acting methadone-type opiates. Because tolerance to clonidine may develop, opiates are discontinued abruptly at the start of treatment. In this way, the peak intensity of withdrawal will occur while clonidine is still maximally effective (Elements Behavioral Health 2013).

One of the most important advantages of clonidine over other treatments for opiate withdrawal detoxification is that it shortens the time for withdrawal to 14 days compared with several weeks or months using standard procedures, such as methadone treatment (O'Shea, Law, and Melichar 2010). The potential disadvantage of taking clonidine is that it can cause serious side effects of its own, the most serious being significantly lowered blood pressure, which can cause fainting and blacking out (Elements Behavioral Health 2013). Overall, its lack of abuse potential makes clonidine particularly useful in rapid treatment of

HERE AND NOW
Dextromethorphan: Nothing to Cough At

Two teenage boys who had purchased dextromethorphan through the Internet were found dead in the bedroom of one of the boys after a sleepover. Next to their bodies was a bag labeled "dextromethorphan, not for human consumption." Dextromethorphan appeared to be the only drug in the boys' bodies. Family members revealed that the boys had a history of recreationally using OTC cough medicine, but the habit escalated to using the "pure" stuff. The conclusion from the autopsy was that two healthy young males died from nonspecific findings such as edema in the lungs, air passages, and on the brain associated with extremely high concentrations of dextromethorphan in their bodies consumed for the hallucinogenic effects of the drug.

Logan, B. K., G. Goldfogel, R. Hamilton, and J. Kuhlman. "Five Deaths Resulting from Abuse of Dextromethorphan Sold Over the Internet." *Journal of Analytical Toxicology.* 33 (2015): 99–103. Available https://www.researchgate.net/publication/24037337_Five_Deaths_Resulting_from_Abuse_of_Dextromethorphan_Sold_Over_the_Internet narcotic dependence; however, the long-term benefit is controversial (Finch 2015).

■ Naloxone/Naltrexone

Naloxone and the related drug naltrexone are relatively pure narcotic antagonists and have short and long half-lives, respectively. These drugs attach to opiate receptors in the brain and throughout the body. They do not activate the receptors but rather prevent narcotic drugs, such as heroin and morphine, from having an effect. By themselves, these antagonists do not cause much change but potently block or reverse the effects of all narcotics.

Because of its antagonistic properties, naloxone is a useful antidote in the treatment of narcotic overdoses; its administration rapidly reverses life-threatening, narcotic-induced effects on breathing and the cardiovascular system (Schumacher et al. 2015). However, if not used carefully, this antagonist will also block the analgesic action of the narcotics and initiate severe withdrawal in narcotic-dependent people (Schumacher et al. 2015). In fact, many individuals dependent on heroin are not interested in using this drug because it can precipitate withdrawal symptoms.

Use of naloxone has been proposed to prevent addicts from experiencing the effects of heroin and other potent opioid narcotics (Schumacher et al. 2015). In fact, as discussed earlier in this chapter, an extended form of naloxone (its effects persist for 1 month) called Vivitrol was approved by the FDA for the treatment of heroin addiction (Rubin 2010). A recent study found that of those heroin addicts who received six monthly injections, 70% did not go back to heroin use (this was twice the success rate of heroin addicts given placebo), and they claimed that the Vivitrol reduced their cravings for the opiate drug (Tabachnick 2015). It is critical to appreciate that Vivitrol is not a cure for heroin or opioid dependence in general and that heroin/opioid addicts must also develop good coping skills in order to stop abusing their narcotic drugs (Tabachnick 2015)

An interesting use of naloxone has been to combine it with buprenorphine in small quantities (Suboxone). As long as this product is taken as prescribed, the quantity of naloxone is too small to have an antagonistic effect; however, if Suboxone is consumed in high doses, such as would occur if it were being abused, there would be sufficient naloxone to block the opioid effect (Mental Health Daily 2015). The FDA also has approved Suboxone to reduce the craving for alcohol in the treatment of chronic alcoholism (*Drug Facts and Comparisons*

2010). Additional reports suggest that opioid receptors may contribute to other drug addictions, such as those caused by nicotine and psychostimulants. At this time it is not clear if an opioid antagonist like naloxone would be effective in treating these other addictions (Ling et al. 2016).

Natural Narcotic Substances

Although many herbal preparations can cause drowsiness or have some analgesic properties, few of these actually contain opioid narcotic drugs. The naturally occurring opioid drugs include morphine, codeine, heroin, papaverine, and thebaine and are found only in the opium poppy, *Papaver somniferum*. Although several varieties of opium-yielding poppies exist, they are typically winter crops in the Southern Hemisphere and do best in climates that have warm days and cool nights. All of the plants thrive in sandy soil. Most of the active drugs are found in the seepage from the seed heads located beneath the flower petals of the poppy flowers, although small amounts of these active ingredients are found in other parts of the plant such as the stem and leaves. Although this species of plant can survive in the United States if the environment is rigidly controlled, the vast majority of the supplies of the naturally occurring narcotic drugs are brought into the country either legally and sold as legitimate pharmaceuticals or smuggled across borders and sold as illicit narcotics.

The sap oozing from this opium poppy pod contains the natural narcotic drugs.

LEARNING PORTFOLIO

Discussion Questions

1. Why do narcotics have high abuse potential?
2. What are the principal clinical uses of the opioid narcotics?
3. What is the relationship between endorphin systems and the opioid narcotics?
4. Why do the opioid pain relievers account for two-thirds of prescription drug abuse?
5. What effect has the rising abuse of prescription narcotic analgesics had on legitimately prescribing these drugs for pain management?
6. What is the difference between opioid addiction and opioid physical dependence?
7. Why was there a substantial increase in heroin abuse in the United States throughout the 1990s?
8. Why does heroin addiction contribute to criminal activity?
9. What are the principal withdrawal effects when heroin use is stopped in addicts?
10. How does methadone maintenance work for the treatment of narcotic dependence? Discuss a possible drawback to this approach.
11. How does buprenorphine compare to methadone as treatment for narcotic addictions?
12. How does naloxone (e.g., Vivitrol) compare to methadone maintenance treatment for heroin/opioid addiction?
13. What is considered to be successful treatment for heroin addiction?
14. How does morphine compare with heroin?
15. How does tramadol compare to other opioid analgesics?
16. Why is dextromethorphan potentially addicting, and what should the federal government do to stop its abuse?
17. What does the fact that naloxone is effective in the treatment of alcoholism suggest about the role of endogenous opioid systems in alcohol dependence?

Key Terms

Summary

1. The term *narcotic* refers to naturally occurring substances derived from the opium poppy and their synthetic substitutes. These drugs are referred to as the opioid (or opiate) narcotics because of their association with opium. For the most part, the opioid narcotics possess abuse potential, but they also have important clinical value and are used to relieve all kinds of pain (they are analgesic), suppress coughing (they are antitussive), and stop diarrhea.

2. The principal side effects of the opioid narcotics, besides their abuse potential, include drowsiness, respiratory depression, nausea and vomiting, constipation, inability to urinate, and sometimes a drop in blood pressure. These side effects can be annoying or even life-threatening, so caution is required when using these drugs.

3. Heroin is the most likely of the opioid narcotics to be severely abused; it is easily prepared from opium and has a rapid, intense effect. It is a Schedule I drug.

4. When narcotics such as heroin are first used by people not experiencing pain, the drugs can cause unpleasant, dysphoric sensations. However, euphoria gradually overcomes the aversive effects. The positive feelings increase with narcotic use, leading to psychological dependence. After psychological dependence, physical dependence occurs with frequent daily use, which reinforces the narcotic abuse. If the user stops taking the drug after physical dependence has occurred, severe withdrawal symptoms result.

5. Tolerance to narcotics can occur rapidly with intense use of these drugs. This tolerance can result in the use of incredibly large doses of narcotics that would be fatal to a nontolerant person.

6. Methadone and buprenorphine are frequently used to help narcotic addicts stop using heroin or one of the other highly addicting drugs. Oral methadone relieves the withdrawal symptoms that would result from discontinuing narcotics. Methadone can also cause psychological and physical dependence, but it is less addicting than heroin and easier to control. Buprenorphine is distinct from methadone in that it has been approved for use in primary care settings and may be safer for treating women who use opioid narcotics during pregnancy.

7. Fentanyls are very potent synthetic opioid narcotics. They can be easily synthesized and converted into drugs that are as much as 3000 to 6000 times more potent than heroin itself. Detection and regulation of these fentanyl derivatives by law enforcement agencies are very difficult. The fentanyl-type drugs are used as heroin substitutes and have killed narcotic addicts because of their unexpected potency.

8. Attempts to create designer narcotics have led to the synthesis of very potent fentanyl-like drugs that are responsible for a number of overdose deaths. In addition, attempts to synthesize a meperidine (Demerol) designer drug resulted in the inadvertent creation of MPTP, a very reactive compound that causes a dramatic onset of Parkinson's disease in its users.

9. Tramadol is an atypical opioid-like analgesic that has some antidepressant actions that might contribute to its effectiveness as a moderately potent pain killer. It likely has less addicting properties than most of the other opioid narcotics, but its dramatic rise in popularity has revealed a potential for causing dependence and withdrawal in some patients. Although not currently scheduled by the federal government, the DEA is considering its addition to the list of controlled substances.

10. Dextromethorphan is a codeine-related drug used as an antitussive in OTC cough medicines. In very high doses, dextromethorphan can cause PCP-like hallucinations and sensory distortions. The abuse of this drug has not been substantial enough to result in its removal or special control by federal agencies.

References

Adams, K. "Search for Answers in Fentanyl Death Raises More Questions." *Virginian-Pilot* (18 May 2010). Available http://hamptonroads.com/2010/05/search-answers-fentanyl-death-raises-more-questions

Addiction Blog. "Is Cocaine a Narcotic?" 2014a. Available drug.addictionblog.org/is-cocaine-a-narcotic

Addiction Blog. "Morphine Overdose: How Much Amount of Morphine to OD?" 9 August 2014b. Available http://drug.addictionblog.org/morphine-overdose-how-much-amount-of-morphine-to-od/

Addiction Blog. "What Is the Difference Between Oxycontin and Oxycodone?" 27 March 2014c. Available http://prescription-drug.addictionblog.org/what-is-the-difference-between-oxycontin-and-oxycodone/

Addiction Center. "Demerol Addiction and Abuse." n.d. Available https://www.addictioncenter.com/painkillers/demerol/

Agence France-Presse. "Afghan Heroin Took Million Lives Last Decade: Russia." 8 June 2010. Available http://www.globalresearch.ca/afghan-heroin-took-million-lives-last-decade-russia/19640

Alford, D. "Opioid Prescribing for Chronic Pain-Achieving the Right Balance Through Education. *New England Journal of Medicine* 374 (2016): 301–303.

American Society of Addiction Medicine (ASAM). "The National Practice Guideline for the Use of Medications in the Treatment of Addiction Involving Opioid Use." 2015. Available http://www.asam.org/docs/default -source/practice-support/guidelines-and-consensus -docs/national-practice-guideline.pdf?sfvrsn=18

American Society of Addiction Medicine (ASAM). "Opioid Addiction 2016 Facts & Figures." 2016. Available http://www.asam.org/docs/default-source/advocacy /opioid-addiction-disease-facts-figures.pdf

Aminoff, M. "Pharmacologic Management of Parkinsonism and Other Movement Disorders." In *Basic and Clinical Pharmacology,* 7th ed., edited by B. Katzung, 450–463. Stamford, CT: Appleton and Lange, 1998.

Bebinger, M. "It's Not Just Heroin: Drug Cocktails Are Fueling the Overdose Crisis." WBUR's Common Health. 13 November 2015. Available http://commonhealth .wbur.org/2015/11/drug-overdose-cocktails

Bennington-Castro, J. "What Is Morphine?" Everyday Health. 2014. Available http://www.everydayhealth .com/drugs/morphine

Bersett, K., and J. Lee. "Dope-Sick: Youths Migrate to Heroin as Deaths Spike." Clayton Behavioral. 2015. Available https://claytonbehavioral.com/dope-sick-youths -migrate-to-heroin-as-deaths-spike-read-more-here/

Bhuvaneswar, C., G. Chang, L. Epstein, and T. Stern. "Cocaine and Opioid Use During Pregnancy: Prevalence and Management." *Primary Care Companion to the Journal of Clinical Psychiatry* 10 (2008): 59–65.

Brecher, E. M. *Licit and Illicit Drugs.* Boston: Little, Brown, 1972.

Bryan, M. "Emergency Rooms Crack Down on Abusers of Pain Pills." NPR. 5 June 2015. Available http://www.npr .org/sections/health-shots/2015/06/03/411560144 /emergency-rooms-crack-down-on-abusers-of-pain-pills

Carbone, A. "Is Heroin Chic Over?" *AfterParty Magazine.* (1 July 2014). Available https://rehabreviews.com /heroin-chic/

Centers for Disease Control and Prevention (CDC). "Today's Heroin Epidemic." 2015. Available http:// www.cdc.gov/vitalsigns/heroin/

Christenson, S. "Heroin Addiction Takes Brutal Toll on Afghanistan." *San Antonio Express-News.* (24 May 2010). Available http://www.mysanantonio.com/news/military /article/Heroin-addiction-takes-brutal-toll-on-Afghanistan -787499.php

Colon, D. "Number of Newborns Addicted to Painkillers Rising." NPR. 16 February 2011. Available http://www .npr.org/2011/02/16/133805289/number-of-newborns -addicted-to-painkillers-rising

Compton, W., C. Jones, and G. Baldwin. "Relationship Between Nonmedical Prescription-Opioid Use and Heroin Use." *New England Journal of Medicine* 373 (2016): 154–163.

Consumer Healthcare Products Association (CHPA). "Dextromethorphan: Preventing Teen Cough Medicine Abuse." n.d. Available http://www.chpa.org/dex.aspx

Cook, L. "The Heroin Epidemic." *U.S. News and World Report.* (10 August 2015). Available http://www .usnews.com/news/blogs/data-mine/2015/08/19 /the-heroin-epidemic-in-9-graphs

Dalrymple, T. "Myths and Realities of Drug Addiction, Consumption and Crime." Library of Law and Liberty. 31 July 2015. Available http://www.libertylawsite .org/2015/07/31/myths-and-realities-of-drug-addiction -consumption-and-crime/

Darke, S., C. Marel, T. Slada, J. Ross, K. Mills, and M. Teesson. "Patterns and Correlates of Sustained Heroin Abstinence: Findings from the 11-Year Follow-up of the Australian Treatment Outcome Study." *Journal of Studies on Alcohol and Drugs* 76 (2015): 909–915.

DiChiara, G., and A. North. "Neurobiology of Opiate Abuse." *Trends in Pharmacological Sciences* 13 (May 1992): 185–193.

Diep, F. "How Do You Make a Painkiller Addiction-Proof?" *Popular Science.* (13 May 2013). Available http://www.popsci.com/science/article/2013-05 /science-un-crushable-oxycontin

Drug Enforcement Administration (DEA). "Tramadol." March 2013. Available http://www.deadiversion.usdoj .gov/drug_chem_info/tramadol.pdf

Drug Enforcement Administration (DEA). "Dextromethorphan." March 2014. Available http://www.deadiversion .usdoj.gov/drug_chem_info/dextro_m.pdf

Drug Enforcement Administration, Office of Diversion Control, U.S. Department of Justice. "Controlled Substance Schedules." 2016. Available http://www.deadiversion .usdoj.gov/schedules/#list

Drugs.com. "Tramadol: Top 8 Things You Need to Know." 2015a. Available http://www.drugs.com/article/tramadol -need-to-know.html

Drugs.com. "Vivitrol." 2015b. Available http://www.drugs .com/vivitrol.html

Drug Facts and Comparisons. St. Louis, MO: Wolters Kluwer, 2010 (Pocket Version): 244–247, 520–590.

Drug War Facts. "Heroin Assisted Treatment/Heroin Management." 2012. Available http://www.drugwarfacts .org/cms/heroin_maintenance#sthash.LJWKNnvQ.dphs

Edwards, M. "Soldiers at Risk of Getting Hooked on Heroin." ABC News. (6 June 2010). Available http:// www.abc.net.au/news/2010-06-03/soldiers-at-risk -of-getting-hooked-on-heroin/853234

Ekern, B. "Abuse of Dextromethorphan: Signs and Symptoms." Addiction Hope. 9 March 2016. Available

http://www.addictionhope.com/blog/abuse-of
-dextromethorphan-signs-and-symptoms

Elements Behavioral Health. "Clonidine Treatment for Opioid Withdrawal." Drug Addiction Treatment. 20 February 2013. Available http://www.drugaddictiontreatment.com/types-of-addiction/prescription-drug-addiction/clonidine-treatment-for-opioid-withdrawal/

Eshkevari, L., and J. Heath. "Use of Acupuncture for Chronic Pain: Optimizing Clinical Practice." *Holistic Nursing Practice* 19 (2005): 217–221.

Feldman, C. "Heroin Quotes." How to Kick Heroin (2015). Available http://www.howtokickheroin.com/heroin-quotes/

Finch, M. "How to Use Clonidine for Opiate Withdrawal." Opiate Addiction Support. 4 March 2015. Available http://opiateaddictionsupport.com/how-to-use-clonidine-for-opiate-withdrawal/

Fisher, J. "Heroin-fueled Crime Wave." *The News Journal* (delawareonline, 14 February 2015). Available http://www.delawareonline.com/story/news/local/2015/02/14/heroin-fueled-crime-wave/23412993/

Fodale, V. "Killer Fentanyl: A Lesson from Anesthesiology." *Lancet* 368 (2006): 1237–1238.

Food and Drug Administration (FDA). "FDA Approves New Formulation for OxyContin." FDA News Release. 5 April 2010. Available http://www.fda.gov/NewsEvents/Newsroom/PressAnnouncements/ucm207480.htm

Gatehouse, J., and N. Macdonald. "Fentanyl: The King of All Opiates, and a Killer Drug Crisis." *Maclean's*. (22 June 2015). Available http://www.macleans.ca/society/health/fentanyl-the-king-of-all-opiates-and-a-killer-drug-crisis/

Golding, A. "Two Hundred Years of Drug Abuse." *Journal of the Royal Society of Medicine* 86 (May 1993): 282–286.

Goldstein, A. *Addiction from Biology to Drug Policy*. New York: Freeman, 1994: 137–154.

Gorner, J. "74 Overdoses in 72 Hours: Laced Heroin May Be to Blame." *Chicago Tribune*. (2 October 2015). Available http://www.chicagotribune.com/news/local/breaking/ct-heroin-overdoses-met-20151002-story.html

Gourlay, G. "Advances in Opioid Pharmacology." *Supportive Care for Cancer* (21 December 2004): 153–159.

Gray, E. "Heroin Gains Popularity as Cheap Doses Flood the U.S." *Time*. (4 February 2014). Available http://time.com/4505/heroin-gains-popularity-as-cheap-doses-flood-the-u-s/

Gulur, P., K. Loury, P. Arnstein, H. Lee, P. McCarthy, C. Coley, and E. Mort. "Morphine Versus Hydromorphone: Does Choice of Opioid Influence Outcomes?" *Pain Research and Treatment* 2015 (2015): article ID 482081.

Gutstein, H., and H. Akil. "Opioid Analgesics." In *The Pharmacological Basis of Therapeutics*, 11th ed., edited by L. Brunton, J. Lazo, and K. Parker, 547–590. New York: McGraw-Hill, 2006.

Hitti, M. "Prescription Painkiller Addiction: 7 Myths." WebMD. 2 August 2010. Available http://www.webmd.com/pain-management/features/prescription-painkiller-addiction-7-myths

Hubbard, R. "Focus on Heroin: Increase in Users and Changing Treatment System Present New Challenges for Services Researchers." *Connection* (a semiannual newsletter published by the Association for Health Services Research) (June 1998): 1–2.

Johnston, L. "Monitoring the Future 2015." 2016. Available http://www.monitoringthefuture.org/data/15data/15drtbl1.pdf

Karch, S. "Narcotics." In *The Pathology of Drug Abuse*, 281–408. New York: CRC, 1996.

Kosten, T., and L. Hollister. "Drugs of Abuse." In *Basic and Clinical Pharmacology*, 7th ed., edited by B. Katzun, 516–531. Stamford, CT: Appleton & Lange, 1998.

Kral, L. and Ghafoor, V. "Pain and Its Management." In *Applied Therapeutics, The Clinical Use of Drugs*, 10th ed., edited by B. Alldredge et al., 112–146. Philadelphia, PA: Wolters Kluwer, 2013.

Kritz, F. "What You Don't Know Unless You've Been There: Heroin." Addiction.com. 5 August 2015. Available https://www.addiction.com/12360/what-you-dont-know-unless-youve-been-there-heroin/

Langston, J., P. Ballard, J. Tetrud, and I. Irwin. "Chronic Parkinsonism in Humans Due to a Product of Meperidine-Analogue Synthesis." *Science* 219 (1983): 979–980.

Leach, B. "Heroin 'Shooting Galleries' Should Be Introduced." *Telegraph*. (14 September 2009). Available http://www.telegraph.co.uk/news/uknews/crime/6185533/Heroin-shooting-galleries-should-be-introduced.html

Ling, W., M. P. Hillhouse, A. J. Saxon, L. J. Mooney, C. M. Thomas, A. Ang, A. Matthews, A. Hasson, J. Annon, S. Sparenborg, D. Liu, J. McCormack, S. Church, W. Swafford, K. Drexler, C. Schuman, S. Ross, K. Wiest, P. T. Korthuis, W. Lawson, G. S. Brigham, P. C. Knox, M. Dawes, and J. Rotrosen. "Buprenorphine + Naloxone Plus Naltrexone for the Treatment of Cocaine Dependence: The Cocaine Use Reduction with Buprenorphine (CURB) Study." *Addiction* 111 (2016): 1416–1427.

Logan, B. K., G. Goldfogel, R. Hamilton, and J. Kuhlman. "Five Deaths Resulting from Abuse of Dextromethorphan Sold Over the Internet." *Journal of Analytical Toxicology*. 33 (2015): 99–103. Available https://www.researchgate.net/publication/24037337_Five_Deaths_Resulting_from_Abuse_of_Dextromethorphan_Sold_Over_the_Internet

Lubran, R. "Fentanyl-Related Overdose Deaths on the Rise." Substance Abuse and Mental Health Services

Administration. 6 October 2015. Available http://blog.samhsa.gov/2015/10/06/fentanyl-related-overdose-deaths-on-the-rise/#.VuMvyqb2aUk

Luscher, C. "Drugs of Abuse." In *Basic and Clinical Pharmacology*, edited by B. Katzung, 565–580. New York: McGraw-Hill, 2012.

March of Dimes. "Heroin and Pregnancy." 2015. Available http://www.marchofdimes.org/pregnancy/heroin-and-pregnancy.aspx#

"Mary." *Rolling Stone* 30 (1996): 42–43.

Maurer, D., and V. Vogel. *Narcotics and Narcotic Addiction*, 3rd ed. Springfield, IL: Thomas, 1967.

McClure, C. "Global Drug Policy and the HIV/IDU Epidemic in Eastern Europe and Central Asia." International AIDS Society. 2009. Available http://www.iasociety.org/Web/WebContent/File/CraigMcClure_SODAK%202009.pdf

McMurran, M. "What Works in Substance Misuse Treatments for Offenders." *Criminal Behavior and Mental Health* 17 (2007): 225–233.

Meader, N. "A Comparison of Methadone, Buprenorphine and Alpha2 Adrenergic Agonists for Opioid Detoxification: A Mixed Comparison Meta-analysis." *Drug and Alcohol Dependence* 108 (2010): 110–114.

Medi-Cal. "Clinical Review: Morphine Equivalent Daily Dose to Prevent Opioid Overuse." 30 September 2015. Available https://files.medical.ca.gov/pubsdoco/dur/Articles/dured_24035.pdf

Medical Discoveries. "Codeine." n.d. Available http://www.discoveriesinmedicine.com/Bar-Cod/Codeine.html

Mental Health Daily. "Methadone vs. Suboxone: Comparison." 10 June 2015. Available http://mentalhealthdaily.com/2015/06/10/methadone-vs-suboxone-comparison/

Morgan, T., M. Porritt, and A. Poling. "Effects of Dextromethorphan on Rats' Acquisition of Responding with Delayed Reinforcement." *Pharmacology and Biochemical Behavior* 85 (2006): 637–642.

Munoz-Manchado, A. J. Villadiego, S. Romo-Madero, N. Suárez-Luna, A. Bermejo-Navas, J. A. Rodríguez-Gómez, P. Garrido-Gil, J. L. Labandeira-García, M. Echevarría, J. López-Barneo, and J. J. Toledo-Aral. "Chronic and Progressive Parkinson's Disease MPTP Model in Adult and Aged Mice." *Journal of Neurochemistry* 136 (2015): 373–387.

Mutschler, J., A. Koopmann, M. Grosshans, D. Hermann, K. Mann, and F. Kiefer. "Dextromethorphan Withdrawal and Dependence Syndrome." *Deutsches Ärzteblatt International* 107 (2010): 537–540.

NAABT.org. "Physical Dependence and Addiction." October 2014. Available http://www.naabt.org/addiction_physical-dependence.cfm

Nakamura, D. "City to Spend $650,000 on Needle Exchange Programs." *Washington Post* (3 January 2008). Available http://www.washingtonpost.com/wp-dyn/content/article/2008/01/02/AR2008010201905.html

Nandi, A., T. Glass, S. Cole, H. Chu, S. Galea, D. Celentano, G. D. Kirk, D. Vlahov, W. W. Latimer, and S. H. Mehta. "Neighborhood Poverty and Injection Cessation in a Sample of Injection Drug Users." *American Journal of Epidemiology* 171 (2010): 391–398.

National Center for Biotechnology Information (NCBI). "Naltrexone (Injection)." PubMed Health. n.d. Available http://www.ncbi.nlm.nih.gov/pubmedhealth/PMHT0011328/

National Institute on Drug Abuse (NIDA). "What Is the History of Opioid Addiction in the United States?" January 2013. NIDA International Program. Available http://www.drugabuse.gov/international/question-2-what-history-opioid-addiction-in-united-states

National Institute on Drug Abuse (NIDA). "Why Does Heroin Use Create Special Risk for Contracting HIV/AIDS and Hepatitis B and C?" 2014a. Available https://www.drugabuse.gov/publications/research-reports/heroin/why-are-heroin-users-special-risk-contracting-hivaids-hepatitis-b-c

National Institute on Drug Abuse (NIDA). "How Does Heroin Use Affect Pregnant Women?" 2014b. Available https://www.drugabuse.gov/publications/research-reports/heroin/how-does-heroin-abuse-affect-pregnant-women

Office of National Drug Control Policy (ONDCP). "The International Heroin Market." 2015. Available https://www.whitehouse.gov/ondcp/global-heroin-market

O'Shea, J., F. Law, and J. Melichar. "Lofexidine/Clonidine for Withdrawal." BMJ Clinical Evidence. 2010. Available http://clinicalevidence.bmj.com/ceweb/conditions/meh/1015/1015_I5.jsp

"'Oxy' Kids Crisis." *New York Post* (18 June 2007). Available http://www.nypost.com/p/news/regional/item_2RyopB29Z8esHu8oe50qkK

Pain Community Centre. "Opioids." n.d. Available http://www.paincommunitycentre.org/article/opioids

Palm Partners. "How Do Methadone Clinics Work?" 11 June 2013. Available http://blog.palmpartners.com/how-do-methadone-clinics-work/

PBS. "Opium Throughout History." *Frontline*. n.d. Available http://www.pbs.org/wgbh/pages/frontline/shows/heroin/etc/history.html

Pietrangelo, A. "Codeine vs. Hydrocodone: Two Ways to Treat Pain." Healthline. 26 March 2015. Available http://www.healthline.com/health/pain-relief/codeine-vs-hydrocodone#Overview1

Polidoro, R. "Infographic: Emergency Rooms See Increase in Heroin Patients." NBC News. (8 April 2014). Available http://www.nbcnews.com/storyline/americas-heroin

-epidemic/infographic-emergency-rooms-see-increase
-heroin-patients-n7431

Powell, A. "Heroin's Descent." *Harvard Gazette* (29 September 2015). Available http://news.harvard.edu/gazette/story/2015/09/heroins-descent/

Preda, A. "Opioid Abuse Treatment & Management." Medscape. 2015. http://emedicine.medscape.com/article/287790-treatment

Ramde, D. "FBI Report Analyzes Wisconsin's Growing Heroin Problem." USA Today Network, thenorthwestern.com. (2 July 2014). Available http://www.thenorthwestern.com/story/news/local/2014/07/02/fbi-prices-purity-drugs-fueling-wisconsins-growing-heroin-problem/12030025/

Recovery Helpdesk. "10 Things You Should Know About Methadone: A Low Methadone Dose Is Not Necessarily the Best Methadone Dose." 2010. Available http://www.recoveryhelpdesk.com/2010/05/14/series-10-things-you-should-know-about-methadone-number-10

Rehab International. "Concerns of IV Drug Use." Drug and Alcohol Rehab Guides. n.d. Available http://rehab-international.org/drug-addiction/concerns-of-iv-drug-use

Rehabs.com. "Street Names for Oxycontin." n.d. Available http://luxury.rehabs.com/oxycontin-addiction/street-names-and-nicknames/

Reid, L., K. Elifson, and C. Sterk. "Ecstasy and Gateway Drugs: Initiating the Use of Ecstasy and Other Drugs." *Annals of Epidemiology* 17 (2007): 74–80.

Robertson, D., and I. Biaggioni. "Adrenoceptor Agonists & Sympathomimetic Drugs." In *Basic and Clinical Pharmacology*, 13th ed., edited by B. Katzung and A. Trevor, 133–151. New York: McGraw-Hill, 2015.

Rolfs, R. "Utah Clinical Guidelines on Prescribing Opioids." 2008. Available http://health.utah.gov/prescription/pdf/Utah_guidelines_pdfs.pdf

RT. "1mn Died from Afghan Heroin, Drug Production '40 Times Higher' Since NATO Operation." 3 April 2013. Available http://rt.com/news/afghanistan-heroin-production-increased-266

Rubin, R. "FDA OKs Vivitrol to Treat Heroin, Narcotic Addictions." *USA Today* (13 October 2010). Available http://www.usatoday.com/yourlife/health/2010-10-14-opioid14_ST_N.htm

Rudd, R., A. Noah, J. Zibbell, and G. Mathew. "Increases in Drug and Opioid Overdose Deaths—United States, 2000–2014." *Morbidity and Mortality Weekly Report* 64 (2016): 1378–1382. Available http://www.cdc.gov/mmwr/preview/mmwrhtml/mm6450a3.htm

Sansone, R., and L. Sansone. "Buprenorphine Treatment for Narcotic Addiction: Not Without Risks." *Innovations in Clinical Neuroscience* 12 (2015): 32–26.

Schumacher, M., A. Basbaum, and K. Naidu. "Opioid Analgesics and Antagonists." In *Basic and Clinical*

Pharmacology, 13th ed., edited by B. Katzung and A. Trevor, 531–551. New York: McGraw-Hill, 2015.

Seelye, K. "In Heroin Crisis, White Families Seek Gentler War on Drugs." *New York Times.* (30 October 2015). Available http://www.nytimes.com/2015/10/31/us/heroin-war-on-drugs-parents.html

Sify News. "Risk Factors for Painkiller Addiction Identified." 28 August 2010. Available http://sify.com/news/risk-factors-for-painkiller-addiction-identified-news-scitech-ki3pEjahbic.html

Simon, D. "Is Methadone an Effective Treatment for Heroin Addiction? Yes!" Addiction Blog. 9 March 2016. Available http://prescription-drug.addictionblog.org/is-methadone-an-effective-treatment-for-heroin-addiction-yes/

Smith, C. "Experts Push for Painkiller Tramadol to Be on Controlled List." *Pittsburgh Tribune-Review.* (28 March 2010). Available http://www.questia.com/library/1P2-21460255/experts-push-for-painkiller-tramadol-to-be-on-controlled

Substance Abuse and Mental Health Services Administration (SAMHSA). "The Costs of Alcohol and Drug Treatment." About.com: Alcoholism. 31 December 2008. Available http://alcoholism.about.com/od/pro/a/blsam040527.htm

Substance Abuse and Mental Health Services Administration (SAMHSA). "Physician Waiver Qualifications." 2010. Available http://buprenorphine.samhsa.gov/waiver_qualifications.html

Substance Abuse and Mental Health Services Administration (SAMHSA). "Medication and Counseling Treatment." 28 September 2015a. Available http://www.samhsa.gov/medication-assisted-treatment/treatment

Substance Abuse and Mental Health Services Administration (SAMHSA). "Substance Use Disorders." 27 October 2015b. Available http://www.samhsa.gov/disorders/substance-use

Svrluga, S. "The Drug Suboxone Could Combat the Heroin Epidemic. So Why Is It So Hard to Get?" *Washington Post.* (13 January 2015). Available https://www.washingtonpost.com/local/a-drug-called-suboxone-could-combat-the-heroin-epidemic-so-why-is-it-so-hard-to-get/2015/01/13/4135d08c-812e-11e4-9f38-95a187e4c1f7_story.html

Tabachnick, C. "Breaking Good: Vivitrol, A New Drug Given as a Monthly Shot, Is Helping Addicts Stay Clean." *Washington Post.* (13 March 2015). Available https://www.washingtonpost.com/lifestyle/magazine/his-last-shot-will-a-monthly-jab-of-a-new-drug-keep-this-addict-out-of-jail/2015/03/05/7f054354-7a4c-11e4-84d4-7c896b90abdc_story.html

The Economist. "How to Smack It Down." 7 November 2015. Available http://www.economist.com/news/leaders/21677641-beat-scourge-heroin-governments-should-deal-drug-themselves-how-smack-it-down

Trigo, J. M., E. Martin-Garcia, F. Berrendero, P. Robledo, and R. Maldonado. "The Endogenous Opioid System: A Common Substrate in Drug Addiction." *Drug and Alcohol Dependence* 108 (2010): 183–194.

Tur, K. "Saving Lives with Heroin Needles." NBC New York. (19 August 2010). Available http://www.nbcnewyork.com/news/local-beat/The-Syringe-Exchange-Saved-My-Life-101112079.html

UNODC. "World Drug Report." United Nations Office on Drugs and Crime (2015). Available https://www.unodc.org/documents/wdr2015/World_Drug_Report_2015.pdf

Valenzuela, B. E. "Heroin Use on the Rise." *Daily Press* (Victorville, CA). (28 August 2010). Available http://www.vvdailypress.com/article/20100828/NEWS/308289996

Vaults of Erowid. "Dextromethorphan." n.d. Available https://www.erowid.org/chemicals/dxm/dxm_basics.shtml

Volkow, N. "America's Addiction to Opioids: Heroin and Prescription Drug Abuse." National Institute on Drug Abuse. 14 May 2014a. Available https://www.drugabuse.gov/about-nida/legislative-activities/testimony-to-congress/2016/americas-addiction-to-opioids-heroin-prescription-drug-abuse

Volkow, N. "Prescription Opioid and Heroin Abuse." National Institute on Drug Abuse. 29 April 2014b. Available www.drugabuse.gov/about-nida/legislative-activities/testimony-to-congress

Wang, M. "Perinatal Drug Abuse and Neonatal Drug Withdrawal." eMedicine from WebMD. 12 April 2010. Available http://emedicine.medscape.com/article/978492-overview

Way, W., H. Fields, and E. L. Way. "Opioid Analgesics and Antagonists." In *Basic and Clinical Pharmacology*, 7th ed., edited by B. Katzung, 496–515. Stamford, CT: Appleton & Lange, 1998.

Willis, M. "OxyContin Users Turning to Heroin." Drug-Rehabs. 2008. Available http://www.drug-rehabs.com/HeroinReplacesOxycontin.htm

Winkler, M., P. Weyers, R. Mucha, B. Stippekohl, and P. Pauli. "Conditioned Cues for Smoking Elicit Preparatory Responses in Healthy Smokers." *Psychopharmacology* (Berl.) 213 (February 2011): 781–789.

Young, R., and J. Hobson. "Pain Specialist: Many Doctors Underprescribe for Chronic Pain." Here and Now, NPR. (16 February 2016). Available http://hereandnow.wbur.org/2016/02/16/underprescribing-opioids-for-pain

Zielinski, N. "Methadone Deaths Increase in the US." Examiner.com. 1 August 2010. Available http://www.examiner.com/article/methadone-deaths-increase-the-us

Zocchi, A., E. Girlanda G. Varnier, I. Sartori, L. Zanetti, G. Wildish, M. Lennon, M. Mugnaini, and C. A. Heidbreder. "Dopamine Responsiveness to Drugs of Abuse: A Shell-Core Investigation in the Nucleus Accumbens of the Mouse." *Synapse* 50 (2003): 293–302.

CHAPTER 10
Stimulants

© GRAZVYDAS/iStockphoto.com.

Did You Know?

▶ The first therapeutic use of amphetamines was in inhalers to treat nasal congestion.

▶ Illegal methamphetamine can be easily made from drugs found in common over-the-counter (OTC) decongestants and some herbal products.

▶ Methylphenidate (Ritalin), a drug prescribed to treat children with attention deficit hyperactivity disorder (ADHD), is sometimes used illegally by college students to suppress fatigue while studying long hours for exams.

▶ Ecstasy has both psychedelic and stimulant properties.

▶ Products such as bath salts, ivory wave, or flakka contain designer amphetamine- and cocaine-like drugs that have not been well studied and are potentially very dangerous.

▶ Smoking "freebased" or "crack" cocaine is more dangerous and more addicting than other forms of administration.

▶ Using high doses of amphetamines or cocaine can cause behavior that resembles schizophrenia.

▶ Caffeine is the most frequently used stimulant in the world.

▶ Caffeine is the principal active ingredient in most "energy drinks."

▶ Herbal stimulants promoted as "natural highs" contain central nervous system stimulants such as caffeine or guaraná.

▶ Ephedrine found in natural herbal products has caused fatal cardiovascular problems in unsuspecting athletes and was removed from the list of approved OTC products by the Food and Drug Administration (FDA).

Learning Objectives

On completing this chapter you should be able to:

❯ Explain how amphetamines work.

❯ Identify the FDA-approved uses for amphetamines.

❯ Recognize the major side effects of amphetamines on brain and cardiovascular functions.

❯ Identify the terms *speed*, *ice*, *run*, *high*, and *tweaking* as they relate to amphetamine use.

❯ Explain what "designer" amphetamines are and how Ecstasy compares to methamphetamine.

❯ Discuss the unique dangers of products such as bath salts.

❯ Explain what "club drugs" are.

❯ Describe why stimulants are used as "performance enhancers" and why they should be considered dangerous.

❯ Explain how methylphenidate (e.g., Ritalin) compares to methamphetamine.

❯ Trace the changes in attitude toward cocaine abuse that occurred in the 1980s, and explain why they occurred.

❯ Compare the effects of cocaine with those of amphetamines.

❯ Identify the different stages of cocaine withdrawal.

❯ Discuss the different approaches to treating cocaine dependence.

❯ Identify and compare the major sources of the caffeine-like xanthine drugs.

❯ List the principal physiological effects of caffeine.

❯ Compare caffeine dependence and withdrawal to that associated with the major stimulants.

❯ Describe the beverages known as "energy drinks" and relate their potential risks.

❯ Understand the potential dangers of using herbal stimulants such as ephedra.

❯ Identify the role of the FDA in regulating herbal stimulants.

Introduction

Stimulants are substances that cause the user to feel energized and experience a sense of increased energy and a state of euphoria, or "high." This effect is likely due to the ability of these drugs to release dopamine (Mental Health Daily 2015a). When used excessively, the user may also feel restless and talkative and have trouble sleeping. High doses administered over the long term can produce personality changes or even induce violent, dangerous, psychotic behavior. Persons addicted to potent stimulants make notoriously bad decisions that hurt them and their loved ones (Miller 2016). The following describes the experiences of a stimulant (i.e., methamphetamine) user:

> Rayda Tegen, a 46-year-old mother, was arrested and sentenced to 3 years of prison for smuggling in a pound of methamphetamine into Juneau, Alaska. As she sat in a yellow prison suit, she deeply regretted her very bad decisions causing her to relapse back to using methamphetamine after being clean for 20 years. She isn't exactly sure how it happened. "It wasn't that I woke up one day and said, 'I have a beautiful family, why don't I screw that up. I have a beautiful marriage . . . why don't I throw that down the tubes.' Rayda blames herself for her predicament. In fact, she admits that it probably was good thing she was arrested. "Maybe someone would have died from the drugs I was bringing into the state and I would have had to live with that. I couldn't live knowing that I gave someone something that killed them. Or I could have ended up dead." (Penn 2016)

Many users self-medicate psychological conditions (e.g., depression or attention deficit hyperactivity disorder [ADHD]) with stimulants. Because the initial effects of stimulants are so pleasant, these drugs are repeatedly abused, leading to dependence.

In this chapter, you will learn about two principal classifications of stimulant drugs. Major stimulants, including amphetamines and cocaine, are addressed first, given their prominent role in current illicit and prescription drug abuse problems in the United States. The chapter concludes with a review of minor stimulants—in particular, caffeine. The stimulant properties of over-the-counter (OTC) sympathomimetics and "herbal highs" also are discussed.

Major Stimulants

All major stimulants increase alertness, excitation, and euphoria; thus, these drugs are referred to as **uppers**. The major stimulants are classified as either Schedule I ("designer" amphetamines or major ingredients in bath salts–like products) or Schedule II (amphetamine, cocaine, and methylphenidate [Ritalin]) controlled substances because of their abuse potential. Although these drugs have properties in common, they also have unique features that distinguish them from one another (OHSU 2015). The similarities and differences of the major stimulants are discussed in the following sections.

■ Amphetamines

Approximately 1% of 18- to 25-year-olds and 0.4% of those 26 years or older used methamphetamine in 2014 (National Institute on Drug Abuse [NIDA] 2015). Amphetamines are potent synthetic central nervous system (CNS) stimulants capable of causing dependence due to their euphorigenic properties and ability to eliminate fatigue. Despite their addicting effects, amphetamines can be legally prescribed by physicians for appetite control in weight loss programs, narcolepsy, and hyperactivity disorders; however, their medical uses are considered to be limited (NIDA 2015). Consequently, amphetamine abuse occurs in people who acquire their drugs by both legitimate and illicit means.

THE HISTORY OF AMPHETAMINES

The first amphetamine was synthesized by the German pharmacologist L. Edeleano in 1887, but it was not until 1910 that this and several related compounds were tested in laboratory animals. Another 17 years passed before Gordon Alles, a researcher looking for a more potent substitute for ephedrine (used as a decongestant at the time), self-administered amphetamine and gave a firsthand account of its effects. Alles found that when inhaled or taken orally amphetamine dramatically reduced fatigue, increased alertness, and caused a sense of confident euphoria (Grinspoon and Bakalar 1978).

Because of Alles's impressive findings, the Benzedrine (amphetamine) inhaler became available in 1932 as a nonprescription medication in

KEY TERM

uppers
CNS stimulants

drugstores across the United States. The Benzedrine inhaler, marketed for nasal congestion, was widely abused for its stimulant action but continued to be available OTC until 1949. Because of a loophole in a law that was passed later, not until 1971 were all potent amphetamine-like compounds in nasal inhalers withdrawn from the market (Grinspoon and Bakalar 1978; McCaffrey 1999).

Owing to the lack of restrictions during this early period, amphetamines were sold to treat a variety of ailments, including obesity, alcoholism, bed-wetting, depression, schizophrenia, morphine and codeine addiction, heart block, head injuries, seasickness, persistent hiccups, and caffeine mania. Today, most of these uses are no longer approved as legitimate therapeutics but would be considered forms of drug abuse.

World War II provided a setting in which both the legal and "black market" use of amphetamines flourished (Grinspoon and Bakalar 1978). Because of their stimulating effects, amphetamines were widely used by the Germans, Japanese, and British in World War II to counteract fatigue. By the end of World War II, large quantities of amphetamines were readily available without prescription in seven types of nasal inhalers (*Frontline* n.d.; Newman 2016).

In spite of warnings about these drugs' addicting properties and serious side effects, the U.S. armed forces issued amphetamines on a regular basis during the Korean War and, in fact, may still make it available to pilots in the Air Force to relieve fatigue. Amphetamine use became widespread among truck drivers making long hauls; it is believed that among the earliest distribution systems for illicit amphetamines were truck stops along major U.S. highways. High achievers under continuous pressure in the fields of entertainment, business, and industry often relied on amphetamines to counteract fatigue (*Frontline* n.d.). Homemakers used them to control weight and to combat boredom from unfulfilled lives. At the height of one U.S. epidemic in 1967, some 31 million prescriptions were written for **anorexiants** (diet pills) alone.

Today, a variety of related drugs and mixtures exist, including amphetamine substances such as dextroamphetamine (Dexedrine), methamphetamine (Desoxyn), and amphetamine itself. Generally, if doses are adjusted, the psychological effects of these various drugs are similar, so they will be discussed as a group. Other drugs with some of the same pharmacological properties are phenmetrazine (Preludin) and methylphenidate (Ritalin). Not only are illicit stimulants a significant drug abuse problem, but legal stimulants are the second most frequently abused drug on college campuses, with 15% to 20% of college students using these drugs. Common slang terms for amphetamines include *bennies, amped, black/blue mollies, jelly beans, speed, uppers, dexies, eyepoppers,* and *lightning* (Amphetamines.com n.d.).

HOW AMPHETAMINES WORK

Amphetamines are synthetic chemicals that are similar to natural neurotransmitters such as norepinephrine (noradrenaline), dopamine, and the stress hormone epinephrine (adrenaline). The amphetamines exert their pharmacological effect by increasing the release and blocking the metabolism of these catecholamine substances, as well as serotonin, both in the brain and in nerves associated with the sympathetic nervous system. Because amphetamines cause release of norepinephrine from sympathetic nerves, they are classified as sympathomimetic drugs. The amphetamines generally cause an arousal or activating response (also called the *fight-or-flight response*) that is similar to the normal reaction to emergency situations, stress, or crises. Amphetamines also cause alertness so that the individual becomes aroused and hypersensitive to stimuli and feels "turned on." These effects occur even without external sensory input. This activation may be a very pleasant experience in itself, but a continual high level of activation may convert to anxiety, severe apprehension, or panic (Luscher 2015).

Amphetamines have potent effects on dopamine in the reward (pleasure) center of the brain. This action probably causes the "flash" or sudden feeling of intense pleasure that occurs when amphetamine is taken intravenously. Some users describe the sensation as a "whole-body orgasm," and many associate intravenous methamphetamine use with sexual feelings. The actual effect of these drugs on sexual behavior is quite variable and dependent on dose (OHSU 2015).

WHAT AMPHETAMINES CAN DO

A curious condition commonly reported with heavy amphetamine use is **behavioral stereotypy**,

KEY TERMS

anorexiants
drugs that suppress the activity of the brain's appetite center, causing reduced food intake

behavioral stereotypy
meaningless repetition of a single activity

or "getting hung up." This term refers to a simple activity that is done repeatedly. An individual who is "hung up" will get caught in a repetitious thought or act for hours. For example, he or she may take objects apart, like radios or clocks, and carefully categorize all the parts, or sit in a tub and bathe all day, persistently sing a note, repeat a phrase of music, or repeatedly clean the same object. This phenomenon seems to be peculiar to potent stimulants such as the amphetamines and cocaine. Similar patterns of repetitive behavior also occur in psychotic conditions, which suggests that the intense use of stimulants such as amphetamines or cocaine alters the brain in a manner like that causing psychotic mental disorders (NIDA 2015) and can lead to violent behavior.

Chronic use of high doses of amphetamines decreases the brain content of the neurotransmitters dopamine and serotonin, which persists for months even after drug use is stopped (Luschner 2015). These decreases have been shown to reflect damage to the CNS neurons that release these transmitters. It is not clear why this neuronal destruction occurs, although there is evidence that the amphetamines can stimulate production of very reactive molecules, called *free radicals*, which, in turn, damage brain cells (NIDA 2015).

APPROVED USES

Until 1970, amphetamines were prescribed for a large number of conditions, including depression, fatigue, and long-term weight reduction. In 1970, the Food and Drug Administration (FDA), acting on the recommendation of the National Academy of Sciences, restricted the legal use of amphetamines to three medical conditions: (1) narcolepsy, (2) ADHD, and (3) short-term weight reduction programs (Newman 2016).

NARCOLEPSY

Amphetamine treatment of narcolepsy is not widespread because this condition is a relatively rare disorder. The term **narcolepsy** comes from the Greek words for "numbness" and "seizure." A person who has narcolepsy falls asleep as frequently as 50 times a day if he or she stays in one position for very long. Taking low doses of amphetamines helps keep narcoleptic people alert.

ATTENTION DEFICIT HYPERACTIVITY DISORDER

ADHD is a common behavioral problem in children and adolescents that involves an abnormally high level of physical activity, an inability to focus attention, and frequent disruptive behavior. Approximately 11% of children aged 4 to 17 years have been diagnosed with ADHD in the United States (Centers for Disease Control and Prevention [CDC] 2016). The drug commonly used to treat children with ADHD is the amphetamine-related methylphenidate, or Ritalin (discussed later in this chapter).

WEIGHT REDUCTION

The most common use of amphetamines is for the treatment of obesity. Amphetamines and chemically similar compounds are used as anorexiants to help obese or severely overweight people control appetite. Amphetamines are thought to act by affecting the appetite center in the hypothalamus of the brain, which causes the user to decrease food intake. The FDA has approved short-term use of amphetamines for weight loss programs but has warned of their potential for abuse. Many experts believe that the euphoric effect of amphetamines is the primary motivation for their continued use in weight reduction programs. It is possible that many obese people have a need for gratification that can be satisfied by the euphoric feeling this drug produces (Ely and Cusack 2015). If the drug is taken away, these individuals return to food to satisfy their need and sometimes experience "rebound," causing them to gain back more weight than they lost. Some persons who become addicted to amphetamine-like substances begin illicit use of these drugs by trying to prevent weight gain or to lose weight on their own without the guidance of a physician (American Psychiatric Association [APA] 2013).

SIDE EFFECTS OF THERAPEUTIC DOSES

The two principal side effects of therapeutic doses of amphetamines are abuse, which has already been discussed, and cardiovascular toxicities. Many of these effects derive from the amphetamine-induced release of epinephrine from the adrenal glands and norepinephrine from the nerves associated with the sympathetic nervous system. The effects include increased heart rate, elevated blood pressure, and damage to vessels, especially small veins and arteries (Newman 2016). In users with a history of heart attack, coronary arrhythmia, or hypertension, amphetamine toxicity can be severe or even fatal.

KEY TERM

narcolepsy
a condition causing spontaneous and uncontrolled sleeping episodes

HERE AND NOW
Meth and Crime

Methamphetamine is all too frequently at the heart of criminal activities committed by gang members involved in illegal drug distribution. For example, an Aryan Brotherhood gang from Central Texas was selling up to 4 kilograms of "meth" or "ice" each month at the expense of the local community. Persons addicted to methamphetamine have very poor judgment and often engage in criminal activity to secure the money required to support their drug habit. This was the case in Waco and Fort Hood, Texas, locations of the Aryan Brotherhood gang. According to law enforcement officials, these areas were tormented with explosions of burglaries, property crime, arsons, assaults, firearms thefts, and even murders associated with the methamphetamine trade. With a major push from law enforcement, almost all of the members of the Aryan Brotherhood were arrested and

charged with meth distribution, putting them behind bars in federal prison. Following the arrests, the affected communities experienced a dramatic drop in property crime as the drug distribution was stopped.

Federal Bureau of Investigation (FBI). "Aryan Brotherhood Methamphetamine Operation Dismantled." 31 December 2015. Available https://www.fbi.gov/news/stories/aryan-brotherhood-methamphetamine-operation-dismantled

CURRENT MISUSE

Because amphetamine drugs can be readily and inexpensively synthesized in makeshift laboratories for illicit sale, can be administered by several routes, and cause a more sustained effect than cocaine, they are more popular than cocaine in many parts of the United States (Johnston 2016). Surveys suggest that there was a decline in the abuse of amphetamines in the late 1980s and early 1990s in parallel with a similar trend in cocaine abuse (Johnston 2016). By 2002, these declines were replaced by a rise in the number of persons abusing amphetamines to 11.1%. However, abuse again declined, as indicated by the finding that 7.7% of high school seniors used amphetamines in 2015 (Johnston 2016). Of those who abuse amphetamines and become addicted, many end up in the criminal justice system (Federal Bureau of Investigation [FBI] 2015; see "Here and Now: Meth and Crime").

Because of the potential for serious side effects, U.S. medical associations have asked all physicians to be more careful about prescribing

amphetamines. Presently, use is recommended only for narcolepsy and some cases of hyperactivity in children (Newman 2016). In spite of FDA approval, most medical associations do not recommend the use of amphetamines for weight loss.

Amphetamine abusers commonly administer a dose of 10 to 30 milligrams. Besides the positive effects of this dose—the "high"—it can cause hyperactive, nervous, or jittery feelings that encourage the use of a depressant such as a benzodiazepine, barbiturate, or alcohol to relieve the discomfort of being "wired" (Mental Health Daily 2015c).

A potent and commonly abused form of amphetamine is **speed**, an illegal methamphetamine available as a white, odorless, bitter-tasting crystalline powder for injection. Methamphetamine is a highly addictive stimulant that is often cheaper and much longer lasting than cocaine. The profit for the speed manufacturer is substantial enough to make illicit production financially attractive at $10 to $20 a dose; it is sometimes known as the "poor man's cocaine" (KCI.org n.d.). Despite this image of being a particular problem of the working class, there are many examples of rich and famous people who also abuse this potent stimulant (see "Here and Now: Agassi Admits Using Meth").

KEY TERM

speed
an injectable methamphetamine used by drug addicts

HERE AND NOW
Agassi Admits Using Meth

The use of meth by former tennis star Andre Agassi is no secret. In his autobiography, Agassi admitted to using crystal methamphetamine and lying about it to tennis authorities after failing a drug test. Agassi said that he was worried about how fans would respond to the revelation that he used drugs, but he claimed the drug helped distract him from his poor tennis performance. This very popular athlete described his methamphetamine experience as follows:

> I snort some. I ease back on the couch and consider the Rubicon I've just crossed. There is a moment of regret, followed by vast sadness. Then comes a tidal wave of euphoria that sweeps away every negative thought in my head. I've never felt so alive, so hopeful—and I've never felt such energy. I'm seized by a desperate desire to clean. I go tearing around my house, cleaning it from top to bottom. I dust the furniture. I scour the tub. I make the beds.

But his use of methamphetamine came at a high cost as it helped to destroy his tennis career and drive away his first wife, Brooke Shields.

Data from Battula, S. "Recounting the Story of Andre Agassi's Crystal Meth Indulgence." *SK Tennis* (26 August 2015); Wyatt, B. "Agassi Admits Using Crystal Meth." CNN.com. 28 October 2009. Available http://www.cnn.com/2009/SPORT/10/28/tennis.agassi.crystal.meth/index.html

Methamphetamine is relatively easy and inexpensive to make. The illicit manufacturers are usually individuals without expertise in chemistry. Such people, referred to as "cookers," can produce methamphetamine batches by using cookbook-style recipes (often obtained in jail or over the Internet). The most popular recipe uses common OTC ingredients—ephedrine, pseudoephedrine, and phenylpropanolamine—as **precursor chemicals** for the methamphetamine. To discourage the illicit manufacture of this potent stimulant, the Comprehensive Methamphetamine Control Act was passed in the United States in October 1996. This law increases penalties for trafficking in methamphetamine and in the precursor chemicals used to create this drug and gives the government authority to regulate and seize these substances (DEA 2015). Despite the success in shutting down larger neighborhood operations with this and similar local laws, there are still drug users who make their own meth in small batches using simpler and cruder methods that consist of what has become known as "one pot" or "shake and bake" approaches. These scaled-down recipes require relatively small numbers of decongestant pills that are crushed and mixed with common household chemicals; the procedure can be done in inconspicuous places such as a bathroom or in a car. Although no flame is required to "cook" the mixture, the procedure sometimes can produce powerful explosions, fires, and toxic waste (Sampson 2016). For example, a man in southeast Missouri was seen jumping from his car with his crotch on fire holding a flaming bottle, which he quickly dumped before immediately returning to his car and driving away. Upon closer inspection, the bottle was a "shake and bake" effort to make methamphetamine (Keybol.org 2009).

Due to the ease of production and the ready availability of chemicals used to prepare methamphetamine, this drug at times has been particularly problematic in the United States. Although the Comprehensive Methamphetamine Control Act has dramatically reduced the number of meth laboratories across the country, pockets of high meth lab activity still exist. Based on meth

KEY TERM

precursor chemicals
chemicals used to produce a drug

HERE AND NOW

Chemical Toxins Associated with Meth Labs

Methamphetamine labs can be set up almost anywhere and pose a serious threat to occupants as well as to law officers and emergency personnel. The following are some of the chemicals often present and their toxic potentials.

Chemicals	Toxic Reactions
Sodium hydroxide	Irritant to skin and eyes
Ammonia	Induces vomiting and nausea
Ether, acetone, and alcohol	Flammable
Chloroform	Carcinogen and volatile
Mercuric chloride	Poisonous (used as insecticide)
Cyanide gas	Extremely poisonous if breathed
Acids	Potent irritants
Iodine	Irritant; causes nausea, headaches, and dizziness
Phosphene gas	Poisonous, flammable (used as nerve gas)

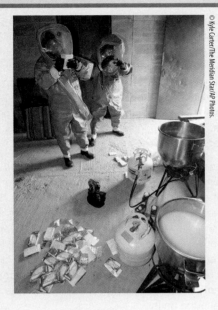

© Kyle Carter/The Meridian Star/AP Photos

Data from Office of National Drug Control Policy (ONDCP). "Synthetic Drug Control Strategy." June 2006. Available http://www.justice.gov/olp/pdf/synthetic_strat2006.pdf

lab busts in 2014, the Midwest has the most meth activity, with Indiana ranking as the worst state for meth activity (DEA 2016). Traditional methamphetamine users in the United States have been white, male, blue-collar workers older than 26 years of age; some adolescents (Johnston 2016); and young adult women.

When discovered, the so-called meth or speed labs are raided by law enforcement agencies. In 2003, the DEA funded the cleanup of approximately 12,000 illegal methamphetamine labs, most of which were in the western United States. This number decreased to 3866 in 2008 (Doyle 2010), but has since increased again (Melnikova, Orr, and Christensen 2015). The laboratory operators are usually well armed, and the facilities are frequently booby-trapped with explosives. Not surprisingly, these operations pose a serious threat to their neighbors and to residents, especially children, in the structure that contains the lab (METH Project 2015). Law enforcement personnel and firefighters are also at risk when dealing

with methamphetamine labs owing to ignitable, corrosive, reactive, and toxic chemicals that might explode, start a fire, emit toxic fumes, or cause serious injury at the site. The toxic chemicals can create fumes that contaminate neighboring buildings, the water supply, or soil. These labs are especially dangerous when they are set up in poorly ventilated rooms (see "Here and Now: Chemical Toxins Associated with Meth Labs").

Although still a problem, as already mentioned, the incidence of "mom and pop" neighborhood methamphetamine labs has dramatically decreased across the nation since 2003. This is mainly due to federal and state laws that limit access to large quantities of precursor drugs found in OTC decongestants. The statutes require that these decongestant products be kept behind the pharmacy counter, and the quantity sold to a customer must be minimal in order to limit access (FDA 2014; see "Holding the Line: Cold Restrictions"). Although successful in decreasing the number of small neighborhood meth labs in the

United States, this strategy unfortunately appears to have had minimal effect on actual supplies of this drug for illegal sales. Methamphetamine is being smuggled across the U.S. border from Mexico and is being manufactured by criminal organizations from chemicals diverted by the ton from Asian pharmaceutical companies (Longmire 2016; Thornton 2015). It is estimated that currently the vast majority of meth is imported, keeping supplies abundant, purity high, and costs low (Thornton 2015). Note, however, that small neighborhood labs are making a significant comeback in some parts of the United States, particularly in the Midwest, due to a strategy referred to as "smurfing." Smurfs are often well organized and enlist the help of many friends and associates to purchase the methamphetamine precursor chemicals such as pseudoephedrine (e.g., in decongestants) in quantities below the legal limits. In this way, large amounts of these chemicals can be accumulated and then sold to methamphetamine producers (Wright 2015).

PATTERNS OF HIGH-DOSE USE

Amphetamines can be taken orally, intravenously, or by smoking. The intensity and duration of effects vary according to the mode of administration. The methamphetamine addict frequently uses chronic, high doses of amphetamines intravenously and can be infected with human immunodeficiency virus (HIV) (Massanella et al. 2015). Another approach to administering amphetamines is smoking **ice**, which can cause effects as potent, but perhaps more prolonged and erratic, than intravenous doses. The initial effect (after 5 to 30 minutes) of these potent stimulants is called the **rush** and includes a racing heartbeat and elevated blood pressure, metabolism, and pulse. During this phase, the user has powerful impressions of pleasure and enthusiasm. The next stage is the **high** (4 to 16 hours after drug use) when the person feels aggressively smarter, energetic, talkative, and powerful and may initiate and complete highly ambitious tasks. The amphetamine addict tries to maintain the high for as long as possible, with continual drug use leading to extended mental and physical hyperactivity; this is referred to as a **run** or **binge** and can persist from 3 to 15 days. Persistent use of these drugs, such as methamphetamine, to maintain the high for long periods of time is called **tweaking**. The tweaker often has neither slept nor eaten much for 3 to 15 days and can be extremely irritable and paranoid and have an elevated body temperature,

a condition known as **hyperpyrexia**. This is a potentially dangerous stage for medical personnel or law enforcement officers because if the tweaker becomes agitated, he or she can respond violently to the efforts of others to help. To relieve some of the side effects of the extensive use of methamphetamine, tweakers often use a depressant such as alcohol, barbiturates, benzodiazepines, or opioid narcotics (Center for Substance Abuse Research [CESAR] 2013). The consequences of such a drug combination are to intensify negative feelings and worsen the dangers of the drug. Tweakers are frequently involved in domestic violence and frequently injure their children and partners. Withdrawal follows for 30 to 90 days, including feelings of depression and lethargy. During this phase, cravings can be intense and the abuser may even become suicidal. Because a dose of methamphetamine often relieves these symptoms, many addicts in treatment return to abusing this stimulant (Narconon 2016a).

After the first day or so of a run, unpleasant symptoms become prominent as the dosage is increased. Symptoms commonly reported at this stage are teeth grinding, disorganized patterns of thought and behavior, stereotypy, irritability, self-consciousness, suspiciousness, and fear. Hallucinations and delusions that are similar to a paranoid psychosis and indistinguishable from schizophrenia can occur (Narconon 2016a). The person is likely to show aggressive and antisocial behavior for no apparent reason, although recent brain

KEY TERMS

ice
a smokable form of methamphetamine

rush
initial pleasure after amphetamine use that includes racing heartbeat and elevated blood pressure

high
lasts for 4 to 16 hours after drug use; includes feelings of energy and power

run
intense use of a stimulant, consisting of multiple administrations over a period of days

binge
similar to a run, but usually of shorter duration

tweaking
repeated administration of methamphetamine to maintain the high

hyperpyrexia
elevated body temperature

imaging studies have revealed that addictions to the amphetamines can cause long-term damage to the brain's inhibitory control centers (NIDA 2014). Severe chest pains, abdominal discomfort that mimics appendicitis, and fainting from overdosage are sometimes reported. "Cocaine bugs" represent one bizarre effect of high doses of potent stimulants such as amphetamines: the user experiences strange feelings, like insects crawling under the skin. The range of physical and mental symptoms experienced from low to high doses is summarized in "Signs and Symptoms: Summary of the Effects of Amphetamines on the Body and Mind."

Toward the end of the run, the adverse symptoms dominate. When the drug is discontinued because the supply is exhausted or the symptoms become too unpleasant, an extreme crash can occur, followed by prolonged sleep, sometimes lasting several days. On awakening, the person is lethargic, hungry, and often severely depressed. The amphetamine user may overcome these unpleasant effects by smoking ice or injecting speed, thereby initiating a new cycle (APA 2013).

Continued use of massive doses of amphetamine often leads to considerable weight loss,

sores on the skin, poor oral hygiene and deterioration of the teeth, nonhealing ulcers, liver disease, hypertensive disorders, cerebral hemorrhage (stroke), heart attack, kidney damage, and seizures (NIDA 2015). For some of these effects, it is impossible to tell if they are caused by the drug, poor eating habits, or other factors associated with the lifestyle of people who inject methamphetamine.

Speed freaks are generally unpopular with the rest of the drug-taking community, especially "acid-heads" (addicts who use lysergic acid diethylamide [LSD]), because of the aggressive, unpredictable behavior associated with use of potent stimulants (Roberts 2015). In general, drug abusers who take high doses of these agents, such as amphetamines or cocaine, are more likely to be involved in violent crimes than those who abuse other drugs (Substance Abuse and Mental Health Services Administration [SAMHSA] 2010). Heavy users are generally unable to hold steady jobs because of their drug habits and often have a parasitic relationship with the rest of the illicit drug-using community.

Although claims have been made that amphetamines do not cause physical dependence, it is

HOLDING THE LINE

Cold Restrictions

Starting on September 30, 2006, it became somewhat more difficult for a person with a cold, and a lot more difficult for persons desiring to make methamphetamine from decongestant ingredients, to readily obtain adequate OTC cold medicine for their needs. This is due to a federal law to stop the manufacture of methamphetamine in illegal meth labs found in homes, garages, or basements. To achieve this objective, the restrictions require customers to show a picture ID to purchase cold medicine such as NyQuil Cold & Flu, Actifed Cold & Allergy, and Claritin-D. These and similar decongestant products that contain drugs that can be converted into methamphetamine must be kept behind the store counters in most states. Customers must sign a logbook identifying what they purchased and where they live. The logbook remains on file for 2 years.

This law restricts purchase to 3 to 6 grams of product per day and 9 grams per month. In Oregon and Mississippi these medicines are only available by prescription.

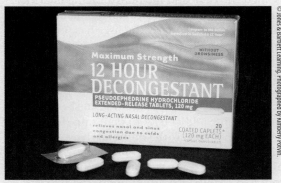

© Jones & Bartlett Learning. Photographed by Kimberly Potvin.

Data from Food and Drug Administration (FDA). "Legal Requirements for the Sale and Purchase of Drug Products Containing Pseudoephedrine, Ephedrine, and Phenylpropanolamine." 2014. Available http://www.fda.gov/drugs/drugsafety/informationbydrugclass/ucm072423.htm; Health & Wellness. "Why Cold Medicines Have Moved Behind the Counter." Women's Health. 2013. Available www.sheknows.com/health-and-wellness/articles/7629/why-some-cold-medicines-have-moved-behind-the-counter;

SIGNS & SYMPTOMS

Summary of the Effects of Amphetamines on the Body and Mind

	Body	Mind
Low dose	Increased heartbeat	Decreased fatigue
	Increased blood pressure	Increased confidence
	Decreased appetite	Increased feeling of alertness
	Increased breathing rate	Restlessness, talkativeness
	Inability to sleep	Increased irritability
	Sweating	Fearfulness, apprehension
	Dry mouth	Distrust of people
	Muscle twitching	Behavioral stereotypy
	Convulsions	Hallucinations
	Fever	Psychosis
High dose	Death due to overdose	

almost certain that depression (sometimes suicidal), lethargy, muscle pains, abnormal sleep patterns, and, in severe cases, suicide attempts occur after high chronic doses as part of withdrawal (Addiction Center 2016c). During withdrawal from amphetamine use, the dependent user often turns to other drugs for relief (Cantwell and McBride 1998). Rebound from the amphetamines is opposite to that experienced with withdrawal from CNS depressants.

Although the effects of amphetamines on the unborn fetus are difficult to evaluate and not fully understood (Davies 2015), some human studies suggest that there is a possibility of serious problems in the offspring. This research shows that babies born to methamphetamine-using mothers are much more likely to be preterm and less likely to survive. In addition, almost 40% of the meth-exposed babies are at least temporarily removed from their mothers to be adopted or placed in Child Protective Services or foster care (Mothers Against Methamphetamine n.d.). Studies on the long-term effects on the offspring of methamphetamine moms have been more difficult to conduct but suggest that brain structures are altered, particularly if these women are also consuming alcohol. These congenital problems could lead to long-term cognitive or behavioral problems (Mothers Against Methamphetamines n.d.). The

methamphetamine-abusing expectant mothers are also vulnerable to serious pregnancy problems of their own such as uncontrolled high blood pressure and delivery complications (Harding 2010).

Evidence suggests that repeated high-dose use of amphetamines, such as methamphetamine, by adolescents or adults causes long-term and perhaps permanent damage to both the dopamine and serotonin neurotransmitter systems of the brain (Northrop and Yamamoto 2015). This brain damage may result in persistent episodes of psychosis as well as long-lasting memory, motor impairment, and cognitive deficits (Recovery.org 2015). Abuse of amphetamines often seriously damages personal relationships with friends, associates, and even family members. Particularly disturbing is the use of methamphetamine by young mothers. Moms on meth have claimed that use of this stimulant makes them feel invincible, and like they can run around the world—and then do it again. They claim to lose weight, but they also can lose their instinct to mother their children as they become obsessed with the drug (Holt 2005). Consequently, children are being exposed to dangerous levels of this drug in many forms (see "Here and Now: Small Town, Big Problems: The Female Methamphetamine Epidemic") at a tremendous emotional cost (see "Signs and Symptoms: A Daughter's Plea to a Meth Mother").

Devastation of oral structures called "meth mouth" sometimes is associated with methamphetamine addiction.

TREATMENT

Admissions for treatment of methamphetamine addiction more than doubled from 2000 to 2005, but since 2013 admissions have decreased by approximately 50% (SAMHSA 2015). This is at least partially due to restricting access to the decongestant drugs used to synthesize methamphetamine (SAMHSA 2015). However, more recent findings suggest that both domestic and Mexican methamphetamine labs are finding ways to get around the laws and avoid detection, resulting in a significant resurgence in methamphetamine supplies and purity in the United States.

HERE AND NOW

Small Town, Big Problems: The Female Methamphetamine Epidemic

Methamphetamine has caused a drug-related epidemic never before experienced in this country. Its abuse and devastating social effects have taxed public social services in unanticipated ways. One of the most striking aspects of this drug's abuse is its appeal to young adult women, many of whom have children or were using methamphetamine when they were pregnant and will have to deal with the potential damage that this drug can cause to their offspring. Typically, the number of women seeking treatment for drug addiction is considerably lower than the number of men in the same situation; however, in many regions roughly equal numbers of men and women seek help for methamphetamine as their primary addiction. Clearly, the destructive influence of methamphetamine abuse is taking an enormous toll on homes and families. Consequently, criminal justice systems for women offenders have been overwhelmed.

Women who are addicted to methamphetamine often do not do well in conventional drug treatment programs. Because of the potent addicting properties of this drug, they typically struggle with the requirements of probation or parole and often end up back in prison, and their children end up in family services and foster care. Although it is not clear why this stimulant is so seductive to young women, women who use methamphetamine typically have:

- A history of chronic unemployment
- A live-in partner who also uses drugs
- A history of physical and sexual abuse
- A history of suicide attempts
- Motivation to use methamphetamine for weight control
- Psychiatric drug-related problems

For female methamphetamine addicts, "this drug is a massive black hole. It's swallowing these people alive and takes a miracle to put these families back together again."

Data from "Escalation in Methamphetamine Use Also Leads to Escalation in Social Service." *Health & Medicine Week* (14 February 2005); Khazan, O. "Into the Body of Another." *The Atlantic* (8 May 2015). Available http://www.theatlantic.com/health/archive/2015/05/into-the-body-of-another/392522/; Rowan-Szal, G., G. Joe, W. Simpson, J. Greener, and J. Vance. "During-Treatment Outcomes Among Female Methamphetamine-Using Offenders in Prison-Based Treatments." *Journal of Offender Rehabilitation* 48 (2009): 388–401

SIGNS & SYMPTOMS

A Daughter's Plea to a Meth Mother

One can only imagine the frustration, anger, and pain that are suffered by the children of mothers who are addicted to methamphetamine. The children's lives are filled with uncertainty, such as the lies of parents who swear that they are clean or will stop their drug habit because they "love their children so much and they don't want to hurt them anymore," but their addiction always seems to crowd out the "love for the child." Often the children try to tough it out and smile on the outside even though on the inside they being torn apart. How long should a child have to tolerate this emotional and even physical abuse? When does it become too much and how can a child escape? Recently a poem was posted on the Internet that beautifully expressed these terrible struggles of a child with a mother who is a drug addict. This poem is entitled "My Mother vs. Meth" and can be accessed at www.familyfriendpoems.com/poem/my-mother-vs-meth.

Currently, 8% of all admissions to treat substance use disorder are linked to the amphetamines and for the most part include persons who are 20 to 44 years of age (SAMHSA 2015).

The dependence disorder caused by the amphetamines is very hard, but not impossible, to treat successfully. Many methamphetamine addicts have significant impairment of their decision-making ability and do not self-refer but are forced into treatment by drug courts and other components of the criminal justice system (National Association of Drug Court Professionals [NADCP] 2015). Presently, the most effective treatments for amphetamine addiction are behavioral interventions to help modify thinking patterns, improve cognitive skills, change expectations, and increase coping with life's stressors. Amphetamine support groups also appear to be successful as adjuncts to behavioral therapies. To date, no well-established pharmacological treatments for amphetamine dependency have been developed (Elkashef et al. 2008; Kishi et al. 2013). Approaches used for cocaine have been tried with some success. Antidepressant medication may help relieve the depression that occurs during early stages of withdrawal (Woolston 2016).

The persistence of the effects of methamphetamine makes this addiction especially difficult to address effectively. The word on the street has been that many of the effects of this stimulant are permanent, and its cognitive damage might be irreversible. Although there is ample evidence that hard-core use of methamphetamine for extended periods has devastating effects on decision-making, impulsivity, memory, and other functions, evidence is accumulating that suggests that recovery from these effects is possible. However, effective treatment is not simple or cheap and typically requires more than a year of intense intervention consisting of drug abstinence; cognitive, emotional, and motivational rehabilitation; and often career and skills development (Woolston 2016).

AMPHETAMINE COMBINATIONS

As previously mentioned, amphetamines are frequently used in conjunction with a variety of other drugs, such as barbiturates, benzodiazepines, alcohol, and heroin (TheGoodDrugsGuide n.d.). Amphetamines intensify, prolong, or otherwise alter the effects of LSD, and the two types of drugs are sometimes combined. The majority of speed users have also had experience with a variety of psychedelics or other drugs. In addition, people dependent on opiate narcotics frequently use amphetamines or cocaine. These combinations are sometimes called **speedballs** (Hawaii Island Recovery 2015).

"DESIGNER" AMPHETAMINES

Underground chemists can readily synthesize drugs that mimic the psychoactive effects of amphetamines. Although the production of such drugs diminished in the early 1990s, their use by American teens surged in the late 1990s and early 2000s, as reflected in the fact that more than 9% of high school seniors used the designer amphetamine known as MDMA (Ecstasy) in 2001. This rate decreased dramatically to 3% in 2005, reflecting a concern about its potential harmful effects. However, the rate of annual use rose to 5.3% in 2011 but dropped back again to 3.6% in 2015,

KEY TERM

speedballs
combinations of amphetamine or cocaine with an opioid narcotic, often heroin

suggesting that the concerns about the risk of recreational use of the designer amphetamines have been vacillating (Johnston 2016).

Designer amphetamines sometimes differ from the parent compound by only a single element. These "synthetic spinoffs" pose a significant abuse problem because often several different designer amphetamines can be made from the parent compound and still retain the abuse potential and physical risks of the original substance (Baumann and Volkow 2016).

For many years, the production and distribution of designer amphetamines were not illegal, even though they were synthesized from controlled substances. In the mid-1980s, however, the DEA actively pursued policies to curb their production and sale. Consequently, many designer amphetamines were outlawed under the Substance Analogue Enforcement Act of 1986, which makes illegal any substance that is similar in structure or psychological effect to any substance already scheduled, if it is manufactured, possessed, or sold with the intention that it be consumed by human beings (Beck 1990).

The principal types of designer amphetamines are the following:

- Derivatives from amphetamine and methamphetamine that retain the CNS stimulatory effects, such as methcathinone ("cat") or mephedrone (methyl-methcathinone)
- Derivatives from amphetamine and methamphetamine that have prominent psychedelic effects in addition to their CNS stimulatory action, such as MDMA (Ecstasy)

Because the basic amphetamine molecule can be easily synthesized and readily modified, hundreds of new amphetamine-like drugs, known as *new psychoactive substances* (NPSs) have appeared on the streets around the world (United Nations Office on Drugs and Crime [UNODC] 2015). Although these designer amphetamines are thought of as new drugs when they first appear, in fact most were originally synthesized from the 1940s to the 1960s by pharmaceutical companies trying to find new decongestant and anorexiant drugs to compete with the other amphetamines. Some of these compounds were found to be too toxic to be marketed but have been rediscovered by "street chemists" and are sold to unsuspecting victims trying to experience a new sensation. **Table 10.1** lists some of these designer amphetamines.

Some designer drugs of abuse that are chemically related to amphetamine include DOM (STP), methcathinone (called *cat* or *bathtub speed*), mephedrone (methylmethcathinone, called *meow meow* or *drone*, and found in products such as ivory wave or bath salts), MDA, and MDMA (or methylenedioxymethamphetamine, called *Ecstasy, X, E, XTC,* or *Adam*). As of 2013, most of these drugs had been classified as Schedule I agents.

MDMA (ECSTASY)

Among the designer amphetamines, MDMA continues to be the most popular. It gained widespread popularity in the United States throughout the 1980s, and its use peaked in 1987 despite its classification as a Schedule I drug in 1985

TABLE 10.1 Designer Amphetamines

Amphetamine Derivative	Properties
Methcathinone ("cat")	Properties like those of methamphetamine and cocaine
Methylenedioxymethamphetamine (MDMA, "Ecstasy")	Stimulant and hallucinogen
Methylenedioxyamphetamine (MDA)	More powerful stimulant and less powerful hallucinogen than MDMA
4-methylaminorex	CNS stimulant like amphetamine
N,N-dimethylamphetamine	One-fifth the potency of amphetamine
4-thiomethyl-2,5-dimethoxyamphetamine	Hallucinogen
Para-methoxymethamphetamine	Weak stimulant
Mephedrone	Potent stimulant and hallucinogen (found in products such as bath salts)
α-Pyrrolidinopentiophenone ("flakka," "5-dollar insanity")	Potent stimulant and hallucinogen

by the DEA. At the height of its use, 39% of the undergraduates at Stanford University reported having used MDMA at least once (Randall 1992a). In the late 1980s and early 1990s, use of MDMA declined in this country, but about this time it was "reformulated." This reformulation was not in a pharmacological sense but in a cultural context.

The "rave" scene in England provided a new showcase for MDMA (Randall 1992a). Partygoers attired in Dr. Seuss–style "Cat in the Hat" hats and psychedelic jumpsuits paid $20 to dance all night to heavy, electronically generated sound mixed with computer-generated video and laser light shows. An Ecstasy tablet could be purchased for the sensory enhancement caused by the drug (Randall 1992b). At one time, it was estimated that as many as 31% of English youth aged 16 to 25 years had used Ecstasy (Grob et al. 1996). The British rave counterculture and its generous use of Ecstasy were exported to the United States in the early 1990s. High-tech music and video trappings were encouraged by low-tech laboratories that illegally manufactured the drug and shipped it into this country. Because of these sensory-enriched environments, Ecstasy became the drug of choice for many young people in the United States (Cloud 2000) and globally (UNODC 2009) looking for a novel "chemical" experience. To this day the rave phenomenon continues to be a major attraction to youthful participants and an excuse for heavy MDMA use and its associated overdose emergencies (Lin 2015).

International seizures of MDMA in 2007 were almost double those reported for 1998 (Power 2015; UNODC 2009). However, compared to methamphetamine, global seizures of Ecstasy have been low and were under 5 tons annually between 2009 to 2013 (UNODC 2015). Currently, more than 90% of these illegal drugs originate in European countries such as the Netherlands and Belgium, which are the principal sources for Ecstasy smuggled into the United States (UNODC 2009). However, recently the number of U.S. homegrown labs that produce MDMA and methamphetamine has increased, despite the fact that the process of making MDMA is very hazardous and the chemicals used for synthesis are difficult to obtain (Friends of Narconon 2010).

Because of its frequent association with raves, clubs, and bars, MDMA is known as a "club drug." At its peak in 2001, Ecstasy was used by 9.2%

of all U.S. high school seniors; since this time, its abuse has been reduced by more than half (Johnston 2016).

Some have compared the rave culture and its use of MDMA to the acid-test parties of the 1960s and the partygoers' use of LSD and amphetamines (*Journal of the American Medical Association* 2010). Some say this drug is not likely to cause significant dependence for most casual users, but intense use appears to be able to lead to addiction. Part of the explanation for the dramatic reduction in MDMA use by young populations is likely a reaction to some highly publicized overdoses of Ecstasy and a perceived increase in the risk of this drug (Johnston 2016).

MDMA was first inadvertently discovered in 1912 by chemists at E. Merck in Darmstadt, Germany (Grob et al. 1996). No pharmaceutical company has ever manufactured MDMA for public marketing, and the FDA has never approved it for therapy. MDMA was first found by the DEA on the streets in 1972 in a drug sample bought in Chicago (Beck 1990). The DEA earnestly began gathering data on MDMA abuse a decade later, which led to its classification as a Schedule I substance in 1985, despite the very vocal opposition of a number of psychiatrists who had been giving MDMA to patients since the late 1970s to facilitate communication, acceptance, and fear reduction (Beck 1990). Some health professionals believe that MDMA should be made available to clinicians for the treatment of some psychiatric disorders such as fear and anxiety (Skomorowsky 2015; Waugh 2015). In fact, with FDA approval, small trial studies have been conducted to test the safety of this drug and its potential value in treating conditions such as posttraumatic stress disorder (PTSD), although the outcome of these clinical trials has yet to be determined.

MDMA and related designer amphetamines are somewhat unique from other amphetamines in that, besides causing excitation, they have prominent psychedelic effects (Drugs.com 2014). These drugs have been characterized as combining the properties of amphetamine and LSD (Drugs.com 2014; Luscher 2015). The psychedelic effects of MDMA are likely caused by release of the neurotransmitter serotonin (Drugs.com 2014). After using hallucinogenic amphetamines, the mind is often flooded with irrelevant and incoherent thoughts and exaggerated sensory experiences and is more receptive to suggestion.

Because of its frequent association with raves, clubs, and bars, MDMA is known as a "club drug."

Dancers at a "rave" often consume Ecstasy for sensory enhancement.

MDMA often is viewed as a "smooth amphetamine" and does not appear to cause the severe depression, "crash," or violent behavior often associated with frequent high doses of the more traditional amphetamines (Drug Policy Alliance 2015b). As mentioned earlier, MDMA was originally thought to be nonaddictive; however, some reports suggest that addiction does occur when high doses of this drug are used (Addiction Center 2016a). Many users tend to be predominantly positive when describing their initial MDMA experiences. They claim the drug causes them to dramatically drop their defense mechanisms or fear responses while they feel an increased empathy for others (Nutt 2015). Combined with its stimulant effects, this action often increases intimate communication and association with others. However, heavy users often experience adverse effects, such as loss of appetite, grinding of teeth, muscle aches and stiffness, sweating, rapid heartbeat, hostility, anxiety, and altered sleep patterns (Davis 2015). In addition, fatigue can be experienced for hours or even days after use. In high doses, MDMA can cause panic attacks and severe anxiety (Davis 2015). Evidence suggests that high doses can significantly damage serotonin neurons or other systems in the brain and cause long-term memory deficits and psychological disturbances in some people (Davis 2015). The duration of these high-dose CNS effects has not been determined and may vary based on the intensity of the bingeing (Hahn 2015).

Recreational use of Ecstasy has been linked to physical emergencies and even occasional fatalities that are similar to those caused by amphetamines and cocaine (Hahn 2015). The leading causes of deaths associated with MDMA use appear to be complications from hyperthermia (related to heatstroke), metabolic problems, or underlying heart problems (Hahn 2015).

Because of its popularity, occasional "spinoff" Ecstasy drugs show up in dance clubs frequented by young people such as *n*-benzylpiperazine, or BZP. This drug is sold in the shape of cartoon characters and has a chemistry that resembles that of MDMA. BZP is not available in pharmacies but can be purchased over the Internet and has been used in the club scene since the 1990s. However, the pharmacology of this drug looks more like that of the amphetamines than MDMA in that it has stimulant effects that cause feelings of euphoria, alertness, and increased energy. With high doses, BZP induces a state of paranoia and anxiety accompanied by increased heart rate, blood pressure, and body temperature (Drug Foundation n.d.). However, when combined with another MDMA-spinoff drug called TFMPP (trifluoromethylphneylpiperazine), it has MDMA-like effects (Keoni 2015).

METHYLPHENIDATE: A SPECIAL AMPHETAMINE

Methylphenidate (Ritalin) is related to the amphetamines but is a relatively mild CNS stimulant, especially when used orally. Although used as a treatment to alleviate depression, research now casts doubt on its effectiveness. It is effective in treating narcolepsy (a sleep disorder). As explained previously, Ritalin has also been found to help calm children and adults suffering from ADHD. ADHD is characterized by an inability to focus attention and increased impulsivity, making it difficult to stay on-task. ADHD can also result in impaired learning abilities and lead to social and personal frustrations (Storebo et al. 2015; WebMD n.d.). Like Adderall (amphetamine) and Provigil (modafinil), Ritalin is routinely used to treat ADHD in both children and adults. Use of these drugs can improve scholastic performance in 70% of those with ADHD. Ritalin is frequently the drug of choice for this indication (Zheng et al. 2015). The stimulant potency of Ritalin lies between that of caffeine and amphetamine. Although it is not used much on the street by hard-core drug addicts, there are increasingly more frequent reports of use by high school and college students because of claims that it helps them to "study better," "party harder," and enhance their "performance" in general (Addiction Center 2016b). It is important that methylphenidate be taken only as prescribed to avoid problems of dependence or addiction (Mayo Clinic 2016). Recent statistics from the Monitoring the Future survey suggest that 2.0% of high school seniors used this drug for nonmedical purposes in 2015 (Johnston 2016). Because of its potential for abuse, some critics claim its medical use in the treatment of childhood ADHD may increase the likelihood that patients will later abuse drugs; however, recent studies have not been able to confirm or disprove these claims, and clearly more research is needed to address this concern (Humphreys, Eng, and Lee 2013).

High doses of Ritalin can cause tremors, seizures, and strokes. Ritalin has been classified as a Schedule II drug, like the other prescribed amphetamines. Its principal mechanism of action is to block the reuptake of dopamine and noradrenaline into their respective neurons; thus, its pharmacological action is more like cocaine than methamphetamine (Learn.Genetics 2016).

PERFORMANCE ENHANCERS

Performance enhancers is a term frequently used to describe stimulants, such as amphetamines or methylphenidate, or other drugs, that are taken to increase physical or mental endurance to embellish one's performance and achieve a more positive outcome (Khazan 2015). As illustrated in the following real-life example, some college students have come to rely on these drugs to get through the stressful challenges of school:

Janell (real name withheld), a college sophomore, is only one of all too many students who pray for a miracle every finals week to help them cram in the studying time to survive this very demanding ritual. The miracle that Janell, and others like her, are hoping for comes from the stimulant effects of drugs such as Ritalin and Adderall. Recognizing the use of these substances comes with significant risk, Janell says, "I am afraid that if I keep taking Adderall during stressful times, I will become addicted." Although these "performance enhancing" drugs can be legally prescribed, the way Janell is using them is not medically sanctioned and can do her great harm. But, despite the potential for very serious consequences for this form of drug abuse, Janell responds, "If you expect me to pass five major tests in one week, you better believe that I am going to take Adderall. I need to get in the zone. Nothing else seems to work for me." (Keenan 2010)

Unfortunately, many students and adults do not appreciate the full adverse potential of this practice, or they choose to ignore the possibility that they might become addicted, experience psychosis, or have a severe cardiovascular reaction if they routinely use the prescription stimulants for illegal nonmedical purposes (Oremus 2013). If these drugs are not being obtained legally by prescription, how do those who use them as performance enhancers obtain them? Often the supply comes from other students who have ADHD and a legitimate prescription and are willing to sell, or sometimes give away, their extra pills (see Prescription for Abuse: Colleges Are Laboratories for Drug Neuroenhancing).

There is no argument that the popularity of these "performance-enhancing" substances has been increasing with many college, and even high school, students (Ricker and Nicolino 2010); however, the value and safety of this practice are being debated (Khazan 2015).

BATH SALTS: A POTPOURRI OF POTENT STIMULANTS

The term *bath salts* is often used to describe a group of stimulant-containing products that frequently include synthetic drugs related to synthetic cathinones (e.g., khat), such as mephedrone, MDPV (methylenedioxypyrovalerone), flakka (α-pyrrolidinopentiophenone [α-PVP]), and other not-yet-identified analogs (NIDAa 2016; Nordrum 2015). Because these designer drugs of the amphetamine class typically have not been well studied in either humans or laboratory animals, their pharmacological

KEY TERM

performance enhancers
drugs taken to increase physical or mental endurance to embellish one's performance

effects are not precisely known. However, recent reports suggest that abuse of bath salts–related products can have both the stimulant and addicting properties of methamphetamine, with the hallucinogenic actions of MDMA or LSD (Hadlock et al. 2011). The following account in the general press illustrates this point. In 2015, a teenager in Florida who had recently taken the amphetamine-like drug flakka ran while naked and covered in blood at police officers screaming that she was both the Devil and God. Another flakka user in Florida tried to climb over a 10-foot fence to get into the Fort Lauderdale police station and slipped and fell, impaling himself through the buttocks on a sharp fence post. It required several hours to remove him from the post (Nordrum 2015).

Bath salts often are packaged in colorful small plastic or foil containers, frequently marketed as "not for human consumption," and labeled as "plant food" or "jewelry cleaner." Buyers typically self-administer the contents of these products by oral, inhalation, or even injection means, even though some of the stimulant ingredients in these products have been classified as Schedule I substances by the federal government, and other ingredients have not even been identified yet. Common product names are Bloom, CloudNine, and Vanilla Sky, just to mention a few (NIDA 2016a). The use of these products has resulted in thousands of alarming visits to emergency rooms across the United States by persons with a syndrome known as *excited delirium* and symptoms including paranoia, hallucinations, psychotic behavior, dehydration, muscle damage, kidney failure, and even death (NIDA 2016a). Government and law enforcement agencies are working hard to develop strategies to address the persistent problems associated with bath salts (NIDA 2016a).

PRESCRIPTION FOR ABUSE

Colleges Are Laboratories for Drug Neuroenhancing

Although everyone agrees that unsupervised use of stimulants to help with studying or to improve one's performance in other intellectual or physical ways is potentially dangerous, does it actually help improve the likelihood of success in the classroom, on the playing field, or in the workplace? The answer to this question is being debated, but there is good evidence that those who have some degree of ADHD do benefit from stimulant medications such as Adderall, Modafinil, or Ritalin and will perform better in academic endeavors (Khazan 2015). But what about everyone else? It is said that college campuses have become laboratories for researching pharmacological neuroenhancement. Although evidence is equivocal, a commentary in 2008 in a prestigious journal called the use of cognitive enhancement drugs inevitable and stated that "Society must respond to the growing demand . . . by rejecting the idea that 'enhancement' is a dirty word." The authors of this article went on to clarify that their statement was intended to encourage a rational and realistic approach to what they perceived as an inevitability; that is, that in the future our society will realize that these cognitive enhancing drugs are "increasingly useful for improved quality of life and extended work productivity" (Sederer 2009). Others counter with the argument that "advocates fail to recognize the severe personal and societal consequences that such availability would generate, looking instead to a pharmaceutical solution that would, in the end, cause more problems than it would solve" (Hessert et al. 2009).

Hessert, A., A. Medvecz, J. Miller, and J. Richard. "The New Performance Enhancing Drugs." Neuroanthropology. 4 June 2009. Available http://neuroanthropology .net/2009/06/04/the-new-performance-enhancing-drugs; Khazan, O. "The Rise of Work-Doping." *The Atlantic* (August 2015). Available http://www.theatlantic .com/health/archive/2015/08/the-rise-of-work-doping/402373/; Sederer, L. "Paying the Piper: Brain 'Neuroenhancers.'" Huffington Post. 1 June 2010. Available http://www.huffingtonpost.com/lloyd-i-sederer-md/paying-the-piper-brain-ne_b_209702.html

■ Cocaine

In the past, cocaine eradication was considered to be a top priority. This cocaine policy reflected the fact that from 1978 to 1987 the United States experienced the largest cocaine epidemic in history. Antisocial and criminal activities related to the effects of this potent stimulant were highly visible and widely publicized.

In the 1980s cocaine use was not believed to cause dependency because it does not cause gross withdrawal effects, as do alcohol and narcotics (Goldstein 1994). In fact, a 1982 article in *Scientific American* stated that cocaine was "no more habit forming than potato chips" (Van Dyck and Byck 1982). This perception has clearly been proven false; cocaine is so highly addictive that it is readily self-administered not only by human beings but also by laboratory animals (Mandt et al. 2015). Surveys suggested that 2.7 million chronic and 3.0 million casual cocaine users lived in the United States as of 2007. There is no better substance than cocaine to illustrate the "love–hate" relationship that people can have with drugs. Many lessons can be learned by understanding the impact of cocaine and the social struggles that have ensued as people and societies have tried to determine their proper relationship with this substance.

THE HISTORY OF COCAINE USE

Cocaine has been used as a stimulant for thousands of years. Its history can be classified into three eras, based on geographic, social, and therapeutic considerations. Learning about these eras can help us understand current attitudes about cocaine (eMedicineHealth 2010).

THE FIRST COCAINE ERA

The first cocaine era was characterized by an almost harmonious use of this stimulant by South American Indians living in the regions of the Andean Mountains and dates back to about 2500 BC in Peru. It is believed that the stimulant properties of cocaine played a major role in the advancement of this isolated civilization, providing its people with the energy and motivation to realize dramatic social and architectural achievements while being able to endure tremendous hardships in barren, inhospitable environments. The *Erythroxylum coca* shrub (cocaine is found in its leaves) was held in religious reverence by these people until the time of the Spanish conquistadors (Drugs Facts 2016).

An Andean Indian chews coca leaves.

The first written description of coca chewing in the New World was by the explorer Amerigo Vespucci in 1499:

> They were very brutish in appearance and behavior, and their cheeks bulged with the leaves of a certain green herb, which they chewed like cattle, so that they could hardly speak. Each had around his neck two dried gourds, one full of that herb in their mouth, the other filled with a white flour-like powdered chalk. . . . [This was lime, which was mixed with the coca to enhance its effects.] When I asked . . . why they carried these leaves in their mouth, which they did not eat, . . . they replied it prevents them from feeling hungry, and gives them great vigor and strength. (Aldrich and Barker 1976, p. 3)

It is ironic that there are no indications that these early South American civilizations had significant social problems with cocaine, considering the difficulty it has caused contemporary civilizations. There are three possible explanations for their lack of significant negative experiences with coca:

1. The Andean Indians maintained control of the use of cocaine. For these people, coca could only be used by the conquering aristocracy, chiefs, royalty, and other designated honorables (Aldrich and Barker 1976).
2. These Indians used the unpurified, and less potent, form of cocaine in the coca plant.
3. Chewing the coca leaf was a slow, sustained form of oral drug administration; therefore, the effect was much less potent, and less likely to cause serious dependence, than the snorting, intravenous injection, or smoking techniques most often used today.

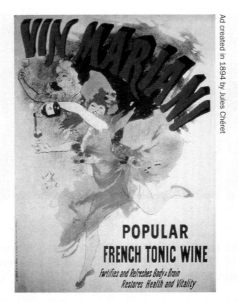

The "refreshing" element in Vin Mariani was coca extract.

Sigmund Freud was an early advocate of cocaine, which he referred to as "cure-all."

THE SECOND COCAINE ERA

A second major cocaine era began in the 19th century. During this period, scientific techniques were used to determine the pharmacology of cocaine and identify its dangerous effects. It was also during this era that the threat of cocaine to society—both its members and institutions—was first recognized (DiChiara 1993; Musto 1998). At about this time, scientists in North America and Europe began experimenting with a purified, white, powdered extract made from the coca plant.

In the last half of the 19th century, Corsican chemist Angelo Mariani removed the active ingredients from the coca leaf and identified cocaine. This purified cocaine was added into cough drops and into a special Bordeaux wine called Vin Mariani (Musto 1998). The Pope gave Mariani a medal in appreciation for the fine work he had done developing this concoction. The cocaine extract was publicized as a magical drug that would free the body from fatigue, lift the spirits, and cause a sense of well-being, and the cocaine-laced wine became widely endorsed throughout the civilized world (Fischman and Johanson 1996). Included in a long list of luminaries who advocated this product for an array of ailments were the Czar and Czarina of Russia; the Prince and Princess of Wales; the kings of Sweden, Norway, and Cambodia; commanders of the French and English armies; President McKinley of the United States; H. G. Wells; August Bartholdi (sculptor of the Statue of Liberty); and some 8000 physicians.

The astounding success of this wine attracted imitators, all making outlandish claims. One of these cocaine tonics was a nonalcoholic beverage named Coca-Cola, which was made from African kola nuts and advertised as the "intellectual beverage and temperance drink"; it contained 4 to 12 milligrams per bottle of the stimulant (DiChiara 1993). By 1906, Coca-Cola no longer contained detectable amounts of cocaine, but caffeine had been substituted in its place. In 1884, the esteemed Sigmund Freud published his findings on cocaine in a report called "Uber Coca." Freud enjoyed the way cocaine made him feel and recommended this "magical drug" for an assortment of medical problems, including depression, hysteria, nervous exhaustion, digestive disorders, hypochondria, "all diseases which involve degeneration of tissue," and drug addiction (PBS Newshour 2011).

In response to a request by Freud, a young Viennese physician, Karl Köller, studied the ability of cocaine to cause numbing effects. He discovered that it was an effective local anesthetic that could be applied to the surface of the eye and permitted painless minor surgery to be conducted. This discovery of the first local anesthetic had tremendous worldwide impact. Orders for the new local anesthetic, cocaine, overwhelmed pharmaceutical companies.

Soon after the initial jubilation over the virtues of cocaine came the sober realization that with its benefits came severe disadvantages. As more people used cocaine, particularly in tonics and patent medicines, the CNS side effects and abuse liability became painfully evident. By the turn of the 20th century, cocaine was being processed from the coca plant and purified routinely by drug companies. People began to snort or inject the purified form of this popular powder, which increased both its effects and its dangers. The controversy over cocaine exploded before the American public in newspapers and magazines.

As medical and police reports of cocaine abuse and toxicities escalated, public opinion demanded that cocaine be banned. In 1914, the Harrison Act misleadingly classified both cocaine and coca as narcotic substances (cocaine is a stimulant) and outlawed their uncontrolled use.

Although prohibited in patent and nonprescription medicines, prescribed medicinal use of cocaine continued into the 1920s. Medicinal texts included descriptions of therapeutic uses for cocaine to treat fatigue, vomiting, seasickness, melancholia, and gastritis. However, they also included lengthy warnings about excessive cocaine use, "the most insidious of all drug habits" (Aldrich and Barker 1976).

Little of medical or social significance occurred for the next few decades (Fischman and Johanson 1996). The medicinal use of cocaine was replaced mostly by the amphetamines during World War II because cocaine could not be supplied from South America. (Cocaine is not easily synthesized, so even today most cocaine, both legal and illegal, continues to come from Columbia, Peru, and Bolivia [*The Economist* 2016]). During this period, cocaine continued to be employed for its local anesthetic action, was available on the "black market," and was used recreationally by musicians, entertainers, and the wealthy. Because of the limited supply, the cost of cocaine was prohibitive for most would-be consumers. Cocaine abuse problems continued as a minor concern until the 1980s.

THE THIRD COCAINE ERA

With the 1980s, came the third major era of cocaine use. This era started much like the second in that the public and even the medical community were naive and misinformed about the drug. Cocaine was viewed as a glamorous substance and portrayed by the media as the drug of celebrities. Its use by prominent actors, athletes, musicians, and other members of a fast-paced, elite society was common knowledge. By 1982, more than 20 million Americans had tried cocaine in one form or another, compared with only 5 million in 1974 (Green 1985).

The following is an example of a report from a Los Angeles television station in the early 1980s, which was typical of the misleading information being released to the public:

> Cocaine may actually be no more harmful to your health than smoking cigarettes or drinking alcohol; at least that's according to a 6-year study of cocaine use [described in *Scientific American*]. It concludes that the drug is relatively safe and, if not taken in large amounts, it is not addictive. (Byck 1987)

With such visibility, an association with prestige and glamour, and what amounted to an indirect endorsement by medical experts, the stage was set for another epidemic of cocaine use. Initially, the high cost of this imported substance limited its use. With increased demand, however, came increased supply, and prices tumbled from an unaffordable $100 per "fix" to an affordable $10. The epidemic began.

By the mid-1980s, cocaine permeated all elements of society. No group of people or part of the country was immune from its effects. Many tragic stories were told of athletes, entertainers, corporate executives, politicians, fathers and mothers, high school students, and even children using and abusing cocaine. It was no longer the drug of the laborer or even the rich and famous. It was everybody's drug and everybody's problem (Golding 1993). As one user recounted,

> It started out with me selling. I loved money; figured I could sell a little cocaine. I didn't use. I had a child to consider. I looked respectable. . . . Then I fell for a customer. A heavy user. I started using with him. Big mistake. . . . Later, when I got honest, I could see he was in love with my cocaine, not me. . . . Soon I didn't take care of my child. . . . I was always in that triple cycle: about to get high, was high, or was crashing. . . . Then my supplier didn't get paid. Dangerous. I wasn't together enough to deal and I owed money everywhere. . . . I wanted to stop, so why couldn't I? What was up with that? Denial, addiction's long shadow, is vital to the addict's psyche. Without it, we quit or commit suicide. . . . I began to look bad, smell bad and talk bad. I couldn't see over the piles of shame to life without coke. . . . I was no longer able to fake normal. I was too scary, a low-bottom addict who didn't have a key to my name (no car, no house, no office). . . . Somehow I go to detox. Somehow, I began the slow climb back to civilization. It was 6 months before the fog

lifted. Six months before I could think in a straight line. I don't refer to myself as normal. Most of the people I sold to are now dead or destroyed. (Barnes 2013)

Cocaine availability decreased sharply in the United States in 2009, resulting in an increase in price for a pure gram of cocaine from about $95 in 2006 to $175 toward the end of 2009. The purity of cocaine also diminished during this time, from 68% to 46%. The reasons for the shortages of cocaine at this time were thought to relate to several factors, including decreased production in Colombia and increased seizures of cocaine destined for Mexico and trafficking into the United States (Beckusen 2013). However, it is important to appreciate that these trends can reverse very quickly and that the United States by far is the largest consumer of cocaine in the world (Central Intelligence Agency [CIA] 2016).

COCAINE PRODUCTION

Because cocaine is derived from the coca plant, which is imported from the Andean countries, the problems with this drug in the United States have had profound effects on several South American countries. With the dramatic rise in U.S. cocaine demand in the early 1980s, coca production in South America increased in tandem. The coca crop is by far the most profitable agricultural venture in some of these countries. In addition, it is easily cultivated and maintained (the coca plant is a perennial and remains productive for decades) and can be harvested several times a year (on average, two to four). The coca harvest has brought many jobs and some prosperity to these struggling economies; however, it has come at a significant environmental cost due to the slash-and-burn techniques used to clear spots for coca bush cultivation resulting in deforestation and damaging soil (UNODC 2015).

It has been claimed that the U.S. coca eradication program has seriously influenced the fragile economies of poor Latin American countries, such as Bolivia and Peru, causing anti-American sentiment, especially in poor rural communities that depend on money from their coca crops (Briceno 2015). This is illustrated by the following account of a very poor coca farmer in Peru:

Duran uses a machete to harvest coca leaves from a plot of small plot of land damaged by a U.S.-backed eradication campaign that affected almost 500,000 Peruvians. "This is what we live off," Duran complains, "Nobody buys anything but coca." Duran and her family tried planting and selling bananas after their coca harvested was destroyed by the eradication effort, but could not make enough money to survive so they returned to planting and selling coca which was much more lucrative and easier to manage. A local counter-narcotics police who is charged with enforcing the coca elimination policies sympathizes with the frustrations of these poor farmers and claims, "They are very poor people. They drop to their knees and beg us to leave them a little (coca), because that's what they live off." (Briceno 2015)

In addition, the spraying of herbicides from U.S.-piloted aircraft to destroy coca harvests is suspected of posing health hazards to the native populations. Because of these problems, there is evidence that the attempts by the U.S. government to control cocaine abuse by eliminating coca crops have been frustrating. Despite this, coca bush cultivation has declined to its lowest level since the mid-1980s. It appears that some of this decline in cocaine cultivation is due to successful law enforcement efforts (UNODC 2015).

Trafficking of illegal cocaine is very profitable and often very dangerous (see "Here and Now: Bloody 'Drug War' Fought in Streets of Mexico"). Because of the highly addictive nature of cocaine and the profits associated with the illegal purchasing and selling of this drug, criminal groups frequently engage in violent struggles for control of the cocaine market For example, Central America has become the location for some of the most deadly cities in the world, causing Honduras to be designated as the country with the highest homicide rate in the world at 82 murders per 100,0000 people (Drug Policy Alliance 2015a). In some ways it is like playing "whack-a-mole." As efforts to shut down drug cartels in Mexico intensify, they tend to pop up elsewhere. As a result, drug-related crime has been increasing in Caribbean countries. For example, with increased cocaine seizures in Mexico, the Dominican Republic has developed into a main transit point for shipping this drug into both the United States and Europe (Voxxi 2013). Solutions are elusive, and it is clear that without a significant reduction in demand the profit from producing, trafficking, and selling cocaine will remain high and attractive to illegal and dangerous groups.

HERE AND NOW
Bloody "Drug War" Fought in Streets of Mexico

Drug cartels ship hundreds of tons of cocaine to the United States. Because of the billions of dollars that can be made from this illegal market, gangs fight each other for control of the production and merchandising of this substance. This competition frequently turns violent. In Mexico, there were approximately 164,000 homicides between 2007 and 2014, with more than half likely associated with the drug wars. Such blatant violence has become almost a way of life in some parts of Mexico, but perhaps the most shocking aspect of these acts of wanton homicide is that most of the victims had nothing whatsoever to do with the drug cartels or the government forces fighting each other over drug-related issues. These people just happened to be in the wrong place at the wrong

time and were innocently killed. Such violence has everyone wondering how this can be stopped. Is victory even possible in the war against the drug cartels?

Data from Grillo (2016) Breslow, J. "The Staggering Death Toll of Mexico's Drug War." *Frontline.* (27 July 2015). Available http://www.pbs.org/wgbh/frontline/article/the-staggering-death-toll-of-mexicos-drug-war/

COCAINE PROCESSING

Cocaine is one of several active ingredients from the leaves of *Erythroxylum coca* (its primary source). The leaves are harvested two or four times per year and used to produce coca paste, which contains as much as 80% cocaine. The paste is processed in clandestine laboratories to form a pure, white hydrochloride salt powder. Often, purified cocaine is **adulterated** (or "cut") with substances such as powdered sugar, talc, arsenic, lidocaine, strychnine, and methamphetamine before it is sold on the streets. Adverse responses to street cocaine are sometimes caused by the additives, not the cocaine itself. The resultant purity of the cut material ranges from 10% to 85% (Stewart 2013).

Cocaine is often sold in the form of little pellets, called *rocks*, or as flakes or powder. If it is in pellet form, it must be crushed before use. Street names used for these cocaine products have included *big flake, crack, gold dust, lime, Snow White, snow cones, white powder,* and *white mosquito* (Buddy 2015).

CURRENT ATTITUDES AND PATTERNS OF ABUSE

Given contemporary medical advances, we now have a greater understanding of the effects of cocaine and its toxicities and the dependence it produces. The reasons that people abuse cocaine are better understood as well. For example, it has

Cocaine is often sold in a form that appears like small rocks.

been suggested that some chronic cocaine users are self-medicating their psychiatric disorders, such as depression, attention deficit disorders, or anxiety (Gorelick 2015). Such knowledge helps in identifying and administering effective treatment. The hope is that society will never again be fooled

KEY TERM

adulterated
contaminating substances are mixed in to dilute the drugs

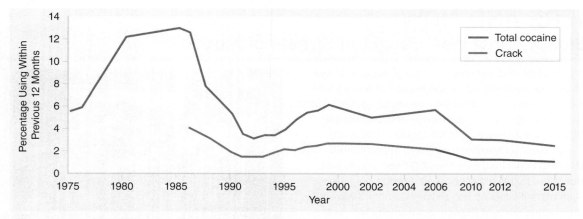

FIGURE 10.1   Trends in cocaine and crack use by high school seniors: 1990–2015. These data represent the percentages of high school seniors surveyed who reported using cocaine during the year.

Data from Johnston, L. "Monitoring the Future 2015." 2016. Available http://www.monitoringthefuture.org/data/15data/15drtbl2.pdf

into thinking that cocaine abuse is glamorous or an acceptable form of entertainment. Attempts are being made to use this understanding (either recently acquired or merely relearned) to educate people about the true nature of cocaine. Surveys have revealed that, in general, cocaine use has become less acceptable (see **Figure 10.1**). From 1992 to 1999 cocaine use rose among high school seniors but leveled off to about 4% to 5% during much of the first decade of the 2000s, dropping to 2.5% by 2015 (Johnston 2016). A recent corresponding reduction in other markers of cocaine use includes decreases in chronic and frequent users, treatment admissions, and accidental overdoses. Possible explanations for this reduction include (1) reduced Colombian coca available for cocaine production, (2) the crackdown on cocaine traffickers in Mexico because of drug-related violence, (3) increased non-U.S. demand for cocaine, and (4) reduced U.S. demand for this potent stimulant (Kilmar, Midgette, and Saloga 2016).

COCAINE ADMINISTRATION

Cocaine can be administered orally, inhaled into the nasal passages, injected intravenously, or smoked. The form of administration is important in determining the intensity of cocaine's effects, its abuse liability, and the likelihood of toxicity (U.S. Department of Justice [USDOJ] 2015).

Oral administration of cocaine produces the least potent effects; most of the drug is destroyed in the gut or liver before it reaches the brain. The result is a slower onset of action with a milder, more sustained stimulation. This form is least likely to cause health problems and dependence. South American Indians still take cocaine orally

to increase their strength and for relief from fatigue. Administration usually involves prolonged chewing of the coca leaf, resulting in the consumption of about 20 to 400 milligrams of the drug (Narconon 2016b). Oral use of cocaine is not common in the United States.

"Snorting" involves inhaling cocaine hydrochloride powder into the nostrils, where deposits form on the lining of the nasal chambers (Narconon 2016b). Substantial CNS stimulation occurs in several minutes, persists for 30 to 40 minutes and then subsides. The effects occur more rapidly and are shorter-lasting and more intense than those achieved with oral administration because more of the drug enters the brain more quickly. Because concentrations of cocaine in the body are higher after snorting than after oral ingestion, the side effects are more severe. One of the most common consequences of snorting cocaine is rebound depression, or "crash," which is of little consequence after oral consumption. As a general rule, the intensity of the depression correlates with the intensity of the euphoria.

According to studies performed by the National Institute on Drug Abuse, 10% to 15% of those who try intranasal (snorting) cocaine go on to heavier forms of dosing, such as intravenous administration. Intravenous administration of cocaine is a relatively recent phenomenon because the hypodermic needle was not widely available until the late 1800s. This form of administration contributed to many of the cocaine problems that appeared at the turn of the 20th century. Intravenous administration allows large amounts of cocaine to be introduced very rapidly into the body and causes severe side effects and dependence. Within seconds after injection, cocaine users experience an incredible state of euphoria. The "high" is intense but short-lived; within 15 to 20 minutes the user experiences dysphoria and is heading for a "crash." To prevent these unpleasant rebound effects, cocaine is readministered every 10 to 30 minutes. Readministration continues as long as there is drug available (NIDA 2013).

This binge activity resembles that seen in the methamphetamine "run," except it is usually shorter in duration. When the cocaine supply is exhausted, the binge is over. Several days of abstinence may separate these episodes. The average cocaine addict binges once to several times a week, with each binge lasting 4 to 24 hours. Cocaine addicts claim that all thoughts turn toward cocaine during binges; everything else loses significance. This pattern of intense use is how some people blow all of their money on cocaine.

Freebasing is a method of reducing impurities in cocaine and preparing the drug for smoking. It produces a type of cocaine that is more powerful than normal cocaine hydrochloride. One way to freebase is to treat the cocaine hydrochloride with a liquid base such as sodium carbonate or ammonium hydroxide. The cocaine dissolves, along with many of the impurities commonly found in it (such as amphetamines, lidocaine, sugars, and others). A solvent, such as petroleum or ethyl ether, is added to the liquid to extract the cocaine. The solvent containing the cocaine floats to the top and is drawn off with an eyedropper; it is placed in an evaporation dish to dry, and crystalized cocaine residue is then crushed into a fine powder, which can be smoked in a special glass pipe (RehabPathway n.d.).

The effects of smoked cocaine are as or more intense than those achieved through intravenous administration. The onset is very rapid, the euphoria is dramatic, the depression is severe, the side effects are dangerous, and the chances of dependence are high. The reason for these intense reactions to inhaling cocaine into the lungs is that the drug passes rapidly through the lining of the lungs and into the many blood vessels present; it is then carried almost directly to the brain, where it accumulates quickly (RehabPathway n.d.).

Freebasing became popular in the United States in the 1980s due to the fear of diseases such as AIDS and hepatitis, which are transmitted by sharing contaminated hypodermic needles. But freebasing involves other dangers. Because the volatile solvents required for freebasing are very explosive, careless people have been seriously burned or

Freebasing paraphernalia. A water pipe is often used to smoke freebased cocaine, or "crack." Cocaine administered by smoking is very potent and fast-acting; the effect lasts for 10 to 15 minutes, after which depression occurs. This is the most addicting form of cocaine.

killed during processing. Street synonyms used for freebased cocaine include *devil's dandruff, Mary White, rock, scramble, sugar, tray, yay,* and *Twinkie* (SoberRecovery 2015).

CRACK COCAINE

Between 1985 and 1986, a special type of freebased cocaine known as **crack** appeared on the streets (RehabPathway n.d.). By 1999, approximately 2.7% of high school seniors had tried crack. As of 2015 this number was down to 1.1% (Johnston 2016). Crack can be smoked without the dangerous explosive solvents mentioned earlier in the discussion of freebasing. It is made by taking powdered cocaine hydrochloride and adding sodium bicarbonate (baking soda) and water. The paste that forms removes impurities as well as the hydrochloride from the cocaine. The substance is then dried into hard pieces called rocks, which may contain as much as 90% pure cocaine.

KEY TERMS

freebasing
conversion of cocaine into its alkaline form for smoking

crack
already processed and inexpensive "freebased" cocaine, ready for smoking

Other slang terms for crack include *big C, blow, nose candy, snow,* and *lady* (SoberRecovery 2015). Like freebased cocaine, crack is usually smoked in a glass water pipe. When the fumes are absorbed into the lungs, they act rapidly, reaching the brain within 8 to 10 seconds. An intense "rush" or "high" results, and later a powerful state of depression, or "crash," occurs. The high may last only 3 to 5 minutes, and the depression may persist from 10 to 40 minutes or longer in some cases. As soon as crack is smoked, the nervous system is greatly stimulated by the release of dopamine, which seems to be involved in the rush. Cocaine prevents resupply of this neurotransmitter, which may trigger the crash.

Because of the abrupt and intense release of dopamine, smoked crack is viewed as a drug with tremendous potential for addiction and antisocial behavior (RehabPathway n.d.); some users consider it to be more enjoyable than cocaine administered intravenously. Crack and cocaine marketing and use are often associated with criminal activity such as robberies and homicides (RehabPathway n.d.).

In general, crack use has been more common among African American and Hispanic populations than among white Americans. Of special concern is the use of crack among women during pregnancy. Children born under these circumstances have been referred to as crack babies. Even though the effects of crack on fetal development are not fully understood, many clinicians and researchers have predicted that these crack babies will impose an enormous social burden as they grow up. However, other experts have expressed concern that the impact of cocaine on the fetus is grossly overstated and have suggested that behavioral problems seen in these children are more a consequence of social environment than direct pharmacological effects. This issue is discussed in greater detail later in this section.

It is not coincidental that the popularity of crack use paralleled the AIDS epidemic in the mid-1980s. Because crack administration does not require injection, theoretically the risk of contracting HIV from contaminated needles is avoided. Even so, HIV infection still occurs in crack users because many crack smokers also use cocaine intravenously, thereby increasing their chances of becoming infected with HIV. Another reason for HIV infection (as well as other sexually transmitted diseases, such as syphilis and gonorrhea) among crack users is the dangerous sexual behaviors in which these people engage (Science Daily 2010). Not only is crack commonly used as payment for sex, but its users are also much less inclined to be cautious about their sexual activities while under the influence of this drug (Ladd and Petry 2003).

MAJOR PHARMACOLOGICAL EFFECTS OF COCAINE

Cocaine can have profound effects on several vital systems in the body (RehabPathway n.d.). With the assistance of modern technology, the mechanisms whereby cocaine alters body functions have become better understood. Such knowledge may eventually lead to better treatment of cocaine dependence.

Most of the pharmacological effects of cocaine use stem from enhanced activity of catecholamine (dopamine, noradrenaline, adrenaline) and serotonin transmitters. It is believed that the principal action of the drug is to block the reuptake and inactivation of these substances following their release from neurons. Such action prolongs the activity of these transmitter substances at their receptors and substantially increases their effects. The summation of cocaine's effects on these four transmitters causes CNS stimulation (RehabPathway n.d.). The increase of noradrenaline activity following cocaine administration increases the effects of the sympathetic nervous system and alters cardiovascular activity.

CNS EFFECTS

Because cocaine has stimulant properties, it has antidepressant effects as well. Some users self-administer cocaine to relieve severe depression or the negative symptoms of schizophrenia, but in general its short-term action and abuse liability make cocaine unsatisfactory for the treatment of depression disorders. The effects of stimulation appear to increase both physical and mental performance while masking fatigue. High doses of cocaine cause euphoria (based on the form of administration) and enhance the sense of strength, energy, and performance. Because of these positive effects, cocaine has intense reinforcing properties, which encourage continual use and dependence (RehabPathway n.d.).

Cocaine addicts can often distinguish between the two phenomena of the rush and the high associated with cocaine administration. Both the rush and the high peak about 3 minutes after use. The rush seems to be associated with elevated heart rate, sweating, and feelings of "speeding" or "being out of control"; the high includes feelings of euphoria, self-confidence, well-being, and sociability. Drug craving also occurs rapidly and is evident as soon as 12 minutes after administration. Interestingly, brain scans of cocaine users have demonstrated that specific brain regions are associated with these drug effects; thus, the rush and craving are linked with different regions of the limbic system in the brain (Stocker 1999).

The feeling of exhilaration and confidence caused by cocaine can easily become transformed into irritable restlessness and confused hyperactivity (APA 2013). In addition, high chronic doses alter personality, frequently causing psychotic behavior that resembles paranoid schizophrenia (RehabPathway n.d.). For example, in an interview with Peter Venturelli, a 17-year-old female explained that a cocaine-abusing friend "was so coked up that he carved the word 'pain' in his arm and poured coke on it. He thought it symbolized something." In addition, cocaine use heightens the risk of suicide, major trauma, and violent crimes (RehabPathway n.d.). In many ways, the CNS effects of cocaine resemble those of amphetamines, although perhaps with a more rapid onset; a more intense high (due partially to the manner in which the drugs are administered); and a shorter duration of action (APA 2013). Besides dependence, other notable CNS toxicities that can be caused by cocaine use include headaches, temporary loss of consciousness, seizures, and death.

CARDIOVASCULAR SYSTEM EFFECTS

Cocaine can initiate pronounced changes in the cardiovascular system by enhancing the sympathetic nervous system, increasing the levels of adrenaline, and causing vasoconstriction (Luscher 2015). The initial effects of cocaine are to increase heart rate and elevate blood pressure. While the heart is being stimulated and working harder, the vasoconstriction effects deprive the cardiac muscle of needed blood (Fischman and Johanson 1996). Such a combination can cause severe heart arrhythmia (an irregular contraction pattern) or heart attack. Other degenerative processes have also been described in the hearts and blood vessels of chronic cocaine users (Kloner and Rezkalla 2003). In addition, the vasoconstrictive action of this sympathomimetic can damage other tissues, leading to stroke, lung damage in those who smoke cocaine, destruction of nasal cartilage in those who snort the drug, and injury to the gastrointestinal tract (Goodger, Wang, and Pogrel 2005).

LOCAL ANESTHETIC EFFECTS

Cocaine was the first local anesthetic used routinely in modern-day medicine (Drasner 2012). Some speculate that in ancient times the Andes Indians of South America used cocaine-filled saliva from chewing coca leaves as a local anesthetic for surgical procedures (Aldrich and Barker 1976); however, this assumption is contested by others (Byck 1987). Even so, cocaine is still used as a local anesthetic for minor pharyngeal (back part of the mouth and upper throat area) surgery due to its good vasoconstriction (reduces bleeding) and topical, local numbing effects. Although relatively safe when applied topically, significant amounts of cocaine can enter the bloodstream and, in sensitive people, cause CNS stimulation, toxic psychosis, or, on rare occasions, death (Mayo Clinic 2010).

COCAINE WITHDRAWAL

Considerable debate has arisen as to whether cocaine withdrawal actually happens and, if so, what it involves. With the most recent cocaine epidemic and the high incidence of intense, chronic use, it has become apparent that nervous systems do become tolerant to cocaine and that, during abstinence, withdrawal symptoms occur (Narconon 2013). In fact, because of CNS dependence, the use of cocaine is less likely to be stopped voluntarily than is the use of many other illicit drugs (Sofuoglu et al. 2003). Certainly, if the withdrawal experience is adverse enough, a user will be encouraged to resume the cocaine habit.

The extent of cocaine withdrawal is proportional to the duration and intensity of use. The physical withdrawal symptoms are relatively minor compared with those caused by long-term use of CNS depressants and by themselves are not considered to be life-threatening (MedlinePlus 2007). Short-term withdrawal symptoms include depression (chronic cocaine users are 60 times more likely to commit suicide than are nonusers), sleep abnormalities, craving for the drug, agitation, and anhedonia (inability to experience pleasure). Long-term withdrawal effects include a return to normal pleasures, accompanied by mood swings and occasional craving triggered by cues in the surroundings (APA 2013; Mendelson and Mello 1996; Narconon 2013).

Of particular importance to the treatment of chronic cocaine users is that abstinence after bingeing appears to follow three unique stages, each of which must be dealt with in a different manner if relapse is to be prevented. These phases are classified as phase 1, or "crash" (occurs 24 hours to 2 days after drug use is stopped); phase 2, or withdrawal (1 to 10 weeks); and phase 3, or extinction (indefinite). The basic features of these phases are outlined in **Table 10.2** (APA 2013).

TABLE 10.2 Cocaine Abstinence Phases

Phase 1: "Crash"	Phase 2: Withdrawal	Phase 3: Extinction
24–48 hours since last binge	1–10 weeks since last binge	Indefinite since last binge
Initial: Agitation, depression, anorexia, suicidal thoughts	*Initial*: Mood swings, sleep returns, some craving, little anxiety	Normal pleasure, mood swings, occasional craving, cues trigger craving
Middle: Fatigue, no craving, insomnia	*Middle and late*: Anhedonia, anxiety, intense craving, obsessed with drug seeking	
Late: Extreme fatigue, no craving, exhaustion		

Data from Garwin, F. "Cocaine addiction: Psychology and Neurophysiology." *Science* 251 (1991): 1580–1586.

TREATMENT OF COCAINE DEPENDENCE

Cocaine dependence is classified as a psychiatric disorder by the American Psychiatric Association (APA 2013) and results in many persons seeking treatment for drug addiction (Platt, Rowlett, and Spealman 2002). Treatment of this condition has improved as experience working with these patients has increased. Even so, success rates vary for different programs. The problem with program assessments is that they often do not take into account patients who drop out. Also, no clear-cut criteria for qualifying success have been established. For example, is success considered to be abstaining from cocaine for 1 year, 2 years, 5 years, or forever?

No one treatment technique has been found to be significantly superior to others or universally effective (MedlinePlus 2010; NIDA 2010), nor is there a particularly effective medication to treat cocaine addiction (Platt et al. 2002). Consequently, substantial disagreement exists as to what is the best strategy for treating cocaine dependency. Efforts are ongoing by federal agencies and scientists to find effective therapy for cocaine addiction. Most treatments are directed at relieving craving. Major differences in treatment approaches include (1) whether outpatient or inpatient status is deemed appropriate, (2) which drugs and what dosages are used to treat patients during the various stages of abstinence, and (3) what length of time the patient is isolated from cocaine-accessible environments.

It is important to treat each individual patient according to his or her unique needs. Some questions that need to be considered when formulating a therapeutic approach include the following:

- Why did the patient begin using cocaine, and why has dependency occurred?
- What is the severity of abuse?
- How has the cocaine been administered?
- What is the psychiatric status of the patient? Are there underlying or coexisting mental disorders, such as depression or attention deficit disorder?
- What other drugs are being abused along with the cocaine?
- What is the patient's motivation for eliminating cocaine dependence?
- What sort of support system (family, friends, coworkers, and so on) will sustain the patient in the abstinence effort?

OUTPATIENT VERSUS INPATIENT APPROACHES

The decision as to whether to treat a patient who is dependent on cocaine as an outpatient or an inpatient is based on a number of factors. For example, inpatient techniques allow greater control than outpatient treatment; thus, the environment can be better regulated, the training of the patient can be more closely supervised, and the patient's responses to treatment can be more closely monitored. In contrast, the advantages of the outpatient approach are that supportive family and friends are better able to encourage the patient, the surroundings are more comfortable and natural, and potential problems that might occur when the patient returns to a normal lifestyle are more likely to be identified. In addition, outpatient treatment is less expensive.

Cocaine-dependent patients should be matched to the most appropriate strategy based on their personality, psychiatric status, and the conditions of their addiction. For instance, a cocaine addict who lives in the inner city, comes from a home with other drug-dependent family members, and has little support probably would do better in the tightly controlled inpatient environment.

However, a highly motivated cocaine addict who comes from a supportive home and a neighborhood that is relatively free of drug problems would probably do better on an outpatient basis.

THERAPEUTIC DRUG TREATMENT

Several drugs have been used to treat cocaine abstinence, some of which are themselves active on dopamine systems, but none has been found to be universally effective (NIDA 2016b). Besides relieving acute problems of anxiety, agitation, and psychosis, drugs can diminish cocaine craving; this effect is achieved by giving drugs such as bromocriptine or levodopa, which stimulate the dopamine transmitter system, or the narcotic buprenorphine. As mentioned, the pleasant aspects of cocaine likely relate to its ability to increase the activity of dopamine in the limbic system. When cocaine is no longer available, the dopamine system becomes less active, causing depression and anhedonia, which result in a tremendous craving for cocaine. The intent of these cocaine substitutes is to stimulate dopamine activity and relieve the cravings. Although this approach sometimes works initially, it is temporary. In the third phase of cocaine abstinence, antidepressants such as desipramine are effective for many cocaine-dependent patients in relieving underlying mood problems and occasional cravings.

The beneficial effects of these drugs are variable and not well studied (NIDA 2016b), and there is some debate over their use. Drugs are, at best, only adjuncts in the treatment of cocaine dependence. Successful treatment of cocaine abuse requires intensive counseling; strong support from family, friends, and coworkers; and a highly motivated patient (NIDA 2016b). It is important to realize that a complete "cure" from cocaine dependence is not likely; ex-addicts cannot return to cocaine and control its use.

RECOVERY FROM COCAINE DEPENDENCE

Although numerous therapeutic approaches exist for treating cocaine addiction, successful recovery is not likely unless the individual will substantially benefit by giving up the drug. Research has shown that treatment is most likely to succeed in patients who are middle-class, employed, and married; for example, 85% of addicted medical professionals recover from cocaine addiction. These people can usually be convinced that they have too much to lose in their personal and professional lives by continuing their cocaine habit. In contrast, a severely dependent crack addict who has no job, family, home, or hope for the future is not likely to be persuaded that abstinence from cocaine would be advantageous, so therapy is rarely successful. As mentioned earlier, there currently is no uniformly effective pharmacological treatment available to deal with long-term cocaine addiction, although intensive research to identify such therapeutic agents is under way (NIDA 2016b).

POLYDRUG USE BY COCAINE ABUSERS

Treatment of most cocaine abusers is complicated by the fact that they are *polydrug* (multiple drug) users. It is unusual to find a person who abuses only cocaine. For example, many cocaine abusers also use alcohol (Pennings, Leccese, and Wolff 2002). In general, the more severe the alcoholism, the greater the severity of the cocaine dependence. Alcohol is used to relieve some of the unpleasant cocaine effects, such as anxiety, insomnia, and mood disturbances (Pennings et al. 2002). This drug combination can be dangerous for several reasons:

- The presence of both cocaine and alcohol (ethanol) in the liver results in the formation of a unique chemical product called cocaethylene, which is created in the reaction of ethanol with a cocaine metabolite. Cocaethylene often is found in high levels in the blood of victims of fatal drug overdoses and appears to enhance the euphoria as well as the cardiovascular toxicity of cocaine (Bazuaye-Ekwuyasi et al. 2015).
- Both cocaine and alcohol can damage the liver; thus, their toxic effects on the liver are likely to add together when the drugs are used in combination (Pennings et al. 2002).
- The likelihood of damaging a fetus is enhanced when both drugs are used together during pregnancy (Pennings et al. 2002).
- Cardiovascular stress is increased in the presence of both drugs (Pennings et al. 2002).

Like users of amphetamines, cocaine abusers frequently coadminister narcotics, such as heroin; this combination is called a *speedball* and has been associated with a high risk for HIV infection (NIDA 2013). Cocaine users sometimes combine their drug with other depressants, such as benzodiazepines, or marijuana to help reduce the severity of the crash after their cocaine binges. Codependence on cocaine and a CNS depressant can complicate treatment but must be considered. Some of the street names for cocaine mixtures include *banana* or *bazooka* (laced marijuana or cigarettes), *bipping* (snorting heroin and cocaine together), *bump* (mix with ketamine), *candy flipping on a string* (mix with methcathinone or inhalants), and *spaceball* (mix with PCP) (SoberRecovery 2015).

COCAINE AND PREGNANCY

One of the consequences of widespread cocaine abuse is that since the mid-1980s many babies in the United States have been born to mothers who used cocaine during pregnancy (Fitzgerald 2013). Cocaine use during pregnancy is highest in poor, inner-city regions. Many of these **cocaine babies** have been abandoned by their mothers and left to the welfare system for care. It is still not clear exactly what types of direct effects cocaine has on the developing fetus (Winkel 2010). Some early studies have been criticized because (1) the pregnant populations examined were not well defined and properly matched, (2) use of other drugs (such as alcohol) with cocaine during pregnancy was often ignored, and (3) the effects of poor nutrition, poor living conditions, and a traumatic lifestyle were not considered when analyzing the results. Due to these problems, much of the earlier work examining prenatal effects of cocaine is flawed, and the conclusions are questionable (Fitzgerald 2013).

It is known that cocaine use during pregnancy can cause vasoconstriction of placental vessels, thereby interfering with oxygen and nutrient exchange between mother and child, or contraction of the uterine muscles, resulting in trauma or premature birth. Even so, recent studies have

Infants born to crack-using mothers are often premature.

© Gert Vrey/Fotolia.

KEY TERM

cocaine babies
infants born to women who used cocaine during their pregnancy

suggested that prenatal cocaine exposure does not cause any long-term specific disorder or condition and its long-term effect is no greater than that of "poverty." However, some suggest that prenatal cocaine exposure may have minor effects on sustained attention and behavioral self-regulation (Fitzgerald 2013; Nonacs 2015). It is likely that this controversy is not yet resolved and will require additional study.

Minor Stimulants

Minor stimulants enjoy widespread use in the United States because of the mild lift in mood provided by their consumption. The most popular of these routinely consumed agents are methylxanthines (commonly called *xanthines*), such as caffeine, which are consumed in beverages made from plants and herbs. On average, in the United States the range of daily caffeine consumption is from 20 milligrams for 2- to 5-year-olds and up to 220 milligrams for 50- to 64-year-olds (Lutz 2015). Other minor stimulants are contained in OTC medications such as cold and hay fever products. Because of their frequent use, some dependence on these drugs can occur; however, serious dysfunction due to dependence is infrequent. Consequently, abuse of xanthines such as caffeine is not viewed as a major health problem by most health experts (Whiteman 2015). However, recently concerns have been raised that many people, especially adolescents and young adults, do not appreciate that caffeine is a drug and consume it more like food, resulting in side effects and even trips to the emergency room (Hitti 2006).

▮ Caffeine-Like Drugs (Xanthines)

Caffeine is a naturally occurring stimulant derived from over 60 different plants (Caffeine Informer 2016) and is the world's most frequently used stimulant and perhaps its most popular drug (Whiteman 2015). Beverages and foods containing caffeine are consumed by almost all adults and children living in the United States today (see **Table 10.3**). Almost 80% of the world's population consumes caffeine daily (MedicineNet 2010). The most common sources of caffeine include coffee beans, tea plants, kola nuts, maté leaves, guaraná paste, yoco bark, and an array of herbal and so-called natural products.

Although the consumption of caffeine-containing drinks can be found throughout history, the active stimulant caffeine was identified by German

TABLE 10.3 Caffeine Content of Beverages and Chocolate

Beverage	Caffeine Content (milligrams/cup)	Amount
Brewed coffee	90–135	5 oz.
Instant coffee	35–164	5 oz.
Decaffeinated coffee	1–6	5 oz.
Tea	25–70	5 oz.
Cocoa	5–25	5 oz.
Coca-Cola	45	12 oz.
Pepsi-Cola	38	12 oz.
Mountain Dew	70	12 oz.
Energy drinks	80–160	8–16 oz.
Excedrin (OTC medication)	65	
NoDoz (OTC medication)	34	
Vivarin (OTC medication)	200	
Chocolate bar	1–35	1 oz.

Reproduced from MedicineNet. "Caffeine." 2010. Available http://www.medicinenet.com/caffeine/article.htm

and French scientists in the early 1820s. Caffeine was described as a substance with alkaloid (basic) properties that was extracted from green coffee beans and referred to as *kaffebase* by Ferdinand Runge in 1820 (Gilbert 1984). In the course of the next 40 to 60 years, caffeine was identified in several other genera of plants that were used as sources for common beverages. These included tea leaves (originally the caffeine-like drug was called *thein*); guaraná paste (originally the drug was called *guaranin*); Paraguay tea, or maté; and kola nuts. Certainly, the popularity of these beverages over the centuries attests to the fact that most consumers find the stimulant effects of this drug desirable.

THE CHEMICAL NATURE OF CAFFEINE

Caffeine belongs to a group of drugs that have similar chemical structures and are known as the **xanthines**. Besides caffeine, other xanthines include theobromine (which means "divine leaf"), discovered in cacao beans (used to make chocolate) in 1842, and theophylline (which means "divine food"), isolated from tea leaves in 1888. These three agents have unique pharmacological properties (which are discussed later), with caffeine being the most potent CNS stimulant.

BEVERAGES CONTAINING CAFFEINE

To understand the unique role that caffeine plays in U.S. society, it is useful to gain perspective on its most common sources: unfermented beverages.

COFFEE

Coffee is derived from the beans of several species of *Coffea*. The most widely grown species, *Coffea arabica*, grows as a shrub or small tree and reaches 4 to 6 meters in height when growing wild. Coffee beans are primarily cultivated in South America and East Africa and constitute the major cash crop for exportation in several developing countries.

The name *coffee* was likely derived from the Arabian word *kahwa* or named after the Ethiopian prince Kaffa. From Ethiopia, the coffee tree was carried to Arabia and cultivated (Kihlman 1977); it became an important element in Arabian civilization and is mentioned in writings dating back to AD 900.

Coffee probably reached Europe through Turkey and was likely used initially as a medicine. By the middle of the 17th century, coffeehouses had sprung up in England and France—places to relax, talk, and learn the news. These coffeehouses turned into the famous "penny universities" of the early 18th century where, for a penny a cup, you could listen to some of the great literary and political figures of the day.

Coffee was originally consumed in the Americas by English colonists, although tea was initially preferred. Tea was replaced by coffee following the Revolutionary War. Because tea had become a symbol of English repression, the switch to coffee was more a political statement than a change in taste. The popularity of coffee grew as U.S. boundaries moved west. In fact, daily coffee intake continued to increase until it peaked in 1986, when annual coffee consumption averaged 10 pounds per person. Although there are concerns about the side effects associated with caffeine, this beverage still plays a major role in the lifestyles of most Americans (Caffeine Informer 2016; MedicineNet 2010), with approximately 56% of adults in the United States being coffee drinkers in 2006 (HealthResearchFunding.org 2014).

KEY TERM

xanthines
the family of drugs that includes caffeine

TEA

Tea is made from the *Camellia sinensis* plant, which is native to China and parts of India, Burma, Thailand, Laos, and Vietnam. Tea contains two xanthines: caffeine and theophylline. As with coffee, the earliest use of tea is not known.

Although apocryphal versions of the origin of tea credit Chinese Emperor Shen Nung for its discovery in 2737 BC, the first reliable account of the use of tea as a medicinal plant appears in an early Chinese manuscript written around 350 AD. The Dutch brought the first tea to Europe in 1610, where it was accepted rather slowly; with time, it was adopted by the British as a favorite beverage and became an integral part of their daily activities. In fact, the tea trade constituted one of the major elements of the English economy. Tea revenues made it possible for England to colonize India and helped to bring on the Opium Wars in the 1800s, which benefited British colonialism.

The British were constantly at odds with the Dutch as they attempted to monopolize the tea trade. Even so, the Dutch introduced the first tea into America at New Amsterdam around 1650. Later, the British gained exclusive rights to sell tea to the American colonies. Because of the high taxes levied by the British government on tea being shipped to America, tea became a symbol of British rule.

SOFT DRINKS

The second most common source of caffeine is soft drinks. In general, the caffeine content per 12-ounce serving ranges from 30 to 60 milligrams (see Table 10.3). Soft drinks account for most of the caffeine consumed by U.S. children and teenagers; for many people, a can of cola has replaced the usual cup of coffee. Recently, because of its general acceptance, caffeine has been added to juices, water, and even combined with alcoholic drinks (Caffeine Informer 2016).

Super-caffeinated energy drinks, with names like 357 Super Magnum, Wired X344, 5-Hour Energy, Adrenalin Shot, All City NRG, and Amp Lightening Charge, have dramatically increased in popularity (Shapefit n.d.). Approximately 30% to 60% of students 12 to 20 years of age regularly consume these energy drinks (Nowak and Jasionowski 2015). Although manufacturers of these high-dose caffeine drinks claim they do not specifically target teenagers in their marketing strategies, most of the advertisements for these products are commonly shown on television stations with a high percentage of adolescents in their viewing base (Edmond 2015).

The reality is that adolescents are heavy consumers of "energy" drinks and do not appreciate how high the caffeine doses are in these caffeine-rich products. This is evident from the reports by poison control systems and emergency rooms of dramatic increases in calls and visits by young people complaining of caffeine-related overdose symptoms such as shakiness, tremors, dizziness, nausea, vomiting, agitation, increased heart rate, and elevated blood pressure (Goodman 2011).

Another concern relates to observations that consumption of these drinks is associated with what has become known as *toxic jock* behavior: a combination of behaviors that reflect an inclination to engage in dangerous risk taking such as unprotected sex, substance abuse, and violence, behaviors perceived as expressions of masculinity. These observations do not mean that the caffeine causes this poor decision making, but it does appear that kids who are heavily involved in consuming these beverages are more likely to ignore basic rules of common sense related to their health and safety (Levant et al. 2015).

As mentioned previously, caffeine also has been added to alcoholic beverages with names such as Four Loco and Joose. Despite claims by the manufacturers that a combination of caffeine and alcohol is "generally recognized as safe," evidence has been accumulating that, especially in underage consumers, these products pose a significant health risk. After a yearlong review of evidence, complaints, and claims, the FDA concluded that this drug combination may mask feelings of drunkenness, prompting consumers to engage in dangerous activities such as driving while under the influence of alcohol. As a result the FDA's conclusion, caffeine–alcohol combination products have been removed from the market (Caffeine Informer 2014).

SOCIAL CONSEQUENCES OF CONSUMING CAFFEINE-BASED BEVERAGES

It is impossible to accurately assess the social impact of consuming beverages containing caffeine, but certainly the subtle (and sometimes not so subtle) stimulant effects of the caffeine present in these drinks have some social influence. These beverages have become integrated into social customs and ceremonies and are recognized as traditional drinks.

Today, drinks containing caffeine are consumed by many people with ritualistic devotion first thing in the morning, following every meal, and at frequent interludes throughout the day known as "coffee breaks" or "tea times." The immense popularity of these products is certainly a consequence of the stimulant actions of caffeine. Both the dependence on the "jump-start" effect of caffeine and the avoidance of unpleasant withdrawal consequences in the frequent user ensure the continual popularity of these products.

OTHER NATURAL CAFFEINE SOURCES

Although coffee and tea are two of the most common sources of natural caffeine in the United States, other caffeine-containing beverages and food are popular in different parts of the world. Some of the most common include guaraná from Brazil; maté from Argentina, southern Brazil, and Paraguay; and kola nuts from West Africa, the West Indies, and South America (Nierenberg 2015).

CHOCOLATE

Although chocolate contains small amounts of caffeine (see Table 10.3), the principal stimulant in chocolate is the alkaloid theobromine, named after the cocoa tree, *Theobroma cacao*. (*Theobroma* is an Aztec word meaning "fruit of the gods.") The Aztecs thought very highly of the fruit and seed pods from the cacao tree, and they used the beans as a medium of exchange in bartering. The Mayans adopted the food and made a warm drink from the beans that they called *chocolatl* (meaning "warm drink"). The original chocolate drink was a very thick concoction that had to be eaten with a spoon. It was unsweetened because the Mayans apparently did not know about sugarcane.

Hernando Cortés, the conqueror of Mexico, took some chocolate cakes back to Spain with him in 1528, but the method of preparing them remained a secret for nearly 100 years. It was not until 1828 that the Dutch worked out a process to remove much of the fat from the kernels to make a chocolate powder that was the forerunner of the cocoa we know today. The cocoa fat, or cocoa butter as it is called, was later mixed with sugar and pressed into bars. In 1847, the first chocolate bars appeared on the market. By 1876, the Swiss had developed milk chocolate, which is highly popular in today's confectioneries.

OTHER SOURCES OF CAFFEINE

Although the consumption of beverages is by far the most common source of xanthines, a number of popular OTC products contain significant quantities of caffeine. For example, many OTC analgesic products (e.g., Anacin and Excedrin) contain approximately 30 to 60 milligrams of caffeine per tablet. Higher doses of 100 to 200 milligrams per tablet are included in stay-awake (NoDoz) and "picker-upper" (Vivarin) products (Kirkwood and Melton 2012; Wilkinson 2012). The use of caffeine in these OTC drugs is highly controversial and has been criticized by clinicians who are unconvinced of caffeine's benefits. Some critics believe that the presence of caffeine in these OTC drugs is nothing more than a psychological gimmick to entice customers through mild euphoric effects provided by this stimulant. Caffeine is also sometimes added to nonbeverage products such as vaporizers, patches, soups, gummy candies, and hot sauces (Ramsey 2015).

Despite this criticism, it is likely that caffeine has some analgesic (pain-relieving) properties of its own (Dunwiddie and Masino 2001). Studies suggest that 130 milligrams, but not 65 milligrams, of caffeine is superior to a placebo in relieving nonmigraine headaches. In addition, the presence of caffeine has been shown to enhance aspirin-medicated relief from surgical pain (such as tooth extraction). Based on such findings, some clinicians recommend the use of caffeine in the management of some types of headaches and minor to moderate pains (Cochrane Review 2015).

PHYSIOLOGICAL EFFECTS OF THE XANTHINES

The xanthines significantly influence several important body functions. Although the effects of these drugs are generally viewed as minor and short-term (Food Insight 2015), when used in high doses or by people who have severe medical problems, these drugs can be dangerous (Nierenberg 2015). The following sections summarize the responses of the major systems to xanthines.

CNS EFFECTS

Among the common xanthines, caffeine has the most potent effect on the CNS, followed by theophylline; for most people, theobromine has relatively little influence. Although the CNS responses of users can vary considerably, in general 100 to 200 milligrams of caffeine enhances alertness, causes arousal, and diminishes fatigue (Galanter and Boushey 2015). Caffeine is often used to block drowsiness and facilitate mental activity, such as when cramming for examinations into the early hours of the morning. In addition, caffeine stimulates the formation of thoughts but does not improve learning ability in the wide-awake student. The effects of caffeine are most pronounced in unstimulated, drowsy consumers

(Food Insight 2015). The CNS effects of caffeine also diminish the sense of boredom (MedicineNet 2010). Thus, people engaged in dull, repetitive tasks, such as assembly-line work, or nonstimulating and laborious exercises, such as listening to a boring professor, often consume caffeinated beverages to help compensate for the tedium. Most certainly, xanthine drinks are popular because they cause these effects on brain activity.

Adverse CNS effects usually occur with doses greater than 300 milligrams per day. Some of these include insomnia, increased tension, anxiety, and initiation of muscle twitches. Doses over 500 milligrams can be dysphoric (unpleasant) and can cause panic sensations, chills, nausea, and clumsiness. Extremely high doses of caffeine, from 5 to 10 grams, frequently result in seizures, respiratory failure, and death (APA 2013).

CARDIOVASCULAR AND RESPIRATORY EFFECTS

Drugs that stimulate the brain usually stimulate the cardiovascular system as well. The response of the heart and blood vessels to xanthines is dependent on dose and previous experience with these mild stimulants. Tolerance to the cardiovascular effects occurs with frequent use (MedicineNet 2010). With low doses (100 to 200 milligrams), heart activity can either increase, decrease, or do nothing; at higher doses (more than 500 milligrams), the rate of contraction of the heart increases. Xanthines usually cause minor vasodilation in most of the body. In contrast, the cerebral blood vessels are vasoconstricted by the action of caffeine. In fact, cerebral vasoconstriction likely accounts for this drug's effectiveness in relieving some minor vascular headaches caused by vasodilation of the cerebral vessels. For most consumers the effects of caffeine on the cardiovascular system are minor, but for some people with underlying heart disease, caffeine can be dangerous (Today Health 2012).

Among the xanthines, theophylline has the greatest effect on the respiratory system, causing air passages to open and facilitate breathing. Because of this effect, tea has often been recommended to relieve breathing difficulties, and theophylline is frequently used to treat asthma-related respiratory problems.

OTC caffeine products frequently contain the equivalent of two to three cups of coffee and are used to stay awake.

OTHER EFFECTS

The xanthines also have noteworthy—albeit mild—effects on other systems in the body. They cause a minor increase in the secretion of digestive juices in the stomach, which can be significant to individuals suffering from stomach ailments such as ulcers. These drugs also increase urine formation (as any heavy tea drinker undoubtedly knows).

CAFFEINE INTOXICATION

Consuming occasional low doses of the xanthines (the equivalent of four to five cups of coffee [around 400 milligrams] per day) is relatively safe for most users (Nierenberg 2015). However, frequent use of high doses causes psychological as well as physical problems called **caffeinism**. This condition is found in about 10% of the adults who consume coffee (APA 2013).

The CNS components of caffeine intoxication are recognized as "caffeine use disorder" in the criteria established by the American Psychiatric Association (2013) in the fifth edition of its *Diagnosis and Statistical Manual of Mental Disorders* (*DSM*-5). The essential features of this disorder are restlessness, nervousness, excitement, insomnia, flushed face, diuresis, muscle twitching, rambling thoughts and speech, and stomach complaints. These symptoms can occur in some sensitive people following a dose as low as 250 milligrams per day. Caffeine doses in excess of 1 gram per day may cause muscle twitching, rambling thoughts and speech, heart arrhythmias, and motor agitation. With higher doses, hearing ringing in the ears and seeing flashes of light can occur. Some researchers suggest consuming large quantities of caffeine is associated with cancers of the bladder, ovaries, colon, and kidneys. These claims have not been reliably substantiated,

KEY TERM

caffeinism
symptoms caused by taking high chronic doses of caffeine

and some evidence suggests that in moderation caffeine may protect against some cancers (Mozes 2015).

One problem with many such studies is that they assess the effect of coffee consumption on cancers rather than the effect of caffeine itself. Because coffee contains so many different chemicals, it is impossible to determine specifically the effect of caffeine in such research. Other reports claim that caffeine promotes cyst formation in women's breasts. Although these conclusions have been challenged, some clinicians advise patients with breast cysts to avoid caffeine (American Cancer Society 2015). Finally, some reports, but not all, indicate that very high doses of caffeine given to pregnant laboratory animals can cause stillbirths. However, studies found that moderate consumption of caffeine (less than 300 milligrams per day) did not significantly affect human fetal development (HealthAssist.net 2016). Generally, expectant mothers are advised to avoid or at least reduce caffeine use during pregnancy just to be safe.

Based on the information available, no strong evidence exists to suggest that moderate use of caffeine leads to disease. In fact, some research has suggested that moderate caffeine consumption may even reduce the risk of degenerative diseases of the brain such as Parkinson's disease and Alzheimer's disease (Van Dam 2015). There are, however, implications that people with existing severe medical problems—psychiatric disorders (such as severe anxiety, panic attacks, and schizophrenia), cardiovascular disease, and possibly breast cysts—may be at greater risk when consuming caffeine. Realistically, other elements, such as alcohol and fat consumption and smoking, are much more likely to cause serious health problems (Van Dam 2015).

CAFFEINE DEPENDENCE

Caffeine causes limited dependence, which, for most people, is relatively minor compared with that of the potent stimulants; thus, the abuse potential of caffeine is much lower and dependence is less likely to interfere with normal daily routines (Food Insight 2015). Despite this, caffeine use is thought to be able be habit-forming in some people (*U.S. News and World Report* 2012). Consequently, 50% of those consuming one to three cups of coffee each day develop headaches when withdrawing, and 10% become significantly depressed, anxious, or fatigued without their coffee. Some people experience elements of withdrawal every morning before their first cup and claim caffeine gives them an edge at work or in

TABLE 10.4 Caffeine Withdrawal Syndrome

Symptom	Duration
Headache	Several days to 1 week
Decreased alertness	2 days
Decreased vigor	2 days
Fatigue and lethargy	2 days
Nervousness	2 days

Bethea, A. "The Duration of Caffeine Withdrawal Symptoms." Livestrong.com. 18 February 2015. Available http://www.livestrong.com/article/399329-the-duration-of-caffeine-withdrawal-symptoms/

school (Hartney 2013). However, caffeine is so readily available and socially accepted (almost expected) that the high quantity of consumption has produced many modestly dependent users and occasionally a trip to the emergency room (see "Here and Now: Caffeine Emergencies").

The degree of physical dependence on caffeine is highly variable but is related to dose. With typical caffeine withdrawal, adverse effects can persist for several days (see **Table 10.4**). Although these symptoms are unpleasant, they usually are not severe enough to prevent most people from giving up their coffee or cola drinks if motivated. It is noteworthy, however, that many of those patients who are treated for caffeinism relapse into their caffeine-consuming habits (Wheeler 2010).

VARIABILITY IN RESPONSES

Caffeine is eventually absorbed entirely from the gastrointestinal tract after oral consumption. In most users, 90% of the drug reaches the bloodstream within 20 minutes and is distributed into the brain and throughout the body very quickly. The rate of absorption of caffeine from the stomach and intestines differs from person to person by as much as sixfold. Because of the wide variations in the rate at which caffeine enters the blood from the stomach, this likely accounts for much of the variability in response to this drug (Mental Health Daily 2015b).

■ OTC Sympathomimetics

Although often overlooked, the sympathomimetic decongestant drugs included in OTC products such as cold, allergy, and diet aid medications have stimulant properties like those of caffeine. For most people, the CNS impact of these drugs is minor, but for those people who are very sensitive

HERE AND NOW

Caffeine Emergencies

Caffeine can easily be purchased online in a pure concentrated powder form. One teaspoon of such a preparation contains a quantity of caffeine comparable to that found in 25 cups of coffee and about four times that considered to be a safe daily dose. Because of this highly concentrated caffeine source, Dr. Glenn Greeting, an emergency physician from Penn State Hershey Medical Center, has been quoted as saying that caffeine powder is even more concerning than powdered alcohol. Proof of this concern includes recent reports that the use of powdered caffeine has caused numerous caffeine overdoses nationwide resulting in hospitalization and in two cases

even death. Signs of the caffeine overdose include symptoms such as rapid, erratic heartbeats; extreme agitation; vomiting; and even seizures. It has been difficult for the FDA to manage these products because powdered caffeine is classified as a dietary supplement and thus not directly regulated by the FDA. However, the FDA has put out an advisory that pure powdered caffeine should be avoided and that its adverse effects are much more severe than consuming too much coffee, tea, or other caffeinated beverage. The FDA has also advised parents that teenagers and young adults are particularly attracted to these products.

Data from Dallas, E. "E.R. Physician Raises Concerns About Powdered Caffeine." HealthDay. 27 February 2015. Available http://consumer.healthday.com /kids-health-information-23/adolescents-and-teen-health-news-719/er-physician-raises-concerns-about-powdered-caffeine-696703.html; Food and Drug Administration (FDA). "FDA Consumer Advice on Pure Powdered Caffeine." 2015. Available http://www.fda.gov/Food/RecallsOutbreaksEmergencies/Safety AlertsAdvisories/ucm405787.htm

---

to these drugs, they can cause jitters and interfere with sleep. For such individuals, OTC products containing the sympathomimetics should be avoided before bedtime (Answers.com 2010).

The common OTC sympathomimetics are shown in **Table 10.5** and include ephedrine, pseudoephedrine, and phenylephrine. In the past, these drugs have been referred to as "look-alikes," suggesting they have effects similar to the more potent stimulants such as amphetamine. Although much less potent than amphetamines (even though they can be used as precursor chemicals to make methamphetamine), these minor stimulants can be abused and have caused deaths (Cucchiara and Levine 2011). Attempts to keep these drugs from being promoted as potent stimulants resulted in passage of the federal and state Imitation Controlled Substances Acts. These statutes prohibit the packaging of OTC sympathomimetics to look like amphetamines.

Despite these laws, occasionally other products containing the OTC sympathomimetics are promoted on the street as "harmless speed" and "OTC uppers." It is likely that use of such products can lead to the abuse of more potent stimulants.

As mentioned earlier in the chapter, some of the sympathomimetics that are included in cold medicines can be readily converted into methamphetamine. For this reason, since 2006 federal statutes have required these products be secured

TABLE 10.5 Common OTC Sympathomimetics

Drug	OTC Product (Form)
Ephedrine	Before being removed from market, was used as a decongestant (oral, nasal spray, or nasal drops) and for weight loss
Naphazoline	Decongestant (nasal spray or nasal drops)
Oxymetazoline	Decongestant (nasal spray or nasal drops)
Phenylephrine	Decongestant (oral, nasal spray, nasal drops, or eye drops)
Pseudoephedrine	Decongestant (oral)
Tetrahydrozoline	Decongestant (eye drops)

Data from Scolaro, K. "Disorders Related to Colds and Allergy." In *Handbook of Nonprescription Drugs*, 17th ed., 179–204. Washington, DC: American Pharmaceutical Association, 2012.

in a locked case behind the counter and sold in limited quantities (Pharmacy Times 2015).

▪ Herbal Stimulants

Some OTC sympathomimetics occur naturally and are also found in herbal stimulants or dietary supplements sold by mail and in novelty stores, beauty salons, health food stores, online, and sometimes

HERE AND NOW
Diet Pills Are Russian Roulette for Athletes

Steve Bechler, a 23-year-old pitcher for the Baltimore Orioles of the American League, died in 2003 after collapsing on the field during running drills due to "multiple organ failure resulting from heat stroke," says the autopsy report. Ephedrine was found in Bechler's body and likely contributed to his death. He was reported to be using an ephedrine supplement called Xenadrine RFA-1. Although advised not to use it by his trainer, Bechler was taking this ephedrine-containing product to get his weight down after being criticized by coaches for being too heavy and not performing well in preseason drills. A teammate explained that heavy athletes like Bechler are under a lot of pressure to control their weight to make big-league teams. Although at the time of Bechler's death use of ephedrine was not prohibited by Major League Baseball, it was prohibited by the National Football League in 2002. The NFL's ban came after Korey Stringer, a lineman for the Minnesota Vikings who was taking an ephedrine product, died after collapsing

during a training camp workout in 2001. In 2004, ephedrine in OTC dietary supplements was made illegal by the FDA due to reports of 22 deaths and 800 incidents of serious toxicity caused by OTC ephedrine.

Data from Mayo Clinic. "Ephedra, Ma Huang." 1 November 2013. Available http://www.mayoclinic.com/health/ephedra/NS_patient-ephedra

by health professionals, including physicians (Myers 2014). (To appreciate this point, perform an Internet search for "herbal stimulant.") These pills have been sold under many names, such as *rave herbal stimulant*, *legal herbal weed*, and *herbal ecstasy*, and often contain stimulants such as ephedrine, ephedra, or ma huang. These products are promoted as natural highs to be used as diet aids, energy boosters, or performance enhancers for athletics (Legal Herbal Drugs 2013). Excessive use of these products can cause seizures, heart attacks, and strokes (Banar 2011). In fact, several deaths and many cases of severe reactions have been reported in the United States from excessive use of these products (FDA 2013). The death of a Major League Baseball player (see "Here and Now: Diet Pills Are Russian Roulette for Athletes") resulted in particularly strong pressure to ban OTC products, including dietary supplements, containing either the herb ephedra or the active ingredient ephedrine (Grace 2006). In response to these pressures, the FDA banned the use of ephedrine or ephedra in OTC products; however, it is difficult to actually remove herbal stimulants from the marketplace because of a 1994 federal

law that prohibits such action until the FDA conclusively proves the dangers of these substances (Miller and Longtin 2010). Numerous lawsuits have been filed against herbal companies that manufactured products containing ma huang and the drug ephedrine. These legal actions claim that such products have caused serious illness and even death. Several of these lawsuits have been settled out of court, reportedly for millions of dollars. Even before the FDA ban, because ephedrine can be converted into methamphetamine, the Comprehensive Methamphetamine Act passed in 1996 regulated the amount of ephedrine that could be purchased or sold at one time (Sprague, Harrod, and Teconchuk 1998).

Global Stimulant Abuse

Like the United States, other countries have been seriously impacted by the abuse of stimulant drugs, causing governments and law enforcement agencies around the world and international organizations such as the United Nations Office on Drugs and Crime to search for solutions (UNODC 2015). For the most part, these drugs are referred to as amphetamine-type stimulants (ATSs) or cocaine and their various forms. The ATS drugs include amphetamines such as methamphetamine, methcathinone, and MDMA and related substances.

■ Stimulant Production

Because most ATS drugs are synthetics, they can be produced anywhere and are relatively inexpensive. As mentioned earlier, for this reason these drugs are often perceived as a "poor-man's cocaine." The global market for ATS drugs continues to be dominated by methamphetamine, and the market for this drug is expanding in East and Southeast Asia. The total quantity of ATS drug seizures is approaching 150 tons per year (UNODC 2015). In contrast, the global market for Ecstasy is smaller, especially in the Americas, and is currently most active in Eastern Asia (UNODC 2015).

In contrast, because cocaine is a natural substance derived from a plant, its production is limited to those regions that have climate and geographic conditions conducive to coca cultivation. The countries that produce the vast majority of the world's cocaine supply are Bolivia, Peru, and Colombia. The global cocaine supply decreased to 845 metric tons in 2008. These recent declines were largely due to a 28% reduction in cocaine production in Colombia as a result of pressure from the United States (UNODC 2009).

© UN Photo/Andrea Brizzi.

Organizations of the United Nations, such as its Office on Drugs and Crime, work with countries around the world to identify critical drug problems and to develop global solutions that cross international borders.

■ Global Stimulant Consumption

It is roughly estimated that globally 27 million persons suffer from substance use disorders, with only one-sixth of those having access to treatment (UNODC 2015). These intense users are likely very dependent on their drug of choice, cause a serious drain on public health and law enforcement resources, and would benefit from proper treatment.

Different drugs tend to cause problems for different global regions. Marijuana is particularly troubling for Africa and Australia; heroin is especially problematic for Asia and Europe; the ATS drugs are a major problem for Asia, North America, and Australia; and cocaine causes the greatest problem in North and South America, with the United States being the largest consumer in absolute numbers. By comparison, the ATS drugs are consumed by almost twice as many people around the world (about 35 million annually) as cocaine (about 17 million). The proliferation of NPSs (new psychoactive substances) pose a special challenge in that little is known regarding their health and social risks. The short- and long-term effects of these drugs often have not been well studied, making it difficult to treat and warn about their use (UNODC 2015).

■ Global Drug Policy

Like the United States, most countries around the world are looking for solutions to the personal and social consequences of drug abuse in general and the stimulant problems in particular. Lively discussions about demand, production, and trafficking occur between countries to try to stem the tide of drug abuse/addiction and its devastating consequences. The causes are many and the solutions are complex and evasive. There are heated discussions between nations on topics such as (1) who is principally at fault for the problems (i.e., the nations that produce or consume), (2) whether these drugs should be legalized or at least be decriminalized, and (3) whether taxing of such drug products be used to raise needed public revenues. The international discussions resemble those occurring throughout the United States. What has become evident to everyone is that although specific solutions are difficult, all nations are in this together. Drug problems and drug policies to address these problems cross national borders, impacting global efforts to find solutions; thus, to be successful in our attempts to mitigate these drug problems, we must have global cooperation and work together.

LEARNING PORTFOLIO

Discussion Questions

1. How are methamphetamine and Ecstasy similar, and how do they differ?
2. Should children be taken from mothers who are addicted to methamphetamine or cocaine?
3. What have past experiences taught us about cocaine? Do you think we have finally learned our lesson concerning this drug?
4. If clinical trials demonstrate that MDMA is effective in the treatment of stress and anxiety, should the FDA approve its use by prescription? What would be the effect on recreational MDMA use by young people if the FDA approved MDMA for treating PTSD?
5. Why does the method of cocaine administration make a difference in how a user is affected by this drug? Use examples to substantiate your conclusions.
6. Why do people smoke cocaine, and what are the major toxicities caused by the use of high doses of this stimulant?
7. How is cocaine dependence treated? What are the rationales for the treatments?
8. How does caffeine compare with cocaine and amphetamine as a CNS stimulant?
9. Because of caffeine's potential for abuse, do you think the FDA should control it more tightly? Defend your answer.
10. Do you feel that herbal stimulants, such as ephedra, should have been removed from OTC products?
11. How do global efforts to address stimulant abuse problems affect the people and policies in the United States?
12. Why is it disturbing to have so many NPSs becoming globally available?

Key Terms

adulterated	341
anorexiants	322
behavioral stereotypy	322
binge	327
caffeinism	352
cocaine babies	348
crack	343
freebasing	343
high	327
hyperpyrexia	327
ice	327
narcolepsy	323
performance enhancers	335
precursor chemicals	325
run	327
rush	327
speed	324
speedballs	331
tweaking	327
uppers	321
xanthines	349

Summary

1. Amphetamines, originally developed as decongestants, are potent stimulants. Some amphetamines have been approved by the FDA as (a) diet aids to treat obesity, (b) treatment for narcolepsy, and (c) treatment for attention deficit hyperactivity disorder in children.
2. In therapeutic doses, amphetamines can cause agitation, anxiety, and panic owing to their effects on the brain; in addition, they can cause an irregular heartbeat, increased blood pressure, heart attack, or stroke. Intense, high-dose abuse of these drugs can cause severe psychotic behavior, stereotypy, and seizures, as well as the severe cardiovascular side effects just mentioned.
3. Speed refers to the use of intravenous methamphetamine. Ice is smoked methamphetamine. A run is a pattern of intense,

multiple dosing over a period of days that can cause serious neurological, psychiatric, and cardiovascular consequences.

4. Tweakers are individuals who repeatedly self-administer methamphetamine to maintain the high. They often have not slept or eaten for days, are very irritable, and sometimes are paranoid or even violent.

5. "Designer" amphetamines are chemical modifications of original amphetamines and are included in the category of NPS (new psychoactive substance). Some designer amphetamines, such as Ecstasy, have some abuse potential and are marketed on the street under exotic and alluring names.

6. Ecstasy and related NPSs have both psychedelic and stimulant properties due to their ability to release serotonin and dopamine in the brain. This combination of pharmacological effects makes these drugs particularly attractive to younger populations engaging in sensory-rich activities, such as dances called raves.

7. In the early 1980s, cocaine was commonly viewed by the U.S. public as a relatively safe drug with glamorous connotations. By the mid-1980s, it became apparent that cocaine was a very addicting drug with dangerous side effects.

8. The CNS and cardiovascular effects of both amphetamines and cocaine are similar. However, the effects of cocaine tend to occur more rapidly, be more intense, and wear off more quickly than those of amphetamines.

9. The intensity of the cocaine effect and the likelihood of dependence occurring are directly related to the means of administration. Going from least to most intense effect, the modes of cocaine administration include chewing, snorting, injecting, and smoking (or freebasing).

10. Crack is cocaine that has been converted into its "freebase" form and is intended for smoking.

11. Cocaine withdrawal goes through three main stages: (a) the "crash," the initial abstinence phase consisting of depression, agitation, suicidal thoughts, and fatigue; (b) withdrawal, including mood swings, craving, anhedonia, and obsession with drug seeking; and (c) extinction, when normal pleasure returns and cues trigger craving and mood swings.

12. Treatment of cocaine dependence is highly individualistic and has variable success. The principal strategies include both inpatient and outpatient programs. Drug therapy often is used to relieve short-term cocaine craving and to alleviate mood problems and long-term craving. Psychological counseling and support therapy are essential components of treatment.

13. Caffeine is the most frequently consumed stimulant in the world. It is classified as a xanthine (methylxanthine) and is added to a number of beverages, including water, and has even been added to alcoholic drinks. It is also included in some OTC medicines such as analgesics and "stay-awake" products. Caffeine causes minor stimulation of cardiovascular activity, kidney function (it is a diuretic), and gastric secretion.

14. Dependence on caffeine can occur in people who regularly consume large doses. Withdrawal can cause headaches, agitation, and tremors. Although unpleasant, withdrawal from caffeine dependence is much less severe than that from amphetamine and cocaine dependence.

15. OTC sympathomimetics such as ephedrine have been consumed in high doses and, although not as potent as the major stimulants, recreational use of these drugs can be dangerous. Because of those potential dangers, the FDA has prohibited the use of ephedrine in OTC products.

16. Stimulant abuse and addiction are problems that are global in nature. Because these drugs are manufactured around the world and trafficked across international borders, it is impossible to find lasting solutions to these problems without working with other countries to help stem the production and smuggling of these illegal substances.

References

Addiction Center. "Ecstasy Addiction and Abuse." 12 April 2016a. Available https://www.addictioncenter.com/drugs/ecstasy/

Addiction Center. "Ritalin Addiction, Abuse and Treatment." 21 January 2016b. Available https://www.addictioncenter.com/stimulants/ritalin/

Addiction Center. "Treatment for Meth Addiction." 22 January 2016c. Available https://www.addictioncenter.com/drugs/meth/withdrawal-detox/

Aldrich, M., and R. Barker. In *Cocaine: Chemical, Biological, Social and Treatment Aspects,* edited by S. J. Mule, 3–10. Cleveland, OH: CRC, 1976.

American Cancer Society (ACS). "Fibrosis and Simple Cysts." 2015. Available http://www.cancer.org/healthy/findcancerearly/womenshealth/non-cancerousbreastconditions/non-cancerous-breast-conditions-fibrocystic-changes

American Psychiatric Association. *Diagnostic and Statistical Manual of Mental Disorders,* 5th ed. Washington, DC: American Psychiatric Association, 2013.

Amphetamines.com. "Amphetamine Street Names." n.d. Available http://amphetamines.com/street-names/

Answers.com. "Decongestant." 2010. Available http://www.answers.com/topic/decongestant

Banar, M. "What Are the Potential Dangers of Herbal Stimulants." Livestrong.com. 7 August 2011. Available http://www.livestrong.com/article/510464-what-are-the-potential-dangers-of-herbal-stimulants

Barnes, L. "An Addict's Story: Cocaine and the Crash." *The Citizen* (Auburn, NY). (1 January 2013). Available http://auburnpub.com/lifestyles/an-addict-s-story-cocaine-and-the-crash/article_aadd6bc1-5678-542a-9cb3-f256a3631981.html

Baumann, M., and N. Volkow. "Abuse of New Psychoactive Substances: Threats and Solutions." *Neuropsychopharm* 41 (2016): 663–665.

Bazuaye-Ekwuyasi, E. A., J. O. Ogunbilege, B. S. Kaphalia, M. A. Eltorky, A. O. Okorodudu. "Comparative Effects of Cocaine and Cocaethylene on Alveolar Epithelial Type II Cells." *Toxicology Mechanisms and Methods* 25 (2015): 604–613.

Beck, J. "The Public Health Implications of MDMA Use." In *Ecstasy,* edited by S. Peroutka, 77–103. Norwell, MA: Kluwer, 1990.

Beckhusen, R. "As Colombian Drug Gangs Collapse, Mexican Cartels Get Tons of Cheap Coke. *WIRED.* (April 2013). Available http://www.wired.com/dangerroom/2013/04/colombian-bacrim-gangs/

Briceno, F. "Eradication Spells Misery for Peru's Coca Farmers." *Salon.* 17 August 2015. Available http://www.salon.com/2015/08/17/eradication_spells_misery_for_perus_coca_farmers/

Buddy, T. "Common Street Names for Cocaine." About Health. 8 July 2015. Available http://alcoholism.about.com/od/coke/a/Common-Street-Names-For-Cocaine.htm

Byck, R. "Cocaine Use and Research: Three Histories." In *Cocaine: Chemical and Behavioral Aspects,* edited by S. Fisher, 3–17. London: Oxford University Press, 1987.

Caffeine Informer. "Caffeine Content of Drinks." 2016. Available http://www.caffeineinformer.com/the-caffeine-database

Caffeine Informer. "Alcohol and Energy Drinks: The Dangers of Mixing." 2014. Available http://www.caffeineinformer.com/alcoholic-energy-drinks-the-list

Cantwell, B., and A. McBride. "Self Detoxification by Amphetamine-Dependent Patients: A Pilot Study." *Drug and Alcohol Dependence* 49 (1998): 157–163.

Center for Substance Abuse Research (CESAR). "Methamphetamine." 29 October 2013. Available http://www.cesar.umd.edu/cesar/drugs/meth.asp

Centers for Disease Control and Prevention (CDC). "New Data: Medication and Behavior Treatment." 2016. Available http://www.cdc.gov/ncbddd/adhd/data.html

Central Intelligence Agency (CIA). "Field Listing, Illicit Drugs." *The World Factbook.* 2016. Available https://www.cia.gov/library/publications/the-world-factbook/fields/2086.html

Cloud, J. "The Lure of Ecstasy." *Time* 155 (5 June 2000): 60.

Cochrane Review. "Caffeine as an Analgesic Adjuvant for Acute Pain in Adults." PubMed Health. 2015. Available http://www.ncbi.nlm.nih.gov/pubmedhealth/PMH0040839/

Cucchiara, B., and S. Levine. "Stroke Associated with Drug Abuse." MedMerits. 2011. Available http://www.medmerits.com/index.php/article/stroke_associated_with_drug_abuse/

Davies, J. "Prenatal Methamphetamine Exposure." RainbowKids, Adoption & Child Welfare Advocacy. 3 September 2015. Available http://www.rainbowkids.com/adoption-stories/prenatal-methamphetamine-exposure-1239

Davis, K. "MDMA (Ecstasy): Facts, Effects and Hazards." MNT. 22 July 2015. Available http://www.medicalnewstoday.com/articles/297064.php

DEA. "Methamphetamine Lab Incidents, 2004-2014." Drug Enforcement Administration (accessed September 26, 2016). Available https://www.dea.gov/resource-center/meth-lab-maps.shtml

DiChiara, G. "Cocaine: Scientific and Social Dimensions." *Trends in Neurological Sciences* 16 (1993): 39.

Doyle, M. "Report: 2006 Anti-meth Law Reduced Number of U.S. Labs." McClatchy. 6 July 2010. Available http://www.mcclatchydc.com/2010/07/06/97092/report-2006-anti-meth-law-reduced.html

Drasner, K. "Local Anesthetics." In *Basic and Clinical Pharmacology*, 12th ed., edited by B. Katzung, S. Masters, and A. Trevor, 449–464. New York: McGraw-Hill Medical, 2012.

Drug Enforcement Administration (DEA). *Drugs of Abuse, a DEA Resource Guide.* 2015. Available https://www.dea.gov/pr/multimedia-library/publications/drug_of_abuse.pdf

Drug Facts. "The Truth About Cocaine." Foundation for a Drug-Free World. 2016. Available http://www.drugfreeworld.org/drugfacts/cocaine/a-short-history.html

Drug Foundation. "BZP and Party Pills." n.d. Available https://www.drugfoundation.org.nz/party-pills

Drug Policy Alliance. "Drug Trafficking in Latin America." 2015a. Available http://www.drugpolicy.org/drug-trafficking-latin-america

Drug Policy Alliance. "10 Facts About MDMA." 2015b. Available http://www.drugpolicy.org/sites/default/files/DPA_Fact_Sheet_10_Facts_about_MDMA.pdf

Drugs.com. "MDMA: What Is MDMA?" 2014. Available http://www.drugs.com/illicit/mdma.html

Dunwiddie, T., and S. Masino. "The Role and Regulation of Adenosine in the Central Nervous System." *Annual Review of Neuroscience* 24 (2001): 31–55.

Edmond, J. "Teenage TV Audiences and Energy Drink Advertisements." Medical Press. 6 March 2015. Available http://medicalxpress.com/news/2015-03-teenage-tv-audiences-energy-advertisements.html

Elkashef, A., F. Vocci, G. Hanson, J. White, W. Wickes, and J. Tiihonen. "Pharmacotherapy of Methamphetamine Addiction: An Update." *Substance Abuse* 29 (2008): 31–49.

Ely, A., and A. Cusack. "The Binge and the Brain." The Dana Foundation. 2015. Available http://www.dana.org/Cerebrum/2015/The_Binge_and_the_Brain/

eMedicineHealth. "Cocaine Abuse." 2010. Available http://www.emedicinehealth.com/cocaine_abuse/article_em.htm

Federal Bureau of Investigation (FBI). "Aryan Brotherhood Methamphetamine Operation Dismantled." 31 December 2015. Available https://www.fbi.gov/news/stories/aryan-brotherhood-methamphetamine-operation-dismantled

Fischman, M., and C. Johanson. "Cocaine." In *Pharmacological Aspects of Drug Dependence: Towards an Integrated Neurobehavior Approach Handbook of Experimental Pharmacology*, edited by C. Schuster and M. Kuhar, 159–195. New York: Springer-Verlag, 1996.

Fitzgerald. S. "'Crack Baby' Study Ends With Unexpected But Clear Results." *The Inquirer* (Philadelphia). (22 July 2013). Available http://articles.philly.com/2013-07-22/news/40709969_1_hallam-hurt-so-called-crack-babies-funded-study

Food and Drug Administration (FDA). "Stimulant Potentially Dangerous to Health, FDA Warns." 2013. Available http://www.fda.gov/ForConsumers/ConsumerUpdates/ucm347270.htm

Food and Drug Administration (FDA). "Legal Requirements for the Sale and Purchase of Drug Products Containing Pseudoephedrine, Ephedrine, and Phenylpropanolamine." 2014. Available http://www.fda.gov/drugs/drugsafety/informationbydrugclass/ucm072423.htm

Food and Drug Administration (FDA). "FDA Consumer Advice on Pure Powdered Caffeine." 2015. Available http://www.fda.gov/Food/RecallsOutbreaksEmergencies/SafetyAlertsAdvisories/ucm405787.htm

Food Insight. "Everything You Need to Know About Caffeine." 27 August 2015. Available http://www.foodinsight.org/everything-about-caffeine-science-amount-safety

Friends of Narconon. "Ecstasy/MDMA Manufacturing and Statistics." 2010. Available http://www.friendsofnarconon.org/drug_education/news/latest_news/ecstasy%10mdma_manufacturing_and_statistics

Frontline. "A Social History of America's Most Popular Drugs." n.d. Available http://www.pbs.org/wgbh/pages/frontline/shows/drugs/buyers/socialhistory.html

Galanter, J., and H. Boushey. "Drugs Used in Asthma." In *Basic and Clinical Pharmacology*, 13th ed., edited by B. Katzung and A. Trevor, 336–351. New York: McGraw-Hill, 2015.

Gilbert, R. "Caffeine Consumption." In *The Methylxanthine Beverages and Foods: Chemistry, Consumption, and Health Effects*, edited by G. Spiller, 185–213. New York: Liss, 1984.

Golding, A. "Two Hundred Years of Drug Abuse." *Journal of the Royal Society of Medicine* 86 (May 1993): 282–286.

Goldstein, A. *Addiction from Biology to Drug Abuse.* New York: Freeman, 1994.

Goodger, N., J. Wang, and M. Pogrel. "Palatal and Nasal Necrosis Resulting from Cocaine Misuse." *British Dental Journal* 198 (2005): 333–334.

Goodman, B. "Energy Drinks Send Thousands to the ER Each Year." WebMD. 22 November 2011. Available http://www.Webmd.com/mental-health/alcohol-abuse/news/20111121/energy-drinks-send-thousands-to-the-er-each-year

Gorelick, D. "Cocaine Use Disorder in Adults: Epidemiology, Pharmacology, Clinical Manifestations, Medical Consequences, and Diagnosis." UpToDate. (7 August 2015). Available http://www.uptodate.com/contents/cocaine-use-disorder-in-adults-epidemiology-pharmacology-clinical-manifestations-medical-consequences-and-diagnosis

Grace, F. "FDA Wants Ephedra Ban Restored." CBS News. 9 May 2006. Available http://www.cbsnews.com/news/fda-wants-ephedra-ban-restored/

Green, E. "Cocaine, Glamorous Status Symbol of the 'Jet Set,' Is Fast Becoming Many Students' Drug of Choice." *Chronicle of Higher Education* 13 (November 1985): 1, 34.

Grillo, I. "Why Cartels Are Killing Mexico's Mayors." *New York Times.* (15 January 2016). Available http://www.nytimes.com/2016/01/17/opinion/sunday/why-cartels-are-killing-mexicos-mayors.html?_r=0

Grinspoon, L., and J. Bakalar. "The Amphetamines: Medical Use and Health Hazards." In *Amphetamines: Use, Misuse and Abuse,* edited by D. Smith, 18–33. Boston: Hall, 1978.

Grob, C., R. Poland, L. Chang, and T. Ernst. "Psychobiological Effects of 3,4-Methylenedioxymethamphetamine in Humans: Methodological Considerations and Preliminary Observations." *Behavioral Brain Research* 73 (1996): 103–107.

Hadlock G., K. Webb, L. McFadden, P. Chu, J. Ellis, S. Allen, D. Andrenyak, et al. "4-Methylmethcathinone (Mephedrone): Neuropharmacological Effects of a Designer Stimulant of Abuse." *Journal of Pharmacology and Experimental Therapeutics* 339 (2011): 530–536.

Hahn, I. "MDMA Toxicity." Medscape. 25 March 2015. Available http://emedicine.medscape.com/article/821572-overview#a5

Harding, A. "Meth Use in Pregnancy Endangers Mom and Baby." Reuters Health. 29 July 2010. Available http://www.reuters.com/article/2010/07/29/us-meth-pregnancy-idUSTRE66S5M720100729

Hartney, E. "What to Expect from Caffeine Withdrawal." About.com Addictions. 20 January 2013. Available http://addictions.about.com/od/Caffeine/a/What-To-Expect-From-Caffeine-Withdrawal.htm

Hawaii Island Recovery. "Speedballs Claim the Life of Baseball Great Ken Caminiti." 2015. Available http://www.hawaiianrecovery.com/speedballs-claim-the-life-of-baseball-great-ken-caminiti.html

HealthAssist.net. "Coffee During Pregnancy." 2016. Available http://www.healthassist.net/blog/general/coffee-pregnancy/

HealthResearchFunding.org. "24 Remarkable Caffeine Consumption Statistics." 2014. Available http://healthresearchfunding.org/remarkable-caffeine-consumption-statistics/

Hessert, A. "The New Performance Enhancing Drugs." Neuroanthropology. 4 June 2009. Available http://neuroanthropology.net/2009/06/04/the-new-performance-enhancing-drugs

Hitti, M. "Caffeine Abuse: Buzz Gone Wrong." WebMD. 16 October 2006. Available http://www.webmd.com/content/article/128/117124

Holt, L. "Former Meth Addicts Jenny Madonecky and Faye Benner Speak About Crystal Meth Addiction." *Saturday Today Show* (NBC). (8 October 2005).

Humphreys, K., T. Eng, and S. Lee. "Stimulant Medication and Substance Use Outcomes." *JAMA Psychiatry.* (29 May 2013). Available https://leelab.psych.ucla.edu/wp-content/uploads/sites/44/2015/10/Humphreys_2013_Stimulant.pdf

Johnston, L. "Monitoring the Future 2015." 2016. Available http://www.monitoringthefuture.org/data/15data/15drtbl2.pdf

Journal of the American Medical Association. "Ecstasy Overdoses at a New Years's Eve Rave Los Angeles, California, 2010." 304 (2010): 629-632.KCI.org. "Methamphetamine FAQ." n.d. Available http://www.kci.org/meth_info/faq_meth.htm

Keenan, B. "Adderall Is 'Secret Miracle' for Illegal Use." The Breeze. 22 April 2010. Available http://www.breezejmu.org/article_8d88baa4-757c-554f-9d36-9e48c47fb35a.html

Keoni, J. "New Synthetic Drug: Trifluoromethylphenylpiperazine (RFMPP)." New Roads. 2015. Available http://newroadstreatment.com/trifluoromethylphenylpiperazine-tfmpp/

Keybol.org. "How to Make Shake and Bake Meth." August 2009. Available http://www.keybol.org/2009/08/how-to-make-shake-and-bake-meth.html

Khazan, O. "The Rise of Work-Doping." *The Atlantic.* (August 2015). Available http://www.theatlantic.com/health/archive/2015/08/the-rise-of-work-doping/402373/

Kihlman, B. *Caffeine and Chromosomes.* Amsterdam: Elsevier, 1977.

Kilmer, B., G. Midgette, and C. Saloga. "Back in the National Spotlight: An Assessment of Recent Changes in Drug Use and Drug Policies in the United States. Improving Global Drug Policy: Comparative Perspectives and UNGASS 2016." Foreign Policy at Brookings. (2016). Available http://www.brookings.edu/~/media/Research/Files/Papers/2015/04/global-drug-policy/Kilmer—United-States-final-2.pdf?la=en

Kirkwood, C., and S. Melton. "Insomnia, Drowsiness and Fatigue." In *Handbook of Nonprescription Drugs,* edited by D. Krinsky, 867–883. Washington, DC: American Pharmacists Association, 2012.

Kishi, T., Y. Matsuda, N. Iwata, and C. Correll. "Antipsy-chotics for Cocaine or Psychostimulant Dependence: Systematic Review and Meta-analysis of Randomized, Placebo-controlled Trials." *Journal of Clinical Psychiatry* 74 (2013): 1169–1180.

Kloner, R., and S. Rezkalla. "Cocaine and the Heart." *New England Journal of Medicine* 348 (2003): 487–488.

Ladd, G., and N. Petry. "Antisocial Personality in Treatment-Seeking Cocaine Abusers: Psychosocial Functioning and HIV Risk." *Journal of Substance Abuse Treatment* 24 (2003): 323–330.

Learn.Genetics. "Ritalin and Cocaine: The Connection and the Controversy." Genetic Science Learning Center, University of Utah. 2016. Available http://learn.genetics.utah.edu/content/addiction/ritalin/

Legal Herbal Drugs. 2013. Available http://legalherbaldrugs.net/

Levant, R., M. Parent, E. McCurdy, and T. Bradstreet. "Moderated Mediation of the Relationships Between Masculinity Ideology, Outcome Expectations, and Energy Drink Use." *Health Psychology* 34 (2015): 1100–1106.

Lin, R. "Q&A ER Doctors: Drug-Fueled Raves Too Dangerous and Should Be Banned." *Los Angeles Times.* (10 August 2015). Available http://www.latimes.com/local/lanow/la-me-ln-why-some-er-doctors-want-to-end-raves-in-los-angeles-county-20150810-story.html

Longmire, S. "Historic METH Bust At Arizona Border Crossing Could Signal Cartel Conflict." Breitbart. 15 February 2016. Available http://www.breitbart.com/big-government/2016/02/15/historic-meth-bust-at-arizona-border-crossing-could-be-major-cartel-signal/

Luscher, C. "Drugs of Abuse." In *Basic & Clinical Pharmacology*, 13th ed., edited by B. Katzung and A. Trevor, 552–566. New York: McGraw Hill Medical, 2015.

Lutz, A. "Here's How Much Caffeine People Consume at Every Age." *Business Insider* (6 April 2015). Available http://www.businessinsider.com/caffeine-consumption-by-age-2015-4

Mandt, B., L. Copenhagen, N. Zahniser, and R. Allen. "Escalation of Cocaine Consumption in Short and Long Access Self-Administration Procedures." *Drug and Alcohol Dependence* 149 (2015): 166–172.

Massanella, M., S. Gianella, R. Schrier, J. M. Dan, J. Pérez-Santiago, M. F. Oliveira, D. D. Richman, S. J. Little, C. A. Benson, E. S. Daar, M. P. Dube, R. H. Haubrich, D. M. Smith, and S. R. Morris. "Methamphetamine use in HIV-Infected Individuals Affects T-Cell Function and Viral Outcome During Suppressive Antiretroviral Therapy." *Scientific Reports* 5 (2015): 13179. Available http://www.nature.com/articles/srep13179

Mayo Clinic. "Cocaine (Topical Route)." 15 December 2010. Available http://www.mayoclinic.com/health/drug-information/DR600467

Mayo Clinic. "Methylphenidate (Oral Route)." 2016. Available http://www.mayoclinic.org/drugs-supplements/methylphenidate-oral-route/proper-use/drg-20068297

McCaffrey, B. "Methamphetamine." ONDCP, Drug Policy Information Clearinghouse. NCJ-1756677 (May 1999): 1–3.

MedicineNet. "Caffeine." 2010. Available http://www.medicinenet.com/caffeine/article.htm

MedlinePlus. "Cocaine Withdrawal." U.S. National Library of Medicine. 2007. Available http://vsearch.nlm.nih.gov/vivisimo/cgi-bin/query-meta?v%3Aproject=medlineplus&query=cocaine+withdrawal+

MedlinePlus. "Cocaine Withdrawal." 15 November 2010. Available http://www.nlm.nih.gov/medlineplus/ency/article/000947.htm

Melnikova, N., M. Orr, J. Wu, B. Christensen. "Injuries from Methamphetamine-Related Chemical Incidents—Five States, 2001–2012." *Morbidity and Mortality Weekly Report* 64 (2015): 909–912. Available http://www.cdc.gov/mmwr/preview/mmwrhtml/mm6433a4.htm

Mendelson, J., and N. Mello. "Management of Cocaine Abuse and Dependence." *New England Journal of Medicine* 334 (1996): 965–972.

Mental Health Daily. "How to Increase Dopamine Levels." 17 April 2015a. Available http://mentalhealthdaily.com/2015/04/17/how-to-increase-dopamine-levels/

Mental Health Daily. "How Long Does Caffeine Stay in Your System?" 21 October 2015b. Available http://mentalhealthdaily.com/2015/10/21/how-long-does-caffeine-stay-in-your-system/

Mental Health Daily. "Stimulant Psychosis: Causes, Symptoms, & Treatment." 20 April 2015c. Available http://mentalhealthdaily.com/2015/04/20/stimulant-psychosis-causes-symptoms-treatment/

METH Project. "Clandestine Laboratories." Southern METH Project. 2015. Available http://somp.kobi5.com/Methamphetamine FAQ

Miller, E. "Addict-Turned-Convict: 'We Are the Unwanted." *Deseret News* 166 (10 January 2016): B4.

Miller, H., and D. Longtin. "Death by Dietary Supplement." Forbes.com. 23 March 2010. Available http://www.forbes.com/2010/03/23/dietary-supplemetns-herbal-fda-opinions-contributors-henry-i-miller-david-longtin.html

Mothers Against Methamphetamine. "Crystal Meth: They Call It Ice." n.d. Available http://www.mamasite.net/index.php?main_page=page&id=53&chapter=0

Mozes, A. "New Findings on Coffee and Cancer Risk." Healthday. 17 August 2015. Available http://www.cbsnews.com/news/new-findings-on-coffee-and-cancer-risk/

Musto, D. "International Traffic in Coca Through the Early 20th Century." *Drug and Alcohol Dependence* 49 (1998): 145–156.

Myers, G. "Top 10 Over-the-Counter Drugs That Will Get You Higher Than Marijuana." TopTenz. 2014. Available http://www.toptenz.net/top-10-over-the-counter-drugs-that-will-get-you-higher-than-marijuana.php

Narconon. "Does Cocaine Have Withdrawal Symptoms?" 2013. Available http://www.narconon.org/drug-rehab/does-cocaine-have-withdrawal-symptoms.html

Narconon. "Methamphetamine/Meth Addiction Info." 2016a. Available http://www.narconon.org/drug-information/methamphetamine-addiction.html

Narconon. "Cocaine Information." 2016b. Available http://www.narconon.org/drug-information/cocaine-coke.html

National Association of Drug Court Professionals (NADCP). "Drug Courts Work." 2015. Available http://www.nadcp.org/learn/facts-and-figures

National Institute on Drug Abuse (NIDA). "Cocaine: Abuse and Addiction." September 2010. Available http://www.drugabuse.gov/publications/research-reports/cocaine-abuse-addiction/what-treatments

National Institute on Drug Abuse (NIDA). "DrugFacts: Cocaine." April 2013. Available https://www.drugabuse.gov/publications/drugfacts/cocaine

National Institute on Drug Abuse (NIDA). "Methamphetamine Alters Brain Structures, Impairs Mental Flexibility.' NIDA Notes (20 March 2014). Available https://www.drugabuse.gov/news-events/nida-notes/2014/03/methamphetamine-alters-brain-structures-impairs-mental-flexibility

National Institute on Drug Abuse (NIDA). "Methamphetamine." 2015. Available https://www.drugabuse.gov/drugs-abuse/methamphetamine

National Institute on Drug Abuse (NIDA). "Bath Salts." 2016a. Available http://teens.drugabuse.gov/drug-facts/bath-salts

National Institute on Drug Abuse (NIDA). "Cocaine: Abuse and Addicting." 2016b. Available http://www.drugabuse.gov/publications/research-reports/cocaine-abuse-addiction

Newman, T. "Amphetamine: Uses, Side Effects and Contraindications." MNT. 18 March 2016. Available http://www.medicalnewstoday.com/articles/221211.php

Nierenberg, C. "10 Interesting Facts About Caffeine." Live Science. 5 October 2015. Available http://www.livescience.com/52383-interesting-facts-about-caffeine.html

Nonacs, R. "Prenatal Cocaine Exposure and Its Effect on the Developing Brain." MGH Center for Women's Mental Health. 12 May 2015. Available https://womensmentalhealth.org/posts/prenatal-cocaine-exposure-and-its-effect-on-the-developing-brain/

Nordrum, A. "Flakka Drug Addiction 2015: Scientists Say Dangerous Recreational Drug Is as Addictive as Bath Salts." International Business Times. (17 November 2015). Available http://www.ibtimes.com/flakka-drug-addiction-2015-scientists-say-dangerous-recreational-drug-addictive-bath-1927327

Northrop, N., and B. Yamamoto. "Methamphetamine Effects on Blood-Brain Barrier Structure and Function." Frontiers of Neuroscience. (4 March 2015). Available http://journal.frontiersin.org/article/10.3389/fnins.2015.00069/full

Nowak, D., and A. Jasionowski. "Analysis of the Consumption of Caffeinated Energy Drinks Among Polish Adolescents." International Journal of Environmental Research and Public Health 12 (2015): 7910–7921.

Nutt, D. "Making a Medicine Out of MDMA." British Journal of Psychiatry 204 (2015): 4–6.

Oregon Health Science University (OHSU). OHSU"Researchers Discover How Cocaine, Amphetamines Disrupt the Brain's Normal Functioning." Oregon Health Science University 2015. Available https://www.ohsu.edu/xd/about/news_events/news/2015/05-11-researchers-discover-how.cfm

Oremus, W. "The New Stimulus Package." Slate. 27 March 2013. Available http://www.slate.com/articles/technology/superman/2013/03/adderall_ritalin_vyvanse_do_smart_pills_work_if_you_don_t_have_adhd.html

PBS Newshour. "Cocaine: How 'Miracle Drug' Nearly Destroyed Sigmund Freund, William Halsted." 17 October 2011. Available http://www.pbs.org/newshour/bb/health-july-dec11-addiction_10-17/

Penn, M. "Addict-Turned-Convict: "We Are the Unwanted." JuneauEmpire.com (2016) Available http://juneauempire.com/state/2015-11-22/addict-turned-convict-we-are-unwanted

Pennings, E., A. Leccese, and F. Wolff. "Effects of Concurrent Use of Alcohol and Cocaine." Addiction 97 (2002): 773–783.

Pharmacy Times. "Reduction in Meth Lab Seizures Following Adoption of Meth-Resistant NEXAFED." 2015. Available http://www.pharmacytimes.com/publications/issue/2015/January2015/R681_January 2015

Platt, D., J. Rowlett, and R. Spealman. "Behavioral Effects of Cocaine and Dopaminergic Strategies for Preclinical Medication Development." Psychopharmacology 163 (2002): 265–282.

Power, M. "Ecstasy in 2015." Mixbag. 2015. Available http://www.mixmag.net/feature/ecstasy-in-2015

Ramsey, L. "9 Crazy Ways to Get a Caffeine Fix Without Taking a Single Sip of Coffee." Business Insider. (21 September 2015). Available http://www.businessinsider.com/ways-to-get-caffeine-without-coffee-2015-9

Randall, T. "Ecstasy-Fueled 'Rave' Parties Become Dances of Death for English Youths." Journal of the American Medical Association 268 (1992a): 1505–1506.

Randall, T. "'Rave' Scene, Ecstasy Use, Leap Atlantic." *Journal of the American Medical Association* 268 (1992b): 1506.

Recovery.org. "Long Term Effects of Crystal Meth Abuse." January 2015. Available http://www.recovery.org/forums /discussion/285/long-term-effects-of-crystal-meth -abuse

RehabPathway. "Crack Addiction and Treatment." n.d. Available https://www.rehabpathway.com/crack/

Ricker, R., and V. Nicolino. "Adderall: The Most Abused Prescription Drug in America." Huffington Post. 21 June 2010. Available http://www.huffingtonpost .com/dr-ronald-ricker-and-dr-venus-nicolino/adderall -the-most-abused_b_619549.html

Roberts, T. "Built for Speed?" The Vaults of Erowid. 2015. Available https://www.erowid.org/chemicals/meth /meth_writings1.shtml

Sampson, Z. "Detectives See More 'One-Pot' Methamphetamine Manufacturing." *Tampa Bay Times.* (29 March 2016). Available http://www.tampabay.com/news /publicsafety/crime/detectives-see-more-one-pot -methamphetamine-manufacturing/2224238

Science Daily. "Crack and Cocaine Use a Significant HIV Risk Factor for Teens." 1 April 2010. Available http://www .sciencedaily.com/releases/2010/03/100331141006 .htm

Shapefit. "Caffeine in Energy Drinks—How Much Caffeine Is in Your Drink?" n.d. Available http://www.shapefit .com/diet/caffeine-energy-drinks.html

Skomorowsky, A. "How Molly Works in the Brain." *Scientific American.* (10 March 2015). Available http://www.scientificamerican.com/article/how -molly-works-in-the-brain/

SoberRecovery. "Cocaine Street Names." 12 March 2015. Available http://www.soberrecovery.com/addiction /cocaine-street-names/

Sofuoglu, M., S. Dudish-Poulsen, S. Brown, and D. Hatsukami. "Association of Cocaine Withdrawal Symptoms with More Severe Dependence and Enhanced Subjective Response to Cocaine." *Drug and Alcohol Dependence* 69 (2003): 273–282.

Sprague, J., A. Harrod, and A. Teconchuk. "The Pharmacology and Abuse Potential of Ephedrine." *Pharmacy Times* (May 1998): 72–80.

Stewart. S. "Mexico's Cartels and the Economics of Cocaine." *Security Weekly* (3 January 2013). Available https://www.stratfor.com/weekly/mexicos-cartels-and -economics-cocaine

Stocker, S. "Cocaine Activates Different Brain Regions for Rush Versus Craving." *NIDA Notes* 13 (1999): 7–10.

Storebo, O. J., H. B. Krogh, E. Ramstad, C. R. Moreira-Maia, M. Holmskov, M. Skoog, T. Danvad Nilausen, F. L. Magnusson, M. Zwi, D. Gillies, S. Rosendal, C. Groth, K. Buch Rasmussen, D. Gauci, R. Kirubakaran, B. Forsbøl, E. Simonsen, and C. Gluud. "Methylphenidate for Attention-Deficit/Hyperactivity Disorder in Children and Adolescents." *BMJ* 351 (2015): 351. Available http://www.bmj.com/content/351/bmj.h5203

Substance Abuse and Mental Health Services Administration (SAMHSA). "Medical Aspects of Stimulant Use Disorders." SAMHSA/CSAT Treatment Protocols. 2010. Available http://www.ncbi.nlm.nih.gov/books/NBK64323/

Substance Abuse and Mental Health Services Administration (SAMHSA). *Treatment Episode Data Set (TEDS): 2003–2013.* National Admissions to Substance Abuse Treatment Services. BHSIS Series X-XX, HHS Publication No. (SMA) XX-XXXX. Rockville, MD: Substance Abuse and Mental Health Services Administration, 2015. Available http://www.samhsa.gov/data/sites /default/files/2003_2013_TEDS_National/2003 _2013_Treatment_Episode_Data_Set_National.pdf

The Economist. "Drug Supplies, Track Marks" (2 April 2016). Available http://www.economist.com/news /science-and-technology/21695861-chemists-find -previously-unknown-sources-cocaine-track-marks

TheGoodDrugsGuide.com. "Mixing." n.d. Available http://www.thegooddrugsguide.com/methamphetamine /mixing.htm

Thornton, K. "Report Finds METH Epidemic in Full Force in San Diego County." United States Department of Justice. (30 November 2015). Available https://www.justice.gov/usao-sdca/pr/report-finds -meth-epidemic-full-force-san-diego-county

Today Health. "Teen Girl Dies of 'Caffeine Toxicity' After Downing 2 Energy Drinks." 21 March 2012. Available http://www.today.com/health/teen-girl-dies-caffeine -toxicity-after-downing-2-energy-drinks-506441

United Nations Office on Drugs and Crime (UNODC). *World Drug Report 2009.* Vienna: United Nations Office on Drugs and Crime, 2009.

United Nations Office on Drugs and Crime (UNODC). *World Drug Report 2015.* Vienna: United Nations Office on Drugs and Crime, 2015. Available https:// www.unodc.org/documents/wdr2015/World_Drug _Report_2015.pdf

U.S. Department of Justice. "Drugs of Abuse: Cocaine." Drug Enforcement Administration (2015). Available https:// www.dea.gov/pr/multimedia-library/publications /drug_of_abuse.pdf#page=47

U.S. News and World Report. "Signs of Caffeine Addiction" (17 April 2012). Available http://health .usnews.com/health-news/articles/2012/04/17 /signs-of-caffeine-addiction

Van Dam, R. "Ask the Expert: Coffee and Health." Harvard School of Public Health. 2015. Available http://www.hsph.harvard.edu/nutritionsource/2015/02/23/ask-the-expert-coffee-and-health-2/

Van Dyck, C., and R. Byck. "Cocaine." *Scientific American* 246 (1982): 128–141.

Voxxi. "Dominican Republic Emerges As Drug Trafficking Center of the Caribbean." Huffington Post. 23 January 2013. Available http://www.huffingtonpost.com/2013/01/23/dominican-republic-emerge_n_2533210.html/

Waugh, R. "MDMA 'Could Be Used to Treat Mental Illness.' Scientists Say." *Metro* (9 September 2015). Available http://metro.co.uk/2015/09/09/mdma-could-be-used-to-treat-mental-illness-scientists-say-5383241/

WebMD. "Ritalin, Uses." n.d. Available http://www.webmd.com/drugs/2/drug-9475/ritalin-oral/details

Wheeler, R. "Hooked on Caffeine?" Everyday Health. 2010. Available http://www.everydayhealth.com/addiction/hooked-on-caffeine.aspx

Whiteman, H. "Caffeine: How Does It Affect Our Health?" MNT. 28 October 2015. Available http://www.medicalnewstoday.com/articles/271707.php

Wilkinson, J. "Headache." In *Handbook of Nonprescription Drugs*, edited by D. Krinsky, 67–86. Washington, DC: American Pharmacists Association, 2012.

Winkel, B. "Real Crack Babies." Treatment Solutions Network, Connections for Recovery. 25 October 2010. Available http://www.treatmentsolutions.com/real-crack-babies/

Woolston, M. "Treatment for Methamphetamine Addiction." HealthDay. 2016. Available http://consumer.healthday.com/encyclopedia/substance-abuse-38/drug-abuse-news-210/treatment-for-methamphetamine-addiction-648262.html

Wright S. "BCSO: Police Busy with Meth 'Smurfers.' *The Daily Times* (Maryville, TN). (15 January 2015). Available http://www.thedailytimes.com/news/bcso-police-busy-with-meth-/smurfers/article_736b28ef-32cf-5439-90ab-77e24f4c8063.html

Wyatt, B. "Agassi Admits Using Crystal Meth." CNN.com. 28 October 2009. Available http://www.cnn.com/2009/SPORT/10/28/tennis.agassi.crystal.meth/index.html

Zheng, Y., et al. "An Open-Label, Self-Control, Prospective Study on Cognitive Function, Academic Performance, and Tolerability of Osmotic-Release Oral System Methylphenidate in Children with Attention-Deficit Hyperactivity Disorder." *Chinese Medical Journal* (Engl.). 128 (2015): 2988–2997.

CHAPTER 11

Tobacco

© Kondrachov Vladimir/Shutterstock, Inc.

Did You Know?

▶ Approximately 25.2% of the U.S. population age 12 or older reports current (past-month) use of a tobacco product.

▶ Tobacco use is the leading preventable cause of death in the United States.

▶ Tobacco kills approximately 480,000 U.S. citizens each year. This represents nearly one in five deaths.

▶ More than 10 times as many U.S. citizens have died prematurely from cigarette smoking than have died in all the wars fought by the United States during its history.

▶ Nicotine is just one of thousands of chemicals found in cigarette smoke.

▶ Approximately 3800 young people in the United States will begin smoking today.

▶ Several smoking cessation aids are available, including nicotine gum, patches, nasal sprays, and inhalers. In addition, newer prescription drugs are now used to help with smoking cessation.

Learning Objectives

On completing this chapter you should be able to:

⟩ Describe the social and economic costs of smoking in the United States.

⟩ Describe the history of tobacco use.

⟩ Explain how the quality of leaf tobacco has changed since the mid-1950s.

⟩ Describe the pharmacological effects of nicotine.

⟩ List several disease states caused by cigarette smoking.

⟩ Explain the consequences of environmental tobacco smoke on nonsmokers.

⟩ List several reasons individuals smoke.

⟩ List several strategies that aid in smoking cessation.

Tobacco Use: Scope of the Problem

Tobacco use is the leading preventable cause of death in the United States, accounting for an estimated 480,000 deaths per year (Centers for Disease Control and Prevention [CDC] 2015b). The impact of nicotine addiction in terms of morbidity, mortality, and economic costs to society is staggering. Smoking-related illness in the United States costs more than $300 billion each year, including nearly $170 billion for direct medical care for adults. Additional costs include more than $156 billion in lost productivity, including $5.6 billion in lost productivity due to secondhand smoke exposure (CDC 2015a). These high costs will likely continue and increase in the future because it is estimated that each day approximately 3800 people younger than age 18 start smoking, and an estimated 2100 become daily smokers (CDC 2015f).

According to the U.S. Surgeon General, every adult who dies prematurely because of smoking is replaced by two, new young smokers. Further, 5.6 million children alive today will ultimately die early from smoking if more is not done to reduce current smoking rates (CDC 2015c).

Although much of this chapter deals with tobacco use in the United States, it is noteworthy that tobacco is used throughout the world and that markets for tobacco sales abroad have expanded in recent years. According to the World Health Organization (WHO 2015b), tobacco is the single largest cause of preventable death. The WHO estimates that tobacco use kills 6 million people each year, of whom 5 million are users or ex-users and more than 600,000 are nonusers exposed to secondhand smoke (WHO 2015b). This is more than all deaths from human immunodeficiency virus (HIV), malaria and tuberculosis combined. If current trends continue, the number of deaths from tobacco use is projected to increase to 8 million by 2030 (WHO 2015a).

■ Current Tobacco Use in the United States

In 2014, 66.9 million Americans, or 25.2% of the population age 12 or older, reported current use of a tobacco product. Among these individuals, 2.2 million smoked tobacco in pipes, 8.7 million used smokeless tobacco, 12.0 million smoked cigars, and 55.2 million smoked cigarettes (Substance Abuse and Mental Health Services

The WHO estimates that tobacco kills 6 million people per year worldwide. Early exposure increases the chance that young people will become regular adult smokers.

Administration [SAMHSA] 2015). Approximately 31.1% of males and 19.7% of females age 12 or older were current users of any tobacco product (SAMHSA 2015).

Current cigarette smoking among individuals age 12 or older by U.S. region is as follows: approximately 23.5% of the population in the Midwest, 22.4% in the South, 16.7% in the West, and 19.8% in the Northeast. Level of educational attainment is also correlated with cigarette smoking: 29.7% of adults age 26 or older who did not complete high school smoke cigarettes, whereas only 10.4% of college graduates smoke (SAMHSA 2015). More than 264 billion cigarettes were purchased in the United States in 2014, with three companies responsible for 85% of sales: Philip Morris, Reynolds American, Inc., and Lorillard (CDC 2015a).

Several investigators have suggested that tobacco can serve as a gateway drug, that is, that its use may lead to the use of other drugs. Although this possibility remains controversial, it is noteworthy that research indicates that cigarette smokers are more likely to use illicit drugs than are nonsmokers. For example, in 2014, among persons age 12 or older, 25.2% of past-month cigarette smokers reported concurrent use of an illicit drug, compared with 6.2% of persons who were not current cigarette smokers. An association also was found with heavy drinking (15.4% of smokers vs. 3.7% of nonsmokers) and binge drinking (43.3% of current cigarette users vs. 17.6% of current nonusers; SAMHSA 2015).

■ Cigarette Smoking: A Costly Addiction

The past 25 years have been marked by a steady decline in cigarette consumption. Still, an estimated 66.9 million Americans age 12 or older smoke cigarettes (SAMHSA 2015), even though

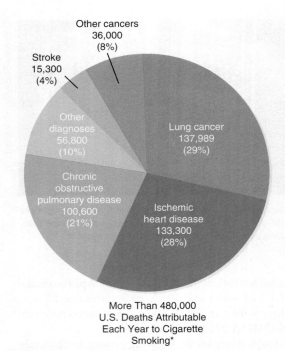

Other cancers
36,000
(8%)

Stroke
15,300
(4%)

Other
diagnoses
56,800
(10%)

Lung cancer
137,989
(29%)

Chronic
obstructive
pulmonary disease
100,600
(21%)

Ischemic
heart disease
133,300
(28%)

More Than 480,000
U.S. Deaths Attributable
Each Year to Cigarette
Smoking*

FIGURE 11.1 Annual deaths attributable to cigarette
smoking, 2005–2009.

*average annual number of deaths 2005–2009

Reproduced from Health Effects Infographics. 2016. Available http://www.cdc.gov/tobacco/infographics
/health-effects/index.htm

this single behavior will result in death or disability for many of its users.

As noted earlier, tobacco use is responsible for
approximately 480,000 deaths each year in the
United States (CDC 2015b). Between 2005 and
2009, cigarette smoking caused approximately
an annual of 133,300 deaths from ischemic heart
disease, 137,989 deaths from lung cancer, 36,000
deaths from other forms of cancer, 100,600 deaths
from chronic pulmonary obstructive disease,
15,300 deaths from stroke, and approximately
36,000 deaths from other cancers (CDC 2016b)
(see **Figure 11.1**). In fact, more deaths are caused
each year by tobacco use than by HIV, illegal drug
use, murders, alcohol use, suicides, and motor
vehicle injuries combined (CDC 2015b).

Overall mortality rates decline the longer
ex-smokers abstain from smoking. Individuals who
quit smoking, regardless of their age, increase
their life expectancy compared to those who continue to smoke. Those who quit between 25 and
34 years of age live approximately 10 years longer.
Individuals who quit between ages 35 and 44 live
approximately 9 years longer. Individuals who quit
between ages 45 and 54 live approximately 6 years
longer, and those who quit between ages 55 and
64 live approximately 4 years longer (National
Cancer Institute [NCI] 2014).

The History of Tobacco Use

Like alcohol, tobacco has a long history of use
in the Americas and is indigenous to the United
States. In fact, tobacco was one of the New World's
contributions to the rest of humanity. The word
tobacco may have come from *tabacco*, which was
a two-pronged tube used by the natives of Central America to take snuff. Columbus reported
receiving tobacco leaves from the natives of San
Salvador in 1492. However, the native peoples had
been smoking the leaves for many centuries before
Columbus arrived. Practically all native people—
from Paraguay to Quebec—used tobacco. The
Mayans regarded tobacco smoke as divine incense
that would bring rain in the dry season. The oldest known representation of a smoker is a stone
carving from a Mayan temple, which shows a priest
puffing on a ceremonial pipe. The Aztecs used
tobacco in folk medicine and religious ritual.

Indeed, Native Americans used tobacco in every
manner known: smoked as cigars and cigarettes
(wrapped in corn husks) and in pipes, as a syrup
to be swallowed or applied to the gums, chewed
and snuffed, and administered rectally as a ceremonial enema (O'Brien et al. 1992; Schultes 1978).

In the 1600s, Turkey, Russia, and China all
imposed death penalties for smoking. In Turkey,
smoking was introduced in the 1600s, spread in
popularity, and instantly created two camps. On
the one hand, poets praised tobacco as one of four
elements of the world of pleasure that also included
opium, coffee, and wine. On the other hand, religious leaders were violently opposed to this substance. They created the legend that tobacco grew
from Mohammed's spittle after he was bitten by a
viper, sucked out the venom, and spat.

Murad (Amurath) IV, known as Murad the
Cruel, who reigned during 1623–1640, executed
many of his subjects caught smoking.

> Whenever the Sultan went on his travels or on
> a military expedition, his halting-places were
> always distinguished by a terrible increase in
> the number of executions. Even on the battle-
> field, he was fond of surprising men in the
> act of smoking … he would punish them by
> beheading, hanging, quartering, or crushing
> their hands and feet and leaving them help-
> less between the lines.… Nevertheless, in
> spite of all the horrors of this lust [smoking]
> that seemed to increase with age, the passion
> for smoking still persisted.… Even the fear of
> death was of no avail with the passionate devo-
> tees of the habit. (Corti 1931)

The Romanov tsars publicly tortured smokers and exiled them to Siberia. The Chinese decapitated anyone caught dealing in tobacco with the "outer barbarians." Yet smoking continued to grow to epidemic proportions. Despite their opposition to anything foreign, the Chinese became the heaviest smokers in Asia, thus facilitating the later spread of opium smoking. Thus, no nation whose population has learned to use tobacco products has been successful in outlawing use or getting people to stop.

Snuffing first became fashionable in France during the reign of Louis XIII and spread throughout the European aristocracy. Snuffing was regarded as daintier and more elegant than constantly exhaling smoke. Louis XIV, however, detested all forms of tobacco, and would not permit its use in his presence. (He would have banned it, but he needed the tax revenue that tobacco brought in.) His sister-in-law, Charlotte of Orleans, was one of the few at court who agreed with him. As she wrote to her sister, "It is better to take no snuff at all than a little; for it is certain that he who takes a little will soon take much, and that is why they call it 'the enchanted herb,' for those who take it are so taken by it that they cannot go without it." Napoleon is said to have used 7 pounds of snuff per month (Corti 1931).

◼ Popularity in the Western World

When tobacco reached Europe, it was at first merely a curiosity, but its use spread rapidly. Europeans had no name for the process of inhaling smoke, so they called this "drinking" smoke. Perhaps the first European to inhale tobacco smoke was Rodrigo de Jerez, a member of Columbus's crew. He had seen people smoking in Cuba and brought the habit to Portugal. When he smoked in Portugal, his friends, seeing smoke coming from his mouth, believed he was possessed by the devil. As a result, he was placed in jail for several years (Heimann 1960; O'Brien et al. 1992).

In 1559, the French ambassador to Portugal, Jean Nicot, grew interested in this novel plant and sent one as a gift to Catherine de Medici, Queen of France. The plant was named *Nicotiana tabacum* after him.

The next several hundred years saw a remarkable increase in the use of tobacco. Portuguese sailors smoked it and left tobacco seeds scattered around the world. Over the next 150 years, the Portuguese introduced tobacco to trade with India, Brazil, Japan, China, Arabia, and Africa. Many large tobacco plantations around the world were started by the Portuguese at this time.

An early Christian religious leader, Bishop Bartolome de las Casas (1474–1566), reported that Spanish settlers in Hispaniola (Haiti) smoked rolled tobacco leaves in cigar form like the natives. When the bishop asked about this disgusting habit, the settlers replied that they found it impossible to give up.

As the use of tobacco spread, so did the controversy about whether it was bad or good. Tobacco use inspired the first major drug controversy of global dimensions. As a medicine, tobacco was at first almost universally accepted. Nicholas Monardes, in his description of New World plants (dated 1574), recommended tobacco as an infallible cure for 36 different maladies. It was described as a holy, healing herb—a special remedy sent by God to humans.

Opponents of tobacco use disputed its medicinal value. They pointed out that tobacco was used in the magic and religion of Native Americans. Tobacco was attacked as an evil plant, an invention of the devil. King James I of England was fanatically opposed to smoking. In an attempt to limit tobacco use, he raised the import tax on tobacco and also sold the right to collect the tax (Austin 1978; O'Brien et al. 1992).

Nevertheless, tobacco use increased. By 1614, the number of tobacco shops in London had mushroomed to more than 7000, and demand for tobacco usually outstripped supply. Tobacco was literally worth its weight in silver; to conserve it, users smoked it in pipes with very small bowls. Use of tobacco grew in other areas of the world as well.

In 1642, Pope Urban VIII issued a formal decree forbidding the use of tobacco in church under penalty of immediate excommunication. This decree was in response to the fact that priests and worshippers had been staining church floors with tobacco juice. One priest in Naples sneezed so hard after taking snuff that he vomited on the altar in full sight of the congregation. In response, Pope Innocent X issued another edict against tobacco use in 1650, but the clergy and the laity continued to take snuff and smoke. Finally, in 1725, Pope Benedict XIII, himself a smoker and "snuff-taker," annulled all previous edicts against tobacco (Austin 1978).

◼ History of Tobacco Use in America

Tobacco played a significant role in the successful colonization of the United States (Langton 1991). In 1610, John Rolfe was sent to Virginia to set up a tobacco industry. At first, the tobacco planted in Virginia was a native species, *Nicotiana rustica*, that was harsh and did not sell well. But in 1612, Rolfe managed to obtain some seeds of the Spanish tobacco species *Nicotiana tabacum*, and by 1613 the success of the tobacco industry and the Virginia colony was ensured.

The history of tobacco smoking in the United States is rich in terms of the tremendous number of laws, rules, regulations, and customs that have arisen around the habit of smoking. Many states have had laws prohibiting the use of tobacco by young people as well as women of any age. In the 1860s, for instance, it was illegal in Florida for anyone younger than the age of 21 to smoke cigarettes. A 20-year-old caught smoking could be taken to court and compelled to reveal his source (the cigarette "pusher"). In Pennsylvania, as in South Carolina, any child not informing on his or her cigarette supplier was a criminal.

Cigars became popular in the United States in the early 1800s. Cigar manufacturers fought the introduction of cigarettes for many years. They spread rumors that cigarettes contained opium, were made with tobacco from discarded cigar butts, were made with paper made by Chinese lepers, and so on. By about 1920, however, cigarette consumption started to exceed that of cigars.

The introduction of the cigarette-rolling machine in 1883 spurred cigarette consumption because cigarettes became less expensive. In 2014, nearly 264 billion cigarettes were sold in the United States, a decrease from 273 billion sold in 2013 (CDC 2015a).

▌ Tobacco Production

Although there are more than 60 species of tobacco, *Nicotiana tabacum* is the primary tobacco species cultivated in the United States. Its mature leaves are 1 to 2.5 feet long. The nicotine content ranges from 0.3% to 7.0%, depending on the variety, leaf position on the stalk (the higher the position, the more nicotine), and growing conditions.

After harvesting and drying, tobacco leaves are shredded, blown clean of foreign matter and stems, remoisturized with glycerine or other chemical agents, and packed in huge tobacco silos. The tobacco is stored for 1 to 2 years to age, during which time the tobacco becomes darker and loses moisture, nicotine, and other volatile substances. When aging has been completed, moisture is again added and the tobacco is blended with other varieties.

There are many types of tobacco, with varying characteristics of harshness, mildness, and flavor. Bright, also called flue-cured or Virginia, has traditionally been among the most common types used in cigarettes. (Flue-cured tobacco is cured with heat transmitted through a flue without exposure to smoke or fumes.) Developed just before the Civil War, this technique made tobacco smoke more readily inhalable.

The amount of leaf tobacco in a cigarette has declined since 1956. There are at least two reasons for this drop. The first reason is the use of reconstituted sheets of tobacco. Parts of the tobacco leaves and stems that were discarded in earlier years are now ground up; combined with many other ingredients to control factors such as moisture, flavor, and color; and then rolled out as a flat, homogenized sheet of reconstituted tobacco. This sheet is then shredded and mixed with regular leaf tobacco, thus reducing production costs. Nearly one-fourth of the tobacco in a cigarette comes from tobacco scraps made into reconstituted sheets. (See "Here and Now: What Is in Tobacco Smoke?")

A second technological advance has further reduced the amount of tobacco needed. This process, called puffing, is based on freeze-drying the tobacco and then blowing air or an inert gas, such as carbon dioxide, into it. The gas expands, or puffs up, the plant cells so they take up more space, are lighter, and can absorb additives better. Additives may include extracts of tobacco, as well as nontobacco flavors such as licorice, cocoa, fruit, spices, and floral compositions. (Licorice was first used in tobacco as a preservative around 1830 and became appreciated only later as a sweetener.) Synthetic flavoring compounds also may be used.

In the 1870s, a "cigarette girl" could roll about four cigarettes per minute by hand. When James

© Kevin Largent/Fotolia.com

Use of spittoons (placed on the floor at the ends of a table) was considered a preferment in public conduct.

Duke leased and improved the first cigarette-rolling machine in 1883, he could make about 200 cigarettes per minute. This advance was the last link in the chain of development leading to the modern American blended cigarette. By 2006, cigarette-rolling machines could roll 20,000 cigarettes per minute (Vox Technology 2015).

Tar and nicotine levels in cigarettes have dropped considerably over the years (Bartecchi, MacKenzie, and Shrier 1995; Palfai and Jankiewicz 1991). Most cigarettes today are low-tar and low-nicotine types. The filter tip, in which the filter is made of cellulose or in some cases charcoal, has also become common; the vast majority of all cigarettes sold currently in the United States have filter tips. The filter does help remove some of the harmful substances in smoke, but most, such as carbon monoxide, pass through into the mouth and lungs. The health consequences of many of the substances found in cigarettes have not been adequately analyzed.

■ Government Regulation

In the early 1960s, attitudes toward tobacco use began to change in the United States. Before this time, tobacco was perceived as being devoid of any negative consequences. After years of study and hundreds of research reports about the effects of smoking, the Advisory Committee to the U.S. Surgeon General reported in 1964 that cigarette smoking is a cause of lung cancer and laryngeal cancer in men, a probable cause of lung cancer in women, and the most important cause of chronic bronchitis. The committee stated, "[C]igarette smoking is a health hazard of sufficient importance in the United States to warrant appropriate remedial action." In 1965, Congress passed legislation setting up the National Clearinghouse for Smoking and Health. This organization had the responsibility of monitoring, compiling, and reviewing the world's medical literature on the health consequences of smoking.

This clearinghouse published reports in 1967, 1968, and 1969. The statistical evidence presented in 1969 made it difficult for Congress to avoid warning the public that smoking was dangerous to their health. Since November 1, 1970, all cigarette packages and cartons have had to carry this label: "Warning: The Surgeon General Has Determined That Cigarette Smoking Is Dangerous to Your Health." In 1984, Congress enacted legislation requiring cigarette advertisements and packages to post four distinct warnings, which were to be rotated every 3 months.

Further pressure on Congress prompted laws to be passed that prohibited advertising tobacco on radio and television after January 2, 1971. The intent was to limit the media's ability to make smoking seem glamorous and sophisticated. The loss in revenue to radio and television was enormous.

The 1979 publication *Smoking and Health: A Report of the Surgeon General* gave what was then up-to-date information on research about the effects of tobacco on cardiovascular disease, bronchopulmonary disease, cancer, peptic ulcer, and pregnancy. It also emphasized the increase in smoking by women and girls over the preceding 15 years. The 1981 U.S. Surgeon General's report, *The Changing Cigarette*, gave further information, and the 1985 report, *The Health Consequences of Smoking*, gave research findings showing the relationship among smoking in the workplace, cancer, and chronic lung disease.

Over the years, private insurance companies, as well as state and federal agencies, have paid billions of dollars to cover healthcare costs presumably resulting from diseases caused by tobacco use. A series of lawsuits has forced large tobacco companies to compensate for some of these losses. In a

HERE AND NOW

What Is in Tobacco Smoke?

Tobacco smoke contains chemicals that are harmful to smokers and nonsmokers alike. Of the more than 7000 chemicals in tobacco smoke, at least 250 are known to be harmful, including hydrogen cyanide, carbon monoxide, and ammonia. Among these 250 harmful chemicals, more than 69 have been found to be carcinogens. These carcinogens include arsenic, benzene, ethylene oxide, and vinyl chloride. Other suspected carcinogens in tobacco include formaldehyde, benzo[α]pyrene, and toluene.

Data from National Cancer Institute (NCI). "Harms of Smoking and Health Benefits of Quitting." 2014. Available http://www.cancer.gov/about-cancer/causes-prevention/risk/tobacco/cessation-fact-sheet

landmark settlement in 1998, 47 states reached an agreement with five major tobacco companies to pay a settlement estimated at exceeding $200 billion. Important features of this "Master Settlement Agreement" include the following (U.S. Department of Agriculture [USDA] 2001):

- Limitations on advertising
- Ban on cartoon characters in advertising
- Ban on "branded" merchandise
- Limitations on sponsorship of sporting events
- Disbanding of tobacco trade organizations
- Funds designated to support antismoking measures and research to reduce youth smoking

All 50 states have enacted laws that restrict the purchase, possession, and/or use of tobacco products by minors. Although no state has completely banned the sale of tobacco products through vending machines, none allow such sales to minors. In fact, many states have created additional restrictions intended to reduce youth access to vending machines. Some have banned the placement of vending machines in areas accessible to young people and allow their placement only in bars, liquor stores, adult clubs, and other adult-oriented establishments.

Since 1985, numerous other reports on smoking and health by the U.S. Surgeon General have been issued; they invariably repeat the assertions about the devastating effects of cigarette smoking.

In June 2009, President Barack Obama signed legislation that granted the Food and Drug Administration (FDA) the authority to regulate tobacco products. This law, the Family Smoking Prevention and Tobacco Control Act (Tobacco Control Act; FDA 2015), put special emphasis on youth because research indicates that most tobacco users become addicted at a young age and when they are too young to understand the risks.

The Tobacco Control Act gave the FDA broad authority over tobacco products, including the authority to regulate the manufacture, distribution, and marketing of tobacco products. Its provisions ban sales to minors, vending machine sales (except in some facilities that are available to adults only), and the sale of packages of fewer than 20 cigarettes. Further, the act banned tobacco-brand sponsorships of sports and entertainment events or other social or cultural events, as well as free giveaways of sample cigarettes and brand-name nontobacco promotional items (FDA 2015).

In August 2016, the FDA finalized a rule that extends its regulatory authority to all tobacco products, including e-cigarettes, cigars, and hookah and pipe tobacco. The rule bans free tobacco samples. It requires health warnings on roll-your-own tobacco and cigarette tobacco (FDA 2016b).

Pharmacology of Nicotine

In 1828, **nicotine** was discovered to be one component of tobacco. This alkaloid is one of more than 7000 chemicals found in the smoke from tobacco products such as cigarettes (NCI 2014). When smoked, nicotine enters the lungs and is then absorbed into the bloodstream. When chewed (**tobacco chewing**) or dipped (**snuff dipping**), nicotine is absorbed through the mucous lining of the mouth.

The amount of nicotine absorbed into the body varies according to several factors:

- The exact composition of the tobacco used
- How densely the tobacco is packed in the cigarette and the length of the cigarette smoked
- Whether a filter is used and the characteristics of the filter
- The volume of smoke inhaled
- The number of cigarettes smoked throughout the day

Depending on how tobacco is taken, the rate at which it enters the bloodstream varies widely. Cigarette smoking results in rapid distribution of nicotine throughout the body; it reaches the brain within 10 seconds of inhalation. A typical smoker will take 10 puffs on a cigarette during the 5 minutes that the cigarette is lit. Thus, a person who smokes 1½ packs (30 cigarettes) each day gets 300 "hits" of nicotine to the brain each day (National Institute on Drug Abuse [NIDA] 2016). In contrast, cigar and pipe smokers typically do not inhale the smoke; nicotine is absorbed more slowly through the lining of the mouth.

KEY TERMS

nicotine
an alkaloid derived from the tobacco plant

tobacco chewing
the absorption of nicotine through the mucous lining of the mouth

snuff dipping
placing a pinch of tobacco between the gums and the cheek

■ Effects of Nicotine on the Central Nervous System

Nicotine produces an intense effect on the central nervous system. Research has demonstrated that nicotine activates the brain circuitry in regions responsible for regulating feelings of pleasure. In particular, nicotine increases the release of the neurotransmitter dopamine in the so-called reward or pleasure pathways of the brain. This effect likely contributes to the abuse potential of the stimulant.

The pharmacokinetic properties of nicotine also enhance its abuse potential. Cigarette smoking allows nicotine to enter the brain rapidly, with drug levels peaking within 10 seconds of inhalation. The acute effects of this rapid increase in brain concentration dissipate within a few minutes, causing the smoker to continue to dose frequently throughout the day in an effort to maintain the pleasurable effects of the drug.

■ Other Effects of Nicotine

In addition to its direct effects in the brain, nicotine increases the respiration rate at low dose levels because it stimulates the receptors in the carotid artery (in the neck) that monitor the brain's need for oxygen. It also stimulates the cardiovascular system by releasing epinephrine, which increases coronary blood flow, heart rate, and blood pressure. The effect is to raise the oxygen requirements of the heart muscle. Initially, nicotine stimulates salivary and bronchial secretions; it then inhibits them.

Nicotine has been used as an insecticide, and at higher concentrations it can be extremely toxic. Symptoms of nicotine poisoning include vomiting, abdominal cramps, mental confusion, and breathing difficulty. Respiratory failure from the paralysis of muscles usually brings on death. The average smoker takes in 1 to 2 milligrams of nicotine from every cigarette (NIDA 2016).

Cigarette Smoking

Smoking leads to disease and damages nearly every organ in the body (CDC 2016a). Cigarette smokers not only tend to die at an earlier age than nonsmokers, but also have a higher probability of developing certain diseases, including cardiovascular disease, cancer, bronchopulmonary disease, and other illnesses, which are described in the following sections.

■ Cardiovascular Disease

Overwhelming evidence shows that cigarette smoking increases the risk of cardiovascular disease. Smoking causes coronary heart disease, a leading cause of death in the United States. In fact, compared with nonsmokers, smoking increases the risk of coronary heart disease two to four times. Smoking damages blood vessels and can make them thicken and grow narrower, thus promoting hypertension. Smoking can promote blood clot formation. A stroke occurs when a clot blocks the blood flow to part of the brain or when a blood vessel in or around the brain bursts; smoking increases the likelihood of a stroke by two to four times (CDC 2015b).

■ Cancer

Smoking causes an estimated 90% of all lung cancer deaths. Cigarette smoking is a major cause of cancers of the bladder, pancreas, cervix, esophagus, stomach, oral cavity, and kidney. The risk of lung cancer in men who smoke is 25 times greater than the risk for nonsmokers; the risk for women smokers is approximately 25.7 times greater than for nonsmokers (CDC 2015b).

■ Bronchopulmonary Disease

Cigarette smoking is the leading cause of bronchopulmonary disease, which includes a host of lung ailments. Lung diseases caused by smoking include chronic obstructive pulmonary disease (COPD), which includes emphysema and chronic bronchitis. Tobacco smoke can trigger asthma attacks. Smokers are 12 to 13 times more likely to die from COPD than nonsmokers (CDC 2015b).

■ Effects on Pregnancy

According to data from 24 states associated with the 2011 Pregnancy Risk Assessment and Monitoring System, approximately 10% of women reported smoking during the last 3 months of pregnancy. Of women who smoked 3 months before pregnancy, 55% quit during pregnancy. Among women who quit smoking during pregnancy, 40% relapsed within 6 months after delivery (CDC 2015e).

Women who smoke during pregnancy are at an increased risk of miscarriage. Smoking during pregnancy can cause a baby to be born prematurely or have low birth weight. It is a risk factor of sudden infant death syndrome (SIDS). Babies born to women who smoke are more likely to have certain birth defects, including a cleft palate or lip (CDC 2015e).

Cigarette smoking is a leading cause of bronchopulmonary disease.

Heavy smoking can severely damage the lungs and cause emphysema. Left, a diseased lung due to smoking. Right, a healthy nonsmoker's lung.

"Light" Cigarettes

Light cigarettes include those with cellulose acetate filters to trap tar, small holes in the filter tip to dilute smoke with air, and pores to allow toxic chemicals to escape. These are no less hazardous than regular cigarettes (NCI 2010b). Smoking machines indicate that they reduce tar levels, and thus should be of some limited benefit. However, many smokers lose this benefit because they often smoke more cigarettes per day, increase the puff number and volume, or block the filter holes with their fingers or lips (see "Here and Now: The Truth About Light Cigarettes").

HERE AND NOW
The Truth About Light Cigarettes

Many smokers choose low-tar, mild, or light cigarettes because they believe that these cigarettes may be less harmful to their health than regular or full-flavor cigarettes. Unfortunately, light cigarettes do not reduce the health risks of smoking. The only way to reduce risk to oneself and others is to stop smoking completely. Common questions concerning light cigarettes include the following:

Q. Are light cigarettes less hazardous than regular cigarettes?

A. No. Light cigarettes are no safer than regular cigarettes. According to the National Cancer Institute, tar exposure from a light cigarette can be just as high as that from a regular cigarette if the smoker takes deeper, longer, or more frequent puffs.

Q. Why would someone smoking a light cigarette take bigger puffs than with a regular cigarette?

A. Features of cigarettes that reduce the yield of machine-measured tar also reduce the yield of nicotine. Thus, smokers may take larger and more frequent puffs, inhale more deeply, or smoke extra cigarettes each day to get enough nicotine to satisfy their craving.

Q. Are machine-measured tar yields misleading?

A. Yes. The ratings cannot be used to predict how much tar a smoker will actually take in because the way the machine smokes a cigarette is not necessarily the same as how an individual smokes. Taking deeper, longer, and more frequent puffs will lead to greater tar exposure.

Q. Do light cigarettes cause cancer?

A. Yes. People who smoke any kind of cigarette are at much greater risk of lung cancer than people who do not smoke.

Data from National Cancer Institute (NCI). "'Light' Cigarettes and Cancer Risk." 2010. Available http://www.cancer.gov/about-cancer/causes-prevention/risk/tobacco/light-cigarettes-fact-sheet

Electronic Cigarettes

Electronic cigarettes (e-cigarettes) are devices designed to deliver nicotine or other substances to a user as a vapor. These products often resemble cigarettes, cigars, or pipes. For individuals who desire to use e-cigarettes without others noticing, some devices are designed to look like pens or USB memory sticks. E-cigarettes are generally composed of a rechargeable battery–operated heating element, a replaceable cartridge that may contain nicotine (or other chemicals), and an atomizer that, when heated, converts the contents of the cartridge into a vapor. The user can then inhale the vapor (FDA 2016a).

E-cigarettes have become increasingly popular among U.S. adolescents relative to regular cigarettes. In 2015, a substantially higher percentage of adolescents and high school students used e-cigarettes in the past 30 days than had smoked regular cigarettes. In particular, in 8th grade, the respective percentages were 9.5% versus 3.6%; in 10th grade, 14.0% versus 6.3%; and in 12th grade, 16.2% versus 11.4%. This is due, in part, to the perception that e-cigarettes do not harm health. Primary reasons for use include curiosity (>50%) and good flavor (40%), while approximately 10% used e-cigarettes to aid in smoking cessation (University of Michigan 2015).

The FDA has not evaluated e-cigarettes for safety or efficacy. However, in a limited study the FDA found significant quality issues that indicate that the quality-control processes used to manufacture these products are "substandard or nonexistent." In particular, the FDA found that cartridges labeled as containing no nicotine contained nicotine and that three different electronic cartridges with the same label emitted a markedly different amount of nicotine with each puff. Concerns have also been raised that any marketing of e-cigarettes to young people may lead them to try other tobacco products and may increase nicotine addiction (FDA 2016a).

Tobacco Use and Exposure Without Smoking

■ Smokeless Tobacco

Although it is customary to associate the effects of tobacco use with smoking, millions of nonsmokers experience tobacco effects through their use of smokeless tobacco products. Approximately 0.3%

of individuals age 12 or older currently use smokeless tobacco.

There are two main forms of smokeless tobacco in the United States. The first, **chewing tobacco**, comes in the form of loose leaf, a plug, or a twist. The second, **snuff**, is finely ground tobacco that can be moist or dry (NCI 2010c). Most smokeless tobacco users place the product in their cheek or between their cheek and gum. Users suck or chew the tobacco and then spit out the juices. Thus, smokeless tobacco is often called spitting tobacco.

Smokeless tobacco contains powerful chemicals that can injure tissues in the mouth and throat. The following findings have been made regarding smokeless tobacco (NCI 2010c):

- Smokeless tobacco use can lead to nicotine addiction and dependence.
- Smokeless tobacco contains at least 28 cancer-causing agents (carcinogens).
- Smokeless tobacco is strongly associated with leukoplakia, a precancerous lesion of the soft tissues in the mouth that consists of a white patch or plaque.
- Smokeless tobacco increases the risk of developing cancer of the oral cavity, esophagus, and pancreas.

Recently, new smokeless tobacco products have entered the U.S. market, including snus (a form of moist snuff) and "dissolvable" products that can take the form of breath mints or strips. These products are available in a range of flavors, which research suggests may make the products more attractive to young adults (Choi et al. 2012). These products can be more appealing than traditional smokeless tobacco products because they do not require spitting and can be used discreetly.

■ Secondhand Smoke

The health of individuals who neither smoke nor chew is also adversely affected by tobacco, specifically, through exposure to **secondhand smoke**,

KEY TERMS

chewing tobacco
tobacco leaves shredded and twisted into strands for chewing purposes

snuff
finely ground smokeless tobacco that can be moist or dry

secondhand smoke
smoke released into the air from a lighted cigarette, cigar, or pipe tip and exhaled mainstream smoke

also known as **environmental tobacco smoke (ETS)**, that is inhaled by passive nonsmokers. Secondhand smoke includes a mixture of smoke that comes directly from the lighted tip of a cigarette, cigar, or pipe and smoke that has been exhaled (CDC 2015d). Passive smoking refers to nonsmokers' inhalation of tobacco smoke. Studies of smoking and its effects have directed increased attention to secondhand smoke because smokers and nonsmokers alike breathe in the burning tobacco smoke that pollutes the air. This type of smoke contains thousands of chemicals, including approximately 70 carcinogens (CDC 2015d).

Exposure to secondhand smoke has serious health consequences. Since 1964, approximately 2,500,000 nonsmokers have died from health problems caused by exposure to secondhand smoke. Breathing secondhand smoke has immediate harmful effects on the cardiovascular system of nonsmokers. It is estimated that secondhand smoke caused nearly 34,000 heart disease deaths each year during 2005–2009 among adult nonsmokers in the United States (CDC 2015d).

In addition to increased risk of cardiovascular disease, secondhand smoke causes significant respiratory problems. During 2005–2009, secondhand smoke exposure caused an estimated 7300 lung cancer deaths annually among adult nonsmokers in the United States (CDC 2015d).

Of note, children are particularly vulnerable to secondhand smoke. In children, it contributes to ear infections, more frequent and severe asthma attacks, and an increased risk for SIDS (CDC 2015d).

Reasons for Smoking and the Motivation to Quit

▪ Reasons for Smoking

Nicotine dependency through cigarette smoking is not only one of the most common forms of drug addiction, but also one responsible for numerous deaths. As noted previously, in the United States more deaths each year are caused by tobacco use than by HIV, illegal drug use, murders, alcohol use, suicides, and motor vehicle injuries

combined. Tobacco use continues despite the fact that, since the 1960s, medical research and government assessments have clearly proved that smoking leads to premature death.

If one asks tobacco users why they smoke, their answers are often quite similar:

- It is relaxing.
- It decreases the unpleasant effects of tension, anxiety, and anger.
- It satisfies the craving.
- It is a habit.
- It provides stimulation, increased energy, and arousal.
- It allows the manipulation of objects that have become satisfying habits (the cigarette, pipe, and so on).

In addition,

- Parents and/or siblings smoke.
- A close friend or boyfriend/girlfriend smokes.

Tobacco use fosters dependence for a number of reasons:

- The habit can be rapidly and frequently reinforced by inhaling tobacco smoke.
- The rapid metabolism and clearance of nicotine allow for frequent and repeated use, which is encouraged by the rapid onset of withdrawal symptoms.
- Smoking has complex pharmacological effects—both central and peripheral—that may satisfy a variety of the needs of the smoker.
- Some groups offer psychological and social rewards for use, especially the peer groups of young people.
- Smoking patterns can be generalized; that is, the smoker becomes conditioned to smoke with specific activities. For example, some smokers feel the need to smoke after a meal, when driving, and so on.
- Smoking is reinforced by both pharmacological effects and ritual.
- No marked impairment in performance occurs. In fact, smoking enhances performance in some cases. (Nicotine produces a state of alertness, prevents deterioration of reaction time, and improves learning.)

These reasons may not only explain why people continue to smoke, but also reveal why it is often difficult for them to stop.

Smokers appear to regulate their intake of nicotine. For example, the smoker of a low-nicotine cigarette often smokes more and inhales more

KEY TERM

environmental tobacco smoke (ETS)
a term referring to secondhand smoke

deeply. The average one-pack-a-day smoker is estimated to self-administer thousands of pulses (one pulse per inhalation) of nicotine to nicotinic receptors in the brain per year. This rate greatly surpasses the stimulation rate of any other known form of substance abuse. A habit that is reinforced as frequently and as easily as smoking is very hard to break.

Other factors responsible for creating the addiction to nicotine follow:

- Cigarettes are readily available.
- No equipment other than a lighter or match is needed.
- Cigarettes are portable and easy to store.
- Cigarettes are legal for individuals 18 years or older.
- Other rewarding behaviors can occur while smoking (e.g., drinking, socializing, and eating).

■ Benefits of Cessation

Individuals who stop smoking greatly reduce their risk for disease and premature death. Although the health benefits are greater for people who stop at earlier ages, cessation is beneficial at all ages. For example, smokers who quit at age 40 reduce their risk of premature death from smoking-related diseases by more than 90%. Individuals who quit between the ages of 45 and 54 reduce their risk of dying prematurely by approximately 67% compared with those who continue to smoke (NCI 2014). According to the National Cancer Institute (2014), immediate health benefits of quitting smoking are significant and include the following:

- A return to normalcy of heart rate and blood pressure (which are abnormally high while smoking)
- A decline of carbon monoxide in the blood within hours
- Improved circulation, production of less phlegm, and decreased rate of coughing and wheezing within weeks
- Substantial improvements in lung function within several months

In addition, according to the CDC (2016c), cessation of smoking is associated with reductions in the following:

- The risk for lung and other types of cancer
- The risk for heart disease, stroke, and peripheral vascular disease
- Respiratory symptoms such as coughing, wheezing, and shortness of breath
- The risk of developing chronic obstructive pulmonary disease
- The risk for infertility in women
- The risk of having a low-birthweight baby

■ The Motivation to Quit

Quitting smoking is easy. I've done it a thousand times.

—Mark Twain

When habitual smokers stop smoking, particularly without the use of smoking cessation aids, they may experience a variety of unpleasant withdrawal effects, including craving for tobacco, irritability, restlessness, sleep disturbances, gastrointestinal disturbances, anxiety, and impaired concentration, judgment, and psychomotor performance. The onset of nicotine withdrawal symptoms may occur within hours or days after quitting and may persist from a few days to several months. Frustration over these symptoms leads many people to start smoking again. The intensity of withdrawal effects may be mild, moderate, or severe; it is not always correlated with the amount smoked.

The National Cancer Institute (2010) has several recommendations of alternative activities that ex-smokers might try as aids to handle the cravings associated with quitting and get through the withdrawal period. These include the following:

- Reminding oneself that cravings will pass
- Avoiding situations and activities that one normally associates with smoking
- Chewing on carrots, pickles, sunflower seeds, apples, celery, or sugarless gum or hard candy as a substitute for smoking so as to keep one's mouth occupied and thus perhaps diminish the psychological craving to smoke
- Repeatedly taking a deep breath through one's nose and exhaling slowly through one's mouth

Of note, studies in two Canadian and 20 U.S. communities demonstrated that employees who work in environments that implemented smoke-free policies—policies that completely eliminate smoking in indoor public places and work areas—were almost twice as likely to stop smoking than those who worked in settings that permitted smoking everywhere. Further, adolescents who work in smoke-free environments are less likely to become smokers (CDC 2016d and references therein).

In addition to behavioral modifications, several pharmacological interventions are available to aid in smoking cessation. These include nicotine replacement therapy (e.g., nicotine gums, patches, lozenges, inhalers, or sprays) and agents such as bupropion (Zyban) and varenicline (Chantix).

NICOTINE GUM

Nicotine gum can be purchased over the counter without a prescription. Chewing the gum allows for the rapid absorption of nicotine through the mucous membranes of the mouth. Users chew the gum until noting a peppery taste, and then hold it against the cheek to permit faster absorption. The user will chew on and off for about 20 to 30 minutes.

Significant advantages afforded by nicotine gum are that it is easy to use and allows the user to control the dose of nicotine by controlling the number of pieces chewed each day. Individuals gradually decrease the number of pieces chewed each day, with a goal of complete abstinence from the drug. Side effects of the gum can include a bad taste, throat irritation, nausea (if the gum is swallowed), jaw discomfort (if chewed too rapidly), and racing heartbeat.

NICOTINE PATCHES

Nicotine patches, also known as *transdermal nicotine systems*, are available without a prescription. The patch, which is directly applied and worn on the skin, releases a continuous flow of small doses of nicotine to quell the desire for cigarette-provided nicotine. The method of delivering nicotine to the skin reduces the withdrawal symptoms as the smoker attempts to quit. As the nicotine doses are lowered over a course of weeks, the smoker is weaned away from nicotine. The most common side effects are mild skin irritations such as redness and itching.

A transdermal patch, an example of a popular therapy for quitting smoking.

NICOTINE NASAL SPRAYS, INHALERS, AND LOZENGES

Nicotine nasal sprays rapidly deliver nicotine to the bloodstream as it is absorbed through the membranous lining of the nasal passages. These are easy to use and give immediate relief of withdrawal symptoms. The most common side effects of using the spray include coughing, sinus irritation, runny nose, watery eyes, sneezing, and throat irritation. It is generally not recommended for individuals with asthma, allergies, or other pulmonary problems.

A nicotine inhaler consists of a small plastic tube that contains a nicotine plug. When the user puffs on the inhaler, the plug provides nicotine vapor into the mouth. One advantage to the inhaler is that the action of puffing mimics some of the behaviors associated with smoking. Side effects associated with its use include coughing and throat irritation.

Nicotine lozenges are alternatives to sprays and inhalers. Potential side effects can include sore throat and heartburn.

Nicotine lozenges are available without a prescription. In the United States, nicotine inhalers and nasal sprays are available by prescription only (U.S. Department of Health and Human Services, 2016).

VARENICLINE AND BUPROPION

Varenicline acts at receptors in the brain affected by nicotine. Common side effects include nausea, constipation, vomiting, difficulty sleeping, and/or strange dreams. Other serious side effects can include changes in behavior, depressed mood, hostility, and suicidal thoughts.

Bupropion also helps patients to abstain from smoking by acting at brain nicotine receptors. Noteworthy, this agent is also used as an antidepressant. Its side effects can include dry mouth, headaches, and dizziness. Other serious potential side effects can include changes in behavior, depressed mood, hostility, suicidal thoughts, seizures, and irregular heartbeat.

Smoking Prohibition Versus Smokers' Rights

In response to the banning of smoking from certain public facilities throughout the United States, people who want to continue smoking have formed action groups to press their right to

HERE AND NOW

Taxing Cigarettes and Saving Lives

State and federal excise taxes on cigarettes increased moderately between 1970 and 2014, but the cost per pack steeply increased during that time period. In 1970, the average cost and tax per pack were $0.38 and $0.18, respectively. In 2014, the average cost per pack was $6.19, and the average tax per pack was $2.56. According to the U.S. Congressional Budget Office (CBO), a $0.50 increase in tax on cigarettes may have a large impact on public health. The CBO estimates that such a hike in the federal cigarette tax could result in an additional 3 million nonsmokers by 2085 by preventing the initiation of smoking or promoting cessation. This figure includes approximately 200,000 people who would have otherwise died from smoking-related causes before 2085.

Data from Centers for Disease Control and Prevention (CDC). "Trends in State and Federal Cigarette Tax and Retail Price—United States, 1970-2014." 2016. Available http://www.cdc.gov/tobacco/data_statistics/tables/economics/infographics/index.htm; and Congressional Budget Office (CBO). "Raising the Excise Tax on Cigarettes: Effects on Health and the Federal Budget. 2012. Available http://www.cbo.gov/sites/default/files/cbofiles/attachments/06-13-Smoking _Reduction.pdf

smoke. Although these groups have made some modest gains, the trend toward restricting and banning cigarette smoking remains very strong. Antismoking groups have been highly successful in their own efforts, and restrictions on the sale of cigarettes and tobacco products remain very tight. Many states ban smoking in worksites, restaurants, and bars.

LEARNING PORTFOLIO

Discussion Questions

1. If smoking is the most preventable cause of disease and premature death in the United States, why do people continue to smoke?
2. How effective are the health warning labels on cigarette packages?
3. List and define the diseases that cigarette smokers are most likely to contract.
4. What effects does maternal smoking have on the fetus?
5. Why is smokeless tobacco perceived as safer than other forms of tobacco?
6. Who is most likely to smoke and why?
7. Why do people who smoke become dependent on tobacco?
8. Assess the major methods for quitting smoking. Which methods are most likely to succeed?
9. Do you think smokers should have the right to smoke in public places? Explain.

Summary

1. Nicotine is a highly addictive substance.
2. Approximately 25.2% of the U.S. population age 12 or older reports current use of a tobacco product.
3. Nicotine is the substance in tobacco that causes dependence. This drug initially stimulates and then depresses the central nervous system.
4. The amount of tobacco absorbed varies according to five factors: (a) the exact composition of the tobacco being used, (b) how densely the tobacco is packed in the cigarette and the length of the cigarette smoked, (c) whether a filter is used and the characteristics of the filter, (d) the volume of the smoke inhaled, and (e) the number of cigarettes smoked throughout the day.
5. Cigarette smoking is an addiction that is costly in several ways. For instance, each year approximately 480,000 deaths in the United States are attributed to cigarette smoking.
6. Chewing tobacco and snuff are types of smokeless tobacco products that are commonly referred to as "spitting tobacco." Chewing tobacco consists of tobacco leaves that are shredded and twisted into strands and then either chewed or placed in the cheek between the lower lip and gum. Snuff is finely ground smokeless tobacco that can be moist or dry.
7. Cigarette smokers tend to die at an earlier age than nonsmokers. They also have a greater probability of contracting various illnesses, including various types of cancers, chronic bronchitis and emphysema, diseases of the cardiovascular system, and peptic ulcers. In addition, smoking has adverse effects on pregnancy and may harm the fetus.

References

Austin, G. A. *Perspectives on the History of Psychoactive Substance Use.* Washington, DC: National Institute on Drug Abuse, 1978.

Bartecchi, C. E., T. D. MacKenzie, and R. W. Shrier. "The Global Tobacco Epidemic." *Scientific American* (May 1995): 49.

Centers for Disease Control and Prevention (CDC). "Economic Facts About U.S. Tobacco Production and Use." 2015a. Available http://www.cdc.gov/tobacco/data_statistics/fact_sheets/economics/econ_facts/index.htm

Centers for Disease Control and Prevention (CDC). "Health Effects of Cigarette Smoking." 2015b. Available http://www.cdc.gov/tobacco/data_statistics/fact_sheets/health_effects/effects_cig_smoking/

Centers for Disease Control and Prevention (CDC). "Let's Make the Next Generation Tobacco-Free. Your Guide to the 50th Anniversary Surgeon General's Report on Smoking and Health." 2015c. Available http://www.surgeongeneral.gov/library/reports/50-years-of-progress/consumer-guide.pdf

Centers for Disease Control and Prevention (CDC). "Secondhand Smoke Facts." 2015d. Available http://www.cdc.gov/tobacco/data_statistics/fact_sheets/secondhand_smoke/general_facts/

Centers for Disease Control and Prevention (CDC). "Tobacco Use and Pregnancy." 2015e. Available http://www.cdc.gov/reproductivehealth/maternalinfanthealth/tobaccousepregnancy/index.htm

Centers for Disease Control and Prevention (CDC). "Youth and Tobacco Use." 2015f. Available http://www.cdc.gov/tobacco/data_statistics/fact_sheets/youth_data/tobacco_use/index.htm

Centers for Disease Control and Prevention (CDC). "Fast Facts." 2016a. Available http://www.cdc.gov/tobacco/data_statistics/fact_sheets/fast_facts/index.htm

Centers for Disease Control and Prevention (CDC). "Health Effects Infographics." 2016b. Available http://www.cdc.gov/tobacco/data_statistics/tables/health/infographics/index.htm

Centers for Disease Control and Prevention (CDC). "Quitting Smoking." 2016c. Available http://www.cdc.gov/tobacco/data_statistics/fact_sheets/cessation/quitting/

Centers for Disease Control and Prevention (CDC). "Smoke-free Polices Reduce Smoking." 2016d. Available http://www.cdc.gov/tobacco/data_statistics/fact_sheets/secondhand_smoke/protection/reduce_smoking/

Choi, K., L. Fabian, N. Mottey, A. Corbett, and J. Forster. "Young Adults' Favorable Perceptions of Snus, Dissolvable Tobacco Products, and Electronic Cigarettes: Findings from a Focus Group Study." *American Journal of Public Health* 102(11) (2012): 2088–2093.

Corti, E. C. *A History of Smoking.* London: Harrap and Company, 1931.

Food and Drug Administration (FDA). "Tobacco Control Act." 2015. Available http://www.fda.gov/TobaccoProducts/GuidanceComplianceRegulatoryInformation/ucm246129.htm

Food and Drug Administration (FDA). "E-Cigarettes: Questions and Answers." 2016a. Available http://www.fda.gov/ForConsumers/ConsumerUpdates/ucm225210.htm

Food and Drug Administration (FDA). "The Facts on the FDA's Final Tobacco Rule." 2016b. Available: http://www.fda.gov/ForConsumers/ConsumerUpdates/ucm506676.htm

Heimann, R. K. *Tobacco and Americans.* New York: McGraw-Hill, 1960.

Langton, P. A. *Drug Use and the Alcohol Dilemma.* Boston: Allyn and Bacon, 1991.

National Cancer Institute (NCI). "How to Handle Withdrawal Symptoms and Triggers When You Decide to Quit Smoking." 2010a. Available http://www.cancer.gov/cancertopics/factsheet/Tobacco/symptoms-triggers-quitting

National Cancer Institute (NCI). "Light Cigarettes and Cancer Risk" 2010b. Available http://www.cancer.gov/about-cancer/causes-prevention/risk/tobacco/light-cigarettes-fact-sheet

National Cancer Institute (NCI). "Smokeless Tobacco and Cancer." 2010c. Available http://www.cancer.gov/cancertopics/factsheet/Tobacco/smokeless

National Cancer Institute (NCI). "Harms of Smoking and Health Benefits of Quitting." 2014. Available http://www.cancer.gov/about-cancer/causes-prevention/risk/tobacco/cessation-fact-sheet; http://www.cancer.gov/cancertopics/factsheet/Tobacco/cessation

National Institute on Drug Abuse (NIDA). "Tobacco/Nicotine." 2016. NIH Publication Number 16-4342. Available https://www.drugabuse.gov/publications/research-reports/tobacco/letter-director

O'Brien, R., S. Cohen, G. Evans, and J. Fine. *The Encyclopedia of Drug Abuse,* 2nd ed. New York: Facts on File and Greenspring, 1992.

Palfai, T., and H. Jankiewicz. *Drugs and Human Behavior.* Dubuque, IA: William C. Brown, 1991.

Schultes, R. E. "Ethnopharmacological Significance of Psychotropic Drugs of Vegetal Origin." In *Principles of Psychopharmacology,* 2nd ed., edited by W. G. Clark and J. del Guidice, 41–70. New York: Academic Press, 1978.

Substance Abuse and Mental Health Services Administration (SAMHSA). "Cigarette Smoking Decreases Among

All Adults Except Those Aged 26 to 34." 2013. Available http://www.samhsa.gov/data/spotlight/Spot100-tobacco .pdf

Substance Abuse and Mental Health Services Administration (SAMHSA), Center for Behavioral Health Statistics and Quality. *Results from the 2014 National Survey on Drug Use and Health: Detailed Tables.* 2015. Available http://www.samhsa.gov/data/sites/default/files/NSDUH -DetTabs2014/NSDUH-DetTabs2014.pdf

U.S. Department of Agriculture (USDA), Economic Research Service. "Trends in the Cigarette Industry After the Master Settlement Agreement." TBS-250-01, 2001.

U.S. Department of Health and Human Services, National Institutes of Health, National Cancer Institute. "Using Nicotine Replacement Therapy." 2016. Available https://smokefree.gov/tools-tips/medications-can-help-you-quit /using-nicotine-replacement-therapy

University of Michigan. "Most Youth Use E-cigarettes for Novelty, Flavors—Not to Quit Smoking." 2015. Available http://ns.umich.edu/new/releases/23371-most-youth-use-e-cigarettes-for-novelty-flavors-not-to-quit-smoking

Vox Technology. "What Everyone Gets Wrong About the History of Cigarettes." 2015. Available http://www.vox .com/2015/3/18/8243707/cigarette-rolling-machines

World Health Organization (WHO). "Raising Taxes on Tobacco Can Save Lives." 2015a. Available ws.com /content/who-raising-taxes-on-tobacoo-can-save-lives /2851676.html

World Health Organization (WHO). "You Hear About Tobacco Control and the WHO FCTC, but What Are They?" 2015b. Available http://http://www.who.int /features/qa/09/en/

© Elfstrom/iStockphoto.com.

CHAPTER **12**

Hallucinogens (Psychedelics)

Did You Know?

▶ Hallucinogens were abused by relatively few people in the United States until the social upheaval of the 1960s.

▶ Some hallucinogens, such as lysergic acid diethylamide (LSD), have been used by psychiatrists to assist in psychotherapy with certain patients.

▶ Ecstasy has been tested in clinical trials for its ability to treat posttraumatic stress disorder.

▶ Hallucinogens such as LSD do not tend to be physically addicting.

▶ Ketamine has been proposed as a unique antidepressant.

▶ The senses are grossly exaggerated and distorted under the influence of hallucinogens.

▶ Abuse of Ecstasy increased dramatically from 1996 to 2000 due to its popularity as a "club drug" and its use at "rave" parties; its use has since declined.

▶ For some users, hallucinogens can cause frightening, nightmarish experiences referred to as "bad trips."

▶ Phencyclidine (PCP) and ketamine were originally developed as general anesthetics, but because of their ability to cause psychosis their use in humans is either prohibited or very limited.

▶ Abuse of high doses of over-the-counter (OTC) cough medicines that contain dextromethorphan is a problem with young populations and can cause a PCP-like hallucinogenic or psychotic effect.

Learning Objectives

On completing this chapter you should be able to:

❯ Explain why hallucinogens became so popular during the 1960s.

❯ Describe how hallucinogens alter the senses.

❯ Outline how psychedelic, stimulant, and anticholinergic effects are expressed in the three principal types of hallucinogens.

❯ Describe why some psychotherapists believe that MDMA may be beneficial for their patients.

❯ Explain the reasons for Ecstasy's recent fluctuations in patterns of use.

❯ Explain how hallucinogens differ from other commonly abused drugs in terms of their addicting properties and their ability to cause dependence.

❯ Describe the effects that environment and personality have on the individual's response to hallucinogens.

❯ Explain what is meant by the term "club drugs," and describe particular problems associated with their use.

❯ Characterize how PCP differs from other hallucinogens and why it is so dangerous.

❯ Explain the similarities between PCP and ketamine.

❯ Describe the recreational and legal status of *Salvia divinorum*.

Introduction

The following is a summary of issues to be considered when caring for someone under the influence of a high dose of a hallucinogen:

> Because persons under the influence of hallucinogens may exhibit very diverse and rapidly changing behaviors ranging from euphoria to agitation and aggression, it is important to be calm and reassuring while trying to "talk them down." Patients presenting with an acute panic reaction should be placed in a quiet nonthreatening environment with minimal stimuli. In extreme situations because of potentially fatal consequences associated with the cardiovascular system, it may even be necessary to either chemically or physically restrain the person to keep him/her from self-injury or from hurting someone nearby. Hospitalization may be necessary in difficult situations to control circumstances and allow for required stabilizing therapy. (D'Orazio 2015b)

This description from an experienced treatment provider illustrates the sensory and emotional distortions that can be caused by using **hallucinogens** or **psychedelics**. The word *psychedelic* comes from the Greek root meaning "mind-revealing." In this chapter, we begin with a brief historical review of the use of hallucinogens, tracing the trend in the United States from the 1960s to today. Next, the nature of hallucinogens and the effects they produce are examined. The rest of the chapter addresses the various types of psychedelic agents—lysergic acid diethylamide (LSD), phenylethylamines (including Ecstasy), anticholinergics, natural products, and other miscellaneous substances.

The History of Hallucinogen Use

People have known and written about drug-related hallucinations for centuries. Throughout the ages, individuals who saw visions or

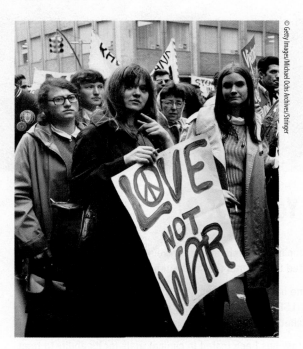

Protests against the Vietnam War in the 1960s and 1970s often included the use of hallucinogens.

experienced hallucinations were perceived as being holy or sacred, as receiving divine messages, or possibly as being bewitched and controlled by the devil. There are many indications that medicine men, shamans, witches, oracles, and perhaps mystics and priests of various groups were familiar with drugs and herbs that caused such experiences, which today are known as hallucinogens (Parrish 2015; Pollan 2015).

Before the 1960s, several psychedelic substances, such as mescaline from the peyote cactus, could be obtained from chemical supply houses with no restriction in the United States. Abuse of hallucinogens did not become a major social problem in this country until this decade of racial struggles, the Vietnam War, and violent demonstrations. Many individuals frustrated with the hypocrisy of "the establishment" tried to "turn on and tune in" by using hallucinogens as pharmacological crutches.

Psychedelic drugs became especially popular when some medical professionals, such as then-Harvard psychology professor Timothy Leary, reported that these drugs allowed users to get in touch with themselves and achieve a peaceful inner serenity. At the same time, it became well publicized that the natural psychedelics (such as mescaline and peyote) for many years had been used routinely by some Native Americans religious

© Getty Images/Michael Ochs Archives/Stringer

KEY TERMS

hallucinogens
substances that alter sensory processing in the brain, causing perceptual disturbances, changes in thought processing, and depersonalization

psychedelics
substances that expand or heighten perception and consciousness

groups for enhancing spiritual experiences. This factor contributed to the mystical, supernatural aura associated with hallucinogenic agents and added to their enticement for the so-called drop-out generation.

Due to their widespread use, it was observed that this and similar drugs may induce a form of psychosis-like schizophrenia (American Psychiatric Association [APA] 2013). The term **psychotomimetic** was coined to describe these compounds; this term means "psychosis mimicking" and is still used in medicine today. The basis for the designation is the effects of these drugs, which induce mental states that impair an individual's ability to recognize and respond appropriately to reality.

By the mid-1960s, federal regulatory agencies had become concerned with the misuse of hallucinogens and the potential emotional damage caused by these drugs. Access to hallucinogenic agents was restricted, and laws against their distribution were passed. Despite the problems associated with these psychedelics, some groups demanded that responsible use with therapeutic benefits was possible and that trained clinicians be allowed legal access to these substances (Pollan 2015). For example, some hallucinogens have been proposed for treatment of patients suffering terminal diseases such as cancer to help them deal with the fear of death (Pollan 2015).

■ The Native American Church

The hallucinogen peyote plays a central role in the ceremonies of Native Americans who follow a religion that is a combination of Christian

Peyote is used as a sacramental plant by members of the Native American Church as part of their religious ceremonies.

doctrine and Native American religious rituals. Members of this church are found as far north as Canada. They believe that God made a special gift of this sacramental plant to them so that they might commune more directly with Him. The first organized peyote church was the First-Born Church of Christ, incorporated in 1914 in Oklahoma. The Native American Church of the United States was chartered in 1918 and is the largest such group at present (approximately 100,000 to 200,000 members) (Dobner 2010; Encyclopedia Britannica 2015).

Because of the religious beliefs of the members of the Native American Church concerning the

KEY TERM

psychotomimetics
substances that cause psychosis-like symptoms

▶ CASE IN POINT

Peyote and the Rights of Native Americans

Two Native Americans living in Oregon worked for a drug rehab facility. They consumed portions of a small cactus referred to as peyote regularly as part of their religious beliefs. The counselors' practice became known by the organization they worked for, resulting in their termination. The Native Americans filed for unemployment benefits, but were denied by the state's unemployment office claiming that they were dismissed due to misconduct. The employees sued the state and lost. The case was appealed to

the U.S. Supreme Court, which ruled against the Native Americans, concluding that an individual's religious affiliation does not exclude him or her from complying with valid laws. Several years later individual states started to pass their own laws that created religious exemptions to this law. This led to the passage of the Religious Freedom Restoration Act, which requires the federal government to "not substantially burden religious exercise without compelling justification."

Sterbenz, C. "Indiana's Religious Freedom Law Was Inspired by Native Americans' Right to Smoke Peyote." *Business Insider* (3 April 2015). Available http://www.businessinsider.com/where-did-indianas-religious-freedom-law-come-from-2015-4

Courtesy of Philip Bailey.

Timothy Leary advocated the legalization of LSD in the 1960s.

powers of peyote, when Congress legislated against its use in 1965, it allowed room for religious use of this psychedelic plant. The American Indian Religious Freedom Act of 1978 was an attempt by Congress to allow the members of the Native American Church access to peyote based on constitutional guarantees of religious freedom. Due to controversy inspired by the original piece of legislation, an amendment to the 1978 act was signed in 1994, which specifically protected the use of peyote in Native American Church ceremonies. This amendment prohibits use of peyote for nonreligious purposes (Native American Church 2008). However, despite these efforts by Congress to resolve this issue, controversies continue to arise (see "Case in Point: Peyote and the Rights of Native Americans").

▌ Timothy Leary and the League of Spiritual Discovery

In 1966, 3 years after being fired by Harvard because of his controversial involvement with hallucinogens (Associated Press 1999), Timothy Leary undertook a strategy based on the right to freedom of religion ensconced in the U.S. Constitution in order to maintain legitimate access to the hallucinogen LSD. He began a religion called the League of Spiritual Discovery; LSD was the sacrament. This unorthodox religious orientation to the LSD experience was presented in a manual called *The Psychedelic Experience* (Leary, Metzner, and Alpert 1964), which was based on the *Tibetan Book of the Dead*. It became the "bible" of the psychedelic drug movement.

The movement grew, but most members used street LSD and did not follow Leary's directions.

Leary believed that the hallucinogenic experience was only beneficial under proper control and guidance. But most members of this so-called religion merely used the organization as a front to gain access to an illegal drug. Federal authorities did not agree with Leary's freedom of religion interpretation and in 1969 convicted him for possession of marijuana and LSD and sentenced him to 20 years in prison (Bio. n.d.). Before being incarcerated, Leary escaped to Algeria and wandered for a couple of years before being extradited to the United States. He served several years in jail and was released in 1976.

Even in his later years, Leary continued to believe that U.S. citizens should be able to use hallucinogens without government regulation. He died in 1996 at the age of 75 years, revered by some but despised by others (Associated Press 1999; "Many Were Lost" 1996).

Hallucinogen Use Today

Today, the use of hallucinogens (excluding marijuana) is mostly a young-adult phenomenon. Although the use rate has not returned to that of the late 1960s and early 1970s (approximately 16%), in high school seniors use in 2015 was 4.8% (Johnston 2016) (see **Table 12.1**).

The Nature of Hallucinogens

Agreement has not been reached on what constitutes a hallucinogenic agent (Cormier 2016), for several reasons. First, a variety of seemingly unrelated drug groups can produce hallucinations, delusions, or sensory disturbances under certain conditions. For example, besides the traditional hallucinogens (such as LSD), high doses of anticholinergics, cocaine, amphetamines, and steroids can also cause hallucinations (Goldsmith 2015).

In addition, responses to even the traditional hallucinogens can vary tremendously from person to person and from experience to experience (see "Signs & Symptoms: Hallucinogens"). Multiple mechanisms are involved in the actions of these drugs, which contribute to the array of responses that they can cause. These drugs most certainly influence the complex inner workings of the human mind and have been described as

TABLE 12.1 Trends in the Use of LSD and All Hallucinogens by 8th, 10th, and 12th Graders: 1994–2015

	Used During Year (%)					
	1994	1996	2006	2010	2012	2015
8th Graders						
LSD	2.4	3.5	0.9	1.2	0.8	0.9
All hallucinogens	2.7	4.1	2.1	2.2	1.6	1.3
10th Graders						
LSD	5.2	6.9	1.7	1.9	1.7	2.0
All hallucinogens	5.8	7.8	4.1	4.2	3.5	3.1
12th Graders						
LSD	6.9	8.8	1.7	2.6	2.4	2.9
All hallucinogens	7.6	10.1	4.9	5.5	4.8	4.2

Data from Johnston, L. D. "Monitoring the Future." 2016. Available http://www.monitoringthefuture.org/

psychedelic, **psychotogenic**, or psychotomimetic (Cormier 2016). The feature of hallucinogens that distinguishes them from other drug groups is their ability to alter perception, thought, and feeling in such a manner that does not normally occur except in dreams or during experiences of extreme religious exaltation (Cormier 2016). We examine these characteristics throughout this chapter.

∎ Sensory and Psychological Effects

In general, LSD is considered the prototype agent against which other hallucinogens are measured (Cormier 2016). Typical users experience several stages of sensory experiences; they can go through all stages during a single "trip" or, more likely,

will pass through only some. These stages are as follows:

1. Heightened, exaggerated senses
2. Loss of control
3. Self-reflection
4. Loss of identity and a sense of cosmic merging

LSD users describe the transitions they experience while under this potent hallucinogen as going from normal, to very colorful, to extremely

KEY TERM

psychotogenics
substances that initiate psychotic behavior

SIGNS & SYMPTOMS

Hallucinogens

Possible Signs of Use	Extreme Reactions
Heightened senses	Increased body temperature (MDMA)
Loss of control	Electrolyte imbalance
Loss of identity	Cardiac arrest
Illusions and hallucinations	A nightmare-like trip (LSD)
Altered perception of time and distance	Unable to direct movement, feel pain, or remember

Hooton, C. "Different Stages of the 9-Hour Trip to Show Its Effects." Independent (August 27, 2015). Available http://www.independent.co.uk/arts-entertainment/art/news/girl-takes-lsd-draws-herself-over-different-stages-of-the-9-hour-trip-to-show-its-effects-10474372.html

emotional and uncontrolled, to demonic, and then to becoming merged with what is outside one's head. This is reflected in a series of facial self-portraits drawn by a young lady on LSD (see Hooton 2015 for an example).

ALTERED SENSES

An associated sensation caused by LSD-like hallucinogens is **synesthesia**, a crossover phenomenon between senses. For example, sound develops visual dimensions, and vice versa, enabling the user to see sounds and hear colors. These altered sensory experiences are described as a heightened sensory awareness and relate to the first component of the psychedelic state (Sapolsky 2015).

LOSS OF CONTROL

The second feature of LSD also relates to altered sensory experiences and a loss of control (Buddy 2012). The user cannot determine whether the psychedelic trip will be a pleasant, relaxing experience or a "bad trip," with recollections of hidden fears and suppressed anxieties that can precipitate neurotic or psychotic responses. The frightening reactions may persist for a few minutes or several

KEY TERMS

synesthesia
a subjective sensation or image of a sense other than the one being stimulated, such as an auditory sensation caused by a visual stimulus

flashbacks
recurrences of earlier drug-induced sensory experiences in the absence of the drug

hours and be mildly agitating or extremely disturbing. Some bad trips can include feelings of panic, confusion, suspicion, helplessness, and a total lack of control. The following example illustrates how terrifying a bad trip can be:

> I was having problems breathing [and] my throat was all screwed up. The things that entered my mind were that I was dead and people were saying good-bye, because they really meant it. I was witnessing my own funeral. I was thinking that I was going to wake either in the back seat of a cop car or in the hospital. *(From Venturelli's files, male, age 19)*

Replays of these frightening experiences can occur at a later time, even though the drug has not been taken again; such recurrences are referred to as **flashbacks**, or hallucinogen persisting perception disorder (GoMentor n.d.). However, the frequency and severity of these experiences are controversial (Ferro 2013).

It is not clear what determines the nature of the sensory response. Perhaps it relates to the state of anxiety and personality of the user or the nature of his or her surroundings. It is interesting that Timothy Leary tried to teach his "drug disciples" that "turning on correctly means to understand the many levels that are brought into focus; it takes years of discipline, training and discipleship" ("Celebration #1" 1966). He apparently felt that, with experience and training, you could control the sensory effects of the hallucinogens. This is an interesting possibility but has never been well demonstrated.

SELF-REFLECTION

During the period when sensory effects predominate, self-reflection also occurs. While in this state, the user becomes aware of thoughts and feelings long hidden beneath the surface, forgotten, and/or repressed. Some claim that this new perspective can lead to valid insights that are useful psychotherapeutic exercises (Johnstad 2015).

Some psychotherapists have used or advocated the use of psychedelics for this purpose since the 1950s, as described many years before by Sigmund Freud, to "make conscious the unconscious" (Snyder 1974, p. 44). Although a case can be made for the psychotherapeutic use of this group of drugs, the Food and Drug Administration (FDA) has not yet approved any of these agents for psychiatric use; it has, however, approved clinical trials to study the psychedelic/stimulant drug Ecstasy

(MDMA) to evaluate if it would be useful in the treatment of posttraumatic stress disorder (PTSD). These studies are supported by an organization known as the Multidisciplinary Association for Psychedelic Studies (MAPS) and are speculated to require 10 years at a cost of $15 million to complete. If approved, the intent is to use MDMA as an adjunct to psychotherapy because of its ability to increase feelings of empathy (Wing 2015).

Although considerable caution is still needed due to the somewhat unpredictable nature of these drugs, other small studies are examining the effects of psychedelic drugs such as psilocybin and LSD to treat emotional problems such as depression in cancer patients, obsessive-compulsive disorder, and end-of-life anxiety. Some of the reported results have been encouraging, but they are very preliminary and still small-scale. Some are concerned that some of the reported benefits have been exaggerated by scientists-turned-evangelists who are anxious to make these drugs routine therapeutics. Only time will tell how, or if, the medical/scientific community will react to the "new science" that is promoted as evidence that psychedelics have an important therapeutic role to play in modern-day medicine. Clearly, this is a controversy that is far from being resolved.

LOSS OF IDENTITY AND COSMIC MERGING

The final features that set the psychedelics apart as unique drugs are the mystical-spiritual aspect of the drug experience (Buxton 2015). Because consumption of hallucinogen-containing plants has often been part of religious ceremonies, it is likely that this sense of cosmic merging and union with all humankind correlates to the exhilaratingly spiritual experiences described by many religious mystics (Buxton 2015).

The loss of identity and personal boundaries caused by hallucinogens is not viewed as being so spiritually enticing by all. In particular, for individuals who have rigid, highly ordered personalities, the dissolution of a well-organized and well-structured world is terrifying because the drug destroys the individual's emotional support. Such an individual finds that the loss of a separate identity can cause extreme panic and anxiety. During these drug-induced panic states, which in some ways are similar to schizophrenia, people have committed suicide and homicide. These tragic reactions are part of the risk of using hallucinogens and explain some of the FDA's hesitancy to legalize or authorize them for psychotherapeutic use (Horgan 2015).

■ Mechanisms of Action

As with most drugs, hallucinogens represent the proverbial "double-edged sword." These drugs may cause potentially useful psychiatric effects for many people. However, the variability in positive versus negative responses, coupled with lack of understanding as to what factors are responsible for the variables, suggests that these drugs may be dangerous for some patients and difficult to manage (Horgan 2015).

Some researchers have suggested that all hallucinogens act at a common central nervous system (CNS) site to exert their psychedelic effects. Although this hypothesis has not been totally disproven, there is little evidence to support it. The fact that so many different types of drugs can cause hallucinogenic effects suggests that multiple mechanisms are likely responsible for their actions.

The most predictable and typical psychedelic experiences are caused by LSD or similar agents. Consequently, these agents have been the primary focus of studies intended to elucidate the nature of hallucinogenic mechanisms. Although LSD has effects at several CNS sites, ranging from the spinal cord to the cortex of the brain, its effects on the neurotransmitter serotonin most likely account for its psychedelic properties. That LSD and similar drugs alter serotonin activity has been proven; how they affect this transmitter is not so readily apparent.

Although many experts believe that changes in serotonin activity are the basis for the psychedelic properties of most hallucinogens, a case can be made for the involvement of norepinephrine, dopamine, acetylcholine, and perhaps other transmitter systems as well. Only additional research will be able to sort out this complex but important issue (Kyzar, Stewart, and Kalueff 2016).

Types of Hallucinogenic Agents

Due to recent technological developments, understanding of hallucinogens has advanced. However, the classification of these drugs remains somewhat arbitrary. Many agents produce some of the pharmacological effects of the traditional psychedelics, such as LSD and mescaline.

A second type of hallucinogen includes those agents that have amphetamine-like molecular structures (referred to as *phenylethylamines*) and that possess some stimulant action. Hallucinogens in this group include drugs such as DOM (dimethoxymethylamphetamine), MDA (methylenedioxyamphetamine), MDMA (methylenedioxymethamphetamine, or Ecstasy), and likely mephedrone (methylmethcathinone). These agents vary in their hallucinogenic or stimulant properties. MDA is more like an amphetamine (stimulant), MDMA is more like LSD (hallucinogen), and the drug mephedrone has potent properties of both (Hadlock et al. 2011). In large doses, however, each of the phenylethylamines causes substantial CNS stimulation (Brock 2012).

The third major group of hallucinogens comprises the anticholinergic (antimuscarinic) drugs, which block some of the receptors for the neurotransmitter acetylcholine. Almost all drugs that antagonize these receptors cause hallucinations in high doses. Many of these potent anticholinergic hallucinogens are naturally occurring and have been known, used, and abused for millennia (D'Orazio 2015a).

❚ Traditional Hallucinogens: LSD Types

The LSD-like drugs are considered to be the prototypical hallucinogens and are used as the basis of comparison for other types of agents with psychedelic properties. Included in this group are LSD itself and some hallucinogens derived from plants, such as mescaline from the peyote cactus, psilocybin from mushrooms, dimethyltryptamine (DMT) from seeds, and myristicin from nutmeg. Because LSD is the principal hallucinogen, its origin, history, and properties are discussed in detail, providing a basis for understanding the other psychedelic drugs.

LYSERGIC ACID DIETHYLAMIDE

Lysergic acid diethylamide (LSD) is a relatively new drug, but similar compounds have existed for a long time. For example, accounts from the Middle Ages tell about a strange affliction that caused pregnant women to abort and others to develop strange burning sensations in their extremities. Today, we call this condition **ergotism** and know it is caused by eating grains contaminated by the ergot fungus. This fungus produces compounds related to LSD called the *ergot alkaloids* (National Institute on Drug Abuse [NIDA] 2007a). Besides

Courtesy of Philip Bailey.

Albert Hofmann first synthesized LSD and later proposed its use in psychotherapy.

the sensory effects, the ergot substances can cause hallucinations, delirium, and psychosis.

In 1938, Albert Hofmann, a scientist for Sandoz Pharmaceutical Laboratories of Basel, Switzerland, worked on a series of ergot compounds in a search for active chemicals that might be of medical value. Lysergic acid was similar in structure to a compound called nikethamide, a stimulant, and Hofmann tried to create slight chemical modifications that might merit further testing. The result of this effort was the production of lysergic acid diethylamide, or LSD. Hofmann's experience with this new compound gave insight into the effects of this drug (Liester 2014).

Soon after LSD was discovered, the similarity of experiences with this agent to the symptoms of schizophrenia were noted, which prompted researchers to investigate correlations between the two (Weber 2006). The hope was to use LSD as a tool for producing an artificial psychosis to aid in understanding the biochemistry of psychosis (NIDA 2001). Interest in this use of LSD has declined because it is generally accepted that LSD effects differ from natural psychoses.

The use of LSD in psychotherapy has also been tried in connection with the treatment of alcoholism, autism, paranoia, schizophrenia, depression, and various other mental and emotional disorders (Devlin 2015; Weber 2006). Even though there continues to be advocates for the therapeutic use of LSD (as discussed earlier in this chapter), the administration of LSD for clinical objectives has not been approved for general use because of its limited proven successes, legal restrictions, difficulty in obtaining the pure drug, adverse reactions to the drug (bad trips can occur under controlled as well as uncontrolled conditions), and rapid tolerance buildup in some patients.

KEY TERM

ergotism
poisoning by toxic substances from the ergot fungus *Claviceps purpurea*

However, there has been a recent resurgence in research on combining low doses of LSD with psychotherapy to treat depression, compulsive disorders, and chronic pain (Penner 2015). Researchers conducting small studies claim that for some patients the drug can be a catalyst to help change perception of problems and make the patient more responsive to the behavioral therapies (Penner 2015). No one believes that this approach will be a panacea or universally effective, and even the strongest of advocates emphasize that it is important to use only low doses for relatively short periods of time (Devlin 2015).

Nonmedical interest in LSD and related drugs began to grow during the 1950s and peaked in the 1960s, when LSD was used by millions of young Americans for chemical escape. On rare occasions, a bad trip would cause a user to feel terror and panic; these experiences resulted in well-publicized tragedies (Harvey 2014).

As with other hallucinogens, the use of LSD by teenagers declined somewhat over the 1970s and 1980s but began to rise again in the early 1990s. The reason for this rise was thought to relate to a decline in the perceived dangers of using LSD and an increase in peer approval. However, the reasons for the recent dramatic drops in LSD use remain unclear (Johnston 2016; see Table 12.1). Of high school seniors sampled in 1975, 11.3% had used LSD sometime during their life; that number declined to 8.6% in 1992, rebounded to 12.2% in 1999, and tumbled to 2.9% in 2015. LSD users are typically college or high school students, white, and middle class and consider themselves to be risk takers (Johnston 2016).

SYNTHESIS AND ADMINISTRATION

LSD is a complex molecule that requires about 1 week to be synthesized. Because of the sophisticated chemistry necessary for its production, LSD is not manufactured by local illicit laboratories but requires the skills of a trained chemist. Because of LSD's potency, it has been difficult to locate illicit LSD labs; small quantities of LSD are sufficient to satisfy the demand and can be easily transported without detection. The last publicized major LSD lab seizure in the United States was in 2000 when a Drug Enforcement Agency (DEA) raid in Kansas resulted in a temporary 95% decrease in LSD supplies (Anders 2015).

The physical properties of LSD are not distinctive. In its purified form, LSD is colorless, odorless, and tasteless. It can be purchased in several

Small quantities of LSD are applied to squares of absorbent blotter paper to be chewed or swallowed.

forms, including tiny tablets (about one-tenth the size of aspirins, called microdots), capsules, thin squares of gelatin called window panes, or more commonly dissolved and applied to paper as "blotter acid" and cut up into 0.25-inch squares for individual dosing (Partnership for Drug-Free Kids n.d.). Each square is swallowed or chewed and represents a single dose. One gram of LSD can provide approximately 10,000 individual doses and be sold on the streets for $10,000 to $100,000. Although LSD usually is taken by mouth, it is sometimes injected. It costs $1 to $10 per dose (Freeman n.d.).

PHYSIOLOGICAL EFFECTS

Like many hallucinogens, LSD is remarkably potent. A common dose today is 10 to 30 micrograms, referred to as *microdosing*, compared with a typical dose of 150 to 300 micrograms in the 1960s (see "Here and Now: Microdosing, the New Hallucinogenic Fad?"). This difference in dose likely explains why today fewer users of LSD are experiencing severe side effects (Smith 2015). In monkeys, the lethal dose has been determined to be about 5 milligrams per kilogram of body weight.

When taken orally, LSD is readily absorbed and diffused into all tissues. It passes through the placenta into the fetus and through the blood–brain barrier. The brain receives about 1% of the total dose. Within the brain, LSD is particularly concentrated in the hypothalamus, the limbic system, and the auditory and visual reflex areas. Electrodes placed in the limbic system show an "electrical storm," or a massive increase in neural activity, which might correlate with the overwhelming flood of sensations and the phenomenon of synesthesia reported by the user (Sample 2016). LSD also activates the

HERE AND NOW

Microdosing, the New Hallucinogenic Fad?

Recently, there has been a new approach to using hallucinogens such as LSD called *microdosing*. This entails the consumption of small quantities of substances like LSD and psilocybin that are 10% to 20% the doses used for typical psychedelic experiences, such as the classic "trip." Users claim that it is best to take the drugs every 4 days in order to experience "subtle internal yet profound shifts." Microdosers have reported improvements in mood, productivity, creativity, and enhanced focusing and decreased reactivity. Some have explained these results as a "rebalancing." Researchers evaluating self-reported testimonies report that the general response of users is that they "feel better and experience an actual movement towards increased health or wellness." However, as of yet there has been no reported peer-reviewed studies that investigate if

and how microdosing works. As of now, all that is known comes from anecdotal stories and personal testimonies.

© CSP_Bialasiewicz/age fotostock

Data from Gregoire, C. "Everything You Wanted to Know About Microdosing (But Were Afraid to Ask)." The Huffington Post. 13 January 2016. Available http://www.huffingtonpost.com/entry/psychedelic-microdosing-research_us_569525afe4b09dbb4bac9db8

sympathetic nervous system; shortly after the drug is taken body temperature, heart rate, and blood pressure rise; the person sweats; and the pupils of the eyes dilate. Its effects on the parasympathetic nervous system increase salivation and nausea (Liester 2014). These systemic effects do not appear to be related to the hallucinogenic properties of the drug.

The effect of LSD begins within 30 to 90 minutes after ingestion and can last up to 12 hours. Tolerance to the effects of LSD develops more rapidly and lasts longer than tolerance to other hallucinogens (Liester 2014). Tolerance develops very quickly to repeated doses, probably because of a change in sensitivity of the target cells in the brain rather than a change in its metabolism. Tolerance wears off within a few days after the drug is discontinued. Because there are no withdrawal symptoms, a person does not become physically dependent, but some psychological dependency on LSD can occur (Liester 2014).

BEHAVIORAL EFFECTS

Because LSD alters a number of systems in the brain, its behavioral effects are many and variable among individuals (Liester 2014). The following sections address common CNS responses to this drug.

Creativity and Insight

Researchers experimenting with LSD are often interested in learning whether LSD helps expand the mind, increasing insight and creativity (Liester 2014). This question is extremely difficult to answer because no one has ever determined the origin of insight and creativity. Moreover, each of us views these qualities differently.

Subjects under the influence of LSD often express the feeling of being more creative, but creative acts such as drawing and painting are hindered by the motor impairment caused by LSD. The products of artists under the influence of the drug usually prove to be inferior to those produced before the drug experience. Paintings done in LSD creativity studies have been described as reminiscent of "schizophrenic art."

In an often-cited study, creativity, attitude, and anxiety tests on 24 college students found that LSD had no objective effect on creativity, although many of the subjects said they felt they were more creative (McGlothin, Cohen, and McGlothin 1967). This paradox is noted in several studies of LSD use. The subjects believe they have more insight and provide better answers to life's problems, but they do not or cannot demonstrate this increase objectively. Overt behavior is not modified, and these new insights are short-lived unless they are reinforced by modified behavior.

In spite of these results, some researchers still contend that LSD can enhance the creative process. For example, Oscar Janigar, a psychiatrist at the University of California, Los Angeles, claimed to have determined that LSD does not produce a tangible alteration in the way a painter paints; thus, it does not turn a poor painter into a good one. However, Janigar claimed that LSD does alter the way the painter appraises the world and allows the artist to "plunge into areas where access was restricted by confines of perceptions" and consequently becomes more creative (Tucker 1987, p. 16).

Adverse Psychedelic Effects

It is important to remember that there is no typical pattern of response to LSD. The experience varies for each user as a function of the person's set, or expectations, and setting, or environment, during the experience (Liester 2014). Two of the major negative responses are described as follows (Liester 2014):

1. The psychotic adverse reaction is an intense, nightmarish experience. The subject may have complete loss of emotional control and experience paranoid delusions, hallucinations, panic attacks, psychosis, and catatonic seizures. In rare instances, some of these reactions are prolonged, lasting days.
2. The nonpsychotic adverse reaction may involve varying degrees of tension, anxiety, fear, depression, and despair but not as intense a response as the "freak-out."

A person with deep psychological problems or a strong need to be in conscious control or one who takes the drug in an unfavorable setting is more likely to have an adverse reaction than a person with a well-integrated personality. Severe LSD behavioral toxicity can be treated with tranquilizers or a sedative such as a benzodiazepine.

Perceptual Effects

Because the brain's sensory processing is altered by a hallucinogenic dose of LSD, many kinds of unusual illusions can occur. Some users report seeing shifting geometrical patterns mixed with intense color perception; others observe the movement of stationary objects, such that a speck on the wall appears as a large blinking eye or an unfolding flower. Interpretation of sounds can also be scrambled; a dropped ashtray may become a gun fired at the user, for instance. In

Courtesy of Dr. Glen Hanson.

This head was sculpted by a university student while under the influence of LSD.

some cases, LSD alters perceptions to the extent that people feel they can walk on water or fly through the air. The sensation that the body is distorted and even coming apart is another common effect, especially for novice users. Thoughts of suicide and sometimes actual attempts can be caused by use of LSD as well (NIDA 2010), although recent studies have challenged these conclusions and suggest that under some conditions LSD may even reduce psychological stress (Hendricks 2015).

Many LSD users find their sense of time distorted, such that hours may be perceived as years or an eternity. As discussed earlier, users may also have a distorted perception of their own knowledge or creativity; for instance, they may feel their ideas or work are especially unique, brilliant, or artistic. When analyzed by a person not on LSD or explained after the trip is over, however, these ideas or creations are almost always quite ordinary.

In sum, LSD alters perception such that any sensation can be perceived in the extreme. An experience can be incredibly beautiful and uplifting.

However, sometimes the experience can be very unpleasant.

Flashbacks

The flashback, or *hallucinogen persisting perception disorder* (HPPD), is an interesting but poorly understood phenomenon of LSD use. Although usually thought of as being adverse, sometimes flashbacks are pleasant and even referred to as "free trips." During a flashback, sensations caused by previous LSD use return, although the subject is not using the drug at the time (Rega 2015).

There are three broad categories of negative LSD-related flashbacks:

1. *Body trip*: Recurrence of an unpleasant physical sensation
2. *Bad mind trip*: Recurrence of a distressing thought or emotion
3. *Altered visual perception*: The most frequent type of recurrence, consisting of seeing dots, flashes, trails of light, halos, false motion in the peripheral field, and other sensations

Flashbacks are most disturbing because they come on unexpectedly. Some have been reported years after use of LSD; for most people, however, flashbacks usually subside within weeks or months after taking LSD. The duration of a flashback is variable, lasting from a few minutes to several hours (NIDA 2009).

Although the precise mechanism of flashbacks is unknown, physical or psychological stresses and some drugs such as marijuana may trigger these experiences (Clark 2015). It has been proposed that flashbacks are an especially vivid form of memory that becomes seared into the subconscious mind due to the effects of LSD on the brain's transmitters.

Treatment consists of reassurance that the condition will go away and use of a sedative such as diazepam (Valium), if necessary, to treat the anxiety or panic that can accompany the flashback experience.

GENETIC DAMAGE AND BIRTH DEFECTS

Experiments conducted in the mid-1960s suggested that LSD could cause birth defects, based on the observation that when LSD was added to a suspension of human white blood cells in a test tube the chromosomes of these cells were damaged. From this finding, it was proposed that when LSD was consumed by humans it could damage the chromosomes of the male sperm or female egg or the cells of the developing infant. Such damage theoretically could result in congenital defects in offspring (Dishotsky et al. 1971).

Carefully controlled studies conducted after news of LSD's chromosomal effects were made public did not support this hypothesis. Experiments revealed that, in contrast to the test tube findings, there is no chromosomal damage to white blood cells or any other cells when LSD is given to a human being (Dishotsky et al. 1971).

Studies have also shown that there are no carcinogenic or mutagenic effects from using LSD in experimental animals or human beings, with the exception of the fruit fly. (LSD is a mutagen in fruit flies if given in doses that are equivalent to 100,000 times the hallucinogenic dose for people.) Teratogenic effects occur in mice if LSD is given early in pregnancy. LSD may be teratogenic in rhesus monkeys if it is injected in doses (based on body weight) exceeding at least 100 times the usual hallucinogenic dose for humans. In other studies, women who took street LSD, but not those given pure LSD, had a higher rate of spontaneous abortions and births of malformed infants; this finding suggests that contaminants in adulterated LSD were responsible for the fetal effects and not the hallucinogen itself (Dishotsky et al. 1971).

EARLY HUMAN RESEARCH

In the 1950s, the U.S. government—specifically, the Central Intelligence Agency (CIA) and the army—became interested in reports of the effects of mind-altering drugs, including LSD. Unknown to the public at the time, these agencies conducted tests on human beings to learn more about such compounds and determine their usefulness in conducting military and clandestine missions. These activities became public when a biochemist, Frank Olson, killed himself in 1953 after being given a drink laced with LSD. Olson had a severe psychotic reaction and was being treated for the condition when he jumped out of a 10th-story window. His family was told only that he had committed suicide. The connection to LSD was not uncovered until 1975. The court awarded Olson's family $750,000 in damages in 1976.

In 1976, the extent of these studies was revealed; nearly 585 soldiers and 900 civilians had been given LSD in poorly organized experiments in which participants were coerced into taking this drug or not told that they were receiving it. Powerful hallucinogens such as LSD can cause serious psychological damage in some subjects, especially when they are unaware of what is happening (OneLuckySoul 2015; Remsberg 2010; Willing 2007).

The legal consequences of these LSD studies continued for years. As recently as 1987, a New York judge awarded $700,000 to the family of a mental patient who killed himself after having been given LSD without an explanation of the drug's nature. The judge said that there was a "conspiracy of silence" among the army, the Department of Justice, and the New York State Attorney General to conceal events surrounding the death of the subject, Harold Blauer (Government Conspiracy 2010).

MESCALINE (PEYOTE)

Mescaline is one of approximately 30 psychoactive chemicals that have been isolated from the peyote cactus and used for centuries in the Americas (see "Here and Now: Peyote: An Ancient Indian Way"). One of the first reports on the peyote plant was made by Francisco Hernandez to the court of King Philip II of Spain. King Philip was interested in reports from the earlier Cortés expedition about strange medicines the natives used and sent Hernandez to collect information about herbs and medicines. Hernandez worked on this project from 1570 to 1575 and reported on the use of more than 1200 plant remedies, as well as the existence of many hallucinogenic plants. He was one of the first to record the eating of parts of the peyote cactus and the resulting visions and mental changes.

In the 17th century, Spanish Catholic priests asked their Indian converts to confess to the use of peyote, which they believed was used to conjure up demons. However, nothing stopped its use. By 1760, use of peyote had spread into what is now the United States. Peyote has been confused with another plant, the mescal shrub, which produces

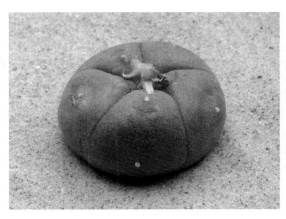

The peyote cactus contains a number of drugs. The best known is mescaline.

dark red beans that contain an extremely toxic alkaloid called *cytisine*. This alkaloid may cause hallucinations, convulsions, and even death. In addition, a mescal liquor is made from the agave cactus. Partly because of misidentification with the toxic mescal beans, the U.S. government outlawed the use of both peyote and mescaline for everyone except members of the Native American Church (Ojibwa 2015). Mescaline has been used for decades by this group as part of their religious sacrament. Research has suggested that long-term religious use of peyote does not have significant psychological effects or cause problems with cognitive performance in Native Americans (Halpern et al. 2005).

Mescaline is the most active drug in peyote and belongs to the family of phenylethylamine compounds such as MDMA (Center for Substance Abuse Research [CESAR] 2013). It induces intensified perception of colors and euphoria in the user.

HERE AND NOW
Peyote: An Ancient Indian Way

Members of the Native American Church use the buttons of the hallucinogenic peyote cactus to brew a sacramental tea as sacred to them as the bread and wine of the Christian Eucharist is to Catholics. As described by one member, "Peyote is a gift given to the Indians, but its ways cannot be obtained overnight. It has to be done with sincerity. It becomes part of your way of life. One has to walk that walk." Those who accept this form of worship believe that respectful use of peyote can be a gateway to the realm of the spirit, visions, and guidance. The use of peyote as part of the latest New Age craze is very disturbing to members of this church and is viewed almost as a form of sacrilege.

Data from Mims, B. "Peyote: When the Ancient Indian Way Collides with a New Age Craze." *Salt Lake Tribune* 258 (1 July 1999): A-10; Native American Church. 2008. Available http://www.nativeamericanchurch.com; Ojibwa. "Suppressing Indian Religions in 1915." Native American Netroots. 1 January 2015. Available http://nativeamericannetroots.net/diary/tag/peyote

However, as Aldous Huxley said in *The Doors of Perception* (1954), his book about his experimentation with mescaline, "Along with the happily transfigured majority of mescaline takers there is a minority that finds in the drug only hell and purgatory." After Huxley related his experiences with mescaline, it was used by an increasing number of people.

PHYSIOLOGICAL EFFECTS

The average dose of mescaline that will cause hallucinations and other physiological effects is from 300 to 600 milligrams. It may take up to 20 peyote (mescal) buttons (ingested orally) to get 600 milligrams of mescaline.

Based on animal studies, scientists estimate that a lethal dosage is 10 to 30 times greater than that which causes behavioral effects in human beings. (About 200 milligrams is the lowest mind-altering dose.) Death in animals results from convulsions and respiratory arrest. Mescaline is perhaps 1000 to 3000 times less potent than LSD and 30 times less potent than another common hallucinogen, psilocybin (Mathias 1993). Psilocybin is discussed later in this chapter.

Mescaline's effects include dilation of the pupils (**mydriasis**), increase in body temperature, anxiety, visual hallucinations, and alteration of body image. The last effect is a type of hallucination in which parts of the body may seem to disappear or to become grossly distorted. Mescaline induces vomiting in many people and some muscular relaxation (sedation). Apparently, there are few aftereffects or drug hangover feelings at low doses. Higher doses of mescaline slow the heart and respiratory rhythm, contract the intestines and the uterus, and cause headache, difficulty in coordination, dry skin with itching, and hypertension (high blood pressure) (DEA 2015).

Mescaline users report that they lose all awareness of time. As with LSD, the setting for the trip influences the user's reactions. Most mescaline users prefer natural settings, most likely due to the historical association of this drug with Native Americans and their nature-related spiritual experiences (often under the influence of this drug). The visual hallucinations achieved depend on the individual. Colors are at first intensified and may be followed by hallucinations of shades, movements, forms, and events. The senses of smell and taste are enhanced. Some people claim (as with LSD) that they can "hear" colors and "see" sounds, such as the wind. Synesthesia occurs naturally in a small percentage of cases. At low to medium doses, a state of euphoria is reported, often followed by a feeling of anxiety and less frequently by depression. Occasionally, users observe themselves as two people and experience the sensation that the mind and the body are separate entities. A number of people have had cosmic experiences that are profound—almost religious—and in which they discover a sense of unity with all creation. People who have this sensation often believe they have discovered the meaning of existence.

MECHANISM OF ACTION

Within 30 to 120 minutes after ingestion, mescaline reaches a maximum concentration in the brain. The effects may persist for as long as 9 or 10 hours. Hallucinations may last up to 2 hours and are usually affected by the dose level. About half the dose is excreted unchanged after 6 hours and can be recovered in the urine for reuse (if peyote is in short supply). A slow tolerance builds up after repeated use, and there is cross-tolerance to LSD. As with LSD, mescaline intoxication can be alleviated or stopped by taking a dose of chlorpromazine (Thorazine), a tranquilizer, and to a lesser extent by taking diazepam (Valium). Like LSD, mescaline probably exerts much of its hallucinogenic effects by altering serotonin systems (Delgado 2013).

Common street names for mescaline include *buttons, cactus, mesc,* and *peyote* (DEA 2015). Analysis of street samples of mescaline obtained in a number of U.S. cities over the past decade shows that the chemical sold rarely is authentic. Regardless of color or appearance, these street drugs are usually other hallucinogens, such as LSD, 2,6-dimethoxy-4-methylamphetamine (DOM), or PCP. If a person decides to take hallucinogenic street drugs, "let the buyer beware." Not only is the actual content often different and potentially much more toxic than bargained for (street drugs are frequently contaminated), but also the dosage is usually unknown even if the drug is genuine.

PSILOCYBIN

The drug psilocybin has a long and colorful history. Its principal source is the *Psilocybe mexicana* mushroom of the "magic" variety (DEA 2015). It was first used by some of the early natives of Central America more than 2000 years ago. In Guatemala, statues of mushrooms that date back to 100 BC have been found. The Aztecs later

KEY TERM

mydriasis
pupil dilation

used the mushrooms for ceremonial rites. When the Spaniards came into Mexico in the 1500s, the natives were calling the *Psilocybe mexicana* mushroom "God's flesh." Because of this seeming sacrilege, the natives were harshly treated by the Spanish priests.

Gordon Wasson identified the *Psilocybe mexicana* mushroom in 1955. The active ingredient was extracted in 1958 by Albert Hofmann, who also synthesized LSD. During research, Hofmann wanted to make certain he would feel the effects of the mushroom, so he ate 32 of them, weighing 2.4 grams (a medium dose by Native American standards), and then recorded his hallucinogenic reactions (Burger 1968).

Timothy Leary also tried some psilocybin mushrooms in Mexico in 1960; apparently, the experience influenced him greatly. On his return to Harvard, he carried out a series of experiments using psilocybin with student groups. Leary was careless in experimental procedures and did some work in uncontrolled situations. His actions caused a major administrative upheaval, ending in his departure from Harvard.

One of Leary's questionable studies was the "Good Friday" experiment in which 20 theological students were given either a placebo or psilocybin in a double-blind study (i.e., neither the researcher nor the subjects know who gets the placebo or the drug), after which all attended the same 2.5-hour Good Friday service. The experimental group reported mystical experiences, whereas the control group did not (Pahnke and Richards 1966). Leary believed that the experience was of value and that, under proper control and guidance, the hallucinatory experience could be beneficial.

Psilocybin is not very common on the street. Generally, it is administered orally and is eaten either fresh or dried. Accidental poisonings are common for those who mistakenly consume poisonous mushrooms rather than the hallucinogenic variety.

The dried form of these mushrooms contains from 0.2% to 0.5% psilocybin. The hallucinogenic effects produced are quite similar to those of LSD, and there is a cross-tolerance among psilocybin, LSD, and mescaline, suggesting they have similar mechanisms of action. The effects caused by psilocybin vary with the dosage taken. Up to 4 milligrams cause a pleasant experience, relaxation, and some body sensation. In some subjects, higher doses cause considerable perceptual and body image changes, accompanied by hallucinations.

The *Psilocybe* mushroom is the source of the hallucinogens psilocybin and psilocin.

Although psilocybin has been reported to be helpful in the treatment of depression for some people (Jacoby 2015), in extreme cases psilocybin can cause mental problems (NIDA 2015). Psilocybin stimulates the autonomic nervous system, dilates the pupils, and increases body temperature. Some evidence suggests that psilocybin is metabolized into psilocin, which is more potent and may be the principal active ingredient. Psilocin is found in mushrooms, albeit in small amounts. Like the other hallucinogens, psilocybin apparently causes no physical dependence (Delgado 2013; NIDA 20010).

TRYPTAMINES

Some compounds related to the tryptamine class of drugs (molecules that resemble the neurotransmitter serotonin) have hallucinogenic properties and can exist naturally in herbs, fungi, and animals or can be synthesized in the laboratory. Some of the newer tryptamines are available for purchase over the Internet, but their effects are not well understood. Many, but not all, of these compounds are Schedule I drugs and illegal (Araujo 2015). Two examples are discussed in this section.

DIMETHYLTRYPTAMINE

Dimethyltryptamine (DMT) is a short-acting hallucinogen found in the seeds of certain leguminous trees native to the West Indies and parts of South America (Schultes 1978) and is reported to occur naturally in the human body in low quantities (Horgan n.d.). It is also prepared synthetically in illicit laboratories and is reported to have both beneficial and terrifying adverse effects (Horgan n.d.). For centuries, the powdered seeds have been used as a snuff called *cohoba* in pipes and snuffing tubes. Haitian natives claim that, under the influence of the drug, they can communicate with their gods. Its effects occur rapidly and may last less than 1 hour, which has earned it the nickname "the businessman's lunch break" (Carollo 2010).

DMT has no effect when taken orally; it is inhaled either as smoke from the burning plant or in vaporized form. DMT is sometimes added to parsley leaves or flakes, tobacco, or marijuana to induce its hallucinogenic effect. The usual dose is 60 to 150 milligrams. In structure and action, it is similar to psilocybin, although it is not as powerful. Like the other hallucinogens discussed, DMT does not cause physical dependence.

FOXY

The synthetic substance 5-methoxy-N,N-diisopropyltryptamine, but more commonly referred to as *Foxy*, is a relatively new hallucinogen. This drug has been used at raves and clubs in Arizona, California, New York, and Florida. It was added to the DEA Schedule I category in 2004. At lower doses, Foxy can cause euphoria; at higher doses, its effects are similar to LSD, causing hallucinations and psychedelic experiences (DEA 2002). Foxy is typically consumed orally in doses of 6 to 20 milligrams, but it may also be smoked (National Drug Intelligence Center [NDIC] n.d.).

NUTMEG

High doses of nutmeg can be intoxicating, causing symptoms such as drowsiness, stupor, delirium, and sleep. Prison inmates have known about this drug for years, so in most prisons use of spices such as nutmeg is restricted. It is typically young people who experiment with nutmeg to get a cheap high, but because of the frequent unpleasant side effects, abusers often end up either in an emergency room or calling a poison control center and usually are not interested in trying nutmeg again. Needless to say, nutmeg is not perceived as a major drug abuse problem by authorities (Szalavitz 2010).

Nutmeg contains 5% to 15% myristica oil, which is responsible for the physical effects. Myristicin (about 4%), which is structurally similar to mescaline, and elemicin are probably the most potent psychoactive ingredients in nutmeg. Myristicin blocks release of serotonin from brain neurons. The exterior covering of the nutmeg seed also contains the hallucinogenic compound myristicin.

Two tablespoons of nutmeg (about 14 grams) taken orally cause a rather unpleasant trip with a dreamlike stage. Rapid heartbeat, dry mouth, and thirst are experienced as well. Agitation,

apprehension, and a sense of impending doom may last about 12 hours, with a sense of unreality persisting for several days (Rahman, Fazilah, and Effarazah 2015).

▌ Phenylethylamine Hallucinogens

The phenylethylamine drugs are chemically related to amphetamines. Phenylethylamines have varying degrees of hallucinogenic and CNS stimulant effects, which are likely related to their ability to release serotonin and dopamine, respectively. Consequently, the phenylethylamines that predominantly release serotonin are dominated by their hallucinogenic action and are more LSD like, whereas those more inclined to release dopamine are dominated by their stimulant effects and are amphetamine like.

DIMETHOXYMETHYLAMPHETAMINE

The basic structure of dimethoxymethylamphetamine (DOM or STP, an acronym for "serenity, tranquility and peace") is amphetamine. Nonetheless, it is a fairly powerful hallucinogen that seems to work through mechanisms similar to those found with mescaline and LSD. In fact, the effects of DOM are similar to those caused by a combination of amphetamine and LSD, with the hallucinogenic effects of the drug overpowering the amphetamine-like physiological effects. Like other hallucinogens, DOM is not considered to be particularly addicting, and users experience tolerance with multiple drug exposures (Leonard 2015). The following is an excerpt from a user who experienced a very bad trip with DOM:

> I like to think of myself as an experienced psychonaut (someone who uses a lot of psychoactive substances)....Yesterday, I took 5 milligrams of DOM.... I was excited to spend the whole day ... exploring new neural connections.... The first 4 hours were enjoyable.... Then all at once, something big shifted ... I found the visual image of myself literally ripped in half.... I felt like I was being dragged down to the very depths of hell. Death was everywhere.... I felt like I was being drenched in blood, almost drowning in it.... My consciousness continued to explode.... I was sobbing hysterically.... I felt my body become a vessel for all pain.... Several times over the next several hours, I was sure that I myself was dying.... Every 15 minutes or so, my body would go into convulsions.... I was convinced that I would never be the same.... I had become self-injurious and suicidal.... Finally around 21 hours, and still going strong,

I (took) a Seroquel which axed the trip ... I certainly will never be taking this chemical again, and am questioning whether or not my journeys with these types of drugs are at an end. I am grateful to be alive and ... have my sanity back. (Psychonaut 2015)

"DESIGNER" AMPHETAMINES

The hybrid actions of "designer amphetamines" as psychedelic stimulants not only make them a particularly fascinating topic for research but also provide a unique experience described by drug abusers as a "smooth amphetamine," or an **entactogen** (implying that the pleasurable sensation of touch is enhanced). This characterization likely accounts for their popularity (Weaver et al. 2015).

3,4-METHYLENEDIOXYAMPHETAMINE

3,4-Methylenedioxyamphetamine (MDA), first synthesized in 1910, is structurally related to both mescaline and amphetamine. Early research found that MDA is an anorexiant (causing loss of appetite), as well as a mood elevator in some people. Further research has shown that the mode of action of MDA is similar to that of amphetamines and a metabolite of MDMA (Zhou 2016). It causes additional release of the neurotransmitters serotonin, dopamine, and norepinephrine (Baggott et al. 2010).

In the past, MDA was used as an adjunct to psychotherapy. In one study, eight volunteers who had previously experienced the effects of LSD under clinical conditions were given 150 milligrams of MDA. Effects of the drug were noted between 40 and 60 minutes following ingestion by all eight subjects. The subjective effects following administration peaked at the end of 90 minutes and persisted for approximately 8 hours. None of the subjects experienced hallucinations, perceptual distortion, or closed-eye imagery, but they reported that the feelings the drug induced had some relationship to those previously experienced with LSD. The subjects found that both drugs induced an intensification of feelings, increased perceptions of self-insight, and heightened empathy with others during the experience. Most of the subjects also felt an increased sense of aesthetic enjoyment at some point during the intoxication. Seven of the eight subjects said they perceived music as "three-dimensional" (Naranjo, Shulgin, and Sargent 1967).

On the street, MDA has been called the *love drug* because of its effects on the sense of touch and the attitudes of the users. Users often report experiencing a sense of well-being (likely a stimulant effect) and heightened tactile sensations (likely a hallucinogenic effect) and thus increased pleasure through sex and expressions of affection. Those under the influence of MDA frequently focus on interpersonal relationships and demonstrate an overwhelming desire or need to be with or talk to people. Some users say they have a very pleasant "body high"—more sensual than cerebral and more empathetic than introverted. For these reasons, MDA is sometimes used by persons attending raves, much like MDMA or Ecstasy (Baggott et al. 2010).

The unpleasant side effects most often reported are nausea, periodic tensing of muscles in the neck, tightening of the jaw and grinding of the teeth, and dilation of the pupils. Street doses of MDA range from 100 to 150 milligrams. Serious convulsions and death have resulted from larger doses, but in these cases the quantity of MDA was not accurately measured. Ingestion of 500 milligrams of pure MDA has been shown to cause death. The only reported adverse reaction to moderate doses is a marked physical exhaustion, lasting as long as 2 days (Marquardt, DiStefano, and Ling 1978).

An unpleasant MDA experience should be treated the same as a bad trip with any hallucinogen. The person should be "talked down" (reassured) in a friendly and supportive manner. The use of other drugs is rarely needed, although medical attention may be necessary.

Under the Comprehensive Drug Abuse Prevention and Control Act of 1970, MDA is classified as a Schedule I substance; illegal possession is a serious offense.

METHYLENEDIOXYMETHAMPHETAMINE

Methylenedioxymethamphetamine (MDMA) is a modification of MDA but is thought to have more psychedelic and less stimulant activity (e.g., euphoria) than its predecessor. MDMA is also structurally similar to mescaline. The popular names for MDMA are *Ecstasy* or *molly*, which is slang for "molecular" (NIDA 2016b).

MDMA was synthesized in 1912 to suppress appetite, but due to bizarre side effects it was withdrawn from development until it became widely used in the 1980s (Adam 2006). This designer

KEY TERM

entactogen
a drug that enhances the sensation and pleasure of touching

Ecstasy is frequently used at "raves" to increase sensory stimulation and the pleasure of touching.

amphetamine can be produced easily, although the process can be hazardous and the chemicals used for the synthesis are difficult to obtain (Plummer et al. 2016). Although the synthesis can be done by local illicit laboratories (Plummer et al. 2016), most of the MDMA supplies in this country are smuggled in from outlaw drug laboratories in European countries such as the Netherlands (Meadow 2015). The unusual psychological effects it produces are part of the reason for its popularity. The drug causes euphoria, increased energy, increased sensitivity to touch, and lowered inhibitions. Many users claim it intensifies emotional feelings without sensory distortion and that it increases empathy and awareness both of the user's body and of the aesthetics of the surroundings. Some consider MDMA to be an aphrodisiac. Because MDMA lowers defense mechanisms and reduces inhibitions, it has even been used during psychoanalysis. In fact, recently there have been reports that an initial FDA-approved clinical trial has demonstrated that MDMA was effective in the treatment of 10 or 12 patients suffering from PTSD. Obviously this represents a very small study, and the results must be confirmed by other, much larger clinical trials (NIDA 2016b).

MDMA—popularized in the 1980s by articles in *Newsweek* (Adler 1985), *Time* (Toufexis 1985), and other magazines—recently was again touted on the national newsstands as a drug with euphoric effects, potential therapeutic value, and lack of serious side effects. MDMA is popular with college-age students and young adults (Johnston 2016). Because of its effect of enhancing sensations, MDMA has been used as part of a countercultural rave scene, including high-tech music and laser light shows. Observers report that MDMA-linked rave parties are reminiscent of the acid parties of the 1960s and 1970s. The latest

cycle of MDMA popularity peaked in 2001, when it was being used by 10% of high school seniors. However, due to reports of MDMA neurotoxicity and persistent negative side effects, use of this drug has decreased dramatically, and by 2015 was being by only 3.6% of high school seniors (Johnston 2016).

Because of the widespread abuse of MDMA, the DEA prohibited its use by formally placing it on the Schedule I list in 1988. At the time of the ban, it was estimated that as many as 200 physicians were using the drug in psychotherapy (Greer and Tolbert 1990) and an estimated 30,000 doses per month were being taken for recreational purposes. MDMA is often referred to as a "club drug" because of its frequent use at rave dances, clubs, and bars. It costs 25 to 50 cents to produce a tablet of Ecstasy in Europe, but on the street that same tablet costs $20 to $30 (Scinto 2013).

MDMA is usually taken orally, but it is sometimes snorted or even occasionally smoked. After the high starts, it may persist for minutes or even an hour, depending on the person, the purity of the drug, and the environment in which it is taken. When coming down from an MDMA-induced high, people often take small oral doses known as "boosters" to get high again. If they take too many boosters, they become very fatigued the next day. The average dose is about 75 to 150 milligrams; toxic effects have been reported at higher doses. Some statistics suggest that almost 50% of the tablets sold as MDMA actually contain other drugs such as aspirin, caffeine, cocaine, methamphetamine, or pseudoephedrine (NIDA 2016b).

A number of possible harmful side effects of MDMA have been reported. Use of high doses can cause psychosis and paranoia (NIDA 2010). Some negative physiological responses caused by recreational doses include dilated pupils, dry mouth and throat, clenching and grinding of teeth (resulting in the use of baby pacifiers), muscle aches and stiffness, fatigue insomnia agitation, and anxiety. Some of these reactions can be intense and unpredictable. Under some conditions, death can be caused by hyperthermia (elevated body temperature), instability of the autonomic nervous system, underlying cardiovascular problems, or kidney failure (NIDA 2016b).

Several studies have demonstrated long-term damage to serotonin neurons in the brain following a single high dose of either MDMA or MDA, which may result in impaired memory, diminished ability to process information, and heightened impulsivity (Rossen 2016). Although the behavioral significance of this damage in people is not clear, at the present time caution using this drug is warranted (DrugDangers 2016).

Experts continue to debate the addictive properties of MDMA. Some claim this drug is like LSD, with little likelihood of causing physical dependence, whereas others claim its properties are likely to be more amphetamine like, and suggest that of those who use MDMA routinely some have developed dependence (NIDA 2010). Part of the difficulty in sorting out this controversy is that most moderate MDMA users also use other drugs, making it difficult to determine which effects are specifically attributable to the MDMA. The potential of MDMA to cause addiction and dependence is likely somewhere between that of amphetamine and LSD. Because of its ability to cause euphoria and release dopamine in the brain, it is very probable that heavy use or administration by smoking or injection can cause significant dependence (NIDA 2016b).

■ Anticholinergic Hallucinogens

The anticholinergic hallucinogens include naturally occurring alkaloid (bitter organic base) substances that are present in plants and herbs found around the world. These drugs are often mentioned in folklore and in early literature as being added to potions. They are thought to have played a role in the death of the Roman emperor Claudius, and Shakespeare refers to them in the poisoning of Hamlet's father. Historically, they have been the favorite drugs used to eliminate inconvenient people. Hallucinogens affecting the cholinergic neurons also have been used by South American Indians for religious ceremonies (Schultes and Hofmann 1980) and were probably used in witchcraft to give the illusion of flying, to prepare sacrificial victims, and even to give some types of marijuana ("superpot") its kick (Black Witch Coven n.d.).

The family of plants that includes potatoes, the Solanaceae, contains most of these mind-altering drugs. The following three potent anticholinergic compounds are commonly found in these plants: (1) scopolamine, or hyoscine; (2) hyoscyamine; and (3) atropine. Scopolamine may produce excitement, hallucinations, and delirium even at therapeutic doses. With atropine, doses bordering on toxic levels are usually required to obtain these effects (Garden Spot 2013). All of these active alkaloid drugs block some acetylcholine receptors.

These alkaloid drugs can be used as ingredients in cold symptom remedies because they have a drying effect and block production of mucus in the nose and throat. They also prevent salivation; therefore, the mouth becomes uncommonly dry and perspiration may stop. Atropine may increase the heart rate by 100% and dilate the pupils markedly, causing inability to focus on nearby objects. Other annoying side effects of these anticholinergic drugs include constipation and difficulty urinating. These inconveniences tend to discourage excessive abuse of these drugs for their hallucinogenic properties. Usually, people who abuse these anticholinergic compounds are receiving the drugs by prescription (Anderson 2016).

Anticholinergics can cause drowsiness by affecting the sleep centers of the brain. At large doses, a condition occurs that is similar to a psychosis, characterized by delirium, loss of attention, mental confusion, and sleepiness (Anderson 2016). Hallucinations may also occur at higher doses. At very high doses, paralysis of the respiratory system may cause death.

Although hundreds of plant species naturally contain anticholinergic substances and consequently can cause psychedelic experiences, only a few of the principal plants are mentioned here.

ATROPA BELLADONNA: *THE DEADLY NIGHTSHADE PLANT*

Knowledge of *Atropa belladonna* is very old, and its use as a drug is reported in early folklore. The name of the genus, *Atropa*, is the origin for the drug name *atropine* and indicates the reverence the Greeks had for the plant. Atropos was one of the three Fates in Greek mythology, whose duty it was to cut the thread of life when the time came. This plant has been used for thousands of years by assassins and murderers. In *Tales of the Arabian Nights*, unsuspecting potentates were poisoned with atropine from the deadly nightshade or one of its relatives. Fourteen berries of the deadly nightshade contain enough drug to cause death.

The species name, *belladonna*, means "beautiful woman." In early Rome and Egypt, girls with large pupils were considered attractive and friendly. To create this condition, they would put a few drops of an extract of this plant into their eyes, causing the pupils to dilate (Garden Spot 2013). Belladonna has also enjoyed a reputation as a love potion.

MANDRAGORA OFFICINARUM: *THE MANDRAKE*

Mandragora officinarum, commonly known as mandrake, contains several active psychedelic alkaloids: hyoscyamine, scopolamine, atropine, and mandragorine. Mandrake has been used as a love potion for centuries but has also been known for its toxic properties. In ancient folk medicine, mandrake was used to treat many ailments in spite of its side effects. It was recommended as a sedative, to relieve nervous conditions, and to relieve pain (University Toronto 2014), as portrayed in the 2006 movie *Pan's Labyrinth*.

The root of the mandrake is forked and, when viewed with a little imagination, may resemble the human body (as portrayed in the *Harry Potter and the Chamber of Secrets* movie in 2002). Because of this resemblance, it has been credited with human attributes, which gave rise to many superstitions in the Middle Ages about its magical powers. Shakespeare referred to this plant in *Romeo and Juliet*. In her farewell speech, Juliet says, "And shrieks like mandrakes torn out of the earth, that living mortals hearing them run mad."

HYOSCYAMUS NIGER: *HENBANE*

Hyoscyamus niger, or henbane, contains both hyoscyamine and scopolamine. In AD 60, Pliny the Elder spoke of henbane: "For this is certainly known, that if one takes it in drink more than four leaves, it will put him beside himself" (Jones 1956). Henbane was also used in the orgies, or *bacchanalias*, of the ancient world.

Although rarely used today, henbane has been given medicinally since early times. It was frequently used to cause sleep, although hallucinations often occurred if given in excess. It was likely included in witches' brews and deadly concoctions during the Dark Ages (WebMD n.d.).

DATURA STRAMONIUM: *JIMSONWEED*

The *Datura* genus of the Solanaceae family includes a large number of related plants found worldwide. The principal active drug in this group is scopolamine; there are also several less active alkaloids.

Throughout history, these plants have been used as hallucinogens by many societies. They are mentioned in early Sanskrit and Chinese writings and were revered by the Buddhists. There is also some indication that the priestess (oracle) at the ancient Greek Temple of Apollo at Delphi was under the influence of this type of plant when she made prophecies (Schultes 1970). Before the supposed divine possession, she appeared to have

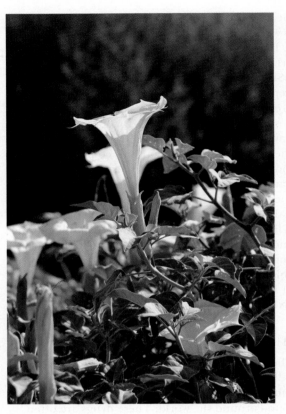

Datura stramonium, or jimsonweed, is a common plant that contains the hallucinogenic drug scopolamine.

chewed leaves of the sacred laurel. A mystic vapor was also reported to have risen from a fissure in the ground. The sacred laurel may have been one of the *Datura* species, and the vapors may have come from burning these plants.

Jimsonweed gets its name from an incident that took place in 17th-century Jamestown and is a contraction of "Jamestown weed." British soldiers ate this weed while trying to capture Nathaniel Bacon, who had made seditious remarks about the king. Jimsonweed is still occasionally consumed by young people who are searching for an inexpensive hallucinogenic experience. Because this wild weed grows in most parts of the United States, it is relatively easy to find and is free. This plant has been referred to by names such as *angel's trumpet*, *locoweed*, and *stinkweed*. The hallucinogenic effects from this plant are mainly due to the presence of the two powerful anticholinergic drugs, atropine and scopolamine, in the roots. Often the person who consumes the jimsonweed in a stew or other brew ends up in the emergency room complaining of hallucinations, confusion, dilated pupils, and rapid heartbeat. Because of the very unpleasant side effects, abuse of jimsonweed is not considered

KEY TERM

jimsonweed
a potent hallucinogenic plant

to be a major drug abuse problem, but most emergency rooms will occasionally see an unsuspecting young person who foolishly experiments with jimsonweed for a cheap and natural high and gets much more than expected (Woolcott 2015).

■ Other Hallucinogens

Technically, any drug that alters perceptions, thoughts, and feelings in a manner that is not normally experienced except in dreams can be classified as a hallucinogen. Because the brain's sensory input is complex and involves several neurotransmitter systems, drugs with many diverse effects can cause hallucinations (Parrish 2015).

Four agents that do not conveniently fit into the principal categories of hallucinogens are discussed in the following sections.

PHENCYCLIDINE

PCP users can be so psychotic when they're brought in that they can't provide any history.... Some PCP users are transferred to the psych unit from the trauma unit, where they had pins put in their legs because they jumped out a window. Some complain of chest pains days after arriving, and when we do an x-ray we find broken ribs. PCP is also an anesthetic, so other injuries often aren't discovered until after it wears off. (Inpatient Director, Einstein Hospital psychiatric unit)

The use of PCP added to marijuana (referred to as wet marijuana) can be particularly destructive causing extreme hyperactivity, physical violence, strokes, cardiac arrests, heart attacks and seizures. (Citizens' Commission 2015)

Phencyclidine (PCP) is considered by many experts as the most dangerous of the

Persons on PCP often have psychotic episodes leading to their admission into psychiatric wards.

hallucinogens. PCP was developed in the late 1950s as an intravenous anesthetic. Although it was found to be effective, it had serious side effects, such as precipitating schizophrenia-like symptoms, which caused it to be discontinued for human use. Sometimes when people were recovering from PCP anesthesia, they experienced delirium and manic states of excitation lasting 18 hours. PCP is currently a Schedule II drug, legitimately available only as an anesthetic for animals, but it has even been banned from veterinary practice since 1985 because of its high theft rate. Most, if not all, PCP used in the United States today is produced illegally (Davis 2016a).

Street PCP is mainly synthesized from readily available chemical precursors in clandestine laboratories. PCP first appeared on the street drug scene in 1967 as the *PeaCe Pill.* In 1968, it reappeared in New York as a substance called *hog.* By 1969, PCP was found under a variety of guises. It was sold as angel dust and sprinkled on parsley for smoking. Today, it is sold on the streets under many different slang names, including *angel dust, supergrass, killer weed, embalming fluid, rocket fuel, wack,* and *ozone,* to mention a few (Partnership for Drug-Free Kids 2013).

In the late 1960s, PCP began to find its way into a variety of street drugs sold as psychedelics. By 1970, authorities observed that phencyclidine was used widely as a main ingredient in psychedelic preparations. It has frequently been used to lace or substitute for LSD, mescaline, marijuana, tobacco, or cocaine (Citizens' Commission 2015; MacLaren n.d.). These drug combinations can cause particularly alarming, and sometimes dangerous, behaviors (Citizens' Commission 2015).

One difficulty in estimating the effects or use patterns of PCP is caused by variance in drug purity. Also, there are about 30 **analogs** of PCP, some of which have appeared on the street. PCP has so many other street names that people may not know they are using it, or they may have been deceived when buying what they thought was LSD or marijuana (Schmetzer 2015). Users may not question the identity of the substances unless they have a bad reaction.

PCP is available as a pure, white crystalline powder; as tablets; or as capsules. However, because it is usually manufactured in makeshift laboratories,

KEY TERM

analogs
drugs with similar structures

it is frequently discolored by contaminants from a tan to brown with a consistency ranging from powder to a gummy mass. PCP can be taken orally, smoked, sniffed, or injected, but currently the preferred form of administration is smoking, often as an additive to marijuana referred to as *wet weed* (Schmetzer 2015). By smoking PCP, the experienced user is better able to limit his or her dosage to a desired level. After smoking, the subjective effects appear within 1 to 5 minutes and peak within the next 5 to 30 minutes. The high lasts about 4 to 6 hours, followed by a 6- to 24-hour "comedown" (APA 2013).

For the past 2 decades, the use of PCP has remained relatively stable, with the reported annual use by high school seniors at 1.4% in 1991 and 2015 (Johnston 2016).

PHYSIOLOGICAL EFFECTS

Although PCP may have hallucinogenic effects, it can cause a host of other physiological actions, including stimulation, depression, anesthesia, and analgesia. The effects of PCP on the CNS vary greatly. At low doses, the most prominent effect is similar to that of alcohol intoxication, with generalized numbness. As the dose of PCP increases, the person becomes even more insensitive and may become fully anesthetized. Large doses can cause coma, convulsions, and death (APA 2013).

The majority of peripheral effects are apparently related to activation of the sympathetic nervous system. Flushing, excess sweating, and a blank stare are common, although the size of the pupils is unaffected. The cardiovascular system reacts by increasing blood pressure and heart rate. Other effects include side-to-side eye movements (called *nystagmus*), muscular incoordination, double vision, dizziness, nausea, and vomiting (NDIC 2004). These symptoms occur in many people who take medium to high doses.

PSYCHOLOGICAL EFFECTS

PCP has unpleasant effects most of the time it is used. Why, then, do people use it repeatedly as their drug of choice?

PCP has the ability to markedly alter the person's subjective feelings; this effect may be reinforcing, even though the alteration is not always positive. Some say use of PCP makes them feel

godlike and powerful (Maier 2003). There is an element of risk, not knowing how the trip will turn out. PCP may give the user feelings of strength, power, and invulnerability (NIDA 2007b). Other positive effects include heightened sensitivity to outside stimuli, a sense of stimulation and mood elevation, and dissociation from surroundings. Also, PCP is a social drug; virtually all users report taking it in groups rather than during a solitary experience. PCP also causes serious perceptual distortions. Users cannot accurately interpret the environment or their own emotions and as a result may do what appears to be absurd things such as throwing themselves at moving police cars, mutilating themselves, or assaulting others without provocation.

Chronic users may take PCP in "runs" extending over 2 to 3 days, during which time they do not sleep or eat. In later stages of chronic administration, users may develop outright paranoia, unpredictable violent behavior, and auditory hallucinations (Davis 2016a). Law enforcement officers claim to be more fearful of suspects on PCP than of suspects on other drugs of abuse. Often such people seem to have superhuman strength and are totally irrational and very difficult—even dangerous—to manage (NIDA 2015).

It is claimed by some that PCP has no equal in its ability to produce brief psychoses similar to schizophrenia The psychoses—induced with moderate doses given to normal, healthy volunteers—last about 2 hours and are characterized by changes in body image, thought disorders, estrangement, autism, and occasionally rigid inability to move (**catatonia**, or catalepsy). Subjects report feeling numb, have great difficulty differentiating between themselves and their surroundings, and complain afterward of feeling extremely isolated and apathetic. They are often violently paranoid during the psychosis (APA 2013).

When PCP was given experimentally to hospitalized chronic schizophrenics, it made them much worse not for a few hours but for 6 weeks. PCP is not just another hallucinogen—many authorities view it as much more dangerous than other drugs of abuse (Maier 2003).

MEDICAL MANAGEMENT

The diagnosis of a PCP overdose is frequently missed because the symptoms often closely resemble those of an acute schizophrenic episode. Simple, uncomplicated PCP intoxication can be managed with the same techniques used

KEY TERM

catatonia
a condition of physical rigidity, excitement, and stupor

in other psychedelic drug cases. It is important to have a quiet environment, limited contact with an empathic person capable of determining any deterioration in the patient's physical state, protection from self-harm, and the availability of hospital facilities. Talking down is not helpful; the patient is better off isolated from external stimuli as much as possible.

Valium is often used for its sedating effect to prevent injury to self and to staff and also to reduce the chance for severe convulsions. An antipsychotic agent (e.g., haloperidol [Haldol]) is frequently administered to make the patient manageable (Schmetzer 2015).

The medical management of a comatose or convulsing patient is more difficult. The patient may need external respiratory assistance and external cooling to reduce fever. Blood pressure may have to be reduced to safe levels and convulsions controlled. Restraints and four to five strong hospital aides are often needed to prevent the patient from injuring him- or herself or the medical staff. After the coma lightens, the patient typically becomes delirious, paranoid, and violently assaultive (see "Case in Point: PCP Use Can Mean Violent Trouble").

EFFECTS OF CHRONIC USE

Chronic PCP users may develop a tolerance to the drug; thus, a decrease in behavioral effects and toxicity can occur with frequent administration. Different forms of dependence may occur when tolerance develops. Users may complain of vague cravings after cessation of the drug. In addition, long-term difficulties in memory, speech, and

Courtesy of Orange County Police Department, Florida.

Ketamine is frequently used as a general anesthetic for veterinary procedures.

thinking persist for 6 to 12 months in the chronic user (MacLaren n.d.). These functional changes are accompanied by personality deficits such as social isolation and states of anxiety, nervousness, and extreme agitation (APA 2013; Farwell 2010).

KETAMINE

Ketamine is considered a club drug (NIDA 2016a). Its annual use in 2012 by high school seniors was 1.4% (Johnston 2016). Almost all persons who abuse ketamine are polydrug users (Bracchi et al. 2015), and those who abuse it chronically lose cognitive function and experience a deteriorating sense of well-being (Morgan, Muetzelfeldt, and Curran 2010). Ketamine, like PCP, was originally

---

▶ CASE IN POINT

PCP Use Can Mean Violent Trouble

Although PCP use has fallen out of favor in recent years, occasionally a PCP-precipitated tragedy occurs that reminds us why this drug is considered to be one of the most dangerous of the substances of abuse. In July 2010 the son of the Dallas police chief was shot and killed by a police officer after he had gunned down two innocent bystanders. The medical examiner discovered PCP in his system. Witnesses related that before the senseless rampage, while humming to himself, the young man had stripped to his boxers, a frequent behavior of PCP users because they have the sensation that bugs are crawling all over their skin. Before shooting the two men, the chief's son manifested considerable aggression and paranoia, which is consistent with the fact that PCP users often become violent because they think that someone is trying to kill them. Accounts such as this are reminders of the terrible consequences of abusing this powerful hallucinogen.

Data from Farwell, S. "Though PCP Use Has Been Falling, Drug Can Still Lead to Violent Trouble." *Dallas Morning News* (9 July 2010). Available http://www .dallasnews.com/sharedcontent/dws/news/localnews/crime/stories/070910dnmetpcp.1cef8c6.html.

developed for its general anesthetic properties. Its effects resemble those of PCP except they are more rapid and less potent (Frohlich and Van Horn 2016). Depending on the dose, ketamine can have many effects, ranging from feelings of weightlessness to out-of-body or near-death experiences. Ketamine, often referred to as *Special K*, has been abused as a date rape drug like other CNS depressants, such as Rohypnol or gamma-hydroxybutyrate (GHB) (Cunha n.d.). Abuse of ketamine has been reported in many cities throughout the United States, and the drug is sometimes snorted as a substitute for cocaine. Several deaths have been linked to ketamine overdoses (Smith 2016).

Despite its potential as a drug of abuse, recent studies have suggested that it may have some potential as an antidepressant. When given to severely depressed patients in a small clinical trial it resulted in a "robust and rapid (within minutes) antidepressant response." This novel use of ketamine has not been well studied or standardized, but the success rate for treating severe depression has been reported to be as high as 75% and often very profound. For example, consider the following report by a depressed patient known as Ted:

> I had situations [of depression] where I just wasn't getting out of bed, I was completely dysfunctional and it was shredding my relationship with my wife.... I'd get hypercritical of myself and my surroundings.... I was prescribed Wellbutrin, a pretty common antidepressant ... (and other antidepressants as well).... Some antidepressants would lift the veil (of depression) a little bit. It would be gray instead of pitch black, ... I was skeptical about ketamine and thought it would also fail ... but I was willing to try almost anything at that point ... (after ketamine infusion the veil) completely goes away.... After my first infusion, when I realized it had worked, I felt so relieved (Landsbaum 2016).

However, the improvement caused by ketamine is temporary, and subsequent ketamine treatments are required every few days or weeks (Landsbaum 2016).

DEXTROMETHORPHAN

Dextromethorphan is the active ingredient used in many OTC cough medicines because of its ability to suppress the cough reflex (Delgado 2013; Schumacher 2012). Although harmless in low recommended doses, if consumed in high quantities (approximately 10 times the recommended dose), it can cause some hallucinogenic effects much like PCP and ketamine do, as well as other symptoms, such as confusion, numbness, disorientation, and stomach pain (Drugs.com n.d.). The effects of dextromethorphan can vary and have been described as ranging from a mild stimulant effect to a complete dissociation from one's body, and they can last for several hours. Abuse of dextromethorphan is typically done by teenagers and is sometimes referred to as *roboing* (CESAR 2005). Recreational use of cough medicines containing this drug reached 5.6% in high school seniors in 2012 (Johnston 2016). This practice of consuming high doses of cough medicine can be extremely dangerous and on occasions even fatal (see "Prescription for Abuse: Cough Medicine Abuse—Nothing to Be Sneezed At"). Most young people who abuse cough medicines are abusing other substances such as marijuana, LSD, or Ecstasy. This surprisingly high rate of abuse for cough medicines has caused some to suggest that these products be removed from shelves and placed behind the pharmacy counters or only be sold to consumers over the age of 18. Laws prohibiting sales of these cough medicines to minors have been passed in states such as California, New Jersey, New York, and several others. However, although the FDA has considered these strategies on the national level, as of yet its advisory panel of medical experts has advised against their implementation (Consumer Healthcare Products Association [CHPA] 2016).

MARIJUANA

Marijuana is known to be the most popular illicit drug of abuse in the United States, with almost 20 million regular users. Whether marijuana should be classified as a hallucinogen is somewhat controversial. Part of this controversy is due to the variable effects caused by smoking marijuana between users. Based on the user and the doses consumed, marijuana can have stimulant, depressant, and/or hallucinogenic effects. This mixture of actions is probably related to the fact that cannabinoid receptors (targets for tetrahydrocannabinol-like ingredients in marijuana) are found in the parts of the brain related to functions such as pleasure, memory, cognitive function, concentration, coordination, and sensory, space, and time perceptions. High doses of tetrahydrocannabinol (THC) or its analogs (the approximately 66 THC-like chemicals found in the marijuana plant) can cause the user to lose contact with reality and result in bizarre and unusual behaviors. In general, marijuana manifests hallucinogenic effects significantly less than those caused by LSD, PCP, or mescaline, but it can distort emotions and sensory perceptions in pleasant or dysphoric ways (Hallucinogens.com

PRESCRIPTION FOR ABUSE

Cough Medicine Abuse—Nothing to Be Sneezed At

Although abuse of cough medicine has not been considered serious enough by the FDA or other federal agencies to do anything more than issue warnings, many parents are concerned because cough syrup abuse seems to be on the rise among teens because it is cheap and readily available. It is generally known by young people that high doses of cough medicines that contain the drug dextromethorphan can cause euphoria, some stimulation, and even hallucinations. However, what is not appreciated by many potential young consumers is that high-dose abuse of these products can have serious negative consequences. For example, some of the cough syrups also contain other ingredients, such as the analgesic drug acetaminophen (the active ingredient in Tylenol). When consumed in high doses (as would be the case if someone were to ingest 10 times the recommended dose of an acetaminophen-containing cough medicine to achieve a high), the high doses of acetaminophen can cause permanent and even fatal damage to the liver. In addition, high doses of dextromethorphan itself cause a dissociative effect (e.g.,

confusion), loss of motor control, nausea, dizziness, fever, hypertension, and difficulty breathing. For long-term abusers, dependence on the dextromethorphan can occur, causing significant withdrawal symptoms, such as insomnia, dysphoria, and depression. Finally, cough medicine overdoses often are accompanied by alcohol use, resulting in potentially life-threatening interactions, such as severe depressed breathing.

Data from Narconon. "Signs and Symptoms of Dextromethorphan Abuse." n.d. Available http://www.narconon.org/drug-abuse/dextromethorphan-signs -symptoms.html

---

n.d.; National Institutes of Health [NIH] 2016). Another controversial issue relates to the claims that marijuana has potential therapeutic benefits in the treatment in conditions such as chronic pain, weight loss, and nausea in people with cancer, acquired immunodeficiency syndrome (AIDS), neurological disorders, PTSD, and anxiety disorders. Although there are many anecdotal reports supporting these and other therapeutic uses for marijuana, most of these claims have not been substantiated by well-conducted, controlled, and peer-reviewed scientific studies (Hallucinogens. com n.d.; NIH 2016).

Natural Substances

■ Naturally Occurring Hallucinogens

Many plants contain naturally occurring hallucinogens. As already discussed, examples of such substances include mescaline from the peyote cactus, psilocybin from *Psilocybe* mushrooms,

and anticholinergic drugs such as atropine from the deadly nightshade plant, mandrake, or jimsonweed. Although some of these plants have been used for medicinal purposes for centuries, typically the therapeutic benefit has not been a consequence of the hallucinogenic effects of the substance. For example, anticholinergic drugs usually cause CNS depression and induce sleep; therefore, herbs that contain these drugs have been used as sleep potions. The hallucinogenic properties of some natural products, such as peyote, are viewed as positive by some cultures. As already mentioned, peyote is employed in a religious context as a sacrament for the Native American Church. In the United States today, the hallucinogen-containing natural substances are generally not viewed as therapeutic and are more likely to be used for their mind-altering properties as recreational drugs by adolescents. Each year thousands of incidents of accidental consumption of these hallucinogenic plants are reported in the United States (see "Case in Point: Jimsonweed Toxicity in Maryland"), most frequently by

► **CASE IN POINT**

Jimsonweed Toxicity in Maryland

Jimsonweed is a natural herb with medicinal purposes that include treatment for asthma, muscle spasms, and whooping cough. It also causes a cluster of very annoying and even dangerous side effects. Because of these toxic effects, intentional and unintentional use of jimsonweed can often result in an unexpected visit to an emergency room. For example, six adults of the same family were admitted to a Maryland hospital emergency room suffering from extreme hallucinations, incoherence, dilated pupils (causing blurred vision), a very rapid heartbeat,

and, in one case, unconsciousness. The symptoms lasted several hours and the patients remained in the hospital 2 to 4 days. Follow-up investigations discovered that all of the patients had consumed a meal of homemade stew that included jimsonweed. The preparer of the stew inadvertently included cuttings from a jimsonweed plant outside the kitchen door without knowledge of the plant's toxic consequences. Such emergency experiences are all too frequent results of ignorance about this natural, but potent, hallucinogen.

Data from Russell, J. "Jimsonweed Poisoning Associated with a Homemade Stew." *Morbidity and Mortality Weekly Report* 59 (2010): 102–104. Available http://www.cdc.gov/mmwr/preview/mmwrhtml/mm5904a3.htm

children and kids trying to get high (Diaz 2016). Some users claim because these are natural rather than synthetic sources of a hallucinogenic episode that somehow it makes the experience more rewarding and desirable. There is no evidence that the natural-versus-synthetic features of a hallucinogen are responsible for the quality of a drug-induced hallucination. Frequently, consumption of these seeds and weeds causes severe hallucinations, dry mouth, hyperthermia, seizures, and occasionally death (Leinwand 2006; Russell 2010; Wagner 2015).

■ Salvia divinorum

Occasionally, obscure hallucinogenic herbs make their way into the culture of hallucinogenic substance users. This migration has become easier because of the Internet and specialized websites that provide information (some accurate and much anecdotal) and the means to acquire these typically natural substances. For example, a relatively recent hallucinogenic fad has been the use of the Mexican herb *Salvia divinorum*, a drug that did not reach the United States until the late 1980s. In 2015, this plant was abused by 1.9% of high school seniors in the United States, a decrease from 5.7% in 2009 (Johnston 2016). This bright, leafy green plant is usually smoked but can also be chewed, crushed, or mixed in a drink (Fernandez 2008). This relatively unknown plant is referred to as *diviner's mint*, and although it has become illegal in many states because of its intense hallucinations, "out-of-body" experiences, and short-term memory loss, the federal government has not yet outlawed this hallucinogenic

plant (Siebert 2015). Promotions for these products include advertising claims such as "The Mazatec people have preserved *Salvia divinorum* and the knowledge surrounding its use for hundreds of years. We are privileged to have them share their sacred herb with us" (Jones 2001, p. A14). The dried herb sells for $10 to $60 a hit depending on the quality and purity of the product (Detrick 2010). The substance typically makes the user introverted while "altering the consciousness in unusual ways" (Vince 2006). The herb can have dramatic effects on perception, similar to those seen with LSD (Johnson et al. 2016), and cause hallucinations when chewed or smoked (Leinwand 2003). It typically is not used in social settings and frequently is used only once because for some people the effects can be quite unpleasant, often triggering a lack of coordination and frightening perceptions (Fernandez 2008). Because of its frequent negative consequences, this herb is not viewed as particularly addicting for most people (Detrick 2010; Pienciak 2003). However, some users describe a pleasant experience that is "almost innocent and quaint," with one teenage user describing the effects of salvia as causing "Ferris wheels, flying pigs, and fairies wearing a green dress" (Fernandez 2008). More recent reports from some scientists researching the active ingredient salvinorum A suggest that this drug may be useful in the treatment of conditions such as depression, stress management, or even drug addiction itself. Much more research needs to be conducted to determine which, if any, of these claims are clinically significant (Davis 2016b; Johnson et al. 2016).

LEARNING PORTFOLIO

Discussion Questions

1. Why were substances with hallucinogenic properties used by ancient religions and cults?
2. Would you expect natural hallucinogens such as peyote to have fewer adverse effects than other hallucinogens? Why or why not?
3. Why would a drug with both stimulant and hallucinogenic effects have peculiar abuse potential, especially to young people?
4. Why do some users find psychedelic experiences terrifying, whereas others find them desirable?
5. Do you think the federal government is justified in covering up information about the benefits of hallucinogens to convince people to stop using these drugs? Defend your answer.
6. How do the side effects of LSD compare with those of the CNS stimulants, especially with regards to addiction?
7. Why has MDMA been so popular, especially among young people?
8. Do you think scientists should research psychedelic drugs such as LSD and MDMA to determine if they have medicinal value? What are the advantages and disadvantages of doing this, and what role should the FDA play?
9. Why is PCP more dangerous than LSD?
10. How do PCP and ketamine compare?
11. Should severe depression be treated with ketamine?
12. What is the best way to convince people that hallucinogenic drugs of abuse can be harmful?
13. What is a flashback, and how is it caused?
14. Should *Salvia divinorum* be more tightly controlled by the federal government?

Key Terms

Summary

1. Many drugs can exert hallucinogenic effects. The principal hallucinogens include LSD types, phenylethylamines, and anticholinergic agents. The four major effects that occur from administering LSD are (a) heightened senses, (b) loss of sensory control, (c) self-reflection or introspection, and (d) loss of identity or sense of cosmic merging.
2. Hallucinogens exaggerate sensory input and cause vivid and unusual visual and auditory effects.
3. The classic hallucinogens, such as LSD, cause predominantly psychedelic effects. Phenylethylamines are related to amphetamines, such as Ecstasy, and cause varying combinations of psychedelic and stimulant effects. Anticholinergic drugs, such as scopolamine or antihistamines, can also produce psychedelic

effects when taken in high doses, but because of their annoying side effects, they are not usually abused recreationally.

4. One of the prominent effects of hallucinogens is self-reflection. The user becomes aware of thoughts and feelings that had been forgotten or repressed. It is claimed that some experiences help to clarify motives and relationships and cause periods of greater openness. These effects have been promoted by some psychiatrists as providing valid insights useful in psychotherapy, especially for managing conditions such as PTSD, anxiety disorders, and depression.

5. The classic hallucinogens do not cause physical dependence. Although some tolerance can build up to the hallucinogenic effects of drugs such as LSD, withdrawal effects are usually minor.

6. The environment plays a major role in determining the sensory response to hallucinogens. Environments that are warm, comfortable, and hospitable tend to create a pleasant sensory response to the psychedelic effects of these drugs. Threatening, hostile environments are likely to lead to intimidating, frightening "bad trips."

7. In some users, high doses of LSD can cause a terrifying destruction of identity, resulting in panic and severe anxiety that resembles schizophrenia. Another psychological feature commonly associated with LSD is the flashback phenomenon. LSD use can cause recurring, unexpected visual and time distortions that last a few minutes to several hours. Although unusual, flashbacks can occur months to years after use of the drug.

8. Designer amphetamines such as MDMA (Ecstasy) have been included in the "club drug" phenomenon. MDMA has been used frequently by young people to enhance the sensory experience of raves and the nightclub scene. Although viewed by some as harmless and even therapeutic, evidence of potentially serious negative physiological and neurological consequences suggests that these drugs can be extremely dangerous in high doses and under some conditions.

9. Hallucinogens purchased on the street are often poorly prepared and contaminated with adulterant substances. This practice of cutting the pure drugs with other stimulant or hallucinogenic substances also makes use of street hallucinogens very dangerous and unpredictable.

10. PCP differs from the other traditional hallucinogens in several ways: (a) it is a general anesthetic in high doses; (b) it causes schizophrenia-like psychosis and can produce incredible strength and extreme violent behavior, making users very difficult and dangerous to manage; (c) management of the severe psychological reactions to PCP requires drug therapy, whereas treatment of other hallucinogens often requires only reassurance, talking down, and supportive therapy; and (d) reactions to overdoses include fever, convulsions, and coma. Ketamine is related to, but less potent than, PCP and shares many of its pharmacological effects.

11. Other substances also abused for their hallucinogenic properties include dextromethorphan, a common OTC anticough medication, and some natural herbs, such as *Salvia divinorum*, that are promoted over the Internet.

References

Adam, D. "Truth About Ecstasy's Unlikely Trip from Lab to Dance Floor." *The Guardian*. (18 August 2006). Available http://guardian.co.uk/uk/2006/aug/18/topstories3 .drugsandalcohol

Adler, J. "Getting High on Ecstasy." *Newsweek*. (15 April 1985): 15.

American Psychiatric Association (APA). *Diagnostic and Statistical Manual of Mental Disorders*, 5th ed. Washington, DC: American Psychiatric Association, 2013.

Anders, C. "There Really Is an LSD Shortage, and Here's Why." io9. 2 January 2015. Available http://io9.gizmodo .com/there-really-is-an-lsd-shortage-and-heres-why -1677123866

Anderson, L. "Anticholinergic Drugs to Avoid in the Elderly." Drugs.com. 10 February 2016. Available http://www.drugs.com/article/anticholinergic-drugs -elderly.html

Araujo, A., F. Carvalho, L. Bastos Mde, P. Guedes de Pinho, and M. Carvalho. "The Hallucinogenic World of Tryptamines: An Updated Review." *Archives of Toxicology* 89 (2015): 1151–1173.

Associated Press. "60s Icon Timothy Leary Cooperated with the FBI." *Salt Lake Tribune* 258 (1 July 1999): A-10.

Baggott, M., J. Siegrist, G. Galloway, L. Robertson, J. Coyle, and J. Mendelson. "Investigating the Mechanisms of Hallucinogen-Induced Visions Using 3,4-Methyleneamphetamine (MDA): A Randomized Controlled Trial in Humans." *PLoS One* 5(12): e14074. doi: 10.1371/journal.pone.001407. Available http://www.plosone.org/article/info%3Adoi%2F10.1371%2Fjournal.pone.0014074

Bio. "Timothy Leary, Psychologist (1920-1996)." The Biography.com website. n.d. Available http://www.biography.com/people/timothy-leary-37330#film-tv-tech

Black Witch Coven. "Belladonna." Blog, Herbs & Oils. n.d. Available http://blackwitchcoven.com/the-most-deadly-magick-herbs-1/

Bracchi, M., D. Stuart, R. Castles, S. Khoo, D. Back, and M. Boffito. "Increasing Use of 'Party Drugs' in People Living with HIV on Antiretrovirals: A Concern for Patient Safety." *AIDS* 29 (2015): 1585–1592.

Brock, T. "Today's Designer Drugs and Recreational Drugs of Abuse." Cayman Chemical. 1 September 2012. Available https://www.caymanchem.com/article/2196

Buddy, T. "What Are the Effects of LSD?" VeryWell. 12 January 2012. Available http://alcoholism.about.com/cs/lsd/f/lsd_faq04.htm

Burger, A., ed. "Quotes from Albert Hofmann." *Drugs Affecting the Central Nervous System. Psychotomimetic Agents*, vol. 2. New York: Dekker, 1968.

Buxton, R. "Neuroscientist Explains the Similarities Between the Brains of Praying Nuns and Psychedelic Drug Users." Huffington Post. 28 May 2015. Available http://www.huffingtonpost.com/2015/05/28/psychedelic-drug-brain-effects_n_7455368.html

Carollo, K. "Georgetown Students Arrested for Manufacturing Illegal Drug in Dorm Room." ABC News. 25 October 2010. Available http://abcnews.go.com/Health/MindMoodNews/georgetown-university-students-busted-illegal-drug-manufacturing/story?id=11963382

"Celebration #1." *New Yorker* 42 (1966): 43.

Center for Substance Abuse Research (CESAR). "Dextromethorphan (DXM)." 2005. Available http://www.cesar.umd.edu/cesar/drugs/dxm.asp

Center for Substance Abuse Research (CESAR). "Peyote." 2013. Available http://www.cesar.umd.edu/cesar/drugs/peyote.asp

Citizens' Commission. "PCP Laced Marijuana: Creating Psychosis and Psychiatric Commitment." Citizens Commission on Human Rights, Florida. 24 March 2015. Available http://www.cchrflorida.org/pcp-laced-marijuana-creating-psychosis-and-psychiatric-commitment/

Clark, C. "LSD Could Take You on a Trip to Alice in Wonderland Syndrome." BrainBlogger. 10 May 2015. Available http://brainblogger.com/2015/05/10/lsd-could-take-you-on-a-trip-to-alice-in-wonderland-syndrome/

Consumer Healthcare Products Association (CHPA). "OTC Cough Medicine Abuse Prevention." February 2016. Available http://www.google.com/url?sa=t&rct=j&q=&esrc=s&source=web&cd=1&ved=0ahUKEwjG6aeq5oTNAhVT2GMKHb2tDIgQFggcMAA&url=http%3A%2F%2Fwww.chpa.org%2FPP_CoughMedAbusePrevention.aspx&usg=AFQjCNHa9n3wY0ktG8HHqiJt3SlFO8jjZQ&bvm=bv.123325700,d.cGc

Cunha, J. "Date Rape Drugs Facts." MedicineNet.com. n.d. Available http://www.medicinenet.com/date_rape_drugs/article.htm

Cormier, Z. "Brain Scans Reveal How LSD Affects Consciousness." *Nature* (2016). Available http://www.nature.com/news/brain-scans-reveal-how-lsd-affects-consciousness-1.19727

Davis, K. "PCP (Phencyclidine): Facts, Effects and Health Risks." MNT. 22 January 2016a. Available http://www.medicalnewstoday.com/articles/305328.php

Davis, K. "What Are the Effects of Using Salvia?" MNT. 2 May 2016b. Available http://www.medicalnewstoday.com/articles/309735.php

DEA. "Drugs of Abuse." Drug Enforcement Administration (2015). Available https://www.dea.gov/pr/multimedia-library/publications/drug_of_abuse.pdf

Delgado, J. "Intoxication from LSD and Other Common Hallucinogens." UpToDate. 2013. Available http://www.uptodate.com/contents/intoxication-from-lsd-and-other-common-hallucinogens

Detrick, B. "Salvia Takes a Starring Role." *New York Times*. (23 December 2010). Available http://www.nytimes.com/2010/12/26/fashion/26noticed.html?_r=1

Devlin, H. "Psychedelic Drugs Like LSD Could Be Used to Treat Depression, Study Suggests." *The Guardian*. (5 March 2015). Available https://www.theguardian.com/science/2015/mar/05/psychedelic-drugs-like-lsd-could-be-used-to-treat-depression-study-suggests

Diaz, J. "Poisoning by Herbs and Plants: Rapid Taxonomic Classification and Diagnosis." *Wilderness & Environmental Medicine* 27 (2016): 136–152.

Dishotsky, N. I., W. D. Loughman, R. E. Mogar, and W. R. Lipscomb. "LSD and Genetic Damage." *Science* 172 (1971): 431–440.

Dobner, J. "American Indian Church Sues Feds over Peyote Use." *Native American Times.* (20 September 2010). Available http://www.nativetimes.com /index.php?option=com_content&view=article&id =4268:american-indian-church-sues-feds-over-peyote -use&catid=51&Itemid=27

D'Orazio, J. "Hallucinogen Toxicity." Medscape. 2015a. Available http://emedicine.medscape.com/article/814848 -overview

D'Orazio, J. "Hallucinogen Toxicity Treatment and Management." Medscape. 2015b. Available http://emedicine .medscape.com/article/814848-treatment#d10

DrugDangers. "MDMA (Molly) Parental Warning." 2016. Available http://www.drugdangers.com/MDMA-molly -parental-warning.htm

Drug Enforcement Administration (DEA). "Trippin on Tryptamine." Intelligence Brief. October 2002. Document No. DEA-02052.

Drugs.com. "Dextromethorphan." n.d. Available http:// www.drugs.com/dextromethorphan.html

Encyclopedia Britannica. "Native American Church." 2015. Available http://www.britannica.com/topic/Native -American-Church

Farwell, S. "Though PCP Use Has Been Falling, Drug Can Still Lead to Violent Trouble." *Dallas Morning News.* (9 July 2010). Available http://www.dallasnews .com/sharedcontent/dws/news/localnews/crime /stories/070910dnmetpcp.1cef8c6.html

Fernandez, D. "Salvia Becoming 'Drug du Jour' for Some Teens; Hallucinogenic Herb Salvia Divinorum Causes Concern as Young Adults Use It to Get a Cheap High." WebMD. 26 June 2008. Available http://www.salvia .net/articles.php?id=29

Ferro, S. "Are Acid Flashbacks a Myth?" *Popular Science.* (August 2013). Available http://www.popsci .com/science/article/2013-08/fyi-can-acid-trip -really-give-you-flashbacks

Freeman, S. "How LSD Works." Howstuffworks. n.d. Available http://www.howstuffworks.com/lsd.htm

Frohlich, J., and J. Van Horn. "Ketamine and Dissociatives: Comparisons with Schizophrenia." In *Neuropathology of Drug Addictions and Substance Misuse,* vol. 2, edited by V. Preedy, 649–657. Cambridge, MA: Elsevier, 2016.

Garden Spot. "Auntie Dogma's Garden Spot." 17 July 2013. Available https://auntiedogmasgardenspot .wordpress.com/2013/07/17/atropa-belladonna -belladonna-nightshade-plant-guide/

Goldsmith, N. "Neurotransmitters and the Integral Approach to Reality." *Psychedelic Press.* (23 January 2015). Available http://psypressuk.com/2015/01/23 /neurotransmitters-and-the-integral-approach-to-reality/

GoMentor.com. "Hallucinogens Persisting Perception Disorder (Flashbacks)." n.d. Available http://www .gomentor.com/articles/hallucinogens-persisting -perception-disorder.aspx

Government Conspiracy. "U.S. Government Research on Psychological and Torture Conspiracy." 18 April 2010. Available http://www.governmentconspiracy.net/tag /mk-ultra/

Greer, G., and R. Tolbert. "The Therapeutic Use of MDMA." In *Ecstasy: The Clinical, Pharmacological and Neurotoxicological Effects of the Drug MDMA,* edited by S. J. Peroutka, 28. Boston: Kluwer, 1990.

Hadlock, G., K. Webb, L. McFadden, P. Chu, J. Ellis, S. C. Allen, D. M. Andrenyak, P. L. Vieira-Brock, C. L. German, K. M. Conrad, A. J. Hoonakker, J. W. Gibb, D G. Wilkins, G. R. Hanson, and A. E. Fleckenstein. "4-Methylmethcathinone (Mephedrone): Neuropharmacological Effects of a Designer Stimulant of Abuse." *Journal of Pharmacology and Experimental Therapeutics* 339 (2011): 530–536.

Halpern, J., A. Sherwood, J. Hudson, D. Yurgelun-Todd, and H. Pope. "Psychological and Cognitive Effects of Long-Term Peyote Use Among Native Americans." *Biological Psychiatry* 58 (2005): 624–631.

Hallucinogens.com. "Is Marijuana a Hallucinogen?" n.d. Available http://hallucinogens.com/what-are -hallucinogens/is-marijuana-a-hallucinogen/

Harvey, M. "The Dreaded 'Bad Trip' on LSD—Researchers Are Starting to Understand What Causes Them." Alternet.org. (2014). Available http://www.alternet.org /drugs/dreaded-bad-trip-lsd-researchers-are-starting -understand-what-causes-them

Hendricks, P. "Psychedelic Drug Use Could Reduce Psychological Distress, Suicidal Thinking." Johns Hopkins Medicine. 9 March 2015. Available http://www .hopkinsmedicine.org/news/media/releases/psyche delic_drug_use_could_reduce_psychological_distress _suicidal_thinking

Hooton, C. "Different Stages of the 9-Hour Trip to Show Its Effects." *Independent.* (27 August 2015). Available http://www.independent.co.uk/arts-entertainment /art/news/girl-takes-lsd-draws-herself-over-different -stages-of-the-9-hour-trip-to-show-its-effects-10474372 .html

Horgan, J. "The Psychedelic Sorcerer." n.d. Available http://www.johnhorgan.org/the_psychedelic_sorcerer _15289.htm

Horgan, J. "Don't Downplay Bad Trips." *Scientific American.* (9 February 2015). Available http://blogs.scientificamerican.com/cross-check/as-psychedelics-revival-rolls -on-don-t-downplay-bad-trips/

Huxley, A. *The Doors of Perception*. New York: Harper, 1954.

Jacoby, S. "How These 4 Illegal Drugs Are Treating Mental Illness." *Refinery* 29 (2015). Available http://www.refinery29.com/2015/03/83909/psychedelics-mental-illness-treatment

Johnson, M., K. MacLean, M., Caspers, T. Prisinzano, and R. Griffiths. "Time Course of Pharmacokinetic and Hormonal Effects of Inhaled High-dose Salvinorin A in Humans." *Psychopharmacology* 30 (2016): 323–329.

Johnstad, P. "User Perceptions of Mental Health Consequences of Hallucinogen Use in Self-identified Spiritual Contexts." NAD Research Report. (2015). Available http://bora.uib.no/bitstream/handle/1956/11901/nsad-2015-0053-1.pdf?sequence=3

Johnston, L. D. "Monitoring the Future." University of Michigan. 2016. Available http://www.monitoringthefuture.org/

Jones, R. "New Cautions About an Herb That's Hip, Hallucinogenic and Legal." *New York Times*. (9 July 2001): A-14.

Jones, W. H. S. *Natural History*. Cambridge, MA: Harvard University Press, 1956.

Kyzar, E. A. Stewart, and A. Kalueff. "Effects of LSD on Grooming Behavior in Serotonin Transporter Heterozygous (Sert +/-) Mice." *Behavioral Brain Research* 296 (2016): 47–52.

Landsbaum, C. "What It's Like to Have Your Severe Depression Treated with a Hallucinogenic Drug." Science of Us. (2016). Available http://nymag.com/scienceofus/2016/03/what-its-like-to-treat-severe-depression-with-a-hallucinogenic-drug.html

Leary, T., R. Metzner, and R. Alpert. *The Psychedelic Experience*. New Hyde Park, NY: University Books, 1964.

Leinwand, D. "Teens, and Now DEA, Are on Trail of Hallucinogenic Herb." *USA Today*. (23 June 2003): 1.

Leinwand, D. "Jimson Weed Users Chase High All the Way to the Hospital." *USA Today*. (1 November 2006). Available http://www.usatoday.com/news/nation/2006-11-01-jimson_x.htm

Leonard, M. "DOM, DOB, STP, 2C-b, 2C-e, 2C-I, MDA." Streetdrugs.org. 2015. Available http://www.streetdrugs.org/dom-dob-stp-2c-b-2c-e-mda/

Liester, M. "A Review of Lysergic Acid Diethylamide (LSD) in the Treatment of Addictions: Historical Perspectives and Future Prospects." *Current Drug Abuse Reviews* 7 (2014): 146–156.

MacLaren, E. "The Effects of PCP Use." DrugAbuse.com. n.d. Available http://drugabuse.com/library/the-effects-of-pcp-use/

Maier, T. "PCP Is Rearing Its Ugly Head Again." *Insight on the News*. (17 February 2003): 4–6.

"Many Were Lost Because of Leary." Letters (to the editor). *USA Today*. (3 June 1996): 12-A.

Marquardt, G. M., V. DiStefano, and L. L. Ling. "Pharmacological Effects of (S)-, and (R)-MDA." In *The Psychopharmacology of Hallucinogens*, edited by R. C. Stillman and R. E. Willette. New York: Pergamon, 1978.

Mathias, R. "NIDA Research Takes a New Look at LSD and Other Hallucinogens." *NIDA Notes* 8 (March/April 1993): 6.

McGlothin, W., S. Cohen, and M. S. McGlothin. "Long-Lasting Effects of LSD on Normals." *Archives of General Psychiatry* 17 (1967): 521–532.

Meadow, M. "European MDMA vs. American Molly: The Winner is Clear." YOUREDM (15 October 2015). Available http://www.youredm.com/2015/10/15/european-mdma-vs-american-molly-the-winner-is-clear/

Morgan, C., L. Muetzelfeldt, and H. Curran. "Consequences of Chronic Ketamine Self-Administration upon Neurocognitive Function and Psychological Wellbeing: A 1-Year Longitudinal Study." *Addiction* 105 (2010): 121–133.

Naranjo, C., A. T. Shulgin, and T. Sargent. "Evaluation of 3,4 Methylenedioxyamphetamine (MDA) as an Adjunct to Psychotherapy." *Medicina et Pharmacologia Experimentalis* 17 (1967): 359–364.

National Drug Intelligence Center (NDIC). "PCP, Increasing Availability and Abuse." Intelligence Bulletin. 2004. DOJ Document ID No. 2004-L0424-002.

National Drug Intelligence Center (NDIC). "Foxy Fast Facts." n.d. Available https://www.justice.gov/archive/ndic/pubs6/6440/6440p.pdf

National Institute on Drug Abuse (NIDA). "Hallucinogens and Dissociative Drugs." NIDA Research Report Series. March 2001. NIH Publication No. 01-4209.

National Institute on Drug Abuse (NIDA). "InfoFacts. LSD." 2007a. Available http://nida.nih.gov/Infofax/lsd.html

National Institute on Drug Abuse (NIDA). "PCP/Phencyclidine." 2007b. Available http://nida.nih.gov/Infofax/pcp.html

National Institute on Drug Abuse (NIDA). "NIDA InfoFacts: LSD." Education.com. December 2010. Available http://www.education.com/reference/article/Ref_NIDA_InfoFacts_LSD

National Institute on Drug Abuse (NIDA). "Hallucinogens and Dissociative Drugs." February 2015. Available https://www.drugabuse.gov/publications/research-reports/hallucinogens-dissociative-drugs/where-can-i-get-more-scientific-information-hallucinogens-diss

National Institute on Drug Abuse (NIDA). "Club Drugs." 2016a. Available https://www.drugabuse.gov/drugs-abuse/club-drugs

National Institute on Drug Abuse (NIDA). "DrugFacts: MDMA (Ecstasy/Molly)." February 2016b. Available https://www.drugabuse.gov/publications/drugfacts /mdma-ecstasymolly

National Institutes of Health (NIH). "Marijuana and Cannabinoids: A Neuroscience Research Summit." 22–23 March 2016. Available http://apps1.seiservices.com /nih/mj/2016/Documents/BriefMJSummitMeeting-Summary.pdf

Native American Church. 2008. Available http://www .nativeamericanchurch.com

Ojibwa. "Suppressing Indian Religions in 1915." Native American Netroots. 1 January 2015. Available http:// nativeamericannetroots.net/diary/tag/peyote

OneLuckySoul. "The LSD Experiments of the 1950s and 60s [Videos & Documentaries]." 2015. Available http:// oneluckysoul.blogspot.com/2015/02/the-lsd-experiments-of-1950s-and-60s.html

Pahnke, W. N., and W. A. Richards. "Implications of LSD and Experimental Mysticism." *Journal of Religion and Health* 5 (1966): 175–208.

Parish, B. "Hallucinogen Use." Medscape. 23 November 2015. Available http://emedicine.medscape.com/article /293752-overview

Partnership for Drug-Free Kids. "PCP." Drugfree.org. 2013. Available www.drugfree.org/drug-guide/pcp

Partnership for Drug-Free Kids. "Drug Guide: LSD." Drugfree.org. n.d. Available http://www.drugfree.org /drug-guide/lsd

Pienciak, R. "DEA Issues Warning for Legal Herb Stronger Than LSD." *Daily News* (New York). (25 July 2003).

Penner, J. "The Rise and Fall of LSD." LARB. 2015. Available https://lareviewofbooks.org/article/the-rise-and -fall-of-lsd/

Plummer, C., T. Breadon, J. Pearson, and O. Jones, "The Synthesis and Characterization of MDMA from a Catalytic Oxidation of Material Isolated from Black Pepper reveals Potential Route Specific Impurities." *Science and Justice* 56 (2016): 223–230.

Pollan, M. "The Trip Treatment." *Annals of Medicine.* (9 February 2015). Available http://www.newyorker.com /magazine/2015/02/09/trip-treatment

Psychonaut. "20 Hours in Waking Hell, or, My Experience with DOM." 2015. Available https://www.reddit .com/r/Psychonaut/comments/2u4i8t/20_hours_in _waking_hell_or_my_experience_with_dom/

Rahman, N., A. Fazilah, and M. Effarizah. "Toxicity of Nutmeg (Myristicin): A Review." *International Journal on Advanced Science Engineering Information Technology* 5 (2015): 61–64. Available http://insightsociety.org/ojaseit /index.php/ijaseit/article/viewFile/518/pdf_20

Rega, P. "LSD Toxicity." Medscape. 2015. Available http:// emedicine.medscape.com/article/1011615-overview

Remsberg, R. "Found in the Archives: Military LSD Testing." NPR. 1 December 2010. Available http://www .npr.org/blogs/pictureshow/2010/12/01/131724898 /lsd-testing

Rossen, J. "The Nighttime Agony of Ecstasy." *Van Winkle's.* (11 February 2016). Available http://vanwinkles.com /the-agony-of-the-ecstasy

Russell, J. "Jimsonweed Poisoning Associated with a Homemade Stew." *Morbidity and Mortality Weekly Report* 59 (2010): 102–104. Available http://www.cdc.gov /mmwr/preview/mmwrhtml/mm5904a3.htm

Sample, I. "LSD's Impact on the Brain Revealed in Groundbreaking Images." *The Guardian.* (11 April 2016). Available https://www.theguardian.com/science/2016/apr/11 /lsd-impact-brain-revealed-groundbreaking-images

Sapolsky, R. "Synesthesia: Tasting Sounds and Smelling Sights." *The Wall Street Journal* (25 March 2015). Available http://www.wsj.com/articles/synesthesia-tasting -sounds-and-smelling-sights-1427298999

Schmetzer, A. "Phencyclidine (PCP)-Related Psychiatric Disorders." Medscape. 29 December 2015. Available http:// emedicine.medscape.com/article/290476-overview

Schultes, R. E. "The Plant Kingdom and Hallucinogens (Part III)." *Bulletin on Narcotics* 22 (1970): 25–53.

Schultes, R. E. "Ethnopharmacological Significance of Psychotropic Drugs of Vegetal Origin." In *Principles of Psychopharmacology*, 2nd ed., edited by W. G. Clark and J. del Giudice. New York: Academic Press, 1978.

Schultes, R. E., and A. Hofmann. *The Botany and Chemistry of Hallucinogens*, 2nd ed. Springfield, IL: Thomas, 1980.

Schumacher, M. "Opioid Analgesics & Antagonists." In: *Basic & Clinical Pharmacology*, 12th ed., edited by B. G. Katzung, S. B. Masters, and A. J. Trevor, 543–564. New York: McGraw-Hill Medical, 2012.

Scinto, M. "Inside the Lucrative World of Ecstasy Smuggling." *New York Post.* (28 January 2013). Available http:// www.nypost.com/p/news/opinion/opedcolumnists /riding_the_train_wxKKIdsE4zYejiWxK5AoUO

Siebert, D. "The Legal Status of Salvia Divinorum." *Salvia divinorum* Research and Information Center. 2015. Available http://www.sagewisdom.org/legalstatus .html

Smith, K. "Ketamine Symptoms and Warning Signs." AddictionCenter. 2016. Available https://www.addictioncenter .com/drugs/hallucinogens/ketamine/

Smith, P. "Microdosing: A New, Low-Key Way to Use Psychedelics." Alternet. 12 June 2015. Available http:// www.alternet.org/drugs/microdosing-new-low-key -way-use-psychedelics

Snyder, S. H. *Madness and the Brain.* New York: McGraw-Hill, 1974.

Szalavitz, M. "Can You Get High on Gingerbread? The Truth About Nutmeg." *Time.* (24 December 2010). Available http://healthland.time.com/2010/12/24/high-on-gingerbread-truth-about-nutmeg/

Toufexis, A. "A Crackdown on Ecstasy." *Time.* (10 June 1985): 64.

Tucker, R. "Acid Test." *Omni.* (November 1987): 16.

University of Toronto. "Contain Powerful Alkaloids ex 6 scopolamine from..." History Drug Discovery (2014). Available https://www.coursehero.com/file/p1vopaq/Contain-powerful-alkaloids-Ex-6-Scopolamine-from-Mandrake-Fascinating-folklore/

Vince, G. "Legally High." *New Scientist.* (30 September 2006): 40–45.

Wagner, R. "Tropane Alkaloid Poisoning." Medscape. 2015. Available http://emedicine.medscape.com/article/816657-overview#a4

Weaver, M., J. Hopper, and E. Gunderson. "Designer Drugs 2015: Assessment and Management." *Addiction Science and Clinical Practice* 10 (2015): 1–9.

Weber, B. "Prairie LSD Studies Coined 'Psychedelic.'" *Toronto Star.* (6 October 2006): A8.

WebMD. "Find a Vitamin or Supplement." n.d. Available http://www.webmd.com/vitamins-supplements/ingredientmono-82-henbane.aspx?activeingredientid=82&activeingredientname=henbane

Willing, R. "Researchers Tested Pot, LSD on Army Volunteers." *USA Today.* (6 April 2007). Available http://www.usatoday.com/news/washington/2007-04-05-army-experiments_N.htm

Wing, N. "DEA Approves Study of Psychedelic Drug MDMA in Treatment of Seriously Ill Patients." Huffington Post (2015). Available http://www.huffingtonpost.com/2015/03/18/dea-mdma-study_n_6888972.html

Woolcott, I. "Jimson Weed Datura Stramonium Poisonous Herbal Medicine." Shamanism. 2015. Available http://www.shamanicjourney.com/jimson-weed-datura-stramonium-poisonous-herbal-medicine

Zhou, S. *Cytochrome P450 2D6, Structure, Function, Regulation and Polymorphism.* Boca Raton, FL: CRC Press, 2016.

CHAPTER 13

Marijuana

© JeremyNathan/iStock/Thinkstock.

Did You Know?

▶ George Washington grew marijuana plants at Mount Vernon for medicine and rope making.

▶ In 2013, out of 19.8 million past-month marijuana users aged 12 and older in the United States, approximately 5.7 million used marijuana on a daily or almost daily basis in the past 12 months. Approximately 64.7% of current illicit drug users only used marijuana, and 15.9% used marijuana and other illicit drugs

▶ In some states, marijuana is one of the largest cash-producing crops. For example, California produces nearly 40% of the marijuana in the United States, worth an estimated $18.8 billion, making it the state's largest cash crop.

▶ Marijuana grows wild in many U.S. states today.

▶ Research shows that many users have difficulty learning and remembering what they have learned when they are "high."

▶ A recent poll indicated that 53% of Americans believe that marijuana should be made legal, compared with 44% who want it to remain illegal.

▶ In 2014, 37% of 8th graders, 67% of 10th graders, and 81% of 12th graders reported marijuana as being fairly or very easy to get. It seems clear that marijuana is a highly accessible drug.

▶ The "high" experienced by using marijuana varies not only according to the quality of the drug, the user's expectations, and the physical surroundings where the drug is taken but also according to how the drug is taken, whether it is smoked, inhaled through a vaporizer, or ingested (eaten).

Learning Objectives

On completing this chapter, you should be able to:

❭ Explain what marijuana is and why it remains so attractive and controversial.

❭ Differentiate between the effects of low and high doses of marijuana.

❭ List the potential effects marijuana use has on the body.

❭ Explain how marijuana use can become psychologically addictive.

❭ Describe how tolerance and dependence affect the response to marijuana and its use.

❭ Describe the medical uses of marijuana.

❭ Identify which age groups are most likely to use marijuana.

❭ Identify the major characteristics of first-time marijuana users.

❭ Explain how the perceived danger of marijuana use has changed with regard to high school seniors and younger age groups.

❭ Differentiate between prior and current beliefs regarding the effects of chronic marijuana use.

Introduction

First interview:

Since I was in college and tried my first hit, I have always been a connoisseur of what we used to call grass, now it's weed or even "the ganja." I first went through a period of using it a lot—it was a different way to get a buzz. Then I got married, and my wife did not like me smoking it, and we had kids, so except for a few occasional puffs from my neighbor, I just about gave it up. Then I got divorced [from my wife] and I married a woman who does not object to me smoking a little weed every now and then, even though she does not do it herself. So sometimes on weekends, I will roll a joint before going to bed and take a few puffs off of it. I know it is illegal, but big deal, who knows about it? I used to watch that program *Cops* and just found it silly when police officers would arrest someone (usually a young kid) for possession. Big bust, I would think. Isn't it silly to charge someone with possession of marijuana? I consider it to be like alcohol and cigarettes. I don't think it should be illegal anymore. I know so many people who do it and there are dozens of people who probably use this drug that I am not even aware of their using it. What happens if two-thirds of our population uses this drug? Are we going to charge and arrest all these people? The whole illegality of it is silly. *(From Venturelli's research files, male restaurant owner, age 48, residing in Reno, Nevada, June 10, 2000)*

Second interview:

My kids know that I still smoke dope, and I know they are used to me doing this since from the day they were born. I never hid this habit of mine. I am now 59, and I never even thought of quitting. You see I started back in the late 60s when I was 17 years old. My wife does not do it as much as I do. Usually a couple of times a week, late at night I go outside on the deck and take a few hits. I don't think it is much different than having a drink. Why I have always done it, so what is the big deal? I have a few friends about my age who do the same thing and we don't bother anyone, we work 5 and often 6 days a week at our full-time jobs, and only do this away from work, and as I said only a few times a week. I ask again, what's the big deal? Now society may look down on me, but at this age, I don't give a rat's ass what society thinks. I don't tell anyone about this long-time habit that brings me relief and relaxation and outside of a few friends, my wife, and kids, no one else knows that I do this. As you asked, I really don't care what the law says; I will always do it until I die. It is so natural for me to do this that I don't even think about breaking drug laws. This is a private matter between my family and me. My kids don't smoke dope, and I never thought I would have kids who would not. Especially when I grew up in the 60s everyone I knew smoked dope and I never thought it would change, but today the world is different so I keep to myself with my habits. To me, honestly professor, if marijuana is outlawed and if I wanted to say smoke oregano then they should outlaw oregano. Outlawing a naturally growing plant is just plain stupid. What threat to the world is my smoking weed? I just think this law making marijuana illegal is ridiculous, especially when smoking it is viewed as a violation of law. What a stupid law it is and how effective this law is in that I have smoked dope all my life. *(From Venturelli's research files, male, living in a Midwestern rural area, August 10, 2010)*

Third interview:

We used to have one great big bong and fill it with dope [referring to marijuana], and all of us in someone's fraternity room would each take hits from the bong. Today, it's a different life altogether. I am working three different jobs, one teaching at a junior high school, [one] working at a film production studio, and my third claim to fame is my job as a part-time waiter. . . . I feel that I wasted many nights by just "smokin'," "dopin'," and "drinkin'" back during those college days. I sometimes think that I could have accomplished a lot more if I would not have inhaled so much dope. If I had to do it over again I would not have wasted so much time. *(From Venturelli's research files, male, age 28, August 9, 1996)*

The preceding interviews illustrate contrasting views regarding marijuana usage as a subcultural phenomenon. The first and second interviews present "die-hard" users who refuse to relinquish their use of this drug. These individuals have been using marijuana for many years and they consider it an essential recreational drug. Conversely, the third interviewee expresses some regret over the time "wasted" while becoming intoxicated with marijuana when he could have been pursuing other, more career-oriented activities.

Although marijuana is potentially less addictive than other drugs, such as cocaine, crack, heroin, and barbiturates (to name a few), it remains one of the few drugs that is controversial. (As an example of the controversy that surrounds this drug, see "Here and Now: Legalizing Recreational and Medicinal Marijuana Use.") It is difficult to wade through the emotion, politics, and rigidity found in the writings on marijuana to tease out the objective, clinical reality. In the United States, extreme views go back to the 1930s, when the film *Reefer Madness* portrayed an after-school marijuana "club" for high school students in suits and

HERE AND NOW

Legalizing Recreational and Medicinal Marijuana Use

Recent developments in legalizing recreational and medical marijuana use include the following:

- An April 2014 Pew Research Center poll found that "[f]or the first time in more than four decades of polling on the issue, a majority of Americans favor legalizing the use of marijuana" (Pew Research Center 2013). The national survey found that 52% said marijuana should be made legal, but 45% said it should not. According to Pew, support for legalizing marijuana has risen 11 points since 2010 (Pew Research Center 2013). A more recent poll in April 2015 indicated that "[a] slim majority (53%) of Americans say the drug [referring to marijuana] . . . should be made legal compared with 44% who want it to be illegal" (Motel 2015).

- "On Tuesday [May 28, 2013], Colorado Gov. John Hickenlooper signed several historic measures to implement marijuana legalization in the state, establishing Colorado as the world's first legal, regulated and taxed marijuana market for adults" (Ferner 2013). Although Governor Hickenlooper is a very vocal opponent of such legalization, he "signed the first bills in history to establish a legal marijuana market as well as starting the development of a regulatory framework for cultivation, distribution, and processing of industrial hemp" (Ferner 2013). At this press conference the governor's chief legal counsel reiterated that "the will of the voters needed to be implemented" (Ferner 2013).

- More recent battleground states where the legalization of marijuana is advancing includes "looking to let either lawmakers or voters decide on cannabis on the 2016 ballot. Four states and Washington, D.C., have passed legislation to permit recreational marijuana entirely, and others are gearing up to consider whether to follow their lead in the new year. At least 10 states are expected to consider whether to legalize marijuana for some degree of use" (Salo 2015). Specifically, the 10 states where legalization of marijuana is gaining momentum are Arizona, California, Florida, Maine, Massachusetts, Michigan, Missouri, Nevada, Rhode Island, and Vermont (Salo 2015). Nevada, for example, has taken "a while to legalize medical marijuana, but now that it's on that path to legalization, it's not stopping 'til the end. Nevada's was the first state campaign to officially gather the required number of signatures to qualify for the 2016 ballot, submitting 170,000 signatures last December. That's about 60,000 more signatures than the 101,667 signatures needed, and nearly two years early. Nevada's already opened a successful medical marijuana program that allows reciprocity without any issues. With any luck, it's locked in on recreational and won't stop until next November" (Rough 2015).

- Finally, another more detailed summation of legislative advances is the state of Connecticut, which "took the plunge for medical marijuana in 2012, and a year after its first dispensaries opened, its program was running smoothly with a patient base of 6700 registrants and six state-licensed dispensaries. Not only that, but a poll from the University of New Haven found residents overwhelming support cannabis, with 56% polled saying they agreed that legalizing marijuana would have a positive impact on Connecticut's economy. There were two legalization initiatives considered during the 2015 legislative session that stalled eventually, and Connecticut cops are already preparing for legalization as an inevitability, so the real question is will 2016 be the year it happens?" (Rough 2015).

- In Salem, Oregon, "[a] legislative budget committee has signed off on a bill that would legalize medical marijuana dispensaries in Oregon" (*The*

(continues)

HERE AND NOW
Legalizing Recreational and Medicinal Marijuana Use (*continued*)

Republic and the Associated Press 2013). This bill was approved and sent to the full House for a vote. If passed, the state's 53,000 medical marijuana cardholders would be able to get their medicine (marijuana).

- [Though] "Alaska law currently allows those with a medicinal marijuana prescription to legally grow up to six plants or have up to one ounce marijuana, . . . [a]n Alaska citizens' group is pushing to legalize recreational marijuana, which would make it the third state to do so after Colorado and Washington . . . [While this initiative to legalize marijuana in Alaska has not yet passed, it is] . . . [d]riven by growing public support, . . . [The] Campaign to Regulate Marijuana submitted more than 45,000 signatures Wednesday to Alaska election

officials. It needs about 30,000 verified signatures to qualify for the August state ballot. 'The proposed initiative will take marijuana sales out of the underground market and put them in legitimate, taxpaying businesses,' . . . [T]he proposal . . . [expected to be voted on in Alaska is] similar to one passed in Colorado, . . . [which] legalizes the growing, buying and consumption of marijuana for adults ages 21 or older. . . . In addition to Colorado and Washington, 18 other states and the District of Columbia allow some legal use of marijuana, primarily for medicinal purposes. Pro-recreational marijuana Initiatives are expected in various states in 2016, including Arizona, California, Maine, Massachusetts, Montana and Nevada, according to Mason Tvert of the Marijuana Policy Project" (Karimi 2014).

Data from Pew Research Center. "Majority Now Supports Legalizing Marijuana." 4 April 2013. Available http://www.people-press.org/2013/04/04/majority-now-supports-legalizing-marijuana/; Motel, S. "6 Facts About Marijuana." Pew Research Center. April 2015. Available http://www.pewresearch.org/fact-tank/2015/04/14/6-facts-about-marijuana/; Flores, E. "Group Works to Legalize Marijuana, Others Fight Against It." KVOA.com (Tucson, AZ), 13 June 2013. Ferner, M. "Marijuana Legalization: Colo. Gov. Hickenlooper Signs First Bills in History to Establish a Legal Regulated Pot Market for Adults." Huffington Post. 28 May 2013 (updated 4 June 2013). Available http://www.huffingtonpost.com/2013/05/28/hickenlooper-signs-colora_n_3346798.html; Rough, L. "Which States Are Most Likely to Legalize Cannabis in 2016." Leafly. (22 December 2015). Available https://www.leafly.com/news/headlines/what-states-are-most-likely-to-legalize-in-2016; Salo, J. "Marijuana Legalization 2016: Which States Will Consider Cannabis This Year?" *International Business Times*. (30 December 2015). Available http://www.ibtimes.com/marijuana-legalization-2016-which-states-will-consider-cannabis-year-2245024; *The Republic* and the Associated Press. "Ore Legislative Panel Signs Off on Bill Legalizing Medical Marijuana Dispensaries," 19 June 2013.

ties who became hallucinatory, homicidal, violent, and suicidal; such symptoms were highly exaggerated. As a complete contradiction, in the same decade, the Rastafarian religion spread among Jamaican agricultural workers, who named marijuana a holy plant:

> [In] *Ganja in Jamaica* (Rubin and Comitas 1975) [the book] focused its findings to refute the claim that marijuana users damaged their productive capability. The study found that most rural Jamaicans who smoked ganja (marijuana) were extraordinarily diligent peasants who invested impressive amounts of time and energy in multiple income-bearing schemes every day of the year. Starting before sunrise, they tended livestock and poultry; farmed gardens; hired out their labor for wages; exchanged goods and services in an indigenous marketing system; maintained churches, self-help associations, political

parties, guilds, schools, and households; and sometimes, at night, clandestinely cleared acres of forest to cultivate marijuana. They listened to the radio, watched television, and read newspapers to perform better as citizens in a modern democracy. These active, clear-sighted economic strategists and community builders depended on a heavy daily intake of ganja for nourishment as "brain food," and relied on it specifically to improve production. Adult Jamaican marijuana smokers consumed some six or more large "spliffs" (hand-rolled cigars) of ganja a day, or a few ounces. They also consumed it in teas, tisanes, and tonics. As employers, they preferred to pay their employees ganja rather than money and encouraged its use in the workplace. (Rubin and Comitas 1975, cited in Hamid 1998, p. 61)

Marijuana consists of the dried and crushed leaves, flowers, stems, and seeds of the *Cannabis*

Close-ups of growing marijuana plants of the *Cannabis indica* strain. This type of marijuana often is used for legal and illegal human consumption as a mind-altering drug.

plant. The two main strains are **Cannabis sativa** and **Cannabis indica**. They differ "in their chemical composition, physiological aesthetic, and medical application" (ProCon.org 2012a). *C. sativa* originates from Colombia, Mexico, Jamaica, South Africa, Thailand, and Southeast Asia and generally causes uplifting and energetic feelings, stimulates the appetite, and provides pain relief from certain ailments (Budfacts.com 2009). Some believe that it enhances creativity:

> *Sativa* dominant marijuana strains tend to have a more grassy type odor to the buds providing an uplifting, energetic and "cerebral" high that is best suited for daytime smoking. A *sativa* high is one filled with creativity and energy as being high on *sativa* can spark new ideas and creations. Many artists take advantage of the creative powers of *Cannabis sativa* [marijuana] to create paintings. (Smoker 2014)

This strain is grown in countries that have hotter climates. It is a brighter green than the *C.*

indica strain and has narrower leaves and reaches an average height of more than 6 feet.

C. indica originates from hash-producing countries (e.g., Afghanistan, Pakistan, India, Turkey, Morocco, and Tibet) (ProCon.org 2012a), and its effects include relaxation of the body, stress relief, and calmness and serenity (Budfacts.com 2009). Some believe that *C. indica* is effective as a pain reliever and as a treatment for insomnia (Smoker 2014). Medical marijuana patients often smoke *C. indica* buds in the late evening or right before bed (Smoker 2014). Unlike *C. sativa*, *C. indica* grows well in warm, not hot, climates, and the plants are shorter (less than 6 feet tall) and a darker green in color with wider leaves (Weedist 2012). The tetrahydrocannabinol (THC) content in the two strains differs; with the *C. indica* strain generally having a lower THC content (Weedist 2012).

Finally, *Cannabis* strains are available across the whole spectrum, from pure *sativas* to pure *indicas*, and in every combination in between, from 30% *sativa*–70% *indica*, 80% *sativa*–20% *indica*, and many, many other combinations (BudFacts.com 2009).

These two main *Cannabis* species have been cultivated for thousands of years. Smoking the dried and crushed leaves, stems, and seeds produces sedative and mind-altering effects, which vary according to the potency of the variety of cannabis used.

Usage in the United States began in the 1920s, rose during the 1960s and 1970s, and fell in every year from 1978 until 1991. From 1991 on, however, usage began to climb. In this chapter, we review the history, past and current usage trends, attitudes, and controversies surrounding marijuana (including the amotivational syndrome and the current debate regarding the legalization of marijuana for medical purposes) and its physiological and behavioral effects on the user.

KEY TERMS

Cannabis sativa
biological name of one of two major species of marijuana that originates from Colombia, Mexico, Thailand, and Southeast Asia; generally causes uplifting and largely psychological and/or mental energetic feelings, as well as providing pain relief for certain ailments

Cannabis indica
biological name of one of two major species of marijuana that originates from hash-producing countries (e.g., Afghanistan, Morocco, and Tibet); its effects include relaxation of the body, stress relief, and calmness and serenity; is known to cause a strong body high

Marijuana: History and Current Trends

As the rich history in this section will reveal, the trends and economic impact of marijuana are noteworthy. Historically, many societies discovered marijuana as a valued crop when they realized that marijuana's woody stems, known as *hemp*, yielded a fiber that could be used to make cloth or rope. The extensive use and economic impact of marijuana continues to the present day, as exemplified by many states using marijuana as a cash crop. In fact, according to the former head of the legalization group NORML, the annual marijuana crop "is now the nation's most valuable, worth more than cultivation of corn and wheat combined" (Join Together Staff 2006). Further, *Reuters* reported "that public-policy analyst Jon Gettman estimated the value of the U.S. marijuana crop at $35 billion annually, with California, Tennessee, Kentucky, Hawaii, and Washington each producing more than $1 billion worth of the illegal drug each year." The market for legal cannabis is growing rapidly, increasing by 74% in 2014 (Ferner 2015). In looking at just one state, estimates put the annual California marijuana crop at $13.8 billion per year (Join Together Staff 2006). By another estimate, "California produces nearly 40 percent of the marijuana in the U.S.; worth an estimated $18.8 billion... [and] by far the state's biggest cash crop" (Jenkins 2011).[1] Other estimates put the value of annual marijuana production in the United States at $35.8 billion, exceeding the combined value of corn ($23.3 billion) and wheat ($7.5 billion) (Venkataraman 2006).

■ Historical Roots of Marijuana

The term *cannabis* comes from the Greek word for hemp. Initially, the Spaniards brought cannabis to the Western Hemisphere as a source of fiber and seeds. For thousands of years, the seeds have been pressed to extract a reddish oil used for medicinal and euphorigenic purposes (Abood and Martin 1992; Iversen 1993). The

plants (both male and female) also produce a resin with active ingredients that affect the central nervous system (CNS). Marijuana contains hundreds of chemical compounds, but only a few found in the resin are responsible for producing the euphoric high.

Even the original uses of marijuana remain controversial. Botanists have never been able to trace cannabis to its origins, although some think it originated in Asia. Ancient Chinese documents contain the earliest recorded name of hemp—*ma*, meaning "fiber-producing plant," as well as "valuable" or "endearing." The term *ma* was still used as late as 1930. In the late 1970s, during an archeological dig in Gansu, the seat of Chinese civilization, workers uncovered cannabis seeds stored in an earthen jar.

Ayurvedic documents from 600 BC describe an intoxicating resin from the plant. The fifth-century BC Greek historian Herodotus recorded that the Scythians burned the tops of the plant, producing a narcotic smoke. A first-century Greek physician wrote that hemp was made into intoxicating cakes, perhaps the forerunners of the marijuana brownies of 1960s fame (Pollan 1998).

Other sources report that the first known record of marijuana use is in the *Book of Drugs*, written about 2737 BC by the Chinese emperor Shen Nung; he prescribed marijuana for treating gout, malaria, gas pains, and absentmindedness. The Chinese apparently had much respect for the plant. They obtained fiber for clothes and medicine from it for thousands of years.

Around 500 BC, another Chinese book of treatments referred to the medical use of marijuana. Nonetheless, the plant got a bad name from the moralists of the day, who claimed that youngsters became wild and disrespectful from the recreational use of *ma*. They called it the "liberator of sin" because, under its influence, the youngsters refused to listen to their elders and did other scandalous things. Although the Chinese recognized *ma*'s medical usefulness, they eventually banned it because of its unpredictable intoxicating effects. Later, because of rampant use, it was legalized again.

India also has a long and varied history of marijuana use. It was an essential part of Indian religious ceremonies for thousands of years. The well-known *Rig Veda* and other chants describe the use of *soma*, which some believe was marijuana. Early writings describe a ritual in which resin was collected from the plants. After fasting and purification, certain men ran naked through the cannabis fields. The clinging resin was scraped off their

---

[1]Note that another assessment regarding the value of marijuana production disagrees with these estimates, stating that "Marijuana's wholesale value as a crop is somewhere between 2 and 4 billion dollars per year, the authors estimate, not $35.8 billion as NORML's John Gettman has said, nor is California's crop worth $17.8 billion, as California's Bureau of Narcotics Enforcement estimates" (Downs 2012; Venkataraman 2006).

bodies, and cakes were made from it and used in feasts. For centuries, missionaries in India tried to ban the use of marijuana, but they were never successful, because its use was too heavily ingrained in the culture. From India, the use of marijuana spread throughout Asia, Africa, Europe, and the Americas, with English settlers bringing it to the American colonies.

Assyrian records dating back to 650 BC refer to a drug called *azulla* that was used for making rope and cloth and was consumed to experience euphoria. The ancient Greeks also knew about marijuana. Galen described the general use of hemp in cakes, which, when eaten in excess, produced narcotic effects. Herodotus described the Scythian custom of burning marijuana seeds and leaves to produce a narcotic smoke in steam baths. It was believed that breathing the smoke from the burning plants would cause frenzied activity. Groups of people stood in the smoke, laughed, and danced as it took effect.

One legend about cannabis is based on the travels of Marco Polo in the 12th century. Marco Polo told of the legendary Hasan Ibn-Sabbah, who terrorized a part of Arabia in the early 1100s. His men were some of the earliest political murderers, and he ordered them to kill under the influence of hashish, a strong, unadulterated cannabis derivative. The cult was called the *hashishiyya*, from which came the word *hashish*. (The word *assassin* may be derived from the name of Sheik Hasan, who was a political leader in the 10th century.) It is unlikely, however, that using hashish can turn people into killers. Experience suggests that people tend to become sleepy and indolent rather than violent after eating or smoking hashish or another of the strong cannabis preparations available in Arabia (Abel 1989).

Napoleon's troops brought hashish to France after their campaign in Egypt at the beginning of the 19th century, despite Napoleon's strict orders to the contrary. By the 1840s, the use of hashish, as well as opium, was widespread in France, and efforts to curb its spread were unsuccessful.

In North America, hemp was planted near Jamestown in 1611 for use in making rope. By 1630, half of the winter clothing at the settlement was made from hemp fibers. There is no evidence that hemp was used medicinally at this time. Hemp was also valuable as a source of fiber for clothing and rope for the Pilgrims at Plymouth. To meet the demand for fiber, a law was passed in Massachusetts in 1639 requiring every household to plant hemp seed. However, it took much manual labor to work the hemp fiber into usable form,

resulting in a chronic shortage of fiber for fishnets and the like (Abel 1989).

George Washington cultivated a field of hemp at Mount Vernon, and there is some indication that it was used for medicine as well as for making rope. In his writings, Washington once mentioned that he forgot to separate the male and female plants, a process usually done because the female plant produces more resin if it remains unpollinated.

In the early 1800s, U.S. physicians used marijuana extracts to produce a tonic intended for both medicinal and recreational purposes. This practice changed in 1937 with passage of the Marijuana Tax Act. The Marijuana Tax Act was modeled after the Harrison Act of 1914 in that marijuana was considered a narcotic and subject to the same legal controls as cocaine and the opiates. Like these opiates, marijuana distributors had to register and pay a tax to legally import, buy, or sell this drug (Musto 1999). As a result, the Marijuana Tax Act prohibited the use of this drug as an intoxicant and regulated its use as a medicine.

Most of the abuse of marijuana in the United States during the early part of the 20th century took place near the Mexican border and in the ghetto areas of major cities. Cannabis was mistakenly considered a narcotic, like opium, and legal authorities treated it as such (Abood and Martin 1992). In 1931, Harry Anslinger, who was the first appointed head of the Bureau of Narcotics and later would become responsible for the enforcement of marijuana laws, believed that the problem was slight (Musto 1999; Venturelli 2016). By 1936, however, he claimed that the increase in the use of marijuana was of great national concern (Anslinger and Cooper 1937) (see **Figure 13.1**).

FIGURE 13.1 This antimarijuana poster was distributed by the Federal Bureau of Narcotics in the late 1930s.

Anslinger set up an informational program that ultimately led to the federal law that banned marijuana. The following sensationalized statement was part of Anslinger's campaign to outlaw the drug:

> What about the alleged connection between drugs and sexual pleasure? . . . What is the real relationship between drugs and sex? There isn't any question about marijuana being a sexual stimulant. It has been used throughout the ages for that: in Egypt, for instance. From what we have seen, it is an aphrodisiac, and I believe that the use in colleges today has sexual connotations. (Anslinger and Cooper 1937, p. 19)

In addition, during this time, some usually accurate magazines reported that marijuana was partly responsible for crimes of violence. In 1936, *Scientific American* reported that "marijuana produces a wide variety of symptoms in the user, including hilarity, swooning, and sexual excitement. Combined with intoxicants, it often makes the smoker vicious, with a desire to fight and kill" ("Marijuana Menaces Youth" 1936, p. 151; Venturelli 2016). A famous poster of the day, called "The Assassination of Youth," was effective in molding attitudes against drug use.

Largely because of the media's influence on public opinion, Congress passed the Marijuana Tax Act in 1937. However, because of the discussions and debates before the passage of the 1970 Comprehensive Drug Abuse Prevention and Control Act, which replaced or updated all other laws concerning narcotics and dangerous drugs, the Marijuana Tax Act of 1937 was declared unconstitutional in 1969 because it classified marijuana as a narcotic. Marijuana has not been classified as a narcotic since 1971 (Venturelli 2016).

In the early 1900s, marijuana was brought across the U.S. border by Mexican laborers who entered the United States seeking jobs. From the border areas of the United States, recreational use of marijuana spread into mainly the southwestern region of the United States. Such use reached major cities in Texas and surrounding states as well as a number of African American communities in these cities. Heavy users of marijuana included a subpopulation of jazz musicians as well as other "bohemian types" who led more of an unstructured existence in unconventional jobs and occupations (e.g., artists, entertainers, poets, criminals). Thus, before the 1960s, marijuana use was largely confined to small segments of African American urban youth, jazz musicians, and artists and writers who belonged to the 1950s Beat Generation. Use rose tremendously in the 1960s,

when it was closely associated with the hippie counterculture, in which marijuana was categorized as a psychedelic (consciousness-expanding) sacrament. It spread into other youth categories during the 1970s, until approximately 1978. In each year from 1978 until 1991, marijuana use fell. After 1991, researchers and prevention specialists were astounded to see a rise in usage among youth (Venturelli 2016).

Marijuana still grows wild in many U.S. states today. Curiously, one reason for the survival of this supply is that, during World War II, the fiber used to make rope (sisal) was hard to import, so the government paid subsidies to farmers who grew hemp. Much of today's crop comes from these same plants. Another reason for the spread of the plants is that, until recently, the seeds were used in birdseed. Leftover seed was discarded in the garbage and thus spread to landfill dumps, where it sprouted. Birdseed containing marijuana seeds is still available, but the seeds are sterilized so that they cannot germinate.

The Indian Hemp Drug Commission Report in the 1890s and the 1930 Panama Canal Zone Report on marijuana stressed that available evidence did not prove marijuana as dangerous as it was popularly thought; these reports were given little publicity, however, and for the most part were disregarded. In 1944, a report was issued by the LaGuardia Committee on Marijuana, which consisted of 31 qualified physicians, psychiatrists, psychologists, pharmacologists, chemists, and sociologists appointed by the New York Academy of Medicine. They stated in one key summary that marijuana was not the killer many thought it to be:

> It was found that marijuana in an effective dose impairs intellectual functioning in general. . . . Marijuana does not change the basic personality structure of the individual. It lessens inhibition and this brings out what is latent in his thoughts and emotions but it does not evoke responses that would otherwise be totally alien to him. . . . Those who have been smoking marijuana for years showed no mental or physical deterioration that may be attributed to the drug. (Solomon 1966, p. 37)

Much of the early research conducted did not consider the potency of marijuana. As a result, findings from various studies are often conflicting and difficult to compare. Because the quality of marijuana varies so greatly, it is impossible to know the amount of drug taken without analyzing the original material and the leftover stub, or "roach." Conditions such as type of seed, soil moisture and fertility, amount of sunlight, and temperature all have an effect on the amounts of active ingredients found in the resulting marijuana plant.

Current Use of Marijuana

The National Survey on Drug Use and Health (NSDUH) reported that among persons aged 12 or older the overall rate of past-month marijuana use was 7.5% in 2013, 7.3% in 2012, and 7.0% in 2011. Throughout these 3 years, the number of people using marijuana slowly increased. **Figure 13.2** shows that in 2013, out of an estimated 19.8 million Americans aged 12 or older who were current marijuana users, the percentage of past-month marijuana users was a staggering 80.6%. An estimated 64.7% of current illicit drug users *used only marijuana*, and 15.9% used marijuana and another illicit drug. This leaves a minority of illicit drug users (19.4%, approximately 8.7 million) who did not use marijuana (Substance Abuse and Mental Health Services Administration [SAMHSA] 2014).

Other current findings regarding marijuana use are as follows (SAMHSA 2014):

- In 2013, 2.4 million persons had used marijuana for the first time within the past

12 months; this averages to approximately 6600 initiates per day! The 2013 estimate was similar to the estimates in 2008 through 2012 (ranging from 2.2 million to 2.6 million) but was higher than the estimates from 2002 through 2007 (ranging from 2.0 million to 2.2 million) (see **Figure 13.3**).

- In 2013, among persons aged 12 or older, an estimated 1.4 million first-time past-year marijuana users initiated prior to the age of 18. This estimate was similar to the corresponding estimate in 2012. The estimated 1.4 million persons in 2013 who initiated

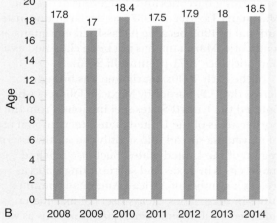

FIGURE 13.3 Past-year marijuana initiates among persons aged 12 or older (A) and mean age at first use of marijuana among past-year initiates (B) aged 12 to 49: 2007–2013.

⁺ Difference between this estimate and the 2011 estimate is statistically significant at the .05 level.

Data from Substance Abuse and Mental Health Services Administration (SAMHSA). *Results from the 2013 National Survey on Drug Use and Health: Summary of National Findings.* NSDUH Series H-48, Publication No. (SMA) 14-4863. Rockville, MD: Substance Abuse and Mental Health Services Administration, 2014.

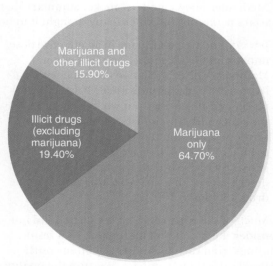

FIGURE 13.2 Types of drugs used in the past month, illicit drug users age 12 or older in 2013.

Data from Substance Abuse and Mental Health Services Administration (SAMHSA). *Results from the 2013 National Survey on Drug Use and Health: Summary of National Findings.* NSDUH Series H-48, Publication No. (SMA) 14-4863. Rockville, MD: Substance Abuse and Mental Health Services Administration, 2014.

TABLE 13.1 Marijuana Use Reported by Americans During Their Lifetime, the Past Year, and the Past Month, According to Age: 2013

Age (Years)	Lifetime (%)	Past Year (%)	Past Month (%)
12-17	16.1	13.3	6.9
18-25	51.9	31.6	19.1
26 or older	48.9	10.3	6.3

Data from Substance Abuse and Mental Health Services Administration, *Results from the 2013 National Survey on Drug Use and Health: Summary of National Findings*, NSDUH Series H-48, HHS Publication No. (SMA) 14-4863. Rockville, MD: Substance Abuse and Mental Health Services Administration, 2014.

prior to the age of 18 represented the majority (56.6%) of the 2.4 million recent marijuana initiates.

- Among all youths aged 12 to 17, an estimated 4.8% had used marijuana for the first time within the past year in 2013, which was similar to the rate in 2012 (5.0%). As a percentage of those aged 12 to 17 who had not used marijuana prior to the past year (i.e., those at risk for initiation), the youth marijuana initiation rate in 2013 (5.5%) was similar to the rate in 2012 (5.7%).
- In 2013, the average age at first marijuana use among recent initiates aged 12 to 49 was 18.0 years, which was similar to the average ages in 2005 through 2008 and 2010 through 2012 but higher than the average ages in 2002 through 2004 and in 2009.
- In 2013, among recent initiates aged 12 or older who initiated marijuana use prior to the age of 21, the mean age at first use was 16.2 years, which was similar to the 2012 estimate of 16.3 years.

As **Table 13.1** shows, the frequency of marijuana use is strongly correlated with age. The age group reporting the highest lifetime (52%), past-year (30.6%), and past-month (18.9%) use is 18- to 25-year-olds. For the 26-and-older age group, marijuana use drops sharply for the past-year (8.8%) and past-month (5.4%) categories.

■ Recent Trends in Use of Marijuana: 8th, 10th, and 12th Graders

In regard to marijuana, in 2014, the percentage of 8th-, 10th-, and 12th-grade students, **Figure 13.4A** shows the percentage who used in the last 12 months. **Figure 13.4B** shows the percentage of grade school students seeing great risk in using

marijuana regularly. **Figure 13.4C** shows the percentage disapproving the use of marijuana on a regular basis. **Figure 13.4D** shows the percentage saying that marijuana is fairly easy or very easy to get.

In looking at the percentage who used in the last 12 months, major findings are the following:[2]

- Annual marijuana prevalence peaked among 12th graders in 1979 at 51%.
- Use declined fairly steadily for 13 years, bottoming at 22% in 1992—a decline of more than half.
- In the 1990s, a resurgence of marijuana use occurred.
- Annual prevalence rates peaked in 1996 at the 8th-grade level and in 1997 at the 10th- and 12th-grade levels. After these peak years, use declined among all three grades through 2006, 2007, and 2008. Since then, there has been an upturn in use in all three grades.
- Annual marijuana prevalence rates among 8th graders increased in use from 2007 to 2010, decreased slightly from 2010 to 2012, and then leveled.
- Among 10th graders, it increased somewhat from 2008 to 2012 and then leveled.
- Daily use increased in all three grades after 2007, reaching peaks in 2011 (at 1.3% in 8th), 2013 (at 4.0% in 10th), and 2011 (at 6.6% in 12th), before declining modestly since. Daily prevalence rates in 2014 for 8th-, 10th-, and 12th-grade students were 1.0%, 3.4%, and 5.8%.
- A more recent study indicates that the prevalence of past-year marijuana/hashish among 12th graders is 34.9% (superseded by alcohol

---

[2]Note that some of the listed findings are not visible in this set of figures (4A-D).

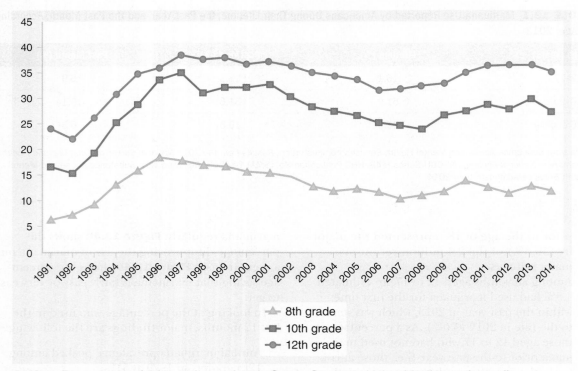

A. Use: Percentage of 8th-, 10th-, and 12th-Grade Students Using Marijuana Annually

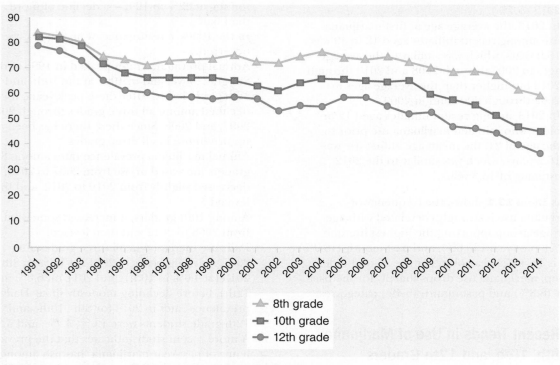

B. Risk: Percentage Seeing "Great Risk" in Using Regularly.

FIGURE 13.4   Marijuana trends: Percentages of marijuana use, risk, disapproval, and availability for 8th-, 10th-, and 12th-grade students. (*continues*)

Data from Johnston, L. D., O'Malley, P. M., Miech, R. A., Bachman, J. G., and J. E. Schulenberg. *Monitoring the Future National Survey Results On Drug Use: 1975–2014: Overview, Key Findings on Adolescent Drug Use.* Ann Arbor: Institute for Social Research, The University of Michigan, 2015.

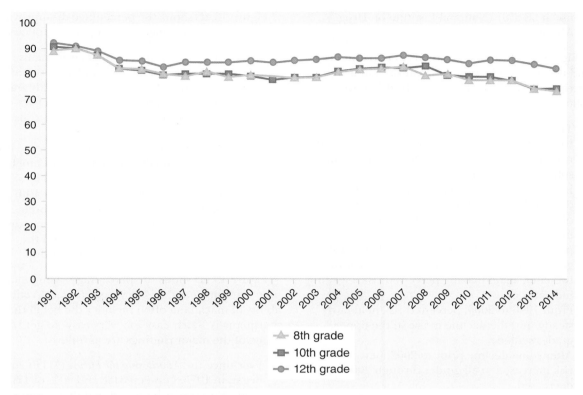

C. Dissaproval: Percentage Disapproving of Using Regularly

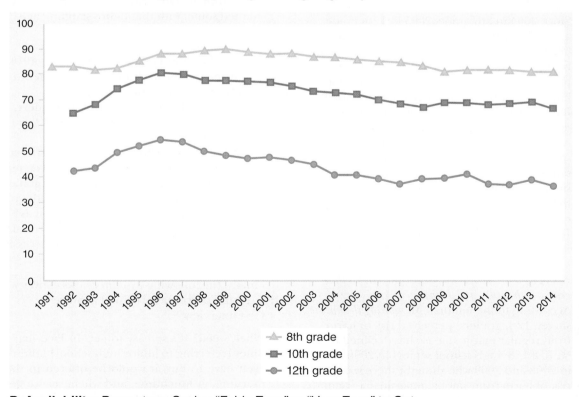

D. Availability: Percentage Saying "Fairly Easy" or "Very Easy" to Get.

FIGURE 13.4 *(continued)*.

Data from Johnston, L. D., O'Malley, P. M., Miech, R. A., Bachman, J. G., and J. E. Schulenberg. *Monitoring the Future National Survey Results On Drug Use: 1975–2014: Overview, Key Findings on Adolescent Drug Use.* Ann Arbor: Institute for Social Research, The University of Michigan, 2015.

use at 58.2%) (National Institute on Drug Abuse [NIDA] 2015).

Figure 13.4B shows the trends in perceived risk and the percentage seeing "great risk" in using marijuana regularly. The major findings are as follows:

- The proportion of students seeing great risk from using marijuana regularly fell during the rise in use in the 1970s and again during the subsequent rise in the 1990s.
- In the 10th and 12th grades, perceived risk declined a year before use rose in the upturn of the 1990s, making perceived risk a leading indicator of change in use. The decline in perceived risk halted in 1996 in 8th and 10th grades; the increases in use ended a year or two later, again making perceived risk a leading indicator of use.
- From 1996 to 2000, perceived risk held fairly steady, and the decline in use in the upper grades stalled.
- After some decline prior to 2002, perceived risk increased in all grades through 2004 as use decreased.
- Perceived risk fell after 2004 in the 8th grade and in 2005 in the 12th grade.
- Since 2004 in 8th grade, 2005 in 12th grade, and 2008 in 10th grade, perceived risk has fallen substantially, presaging the more recent resurgence in marijuana use, but no increase in perceived risk preceded either the recent leveling of use or the modest decline in use in 2014. Rather, perceived risk has continued a steep decline since the mid-2000s.
- According to the national *Monitoring the Future* survey in 2014, the majority of high school seniors do not think occasional marijuana smoking is harmful, with only 36.1% saying that regular use puts the user at great risk, compared to 39.5% in 2013 and 52.4% in 2009 (Johnston et al. 2015). In summation, *although use of marijuana declined in 2014, youth marijuana attitudes moved toward greater acceptance. Perceived risk of regular marijuana use declined in all three grades (8th, 10th, and 12th).*
- According to the national *Monitoring the Future* survey, 12th graders' perceived risk of harm from regular marijuana use has declined from 58% of U.S. high school seniors in 2006 to 52% in 2008 and 2009 who thought there was great risk of harm from smoking marijuana (Center for Substance Abuse Research [CESAR] 2010b).

Figure 13.4C shows the percentage disapproving of regular use. The major findings are as follows:

- Personal disapproval of trying marijuana use fell considerably among 8th graders between 1991 and 1996 and among 10th and 12th graders between 1992 and 1997—by 17%, 21%, and 19%, respectively—which were intervals of increasing use.
- After 1997, there was some modest increase in disapproval among 8th graders but not much among 10th and 12th graders until 2004.
- From 2003 to 2007 (2008 in the case of 10th graders), disapproval increased in all three grades but has declined some since then, particularly in the lower grades. As is often the case, perceived risk fell before disapproval.

Figure 13.4D shows the percentage saying marijuana is "fairly easy" or "very easy" to get. (Availability of marijuana often includes the belief that marijuana is "fairly easy" or "very easy" to get.) Some of the major findings are as follows:

- Ever since the *Monitoring the Future* (MTF) study began in 1975, between 81% and 90% of 12th graders each year have said that they could get marijuana fairly easily or very easily if they wanted some, with that figure standing at 81% in 2014.
- Marijuana has been considerably less readily available to 8th graders, with 37% in 2014 reporting it to be fairly or very easy to get (a significant decline from 2013).
- Availability is intermediate for 10th graders, with 67% reporting easy access in 2014 (also a significant decline from 2013).
- Availability has declined appreciably, especially among the younger adolescents; however, marijuana remains readily available to 12th graders.
- In 2011, 38% of 8th graders, 68% of 10th graders, and 82% of 12th graders reported it as being fairly or very easy to get. It seems clear that marijuana has remained a highly accessible drug.

Finally, the following two interviews convey what figures and percentages cannot capture:
First interview:

What, weed? It's so easy to get. In fact, many times [referring to junior high school] I didn't even have to buy, it would be offered in the morning, at lunchtime, and whenever we get together, even after school it is there. Among the users (and we know each other real well), it's as common as sharing candy. *(From Venturelli's research files, male first-year high school student in a medium-sized town in the Midwest, age 15, June 19, 2000)*

Second interview:

No, I don't smoke it often, but I know over half my friends smoke it two or three times a week and on weekend nights. It's not unusual for several of my friends to smoke up before partying. I usually take a hit or two, but I wouldn't even do that if it weren't for my friends always having it. *(From Venturelli's research files, male senior in high school in a medium-sized town in the Midwest, age 17, July 16, 2010)*

Marijuana: Is It the Assassin of Youth?

In the late 1930s, the poster "Marijuana: Assassin of Youth" made a clever play on words, bringing up reminders of the Middle Eastern *hashashin* cult, whose terrible exploits were attributed to their use of hashish (marijuana resin). At the time, marijuana was incorrectly classified as a narcotic, like opium and morphine. Amotivational syndrome, lassitude, poor driving skills the day after smoking, educational failure, and dependence may not quite add up to "assassination," as wildly exaggerated in *Reefer Madness*. The poster was right, however, in associating use of this drug with young people, among whom marijuana is popular in both local peer groups and broad youth cultures.

■ Major Factors Affecting Marijuana Use

The mass media, parental role models, perceived risk, availability, and peers have the most direct influence on the development of youth's attitudes regarding drug use. An estimated 8.3 million children—11.9%—live with at least one parent (biological, step, adoptive, or foster) who had abused or was dependent on alcohol or an illicit drug in the past year (CESAR 2010a). These findings become worrisome when we consider that marijuana is the most frequently used illicit drug and that parental use of marijuana is a significant influence on teens' use of this drug.

In a study by Kandel et al. (2001), when parents had used marijuana at some time in their lives, their teen children were 40% more likely to have used the drug in their lifetime than teens whose

parents had never used marijuana. Moreover, when parents had used marijuana in the past year, their children were twice as likely to have used in the same time period, as were teens whose parents had not used in the past year. This same study also found that when parents had used marijuana in the past year, their teen children were more likely to have used marijuana in the past year compared with the children of parents who had used at some time in their life but not in the last year. Similarly, parental use of other drugs, such as alcohol, nicotine, and cocaine, was also found to have an impact on their teen children's use of marijuana. More important, the perceived risk is the most important influence on teen marijuana use. In the Kandel et al. (2001) study, it was found to be five times more important than parental use.

As shown in Figure 13.4A, when comparisons are made among 8th, 10th, and 12th graders, marijuana use rises sharply by 12th grade. One main reason for this is because children in lower grades are less likely to have friends and access to friends who use marijuana (as well as access to other major drugs of abuse). Marijuana has been almost universally available to U.S. high school seniors (from 83% to 90%) over at least the past 30 years (Johnston et al. 2009), and nearly half of youth aged 12 to 17 reported easy access to marijuana (Johnston et al. 2013). With easy access to marijuana, it is not surprising that "[n]early 80% of high school seniors don't consider occasional marijuana use harmful—the highest rate since 1983—and 1 in 15 smoke nearly every day" (Leger 2012).

Beginning several years before age 13 (early adolescence), peers and peer groups begin to exert the most influence (Bauman and Ennett 1996; Greenblatt 1999; Heitzeg 1996; Scholastic Inc. 2016; Steinberg 2011; Tudor, Petersen, and Elifson 1987; Venturelli 2000). In fact, even in acquiring the drug, one finding stated that "[m]arijuana distribution relies primarily on informal dealing through social networks" (CESAR 2007). More than one-half (58%) of household residents who had used marijuana in the past year reported that they most recently obtained their marijuana for free, compared to 39% who reported purchasing it. Nearly all marijuana users (89%) reported getting their most recent acquisition from a friend or relative. Unlike users of more expensive drugs, such as cocaine and heroin, the majority of people who used marijuana in the past year (58%) gave away or shared some of their most recent acquisition (CESAR 2007).

Research shows that it is unlikely that an individual will use drugs when his or her peers do not use them. Marijuana use, in particular, is a group-motivated behavior that is strongly affected by peer pressure and influence. In effect, habitual drug users are likely to belong to drug-using groups. In contrast, people who do not use drugs belong to groups in which drug use is perceived as an unacceptable and devious form of social recreation. Learning theory explains how peers can influence one another; drug-using peer members serve as role models, legitimizing use. Peers in such groups are saying, in essence, "It's perfectly normal to use drugs"; in turn, this justifies usage.

In addition to these major factors (the mass media, parental role models, perceived risk, availability, and peer influences), six other factors must be taken into account as influencing drug use:

1. Structural factors, such as age, gender, family background, and religious beliefs.
2. Social and interactional factors, such as the type of interpersonal relationships, friendship cliques, and drug use within the peer group setting.
3. Setting, such as the type of community and neighborhood (physical location where drugs are used).
4. Attitudinal factors, such as personal beliefs and attitudes regarding drug use, and personality factors, such as self-esteem, level of security versus insecurity, and maturation level.
5. Participation in after-school activities is associated with higher levels of academic achievement and self-esteem, as well as lower levels of substance use (SAMHSA 2007b). Regardless of family income, youth ages 12 to 17 who did not participate in any activities had higher rates of past-month cigarette and illicit drug use than those who participated in four, six, seven, or more activities (SAMHSA 2007b, 2016).
6. Finally, even the amount of religious involvement affects illicit drug use (which includes marijuana use). With regard to religious involvement and substance use, adults who reported that religious beliefs are a very important part of their lives were less likely to use illicit drugs in the past month than those who reported that religious beliefs are not a very important part of their lives (6.1% vs. 14.3%) (SAMHSA 2007a, 2016). Other researchers have also identified religiosity as

an important protective factor against substance use (Brigham Young University 2008; Kendler, Gardner, and Prescott 1997; National Center on Addiction and Substance Abuse 2001; SAMHSA 2016; Wallace, Myers, and Osai 2004).

Keep in mind these factors can easily overlap; they are not separate and distinct. Sociologists have long studied "youth cultures" (Coleman 1961). In the 1970s, sociologists began to examine different subcultures of youth in terms of the behaviors that symbolically represent the group, in which participation in drug use is a ritual that marks off entrance into the group and out of childhood—a rite of passage. Typically, U.S. high school culture includes a leading clique, often associated with team sports, whose members might be called "jocks," and a marginal, deviant, or rebellious group (Eckert 1989). In some cases, the latter group is associated with marijuana use. In the mid-1960s, hippies were perceived as a group whose members were part of a counterculture committed to unconventional values, pacifism, and communalism, in addition to psychedelic drugs. By 1970, this name denoted broader segments of youth who adhered merely to hippie styles of clothing and drug use (Buff 1970). By the 1980s, marijuana use was identified with subgroups of youth often called "burnouts." In many communities that were studied by sociologists, burnouts came from all social levels, but were often overrepresented in upper-middle classes, and they were marginal and/or rebellious within the educational system, if not dropouts (Eckert 1989; Gaines 1992). Membership in such marijuana-using subcultures often bonds the youth to ongoing and persistent drug use.

A common example of polydrug use (alcohol and marijuana).

Is Marijuana Really a Gateway Drug?

Gateway drugs are drugs that serve as the gate or path that usually precedes the use of illicit drugs, such as tobacco, marijuana, heroin, and LSD. This concept is often referred to as the *gateway theory*, the *gateway hypothesis*, or the *gateway effect*. Gateway drugs, or drugs of entry, serve to initiate a novice user into the drug-using world. Although the linkage is not biochemical, common gateway drugs include tobacco, inhalants, alcohol, anabolic steroids, Ritalin, and prescription painkillers (i.e., prescription opioid medications) (Benson 2010; NIDA 2011).

The claim that marijuana use often leads to the use of other more serious drugs, such as heroin, remains controversial (Gardner 1992). A Rand press release reported that the gateway theory does not explain the progression to other more addictive drugs; instead, "[t]he people who are predisposed to use drugs and have the opportunity to use drugs *are more likely* than others to use both marijuana and harder drugs. . . . Marijuana typically comes first because it is more available" (Rand Drug Policy Research Center 2002). Thus, instead of assuming that marijuana, alcohol, and other more commonly used drugs are simply gateway drugs responsible for leading to more serious drugs, it is more likely that factors such as (1) the age when teens have opportunities to use marijuana and other drugs, (2) associated opportunities, and (3) the willingness, mindset, or predisposition to use drugs may be better predictors of the progression from less addictive to more addictive and powerful types of drugs.

For example, the gateway theory cannot explain the fact that although it is true that many heroin addicts began drug use with marijuana, it is also true that many, if not most, also used coffee and cigarettes. Millions of marijuana users never go beyond the gateway drugs used: "There are only a few thousand opiate addicts in Great Britain, yet there are millions who have tried cannabis" (Gossop 1987, p. 9).

Nevertheless, the gateway theory may offer a plausible explanation as to why a small percentage of marijuana users progress to hard drugs such as cocaine or heroin. In many cases, it may be unlikely that the use of marijuana as well as other drugs considered to be gateway drugs would be the *principal cause* for progressing to harder and more addictive types of drugs.

Youth who turn to drugs are usually seriously alienated individuals. Thus, progression from marijuana to other drugs is more likely to depend on peer-group composition, family relationships, social class, and the age at which drug use begins (Indiana Prevention Resource Center 1996).

It is important to note, however, that many, if not most, young drug users do eventually leave drug-using groups and abandon their drug-using behavior, a process sometimes called *maturing out*. An example that often typifies maturing out is found in the following interviews:

First interview:

Up until I started my full-time job after graduation from college I was smoking weed and at parties using other even worse types of drugs without any hesitation. Even during my senior year in high school I was smoking weed nearly every day and graduated with a B average. But then, once I joined this company I am still working at today, they were drug testing, so I quit everything. I just did not want to risk a good paying job that I liked for drugs. Plus the embarrassment of not passing a drug test, when my dad is a CEO in the company I am working at. Now, I am even a Boy Scout leader and known as the Scout who is totally against any unnecessary drug use. What a change from those younger days! *(From Venturelli's research files, male working for a major corporation in Chicago, age 29, May 12, 2010)*

Second interview:

I first started with marijuana when I was 13. Friends of mine were also smoking cigarettes whenever we got together to smoke weed. It was easy to try cigarettes after smoking weed so at around age 14 or 15 I added cigarettes to my weed smoking. From there and in enjoying the highs alcohol was my next drug of choice. Pills and snorting my best friend's Ritalin crushed into power was added to my favorite drugs. I guess you could say that one led to another, but I never went to snorting coke because it was so expensive and I figured I progressed enough in my drug usage and didn't need to add yet another drug to my drugs of choice. I was 24 when I decided to quit playing around with all these drugs and only drink alcohol occasionally now. *(From Venturelli's research files, male working at a health club in Valparaiso, Indiana, age 29, April 6, 2013)*

Misperceptions of Marijuana Use

In a world in which marijuana can be considered either an assassin or a sacrament, and in which it is associated with membership in prized or despised peer groups, it is not surprising that estimates of its use vary widely and are often inaccurate. Parents, for example, tend to underestimate their children's use of drugs. Findings from one study indicated that "only 14% of the parents interviewed thought their children had experimented with marijuana while 38% of the teenagers said they had tried it" (Wren 1996, p. 1). In the same survey, 52% of teenagers reported having been offered drugs, whereas 34% of the parents thought their children might have been offered drugs. Another more recent study indicated that "[o]nly 10% of parents think their own teens drank alcohol within the last year, and 5% believe their teens smoked marijuana in the last year, according to the latest poll by the University of Michigan's C.S. Mott Children's Hospital" (Melina 2011). Reports from the 2010 Monitoring the Future survey reported that 29% of 10th graders had used marijuana within the past year (Johnston et al. 2012).

Other recent research indicates that parents who more carefully and consistently monitor their children and maintain more open communication are more likely to underestimate their children's risky behavior. "[Further,] parents of adolescents who perceived themselves as better than average in school performance and who participated in religious services were more likely to underestimate adolescents' substance use" (Hongmei et al. 2006, p. 1).

Interestingly, another report by the former president of the National Center on Addiction and Substance Abuse at Columbia University stated the following with regard to baby-boomer parents (parents born between 1946 through 1964):

> Almost half know someone who uses illegal drugs; a third have friends who use marijuana. Almost half expect their children to try illegal drugs, and 65 percent of those who smoked pot regularly when young believe their kids will try drugs . . . almost half of the parents don't think they can have much influence on whether their kids will use drugs. (Califano 1996, p. 19)

Even with regard to users' perceptions of other users, beliefs about marijuana remain distorted. College students tend to have exaggerated misperceptions of use, believing that their peers use marijuana much more than is true (Berkowitz 1991; Johnston et al. 2009; Sorden 2011). For example, at one campus in northern New Jersey, two-thirds of students reported never using marijuana, yet most students polled believed that the average student uses marijuana once per week. Other research also shows a widespread misperception in usage of marijuana. In 2005, in a randomly selected sample of 3639 college students, a large proportion (51%) of undergraduate students overestimated the use of marijuana among their peers on campus (McCabe 2008).

These findings of misperception in the use of marijuana are important because actual marijuana usage remains high for the time being. Recent findings show that marijuana continues to be the most commonly used illicit drug. An estimated 19.8 million Americans aged 12 or older have tried marijuana at least once past month, representing 7.5% of the U.S. population in that age group. Daily or almost daily use of marijuana (used on 20 or more days in the past month) increased from 5.1 million persons in 2005 to 2007 to 8.1 million persons in 2013 (SAMHSA 2014).

Characteristics of Cannabis

In 1753, Carolus Linnaeus, a Swedish botanist, classified marijuana as *Cannabis sativa* (see **Figure 13.5**). Some botanists believe that *C. sativa* is the only one species and that the other species are merely variants (Schultes 1978). Other botanists think that there are three distinct species, namely, *C. sativa*, *C. indica*, and *C. ruderalis*.

Cannabis sativa grows well in many parts of the world. It is the tallest of the three *Cannabis* species and can reach 20 to 25 feet high when grown outdoors. Because of its height, it has long been cultivated for its very long fibers, which can be used to make rope or cloth. It is not as bushy as *C. indica*, and thus plants can be cultivated more closely together (MMJ-Guide.com 2010).

C. indica is the bushiest of the three *Cannabis* species and in the middle with regard to height, rarely exceeding 10 feet. *C. indica* has a higher THC-to-cannabidiol (CBD) ratio than *C. sativa*. This means that it produces a much heavier "stone" and more of a body high compared to *C. sativa*. The resin of *C. indica* is thought to be the most potent, but potency is influenced by climate, soil, and breeding. *C. indica* produces a higher yield than *C. sativa* and reaches maturity more quickly (MMJ-Guide.com 2010).

© skydie/Shutterstock

FIGURE 13.5 Marijuana plants.

The Russian botanist D. E. Janichevsky discovered *C. ruderalis* in Eastern Europe. It is the shortest of the three species, reaching 24 inches at most, and is able to grow in cold climates. Unlike the other two varieties, it is able to switch from vegetative growth to flowering once it has grown five to seven sets of leaves. This is important because it means that flowering in this species is not affected by day length. Breeders have crossed *C. ruderalis* with the other two varieties to create a heavy budding plant that will grow in cooler conditions. The hybrid plants are shorter and mature more quickly that *C. sativa* and *C. indica* but have a lower THC content (MMJ-Guide.com 2010).

Cannabis is *dioecious*, meaning that there are male and female plants. After the male plant releases its pollen, it usually dies. In any case, even before the male plant dies, cultivators of marijuana often eliminate or remove the male plants before the female plant has been pollinated.

Cannabis plants produce more than 421 different chemicals, many of which have not yet been identified. Tetrahydrocannabinol, or THC, is the primary mind-altering (psychoactive) agent in marijuana (Abood and Martin 1996; NIDA 2009; Swan 1996) and appears to be important for the reinforcing properties of this substance (Kelly et al. 1994). THC is most highly concentrated in the flowering tops and upper leaves of the female plant. The flowering tops, or "buds," when crushed, produce a resin that contains the THC. THC concentrations are usually highest in the buds of the female *Cannabis* plant, followed by the leaves. The seeds and stalks have much lower THC levels and are of limited commercial value (National Cannabis Prevention and Information Centre [NCPIC] 2013).

In cultivated marijuana crops, as mentioned earlier, male plants are eradicated from the growing fields so that they cannot pollinate the female plants. The lack of pollination makes the potency of female plants increase dramatically.

There are approximately four derivatives (or "spin-offs") from marijuana plants. The first derivative, **sinsemilla** (meaning "without seeds" in Spanish), is one of the most potent types of marijuana in the United States, with an average THC content of 9.6% but reaching as high as 24%. *Sinsemilla* is produced from the buds of the flowering tops of female plants (NIDA 1998). Varieties of *sinsemilla* that have a high THC content include "hydro" (which means grown in water), "blueberry," and "kind bud." Through selective breeding, breeders have developed new strains of marijuana, such as 8 Miles High, Albert Walker, Black Pineapple Kush, Cantatonic Incognito, Diesel Mange Haze, Girl Scout Cookies, Elephant Stomper, Snowcap, Satori, Purple Urkle, Big Budda Cheese, Trainwreck, Trinity, and GDP Grand Daddy Purple. Many of these new varieties have much higher THC content (MMJ-Guide.com 2010).

One interviewee provided noteworthy insight regarding comparing these more potent varieties with more generic types of marijuana by stating the following:

> Smoking those *primo* buds [referring to the more potent types of marijuana] ... is like the difference between eating strip steak versus filet mignon. The THC content of these more specialized types of marijuana is more like a quantum leap in the quality of marijuana. These strains are very mellow in taste and they are potent as hell.... [The interviewee also humorously added] and the cost difference is every bit like paying for filet mignon, but this upgrade in quality is totally worth the extra cost. (*From Venturelli's research files, male, commodities stock broker, age 36, residing in Chicago, February 28, 2016*)

In a report by the University of Mississippi Potency Monitoring Project, dated December 2008 through March 2009, the average potency of all marijuana in the United States was 8.52%

KEY TERM

sinsemilla
meaning "without seeds," this marijuana is made from the buds and flowering tops of female plants and is one of the most potent types

(5.62% domestic and 9.57% nondomestic). Non-domestic varieties include Jamaican, Colombian, Mexican, and Canadian, which averaged 9.57% THC. "Out of 788 domestic and nondomestic samples seized between 2008 and 2009 the average was 8.52% THC" (ElSohly 2009, p. 6). "For comparison, the national average of marijuana's THC content in 1978 was 1.37%, in 1988 it was 3.59%, in 1998 4.43%, and in 2008 8.49%" (ProCon 2012b).

Other more recent research, presented at a meeting of the American Chemical Society (ACS) in Denver reported that the potency (THC content) is continually increasing.

The main finding of the new analysis was that potency has risen by a factor of three in the last few decades. "As far as potency goes, it's been surprising how strong a lot of the marijuana is," says researcher and study lead Andy LaFrate. "We've seen potency values close to 30 percent THC, which is huge." Potency used to be around 10% or less, but it's been bred upwards over the years, presumably because the market has demanded it (Walton 2015).

This dramatic increase in the potency of marijuana results from "[m]ore efficient agriculture—new methods of harvesting and processing marijuana plants—has made pot about 20 times more potent than the marijuana on the street in the 1960s and 1970s, drug treatment experts and law officials say" (Henneberger 1994, p. F-18). Further, the quantities of other, more potent types of marijuana such as *sinsemilla* and hydro are increasingly readily available in illegal drug markets. In addition, recently developed **drug trafficking organizations (DTOs)**—which are complex illegal organizations with highly defined command-and-control structures—produce, transport, and/or distribute large quantities of one or more illicit drugs.

Another finding is the following:

Marijuana produced in Mexico remains the most widely available in the United States. High potency marijuana has also entered

the U.S. drug market from Canada. Another source for marijuana in the United States is domestically grown marijuana, which includes both indoor and outdoor operations. Groups [such as identified DTOs] operating from Mexico employ a variety of transportation and concealment methods to smuggle marijuana into the United States. Most of the marijuana smuggled into the United States is concealed in vehicles—often in false compartments—or hidden in shipments of legitimate agricultural or industrial products. Marijuana is also smuggled across the border by rail, horse, raft, and backpack. Canada is becoming a source country for indoor-grown, high potency (15% to 25% THC) marijuana destined for the United States. Such indoor-grow operations have become an enormous and lucrative illicit industry, producing a potent form of marijuana that has come to be known as "BC Bud." (Office of National Drug Control Policy [ONDCP] 2003)

Finally, not only are there many more types of marijuana available today in comparison to 20 years ago from illegal drug markets, but also the types and quality of marijuana seeds for growing marijuana plants have multiplied. One website among many devoted to selling high-quality marijuana seeds on the internet is BC Bud Depot in Ontario, Canada, which greets shoppers with the following:

Welcome to the BC Bud Depot. View our entire seed bank listing here. Along with breeding the world's best marijuana seeds for fast and discreet delivery worldwide, the BC Bud Depot also collaborates with other world renowned breeders to bring you the very best and most comprehensive marijuana seed bank in the world today. Find everything you need here, from CC Bud Depot and Reeferman seeds, to European breeders like T.H. Seeds, Soma, DNA Genetics and Delta-9 Labs. Take a look at our awards cabinet and sign up for our newsletter for amazing monthly specials and limited time offers. (BC Bud Depot n.d.)

Hashish (or hasheesh) is the second cannabis derivative; it contains a very pure form of resin. This type of marijuana consists of the sticky resin from the flowers of the female plant. Domestic samples of resin had an average of 12.14% THC, nondomestic had 7.03% THC, and the average of all samples seized, which includes samples with much higher amounts of THC, was 20.76% THC (ElSohly 2009). Historically, hashish users have

KEY TERMS

drug trafficking organizations (DTOs)
complex organizations with highly defined command-and-control structures that produce, transport, and/or distribute large quantities of one or more illicit drugs

hashish
a cannabis product produced from the pure resin from the flowers of female plants with high amount of THC (the average THC content of all samples seized was 12.14% and often ranges from 7.03% [nondomestic] to 20.76%)

represented a somewhat small percentage of the cannabis user population in the United States compared to Europe, where its use is much more prevalent. Hashish often is produced in Lebanon, Afghanistan, and Pakistan.

The third cannabis derivative is **marijuana wax**, which is also known as *wax, ear wax, butter, honey oil, shatter, BHO* (which stands for "butane honey oil" or "butane hash oil"), and *dabs*. To date, this is one of the most powerful and the most potent (80% pure THC) types of marijuana on both the illegal and legal drug markets (in states where marijuana has either been decriminalized or medically sanctioned). Smoking or vaporizing this type of marijuana "leads to a quicker, stronger high," and "wax is said to be the strongest form of marijuana on the market" (Kimble 2013). However, making marijuana wax is no easy task:

> Amateur chemists be warned: making marijuana wax is not a kitchen-friendly (or, for that matter, user-friendly) activity. The marijuana is placed into a long tube or pipe, which is then hit with a rush of highly flammable butane—yes, like lighter fluid. The butane is used to extract THC, marijuana's active ingredient, in a hardened, extremely potent form that resembles wax, hence the name. For anyone familiar with how hash is made, it's a similar, yet more dangerous, process. (Kimble 2013)

Reports from users indicate that marijuana wax is highly hallucinogenic in comparison to smoking common marijuana plant leaves and flowering buds. Some say that the effects also include intense visions and intense physical effects (Ghaly 2015), passing out, and high levels of impairment. Wax sells for approximately $45 a gram on the street, "compared to $20 to $60 for an eighth of an ounce, roughly 3.5 grams, of plant marijuana depending the quality" (Pinto 2016).

A fourth cannabis derivative is *ganja*, which is produced in India. This preparation consists of the dried tops of female plants. *Ganja* is also used as a slang term for marijuana (as are *pot, herb,* *weed, grass, boom, Mary Jane, gangster,* or *chronic*). In fact, there are more than 200 slang terms for marijuana.

Synthetic Marijuana

In recent years, psychoactive drugs such as Spice and K-2 have become available. Such drugs are referred as **synthetic marijuana** because they are composed of herbal materials that have been sprayed with one or more of the designer chemicals that fall into the cannabinoid family (i.e., they are related to chemicals found in the marijuana plant). The synthetic cannabinoids are often marketed as "fake weed" and as a safe, legal alternative to marijuana. Users smoke the dried plant material that has been sprayed with synthetic cannabinoids or mix the sprayed plant material with marijuana or brew it as tea. Other users buy synthetic cannabinoid products as liquids that can be vaporized in e-cigarettes. Some experts think that synthetic cannabinoids have much more powerful, and unpredictable, effects. In some instances, the effects may even be life-threatening (NIH 2015a).

Other important findings include the following (NIH 2015a):

- The dried plant materials are the only part of synthetic cannabinoid products that are "natural." The active ingredients are manmade cannabinoid compounds.
- The effects of synthetic cannabinoids are similar to those produced by marijuana, such as elevated mood, relaxation, altered perception, and symptoms of psychosis.
- Use of synthetic cannabinoids can cause serious mental and physical health problems, such

Marijuana wax.

© Canna Obscura/Shutterstock

KEY TERMS

marijuana wax
extremely potent cannabis spin-off made by using butane to extract the THC content, producing a "waxy" residue that is smoked or vaporized; has THC levels of approximately 80% and is highly hallucinogenic, often resulting in high levels of physical and mental impairment

synthetic marijuana
also known as "fake weed," refers to manmade mind-altering chemicals that are either sprayed on dried, shredded plant material so they can be smoked (herbal incense) or sold as liquids to be vaporized and inhaled in e-cigarettes and other devices (liquid incense)

as rapid heart rate, vomiting, violent behavior, and suicidal thoughts.

- Synthetic cannabinoids can be addictive, and behavioral therapies and medications have not been tested for treatment of addiction to these products.
- The psychotic effects from synthetic cannabinoids include extreme anxiety, confusion, paranoia, and hallucinations.

Until March 2011, these drugs were not scheduled by the Drug Enforcement Administration (DEA), so they were readily and legally available on the Internet and in head shops, gas stations, and so on. However, the DEA scheduled some of the most widely used chemicals beginning March 1, 2011, making their possession and sale illegal. Subsequent laws have expanded the list of banned chemicals (Johnston et al. 2015).

■ Trends in Use

The Monitoring the Future (MTF) study first addressed the use of synthetic marijuana in its 2011 survey by asking 12th graders about their use of such products in the prior 12 months (which would have covered a considerable period of time prior to the drugs being scheduled) (Johnston et al. 2015). Annual prevalence was found to be 11.4%, making synthetic marijuana the second most widely used class of illicit drug after marijuana among 12th graders. Despite the DEA's intervention, use among 12th graders remained unchanged in 2012 at 11.3%, which suggested that either compliance with the new scheduling had been limited or that producers of these products succeeded in continuing to change their chemical formulas to avoid using the ingredients that had been scheduled. In 2012, for the first time, 8th and 10th graders were asked about their use of synthetic marijuana; annual prevalence rates were 4.4% and 8.8%, respectively. Use by 8th, 10th, and 12th graders dropped in 2013, and the decline was sharp and significant among 12th graders. The declines continued into 2014 and were significant for both 10th and 12th graders (Johnston et al. 2015).

■ Perceived Risk

The 2012 survey (Johnston et al. 2015) also asked 8th, 10th, and 12th graders whether they associated great risk with trying synthetic marijuana once or twice. The level of perceived risk for experimental use was quite low (between 24% and 33%) but has been rising some among 12th

graders. Likely, the over-the-counter availability of these drugs has had the effect of communicating to teens that they must be safe, even though they are not.

The Behavioral Effects of Marijuana Use

This section will discuss the "high" experienced from marijuana, the subjective euphoric effects of this drug, how the use of marijuana affects driving performance and critical-thinking skills, and the amotivational syndrome that appears to be a characteristic effect of marijuana use.

■ The "High"

The widely held belief of the 1930s that marijuana was a destructive assassin of youth is no longer considered valid for casual or occasional users of this drug. In most individuals, low to moderate doses of cannabis produce euphoria and a pleasant state of relaxation (Goldstein 1994). What are the common effects experienced from marijuana use? After a few delayed moments of forcibly holding the smoke in the lungs, most users suddenly experience the high. In this state of euphoria, the user experiences a dry mouth, elevated heartbeat, and some loss of coordination and balance, coupled with slower reaction times and a feeling of euphoria (mild to elevated intoxication). Blood vessels in the eyes expand, which accounts for reddening of the eyes. Some people experience slightly elevated blood pressure, which can double the normal heart rate. These effects can become intensified when other drugs, such as LSD and/or psychedelic ("magic") mushrooms, are combined with the marijuana.

The state of euphoria that results from the high is usually mild and short-lived; a typical high from one joint may last from 2 to 3 hours. Subjectively, the user experiences altered perception of space and time, impaired memory of recent events, and impaired physical coordination (Abood and Martin 1992). (More of these subjective effects are discussed at length in the next section.) An occasional high is not usually hazardous unless the person attempts to drive a car, operate heavy machinery, fly a plane, or function in similar ways requiring coordination, good reflexes, or quick judgment (Nahas and Latour 1992). Even low doses of marijuana alter perception, such as being able to judge the speed of an approaching vehicle or how much to slow down on an exit ramp. According to one user,

> In trying to describe the high, it's not like an alcohol high. In an alcohol high, you are a lot more uncoordinated if drinking a lot. With weed, it's like reality changes—you add a lot more bass so-to-speak to what you see, hear, think, and feel. The reality is tempered with some distortion that to me and many others is pleasurable. You know how you feel after three or four very strong drinks [referring to alcoholic beverages]. Well take two more of those drinks and then look around the room you are in. Now, the difference between alcohol and weed is that you can walk to the bathroom quite well while under the influence of weed, while with alcohol you walk carefully so that no one notices that you are just about drunk. Weed is a mind high while alcohol is more of a body high. *(Venturelli's research files, female professionally employed and residing in San Francisco, age 23, May 19, 2000)*

Three additional interviews attempted to compare the high from marijuana with the effects of alcohol.

First interview:

> The marijuana high is also not nearly as harsh on the body. Being high doesn't give you that painful hangover as alcohol does. The actual high is very functional; I tend to do some of my best work (after burning a "dubbie") in that state [of mind]. It is part of the lifestyle of marijuana. [In contrast], alcohol makes me (and most people I know) very unproductive when the "buzz" is reached. *(From Venturelli's research files, male undergraduate student at a Midwestern university, age 21, August 10, 2000)*

Second interview with the same person a day later:

> There seems to be a small misconception about the effects of marijuana and alcohol. For me, anyway, in looking at the physical "buzz" you get from alcohol, it is very physically disabling. You get drunk and stumble around, your lips loosen up, and you say things that you would not normally say. I find that marijuana has more of a calming effect. It makes you relaxed, a little more perceptive to some stimuli, and obviously less perceptive to other stimuli. It is a light feeling, but not overwhelming to the equilibrium. *(From Venturelli's research files, same student as above, August 11, 2000)*

Third interview:

> I can't drink much, because I feel the effects of alcohol more than the average person. I also don't like the effects of being high on alcohol. I feel very loopy and uncoordinated. Then, the next morning after drinking the night before is very unpleasant for me with headaches and sometimes even nausea. This is why I like to smoke weed. With weed you don't have all the impairment, the sick feelings, and you don't wake all messed up. I also have great conversations with people who are high on marijuana and find myself in a good mood while high. Also with regard to impairment, I would never drive under the influence of alcohol, but with marijuana, I have no problem driving. I even had a police officer stop me one night when my tail light was out on one side while on weed, and he never detected my marijuana high. He just wrote me a warning notice. Now, if it were alcohol, he probably would have become suspicious. Everyone is different, and this is my take on comparing these two drugs. *(From Venturelli's research files, female student at a Midwestern university, age 22, September 9, 2010)*

In describing how the effects of THC in marijuana can enhance feelings, one source provided the following:

> *Cannabis* use can increase focus and concentration, making a person's moods, sensations, and experience seem more intense. Your heart may feel like it's pounding, the music is fantastic, this is the best dessert you've ever eaten and, wow, get a load of how beautiful nature is. The problem is that if you're concentrating on something that's negative, you can intensify that feeling, as well. Fortunately, something else will come along and distract you with another thought to pursue, if you so choose. And if your fleeting idea feels like the answer to the world's problems, please write it down. It's profundity might escape you later, but it will feel good if it turns out you're right (Norris and Conrad n.d)

An acute dose of cannabis can produce adverse reactions, ranging from mild anxiety to panic and paranoia in some users. These reactions occur most frequently in individuals who are under stress or who are anxious, depressed, or borderline schizophrenic (Nahas and Latour 1992). Documented research indicates the following:

Acute cannabis toxicity results in difficulty with coordination, decreased muscle strength, decreased hand steadiness, postural hypotension, lethargy, decreased concentration, slowed reaction time, slurred speech, and conjunctival injection. Large doses of THC may produce confusion, amnesia, delusions, hallucinations, anxiety, and agitation, but most episodes remit rapidly. Chronic users may experience paranoia, panic disorder, fear, or dysphoria. (Aydin and Fulton 2015)

Such effects also may also be experienced by users who accidentally take much more than they feel they can handle.

Although the more potent varieties can cause acute cannabis toxicity, extreme reactions can also occur because of ingesting marijuana treated (or "laced") with such things as opium, PCP, or other additives. Based on limited evidence from survey studies, mild or often adverse reactions can be experienced by regular users that are mainly self-treated and usually go unreported (see "Signs and Symptoms: Specific Indicators of Marijuana Use").

▪ Subjective Euphoric Effects

Subjective euphoric effects associated with marijuana use refer to the ongoing social and psychological experiences incurred while intoxicated by marijuana. These effects of intoxication include both the user's altered state of consciousness and his or her perceptions. Subjective effects in experienced users include a general sense of relaxation and tranquility, coupled with heightened sensitivity to sound, taste, and emotionality. For inexperienced users the subjective effects can vary from very similar experiences that experienced users have to some anxiety from anticipation of the effects. Often, it depends on the **set and setting** (Goode 1999; Zinberg 1984; Zinberg and Robertson 1972). *Set* is the individual's expectation of what a drug will do to his or her personality (state of mind and mood). *Setting* is both the physical and the social environment

KEY TERMS

subjective euphoric effects
ongoing social and psychological experiences incurred while intoxicated with marijuana

set and setting
set refers to the individual's expectation of what a drug will do to his or her personality; *setting* is the physical and social environments where the drug is consumed

in which the drug is consumed (surroundings where the drug is taken, including the people in the immediate environment when the drug is consumed). Some users report occasional similarities to the typical hallucinogenic high, emphasizing much less intensity. How closely the marijuana high resembles a hallucinogenic high depends on the amount of THC absorbed from marijuana. For example, higher amounts of THC found in more potent types of marijuana, like *sinsemilla*, hydro, and kind bud, more clearly mimic a hallucinogenic high. These effects are especially evident when considering the extent to which the senses of hearing, vision, sound, and taste are distorted by use of highly potent forms of marijuana. As mentioned previously, recent, potent varieties of marijuana with higher than usual THC content include 8 Miles High, Albert Walker, Black Pineapple Kush, Cantatonic Incognito, Diesel Mange Haze, Girl Scout Cookies, Elephant Stomper, Snowcap, Satori, Purple Urkle, Big Budda Cheese, Trainwreck, Trinity, and GDP Grand Daddy Purple (MMJ-Guide.com 2010). Some marijuana users become very attached to these euphoric effects by desiring and looking forward to repeating these effects. Such users often pride themselves on their extensive knowledge of this drug and maintain interest in discussing past experiences of "when I was really high" or "let me tell you about that night we smoked hydro. . . ." Devotees stay current with developments in the marijuana field by avidly reading monthly issues of magazines devoted to marijuana (the art of marijuana use) and frequently scan the Internet for information and conversations in chat rooms about the best varieties of marijuana, the best growing techniques, announcements of hemp festivals, advice, and information regarding current laws, fines, and other information. A vivid example of such an enthusiast is recalled in the following observation:

This author recalls visiting a neighbor one evening and noticing that one of the visitors sat very quietly with a pleasant smile while several intense conversations were occurring. I recall noticing this student because he sat very quietly appearing somewhat distant and occasionally displaying several facial gestures in either approval or disapproval of comments and suggestions during the ongoing conversations. About 1 hour into my visit, while others continued having multiple conversations, I directed my attention to this "quiet" individual with some introductory comments. He made minimal responses in the conversation. As others

SIGNS & SYMPTOMS

Specific Indicators of Marijuana Use

A sweet odor similar to burnt rope in room, on clothes, and so on.

Roach: The small butt end of a marijuana cigarette.

Joint: Looks like a hand-rolled cigarette; usually the ends are twisted or crimped.

Roach clips: Holders for the roach could be any number of common items such as paper clips, bobby pins, or hemostats. They also could be of a store-bought variety in a number of shapes and disguises.

Herb/marijuana grinder: Usually a round device in which solid marijuana is placed that can grind the bud into fine bits so that marijuana joints or blunts can be made.

© iStock/Thinkstock

Seeds or leaves in pockets or possession.

Plastic baggies, either with some amount of marijuana inside the baggie or an empty baggie often found in pant or shirt pockets.

Rolling papers or pipes, usually hidden somewhere.

Eye drops: For disguising red eyes.

Excessive use of incense, room deodorizers, or breath fresheners.

Devices for storing the substance, such as film canisters, boxes or cans, a dugout (containing a one hitter device), pill bottles (fully formed buds of marijuana or high-end strains may be distributed in pill bottles to protect their shape and size).

Eating binges: An after effect for some marijuana users.

Appearance of intoxication, yet no smell of alcohol.

Excessive laughter.

Initial use (first hour): Animated behavior (loud or excessive talking).

Hours later: Fatigue or drowsiness.

---

were discussing multiple topics, several of the guests began talking about drug use. Immediately, this quiet and reserved individual became very lively and began talking about the best types of marijuana on campus. Within several minutes, I literally saw a transformation in his involvement with the ongoing conversation. He was incessantly talking about marijuana and dominated the conversation with his many insights about the drug. I realized, prior to the topic of drug use and marijuana, he probably did not have much interest in the other topics. However, when we "hit" what appeared to be an interesting topic, which was a passion for marijuana use, an intensive amount of enthusiasm emerged. Clearly, this former "quiet young man" had transformed and clearly appeared to be quite a connoisseur about the varieties and the subjective euphoric effects of marijuana. By his overall conversational enthusiasm, he appeared quite content in letting us know how much he knew about this topic—and it was an extensive amount of knowledge. *(Observation from Venturelli visiting a neighbor's home in a small Midwestern town, June 9, 2010)*

Why is marijuana so attractive to many individuals? One quote from an interview illustrates the extensive psychological and social reinforcement experienced by marijuana users:

It's the high that I particularly like. Everything becomes mellower. Everyday tensions are released or submerged by more inner-like experiences. I can review the day and how happy or miserable I feel. Actually, when I am thinking and I am high on grass, I always feel that my thoughts are profound. You think from another perspective, one that numbs the more reality-based everyday strains. On the other hand, there are moments when this drug affects your mood and channels it [in] different ways. You have moments when you either feel sad, happy, angry (in a more contemplative way), or worried. These moods are both good and bad. If for the moment you feel good, then your mood is positive. If you feel down, your mood is negative in a particular way. If I am with friends and we are all sharing the bong or joint or pipe, we laugh a lot together. It's a type of drug that makes you more jovial, more introspective, and friendly, gregarious *(From Venturelli's research files, male personnel manager, age 40, August 20, 1996)*

As documented, marijuana enthusiasts have a strong attachment to their passionate feelings surrounding the use of marijuana. Psychologists believe the drug user becomes attached and habituated to the drug largely through the reinforcement of pleasurable feelings. If these subjective euphoric experiences were to become largely negative, attachment to and repeated use of this drug would cease. Thus, the theory of differential association applies. This theory, developed by Edwin H. Sutherland in his classic publication in 1939 (revised in 1947), attempts to explain the causes of delinquent behavior. Sociologists define the term **differential association** as the process by which individuals become socialized into the

perceptions and values of a group. Differential association can apply to drug use. In using this drug, the *camaraderie*, the conversations and banter that often occur among friends, is often perceived as a fun activity. It can include the perception that marijuana relieves boredom or stress or is the perfect drug for just hanging out, chilling, partying, and getting high together. Specifically, the definition of differential association can include the behavioral satisfaction derived from friends who use marijuana. In this situation, getting high with others is the positive reward that solidifies the user to his or her friends and the drug.

■ Driving Performance

Some evidence[3] shows that the ability to perform complex tasks, such as driving, can be impaired while under the influence of marijuana (Couper and Logan 2004; Goldstein 1994; Mathias 1996; NIH 2015b; TheWeek.com 2010). Research indicates that "*Cannabis* consumption impairs motor coordination, reaction time, sensory perceptions and glare recovery" (Teen Challenge 2000, p. 1). This effect has been demonstrated in laboratory assessments of driving-related skills such as eye–hand coordination and reaction time, in driver simulator studies, in test course performance, and in actual street driving situations (Chait and Pierri 1992; Couper and Logan 2004; Mathias 1996; NIH 2015b; Teen Challenge 2000). Other research summarizes the key impairments with driving under the influence of marijuana as deficiencies in "attentiveness, vigilance, perception of time and speed, and use of acquired knowledge" (Sewell, Poling, and Sofuoglu 2009).

One study tested the effects of known amounts of marijuana, alcohol, or both on driving. The subjects drove a course rigged with various traffic problems. Driving skills deteriorated among those who had used either drug, but the greatest deterioration was observed in subjects who had taken both. In another test, 59 subjects smoked marijuana until they were intoxicated and then were given sobriety tests on the roadside by highway patrol officers. Overall, 94% of the subjects did not pass the test 90 minutes after smoking, and 60% failed at 150 minutes, even though the blood THC was much lower at this time (Hollister 1986). Another, more recent study indicated

KEY TERM

differential association
process by which individuals become socialized into the perceptions and values of a group

[3]Other, more recent published research contradicts impaired driving under the influence of marijuana; see Ghose (2015) and Norml (2016).

that "[m]arijuana significantly impairs judgment, motor coordination, and reaction time, and studies have found a direct relationship between blood THC concentration and impaired driving ability" (NIDA 2016).

Another study detailing results from driving performance found that the short-term effects of marijuana use include problems with memory and learning, distorted perception, difficulty in thinking and problem-solving, and loss of coordination (National Highway Transportation Association [NHTSA] 2004). Heavy users may have increased difficulty sustaining attention, shifting attention to meet the demands of changes in the environment, and registering, processing, and using information. In general, laboratory performance studies indicate that sensory functions are not highly impaired, but perceptual functions are significantly affected. The ability to concentrate and maintain attention is decreased during marijuana use, and impairment of hand–eye coordination is dose related over a wide range of dosages. Impairment in retention time and tracking, subjective sleepiness, distortion of time and distance, vigilance, and loss of coordination in divided attention tasks have been reported. Note, however, that subjects can often "pull themselves together" to concentrate on simple tasks for brief periods of time, but that significant performance impairments are usually observed for at least 1 to 2 hours following marijuana use, and residual effects have been reported for up to 24 hours (Couper and Logan 2004; see also NIDA 2010b).

Another, slightly less critical study of city driving

> showed that drivers who drank alcohol overestimated their performance quality [often by speeding and overconfidence] whereas those who smoked marijuana under-estimated it [slower speed and more cautious driving]. . . . Drivers under the influence of marijuana retain insight in their performance and will compensate where they can, for example, by slowing down or increasing effort. As a consequence, THC's adverse effects on driving performance appear relatively small. Still we can easily imagine situations where the influence of marijuana smoking might have an exceedingly dangerous effect; i.e., emergency situations which put high demands on the driver's information processing capacity, prolonged monotonous driving, and after THC has been taken with other drugs, especially alcohol. (U.S. Department of Transportation 1993)

Research reported by the DEA (2013) indicates the following:

- "[O]ver 3000 fatally-injured drivers in Australia showed that when marijuana was present in the blood of the driver they were much more likely to be at fault for the accident. And the higher the THC concentration, the more likely they were to be culpable" (p. 43).
- "A study in the *British Medical Journal* on the consequences of cannabis impaired driving found that drivers who consume cannabis within 3 hours of driving are nearly twice as likely to cause a vehicle collision as those who are not under the influence of drugs or alcohol" (p. 41).
- "A study in the *Epidemiologic Reviews* by researchers from Columbia University found that drivers who get behind the wheel after smoking pot run more than twice the risk of getting into an accident" (p. 42).
- "In 2009, marijuana was the most prevalent drug found in this population—approximately 28% of fatally injured drivers who tested positive tested positive for marijuana" (p. 42).

Other, more recent findings by the Canadian Centre on Substance Abuse (CCSA) include the following (Beirness and Porath-Waller 2015):

- Among young drivers, driving after using cannabis is more prevalent than driving after drinking.
- Cannabis impairs the cognitive and motor abilities necessary to operate a motor vehicle and doubles the risk of crash involvement.
- After alcohol, cannabis is the most commonly detected substance among drivers who die in traffic crashes.
- Cannabis use is not uncommon among drivers involved in collisions.
- The police have the tools and authority required to detect and arrest drivers who are impaired by cannabis.

Other research regarding drug-impaired driving indicated that U.S. Census data found that "there are 13 million driving-aged teenagers and, with 23 percent of teens admitting to driving under the influence of alcohol, marijuana or other drugs" (Liberty Mutual Insurance 2013). This same study revealed that 75% of teens claimed marijuana use has no impact on their driving ability. Another interesting report pointing to the severity of teens driving under the influence stated that in 2007 the State of Maryland Adolescent Survey indicated that 11.1% of the state's licensed adolescent drivers reported driving under the influence of marijuana on three or more occasions, and 10% reported driving while using a drug other than marijuana (not including alcohol) (NIDA 2010b).

Drugged driving is defined as operating a motor vehicle with a measurable quantity (or quantities) of a legal and/or an illegal drug in the driver's body, which most often results in impaired driving. Medical data indicate a connection between drugged driving and accidents—a study of patients in a shock trauma unit who had been in collisions revealed that 15% of those who had been driving a car or motorcycle had been smoking marijuana, and another 17% had both THC and alcohol in their blood. In 2009, an estimated 12% of persons aged 12 or older (30.2 million persons) drove under the influence of alcohol at least once in the past year (NIDA 2010b), and another major study found that 33% of fatally injured drivers with known test results tested positive for at least one drug (Dupont 2011).

Research conducted by the University of Auckland, New Zealand, proves the link between marijuana use and car accidents. The research found that habitual cannabis users were 9.5 times more likely to be involved in crashes, with 5.6% of people who had crashed having taken the drug, compared to 0.5% of the control group (Blows et al. 2005).

A study published by researchers at the University of Maryland Medical Center Shock Trauma Center indicated that during the 90-day study about half of the drivers admitted to the shock trauma center tested positive for drugs other than alcohol. Additionally, one in four drivers admitted to the shock trauma unit tested positive for marijuana. According to the researchers,

> This population-based case–control study indicates that habitual use of marijuana is strongly associated with car crash injury. The nature of the relationship between marijuana use and risk-taking is unclear and needs further research. The prevalence of marijuana use in this driving population was low, and acute use was associated with habitual marijuana use, suggesting that intervention strategies may be

more effective if they are targeted towards high use groups. (Blows et al. 2005, p. 605)

One notable interview presents us with a negative experience regarding use of marijuana and driving experiences:

> One time I smoked some real strong dope at my friend's house, then had to drive back home, which was 2 miles in one direction. I remember wigging out [panicking] in trying to get home. There were moments when I did not know where I was until I would see the next marker of my neighborhood. I remember having seconds of panic because I did not know where I was; then suddenly, I would notice a neighborhood restaurant or some other marker that said I was right around my neighborhood. I took smaller streets on the way home and even took a longer way home because I was freaking out about the cops—what if one would spot me? This was bogus thinking because how the hell would anyone suddenly spot me while driving home? Well, that's an example of wigging out on weed. But, I still don't think that even that time I would be getting into an accident. I was so freaked out that I was extra careful not to speed, pass stop signs, or violate any law for fear of being seen. If anything, I drive slower when I am really high, not more dangerously.
> *(From Venturelli's research files, male college student in a Midwestern town, age 20, July 19, 2000)*

In contrast to this student's beliefs, scientific research indicates that some perceptual or other performance deficits resulting from marijuana use may persist for some time after the high, and users who attempt to drive, fly, operate heavy machinery, perform surgery, and so on may not recognize their impairment because they do not feel intoxicated. States such as California have established testing procedures to detect the presence of THC in urine or blood samples from apparently intoxicated drivers.

If the use of marijuana becomes more socially acceptable (or perhaps even legal) and penalties for simple possession become more lenient, it is likely that individuals will feel less inclined to hide their drug use. Unfortunately, it follows that these individuals may also be more inclined to drive while high, endangering themselves and others.

▪ Critical-Thinking Skills

Marijuana has been found to have a negative impact on critical-thinking skills. Research by NIDA shows that heavy marijuana use impairs

KEY TERM

drugged driving
operating a motor vehicle with a measurable quantity or quantities of a legal and/or an illegal drug in the driver's body, which most often results in impaired driving

critical skills related to attention, memory, and learning. Another study showed that even alertness, coordination, and reaction time were impaired by marijuana usage (Couper and Logan 2004; National Clearinghouse on Alcohol and Drug Information [NCADI] 1998; NIDA 2010a). Impairment from marijuana continues even after discontinuing use of the drug for at least 24 hours (Brown and Massaro 1996).

In the same study (Brown and Massaro 1996), researchers compared 65 heavy users (using approximately every other day) with light users (using once or twice per week). Heavy users made more mistakes and had greater difficulty sustaining attention, shifting attention to meet the demands of challenges in the environment, and registering, processing, and using information (Brown and Massaro 1996; Fuller 2008; Norton 2009) compared with light users. In addition, heavy users had greater difficulty completing the tests, which specifically measured aspects of attention, memory, and learning, such as intellectual functioning, abstraction ability, attention span, verbal fluency, and learning and recalling abilities (Brown and Massaro 1996; Teen Challenge 2000). One researcher stated, "If you could get heavy users to learn an item, then they could remember it; the problem was getting them to learn it in the first place" (Brown and Massaro 1996, p. 3). The researchers surmised that marijuana alters brain activity because residues of the drug persist in the brain or because a withdrawal syndrome follows the euphoric effects of the marijuana.

In another study, researchers tested the cognitive functioning of 65 marijuana-using college students. Residual impairments were seen in the 24 hours after use in terms of sustaining attention and shifting attention and hence in registering, organizing, and using information (NIDA 2010a; Pope and Yurgulen-Todd 1996). This study, which was undertaken during the 1990s, is significant because it was carefully controlled. The unresolved question is whether these memory impairments are short term or long term. These noteworthy findings complement many other similar findings that identified protracted cognitive impairment among heavy users of marijuana (Fuller 2008; NCADI 1998; Norton 2009).

■ Amotivational Syndrome

The so-called **amotivational syndrome** (sometimes referred to as *antimotivational syndrome*) is a flashpoint of controversy about marijuana although not as newsworthy as that regarding medical legalization. Amotivational syndrome refers to a belief that heavy use of marijuana causes a lack of motivation or "impaired desire" and reduced productivity. Specifically, users show apathy, poor short-term memory, difficulty in concentration, and a lingering disinterest in pursuing goals (Abood and Martin 1992; Right Diagnosis 2010).

In the past, this syndrome received considerable attention. People who are high, or stoned, lack the desire to perform hard work and are not interested in doing difficult tasks. There is some evidence of this behavior in regular marijuana users (Nahas and Latour 1992). Overall, although not solely the result of cannabis use, chronic users have lower grades in school, are more likely to be absent from classes, and are likely not to complete assignments and to drop out of school (Hardcastle 2007; Henneberger 1994; Liska 1997). In terms of age, the earlier someone begins smoking marijuana, coupled with heavier use, the more likely the amotivational characteristics will prevail and the more difficult it will be to cease using this drug.

Although the effects of marijuana per se are somewhat responsible for creating this syndrome, other factors contribute as well. For instance, is the lack of motivation caused by the drug itself, or is it that poorly motivated people begin using marijuana, which then further exacerbates their lack of motivation? Surveys show that a sizable number of marijuana users and their peer groups tend to be alienated from society and are likely to be classified as nonconformists and/or rebellious youth. They may, in fact, select to emphasize pleasure and nonconformity rather than goal-directed behavior. Another challenge to the concept of amotivational syndrome argues that the lack of motivation may simply be due to the effects of marijuana while under its influence and not any type of longer term or unique syndrome (Iverson 2005; Johns 2001).

Advocates of marijuana legalization stress data that tend to debunk research on amotivational syndrome. One institute that supports legalization, the Lindesmith Center, published a study asserting that college students who are users have higher grades than nonusers (Zimmer and Morgan 1997). How can we account for the discrepancies between this study and others, not to

KEY TERM

amotivational syndrome
a controversial syndrome whose proponents claim that heavy use of marijuana causes a lack of motivation and reduced productivity

mention the clinical experiences of students, who often report academic repercussions of heavy use? One factor in the explanation is sociocultural:

> In the New York–New Jersey metro region, there are "druggy" schools and "drinking" schools. The "druggy" schools are more upper-middle class, liberal arts schools, artsy types, latter-day hippies, etc. The boozer campuses are filled with blue-collar and lower-middle-class kids— sometimes big fraternity schools. Frontloading at basketball games, comas after pledge parties. . . . Not as good educational backgrounds as the artsy potheads, who went to better schools, private schools, read a lot, or heard a lot at dinner before college, so they get by with their profs. However, the potheads ratchet down into easier majors, and they get crummier grades as they get into regular use. *(Interview with Pearl Mott for a prevention newsletter, prevention specialist, Drug Prevention Programs in Higher Education, Washington, D.C., October 1994)*

A second methodological factor complicating drug research among such students is simply that academic failures stay in "F" categories for only one or two semesters. Many then disappear from statistics entirely, via academic attrition.

A more serious challenge to the notion of amotivational syndrome comes from the same ethnographic research that was mentioned at the beginning of this chapter. The most well-known of these investigations was carried out by Vera Rubin and Labros Comitas, as reported in their book *Ganja in Jamaica* (1975). Follow-up studies were done in Jamaica (Dreher 1982; Hamid 1998) and Costa Rica (Carter 1980; Pollan 1998). None of these works found that chronic use impaired occupational or other functioning; in fact, the main point of the Jamaican studies was that users defined this drug as helpful and motivating for work—a "motivational syndrome." This work is often cited to counter amotivational syndrome claims. By this logic, dropping out of the rat race is a cultural posture, with marijuana being secondary to or, at most, reinforcing the drift away from a mainstream lifestyle.

The Jamaican and Costa Rican subjects, however, were not observed engaging in an academic, cognitively complex, or rapid reflex activity, nor

Typical effects of amotivational syndrome.

were they found in occupations that were competitive and striving for mobility. Rather, these subjects were involved in repetitive, physical labor involving cutting of sugarcane. In such a context, marijuana drug use functions to provide a pleasant stimulation that counters the monotony and physical discomfort of such labor.

When studies in other cultures contradict the American notion of amotivational syndrome, we are left to be cautious in making a direct assumption that marijuana use per se leads to such a syndrome, especially given that one strain of marijuana, *C. indica*, causes sedation, whereas the other strain, *C. sativa*, causes stimulation. More than likely, if we agree that the amotivational syndrome does manifest itself in marijuana users, it may be a direct result of a particular strain of marijuana. As discussed previously, it is important to keep in mind that *C. indica* differs from *C. sativa*. Also, there is great likelihood that in Jamaica, the stimulation caused by *C. sativa* (which is the most common variety of marijuana in Jamaica) may explain why these sugarcane field workers under the effects of this particular strain of marijuana are able to work long hours. (For additional information on how marijuana affects personality, see "Case in Point: A Letter to an Editor: No Valid Reason to Ban Marijuana.")

Therapeutic Uses and the Controversy over Medical Marijuana Use

Although the use of marijuana for medical purposes is far more accepted than it was ten years ago, the controversy about the medical uses of marijuana remains. Basically, **medical marijuana**

© Sanjmur/Dreamstime.com.

KEY TERM

medical marijuana
use of the THC in cannabis as a drug to calm or to relieve symptoms of an illness

use involves using cannabis, primarily the THC from the *Cannabis* plant, as a drug to calm or to relieve symptoms of an illness. At the heart of this controversy is the use of an illicit drug for medical purposes. However, the desire to use cannabis in this fashion is nothing new. Between 1840 and

1900, European and American medical journals published more than 100 articles on the therapeutic use of the drug known then as *Cannabis indica* (or Indian hemp) and now as marijuana. It was recommended as an appetite stimulant, muscle relaxant, analgesic, hypnotic, and anticonvulsant.

▶ CASE IN POINT

A Letter to an Editor: No Valid Reason to Ban Marijuana

An Associated Press release printed in the *Kentucky Enquirer* had the head of the White House Office of Drug Control Policy, Gil Kerlikowske, President Obama's Drug Czar, extolling the necessity of continuing the prohibition of marijuana. The reasons he cites for continuing the 70-year war on marijuana smokers are a clear indication that history is correct in judging marijuana prohibition as one of the greatest policy failures in the history of the federal government. The letter is as follows:

Below is a veteran soldier responding to Gil Kerlikowske.

Those who support prohibition started in 1933 at the end of alcohol prohibition to shift all the bad outcomes of alcohol use to marijuana. The films and newspaper stories of the day claimed that using marijuana leads to violence, murder, and insanity. Think of the movie, "Reefer Madness." Cut to the present and the Drug Czar is reduced to claiming that marijuana causes lung cancer, and that marijuana use is the cause of a significant amount of traffic accidents. The lung cancer, marijuana connection is a myth that grows out of the fact that tobacco smoking causes lung cancer therefore marijuana smoking should too. With this in mind, the Government originally supported the work of Dr. Donald Tashkin. His study on marijuana smoking and head, neck, and lung cancer was expected to be a slam-dunk for the Government. The problem is that the results of Dr. Tashkin's and other studies is that the opposite is true. Dr. Tashkin's study showed that people who regularly use marijuana get head, neck, and lung cancer at the same rate as people who do not smoke at all. He reported that marijuana seemed to have an anti-cancer effect and acted as a cancer preventer. One would think medical researchers would be all over this like "stink on poopy" looking for a cancer cure, but the forces

of prohibition continue to block research, even though compassion for one's fellow men and the saving of lives would indicate the opposite.

Mr. Kerlikowske's claim about marijuana being the cause of a significant amount of traffic accidents is a "fact" that he must have pulled out of a lower opening. There is no data to support this. Again, what studies have been done on this angle do not support his claim. Studies have found that marijuana smokers get into accidents as often as those who do not use marijuana. Think about it! I returned to Northern Kentucky in 1996. I watch local news at least once a day and read the paper every day.

In the 14 years since 1996, I have seen only one report of a marijuana caused traffic accident. If I remember right, a young man had blown through an intersection and someone was killed in the resulting accident. The local media reported that the driver had been smoking marijuana and that was the cause of the accident. A follow up report later claimed the driver was texting when he blew the intersection. You have to ask yourself that if there are so many marijuana's caused accidents, where are all the marijuana accident stories, arrests, trials, and incarcerations.

Marijuana prohibition is an idea that has lived long past the point of being something that is "good" for America. Marijuana use is not as Reagan said that it's the greatest threat faced by America. The end of the federal ban on marijuana is long overdue. It has no basis in science or logic, costs billions of tax dollars, and causes more harm than good. At a time when Americans need jobs and economic growth, we are shooting ourselves in the foot by continuing to suppress the marijuana/hemp industry, an industry that could go a long way in creating jobs and economic activity worth billions of dollars.

M.Sgt. Thomas Vance, USAF Ret., Alexandria

(continues)

► **CASE IN POINT**

A Letter to an Editor: No Valid Reason to Ban Marijuana (*continued*)

Questions to Consider

1. What is your initial reaction to this letter?

2. Like the firmly established link between lung cancer and smoking tobacco, do you think a similar argument can be made between smoking marijuana and lung cancer? Explain.

3. Do you think the "forces of prohibition" are masking potential benefits of using marijuana, as the writer claims? Explain.

4. What is your opinion about using marijuana and driving? Do you think drivers under the influence are adversely affected by the effects of this drug? Explain.

5. How do you generally feel about people who use marijuana?

6. How much of a threat to society is marijuana use? Should marijuana be decriminalized? If yes, why? Should it remain illegal? If so, what penalties should apply and why?

Data from Cincinnati.com. Letters to the Editor, "No Valid Reason to Ban Marijuana." *The Enquirer*. (9 August 2010). Available http://cincinnati.com /blogs/letters/2010/08/09/no-valid-reason-to-ban-marijuana

As late as 1913, Sir William Osler recommended it as the most satisfactory remedy for migraines (Grinspoon and Bakalar 1995).

Marijuana was used to treat a variety of human ills in folk and formal medicine for thousands of years in South Africa, Turkey, South America, and Egypt, as well as such Asian countries as India, Malaysia, Myanmar, and Siam. Thus, marijuana, known as *cannabis* back then, has a 5000-year medical history that came to an abrupt end in the United States by passage of the Marijuana Tax Act of 1937. When the Marijuana Tax Act became law, marijuana was legally classified as a narcotic, and at that time medical use of this substance effectively ceased. Only in the past 2 decades has there been organized renewed interest in possible medical uses for cannabis. Because of potential clinical uses for marijuana, enforcement of laws prohibiting the use of this substance has been very controversial (see "Holding the Line: Despite Federal Drug Laws Prohibiting the Cultivation, Possession, Use, and the Sale of Marijuana, States Sanction Cannabis Buyers' Clubs").

Marijuana has been shown to be effective in the treatment of certain types of medical conditions. However, because medications exist that are at least as effective and without abuse potential, such as legally approved **Marinol** (dronabinol), to date, none of these applications have been approved by the Food and Drug Administration (FDA). The potential medical uses that have been described by researchers (Abood and Martin 1992; Consroe and Sandyk 1992; Iversen 1993) and proponents (ProCon.org 2012a) for the medical uses of marijuana are described in the following sections.

▪ Reduction in Intraocular (Eye) Pressure

Glaucoma, the second-leading cause of blindness, is caused by uncontrollable eye pressure (Julian 1994; National Eye Institute 2010). Marijuana lowers glaucoma-associated intraocular pressure, even though it does not cure the condition or reverse blindness (Goldstein 1995; Green 2006; NIDA 2010c).

▪ Cancer

Recent animal studies have shown that marijuana extracts may help kill certain cancer cells and reduce the size of others. Evidence from one cell culture study suggests that purified extracts from whole-plant marijuana can slow the growth of cancer cells from one of the most serious types of brain tumors. Research in mice showed that treatment with purified extracts of THC and CBD, when used with radiation, increased the cancer-killing effects of the radiation (NIH 2015c; Scott, Dalgleish, and Liu 2014).

KEY TERMS

Marinol
FDA-approved synthesized THC in capsule form (dronabinol); primarily used to treat nausea and vomiting, often prescribed to people diagnosed with acquired immune deficiency syndrome (AIDS)

glaucoma
potentially blinding eye disease causing continual and increasing intraocular pressure

HOLDING THE LINE

Despite Federal Drug Laws Prohibiting the Cultivation, Possession, Use, and Sale of Marijuana, States Sanction Cannabis Buyers' Clubs

Currently, 28 states plus the District of Columbia (DC) are medical marijuana states that have enacted laws to legalize medical marijuana. The 28 states are Alaska, Arizona, Arkansas, California, Colorado, Connecticut, Delaware, Florida, Hawaii, Illinois, Maine, Maryland, Massachusetts, Michigan, Minnesota, Montana, Nevada, New Hampshire, New Jersey, New Mexico, New York, North Dakota, Ohio, Oregon, Pennsylvania, Rhode Island, Vermont, and Washington (ProCon.org 2016ba). Out of 323,086,768 of U.S. population as of March 1, 2016 (ProCon.org 2016b), the *estimated* number of medical marijuana users would be 2,604,079 medical marijuana users" (ProCon.org 2016a).

Why should medically ill patients, those afflicted with AIDS and AIDS wasting, lack of appetite, nausea, arthritis, hepatitis C, migraines, multiple sclerosis, muscle spasms, chronic pain, glaucoma, and other illnesses (such as posttraumatic stress disorder [PTSD], depression, or bipolar disorder) or those suffering the deleterious effects of chemotherapy and/or radiation not be able to legally purchase marijuana if they find relief from the effects of their illnesses? The first cannabis buyers' club began in 1996, when the voting citizens of Marin County, California, passed "Proposition 215, which authorized the use of medical marijuana . . . for those who have a doctor's recommendation" (*Cannabis News* 2002). The main problem facing this club in Marin County, and all the other cannabis buyers' clubs throughout the United States, is that although these 23 states and DC have legalized such enterprises, they continue to violate federal drug laws, causing a conflict between federal and state law. At times, the clubs can be ordered closed by a superior court judge, resulting in federal agents raiding the clubs, confiscating the marijuana, and arresting the owners and operators of these establishments.

To date, this cyclical pattern of raids and arrests by federal officials continues to sporadically occur because of this rift between state and federal laws. The clubs are either for-profit or nonprofit organizations whose sole intent is to distribute marijuana for medicinal purposes when prescribed by a licensed physician. Many of the buyers (known as patients) report relief and satisfaction from their use of marijuana. For example, a man by the name of Clay Shinn, 46, was diagnosed with AIDS in 1992. At the time of his interview, he had been going to the Marin Alliance's Cannabis Buyers' Club for 5 years. "It's made a major difference in my life," he said. After taking his [AIDS] medication morning, afternoon, and evening, he said, "I was always getting nauseated . . . I could set my watch by it. I hate it. God, it's awful. Now I don't barf anymore" (*Cannabis News* 2002). Another interviewee, who is an arthritic, HIV-positive cabaret performer, said, "After I leave here . . . I won't feel my pain" (Goldberg 1996). Another man, the club's director, reiterated that, "'You have to be sick or dying' . . . If you are, with a doctor's note to prove that you have AIDS or cancer or another condition with symptoms that marijuana is known to alleviate, Mr. Peron [the club's director] is willing to sell some relief" (Goldberg 1996). Finally, Dennis Peron, the founder of the San Francisco Buyers' Club, stated that "We have over 400 senior citizens that come here for arthritis, glaucoma, pain, etc. We have an old woman trapped in her wheelchair, day in and day out. Marijuana makes her feel a little bit better. I don't require a letter of diagnosis for people 65 or older—things wear out—or for people who are blind or deaf, as they say it helps their other senses" (Fuhrman 1995).

What are your views regarding the prescribed use of marijuana, especially when these clubs or cooperatives provide seriously ill patients with a safe and reliable source of medical cannabis information and patient support? Would you support a cannabis buyers club or cooperative in your community? What are your views regarding federal laws that prohibit such establishments while states pass laws allowing these establishments to legally operate? How do you think this current problem of the illegality on the federal level should be resolved? Finally, how do you think this dilemma will be resolved in your lifetime?

Data from *Cannabis News*. "Medical Pot War Rages On." *Marin Independent Journal*. (1 July 2002). Available http://cannabisnews.com/news/13/thread13278.shtml; Fuhrman, R. A. "Cannabis Buyers' Club Flourishes in 'Frisco." San Francisco: Cannabis Buyers' Club, 1995; Goldberg, C. "Marijuana Club Helps Those in Pain." *New York Times*. (26 February 1996). Available http://query.nytimes.com/gst/fullpage.html?res=9C06E6DF1139F936A1575 1C0A960958260&sec=&spon=&pagewanted=all; ProCon.org. "How Many People in the United State Use Medical Marijuana?" Santa Monica: CA, 2013. Available http://medicalmarijuana.procon.org/view.answers.php?questionID=001199; ProCon.org. "28 Legal Marijuana States and DC: Laws, Fees, and Possession Limits." Santa Monica, CA: ProCon.org, 9 November 2016a. Available http://medicalmarijuana.procon.org/view.resource.php?resourceID= 000881 ProCon.org. "Number of Legal Medical Marijuana Patients." Santa Monica, CA: ProCon.org, 3 March 2016b. Available http://medicalmarijuana. procon.org/view.resource.php?resourceID=005889

In November 2010, Arizona began to issue cards that allow the users to purchase marijuana for medicinal purposes.

▪ Antiasthmatic Effect

Some research indicates that short-term smoking of marijuana improves breathing for asthma patients. Marijuana smoke dilates the lungs' air passages (bronchodilation). Other findings also show, however, that the lung-irritating properties of marijuana smoke seem to offset its benefits. The adverse effects of marijuana smoke remain controversial (NIDA 2006, 2010c). Regardless, marijuana may still prove useful when other drugs are not effective because of the different mode of action in causing bronchodilation.

Another study made a distinction between short-term and long-term marijuana smoking, emphasizing a distinction: "Short-term exposure to marijuana is associated with bronchodilation. However, physiologic data were inconclusive regarding an association between long-term marijuana smoking and airflow obstruction measures. Long-term marijuana smoking is associated with increased respiratory symptoms suggestive of obstructive lung disease" (Barclay and Vega 2007).

▪ Muscle-Relaxant Effect

Some studies indicate that muscle spasms are relieved when patients with muscle disorders, such as multiple sclerosis, use marijuana. Researchers have found that the key medicinal ingredients of cannabis, THC and CBD, have beneficial effects in the treatment of muscle spasms and spasticity. "Many patients report that medical cannabis is effective in relieving their muscle spasms. Medical cannabis may also be effective in alleviating uncontrollable and debilitating muscle tremors. Some patients with severe spasticity report that medical cannabis is the only treatment that allows them to function" (Medical Marijuana Education Center 2012).

▪ Antiseizure Effect

Marijuana has both convulsing and anticonvulsant properties and has been considered for use in preventing seizures associated with epilepsy. In studies with animal models, the cannabinoids reduced or increased seizure activities, depending on how the experiments were conducted. One or more of the components of marijuana may be useful in combination with other standard antiseizure medication. "New evidence suggests that a chemical derived from marijuana may be an effective treatment for patients with drug-resistant forms of epilepsy" (Kwon 2016). The Epilepsy Foundation, comprised of parent advocates, advocates the belief that cannabis should a legalized treatment option for physicians and patients dealing with epilepsy (Rabinski 2015).

▪ Antidepressant Effect

Some research studies have suggested that cannabis is a promising remedy for treating physical and mental conditions. "Neuroscientists from the University of Buffalo's Research Institute on Addictions found that endocannabinoids—chemical compounds in the brain that activate the same receptors as THC, an active compound in marijuana—may be helpful in treating depression that results from chronic stress" (Gregoire 2015). The use of cannabis—marijuana—stabilized moods and reduced symptoms of depression (Gregoire 2015; Wilde 2015).

▪ Analgesic Effect

Published testimonials have reported that marijuana can relieve the intense pain associated with migraine and chronic headaches or inflammation (Green 2006; Grinspoon and Bakalar 1995). Among chronic pain populations, survey data indicate that use of cannabis is common, and clinical trials have indicated that inhaled marijuana can alleviate neuropathic pain (Cone et al. 2008; Gardner 2010; Green 2006; NORML 2013). In South Africa, native women smoke cannabis to dull the pain of childbirth (Hamid 1998; Solomon 1966). The pain-relieving potency of marijuana has not been carefully studied and compared with other analgesics, such as narcotics or aspirin-type drugs.

▪ Antinauseant

Marijuana can relieve the nausea that accompanies chemotherapy for cancer treatment (NIDA 2010c; Robson 2001).

■ Appetite Stimulant

Marijuana is also a powerful appetite stimulant (NIDA 2010c; NORML n.d.). The stimulant effects on appetite are seen as useful for patients with human immunodeficiency virus (HIV), AIDS wasting syndrome, or dementia, as well as those with eating disorders (NORML n.d.; Sewester 1993).

Short-Term Consequences of Smoking Marijuana

Discomforts associated with smoking marijuana include dry mouth, dry eyes, increased heart rate, and visible signs of intoxication such as bloodshot eyes and puffy eyelids (Brown University Health Education 2007). Marijuana overactivates the parts of the brain that contain receptors (a protein molecule that receives chemical signals from outside a cell). In cell biology, a receptor is a structure on the surface of a cell (or inside a cell) that selectively receives and binds a specific substance. The high (altered state of consciousness) occurs when receptors in the brain are affected by the THC in marijuana(NIH 2015d). Other short-term effects of marijuana use include the following (NIH 2015d):

- Altered senses (e.g., seeing brighter colors)
- Altered sense of time
- Changes in mood
- Impaired body movement
- Difficulty with thinking and problem-solving
- Impaired memory

Long-Term Consequences of Smoking Marijuana

Marijuana affects brain development. When marijuana users begin using as teenagers, the drug may reduce thinking, memory, and learning functions and affect how the brain builds connections between the areas necessary for these functions. Marijuana's effects on these abilities may last a long time or may even be permanent (NIH 2015d).

Long-term consequences, lasting longer than intoxication, and cumulative effects of chronic abuse of smoking marijuana include the following:

- *Respiratory problems*: Many of these problems are the same as for cigarette smokers. Persistent coughing, symptoms of bronchitis, and more frequent chest colds are possible symptoms from the 400-plus chemicals (some carcinogenic) in marijuana smoke. "Researchers report that marijuana cigarettes release five times as much carbon monoxide into the bloodstream and three times as much tar into the lungs of smokers as tobacco cigarettes" (MarijuanaDetox.com 2008; NIDA 2010c).
- *Memory and learning*: Regular marijuana use compromises the ability to learn and to remember information by impairing the ability to focus, sustain, and shift attention. One study also found that long-term use reduces the ability to organize and integrate complex information. Marijuana impairs short-term memory and decreases motivation to accomplish tasks, even after the high is over.
- *Fertility*: Long-term marijuana use suppresses the production of hormones that help regulate the reproductive system. For men, this can cause decreased sperm counts, and very heavy users can experience erectile dysfunction. Women may experience irregular periods from heavy marijuana use.
- *Mental effects:* Long-term marijuana use has been linked to mental illness in some users, such as temporary hallucinations, temporary paranoia, and worsening symptoms in patients with schizophrenia (NIH 2015d).
- *Addictive properties*: For a small percentage of people who use it, long-term marijuana use can lead to addiction (NIDA 2010c). Researchers estimate that about 9% of marijuana users become addicted and that this number is higher among those who start their marijuana use at a young age (about 17%) and among daily users (25% to 50%) (NIDA 2012; NIH 2015). Both animal and human studies show physical and psychological withdrawal symptoms from marijuana, including irritability, restlessness, insomnia, nausea, and intense dreams. The withdrawal syndrome has been described as being similar to that of nicotine withdrawal, with people trying to quit reporting irritability, sleeping difficulties, craving, and anxiety (NIDA 2010c; NIH 2015e). Tolerance to marijuana also builds up rapidly. Heavy users need eight times higher doses to get the same effects as infrequent users. It is estimated that 10% to 14% of users will become *heavily* dependent during the addiction process. More

than 120,000 people in the United States seek treatment for marijuana addiction every year (Brown University Health Education 2007).

All of these effects have either been disputed or been shown to be exaggerated by proponents who are in favor of medical marijuana. Proponents for medical marijuana argue that "its illegality [marijuana] . . . imposes much anxiety and expense on suffering people, forces them to bargain with illicit drug dealers, and exposes them to the threat of criminal prosecution" (Grinspoon and Bakalar 1995, p. 1876). For a list of states currently allowing the use of marijuana for medical purposes, see the "Holding the Line" feature earlier in this chapter.

The Physiological Effects of Marijuana Use

Although the literature on marijuana use repeatedly states that "in 5,000 years of medical and non-medical use, marijuana has not caused a single overdose death" (Grinspoon and Bakalar 1995, p. 1875), the effects of marijuana use should not be overlooked. We begin by examining the effects of marijuana on the lungs.

When marijuana smoke is inhaled into the lungs, THC, the psychoactive ingredient, leaves the blood rapidly through metabolism and efficient uptake into the tissues. THC and its metabolites tend to bind to proteins in the blood and remain stored for long periods in body fat. Five days after a single dosage of THC, 20% remains stored, whereas 20% of its metabolites remain in the blood (Indiana Prevention Resource Center 1996; Kryger 1995). Complete elimination of a single dose can take up to 30 days. Measurable levels of THC in blood from chronic users often can be detected for several days or even weeks after their last marijuana cigarette (joint).

When marijuana is smoked, THC is rapidly absorbed into the lungs and transported to the brain, with THC reaching the brain within as little as 14 seconds after inhalation. Marijuana is metabolized more efficiently through smoking than via intravenous injection or oral ingestion. Smoking is also three to five times more potent than these two methods (Jones 1980; Kaplan and Whitmire 1995; Kryger 1995). Other findings that compare the amounts of marijuana with tobacco conclude, "three to four joints a day is about as harmful to your lungs as smoking a pack of cigarettes a day" (Reaney 2000, p. 1).

Some of the effects of cannabis described in the following sections are unquestionably toxic in that they can either directly or indirectly produce adverse health effects. Other effects may be beneficial in treating some medical conditions. The use of marijuana, THC, and synthetic cannabinoids, either alone or in combination with other drugs, continues to be discussed and investigated for treating pain, inflammation, glaucoma, nausea, and muscle spasms (Iversen 1993; NIDA 2010c).

▌ Effects on the Brain

As THC enters the brain, it causes the user to feel euphoric—or high—by acting on the brain's reward system, which is made up of regions that govern the response to pleasurable things like sex and chocolate, as well as to most drugs of abuse. THC activates the reward system in the same way that nearly all drugs of abuse do: by stimulating brain cells to release the chemical dopamine (NIDA 2010c). THC affects the nerve cells in the part of the brain where memories are formed. This makes it hard for the user to recall recent events (such as what happened a few minutes ago). It is hard to learn while high—a working short-term memory is required for learning and performing tasks that call for more than one or two steps (NIDA 2007, 2010c).

An interesting finding reported that among a group of long time heavy marijuana users in Costa Rica, researchers found that the people had great trouble when asked to recall a short list of words (a standard test of memory). People in that study group also found it very hard to focus their attention on the tests given to them.

As people age, they normally lose nerve cells in a region of the brain that is important for remembering events. Chronic exposure to THC may hasten the age-related loss of these nerve cells. In one study, researchers found that rats exposed to THC every day for 8 months (about one-third of their lifespan) showed a loss of brain cells comparable to rats that were twice their age. It is not known whether a similar effect occurs in humans. Researchers are still learning about the many ways that marijuana could affect the brain (NIDA 2007).

When someone smokes marijuana, THC stimulates the cannabinoid receptors (CBRs) artificially, disrupting the function of the natural, or endogenous, cannabinoids. An overstimulation of these receptors in key brain areas produces the marijuana high, as well as having other effects on mental processes. Over time, this overstimulation can alter the function of CBRs, which, along with other changes in the brain, can lead to addiction and to withdrawal symptoms when drug use stops (NIDA 2010c).

∎ Effects on the Central Nervous System

The primary effects of marijuana—specifically, of THC—are on CNS functions. The precise CNS effects of consuming marijuana or administering THC can vary according to the expectations of the user, the social setting, the route of administration, and previous experiences (Abood and Martin 1992; Jaffe 1990). Smoking a marijuana cigarette can alter mood, coordination, memory, and self-perception. Usually, such exposure causes some euphoria, a sense of well-being, and relaxation. Marijuana smokers often claim heightened sensory awareness and **altered perceptions** (particularly a slowing of time), symptoms associated with hunger (the **munchies**), and a dry mouth (Hubbard, Franco, and Onaivi 1999; Swan 1994). High doses of THC or greater exposure to marijuana can cause hallucinations, delusions, and paranoia (American Psychiatric Association [APA] 1994; Goldstein 1995; Hubbard et al. 1999; NIDA 2007). Some users describe anxiety after high-dose exposure. Due to the availability and widespread use of marijuana, psychiatric emergencies from marijuana overdose are becoming somewhat common. Long-term, chronic users often show decreased interest in personal appearance or goals (part of the amotivational syndrome, discussed earlier in this chapter) as well as an inability to concentrate, make appropriate decisions, and recall information from short-term memory (Abood and Martin 1992; Block 1996).

The precise classification of THC is uncertain because the responses to marijuana are highly variable and appear to have elements of all three major groups of drugs of abuse. Consequently, marijuana use can cause euphoria and paranoia (like stimulants), drowsiness and sedation (like depressants), and hallucinations (like psychedelics). It is possible that THC alters several receptor or transmitter systems in the brain; this action would account for its diverse and somewhat unpredictable effects.

The dramatic discovery of a specific receptor site in the brain for THC, the cannabinoid receptor (mentioned earlier), suggests that a selective endogenous marijuana system exists in the brain and is activated by THC when marijuana is consumed (Hudson 1990; NIDA 2007). Some researchers speculate that an endogenous fatty acid–like substance called *anandamide* naturally works at these marijuana sites; efforts are being made to characterize this substance, which is a neurotransmitter (Iversen 1993; NIDA 2010c). It is possible that, from this discovery, a group of new therapeutic agents will be developed that can selectively interact with the marijuana receptors, resulting in medical benefits without the side effects that generally accompany marijuana use (Iversen 1993; Swan 1993).

∎ Effects on the Respiratory System: Smoking Marijuana

Marijuana is often smoked like tobacco and, like tobacco, it can cause damage to the lungs (Adams and Martin 1996; Consroe and Sandyk 1992; NIDA 2010c). When smoking tobacco, nearly 70% of the total suspended particles in the smoke are retained in the lungs. Because marijuana smoke is inhaled more deeply than tobacco smoke, even more tar residues may be retained with its use.

Smoke is a mixture of tiny particles suspended in gas, mostly carbon monoxide. These solid particles combine to form a residue called tar. Cannabis produces more tar (as much as 50% more) than an equivalent weight of tobacco and is smoked in a way that increases the accumulation of tar (Jones 1980).

More than 140 chemicals have been identified in marijuana smoke and tar. A few are proven carcinogens; many others have not yet been tested for carcinogenicity. The carcinogen benzopyrene, for example, is 70% more abundant in marijuana smoke than in tobacco smoke. When cannabis tar is applied to the skin of experimental animals, it causes precancerous lesions similar to those caused by tobacco tar. Similarly, whenever isolated lung tissue is exposed to these same tars, precancerous changes result (Hollister 1986; Jones 1980; Turner 1980).

Special white blood cells in living lung tissue—alveolar macrophages—play a role in removing debris from the lungs. When exposed to smoke

KEY TERMS

altered perceptions
changes in the interpretation of stimuli resulting from marijuana

munchies
hunger experienced while under the effects of marijuana

from cannabis, these cells are less able to remove bacteria and other foreign debris.

Smoking only a few marijuana cigarettes a day for 6 to 8 weeks can significantly impair pulmonary function. Laboratory and clinical evidence often indicate that heavy use of marijuana causes cellular changes, and those heavy users have a higher incidence of such respiratory problems as laryngitis, pharyngitis, bronchitis, asthma-like conditions, cough, hoarseness, and dry throat (Goldstein 1995; Hollister 1986). Some reports emphasize the potential damage to pulmonary function that can occur from chronic marijuana use (NIDA 1991). Evidence suggests that many 20-year-old smokers of both hashish and tobacco have lung damage comparable to that found in heavy tobacco smokers older than 40 years of age. It is believed that the tar from tobacco and marijuana has damaging effects, but it is not known whether smokers who use both products suffer synergistic or additive effects (Hollister 1986; Jones 1980).

∎ Effects on the Respiratory System: Vaporizing Marijuana

As just presented, the evidence shows that smoking marijuana clearly appears to be hazardous to the respiratory system, having the most negative impact on the lungs. A newer method of use, known as vaporizing marijuana, is slowly increasing among users, even though one major study of 6883 people surveyed showed that "only 152 participants (2.2%) reported vaporizing as their primary method for cannabis use" (Earleywine and Smucker Barnwell 2007, p. 3). However, another survey found that 18% of e-cigarette users in Connecticut high schools had "vaped" marijuana or used an e-cigarette to get high and that more than one-quarter those students who described themselves as dual users of e-cigarettes and marijuana had used the devices get high (Thompson 2015).

Cannabis smoke contains gaseous and particulate matter with the potential to create symptoms of respiratory problems. Although cannabis smoke creates fewer problems than cigarette smoke, increasing its safety has the potential to improve quality of life. One step toward increasing the safety of cannabis involves the use of vaporizers. Vaporizers heat cannabis to temperatures that cause the release of cannabinoids in a fine mist without creating the toxins associated with combustion. Although vaporizers are not common knowledge in popular culture, a recent photograph of one appeared in the *New England*

Journal of Medicine, and information about the machine is becoming more available. A vaporizer has the potential to increase the safety of cannabis use, but data from human users appear only rarely (Earleywine and Smucker Barnwell 2007). Research suggests that "the respiratory effects of cannabis can decrease with the use of a vaporizer. The data reveal that respiratory symptoms like cough, phlegm, and tightness in the chest increase with cigarette use and cannabis use, but are less severe among users of a vaporizer" (Earleywine and Smucker Barnwell 2007, p. 3).

The cost of a vaporizer unit can usually run several hundred dollars and above. Using a vaporizer for marijuana use may decrease respiratory problems; however, other hazards continue to exist. Users who replace smoking marijuana with vaporizing marijuana continue to run the risk of marijuana dependence (addiction), impaired driving skills, and cognitive, mainly short-term memory, impairment. Also, users often mix smoking with vaporizing, resulting in increased usage. Thus, although pulmonary damage is likely to be minimized when using a vaporizer, other deleterious consequences from marijuana use are continued and even increased.

∎ Effects on the Cardiovascular System

In human beings, cannabis causes both *vasodilation* (enlarged blood vessels) and an increase in heart rate related to the amount of THC consumed (Abood and Martin 1992; NIDA 2000, 2010c). The vasodilation is responsible for the reddening of the eyes often seen in marijuana smokers. In physically healthy users, these effects, as well as slight changes in heart rhythm, are transitory and do not appear to be significant. In patients with heart disease, however, the increased oxygen requirement due to the accelerated heart rate may have serious consequences. The effect of cannabis on people with heart rhythm irregularities is not known. Because of vasodilation caused by marijuana use, abnormally low blood pressure can occur when standing. In addition, if a user stands up quickly after smoking, a feeling of lightheadedness or fainting may result. Chronic administration of large doses of THC to healthy volunteers shows that tolerance develops to the increase in heart rate and vasodilation.

People with cardiovascular problems seem to be at an increased risk when smoking marijuana (Hollister 1986; NIDA 2010c). Marijuana products also bind hemoglobin, limiting the amount of oxygen that can be carried to the

A demonstration of a marijuana vaporizer.

heart tissue. In a few cases, this deficiency could trigger heart attacks in susceptible people (Palfai and Jankiewicz 1991). The National Academy of Sciences' Institute of Medicine recommends that people with cardiovascular disease avoid marijuana use because there are still many unanswered questions about its effects on the cardiovascular system (Mack and Joy 2001).

■ Effects on Sexual Performance and Reproduction

Drugs may interfere with sexual performance and reproduction in several ways (Hanson 2011). They may alter sexual behavior, affect fertility, damage the chromosomes of germ cells in the male or female, or adversely affect fetal growth and development.

The Indian Hemp Commission (Taylor 1963, 1966), which wrote the first scientific report on cannabis, commented that it had a sexually stimulating effect, like alcohol. However, the report also said that cannabis was used by Asian Indian ascetics to destroy the sexual appetite. This apparent discrepancy may be a dose-related effect. Used occasionally over the short term, marijuana may act as an **aphrodisiac** by decreasing CNS inhibitions. In addition, the altered perception of time under the influence of the drug could make the pleasurable sensations appear to last longer than they actually do.

Marijuana affects the sympathetic nervous system, increasing vasodilation in the genitals and delaying ejaculation. High doses over a period of time lead to depression of libido and impotence— possibly due to the decreased amount of testosterone, the male sex hormone. "Some research has found a relationship between long-term use of marijuana . . . [and] increased erectile dysfunction" (Silverberg 2007).

Cannabis has several effects on semen (Cadena 2007). The total number of sperm cells and the concentration of sperm per unit volume are decreased during ejaculation (Cadena 2007). Moreover, there is an increase in the proportion of sperm with abnormal appearance and reduced motility. These qualities are usually associated with lower fertility and a higher probability of producing an abnormal embryo should fertilization take place.

Despite these effects, there are no documented reports of children with birth defects in which the abnormality was linked to the father's smoking marijuana. It is possible that damaged sperm cells are incapable of fertilization (so that only normal sperm cells reach the egg) or that the abnormal sperm appearance is meaningless in terms of predicting birth defects. When marijuana use stops, the quality of sperm gradually returns to normal over several months.

Less reliable data are available on the effects of cannabis on female libido, sexual response (ability to respond to sexual stimulation with vaginal lubrication and orgasm), and fertile reproductive (menstrual) cycles (Consroe and Sandyk 1992; Grinspoon 1987). However, some researchers have found that heavy marijuana use in women may inhibit ovulation and that use during pregnancy can harm the development of the fetus, resulting in neurobehavioral and physical abnormalities, and increase the chance of a premature birth (Silverberg 2007). Data from the Reproductive Biology Research Foundation show that chronic smoking of cannabis (at least three times per week for the preceding 6 months) adversely affects the female reproductive cycle. Results with women were correlated with work in rhesus monkeys; it was found that THC blocks ovulation (due to effects on female sex hormones).

Data on the effects of marijuana use during pregnancy and lactation are inconclusive. Some evidence suggests that the use of this drug by pregnant women can result in intrauterine growth retardation, which is characterized by increased fetal mortality, prolonged labor, low-birth-weight babies (Foley 2007), and behavioral abnormalities in newborns (Fernandez-Ruiz et al. 1992; Nahas and Latour 1992; Roffman and George 1988).

KEY TERM

aphrodisiac
a compound that is believed to be the cause of sexual arousal

THC and other cannabinoids pass through the blood–placenta barrier and concentrate in the fetus's fatty tissue, including its brain. Ethical considerations prevent duplication of the experiment in humans.

Women who smoke marijuana during pregnancy also often use other drugs—such as alcohol, tobacco, and cocaine—that are known to have adverse effects on the developing fetus. Because multiple drugs are used, it is difficult to isolate the specific effects of marijuana during pregnancy. Like many other substances, THC is taken up by the mammary glands in lactating women and is excreted in the breast milk. Effects of marijuana in the breast milk on human infants have not been determined (Christina 1994; Murphy and Bartke 1992).

In studies on mice and rats (but not humans), the addition of THC to pregnant animals decreased litter size, increased fetal reabsorption, and increased the number of reproductive abnormalities in the surviving offspring (Dewey 1986). The offspring of the drug-treated animal mothers had reduced fertility and more testicular abnormalities. The dose of cannabinoids used in these studies was higher than that used by humans. Clearly, pregnant women should be advised against using marijuana, even though there are few direct data on its prenatal effects in humans (Dewey 1986; Foley 2007; Murphy and Bartke 1992).

▪ Tolerance and Dependence

It has been known for many years that tolerance to some effects of cannabis builds rapidly in animals—namely, the drug effect becomes less intense with repeated administration. Frequent use of high doses of marijuana or THC in humans produces similar tolerance. For example, increasingly higher doses must be given to obtain the same intensity of subjective effects and increased heart rate that occur initially with small doses (Abood and Martin 1992; NIDA 2010c).

Frequent high doses of THC also can produce mild physical dependence. Healthy subjects who smoke several joints a day or who are given comparable amounts of THC orally experience irritability, sleep disturbances, weight loss, loss of appetite, sweating, and gastrointestinal upsets when drug use is stopped abruptly. However, not all subjects experience this mild form of withdrawal.

It is much easier to show psychological dependence in heavy users of marijuana (Abood and Martin 1992; Hollister 1986; NIDA 2010c).

Psychological dependence involves an attachment to the euphoric effects of the THC content in marijuana and may include craving for the drug. The subjective psychological effects of marijuana intoxication include a heightened sensitivity to and distortion of sight, smell, taste, and sound; mood alteration; and diminished reaction time.

DIAGNOSIS: CANNABIS DEPENDENCE

In general, outright cannabis addiction, with obsessive drug-seeking and compulsive drug-taking behavior, is relatively rare with low-THC cannabis. Contributing to this is the fact that the less potent forms of marijuana are the most readily available in the United States, resulting in most chronic users in this country having little problem controlling or eliminating their cannabis habit if they so desire.

The Diagnostic and Statistical Manual of Mental Disorders, fifth edition (*DSM-5*), recognizes a diagnosis of cannabis dependence. It is characterized by compulsive use and hours per day spent acquiring and using the substance. Compulsive users persist in their use despite knowledge of physical problems (e.g., chronic cough related to smoking) or psychological problems (e.g., excessive sedation resulting from repeated use of high doses) (APA 2013).

▪ Chronic Use

Research on chronic use of marijuana (repeated daily use of this drug) in the 1970s indicated the possibility of three types of damage: (1) chromosomal damage (Stenchever, Kunysz, and Allen 1974), (2) cerebral atrophy (shrinking of the brain) (Campbell et al. 1971), and (3) lowered capacity of white blood cells to fight disease (Suciu-Foca, Armand, and Morishima 1974). These findings have all been contradicted or refuted by subsequent research. The only finding that appears very credible is that heavy use of this drug impairs lung capacity (Bloodworth 1987; Henneberger 1994; Kaplan and Whitmire 1995; NIDA 2010c; Oliwenstein 1988; Swan 1994). Other evidence indicates that chronic, heavy use of cannabis can lead to unforeseen calamities in some users (see "Case in Point: Chronic Marijuana Use").

We have pointed out that marijuana produces a variety of psychoactive effects. One of those effects is sedation of unwanted emotional states, such as anxiety, which are inevitable given the conflicts and turmoil of living in our fast-paced society today. As with the chronic use of any psychoactive drug that produces sedating effects, normal emotional and psychosocial development can be arrested by heavy marijuana consumption. For example, a youth who is usually high at a party avoids the anxieties and embarrassments of introspective and critical interpersonal interactions but instead will be interested in thrill-seeking behavior, such as romantic and sexual involvements, experimentation with and heavy use of other drugs, and other types of more daring experiences.

From years of research with this drug, we find that heavy and chronic use of marijuana can very easily compromise cognitive functions, such as short-term memory, concentration, moderately taxing problem-solving, and even spiritual growth and development. Often, the more serious costs in using this drug are that the individual acquires a poor record for development and advancement of learning, as is often expected in educational settings (schools, colleges, trade schools, and universities). Another cost that is more serious is the retardation in emotional development. Such types of development are often obscured by being high all the time. Further, in such chronic use cases, much time is wasted seeking the pleasures and

sometimes the longed-for thrills derived from the habitual use of marijuana.

The amotivational syndrome, in fact, can be deconstructed into the sedation, depression, and cognitive impairment discussed throughout this chapter. The user who is experiencing a subjective euphoric effect, enjoying the presence and social reinforcement of peers, feeling no pain, and remaining cognitively unfocused finds it difficult to intellectually grasp the learned experiences from such developmental delays. Although many do mature out of use, this step may occur only after years of development have slipped away, never to be regained. Sometimes treatment interventions are necessary to get the subject into a drug-free state and reunited with non-drug-using peer groups.

In concluding this chapter, we note that the history of this drug indicates that usage and availability will remain widespread despite all the efforts to eradicate its existence. Despite all the prevention efforts to date, marijuana remains the most popular illicit drug, topped only by alcohol and tobacco, which are licit drugs.

► **CASE IN POINT**

Chronic Marijuana Use

The following comments show how marijuana use can become a disturbing habit:

I guess you could say it was peer pressure. Back in 1969, I was a sophomore in college, and everyone was smoking "dope." The Vietnam War was in progress, and most students on college campuses were heavily involved in the drug scene. I first started smoking marijuana when my closest friends did. I was taught by other students who already knew how to enjoy the effects of "pot."

I recall that one of my fellow students used to supply me with "nickel bags," and many users nicknamed him "God." How did he get such a name? Because he sold some very potent marijuana that at times caused us to hallucinate.

I used pot nearly every day for about a year and a half, and hardly an evening would pass without smoking dope and listening to music. Smoking marijuana became as common as drinking alcohol. I used it in the same manner a person has a cocktail after a long day. At first, I liked the effects of being "high," but later I became so accustomed to the stuff that life appeared boring without it.

After graduating, my college friends went their separate ways, and I stopped using marijuana for a few years. A year later, in graduate school, a neighborhood friend reintroduced me to the pleasure of smoking pot. I began to use it again but not as often. Whenever I experienced some pressure, I would use a little to relax.

After finishing my degree, I found myself employed at an institution that at times was boring. Again, I started using pot at night to relax, and somehow it got out of control. I used to smoke a little before work and sometimes during lunch. I thought all was well until one day I got fired because someone accused me of being high on the job.

Soon afterward, I came to the realization that the use of marijuana can be very insidious. It has a way of becoming psychologically addictive, and you don't even realize it. When I was high, I thought that no one knew, and that I was even more effective with others. Little did I know, I was dead wrong and fooling no one. *(From Venturelli's research files, male, age 39, May 1990)*

(continues)

► CASE IN POINT

Chronic Marijuana Use (*continued*)

In May 2013, this same interviewee, now 62 years of age, was asked if he had any additional remarks about the interview he gave in May 1990. He said the following:

How time flies! Now it's been 23 years since I was interviewed. I can say that as a very recent retired man I still occasionally dabble in pot smoking and still enjoy it. I did quit for many years, but about 9 years ago, a lifelong friend of mine was visiting and I asked him to get me some so we could "fire one up after a long time." We did that and it was nothing but memory lane while we were smoking it. We had a good time talking and laughing about things we did during those as you say [referring to the interviewer] days of chronic marijuana use.

What I really like about the pot these days is that you have real quality and really powerful stuff. Several puffs and you can get really stoned. My friend picked up some blueberry marijuana and it was really powerful. I only had a few puffs during the first few hours I tried it with him and I was really high. Very potent stuff for sure. Thank God we did not have this stuff when I was doing it a lot in my younger days. I think I really would have been totally addicted. Back when I was young, we had stuff that was effective in achieving a buzz but not feeling it so strongly as the stuff my friend brought me. Get this: he got it from his grandchild when he told him to get him some because he was visiting me.

I want to emphasize, I only smoke marijuana about once or twice a month now and I am very careful to not like it too much because as I said in my first interview back in 1990, I really had a problem years ago. It's real good today and think that there must be a lot more addiction to this drug today in comparison to when I was young when we did not have such potent stuff. *(Second interview with same interviewee on May 12, 2013, from Venturelli's research files, male, age 62)*

LEARNING PORTFOLIO

Discussion Questions

1. What are the sociological and psychological reasons why the very young continue to use marijuana at alarming rates despite the illegality of usage?

2. Do you believe that prosecution for marijuana where marijuana is prohibited should be more or less rigid than it currently is? Explain.

3. Debate whether marijuana use adversely affects driving capabilities.

4. Either directly interview or imagine interviews with several users and nonusers of marijuana. How do you think they would answer the question of whether their critical-thinking skills are adversely affected by this drug?

5. Among marijuana users, do you believe that the amotivational syndrome exists as a syndrome? Interview several users and try to either add to the characteristics of this syndrome from your interviews or modify the syndrome as discussed in this chapter.

6. In light of the information in "Holding the Line," do you believe the sale of marijuana for medical and/or for recreational purposes will ever be completely legalized at the state and federal levels in all 50 states? Why or why not for medical purposes, and why or why not for recreational purposes?

7. What is your reaction to legalizing marijuana as a controlled substance? Give reasons either for or against legalization.

8. Do you believe consistent use of marijuana changes the user's personality? If so, how?

9. Summarize how marijuana affects the brain, CNS, respiratory system, cardiovascular system, and sexual performance and reproduction.

10. Debate how much family upbringing and attachment to a religion affect later drug use.

11. From reading this chapter, try to explain why most heroin users have used marijuana, whereas the vast majority of marijuana users never advance to such highly addictive drugs.

12. Explain how a user of cannabis might develop psychological dependence.

13. Do you believe that use of marijuana is more or less harmful than use of tobacco products? Should they be regulated differently?

14. Why do you think that in 2014 youth marijuana attitudes were more accepting of marijuana use and that perceived risk of regular marijuana use declined in all three grades (8th, 10th, and 12th) (Johnston et al. 2015)?

Key Terms

altered perceptions	451
amotivational syndrome	443
aphrodisiac	453
Cannabis indica	420
Cannabis sativa	420
differential association	440
drugged driving	442
drug trafficking organizations (DTOs)	434
glaucoma	446
hashish	434
marijuana wax	435
Marinol	446
medical marijuana	444
munchies	451
set and setting	438
sinsemilla	433
subjective euphoric effects	438
synthetic marijuana	435

Summary

1. Marijuana consists of the dried and crushed leaves, flowers, stems, and seeds of the *Cannabis* plant. Tetrahydrocannabinol (THC) is the primary mind-altering (psychoactive) ingredient in marijuana. There are two main strains: *Cannabis sativa* and *Cannabis indica*. They differ "in their chemical composition, physiological aesthetic, and medical application" (ProCon.org 2012a). *C. sativa* originates from Colombia, Mexico, Jamaica, South Africa, Thailand, and Southeast Asia and generally causes uplifting and energetic feelings, stimulates the appetite, and provides pain relief from certain ailments (Budfacts.com 2009). It is cultivated in hot climates. It is a brighter green than the *C. indica* strain and has narrower leaves. It reaches an average height of over 6 feet when grown outdoors. *C. indica* originates from hash-producing countries (e.g., Afghanistan, Pakistan, India, Turkey, Morocco, and Tibet) (ProCon.org 2012a), and its effects include body relaxation, stress relief, and calmness and serenity (Budfacts.com 2009). *C. indica* is grown in warm, not hot, climates; the plants are shorter (under 6 feet tall) and a darker green in color with wider leaves (Weedist 2012). The THC content in the two strains differs, with *C. indica* generally having a lower THC content (Weedist 2012).

2. There are approximately four cannabis derivatives (or spin-offs). The first derivative, *sinsemilla*, includes the more potent strains that are available today. Hashish is the second derivative; it contains a very pure form of resin produced from the flowers of female cannabis plants. A third, more recent derivative from cannabis is *marijuana wax*. To date, this is one of the most powerful and most potent (80% pure THC) types of marijuana on the illegal and legal drug markets. Smoking or vaporizing this type of marijuana "leads to a quicker, stronger high" (Kimble 2013). It is thought to be the strongest form of marijuana on the market. A fourth derivative is *ganja*, which is produced in India. This preparation consists of the dried tops of female plants. *Ganja* is also used as a slang term for marijuana. There are more than 200 slang terms for marijuana.

3. Marijuana remains very controversial for the following reasons: (a) a high percentage of the U.S. population uses this drug; (b) it continues to be illegal in most states; (c) 23 states and the District of Columbia have legalized the sale of marijuana for medical purposes, although the use and sale of marijuana in these states remains illegal at the federal level; (d) marijuana accounts for a large number of arrests for simple possession; (e) it is one of the least addictive types of drugs; and (f) most marijuana users do not graduate to other, more addictive illicit drugs.

4. The effects of marijuana can vary according to the user's expectations and where the drug is consumed (surroundings). At low doses, such as when smoked, ingested (eaten), or vaporized, the *C. indica* strain often has a sedative effect. At higher doses, it can produce hallucinations and delusions.

5. As with tobacco, heavy use of marijuana can impair pulmonary function, cause chronic respiratory diseases (such as bronchitis and asthma), and promote lung cancer. Marijuana causes vasodilation and a compensatory increase in heart rate. The effects of marijuana on sexual performance and reproduction are controversial. Some studies have indicated this substance enhances sexual arousal.

6. Tolerance to the CNS and cardiovascular effects of marijuana develops rapidly with repeated use. Although physical dependence and associated withdrawal are minor, psychological dependence can be significant in chronic, heavy users.

7. THC (tetrahydrocannabinol), the active ingredient in marijuana, has been used for treating a variety of seemingly unrelated medical conditions. This drug is indicated for treatment of nausea and vomiting in cancer patients receiving chemotherapy and for treatment of anorexia (lack of appetite) in AIDS patients. Other potential therapeutic uses for THC include relief of intraocular pressure associated with glaucoma, as an antiasthmatic drug, as a muscle relaxant, as an antiseizure drug, as an antidepressant, as a

tumor-reducing agent, and as an analgesic to relieve migraines and other types of pain.

8. The age groups most likely to use marijuana are the following: (a) highest lifetime use, adults between 18 and 25 years of age (51.9%), and (b) highest past-year (31.6%) and past-month (19.1%) use in the 18- to 25-year age category. There is a sharp drop in past-year and past-month use in the 26-and-older age group.

9. The National Survey on Drug Use and Health (NSDUH) reported that among persons aged 12 or older, the overall rate of past-month marijuana use in 2013 was 7.5%, 7.3% in 2012, and 7.0% in 2011. Over these 3 years, the number of marijuana users has been slowly increasing (SAMHSA 2014).

10. Drugged driving is defined as operating a motor vehicle with a measurable quantity (or quantities) of a legal and/or an illegal drug in the driver's body, which most often results in impaired driving. Recent findings reported by the Canadian Centre on Substance Abuse (CCSA) note that (a) among young drivers, driving after using cannabis is more prevalent than driving after drinking; (b) cannabis impairs the cognitive and motor abilities necessary to operate a motor vehicle and doubles the risk of crash involvement; (c) after alcohol, cannabis is the most commonly detected substance among drivers who die in traffic crashes; (d) cannabis use is not uncommon among drivers involved in collisions; and (e) the police have the tools and authority required to detect and arrest drivers who are impaired by cannabis (Beirness and Porath-Waller 2015).

11. Currently, 25 states plus the District of Columbia are medical marijuana states that have enacted laws to legalize medical marijuana. The 25 states are Alaska, Arizona, California, Colorado, Connecticut, Delaware, Hawaii, Illinois, Maine, Maryland, Massachusetts, Michigan, Minnesota, Montana, Nevada, New Hampshire, New Jersey, New Mexico, New York, Ohio, Oregon, Pennsylvania, Rhode Island, Vermont, and Washington (ProCon.org 2016ba). Out of 323,086,768 of U.S. population as of March 1, 2016 (ProCon.org 2016b), the *estimated* number of medical marijuana users would be 2,604,079 medical marijuana users (ProCon.org 2016a).

12. Marijuana affects brain development. When marijuana users begin using as teenagers, the drug may reduce thinking, memory, and learning functions and affect how the brain builds connections between the areas necessary for these functions. Marijuana's effects on these abilities may last a long time or even be permanent (NIH 2015d).

13. Long-term consequences of regularly using marijuana include respiratory problems, memory and learning impairments, problems with fertility, mental effects (hallucinations, paranoia, and disorganized thinking). Marijuana can become an addictive drug.

14. Legalization of the medical use of marijuana entails permitting physicians to prescribe marijuana for medical problems, with the idea that terminally ill as well as other types of sick patients could be given the option of smoking marijuana as opposed to taking the already-approved Marinol (dronabinol), an FDA-approved version of THC in capsule form.

References

Abel, E. L. *Marijuana: The First Twelve Thousand Years.* New York: Plenum, 1989.

Abood, M., and B. Martin. "Neurobiology of Marijuana Abuse." *Trends in Pharmacological Sciences* 13 (May 1992): 201–206.

Abood, M. E., and B. R. Martin. "Molecular Neurobiology of the Cannabinoid Receptor." *International Review of Neurobiology* 39 (May 1996): 197–219.

Adams, I. B., and B. R. Martin. "Cannabis: Pharmacology and Toxicology in Animals and Humans." *Addiction* 91 (1996): 1585–1614.

American Psychiatric Association (APA). *Diagnostic and Statistical Manual of Mental Disorders,* 4th ed. Washington, DC: American Psychiatric Association, 1994.

American Psychiatric Association (APA). *Diagnostic and Statistical Manual of Mental Disorders,* 5th ed. Washington, DC: American Psychiatric Association, 2013.

Anslinger, H. J., and C. R. Cooper. "Marijuana: Assassin of Youth." *American Magazine* 124 (July 1937): 19–20, 150–153.

Aydin A., and J. A. Fulton. "Cannabinoid Poisoning." Medscape. 12 August 2015. Available http://emedicine.medscape.com/article/833828-overview

Barclay, L., and C. Vega. "Marijuana Use Linked to Bron-chodilation and Respiratory Symptoms." Medscape. 19 February 2007. Available http://www.medscape.org /viewarticle/552405

Bauman, K. E., and S. T. Ennett. "On the Importance of Peer Influence for Adolescent Drug Use: Commonly Neglected Considerations." *Addiction* 91 (February 1996): 185–198.

BC Bud Depot. "Welcome to the BC Bud Depot." Available https://www.bcbuddepot.com

Beirness, D. J., and A. J. Porath-Waller. "Clearing the Smoke on Cannabis." Ottawa: Canadian Centre on Substance Abuse, 2015. Available http://www.ccsa.ca/Resource%20 Library/CCSA-Cannabis-Use-and-Driving-Report-2015 -en.pdf

Benson, J. "Prescription Painkillers Now Gateway Drugs to Hard Drug Use." NaturalNews.com. 30 August 2010. Available http://www.naturalnews.com/029606_prescription _opioids_gateway_drugs.html

Berkowitz, A. "Following Imaginary Peers: How Norm Misperceptions Influence Student Substance Abuse." In *Project Direction*, edited by G. Lindsay and G. Rulf, 12–15 (Module No. 2). Muncie, IN: Ball State University, 1991.

Block, R. I. "Does Heavy Marijuana Use Impair Human Cognition and Brain Function?" *Journal of the American Medical Association* 275 (1996): 560–561.

Bloodworth, R. C. "Major Problems Associated with Marijuana Use." *Psychiatric Medicine* 3 (1987): 173–184.

Blows, S., R. Q. Ivers, J. Connor, S. Ameratunga, M. Woodward, and R. Norton. "Marijuana Use and Car Crash Injury." *Society for the Study of Addiction* 100 (2005): 605–611.

Brigham Young University. "News Release: National Study Finds Religiosity Curbs Teen Marijuana Use by Half." 1 October 2008. Available http://news.byu.edu/archive08-oct -religiosity.aspx

Brown, M. W., and S. Massaro. *Attention and Memory Impaired in Heavy Users of Marijuana*. Rockville, MD: National Institute on Drug Abuse, 20 February 1996.

Brown University Health Education. "Marijuana." 2007. Available http://brown.edu/Student_Services/Health _Services/Health_Education/alcohol,_tobacco,_& _other_drugs/marijuana.php

BudFacts.com. "Types of Medical Marijuana." 26 June 2009. Available http://budfacts.com/126/types-of-medical -marijuana/

Buff, J. "Greasers, Dopers, and Hippies: Three Responses to the Adult World." In *The White Majority*, edited by L. Howe, 60–70. New York: Random House, 1970.

Cadena, C. "Marijuana Promotes Relaxation in Sexual Activity but Depresses Libido." Yahoo! Voices. 13 November 2007. Available http://www.associatedcontent.com/article /443811/marijuana_promotes_relaxation_in_sexual .html

Califano, J. A. "Dangerous Indifference to Drugs." *Washington Post*. (23 September 1996): A-19.

Campbell, A. G., M. Evans, J. L. Thomson, and M. J. Williams. "Cerebral Atrophy in Young Cannabis Smokers." *Lancet* 19 (1971): 1219–1225.

Carter, E. *Cannabis in Costa Rica*. Philadelphia, PA: Institute for the Study of Human Issues, 1980.

Center for Substance Abuse Research (CESAR). "Marijuana Distribution Relies Primarily on Generosity of Friends and Family." CESAR FAX 16. (19 March 2007). Available http://www.cesar.umd.edu/cesar/cesarfax /vol16/16-11.pdf

Center for Substance Abuse Research (CESAR). "More Than One in Ten Children in the U.S. Live with Substance-Abusing or Substance-Dependent Parent." CESAR FAX 18. (11 May 2010a). Available http://www .cesar.umd.edu/cesar/cesarfax/vol18/18-18.pdf

Center for Substance Abuse Research (CESAR). "U.S. High School Seniors' Perception of Harm from Regular Marijuana Use Decreasing." CESAR FAX 19. (19 January 2010b). Available http://www.cesar.umd.edu/cesar /cesarfax/vol19/19-02.pdf

Chait, L., and J. Pierri. "Effect of Smoked Marijuana on Human Performance: A Critical Review." In *Marijuana/ Cannabinoids, Neurobiology and Neurophysiology*, edited by L. Murphy and A. Bartke, 387–424. Boca Raton, FL: CRC Press, 1992.

Christina, D. *Marijuana: Personality and Behavior*. Tempe, AZ: Do It Now, 1994.

Coleman, J. S. *The Adolescent Society*. New York: Free Press of Glencoe, 1961.

Cone, E. J., Y. H. Kaplan, D. L. Black, T. Robert, and F. Moser. "Urine Drug Testing of Chronic Pain Patients: Licit and Illicit Drug Patterns." *Journal of Analytic Toxicology* 32 (2008): 532–543.

Consroe, P., and R. Sandyk. "Potential Role of Cannabinoids for Therapy of Neurological Disorders." In *Marijuana/ Cannabinoids, Neurobiology and Neurophysiology*, edited by L. Murphy and A. Bartke, 459–524. Boca Raton, FL: CRC Press, 1992.

Couper, F. J., and B. K. Logan. *Cannabis/Marijuana (Δ^9 Tetrahydro-cannabinol, THC)*. Drugs and Human Performance Fact Sheets. Washington, DC: National Highway Traffic Safety Administration, March 2004.

Dewey, W. L. "Cannabinoid Pharmacology." *Pharmacological Reviews* 38 (1986): 48–50.

Downs, D. "Is Marijuana the U.S.'s Top Cash Crop?" SFGATE. 14 August 2014. Available http://blog.sfgate.com /smellthetruth/2012/08/14/is-marijuana-the-u-s-s -top-cash-crop/

Dreher, M. C. *Working Men and Ganja: Marijuana Use in Rural Jamaica*. Philadelphia, PA: Institute for the Study of Human Issues, 1982.

Drug Enforcement Administration (DEA). "The DEA Position on Marijuana." Washington, DC: Drug Enforcement Administration, April 2013. Available http://www.justice.gov/dea/docs/marijuana_position_2011.pdf

Dupont, R. L. "Drugged Driving Research: A White Paper." Rockville, MD: Institute for Behavior and Health, Inc. Drugged Driving Committee, 31 March 2011. Available http://www.whitehouse.gov/sites/default/files/ondcp/issues-content/drugged-driving/nida_dd_paper.pdf

Earleywine M., and S. Smucker Barnwell. "Decreased Respiratory Symptoms in Cannabis Users Who Vaporize." *Harm Reduction Journal* 4 (16 April 2007): 1–6.

Eckert, P. *Jocks and Burnouts: Social Categories and Identity in the High School*. New York: Teachers College, Columbia University, 1989.

ElSohly, M. *Quarterly Report: Potency Monitoring Projected, Report 104, December 16, 2008 thru March 15, 2009*. National Institute on Drug Abuse (NIDA). Oxford, MS: National Center for Natural Products Research, Research Institute of Pharmaceutical Sciences, School of Pharmacy, University of Mississippi, 2009.

Fernandez-Ruiz, J., F. Rodriguez de Fonseca, M. Navarro, and J. Ramos. "Maternal Cannabinoid Exposure and Brain Development: Changes in the Ontogeny of Dopaminergic Neurons." In *Marijuana/Cannabinoids, Neurobiology and Neurophysiology*, edited by L. Murphy and A. Bartke, 118–164. Boca Raton, FL: CRC Press, 1992.

Ferner M. "Legal Marijuana Is the Fastest-Growing Industry in the U.S.: Report." Huffington Post. 28 January 2015. Available http://www.huffingtonpost.com/2015/01/26/marijuana-industry-fastest-growing_n_6540166.html

Foley, M. R. "Drug Use During Pregnancy." *Merck Manuals Online Edition*. Whitehouse Station, NJ: Merck & Co, 2007. Available http://www.merck.com/mmhe/sec22/ch259/ch259a.html

Fuller, D. "Adolescent Brain Function Adversely Affected by Marijuana Use." Medical News Today. October 2008. Available http://www.medicalnewstoday.com/articles/125443.php

Gaines, G. *Teenage Wasteland: Suburbia's Dead-End Kids*. New York: Harper Perennial, 1992.

Gardner, A. "Study: Smoking Pot May Ease Chronic Pain." CNN.com, Health Magazine. 30 August 2010. Available http://www.cnn.com/2010/HEALTH/08/30/health.pot.reduce.pain/index.html

Gardner, E. "Cannabinoid Interaction with Brain Reward Systems: The Neurobiological Basis of Cannabinoid Abuse." In *Marijuana/Cannabinoids, Neurobiology and Neurophysiology*, edited by L. Murphy and A. Bartke, 275–335. Boca Raton, FL: CRC Press, 1992.

Ghaly, S. J. "What Is Marijuana Wax?" The Stoner's Cookbook. 31 October 2015. Available http://www.thestonerscookbook.com/2015/10/31/what-is-marijuana-wax/

Ghose, T. "Driving with a Marijuana High: How Dangerous Is It?" Live Science. 6 July 2015. Available http://www.livescience.com/51450-driving-on-marijuana-alcohol-dangerous.html

Goldstein, A. *Addiction from Biology to Drug Policy*. New York: Freeman, 1994.

Goldstein, F. "Pharmacological Aspects of Substance Abuse." In *Remington's Pharmaceutical Sciences*, 19th ed. Easton, PA: Mack, 1995.

Goode, E. *Drugs in American Society*. Boston: McGraw-Hill, 1999.

Gossop, M. *Living with Drugs*, 2nd ed. Aldershot, England: Wildwood House, 1987.

Green, C. A. "Gender and Use of Substance Abuse Treatment Services." *Alcohol Research and Health* 29 (2006): 55–62.

Greenblatt, J. C. *Adolescent Self-Reported Behaviors and Their Association with Marijuana Use*. Office of Applied Studies, Substance Abuse and Mental Health Services Administration. Rockville, MD: National Clearinghouse for Alcohol and Drug Information, July 1999.

Gregoire, C. "New Study Finds Marijuana to be Effective Against Depression." *Huffington Post*, 6 February 2015. Available http://www.huffingtonpost.com/2015/02/06/marijauna-depression_n_6622126.html

Grinspoon, L. "Marijuana." *Harvard Medical School Mental Health Letter* 4 (November 1987): 1–4.

Grinspoon, L., and J. B. Bakalar. "Commentary, Marijuana as Medicine: A Plea for Reconsideration." *Journal of the American Medical Association* 273 (1995): 1875–1876.

Hamid, A. *Drugs in America: Sociology, Economics, and Politics*. Gaithersburg, MD: Aspen, 1998.

Hanson, D. "Sex, Drugs, and . . . Sex: Pharmaceuticals and Sexual Performance." Addiction Inbox, The Science of Substance Abuse. 28 July 2011. Available http://addiction-dirkh.blogspot.com/2010/09/sex-drugs-and-sex.html

Hardcastle, M. "Marijuana Use Can Threaten Teen's Academic Success." About.com. 15 March 2007. Available http://teenadvice.about.com/od/marijuanause/a/marijana1.htm

Heitzeg, N. *Deviance: Rulemakers and Rulebreakers*. St. Paul, MN: West Publishing, 1996.

Henneberger, M. "Pot Surges Back, It's Like a Whole New World." *New York Times*. (6 February 1994): C19.

Hollister, L. E. "Health Aspects of *Cannabis*." *Pharmacological Reviews* 38 (1986): 39–42.

Hongmei, Y., B. Stanton, L. Cottrel, L. Kaljee, J. Galbraith, X. Li, M. Cole, C. Harris, and Y. Wu. "Parental Awareness of Adolescent Risk Involvement: Implications of Overestimates and Underestimates." *Journal of Adolescent Health* 39 (September 2006): 353–361.

Hubbard, J. R., S. E. Franco, and E. S. Onaivi. "Marijuana: Medical Implications." *American Family Physician* 283 (1999): 231–240.

Hudson, R. "Researchers Identify Gene That Triggers Marijuana's 'High.'" *Wall Street Journal* (9 August 1990): B2.

Indiana Prevention Resource Center. *Factline on: Marijuana.* Bloomington: Indiana Prevention Resource Center, 1996.

Iversen, L. "Medicinal Use of Marijuana." *Nature* 365 (1993): 12–13.

Iverson, L. "Long-Term Effects of Exposure to *Cannabis.*" *Current Opinion in Pharmacology* 5 (2005): 69–72.

Jaffe, J. H. "Drug Addiction and Drug Abuse." In *The Pharmacological Basis of Therapeutics*, 8th ed., edited by A. Gilman, T. Rall, A. Nies, and P. Taylor, 522–575. New York: Pergamon, 1990.

Jenkins, M. "Ganjanomics: Bringing Humboldt's Shadow Economy into the Light." *High Country News.* (8 August 2011). Available http://www.hcn.org/issues/43.13/ganjanomics-bringing-humbolts-shadow-economy-into-the-light?gclid=CODc-56K-bcCFe9cMgodihMAmg

Johns, A. "Psychiatric Effects of *Cannabis.*" *British Journal of Psychiatry* 178 (2001): 116–122.

Johnston, L. D., P. M. O'Malley, J. G. Bachman, and J. E. Schulenberg. *Monitoring the Future: National Survey Results on Drug Use.* Bethesda, MD: National Institute on Drug Abuse, 2009.

Johnston, L. D., P. M. O'Malley, J. G. Bachman, and J. E. Schulenberg. *Monitoring the Future: National Survey Results on Drug Use, 1975–2011: Volume I, Secondary School Students.* Ann Arbor: Institute for Social Research, University of Michigan, 2012.

Johnston, L. D., P. M. O'Malley, J. G. Bachman, and J. E. Schulenberg. *Monitoring the Future: National Survey Results on Drug Use, 1975–2012: Volume I, Secondary School Students.* Ann Arbor: Institute for Social Research, University of Michigan, 2013.

Johnston, L. D., P. M. O'Malley, R. A. Miech, Bachman J. G., and J. E. Schulenberg. *Monitoring the Future National Survey Results on Drug Use: 1975–2014: Overview of Key Findings on Adolescent Drug Use.* Ann Arbor: Institute for Social Research, The University of Michigan, 2015.

Join Together Staff. "Biggest U.S. Cash Crop: Marijuana." Partnership for Drug-Free Kids. 19 December 2006. Available http://www.drugfree.org/join-together/drugs/biggest-us-cash-crop

Jones, R. T. "Human Effects: An Overview." In *Marijuana Research Findings: 1980.* NIDA Research Monograph No. 31. Washington, DC: National Institute on Drug Abuse, 1980.

Julian, B. S. "alt.hemp *Cannabis*/Marijuana FAQ." University of Massachusetts at Amherst. 1994. Available http://www.faqs.org/faqs/drugs/hemp-marijuana

Kandel, D. B., P. C. Griesler, G. Lee, M. Davies, and C. Shaffsan. *Parental Influences on Adolescent Marijuana Use and the Baby Boom Generation: Findings from the 1995–1996 National Household Surveys on Drug Abuse.* Rockville, MD: Substance Abuse and Mental Health Services Administration, 2001.

Kaplan, L. F., and R. Whitmire. "Pot—It's Potent, Prevalent and Preventable." *Salt Lake Tribune* 250 (21 May 1995): 9.

Kelly, T., R. Foltin, C. Enurian, and M. Fischman. "Effects of THC on Marijuana Smoking, Drug Choice and Verbal Report of Drug Liking." *Journal of Experimental Analysis of Behavior* 61 (1994): 203–211.

Kendler, K. S., C. O. Gardner, and C. A. Prescott. "Religion, Psychopathology, and Substance Use and Abuse: A Multimeasure, Genetic-Epidemiologic Study." *American Journal of Psychiatry* 154 (1997): 322–329.

Kimble, J. "Everything You Need to Know About Marijuana Wax." Complex. 22 October 2013. Available http://www.complex.com/pop-culture/2013/10/marijuana-wax-facts-info/marijuana-wax-nicknames

Kryger, A. H. "Preventive Medicine Clinic of Monterey: Marijuana Mental Disturbances." Virtual Hospital Home Page. 24 October 1995. Available http://vh.radiology.uiowa.edu

Kwon, D. "Can Cannabis Treat Epileptic Seizures?" *Scientific American*, 22 January 2016. Available https://www.scientificamerican.com/article/can-cannabis-treat-epileptic-seizures/

Leger, D. L. "Survey: 1 in 15 High School Students Smoking Pot." *USA Today.* (20 December 2012). Available http://www.usatoday.com/story/news/nation/2012/12/19/national-drug-survey-youth-marijuana/1779563/

Liberty Mutual Insurance. "Liberty Mutual Insurance News Release." Boston, MA, 24 April 2013. Available https://www.libertymutualgroup.com/about-lm/news/news-release-archive/articles/one-in-four-teens-admits-to-driving-under-the-influence-and-many-believe-it-does-not-impact-their-safety

Liska, K. *Drugs and the Human Body*, 5th ed. Upper Saddle River, NJ: Prentice Hall, 1997.

Mack, A. and J. Joy. *Marijuana as Medicine? The Science Beyond the Controversy.* Washington, DC: National Academy Press, 2001.

MarijuanaDetox.com. "Marijuana Detox." 2008. Available http://www.marijuana-detox.com/m-facts.htm

"Marijuana Menaces Youth." *Scientific American* 154 (1936): 151.

Mathias, R. "Marijuana Impairs Driving-Related Skills and Workplace Performance." *NIDA Notes* 11 (January/February 1996): 6.

McCabe, S. E. "Misperceptions of Nonmedical Prescription Drug Use: A Web Survey of College Students." *Addictive Behavior* 33 (May 2008): 713–724.

Medical Marijuana Education Center. "Medical Cannabis and Muscle Spasms." Centric Wellness. 3 July 2012. Available http://medicalmarijuanaeducationcenter.com/2012/07/03/medical-cannabis-and-muscle-spams/

Melina, R. "Not My Kid: Parents Severely Underestimate Teens' Drug and Alcohol Use." Live Science. 13 September 2011. Available http://www.livescience.com/16037-parents-underestimate-kids-substance.html

MMJ-Guide.com. "Cannabis Varieties." 2010. Available http://www.mmj-guide.com/Cannabis-Varieties.html

Murphy, L., and A. Bartke. "Effects of THC on Pregnancy, Puberty, and the Neuroendocrine System." In *Marijuana/Cannabinoids, Neurobiology and Neurophysiology*, edited by L. Murphy and A. Bartke, 539. Boca Raton, FL: CRC Press, 1992.

Musto, D. F. *The American Disease: Origins of Narcotic Control*, 3rd ed. New York: Oxford University Press, 1999.

Nahas, G., and C. Latour. "The Human Toxicity of Marijuana." *Medical Journal of Australia* 156 (1992): 495–497.

National Cannabis Prevention and Information Centre (NCPIC). "Cannabis Potency." 1 April 2013. Available http://ncpic.org.au/ncpic/publications/factsheets/article/cannabis-potency

National Center on Addiction and Substance Abuse at Columbia University. "Casa Report: Spirituality and Religion Reduce Risk of Substance Abuse." 2001. Available http://www.casacolumbia.org/absolutenm/templates/PressReleases.aspx?articleid=115&zoneid=48

National Clearinghouse on Alcohol and Drug Information (NCADI). *Marijuana: Facts Parents Need to Know. Quick Screen, At Home Drug Test*. Rockville, MD: National Clearinghouse on Alcohol and Drug Information, November 1998.

National Eye Institute. *Facts About Glaucoma*. Bethesda, MD: U.S. Department of Health and Human Services and National Institutes of Health, 2010.

National Highway Traffic Safety Administration (NHTSA). "Cannabis/Marijuana." In *Drugs and Human Performance Fact Sheets*, edited by F. J. Couper and B. K Logan. Washington, DC: National Highway Traffic Safety Administration, 2004.

National Institute on Drug Abuse (NIDA). *Drug Abuse and Drug Abuse Research*. DHHS Pub. No. 91-1704. Washington, DC: U.S. Department of Health and Human Services, 1991.

National Institute on Drug Abuse (NIDA). *Marijuana: Facts Parents Need to Know*. NIH Pub. No. 95-4037. Rockville, MD: National Clearinghouse on Alcohol and Drug Information, 1998.

National Institute on Drug Abuse (NIDA). *DrugFacts: Marijuana*. Bethesda, MD: U.S. Department of Health and Human Services, 29 March 2000. Available http://www.nida.nih.gov/infofax/marijuana.html

National Institute on Drug Abuse (NIDA). *Marijuana Smoking Is Associated with a Spectrum of Respiratory Disorders*. Bethesda, MD: National Institute on Drug Abuse and National Institutes of Health, 21 October 2006.

National Institute on Drug Abuse (NIDA). *Marijuana: Facts Parents Need to Know*. Bethesda, MD: National Institute on Drug Abuse and National Institutes of Health, August 2007.

National Institute on Drug Abuse (NIDA). *InfoFacts: Marijuana*. Bethesda, MD: National Institute on Drug Abuse and National Institutes of Health, 2009.

National Institute on Drug Abuse (NIDA). "Does Marijuana Use Affect Driving?" Bethesda, MD: National Institute on Drug Abuse, December 2010a. Available http://www.drugabuse.gov/publications/marijuana-abuse/does-marijuana-use-affect-driving

National Institute on Drug Abuse (NIDA). "DrugFacts: Drugged Driving." Bethesda, MD: National Institute on Drug Abuse, December 2010b. Available http://www.drugabuse.gov/publications/drugfacts/drugged-driving

National Institute on Drug Abuse (NIDA). "Research Report Series: Marijuana Abuse." Bethesda, MD: U.S. Department of Health and Human Services and National Institutes of Health, September 2010c. Available http://www.drugabuse.gov/PDF/RRMarijuana.pdf

National Institute on Drug Abuse (NIDA). "NIH Study Examines Nicotine as a Gateway Drug." NIH News, National Institutes of Health. Bethesda, MD: U.S. Department of Health and Human Services. 2 November 2011. Available http://www.nih.gov/news/health/nov2011/nida-02.htm

National Institute on Drug Abuse (NIDA). "Drug Facts: Marijuana." Bethesda, MD: National Institute on Drug Abuse, December 2012.

National Institute on Drug Abuse (NIDA). "Monitoring the Future Study, Overview of Findings 2015." Bethesda, MD: National Institute on Drug Abuse, December 2015. Available https://www.drugabuse.gov/related-topics/trends-statistics/monitoring-future/monitoring-future-survey-overview-findings-2015

National Institute on Drug Abuse (NIDA). "Does Marijuana Use Affect Driving? Bethesda, MD: National Institute on Drug Abuse, August 2016.

National Institutes of Health (NIH). "Drug Facts: Synthetic Cannabinoids." Bethesda, MD: U.S. Department of Health and Human Services, National Institutes of Health, 2015a.

National Institutes of Health (NIH). "Effects of Marijuana—With and Without Alcohol—On Driving Performance." Bethesda, MD: U.S. Department of Health and Human Services, National Institutes of Health, June 23, 2015b. Available https://www.drugabuse.gov/news-events/news-releases/2015/06/effects-marijuana-without-alcohol-driving-performance

National Institutes of Health (NIH). "Drug Facts: Is Marijuana Medicine?" Bethesda, MD: U.S. Department of Health and Human Services, National Institute of Health, July 2015c. Available https://www.drugabuse.gov/publications/drugfacts/marijuana-medicine

National Institutes of Health (NIH). "Drug Facts: Marijuana." Bethesda, MD: U.S. Department of Health and Human Services, National Institute of Health, September 2015d. Available https://www.drugabuse.gov/publications/drugfacts/marijuana

National Institutes of Health (NIH). "Marijuana: Is Marijuana Addictive?" Bethesda, MD: U.S. Department of Health and Human Services, National Institute of Health, September 2015e. Available https://www.drugabuse.gov/publications/research-reports/marijuana/marijuana-addictive

National Organization for the Reform of Marijuana Laws (NORML). "Chronic Pain." 30 January 2013. http://norml.org/library/item/chronic-pain

National Organization for the Reform of Marijuana Laws (NORML). "Medical Use." n.d. Available http://norml.org/marijuana/medical

National Organization for the Reform of Marijuana Laws (NORML). "Marijuana and Driving: A Review of the Scientific Evidence." Washington, DC: NORML and the NORML Foundation, 2016.

New York Times. "U.S. Marijuana Is Getting More Potent and More Dangerous, Study Contends." (12 June 2008). Available http://www.nytimes.com/2008/06/12/world/americas/12iht-pot.1.13656558.html

Norris, M. with C. Conrad. "The Experience of Getting High." 1012 DV Amsterdam, The Netherlands: Hemp Museum of Amsterdam, n.d. Available http://cannabisconsumers.org/reports/gettinghigh.php

Norton, A. "Address Client Myths About Marijuana: Professionals Can Counteract Mixed Messages in Society That Impede Healing." *Addiction Professional* 4 (July/August 2009): 32–34.

Office of National Drug Control Policy (ONDCP). "Drug Facts: Marijuana." Washington, DC: Office of National Drug Control, 2003.

Oliwenstein, L. "The Perils of Pot." *Discover* 9 (1988): 18.

Palfai, T., and H. Jankiewicz. *Drugs and Human Behavior.* Dubuque, IA: William C. Brown, 1991.

Pew Research Center. "Majority Now Supports Legalizing Marijuana." 4 April 2013. Available http://www.people-press.org/2013/04/04/majority-now-supports-legalizing-marijuana/

Pinto, F. G., "What Is Marijuana Wax? 7 Things You May Not Know About Dabs, Shatter, and Honey Oil." NJ.com. 4 February 2016. Available http://www.nj.com/news/index.ssf/2016/02/pro-marijuana_advocates_debate_officials_warnings.html

Pollan, M. "Medical Marijuana: Can It Help You? Should It Be Legal? A Report from California." *Herbs for Health* (March/April 1998): 38–50.

Pope, H. G., Jr., and D. Yurgulen-Todd. "The Residual Cognitive Effects of Heavy Marijuana Use in College Students." *Journal of the American Medical Association* 275 (1996): 521–527.

ProCon.org. "Medical Marijuana: What Are the Differences Between Cannabis Indica and Cannabis Sativa, and How Do They Vary in Their Potential Medical Utility?" 11 June 2012a. Available http://medicalmarijuana.procon.org/view.answers.php?questionID=000638#answer-id-011092

ProCon.org. "Is Marijuana Significantly More Potent Now Than in the Past?" 7 February 2012b. Available http://medicalmarijuana.procon.org/view.answers.php?questionID=000336

ProCon.org. "How Many People in the United States Use Medical Marijuana?" 31 December 2012c. Available http://medicalmarijuana.procon.org/view.answers.php?questionID=001199

ProCon.org. "20 Legal Medical Marijuana States and DC." 2013. Available http://medicalmarijuana.procon.org/view.resource.php?resourceID=000881

ProCon.org. "23 Legal Medical Marijuana States and DC." Santa Monica, CA: *ProCon.org*, 3 March 2016.

Rabinski, G. "How Does Cannabis Treat Epilepsy?" *Whaxy*, 14 September 2015. Available https://www.whaxy.com/learn/does-cannabis-treat-epilepsy

Rand Drug Policy Research Center. "Rand Releases Study on Marijuana 'Gateway Effect.'" Press Release. 26 December 2002. Available http://www.jointogether.org

Reaney, P. "Getting High May Not Be So Harmless After All." Reuters Limited. (20 March 2000).

Right Diagnosis. "Amotivational Syndrome." Health Grades Inc. August 2010. Available http://www.wrongdiagnosis.com/a/amotivational_syndrome/intro.htm#whatis

Robson, P. "Therapeutic Aspects of Cannabis and Cannabinoids." *British Journal of Psychiatry* 178 (2001): 107–115.

Roffman, R. A., and W. H. George. "Cannabis Abuse." In *Assessment of Addictive Behaviors*, edited by D. M. Donovan and G. A. Marlatt, 78–86. New York: Guilford, 1988.

Rough, L. "Which States Are Most Likely to Legalize Cannabis in 2016." *Leafly.* (22 December 2015). Available https://www.leafly.com/news/headlines/what-states-are-most-likely-to-legalize-in-2016

Rubin, V., and L. Comitas. *Ganja in Jamaica: A Medical Anthropological Study of Chronic Marijuana Use.* Paris: Mouton, 1975.

Salo J. "Marijuana Legalization 2016: Which States Will Consider Cannabis This Year?" *International Business Times.* (30 December 2015). Available http://www.ibtimes.com/marijuana-legalization-2016-which-states-will-consider-cannabis-year-2245024

Scholastic, Inc. "Peer Pressure: Its Influence on Teens and Decision Making." 2016. Available http://headsup.scholastic.com/students/peer-pressure-its-influence-on-teens-and-decision-making

Scott K. A, A. G. Dalgleish, W. M. Liu. "The Combination of Cannabidiol and Δ9-Tetrahydrocannabinol Enhances The Anticancer Effects of Radiation in an Orthotopic Murine Glioma Model." *Molecular Cancer Therapy* 13 (2014): 2955–2967.

Schultes, R. E. "Ethnopharmacological Significance of Psychotropic Drugs of Vegetal Origin." *Principles of Psychopharmacology*, 2nd ed., edited by W. G. Clark and J. del Giudice. New York: Academic Press, 1978.

Sewell. R. A., J. Poling, and M. Sofuoglu. "The Effect of Cannabis Compared with Alcohol on Driving." *American Journal of Addictions* 18 (2009): 185–193. Available http://www.ncbi.nlm.nih.gov/pmc/articles/PMC2722956/

Sewester, S. *Drug Facts and Comparisons.* St. Louis, MO: Kluwer, 1993, 259h–259k.

Silverberg, C. "Sex and Marijuana." About.com Sexuality. 5 July 2007. Available http://sexuality.about.com/od/sex_and_drugs/a/marijuana_sex.htm

Smoker, J. "What Is the Difference Between Indica and Sativa Marijuana Plants?" The Weedblog. 20 April 2014. Available http://www.theweedblog.com/the-difference-between-indica-and-sativa-marijuana-plants/

Solomon, D., ed. *The Marihuana Papers.* New York: New American Library, 1966.

Sorden, S. "The Promise of Social Norming." John's Addiction. 7 October 2011. Available http://johnsaddiction.com/911-social-norming-drinking/

Steinberg, L. "How Peers Affect the Teenage Brain." *Psychology Today*, 3 February 2013.

Stenchever, M. A., T. J. Kunysz, and M. A. Allen. "Chromosome Breakage in Users of Marijuana." *American Journal of Obstetrics and Gynecology* 118 (January 1974): 106–113.

Substance Abuse and Mental Health Services Administration (SAMHSA), Office of Applied Studies. "The NHSDA Report. Religious Involvement and Substance Use Among Adults." 23 March 2007a. Available http://www.oas.samhsa.gov

Substance Abuse and Mental Health Services Administration (SAMHSA), Office of Applied Studies. "The NHSDA Report. Youth Activities, Substance Use, and Family Income." 19 April 2007b. Available http://www.oas.samhsa.gov

Substance Abuse and Mental Health Services Administration (SAMHSA), Office of Applied Studies. *Results from the 2011 National Survey on Drug Use and Health: Detailed Tables.* HHS Pub. No. SMA 12-4713, NSDUH Series H-44. Rockville, MD: Substance Abuse and Mental Health Services Administration, 2012.

Substance Abuse and Mental Health Services Administration (SAMHSA). *Results from the 2013 National Survey on Drug Use and Health: Summary of National Findings.* NSDUH Series H-48, HHS Publication No. (SMA) 14-4863. Rockville, MD: Substance Abuse and Mental Health Services Administration, 2014.

Substance Abuse and Mental Health Services (SAMHSA). *Building on Strengths: Tools for Improving Positive Outcomes Among Boys and Young Men of Color: Executive Summary: Main Findings on Protective Factors and Programs.* Rockville, MD: SAMHSA's Center for the Application of Prevention Technologies, January 2016. Available http://www.samhsa.gov/capt/sites/default/files/resources/executive-summary-main-findings-protective-factors-programs.pdf

Suciu-Foca, N., J. P. Armand, and A. Morishima. "Inhibition of Cellular Immunity in Marijuana Smokers." *Science* 183 (1974): 419–420.

Sutherland, Edwin H. *Principles of Criminology*, 3rd ed. Philadelphia: Lippincott, 1939; 4th ed., 1947.

Swan, N. "A Look at Marijuana's Harmful Effects." *NIDA Notes* 9 (February/March 1994): 3–4.

Swan, N. "Facts About Marijuana and Marijuana Abuse." *NIDA Notes* 11 (March/April 1996): 15.

Taylor, N. *Narcotics: Nature's Dangerous Gifts.* New York: Dell, 1963.

Taylor, N. "The Pleasant Assassin: The Story of Marijuana." In *The Marihuana Papers*, edited by D. Solomon. New York: Signet Books, 1966.

Teen Challenge. *Drugs: Frequently Asked Questions.* South Australia: Pragin Press, 2000.

TheWeek.com. "Do Marijuana and Driving Mix?" 7 June 2010. Available http://theweek.com/article/index/203778/do-marijuana-and-driving-mix

Thompson, D. "Teens Using E-Cigarettes to 'Vape' Pot, Survey Finds." HealthDay. 7 September 2015. Available http://consumer.healthday.com/public-health-information-30/marijuana-news-759/teens-using-e-cigarettes-to-smoke-pot-survey-finds-703025.html

Tudor, C. G., D. M. Petersen, and K. W. Elifson. "An Examination of the Relationships Between Peer and Parental Influences and Adolescent Drug Use." In *Chemical Dependencies: Patterns, Costs, and Consequences*, edited by C. D. Chambers, J. A. Inciardi, D. M. Petersen, H. A. Siegal, and O. Z. White. Athens: Ohio University Press, 1987.

Turner, C. E. "Chemistry and Metabolism." In *Marijuana Research Findings: 1980.* NIDA Research Monograph No. 31. Washington, DC: National Institute on Drug Abuse, 1980.

U.S. Department of Transportation. *Marijuana and Actual Driving Performance: Effects of THC on Driving Performance.* DOT HS 808 078. Washington, DC: National Highway Traffic Safety Administration, November 1993.

Venkataraman, N. "Marijuana Called Top U.S. Cash Crop." ABC News Internet Ventures. (18 December 2006). Available http://abcnews.go.com/Business/story?id=2735017

Venturelli, P. J. "Drugs in Schools: Myths and Reality." In *The Annals of the American Academy of Political and Social Science,* edited by W. Hinkle and S. Henry, 72–87. Thousand Oaks, CA: Sage Publications, 2000.

Venturelli, P. J. "Drug Use as a Socially Constructed Problem." In *The Handbook of Drugs and Society,* edited by H. H. Brownstein, 177–196. West Sussex, UK: John Wiley and Sons 2016.

Wallace, J. M., V. L. Myers, and E. R. Osai. *Faith Matters: Race/Ethnicity, Religion and Substance Use.* Baltimore, MD: Annie E. Casey Foundation, 2004.

Walton, A. G. "New Study Shows How Marijuana's Potency Has Changed over Time." Forbes/Pharma & Healthcare. 25 March 2015. Available http://www.forbes.com /sites/alicegwalton/2015/03/23/pot-evolution-how-the -makeup-of-marijuana-has-changed-over-time /#3b8c32745579

Weedist. "Cannabis 101: Differences Between Sativa and Indica Marijuana." 17 August 2012. Available http:// www.weedist.com/2012/08/differences-between -sativa-and-indica-marijuana/

Wilde C. "RIA Neuroscience Study Points to Possible Use of Medical Marijuana for Depression." Buffalo, NY: News Center, University of Buffalo, 4 February 2015. Available http://www.buffalo.edu/news/releases/2015/02/004 .html

Wren, C. S. "Youth Marijuana Use Rises." *New York Times.* (20 February 1996): 1.

Zimmer, L., and J. P. Morgan. *Marijuana Myths, Marijuana Facts: A Review of the Scientific Evidence.* New York: Lindesmith Center, 1997.

Zinberg, N. E., and J. A. Robertson. *Drugs and the Public.* New York: Simon & Schuster, 1972.

© Marmaduke St. John/Alamy.

Did You Know?

▶ More than 1000 different commercial and household products are commonly abused in the United States.

▶ Ordinary household products are misused as inhalants: glues/adhesives, nail polish remover, gasoline, paint thinner, spray paint, butane lighter fluid, propane gas, typewriter correction fluid, household cleaners, cooking sprays, deodorants, whipping cream aerosols, marking pens, and air conditioning coolants.

▶ Inhalant abuse is typically a problem of adolescents and teenagers. By the time children reach 8th grade, approximately 9% will have misused inhalants.

▶ Each year, young people in this country die of inhalant abuse or suffer severe consequences, including permanent brain damage and damage to the heart, kidneys, and liver.

▶ Inhalant abusers can die suddenly and without warning; even first-time abusers have died from sniffing inhalants.

Learning Objectives

On completing this chapter you should be able to:

❭ Understand that inhalant use is not harmless and that even one-time use could lead to sudden sniffing death syndrome.

❭ List the household and commercial products that are most often abused as inhalants.

❭ Describe the principal means of using household and commercial products as inhalants.

❭ Identify signs of abuse.

❭ Examine the current patterns of abuse among various groups.

❭ List the dangers of inhalant abuse.

Introduction

Inhalants are **volatile** substances that elicit psychological or physiological changes when introduced into the body via the lungs. They are rarely administered by any other route. Most cause intoxicating and/or **euphorigenic** effects. Many of these substances were never intended to be used by humans as drugs; consequently, they are not often thought of as having abuse potential. However, abuse of inhalants is a serious public health problem; according to data obtained from the National Institute on Drug Abuse (NIDA)–sponsored *Monitoring the Future* study, 9.4% of 8th graders have misused an inhalant at least once in their lifetime. Among 10th and 12th graders, lifetime reported use was 7.2% and 5.7%, respectively (Meich et al. 2016). This lifetime frequency of inhalant abuse among 8th graders surpasses the frequency of abuse of such highly publicized drugs as cocaine (1.6%) and amphetamines (6.8%). For comparison, lifetime marijuana/hashish use was 15.5% in this age group (Meich et al. 2016). Noteworthy, in 2013, of the estimated 2.8 million individuals aged 12 or older who used illicit drugs for the first time within the past 12 months, 6.3% reported inhalants as their first illicit drug (Substance Abuse and Mental Health Services Administration [SAMHSA] 2014). The average age of first use of inhalants was 19.2 years (SAMHSA 2014).

A widespread misconception is that inhalant abuse is a harmless phase that occurs commonly during normal childhood and teenage development and as such is not worthy of significant concern because young people will grow out of it without experiencing harm. On the contrary, numerous adolescents and teenagers in the United States die or are seriously injured each year as a result of inhalant abuse. Even first-time users may die from sudden sniffing death syndrome (SSDS), a condition characterized by serious cardiac **arrhythmia** occurring during or immediately after inhaling. Accurate statistics regarding the number of inhalant-associated deaths and injuries each year are unavailable, in part because medical examiners often attribute deaths from inhalant use to suicide, suffocation, or accidents. Nevertheless, every year young people in the United States die from inhalant abuse, and many more suffer severe consequences, such as damage to the brain, heart, kidneys, and liver (U.S. Consumer Product Safety Commission n.d.).

Most inhalants are household or commercial products composed of several different chemicals. These compounds can act alone or synergistically to exert toxic effects. The potential of these agents to cause harm is compounded by the high concentrations of these substances absorbed in the body by inhalation and the tendency for these often lipid-rich (oily or fatty) substances to be retained in lipid-containing vital organs. Another important consideration is that the users are often developmentally immature and as such can be more susceptible to the toxic effects of inhalants. The summation of these factors makes inhalants dangerous substances of abuse.

History of Inhalants

The modern era of inhalant abuse can be traced to 1776, when British chemist Joseph Priestley synthesized nitrous oxide (Kennedy and Longnecker 1990), a colorless gas with a slightly sweet odor and no noticeable taste. Roughly 20 years later, he and Humphry Davy suggested correctly that the gas might be useful as an anesthetic, and experiments were conducted to test this possibility.

Dentists contributed greatly to the introduction of nitrous oxide as an anesthetic. At a stage show in the 1840s, Horace Wells, a dentist, noticed that one of the persons involved in the show injured himself while under the influence of nitrous oxide yet felt no pain. Wells was so impressed by this anesthetic effect that he subsequently allowed his own tooth to be extracted while under the influence of the gas. His experiment was a success; Wells did not experience pain. He went on to attempt to demonstrate his discovery at Massachusetts General Hospital in Boston; unfortunately, the patient cried out during the procedure and the experiment was deemed unsuccessful (Kennedy and Longnecker 1990). Nevertheless, word of this demonstration and others like it spread, ultimately leading to the use of nitrous

KEY TERMS

volatile
readily evaporated at low temperatures

euphorigenic
having the ability to cause feelings of pleasure and well-being

arrhythmia
an irregular heartbeat

oxide and other volatile anesthetics as legitimate medical therapy.

Over the years, it was discovered that many chemicals, in addition to nitrous oxide, could be inhaled so as to alter psychological function. Such abuse of inhalants came to public attention in the 1950s when the news media reported that young people were getting high from sniffing glue. The term *glue sniffing* is still used today, but it is often used to describe inhalation of many products besides glue. In fact, more than 1000 different products are misused as inhalants (U.S. Consumer Product Safety Commission n.d.). These chemicals are not regulated like other drugs of abuse; hence, they are readily available to young people. This category of drugs can be classified into three major groups: volatile substances, anesthetics, and nitrites.

Types of Inhalants

■ Volatile Substances

Over the past 50 years, the number of products containing volatile substances has increased substantially. This category of agents includes aerosols (e.g., spray paints, hair sprays, deodorants, vegetable oil sprays), art or office supplies (e.g., correction fluids, felt-tip marker fluids), adhesives (e.g., airplane and other glues), fuels (e.g., propane, gasoline), and industrial or household solvents (e.g., nail polish remover, paint thinners, dry-cleaning fluids). Some volatile substances exist as gases (e.g., nitrous oxide, the propellant in whipping cream cans), whereas others are liquids that vaporize at room temperature (e.g., gasoline). In some cases, the abuser inhales vapors directly from their original containers (called *sniffing* or *snorting*). Still others inhale volatile solvents from plastic bags (called *bagging*) or from old rags or bandannas soaked in the solvent fluid and held over the mouth (called *huffing*).

Acute effects of the volatile chemicals that are commonly abused include initial nausea with some irritation of airways causing coughing and sneezing. Low doses often bring a brief feeling of lightheadedness, mild stimulation followed by a loss of control, lack of coordination, and disorientation accompanied by dizziness and possible hallucinations. In some instances, higher doses can produce relaxation, sleep, or even coma. If inhalation is continued, dangerous **hypoxia** may occur and cause brain damage or death. In other cases, SSDS can occur. Other potential toxic

consequences of inhaling such substances include hypertension and damage to the cardiac muscle, peripheral nerves, brain, and kidneys. In addition, chronic users of inhalants frequently lose their appetite, are continually tired, and experience nosebleeds. If use of inhalants persists, some of the damage may become irreversible (see "Here and Now: Chronic Solvent Abuse, Brain Abnormalities, and Cognitive Deficits").

AEROSOLS

Chemicals associated with aerosol sprays are popular among young inhalant abusers. They include spray paints, deodorant and hair sprays, vegetable oil sprays for cooking, and fabric protector sprays (NIDA 2012). Aerosol sprays are often abused not because of the effects produced by their principal ingredients, but rather because of the effects of their propellant gases. Inhalation of aerosol preparations can be dangerous because these devices are capable of generating very high concentrations of the inhaled chemicals, much greater than those released more slowly from liquid products.

TOLUENE

Toluene is a chemical found in some glues, paints, thinners, nail polishes, and typewriter correction fluid. It is a principal ingredient in "Texas shoe shine" (a shoe spray) (NIDA 2012). Toluene is detectable in the arterial blood within 10 seconds of inhalation exposure (National Highway Traffic Safety Administration [NHTSA] n.d.). Because this molecule is highly lipid soluble, it is rapidly absorbed by the brain, heart, and liver. Accordingly, toluene abuse can cause brain damage. Other damage can include impaired cognition and gait disturbances. Loss of coordination, equilibrium, hearing, and vision can also occur. Liver and kidney damage have also been reported (NIDA 2012). Of note, at least one study indicates that toluene activates dopaminergic activity in the brain (NIDA 2012). The dopamine system is important for the rewarding effects of nearly all drugs of abuse.

BUTANE AND PROPANE

Butane and propane are found commonly in hair and paint sprays and lighter fluid. Serious burn

KEY TERM

hypoxia
a state of oxygen deficiency

HERE AND NOW

Chronic Solvent Abuse, Brain Abnormalities, and Cognitive Deficits

Chronic inhalant abuse has long been associated with neurological damage and cognitive abnormalities that can range from mild impairment to severe dementia. In fact, the severity of these problems can be greater than for drugs often considered by the general population as being more harmful. For example, a 2002 report published by Neil Rosenberg of the University of Colorado Health Sciences Center found that chronic solvent abusers performed worse than chronic users of other drugs (especially cocaine and alcohol) on tests of working memory and executive function. In this study, abusers inhaled primarily vapors from spray paint containing toluene, and averaged more than 10 years of abuse. More than half of the group reported near-daily inhalant intoxication.

According to Rosenberg,

[T]he extensive neurological damage and cognitive impairments we found among chronic solvent abusers in our study could limit their ability to control their behavior and perceive problems associated with their substance abuse.... Some of the

brain damage and cognitive deficits seen in both primary inhalant and cocaine abusers in the study could stem from the heavy use of alcohol that was common among both groups.... However, the diffuse white matter changes and abnormalities found in the thalamus have not been seen in alcohol abusers and are clearly from solvent abuse.

Data from Mathias, R. "Chronic Solvent Abusers Have More Brain Abnormalities and Cognitive Impairments Than Cocaine Abusers." *NIDA Notes* 17 (4). (November 2002). Available http://archives.drugabuse.gov/NIDA_notes/NNVol17N4/Chronic.html; Rosenberg, N. L., J. Grigsby, J. Dreisbach, D. Busenbark, and P. Grisby. "Neuropsychologic Impairment and MRI Abnormalities with Chronic Solvent Abuse." *Journal of Clinical Toxicology* 40 (2002): 21–34.

injuries (because of flammability) and SSDS have resulted from their abuse (NIDA 2012).

GASOLINE

Because of its widespread availability, young people, often in rural settings, sometimes abuse gasoline. Gasoline is a mixture of volatile chemicals, including toluene, benzene, and triorthocresyl phosphate (TCP). Because it is a mixture of chemicals, the intentional inhalation of gasoline can be especially dangerous. Benzene is an organic compound that causes impaired immunologic function, bone marrow injury, increased risk of leukemia, and reproductive system toxicity (NIDA 2012). TCP is a fuel additive that causes degeneration of motor neurons (Scatterday n.d.). Furthermore, gasoline is highly flammable; as with butane and propane, fires and serious burn injuries have resulted when gasoline inhalation has been combined with smoking of marijuana, tobacco, or other drugs.

FREON

Freon and other related agents are used in a number of products, including refrigerators, air conditioners, and airbrushes. Their inhalation can cause not only serious liver damage, but also SSDS (NIDA 2012). Inhaling these agents also poses other dangers; freeze injuries can occur when individuals inhaling Freon lose consciousness, leaving unprotected skin in close proximity to cold. In one serious but rare case, a 16-year-old male attempted to get high by inhaling airbrush propellant. The patient lost consciousness. When he awoke, he discovered that his tongue and lips were frozen and that he had suffered serious burns on his larynx, vocal cords, trachea, bronchi, and esophagus (Kuspis and Krenzelok 1999).

■ Anesthetics

When used properly, other forms of inhalants with abuse potential are important therapeutic agents.

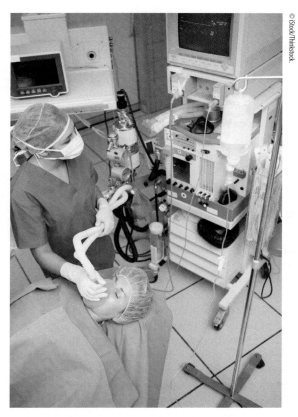

Anesthetics are an example of an inhalant.

Included in this category are anesthetics such as ether, chloroform, halothane, and nitrous oxide. Only nitrous oxide is available widely enough to be a significant abuse concern. Nitrous oxide is a colorless gas that is used for minor outpatient procedures in offices of both physicians and dentists. It is often referred to as "laughing gas" because it can cause giggling and laughter in the patient receiving it. It is also found in products used in cars to boost octane levels (NIDA 2012). Because it is readily accessible, health professionals themselves or their staff are most likely to abuse nitrous oxide.

In addition to being found in a clinical setting, nitrous oxide can also be sold in large balloons from which the gas is released and inhaled for its mind-altering effects. It is also found in small cylindrical cartridges used as charges for whipped cream dispensers. These cylinders and other plastic containers filled with nitrous oxide are referred to as "whippets." Although significant abuse problems of nitrous oxide are infrequent, there are occasional reports of severe hypoxia (i.e., a lack of oxygen) or death due to acute overdoses. Nitrous oxide can also cause loss of sensation, limb spasms, altered perception and motor coordination, blackouts resulting from blood pressure changes, and reduced cardiac function (NIDA 2012).

■ Nitrites

Nitrites are chemicals that cause vasodilation. Owing to this property, the prototype of this group, amyl nitrite, has been used in the past to treat angina. Nitrites have been abused most commonly as sexual enhancers. Nitrites were first abused in the 1960s when ampules of the compound were available over the counter (OTC). The ampules were popped between the fingers (hence, the name "poppers") and held to the nostrils for inhalation.

Although the use of nitrites is now prohibited by the Consumer Product Safety Commission, they can still be obtained in small bottles labeled as "video head cleaner," "room odorizer," "leather cleaner," or "liquid aroma" (NIDA 2012). The use of amyl and the related butyl, nitrite has decreased dramatically from an annual use among 12th graders of 6.5% in 1979 to only 0.9% in 2009; since then, the Monitoring the Future study (an ongoing series of national surveys of American adolescents and adults that has provided important data concerning drug usage for over 30 years; Meich et al. 2016) has ceased to monitor usage because of this low prevalence.

Legislation

Inhalants of abuse are generally not regulated as controlled substances. However, at least 37 states have enacted laws regulating inhalant and aerosol sales and/or abuse (National Inhalant Prevention Coalition [NIPC] n.d.).

Current Patterns and Signs of Abuse

Inhalants, particularly gases and aerosols, are often among the first drugs that young children misuse. The inhalants are popular for several reasons:

- They are legally obtained.
- They are readily available in most households and workplaces.
- They are inexpensive.
- They are easy to conceal.

• Most users are uninformed about the potential dangers.

In addition, inhalation is popular because it causes feelings of intoxication and euphoria much more rapidly than does the consumption of agents such as alcohol.

■ Adolescent and Teenage Usage

Adolescents most commonly use inhalants, with usage decreasing as students grow older. For example, according to the 2015 Monitoring the Future study (Meich et al. 2016), 2.0% of 8th graders reported using inhalants within the past month, whereas only 1.2% of 10th graders and 0.7% of high school seniors reported a similar pattern of use (see **Table 14.1**). By comparison, in 2015, past-month use among college students was 0.2%. One reason for this age difference is that older individuals often view use of inhalants with disdain and consider it unsophisticated and a "kid's habit."

Lifetime inhalant use among 12th graders in 2015 was 5.7%, compared with 7.2% among 10th graders. Of considerable concern are reports that inhalant abuse can begin in very young children (Spiller and Krenzelok 1997). Researchers and poison information centers have described cases of 2- to 6-year-old children inhaling gasoline vapors. Imitation of older siblings or neighbors often accounts for this initial exposure. Hence, education efforts should be directed at very young children as well as adolescents and their parents.

■ Gender, Race, Socioeconomics, and Abuse

According to the 2014 National Survey on Drug Use and Health, a greater percentage of men (0.8%) than women (0.4%) aged 12 or older have used an inhalant during the past year. However, that gender difference is diminishing, as evidenced by recent findings that rates of past-year inhalant use were greater among females (2.4%) than males (1.7%) ages 12 to 17. Approximately 6% of American Indian or Alaskan Natives ages 12 to 17 have abused an inhalant at least once. White, non-Hispanic; Hispanic; black or African American; and Asian individuals ages 12 to 17 abused inhalants at least once in their lifetime at rates of 4.9%, 5.8%, 5.9%, and 3.4%, respectively (SAMHSA 2015).

■ Signs of Inhalant Abuse

Individuals under the influence of inhalants are often uncoordinated and disoriented and appear drunken, as if having consumed alcohol. Red and watery eyes, slurred speech, nausea, headaches, and nosebleeds are also common. Rashes around the nose and mouth or unexplained paint on the hands and mouth can be signs of inhalant abuse. Other signs include smelling a chemical odor in the room or in unusual containers (e.g., soda cans, plastic bags), finding cans of aerosol whipped cream that will not foam, or discovering air conditioners that do not work. In addition, children who are frequent users of inhalants have the following characteristics:

• Often collect an unusual assortment of chemicals (such as glues, paints, thinners and solvents, nail polish, liquid eraser, and cleaning fluids) in bedrooms or with belongings
• Have breath that occasionally smells of solvents
• Often have the sniffles similar to a cold but without other symptoms of the ailment
• Appear drunk for short periods of time (15 to 60 minutes) but recover quickly
• Do not do well in school and are often unkempt

TABLE 14.1 Inhalant Use Among 8th, 10th, and 12th Graders

	8th Graders (%)			10th Graders (%)			12th Graders (%)		
	2013	2014	2015	2013	2014	2015	2013	2014	2015
Lifetime	10.8	10.8	9.4	8.7	8.7	7.2	6.9	6.5	5.7
Annual	5.2	5.3	4.6	3.5	3.3	2.9	2.5	1.9	1.9
30 day	2.3	2.2	2.0	1.3	1.1	1.2	1.0	0.7	0.7

Data from Miech, R. A., L. D. Johnston, P. M. O'Mailey, J. G. Bachman, and J. E. Schulenberg. *Monitoring the Future National Survey Results on Drug Use, 1975–2015. Volume I, Secondary School Students.* Ann Arbor: Institute for Social Research, University of Michigan, 2016.

Other signs of inhalant abuse can include the following:

- Sitting with a pen or marker near nose
- Constantly smelling clothing sleeves
- Hiding rags, clothes, or empty containers of the potentially abused products in closets, boxes, and other places
- Possessing chemical-soaked rags, bags, or socks
- Abusable household items missing

Dangers of Inhalant Abuse

The dangers of inhalant abuse stretch beyond simply the direct physical damage to the heart, lungs, liver, and brain. Other dangers can include death by choking on their own vomit or by fatal injury from accidents, including car crashes (NIDA 2012).

Use of inhalants by pregnant women also may put newborns at risk of developmental deficits. Although it is not yet possible to link prenatal exposure to specific inhalants with a specific birth defect, case reports have documented developmental abnormalities in offspring of mothers who chronically abuse inhalants (NIDA 2012).

According to NIDA (2012), many individuals who have abused inhalants for prolonged periods over many days report a strong need to continue inhalant use. A mild withdrawal syndrome and compulsive use can occur with long-term inhalant abuse.

A recent survey of 43,000 U.S. adults indicates that inhalant users, on average, initiate use of alcohol, cigarettes, and almost all other drugs at younger ages than those who do not abuse inhalants. Further, these individuals display a higher lifetime prevalence of substance use disorders, including prescription drug abuse, when compared with substance abusers without a history of inhalant use (NIDA 2012).

Of note, between 2006 and 2008, nearly 1 in 20 adolescents with at least one of four respiratory conditions (asthma, bronchitis, pneumonia, or sinusitis) also reported past-year use of an inhalant. This is significant because inhalant use may exacerbate existing medical conditions, including respiratory conditions. Still, adolescents with respiratory conditions are no less likely to use inhalants than those in the general population. Thus, continuing efforts are needed to educate individuals about the health risks of inhalant abuse (SAMHSA 2010).

LEARNING PORTFOLIO

Key Terms

Discussion Questions

1. Name the three types of inhalants and list examples of each type. List the dangerous side effects associated with the misuse of each type of inhalant.
2. Why are inhalants widely abused?
3. What is sudden sniffing death syndrome?
4. What chemical properties of inhalants make these agents particularly dangerous?
5. Who is most likely to abuse inhalants?
6. List several signs of inhalant abuse.
7. List several dangers of inhalant abuse other than the direct physical damage done by the chemical itself.

Summary

1. Inhalants are volatile substances that cause intoxicating and/or euphorigenic effects. Most were never intended to be used as drugs and are not often thought of as having abuse potential. However, inhalant abuse is a serious public health problem. Hundreds of adolescents and teenagers in the United States die or are seriously injured each year as a result of inhalant abuse. Even first-time users can die from a condition referred to as sudden sniffing death syndrome (SSDS).
2. Most inhalants are household or commercial products composed of several different fat-soluble chemicals that can act alone or synergistically to exert toxic effects. These agents can be classified into three groups: volatile substances, anesthetics, and nitrites.
3. Volatile substances include aerosols, adhesives, fuels, and household solvents. Abusers inhale vapors directly from their original containers (called sniffing or snorting), from plastic bags (called bagging), or from old rags or bandannas soaked in the solvent fluid and held over the mouth (called huffing). Abuse of these agents can cause damage to the liver, brain, kidneys, and immune system, as well as SSDS.
4. Anesthetics include ether, chloroform, halothane, and nitrous oxide. When used properly, these forms of inhalants are important therapeutic agents; however, their misuse can cause severe hypoxia and death.
5. Inhalants are popular because they are legally obtained, readily available, inexpensive, and easy to conceal.
6. Inhalant abuse is typically a problem of adolescents and teenagers.
7. Signs of inhalant abuse include a drunken appearance, watery eyes, nausea, headaches, and nosebleeds. Rashes around the nose and mouth or unexplained paint on the hands and mouth

can be signs of inhalant abuse. Other signs can include smelling a chemical odor in the room or in unusual containers (e.g., soda cans, plastic bags), finding cans of aerosol whipped cream that will not foam, or discovering air conditioners that do not work.

References

Kennedy, S. K., and D. E. Longnecker. "History and Principles of Anesthesiology." In *The Pharmacological Basis of Therapeutics*, edited by A. G. Gilman, T. W. Rall, A. S. Nies, and P. Taylor, 269. New York: Pergamon Press, 1990.

Kuspis, D. A., and E. P. Krenzelok. "Oral Frostbite Injury from Intentional Abuse of a Fluorinated Hydrocarbon." *Journal of Toxicology and Clinical Toxicology* 37 (1999): 873–875.

Miech, R. A., L. D. Johnston, P. M. O'Mailey, J. G. Bachman, and J. E. Schulenberg. *Monitoring the Future National Survey Results on Drug Use, 1975–2015. Volume I, Secondary School Students.* Ann Arbor: Institute for Social Research, University of Michigan, 2016.

National Highway Traffic Safety Administration (NHTSA). "Drug and Human Performance Fact Sheets: Toluene." n.d. Available http://www.nhtsa.gov/people/injury/research/job185drugs/toluene.htm

National Inhalant Prevention Coalition (NIPC). "State Inhalant Legislation." n.d. Available http://www.inhalants.org/laws.htm

National Institute on Drug Abuse (NIDA). *Research Report Series: Inhalant Abuse.* NIH Pub. No. 12-3818. July 2012. Available http://www.drugabuse.gov/publications/research-reports/inhalant-abuse

Scatterday, R. "Commonly Abused Products and Chemical Effects." n.d. Available http://www.inhalants.org/scatter.htm

Spiller, H. A., and E. P. Krenzelok. "Epidemiology of Inhalant Abuse Reported to Two Regional Poison Centers." *Clinical Toxicology* 35 (1997): 167–173.

Substance Abuse and Mental Health Service Administration (SAMHSA). "Adolescent Inhalant Use and Selected Respiratory Conditions." 2010. Available http://oas.samhsa.gov/2k10/175/175RespiratoryCond.htm

Substance Abuse and Mental Health Services Administration (SAMHSA). *Results from the 2013 National Survey on Drug Use and Health: Summary of National Findings.* NSDUH Series H-48, HHS Pub. No. (SMA) 14-4863. Rockville, MD: Substance Abuse and Mental Health Services Administration, 2014.

Substance Abuse and Mental Health Services Administration (SAMHSA). *Results from the 2014 National Survey on Drug Use and Health: Detailed Tables.* Center for Behavioral Health Statistics and Quality, Substance Abuse and Mental Health Services Administration, Rockville MD, 2015.

U.S. Consumer Product Safety Commission. "A Parent's Guide to Preventing Inhalant Abuse." n.d. Document #389. Available http://www.cpsc.gov/cpscpub/pubs/389gph.html

CHAPTER 15

Over-the-Counter, Prescription, and Herbal Drugs

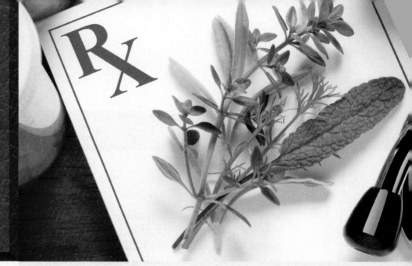

© DNY59/iStockphoto/Getty Images

Did You Know?

▶ More than 100 ingredients and 700 drug products that are currently available over-the-counter (OTC) were available only by prescription 30 years ago.

▶ Pharmacists can provide useful counseling in selecting appropriate OTC products.

▶ Careless, excessive use of some OTC medications can cause addiction, physical dependence, tolerance, and withdrawal symptoms.

▶ When used together, prescription drugs or drugs of abuse can interact with OTC or herbal drugs in a dangerous and sometimes even lethal manner.

▶ Most herbal (natural) remedies are very popular products that, despite containing drugs, are available without a pre-scription and by law are excluded from routine OTC regula-tion by the Food and Drug Administration (FDA).

▶ More people die in the United States from adverse reactions to legal medications than succumb to all illegal drug use.

▶ Every day more than 70 deaths occur in the United States due to prescription drugs, the majority of which are linked to opioid painkillers.

▶ One-third of college students take stimulant prescrip-tion drugs to either get high or enhance their academic performance.

▶ Most generic drugs are as effective as but substantially less expensive than their proprietary counterparts.

Learning Objectives

On completing this chapter you should be able to:

〉 Outline the general differences between prescription and nonprescription drugs.

〉 Explain why the Food and Drug Administration (FDA) occasionally switches prescription drugs to over-the-counter (OTC) status.

〉 Describe potential abuse problems with OTC, prescription, and herbal drugs.

〉 Identify some of the most popular drugs that have been switched to OTC.

〉 Discuss the potential problems of making more effective OTC drugs available to the public for self-care.

〉 Describe the type of information that is included on the labels of nonprescription medicines.

〉 Discuss the rules for safe use of nonprescription drugs.

〉 Determine the difference between herbal products and OTC medications.

〉 Explain why the FDA has removed ephedrine and ephedra from its list of approved OTC products.

〉 Compare problems of abuse/addiction of illicit and prescription drugs, and explain why prescription abuse has become so widespread.

〉 Discuss the type of information that should be communicated between doctor and patient to avoid unnecessary drug side effects.

〉 Explain how prescription drugs should be disposed of properly.

〉 Explain the advantages and disadvantages of generic and proprietary drugs.

〉 Explain which prescription drugs are most likely to be abused and why.

Introduction

Prescription drug costs approach 10% of overall health spending in the United States (Centers for Disease Control and Prevention [CDC] 2016). Clinicians are able to prescribe in excess of 10,000 different prescription medications, with more than 30% of U.S. adults consuming at least five medications. While drugs properly prescribed have dramatically improved the management of many minor and serious diseases, their frequent use also comes with significant risks referred to as *adverse drug events* (ADE). Each year these ADEs result in approximately 700,000 visits to emergency departments and 100,000 hospitalizations (PSNet 2015), underscoring the need for careful management of these medications and consideration of their benefit-to-risk ratio.

Over-the-counter (OTC) and prescription drugs have been viewed differently by the public since these classifications were formally established by the Durham–Humphrey Amendment of 1951. In general, we view OTC medications as less effective, relatively free from side effects, and rarely abused; in contrast, we often consider prescription drugs as much more potent, typically used for more serious medical conditions, and frequently dangerous.

However, distinctions between prescription and nonprescription drugs, which at one time appeared to be obvious, have become blurred by changes in public demand and federal policies. Because of escalating health costs and a growing interest in self-care, people today want access to effective medications, and government agencies such as the Food and Drug Administration (FDA) are responding to their demands. Consequently, the FDA has been involved in switching some 106 effective and relatively safe prescription medications to OTC status. In fact, more than 700 drug products sold OTC today were available only by prescription 30 years ago (FDA 2016c). Overall, OTC drugs make up approximately 10% of the total U.S. drug sales, with sales of OTC drugs totaling approximately $30 to $40 billion per year (Consumer Healthcare Products Association [CHPA] 2016a).

It is likely that in the future other drugs will be removed from behind the pharmacist's counter and made available for public access as nonprescription medications. Some possibilities for switching from prescription to OTC that have been suggested by health experts include drugs to treat migraine headaches, high cholesterol, and benign enlarged prostate glands (Page 2015). These changes of shifting drugs between prescription and nonprescription status emphasize the somewhat arbitrary nature of classifying drugs as prescription and OTC and remind us that similar care should be taken with all medications to achieve maximal benefit and minimal risk.

In this chapter, we begin by discussing OTC (nonprescription) drugs. The first topic encompasses policies regarding OTC drug regulation and is followed by a discussion of safe self-care with nonprescription drug products. Explanations of some of the most common medications in this category, including herbal (natural) remedies, conclude the section on OTC drugs. The second part of this chapter provides a general overview of prescription drugs. The consequences of misusing prescription drugs, as well as ways for you to avoid such problems, are discussed. A brief presentation of some of the most commonly prescribed drugs ends the chapter.

OTC Drugs

Today, more than 100,000 different OTC products including more than 1500 active ingredients are available to treat everything from age spots to halitosis; they account for 60% of the annual drug purchases in this country (CHPA 2016b). An estimated 60% of the population routinely self-medicates with these drug products (CHPA 2016a). The top five OTC categories by sales account for approximately 60% of the total OTC purchases: respiratory drugs ($7.7 billion), oral care products ($4.2 billion), drugs for gastrointestinal ailments ($4.2 billion), internal analgesics ($3.8 billion), and eye care ($1.7 billion) (CHPA 2016a).

Some of the 80 major drug classes currently approved for OTC status are shown in **Table 15.1**. OTC remedies are nonprescription drugs that may be obtained and used without the supervision of a physician or other health professional. Nevertheless, for some people, certain OTC products can be dangerous when used alone or in combination with other drugs. Although some OTC drugs are very beneficial in the self-treatment of minor to moderate uncomplicated health problems, others are of questionable therapeutic value, and their usefulness is often misrepresented by manufacturers.

TABLE 15.1 Some Major Drug Classes Approved by the FDA for OTC Status

Drug Class	Effects
Analgesics and anti-inflammatories	Relieve pain, fever, and inflammation
Cold remedies	Relieve cold symptoms
Antihistamines and allergy products	Relieve allergy symptoms
Stimulants	Diminish fatigue and drowsiness
Sedatives and sleep aids	Promote sleep
Antacids	Relieve indigestion from rebound activity
Laxatives	Relieve self-limiting constipation
Antidiarrheals	Relieve minor, self-limiting diarrhea
Gastric secretion blockers	Relieve heartburn
Topical antimicrobials	Treat skin infections
Bronchodilators and antiasthmatics	Assist breathing
Dentifrices and dental products	Promote oral hygiene
Acne medications	Treat and prevent acne
Sunburn treatments and sunscreens	Treat and prevent skin damage from ultraviolet rays
Dandruff and athlete's foot medications	Treat and prevent specific skin conditions
Contraceptives and vaginal products	Prevent pregnancy and treat vaginal infections
Ophthalmics	Promote eye hygiene and treat eye infections
Vitamins and minerals	Provide diet supplements
Antiperspirants	Promote body hygiene
Hair growth stimulators	Promote hair growth

Data from Consumer Healthcare Products Association (CHPA). "OTC Review/Drug Monographs." 2016. Available http://www.chpa.org/OTCReview.aspx

▌ Abuse of OTC Drugs

Although the consequences of abusing OTC drugs can be substantial, relatively speaking, the occurrence rate of such abuse is low; however, there are some notable exceptions, such as cough medicines and decongestants (Disabled World 2013).

Because these drugs are usually available on demand, perceived as being exceptionally safe, and poorly understood by the general public, their abuse patterns differ somewhat from those seen with the so-called hard-core drugs of abuse; nevertheless, they can be equally harmful. Even though the OTC products generally have a greater margin of safety than their prescription counterparts, issues of abuse need to be considered (Disabled World 2013). For example, many OTC drugs, when misused, can cause physical and psychological dependence. Nonprescription products that can be severely habit-forming include nasal and ophthalmic (eye) decongestants, laxatives, antihistamines, sleep aids, and antacids. Of particular abuse concern are OTC stimulants, such as ephedrine, that can be severely toxic by themselves or can be used as precursors to the synthesis of the extremely addicting and dangerous amphetamines. In fact, because of these concerns, the FDA has ruled that ephedrine no longer can be included in OTC or herbal products, and most states require that cold products containing amphetamine precursors be safeguarded behind the counter (Cunningham et al. 2012).

Because use of OTC products is unrestricted, the patterns of abuse are impossible to determine accurately. However, these products are more likely to be abused by members of the unsuspecting general public who inadvertently become dependent due to excessive self-medication than by hard-core drug addicts who obtain the most potent drugs of abuse by illicit means.

■ Federal Regulation of OTC Drugs

In the United States, the FDA is responsible for regulating OTC drugs through the Center for Drug Evaluation and Research (CDER). Under the direction of the FDA, the active ingredients in OTC drugs have been, and continue to be, evaluated and classified according to their effectiveness and safety.

The FDA has attempted to make even more drugs available to the general public by switching some frequently used and safe prescription medications to OTC status. This policy is in response to public demand to have access to effective drugs for self-medication and has resulted in approximately 106 successful switches, leading to 700 new OTC products (FDA 2016c, 2016d). This policy helps to cut medical costs by eliminating the need for costly visits to healthcare providers for treatment of minor, self-limiting ailments (CHPA 2016a). A few of the more notable drugs that have been switched from prescription to nonprescription status since 1985 are naproxen (analgesic, anti-inflammatory; Aleve), hydrocortisone (anti-inflammatory steroid; Cortaid), loperamide (antidiarrheal; Imodium), miconazole (antifungal; Monistat 7), cimetidine (heartburn medication; Tagamet), increased-strength minoxidil (hair growth stimulant; Rogaine), nicotine patch (smoking cessation aid; Nicotrol), orlistat (weight loss; Alli), lansoprazole (gastric acid reducer; Prevacid), diphenhydramine (sleep aid; Sominex), levonorgestrel (contraception; Plan B), cetirizine (allergy; Zyrtec), triamcionolone (24-hour corticosteroid nasal spray for allergies; Nasocort Allergy 24 HR), oxybutynin (overactive bladder for women; Oxytrol), and esomeprozole (24-hour relief of esophageal reflux; Nexium 24 HR) (FDA 2016c, 2016d).

A major concern of health professionals is that reclassification of safe prescription drugs to OTC status will result in overuse or misuse of these agents. The reclassified drugs may tempt individuals to self-medicate rather than seek medical care for potentially serious health problems or encourage the use of multiple drugs at the same time, increasing the likelihood of dangerous interactions (CHPA 2016a; FDA 2016c).

However, because there has been no evidence of significant problems, it is likely that effective and safe prescription drugs will continue to be made available OTC, although the rate of switching prescription drugs to OTC status does appear to be slowing.

■ OTC Drugs and Self-Care

Of the approximately 3.5 billion health problems treated in the United States annually, almost 2 billion can be treated with an OTC drug (CHPA 2016a). This fact demonstrates that the public frequently engages in medical self-care with OTC products. Self-care with nonprescription medications occurs because we decide that we have a health problem that can be adequately self-medicated without involving a health professional. Proper self-care assumes that the individual has made a correct diagnosis of the health problem and is informed enough to select the appropriate OTC product. If done correctly, self-care with OTC medications can provide significant relief from minor, self-limiting health problems at minimal cost and can save billions of dollars that would otherwise be spent on expensive health care and prescription drugs (CHPA 2016a). However, a lack of understanding about the nature of the OTC products—what they can and cannot do—and their potential side effects can result in harmful misuse. For this reason, it is important that those who consume OTC medications be fully aware of their proper use. This goal usually can be achieved by reading product labels carefully and asking questions of health professionals such as pharmacists and physicians. Potential problems associated with the use of OTC medicines include (1) delay in seeking proper medical care for serious illnesses, (2) risk of drug or herbal interactions, (3) unassessed potential for adverse effects in individual users, and (4) potential for abuse, dependence, and misuse (American College of Preventive Medicine [ACPM] 2016).

OTC LABELS

Information about proper use of OTC medications is required to be cited on the drug label and is regulated by the FDA. Required label information includes (1) approved uses of the product, (2) detailed instructions on safe and effective use, and (3) cautions or warnings to those at greatest risk when taking the medication. FDA regulations require that this information be readily intelligible to the lay public and easily read (Henderson 2012) (see **Figure 15.1**). Many consumers

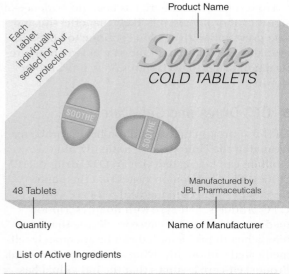

Product Name

Each tablet individually sealed for your protection

Soothe
COLD TABLETS

48 Tablets

Manufactured by
JBL Pharmaceuticals

Quantity

Name of Manufacturer

List of Active Ingredients

Drug Facts

Active ingredient (in each tablet) .... **Purpose**
Chlorpheniramine maleate 2 mg .... Antihistamine

Uses: temporarily relieves these symptoms due to hay fever or other upper respiratory allergies:
• sneezing • runny nose • itchy, watery eyes • itchy throat

Warnings: Ask a doctor before use if you have: • glaucoma • a breathing problem such as emphysema or chronic bronchitis • trouble urinating due to an enlarged prostate gland

Ask a doctor or pharmacist before use if you are taking tranquilizers or sedatives

When using this product: • you may get drowsy • avoid alcoholic drinks • alcohol, sedatives, and tranquilizers may increase drowsiness • be careful when driving a motor vehicle or operating machinery • excitability may occur, especially in children

If pregnant or breast-feeding, ask a health professional before use. *Keep out of reach of children.* In case of overdose, get medical help or contact a Poison Control Center right away.

Directions

adults and children 12 years and over	take 2 tablets every 4 to 6 hours; not more than 12 tablets in 24 hours
children 6 years to under 12 years	take 1 tablet every 4 to 6 hours; not more than 6 tablets in 24 hours
children under 6 years	ask a doctor

Other Information: • store at 20-25C (68-77F) • protect from excessive moisture

Inactive Ingredients: D&C yellow no. 10, lactose, magnesium stearate, microcrystalline cellulose, pregelatinized starch

Directions Warnings   Indications for Use

FIGURE 15.1 OTC label. Certain information must appear on the labels of OTC medicinal products.

experience adverse side effects because they either choose to ignore the warnings on OTC labels or simply do not bother to read them. For example, as previously mentioned, excessive or inappropriate use of some nonprescription drugs can cause drug dependence; consequently, people who are always dropping medication in the eyes "to get the red out" or popping antacids like dessert after every meal are likely dependent. They continue to use OTC products to avoid unpleasant eye redness or stomach acidity, which are likely withdrawal consequences of excessive use of these medications (WebMD 2016b).

RULES FOR PROPER OTC DRUG USE

The OTC marketplace for drugs operates differently than does its prescription counterpart. The use of OTC drugs is not restricted, and consumers are responsible for making correct decisions about

these products. Thus, to a large degree, the consumer sets policy and determines use patterns.

Because there are no formal controls over the use of OTC drugs, abuse often occurs. In extreme situations, the abuse of OTC medication can be very troublesome, even causing structural damage to the body and, on rare occasions, death. Proper education about the pharmacological features of these agents is necessary if consumers are to make intelligent and informed decisions about OTC drug use. To reduce the incidence of problems, the following rules should be observed when using nonprescription products (Hussar 2016):

- Make sure your self-diagnosis is accurate.
- Chose products with the fewest appropriate ingredients.
- Always know what you are taking. Identify the active ingredients in the product.
- Know the effects. Be sure you know both the desired and potential undesired effects of each active ingredient.
- Read and heed the warnings and cautions.
- The warnings are not intended to scare but to protect.
- Do not use OTC drug products for more than 1 to 2 weeks. If the problem being treated persists beyond this time, consult a health professional.
- Be particularly cautious if you are also taking prescription or herbal drugs. Serious interactions between OTC drugs and these medications frequently occur. If you have a question, be sure to find out the answer.
- If you have questions, ask a pharmacist. Pharmacists are excellent sources of information about OTC drugs. They possess up-to-date knowledge of OTC products and can assist consumers in selecting correct medications for their health needs. Ask them to help you.
- Most important, if you don't need it, don't use it!

▎ Types of OTC Drugs

It is impossible to provide a detailed description of the hundreds of active ingredients approved by the FDA for OTC distribution; however, the following includes a brief discussion of the most common OTC drugs available in the United States.

INTERNAL ANALGESICS

Each year Americans spend more than $3.8 billion on internal (taken by mouth) analgesics (CHPA 2016a). Most of this is spent on salicylates (aspirin products; Anacin, Bayer), acetaminophen

TABLE 15.2 Compositions of OTC Internal Analgesics (dose per unit)

Product	Aspirin (mg)	Acetaminophen (mg)	Ibuprofen (mg)	Other
Bayer Aspirin	325	–	–	–
Ecotrin	325	–	–	Coated tablet
Tylenol, Children's	–	80	–	–
Advil	–	–	200	–
Motrin IB	–	–	200	–
Motrin, Children's	–	–	200	–
Aleve	–	–	–	Naproxen (220 mg)

Data from Wilkinson, J. "Headache." In *Handbook of Nonprescription Drugs*, 17th ed., edited by D. Krinsky, R. Beradi, S. Ferreri, A. Hume, G. Newton, C. Rollins, and K. Tietze, 67–86. Washington, DC: American Pharmacists Association, 2012.

(Tylenol, Datril, Pamprin, Panadol), ibuprofen (Advil, Nuprin), and ibuprofen-like drugs such as naproxen (Aleve). The compositions of common OTC internal analgesics are provided in **Table 15.2**.

THERAPEUTIC CONSIDERATIONS

The internal analgesic products are effective in treating several common ailments (Borazan and Furst 2015):

- *Analgesic action*: The OTC analgesics effectively relieve mild to moderate somatic pain associated with musculoskeletal structures such as bones, skin, teeth, joints, and ligaments. Pains that are relieved by the use of these drugs include headaches, toothaches, earaches, and muscle strains. In contrast, these drugs are not effective in the treatment of severe pain or pain associated with internal organs, such as the heart, stomach, and intestines.
- *Anti-inflammatory effects*: Use of high doses (two to three times the analgesic dose) of the salicylates and ibuprofen relieves the symptoms of inflammation such as those associated with arthritis. In contrast, even high doses of acetaminophen have little anti-inflammatory action. Because of this anti-inflammatory effect, these drugs are frequently compared with a group of natural, very potent anti-inflammatory compounds, the steroids. To distinguish drugs such as the salicylates and ibuprofen from steroids, these drugs are often called *nonsteroidal anti-inflammatory drugs* (NSAIDs).
- *Antipyretic effects*: The OTC analgesics, such as aspirin and acetaminophen, reduce fever but do not alter normal body temperature. Such

drugs are called *antipyretics*. The frequent use of these drugs to eliminate fevers is very controversial. Some clinicians believe that low-grade fever may be a defense mechanism that helps destroy infecting microorganisms such as bacteria and viruses; thus, interfering with fevers may hamper the body's ability to rid itself of infection-causing microorganisms. Because no serious problems are associated with fevers of 102°F or lower, they are probably better left unmedicated.

- *Side effects*: When selecting an OTC analgesic drug for relief of pain, inflammation, or fever, possible side effects should be considered. Although salicylates such as aspirin are frequently used, they can cause problems for both children and adults (see "Signs & Symptoms: Common Side Effects of OTC NSAIDs"). Because of their side effects, salicylates are not recommended for (1) children, because of the potential for Reye's syndrome; (2) people suffering from gastrointestinal problems, such as ulcers; or (3) people with bleeding problems, who are taking anticlot medication, who are scheduled for surgery, or who are near term in pregnancy, because salicylates interfere with blood clotting and prolong bleeding.

For minor aches and pains, acetaminophen substitutes adequately for salicylates, has no effect on blood clotting, and does not cause stomach irritation. In addition, acetaminophen does not influence the occurrence of Reye's syndrome, a potentially deadly complication of colds, flu, and chickenpox in children up to the age of 18 years who are using salicylates (Wilkinson 2012). However, even acetaminophen, if used in high doses, can have serious health consequences. Concern that excessive use of acetaminophen can cause permanent and even fatal liver damage has caused the FDA to put out warnings to consumers of acetaminophen-containing products to avoid the use of high doses of this drug (Brennan 2015).

CAFFEINE AND OTHER ADDITIVES

A number of OTC analgesic products contain caffeine. Caffeine may relieve the negative element of pain due to its stimulant effect, which may be perceived as pleasant and energizing. The combination of caffeine with OTC analgesics may enhance pain relief (Baratloo et al. 2016) and be especially useful in treating vascular headaches because of the vasoconstrictive properties on cerebral blood vessels caused by this stimulant. In most OTC analgesic products—for example, Anacin or Excedrin—the amount of caffeine is less than that found in one-fourth to one-half cup of coffee (about 30 milligrams/tablet). Other ingredients—such as antacids, antihistamines, and decongestants—sometimes included in OTC pain-relieving products have little or no analgesic action and usually add little to the therapeutic value of the medication. A recent development for OTC analgesic products was FDA permission to advertise pain-relieving products effective in the relief of migraine headaches. Although these products have been found to provide relief from minor migraine headaches, they do not contain any new breakthrough drugs; these products contain previously available ingredients, such as aspirin, ibuprofen, and caffeine, just in higher doses (e.g., Migraine Extra Strength Excedrin).

COLD, ALLERGY, AND COUGH REMEDIES

More than 50% of the population routinely uses OTC medicines to treat cold symptoms (CHPA 2010). The incidence of the common cold varies with age. Children between 1 and 5 years are most susceptible; each child averages 6 to 12 respiratory illnesses per year, most of which are common colds. Individuals 25 to 30 years old average about six respiratory illnesses a year, and older adults average two or three. The declining incidence of colds with age is owing to the immunity that occurs after each infection with a cold virus; thus, if reinfected with the same virus, the microorganism is rapidly destroyed by the body's defense system and the full-blown symptoms of a cold do not occur (*New York Times* 2016).

Most colds have similar general symptoms. In the first stage, the throat and nose are dry and scratchy; in the second stage, secretions accumulate in the air passages, nose, throat, and bronchial tubes. The second stage is marked by continuous sneezing, nasal obstruction, sore throat, coughing, and nasal discharge. There may be watering and redness of the eyes and pain in the face (particularly near the sinuses) and ears. One of the most bothersome symptoms of the

SIGNS & SYMPTOMS

Common Side Effects of OTC NSAIDs

Drugs	System Affected	Side Effects
Salicylates	Gastrointestinal	Can cause irritation, bleeding; aggravate ulcers
	Blood	Interfere with clotting; prolong bleeding
	Ears	Chronic high doses cause ringing (tinnitus) and hearing loss
	Pediatric	Can cause Reye's syndrome
Acetaminophen	Liver	High acute doses or chronic exposure can cause severe damage
Ibuprofen (includes other, newer NSAIDs)	Gastrointestinal	Similar to salicylates but less severe
	Blood	Similar to salicylates but less severe
	Kidneys	Damage in elderly or those with existing kidney disease

Data from Borazan, N., and D. Furst. "Nonsteroidal Anti-inflammatory Drugs, Disease-Modifying Antirheumatic Drugs, Nonopioid Analgesics, and Drugs Used in Gout." In *Basic and Clinical Pharmacology*, 13th ed., edited by B. Katzung and A. Trevor, 618–641. New York: McGraw-Hill, 2015.

TABLE 15.3 Compositions of Common OTC Cold and Allergy Products (dose per tablet)

Product	Sympathomimetic	Analgesic
Afrin	Oxymetazoline (0.05%)	—
Alka-Seltzer Plus	Phenylephrine (7.8 mg)	Aspirin (325 mg)
Tylenol Cold	Pseudoephedrine (5 mg)	Acetaminophen (325 mg)
Aleve-D Sinus	Pseudoephedrine (120 mg)	Naproxen (220 mg)

Data from Scolaro, K. "Disorders Related to Colds and Allergies." In *Handbook of Nonprescription Drugs*, 17th ed., edited by D. Krinsky, R. Beradi, S. Ferreri, A. Hume, G. Newton, C. Rollins, and K. Tietze, 180–204. Washington, DC: American Pharmacists Association, 2012.

common cold is the congestion of the mucous membranes of the nasal passages, due in part to capillary dilation, which causes these blood vessels to enlarge and become more permeable. Such vascular changes allow fluids to escape, resulting in drainage and also inflammation due to fluid-swollen tissues (WebMD 2016b).

There has been a growing problem of young people abusing these OTC products. Recent surveys suggest that up to 4.6% of high school seniors used cough medicine with dextromethorphan to get high in 2015 (Johnston 2016). This practice is sometimes referred to as *robo-tripping* or *skittling*. Common side effects include confusion, dizziness, excessive sweating, stomach pain, numbness, and blurred vision.

DECONGESTANTS

The cold and allergy products we use are principally formulated with such drugs as decongestants (sympathomimetics), antihistamines (chlorpheniramine and pheniramine), and analgesics (aspirin, acetaminophen, and naproxen). **Table 15.3** lists the ingredients found in many common OTC cold and allergy products.

Antihistamines reduce congestion caused by allergies, but their effectiveness in the treatment of virus-induced colds is controversial. In high doses, the anticholinergic action of antihistamines also decreases the secretion of mucus, relieving the runny nose; however, this action is probably insignificant at the lower recommended doses of OTC preparations (Stoppler 2016). An anticholinergic drying action may actually be harmful because it can lead to a serious coughing response. Due to anticholinergic effects, antihistamines also may cause dizziness, drowsiness, impaired judgment, constipation, and dry mouth; they sometimes are abused because of psychedelic effects resulting from high-dose consumption. Because of the limited usefulness and the side effects of antihistamines for treating colds,

decongestant products without such agents are usually preferred for these viral infections. In contrast, antihistamines are very useful in relieving allergy-related congestion and symptoms.

The sympathomimetic drugs used as decongestants cause nasal membranes to shrink because of their vasoconstrictive effect, which reduces the congestion caused by both colds and allergies. Such drugs can be used in the form of sprays or drops (topical decongestants) or systemically (oral decongestants) (see **Table 15.4**). FDA-approved sympathomimetics include pseudoephedrine, phenylephrine (probably the most effective topical), and oxymetazoline (Scolaro 2012). A substantial problem associated with the sympathomimetic decongestant ingredients in cold medicines is that they can easily be chemically converted into methamphetamine. For this reason the federal government passed the Combat Methamphetamine Epidemic Acts of 2005 and 2010, which require these decongestant products to be kept behind the counter and records to be kept of those who purchase these medications (see "Here and Now: Fighting the 'Common Cold' Pills"). In addition to the federal laws, many states have also passed their own statutes to regulate the sale of precursors used to make methamphetamine. The control

TABLE 15.4 Compositions of OTC Topical Decongestants (drug concentrations)

Product	Sympathomimetic
Afrin	Oxymetazoline (0.05%)
Neo-Synephrine	Phenylephrine (0.5%)
Vicks Sinex	Oxymetazoline (0.05%)

Data from Scolaro, K. "Disorders Related to Colds and Allergies." In *Handbook of Nonprescription Drugs*, 17th ed., edited by D. Krinsky, R. Beradi, S. Ferreri, A. Hume, G. Newton, C. Rollins, and K. Tietze, 180–204. Washington, DC: American Pharmacists Association, 2012.

varies from state to state, and many of these local laws are more rigid than the federal regulations (FDA 2016b; NIDA 2016b).

Someone using decongestant nasal sprays frequently can experience **congestion rebound** due to tissue dependence. After using a nasal spray regularly for longer than the recommended period of time, the nasal membranes adjust to the effect of the vasoconstrictor and become very congested when the drug is not present. One can become hooked and use the spray more and more with less and less relief until one's tissues no longer respond and the sinus passages become almost completely obstructed (FamilyDoctor.org 2016). Allergists frequently see new patients who are addicted to nasal decongestant sprays and are desperate for relief from congestion. This problem can be prevented by using nasal sprays sparingly and for no longer than the recommended time.

Orally ingested sympathomimetic drugs give less relief from congestion than the topical medications but are less likely to cause rebound effects. In contrast, systemic administration of these drugs is more likely to cause cardiovascular problems (i.e., stimulate the heart, cause arrhythmia, increase blood pressure, and cause stroke).

ANTITUSSIVES

Other drugs used to relieve the common cold are intended to treat coughing. The cough reflex helps clear the lower respiratory tract of foreign matter, particularly in the later stages of a cold. There are two types of cough: productive and nonproductive. A *productive cough* removes mucous secretions and foreign matter so that breathing becomes easier and the infection clears up. A *nonproductive*, or *dry, cough* causes throat irritation; this type of cough is of little cleansing value. Some types of cough suppressant (antitussive) medication are useful for treating a nonproductive cough but should not be used to suppress a productive cough (ePainAssist 2016).

The common cold accounts for 20% of all acute illnesses in the United States.

Two kinds of OTC preparations are available to treat coughing:

- **Antitussives**, such as codeine, dextromethorphan, and diphenhydramine (an antihistamine), that act on the central nervous system (CNS) to raise the threshold of the cough-coordinating center, thereby reducing the frequency and intensity of a cough
- **Expectorants**, such as guaifenesin and terpin hydrate, which theoretically (but not very effectively) increase and thin the fluids of the respiratory tract in an attempt to soothe the irritated respiratory tract membranes and decrease the thickness of the accumulated secretions so that coughing becomes more productive

Table 15.5 lists commonly used OTC antitussives and their compositions. Often, the tickling sensation in the throat that triggers a cough can be eased by sucking on a cough drop or hard candy, which stimulates saliva flow to soothe the irritated membranes. Unless the cough is severe, sour hard candy often works just as well as more expensive cough lozenges.

Cough remedies, like other medications, have a psychological value. Many patients with respiratory tract infections claim that they cough less after using cough remedies, even when it is objectively demonstrated that the remedies reduce neither the frequency nor the intensity of the

© Leah-Anne Thompson/ShutterStock, Inc.

KEY TERMS

congestion rebound
withdrawal from excessive use of a decongestant, resulting in congestion

antitussives
drugs that block the coughing reflex

expectorants
substances that stimulate secretion of mucus and diminish its viscosity

HERE AND NOW
Fighting the "Common Cold" Pills

It is becoming harder and harder to get those pills we all buy to fight the common cold. This problem is not because drugs like Sudafed are themselves particularly addicting; rather, the concern arises because of what they can become, and this is leading to the imposition of tighter controls on these popular decongestants. Because ingredients in OTC cold medicines, such as pseudoephedrine, can easily be converted into methamphetamine, these products have been bought in large quantities to be used in makeshift meth labs across the country. As a result, law enforcement agencies and even Congress itself have pointed out these drugs' potential dangers. Besides requiring that these OTC products be kept behind the counter in pharmacies, there have been attempts to pass local and national legislation to limit purchases of these drugs to about 9 grams (roughly 300 pills) in a 30-day period. This quantity of pseudoephedrine can be turned into approximately 25 doses of methamphetamine. Such restrictions have made it difficult, although not impossible, for small neighborhood meth labs to cook their dangerous brew. However, as the local "mom-and-pop" domestic producers have been significantly curtailed, Mexican drug cartels have filled the gap with large

quantities of methamphetamine manufactured in Mexico and smuggled across the border. The cartels are using dummy corporations and false labeling to bring ordinary cold, flu, and allergy medicines into Mexico from China, India, and Belgium and converting the ingredients from these common decongestants into large quantities of methamphetamine for illicit sale. Despite efforts by both the Mexican and U.S. governments, these trafficking groups are very resilient, keeping ahead of the law, and have become the primary source for illegal U.S. methamphetamine.

Data from Booth, W., and A. O'Connor. "Mexican Cartels Emerge as Top Source for U.S. Meth." *The* Washington Post. (28 November 2010). Available http://www.washingtonpost.com/wp-dyn/content/article/2010/11/23/AR2010112303703.html?sid=ST2010112303730; Cooper, C. "Methamphetamine Abuse and Illegal Trafficking Remain a Persistent Threat Across the State." CN Cronkite News. 31 March 2016. Available https://cronkitenews.azpbs.org/2016/03/31/methamphetamine-abuse-and-illegal-trafficking-remain-a-persistent-threat-across-the-state/; Elena, M. "Mexican Drug Cartel's Crystal Meth Ingredient May be From Belgian Pharma Execs." *Latin Post.* (10 March 2016). Available http://www.latinpost.com/articles/118030/20160310/mexican-drug-cartels-crystal-meth-ingredient-belgian-pharma-execs.htm

TABLE 15.5 Compositions of Common OTC Antitussives

Product	Antitussive	Expectorant
Delsym	Dextromethorphan	—
Humibid	—	Guaifen
Vicks Cough Drops	—	Guaifen
Robitussin DM Cough	Dextromethorphan	Guaifen

Data from Scolaro, K. "Disorders Related to Colds and Allergies." In *Handbook of Nonprescription Drugs*, 17th ed., edited by D. Krinsky, R. Beradi, S. Ferreri, A. Hume, G. Newton, C. Rollins, and K. Tietze, 180–204. Washington, DC: American Pharmacists Association, 2012.

cough. Cough remedies work, in part, by reducing patients' anxiety about the cough and causing them to believe that their cough is lessening. If one believes in the remedy, one often can get as much relief from a simple, inexpensive product as from the most sophisticated and costly one. If a cough does not ease in a few days, one should consult a doctor (ePainAssist 2016).

As mentioned earlier, abuse of antitussive products by teenagers is a significant problem in some regions of this country. This abuse likely relates to the fact that in high doses the antitussive ingredient dextromethorphan can have a phencyclidine (PCP)–like effect (see "Here and Now: The Dextromethorphan Trip"). Up to 10% of young people use high doses of antitussives that contain dextromethorphan to get high (Johnston 2016). Even though possession of cough medicines is not controlled, the National Institute on Drug Abuse advises parents to control access to cough and cold medications at home to prevent this potential problem (NIDA 2016a).

WHAT REALLY WORKS?

With all the advances in medicine today, there is still no cure for the common cold. In most cases, the best treatment is plenty of rest, increased fluid intake to prevent dehydration and to facilitate productive coughing, humidification of the air if it is dry, gargling with diluted salt water (2 teaspoons per quart), an analgesic to relieve the accompanying headache or muscle ache, and perhaps an occasional decongestant if nasal stuffiness is unbearable. Allergy symptoms, in contrast, are best relieved by antihistamines.

SLEEP AIDS

The inability to sleep, or insomnia, is a major problem in the United States, as illustrated by the following facts (The Better Sleep Guide 2016):

* People today sleep 20% less than they did a century ago.
* Approximately one-third of the population will suffer from some form of insomnia during their lifetime.
* The majority of Americans lose sleep because of stress and anxiety.
* Women are twice as likely to have problems sleeping than men.
* Some forms of insomnia have a genetic basis.
* Approximately 90% of the people who suffer from depression also have sleep problems.
* Approximately 10 million Americans use sleep aids.
* People suffering from sleep deprivation are more likely to become overweight or obese.
* The U.S. Surgeon General's office reports that sleep disorders cost our economy more than $15 billion per year in additional health costs.
* Each employee with sleep problems cost his or her employer approximately $3200 more in healthcare costs than those employees who

HERE AND NOW
The Dextromethorphan Trip

Dextromethorphan is the antitussive ingredient frequently found in nonprescription cough medicine. Because of pharmacological properties that resemble those of PCP, OTC cough medicines are sometimes abused by teenagers and young adults. The following was a posting on "BlueLight" with "advice" by a so-called experienced dextromethorphan user to the "beginner" illustrating the unpredictability and potential dangers of abusing this drug:

Don't start getting anxious before your first "trip." Use the search engine and look up dextromethorphan.... There are a few things you need to know.... It can be enlightening, scary, dull, crazy.... It is not a classical psychedelic. Mixing different things will give you different results. Tripping with some friends, listening to a Dead album might be perfect. Spazzing out to EMTs and police,

because you don't understand what's going on is quite different.... I don't recommend mixing other drugs [the] first time.... Don't drink ALCOHOL.... Everyone is different. My "good time" could suck for you.

© Cheryl Casey/Shutterstock

Data from BlueLight. "Speed King" 2016. Available http://www.bluelight.org/vb/threads/785632-Dxm-trip

have normal sleep patterns, resulting in a total expense of about $150 billion.

These drugs should not be used as a sleep aid for young children because they can be unpredictable or even dangerous in this population. For example, the parents of a young child were traveling cross-country. They knew the trip would be long and the child would likely grow tired and cranky. To keep the child quiet and manageable, the parents used Benadryl, an allergy medication, which contains an antihistamine to cause sedation. Instead of going to sleep, the medicated child became excited and uncontrollable resulting in a very difficult journey for the rest of the family. (personal communication to Hanson 2016). The drugs commonly used in OTC sleep aids are antihistamines, particularly diphenhydramine (Soong 2016). Although antihistamines have been classified as OTC category I sleep aid ingredients, their usefulness in treating significant sleep disorders is limited. At best, some people who suffer mild, temporary sleep disturbances caused by problems such as physical discomfort, short-term disruption in daily routines (such as jet lag), and extreme emotional upset might experience temporary relief. However, even for those few who initially benefit from these agents, tolerance develops within 4 days. For long-term sleep problems, OTC sleep aids are of no therapeutic value and are rarely recommended by health professionals (Soong 2016). Actually, their placebo benefit is likely more significant than their actual pharmacological benefit. Usually counseling and psychotherapy are more effective approaches for resolving chronic insomnia than OTC or even prescription sleep aid drugs (Bushak 2016).

Because antihistamines are CNS depressants, in low doses they can cause sedation and antianxiety action. Although in the past some OTC products containing antihistamines were promoted for their relaxing effects (e.g., Quietworld, Compoz), currently, no sedatives are approved for OTC marketing. The FDA decided that the earlier products relieved anxiety by causing drowsiness, and thus were not legitimate sedatives. Because of this ruling, medications that are promoted as antianxiety products are no longer available without a prescription. However, antihistamines have been added to an array of other OTC drug products marketed for the purpose of causing relaxation or promoting sleep; such products include analgesics (e.g., Excedrin PM), cold medicines (e.g., Tylenol Cold Multisymptom Nighttime), Midol Complete, and many others (Kirkwood and Melton 2012;

Scolaro 2012; Shimp 2012). The rationale for such combinations is questionable and their therapeutic value unsubstantiated.

MELATONIN

The hormone melatonin is currently being used by millions to induce sleep or to help the body's natural clock readjust after the effects of jet lag. Melatonin was referred to as the "all-natural nightcap of the 1990s." Although most users of this hormone want assistance in falling asleep, some people claim that melatonin also slows the aging process, stimulates the immune system, and enhances the sex drive. Melatonin is a naturally occurring hormone and is also found in some foods. Under the 1994 Dietary Supplement and Education Act, melatonin is considered a dietary supplement and is not regulated by the FDA. Despite the popularity of melatonin products, the efficacy of supplemental melatonin as a sleep aid or to help with jet lag is minimal at best (Bonnet and Arand 2016). Products containing melatonin should be used cautiously, if at all (van den Heuval et al. 2005).

STIMULANTS

Some OTC drugs are promoted as stay-awake (e.g., NoDoz) or energy-promoting (e.g., Vivarin) products (Kirkwood and Melton 2012). In general, these medications contain high doses of caffeine (100 to 200 milligrams per tablet). Although it is true that CNS stimulation by ingesting significant doses of caffeine can increase the state of alertness during periods of drowsiness, the repeated use of such an approach is highly suspect.

For example, college students sometimes rely on such products to repeatedly enhance mental endurance during cramming sessions for examinations. In fact, at one western U.S. university, the back page of a quarterly class schedule, printed and distributed by the university, included a full-page advertisement for the OTC stimulant Vivarin with the caption, "Exam Survival Kit." The implications of such promotions are obvious and disturbing. Due to the objections of the faculty, the advertisement was not run again at the university. While moderate doses (around 200 milligrams) may help on test scores, excessive caffeine (more than 400 milligrams) causes anxiety and actually can significantly impair memory (Miller 2016).

Routine use of stay-awake or energy-promoting products to enhance performance at work or in school can lead to dependence, resulting in withdrawal when the person stops using the drug.

Most health professionals agree that there are more effective and safer ways to deal with fatigue and drowsiness—for example, managing time efficiently and getting plenty of rest (Kirkwood and Melton 2012).

SYMPATHOMIMETICS

Mild OTC sympathomimetics have been marketed as safe stimulants and as legal alternatives to cocaine and other illicit stimulants. The principal ingredients found in the mild stimulants are drugs such as phenylephrine and caffeine. The same drugs are also found in OTC decongestants and diet aids (Miller and Bartels 2012; Scolaro 2012). Ephedrine, a naturally occurring stimulant (i.e., from the ephedra plant), and phenylpropanolamine were withdrawn from OTC use due to their potential toxicity on the cardiovascular system (Cleveland Clinic 2016).

Although much less potent than amphetamines, when used in high doses, the OTC stimulants can cause anxiety, restlessness, throbbing headaches, breathing problems, and tachycardia (rapid heartbeat). There have been reports of death due to heart arrhythmia, cerebral hemorrhaging, and strokes, as discussed earlier, from excessive ephedrine use.

GASTROINTESTINAL MEDICATIONS

The gastrointestinal (GI) system consists principally of the esophagus, stomach, and intestines and is responsible for the absorption of nutrients and water into the body, as well as the elimination of body wastes. The function of the GI system can be altered by changes in eating habits, stress, infection, and diseases such as ulcers and cancers. Such problems may affect appetite, cause discomfort or pain, result in nausea and vomiting, and alter the formation and passage of stools from the intestines.

A variety of OTC medications are available to treat GI disorders such as indigestion (antacids), heartburn (gastric secretion blockers), constipation (laxatives), and diarrhea (antidiarrheals) (*U.S. News and World Report* 2016). However, before individuals self-medicate with nonprescription drugs, they should be certain that the cause of their GI problem is minor, is self-limiting, and does not require professional care. Because

antacids are the most frequently used of the GI nonprescription drugs, they are discussed next.

ANTACIDS AND ANTIHEARTBURN MEDICATION

Almost $2 billion is spent each year on antacids and heartburn medications that claim to give relief from heartburn and indigestion caused by excessive eating or drinking and to provide long-term treatment of chronic peptic ulcer disease (Sandi 2016). It is estimated that as much as 50% of the population has had one or more attacks of **gastritis**, often referred to as *acid indigestion, heartburn, upset stomach,* and *sour* or *acid stomach.* These attacks are often due to acid rebound, occurring 1 to 2 hours after eating; by this time, the stomach contents have passed into the small intestine, leaving the gastric acids to irritate or damage the lining of the empty stomach. Heartburn, or gastroesophageal reflux, occurs after exposure of the lower esophagus to these very irritating gastric chemicals.

Some cases of severe, chronic acid indigestion may progress to peptic ulcer disease. Peptic ulcers (open sores) most frequently affect the duodenum (first part of the intestine) and the stomach. Although this condition is serious, it can be treated effectively with antacids, which are often combined with drugs available OTC or by prescription such as cimetidine (Tagamet), ranitidine (Zantac), and famotidine (Pepcid). A person with acute, severe stomach pain; chronic gastritis; blood in the stools (common ulcer symptoms); diarrhea; or vomiting should see a physician promptly and should not attempt to self-medicate with OTC antacids (Sandi 2016).

Most bouts of acid rebound, however, are associated with overeating or consuming irritating foods or drinks; these self-limiting cases can usually be managed safely with OTC antacids

More than $2 billion is spent each year on antacid products such as this in the United States.

KEY TERM

gastritis
inflammation or irritation of the gut

(such as sodium bicarbonate, calcium carbonate, aluminum salts, and magnesium salts). Because of their alkaline (opposite of acidic) nature, the nonprescription products neutralize gastric acids and give relief.

Generally speaking, OTC antacid preparations are safe for occasional use at low recommended doses, but excessive use can cause serious problems.

In addition, all antacids can interact with other drugs; they may alter the GI absorption or renal elimination of other medications. For example, some antacids inhibit the absorption of some vitamins and the minerals calcium and iron; thus, these products should not be taken at the same time. Consequently, patients using prescription drugs should consult with their physicians before taking OTC antacids (Sandi 2016).

Heartburn can be treated effectively with low doses of Tagamet, Zantac, or Pepcid. These drugs were switched to OTC status in the mid-1990s and help reduce gastric secretions (Zweber and Berardi 2012).

DIET AIDS

In U.S. society, being slim and trim are prerequisites to being attractive. It is estimated that in the United States two-thirds of adults and one-third of children and adolescents are obese or overweight (The State of Obesity 2016). Being obese has been linked to cardiovascular disease, some cancers, diabetes, chronic fatigue, and an array of aches and

Approximately 25% to 30% of the people in the United States are obese and 50% are overweight.

pains, not to mention psychological disorders such as depression (DerSarkissian 2016). Popular remedies for losing weight often include fad diets advertised in supermarket journals, expensive weight loss programs, or prescription or OTC diet aids.

Using drugs as diet aids is highly controversial (Anderson 2016). Many experts view them as useless or even dangerous. Drugs marketed as diet aids are supposed to depress the appetite, which helps users maintain low-calorie diets. The most effective of these agents are called **anorexiants**. Potent anorexiants, such as amphetamine-like drugs (including the once-popular diet aid fen-phen), can cause dangerous side effects and are available only by prescription. The appetite suppression effects of prescription anorexiants are usually temporary, after which tolerance often builds. Thus, even prescription diet aid drugs are usually effective for only a short period. There are no wonder drugs to help the obese lose weight permanently.

The most potent and most frequently used OTC diet aid ingredients were the sympathomimetic drugs phenylpropanolamine and ephedrine, but several years ago the FDA removed both drugs from all OTC products (About.com 2010). The current OTC diet aids are minimally effective and of no value in the treatment of significant obesity; they typically contain high doses of caffeine and sometimes natural ingredients such as "bitter orange," which contains the mild sympathomimetic synephrine. Despite their minimal value, frequent use of high doses of the OTC diet aid products is a common practice by weight-conscious female high school and college students. As one college sophomore who routinely carried a package of Dexatrim in her purse said, "Popping two or three of these before an important date helps me to eat like a bird and appear more petite" (personal communication to Hanson). Interestingly, this same woman also occasionally induced vomiting after eating because of her fear that she was gaining weight. Such weight-management practices are extremely worrisome and may be part of strategies of young people suffering from eating disorders such as anorexia and bulimia (Mayo Clinic 2016).

KEY TERM

anorexiants
drugs that suppress the activity of the brain's appetite center, causing reduced food intake

SKIN PRODUCTS

Because the skin is so accessible and readily visible, most people are sensitive about its appearance. These cosmetic concerns are motivated by attempts to look good and preserve youth. Almost 5% of the U.S. population reports having a chronic skin problem; many others suffer from seasonal or acute skin disorders (Scott and Martin 2006). Only a few of the most commonly used products are mentioned here: acne medications, sun products, and basic first-aid products.

ACNE MEDICATIONS

Acne is the most common skin disorder that affects adolescents. It typically occurs during puberty in response to the secretion of the male hormone androgen, which is produced by both males and females. Acne is typically a chronic inflammation caused by bacteria trapped in plugged sebaceous (oil) glands and hair follicles. This condition consists of whiteheads, pimples, nodules, and, in more severe cases, pustules, cysts, and abscesses. Moderate to severe acne can cause unsightly scarring on the face, back, chest, and arms and should be treated aggressively by a dermatologist with drugs such as antibiotics (tetracycline) and potent **keratolytics**, such as Retin-A (retinoic acid), vitamin A, or Accutane (isotretinoin). Usually, minor to moderate acne does not cause scarring or permanent skin damage and often can be safely self-medicated with OTC acne medications (Lynn et al. 2016).

Several nonprescription approaches to treating mild acne are available, including the following:

- *Sebum removal*: Oil and fatty chemicals (sebum) can accumulate on the skin and plug the sebaceous glands and hair follicles. Use of OTC products such as alcohol wipes (e.g., Stri-Dex) can help remove such accumulations.
- *Peeling agents*: The FDA found several keratolytic agents safe and effective for treatment of minor acne: benzoyl peroxide (Oxy 10 Daily Wash), salicylic acid (Neutrogena Rapid Defense),

KEY TERMS

keratolytics
caustic agents that cause the keratin skin layer to peel

keratin layer
outermost protective layer of the skin

SPF (sun protection factor) number
designation to indicate a product's ability to screen ultraviolet rays

resorcinol, and sulfur (DDF Sulfur), alone or in combination. These drugs help to prevent acne eruptions by causing the **keratin layer** of the skin to peel or by killing the bacteria that cause inflammation associated with acne. If multiple concentrations of a keratolytic are available, it is better to start with a lower concentration and move up to the higher one, allowing the skin to become accustomed to the caustic action of these products. The initial exposure may worsen the appearance of acne temporarily; however, with continual use, the acne usually improves.

SUN PRODUCTS

The damaging effects of sun exposure on the skin have been well publicized in recent years. It is now clear that the ultraviolet (UV) rays associated with sunlight have several adverse effects on the skin. Skin cancer is the most common cancer in the United States. Most cases are a direct consequence of exposure to UV rays, which cause cumulative skin damage over time (American Academy of Dermatology 2016a).

The majority of cases will be cancers of skin cells called *basal cell* or *squamous cell carcinomas* (Crosby and O'Neal 2012). These cancers usually are easily removed by minor surgery, and patients have a good prognosis for recovery. However, about 0.5% of the population will suffer a much more deadly form of skin cancer called *melanoma*. Melanomas are cancers of the pigment-forming cells of the skin, called *melanocytes*, and spread rapidly from the skin throughout the body, ultimately causing 75% of skin cancer–related deaths. Almost 10,000 deaths occur from melanomas each year (American Academy of Dermatology 2016a).

Another long-term concern related to UV exposure is premature aging. Skin frequently exposed to UV rays, such as during routine tanning, experiences deterioration associated with the aging process. Elastin and collagen fibers are damaged, causing a loss of pliability and elasticity in the skin and resulting in a leathery, wrinkled appearance (American Academy of Dermatology 2016b).

Because of these damaging effects of sun exposure, an array of protective sunscreen products is available OTC. Most sunscreens are formulated to screen out the shorter UVB rays. Due to their deep penetration in the skin, the longer UVA rays likely contribute to melanoma as well as chronic skin damage, causing skin to wrinkle, sag, and lose tone; consequently, many of the newer sunscreens block the UVA rays as well (Epstein and Wang 2013).

The protection afforded by sunscreens is designated by an **SPF (sun protection factor) number**.

This designation tells users the relative length of time they can stay in the sun before burning, and includes ratings of 2 to 11 (minimum), 12 to 30 (moderate), and greater than 30 (high) (Crosby and O'Neal 2012). For example, proper application of a product with an SPF of 10 allows users to remain in the sun without burning 10 times longer than if it was not applied. It is important to remember that the SPF designation does not indicate protection against UVA rays. Although there currently is no convenient rating system to assess UVA screening, products with SPF ratings of 15 or greater usually offer some protection against the longer UV radiation. In addition, a compound called avobenzone appears to offer the fullest protection against UVA rays. Because the natural pigment in the skin affords some UV protection, people with fair complexions (less skin pigmentation) require products with higher SPF numbers than do darker-skinned people.

People who want complete protection from UVB exposure can use OTC sunblockers, which prevent any tanning. Sunscreen ingredients in high concentrations essentially become sunblockers. In addition, an opaque zinc oxide ointment is a highly effective and inexpensive sun-blocking product and is available OTC.

SKIN FIRST-AID PRODUCTS

A variety of unrelated OTC drugs are available as first-aid products for the self-treatment of minor skin problems, such as burns, sunburns, and wounds (Drugs.com 2016). Included in this category of agents are the following products:

- Local anesthetics, such as benzocaine (e.g., Dermoplast) to relieve the discomfort and pain of burns or trauma
- Antibiotics and antiseptics, such as bacitracin (Polysporin), neomycin (Neosporin), betadine, and tincture of iodine to treat or prevent skin infections
- Antihistamines (Benadryl) or corticosteroids (hydrocortisone [Cortaid]) to relieve itching or inflammation associated with skin rashes, allergies, or insect bites

These first-aid skin products can be effective when used properly. In general, side effects to such topical products are few and minor when they do occur.

■ OTC Herbal (Natural) Products

The World Health Organization (WHO) reports that 80% of people worldwide use herbal products as part of their primary health care (University of Maryland Medical Center 2015). Herbal products are a unique category of OTC remedies that account for almost $5 billion a year in U.S. sales (Nutraceuticals World 2011). They are unique because, despite the presence of active ingredients, there is little or no federal regulation (Drugs.com 2015) due to a 1994 law, supported by the dietary supplement industry, called the Dietary Supplement Health and Education Act (National Library of Medicine 2010). This law requires the government to demonstrate that substances in the herbal products are harmful before such products can be removed from the market; thus, the burden of proof lies with the FDA, not the manufacturer (Rickert 2012).

This act also (1) makes the manufacturer responsible for its product's safety, (2) explains how product literature is used for product promotion, and (3) describes what can be included on labels. Due to these regulations, manufacturers cannot use terms such as *diagnose, treat, prevent,* or *cure* to describe their herbal products. Companies can, however, make claims about affecting body function. For example, manufacturers of glucosamine cannot claim their product helps cure arthritis, but they can say products with glucosamine help the joints function better (National Library of Medicine 2010). Because of the lack of regulation, these products often are not scientifically tested, and they vary considerably in both the quantity and quality of active ingredients (National Library of Medicine 2010). Herbal products have been viewed with considerable skepticism by many experts who argue that "assertions, speculation and testimonials do not substitute for evidence" when it comes to establishing the value of a drug (McQueen and Orr 2012).

This skin cancer is melanoma and is caused by excessive exposure to ultraviolet light.

© Nasekomoe/Shutterstock

Herbal products have become very popular and widely accepted.

In the past few years, some changes in attitude toward herbal products have occurred. More people, including a few traditional health professionals, believe that some herbs may be useful in the treatment of minor health problems (McQueen and Orr 2012). However, physicians are typically not taught about herbal medicines in medical school and are generally perceived as being ignorant about herbal products and knowing little about their therapeutic value or their ability to interact with prescribed drugs (Medical News Today 2010). Despite greater acceptance, the fact that most people who use herbs to treat medical conditions still consider prescription drugs to be considerably more effective suggests there exists persistent skepticism regarding these products, even among consumers (Lampert 2013).

Frequent uses of herbal products include treatment of anxiety, chronic fatigue, arthritis, and digestive problems (University of Maryland Medical Center 2015). Another common use of these natural products is to elevate mood. The most popular herbs for these purposes are St. John's wort, S-adenosylmethionine (SAM-e), and kava

HERE AND NOW
Herbal Options

With the increasing popularity of herbal products, an array of choices has become available for dealing with many common, usually self-limiting health problems. The following is a list of some of the most popular of these medicinal herbs.

Echinacea

Common claim: Stimulates immune system and helps fight infections.

Common use: Reduce cold symptoms and help accelerate recovery.

Effectiveness: May shorten the duration of a cold, but does not prevent it; however, even this is controversial.

Concerns: Relatively well tolerated, but fatigue and sleepiness occasionally occur.

Garlic

Common claim: Inhibits production of cholesterol and reduces blood sugar.

Common use: Treat diabetes and prevent cardiovascular disease.

Effectiveness: Most studies do not find garlic effective against serious diseases.

Concerns: Mild stomach discomfort and possible interaction with blood-thinning (anticlotting) prescription drugs occur.

Ginkgo Biloba

Common claim: Improves memory.

Common use: Often promoted to enhance memory for patients with Alzheimer's disease.

Effectiveness: At best helps to prevent some mental decline in Alzheimer's patients but does not appear to reverse memory loss or help normal or age-related memory losses.

Concerns: Can interact with blood-thinning medications such as aspirin.

Glucosamine and Chondroitin

Common claim: Contributes to joint strength.

Common use: Relieve the discomfort of arthritis.

Effectiveness: Provides moderate relief from the pain of arthritis and may help to slow progress of the disease.

Concerns: May interact with blood thinners and adversely affect adult-onset diabetes.

Saw Palmetto

Common claim: Relieves discomforts associated with prostate gland.

Common use: Shrink enlarged prostate and facilitate urination.

HERE AND NOW
Herbal Options (*continued*)

Effectiveness: Provides relief for most men within a month of use.

Concerns: Well tolerated by most men.

SAM-e

Common claim: Helps regulate brain transmitters such as dopamine.

Common use: Relieve symptoms of depression.

Effectiveness: Some evidence that it relieves moderate depression.

Concerns: Side effects are typically mild, such as stomach upset, insomnia, and nervousness. Can be very expensive, ranging from $55 to $260 per month.

St. John's Wort

Common claim: Elevates mood.

Common use: Treat mild to moderate depression.

Effectiveness: Appears to relieve some cases of mild depression for the short term.

Concerns: Recent alert from the FDA warns about interactions with numerous medications, such as other antidepressants and birth-control pills.

Ginseng

Common claim: Increases energy.

Common use: Treat fatigue and enhance performance.

Effectiveness: There may be some mild stimulation, but there is no evidence of enhanced performance.

Concerns: Well tolerated for the most part, although there are some reports of minor addiction.

Data from McQueen, C. and K. Orr. "Natural Products." In *Handbook of Nonprescription Drugs,* 17th ed., edited by D. Krinsky, 967-1006. Washington, DC: American Pharmacists Association, 2012; and National Center for Complementary and Aternative Medicine (NCCAM). "Herbs at a Glance." June 2013. Available http://nccam.nih.gov/health/herbsataglance.htm

kava (Hume and Strong 2006; Williams et al. 2005; see "Here and Now: Herbal Options"). It is generally thought that although these products do have some effect in the treatment of minor to moderate depression and anxiety, there is no evidence they elevate a normal, undisturbed mood or that they are particularly effective against severe mood disturbances (National Center for Complementary and Alternative Medicine [NCCAM] 2013). A major risk of self-administering these remedies for mood disorders is that some of the people self-treating their depression are severely emotionally unstable. Overall, depression leads to approximately 20,000 suicides in this country each year. Another considerable problem of self-medicating with herbal products for mood disorders is the lack of standardization for these substances. A recent survey revealed that the actual amount of active SAM-e per pill in products claiming to contain 200 milligrams of active ingredient ranged from 80 to 250 milligrams. For these reasons, it is almost universally recommended that patients with serious emotional disturbances, especially depression, be diagnosed by a mental health professional even though some of these professionals may find use of the natural products to be acceptable for treatment of mild emotional problems.

Other concerns with herbal products include the possibility of interaction with other OTC and prescription medications, especially in the elderly population (Landro 2016; NCCAM 2013). This is becoming more problematic as the routine use of herbs becomes common, especially because unscrupulous manufacturers may deceive customers into thinking that these products are perfectly safe and do not really contain any drugs but "only natural ingredients." Products containing herbs such as garlic, ginkgo biloba, and ginseng have been shown to interact with some drugs . A notable example of drug interactions has been reported with St. John's wort, kava, and Echinacea, which alter the metabolism of drugs used to treat heart failure, asthma, infections, blood clots, and cancer (Landro 2016). Despite such potentially dangerous interactions with prescriptions, 70% of patients claim they do not advise physicians that they regularly use herbal products (Landro 2016).

Finally, lack of regulation has encouraged such a lackadaisical attitude concerning herbs that their use has been trivialized to the extent that they and their associated active drugs are now being included in foods and marketed in both health-food stores and supermarkets. Recent snacks, cereals, and beverages spiked with medicinal herbs include ginseng ginger ale, kava kava corn chips, Echinacea fruit drinks, and ginkgo biloba chocolate bars. These products, sometimes referred to as "functional foods," are typically packaged in colorful containers with cartoon figures that are likely to appeal to kids and accompanied by subtle suggestive promotions implying that they can "support emotional and mental balance." The exact quantities of herbal substances added to such food and snack products and their actual effects (if any) are difficult to monitor. Although concerned, regulatory agencies are uncertain as to how to deal with the potential problems associated with this marketing strategy (Brophy and Schardt 2010).

HERBALS AND ABUSE

Despite the lack of governmental control, drugs found naturally in plants or herbs can have serious side effects or can be abused. In fact, some of the most powerful substances of abuse are extracted from plants, including drugs such as cocaine (*Erythroxylum coca*), marijuana (*Cannabis sativa*), peyote (*Lophophora williamsii*), and tobacco (*Nicotiana tabacum*). These substances are mentioned to emphasize the point that being associated with herbs and natural products does not exclude a drug from being abused. Of concern in this section are unregulated herbal products and their potential for abuse and addiction. As a general rule, if a substance (including a natural product) elevates mood, causes a feeling of energy, or brings on a feeling of relaxation and relief from stress, it likely has potential for abuse. Based on these principles, the herbal products most likely to be abused include those containing ma huang, ginseng, kava kava, and ephedrine (NCCAM 2013). Of course, with addiction typically comes high-quantity use and a greater chance of serious side effects. Even though serious abuse of herbal products is possible, it does not occur frequently and, when it does occur, it is generally relatively easy to treat.

Prescription Drugs

The Durham–Humphrey Amendment of 1951 established the criteria that are still used today to determine whether a drug should be used only under the direction of a licensed health professional, such as a physician. According to this piece of legislation, drugs are controlled with

prescriptions if they are (1) habit-forming, (2) not safe for self-medication, (3) intended to treat ailments that require the supervision of a health professional, or (4) new and without an established safe track record (Katzung 2015b). Currently more than 10,000 prescription products are sold in the United States, representing approximately 1500 different drugs, with 20 to 50 new medications approved each year by the FDA (Borgsdorf 2007; Drugs.com 2013). In 2009, 3.9 billion drug prescriptions were written at a cost of about $300 billion; this cost was expected to rise soon to $400 billion (Bartholow 2010; Kaiser Family Foundation 2010). With statistics like these, it is not surprising that the United States leads the world in prescription drug consumption on a per capita basis (Hanson 2010).

Because of their specialized training, physicians, dentists, and, under certain conditions, podiatrists, physician assistants, nurse practitioners, pharmacists, and optometrists are granted drug-prescribing privileges. The health professionals who write prescriptions are expected to accurately diagnose medical conditions requiring therapy, consider the benefits and risks of drug treatment for the patient, and identify the best drug and safest manner of administering it. The responsibility of the health professional does not conclude with the writing of a prescription; in many ways, it only just begins. Professional monitoring to ensure proper drug use and to evaluate the patient's response is crucial for successful therapy.

▍ Prescription Drug Abuse

Daniel had been sober for a year and half, and his parents thought he had finally gotten his addiction to painkiller prescription drugs under control after multiple attempts at treatment. But for no apparent reason, his drug problems all came back and spiraled out of control. Daniel, a well-liked former hockey player, died at his best friend's house after overdosing on OxyContin and cocaine. "We heard that he had told his girlfriend that he wanted to start again and turn his life around, and that night he overdosed," said his mother (Thomas 2010).

In many places, abuse of prescription drugs is a greater problem than use of illicit drugs. This is supported by the following:

- The overall cost of prescription painkiller abuse is $70 billion per year (O'Toole 2012).
- More than 70 deaths occur each day in the United States due to prescription drugs, the

majority of which are related to use of opioid pain relievers (National Institute on Drug Abuse [NIDA] 2016a).

- More accidental deaths occur from medication overdoses than from car crashes (Biekiempis 2012; Kerlikowske 2012).
- In the past decade, death from overdoses of prescription drugs has increased fivefold in women (Waseem 2013).
- Admissions for treatment of persons addicted to prescription drugs has increased fourfold (Stetka and McCance-Katz 2012; Thomas 2010).
- An average of 5500 people per day use prescription painkillers nonmedically for the first time (Stack 2012).
- The number of emergency department visits for nonmedical use of prescription opioid analgesics has doubled (Quest Diagnostics 2010); specifically, in 2004, 627,000 persons went to emergency rooms due to problems with pharmaceutical drugs, compared to 1.2 million in 2009 (Goodnough 2011).

- Two-thirds of college students have been offered prescription stimulants and on-third have used them for non-medical purposes such as "performance-enhancing" or to lose weight (Brennan 2015)
- Nearly 70% of those who misuse prescription painkillers obtain their drugs from friends or relatives (free, paid for, or stolen) and not from a legitimate prescriber (Stack 2012).
- In the United States, we prescribe enough opioid narcotics each year to medicate every adult around the clock for 1 month (Stack 2012).

The three classes of prescription drugs most likely to be abused, in order of their abuse frequency, are narcotic analgesics, CNS depressants, and stimulants (used to treat obesity and attention deficit hyperactivity disorder [ADHD]). Particularly troubling is what appears to be an exploding epidemic of abusing prescription narcotic painkilling drugs such as OxyContin and Vicodin (Johnston 2016; U.S. Department of Health and Human Services [HHS] 2016). Headlines

HERE AND NOW

Another Celebrity Death from Prescription Drug Abuse

The music megastar known as Prince (Prince Rogers Nelson) died from a prescription overdose on April 21, 2016. Authorities confirmed that the 57-year-old rock star was addicted to pain medications. However, at his death little was known about his past use of these drugs or how he was able to obtain them. An autopsy revealed no trauma and no evidence of foul play. It was also concluded that his death was not an act of suicide but rather accidental. It is believed his abuse of these opioid analgesics began after a hip surgery several years prior due to his energetic stage performances. Friends have revealed that at the time of death attempts were being made to persuade Prince to enroll in a treatment program to deal with his opioid drug addiction. Reports from the Medical Examiner's office claim that the cause of Prince's death was self-administration of the powerful opioid narcotic fentanyl. This opioid analgesic is the most potent (approximately 100 times more potent than morphine and 20 to 40 times more potent than heroin) of all the opioid drugs prescribed for pain relief. Although it is often used to manage cancer-related pain, because

of its potency and rapid action it has become a favorite drug for narcotic abusers. Because of fentanyl's potency and low cost (it is cheaper than heroin), drug dealers often add it to their street drugs to enhance their effects. In high doses or in combination with other CNS-depressing drugs, fentanyl can kill in seconds. This certainly is not the first time that fentanyl has contributed to the narcotic overdose death of an unsuspecting user, and certainly will not be the last.

© Anthony Correia/Shutterstock

Data from Hayes, A. "Prince Died from Fentanyl Overdose." WebMD Magazine. 2016. Available http://www.webmd.com/mental-health/addiction/news /20160602/prince-fentanyl-overdose; Sickles, J. "Prince Cause of Death: Opioid Overdose, Tests Reportedly Show." Yahoo News. 2016. Available https://www .yahoo.com/news/prince-cause-death-000000903.html announcing a celebrity seeking treatment for dependence on, or even death because of, these drugs are becoming disturbingly routine (see "Here and Now: Another Celebrity Death from Prescription Drug Abuse"). In fact, as mentioned earlier, abuse of prescription narcotics appears to be the leading problem with prescription drugs (Waseem 2013). Often young people abuse a combination of these prescribed drugs, and their sources include the medicine cabinets in their parents' or friends' homes or the Internet from "web pharmacies" that do not require legitimate prescriptions (Twelve Keys 2015). This is a problem with youth and adults from all backgrounds.

In order to deal with this escalating problem, it is important to determine why nonmedical prescription drug abuse occurs. Although there are many general and personal explanations for why a person takes medications that were not prescribed for them, the most frequent are as follows (Health Day News 2012; McCabe, Boyd, and Teter 2009):

- 13% abuse the prescription drugs for recreation, usually to get high or to try to feel better.
- 39% try to self-medicate a preexisting medical/emotional problem with someone else's prescription medication (e.g., use a benzodiazepine to relieve anxiety).
- 48% have elements of both of the above explanations.
- Prescription abuse can be part of a bigger picture of substance abuse that includes the abuse of other drugs (both licit and illicit). One drug may be used to either embellish or relieve withdrawal from another drug of abuse (e.g., benzodiazepines taken to relieve the withdrawal from alcohol) (NIDA 2016c).

HERE AND NOW
Pharm Parties and Russian Roulette

One expression of prescription drug abuse is seen with high school students who bring samples of prescription drugs from home and dump them into a common bowl. The teens then grab a handful and pop them into their mouths like trail mix and swallow. The objective is to try to produce bizarre feelings and unusual highs. The mixtures often include medications such as antidepressants, stimulants, sleeping pills, antianxiety drugs, and narcotic pain relievers. One doctor described the activity as "Russian roulette," only with pills instead of bullets. The source of the drugs is often parents' or grandparents' medicine cabinets that frequently are filled with years of drug accumulation. For example, one 15-year-old said he wanted to be "cool" and told his friends that he could get some Percocets out of his stepdad's bottle. He explained that his stepdad had undergone many surgeries, so he had a lot of pills. The young man explained that the pills went down quick and the smooth buzz was free and everyone thought it was safe. Soon other friends joined the group and each would bring medicines from their own homes—a little Vicodin here, some OxyContin there, usually with some whiskey and vodka to wash it down. As word got around, other friends joined the "cool" group and more prescription drugs were pooled and the activity had escalated into a "pharm party." Although at first everything seemed innocent and fun, the group soon learned that use of high quantities and mixed assortments of drugs that belong to someone else can be disastrous and even deadly.

Data from Fagan, K. "'Pharma Parties: A Troubling Trend Among Youths." *San Francisco Chronicle*. (16 March 2010). Available http://www.sfgate.com/bayarea/article/Pharma-parties-a-troubling-trend-among-youths-3270176.php; Negrete, D. "Pharm Parties, Finds Place Among Teens." STJOECHANNEL.com. 2016. Available http://www.stjoechannel.com/news/local-news/pharm-parties-finds-place-among-teens; Valley, J. "'Pharm Parties,' Designer Drugs Among Trends for High Schoolers." *Las Vegas Sun*. (19 April 2012). Available http://www.lasvegassun.com/news/2012/apr/19/pharm-parties-designer-drugs-among-trends-high-sch/#axzz2XuZw4jK2; WIXT/WSYR, TV ABC 9. "Pharm Parties. Popping Prescriptions." Syracuse. 18 May 2007.

Dealing with suspected abuse of prescription medication can pose a difficult management problem for physicians and pharmacists. It has become such a major issue that some third-party payers (i.e., health insurance companies) have implemented tight monitoring procedures. Those who try to fraudulently obtain controlled substances with valid and invalid prescriptions include persons from all walks of life.

In the United States, young people frequently abuse prescription drugs. One trend is called "pharm parties," where high school students get together and try to get high on a mixture of prescription drugs followed by a chaser of alcohol (Valley 2012; see "Here and Now: Pharm Parties and Russian Roulette"). However, young people rarely obtain the drugs by theft, fraud, or doctor shopping, although occasionally unscrupulous doctors will write prescriptions without questions for money (Negrete 2016). Instead, they usually obtain their prescription drugs from peers, friends, or family members or sometimes purchase them from rogue Internet pharmacies (Negrete 2016). In some areas, the problem is so severe that high schools have implemented programs to prevent such sharing.

Abusers of prescription drugs often have multiple addictions, including dependence on caffeine, alcohol, or nicotine. In addition, once a pharmacy is recognized as an easy target, word spreads and other abusers often begin to frequent the same store. Signs of patients with drug-seeking behavior include the following:

- Use of altered or forged prescriptions
- Claims that a prescription has been lost and a physician is unavailable for confirmation
- Frequent visits to emergency rooms or clinics for poorly defined health problems
- Visits made to a pharmacy late in the day, on weekends, or just before closing
- Alteration of doses on a legitimate prescription
- Loud, abusive, and insulting behavior
- Use of several names
- Being particularly knowledgeable about drugs

■ Prescription Abuse and Pregnancy

It has been said that babies born to mothers addicted to prescription drugs have become the youngest victims of the prescription abuse epidemic. In excess of 22,000 babies are born annually who are physically dependent on the prescription analgesics to which their mothers are addicted and experience withdrawal after birth (NIDA 2015). This disturbing outcome includes a newborn who within days after birth, for no apparent reason, experienced vomiting with diarrhea, extreme irritability and shaking, inability to sleep, trouble eating, and frequent shrieking from pain. Infants such as this are manifesting withdrawal symptoms caused by their in utero exposure to the drugs (usually prescription narcotics) the mother consumed in large quantities during pregnancy. Although these infants are sometimes described as addicted to their mothers' drugs, this is inaccurate. Their bodies have become physically dependent on the substances the newborns were exposed to during development; after birth their bodies are abruptly removed from drug exposure and thrown into a withdrawal reaction. These drug-dependent babies should remain in the hospital for weeks or months while they are gradually weaned from the drug on which they are physically dependent. These babies put a tremendous financial strain on our healthcare systems, costing an average of about $50,000 per child. As stated by a maternal–fetal medicine specialist, "They are the innocent victims. They had no control over it and yet they suffer tremendously for it" (Olian 2012).

■ Necessary Drug Information for Healthcare Providers

Many unnecessary side effects and delays in proper care are caused by poor communication between the health professional and the patient or by a doctor's lack of knowledge concerning the patient's medical history when a drug is prescribed. The smaller a drug's margin of safety (i.e., the difference between therapeutic and toxic doses), the more critical it becomes that the doctor has all relevant information regarding the patient's medical needs and vulnerabilities. The following is a brief overview of principles to help ensure that the health professional has the necessary information to properly prescribe and manage drug use for the patient.

Doctor–patient communication must be reciprocal. We tend to think that patients listen while doctors talk when it comes to deciding on the best medication for treatment. To ensure a proper diagnosis, precise and complete information from the patient is also essential. In fact, if a doctor is to select the best and safest drug for a patient, he or she needs to know everything possible about the medical problems to be treated. In addition, the patient should provide the doctor with a complete medical and drug history, particularly if there has been a problem with the patient's cardiovascular system, kidneys, liver, or mental functions. Other information that should be shared with the doctor includes previous drug reactions as well as a complete list of drugs routinely being used, including prescription, nonprescription, and herbal products. In this regard, more and more states are establishing database systems that include up-to-date information concerning prescription drug histories that allow monitoring of what has been prescribed and dispensed to individual patients. Currently, most states have passed legislation authorizing, and in some cases mandating, such programs, but making these databases real-time can be extremely expensive and must adequately address issues such as patient confidentiality (Small 2013; Vestal 2016). However, it is hoped that eventually there will be a nationwide program that allows pharmacies, doctors, and other medical personnel to contribute to and access information from the prescription drug history of their patients in order to avoid dangerous and unnecessary prescribing practices and to be aware of potential prescription abuse problems.

The patient needs to be educated about proper drug use. If the doctor does not volunteer this information, the patient should insist on answers to the following questions:

- *What is being treated?* This question does not require a long, unintelligible scientific answer.

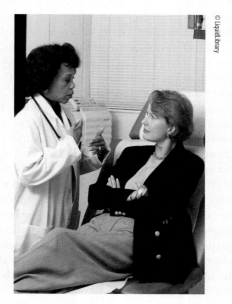

In order to maximize benefit and minimize risk, there must be proper doctor–patient communication.

It should include an easy-to-understand explanation of the medical problem.

- *What is the desired outcome?* The patient should know why the drug is being prescribed and what the drug treatment is intended to accomplish. It is difficult for the patient to become involved in therapy if he or she is not aware of its objectives.
- *What are the possible side effects of the drug?* This answer does not necessitate an exhaustive list of every adverse reaction ever recorded in the medical literature; however, it is important to realize that adverse drug reactions to prescription drugs are very common. In the United States, more people die from adverse reactions to legal medications than succumb to all illegal drug use. It is estimated that approximately 20,000 people die while another 2.1 million are seriously injured in this country each year from reactions to legal medications (Alton 2016). In general, if adverse reactions occur in more than 1% of users, this should be mentioned to the patient. In addition, the patient should be made aware of ways to minimize the occurrence of side effects (e.g., an irritating drug should not be taken on an empty stomach, to minimize nausea), as well as what to do if a side effect occurs (e.g., if a rash occurs, call the doctor immediately).
- *How should the drug be taken to minimize problems and maximize benefits?* This answer should include details on how much, how often, and how long the drug should be taken.
- *How should the drug be disposed of?* This should include a discussion of the facts concerning proper and safe elimination of prescription drugs (see "Here and Now: Do Not Flush! Do Not Pour!").

Although it is a health professional's legal and professional obligation to communicate this information, patients frequently leave the doctor's office with a prescription that gives them legal permission to use a drug but without the knowledge of how to use it properly. Because of this all-too-common problem, pharmacists have been mandated by legislation referred to as the Omnibus Budget Reconciliation Act of 1990 to provide the necessary information to patients on proper drug use (Centers for Medicare and Medicaid Services [CMS] 2016; see "Here and Now: OBRA '90: The Evolving Role of Pharmacists in Drug Management"). Patients should be encouraged to ask questions of those who write and fill prescriptions.

HERE AND NOW
Do Not Flush! Do Not Pour!

Most of us have prescription drugs we no longer need sitting in our medicine cabinets or in other unsecured places. Often these medications have long passed their recommended expiration dates or intended use, but due to ignorance or neglect they become forgotten and a potential risk to an inquisitive child, to someone who is tempted to use them for medical purposes other than those for which they were prescribed, or to someone who is desperately looking to steal drugs to satisfy a substance abuse problem. To avoid these undesirable outcomes, along with water pollution, it is important for patients to be educated about the proper use and disposal of their prescription drugs. For safe management of prescription drugs, the following guidelines should be observed:

- *Don't flush unused prescription drugs down the toilet or pour them down the drain.* Some drugs that are disposed of in our sewers end up in our water systems, causing pollution and damaging the environment. This is not a desirable method of disposing of prescription substances.

- *Don't throw unused prescription drugs into the garbage.* Because abuse of some of the prescription drugs such as opioid painkillers is very common, often persons with substance abuse problems check the garbage cans of acquaintances and strangers alike for unused drugs that satisfy their intense cravings.

- *Prescription drugs still being used should be safely secured.* Keeping in mind the potential danger and abuse of many prescription drugs, it is important that these substances be stored in a secure place that can be locked and is inaccessible to children and unintended users.

- *Disposal of unused prescription drugs at approved permanent collection sites is preferred.* Steel-mounted metal drug disposal bins are usually available at approved law enforcement stations or offices. The prescription drugs can be anonymously deposited in the bins for frequent removal by law enforcement officers and then transferred to special facilities for incineration.

- *Prescription medicines can be safely disposed of at home.* If there is not access to a permanent collection site, safe disposal at home can be achieved by mixing all unused drugs with an undesirable substance such as coffee grounds, moist unused cat litter, or spoiled food and putting it into a sealable plastic bag. The bag should be wrapped with duct tape or placed in a solid container. If the medications are solid, water should be added to dissolve them before mixing. The container should then be thrown away on the day of garbage collection. When disposing of the drug container, be sure all identifying personal information has been removed or destroyed.

In 2014 the Drug Enforcement Administration (DEA) posted a final ruling for the public entitled the Disposal Act, which gives the DEA authority to create and enforce regulations that allow prescription drug users to deliver unused pharmaceutical controlled substances to appropriate facilities (such as pharmacies) for safe and effective disposal. The objective is to encourage public and private users of these drugs to eliminate unnecessary controlled medications in an efficient, secure, and convenient manner, thereby minimizing the likelihood of illegal diversion and abuse of these products.

This is a secure drug disposal box now available in some pharmacies throughout the country for secure disposal of unused controlled prescription substances.

Data from Drug Enforcement Administration (DEA). "Disposal of Controlled Substances; Final Rule. 21 CFR Parts 1300, 1301, 1304 et al." *Federal Register* 79 (2014). Available http://www.deadiversion.usdoj.gov/fed_regs/rules/2014/2014-20926.pdf; Use Only As Directed. "Safe Disposal: Learn the Facts." Utah State Division of Substance Abuse. 24 June 2013. Available http://www.useonlyasdirected.org/safe-disposal; Disposal Act 2016.

HERE AND NOW

OBRA '90: The Evolving Role of Pharmacists in Drug Management

In 1990, the U.S. Congress passed section 4401 of the Omnibus Budget Reconciliation Act (commonly referred to as OBRA '90), which substantially altered the role of pharmacists in drug management. This act designated the pharmacist as the key player in improving the quality of drug care for patients in this country. Because OBRA '90 is federal legislation, it can require drug-related services for Medicare patients only; however, most states have recognized that similar services should be made available to all patients and have enacted legislation to that end. OBRA '90 requires pharmacists to conduct a drug use review (DUR) for each prescription to improve the outcome of drug therapy and reduce adverse side effects. The DUR program describes four basic professional services that a pharmacist must render whenever a drug prescription is filled:

1. Prescriptions and patients' records must be screened to avoid problems caused by drug duplications, adverse drug–drug interactions, medical complications, incorrect drug doses, and incorrect duration of drug treatment.

2. Patients should be counseled regarding the following:
   - How to safely and effectively administer the drug
   - Common adverse effects and interactions with other drugs, food, and so forth
   - How to avoid problems with the drug
   - How to monitor the progress of drug therapy
   - How to store the drug properly
   - Whether a refill is intended
   - What to do if a dose is missed

3. Patient profiles, including information on disease, a list of medications, and the pharmacist's comments relevant to drug therapy, must be maintained. This information should be stored in computer files for future reference.

4. Documentation must record if the patient refuses consultation from the pharmacist or if a potential drug therapy problem is identified and the patient is warned.

   Note: In 2016, the OBRA '90 act was still being enforced.

Data from Abood, R. "OBRA '90: Implementation and Enforcement." *NABP U.S. Pharmacists, State Boards—A Continuing Education Series*. Park Ridge, IL: National Association of Pharmacy, 1992.

▮ Drug Selection: Generic Versus Proprietary

Although it is the primary responsibility of the doctor or healthcare provider to decide which drug is most suitable for a treatment, often an inexpensive choice can be as effective and as safe as a more costly option. This statement frequently is true when choosing between generic and proprietary drugs. The term **generic** refers to the common name of a drug that is not subject to trademark rights; in contrast, **proprietary** denotes medications marketed under specific brand

KEY TERMS

generic
official, nonpatented, nonproprietary name of a drug

proprietary
brand or trademark name that is registered with the U.S. Patent Office

names (FDA 2016a). For example, diazepam is the generic designation for the proprietary name Valium. Often, the most common proprietary name associated with a drug is the name given when it is initially released for marketing. Because such drugs are almost always covered by patent restrictions for several years when first sold to the public, they become identified with their first proprietary names. After the patent lapses, the same drug often is also marketed by its less known generic designation (Stoppler and Hecht 2010).

Because the pharmaceutical companies that market the generic products usually have not invested in the discovery or development of the drug, they often charge much less for their version of the medication. This situation contrasts with that of the original drug manufacturer, which may have invested as much as $2.6 billion for research and development. Even though the generic product frequently is less expensive, because of FDA regulations the quality is not inferior to the related proprietary drug; thus, substitution of generic for proprietary products usually does not compromise therapy (eMedExpert 2016).

Because of reduced cost, generic products have become very popular. Currently, generic drugs account for approximately 80% of prescriptions dispensed (Stone 2013), up from 57% in 2004, and they cost approximately 80% less than corresponding proprietary drugs (FDA 2016a). Due to the high demand, all states have laws that govern the use and substitution of generic drugs; unfortunately, the laws are not all the same. Some states have positive laws that require pharmacists to substitute a generic product unless the physician gives specific instructions not to do so. Other states have negative laws that forbid substitution without the physician's permission. Some physicians use convenient prescription forms with "May" or "May

Not" substitution boxes that can be checked when the prescription is filled out.

■ Common Categories of Prescription Drugs

Of the approximately 10,000 different prescription drugs available in the United States, the top 50 drugs in sales account for almost 30% of all new and refilled prescriptions. As an example, a list of the 20 top-selling prescription drugs for the first quarter of 2015 is shown in **Table 15.6**. The following includes a brief discussion of some of the more popular prescription drug groups used in the United States. This list is not intended to be all-inclusive, but gives only a sampling of common prescription products.

TABLE 15.6 The Top 20 Prescription Drugs by U.S. Sales: 2015

Rank	Proprietary Name	Generic Name	Principal Clinical Use	Sales ($ billion)
1	Harvoni	Ledipasvir	Treat hepatitis C	14.3
2	Humira	Adalimumab	Reduce swelling	10.6
3	Enbrel	Etanercept	Treat autoimmune disease	6.6
4	Crestor	Rosuvastatin	Reduce cholesterol	6.3
5	Lantus Solostar	Human (long-lasting) insulin	Treat diabetes	5.8
6	Remicade	Infliximab	Treat Crohn's disease	5.0
7	Adair Discus	Salmeterol	Bronchodilator/asthma	4.7
8	Abilify	Aripiprazole	Antipsychotic	4.4
9	Copaxone	Glatiramer	Treat multiple sclerosis	4.4
10	Januvia	Sitagliptin	Treat type 2 diabetes	4.2
11	Neulasta	Pegfilgrastim	Treat neutropenia	4.1
12	Lyrica	Gabapentin	Treat pain (fibromyalgia)	3.8
13	Lantes	Human insulin	Treat diabetes	3.8
14	Rituxan	Rituximab	Suppress immune system	3.6
15	Nexium	Esomeprazole	Relieve ulcers	3.5
16	Tecfidera	Dimethyl Fumarate	Treat multiple sclerosis	3.5
17	Spiriva	Tiotropium	Treat emphysema	3.4
18	Avastin	Bevacizumab	Treat cancer	3.1
19	Sovaldi	Sofosbuvir	Treat Hepatitis C	3.0
20	Atripla	efavirenz	Treat AIDS	2.9

Data from Statista. "Top 20 Prescription Drugs Based on U.S. Sales in 2015." The Statistical Portal. 2016. Available http://www .statista.com/statistics/258010/top-branded-drugs-based-on-retail-sales-in-the-us/

ANALGESICS

The prescription analgesics consist mainly of narcotic and NSAID types. The narcotic analgesics most often dispensed to patients by prescription are (1) codeine and hydrocodone (e.g., Lortab, Vicodin), (2) the moderate-potency agents pentazocine (e.g., Talwin) and oxycodone (e.g., Percodan), and (3) the high-potency drug morphine. All narcotic analgesics are scheduled drugs because of their abuse potential and are effective against most types of pain. The narcotic analgesic products are often combined with aspirin or acetaminophen (e.g., Lortab and Vicodin are combinations of hydrocodone and acetaminophen) to enhance their pain-relieving actions. These are the most likely prescription drugs to be abused and can cause severe substance dependence and devastate lives when not managed properly (see "Here and Now: A Blackbox for Painkillers"). Unfortunately, because of concern about abuse of the prescription painkillers, many patients with legitimate pain symptoms are inadequately treated to relieve their extreme discomfort for fear by the prescribers that they may be contributing to the development of a narcotic addict (Dowell, Haegerich, and Chou 2016).

The NSAIDs constitute the other major group of analgesics available by prescription. The pharmacology of these drugs is very similar to that of the OTC compound ibuprofen, discussed earlier in this chapter. These medications are used to relieve inflammatory conditions such as arthritis and are effective in relieving minor to moderate musculoskeletal pain (pain associated with body structures such as muscles, ligaments, bones, teeth, and skin). These drugs have no abuse potential and are not scheduled; several are also available OTC (see the discussion of OTC analgesics). Their principal adverse side effects include stomach irritation, kidney damage, tinnitus (ringing in the ears), dizziness, and swelling from fluid retention. Most prescription NSAIDs have similar pharmacological and side effects. Included in the group of prescription NSAIDs are ibuprofen (e.g., Motrin), naproxen (e.g., Anaprox), indomethacin (e.g., Indocin),

sulindac (e.g., Clinoril), mefenamic acid (e.g., Ponstel), tolmetin (e.g., Tolectin), piroxicam (e.g., Feldene), and ketoprofen (e.g., Orudis) (Borazan and Furst 2015).

ANTIBIOTICS

Drugs referred to by the layperson as "antibiotics" are more accurately described by the term *antibacterials*, although the more common term will be used here. For the most part, antibiotics are effective in treating infections caused by microorganisms classified as bacteria. Bacterial infections can occur anywhere in the body, resulting in tissue damage, loss of function, and, if untreated, ultimately death. Even though bacterial infections continue to be the most common serious diseases in the United States and throughout the world today, the vast majority of these can be cured with antibiotic treatment.

Close to 100 different antibiotic drugs are available, which differ from one another in (1) whether they kill bacteria (*bactericidal*) or stop their growth (*bacteriostatic*) and (2) the species of bacteria that are sensitive to their antibacterial action. Antibiotics that are effective against many species of bacteria are classified as *broad-spectrum types*, whereas those antibiotics that are relatively selective and effective against only a few species of bacteria are considered *narrow-spectrum types*.

Although most antibiotics are well tolerated by patients, they can cause very serious side effects, especially if not used properly. For example, the penicillins have a very wide margin of safety for most patients, but 5% to 10% of the population is allergic to these drugs, and life-threatening reactions can occur in sensitized patients if penicillins are used.

The most common groups of antibiotics include penicillins (e.g., amoxicillin [Amoxil, Augmentin, and Trimox]), cephalosporins (e.g., cephalexin), fluoroquinolones (e.g., ciprofloxacin [Cipro]), tetracyclines (e.g., minocycline [Minocin]), aminoglycosides (e.g., streptomycin), sulfonamides (e.g., sulfamethoxazole [Bactrim and Septra]), and macrolides (e.g., erythromycin [E-Mycin]) (Chemotherapeutic Drugs 2015).

HERE AND NOW
A Black Box for Opioid Painkillers

Experts and government officials claim that opioid abuse, severe dependence, and overdose consequences have reached epidemic levels in the United States and elsewhere. Consequently, the FDA has been called upon to do its part to reverse these very disturbing trends. In response to these expectations,

HERE AND NOW
A Black Box for Opioid Painkillers (*continued*)

the FDA has announced label changes on prescription opioid medications that are designed to educate prescribers and patients about the potential dangers related to use of both extended-release/long-acting (ER/LA) opioids intended for use once or twice a day and immediate-release (IR) opioids intended for use every 4 to 6 hours. The FDA has mandated two types of label changes. First, the FDA now requires the placement of a "black box" advisory on all single-drug opioid analgesics that includes precautions about the potentially serious consequences of misuse, abuse, addiction and overdose deaths, as well as warnings about the risks of chronic use of opioids during pregnancy and the association with neonatal withdrawal syndrome [NOWS]). Second, the FDA has mandated changes in the labeling of opioid analgesics so that labels now include information related to a drug's (1) indications, (2) limitations of use, (3) serious risks, and (4) safety information concerning potentially harmful drug interactions that can affect the CNS, adrenal glands and sex hormone levels. Although not yet included, it is anticipated that after review of causes for life-threatening opioid overdose

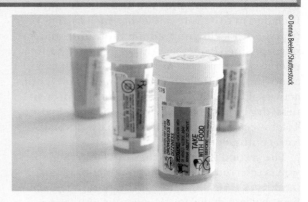

consequences the FDA also will require the addition of label information on the potentially serious outcomes related to opioid interactions with antianxiety drugs (e.g., benzodiazepines). In addition to these required label changes for opioid painkiller products, the FDA is also considering its role in promoting the use of the opioid antagonist drug naloxone as a rescue medication to prevent opioid overdose death and expanding access to the use of medication-assisted treatment with drugs such as methadone and buprenorphine.

Data from Food and Drug Administration (FDA). "FDA Announces Enhanced Warnings for Immediate-Release Opioid Pain Medications." FDA News Release. 22 March 2016. Available http://www.fda.gov/NewsEvents/Newsroom/PressAnnouncements/ucm491739.htm

ANTIDEPRESSANTS

Severe depression is characterized by diminished interest or pleasure in normal activities accompanied by feelings of fatigue, pessimism, and guilt, as well as sleep and appetite disturbances and suicidal desires (American Psychiatric Association [APA] 2013). Major depression afflicts approximately 6% to 7% of the population at any one time, and it is estimated that about 23% of the population will become severely depressed during their life (National Center for Health Statistics [NCHS] 2016). This high prevalence makes depression the most common psychiatric disorder. According to the American Psychiatric Association's (2013) classification in the *Diagnostic and Statistical Manual of Mental Disorders*, fifth edition, several types of depression exist, based on their origin:

- *Endogenous major depression*: A genetic disorder that can occur spontaneously and is due to transmitter imbalances in the brain.

- *Depression associated with bipolar mood disorder*: That is, manic-depressive disorder.
- *Drug-induced depression*: The depressive symptoms are associated with the ingestion, injection, or inhalation of a substance (e.g., drug abuse, toxin, psychotropic medication, or other medication), and the symptoms persist beyond the expected length of physiological effects, intoxication, or withdrawal period. The relevant depressive disorder should have developed during or within 1 month after use of the depression-inducing substance.
- *Reactive depression*: The most common form of depression, which is a response to situations of grief, personal loss, illness, or other very stressful situations.

Antidepressant medication is typically used to treat endogenous major depression, although on occasion these drugs are used to treat other forms of depression if they are resistant to conventional therapy (DeBatista 2015).

Several groups of prescription antidepressant medications are approved for use in the United States (DeBatista 2015). The most commonly used category is the **tricyclic antidepressants**. Included in this group are drugs such as amitriptyline (Elavil), imipramine (Tofranil), and nortriptyline (Pamelor). Although usually well tolerated, the tricyclic antidepressants can cause annoying side effects due to their anticholinergic activity. These adverse reactions include drowsiness, dry mouth, blurred vision, and constipation. Tolerance to these side effects usually develops with continued use.

The second group of drugs used to treat depression is referred to as the **monoamine oxidase inhibitors (MAOIs)**. Historically, these agents have been backup drugs for the tricyclic antidepressants. Because of their annoying and sometimes dangerous side effects, as well as problems interacting with other drugs or even food, the MAOIs have become less popular with clinicians. These drugs can have deadly interactions with many of the stimulants of abuse, such as methamphetamine, cocaine, and Ecstasy. Drugs belonging to this group include phenelzine (Nardil) and tranylcypromine (Parnate).

Agents from a third, somewhat disparate group of antidepressants that are safer and have fewer side effects than the tricyclic or MAOI antidepressants are very popular. They include fluoxetine (Prozac), sertraline (Zoloft), paroxetine (Paxil), uvoxamine (Luvox), bupropion (Wellbutrin), trazodone (Desyrel), and duloxetine (Cymbalta). Although the side effects and margin of safety of these groups of antidepressants may differ, in general they all appear to have similar therapeutic benefits. Of this third group of antidepressants, Prozac is the best known and used to be the most frequently prescribed antidepressant; in 2003 it was the 11th most frequently prescribed drug in the United States. However, by 2009 it had been replaced by other antidepressants such as Lexapro (escitalopram). Although most commonly used to treat depression, Prozac has also been prescribed by physicians to treat more than 30 other conditions ranging from drug addiction (although not found to be generally effective) to kleptomania. The vast majority of these uses are not proven to be effective nor are they approved by the FDA.

ANTIDIABETIC DRUGS

Diabetes mellitus is likely the leading metabolic endocrine disease in this country; it afflicts approximately 29 million people in the United States (21 million diagnosed and 8 million undiagnosed), with 86 million Americans considered "prediabetic" (i.e., in early stages but likely to progress to full expression) (American Diabetes Association [ADA] 2016). Of the 20 top-selling prescription drugs, three are for the treatment of diabetes (see Table 15.6). It is the result of insufficient or ineffective activity of insulin, a hormone secreted from the pancreas (Kennedy and Mashirani 2015). Due to the lack of insulin, untreated diabetics have severe problems with cellular and systemic metabolism and elevated blood sugar (called **hyperglycemia**). The two major types of diabetes are type 1 and type 2. **Type 1 diabetes** is caused by total destruction of the insulin-producing cells in the pancreas and

Insulin is self-administered by diabetic patients in subcutaneous injections.

© Photodisc

KEY TERMS

tricyclic antidepressants
most commonly used group of drugs to treat severe depression

monoamine oxidase inhibitors (MAOIs)
drugs used to treat severe depression

diabetes mellitus
disease caused by elevated blood sugar due to insufficient insulin

hyperglycemia
elevated blood sugar

type 1 diabetes
disease associated with complete loss of insulin-producing cells in the pancreas

Obesity in young children has reached epidemic status and is causing type 2 diabetes to occur at a younger age.

usually begins in juveniles, although it occasionally begins during adulthood. In contrast, **type 2 diabetes**, which used to be called *adult-onset diabetes*, typically occurs after age 40 and is frequently associated with obesity. Recently, however, because severe obesity is occurring more often in younger persons (about 17% of Americans), an epidemic of type 2 diabetes has erupted in adolescents (Woolston 2016), making the term *adult-onset diabetes* less meaningful. In type 2 diabetes, the pancreas is able to produce insulin, but insulin receptors no longer respond normally to this hormone (Woolston 2016). In both types of diabetes mellitus, drugs are administered to restore proper insulin function.

Because people with type 1 diabetes are unable to produce or release insulin, these patients are universally treated with subcutaneous injections of insulin one to three times per day, depending on their needs. Usually the levels of sugar (glucose) in the blood are evaluated to determine the effectiveness of treatment. Insulin products are characterized by their onset of action (either rapid or delayed onset) and duration (short to long) (Kennedy and Masharani 2015).

The strategy for treating type 2 diabetics is somewhat different. For many of these patients, the symptoms of diabetes and problems of insufficient insulin function subside with proper diet, weight, and exercise management. If an appropriate change in lifestyle does not correct the diabetes-associated problems, drugs called **oral hypoglycemic** (meaning they are taken by mouth and lower blood sugar) are often prescribed. These drugs, which stimulate the release of additional insulin from the pancreas, include popular drugs such as rosiglitazone (Avandia). Recently, however, concerns have been raised that although

these drugs are effective in controlling glucose levels, some of them might increase the incidence of cardiovascular disease (Kennedy 2012). If the diabetic symptoms are not adequately controlled with the oral hypoglycemic drugs, type 2 diabetics are treated with insulin injections, as are type 1 patients. The treatment of diabetes has improved substantially in recent years due to new, more selective and effective drugs that control glucose blood levels (Kennedy and Masharani 2015).

ANTIULCER DRUGS

Peptic ulcers are sores that recur in the lining of the lower stomach (gastric ulcer) or most often in the upper portion of the small intestine (duodenal ulcer). It is apparent that secretions of gastric acids and digestive enzymes are necessary for ulcer development. Because gastric secretions are involved in developing peptic ulcers, several drug types are useful in ulcer treatment.

Antacids help to relieve acute discomfort due to ulcers by neutralizing gastric acidity. These drugs are discussed in greater detail in the OTC section of this chapter. Prescription drugs that block gastric secretion have been the mainstay of ulcer treatment. Because the endogenous chemical histamine is important in regulating gastric secretions, drugs that selectively block the activity of gastric histamine (called H2 blockers) substantially reduce secretion of gastric acids and digestive enzymes. The very popular drugs cimetidine (Tagamet), ranitidine (Zantac), and famotidine (Pepcid) function in this manner. Because Tagamet, Zantac, and Pepcid are used so frequently, that they have been switched to OTC status by the FDA—not to treat ulcers but to relieve heartburn (esophageal reflux) (McQuaid 2015).

Although the exact causes of peptic ulcers are not completely understood, it is widely accepted that the bacteria *Helicobacter pylori* play a role. Because of the involvement of these microorganisms, most clinicians treat patients with recurring

KEY TERMS

type 2 diabetes
disease usually associated with obesity; does not involve a loss of insulin-producing cells

oral hypoglycemics
drugs taken by mouth to treat type 2 diabetes

peptic ulcers
open sores that occur in the stomach or upper segment of the small intestine

ulcers with multiple antibiotics to eliminate these bacteria (McQuaid 2015).

BRONCHODILATORS

Drugs that widen air passages (bronchi) facilitate breathing in patients with air passage constriction or obstruction. Such drugs are called **bronchodilators** and are particularly useful in relieving respiratory difficulty associated with asthma. Asthmatic patients frequently experience bouts of intense coughing, shortness of breath, tightness in the chest, and wheezing resulting in breathing difficulties. Many of the symptoms of asthma are due to an increased sensitivity of the airways to irritating substances and can result in serious asthma attacks that are life-threatening if not treated promptly (Galanter and Boushey 2015). Two major categories of bronchodilators are the sympathomimetics known as **beta-adrenergic stimulants**—for example, isoproterenol (Isuprel) and albuterol (Proventil, Ventolin)—and xanthines (caffeine-like drugs) such as theophylline and its derivatives. These drugs relax the muscles of the air passages, cause bronchodilation, and facilitate breathing. In the early 1990s, some bronchodilators were switched to OTC status, such as Bronkaid Mist and Primatene Mist. These contain relatively low amounts of epinephrine and are safe and effective when used for mild, intermittent disease. Typically these OTC medications should not be used by patients with cardiovascular disease (MedicineNet 2013) and may dangerously interact with sympathomimetic stimulants of abuse such as cocaine and the amphetamines.

CARDIOVASCULAR DRUGS

Cardiovascular disease has been the number one cause of death in the United States for the past several decades. Consequently, of the 20 top-selling drugs in this country, two are medications for diseases related to the cardiovascular system (see Table 15.6). The following are brief discussions of the major categories of cardiovascular drugs (National Heart, Lung, and Blood Institute [NHLBI] 2016).

ANTIHYPERTENSIVE AGENTS

It is estimated that about 29% of U.S. adults have **hypertension** (persistent elevated high blood pressure) (Benowitz 2012). Because hypertension can result in serious damage to the heart, kidneys, and brain, this condition needs to be treated aggressively. Treatment should consist of changes in lifestyle, including exercise and diet, but usually also requires drug therapy. Two of the principal classes of antihypertensive agents are diuretics and direct vasodilators (Benowitz 2015):

- *Diuretics* lower blood pressure by eliminating sodium and excess water from the body. Included in this category is hydrochlorothiazide.
- *Direct vasodilators* reduce blood pressure by relaxing the muscles in the walls of blood vessels that cause vasoconstriction, thereby dilating the blood vessels and decreasing their resistance to the flow of blood. Drugs included in this category are calcium-channel blockers (diltiazem [Cardizem], verapamil [Calan], nifedipine [Procardia]); inhibitors of the enzyme that synthesizes the vasoconstricting hormone, angiotensin II (enalapril [Vasotec]); and drugs that block the vasoconstricting action of the sympathetic nervous system (clonidine [Catapres] and prazosin [Minipress]).

ANTIANGINAL AGENTS

When the heart is deprived of sufficient blood (a condition called **ischemia**), the oxygen requirements of the cardiac muscle are not met and the breakdown of chemicals caused by the continual activity of the heart results in pain; this viselike chest pain is called **angina pectoris**. The most frequent cause of angina is obstruction of the coronary vessels (Katzung 2015a). Angina pectoris frequently occurs in patients with hypertension; left untreated, the underlying blockage of coronary vessels can result in heart attacks. All the drugs used to relieve or prevent angina decrease the oxygen deficit of the heart either by decreasing the amount of work required of the heart during normal functioning or by increasing the blood supply

KEY TERMS

bronchodilators
drugs that widen air passages

beta-adrenergic stimulants
drugs that stimulate a subtype of adrenaline and noradrenaline receptors

hypertension
elevated blood pressure

ischemia
tissue deprived of sufficient blood and oxygen

angina pectoris
severe chest pain usually caused by a deficiency of blood to the heart muscle

to the heart (Katzung 2015a). The three types of drugs prescribed for treating angina pectoris are (1) calcium-channel blockers (e.g., verapamil [Calan], diltiazem [Cardizem]), (2) nitrates and nitrites (e.g., amylnitrite [Vaporate], nitroglycerin [Transderm-Nitro]), and (3) blockers of the sympathetic nervous system, specifically classified as beta-adrenergic blockers (e.g., atenolol [Tenormin], propranolol [Inderal]) (Katzung 2012c).

DRUGS TO TREAT CONGESTIVE HEART FAILURE

When the cardiac muscle is unable to pump sufficient blood to satisfy the oxygen needs of the body, **congestive heart failure** occurs. This condition causes an enlarged heart, decreased ability to exercise, shortness of breath, and accumulation of fluid (**edema**) in the lungs and limbs (Katzung 2015c). The principal treatment for congestive heart failure consists of drugs that improve the heart's efficiency, such as digoxin (Lanoxin) (Katzung 2015c).

Drugs that cause vasodilation are also sometimes used successfully to reduce the work required of the heart as it pumps blood through the body. Among the drugs causing vasodilation are those already discussed in conjunction with other heart conditions such as hypertension and angina pectoris (e.g., enalapril [Vasotec]).

CHOLESTEROL- AND LIPID-LOWERING DRUGS

Cholesterol and some types of fatty (lipid) molecules can accumulate in the walls of arteries and narrow the openings of these blood vessels. Such arterial changes cause hypertension, heart attacks, strokes, and heart failure and are the leading cause of death in the United States, costing about $380 billion annually (Pharmaletter 2016). These health problems can often be avoided by adopting a lifestyle that includes a low-fat and low-cholesterol diet combined with regular, appropriate exercise (Malloy and Kane 2012). However, sometimes lifestyle changes are insufficient; in such cases, cholesterol-lowering drugs can be used to prevent the damaging changes in blood vessel walls. The drugs most often used include lovastatin (Mevacor), cholestyramine (Questran), and niacin (vitamin B3) (Malloy and Kane 2015).

HORMONE-RELATED DRUGS

Hormones are released from endocrine (ductless) glands and are important in regulating metabolism, growth, tissue repair, reproduction, and other vital functions. When there is a deficiency or excess of specific hormones, body functions can be impaired, causing abnormal growth, imbalance in metabolism, disease, and often death. Hormones, or hormone-like substances, are sometimes administered as drugs to compensate for an endocrine deficiency and to restore normal function. This is the case for (1) insulin used to treat diabetes (see the earlier discussion for more details), (2) levothyroxine (Synthroid, an artificial thyroid hormone) to treat **hypothyroidism** (insufficient activity of the thyroid gland), and (3) conjugated estrogens (Premarin) to relieve the symptoms caused by estrogen deficiency during menopause.

Hormones also can be administered as drugs to alter normal body processes. Thus, drugs containing the female hormones, estrogen and progesterone (norethindrone, ethinyl estradiol [Ortho Novum]), can be used as contraceptives to alter the female reproductive cycles and prevent pregnancy. Another example involves drugs related to corticosteroids (hormones from the cortex of the adrenal glands), which are often prescribed because of their immune-suppressing effects. In high doses, the corticosteroid drugs (e.g., triamcinolone [Kenalog]) reduce symptoms of inflammation and are used to treat severe forms of inflammatory diseases, such as arthritis (Ogbru 2016). Finally, hormone-linked drugs such as etanercept (Enbrel), which depress the important immune mediator, tissue necrosis factor (TNF), have also become very popular for suppressing serious inflammatory diseases such as arthritis (see Table 15.6).

SEDATIVE-HYPNOTIC AGENTS

About 12.5% of U.S. adults use sedative-hypnotics annually, and 2% use them daily (Sola 2010). Some popular sleeping medications include Ambien (zolpidem), Lunesta (eszopiclone), Rozerem (ramelteon), Sona (carisoprodol), and Silenor (doxepin). If one is not careful, these drugs can be used excessively for reducing stress and aiding sleep, leading to addictions and adverse consequences. Benzodiazepines commonly prescribed for these purposes are

KEY TERMS

congestive heart failure
the heart is unable to pump sufficient blood for the body's needs

edema
swollen tissue due to an accumulation of fluid

hypothyroidism
thyroid gland does not produce sufficient hormone

clonazepam (Klonopin) and lorazepam (Ativan) (Trevor 2015).

STIMULANTS

One of the most common uses for prescription stimulants is the treatment of attention deficit hyperactivity disorder (ADHD). This neurobehavioral disorder is the most common mental health problem in children, affecting approximately 10% of all school-aged children in the United States (CDC 2016), the majority of which are male (Quinlan 2016). Of those children diagnosed with ADHD, many will continue to manifest associated impairment into adolescence and even adulthood, although the expression of the symptoms of hyperactivity may be replaced with inattention (National Institute of Mental Health [NIMH] 2016). The most frequent treatments for ADHD include (1) stimulants such as methylphenidate (Ritalin) and amphetamine (Adderall), which have been proven to improve attention while controlling impulsivity and disruptive behaviors; (2) nonstimulants (such as Atomoxetine-Strattera), which are typically used as a backup for the stimulants because of fewer side effects; and, less often, (3) antidepressants that affect the neurotransmitters norepinephrine and dopamine. Of some concern is the dramatic increase in stimulant prescriptions for ADHD treatment and whether they are the best drug choice for treating ADHD patients (Keshavan 2016). This rise in ADHD-related medication use has corresponded with a disturbing increase in the use of these stimulants without prescriptions. It has been estimated that approximately 21 million people aged 12 or older in the United States are prescribed these stimulants annually, and in 2015 these drugs were abused by approximately 7% of high school seniors, many of whom were not the legal recipients of the prescriptions (Johnston 2016).

Perhaps the most troubling issue is the trend for college students to abuse these short-acting stimulants to enhance performance while studying to prepare for examinations or stay awake to party well into the night (Awad 2013). Another common reason for this group to abuse these drugs is to lose weight due to their appetite-suppressing actions. It is likely that the increase of stimulant abuse by college students reflects an assumption that these agents must be safe or they would not be prescribed by physicians. Due to this growing problem, scientists and drug companies are working to develop nonaddicting medications to treat ADHD.

DRUGS TO TREAT HIV

The top-20 list of prescription drugs (see Table 15.6) includes a number of medications used to treat or to prevent HIV infection. Of relevance to our discussion on prescription drugs are recent advances in pharmacological management of this disease. Although no cure for HIV or immunization against this virus is available yet, some drug therapies can delay the onset or dramatically slow the progression of this infection. The first drugs to be used effectively in AIDS therapy were the transcriptase inhibitors such as zidovudine (AZT) and stavudine (Zerit), which block a unique enzyme essential for HIV replication (Flexner 2006). Another group of anti-AIDS drugs called the *protease inhibitors* prevent HIV maturation; they include aquinavir. The protease inhibitors are particularly effective when used in combination with the transcriptase inhibitor drugs (Flexner 2006). Most current strategies for AIDS therapy include drug combinations based on issues such as viral susceptibility, drug toxicity, drug metabolism, drug interaction potential, and medical conditions of the patient. More than 20 anti-HIV drugs from six different mechanistic classes can be used in combination-drug treatments. These include drug categories such as the transcriptase inhibitors, protease inhibitors, fusion inhibitors, and CCR5 antagonists. Strategies for more effective drug treatments are continually being developed. Research suggests that, if done properly, antiviral treatment is more than 80% effective in suppressing the symptoms of AIDS and preventing death (Panel on Antiretroviral Guidelines for Adults and Adolescent 2016).

Common Principles of Drug Use

Probably the most effective way to teach people not to use drugs improperly is to help them understand how to use drugs correctly. This goal can be achieved by educating the drug-using public about prescription, OTC, and herbal drug products. If people can appreciate the difference between the benefits of therapeutic drug use and the negative consequences of drug misuse or abuse, they will be more likely to use medications in a cautious and thoughtful manner. To reach this level of understanding, patients must be able to communicate freely with health professionals. Before prescription or OTC drugs are purchased and used, patients should have all questions answered about the therapeutic objective, the most effective

PRESCRIPTION FOR ABUSE

Invitation for Prescription Abuse

Michael was polite, clean-cut, and a typical white-collar professional. To consider him a drug addict would be unthinkable, and yet Michael would be the first to admit his drug addiction on prescription medication is as strong and debilitating as an addiction to illegal drugs such as cocaine and heroin. Michael became extremely skilled in his ability to feign back pain in a doctor's office or emergency room so he could walk away with a prescription for potent narcotic painkillers. When asked if he drove himself to the office, Michael would always say no, so he could also get an injection of the potent narcotic Demerol. If he had difficulty getting a medication from legitimate or forged prescriptions, Michael would steal pills from easy targets in the suburbs. For example, at garage sales he would ask to use the bathroom, and unsuspecting homeowners would nicely open their houses to him and leave him unsupervised. People trying to sell their house would usually invite him in as a prospective buyer, and, as he looked around unattended, he would sneak into a bathroom or bedroom and rifle through medicine cabinets and dresser drawers for drugs to satisfy his cravings. Michael tells of one experience when he went to an open house pretending to be an interested buyer. When the owner wasn't looking, Michael slipped into a bedroom and snatched a large bottle of Vicodin and an unfilled prescription next to a wheelchair and crutches. At the peak of

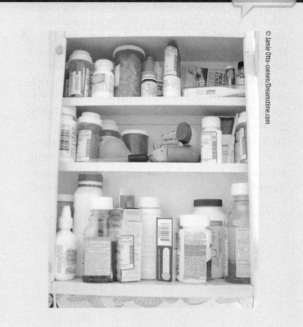

his addiction, Michael was consuming up to 120 narcotic painkillers a day. Michael explains that using large quantities of these prescriptions was not all that difficult. He claims that "doctors and psychiatrists would hand out drugs like candy" and people were so unsuspecting that it was easy to take unsecured prescription drugs from bathrooms and bedrooms.

Data from Sotonoff, J. "Addiction Began with Prescription Drugs He Got from Your Homes." *Chicago Daily Herald.* (26 July 2010). Available http://prev.dailyherald.com/story/?id=396310

mode of administration, and side effects. Education about proper drug use greatly diminishes drug-related problems and unnecessary health-care costs.

To minimize problems, before using any drug product, the patient should be able to answer the following questions:

- Why am I using this drug?
- How should I be taking this drug?
- What are the active ingredients in this drug product?
- What are the most likely side effects of this drug?
- How long should this drug be used?
- How should this drug be disposed of?

A major factor in the escalation of prescription drug misuse is that excess unused medications are not dealt with appropriately and are readily available to those who would abuse them or use them in a dangerous fashion. This problem can be prevented by complying with the following guidelines from the Office of National Drug Control Policy (ONDCP) that explain how to manage and dispose of these extra drugs (Siler et al. n.d.):

- Do not flush medications. The Environmental Protection Agency (EPA) has declared that flushing drugs down the toilet results in high levels of many medications in community water supplies, causing health problems for people, animals, and the environment.

- Realize that many of these prescription medications are in high demand on the Internet and the street, are often sold for a considerable amount of money, and can be very tempting to young people. Consequently, teens frequently raid home medicine cabinets to use these drugs for "pharm parties," where the pills are mixed together and shared or sold to friends and acquaintances. For these reasons, all prescription drugs should be stored in a secure (even locked) place (*Alcoholism & Drug Abuse Weekly* 2010).
- Do not dispose of your medications or their containers with labels in the trash. The bright labels of these bottles are highly visible in garbage cans and landfills and contain important personal information that can be used to steal your identity.
- The FDA recommends placing unused prescription medications into a plastic bag with moist coffee grounds or cat litter before disposing of the pills/tablets in the garbage. The moisture from the coffee grounds or cat litter will help dissolve the capsules, pills, or tablets, making them unusable.
- Many communities have secured drop-off boxes that are attended by certified law-enforcement personnel. Medications left in these boxes are collected by authorized personnel and properly disposed of. Locations of these drop-off containers can usually be determined by checking with local police.

LEARNING PORTFOLIO

Discussion Questions

1. Why are some prescription drugs appropriate for switching to OTC status?
2. What should the FDA use as a standard of safety when evaluating OTC and prescription drugs?
3. What role should the pharmacist play in providing information about OTC and prescription drugs to patients?
4. What type of formal training should be required before a health professional is allowed to prescribe drugs?
5. What kinds of questions should be asked by a health professional to ensure that a patient has sufficient understanding concerning a drug to use it properly and safely?
6. What are the basic rules for using OTC drugs properly?
7. Why is abuse of prescription drugs such a common problem?
8. Why are the opioid painkillers the most frequently abused of the prescription drugs?
9. How should users of prescription drugs handle their medications to prevent their abuse by others?
10. Why are some people more likely to abuse prescription drugs than illegal substances?
11. Even though some antibiotics have a wide margin of safety, currently there is no systemic antibiotic available OTC. Why is the FDA not willing to make some of these drugs available on a nonprescription basis?
12. Should herbal remedies be required to be safe and effective by the FDA like other OTC drug products?
13. What role, if any, should the FDA have in regulating herbal products?

Summary

1. Prescription drugs are available only by recommendation of an authorized health professional, such as a physician. Non-prescription (OTC) drugs are available on request and do not require approval by a health professional. In general, OTC medications are safer than their prescription counterparts, but often are less effective.
2. The FDA's switching policy is an attempt to make available more effective medications to the general public on a nonprescription basis. This policy has been implemented in response to the interest in self-treatment by the public and in an attempt to reduce healthcare costs.
3. Drugs switched by the FDA to OTC status include ulcer medications, such as cimetidine (Tagamet) and ranitidine (Zantac); medications for asthma and allergies; the contraceptive levonorgestrel (Plan B); and the weight loss drug orlistat (Ally).

Key Terms

angina pectoris	506
anorexiants	489
antitussives	484
beta-adrenergic stimulants	506
bronchodilators	506
congestion rebound	484
congestive heart failure	507
diabetes mellitus	504
edema	507
expectorants	484
gastritis	488
generic	500
hyperglycemia	504
hypertension	506
hypothyroidism	507
ischemia	506
keratin layer	490
keratolytics	490
monoamine oxidase inhibitors (MAOIs)	504
oral hypoglycemics	505
peptic ulcers	505
proprietary	500
SPF (sun protection factor) number	490
tricyclic antidepressants	504
type 1 diabetes	504
type 2 diabetes	505

4. Potential problems caused by making more effective drugs available OTC include overuse and inappropriate use, leading to dependence and other undesirable side effects. For example, these more effective drugs could encourage self-treatment of medical problems that usually require professional care.

5. Information on OTC product labels is crucial for proper use of these drugs and thus is regulated by the FDA. Product labels must list the active ingredients and their quantities in the product. Labels must also provide instructions for safe and effective treatment with the drug, as well as cautions and warnings.

6. Many herbal products contain active drugs and have become very popular. The lack of regulation makes these remedies difficult to assess for either efficacy or safety.

7. Although OTC drug products can be useful for treatment of many minor to moderate self-limiting medical problems, when used without proper precautions they can cause problems.

8. The principal drug groups available OTC are used in the treatment of common, minor medical problems and include analgesics, cold remedies, allergy products, mild stimulants, sleep aids, antacids, laxatives, antidiarrheals, antiasthmatics, acne medications, sunscreens, contraceptives, and nutrients.

9. For drugs to be prescribed properly, patients need to provide complete and accurate information about their medical condition and medical history to their physicians. In turn, providers need to communicate to patients what is being treated, why the drug is being used, how it should be used for maximum benefit, and what potential side effects can occur.

10. Proprietary drug names can be used legally only by the drug company that has trademark rights. Often, the original proprietary name becomes the popular name associated with the drug. Because the pharmaceutical company that develops a drug is trying to recover its investment, a newly marketed proprietary drug is expensive. Once the patent rights expire, other drug companies can also market

the drug but under a different name; often, the common, generic name is used because it cannot be trademarked. The generic drugs are less expensive because the manufacturers do not need to recover any significant investment. The FDA requires the less expensive generic drug to be as effective and safe as the proprietary counterpart.

11. Of the approximately 1500 different prescription drugs currently available in the United States, the most commonly prescribed groups are analgesics, antibiotics, antidepressants, drugs used for diabetes, antiulcer drugs, bronchodilators, drugs used to treat cardiovascular diseases, hormone-related drugs, and sedative-hypnotics.

12. Abuse of prescription drugs is a serious problem in the United States. Some patients try to persuade clinicians or pharmacists to make prescription medications available by using deceit or intimidation. Legal drugs obtained in this manner are often used to relieve drug dependence or to reduce withdrawal symptoms from illicit substances. Those who abuse prescription drugs often abuse other substances as well, such as alcohol, tobacco, or even illicit drugs.

13. To help reduce prescription abuse, those who use these drugs legitimately should make sure their medications are securely stored and that unused prescriptions are disposed of properly.

References

About.com. "Urban Legends: Phenylpropanolamine Recall." 2010. Available http://urbanlegends.about.com/library/blppa.htm

Alcoholism & Drug Abuse Weekly. "Only Federal Prevention Message About Prescription Drugs: Lock Up or Throw Out." 15 March 2010. Available http://onlinelibrary.wiley.com/doi/10.1002/adaw.20225/abstract

Alton, L. "FDA Warns: Drugs Cause Over 2 Million 'Adverse' Reactions Per Year." *Natural Health* 365 (2016). Available http://www.naturalhealth365.com/fda-big-pharma-drug-interaction-1736.html

American Academy of Dermatology. "Skin Cancer, Incidence Rates." 2016a. Available https://www.aad.org/media/stats/conditions/skin-cancer

American Academy of Dermatology. "What Causes Our Skin to Age?" 2016b. Available https://www.aad.org/public/skin-hair-nails/younger-skin

American College of Preventive Medicine (ACPM). "Over-the-Counter Medications Time Tool." 2016. Available http://www.acpm.org/page/OTCMeds_clinicians

American Diabetes Association (ADA). "Statistics About Diabetes." 2016. Available http://www.diabetes.org/diabetes-basics/statistics/

American Psychiatric Association. *Diagnostic and Statistical Manual of Mental Disorders*, 5th ed. Washington, DC: American Psychiatric Association, 2013.

Anderson, W. "Can a Drug or Surgery Solve Your Weight Problem?" The Huffington Post. 2016. Available http://www.huffingtonpost.com/william-anderson-ma-lmhc/can-a-drug-or-surgery-sol_b_7486428.html

Awad, S. "ADHD Medication Stimulates Controversy." Technician Online. 17 April 2013. Available http://www.technicianonline.com/article_c5a144c6-a004-11e2-9ff0-0019bb30f31a.html

Baratloo, A. A. Rouhipour, M. Forouzanfar, S. Safari, M. Amiri, and A. Negida. "The Role of Caffeine in Pain Management: A Brief Literature Review." *Anesthesiology and Pain Medicine* 6 (2016): e33139.

Bartholow, M. "Top 200 Prescription Drugs of 2009." *Pharmacy Times*. 11 May 2010. Available http://www.pharmacytimes.com/issue/pharmacy/2010/May2010/RxFocusTopDrugs-0510

Benowitz, N. "Antihypertensive Agents." In *Basic and Clinical Pharmacology*, 13th ed., edited by B. Katzung and A Trevor, 169–190. New York: McGraw-Hill, 2015.

The Better Sleep Guide. "Insomnia Statistics." 2016. Available http://www.better-sleep-better-life.com/insomnia-statistics.html

Biekiempis, V. "America's Prescription Addiction Suggests a Sick Nation." *The Guardian* (9 April 2012). Available http://www.guardian.co.uk/commentisfree/2012/apr/09/america-prescription-drug-addiction

Bonnet, M., and D. Arand. "Treatment of Insomnia." UpToDate. 2016. Available http://www.uptodate.com/contents/treatment-of-insomnia

Borazan, N., and D. Furst. "Nonsteroidal Anti-inflammatory Drugs, Disease-Modifying Antirheumatic Drugs, Nonopioid Analgesics, and Drugs Used in Gout." In *Basic and Clinical Pharmacology*, 13th ed., edited by B. Katzung and A. Trevor, 618–641. New York: McGraw-Hill, 2015.

Borgsdorf, L. "Preface." In *Drug Facts and Comparisons*, edited by L. Borgsdorf, et al., xi. St. Louis, MO: Wolters & Kluwer, 2007.

Brennan, C. "Popping Pills: Examining the Use of 'Study Drugs' During Finals." *USA Today College*. (15 December 2015). Available http://college.usatoday.com/2015/12/16/popping-pills-examining-the-use-of-study-drugs-during-fnals/

Brennan, Z. "FDA Amends Liver Warning Labeling Guidance for Some OTC Drugs Containing Acetaminophen." Regulatory Affairs Professionals Society (RAPS). 2015. Available http://www.raps.org/Regulatory-Focus/News/2015/11/16/23608/FDA-Amends-Liver-Warning-Labeling-Guidance-for-Some-OTC-Drugs-Containing-Acetaminophen/

Brophy, B., and D. Schardt. "Functional Foods." HighBeam Research. 2011. Available http://www.highbeam.com/doc/1G1-54271809.html

Bushak, L. "Psychotherapy Is Better Than Sleeping Pills for Insomnia Treatment: Report." Medical Daily. 2016. Available http://www.medicaldaily.com/insomnia-treatment-psychotherapy-sleeping-pills-384574

Centers for Disease Control and Prevention (CDC). "Health Expenditures." 2015. Available http://www.cdc.gov/nchs/fastats/health-expenditures.htm

Centers for Disease Control and Prevention (CDC). "Attention-Deficit/Hyperactivity Disorder (ADHD)." 2016. Available http://www.cdc.gov/ncbddd/adhd/data.html

Centers for Medicare and Medicaid Services (CMS). "Drug Diversion Toolkit, Patient Counseling." 2016. Available https://www.cms.gov/Medicare-Medicaid-Coordination/Fraud-Prevention/Medicaid-Integrity-Education/Downloads/drugdiversion-patientcounseling-booklet.pdf

Chemotherapeutic Drugs. *Basic and Clinical Pharmacology*, 13th ed., edited by B. Katzung and A. Trevor, 767–970. New York: McGraw-Hill, 2015.

Cleveland Clinic. "Over-the-Counter & Herbal Remedies for Weight Loss." 2016. Available http://my.clevelandclinic.org/health/healthy_living/getting_fit/hic_Maintaining_a_Healthy_Weight/hic_Over-the-Counter_and_Herbal_Remedies_for_Weight_Loss

Colliver, V. "Curbing Cough Medicine Abuse Target of Calif. Law." *SF Gate*. (28 December 2011). Available http://www.sfgate.com/cgi-bin/article.cgi?f=/c/a/2011/12/28/MNQE1MAS92.DTL&type=science

Consumer Healthcare Products Association (CHPA). "White Paper on the Benefits of OTC Medicines in the United States." 2010. Available http://www.yourhealthathand.org/images/uploads/r_6842.pdf

Consumer Healthcare Products Association (CHPA). "Statistics on OTC Use." 2016a. Available http://www.chpa.org/marketstats.aspx

Consumer Healthcare Products Association (CHPA). "OTC Review/Drug Monographs." 2016b. Available http://www.chpa.org/OTCReview.aspx

Crosby, K., and O'Neal, K. "Prevention of Sun-Induced Skin Disorders." In *Handbook of Nonprescription Drugs*, 17th ed., edited by D. Krinsky, R. Beradi, S. Ferreri, A. Hume, G. Newton, C. Rollins, and K. Tietze, 707–722. Washington, DC: American Pharmacists Association, 2012.

Cunningham, J. K., R. C. Callaghan, D. Tong, L. M. Liu, H. Y. Li, and W. J. Lattyak. "Changing Over-the-Counter Ephedrine and Pseudoephedrine Products to Prescription Only: Impacts on Methamphetamine Clandestine Laboratory Seizures." *Drug and Alcohol Dependency* 126 (2012): 55–64.

DeBatista, C. "Antidepressant Agents." In *Basic and Clinical Pharmacology*, 13th ed., edited by B. Katzung and A. Trevor, 510–527. New York: McGraw-Hill, 2015.

DerSarkissian, C. "Health Risks Linked to Obesity." WebMD. 2016. Available http://www.webmd.com /diet/obesity/obesity-health-risks

Disabled World. "Abuse of Over-the-Counter Medications." 2013. Available http://www.disabled-world.com/medical /pharmaceutical/addiction/ocm.php

Dowell, D., T. Haegerich, and R. Chou. "CDC Guideline for Prescribing Opioids for Chronic Pain—United States, 2016." *Morbidity and Mortality Weekly Report* 65 (2016): 1–49. Available http://www.cdc.gov/mmwr /volumes/65/rr/rr6501e1.htm

Drug Enforcement Administration (DEA). "Disposal of Controlled Substances; Final Rule. 21 CFR Parts 1300, 1301, 1304 et al." *Federal Register* 79 (2014). Available http:// www.deadiversion.usdoj.gov/fed_regs/rules/2014 /2014-20926.pdf

Drugs.com. "New Drug Approvals." 2013. Available http:// www.drugs.com/newdrugs.html

Drugs.com. "18 Herbal Supplements with Risky Drug Interactions." 2015. Available http://www.drugs.com /slideshow/herb-drug-interactions-1069

Drugs.com. "Over-the-Counter Medications." 2016. Available https://www.drugs.com/otc/

eMedExpert. "Brand-Name Drugs vs. Generic Drugs." 2016. Available http://www.emedexpert.com/tips /brand-vs-generic-drugs.shtml

ePainAssist. "Differentiating Dry Cough and Wet Cough Based on Causes, Symptoms, Treatment." 2016. Available http:// www.epainassist.com/chest-pain/lungs/differentiating -dry-cough-and-wet-cough

Epstein, J., and S. Wang. "UVA & UVB." Skin Cancer Foundation. 24 May 2013. Available http://www.skincancer .org/prevention/uva-and-uvb

FamilyDoctor.org. "Decongestants: OTC Relief for Congestion." October 2013. Available http://familydoctor .org/familydoctor/en/drugs-procedures-devices/over

-the-counter/decongestants-otc-relief-for-congestion .html

Flexner, C. "Antiretroviral Agents and Treatment of HIV Infection." In *The Pharmacological Basis of Therapeutics*, 11th ed., edited by L. Brunton, J. Lazo, and K. Parker, 1273–1314. New York: McGraw-Hill, 2006.

Food and Drug Administration (FDA). "Facts About Generic Drugs." 2016a. Available http://www.fda.gov/drugs /resourcesforyou/consumers/buyingusingmedicinesafely /understandinggenericdrugs/ucm167991.htm

Food and Drug Administration (FDA). "Legal Requirements for the Sale and Purchase of Drug Products Containing Pseudoephedrine, Ephedrine, and Phenylpropanolamine." 2016b. Available http://www.fda.gov /MedicalDevices/default.htm

Food and Drug Administration (FDA). "Now Available Without a Prescription." 2016c. Available http:// www.fda.gov/Drugs/ResourcesForYou/Consumers /ucm143547.htm

Food and Drug Administration (FDA). "Prescription to Over-the-Counter (OTC) Switch List." 2016d. Available http://www.fda.gov/AboutFDA/CentersOffices/Office ofMedicalProductsandTobacco/CDER/ucm106378 .htm

Freundlich, N. "Illicit Drugs on Campus Are Increasingly the Rx Variety." Health Beat. 12 July 2010. Available http://www.healthbeatblog.com/2010/07/illicit-drugs -on-campus-are-increasingly-the-rx-variety/

Galanter, J., and H. Boushey. "Drugs Used in Asthma." In *Basic and Clinical Pharmacology*, 13th ed., edited by B. Katzung and A. Trevor, 336–353. New York: McGraw-Hill, 2015.

Goodnough, A. "Prescription Drug Abuse Sends More People to the Hospital." *New York Times*. (5 January 2011). Available http://www.nytimes.com/2011/01/06 /health/06drugs.html

Hanson, D. "U.S. Leads World in Prescription Drug Use." Addiction Inbox. 28 July 2010. Available http://addiction -dirkh.blogspot.com/2010/07/us-leads-world-in -prescription-drug-use.html

Health Day News. "More Mental Health Woes in College Kids Who Abuse Prescription Drugs." *U.S. News and World Report* (19 June 2012). Available https:// consumer.healthday.com/mental-health-information -25/depression-news-176/more-mental-health-woes-in -college-kids-who-abuse-prescription-drugs-665719.html

Henderson, M. "Self-Care and Nonprescription Pharmacotherapy." In *Handbook of Nonprescription Drugs*, 17th ed., edited by D. Krinsky, R. Beradi, S. Ferreri, A. Hume, G. Newton, C. Rollins, and K. Tietze, 3–36. Washington, DC: American Pharmacists Association, 2012.

Hume, A., and K. Strong. "Botanical Medicines." In *Handbook of Nonprescription Drugs*, 15th ed., edited by I. Bernardi, 1103–1136. Washington, DC: American Pharmacists Association, 2006.

Hussar, D. "Overview of Over-the-Counter Drugs." Merck Manual Consumer Version. (2016). Available http://www.merckmanuals.com/home/drugs/over-the-counter-drugs/overview-of-over-the-counter-drugs

Johnston, L. "Monitoring the Future." 2016. Available http://www.monitoringthefuture.org/data/15data/15drtbl2.pdf

Kaiser Family Foundation. "Prescription Drug Trends." May 2010. Available http://www.kff.org/rxdrugs/upload/3057-08.pdf

Katzung, B. "Vasodilators & the Treatment of Angina Pectoris." In *Basic and Clinical Pharmacology*, 13th ed., edited by B. Katzung and A. Trevor, 191–207. New York: McGraw-Hill, 2015a.

Katzung, B. "Development and Regulation of Drugs." In *Basic and Clinical Pharmacology*, 13th ed., edited by B. Katzung and A. Trevor, 69–77. New York: McGraw-Hill, 2015b.

Katzung. B. "Drugs Used in Heart Failure." In *Basic and Clinical Pharmacology*, 13th ed., edited by B. Katzung and A. Trevor, 209–223. New York: McGraw-Hill, 2015c.

Kennedy, M. "Pancreatic Hormones and Antidiabetes Drugs." In *Basic and Clinical Pharmacology*, 12th ed., edited by B. Katzung, 743–768. New York: McGraw-Hill Medical, 2012.

Kennedy, M. S., and U. Masharani. "Pancreatic Hormones & Antidiabetic Drugs." In *Basic and Clinical Pharmacology*, 13th ed., edited by B. Katzung and A. Trevor, 723–746. New York: McGraw-Hill, 2015.

Kerlikowske, G. "Setting the Record Straight: Responding to the Prescription Drug Abuse Epidemic." Huffington Post. 22 March 2012. Available http://www.huffingtonpost.com/r-gil-kerlikowske/prescription-drug-abuse_b_1365785.html

Keshavan, M. "Tasty and Easy to Take, A New ADHD Alarms Some Psychiatrist." Health 2016. Available https://www.statnews.com/2016/05/23/adhd-drug-concerns/

Kirkwood, C., and S. Melton. "Insomnia, Drowsiness, and Fatigue." In *Handbook of Nonprescription Drugs*, 17th ed., edited by D. Krinsky, R. Beradi, S. Ferreri, A. Hume, G. Newton, C. Rollins, and K. Tietze, 867–883. Washington, DC: American Pharmacists Association, 2012.

Lampert, P. "Consumer Skepticism Growing Regarding 'All Natural' Food Claims." PR Newswire. 14 May 2013. Available http://www.prnewswire.com/news-releases/consumer-skepticism-growing-regarding-all-natural-food-claims-207362511.html

Landro, L. "How Your Supplements Interact with Prescription Drugs." *Wall Street Journal.* (29 February 2016). Available http://www.wsj.com/articles/what-you-should-know-about-how-your-supplements-interact-with-prescription-drugs-1456777548.

Lynn, D. T. Umari, C. Dunnick, and R. Dellavalle. "The Epidemiology of Acne Vulgaris in Late Adolescence." *Adolescent Health, Medicine, and Therapeutics* 7 (2016): 13–25.

Malloy, M., and J. Kane. "Agents Used in Dyslipidemia." In *Basic and Clinical Pharmacology*, 13th ed., edited by B. Katzung and A. Trevor, 602–615. New York: McGraw-Hill, 2015.

Mayo Clinic. "Eating Disorders." 2016. Available http://www.mayoclinic.org/diseases-conditions/eating-disorders/symptoms-causes/dxc-20182875

McCabe, S., C. Boyd, and C. Teter. "Subtypes of Nonmedical Prescription Drug Misuse." *Drug and Alcohol Dependence* 102 (2009): 63–70.

McQuaid, K. "Drugs Used in the Treatment of Gastrointestinal Diseases." In *Basic and Clinical Pharmacology*, 13th ed., edited by B. Katzung and A. Trevor, 1052–1083. New York: McGraw-Hill, 2015.

McQueen, C., and R. Orr. "Natural Products." In *Handbook of Nonprescription Drugs*, 17th ed., edited by D. Krinsky, R. Beradi, S. Ferreri, A. Hume, G. Newton, C. Rollins, and K. Tietze, 967–1006. Washington, DC: American Pharmacists Association, 2012.

Medical News Today. "Are Doctors Knowledgeable About Herbal Medicines?" 2010. Available http://www.medicalnewstoday.com/articles/184716.php

MedicineNet. "Asthma: Over-the-Counter Treatment." 2013. Available http://www.medicinenet.com/asthma_over_the_counter_treatment/article.htm

Miller, M. "Is Caffeine Before an Exam a Good or Bad Idea?" Viter.com. 2016. Available http://goviter.com/blog/is-caffeine-before-an-exam-a-good-or-bad-idea/

Miller, S., and C. Bartels. "Overweight and Obesity." In *Handbook of Nonprescription Drugs*, 17th ed., edited by D. Krinsky, R. Beradi, S. Ferreri, A. Hume, G. Newton, C. Rollins, and K. Tietze, 488–505. Washington, DC: American Pharmacists Association, 2012.

Mitchell, D. "Is Your Child Abusing Cough and Cold Medications?" EmaxHealth.com. 2010. Available http://www.emaxhealth.com/1275/your-child-abusing-cough-and-cold-medications

National Center for Complementary and Alternative Medicine (NCCAM). "Herbs at a Glance." 10 June 2013. Available http://nccam.nih.gov/health/herbsataglance.htm

National Center for Health Statistics. "Depression in the U.S. Household Population 2009–2012." Centers for

Disease Control and Prevention. 2016. Available http://www.cdc.gov/nchs/data/databriefs/db172.htm

National Heart, Lung, and Blood Institute (NHLBI). "Other Names for Coronary Heart Disease." 2016. Available http://www.nhlbi.nih.gov/health/health-topics/topics/cad/names

National Institute of Mental Health (NIMH). "Attention Deficit Hyperactivity Disorder (ADHD)." 2010. Available http://www.nimh.nih.gov/health/publications/attention-deficit-hyperactivity-disorder/complete-index.shtml

National Institute on Drug Abuse (NIDA). "Dramatic Increases in Maternal Opioid Use and Neonatal Abstinence Syndrome." 2015. Available https://www.drugabuse.gov/related-topics/trends-statistics/infographics/dramatic-increases-in-maternal-opioid-use-neonatal-abstinence-syndrome

National Institute on Drug Abuse (NIDA). "Overdose Death Rates." 2016a. Available https://www.drugabuse.gov/related-topics/trends-statistics/overdose-death-rates

National Institute on Drug Abuse (NIDA). "DrugFacts: Cough and Cold Medicine Abuse." 2016b. Available https://www.drugabuse.gov/publications/drugfacts/cough-cold-medicine-abuse

National Institute on Drug Abuse (NIDA). "Popping Pills: Prescription Drug Abuse in America." 2016c. Available https://www.drugabuse.gov/news-events/news-releases/2016/03/extended-release-naltrexone-lowers-relapse-rates-in-ex-offenders

National Institute of Mental Health (NIMH). "Attention Deficit Hyperactivity Disorder." 2016. Available http://www.nimh.nih.gov/health/topics/attention-deficit-hyperactivity-disorder-adhd/index.shtml

National Library of Medicine. "Dietary Supplement Labels Database." 2010. Available http://www.dsld.nlm.nih.gov/dsld/

Negrete, D. "Pharm Parties, Finds Place Among Teens." STJOECHANNEL.com. 2016. Available http://www.stjoechannel.com/news/local-news/pharm-parties-finds-place-among-teens

New York Times. "Common Cold Risk Factors." Health Guide. (June 14, 2016). Available. http://www.nytimes.com/health/guides/disease/common-cold/risk-factors.html

Nutraceuticals World. "Herbal Supplement Sales Increase to $5 Billion in Sales in the U.S." 2011. Available http://www.nutraceuticalsworld.com/issues/2010-06/view_industry-news/u-s-herbal-supplement-sales-reach-5-billion

Ogbru, O. "Corticosteroids Systemic (Oral and Injectable)." MedicineNet.com. 2016. Available http://www.medicinenet.com/corticosteroids-oral/article.htm

Olian, K. "Prescription Drug Addiction Among Women Becoming 'Monstrous Tidal Wave.'" NBC News. 5 July 2012. Available http://rockcenter.nbcnews.com/_news/2012/07/05/12570381-prescription-drug-addiction-among-pregnant-women-becoming-monstrous-tidal-wave?lite

O'Toole, J. "How Prescription Drug Abuse Costs You Money." CNN. 24 February 2012. Available http://money.cnn.com/2012/02/22/news/economy/prescription_drug_abuse/index.htm

Page, M. "Rx-to-OTC Switches: Trends to Watch." Pharmacy Times. February 2015. Available http://www.pharmacytimes.com/publications/issue/2015/february2015/rx-to-otc-switches-trends-to-watch/p-2

Panel on Antiretroviral Guidelines for Adults and Adolescents. "Guidelines for the Use of Antiretroviral Agents in HIV-1-Infected Adults and Adolescents." Department of Health and Human Services. 2016. Available at http://www.aidsinfo.nih.gov/ContentFiles/AdultandAdolescentGL.pdf

Pharmaletter. "Costs and Consequences of Not Treating High Cholesterol in the USA." 2016. Available http://www.thepharmaletter.com/article/costs-and-consequences-of-not-treating-high-cholesterol-in-the-usa

PSNet. "Medication Errors." Agency for Healthcare Research and Quality. 2015. Available https://psnet.ahrq.gov/primers/primer/23/medication-errors

Quest Diagnostics. "U.S. Worker Use of Prescription Opiates Climbing, Shows Quest Diagnostics Drug Testing Index." 2 September 2010. Available http://newsroom.questdiagnostics.com/index.php?s=30649&item=94682

Quinlan, C. "Our Understanding of ADHD Is Changing. Here's Why That Matters for Girls and Women." ThinkProgress.org. 2016. Available http://thinkprogress.org/education/2016/01/21/3741518/adhd-in-girls/

Rickert, E. "Legal and Regulatory Issues in Self-Care Pharmacy Practice." In *Handbook of Nonprescription Drugs*, 17th ed., edited by D. Krinsky, R. Beradi, S. Ferreri, A. Hume, G. Newton, C. Rollins, and K. Tietze, 53–64. Washington, DC: American Pharmacists Association, 2012.

Sandi, B. "OTC Reflux Medications: Concerns for Patients and Proactive Roles for Compounding Pharmacists." Pharmaceutica North America, Inc. 2016. Available http://www.pnarx.com/index.php/blog/otc-reflux

-medications-concerns-patients-proactive-roles-compounding-pharmacists/

Scolaro, K. "Disorders Related to Colds and Allergies." In *Handbook of Nonprescription Drugs*, 17th ed., edited by D. Krinsky, R. Beradi, S. Ferreri, A. Hume, G. Newton, C. Rollins, and K. Tietze, 180–204. Washington, DC: American Pharmacists Association, 2012.

Scott, S., and R. Martin. "Atopic Dermatitis and Dry Skin." In *Handbook of Nonprescription Drugs*, 15th ed., edited by I. Bernardi, 711–728. Washington, DC: American Pharmacists Association, 2006.

Shimp, L. "Disorders Related to Menstruation." In *Handbook of Nonprescription Drugs*, 17th ed., edited by D. Krinsky, R. Beradi, S. Ferreri, A. Hume, G. Newton, C. Rollins, and K. Tietze, 139–158. Washington, DC: American Pharmacists Association, 2012.

Siler, S., S. Duda, R. Brown, J. Gbemudu, S. Weier, and J. Glaudemans. "Safe Disposal of Unused Controlled Substances." Avalere, prepared for the King Pharmaceuticals, Inc. n.d. Available http://www.ncdoi.com/osfm/safekids/Documents/OMD/SafeDisposalOfUnusedControlledSubstancesReport.pdf

Small, J. "Funds to Run Out for Database That Monitors Prescription Drug Usage." 89.3 KPCC Southern California Public Radio. 15 April 2013. Available http://www.scpr.org/news/2013/04/15/36829/funds-to-run-out-for-database-that-monitors-prescr/

Sola, C. "Sedative, Hypnotic, Anxiolytic Use Disorders." eMedicine from WebMD. 2010. Available http://emedicine.medscape.com/article/290585-overview

Soong, J. "Living with Insomnia: Get a Good Night's Sleep." WebMD. 2016. Available http://www.webmd.com/sleep-disorders/living-with-insomnia-11/sleeping-pills

Stack, S. "Prescription Abuse Laws Can Create a No-Win Situation for Doctors." American Medical News. 13 August 2012. Available http://www.amednews.com/article/20120813/opinion/308139962/5/

The State of Obesity. "Obesity Rates & Trends." 2016. Available http://stateofobesity.org/rates/

Statista. "Top 20 Prescription Drugs Based on U.S. Sales in 2015." The Statistical Portal. 2016. Available http://www.statista.com/statistics/258010/top-branded-drugs-based-on-retail-sales-in-the-us/

Stetka, B., and E. McCance-Katz. "Two New Resources to Curb Prescription Drug Abuse." Medscape. 8 May 2012. Available http://www.medscape.com/viewarticle/763209

Stone, K. "Top Generic Drug Companies." About.com Pharma. 2013. Available http://pharma.about.com/od/Generics/a/Top-Generic-Drug-Companies.htm

Stoppler, M. "Cold, Flu, Allergy Treatments." MedicineNet.com. 2016. Available http://www.medicinenet.com/cold_flu_allergy/article.htm

Stoppler, M., and B. Hecht. "Generic Drugs, Are They as Good as Brand Names?" MedicineNet.com. 29 December 2010. Available http://www.medicinenet.com/script/main/art.asp?articlekey=46204

Thomas, M. "Prescription Drug Abuse Is Fastest-Growing Drug Problem in Country." *Chicago Sun-Times*. (26 December 2010). Available http://www.new-hope-recovery.com/center/2012/01/16/prescription-drug-abuse-is-fastest-growing-drug-problem-in-country/

Trevor, A. "Sedative-Hypnotic Drugs." In *Basic and Clinical Pharmacology*, 13th ed., edited by B. Katzung and A. Trevor, 369–381. New York: McGraw-Hill, 2015.

Twelve Keys. "The Dangers of Pharm Parties." 12 Keys Rehab. 2015. Available http://www.12keysrehab.com/blog/dangers-of-pharm-parties

University of Maryland Medical Center. "Herbal Medicine." 2015. Available http://umm.edu/health/medical/altmed/treatment/herbal-medicine

U.S. Department of Health and Human Services (HHS). "The U.S. Opioid Epidemic." 2016. Available http://www.hhs.gov/opioids/about-the-epidemic/#

U.S. News and World Report. "Stomach and GI." 2016. Available http://health.usnews.com/health-products/stomach-and-gi-10

Valley, J. "'Pharm Parties,' Designer Drugs Among Trends for High Schoolers." *Las Vegas Sun*. (19 April 2012). Available http://www.lasvegassun.com/news/2012/apr/19/pharm-parties-designer-drugs-among-trends-high-sch/#axzz2XuZw4jK2

van den Heuval, C., S. Ferguson, M. Macchiand, and D. Dawson. "Melatonin as a Hypnotic: Con." *Sleep Medicine Review* 9 (2005): 71–80.

Vestal, C. "States Require Opioid Prescribers to Check for 'Doctor Shopping.'" Stateline. 2016. Available http://www.pewtrusts.org/en/research-and-analysis/blogs/stateline/2016/05/09/states-require-opioid-prescribers-to-check-for-doctor-shopping

Waseem, F. "Drug Overdose Deaths Spike Among Middle-Aged Women." *USA Today*. (3 July 2013). Available http://www.usatoday.com/story/news/nation/2013/07/02/drug-overdose-deaths-women/2483169/

WebMD. "The New Over-the-Counter Medicine Label: Take a Look." 2016a. Available http://www.webmd.com/a-to-z-guides/the-new-over-the-counter-medicine-label-take-a-look

WebMD. "Cold, Flu & Cough Health Center." 2016b. Available http://www.webmd.com/cold-and-flu/

Wilkinson, J. "Headache." In *Handbook of Nonprescription Drugs*, 17th ed., edited by D. Krinsky, R. Beradi, S. Ferreri, A. Hume, G. Newton, C. Rollins, and K. Tietze, 67–86. Washington, DC: American Pharmacists Association, 2012.

Williams, A., C. Girard, D. Jui, A. Sabina, and D. Katz. "SAMe as Treatment for Depression: A Systemic Review." *Clinical Investigation of Medicine* 28 (2005): 132–139.

Woolston, M. "Type 2 Diabetes and Kids: The Growing Epidemic." HealthDay (2016). Available https://consumer.healthday.com/encyclopedia/diabetes-13/misc-diabetes-news-181/type-2-diabetes-and-kids-the-growing-epidemic-644152.html

Zweber, A., and R. Berardi. "Heartburn and Dyspepsia." In *Handbook of Nonprescription Drugs*, 17th ed., edited by D. Krinsky, R. Beradi, S. Ferreri, A. Hume, G. Newton, C. Rollins, and K. Tietze, 221–235. Washington, DC: American Pharmacists Association, 2012.

© Deco Images/Alamy.

Did You Know?

▶ As a subcultural group, athletes are much more likely to abuse performance-enhancing (erogenic drugs) to enhance athletic performance.

▶ In the United States, approximately 500,000 teenagers and 52,000 children aged 12 and younger use anabolic steroids.

▶ In general, men tend to use drugs more than women, yet women are more likely to become addicted to drugs.

▶ In comparison to men, women are more reluctant to seek substance abuse treatment.

▶ Approximately 70% of women in drug abuse treatment report histories of physical and sexual abuse, with victimization beginning before 11 years of age and occurring repeatedly.

▶ Adolescents who abuse drugs often have other co-occurring mental health problems.

▶ The major reasons adolescents use drugs are to cope with boredom, unpleasant feelings, emotions, and stress or to relieve depression and reduce tension and alienation.

▶ Prescription and over-the-counter drugs are the most commonly abused substances by Americans aged 14 and older, after marijuana and alcohol.

▶ Suicide is more likely to be attempted by those adolescents who turn to alcohol and other drugs to help them cope with serious emotional and personality conflicts and frustrations.

▶ Street gangs, outlaw motorcycle gangs, and prison gangs are the primary distributors of illegal drugs in the United States.

▶ Alcohol use is implicated in one-third to two-thirds of sexual assaults and acquaintance or date rapes among teens and college students.

▶ According to a national survey, almost 60% of college students aged 18 to 22 years drank alcohol in the past month, and more than 60% of those who drank engaged in binge drinking during that same time frame.

▶ More than 1.2 million people in the United States are living with HIV infection, and almost 12.8% are unaware of their infection.

▶ Gay, bisexual, and other men who have sex with men (MSM) of all races and ethnicities remain the population most profoundly affected by HIV.

▶ An HIV-infected individual may not manifest symptoms of AIDS for as many as 10 to 12 years after the initial infection, and during this dormant period the person is highly contagious.

▶ Licit and illicit drugs can easily be purchased via Internet websites.

Learning Objectives

On completing this chapter, you should be able to:

❯ Know which drugs are most likely to be abused by athletes and why.

❯ Describe the use of drug testing in athletic competitions.

❯ Identify where users obtain anabolic steroids.

❯ Describe the purpose and goals of the Adolescents Training and Learning to Avoid Steroids (ATLAS) prevention program.

❯ Explain two major ways the history of drug abuse among women differs from that of men.

❯ Explain the major reasons why adolescents use substances of abuse.

❯ Explain which types of parents are more likely to raise drug-abusing adolescents.

❯ List the types of drugs adolescents are most likely to abuse.

❯ List two major findings from research regarding drug use by college students.

❯ Know what "club drugs" are and how they are used.

❯ Explain how drug abuse contributes to the spread of HIV/AIDS.

❯ Know the key statistics regarding HIV/AIDS.

❯ List the major strategies to prevent HIV infection.

❯ Know how the use of alcohol and other drugs is presented in popular movies and songs.

❯ Understand how users can access the Internet to purchase licit and illicit types of drugs.

Introduction

Although similarities appear in the patterns of addiction among drug users, the development of, initial use, dependence, and oftentimes eventual abuse of drugs varies from individual to individual. When attempting to understand common patterns and possible causes of drug use, examining the subcultures of special populations provides a more organized grasp of commonalities within such groups. A **subculture** is defined as a special population or subgroup whose members share similar values, attitudes, and patterns of related behaviors that differ from those of other subcultures in the larger population. For example, from a subcultural perspective, a group of drug-using adolescents from a particular locality in a city or town is not much different from a group of divorced women meeting to discuss coping with separation and suddenly being single. Both of these are distinct subcultures in that their members are involved with similar goals and ambitions. They have patterns of similar attitudes and goal-seeking behaviors.

Even though many subcultures are so broad and diverse that not all members may be consciously aware of one another, from an **outsider's perspective** they can be perceived as subcultures because each subculture shares a set of similar behavior patterns. For example, when drug-using subcultures are viewed from an outsider's perspective, a set complementary behaviors can be identified.

An **insider's perspective** refers to participants who use drugs within their group as insiders. The members of a drug-using subculture are experiencing ongoing activity within their group. Group members maintain an insiders' perspective and are often surrounded by other group members who also maintain an insiders' perspective. Outsiders such as conventional members of society and law enforcement officials are composed of groups who challenge and largely oppose drug use and perceive drug use as deviant behavior. In summary, *insiders are looking at their drug use behavior from inside the group and outsiders are looking at this same group outside the boundaries of the group.* This distinction between insiders and outsiders is important for understanding drug use because the often clashing perspectives result in vastly different perspectives and, by extension, vastly different beliefs about this type of behavior.

Sociologists often refer to a subculture as a "world within a world." Subcultures create and provide their members with lifestyle patterns that are observable, fairly consistent, and interwoven. Viewing a drug-using group as a subculture offers a way to look for more generalized and distinctive patterns of drug use. In looking at the subcultures of drug users, we can begin to logically and methodically examine the reasons why individuals within various subcultures might initially use and persist in using drugs. The two types of forces that affect members of a subculture are internal and external, both of which affect these individuals' drug use behavior.

Internal subcultural forces affecting drug users include the following:

- Shared in-group attitudes about people who do and do not use drugs (drug users versus nonusers)
- Compatibility with other members of the peer group (often peer members share complementary personality traits)
- Shared attitudes favorable to drug use despite conventional society's view that such behavior is deviant
- Addiction to drugs or, at minimum, habitual drug usage
- A common secrecy about drug use (who you can and cannot trust in knowing about your drug usage)

External subcultural forces affecting drug users include the following:

- Preoccupation with law enforcement while procuring the drugs and while under the effects of illicit drugs
- A desire to identify other users and dealers of illicit drugs, such as verifying the dependability of the drug dealer (who best to deal drugs with and who has the best quality drugs)

KEY TERMS

subculture
subgroup within the population whose members share similar values and patterns of related behaviors that differ from other subcultures and the larger population

outsider's perspective
viewing a group or subculture from outside the group and viewing the group and its members as an observer; looking "in" at the members

insider's perspective
viewing a group or subculture from inside the group; seeing members as they perceive themselves

- Constant preoccupation regarding drug supply and when to keep in touch with drug dealer(s) and concern about acquiring a new supply of their drug of choice
- Some preoccupation with being viewed and/or observed using or acting "high" in public, at work, at school, or at a social function where drug use would be perceived as deviant social behavior

To further understand how similar patterns of drug use and/or abuse occur, in this chapter we look at drug use and users from both outsiders' and insiders' perspectives, from the vantage point of the members belonging to a distinct subculture and how they are perceived by society. This chapter focuses on and examines drug use, drug dependence, and drug abuse in the following seven drug-using subcultures:

1. Athletes/those involved in sports
2. Women
3. Adolescents
4. College students
5. Those affected by HIV/AIDS
6. A certain percentage of professional actors, actresses, and music celebrities
7. Internet users who are seeking and purchasing illicit drugs

Athletes and Drug Abuse

Drug abuse among athletes has been reported as far back as the Greek Olympics in 776 BC, when it was noted that competitors were ingesting certain substances to gain ground against their fellow competitors (Lajis 2007).

Using performance-enhancing drugs for increased athletic ability is known as **doping** (National Institute on Drug Abuse [NIDA] 2009). In sport, doping

is the deliberate or inadvertent use by an athlete of a substance or method banned by the International Olympic Committee (IOC). FIMS [International Federation of Sports Medicine] supports the prohibition of doping to protect athletes from the:

- unfair advantage, which may be gained by those athletes who use banned substances or methods to enhance performance,
- possible harmful side effects, which some substances or methods can produce. (Technische Univerisität München n.d.)

In the past, reports revealed that "'Doping' among world-class competitors is rampant ... and the governing bodies of individual sports, as well as the International Olympic Committee, turn a blind eye" (Begley et al. 1999, p. 49). The reasons boil down to winning in sports, especially when millisecond differences exist between gold and silver medals. The differences between the two medals "can amount to millions in endorsement contract and appearance fees" (p. 49), and apparently the world of professional sports and "drugs [performance-enhancing drugs] go together like socks and sweat" (p. 49). Charles Yesalis, an epidemiologist at Pennsylvania State University at University Park, stated,

Elite athletes stay away from traditional anabolic steroids. They use testosterone creams or gels, which dramatically reduce the chance of being caught, in conjunction with insulin or insulin-like growth factor.... The supplement industry has exploded since the passage of the Dietary Supplement Health and Education Act in 1994. ... Anyone can buy substances like testosterone, human-growth hormone (HGH), and insulin-like growth factor over the Internet. One site requires a doctor's prescription, but will sell one to any customer for $100 or someone can just walk down to the local GNC, like Mr. Jackson's teammates at Florida State. There, one can buy muscle-building steroid "precursors" like androstenedione and creatine monohydrate. (Suggs 2003, p. 36)

More recently, however, findings indicate that since 2007

anti-doping agencies introduced the concept of a "biological passport," a record of the substances found normally in an athlete's blood and urine, created by repeated sampling over time. By comparing the results of a blood test administered right before a competition to the passport, officials can determine if an athlete has been using EPO or other performance-enhancing drugs. (Harris 2013)

As a result, the use of muscle-building steroid "precursors" like androstenedione and creatine monohydrage are now detectable in drug testing.

KEY TERM

doping
the use of performance-enhancing drugs to increase athletic ability

Athletes may come into contact with performance-enhancing substances inadvertently or intentionally. For example, some athletes may inadvertently (or allegedly inadvertently) consume a pharmaceutical that is banned from competition, either because the ingredients or manufacturing method are kept secret or because it is protected by trademark or copyright (also known as a **proprietary medicine**). Other athletes may deliberately consume such substances for misuse as a recreational drug or deliberately consume them to enhance their performance (Docherty 2008).

To further our understanding of why athletes are willing to risk using these drugs, it is necessary to further explore their mind-set.

To excel in athletic competition is admirable. Most high school, college, amateur, and professional athletes participate in sports for the opportunity to pit their abilities against those of their peers and to experience the satisfaction that comes from playing to their potential. Others do so to satisfy a desire for recognition and fame. Unfortunately, that creates some athletes who are determined to win at any cost. And they may use that determination to justify the use of anabolic steroids despite evidence that these drugs can inflict irreversible physical harm and have significant side effects (New York State Department of Health 2010).

Young athletes receive exaggerated attention and prestige in almost every university, college, high school, and junior high school in the United States. Pressure to excel or be the best is placed on athletes by parents, peers, teachers, coaches, school administrators, the media, and the surrounding community. The importance of sports is frequently distorted and even used by some to evaluate the quality of educational institutions (Lawn 1984; New York State Department of Health 2010) or the quality of living conditions in a city. Athletic success can determine the level of financial support these institutions receive from local and state governments, alumni, and other private donors; thus, winning in athletics often translates into fiscal stability and institutional prosperity.

KEY TERM

proprietary medicine
pharmaceutical medicine that is protected from commercial competition because the ingredients or manufacturing method is kept secret or because it is protected by trademark or copyright

For the athlete, success in sports means psychological rewards such as the admiration of peers, school officials, family, and the community. In addition, athletic success can mean financial rewards such as scholarships, paid living expenses in college, advertising endorsement opportunities, and, for a few, incredible salaries as professional athletes. With the rewards of winning, athletes have to deal with the added pressures of not winning: "What will people think of me if I lose?" "When I lose, I let everybody down." "Losing shows that I am not as good as everyone thinks." These pressures on young, immature athletes can result in poor coping responses. Being better than competitors, no matter the cost, becomes the driving motivation, and doing one's best is no longer sufficient. Such attitudes may lead to serious risk-taking behavior in an attempt to develop an advantage over the competition; this situation can include using drugs to improve performance.

The Canadian sprinter Ben Johnson, once known as the fastest human in history, was banned for life from competitive running in March 1993 (Begley et al. 1999; Hoberman and Yesalis 1995). Five years earlier, at the 1988 Seoul Olympics, Johnson was stripped of a world record for the 100-meter dash and forfeited the gold medal when his urine tested positive for steroids. Because of the first incident, Johnson was suspended from competition for 2 years. However, in 1992, the 31-year-old sprinter was attempting a comeback, with speeds that approached his world record times. In January 1993, a routine urine test determined Johnson was again using steroids to enhance his athletic performance (Ferrente 1993). More recently, "Johnson, 51, has admitted to years of steroid use, but still feels he was unfairly picked out for vilification at a time of widespread drug use in athletics. 'I was nailed on a cross, and 25 years later I'm still being punished,' he [Johnson] … said" (*Telegraph Sport*, and Agencies 2013).

Another incident involving the use of steroids that ended in shocking tragedy was the case of wrestler Chris Benoit's double murder–suicide. Evidence proved that the pro wrestler asphyxiated his son and wife before he hanged himself in a basement weight room using a cord from one of the weight machines (ESPN.com 2007). When going through Benoit's house, investigators found a number of prescription steroid medications (Donaldson-Evans 2007). One of the side effects of anabolic steroids is extreme anger (Donaldson-Evans 2007).

After Major League Baseball (MLB) implemented a new steroid policy, 83 players were suspended. "Guys did steroids because it was easy to get away with" (Anonymous, as told by Penn 2005, p. 292). According to a player who chose to remain anonymous, "So many people were doing it that it didn't feel like cheating. If anything, it felt like leveling the field.... I juiced because I love playing more than anything else in the world, and I would have pretty much done anything to keep my career going" (Anonymous 2005, p. 297).

Widely publicized incidents such as these concerning illicit use of so-called **ergogenic** (performance-enhancing) drugs by professional and amateur athletes have created intense interest in the problem of drug abuse in sport (Begley et al. 1999; Merchant 1992; see "Point/Counterpoint: How the 'Juice' Was and Is Flowing in Baseball").

A more recent case of steroid use in professional sports involves Alexander Emmanuel "Alex" Rodriguez. Rodriguez (born in 1975) is currently a U.S. Major League Baseball player for the New York Yankees. He is considered one of the youngest best players in baseball history, and in 2007 he signed a 10-year, $252 million contract (Britannica.com 2010). However, Rodriguez has been dogged by accusations of steroid use:

> The Slugger [Rodriguez] who might some-day become baseball's all-time home run king remembered more details about performance-enhancing drugs Tuesday, saying his cousin repeatedly injected him from 2001–03 with a mysterious substance from the Dominican Republic. "I didn't think they were steroids" the New York Yankees star said. Later, he admitted, "I knew we weren't taking Tic Tacs." (Blum 2009, p. A11)

It was at this press conference that Rodriguez made "his second public attempt to explain a 2003 positive drug test while with Texas ... while his cousin persuaded him to use 'boli'—a substance he said the cousin obtained without a prescription and without consulting doctors or trainers" (Blum 2009, p. A11).

Rodriguez was suspended from the MLB for steroid use, but recently

> in an effort to reverse the suspension, the three-time American League Most Valuable Player sued MLB, its players' union and a Yankees team physician. The Yankees and Rodriguez issued a joint statement on Tuesday [referring to February 10, 2015].... "Alex initiated the meeting and apologized to the organization for his actions over the past several years," the statement said. "There was an honest and frank discussion on all of the issues. As far as the Yankees are concerned, the next step is to play baseball in spring training." Rodriguez, who turns 40 in July, is set to make $61 million over the next three years, thanks to a 10-year $275 million contract he signed in 2007. (McSpadden 2015)

Finally, one of the most shocking cases was that of Lance Armstrong, who, because of doping, was stripped of his record-holding *seven* Tour de

KEY TERM

ergogenic
drugs that enhance athletic performance

▶ POINT/COUNTERPOINT

How the "Juice" Was and Is Flowing in Baseball

We embrace instant gratification in the United States. We are a society that embraces "bigger, faster, stronger" and winning at all costs (Dvorchak 2005). This concept now applies to professional sports. A sampling from news sources reveals the following:

- "Jose Canseco, a Major League Baseball player for the Oakland Athletics and Texas Rangers (among other teams), wrote a tell-all book titled *Juiced*, in which he exposed not only the rampant use of

performance-enhancing substances in baseball.... A steroid devotee since the age of 20, Conseco goes beyond admitting his own usage ... [to claiming that] he often injected [Mark] McGwire while they were teammates.... According to Canseco, steroids and human growth hormone gave McGwire and Sammy Sosa (whose own usage was 'so obvious, it was a joke') the strength, stamina, regenerative ability, and confidence they needed for [the] record setting home run duels often credited with restoring baseball's popularity after the 1994 strike" (Amazon.com 2005).

- "[S]everal star athletes, including New York Yankees slugger Jason Giambi, have reportedly

(continues)

►POINT/COUNTERPOINT

How the "Juice" Was and Is Flowing in Baseball (*continued*)

told a federal grand jury investigating the [Balco] lab that they used illegal steroids, prompting Congress to hold hearings on the testing policies of all the major sports leagues" (Coile 2005).

- "Seattle Mariners minor-league outfielder Jamal Strong was suspended for 10 days ... making him the fourth player to test positive under Major League Baseball's new policy on performance-enhancing drugs" (Associated Press 2005).

- "McGwire's shameful refusal to answer questions about his alleged steroid use before a congressional committee and Bonds' unbelievable claim that he did not know that substances rubbed into his body were steroids clearly suggest deceit and dishonesty" (Eilek 2005).

- "Performance enhancing drugs (PEDs) have once again taken a toll on the professional sports world with yesterday's suspensions of 13 Major League Baseball players, including Alex Rodriguez—the highest paid player in professional baseball" (Woemer 2013).

- "Rodriguez was suspended in August for an unprecedented 211 games for his connection to the now defunct Biogenesis anti-aging clinic linked to providing 14 players with performance enhancing drugs. His suspension came since he violated the joint drug agreement and the collective bargaining agreement. A-Rod had the harshest punishment of all the players as Ryan Braun received a 65-game ban while the other 12 players each accepted and served 50-game suspensions" (Smollins 2013).

- "According to Ken Rosenthal, Major League Baseball has suspended 12 players in relation to the Biogenesis case.... [Biogenesis case occurred in 2013 involving a recent defunct clinic, Biogenesis of America, provided performance-enhancing drugs

("PEDs") to MLB players] ... Nelson Cruz, Jhonny Peralta, Antonio Bastardo, Jordany Valdespin, Everth Cabrera, Francisco Cervelli, Jesus Montero, Sergio Escalona, Fautino De Los Santos, Cesar Puello, Fernando Martinez, and Jordan Norberto will all be suspended. All 12 players have accepted their 50-game suspensions" (TheScore.com 2013).

Questions to Consider

1. Are professional sports players entitled to claim records set if they were on drugs during their successful career? If they are entitled to their accomplishments regardless of their drug usage, how would it affect non–drug-using players? Is it fair to the sport and to the fans supporting the players? If they are not entitled to their accomplishments under drugged conditions, what should the penalty be?

2. Do you think that all players in professional sports should be continuously tested for drugs? Should this policy be extended to high school and college sports players as well? If so, what should the penalties for drug violations be?

3. What if we find clear evidence that some currently admired major sports figures who scored big-time records in the past were using steroids or other performance-enhancing drugs while setting new and impressive records? Should anything be done about such evidence? If so, what penalties should the athletes receive? If not, why should we let them remain unblemished?

4. Are the real victims of this tragedy America's youth? Have athletes such as McGwire and Rodriguez betrayed the young people who admire and emulate them? Do you think America's youth are affected by their drug use in professional sports?

5. Does this scandal about professional sports and drug use suggest anything about the findings by the Centers for Disease Control and Prevention that steroid use among high school students more than doubled from 1991 to 2003?

Data form Amazon.com. "Editorial Reviews." 2005. Available http://www.amazon.com/exec/obidos/asin/0060746408/ref=bxgy; Associated Press. "Strong Suspended for Performance-Enhancing Drugs." Sports ESPN. 26 April 2005. Available http://sports.espn.go.com/mlb/news/story?id=2046762; Coile, Z. "House Bill Seeks to Toughen Steroid Rules: Athletes in All Leagues Would Be Held to the Strict Standards Used in Olympics." *San Francisco Chronicle.* (27 April 2005): 1–2; Dvorchak, R. "Former Steeler Courson Outlines Solutions for Steroid Use." Black and Gold. 27 April 2005. Available http://blackandgold world.blogspot.com/2005/04/robert-dvorchak-courson-outlines.html; Eilek, R. "Pro Sports Keep Heads in Sand on Steroids." *San Diego Union Tribune.* (17 April 2005). Smollins, M. "Alex Rodriguez Biogenesis Case: MLB CEO Rob Manfred Calls A-Rod Career 'Sad and Tarnished,' Claims Rodriguez PED Use 'Longer Than Any Other Player.'" *Sports World News.* (1 November 2013). Available http://www.sportsworldnews.com/articles/6205/20131101/alex-rodriguez -biogenesis-case-mlb-ceo-rob-manfred-calls-a-rod-career-sad-tarnished-claims-rodriguez-ped-use-longer-than-any-other-player.htm; TheScore.com. "MLB Suspends 12 Players in Biogenesis Case." 5 August 2013. Woemer, A. "MLB Players' Use of Performance Enhancing Drugs Comes with Serious Health Risks." FoxNews.com. 6 August 2013. Available http://www.foxnews.com/health/2013/08/06/mlb-players-use-performance-enhancing-drugs-comes-with -serious-health-risks/

France titles that he received from 1999 to 2005. Armstrong stated that in order to be a record holder, doping is needed to win (Leicester 2013). Armstrong also stated that "his life has been ruined by the U.S. Anti-Doping Agency investigation that exposed as lies his years of denials that he and his teammates doped" (Leicester 2013).

■ Laws Intended to Stop the Use of Performance-Enhancing Drugs in Professional Sports

In 2003, the first **World Anti-Doping Code** was approved and remained in effect from January 1, 2004, to December 31, 2008. In November 2007, revisions were made to the code that took effect in 2009 and in 2011. It was again revised in 2013 and remains in effect (WADA 2016). According to the World Anti-Doping Agency (WADA 2016),

> The World Anti-Doping Code (Code) is the core document that harmonizes anti-doping policies, rules and regulations within sport organizations and among public authorities around the world. It works in conjunction with five International Standards which aim to foster consistency among anti-doping organizations in various areas: testing; laboratories; Therapeutic Use Exemptions (TUEs); the List of Prohibited Substances and Methods; and the protection of privacy and personal information.

This code has proven to be a very powerful and effective tool in the harmonization of anti-doping efforts worldwide since it came into force on January 1, 2004 (WADA 2009).

One revision of the code provides provisions for increased sanctions, greater flexibility (the accused athlete has the option to provide evidence that the substance used was not intended to enhance performance), clear listing and definition of specified substances violating the rules, incentives to come forward and report personal usage or use by other athletes of performance-enhancing drugs, financial sanctions (including clearly specified periods of ineligibility), and WADA's right to appeal to a Court of Sport Arbitration (WADA 2009). Another more recent revision strengthened the code to be a more vigorous tool protecting the rights of the clean athlete worldwide (WADA 2015).

In 2015, the World Anti-Doping Agency (WADA) stipulated a revised Code Compliance listing the following (WADA 2015 unless otherwise noted):

- "To date, more than 660 sport organizations have accepted the World Anti-Doping Code. These organizations include the International Olympic Committee (IOC), the International Paralympic Committee (IPC), all Olympic Sport International Federations (IFs) and all IOC-recognized IFs, National Olympic and Paralympic Committees, National Anti-Doping Organizations."
- "Sports are required to undertake three steps in order to be fully compliant with the Code: acceptance, implementation, and enforcement."
- "Code acceptance means that a sport organization agrees to the principles of the Code and agrees to implement and comply with the Code."
- "Once a sport organization accepts the Code, it must then implement it. The implementation of the Code is the process that an anti-doping organization goes through to amend its rules and policies so that all mandatory articles and principles of the Code are included."
- "Finally, enforcement refers to the sport organization actually enforcing its amended rules and policies in accordance with the Code."
- WADA monitors implementation of and compliance with the Code. (WADA 2016)

■ Drugs Used by Athletes

A very memorable interview:

> Yes, the steroids I used certainly made me get bigger. I was going out for football and I had just made the team, so I kept using them and the results were phenomenal. Now, 2 years later, I won't be graduating. Several months ago, they removed a tumor on my liver, but they didn't get all the cancer. I am going home at the end of this semester. My parents want me to stay with them for the time I have left. When I go, I only have one wish—I want to die big and always be known as Big Jim. *(From Venturelli's research files, male, age 20, December 13, 1996)*

Studies have shown that athletes are less likely than nonathletes to use other drugs of abuse such as marijuana, alcohol, barbiturates, cocaine, and hallucinogens (Hoberman and Yesalis 1995; Substance Abuse and Mental Health Services

KEY TERM

World Anti-Doping Code
the core document providing a framework for harmonized antidoping policies, rules, and regulations within sport organizations and among public authorities

Administration [SAMHSA] 2007). However, with regard to the types of drugs athletes are prone to use and abuse, there is some disagreement. A study by Yusko et al. (2008, p. 281) found that "[m]ale student athletes were at high risk for heavy drinking and performance-enhancing drug use. Considerable in-season versus out-of-season substance use fluctuations were identified in male and female student athletes."

Regardless of whether alcohol use and abuse is or is not more likely in college athletes, athletes *are* much more likely than other populations to take drugs that enhance (physically or psychologically), or are thought to enhance, competitive performance. These drugs include stimulants such as amphetamines and cocaine and an array of drugs with presumed ergogenic effects, such as anabolic steroids (Bell 1987; NIDA 2006b). Some of the major drugs abused by athletes are listed in **Table 16.1**, along with their desired effects. The sections that follow discuss the drugs that are most frequently self-administered by athletes in an effort to improve their competitive performance.

TABLE 16.1 Partial List of Ergogenic Substances* and Expected Effects

Drugs	Expected Results
Amino acids	Stimulate natural production of growth hormone and increase strength
Amphetamines and cocaine	Increase strength, alertness, and endurance
Anabolic steroids	Increase muscle mass and strength
Androl-50 (Oxymetholone)	Increase the amount of the hormone (erythropoietin) involved in production of red blood cells
Asthma medication	Improve breathing
B-complex vitamins	Enhance body metabolism and increase energy
Beta-blockers	Reduce hand tremor and stimulate growth hormone
Caffeine	Reduce fatigue
Chromium	Enhance carbohydrate metabolism
Creatine	Increase strength, gain weight, increase muscle mass
Dianabol (methandrostenolone)	Increase muscle mass and fat reduction
Ephedrine	Improve breathing/increase energy
Equipoise (boldenone undecylenate)	Increase endurance, muscle mass, and the production of red blood cells in the body
Furosemide	Mask steroid use and enable rapid weight loss
Methylphenidate	Enhance alertness and endurance
Deca-Durabolin (nandrolone decanoate)	Increase muscle mass
Over-the-counter decongestants	Increase endurance and energy
Oxandrin (oxandrolone)	Promote growth of muscle tissue
Protein powders	Gain more muscle, gain weight, maintain weight, recover from workouts
Testosterone (testosterone cypionate)	Replace testosterone that the body is missing
Tetrahydrogestrinone (THG)	A difficult-to-detect designer steroid used to increase muscle bulk and muscle strength and speed muscle recovery
Thyroid hormone	Enhance metabolism

*Ergogenic drugs are substances that are used to enhance athletic performance.

Data from Brandenburg, J. R. "The Use of Ergogenic Aids Among High School Athletes in Eastern Kentucky." Theses, Dissertations, and Capstones, Paper 508, Marshall University, Huntington, West Virginia. 1 January 2004. Available http://mds.marshall.edu/cgi /viewcontent.cgi?article=1509&context=etd; Harlan, R., and M. Garcia. "Neurobiology of Androgen Abuse." *Drugs of Abuse and Neurobiology,* edited by R. Watson, 185–201. Boca Raton, FL: CRC Press, 1992; National Institute on Drug Abuse (NIDA). "DrugFacts: What Are Anabolic Steroids?" March 2016. Available https://www.drugabuse.gov/publications/drugfacts/anabolic-steroids

ANABOLIC STEROIDS

Anabolic steroids are a group of natural or synthetic drugs that are chemically similar to cholesterol and related to the male hormone testosterone (Guide4living.com 2005; Lukas 1993) and its artificial derivatives. A more recent definition states that "[a]nabolic steroids are synthetic variations of the male sex hormone testosterone. The proper term for these compounds is *anabolic-androgenic steroids.* 'Anabolic' refers to muscle building, and 'androgenic' refers to increased male sex characteristics" (NIDA 2016). Common names for anabolic steroids include *gear, juice, roids,* and *stackers* (NIDA 2016).

Steroids are used medically for treatment of certain diseases, such as certain types of anemia; treatment of hormonal issues, such as delayed puberty; diseases that cause muscle loss, such as cancer and AIDS; some breast cancers; and testosterone deficiency (NIDA 2016). Although illegal when taken for nonmedical purposes, steroids have been used illegally by both athletes and nonathletes since the late 1950s to improve athletic ability and physical appearance because steroids have performance-enhancing and bodybuilding properties. Steroids are taken orally or injected into the muscles. Although males and females both use steroids, males have higher rates of use (NIDA 2009, 2016; SAMHSA 1999b).

Naturally occurring male hormones, or androgens, are produced by the testes in males. These hormones are essential for normal growth and development of male sex organs as well as secondary sex characteristics such as muscular development, male hair patterns, voice changes, and fat distribution. The androgens are also necessary for appropriate growth spurts during adolescence (Olin 1994). The principal accepted therapeutic use for androgens is for hormone replacement in males with abnormally functioning testes. In such cases, the androgens are administered before puberty and for prolonged periods during puberty to stimulate proper male development (Olin 1994).

THE MAJOR REASONS FOR THE ABUSE OF ANABOLIC STEROIDS

In light of a finding on the sources of banned substances in sports it was reported that "Athletes may obtain banned medicines from physicians, pharmacists, retail outlets, health and lifestyle magazines, gymnasiums, coaches, family members, fellow athletes, the Internet and the black market" (TheAthlete.org 2011). The major reason for the use and abuse of anabolic steroids is that many athletes use them to improve athletic performance (Burke and Davis 1992; NIDA 2006b, 2016). Under some conditions, androgen-like drugs can increase muscle mass and strength. Athletes may also use steroids to increase their muscle size or to reduce their body fat (NIDA 2006b).

Studies have found that some athletes who abuse steroids in order to boost their muscle size have experienced physical or sexual abuse. In one series of interviews with male weightlifters, 25% who abused steroids reported memories of childhood physical or sexual abuse. Similarly, female weightlifters who had been raped were found to be twice as likely to report use of anabolic steroids or another purported muscle-building drug, compared with those women who had not been raped. Moreover, almost all of those who had been raped reported that they markedly increased their bodybuilding activities after the attack (NIDA 2006b).

Adolescent steroid abuse has been found to be part of a pattern of high-risk behaviors. Steroid-abusing adolescents have also been found to take risks such as drinking and driving, carrying a gun, driving a motorcycle without a helmet, and abusing other illicit drugs.

In conclusion, conditions such as **muscle dysmorphia** (a behavioral syndrome that causes individuals to have a distorted image of their bodies, perceiving themselves as looking small and weak, even when they may be large and muscular), a history of physical or sexual abuse, or a history of engaging in high-risk behaviors have all been associated with an increased risk of initiating or continuing steroid abuse.

A more recent study from the *American Journal of Sports Medicine* reported that the number of anabolic steroid users in the United States is *estimated* at approximately 3 million people. This number has increased dramatically since 1991 when data from the National Household Survey on Drug Abuse estimated the number of anabolic steroid users in the United States to be more than 1 million (1,084,000) (e-Steroid.com 2013) (see **Figure 16.1**).

KEY TERM

muscle dysmorphia
behavioral syndrome that causes men to have a distorted image of their bodies, perceiving themselves as looking small and weak, even when they may be large and muscular; women with this condition think they look fat and flabby, even though they may actually be lean and muscular

FIGURE 16.1 Reasons for nonmedical steroid use by college students.

Reproduced with permission from Harlan, R., and M. Garcia. "Neurobiology of Androgen Abuse," *Drugs of Abuse and Neurobiology*, edited by R. Watson, 186, Boca Raton, FL: CRC Press, 1992.

The most commonly abused steroids are in two categories: oral and injectable. Oral steroids include the following:

- Anadrol (oxymetholone)
- Oxandrin (oxandrolone)
- Dianabol (methandrostenolone)
- Winstrol (stanozolol)

Injectable steroids include the following:

- Deca-Durabolin (nandrolone decanoate)
- Durabolin (nandrolone phenylpropionate)

Besides risking their health, athletes who choose to dope should remember that they are role models. Seventy-three percent of youth want to be like a famous athlete; 53% of youth say it is common for famous athletes to use banned substances to get ahead.

- Depo-Testosterone (testosterone cypionate)
- Equipoise (boldenone undecylenate)
- Tetrahydrogestrinone (THG)

Competition for scholarships and entry into professional sports are major factors that influence young athletes to use steroids (Scott, Wagner, and Barlow 1996). However, a 2015 Monitoring the Future Study funded by the National Institute on Drug Abuse found that only 1% of 8th graders, 1.2% of 10th graders, and 2.3% of 12th graders had used steroids (Johnston et al. 2016b). Another study, from 2012, found that approximately 5% of middle and high school students had used anabolic steroids to add muscle, with almost one-third of boys and one-fifth of girls consuming protein powder or shakes. Between 5% and 10% reported use of nonsteroid muscle-enhancing substances such as creatine (Alvarez 2012). In a prior nationwide study, in 2005, annual use rates were 1.2%, 1.8%, and 2.6% for boys in grades 8, 10, and 12, respectively, compared with 0.9%, 0.7%, and 0.4% for girls in those grades (Johnston et al. 2006). Encouraging results indicate that steroid use among adolescents in 8th, 10th, and 12th grade is significantly lower than in previous years (Johnston et al. 2006).

While a vast majority of anabolic steroid users are male, women involved in bodybuilding and strength and endurance sports also abuse these drugs. In another study, among high school seniors, 3.2% of the males reported steroid use in the past year compared with 1.1% of the females. These statistics are much lower among 19- to 32-year-olds (0.4%), with males accounting for all steroid use (Johnston et al. 2006).

A 2014 college survey by the National Collegiate Athletic Association (NCAA) found that usage of stimulants, including ephedrine and amphetamines, and anabolic steroids had risen slightly during survey years 2009 and 2013. In 2009, the overall percentage of anabolic steroids used by females within the last 12 months was 0.2% and males was 0.5%. In 2013, 0.1% of females and 0.7% of males used anabolic steroids (NCAA Research 2014). The following are more recent findings regarding NCAA students:

- Substance use is typically highest among Division III student athletes and for most substances appears to be on the rise relative to trends in Division I and Division II.
- With the exception of alcohol use, substance use is higher among male student-athletes.
- Excessive drinking (10+ drinks in one sitting) is six times higher in male student-athletes than female student-athletes.

- Contrary to popular belief, excessive drinking overall is going down among student-athletes. Spit tobacco use has remained relatively consistent and is currently being used at a higher level than cigarettes. Cigarette use is declining.
- Marijuana is used most among Division III student-athletes, at a rate approximately 10% higher than Division I and Division II student-athletes.
- Compared with general college student cohorts, student-athletes are using cigarettes, marijuana, amphetamines, cocaine and synthetic marijuana at a lower rate. (NCAA Research 2014)

PATTERNS OF ABUSE

Geographical factors appear to have little to do with the use of anabolic steroids among athletes. In both inner city and suburban schools, all are equally attracted to these drugs. However, some athletes are more inclined to abuse anabolic steroids than others. For example, football players have the highest rate of abuse and track athletes have one of the lowest (NCAA Research 2014).[1] In a survey conducted by the NCAA of 11 NCAA colleges and universities, 9% of football players self-reported abuse of steroids compared to only 4% of track and field athletes (National Institutes of Health [NIH] and NIDA 1998). A study by WADA that examined blood samples taken between 2003 and 2008 across all professional sports found the following (Burn-Murdoch 2012):

- Of the 26 sports included in the 2012 Games, the worst offender in terms of the rate of findings per sample (averaged across all 8 years) is cycling, 3.71%.
- The second highest rate—3.05%—was found among boxers. Badminton had the lowest rate of usage-indication findings per sample, at 0.87%.
- Footballers were the most tested athletes in terms of the total number of samples (30,398), followed by athletics (competitive running, jumping, throwing, and walking) (25,013), cycling (21,427), and aquatics (13,138).

---

[1] Even the usage rates of other major drugs such as alcohol, marijuana, and cocaine within the three divisions at educational institutions are noteworthy and problematic. The National Collegiate Athletic Association (NCAA) reports the following usage rates among college athletes: Division I: 78% alcohol, 16% marijuana, and 1.5% cocaine usage. Division II: 79% alcohol, 20% marijuana, and 1.3% cocaine usage. Division III: 83% alcohol, 29% marijuana, and 2.6% cocaine usage (NCAA 2014).

Another study using a more indirect method of interviewing (known as self-reporting) found rates three times higher than the percentages just reported (Burn-Murdoch 2012). In addition, the likelihood of abusing these drugs increases as the level of competition increases. Colleges and universities are either Division I, II, or III. Educational institutions in Division I "have to sponsor at least seven sports for men and seven for women (or six for men and eight for women) with two team sports for each gender. Each playing season has to be represented by each gender as well" (NCAA 2015).

Educational institutions in Division II "have to sponsor at least five sports for men and five for women (or four for men and six for women), with two team sports for each gender, and each playing season represented by each gender" (NCAA 2015). "Division III institutions have to sponsor at least five sports for men and five for women, with two team sports for each gender, and each playing season represented by each gender. There are minimum contest and participant minimums for each sport. Division III athletics features student-athletes who receive no financial aid related to their athletic ability and athletic departments are staffed and funded like any other department in the university. Division III athletics departments place special importance on the impact of athletics on the participants rather than on the spectators" (NCAA 2015).

In general, usage patterns for anabolic steroids vary considerably according to athletes' motivation, the level of competition, the type of sport, and the pressure for winning.

The pattern of use usually consists of self-administering doses that are 1 to 100 times greater than dosages used for legitimate medical conditions (U.S. Department of Justice 2004). Users take nonmedical anabolic-androgenic steroids in cycles, which are periods of use lasting 6 to 12 weeks or longer. **Stacking** these drugs means taking two or more types of steroids, which is common. The use of different steroids taken singly but in sequence is called **cycling**. **Plateauing** steroids is a process where athletes develop tolerance to

KEY TERMS

stacking
combining two or more different types of steroids

cycling
taking doses of steroid for a period of time, stopping for a time, and then restarting

plateauing
developing tolerance to the effects of anabolic steroids

the effects of anabolic steroids by staggering various drugs, sometimes taking them in overlapping patterns or alternately (NIDA 2016). Users often move from a low daily dose at the beginning of a cycle to a higher dose, then reduce their use toward the end of the cycle (**pyramiding**) (NIDA 2016). To combat the unwanted side effects of steroids, such as severe skin rashes and development of irreversible masculine traits in women, as well as sudden anger and explosive physical aggressiveness (known as "roid rage" in men), other drugs, such as diuretics, antiestrogens, human chorionic gonadotropin, and antiacne medication, are often taken concurrently. This pattern of use is referred to by users as an **array**. In general, power athletes prefer stacking, whereas bodybuilders prefer cycling. (See **Table 16.2**, which lists classes of drugs banned by the NCAA, drugs and procedures subject to restrictions, and some examples of NCAA banned substances in each drug class.)

Because steroid use has been prohibited by all legitimate sporting organizations, urine testing just before the athletic event has become commonplace (Lukas 1993). Steroid-using athletes attempt to avoid detection by trying to fool the tests. These highly questionable strategies include the following (Lukas 1993; Merchant 1992):

- Using the steroid only during training for the athletic events, but discontinuing its use several weeks before the competition to allow the drug to disappear from the body. Because oral steroids are cleared from the body faster than the injectable types, they are usually discontinued 2 to 4 weeks prior to competition, and the injection steroids are stopped 3 to 6 weeks before competition.
- Taking drugs, such as probenecid, that block the excretion of steroids in the urine. Probenecid often is used in an attempt to mask (cover up) anabolic steroids when drug tests are taken. Probenecid "[d]ecreases entry of steroids into the urine" (U.S. Department of Justice 2004). Current drug testing can detect the use of these drugs.

KEY TERMS

pyramiding
slowly increasing the dose or frequency of steroid abuse, reaching a peak amount, and then gradually tapering off

array
use of other drugs while taking anabolic steroids to avoid possible side effects

- Adding adulterant chemicals to the urine, such as Drano, Clorox, ammonia, or eye drops in order to invalidate the tests.

Some of the most recent types of drugs that athletes use, even though they are all banned by WADA, are listed in **Table 16.3**. This table summarizes the 2013 list of prohibited performance-enhancing substances banned by the World Anti-Doping Code—International Standard.

EFFECTS OF ANABOLIC STEROIDS

Low to moderate doses of anabolic steroids have little effect on the strength or athletic skills of the average adult. However, when high doses are used by athletes during intense training programs, these drugs cause significant gains in lean body mass (i.e., muscle) and strength while decreasing fat (Lukas 1993). Because most of these effects are transient and will disappear when steroid use is stopped, athletes feel compelled to continue using them and become psychologically hooked (Toronto 1992). The drugs are most likely to benefit athletes in contact and strength sports in which increased muscle mass provides an advantage, such as weightlifting and football; anabolic steroids are less likely to benefit athletes involved in sports requiring dexterity and agility, such as baseball or tennis.

The risks associated with anabolic steroids are not completely understood. Most certainly, the higher the doses and the longer the use, the greater the potential damage these drugs can do to the body. Adverse effects largely depend on "[a]ge, sex, the anabolic steroid used, amount used, and duration of use" (Drug Enforcement Administration [DEA] 2015, p. 77). The following adverse effects are associated with heavy steroid use (10 to 30 times the theurapeutic dose):

- Anabolic steroid use can stunt the ultimate height that an individual achieves.
- In boys, steroid use can cause early sexual development, acne, and stunted growth (if adolescents use steroids before their growth spurt).
- In adolescent girls and women, anabolic steroid use can induce permanent physical changes, such as deepening of the voice, increased facial and body hair growth, menstrual irregularities, male pattern baldness, and lengthening of the clitoris.
- In men, anabolic steroid use can cause shrinkage of the testicles, reduced sperm count, enlargement of the male breast tissue, sterility, and an increased risk of prostate cancer.

TABLE 16.2 NCAA Banned Drug List

The NCAA bans the following classes of drugs:

1. Stimulants
2. Anabolic Agents
3. Alcohol and Beta Blockers (banned for rifle only)
4. Diuretics and Other Masking Agents
5. Street Drugs
6. Peptide Hormones and Analogues
7. Anti-estrogens
8. Beta-2 Agonists

Note: Any substance chemically related to these classes is also banned.

The institution and the student-athlete shall be held accountable for all drugs within the banned drug class regardless of whether they have been specifically identified.

Drugs and Procedures Subject to Restrictions:

1. Blood doping
2. Gene doping
3. Local anesthetics (under some conditions)
4. Manipulation of urine samples.
5. Beta-2 agonists permitted only by prescription and inhalation

NCAA Nutritional/Dietary Supplements Warning:

Before consuming any nutritional/dietary supplement product, review the product with the appropriate or designated athletics department staff. There are no NCAA approved supplement products.

1. Dietary supplements, including vitamins and minerals, are not well regulated and may cause a positive drug test result.
2. Student-athletes have tested positive and lost their eligibility from using dietary supplements.
3. Many dietary supplements are contaminated with banned drugs not listed on the label.
4. Any product containing a dietary supplement ingredient is taken at your own risk. Check with your athletics department staff prior to using a supplement.

Examples of NCAA Banned Substances in Each Drug Class

Note to Student-Athletes: There is NO complete list of banned substances.

Do not rely on this list to rule out any label ingredient.

1. Stimulants—Amphetamine (Adderall); caffeine (guarana); cocaine; ephedrine; fenfluramine (Fen); methamphetamine; methylphenidate (Ritalin); phentermine (Phen); synephrine (bitter orange); methylhexaneamine, "bath salts" (mephedrone); octopamne; DMBA; etc. Exceptions: phenylephrine and pseudoephedrine are not banned.
2. Anabolic Agents (sometimes listed as a chemical formula, such as 3,6,17-androstenetrione)—Androstenedione; boldenone; clenbuterol; DHEA (7-Keto); epi-trenbolone; etiocholanolone; methasterone; methandienone; nandrolone; norandrostenedione; ostarine, stanozolol; stenbolone; testosterone; trenbolone; SARMS (ostarine); etc.
3. Alcohol and Beta Blockers (banned for rifle only)—Alcohol; atenolol; metoprolol; nadolol; pindolol; propranolol; timolol; etc.
4. Diuretics (water pills) and Other Masking Agents—Bumetanide; chlorothiazide; furosemide; hydrochlorothiazide; probenecid; spironolactone (canrenone); triamerene; trichlormethiazide; etc.
5. Street Drugs—Heroin; marijuana; tetrahydrocannabinol (THC); synthetic cannabinoids (e.g., spice, K2, JWH-018, JWH-073).
6. Peptide Hormones and Analogues—Growth hormone (hGH); human chorionic gonadotropin (hCG); erythropoietin (EPO); IGF-1; etc.
7. Anti-Estrogens—Anastrozole; tamoxifen; formestane; ATD; clomiphene; SERMS (nolvadex); etc.
8. Beta-2 Agonists—Bambuterol; formoterol; salbutamol; salmeterol; higenamine; norcoclaurine; etc.

Any substance that is chemically related to the class, even if it is not listed as an example, is also banned!

It is your responsibility to check with the appropriate or designated athletics staff before using any substance.

Reproduced with permission from The National Collegiate Athletic Association (NCAA). "2015–16 NCAA Banned Drugs." 7 November 2016. Available http://www.ncaa.org/sites/default/files/2015-16%20NCAA%20Banned%20Drugs.pdf

TABLE 16.3 World Anti-Doping Code 2016 List of Prohibited Substances and Methods*
SUBSTANCES AND METHODS PROHIBITED AT ALL TIMES (In- and Out-of-Competition)

Prohibited Substances

S0 Non-Approved Substances

Any pharmacological substance which is not addressed by any of the subsequent sections of the List and with no current approval by any governmental regulatory health authority for human therapeutic use (e.g. drugs under pre-clinical or clinical development or discontinued, designer drugs, substances approved only for veterinary use) is prohibited at all times.

S1 Anabolic Agents

Anabolic agents are prohibited.

1. Anabolic Androgenic Steroids (Aas)

    a. Exogenous[1] AAS, including: (e.g. 1-Androstenediol (5α-androst-1-ene-3β,17β-diol); 1-Androstenedione (5α-androst-1-ene-3,17-dione); 1-Testosterone (17β-hydroxy-5α-androst-1-en-3-one); 4-Hydroxytestosterone (4,17β-dihydroxyandrost-4-en-3-one); 19-Norandrostenedione (estr-4-ene-3,17-dione); Bolandiol (estr-4-ene-3β,17β-diol); Bolasterone, etc., etc.

    b. Endogenous[2] AAS when administered exogenously: Androstenediol (androst-5-ene-3β,17β-diol); Androstenedione (androst-4-ene-3,17-dione); Dihydrotestosterone (17β-hydroxy-5α-androstan-3-one); Prasterone (dehydroepiandrosterone, DHEA, 3β-hydroxyandrost-5-en-17-one); etc., etc.

2. Other Anabolic Agents Including, but not limited to: Clenbuterol, selective androgen receptor modulators (SARMs, e.g. andarine and ostarine), tibolone, zeranol and zilpaterol, etc., etc.

S2 Peptide Hormones, Growth Factors, Related Substances and Mimetics

The following substances, and other substances with similar chemical structure or similar biological effect(s), are prohibited:

1. Erythropoietin-Receptor agonists: 1.1 Erythropoiesis-Stimulating Agents (ESAs) including e.g. Darbepoietin (dEPO); Erythropoietins (EPO); EPO-Fc; EPO-mimetic peptides (EMP), e.g. CNTO 530 and peginesatide; methoxy polyethylene glycol-epoetin beta (CERA), etc., etc.

S3 Beta-2 Agonists

All beta-2 agonists, including all optical isomers, e.g. d- and l- where relevant, are prohibited.

Except:

* Inhaled salbutamol (maximum 1600 micrograms over 24 hours);

* Inhaled formoterol (maximum delivered dose 54 micrograms over 24 hours); and

* Inhaled salmeterol in accordance with the manufacturers' recommended therapeutic regimen.

The presence in urine of salbutamol in excess of 1000 ng/mL or formoterol in excess of 40 ng/mL is presumed not to be an intended therapeutic use of the substance and will be considered as an Adverse Analytical Finding (AAF) unless the Athlete proves, through a controlled pharmacokinetic study, that the abnormal result was the consequence of the use of the therapeutic inhaled dose up to the maximum indicated above.

S4 Hormone and Metabolic Modulators

The following hormone and metabolic modulators are prohibited:

1. Aromatase inhibitors including, but not limited to: 4-Androstene-3,6,17 trione (6-oxo); Aminoglutethimide; Anastrozole; Androsta-1,4,6-triene-3,17-dione (androstatrienedione); Exemestane; Formestane; Letrozole; Testolactone.

2. Selective estrogen receptor modulators (SERMs) including, but not limited to: Raloxifene; Tamoxifen; Toremifene.

3. Other anti-estrogenic substances including, but not limited to: Clomiphene; Cyclofenil; Fulvestrant, etc., etc.

S5 Diuretics and Masking Agents

The following diuretics and masking agents are prohibited, as are other substances with a similar chemical structure or similar biological effect(s).

Including, but not limited to:

* Desmopressin; probenecid; plasma expanders, e.g. glycerol and intravenous administration of albumin, dextran, hydroxyethyl starch and mannitol.

* Acetazolamide; amiloride; bumetanide; canrenone; chlortalidone; etacrynic acid; furosemide; indapamide; metolazone; spironolactone; thiazides, e.g. bendroflumethiazide, chlorothiazide and hydrochlorothiazide; triamterene and vaptans, e.g. tolvaptan.

TABLE 16.3 World Anti-Doping Code 2016 List of Prohibited Substances and Methods*
SUBSTANCES AND METHODS PROHIBITED AT ALL TIMES (In- and Out-of-Competition) (*continued*)

Except:

- Drospirenone; pamabrom; and ophthalmic use of carbonic anhydrase inhibitors (e.g. dorzolamide, brinzolamide).

- Local administration of felypressin in dental anaesthesia.

The detection in an Athlete's Sample at all times or In-Competition, as applicable, of any quantity of the following substances subject to threshold limits: formoterol, salbutamol, cathine, ephedrine, methylephedrine and pseudoephedrine, in conjunction with a diuretic or masking agent, will be considered as an Adverse Analytical Finding unless the Athlete has an approved TUE for that substance in addition to the one granted for the diuretic or masking agent.

Prohibited Methods

M1 Manipulation Of Blood And Blood Components

The following are prohibited:

1. The Administration or reintroduction of any quantity of autologous, allogenic (homologous) or heterologous blood, or red blood cell products of any origin into the circulatory system.

2. Artificially enhancing the uptake, transport or delivery of oxygen. Including, but not limited to: Perfluorochemicals; efaproxiral (RSR13) and modified haemoglobin products, e.g. haemoglobin-based blood substitutes and microencapsulated haemoglobin products, excluding supplemental oxygen.

3. Any form of intravascular manipulation of the blood or blood components by physical or chemical means.

M2 Chemical And Physical Manipulation

The following are prohibited:

1. Tampering, or Attempting to Tamper, to alter the integrity and validity of Samples collected during Doping Control. Including, but not limited to: Urine substitution and/or adulteration, e.g. proteases.

2. Intravenous infusions and/or injections of more than 50 mL per 6 hour period except for those legitimately received in the course of hospital admissions, surgical procedures or clinical investigations.

M3 Gene Doping

The following, with the potential to enhance sport performance, are prohibited:

1. The transfer of polymers of nucleic acids or nucleic acid analogues;

2. The use of normal or genetically modified cells.

[1] "exogenous" refers to a substance which is not ordinarily produced by the body naturally.

[2] "endogenous" refers to a substance which is ordinarily produced by the body naturally.

*This table has been abbreviated from WADA's 2016 Prohibited List The List of Prohibited Substances and Methods is the World Anti-Doping Agency's (WADA) International Standard identifying substances and methods prohibited in-competition, out-of-competition, and in particular sports. The complete and current List can be found on WADA's website at http://www.usada.org/wp-content/uploads/wada-2016-prohibited-list-en.pdf. Please be advised that the official text of the List shall be maintained by WADA and, in the event of any discrepancy between this extract and the List, the official WADA List shall prevail.

Data from World Anti-Doping Code. *International Standard: Prohibited List.* Montreal, Canada: World Anti-Doping Agency (WADA), 1 January 2016. Available http://www.usada.org/wp-content/uploads/wada-2016-prohibited-list-en.pdf

- In both men and women, anabolic steroid use can cause high cholesterol levels, which may increase the risk of coronary artery disease, strokes, and heart attacks.
- Anabolic steroid use can also cause acne and fluid retention.
- Oral preparations of anabolic steroids, in particular, can damage the liver.
- Abusers who inject steroids run the risk of contracting various infections due to non-sterile injection techniques, sharing of contaminated needles, and the use of steroid preparations manufactured in non-sterile environments. All these factors put users at risk for contracting viral infections such as HIV/AIDS or hepatitis B or C, and bacterial infections at the sight of injection.
- Abusers may also develop endocarditis, a bacterial infection that causes a potentially fatal inflammation of the heart lining. (DEA 2015, p. 77)

Additional adverse side effects include the following:

- Psychological side effects, including irritability, outbursts of anger, mania, psychosis, and major depression

- Persistent unpleasant breath odor
  (NCADI 1999)
- Swelling of the feet or lower limbs
  (NCADI 1999)

People who abuse steroids may experience withdrawal symptoms when they stop use, including mood swings, fatigue, restlessness, loss of appetite, sleep problems, decreased sex drive, and steroid cravings (NIDA 2016).

Finally, several substances produce effects similar to those of anabolic steroids. These include human growth hormone (hHG), clenbuterol, gonadotropins, and erythropoietin (DEA 2015).

LAWS AND PENALTIES FOR ANABOLIC STEROID ABUSE

The first report of use of anabolic steroids to improve athletic performance was in 1954 by the Russian weightlifting team. These drugs' performance-enhancing advantages were quickly recognized by other athletes, and it has been estimated that as many as 90% of weightlifting competitors in the 1960 Olympic Games used some form of steroid (Toronto 1992). Because of the widespread misuse and associated problems with the use of these drugs, in the United States anabolic steroids were classified as Schedule III controlled drugs in 1991 (Merchant 1992).

The Anabolic Steroids Control Act of 1990 placed anabolic steroids into Schedule III of the Controlled Substances Act (CSA) as of February 27, 1991. Under this legislation, anabolic steroids are defined as any drug or hormonal substance chemically and pharmacologically related to testosterone (other than estrogens, progestin's, and corticosteroids) that promotes muscle growth.

The possession or sale of anabolic steroids without a valid prescription is illegal. Federal law states that simple possession of illicitly obtained anabolic steroids carries a maximum penalty of 1 year in prison and a minimum $1000 fine if it is an individual's first drug offense. Second-time offenders face fines of $2500 and a maximum of 2 years in prison. For individuals with more than two prior convictions, the fine is doubled to a minimum of $5000 and a possible 3-year prison term. It is important to note that simple possession is any amount. The maximum penalty for trafficking anabolic steroids is 5 years in prison and a fine of $250,000 if it is the individual's first felony drug offense. If it is the person's second felony drug offense, the maximum period of imprisonment and the maximum fine both double (Anabolics. com 2016; U.S. Department of Justice 2004).

The penalties described above are for federal offenses; individual states also impose fines and penalties for illegal use of anabolic steroids. State executive offices have also recognized the seriousness of steroid abuse and other drugs of abuse in schools. For example, the State of Virginia enacted a new law that will allow student drug testing as a legitimate school drug prevention program. Other states and individual school districts are considering implementing similar measures (Anabolics.com 2016; U.S. Department of Justice 2004).

SOURCES OF STEROIDS

Where do the anabolic steroids come from? About 50% of the anabolic steroids used in the United States are prescribed by doctors; the other 50% are obtained from the black market. Black market sources of steroids include drugs diverted from legitimate channels, smuggled from foreign countries—including Brazil, Italy, Mexico, Great Britain, Portugal, France, and Peru (NIDA 1996)—that are designated for veterinarian use, or inactive counterfeits (U.S. Department of Justice 1991–1992). A primary source for steroids in the United States is the Baja, California, area of Mexico (Yesalis and Cowart 1998). The steroids are manufactured in Mexico City and shipped to pharmacies in the Baja region. Some health food stores and mail-order firms also offer products with names similar to the prescription anabolic steroids, such as Dynabdin, Metrobolin, and Diostero. These sham steroids contain only vitamins, amino acids, or micronutrients (Merchant 1992; NIDA 2006b). More recent findings regarding the origins of steroids indicate that "[m]ost illicit steroids are smuggled into the U.S. from abroad. Steroids are also illegally diverted from legitimate sources (theft or inappropriate prescribing). The Internet is the most widely used means of buying and selling anabolic steroids. Steroids are also bought and sold at gyms, bodybuilding competitions, and schools from teammates, coaches, and trainers" (DEA 2015).

Most steroids used for nonmedical purposes are obtained illegally. A major federal report indicates that sources of illicit steroids fall into three rough categories: (1) smuggled steroids manufactured licitly or illicitly abroad, (2) drugs legally manufactured in this country and diverted to illicit sales at various places in the distribution chain, and (3) drugs clandestinely produced domestically. Small minorities of users obtain their drugs by prescription. Actual doses are often difficult to estimate because the product may have been produced in an uncontrolled laboratory with unknown quality control, may have been intended for veterinary use with its human equivalent doses not known, or may be counterfeit (NIH and NIDA 1998). Another source noted that the majority of young people report that steroids are easily available through their friends and coaches (McCaffrey 1999).

STIMULANT USE AMONG ATHLETES

Reports often appear in the media of football, basketball, or baseball players who have tested positive in a drug-screening evaluation or who have been suspended from competition due to drug abuse. In 1986, reports of cocaine-related deaths of sports figures included basketball star Len Bias and professional football player Don Rogers. Perhaps such sports tragedies helped convince some U.S. youth of the dangers of stimulant abuse and contributed to the decline in drug abuse in the late 1980s (Johnston et al. 1993). Clearly, no one—not even an athlete—is immune from the risks of these drugs (see "Case in Point: When Drugs Enter the Boxing Ring").

Amphetamines and cocaine are abused to improve athletic skills (McDonald 1995). However, it is not clear if stimulants actually enhance athletic performance or merely the athlete's perception of performance. Many athletes believe these drugs promote quickness, enhance endurance, delay fatigue, increase self-confidence and aggression, and mask pain (Hoberman and Yesalis 1995). In fact, some studies have shown that stimulants can improve some aspects of athletic performance, especially in the presence of fatigue (NIDA 1996).

Although some athletes would never consider using the hard stimulants, such as cocaine and amphetamines, milder stimulants that are legal and available over-the-counter (OTC) may be thought to be acceptable. Such stimulants include caffeine and OTC decongestants (e.g., phenylpropanolamine and phenylephrine). These drugs can be a double-edged sword for the athlete. Their use can reduce fatigue, give a sense of energy, and even mask pain. Nevertheless, in high doses, especially when combined, they can cause nervousness, tremors, and restlessness; impair concentration; accelerate dehydration; and interfere with sleep ("OTC Drugs and Athletes" 1992). Some athletic competitions limit permissible blood levels of caffeine and do not allow the use of OTC stimulants such as decongestant drugs.

MISCELLANEOUS ERGOGENIC DRUGS

Most athletic organizations have banned the use of anabolic steroids and stimulants and are using more effective screening procedures to detect offenders. A result of this clampdown has been

► CASE IN POINT
When Drugs Enter the Boxing Ring

Former heavyweight champion Mike Tyson (now retired from boxing) admitted to being under the influence of illicit drugs during major fights and even admitted to using "a fake penis to avoid detection" (Swaine 2013) in order to pass drug testing. In his tell-all memoir, Tyson writes, "I was a full-blown coke-head" and that he "was high before taking to the ring for a match against Lou Savarese in Glasgow in June 2000"(Swaine 2013). Further, "Tyson explained he had taken cocaine before a notorious televised press conference with Lennox Lewis in New York in January 2002, which descended into an onstage brawl between the rival camps" (Swaine 2013). During this event he writes that he lost his mind

and recalled that he was so drugged up that he lost control and attacked another heavyweight (Lewis) that resulted in him biting into "one of Lewis's legs" (Swaine 2013).

Tyson, the youngest boxer ever to win the WBC, WBA and IBF heavyweight titles, said he regrets that his drug use led to "Herculean" mood swings. After several years of rehabilitation treatment—between staging a one-man show, appearing in the film *The Hangover* and socializing with A-list celebrities such as Victoria Beckham—Tyson said in August this year that he was close to death due to his chronic alcoholism. (Swaine 2013)

Swaine, J. "Mike Tyson Admits to Being High on Drugs During Major Fights, and Using a Fake Penis to Avoid Detection." *The Telegraph.* (12 November 2013). Available http://www.telegraph.co.uk/sport/othersports/boxing/10444998/Mike-Tyson-admits-to-being-high-on-drugs-during-major-fights-and-using-a-fake-penis-to-avoid-detection.html the search for alternative performance-enhancing drugs by athletes who feel a need for such pharmacological assistance. The following are brief discussions of a few of these substitute ergogenic substances.

CLENBUTEROL

At the 1992 Olympic Games in Barcelona, Spain, at least four athletes, including German world sprint champion Katrina Krabbe, were disqualified from competition for using the drug clenbuterol to enhance their athletic performance (Merchant 1992). Not legally available in the United States, this drug is known as "Doper's Delight" and is supposed to improve breathing and increase strength. Currently, most athletic urine examinations test for it.

ERYTHROPOIETIN

Clinically, erythropoietin (EPO) is a drug used to treat patients with anemia (Kennedy 2000). Because it stimulates the production of red blood cells (the oxygen-carrying cells in the blood), it is thought that this drug enhances oxygen use and produces additional energy. EPO was used as a substitute for blood doping when it was undetectable (today it is detectable). *Blood doping* is when athletes attempt to increase their number of red blood cells by reinfusing some of their own blood (which has been stored) before an athletic event. EPO can now be detected through testing. In the past, it was reportedly used by athletes engaged in endurance activities such as long-distance cycling.

The drug is not without dangers. Use of EPO thickens the blood due to the increase in the number of red blood cells. The increased thickness of the blood increases risk of blood clots, heart attacks, and strokes. It can also cause problems when the heart rate slows down, such as during sleep (Quinn 2016).

HUMAN GROWTH FACTOR AND HUMAN GROWTH HORMONE

Athletes sometimes abuse hormones such as **human growth factor (HGF)** or its synthetic version, **human growth hormone (HGH)**. HGH also is

referred to simply as *GH* (growth hormone). HGF, also known as *somatotropin*, is a hormone naturally secreted by the pituitary gland at the base of the brain that helps to achieve normal growth potential of muscles, bones, and internal organs. Some athletes claim that release of natural HGF can be simulated by using drugs such as levodopa (used to treat Parkinson's disease), clonidine (used to treat hypertension), and amino acids. Athletes use commercially prepared HGH because it cannot be distinguished from naturally occurring HGF (Kennedy 2000).

Use of this hormone by athletes is limited, however, by its high cost. The benefits of HGF to athletic performance are very controversial, although the potential side effects are substantial, including abnormal growth patterns (called acromegaly), diabetes, thyroid gland problems, heart disease, and loss of sex drive (Merchant 1992).

The synthetic HGH is available in the form of a structured steroid-type analog sold in vials; this product is used to build muscle tissue, with corresponding decreases in body fat, without exercise (McDonald 1995). HGH is probably the most potent anabolic agent ever discovered, but it is also one of the most expensive. In fact, HGH is so expensive that until the mid-1990s "its use in the United States was confined to pediatric endocrinologists who used it to treat undersized children" (McDonald 1995, p. C1). To date, tests are capable of detecting HGH in the blood (WebMD.com 2008). In addition, the side effects of this drug remain largely unknown. As a result, this drug is highly vulnerable to abuse.

BETA (β)-ADRENERGIC BLOCKERS

The β-adrenergic blockers are drugs that affect the cardiovascular system and are frequently used to treat hypertension. They have been used in sports because they reduce heart rate and signs of nervousness, which, in turn, quiets hand tremors. Consequently, these drugs are most likely to be used by individuals participating in sports that require steady hands, such as competitive shooting. The use of these drugs is prohibited by most athletic organizations (Kennedy 2000; Merchant 1992).

GAMMA-HYDROXYBUTYRATE

The substance gamma-hydroxybutyrate (GHB) is found naturally in the brain and has been used in England to treat insomnia. Athletes and bodybuilders have used GHB to increase muscle mass and strength (Kennedy 2000). Although the actual effects of the compound are not known, it has been reported to cause euphoria and increase

KEY TERMS

human growth factor (HGF)
a natural hormone that stimulates normal growth

human growth hormone (HGH)
a designer drug synthetic version of HGF; also referred to as simply *GH* (growth hormone)

the release of growth hormone. Acute poisoning with GHB has occurred, causing hospitalization; other adverse effects can include headaches, nausea, vomiting, muscle jerking, and even short-term coma, though full recovery has been universal ("Bodybuilding Drug" 1992; "Multistate Outbreak" 1994). Prolonged use may cause withdrawal (insomnia, anxiety, and tremor). GHB is especially dangerous when combined with central nervous system (CNS) stimulants such as amphetamines and cocaine (U.S. Department of Justice 2004).

■ Prevention of Abuse

If the problem of drug abuse among athletes is to be dealt with effectively, sport programs must be designed to discourage inappropriate drug use and assist athletes who have developed drug abuse problems. Coaches and administrators should make it clear to sport participants that substance abuse will never give an athlete a competitive advantage in their programs and will not be tolerated. The **Adolescents Training and Learning to Avoid Steroids (ATLAS) program**, which was developed by Dr. Linn Goldberg of Oregon Health Sciences at the University of Portland, is one of the most successful prevention programs for steroid abuse:

> The Adolescent[s] Training and Learning to Avoid Steroids Program (ATLAS) was designed to lower the use of anabolic steroids among high school athletes. The program combined classroom and weight-training sessions, to teach students about strength training, nutrition, and risk factors for steroid use. Overall, the ATLAS program was found to reduce the use of steroids. (Child Trends 2009)

More specifically,

> Athletes Training and Learning to Avoid Steroids (ATLAS) is a drug prevention and health promotion program for adolescent high school athletes that emphasizes the negative impact of anabolic steroids, alcohol, and other drugs on immediate sports performance. The program is integrated into team practice sessions and consists of a seven-session classroom curriculum and seven weight room skill training sessions. Coaching staff or surrogates administer the classroom curriculum which includes subjects such as risk factors of steroid use, strength training and sports nutrition, as well as skills to refuse steroids and other substances. In addition, nutritional recommendations and false claims of over the counter supplements

are discussed. Parents attend a single evening meeting centered on program goals. (Blueprints for Healthy Youth Development 2016)

Athletes, coaches, and team leaders are trained to educate team members about the effects of anabolic steroid abuse. Because adolescents already know that anabolic steroids build muscles and can increase athletic abilities, both desirable and adverse effects of steroid use are taught. Research has shown that information about anabolic steroids that fails to acknowledge potential benefits creates a credibility gap that can make youth distrustful of the prevention program. The program consists of three components—classroom, weight training, and parent information—to "give the student athletes the knowledge and skills to resist steroid use and achieve their athletic goals in more effective, healthier ways" (Goldberg et al. 1996, p. 1555):

1. The classroom component consists of football coaches and student leaders conducting highly interactive sessions that explore the effects of steroids, the elements of sports nutrition, and strength training alternatives to steroid use. In this setting, while the coaches introduce topics and act as leaders, the students are exploring and learning from one another (Goldberg et al. 1996).

2. In the weight-training component, research staff members conduct seven hands-on sessions that teach the students proper weight-training techniques (Goldberg et al. 1996).

3. The parent information component consists of discussions and information sessions with parents. The staff provides nutrition guidelines and seeks compliance while stressing the very best nutrition for the athletes and their families. Parents become more vigilant against steroid use and learn to enjoy well-balanced, nutritious meals (Goldberg et al. 1996).

Briefly summarized, results indicate that the students who participated in this program in comparison with a control group (a group of students

---

KEY TERM

Adolescents Training and Learning to Avoid Steroids (ATLAS) program
an anabolic abuse prevention educational program that empowers student athletes to make the right choices about steroid use

not participating in the program) (1) knew more about proper exercise, (2) had a clear understanding of the dangers of using steroids and had become much more sensitized to the harmful effects of such drugs, (3) held more unfavorable views of others' use of anabolic steroids, and (4) were more likely to avoid unhealthy eating (such as frequenting fast-food restaurants) (Child Trends 2009; Goldberg et al. 1996).

Major outcomes to date include the following:

Drug use intentions and behaviors:

- Decreased likelihood of lifetime steroid use at posttest and 1-year follow-up, but differences not significant.
- Decreased likelihood of alcohol and other drug use at the 1-year follow-up.
- Decreased likelihood of new occurrences of drinking and driving at 1-year follow-up.

Health promotion behaviors found at posttest and 1-year follow-up:

- Heightened perception of coach intolerance to drug use.
- Improved nutrition knowledge and behaviors.
- Enhanced strength training self-efficacy.
- Less likely to believe advertisements for sports supplements and positive steroid use images.
- Reduction in sport supplement use at 1-year follow-up.

Significant program effects on risk and protective factors:

- Greater self-reported ability to refuse drug offers from peers.
- Greater knowledge of the effects of steroids and alcohol.
- Stronger beliefs about the harmful effects of anabolic steroid use and perceived greater susceptibility to their effects. (Blueprints for Healthy Youth Development 2016)

Drug Use Among Women

In the recent past, little was known about the patterns of female drug abuse. In general, most clinical drug abuse research, including treatment and rehabilitation outcomes, was either conducted in male populations and the results were extrapolated to women or the research was done in general populations with little regard to gender influences (Chilet-Rosell 2014; Dicker

and Leighton 1994; Klee and Jackson 2002; Lin 1994; NIDA 2006a; U.S. Department of Health and Human Services [USDHHS] and NIDA 1999). Most researchers considered drug abuse to be a male problem. Today, the research focusing on women and drug use is better, but a greater amount of study is still needed. Even today, scientists performing even basic research with animals generally prefer male animal models to avoid the hormonal complexities of female animals. However, a growing concern for the importance of the unique emotional, social, biochemical, and hormonal features in females has caused researchers to acknowledge the importance of gender differences. Further, women and men may face unique issues when it comes to substance use, as a result of both sex and gender. *Sex differences* result from biology, or being genetically female or male, whereas *gender differences* are based on culturally defined roles for men and women, as well as those who feel uncomfortable identifying with either category. Gender roles influence how people perceive themselves and how they interact with others. Sex and gender can also interact with each other to create even more complex differences between men and women (NIDA 2015b).

Scientists who study substance use have discovered special sex-related issues related to hormones, menstrual cycle, fertility, pregnancy, breastfeeding, and menopause that can impact women's struggles with drug use. In addition, women themselves experience unique gender issues and reasons for using drugs that may include, for example, controlling weight, fighting exhaustion, coping with menstrual and pregnancy pain, and self-treating mental health problems (NIDA 2015b).

▪ Women Are More Concerned About Drug Use Than Men

Women express greater initial concerns about drug use than men, although "most recent studies suggest that gender either has no effect on treatment initiation, or, if it has an effect, women are more likely than men to initiate treatment" (Green 2006, p. 6). When asked whether drug abuse is a greater problem now than 5 years earlier, 51% of women and 42% of men answered "yes" (Drug Strategies 1998). When asked whether drug use is a big concern among youth, 58% of women and 48% of men answered "yes" (Drug Strategies 1998). Further, 58% of women and 50% of men thought it was wrong to reduce prevention funds while increasing prison funds (Drug

Strategies 1998). One reason for this discrepancy may be that women traditionally have been primary caregivers; therefore, they feel more responsible about issues that can plague their communities and their families and often feel the need to be more vocal and be in positions that maintain harmony within the family setting (Green 2006). Women also generally express more concerns about safety issues than men because they are more likely to be victims of violent crimes, such as muggings or sexual assaults.

■ Patterns of Drug Use: Comparing Females with Males

Recent surveys comparing male and female drug use patterns confirm that differences exist among the licit and illicit drug-using populations. **Table 16.4** compares annual female and male drug use among respondents aged 19 to 30 years in 2014. The research findings in this table indicate the following gender-related differences in drug use (Johnston et al. 2015a):

- Overall, use of illicit drugs is consistently lower in females (34.4%) than in males (39.8%).
- The most common types of abused drugs (in descending order) for females were as follows: alcohol (82.9%), flavored alcoholic beverages (53.8%), any illicit drug use (34.4%), marijuana (27.8%), cigarettes (26.9%), binge drinking (five or more drinks in a row in last 2 weeks) (26.4%), and any illicit drug other than marijuana (19.2%).
- Males have higher annual prevalence rates for nearly all illicit drugs. They are twice as likely or more to use synthetic marijuana (not shown in table), hallucinogens, LSD, hallucinogens other than LSD, salvia (not shown in table), heroin, heroin with a needle, GHB (not shown in table), ketamine (not shown in table), bath salts (not shown in table), and steroids.
- All three measures of cocaine use showed higher rates of use by male than female 19- to 30-year-olds. Annual cocaine use was reported by 6.9% of males and 3.6% of females, powder cocaine use by 6.3% of males and 3.6% of females, and crack use by 0.5% of males and 0.4% of females.
- Other large gender differences among those aged 19 to 30 were found in daily marijuana use (9.0% for males vs. 5.2% for females), daily alcohol use (7.4% vs. 4.1%), and occasions of drinking five or more drinks in a row in the prior 2 weeks (43% vs. 26%).

TABLE 16.4 Annual Percentage Use of Various Types of Drugs by Gender Among Respondents Aged 19 to 30 Years, 2014.

	Males (%)	Females (%)	Total (%)
Any illicit drug use (nonmedical use)*	39.8	34.4	36.6
Alcohol	83.1	82.9	83.0
Flavored alcoholic beverages	53.0	53.8	53.5
Binge drinking (five or more drinks in a row in last 2 weeks)	42.9	26.4	33.1
Cigarettes	31.1	24.1	26.9
Marijuana	34.2	27.8	30.4
Any illicit drug other than marijuana	23.6	19.2	21.0
Narcotics other than heroin**	7.4	5.5	6.3
Amphetamines, adjusted**	8.8	6.8	7.6
Tranquilizers**	4.8	5.0	4.9
Other cocaine	6.3	3.6	4.7
Cocaine	6.9	3.6	4.9
Sedatives (barbiturates)**	2.9	3.4	3.2
MDMA (Ecstasy)	5.4	3.4	4.2
Hallucinogens	5.9	2.4	3.9
Hallucinogens other than LSD	4.7	1.7	2.9
LSD	2.9	1.3	2.0
Inhalants	1.1	0.9	1.0
Methamphetamines	0.8	0.6	0.7
Crack	0.5	0.4	0.4
Crystal methamphetamine (ice)	0.3	0.4	0.4
Heroin	0.4	0.3	0.4
PCP	0.1	0.2	0.2
Heroin (with a needle)	0.2	0.2	0.2
Steroids	1.1	0.3	0.6
Heroin (without a needle)	0.5	0.2	0.3

* Use of any illicit drug includes any use of marijuana, hallucinogens, cocaine, heroin or other narcotics, amphetamines, sedatives (barbiturates), or tranquilizers not under a doctor's orders

** Nonprescription use.

Data from Johnston, L. D., O'Malley, P. M., Bachman, J. G., Schulenberg, J. E., and Miech, R. A. *Monitoring the Future National Survey Results on Drug Use, 1975–2014: Volume 2, College Students and Adults Ages 19–55.* Ann Arbor: Institute for Social Research, The University of Michigan, 2015.

- A particularly large gender difference exists in measures of extreme binge drinking based on years 2005–2014 combined: the rate for having 10 or more drinks on at least one occasion in the prior 2 weeks was 17.2% for males versus 5.7% for females. The rate for having 15 or more drinks in that interval was 7.0% for males and 1.4% for females.
- Ecstasy (MDMA) use was slightly higher among males than among females, with an annual prevalence of 5.4% and 3.4%, respectively.
- Annual prevalence of use of narcotics other than heroin outside of medical supervision was also slightly higher among males than females (7.4% vs. 5.5%). Use of Vicodin, one of the most widely used drugs in the class was 7.0% for males versus and 3.9% for females. The gender difference for OxyContin was 3.0% for males versus 2.3% for females.
- The use of amphetamines was slightly higher among males than among females, with annual prevalences of 8.8% and 6.8%, respectively.
- Among young adults there was a large gender difference in 2014 in the use of smokeless tobacco, with males much more likely than females to have used in the prior month (16.2% vs. 3.8%). Almost all past-year use of snus occurred among males (9.7%) compared to females (1.5%), as was also the case for dissolvable tobacco (1.6% in males vs. <0.5% in females).
- Steroid use among young adults was much more prevalent among males than females, as was true for 12th graders. Among 12th graders in 2014, 2.0% of males reported steroid use in the past year versus 0.7% of females. These statistics were much lower among 19- to 30-year-olds, but use by males remained higher (1.1% for males vs. 0.3% for females).

Recent findings regarding gender differences among 8th, 10th, and 12th graders in 2015 are as follows (Johnston et al. 2016b):

- Similar to adult males and females, males have somewhat higher rates of illicit drug use than females (especially higher rates of frequent use), most notably by 12th grade. This also includes much higher rates of smokeless tobacco and steroid use.
- The primary exception with regard to gender differences among 12th graders may be found in the misuse of prescription drugs such as amphetamines, sedatives, and tranquilizers, where females currently tend to have higher rates of use than males, particularly in the early grades (8th, 10th, and 12th graders).
- Twelfth-grade males also currently have higher levels of inhalants and synthetic marijuana use than in 8th-grade males.
- For most drugs, gender differences among 8th graders are very small, with females fairly consistently reporting slightly higher rates of use than males since 2002.
- Among 10th graders, males have generally, though not always, reported higher rates of illicit drug use than females; males consistently were slightly higher in use than females between 2009 and 2013, but females were slightly higher in 2014.
- Among 12th graders, for many years males have consistently reported distinctly higher 30-day alcohol usage rates than females; however, the differences have been narrowing, and in 2015 females had slightly higher prevalences in 8th and 10th grades and only a slightly lower one in 12th grade (35% female vs. 36% male).
- Gender differences in binge drinking have followed a similar pattern—females report higher or the same rates in 8th grade, males somewhat higher rates in 10th grade, and males distinctly higher rates in 12th grade (though the gap is narrowing).
- Among 12th graders, females generally had higher rates of smoking than males through 1990, but since then, males have generally had the higher rates (13% vs. 9% in 2015).
- The various gender differences in substance use appear to emerge for many drugs as students grow older.

The following findings are pertinent to adults and gender differences in substance use/abuse:

To date, there is extensive evidence of the differences between women and men regarding substance use. Epidemiological studies show that even though women are less likely to initiate drug use than men, they start earlier and are more susceptible to develop an addiction. Women are also more vulnerable to drug-related pathologies, such as liver and cardiovascular diseases, and are more exposed to sexual and physical abuse and violence and to sexually transmitted diseases. At the same time studies of gender differences in drug treatment show that reasons why women and men seek help are often dissimilar, and that psychological, biological and social gender differences are important factors for the success of diverse types of treatment and for retention into treatment. (UNICRI 2013, p. 1)

Although some similarities appear between genders in drug usage rates for specific types of drugs, the general differences in the prevalence rates for females and males compel researchers to look for explanations so that we can better understand and deal with gender-related drug abuse problems.

■ Female Roles, Seeking Treatment, and Drug Addiction

Women are expected to take on more responsibilities than in my mother's day. Not only are we expected to work like men, but we also take care of the house, worry about the children, and get dinner on the table. If the house needs cleaning, everyone looks at the woman of the house. Men still have these expectations. I know things are changing with more equality between the sexes, but real equality of responsibilities has yet to occur. After everyone gets to bed on weekdays, I have a few drinks in order to calm me down before I go to bed. *(From Venturelli's research files, female employed full-time, age 43, June 30, 1996)*

Another interview revealed the following:

When we first married my husband used to help me with housework. However, several years later he gradually slacked off with helping me with house cleaning. I really cannot fully blame him because this happened when his job become increasingly demanding and on weekends he had to catch up with his loss of sleep during his demanding workweek. I complained at the time that it was a lot of work doing it all alone. Shortly after I continually complained we decide to hire a cleaning service. However, I have to admit, whenever we have company over, the pressure to make the house look good is always on me and even most guests look at me when they complement how nice and clean our house is. So, it's not just who does the housework and how we divide the work to maintain it, it's how people traditionally look at women as being responsible for cleanliness and order inside the home *(From Venturelli's research files, female nurse practitioner, age 41, residing in Chesterton, Indiana, March 2016)*

Data from the 2014 *National Survey on Drug Use and Health* (CBHSQ 2015) show that rates of substance use disorders differ between men and women. For instance:

- The percentage of women aged 18 and older who had five or more drinks in 1 day at least once in the past year was 17.4%. The percentage was higher for men in this age group at 32.6%.
- Men aged 12 or older are more likely than women to report illegal drug use (12.8% vs. 7.3%).
- More men than women aged 12 and older reported using marijuana (10.9% vs. 6%), cocaine (0.8% vs. 0.4%), and hallucinogens (0.6% vs. 0.3%).
- The rate of substance dependence or abuse for males aged 12 and older was greater than the rate for females (10.7% vs. 5.7%).

Women's drinking patterns are different from men's. They face greater risks than men because of the following (CBHSQ 2015):

- Women typically start to have alcohol-related problems at lower drinking levels than men.
- Women typically weigh less than men.
- Pound for pound, women have less water in their bodies than men do, and alcohol resides predominantly in body water.

Recent research indicates that most people who have a substance use problem do not receive treatment. In comparing men with women, women are at a greater disadvantage for receiving substance abuse treatment:

Although males abuse drugs at an earlier age and more frequently than females, females tend to become addicted more quickly once they are introduced to drugs—a phenomenon known as "telescoping." Women tend to relapse at higher rates than men after going through rehab, and they tend to suffer from more serious consequences to their health, occupational status, relationships, and finances. (The Recovery Village 2016)

Further, males are more likely than females to report marijuana and alcohol use, whereas females are more likely than males to report nonmedical use of prescription drugs. Also, differences in substance abuse patterns among men and women vary by age. Data from the 2011 National Survey on Drug Use and Health show that men aged 18 or older have almost twice the rate of substance dependence as adult women, but among youths aged 12 to 17, the rate of substance dependence for both genders is the same (6.9%) (SAMHSA 2014b).

In 2011, about 609,000 of the 1.84 million admissions to substance abuse treatment were female (33.1%), and 1.23 million were male (66.9%). In general, the proportions of female and male admissions were similar for each of the seven age categories examined. Other major findings regarding female substance abuse treatment include the following:

• No meaningful gender differences were found by race/ethnicity. Specifically, the majority of female and male admissions (66.4 and 58.2%, respectively) were non-Hispanic White. The percentages of female and male admissions that were non-Hispanic Black and Hispanic were similar (SAMHSA 2014a).

• Alcohol was the most commonly reported primary substance of abuse by female (33.3%) and male (42.3%) admissions. Among females, alcohol was followed by heroin (15.3%), marijuana (14.6%), and prescription pain relievers (13.8%); among males, the next most frequently reported substances were marijuana (19.9%), heroin (15.0%), and prescription pain relievers (7.8%) (SAMHSA 2014b).

• Marijuana was reported as the primary substance of abuse less frequently by females than males among admissions aged 12 to 17 (60.8 vs. 80.7%) and 18 to 24 (22.1 vs. 33.4%). There was no variation by gender in primary marijuana abuse among admissions aged 25 or older (SAMHSA 2014a).

• The proportions of female and male admissions reporting methamphetamine/amphetamines as their primary substance of abuse were similar across all age groups with the exception of those aged 18 to 24. Specifically, among admissions aged 18 to 24, 8.9% of female admissions reported primary methamphetamine/amphetamine abuse compared with 3.7% of male admissions (SAMHSA 2014a).

• The highest proportions of primary abuse of prescription pain relievers (e.g., oxycodone) were found among admissions aged 18 to 24 and 25 to 34. In the 25 to 34 age group, 19.0% of female admissions and 12.2% of male admissions reported prescription pain relievers as their primary substance of abuse. In terms of the effect size, however, the differences between male and female admissions in these age groups were negligible. The only meaningful difference by effect size between males and

females was observed among admissions aged 65 or older. Within the 65 or older age group, the proportion of female admissions reporting primary abuse of prescription pain relievers was nearly 3 times that of their male counterparts (7.2 vs. 2.8%) (SAMHSA 2014b).

Another study indicated that the major reasons reported why women ages 18 to 49 who needed treatment did not receive it were as follows (NSDUH 2007; SAMHSA 2010):

• Not ready to stop using (36%)
• Cost/insurance barriers (34%)
• Social stigma (29%)
• Did not feel need for treatment/could handle the problem without treatment (15.5%)
• Did not know where to go for treatment (13.2%)
• Did not have the time (4.7%)
• Treatment would not help (2.7%)
• Other access barriers (15.7%)

To appreciate the impact of drug abuse on women and the reasons why they are more reluctant to seek substance abuse treatment, it is necessary to understand the uniqueness of female roles in our society. Relative to drug abuse problems, women today often experience a double standard. Women suffering from drug addictions are often perceived less tolerant than comparably addicted men (Erickson and Murray 1989). Because of these social biases, women are afraid of being condemned and are less likely to seek professional help for their own personal drug abuse problems; they also are more likely to report feeling shame or embarrassment because they are in substance abuse treatment (Green 2006). In addition, family, friends, and associates are less inclined to provide drug-dependent women with important emotional support (Klee and Jackson 2002; NSDUH 2007; USDHHS and NIDA 1999).

The image of the alcoholic woman has always been that of one who is boisterous, flirtatious, effusive, and, sometimes, loudmouthed. This may be the person she might become on occasion, but more often she is secluded in the privacy of her apartment or home after getting the kids off to school or having just come home from the office, classroom, or business. She is shy, reclusive to a point, alienated, retrospective, and lacking in self-esteem. Later in her drinking, she may become self-pitying, resentful, and even childishly cruel because of alcohol usage (Kirkpatrick 1999).

Due to their unique socioeconomic and family roles, women are especially vulnerable to emotional disruptions resulting from divorce, loneliness, and professional failures. Studies suggest that such stresses aggravate tendencies for women to abuse alcohol and other substances (Brady and Ashley 2005; Kirkpatrick 1999; Korolenko and Donskih 1990). More specifically, "women drink from a feeling of inadequacy and from a need for love, the kind of love not found within a sexual relationship but, rather, a love that is deeper and more primal" (Kirkpatrick 1999, p. 1; see also Verhaak et al. 2010).

In addition, drug addiction can occur in some women as a result of domestic adversities. Consequently, there is a high prevalence of drug dependence in women who are victims of sexual and/or physical abuse (Ladwig and Anderson 1989). "Approximately 70% of women in drug abuse treatment report histories of physical and sexual abuse, with victimization beginning before 11 years of age and occurring repeatedly" (SAMHSA 1999a, p. 1). These physical and emotional traumas result in, or are precursors to, factors leading to drug abuse, such as low self-esteem, self-condemnation, anxiety and personal conflicts, dysfunctional dependencies, and overwhelming feelings of guilt (Kirkpatrick 1999; Verhaak et al. 2010). In addition, because of the crucial nurturing roles women hold, drug abuse problems can be particularly damaging to family stability.

Another unique role for women in drug abuse situations is that of a spouse, significant other, or mother to a drug addict. Often, in both traditional and nontraditional family relationships, women are expected to be nurturing, understanding, and willing to sacrifice to preserve the integrity of the family. If a family member becomes afflicted by drug dependence, the wife or mother is viewed as a failure. In other words, if the woman had maintained a good home and conducted her domestic chores properly, the family member would not have been driven to drugs (Green 2006; Klee and Jackson 2002; USDHHS and NIDA 1999).

Despite the disruption and considerable stress caused by drug addiction in the home, women continue to bear the burden of raising children, performing domestic chores, and keeping the family together. In addition, women in such circumstances are frequently put at great physical risk. The risk is from an addicted spouse who becomes abusive to his partner or from exposure to sexually transmitted infections, such as HIV or hepatitis, transmitted by a careless infected partner. The anxiety and frustrations resulting from these stressful circumstances can encourage women themselves to become dependent as they seek emotional relief by using drugs.

■ Women's Responses to Drugs

Research continues to lag regarding how women respond to substances of abuse. "Women have traditionally been underrepresented in clinical trials. In order to translate recent advances in our understanding of the molecular and physiological bases of sex differences into new therapeutics and health practices, sound sex-specific clinical data are imperative" (Schiebinger 2003). Although the situation is slowly changing, the trend in drug abuse studies is still to avoid female populations; the effects of the drugs in men are still extrapolated to women. Even when drug abuse research is conducted on women, frequently the woman's response is not the primary concern; rather, the objective is to determine the effects of a drug on a fetus during pregnancy or an infant during nursing (Klee and Jackson 2002; NSDUH 2007; USDHHS and NIDA 1999).

Although it generally can be assumed that the physiological and drug responses of men and women are similar, some distinctions should be recognized. For example, one study compared the risk for lung cancer in men and women after a lifetime of cigarette smoking. It was found that female smokers were twice as likely to get lung cancer as males who had smoked an identical number of cigarettes in their lifetimes ("Women Smokers" 1994). Another study indicated that women are *three* times more likely to contract lung cancer than men when smoking the same amount of cigarettes (Kirkpatrick 1999). These differences clearly indicate that cigarette smoking is far more dangerous for women than for men. Finally, women's unique responses to drugs includes a finding discovered by researchers at the University of California at San Francisco that women respond to a class of painkillers called kappa-opioids, which are ineffective in men (*Science Daily* 2000).

DRUG ABUSE AND REPRODUCTIVE HEALTH

A very important physiological distinction that sets women apart from men in terms of taking drugs is their ability to bear children. Because of this unique function, men and women have different endocrine (hormone) systems and reproductive organs and structures and women have varied drug responses based on their reproductive state. The unique features of women have a substantial impact on the response to drug abuse in the presence and absence of pregnancy:

Long term drug abuse may make it difficult to have children in the future and cause short term hormone problems. Worse yet, long term drug abuse can cause difficulty having children later in life. The effects of drug abuse on your reproductive system are numerous. Drug use during pregnancy or conception may cause a baby to be born with an addiction or cause physical and mental disabilities. (Drug and Alcohol Rehab Florida 2012)

Drug abuse patterns can influence the outcome of pregnancy even if they occur before a woman becomes pregnant. For example, women who are addicted to heroin are more likely to have poor health, including chronic infections, poor nutrition, and sexually transmitted infections such as human immunodeficiency virus (HIV), which can damage the offspring if pregnancy occurs. If substances are abused during pregnancy, they may directly affect the fetus and adversely alter its growth and development. The incidence of substance abuse during pregnancy is not known precisely, but undoubtedly hundreds of thousands of children have been exposed to drugs in utero. The effects of individual drugs of abuse taken during pregnancy are not discussed in depth in this chapter, but several specific observations merit reiteration here (CDC 2015a, unless otherwise noted):

- Cocaine is a substantial threat for both the pregnant woman and the fetus. Although a number of specific claims for the fetal effects of cocaine are controversial, several observations appear legitimate: cocaine use increases the likelihood of miscarriage when used during pregnancy (Drug and Alcohol Rehab Florida 2012), cocaine use in the late stages of pregnancy can cause cardiovascular or CNS complications in the baby at birth and immediately thereafter, and, due to its vasoconstrictor effects, cocaine may deprive the fetal brain of oxygen, resulting in strokes and permanent physical and mental damage to the child.
- The impact of alcohol consumption during pregnancy has been well documented and publicized (Mathias 1995). When alcohol is consumed by the mother, it crosses the placenta, but the effect of this drug on the fetus is highly variable and depends on the quantity of alcohol consumed, timing of exposure, maternal drug metabolism, maternal state of health, and presence of other drugs. A particularly alarming consequence of high alcohol intake during pregnancy is an aggregate of physical and mental defects called *fetal alcohol syndrome* (FAS).

Characteristics of this syndrome include low birth weight, abnormal facial features, mental retardation, and retarded sensorimotor development. In addition to its direct effects on the fetus, alcohol has played a major role in many unwanted pregnancies or has resulted in women's exposure to sexually transmitted infections. As a CNS depressant, alcohol impairs judgment and reason and, in turn, encourages sexual risk taking that normally would not occur. The results are all too frequently tragic for women (SAMHSA 1999a).

- Tobacco use, primarily smoking, during pregnancy is an avoidable health hazard in the United States.
- Some experts suggest smoking cigarettes during pregnancy may pose a greater risk to the fetus than taking cocaine. Tobacco use by pregnant women may interfere with blood flow to the fetus, deprive it of oxygen and nutrition, and disrupt development of its organs—particularly the brain. Smoking harms many aspects and every phase of reproduction. Despite having greater increased knowledge of the adverse health effects of smoking during pregnancy, many pregnant women and girls continue to smoke.
- Of women who smoked 3 months before pregnancy, 55% quit during pregnancy. Among women who quit smoking during pregnancy, 40% relapsed within 6 months after delivery.
- Approximately 10% of women reported smoking during the last 3 months of pregnancy.
- Smoking during pregnancy can cause a baby to be born too early or to have low birth weight—making it more likely the baby will be sick and have to stay in the hospital longer. A few babies may even die.
- Smoking during and after pregnancy is a risk factor of sudden infant death syndrome (SIDS). SIDS is an infant death for which a cause of the death cannot be determined.
- Babies born to women who smoke are more likely to have certain birth defects, such as a cleft lip or cleft palate.
- Also of significant concern is the possibility that exposure of nonsmoking pregnant women to secondhand tobacco smoke may be damaging to the fetus.
- Drugs of abuse that have been associated with abnormal fetal development when used during pregnancy include alcohol, barbiturates,

benzodiazepines, amphetamines, marijuana, methamphetamine, and cocaine, and even caffeine when consumed in high doses.

Clearly, women should be strongly urged to avoid all substances of abuse, especially during pregnancy.

WOMEN AND ALCOHOL

Alcohol is the drug most widely used and abused by women in the United States. According to the 2013 National Household Survey on Drug Use and Health, among women aged 12 or older, 47.5% used alcohol in the past month (current drinkers) and 31.4% reported binge drinking (SAMHSA 2014). Alcohol abuse is also a major problem for women on college campuses, even though male college students are more likely than their female counterparts to use alcohol on a daily basis.

As a rule, women are less likely than men to develop severe alcohol dependence; thus, only 25% of the alcoholics in the United States are female. Women are also likely to initiate their drinking patterns later in life than men (Green 2006; SAMHSA 2014). "Women are older than men are when they begin drinking to intoxication, but once they develop a pattern of regular intoxication, they: encounter drinking-related problems more quickly than men and lose control over their drinking more quickly than men" (Green 2006). Interesting ethnic patterns of alcohol consumption have been reported in females, with black and white women manifesting similar drinking patterns. Although the proportions are similar, black women are more likely to completely abstain from alcohol than white women are.

Women who are dependent on alcohol are usually judged more harshly than men with similar difficulties. Alcoholic males are more likely to be excused because their drinking problems are often perceived as being caused by frustrating work conditions, family demands, economic pressures, or so-called nagging wives and children. In contrast, women with drinking problems are often perceived as spoiled or pampered, weak, deviant, or immoral. Such stigmas cause women to experience more guilt and anxiety about their alcohol dependence and discourage them from admitting their drug problems and seeking professional help (Kirkpatrick 1999).

The principal reasons for excessive alcohol consumption in women range from loneliness, boredom, and domestic stress in the housewife drinker to financial problems, sexual harassment, lack of challenge, discrimination, and powerlessness in the career woman. Depression is often associated with alcohol problems in women, although it is not clear whether this condition is a cause or an effect of the excessive use.

WOMEN'S PHYSIOLOGICAL RESPONSES TO ALCOHOL

Health consequences for excessive alcohol consumption appear to be more severe for women than for men. For example, alcoholic women are more likely to suffer premature death than alcoholic men. In addition, liver disease is more common and occurs at a younger age in female drinkers than in male alcoholics. In general, higher morbidity rates are experienced by alcoholic women than by their male counterparts.

Several explanations have been suggested for the higher rate of adverse effects seen in female alcoholics. Their higher blood alcohol concentrations may be due to a smaller blood volume and more rapid absorption into the bloodstream after drinking. Alternatively, slower alcohol metabolism in the stomach and liver might cause more alcohol to reach the brain and other organs as well as prolong exposure to the drug following consumption (Goldstein 1995). Studies have shown that for a woman of average size, one alcoholic drink has effects equivalent to two drinks in an average-size man.

DEALING WITH WOMEN'S ALCOHOL PROBLEMS

Alcohol consumption varies considerably in women, ranging from total abstinence or an occasional drink to daily intake of large amounts of alcohol. Clearly, much is yet to be learned about the cause of some women's excessive drinking and dependence on alcohol. The role of genetic factors in predisposing women to alcohol-related problems is still unclear. The environment is certainly a major factor contributing to excessive alcohol consumption in women. It is well established that depression, stress, and trauma encourage alcohol consumption because of the antianxiety and amnesic properties of this drug. Because of unreasonable societal expectations and numerous socioeconomic disadvantages, women are especially vulnerable to the emotional upheavals that encourage excessive alcohol consumption.

As with all drug dependence problems, prevention is the preferred solution to alcohol abuse by women. Alcohol usually becomes problematic when it is no longer used occasionally to enhance social events but used daily to deal with personal problems. Such alcohol dependence can best be avoided by using constructive techniques to manage stress and frustrations. Because of unique female roles and society's expectations, women especially need to learn to be assertive with family members, associates in the workplace (including bosses), and other contacts in their daily routines. By expecting and demanding equitable treatment and consideration in personal and professional activities, stress and anxiety can often be reduced. Education, career training, and development of communication abilities can be particularly important in establishing a sense of self-worth. With these skills and confidence, women are better able to manage problems associated with their lives and less likely to resort to drugs for an escape.

WOMEN AND PRESCRIPTION DRUGS

A recent report states,

> Misuse of, abuse of and dependence on pre-scription drugs are major health problems for women. Two-thirds of all tranquilizers, such as diazepam (Valium), chlordiazepoxide (Librium) and alprazolam (Xanax), are pre-scribed to women. Other examples of prescrip-tion drugs used frequently by women include sedatives such as triazolam (Halcion) and estazolam (ProSom); analgesics like meperi-dine (Demerol) or other types of painkillers such as oxycodone mixed with aspirin (Perco-dan) or guaifenesin mixed with codeine (Bron-tex); and stimulants such as methylphenidate (Ritalin), sibutramine (Meridia) and dextro-amphetamine (Dexedrine). (HealthyWomen .org 2016)

Women are more likely than men to suffer depression, anxiety, and panic attacks (ADAA 2016); be unable to express anger; be victims of physical and sexual abuse; and be subject to overwhelming guilt feelings (Kirkpatrick 1999). Consequently, they are also more likely to take and become addicted to the prescription drugs used in treating these disorders. Because these drugs are used as part of psychiatric therapy and under the supervision of a physician, drug dependence frequently is not recognized and may be ignored for months or even years. This type of legitimate drug abuse occurs most often in elderly women and includes the use of sedatives, antidepressants, and antianxiety medications. A recent study found that one in four women older than age 60 takes at least one of these drugs daily and that some of them develop serious drug problems (Drug Strate-gies 1998). Excessive use of these drugs by older women results in side effects such as insomnia,

mood fluctuations, and disruption of cognitive and motor functions that can substantially compromise the quality of life.

▪ Treatment of Drug Dependence in Women

As previously discussed, women are less likely than men to seek treatment for, and rehabilitation from, drug dependence (Kirkpatrick 1999; SAM-HSA 2010). Possible reasons for their reluctance are as follows:

- In more traditional families, women have unique roles with high expectations. They are expected to assume demanding and ongoing responsibilities, such as motherhood, child rearing, and family maintenance, that cannot be postponed and often cannot be delegated, even temporarily, to others. Consequently, many women feel that they are too essential for the well-being of other family members to leave the home and seek time-consuming treatment for drug abuse problems.
- Drug treatment centers often are not very well designed to handle the unique health require-ments of females—thus, women face more obstacles. These obstacles involve barriers to treatment entry, treatment engagement, and long-term recovery (Holdcroft 2007; NIDA 1999). Women have been shown to have greater health needs than men due to more frequent respiratory, genitourinary (associated with the sex and urinary organs), and circula-tory problems. If drug treatment centers are not capable of providing the necessary physi-cal care, women are less likely to participate in associated drug abuse programs.
- Women are also more likely to relapse when their romantic partners are substance users (Rubin, Stout, and Longabaugh 1996).
- Drug-dependent women are more inclined to be unemployed than their male counterparts and more likely to be receiving public support. The implications of this difference are twofold. First, because concerns about one's job often motivate drug-dependent workers to seek treatment, this issue is less likely to be a factor in unemployed women. Second, without the financial security of a job, unemployed women may feel that good treatment for their drug problems is unaffordable.

The unique female requirements must be rec-ognized and considered if women are to receive adequate treatment for drug dependence. Some considerations on how to achieve this objective include the following (Futures 2016, unless otherwise noted):

- Availability of female-sensitive services
- Nonpunitive and noncoercive treatment that incorporates supportive behavior change approaches
- Treatment for a wide range of medical problems, mental disorders, and psychosocial problems (NIDA 1999)
- Provision of childcare during treatment because many women drug abusers are likely to be the primary caregivers for their children
- Offering supportive network-based therapy rather than confrontational therapy
- Inclusion of alternative therapies that focus on creativity, such as art or music therapy

The role of motherhood needs to be used in a positive manner in drug treatment strategies. For most women, motherhood is viewed with high regard and linked to self-esteem. Approximately 90% of female drug abusers are in their childbearing years, and many have family responsibilities. Consequently, treatment approaches need to be tailored to allow women to fulfill their domestic responsibilities and satisfy their female and maternal motivations and obligations.

Women dependent on drugs often lack important coping skills. Even today, a significant percentage of women lead restricted, almost isolated, lives that focus entirely on domestic responsibilities, and thus face limited alternatives for dealing with stressful situations. Under these restrictive circumstances, the use of drugs to cope with anxieties and frustrations is very appealing. To enhance their ability to cope, drug-dependent women need to develop communication and assertiveness skills. Further, many need to be encouraged to control situations rather than allowing themselves to be controlled by the situation. Specific techniques that have proven useful in coping management are exercise (particularly relaxation types), relaxing visual imagery, personal hobbies, and outside interests that require active participation. Many drug-dependent women require experiences that divert their attention from the source of their frustrations while affording them an opportunity to succeed and develop a sense of self-worth.

Finally, one research study found that the most effective treatment for women included a mutually supportive therapeutic environment that addressed the following issues: psychopathology (such as depression), a woman's role as mother,

interpersonal relationships, and the need for parenting education (Werner et al. 2007). Another study found that cocaine-using women whose children were living with them during residential treatment remained in the treatment programs significantly longer than women whose children were not living with them at the facility. Thus, having the children in the treatment facility provides opportunities to assess and meet women's needs, which in turn affects the women's prognosis (Holdcroft 2007; NIDA 1999).

■ Prevention of Drug Dependence in Women

The best treatment for drug addiction is prevention. To help prevent drug problems in women, as opposed to men, socioeconomic disadvantages need to be recognized as factors that make women more vulnerable to drug dependence, especially dependence on prescription medication. Women need to learn that nondrug approaches are often more desirable for dealing with situational problems than prescribed medications. For example, for older women suffering loneliness, isolation, or depression, it is better to encourage participation in outside interests, such as hobbies and service activities. In addition, social support and concern should be encouraged from family, friends, and neighbors. Such nonmedicinal approaches are preferred over prescribing sedatives and hypnotics to cope with emotional distresses. Similarly, medical conditions such as obesity, constipation, or insomnia should be treated by changing lifestyle, eating, and exercise habits rather than using drug "bandage therapy."

When women are prescribed drugs, they should ask about the associated risks, especially as they relate to drug abuse potential. Frequently, drug dependency develops insidiously and is not recognized by either the patient or the attending physician until it is already firmly established. If a woman taking medication is aware of the potential for becoming dependent and is instructed on how to avoid its occurrence, the problems of dependence and abuse can frequently be averted.

Drug Use Among Adolescents

I love waking up in the morning and smoking a nice fat joint. I live above the garage now, and my mom lives across the yard from the garage.

This is a great living arrangement! I go to my room a few hours before crashing on many school nights, get high, drink some vodka that my older brother buys for me, then finally crash. In the morning, I always wake myself up so my mom stays away from my room, and my hide-away stash box is always locked. I roll me a joint and get a little high before I greet mom in the morning for a quick breakfast. I think she gets high too, but if I ask her and she says "no," what if she then asks me and gets all suspicious and shit? Besides, my Uncle Prentice always gets high with me, so I still think my mom really does not care about smoking weed. In fact, I know she is more worried about me drinking and driving than my friend "Mary Jane" [nickname for marijuana]. That's just my private life and no one needs to know. *(From Venturelli's research files, male residing in Chicago, age 18, July 10, 2000)*

From ages 13 through 18, adolescents are more likely to experience heightened psychological, social, and biological changes (Office of the Surgeon General 2007; NIMH 2012). Often, such internal and external changes are manifested by emotional outbursts. Why do such changes and urges arise? The adolescent's body is stretching, growing, and sometimes appearing out of control due to the hormonal changes of puberty. These changes have an impact on drug use and abuse by adolescents:

> Adolescent drug abusers have unique needs stemming from their immature neurocognitive and psychosocial stage of development. Research has demonstrated that the brain undergoes a prolonged process of development and refinement from birth through early adulthood. Over the course of this developmental period, a young person's actions go from being more impulsive to being more reasoned and reflective. In fact, the brain areas most closely associated with aspects of behavior such as decision-making, judgment, planning, and self-control undergo a period of rapid development during adolescence and young adulthood. (NIDA 2012)

Adolescents who abuse drugs often have other co-occurring mental health problems. These disorders can include any one or combination of the following: attention deficit hyperactivity disorder (ADHD), oppositional defiant disorder, conduct problems, and depressive and anxiety disorders (NIDA 2012).

One perspective regarding early adolescent identity formation characterizes it as a developmental stage teeming with storm and stress, where adolescents are uncertain and confused about who or what they are becoming. They often are confused as to their worth to family, peers, society, and even to themselves (Kantrowitz and Wingert 1999). Adding to the frustration of growing up, the cultural status of adolescents is poorly defined. They find themselves trapped in a "no man's land" between the acceptance, simplicity, and security of childhood and the stress, complexities, expectations, independence, and responsibilities of adulthood. Not only do adolescents have difficulty deciding who and what they are, but adults are equally unsure as to how to deal with these transitional human beings. Although the grown-up world tries to push adolescents out of the secure nest of childhood, it is not willing to bestow the full membership and rights of adulthood upon them (Johnson, Hoffmann, and Gerstein 1996; Kantrowitz and Wingert 1999).

Because of their uniquely rapid development, several developmental issues are particularly important to evolving adolescents (Elmen and Offer 1993; Johnson, Hoffman, and Gerstein 1996; Kantrowitz and Wingert 1999; Office of the Surgeon General 2007; Von Der Haar 2005):

- Discovering and understanding their distinctive identities
- "Feeling awkward or strange about one's self and one's body" (American Academy of Child and Adolescent Psychiatry 2006)
- Forming more intimate and caring relationships with others
- Conflicts with parents over the need for independence
- Increased interest in sexuality and concern with heterosexual versus homosexual identities
- "Experimentation with sex and drugs (cigarettes, alcohol, and marijuana)" (American Academy of Child and Adolescent Psychiatry 2006)
- Establishing a sense of autonomy
- Coming to terms with the hormone-related feelings of puberty and expressing their sexuality
- Learning to become productive contributors to society
- Feeling alone and alienated

Due to all of this developmental confusion, "normal" behavior for the adolescent is difficult to define precisely. Experts generally agree that persistent low self-esteem, depression, feelings of alienation, and other emotional disturbances can be troublesome for teenagers (Von Der Haar 2005). However, most adolescents are relatively well adjusted and are able to cope with **sociobiological changes**.

Emotionally stable adolescents relate well to family and peers and function productively within their schools, neighborhoods, and communities. The majority of adolescents experience transient problems, which they are able to resolve, but some become deeply disturbed and are unable to grow out of their problems without counseling and therapy. Those adolescents who are unable or unwilling to ask for assistance often turn to destructive devices, such as drugs, juvenile delinquency, or violence (Kantrowitz and Wingert 1999), for relief from their emotional dilemmas.

Another perspective regarding adolescent identity development outlines specific stages and statuses regarding identity development (Butler 2010). Butler (2010) identifies the following major developmental stages for drug-using adolescents:

- "*Identity diffusion* is the status of adolescents who have not made a commitment to a particular identity." Often these adolescents drift in and out of drug use because of their attachment to drug-using peers.
- "*Identity foreclosure* involves committing to an identity prematurely without exploration or choice." For example, this might occur when adolescents join drug-using or drug-dealing gangs and foreclose on drug usage largely because drugs are viewed positively. For example, such adolescents foreclose by identifying when higher-status gang members who are insistent on drug use and/or drug dealing.
- "*Identity moratorium* is a stage of active exploration coupled with low commitment to a particular identity." This can be an interesting, exciting, and potentially dangerous time for an adolescent who identifies with drug users/dealers, resulting in conflict with parents and/or authority figures. Adolescents in this stage of identity development have freedom to explore and develop their identities with drug users/dealers.
- "*Identity achievement* is said to occur when the adolescent, having had the opportunity to closely explore an identity, chooses that identity with a high degree of commitment." An example would be gang members who are accepted as members of a gang or social group involved in drug use and/or drug dealing.

Adolescents living in neighborhoods infested with drugs, who have fellow gang members involved in drug use, or associate with drug-using friends in neighborhoods where drug use is not common can experience each of these stages in their drug use and abuse.

■ Consequences of Underage Drug Use

Some of the well-known consequences of underage drug use by adolescents are presented below (Office of the Surgeon General 2007, unless noted otherwise):

- Alcohol poses a greater risk than any other drug, including marijuana, to the largest number of teens, largely because of alcohol's availability.
- Underage alcohol use is the major cause of death from injuries among young people. Each year approximately 5000 people under the age of 21 die as a result of underage drinking; this includes about 1900 deaths from motor vehicle crashes, 1600 as a result of homicides, and 300 from suicide, as well as hundreds from other injuries such as falls, burns, and drowning.
- Alcohol use increases the risk of carrying out, or being a victim of, a physical or sexual assault.
- Underage alcohol use can affect the body in many ways. The effects of alcohol and other drug use ranges from hangovers to death from alcohol and/or other drug abuse.
- Alcohol and other drugs can lead to other problems such as bad grades in school and run-ins with the law.
- Alcohol and other drugs affect how well a young person judges risk and makes sound decisions, such as driving while under the influence and riding with a driver under the influence.
- Alcohol and other drugs play a role in risky sexual activity, which can increase the chance of teen pregnancy and sexually transmitted infections (STIs), including HIV.
- Alcohol can harm the growing brain. (Current research clearly shows that the brain continually develops from birth through the teen years into the mid-20s.)

KEY TERM

sociobiological changes
belief that biological forces (largely genes) have a direct influence on the root causes of social psychological behavior

■ Why Adolescents Use Drugs

Although there is no such thing as a typical substance-abusing adolescent, certain physiological, psychological, and sociological factors are often associated with drug problems in this subculture (Johnson et al., 1996; Johnston et al. 2009a). In looking at an array of explanations regarding why adolescents use drugs, one study by Columbia University's National Center on Addiction and Substance Abuse found that children ages 12 to 17 who are frequently bored are 50% more likely to smoke, drink, get drunk, and use illegal drugs. In addition, kids with $25 or more a week in spending money are nearly twice as likely to smoke, drink, or use drugs as children with less money. Anxiety is another risk factor. The study found that youngsters who said that they were highly stressed were twice as likely as low-stress kids to smoke, drink, or use drugs (Associated Press 2003).

It is important to remember that not all drug use by adolescents means therapy is necessary or even desirable. More traditional proven and accepted explanations stress that most excessive drug use that often leads to abuse by adolescents results from the desire to experience new behaviors and sensations, a passing fancy of maturation, an attempt to relieve peer pressure, feelings of alienation, or an inclination to enhance a social setting with chemistry (Jayson 2007; Kantrowitz and Wingert 1999). Most of these adolescent users will not go on to develop problematic dependence on drugs and, for the most part, should be watched but not aggressively confronted or treated. The adolescents who usually have significant difficulty with drug use are those who turn to drugs for extended support as coping devices and become drug reliant because they are unable to find alternative, less destructive solutions to their problems. Several major factors can contribute to serious drug dependence in adolescents (Archambault 1992; Johnson et al. 1996; Walsh and Shenkman 1992).

Research indicates that the most important factor influencing drug use among adolescents is peer drug use (Bahr, Marcos, and Maughan 1995; Yoder 2015; Jayson 2007; Kandel 1980; NIDA 1999; Swadi 1992; Winters 1997). Other primary factors that can either increase or decrease drug use include how teens perceive the risk of drug use, perceive social approval, and perceive the availability of drugs (CRC Health Group 2007).

Consequently, eventual transition to heavier substance use also directly correlates with peer use (Steinberg, Fletcher, and Darling 1994). Conversely, individuals whose peer groups do not use or abuse drugs are less likely to use drugs themselves (Venturelli 2000). Research has identified a correlation between strong family bonds and non–drug-using peer groups (NIDA 1999). "Adolescents with higher [stronger] family bonds are less likely than adolescents with lower [weaker] bonds to have close friends who use drugs" (Bahr et al. 1995, p. 466). In addition, family bonding is highly correlated with educational commitment. In essence, family bonding influences choice of friends and educational goals and aspirations (Bahr et al. 1995). However, three noteworthy differences exist between male and female adolescents (Teen Challenge 2000):

1. Males demonstrate a stronger association between educational achievement and family bonds.
2. Among females, peer drug use is negatively associated with family bonds, so peer drug use and family bonds are not likely to influence the use of licit and illicit drugs by females.
3. The impact of age on peer drug use (the younger the age, the more vulnerable to peer pressure) and on the amount of alcohol consumed can be predicted with slightly greater accuracy for males than females.

Many adolescents use drugs to help cope with boredom, unpleasant feelings, emotions, and stress or to relieve depression, reduce tension, and reduce alienation (Teen Challenge 2000). Psychological differences among adolescents who are frequent drug users, experimenters, and abstainers often can be traced to early childhood, the quality of parenting in their homes, and their home environment. It has been suggested that certain types of parents are more likely to raise children at high risk for substance abuse (Archambault 1992). Children from families where a parent or caregiver is suffering from alcohol abuse often suffer from guilt, anxiety, embarrassment, inability to have close relationships, confusion, anger, and depression (American Academy of Child and Adolescent Psychiatry 2011).

For example, an alcoholic adolescent usually has at least one parent of the following types:

- *Alcoholic:* This parent serves as a negative role model for the adolescent. The child sees the parent dealing with problems by consuming drugs. Even though drinking alcohol is not illegal for adults, it sends the message that drugs can solve problems. The guilt-ridden alcoholic parent is unable to provide the child with a loving, supportive relationship. In addition, the presence of the alcoholic parent is often disruptive or abusive to the family and creates fear or embarrassment in the child.

- *Nonconsuming and condemning*: This type of parent not only chooses to abstain from drinking, but also is very judgmental about drinkers and condemns them for their behavior. Such persons, who are often referred to as teetotalers, have a rigid, moralistic approach to life. Their black-and-white attitudes frequently prove inadequate and unforgiving in an imperfect, gray world. Children in these families can feel inferior and guilty when they are unable to live up to parental expectations, and they may resort to drugs to cope with their frustrations.

- *Overly demanding*: This type of parent forces unrealistic expectations on his or her children. These parents often live vicariously through their children and require sons and daughters to pursue endeavors in which the parents were unable to succeed. Particular emphasis may be placed on achievements in athletics, academics, or career selections. Even though the parents' efforts may be well intended, the children get the message that their parents are more concerned about what they are than who they are. These parents frequently encourage sibling rivalries to enhance performance, but such competitions always yield a loser.

- *Overly protective*: These types of parents do not give their children a chance to develop a sense of self-worth and independence. Because the parents deprive their children of the opportunities to learn how to master their abilities within their surroundings, the children are not able to develop confidence and a positive self-image. Such children are frequently unsure about who they are and what they are capable of achieving. Parents who use children to satisfy their own ego needs or who are trying to convince themselves that they really do like their children tend to be overly protective.

The principal influence for learned behavior is usually the home; therefore, several other family-related variables can significantly affect an adolescent's decision to start, maintain, or cease a drug habit (Kinney 2000; Lawson and Lawson 1992). For example, adolescents usually learn their attitudes about drug use from family models. In other words, what are the drug-consuming patterns of parents and siblings? Adolescents are more likely to develop drug problems if other members of

the family (1) are excessive in their drug (legal or illegal) consumption, (2) approve of the use of illicit drugs, or (3) use drugs as a problem-solving strategy.

Sociological factors that damage self-image can also encourage adolescent drug use. Feelings of rejection may cause poor relationships with family members, peers, school personnel, or coworkers.

Ethnic differences sometimes contribute to a poor self-image because people of minority races or cultures are frequently socially excluded and are sometimes viewed as being inferior and undesirable by the majority population. This type of negative message is very difficult for adolescents to deal with. Sometimes, to ensure acceptance, adolescents adopt the attitudes and behaviors of their affiliated groups. If a peer group, or a gang, views drug use as cool, desirable, or even necessary, members (or those desiring membership) feel compelled to conform and become involved in drugs.

▪ Patterns of Drug Use in Families of Adolescents

Growing minorities of younger teenagers are being exposed to drug use within their own families. One study reported that "20% of ... 600 teens in drug treatment in New York, Texas, Florida and California said they have shared drugs other than alcohol with their parents, and that about 5% of the teens actually were introduced to drugs—usually marijuana—by their moms and dads" (Leinwand 2000, p. 1). In 1999, Partnership for a Drug-Free America reported similar alarming findings (Leinwand 2000).

Years ago, alcohol may have been shared between parents and their children in a low percentage of cases; however, today there are parents who either have been or are currently using illicit drugs and they appear to be influencing their children in the use of these drugs. Currently, this occurs in a small minority of families; nevertheless, it remains shocking.

Jason, 17, a recovering addict from an upper-middle-class family in Simi Valley, California, says he wishes his father had been more of a parent and less of a buddy when it came to marijuana:

[Jason] made his drug purchase: a $5 bag of pot. Jason says his father walked by his room's open door as he was stashing it in a dresser drawer. [His father then] "told about his marijuana use," Jason says. "We went into his [dad's] office, and he had a (water pipe) and we got high together." [Jason reports that at the time, he] "thought it was sooo cool." (Leinwand 2000, p. 2)

In another example, La'kiesha, 15, of southern California, is the third generation of a family in which members have become addicted to drugs. La'kiesha said her grandmother smoked pot regularly and gave her a few puffs when she was 5 years old to settle her down before bedtime (Leinwand 2000).

In a more recent survey of participants in 70 Phoenix House drug treatment programs in the United States, researchers found that "[o]ne in five drug abusers in some treatment programs in the United States received their first taste of these illegal substances from their parents, usually before the age of 18" (Livni 2013). Drug treatment candidates completing the survey were "19 times more likely to have been introduced to illicit drugs by a family member than a professional drug dealer," with 20% obtaining the drugs from their parents, and, of these, 6% using heroin with them (Livni 2013).

■ Noteworthy Findings Regarding Teen Drug Use

Recent surveys regarding drug use patterns found that, in 2014, by the 12th grade approximately 66.0% of the teens had used alcohol, approximately 34.4% had used cigarettes, approximately 44.4% had used marijuana, and 6.5% had used inhalants. See **Table 16.5**, which details 8th, 10th, and 12th graders' use of drugs from 2011 through 2014.

TABLE 16.5 Drug Use Among 8th, 10th, and 12th Graders: 2011–2014*

	8TH GRADERS				10TH GRADERS				12TH GRADERS			
	2011	2012	2013	2014	2011	2012	2013	2014	2011	2012	2013	2014
Any illicit drug												
Lifetime	20.1	18.5	21.1	20.3	37.7	36.8	39.1	37.4	49.9	49.1	49.8	49.1
Annual	14.7	13.4	15.2	14.6	31.1	30.1	32.1	29.9	40.0	39.7	40.1	38.7
30-day	8.5	7.7	8.7	8.3	19.2	18.6	19.2	18.5	25.2	25.2	25.2	23.7
Alcohol												
Lifetime	33.1	29.5	27.8	26.8	56.0	54.0	52.1	49.3	70.0	69.4	68.2	66.0
Annual	26.9	23.6	22.1	20.8	49.8	48.5	47.1	44.0	63.5	63.5	62.0	60.2
30-day	12.7	11.0	10.2	9.0	27.2	27.6	25.7	23.5	40.0	41.5	39.2	37.4
Cigarettes (Any Use)												
Lifetime	18.4	15.5	14.8	13.5	30.4	27.7	25.7	22.6	40.0	39.5	38.1	34.4
Annual**	–	–	–	–	–	–	–	–	–	–	–	–
30-day	6.1	4.9	4.5	4.0	11.8	10.8	9.1	7.2	18.7	17.1	16.3	13.6
Marijuana/Hashish												
Lifetime	16.4	15.2	16.5	15.6	34.5	33.8	35.8	33.7	45.5	45.2	45.5	44.4
Annual	12.5	11.4	12.7	11.7	28.8	28.0	29.8	27.3	36.4	36.4	36.4	35.1
30-day	7.2	6.5	7.0	6.5	17.6	17.0	18.0	16.6	22.6	22.9	22.7	21.2
Inhalants												
Lifetime	13.1	11.8	10.8	10.8	10.1	9.9	8.7	8.7	8.1	7.9	6.9	6.5
Annual	7.0	6.2	5.2	5.3	4.5	4.1	3.5	3.3	3.2	2.9	2.5	1.9
30-day	3.2	2.7	2.3	2.2	1.7	1.4	1.3	1.1	1.0	0.9	1.0	0.7

TABLE 16.5 Drug Use Among 8th, 10th, and 12th Graders: 2011–2014* *(continued)*

	8TH GRADERS				10TH GRADERS				12TH GRADERS			
	2011	2012	2013	2014	2011	2012	2013	2014	2011	2012	2013	2014
Amphetamines												
Lifetime	5.2	4.5	6.9	6.7	9.0	8.9	11.2	10.6	12.2	12.0	13.8	12.1
Annual	3.5	2.9	4.2	4.3	6.6	6.5	7.9	7.6	8.2	7.9	9.2	8.1
30-day	1.8	1.3	2.3	2.1	3.1	2.8	3.3	3.7	3.7	3.3	4.2	3.8
Hallucinogens												
Lifetime	3.3	2.8	2.5	2.0	6.0	5.2	5.4	5.0	8.3	7.5	7.6	6.3
Annual	2.2	1.6	1.6	1.3	4.1	3.5	3.4	3.3	5.2	4.8	4.5	4.0
30-day	1.0	0.6	0.8	0.5	1.4	1.2	1.1	1.2	1.6	1.6	1.4	1.5
Cocaine												
Lifetime	2.2	1.9	1.7	1.8	3.3	3.3	3.3	2.6	5.2	4.9	4.5	4.6
Annual	1.4	1.2	1.0	1.0	1.9	2.0	1.9	1.5	2.9	2.7	2.6	2.6
30-day	0.8	0.5	0.5	0.5	0.7	0.8	0.8	0.6	1.1	1.1	1.1	1.0
Crack												
Lifetime	1.5	1.0	1.2	1.2	1.6	1.4	1.5	1.0	1.9	2.1	1.8	1.8
Annual	0.9	0.6	0.6	0.7	0.9	0.6	0.6	0.7	1.0	1.2	1.1	1.1
30-day	0.5	0.3	0.3	0.3	0.4	0.4	0.4	0.3	0.5	0.6	0.6	0.7
Steroids												
Lifetime	1.2	1.2	1.1	1.0	1.4	1.3	1.3	1.4	1.8	1.8	2.1	1.9
Annual	0.7	0.6	0.6	0.6	0.9	0.8	0.8	0.8	1.2	1.3	1.5	1.5
30-day	0.4	0.3	0.3	0.2	0.5	0.4	0.4	0.4	0.7	0.9	1.0	0.9
Heroin												
Lifetime	1.2	0.8	1.0	0.9	1.2	1.1	1.0	0.9	1.4	1.1	1.0	1.0
Annual	0.7	0.5	0.5	0.5	0.8	0.6	0.6	0.5	0.8	0.6	0.6	0.6
30-day	0.4	0.2	0.3	0.3	0.4	0.4	0.3	0.4	0.4	0.3	0.3	0.4

* Data show the percentages of 8th, 10th, and 12th graders who used both licit and illicit types of drugs in 2011, 2012, 2013, and 2014.

** Not available at time of printing

Data from Johnston, L. D., O'Malley, P. M., Miech, R. A., Bachman, J. G., & Schulenberg, J.E. *Monitoring The Future National Survey Results on Drug Use: 1975–2014: Overview, Key Findings on Adolescent Drug Use.* Ann Arbor: Institute for Social Research, The University of Michigan, 2015.

In addition, a recent Monitoring the Future study indicated that, in 2015, 18.30% of 12th graders had abused prescription drugs and that both "prescription and over-the-counter drugs are the most commonly abused substances by Americans age 14 and older, after marijuana and alcohol" (NIDA for Teens 2016a). Teens are turning away from street drugs and the stigma that goes along with using them, and abusing prescription drugs to get the same type of high. Many young people are under the false notion that prescription and OTC drugs are medically safer, when in fact, they can be just as dangerous and addictive as street drugs (NEAHIN 2013).

In a 2007 press conference, White House drug czar John Walters stated, "The drug dealer is us" (*USA Today* 2007). What the national drug policy director was alluding to was that "many teenagers are obtaining drugs over the Internet, getting them free from their family members, friends, or taking them from other people's medicine cabinet" and that "2.1 million teenagers abused prescription drugs in 2005" (*USA Today* 2007). A recent report found that

> [e]very day in the United States, an average of 2,000 teenagers use prescription drugs without a doctor's guidance for the first time. Among youth who are 12 to 17 years old, 2.8% reported past-month nonmedical use of prescription medications. According to the 2012 Monitoring the Future survey, prescription and over-the-counter drugs are among the most commonly abused drugs by 12th graders, after alcohol, marijuana, synthetic marijuana (e.g., "Spice"), and tobacco. Youth who abuse prescription medications are also more likely to report use of other drugs. (NIDA for Teens 2013)

The four most common sources for obtaining prescription drugs (namely, amphetamines, tranquilizers, and narcotics other than heroin) from 2009 through 2013 for 12th graders were as follows:

- "Given for free by a friend or relative" (60.7%)
- "Bought from a friend or relative" (39.2%)
- "Bought from drug dealer/stranger" (20.6%)
- "Took from friend/relative without asking" (16.1%)

Surprisingly, only 3.8% of adolescents "bought prescription drugs on the Internet" (Johnston et al. 2014). Clearly, the informal network of family and friends is a major source of these drugs for adolescents.

Finally, "Teens are also abusing stimulants like Adderall and anti-anxiety drugs like Xanax because they are readily available and perceived as safer than street drugs," says White House drug czar Walters (*USA Today* 2007). The extent of naiveté is best illustrated by the interview of one female in Indiana, as stated in the *Daily News*, Muncie, on November 6, 2006: "It's not like I'm taking cocaine or crack—it's OK, these are pharmaceutical drugs made by professionals who know what they are doing" (National Youth Anti-Drug Media Campaign 2007). Another study found that

[t]he classes of prescription drugs most commonly abused are: opioid pain relievers, such as Vicodin or Oxycontin; stimulants for treating Attention Deficit Hyperactivity Disorder (ADHD), such as Adderall, Concerta, or Ritalin; and central nervous system (CNS) depressants for relieving anxiety, such as Valium or Xanax. The most commonly abused OTC drugs are cough and cold remedies containing dextromethorphan. (NIDA 2013)

The use of drugs for recreational purposes by young people is of special concern. In looking at drug use by adolescents, the following findings are noteworthy (CBHSQ 2015, unless otherwise noted):

- The percentage of adolescents aged 12 to 17 who were current alcohol users was 11.5% in 2014, totaling 2.9 million adolescents.
- In 2014, about 6.1% adolescents (1.5 million) aged 12 to 17 were past-month binge alcohol users.
- An estimated 1.3 million adolescents aged 12 to 17 had substance abuse disorders (SUDs) in 2014, representing 5.0% of adolescents.
- In 2014, slightly more than 2.3 million adolescents aged 12 to 17 were current users of illicit drugs, which represents 9.4% of adolescents.
- In 2014, 7.4% of adolescents aged 12 to 17 were current users of marijuana. This means that approximately 1.8 million adolescents used marijuana in the past month.
- In 2014, an estimated 467,000 adolescents aged 12 to 17 were current nonmedical users of pain relievers, which corresponds to 1.9% of adolescents.
- Current use of inhalants in 2014 was more common among adolescents aged 12 to 17 (0.6%) than among people in other age groups.
- Among adolescents aged 12 to 17 in 2014, 1.7 million used tobacco products in the past month, including 1.2 million current cigarette smokers. These 2014 numbers represent 7.0% of adolescents who were current tobacco users and 4.9% who were current cigarette smokers.
- In 2014, use of electronic cigarettes (e-cigarettes) was high among teens, with 9.5% of 8th graders, 14% of 10th graders, and 16.2% of 12th graders using e-cigarettes in the past month (Johnston et al. 2016b). Only 14.2% of 12th graders viewed regular e-cigarette use as harmful. The nicotine in e-cigarettes is vaporized and inhaled (not smoked); however, the health

impact of e-cigarette use is not yet known (NIDA 2014a).

- A significant majority (over 60% across all grades) reported vaporizing "just flavoring." Among high school seniors, 22.2% reported inhaling nicotine, 6.1% reported inhaling marijuana or hash oil, and 6.3% indicated that they did not know what they inhaled. Early evidence suggests that e-cigarette use may serve as an introductory product for youth who then go on to use other tobacco products, including conventional cigarettes (Johnston et al. 2016b).

- Past-month marijuana use continues to exceed cigarette use among high school seniors. In 2015, 21.3% of high school seniors used marijuana in the past 30 days, compared with 11.4% who smoked cigarettes (Johnston et al. 2016b).

- In 2015, for the first time, daily cigarette use (5.5%) was lower than daily marijuana use (6%) among high school seniors. Among high school seniors, 79.5% say it is easy to get marijuana (Johnston et al. 2016b).

- While marijuana use has remained relatively stable over the past few years, there continues to be a changing of attitudes about the perceived risk of harm associated with marijuana use. The majority of high school seniors do not think regular marijuana smoking is harmful, with only 36.1% saying that regular use puts the user at great risk, compared to 52.4% 5 years ago. However, 56.7% of seniors say they disapprove of occasional marijuana smoking, and 73.4% say they disapprove of regular marijuana smoking, down from 65.6% and 80.3%, respectively, in 2009. Eighty-one percent of seniors say it is easy to get marijuana (NIDA 2014a).

- Past-year hookah use continued to increase among 12th graders to 22.9%—the highest rate since 2010, when the survey started capturing this type of tobacco use (NIDA 2014a).

- Changing attitudes toward substance abuse often precede changes in reported use. The perceived risk of harm of regularly smoking marijuana and taking prescription stimulants, including amphetamines, has continued to decline among 12th graders (NIDA 2014a).

As we can see from above, the use of alcohol and marijuana is more widespread than the use of other drugs. Of greater concern than just any use of alcohol is its use to the point of inebriation: 18% of 8th graders, 37% of 10th graders, and 54.2% of 12th graders said they had been drunk at least once in their lifetime.

TEEN DRUG USE OF OVER-THE-COUNTER AND PRESCRIPTION DRUGS

Each year, "more teens die from prescription drugs than heroin/cocaine combined" (Teen-drugsrehabs.com 2015). Some over-the-counter (OTC) and prescription cough and cold medicines contain active ingredients that are psychoactive (mind-altering) at higher-than-recommended dosages and are frequently abused for this purpose. These products may also contain other drugs, such as expectorants and antihistamines, which are dangerous at high doses and compound the dangers of abuse. When teens were asked about past-year cough medicine drug use by the 2015 Monitoring the Future survey, researchers found that 1.60% of 8th graders, 3.30% of 10th graders, and 4.60% of 12th graders used cough and cold medicine (most often Dextromethorphan, or DXM) and codeine syrup (most often promethazine-codeine cough syrup) to get high (NIDA for Teens 2016b). Products with DXM include Alka Selter Plus, Coricidin, Dimtapp, Mucinex DM, Robitussin NyQuil, Coricidin, and Robitussin, among others.

Cough and cold medicines are usually consumed orally in tablet, capsule, or syrup form. They may be mixed with soda for flavor and are often abused in combination with other drugs, such as alcohol or marijuana. Because they are easily purchased in drugstores without a prescription, cough syrups, pills, and gel capsules containing DXM—particularly "extra-strength" forms—are frequently abused by young people (who refer to the practice as *robo-tripping* or *skittling*) (NIDA 2014b).

This type of drug abuse is a particular concern, given the easy access teens have to these products. Teens who abuse prescription or OTC drugs may be abusing other substances as well. Sometimes they abuse prescription and OTC drugs together with alcohol or other drugs, which can lead to dangerous consequences, including death. Teens are abusing prescription drugs because they are widely available, free or inexpensive, and they believe they are not as risky as street drugs. The majority of teens who abuse these products say they get them for free, usually from friends and relatives, and often without their knowledge. Because these drugs are so readily available, teens who otherwise would not touch street drugs might abuse prescription drugs.

■ Adolescent Versus Adult Drug Abuse

Adolescent patterns of drug abuse are very different from drug use patterns in adults (Moss et al.

1994). The uniqueness of adolescent drug abuse means that drug-dependent teenagers usually are not successfully treated with adult-directed therapy. For example, compared with adults who abuse drugs, drug-using adolescents are (1) more likely to be involved in criminal activity and at earlier ages, (2) more likely to have other members of the family who abuse drugs, (3) more likely to be associated with a dysfunctional family that engages in emotional and/or physical abuse of its members, and (4) more likely to begin drug use because of curiosity or peer pressure (Bahr et al. 1995; Daily 1992b; Hoshino 1992; Steinberg et al. 1994; Teen Challenge 2000). Such differences need to be considered when developing adolescent-targeted treatment programs.

▌ Consequences and Coincidental Problems

Researchers have concluded that the problem of adolescent drug use is a symptom and not a cause of personal social maladjustment. Even so, because of the pharmacological actions of drugs, routine use can contribute to school and social failures, unintended injuries (usually automobile-related), criminal and violent behavior, sexual risk taking, depression, and suicide (Curry and Spergel 1997).

It is important to realize that, because serious drug abuse is usually the result of emotional instability, consequences of the underlying disorders may be expressed with chemical dependence, making diagnosis and treatment more difficult. The undesirable coincidental problems may include self-destruction, risk taking, abuse, or negative group behaviors. Some of these adolescent problems and their relationship to drug abuse are discussed in the following sections.

ADOLESCENT SUICIDE

Current research shows that although no cause-and-effect relationship exists between use of alcohol and/or other drugs and suicide, such drugs are often contributing factors (Destinations to Recovery 2014; see also American Academy of Child and Adolescent Psychiatry 2013; Minnesota Institute of Public Health 1995). Adolescents are particularly vulnerable to suicide actions; in fact, white males between 14 and 20 years are the most likely to commit suicide in the United States (Daily 1992b). Further, the teenage suicide rate has doubled since 1980 (Siegel and Senna 1997; Siegel and Welsh 2009). "Suicides among young people continue to be a serious problem. Each

year in the U.S., thousands of teenagers commit suicide. Suicide is the third leading cause of death for 15- to-24-year-olds, and the sixth leading cause of death for 5- to-14-year-olds" (American Academy of Child and Adolescent Psychiatry 2004). Twenty percent to 36% of suicide victims have a history of alcohol abuse or were drinking shortly before their suicide. Some experts have described severe chemical dependence as a form of slow, drug-related suicide. For clinicians, every case of serious drug addiction conceals a suicidal individual because all drug abuse inevitably constitutes a game of life and death very similar to "Russian roulette," which comes back into fashion at certain times and under certain circumstances (Bergeret 1981).

Clearly, many teenagers who abuse alcohol and other drugs possess a self-destructive attitude (Destinations to Recovery 2014), as this quote from an online chat with Dr. David Shaefer, a teen suicide expert, demonstrates: "[T]wo-thirds of all suicides amongst boys occur in boys who are abusing alcohol or other drugs; so the link between suicide and alcohol and certain drugs, like cocaine and Ecstasy and other stimulant drugs, is a very close one" (Schaefer et al. 1993, p. 39). According to Shaeffer, adolescents who attempt suicide are more likely to (1) have disciplinary problems, then abuse alcohol and feel even more depressed; (2) be very anxious and not display any bad behavior problems; or (3) have a perfectionist attitude and never be satisfied with their outcomes. Nearly all suffer from depression before their suicide attempts. Females generally differ from males in that they are prone to even greater amounts of depression with fewer cases of alcohol or other drug abuse. Finally, another study based on extensive survey data suggests that "between 12 and 25 percent of school age youth consider suicide or make plans to commit suicide … [and that] the rate of youth suicide is on an upward path, tripling between 1950 and 1990" (Bussing-Burks 2013). This research also states that alcohol and drug use increases the likelihood of suicidal thoughts and attempts (Bussing-Burks 2013).

Besides posing a direct health threat because of their physiological effects, drugs of abuse can precipitate suicide attempts due to their pharmacological impact. A number of studies have found a very high correlation between acute suicidal behavior and drug use (Destinations to Recovery 2014; Buckstein et al. 1993). One report noted that adolescent alcoholics have a suicide rate 58 times greater than the national average (Buckstein et al. 1993). In another study, 30% of adolescent alcoholics had made suicide attempts, although 92% admitted to a history of having suicidal thoughts (Daily 1992b). It has been speculated that the incidence of suicide in drug-consuming adolescents is high because both types of behavior are the consequence of an inability to develop fundamental adult attributes of confidence, self-esteem, and independence. When drug use does not make up for their need for these characteristics, the resulting frustrations are intensified and ultimately played out in the suicide act.

Most adolescents experiment with drugs for reasons not related to antisocial or deviant behavior but rather due to curiosity, desire for recreation, boredom, peer pressure, desire to gain new insights and experiences, or urge to heighten social interactions. These adolescents are not likely to engage in self-destructive behavior. In addition, adolescents from "healthy" family environments are not likely to attempt suicide. Specifically, Daily (1992b) stated that the families least likely to have suicidal members are those that do the following:

- Express love and show mutual concern
- Are tolerant of differences and overlook failings
- Encourage the development of self-confidence and self-expression
- Have parents who assume strong leadership roles but are not autocratic
- Have interaction characterized by humor and good-natured teasing
- Are able to serve as a source of joy and happiness to their members

Suicide is more likely to be attempted by those adolescents who turn to alcohol and other drugs to help them cope with serious emotional and personality conflicts and frustrations. These susceptible teenagers represent approximately 5% of the adolescent population (American Academy of Child and Adolescent Psychiatry 2013; Beschner and Friedman 1985; Siegel and Senna 1997; Siegel and Welsh 2009). Wright (1985) found that four features significantly contribute to the likelihood of suicidal thought in high school students:

1. Parents with interpersonal conflicts who often use an adolescent child with drug problems as the scapegoat for family problems
2. Fathers who have poor and often confrontational relationships with their children
3. Parents who are viewed by their adolescent children as being emotionally unstable, usually suffering from perpetual anger and depression

4. A sense of frustration, desperation, and inability to resolve personal and emotional difficulties through traditional means

Clearly, it is important to identify those adolescents who are at risk for suicide and to provide immediate care and appropriate emotional support.

SEXUAL VIOLENCE AND DRUGS

Alcohol use has been closely associated with almost every type of sexual abuse in which the adolescent is victimized. "For the perpetrator, being under the influence may remove both physical and psychological inhibitors which keep people from acting out violently. They may also use alcohol or drugs as an excuse for criminal behavior" (Wisconsin Coalition Against Sexual Assault [WCASA] 1997, p. 13). For example, alcohol is by far the most significant factor in date, acquaintance, and gang rapes involving teenagers (Office of the Surgeon General 2007; Parrot 1988; Prendergast 1994). The evidence for alcohol involvement in incest is particularly overwhelming. Approximately 4 million children in the United States live in incestuous homes with alcoholic parents. In addition, 42% of drug-abusing female adolescents have been victims of sexual abuse (Daily 1992a). It is estimated that almost half of the offenders consume alcohol before molesting a child and at least one-third of the perpetrators are chronic alcoholics (Baltieri and de Andrad 2008). Finally, 85% of child molesters were sexually abused themselves as children, usually at the same age as their victims, and the vast majority of these molesters abused drugs as adolescents (Daily 1992a).

These very disturbing associations illustrate the relationship between drugs and violent sexual behavior both in terms of initiating the act and because of the act. The effects of such sexual violence are devastating and far-reaching. Thus, incest victims are more likely than the general population to abuse drugs as adolescents and to engage in antisocial delinquency, prostitution, depression, and suicide (Daily 1992a).

GANGS AND DRUGS

The very disturbing involvement of adolescents in gangs and gang-related activities and violence is a social phenomenon that first became widely recognized in the 1950s and 1960s. Hollywood, for example, introduced America to the problems of adolescent gangs in the classic movies *Blackboard Jungle* and *West Side Story*. Although the basis for gang involvement has not changed over the years, the levels of violence and public concern have increased dramatically. Many communities consider gang-related problems to be their number one social issue (Henslin 2014). Access to sophisticated weaponry and greater mobility have drawn unsuspecting neighborhoods and innocent bystanders into the often-violent clashes of **intragang** and **intergang** warfare. Individuals and communities have been reacting angrily to this growing menace. To deal effectively with the threats of gang-initiated violence and crime, however, it is important to understand why gangs form, what their objectives are, how they are structured, and how to discourage adolescent involvement.

Children often join gangs because they are neglected by their parents, lack positive role models, and fail to receive adequate adult supervision. Other motivations for joining a gang include peer pressure, low self-esteem, and the perceived easy acquisition of money from gang-related drug dealing and other criminal activities

In comparison to traditional, formal youth organizations, juvenile gangs may appear disorganized. Research shows, however, that verbal rules, policies, customs, and hierarchies of command are rigidly observed within the gang. Thus, common values and attitudes exist:

- Gang membership is usually defined in socioeconomic, racial, and ethnic terms, and adolescents involved have similar backgrounds.
- Gang members are distinguished by a distinctive and well-defined dress code. Violation of this code by members, or mimicking of the dress code by nongang members, can result in ostracism, ridicule, physical abuse, and violence.
- Leadership and seniority within the gang are defined by vested time in belonging to the gang, age, loyalty, and demonstrated delinquent cleverness (often related to drug dealing and other crimes).
- Gang members use gang slang to ensure camaraderie and group loyalty.

Although a stable home life does not ensure that an adolescent will not become involved with

gang-related activity, a strong family environment and guidance from respected parents and guardians are clearly deterrents (Lale 1992). Many gang members are children from dysfunctional, broken, or single-parent homes. Many parents are aware of their children's gang involvement but they lack the skill, confidence, and authority to deter the gang or curtail drug involvement of their teenagers. To make matters worse, ineffective parents often discourage or even interfere with involvement by outside authorities due to misdirected loyalty to their children and/or to avoid embarrassment to their family and community.

Because troubled adolescents are often estranged from their families, they are particularly influenced by their peer groups. These teenagers are most likely to associate with groups whose members have similar backgrounds and problems and who make them feel accepted. Because of this vulnerability, adolescents may become involved with local gangs. In summary, gangs offer the following:

- Fellowship and camaraderie
- Identity and recognition
- Membership and belonging
- Family substitution and role models
- Security and protection
- Diversion and excitement
- Friendships and structure
- Money and financial gain for relatively little effort
- Ability to live the crazy life (*vida loca*) (Sanders 1994; Shelden, Tracy, and Brown 2001) or *locura* (craziness) (Shelden et al. 2004)

In the United States, estimates of the total number of existing gangs vary widely. There are at least 30,000 gangs and more than 800,000 active gang members in the United States. Gangs conduct criminal activity in all 50 states and the U.S. territories. Although most gang activity is concentrated in major urban areas, gangs also are proliferating in rural and suburban areas of the country as gang members flee increasing law enforcement pressure in urban areas or seek more lucrative drug markets. This proliferation in nonurban areas increasingly is accompanied by violence and is threatening society in general (National Drug Intelligence Center [NDIC] 2009).

Sadly, despite recent declines, gangs have a strong presence in schools:

In 2009, about 20 percent of students ages 12–18 reported that gangs were present at

KEY TERMS

intragang
between members of the same gang

intergang
between members of different gangs

their school during the school year. This was a decrease from the 23 percent of students who reported a gang presence in 2007. A higher percentage of students from urban schools (31 percent) reported a gang presence at their school in 2009 than students from suburban and rural schools (17 percent and 16 percent, respectively). (National Center for Education Statistics 2011)

In Chicago alone, estimates have ranged from 12,000 to 120,000 gang members. In 2012 it was reported that "Chicago is the gang capital of the United States. According to the Chicago Crime Commission, a 2012 Chicago Police Department gang audit found there are more than 600 gang factions in the city, with a minimum combined membership of 70,000" (CBS News 2013). Spergel (1990) provided the following percentages of those who are reportedly in gangs within a particular school population in the Chicago area: "5% of the elementary school youths, 10% of all high school youths, 20% of those in special school programs, and, more alarmingly perhaps, 35% of those between 16 and 19 years of age who have dropped out of school" (Shelden et al. 2004, p. 29). Keep in mind that these data are for just one city.

Street gangs, outlaw motorcycle gangs (OMGs), and prison gangs in prisons are the primary distributors of illegal drugs in the United States. Gangs also smuggle drugs into the United States and produce and transport drugs within the country, supplying most major drug dealers.

Street gang members convert powdered cocaine into crack cocaine and produce most of the phencyclidine (PCP) available in the United States. Gangs, primarily OMGs, also produce marijuana and methamphetamine. In addition, gangs increasingly are involved in smuggling large quantities of cocaine and marijuana and lesser quantities of heroin, methamphetamine, and MDMA (also known as Ecstasy) into the United States from foreign sources of supply. Gangs primarily transport and distribute powdered cocaine, crack cocaine, heroin, marijuana, methamphetamine, MDMA, and PCP in the United States.

Located throughout the country, street gangs vary in size, composition, and structure. Large, nationally affiliated street gangs pose the greatest threat because they smuggle, produce, transport, and distribute large quantities of illicit drugs throughout the country and are extremely violent. As mentioned earlier, local street gangs in rural, suburban, and urban areas pose a growing threat (NDIC 2009).

A recent survey claims that 27% of public school students ages 12 to 17 attend schools that are both gang and drug infested. That means 5.7 million students attend schools that are both gang and drug dominated. Nearly 50% of all public school students report drug use or sales on school grounds (Funk 2010). Research shows that teenage gangs are becoming major players in the drug trade (Siegel and Senna 1997; Siegel and Welsh 2009). Two of the largest gangs in Los Angeles, the Bloods and the Crips, are examples of this trend. Estimated membership in these two gangs exceeds 20,000. In the past, organized crime families maintained a monopoly on the Asian heroin market. Today, youth gangs have entered this trade, for two reasons: (1) recent efforts and successes in prosecuting top mob bosses by criminal justice officials have created opportunities for new players and (2) demand has grown for cocaine and synthetic drugs that are produced locally in many U.S. cities. In Los Angeles and most major large cities, drug-dealing gangs maintain "rock houses" or "stash houses" (where crack cocaine is used and sold) that serve as selling and distribution centers for hard drugs. The crack cocaine found in these rock houses is often supplied or run by gang members (Siegel and Senna 1997; Siegel and Welsh 2009).

To a lesser extent, other, less violent gangs with smaller memberships are also involved in drug dealing. However, research shows that the media may exaggerate the percentage of gangs involved in drug dealing. In the past, citywide drug dealing by tightly organized "super" gangs appeared to be on the decline and was being superseded by the activities of loosely organized, neighborhood-based groups (Siegel and Senna 1997). In the past, the main reason for this shift was that federal and state law enforcement of drug laws have forced drug dealers to become "flexible, informal organizations [rather] than rigid vertically organized gangs with … [leaders] who are far removed from day-to-day action [on the street]" (Siegel and Senna 1997, p. 409).

Other past findings were that

[l]arge trafficking organizations dominate the illicit drug market. These groups include the "families" of America's La Cosa Nostra, as well as an array of more recently identified crime groups such as the Sicilian "Mafia," outlaw motorcycle gangs and groups based in the Nigerian and Colombian communities. …

Organized crime groups involved in drug trafficking, however, share a central feature with other organized crime groups in that they consist of a core criminal group and a specialized criminal support designed to facilitate illicit activity. (Gonzales et. al 1986, 71)

Levitt and Venkatesh's (2000) research involving criminal gangs in Chicago revealed that the gang's turf they studied

for most of the time period examined is a twelve-square block area bordered by major thoroughfares on all sides. Most of the drug-dealing is conducted along the edges of the territory on or near one of the major streets. The gang sells perhaps 30 percent of the drugs to those living within the twelve-block area— most of the remaining purchasers come from a relatively limited geographic range. In this particular area, few buyers come from the suburbs. (p. 763)

Drug use and gang-related activities are often linked, but the relationship is highly variable (Curry and Spergel 1997; Fagan 1990). Clearly, problems with drugs exist without gangs, and gang-related activities can occur despite the absence of drugs; however, because they have common etiologies, their occurrences are often intertwined. Most adolescents who are associated with gangs are knowledgeable about drugs. Many gang members have experimented with drugs, much like other adolescents their age. However, the hard-core gang members are more likely to be engaged not only in drug use, but also in drug dealing as a source of revenue to support the gang-related activities (Lale 1992; Siegel and Senna 1997). The types of drugs used and their significance and functions vary from gang to gang (Fagan 1990; Siegel and Senna 1997). For example, many Latino gangs do not profit from drug trafficking but are primarily interested in using hard-core drugs such as heroin and PCP. In contrast, African American gangs tend to be more interested in the illicit commercial value of drugs and often engage in dealing crack and other cocaine forms.

PREVENTING ADOLESCENT GANG INVOLVEMENT

The most effective way to prevent adolescent gang involvement is to identify, at an early age, those children at risk and provide them with lifestyle alternatives. Important components of such strategies are as follows:

- Encourage parental awareness of gangs and teach parents how to address problems in

their own families that may encourage gang involvement.
- Provide teenagers with alternative participation in organizations or groups that satisfy their needs for camaraderie, participation, and emotional security in a constructive way. These groups can be organized around athletics, school activities, career development, or service rendering.
- Help children to develop coping skills that will enable them to deal with the frustration and stress in their personal lives.
- Educate children about gang-related problems and help them understand that, like drugs, young people who join gangs create more problems for themselves, and gang membership is not a solution to their personal or family problems.

▌ Prevention, Intervention, and Treatment of Adolescent Drug Problems

As with most health problems, the sooner drug abuse is identified in the adolescent, the greater the likelihood that the problem can be resolved. It can be difficult to recognize signs of drug abuse in teenagers because their behavior can be erratic and unpredictable even under the best of circumstances. In fact, many of the behavioral patterns that occur coincidentally with drug problems are also present when drugs are not a problem. However, frequent occurrence or clustering of these behaviors may indicate the presence of substance abuse. The behaviors that can be warning signs include the following (Archambault 1992):

- Abruptly changing their circle of friends
- Experiencing major mood swings
- Continually challenging rules and regulations
- Overreacting to frustrations
- Being particularly submissive to peer pressures
- Sleeping excessively
- Keeping very late hours
- Withdrawing from family involvement
- Letting personal hygiene deteriorate
- Becoming isolated
- Engaging in unusual selling of possessions
- Manipulating family members
- Becoming abusive toward other members of the family
- Frequently coming home at night high

PREVENTION OF ADOLESCENT DRUG ABUSE

Logically, the best treatment for drug abuse is to prevent the problem from starting. This approach, referred to as **primary prevention**, typically has been viewed as total abstinence from drug use. Informational scare tactics are frequently used as a component of primary prevention strategies. These messages often focus on a dangerous (although in some cases rare) potential side effect and present the warning against drug use in a graphic and frightening fashion. Although this approach may scare naive adolescents away from drugs, many adolescents today, especially if they are experienced, question the validity of the scare tactics and ignore the message.

Another form of primary prevention is to encourage adolescents to become involved in formal groups, such as structured clubs or organizations, in an effort to reduce the likelihood of substance abuse (Howard 1992). Group memberships can help adolescents develop a sense of belonging and contributing to a productive, desirable objective. This involvement can also provide the adolescent with the strength to resist undesirable peer pressures. In contrast, belonging to informal groups such as gangs— groups with loose structures and ill-defined, often antisocial objectives—can lead to participation in poorly chaperoned parties, excessive sexual involvement, and nonproductive activities. Adolescent members of such poorly defined organizations tend to drink alcohol at an earlier age and are more likely to use other substances of abuse.

Some experts claim that primary prevention against drug use is unrealistic for many adolescents. They believe that no strategy is likely to stop adolescents from experimenting with alcohol or other drugs of abuse, especially if these substances are part of their home environment (e.g., if alcohol or tobacco is routinely used) and are viewed as normal, acceptable, and even expected behaviors (Howard 1992). For these adolescents, it is important to recognize when drug use moves from experimentation or a social exercise to early stages of a problem and to prevent serious dependence from developing. This approach, referred to as **secondary prevention**, consists of (1) teaching adolescents about the early signs of abuse, (2) teaching adolescents how to assist peers and family members with drug problems, and (3) teaching adolescents how and where help is available for people with drug problems (Archambault 1992). Regardless of the prevention approach used, adolescents need to understand that drugs are never the solution for emotional difficulties, nor are they useful for long-term coping.

TREATMENT OF ADOLESCENT DRUG ABUSE

To provide appropriate treatment for adolescent drug abuse, the severity of the problem must be ascertained. The criteria for such assessments include the following:

- Differentiating between abuse and normal adolescent experimentation with drugs
- Distinguishing between minor abuse and severe dependency on drugs
- Distinguishing among behavioral problems resulting from (1) general behavioral disorders, such as juvenile delinquency; (2) intellectual disability; and (3) drugs of abuse

There is no single best approach for treating adolescent substance abuse. Occasionally, the troubled adolescent is admitted to a clinic and treated on an inpatient basis. The inpatient approach is very expensive and creates a temporary artificial environment that may be of limited value in preparing adolescents for the problems to be faced in their real homes and neighborhoods. However, the advantage of an inpatient approach is that adolescents can be managed better and their behavior can be more tightly monitored and controlled (Hoshino 1992). A more practical and routine treatment approach is to allow adolescents to remain in their natural environment and to provide the necessary life skills to be successful at home, in school, and in the community. For example, adolescents being treated for drug dependence should be helped with:

- Schoolwork, so that appropriate progress toward high school graduation occurs
- Career skills, so that they can become self-reliant and learn to care for themselves and others
- Family problems and learning to communicate and resolve conflicts

If therapy is to be successful, it is important to improve the environment of the drug-abusing adolescent. This aspect of treatment includes disassociation of the adolescent from groups (such as gangs) or surroundings that encourage drug use

KEY TERMS

primary prevention
preventing the use of any drug (total abstinence)

secondary prevention
preventing casual and/or recreational drug use from advancing to drug dependence

and promoting association with healthy and supportive groups (such as a nurturing family) and experiences (such as athletics and school activities). Although desirable, such separation is not always possible, especially if the family and home environment are factors that encourage abuse; the likelihood of therapeutic success is substantially diminished under these circumstances.

Often, therapeutic objectives are facilitated by positive reinforcement that encourages life changes that eliminate access to and use of drugs. This goal frequently can be achieved by association with peers who have similar drug and social problems but are motivated to make positive changes in their life. Group sessions with such peers are held under the supervision of a trained therapist and consist of members sharing problems and solutions (Hoshino 1992). Some other options include holistic therapies such as acupuncture, homeotherapy, massage therapy, aromatherapy, yoga, nutrition therapy, and many more alternatives that were once marginalized by the medical profession (Apostolides 1996).

Another useful approach is to discourage use of drugs by reducing their reinforcing effects. This result can sometimes be achieved by substituting a stronger positive or negative reinforcer. For example, if adolescents use drugs because they believe these substances cause good feelings and help them cope with emotional problems, it may be necessary to replace the drug-taking behavior with other activities that make the adolescent feel good without the drug (such as participation in sports or recreational activities). Negative reinforcers, such as parental discovery and punishment or police apprehension, may discourage drug use by teenagers who are willing to conform and respect authorities; however, negative approaches are ineffective deterrents for nonconforming, rebellious adolescents. Negative reinforcers also do not tend to discourage adolescent use of substances that are more socially acceptable, such as alcohol, tobacco, and even marijuana (Howard 1992).

Regardless of the treatment approach, adolescents must meet several basic objectives if therapy for their drug dependence is to be successful (Daily 1992b):

- Realize that drugs do not solve problems—they only make the problems worse.
- Understand why they turned to drugs in the first place.
- Be convinced that abandoning drugs grants them greater independence and control over their own lives.

- Understand that drug abuse is a symptom of underlying problems that need to be resolved.

▪ Summary of Adolescent Drug Abuse

Drug abuse by adolescents is particularly problematic in the United States. The teenage years are filled with experimentation, searching, confusion, rebellion, poor self-image, and insecurity. These attributes, if not managed properly, can cause inappropriate coping and lead to problems such as drug dependence, gang involvement, violence, criminal behavior, and suicide. Clearly, early detection of severe underlying emotional problems and application of effective early preventive therapy are important for proper management. Approaches to treatment of drug abuse problems must be individualized because each adolescent is a unique product of physiological, psychological, and environmental factors.

Almost as important as early intervention for adolescent drug abuse problems is recognizing when treatment is unnecessary. We should not be too quick to label all young drug users as antisocial and emotionally unstable. In most cases, teenagers who have used drugs are merely experimenting with new emotions or exercising their newfound freedom. In such situations, nonintervention is usually better than therapeutic meddling. For the most part, if adolescents are given the opportunity, they will work through their own feelings, conflicts, and attitudes about substance abuse, and they will develop a responsible philosophy concerning the use of these drugs.

Drug Use Among College Students

This section focuses on college undergraduate use of alcohol, with additional emphasis on the use and abuse of illicit drugs by college students currently attending institutions of higher education.

Table 16.6 compares trends in the annual use of various types of licit and illicit drugs by full-time college students with annual usage by others who are the same age (1 to 4 years beyond high school) but are not attending college. Overall, Table 16.6 shows the following noteworthy prevalence trends (Johnston et al. 2015):

- It is clear that use of a number of illicit drugs other than marijuana tended to be distinctly higher among those not in college. In 2014, 38.6% of full-time college students and 44.1% of noncollege students used illicit drugs. The

TABLE 16.6 Annual Prevalence of Drug Use for Full-Time College Students Versus Others, 1 to 4 Years Beyond High School: 2014*

	Full-Time College Students (%)	Others, 1 to 4 Years Beyond High School (%)
Any illicit drug**	38.6	44.1
Any illicit drug** other than marijuana	20.8	24.5
Alcohol	76.1	74.5
Marijuana	34.4	39.7
Cigarettes	22.6	34.7
Amphetamines+	10.1	9.2
Ritalin	1.6	2.6
Methamphetamine	0.1	0.9
Crystal methamphetamine (ice)	0.1	0.8
Synthetic marijuana	0.9	3.4
Other narcotics+	4.8	7.8
OxyContin	1.3	3.7
Vicodin	2.8	6.5
MDMA (Ecstasy)	5.0	6.5
Tranquilizers	3.5	6.0
Hallucinogens	4.0	7.0
LSD	2.2	4.5
Cocaine	4.4	5.1
Crack	0.8	0.3
Sedatives+ (barbiturates)	3.1	4.7
Inhalants	1.3	1.2
Ketamine	0.1	0.2
Heroin	0.1	0.6
GHBs	0.2	0.6

*All full-time college entries, except for the first two percentage entries, are college from highest to lowest

**Use of any illicit drug includes use of marijuana, hallucinogens, cocaine, or heroin, or any use of other narcotics, amphetamines, sedatives (barbiturates), or tranquilizers not under a doctor's orders.

+Only drug use that was not under a doctor's orders is included here.

Data from Johnston, L. D., P. M. O'Malley, J. G. Bachman, J. E. Schulenberg, and R. A. Miech. *Monitoring the Future, National Survey Results on Drug Use, 1975–2014. Volume II: College Students and Adults Ages 19–55.* Ann Arbor: Institute for Social Research, University of Michigan, 2015. Available http://www.monitoringthefuture.org/pubs/monographs/mtf-vol2_2014.pdf

annual prevalence of use of any illicit drug *other than marijuana* was 20.8% for college students versus 24.5% for noncollege students. (Such differences would likely be even larger if the noncollege sample included high school dropouts.) In fact, several drugs showed annual use rates for noncollege respondents in 2014 that were two or more times those for college students, including synthetic marijuana, LSD, salvia, heroin, heroin with a needle, heroin without a needle, OxyContin, Vicodin, 357 methamphetamine, crystal methamphetamine, bath salts (synthetic stimulants), GHB, and ketamine.

- The gap between prevalence rates for a few drugs widened in 2014, whereas four specific drugs showed similar annual prevalence rates for the college student segment versus noncollege segment: hallucinogens other than LSD (3.2% vs. 4.9%), Ecstasy (5.0% vs. 6.5%), methamphetamine (0.1% vs. 0.9%), and ketamine (0.1% vs. 0.2%). Inhalant use (1.3% vs. 1.2%) was also nearly equivalent.
- In 2014, college students (76.1%) were moderately higher in annual use of alcohol than the noncollege group (74.5%).
- College students had a higher prevalence of occasions of being drunk (42.6%) versus their age peers (34.1%; not shown in this table). Indeed, 4 in every 10 college students (40%) reported having been drunk in the prior 30 days, compared to 36% of the noncollege respondents. The groups differed in rates of daily drinking (not shown in this table), at 3.8% versus 4.9%. In high school, college-bound students, especially in earlier grades, were far less likely to drink alcohol at any level compared to their non-college-bound peers; thus, the relative and absolute increases in alcohol use among college students in the first few years following high school are quite striking.
- Annual marijuana use was somewhat similar among college students and high school graduates of the same age who were not in college (34.4% vs. 39.7%). However, the rate of current daily marijuana use (not shown in this table) was lower among college students than among their out-of-school counterparts (19.6% vs. 24.4%).
- In 2014, notably significant differences in usage of narcotics other than heroin between the noncollege group (7.8%) and college students (4.8%) (not shown in this table) was reported.
- Annual prevalence of use of the amphetamine-type drug Adderall was somewhat higher

among college students (9.6%) than among noncollege respondents (7.2%), as was the case for the 2 years prior to this study. The higher use by college students is very likely because this amphetamine drug, intended for the treatment of attention deficit hyperactivity disorder (ADHD), is sometimes used by students to stay awake and alert in order to complete course work and to study for exams.

- Among all substances studied, the largest differences for annual, 30-day, and daily prevalence rates (not shown in this table) between the two groups are for cigarette smoking. For example, the prevalence of daily smoking for college students was 5% versus 16% for noncollege respondents in 2014. Smoking at the rate of a half pack or more per day stood at 2% versus 10% for these two groups, respectively.
- Although not shown in Table 16.6, in comparing male and female college students with noncollege peers, the findings indicate that male college students tend to use most substances, licit and illicit, more than their female counterparts, with the greatest proportional differences occurring for various hallucinogens. Compared with college females and with noncollege peers, college males are also more frequent users of alcohol and marijuana and more likely to use Adderall outside of medical supervision.

In summary, the noncollege segment is generally more drug-involved than the college student segment. This pattern is a continuation of the high school scenario in which those without college plans are more likely to use drugs. The only substances that college students were appreciably more likely to use than their noncollege peers were amphetamines (including Adderall specifically) and alcohol (particularly getting drunk and binge drinking). The higher rates of alcohol use among college students emerged only after high school; during high school alcohol use was lower among those planning to go to college.

Table 16.7 shows yearly trends in drug use among U.S. college students from 2011 through 2014 (Johnston et al. 2015a). This table details the percentages of college students who used drugs in the past 12 months before the surveys were administered. The main finding is that the overall use of any illicit drugs remained fairly constant from 2011 to 2014—approximately 38.1%, when averaging the 4 years of surveying. The following list shows that drug usage is either declining, holding steady, or decreasing in usage.

Drugs declining in use from 2011 to 2014:

- Cigarettes
- Heroin
- Narcotics (other than heroin)
- Oxycontin

Drugs holding relatively steady from 2011 to 2014:

- Any illicit drug
- Alcohol
- Inhalants
- Marijuana
- Hallucinogens
- Amphetamines
- LSD
- Adderall
- MDMA (Ecstasy)
- Crystal methamphetamine (ice)
- Vicodin/
- Tranquilizers
- Cocaine
- Crack
- Oxycontin

Drugs increasing in use from 2011 to 2014:

- Any illicit drug other than marijuana
- Ritalin
- Sedatives (barbiturates)

▪ Reasons for College Students' Drug Use

Figure 16.2A shows the primary reasons why a sample survey of 53,622 male and female college students used alcohol and other drugs (38.8% were male and 63.2% were female). The major reasons cited in this sample survey were (1) breaks the ice (75.1%), (2) enhances social activity (74.6%), (3) gives people something to do (73.0%), (4) gives people something to talk about (67.3%), (5) allows people to have more fun (62.5%), (6) peer bonding (62.4%), (7) male bonding (60.6%), (8) facilitates sex (51.2%), (9) female bonding (52.9%), and (10) makes it easier to deal with stress (43.6%) (Southern Illinois University Carbondale [SIUC]/Core Institute 2014, p. 5) (see **Figure 16.2B**). Although not shown in this figure, this same survey revealed the following regarding alcohol (SIUC/Core Institute 2014, p. 1):

- 81.3% of the students consumed alcohol in the past year ("annual prevalence").

TABLE 16.7 Trends in Annual Use of Drugs Among College Students 1 to 4 Years Beyond High School (Percentage Who Used in the Past 12 Months Except as Noted): 2011–2014

	2011	2012	2013	2014
Approximate weighted N	1230	1150	1090	1030
Any illicit drug*	36.3	37.3	40.5	38.6
Any illicit drug other than marijuana*	16.8	17.1	19.3	20.8
Alcohol	77.4	79.2	75.6	76.1
Cigarettes	25.8	23.4	23.2	22.6
Marijuana	33.2	34.9	35.5	34.4
Hallucinogens	4.1	4.5	4.5	4.0
LSD	2.0	1.9	2.6	2.2
MDMA (Ecstasy)	3.4	3.9	3.7	3.2
Amphetamines[+]	9.3	11.1	9.6	10.1
Ritalin	2.3	1.8	3.6	1.6
Adderall	9.8	9.0	10.7	9.6
Provigil	—	—	—	—
Methamphetamine	0.2	0.0	0.4	0.1
Crystal methamphetamine (ice)	0.1	0.6	0.6	0.6
Cocaine	3.3	3.1	2.7	4.4
Crack	0.3	0.3	0.3	0.8
Narcotics (other than heroin)	6.2	5.4	5.4	4.8
OxyContin	2.4	1.2	2.3	1.3
Vicodin	5.8	3.8	4.4	2.8
Tranquilizers	4.2	3.4	4.4	3.5
Sedatives (barbiturates)[+]	1.7	2.2	2.7	3.1
Inhalants	0.9	1.5	0.5	1.3
Heroin	0.1	0.1	0.3	0.0
GHB	0.1	0.1	0.1	0.2
Ketamine	0.6	0.4	0.9	0.1

*Use of any illicit drug includes any use of marijuana, hallucinogens, cocaine, or heroin, or any use of other narcotics, amphetamines, sedatives (barbiturates), or tranquilizers not under a doctor's orders.

[+]Only drug use that was not under a doctor's orders is included here.

— no data available

Data from Johnston, L. D., O'Malley, P. M., Bachman, J. G., Schulenberg, J. E. and Miech, R. A. *Monitoring the Future: National Survey Results on Drug Use, 1975–2014, Volume II: College Students and Adults, Ages 19–55.* Ann Arbor: Institute for Social Research, University of Michigan, 2015.

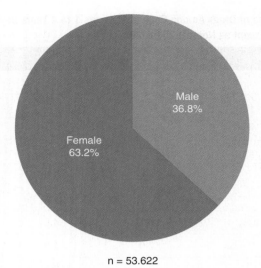

n = 53.622

A. Gender (Students Completing Survey)

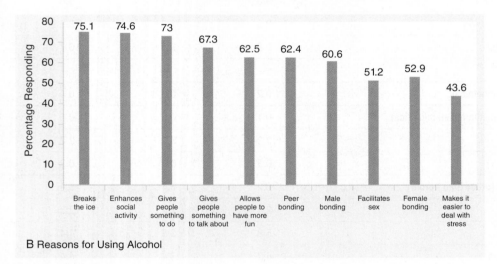

B Reasons for Using Alcohol

FIGURE 16.2 Sample of major reasons for using alcohol and other drugs.

Adapted from Southern Illinois University/Core Institute. *2012 Annual Reference Group, Core Alcohol and Drug Survey Long Form-Form 194, Executive Summary.* Carbondale, IL: Southern Illinois University/Core Institute, April 23, 2014.

- 68.4% of the students consumed alcohol in the past 30 days ("30-day prevalence").
- 61.3% of underage students (younger than 21) consumed alcohol in the previous 30 days.
- 43.9% of students reported binge drinking in the previous 2 weeks. (A binge is defined as consuming five or more drinks in one sitting.)

Key findings on the use of illegal drugs included the following (SIUC/Core Institute 2014, p. 1):

- 32.8% of the students have used marijuana in the past year ("annual prevalence").
- 19.5% of the students are current marijuana users ("30-day prevalence").

- 11.8% of the students have used an illegal drug other than marijuana in the past year ("annual prevalence").
- 6.2% of the students are current users of illegal drugs other than marijuana ("30-day prevalence")

The most frequently reported illegal drugs used in the past 30 days were the following (SIUC/Core Institute 2014, p. 1):

- 19.5% marijuana (pot, hash, hash oil)
- 2.9% amphetamines (diet pills, speed)
- 1.7% designer drugs (Ecstasy, MDMA)

Demographically, approximately 83.3% of the students taking this survey were between the ages of 18 and 22, and 93.3% were full-time students. Approximately 28.4% were freshmen, 21.8% were sophomores, 22.9% were juniors, 22.4% were seniors, 3.6% were graduates, and 0.9% were other.

In addition, 49.5% lived off campus, and 54.5% worked part time or full time. It is likely that these results regarding college students' use of alcohol and other drugs would be similar to those found on other larger state university campuses in the United States.

■ Additional Noteworthy Findings Regarding Drug Use by College Students

The following sections describe the most recent significant studies and findings regarding the use of drugs by college students.

PATTERNS OF ALCOHOL AND OTHER DRUG USE

Research reviews of undergraduates' substance use and abuse and the prevalence patterns of alcohol and other drug use found that the most popular substance used by undergraduates is alcohol (Johnston et al. 2015a; Leinwand 2007b; SIUC/ Core Institute 2014). According to McMurtrie (2014), "[T]he binge-drinking rate among college students has hovered above 40 percent for two decades, and signs are that partying is getting even harder. More students now drink to get drunk, choose hard liquor over beer and drink in advance of social events. For many the goal is to black out." Another report indicated that "According to a national survey, almost 60 percent of college students ages 18–22 drank alcohol in the past month, and almost 2 out of 3 (over 60%) of them engaged in binge drinking during that same timeframe" (NIDA 2015c).

Common heavy drinking settings include the following (Stewart 2013):

- Fraternity parties
- Drinking in conjunction with athletic events
- Drinking in residence halls
- Drinking in off-campus housing areas with a high proportion of students
- Drinking in bars adjacent to campus

Alcohol use has been found to be associated with serious and acute problems such as alcoholism, poor academic performance, drinking and driving, and criminalistic behavior (e.g., driving while intoxicated, vandalism, violence) (Center for Science in the Public Interest 2007; NIDA 2015c).

College students vary greatly in their use of alcohol and their beliefs about its positive and negative effects. Studies show that two major drinking patterns appear dominant among college students: (1) drinking related to impulsivity, disinhibition, and sensation-seeking and (2) drinking to manage negative emotional states, such as depression (National Institute on Alcohol Abuse and Alcoholism [NIAAA] 2005a).

Summarized in the following list are other significant findings regarding alcohol and other drug use:

- *High-risk drinking*: Studies show that about 43% of all students report drinking in a high-risk manner at some point in their college career. Twenty percent of students report drinking in a high-risk manner often (Gloucester County College 2013).
- *Poor grades*: College students who received grades of D or below were more likely than those with higher grades to have used cigarettes, alcohol, or illicit drugs during the past month (SAMHSA 2011).
- *Death*: Each year, 1825 college students between the ages of 18 and 24 die from alcohol-related unintentional injuries, including motor vehicle crashes (Hingson, Zha, and Weitzman 2009; NIAAA 2005a; NIDA 2015c).
- *Injury*: Each year, 599,000 students between the ages of 18 and 24 are unintentionally injured under the influence of alcohol (Hingson et al. 2009; NIAAA 2005a).
- *Assault*: Each year, 696,000 students between the ages of 18 and 24 are assaulted by another student who has been drinking (Hingson et al. 2009; NIAAA 2005b; NIDA 2015c).
- *Sexual assault*: Each year, 97,000 students between the ages of 18 and 24 are victims of alcohol-related sexual assault or date rape (NIAAA 2005b; NIDA 2015). Researchers estimate that alcohol use is implicated in one-third to two-thirds of sexual assault and acquaintance or date rape cases among teens and college students.
- *Unsafe sex*: Each year, 400,000 students between the ages of 18 and 24 have unprotected sex, and more than 100,000 students between the ages of 18 and 24 report having been too intoxicated to know if they consented to having sex (NIAAA 2005a).
- *Academic problems*: About one in four college students report academic consequences from drinking, including missing class, falling behind in class, doing poorly on exams

or papers, and receiving lower grades over-all. In a national survey of college students, binge drinkers who consumed alcohol at least three times per week were roughly six times more likely than those who drank but never binged to perform poorly on a test or project as a result of drinking (40% vs. 7%) and five times more likely to have missed a class (64% vs. 12%) (NIAAA 2005a; NIDA 2015).

- *Health problems/suicide attempts*: More than 150,000 students develop an alcohol-related health problem each year (Hingson et al. 2009), and between 1.2% and 1.5% of students indicate that they tried to commit suicide within the past year due to drinking or drug use (NIAAA 2005a).
- *Drunk driving*: Each year, 3,360,000 students between the ages of 18 and 24 drive under the influence of alcohol (Hingson et al. 2009; NIAAA 2005a).
- *Vandalism:* About 11% of college student drinkers report that they have damaged property while under the influence of alcohol (SAMHSA 2011).
- *Property damage*: More than 25% of administrators from schools with relatively low drinking levels and over 50% from schools with high drinking levels say their campuses have a "moderate" or "major" problem with alcohol-related property damage (SAMHSA 2011).
- *Police involvement*: About 5% of 4-year college students are involved with the police or campus security as a result of their drinking (Wechsler et al. 2002), and 110,000 students between the ages of 18 and 24 are arrested each year for an alcohol-related violation such as public drunkenness or driving under the influence (SAMHSA 2011).
- *Alcohol abuse and dependence*: In the past 12 months, 31% of college students met criteria for a diagnosis of alcohol abuse and 6% for a diagnosis of alcohol dependence, according to questionnaire-based self-reports about their drinking (NIAAA 2005a).
- *Alcohol use disorder (AUD)*: About 20% of college students meet the criteria for an AUD (NIDA 2015c).
- *Binge drinking*: Young adults ages 18 to 25 are most likely to binge or drink heavily; 54% of the drinkers in this age group binge and about one in four are heavy drinkers (SAMHSA 2011).
- *Victimization*: About 4 in 10 violent crimes against college students were committed by offenders who were perceived by victims to

be using drugs or alcohol (NCVRW Resource Guide 2007).

- *Housing:* The amount and proportion of alcohol consumed by college students varies depending on where they live. Drinking rates are highest in fraternities and sororities, followed by on-campus housing (e.g., dormitories, residence halls). Students who live independently off-site (e.g., in apartments) drink less, and commuting students who live with their families drink the least (NIAAA 2005b).

PREDICTING DRUG USE FOR FIRST-YEAR COLLEGE STUDENTS

One of the best predictors of drug use for first-year college students was drug use during a typical month in the senior year of high school. Overall, college students responding to a questionnaire were found to use marijuana less frequently than they did in high school. Further, alcohol use increased early in the college years. Although the frequency of alcohol use increased, the number of times that college students got drunk did not rise. Most of these students found new friends in college with whom they got drunk. Alcohol and drug use depended on the choice of new college friends (Leibsohn 1994).

A more recent study examined personality disposition to risky behavior as a predictor of first-year college drinking. A survey of 418 first-year college students at the University of Kentucky revealed that students with a preponderance of sensation-seeking predispositions (risk taking) were more likely to drink more frequently, consume greater quantities of alcohol, and experience negative outcomes from drinking than those students scoring significantly lower on the UPPS-R Impulsive Behavior Scale, the positive urgency measure (PUM), and the Drinking Styles Questionnaire (DSQ). Sensation-seeking students experienced more lack of control (i.e., dyscontrol) stemming from extreme positive mood swings, and it was during these periods that alcohol consumption rapidly increased (Cyders et al. 2009).

DORMITORIES FOR NON–DRUG-USING STUDENTS

In 1988, Rutgers University was one of the first universities to create a dormitory for students who were recovering addicts and who wanted to stay away from the alcohol-charged atmosphere of conventional dormitories. The dormitory at Rutgers maintains strict rules and careful management (Witham 1995). Other universities offer similar variations for on-campus living. In 1989, the University of Michigan opened a substance-free housing facility and set aside 500 dormitory spaces; 1200 students applied for these spaces (Belsie 1995). More recent findings indicate that "[N]ow that substance-free housing is commonplace, a handful of campuses, including Rutgers, have gone [even] further, offering 'recovery' housing for students who have been in treatment for addiction" (Lewin 2005). Today, substance-free housing has become a nationwide choice. This type of housing is found "at dozens of campuses nationwide, from huge state universities like the University of Michigan to Ivy League schools like Dartmouth and small liberal arts colleges like Vassar" (Lewin 2005). For example,

> a junior at Earlham College who asked that his name not be used … [said] "When I got to college, I didn't want to have to worry about having all that stuff in my face [in reference to having to live with drunk and drugged students in the dorm]. I've been in wellness housing my whole time here. I could handle normal housing now, but I like the people I live with, and there's a very good atmosphere. (Lewin 2005)

Further, on some campuses, large numbers of entering freshmen prefer substance-free living accommodations, mainly dormitories as well as other types of housing. "At Dartmouth, for example, about 400 of the 1075 incoming freshmen requested it, compared with only about 200 of the 2200 sophomores, juniors and seniors who live on campus" (Lewin 2005). A recent online search in 2016 by the author for substance-free dormitories on college campuses listed approximately 40 U.S. colleges and universities offering such housing, including Bucknell University, California State University–Monterey Bay, Colby-Sawyer College, Indiana University of Pennsylvania, James Madison, Julliard School, Rutgers, the State University of New Jersey–New Brunswick, and University of New Hampshire (CollegeXpress.com 2016).

REMAINING POPULARITY OF CERTAIN TYPES DRUGS AMONG COLLEGE, NONCOLLEGE, AND 12TH GRADERS

Marijuana and psilocybin mushrooms are two types of illicit recreational drugs whose popularity appeared to grow in the 1990s and that, to date, remain popular on most college campuses. Referred to as "soft drugs," these substances are commonly used on most college campuses (Ravid 1995).

I know my older brothers told me that when they were at this same college I am now attending "shrooms" [referring to psilocybin mushrooms] were not that easy to get and the better types of weed were very infrequent back 7 years ago. Well, today it's really different! Even at this smaller university it's all a matter of finding the right dude to hook you up. I have a hook-up that always has blueberry, which is a small percentage *Sativa* and nearly all *Indica*. He is in partnership with a friend in Michigan who grows only this kind. It is expensive but oh is it worth it. You certainly don't need much like the other stuff that is weaker. It is awesome stuff. The "shrooms" are not as frequent and several times I had to go to another friend's campus to get them. (*From Venturelli's research files, male attending a smaller comprehensive university in the Midwest, age 22, June 12, 2013*)

Nationwide surveys studying yearly drug use averages from 1984 through 1999 showed a steady, progressive increase in the use of hallucinogens, which include psilocybin mushrooms, Ecstasy, and LSD. In 1984 (the first year of the survey), 3.7% of college students used LSD, and 5.4% used this same drug in 1999. Similarly, in 1984, 6.2% used hallucinogens (excluding LSD), and, in 1999, 7.8% used these same hallucinogenic-type drugs (Johnston et al. 2000a, 2000b). Other findings show hallucinogen use has been dropping, from 7.4% in 2003 to 5.1% in 2008. One noteworthy finding is that the use of LSD increased slightly from 2007 (1.3%) to 2008 (2.6%) (a 1.3% increase over a 2-year period) (Johnston et al. 2009b). Concerning college students' use of MDMA (Ecstasy), the annual use was 9.1% in 2000, 4.4% in 2003, dropping to 2.2% in 2007, then rising to 3.7% in 2008 (an increase of 1.6% over a 2-year period) (Johnston et al. 2009b). More recent findings regarding MDMA (Ecstasy) show an average of 3.6% of college students using the drug from 2011 through 2014 (Johnson et al. 2015). The annual prevalence of LSD remained fairly low among college students in 2012. In 2012 annual prevalence of LSD use was 1.9% among college students and 2.2% in the noncollege group (after a significant drop of 1.6% in 2012). Recent prevalence of LSD findings among college students from 2011 through 2014 averaged 2.1%. Among 12th graders, from 2009 through 2012 annual hallucinogen use, which includes LSD and MDMA (Ecstasy) was 4.5% (Johnston et al. 2013) and more recent findings from 2011 through 2014 averaged 4.6% (Johnston et al. 2015a).

Both the college and noncollege groups showed very slight decreases in MDMA (Ecstasy) use in 2011, averaging 4.2% in college students and 5.7% in the noncollege group (Johnston et al. 2012). More recent findings regarding the use of this drug in 2014 is 5.0% for full-time college students and 6.5% in noncollege students (Johnston et al. 2015), which indicates an increase in the percentage using MDMA (Ecstasy) in both groups (college and noncollege groups).

Finally, in the college group daily marijuana smoking was 1.8% in 1994 and 5.9% in 2014, showing a noteworthy increase, with other findings indicating that "[c]ollege students now smoke marijuana daily more than they drink alcohol daily" (NIDA 2015d). Other significant findings regarding the *2014 Monitoring the Future College Students and Adults Survey Results* include the following (NIDA 2015d):

- Daily drinking: 3.7% in 1994 and 4.3% in 2014.
- Intoxication (past month): 42.6% of college students and 34.1% of noncollege peers.
- Cigarettes (past month): 12.9% of college students and 24.6% of noncollege peers
- E-cigarettes (past month): 9.7% of college students and 15.4% of noncollege peers
- Stimulant use in full-time college students: Adderall use decreased from 10.7% in 2013 to 9.6% in 2014, but cocaine use increased from 2.7% in 2013 to 4.4% in 2014.

ROHYPNOL AND DATE RAPE

Rohypnol, also known as the "date-rape drug," is one of six drugs referred to as "club drugs." The other club drugs are MDMA (Ecstasy), gamma-hydroxybutyrate (GHB), ketamine, methamphetamine, and LSD. Club drugs are used by individuals at all-night dance parties such as raves or trances, dance clubs, and bars. All of these drugs are colorless, tasteless, and odorless. They can be added unobtrusively to beverages by individuals who may want to intoxicate or sedate others (NIDA 2000, 2015d). In cases of sexual assault or rape, the small white Rohypnol pills are slipped into a person's drink, causing the person to black out and have no memories of events that occurred

KEY TERM

Rohypnol
the "date-rape drug" that is used on some college campuses to commit sexual assault; the three most common date rape drugs are Rohypnol (flunitrazepam), GHB (gamma-hydroxybutyrate), and ketamine.

while he or she was under the influence of the drug. A minority of undergraduates also use the drug to intensify the effects of marijuana and alcohol. One problem with identifying whether this drug has been given to an unwilling recipient is that Rohypnol can be detected only for 60 hours after ingestion (Lively 1996).

Rohypnol (flunitrazepam) belongs to a class of drugs known as benzodiazepines (such as Valium and Xanax). Although this drug is not approved for prescription use in the United States, it is approved and used in more than 60 countries as a treatment for insomnia, as a sedative, and as a presurgery anesthetic (NIDA 2000).

▋ Recommendations for Reducing Drug Use and Abuse on College Campuses

There is an elevated risk of increased drug use and abuse when students move to a college campus. Approaches to minimize increased drug use include the following (Ross and Dejong 2008, p. 3):

- *Alcohol-free options*: "offer and promote social, recreational, extracurricular, and public service options that do not include alcohol and other drugs."
- *Normative environment*: "create a social, academic, and residential environment that supports health-promoting norms."
- *Alcohol availability*: "limit alcohol availability both on and off campus."
- *Alcohol marketing and promotion*: "restrict marketing and promotion of alcohol beverages both on and off campus."
- *Policy development and enforcement*: "develop and enforce campus policies and enforce local, state, and federal laws, and make sure everyone knows what the policies are."

HIV and AIDS

Acquired immune deficiency syndrome (AIDS) came to the attention of medical authorities in the United States on June 4, 1981, in a newsletter from the Centers for Disease Control and Prevention (CDC) in Atlanta, Georgia (Zuger 2000). Human immunodeficiency virus (HIV), the virus that causes AIDS, was not discovered until 1983. The following is the current state of the HIV/AIDS epidemic:

- More than 35 million people worldwide are living with HIV since the first cases were reported in 1981 (CDC 2015b).

- In 2015, globally, 2 million people were newly infected with HIV (CDC 2015b).
- Globally, each year 1.2 million die of AIDS each year (CDC 2015b).
- The number of people living with HIV included 2.6 million children younger than 15 years of age, 17.4 million women, and 34.5 million adults, for a total of 36.9 million people living with HIV in 2014 (WHO 2015).
- AIDS deaths in 2014 numbered 150,000 children younger than 15 years of age and 1.0 million adults, for a total of 1.2 million AIDS deaths (WHO 2015).

The regions of the world with the highest incidence of new HIV infections are the following (from highest to lowest) (UNAIDS 2015a):

- *Sub-Saharan Africa*: 1.4 million new cases in 2014, a 41% drop from 2.3 million new cases in 2000.
- *Asia and the Pacific*: 340,000 new cases in 2014, a 31% drop from 500,000 new cases in 2000.
- *Eastern Europe and central Asia*: 140,000 new cases in 2014, a 30% increase from 100,000 new cases in 2014.
- *Latin America*: 87,000 new cases in 2014, a 17% decrease from 100,000 new cases in 2000.
- *Western and central Europe and North America*: 85,000 new cases in 2014, roughly the same as the number of new cases in 2000 (87,000).
- *Caribbean*: 13,000 new cases in 2014, a 50% decrease from 27,000 new cases in 2000.
- *Middle East and North Africa*: 22,000 new cases in 2014, a 26% increase from 18,000 new cases in 2000.

Although cases have been reported in all regions of the world, almost all those living with HIV (97%) reside in low- and middle-income countries, particularly in sub-Saharan Africa. The HIV epidemic not only affects the health of individuals but also impacts households, communities, and the development and economic growth of nations. Many of the countries hardest hit by HIV also suffer from other infectious diseases, food insecurity, and other serious problems. According to the World Health Organization (WHO), most people living with HIV or at risk for HIV do not have access to prevention, care, or treatment, and there is still no cure (UNAIDS 2015b).

Despite these challenges, there have been successes and promising signs. New global efforts have been mounted to address the epidemic, particularly in the last decade. Prevention has helped to reduce HIV prevalence rates in a small but growing number of countries, and new HIV infections are declining. In addition, the number of people with HIV receiving antiretroviral therapy treatment in resource-poor countries has increased 10-fold since 2002, reaching an estimated 15.8 million people living with HIV as of June 2015 (in 2014 13.6 million were receiving antiretroviral therapy) (UNAIDS 2015b).

As of June 2015, trends in treatment were as follows:

- 41% of all adults living with HIV were accessing treatment in 2014, up from 23% in 2010 (CDC 2015b).
- 32% of all children living with HIV were accessing treatment in 2014, up from 14% in 2010 (CDC 2015c).
- 73% of pregnant women living with HIV had access to antiretroviral medicines to prevent transmission of HIV to their babies in 2014, and new HIV infections among children were reduced by 58% from 2000 to 2014 (CDC 2015c).

■ Major U.S. Statistics and Trends in Specific Populations Living with HIV/AIDS

In the United States, the CDC (2015c) provides the following estimates with regard to populations with HIV/AIDS:

- In 2013, an estimated 47,352 people were newly diagnosed with HIV infection. In that same year, an estimated 26,688 people were diagnosed with AIDS. Overall, an estimated 1,194,039 people in the United States have been diagnosed with AIDS.
- More than 1.2 million people aged 13 years and older are living with HIV infection, including 156,300 (12.8%) who are unaware of their infection. Over the past decade, the number of people living with HIV has increased, while the annual number of new HIV infections has remained relatively stable. The pace of new infections continues at far too high a level, particularly among certain groups.
- Gay, bisexual, and other men who have sex with men (MSM), particularly young black/African American MSM, are most seriously affected by HIV.
- By race, blacks/African Americans face the most severe burden of HIV.
- The estimated incidence of HIV has remained stable overall in recent years, at about 50,000 new HIV infections per year.

- An estimated 13,712 people with an AIDS diagnosis died in 2012, and approximately 658,507 people in the United States with an AIDS diagnosis have died overall. The deaths of persons with an AIDS diagnosis can be due to any cause (i.e., the death may or may not be related to AIDS).

By Risk Group

- *Gay, bisexual, and other men who have sex with men (MSM)* of all races and ethnicities remain the population most profoundly affected by HIV.

  ○ Men aged 40 years and older are more likely to have HIV than men aged 18 to 39. Young black MSM are more likely to have older sex partners and therefore are more likely to encounter an HIV-positive partner. Thus, sexual relationships with older men may increase risk of exposure to HIV.

  ○ In 2010, the estimated number of new HIV infections among MSM was 29,800, a significant 12% increase from the 26,700 new infections among MSM in 2008.

  ○ Although MSM represent about 4% of the male population in the United States, in 2010 MSM accounted for 78% of new HIV infections among males and 63% of all new infections. MSM accounted for 54% of all people living with HIV infection in 2011, the most recent year these data are available.

  ○ In 2010, white MSM continued to account for the largest number of new HIV infections (11,200), by transmission category, followed closely by black MSM (10,600).

  ○ The estimated number of new HIV infections was greatest among MSM in the youngest age group. In 2010, the greatest number of new HIV infections (4800) among MSM occurred in young black/African American MSM aged 13 to 24. Young black MSM accounted for 45% of new HIV infections among black MSM and 55% of new HIV infections among young MSM overall.

  ○ Since the epidemic began, an estimated 311,087 MSM with an AIDS diagnosis have died, including an estimated 5380 in 2012.

- *Heterosexuals and injection drug users* also continue to be affected by HIV.

  ○ Since the epidemic began, almost 92,613 persons with AIDS that were infected through heterosexual sex have died, including an estimated 4550 in 2012.

  ○ New HIV infections among women are primarily attributed to heterosexual contact (84% in 2010) or injection drug use (16% in 2010). Women accounted for 20% of estimated new HIV infections in 2010 and 23% of those living with HIV infection in 2011. The 9500 new infections among women in 2010 reflect a significant 21% decrease from the 12,000 new infections that occurred among this group in 2008.

  ○ Injection drug users represented 8% of new HIV infections in 2010 and 15% of those living with HIV in 2011.

  ○ Since the epidemic began, nearly 186,728 people with AIDS who inject drugs have died, including an estimated 3514 in 2012.

By Race/Ethnicity

- *Blacks/African Americans* continue to experience the most severe burden of HIV, compared with other races and ethnicities.

  ○ Blacks represent approximately 12% of the U.S. population, but accounted for an estimated 44% of new HIV infections in 2010. They also accounted for 41% of people living with HIV infection in 2011.

  ○ Since the epidemic began, an estimated 270,726 blacks with AIDS have died, including an estimated 6540 in 2012.

- *Hispanics/Latinos* are also disproportionately affected by HIV.

  ○ Hispanics/Latinos represented 16% of the population but accounted for 21% of new HIV infections in 2010. Hispanics/Latinos accounted for 20% of people living with HIV infection in 2011.

  ○ Disparities persist in the estimated rate of new HIV infections in Hispanics/Latinos. In 2010, the rate of new HIV infections for Latino males was 2.9 times that for white males, and the rate of new infections for Latinas was 4.2 times that for white females.

  ○ Since the epidemic began, more than 100,888 Hispanics/Latinos with an AIDS diagnosis have died, including 2155 in 2012.

▌ The Nature of HIV Infection and Related Symptoms

AIDS, which is caused by HIV, is a disease in which the body's immune system breaks down and is unable to fight off certain infections, known as *opportunistic infections*, and other illnesses that take advantage of a weakened immune system.

In the early stage of HIV infection, often referred to as the *HIV syndrome*, the symptoms can include the following (TreatHIVNow 2013):

- Fever
- Headache

- Fatigue
- Swollen lymph glands
- Sore throat
- Skin rash

Be aware that many of these symptoms can also be symptoms of mononucleosis (mono), other STIs, or viral hepatitis. Only an HIV test can determine if a person displaying any combination of these symptoms has contracted HIV. Symptoms for HIV as it advances and worsens include the following (AIDS.gov 2012; TreatHIVNow 2013):

- Swollen lymph glands
- Diarrhea that is frequent or ongoing

- Frequent high fevers (over 100°F)
- Shaking chills
- Shortness of breath
- Blurred and distorted vision
- Unplanned or rapid weight loss
- Ongoing fatigue
- Ulcerated skin in the mouth
- Soaking night sweats
- Cough
- Headaches
- Skin rashes or bumps

When a person is infected with HIV, the virus enters the body and lives and multiplies primarily in the white blood cells (see **Figure 16.3**). These

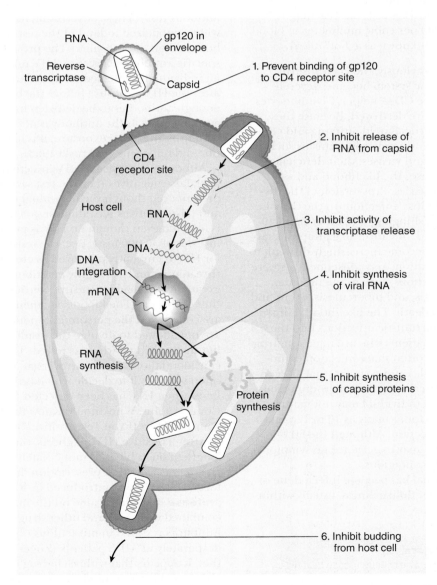

FIGURE 16.3 Disrupting the assembly line, HIV survives by invading white blood cells and turning them into virus factories. Approaches for developing anti-HIV therapies focus on interfering with the replication of HIV.

immune cells normally protect us from disease. The hallmark of HIV infection is the progressive loss of a specific type of immune cells called T-helper or CD4+ cells.

As the virus multiplies, it damages or kills CD4+ and other cells, weakening the immune system and leaving the individual vulnerable to numerous opportunistic infections and other illnesses, ranging from pneumonia to cancer. The CDC defines someone as having a clinical diagnosis of AIDS if he or she has tested positive for HIV and has one or both of the following conditions (Schernoff and Smith 2001):

- The person has experienced at least one AIDS-related infection or illness.
- The number of CD4+ cells has reached or fallen below 200 per cubic millimeter of blood (a measurement known as a *T-cell count*).

As mentioned previously, the HIV-positive individual's immune system becomes severely compromised as the CD4+ helper T lymphocytes and macrophages are destroyed. Because these immune cells are crucial in identifying and eliminating infection-causing microorganisms such as bacteria, fungi, and viruses, their deficiency substantially increases the likelihood and severity of infectious diseases. Progression of the disease brings weight loss, infections in the throat (thrush) and skin (shingles), and other opportunistic infections and/or cancer (e.g., Kaposi's sarcoma). Infections become increasingly difficult to control with medication, and consequently severe opportunistic infections, such as pneumonia, meningitis, hepatitis, and tuberculosis, occur and eventually lead to death. The likelihood of introducing these opportunistic infections into the body increases in patients who are injection drug users because they often share injection equipment, such as needles and syringes, that are contaminated with disease-causing microorganisms.

An HIV-infected individual may not manifest symptoms of AIDS for as many as 10 to 12 years after the initial infection. Although the HIV-infected individual may experience no symptoms, he or she is highly contagious.

After an individual has become infected, he or she may have a brief flulike illness, usually within

6 to 12 weeks. It is not known what determines the length of the latency period, when symptoms are not present. The asymptomatic period eventually ends, however, and signs of immune disorder appear.

■ Diagnosis and Treatment

It is crucial that HIV-infected people be aware of their condition to avoid activities that might transmit the infection to others. Testing for the presence of infection has been available since 1985 and is done by determining whether the body is producing antibodies against HIV. Further, since 1996, newspapers, magazines, radio, and television have been advertising a take-at-home HIV antibody test. (These advertisements are not as widely publicized today, but the test can readily be found on the Internet.) The presence of these specific antibodies indicates HIV infection. If an individual is infected, it takes 6 to 12 weeks after the HIV exposure before the body produces enough antibodies to be detected in currently available tests. If the antibody is not present within 6 months after HIV exposure, it is likely that infection did not occur (Pietroski 1993).

Although the tests for HIV infection are reliable, false negatives (i.e., the test says no HIV is present even though the individual is infected) and false positives (i.e., the test says the individual is infected even though no HIV is present) occur in 1 out of 30,000 tests. Because testing positive for HIV is currently perceived as eventually life-threatening and is a highly emotional diagnosis, great effort is made to ensure confidentiality of the test results. The blood specimens to be tested are coded, and the personnel conducting the tests are not allowed to divulge the results to anyone but the individual who was tested. The issue of confidentiality is very controversial, however. It often is difficult to decide who has the right to know when HIV has been detected (see "Point/Counterpoint: Who Should Know the Results of Your HIV Test If You Test Positive?").

After a positive HIV diagnosis, the best way to lengthen one's life is to immediately begin drug treatments. The first prescription drug treatment for AIDS, AZT, was introduced in 1987. In 1996, **protease inhibitors** came on the market. When combined with AZT and other drugs, protease inhibitors resulted in miraculous remissions of desperately ill AIDS patients (Zuger 2000). Further, it appears that with such drug combinations HIV blood levels in newly infected patients remain exceedingly low (Zuger 2000). Although the drug

KEY TERM

protease inhibitors
a major breakthrough class of drugs used to treat HIV-infected individuals

►POINT/COUNTERPOINT

Who Should Know the Results of Your HIV Test If You Test Positive?

Most people would probably want to keep such results private, but would your opinion about HIV-positive people keeping their results confidential change in the following circumstances?

- You require first aid after a serious auto accident, and the emergency medical technician assisting is HIV positive.
- Your doctor is HIV positive.
- Your dentist is HIV positive.
- Your manicurist is HIV positive.
- Your massage therapist is HIV positive.
- Your severely handicapped daughter's elementary school teacher is HIV positive.
- Your lover is HIV positive.
- Your tattoo artist is HIV positive.
- Your jeweler who is about to pierce your daughter's ears is HIV positive.
- Your boxing partner is HIV positive.
- Your jail cellmate is HIV positive.

Arguments for not disclosing HIV-positive results to anyone other than the person undergoing HIV screening are that reporting such results to others would (1) cause many people not to take the test for fear of disclosure to others; (2) possibly cause loss of employment (if the results require mandatory reporting to supervisors or managers);

(3) unnecessarily stigmatize the HIV-positive person, exposing an infected person to social ostracism and gossip and potentially creating fear and panic in others; and (4) potentially destroy a partner or marriage relationship if the significant other or spouse is notified.

Arguments for mandatory disclosure to others potentially affected by the results of this disease include (1) to protect domestic or marital partners, (2) to protect others from HIV-positive workers who could infect them (such as surgeons who are involved in invasive bodily care or procedures), and (3) to honor the public's right to know of the threat of contracting this terminal disease.

Currently, employers cannot legally terminate a worker for being HIV positive. In cases of direct potential threat to the public, an HIV-positive worker can be reassigned to a different position. Also, in most cases, employers cannot legally inquire about HIV test results. An exception to this is the military and prison, where mandatory testing is required. What is your opinion about this issue?

The sooner an HIV-positive person begins drug treatment, the more effective the treatment may be. Knowing this, should HIV-positive individuals be required to inform past sexual partners and people with whom they have shared needles so that these people can be tested (known as *partner notification* or *contact tracing*)?

If an HIV-positive surgeon is going to operate on you, your mother, your father, or your child, do you have the right to know? What are the rights of the HIV-positive individual versus the rights of the public?

---

combinations do not rid the body of infected cells, results indicate that HIV infections could become as manageable as diabetes (Crowley 1996).

Today, people in the United States and other developed countries can use a number of drugs to treat HIV infection and AIDS. Some of these are designed to treat the opportunistic infections and illnesses that affect people with HIV/AIDS. In addition, several types of drugs seek to prevent HIV from reproducing and destroying the body's immune system. Reverse transcriptase inhibitors attach to an HIV enzyme called *reverse transcriptase*. The two major categories of reverse transcriptase inhibitors are nucleoside/nucleotide reverse transcriptase inhibitors (NRTIs) and

non-nucleoside reverse transcriptase inhibitors (NNRTIs) (EBSCO 2013). The following NRTIs and NNRTIs are currently used in the treatment of HIV/AIDS (EBSCO 2013):

- Combivir (lamivudine and zidovudine [AZT])
- Emtriva (emtricitabine)
- Epivir (lamivudine)
- Epzicom (abacavir and lamivudine)
- Hivid (zalcitabine)
- Rescriptor (delavirdine)
- Retrovir (AZT and zidovudine)
- Trizivir (abacavir, lamivudine, and zidovudine)
- Truvada (emtricitabine and tenofovir)
- Videx (didanosine)

- Viramune (nevirapine)
- Viread (tenofovir)
- Zerit (stavudine)
- Ziagen (abacavir)

Medications used to treat HIV infection (antiretroviral drugs) help many people with HIV to lower the levels of virus in their blood (viral load) to undetectable levels. Treatment with combinations of these medications, which is often referred to as **antiretroviral therapy (ART)**, slows the rate at which HIV multiplies in the body and may decrease the chance that an infected person will transmit HIV to others through sex. However, the risk of spreading infection is still not zero, which means that persons with HIV who are taking ART, or persons who are in a relationship with someone who has HIV and is taking ART, should still use proven prevention methods, such as condoms (CDC 2010d).

Many HIV patients are taking several of these drugs in combination, a form of ART known as **highly active antiretroviral therapy (HAART)**. When successful, combinations or "cocktail" therapy can reduce the level of HIV in the bloodstream to very low—even undetectable—levels and sometimes enable the body's CD4+ immune cells to rebound to normal levels (American Foundation for AIDS Research [amfAR] 2001). Less than 15 years ago the drug regimen was quite difficult:

I take the famous drug "cocktail" and have to wake myself up in the middle of the night around 4 in the morning, then go back to sleep. I am used to it. I know it is a pain in the neck, but I think that despite this, the side effects can even be worse at times. I really don't want to go into it; it's depressing. The bright side: I am still alive after 9 years since diagnosed with AIDS; I am not dead yet. *(From Venturelli's research files, male bartender in Chicago, age 52, May 18, 2000)*

KEY TERMS

antiretroviral therapy (ART)
refers to maintaining a regimen of taking a combination of several antiretroviral medicines to slow the rate at which HIV multiplies in the body

highly active antiretroviral therapy (HAART)
maintaining a regimen of more recent types of medications to slow the rate at which HIV multiplies in the body

An update regarding the treatment of HIV/AIDS reveals that

[i]t wasn't until 1995, with the development of a second class of anti-HIV drugs, that we began to make real progress in controlling the pandemic. These drugs target the HIV protease, an enzyme involved in processing HIV proteins into their functional forms. Today, 20 out of the 21 USDA-approved antiretroviral drugs target either the reverse transcriptase or the viral protease. With the introduction of multiple antiretroviral therapies, clinicians began a treatment regime known as HAART (Highly Active Antiretroviral Therapy) that involves combinations of 3–4 drugs at once. Despite the fact that there might be viruses resistant to one drug, they can still be suppressed by one of the other drugs being used. Just as the probability of getting struck by lightning twice in a row is much lower than getting struck once, the probability of finding a virus resistant to multiple drugs is much lower than being resistant to one. By reducing the probability of resistance, HAART was finally able to increase patient lifespan by suppressing viral replication and curbing immune cell loss. Although HAART has been very successful in preventing those infected with HIV from progressing to AIDS, it is not a cure, thus making prevention of new HIV cases a critical component of the strategy against HIV/AIDS. (Clark 2010)

As a therapy regimen, HAART results in a dramatic reduction in the incidence of AIDS and death in individuals infected with HIV (MyDNA.com 2005). Less than 15 years ago, patients took approximately 37 pills per day; a few years later it was a 14-pill-a-day regimen. Today, in the majority of cases, only three pills have to be taken each day (Scripps Howard News Service 2003). One source estimated the annual cost of care with HAART at about $10,000 to $15,000 per year (AVERT.org 2011). However, in a recent review of the cost of 24 major HIV medications by this author, the average yearly cost was approximately $8000 for each of the medications taken. If, for example, three types of HIV drugs are required, then the average amount is approximately $24,000 per year. Note, however, this approximate cost can *vary significantly* depending on what combinations of the 28 major HIV drugs are prescribed on a daily basis. For example, in 2008 Aptivus cost $1071 monthly, whereas another HIV drug, Videx or Videx EC, cost $368 monthly (Diaz-Linares et al. 2008). Another recent estimate indicates that "[m]onthly

HIV treatment regimens range from $2,000 to $5,000—much of it for drugs. With the life expectancy for HIV patients increasing, the lifetime cost of treatment in today's terms is estimated at more than half-million dollars (Aguirre 2012).

Recently, a new class of medicines known as *integrase inhibitors* was discovered that is very efficient in controlling HIV (Chong 2006). "Integrase inhibitors prevent HIV, or human immunodeficiency virus, from replicating by blocking its ability to patch its DNA onto cells" (Chong 2006, p. A9). When combined with two other drugs, tenoflovir and lamivudine, it appears promising. Used as part of a drug cocktail, "the amount of HIV in 90% of patients … [was reduced to] undetectable levels in 24 weeks" (Chong 2006, p. A9).

Newer AIDS drugs include the following findings:

- "Entry inhibitors that work by preventing HIV from entering healthy CD4 cells (T-cells) in the body" (AIDSMEDS 2011).
- Entry inhibitors (including fusion inhibitors) "work differently than many of the approved anti-HIV drugs—the protease inhibitors (PIs), the nucleoside reverse transcriptase inhibitors (NRTIs), and the non-nucleoside reverse transcriptase inhibitors (NNRTIs)—which are active against HIV after it has infected a CD4 cell" (AIDSMEDS 2011).
- "Entry/fusion inhibitors…stops the virus from entering cells. Two drugs in this class have been approved by the Food and Drug Administration (FDA): maraviroc, an entry inhibitor, and enfuvirtide, a fusion inhibitor" (amfAR 2010).
- "Integrase inhibitors prevent an HIV enzyme called integrase from inserting HIV's genetic information into the virus's target cell. To date, only one integrase inhibitor, reltegravir, has been approved by the FDA" (amfAR 2010).

Because these newer drugs halt the progression of HIV to AIDS, the rate of new AIDS cases fell 25% by 1998 (Zuger 2000). Today, there is approximately a 70% survival rate for those on daily medication (CDC 2010d).

Unfortunately, many health insurance companies continue to actively issue restrictive amendments on their policies that cap reimbursement for such expensive drug therapies. As a result, infected individuals with extensive debt obligations and patients without health insurance are often unable to afford the latest drug therapy.

A successful prognosis for HIV infection and AIDS relies on three factors: (1) initiation of a drug regimen as soon as possible after an HIV-positive diagnosis, (2) strict adherence to medical advice and treatment, and (3) maintenance of a healthy diet without drug use or abuse in order to avoid taxing the immune system.

■ Who Is at Risk for AIDS?

Although anyone can become infected with HIV, its routes of transmission are limited to blood, semen, vaginal fluid, and possibly some other body fluids (Grinspoon 1994). Before the advent of AZT, mothers were more likely to pass the virus to their children prenatally or through breast milk. HIV is a virus that is not likely to survive outside of the body. Consequently, it is not spread by casual contact, such as by shaking hands, touching, hugging, or kissing (although "deep" kissing with an infected person is not recommended). In addition, it is not spread through food or water, by sharing cups or glasses, by coughing and sneezing, or by using common toilets. It is not spread by mosquitoes or other insects.

The following populations are at greatest risk for contracting HIV:

- Men with a history of having had multiple homosexual or bisexual partners. Men who have sex with men (MSM) account for more than half of all new HIV infections in the United States each year (53%), as well as nearly half of people living with HIV (48%) (CDC 2010a). Although new HIV infections have declined among both heterosexuals and injection drug users, infections among MSM have been steadily increasing since the early 1990s (CDC 2010a).
- Injecting drug users and their sexual partners.
- Heterosexuals with multiple partners.
- Infants born to HIV-infected women (approximately 10% of all HIV-positive mothers have HIV-positive babies).
- People who receive contaminated blood products, such as for transfusions or treatment of blood disorders. (Blood banks have improved the screening of their blood supplies in the last decade.)

See **Figures 16.4** and **16.5** for a detailed breakdown of categories of estimated new HIV infections by transmission category by type of exposure for men and adult and adolescent females by transmission category in 2014. Figure 16.4 shows that approximately 67% of men with AIDS reported sex with men, and approximately 6% of people reported injection drug use. An estimated

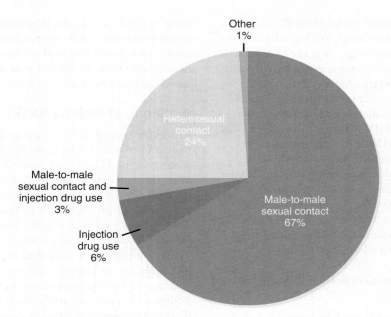

FIGURE 16.4 Estimated new HIV infections by transmission category: 2014 (*n* = 44,073).

Data from Centers for Disease Control and Prevention (CDC). *HIV/AIDS Statistics and Surveillance Report, 2014.* Atlanta, GA: U.S. Department of Health and Human Services, 2014.

3% of cases were attributed to male-to-male sexual contact and injection drug use, 24% were attributed to heterosexual contact, and other risk exposures accounted for the remaining 1% of cases. Figure 16.5 shows that in 2014 the majority of diagnoses of HIV infection (87%) among females aged 13 or older were attributed to heterosexual contact, regardless of age group; 12% attributed to their exposure to injection drug use; and 1%

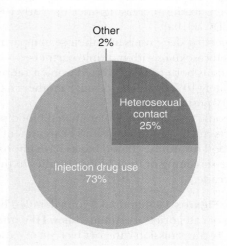

FIGURE 16.5 Percentage diagnoses of HIV infection among adult and adolescent females by transmission category: 2014 (*n* = 8472).

Data from Centers for Disease Control and Prevention (CDC). *HIV/AIDS Surveillance Report,* 2014. Atlanta, GA: U.S. Department of Health and Human Services, 2014.

reported another type of exposure. Heterosexual contact is with a person known to have, or to be at high risk for, HIV infection. Other transmission categories include blood transfusion, perinatal exposure, and risk factor not reported or not identified (CDC 2014).

Although not shown in this figure, the percentages attributed to heterosexual contact were higher among females aged 20 to 24 years (89.6%) than among other age groups. In addition, an estimated 14.5% of diagnosed HIV infections among females aged 45 years and older were attributed to injection drug use, compared with 9.0% in females aged 13 to 19 years, 9.8% in females aged 20 to 24 years, 11.8% in females aged 25 to 34 years, and 12.3% in females aged 35 to 44 years (CDC 2014).

▌ Women and Men Acquiring HIV and Drugs of Abuse

Contracting HIV is closely associated with drug abuse problems. As mentioned earlier, individuals addicted to illicit drugs are currently the second largest risk group for contracting HIV. As Figure 16.5 shows, at the end of 2014 an estimated 87% of adult and adolescent females aged 13 years or older living with a diagnosis of HIV in the United States were women who were infected with HIV through heterosexual contact, and 12% of adults and adolescent females contracted

HIV from injection drug use. In 2014, women accounted for an estimated 8472, or approximately 19%, of the estimated total of 52,545 new HIV infections in the United States between males and females. (heterosexual realationships). Regarding men, Figure 16.4 shows that 67% contracted HIV as a result of male-to-male sexual contact, 24% acquired HIV through heterosexual contact, and 6% acquired HIV from injection drug use.

HIV infections among women are attributable to injection drug and other substance use, either directly, through sharing drug injection equipment contaminated with HIV, or indirectly, through engaging in high-risk behaviors such as unprotected sex, while under the influence of drugs or alcohol (CDC 2013e). Several reasons account for the high incidence of this deadly infection in the drug-abusing population.

INTRAVENOUS DRUGS

Injected drugs are drugs that are introduced into the bloodstream using a needle and syringe. Sharing drug preparation or injecting equipment increases the risk of exposure to HIV-infected blood. If an injection-drug user shares injecting equipment with a person who is HIV positive, that person's blood, and the HIV virus, can contaminate the needle or spread to the drug solution. The HIV virus can then be injected directly into the user's body if the infected needle and syringe are reused (AIDS.gov 2014).

HIV-infected blood can also get into drug solutions through the following (AIDS.gov 2014):

- Using blood-contaminated syringes to prepare drugs
- Reusing water
- Reusing bottle caps, spoons, or other containers ("cookers") to dissolve drugs into water and to heat drugs solutions
- Reusing small pieces of cotton or cigarette filters ("cottons") to filter out particles that could block the needle

Intravenous drug use has become an important factor in the spread of AIDS in the United States. It is responsible for approximately 10% of new HIV cases each year (AIDS.gov 2014). "Drugs can be taken in a variety of ways including drinking, smoking, snorting, and rubbing, but it is the injection of drugs that creates the biggest risk of HIV transmission" (AVERT.org 2013). Among severely addicted populations, intravenous drug use is often undertaken with little regard to hygiene,

and injection paraphernalia such as needles, syringes, and cotton are frequently shared with other drug addicts (Millstein 1993). Sharing HIV-contaminated injection equipment can easily result in the transmission of this virus. The likelihood of an intravenous drug user contracting AIDS is directly correlated with (1) the frequency of drug injections, (2) the number of partners with whom injection equipment is shared, (3) the frequency of needle sharing, and (4) the frequency of injections in locations where there are high AIDS infection rates, such as in shooting galleries or crack houses (AIDS.gov 2014; Booth, Watters, and Chitwood 1993).

CRACK COCAINE

Cocaine is a powerfully addictive stimulant drug. The powdered form of cocaine is either inhaled through the nose (snorted) or dissolved in water and injected into the bloodstream. Crack is a form of cocaine that has been processed to make a rock crystal that users smoke. Use of crack increases the risk of contracting HIV because it can cause users to engage in risky sexual behaviors. When their financial resources are exhausted due to their purchase of the drug, users may turn to other ways to get the drug, such as trading sex for drugs or money, increasing their HIV infection risk (AIDS.gov 2014).

Compared to nonusers, crack cocaine users report the following:

- A greater number of recent and lifetime sexual partners
- Infrequent condom use
- Using more than one substance
- Being less responsive to HIV prevention programs

Use of crack (Ciba Foundation 1992), as well as other substances, such as alcohol, methamphetamine, Ecstasy, ketamine, GHB, and poppers, can alter the user's judgment and impair decisions about sex or other drug use, resulting in poor judgment and increased engagement in high-risk activities such as injection drug use or sexual risk taking (AIDS.gov 2014; Beard and Kunsman 1993; Inciardi, Lockwood, and Pottieger 1993). In particular, the use of crack and methamphetamine continue to be associated with high rates of HIV infection (AIDS.gov 2014; Campsmith, Nakashima, and Jones 2000). One study found that "[i]n poor, inner-city communities young smokers of crack cocaine, particularly women who have sex in exchange for money or drugs, are at a high risk for HIV infection. Crack use promotes the heterosexual transmission of HIV" (Edlin et al. 1994). As mentioned earlier, crack addicts often exchange sex for drugs or money to purchase drugs (Inciardi et al. 1993; Mathias 1993). These dangerous activities frequently occur in populations with an already high rate of HIV infection. Once infected, almost half of crack users continue to use sex to obtain their drugs, and thus become a source of HIV infection for others (Diaz and Chu 1993).

■ Youth and HIV/AIDS

The CDC reports that young people in the United States are at persistent risk for HIV infection. The following are the numbers regarding HIV/AIDS diagnoses in young people (CDC 2016):

- An estimated 9731 youth aged 13 to 24 were diagnosed with HIV in 2014 in the United States, with 81% (7868) of cases occurring in persons aged 20 to 24.
- Among youth aged 13 to 24 diagnosed with HIV in 2014, 80% (7828) were gay and bisexual males. Of those young gay and bisexual males who were newly diagnosed, 55% (4321) were black, 23% (1786) were Hispanic/Latino, and 16% (1291) were white.
- From 2005 to 2014, HIV diagnoses among both black and Hispanic/Latino gay and bisexual men aged 13 to 24 increased about 87%. Among young white gay and bisexual men, HIV diagnoses increased 56%. However, the most recent 5 years of data (2010 to 2014) indicate that diagnoses among black and white gay and bisexual men aged 13 to 24 have stabilized, and the increase slowed to 16% among Hispanic/Latinos.
- In 2014, an estimated 1716 youth aged 13 to 24 were diagnosed with AIDS, representing 8% of total AIDS diagnoses that year.

The following are the main findings with regard to young people living with HIV and deaths among young people due to AIDS (CDC 2016):

- At the end of 2012, an estimated 57,200 youth aged 18 to 24 were living with HIV in the United States. Of these, 25,300 were living with undiagnosed HIV—the highest rate of undiagnosed HIV in any age group.
- Among youth aged 13 to 24 who were diagnosed with HIV in 2013, 78% were linked to care within 3 months—the lowest rate of any age group.

- Among youth diagnosed with HIV in 2011 or earlier, 52% were retained in HIV care at the end of 2012.
- Among youth aged 18 to 24 who were living with HIV in 2012, 21% were prescribed HIV medicines (i.e., ART) and 16% had a suppressed viral load—the lowest rates of any age group.
- In 2013, 109 youth aged 15 to 24 died of HIV or AIDS.

Data from the 2013 Youth Risk Behavior Surveillance System (YRBS), which monitors health risk behaviors that contribute to the leading causes of death and disability among youth, revealed the following (CDC 2016):

- *Low rates of testing.* Only 22% of high school students who had ever had sexual intercourse had been tested for HIV.
- *Low rates of condom use.* Of the 34% of high school students reporting sexual intercourse during the previous 3 months, 41% did not use a condom the last time they had sexual intercourse.
- *Substance use.* Among the 34% of currently sexually active students nationwide, 22% had drunk alcohol or used drugs before their most recent sexual intercourse.

The risk of HIV/AIDS is especially notable for youth of minority races and ethnicities. Continual HIV prevention outreach and education efforts, including programs on abstinence and on delaying the initiation of sex, are required as new generations replace the generations that benefited from earlier prevention strategies.

In 2011, adolescent males (13 to 19 years of age) and young adult males (20 to 24 years of age) who were diagnosed with AIDS contracted the disease in the following ways (CDC 2013c):

- Male-to-male sexual contact: 91.8%
- Heterosexual contact: 4%
- Male-to-male sexual contact and injection drug use: 2.7%
- Injection drug use (IDU): 1.5%

Regarding race and ethnicity, this group was composed of the following (CDC 2013):

- 62% of males and 64% of females were black/African American.
- 19% of males and 18% of females were Hispanic/Latino.
- 16% of males and 14% of females were white.
- 2% of males and 2% of females were from multiple races.

Other important findings include the following (CDC 2010b), unless otherwise noted):

- An estimated 4883 young people received a diagnosis of HIV infection or AIDS, representing about 13% of the persons given a diagnosis within a year of initial sexual contact.
- HIV infection progressed to AIDS more slowly among young people than among all other persons with a diagnosis of HIV infection. The following are the proportions of persons in whom HIV infection did not progress to AIDS within 12 months after diagnosis of HIV infection:
  - 81% of persons aged 15 to 24
  - 70% of persons aged 13 to 14
  - 61% of all persons
- African Americans were disproportionately affected by HIV infection, accounting for 55% of all HIV infections reported among all other persons aged 13 to 24.
- Young men who have sex with men (MSM), especially those of minority races or ethnicities, were at high risk for HIV infection. In the seven cities that participated in the CDC's Young Men's Survey from 1994 to 1998, 14% of African American MSM and 7% of Hispanic MSM aged 15 to 22 years were infected with HIV.
- From 2001 to 2004, in the 33 states with long-term, confidential name-based HIV reporting, 62% of the 17,824 persons aged 13 to 24 years who were given a diagnosis of HIV/AIDS were male, and 38% were female.
- "It is estimated that 50% of all new HIV infections are among young people (about 7,000 young people become infected every day), and that 30% of the 40 million people living with HIV/AIDS are in the 15–24 age group" (WHO 2005). Equally serious is the fact that "[t]he vast majority of young people who are HIV positive do not know that they are infected, and few young people who are engaging in sex know the HIV status of their partners" (WHO 2005).
- Approximately 68,600 young people aged 13 to 24 years were living with HIV infection at the end of 2008; of those, nearly 60% did not know they were infected (CDC 2010c).
- Young people in the United States use alcohol, tobacco, and other drugs at high rates. Both casual and chronic substance users are more likely to engage in high-risk behaviors, such as unprotected sex, when they are under the influence of drugs or alcohol. Runaways and other homeless people are at high risk for HIV infection if they are exchanging sex for drugs or money (CDC 2007).
- Approximately two-thirds of AIDS cases among adolescent and young adult women were attributed to heterosexual contact as the mode of exposure to HIV. Cases among young women aged 13 to 19 years were less likely to be attributed to injection drug use (19%) than were cases among women aged 20 to 24 years (29%).
- Most 13- to 19-year-old females reported contracting HIV followed by AIDS through heterosexual contact (66%), injection drug use (19%), and other/not identified causes (15%) (CDC 2004a).
- A recent UNAIDS report estimated that throughout the world "one-third of those living with AIDS are aged 15–24" (MSNBC 2004). Further, most of these individuals who contract HIV do not even know they have the disease.
- HIV infection is spreading rapidly among younger urban gay men who are too young to recall the beginning of the AIDS epidemic two decades ago.
- Nearly half of the roughly 40,000 Americans who become newly infected with HIV each year are younger than the age of 25. Approximately 25% of the people now living with HIV in this country became infected when they were teenagers. More important, many young people also use drugs and alcohol, which can increase the likelihood that they will engage in high-risk sexual behavior.
- Adolescents who are most vulnerable to HIV infection include those who are homeless or runaways, juvenile offenders, and school dropouts.
- Worldwide, sexual intercourse is by far the most common mode of HIV transmission. In the United States, however, as many as half of all new HIV infections are associated either directly or indirectly with injection drug use (i.e., using HIV-contaminated needles to inject drugs or having sexual contact with an HIV-infected drug user) (amFAR 2010).

Three of the principal ways adolescents become infected with HIV are as follows: (1) high-risk sexual activity (unprotected sexual intercourse is reported by more than half of adolescents by the age of 17 years), (2) injection of substances of abuse, and (3) sex with multiple partners (CDC 2004b, 2004c, 2010b, 2016; Schaefer et al. 1993). Clearly, young people must be better educated about HIV, its transmission, and potential consequences before this epidemic becomes even more disastrous in adolescents.

▪ What to Do About HIV and AIDS

Yep, I live with it [being HIV positive] and my partner is HIV negative. We are pretty careful with sex. The drugs they have today are really effective. Luckily I did not contract HIV until two years ago before I met my current partner. I had older friends who did not make it twelve years ago while others I knew had this disease and were able to survive until the medication became a lot more effective. I do give presentations about having HIV/AIDS to organizations that have a majority of their members who are either gay or bisexual. I figure, why not do some good for the world and help others understand that safe sex is the only way to have sex. I have written pamphlets on safe sex from an insider's perspective and give out these pamphlets and other written material each time I make a presentation. *(From Venturelli's research files, male pharmacist, age 29, June 10, 2013)*

To date, the combination of various types of protease inhibitors and antiretroviral therapy medications is the most promising treatment for remaining relatively healthy with HIV. Although protease inhibitors do not completely rid the body of HIV antibodies, this category of drugs is usually successful in holding the virus at low levels in the bloodstream. The current lack of a permanent cure makes prevention the most important element in dealing with the AIDS problem. There are two main strategies for preventing HIV:

- *People should be encouraged to adopt safer sexual behavior.* Some of the steps to help achieve this include (1) avoiding multiple sex partners, especially if they are strangers or only casual acquaintances; (2) avoiding risk-taking sexual behavior that may allow HIV transmission, such as unprotected vaginal, oral, and anal intercourse; and (3) encouraging individuals who choose to continue high-risk sexual behaviors to use condoms or insist that their sexual partner use a condom.
- *Drug abusers should be educated about their risk of contracting AIDS.* They should be encouraged to reduce their risk by (1) abstaining from injecting drugs, (2) not sharing injection paraphernalia or always using clean needles (if available through needle exchange programs), (3) not sharing drugs with groups with high rates of HIV infection such as those in shooting galleries or crack houses, and (4) disinfecting the equipment (cleaning and boiling equipment for at least 15 minutes) between uses if they continue to share injection equipment.

One of the major difficulties in controlling the AIDS epidemic is identifying where preventive efforts should be focused. Because of limited resources, it is impossible to personally educate everyone in this country about HIV and AIDS. Consequently, our most intense efforts must be targeted at populations, neighborhoods, and areas with particularly high HIV infection rates. At the end of 2010, the South accounted for 45% of the estimated 33,015 new AIDS diagnoses in the 50 states and the District of Columbia, followed by the Northeast (24%), the West (19%), and the Midwest (13%). In 2010, the Northeast reported the highest rate of new AIDS diagnoses (14.2%/100,000), followed by the South (13.0%/100,000), the West (8.8%/100,000), and the Midwest (6.3%/100,000). In addition, HIV/AIDS is generally concentrated in urban areas in the United States (CDC 2013f).

It has also been proposed that AIDS prevention efforts particularly be focused on younger gay men and injection drug users who have multiple sex partners in the high-density AIDS neighborhoods found in many large metropolitan cities throughout the United States. Even with this focused approach, no one should be fooled into thinking that the HIV/AIDS problem will be eliminated. Everyone should approach potential sexual partners with some degree of caution, especially because the carrier of HIV may be unaware of infection or be reluctant to admit being a carrier for fear of abandonment. One thing is evident: If any doubt exists, we strongly recommend both partners being tested several times in a row before engaging in potentially life-threatening sexual contact.

The Entertainment Industry and Drug Use

Musicians sing about guzzling liquor and movie stars puff cigarettes and take drugs on the big screen. However, federal officials ask, Where is the unglamorous side of substance use—like hangovers, slurred speech, or trouble with the law (*News Tribune* 1999)? Drug use has a tendency to be displayed or fueled (depending on your perspective) by popular culture. In this section, we discuss two important genres of popular culture—movies and music—as one electronic subculture that depicts and promotes drug use.

At the Lollapalooza music festival held in July 1997 in an amphitheater in Massachusetts, the mostly white, suburban teen crowd cheered wildly when rap group Cypress Hill pushed a 6-foot-tall bong, or water pipe, onstage. The group sold 5 million copies of its first two albums, one of which included songs titled "Legalize It," "Hits from the Bong," and "I Wanna Get High" (Winters 1997).

In a research study for Columbia's Center on Addiction and Substance Abuse, 76% of 12- to 17-year-olds indicated that the entertainment industry encouraged illegal drug use. One 16-year-old daily marijuana user said, "All I know is that almost every song you listen to says something about [drug use]. It puts it into your mind constantly.... When you see the celebrities doing it, it makes it seem okay" (Winters 1997, p. 41).

About 20 years ago, the rock and rap music industries experienced a heroin epidemic. Although many other rock stars before Kurt Cobain used and abused drugs, Cobain's struggle with heroin and his 1994 suicide appear to have glamorized the use of this drug. "The number of top alternative bands that have been linked to heroin through a member's overdose, arrest, admitted use, or recovery is staggering: Nirvana, Hole, Smashing Pumpkins, Everclear, Blind Melon, Skinny Puppy, 7 Year Bitch, Red Hot Chili Peppers, Stone Temple Pilots, Breeders, Alice in Chains, Sublime, Sex Pistols, Porno for Pyros, and Depeche Mode" (Schoemer 1996, p. 50). Together these bands have sold more than 60 million albums—"that's a heck of a lot of white, middle-class kids in the heartland" (Schoemer 1996, p. 50).

Despite such excessive drug use and glamorization of drug use in the past, more recent commentary notes that

[s]ince the 1970s, addiction has become something which the music industry has, in the main, been happy to see swept under the carpet. Perhaps partly because the drug of choice during the "great rave explosion" of the late 1980s and 1990s was Ecstasy, which is not considered physically addictive, the last few decades have been short on songs about addiction. There is a sizeable tranche celebrating drug indulgence, from bands like Happy Mondays, Black Grape, and Primal Scream, but the only one I can recall confronting the possibility of addiction is Oasis's "Morning Glory,"

which deals with the need for artificial energy in ambivalent fashion. (*Independent* 2013)

And with regard to rap music in particular, the following has been noted:

Rap music has been shown to be a particular problem when it comes to the promotion of drugs. A study conducted by researchers at the University of California, Berkeley, found that there has been a six-fold increase in the number of references to drugs in the lyrics of rap songs over the past 20 years. Denise Herd, associate dean of students at the School of Public Health and the author of the study, says it is an alarming trend considering that rap artists are role models for so many young people. In addition, the discussion of drug use in these song lyrics is often in code, which means kids understand them and parents do not. (Ridings 2014)

Other music genres also promote the use of drugs:

In a surprise appearance at the Deadmau5 music festival in 2012, Madonna asked the crowd if anyone had seen Molly, which is another name for MDMA or ecstasy. Music videos are also a culprit in promoting drug use, including videos such as Black Mountain's "Old Fangs," The Dandy Warhols' "Not If You Were the Last Junkie on Earth," Jarvis Cocker's "Synchronize," and Wavves' "No Hope Kids." (Ridings 2014)

Some reports regarding drug use in the music industry show some change. The past president of CBS Records International and CBS Records reiterates that "[i]n the '80s, drug use was more prevalent, ... [t]oday, it's more spotty" (Paoletta 2004). Reasons cited for this change in drug use include growing awareness of the numbers of tragic drug overdoses and deaths of past musicians coupled with increasing pressures, demands, and "cut-throat" competition to remain musically successful. "Today, there is a lot more demand for an artist's time," says Flom, who has been sober since 1987. "Artists must perform at the top of their game at all times." Further, according to Warner Bros. senior VP Liz Rosenberg "artists on drugs can definitely slow down the promotional process. In the publicity world, this has a very strong impact" (Paoletta 2004).

Finally, more so today, "in the ever-changing addiction scene, alcohol is a continuing problem. But doctors and counselors say such prescription painkillers as Vicodin and OxyContin have eclipsed street drugs (cocaine, heroin) during the past five years" (Paoletta 2004).

How pervasive is drug use in today's popular movies and music? Research indicates that there is much substance abuse in popular movies and music. Studies revealed that 98% of movies reviewed depicted illicit drugs, alcohol, tobacco, or OTC and prescription medicines. Alcohol and tobacco appeared in more than 90% of movies, and illicit drugs appeared in 22%. About one-fourth (26%) of the movies that depicted illicit drugs contained explicit, graphic portrayals of their preparation and/or ingestion. Substance use was almost never a central theme, and very few movies ever specified motivations for use. Less than one-half (49%) of the movies portrayed short-term consequences of substance use, and about 12% depicted long-term consequences. Of the 669 adult major characters featured in the 200 movies studied, 5% used illicit drugs, 25% smoked tobacco, and 65% consumed alcohol. At least two major characters used illicit drugs in 12% of the movies, tobacco in 44%, and alcohol

in 85% (Office of National Drug Control Policy [ONDCP] 1999).

One list of the 10 top drinking movies included *Barfly* (1987), *Dazed and Confused* (1993), *Animal House* (1978), *The Thin Man* (1934), *Old School* (2003), *Arthur* (1981), *The Hangover* (2009), *The Lost Weekend* (1945), *The Big Lebowski* (1998), and *Who's Afraid of Virginia Woolf* (1966) (Goodykoontz 2011). Other movies about drugs and addiction include *Limitless* (2011), *Pineapple Express* (2008), *Thirteen* (2013), *Scarface* (1983), *The Wolf of Wall Street* (2013), *Traffic* (2000), *Enter the Void* (2009), and *Human Traffic* (1999), to name a few (WhatCulture.com 2016).

In all of these movies, which spanned the 20th and 21st centuries, "[l]ots of people drink lots of alcohol" (Goodykoontz 2011). A good number of these movies remain popular with movie buffs. Another news article discussing cocaine use on film sets noted that author Bob Woodward, who with Carl Bernstein first chronicled the Watergate scandal that brought down President Nixon, wrote a "detailed biography of [John] Belushi (*Wired: The Short Life and Fast Times of John Belushi*), [and] 'lots of cocaine' was used on set both by some of the actors and members of the production team. Then, when the film came to be released, the mostly negative reviews couldn't help making indirect references to drugs" (Brown 2013).

Findings from a study published in the *Journal of the American Medical Association* (*JAMA*) noted the following with regard to the depiction of drugs and alcohol in music and film (Primack et al. 2008):

- "explicit substance use is represented in about one-third of the most popular songs in the United States, with alcohol and marijuana referenced most frequently."
- "different genres …[of music] portray different (1) substances, (2) amounts of substances, and (3) motivations for, associations with, and consequences of use."
- "Overall, explicit substance use is portrayed most frequently in rap music (48 of 62 songs [77%]) and least frequently in pop music (3 of 35 songs [9%])."
- "Substance use is most commonly motivated by peer/social pressure and sex, and it is associated with partying and sex."
- "The social, sexual, emotional, and financial consequences of use are more commonly depicted as positive than negative, whereas the legal and physical consequences of use are generally depicted as more negative than positive."

© s_bukley/Shutterstock, Inc.

Snoop Dogg consuming a drug. Do such pictures have any effect on viewers?

- "alcohol and marijuana use are far more common than tobacco use in popular music."
- "children and adolescents are heavily exposed to substance use in popular music, and this exposure varies widely by genre."
- "Substance use in music is frequently motivated by peer acceptance and sex, and it has highly positive associations and consequences."

These findings clearly indicate that both movies and songs continue to reflect widespread use of alcohol and other drugs in our culture. Furthermore, their influence on the public viewing audiences continues to have an impact on values and attitudes about the use and/or abuse of drugs. One executive director of a Washington, D.C., area youth group, said, "It's becoming increasingly difficult to administer our preventive drug programs because the youth culture has changed in a manner that a lot more of popular music idolizes the use of marijuana and hallucinogens and that has a profound effect on young people" (Haywood 1996, p. 14).

Another top administrator at the Center for Substance Abuse Prevention of the Substance Abuse and Mental Health Services Administration agreed, "Our pop culture is sending a lot of pro-drug messages" (Haywood 1996). A more recent study supporting alcohol use in popular music found that

> [t]oday's popular music often celebrates excessive drinking as a fun, beneficial pastime, even highlighting select booze brands in many lyrics, a new study finds. Hip-hop, rap, R&B and country songs included references to Patron tequila, Hennessy cognac, Grey Goose vodka, and Jack Daniel's whiskey, which is featured in half of the songs that mentioned alcohol. ... Music can have a particularly powerful influence, the researchers said, because American teens spend about two and a half hours each day listening to music. (Drugs.com 2013)

In addition to these observations and findings, the major findings noted earlier with regard to substance use in movies and songs support the amount of alcohol and other drugs used in these two major types of electronic and audio media.

Promoter of Drug Use: The Internet

As of 2015, 84% of Americans and 96% of young adults aged 18 to 29 years used the Internet (Perrin and Duggan 2015). Of those adults online, 72% used social networking sites, 18% used Twitter, and 6% used reddit (Brenner 2013). There is no question that prodrug messages and detailed information are readily available over the Internet. The Internet maintains a unique subculture of drug enthusiasts. Drug use information found online includes how to roll super-joints, bake marijuana-laced brownies, grow "magic" psilocybin mushrooms, and create formulas for making amphetamine-like drugs; where to purchase the latest equipment for indoor growing of marijuana; and where to obtain catalogs that offer drug paraphernalia for sale. Similarly, magazines such as *High Times* and *Hemp Times* claim growing numbers of subscribers. These magazines devote most of their articles, features, advice columns, hemp festival information, and advertisements to the pleasures of drug consumption. Further, chat rooms devoted to finding, growing, purchasing, and making drug substances are growing in popularity. Those who do not use illicit drugs are often oblivious to the chat rooms and exchange of information found on the Internet:

> "The Internet is great at proliferating this sort of [drug] information almost faster than law enforcement can really keep track of it," says Robert J. Bell, a coordinator inside the DEA's synthetic drug department. Once the recipe makes its way online, anyone with the financial means can order chemicals in bulk, usually from China and Southeast Asia. (Vargas-Cooper 2012, p. 64)

A more recent and alarming occurrence is the boom in illicit drug sales online. Prescription drugs are being sold without a prescription over the Internet. Often solicitations are in the form of spam (unsolicited emails), with some people receiving multiple offers each day. The International Narcotics Control Board (INCB) reported recently that "90% of online drug sales take place without a medical prescription" and that "[t]he illicit trade over the Internet has been identified as one of the major sources for prescription medicines abused by children and adolescents in certain countries such as the United States" (Join Together Online and BBC News 2005). In addition,

> Billions of [doses of] controlled substances—some of them highly potent drugs such as oxycodone, equivalent to morphine, and fentanyl, which is many times stronger than morphine [as well as Viagra, Xanax, and OxyContin (to name a few)]—are being sold by unlicensed Internet pharmacies. (Join Together Online and BBC News 2005)

Other reports indicated the following:

Despite new efforts to regulate Internet pharmacies, 85% of sites selling controlled drugs do not require a prescription. Most orders filled by the 365 Internet pharmacies examined were for controlled substances, especially benzodiazepines like Xanax and Valium, according to the report by the National Center on Addiction and Substance Abuse at Columbia University in New York. (Seetharaman 2008)

According to the *Global Drugs Survey* 2015, which examines data from 100,000 responses across 50 countries, one quarter of the 11,750 people who said they had bought drugs online had done so in 2014, more than any other year. ... The report states: "As we suspected, access to lots of drugs for some ... leads to experimentation with new drugs and extended drug repertoires which may not be a good thing for some people. (Palmer 2015)

MDMA, LSD and forms of cannabis such as hydro or herbal are the most popular drugs purchased online. According to the Global Drugs Survey noted above, when given access to drugs to buy online, the ones people appear to choose are the "traditional illicit" drugs that are "tried, tested, desirable, familiar and probably safer" (Palmer 2015). Overall, the Global Drugs Survey states that "reduced rates of exposure to violence, less adulterated drugs, more confidence in product quality and removal from street dealing were clear benefits" of using the dark Web to purchase drugs (Palmer 2015).

In addition, *USA Today* reported that "more than 10 million online messages written by teens in the past year shows they regularly chat about drinking alcohol, smoking pot, partying and hooking up" (Leinwand 2007a). "Many of the teens who posted messages about drugs or alcohol often traded information about using illicit substances without getting hurt or caught. Some teens debated drug legalization and the drinking age. Other teens recounted their partying experiences, including sexual liaisons while drunk or high" (Leinwand 2007a).

More recently, a yearly study by the National Center on Addiction and Substance Abuse at Columbia University, which studies situations, circumstances, and factors associated with teen substance abuse, found that

75 percent of teens said that seeing pictures on social networks of peers partying with alcohol or marijuana encourages other teens to want to party like that as well. Nearly half of teens surveyed said they have seen pictures on Facebook or other social networking sites of kids getting drunk, passing out, or using drugs. Among teens who have seen the pictures, 47 percent said that it seems like those pictured are having a good time. (Duncan 2012)

■ Social Networking Motivating Drug Use

A new form of peer pressure has emerged. *Peer pressure* has been defined as collective human behavior where the norms of a group persuade and motivate naive group members to seek and act out certain forms of behavior in order to achieve peer acceptance and approval. There now appears to be an additional form of peer pressure to recreationally use drugs. The National Center on Addiction and Substance Abuse at Columbia University conducted a survey of 12- to 17-year-olds asking whether they spent any time on social media sites. They found that the vast majority (70%) of the teens surveyed used the sites and that 40% of all teens had "seen pictures on those sites of kids drinking or using drugs and that half of those teens were not yet teens—they were 13 years old or younger" (Reuters and Fox News Network 2011).

According to a National Center on Addiction and Substance Abuse study,

90% of teens are initially exposed to pictures of their peers drinking, using drugs or passing out on social media before they reach the age of 15 years old. Teens who are exposed to these types of images are three times likelier to consume alcohol, and it's four times as likely that they'll use marijuana. Just as disturbingly, these teens are able to access mind-altering substances, including prescription drugs, more readily than teens who don't use social media. These teenagers are also more likely to have friends who abuse prescription and illegal drugs. (12 Keys Rehab 2016)

It appears that the popularity and use of drugs largely through peer pressure can be linked to teen social media websites. Research shows that as result of smartphones "24% of teen go online 'almost constantly'" (Lenhart 2015). The top social media platforms for American teens are Facebook (71%), Instagram (52%), Snapchat (41%), and Twitter (33%).

■ The Dark Web: The Place to Go to Anonymously Purchase Illicit Drugs?

The Internet has different layers, but most Internet users are only aware of websites that they can navigate to via Google or Bing or online databases and academic journals. In reality, most search engines just scrape the surface of the World Wide Web. There is actually much more to the Web:

> When you surf the Web, you really are just floating at the surface. Dive below and there are tens of trillions of pages—an unfathomable number—that most people have never seen. They include everything from boring statistics to human body parts for sale (illegally). (CNN Money 2014)

How can you access and dip below the surface of the World Wide Web? A vast network is accessible once a user installs the **Tor browser** on his or her computer. With the Tor browser, users can browse the Web anonymously, including the most hidden section of the Web that can only be accessed with software that that makes the user's location anonymous (CNN Money 2014). The Tor browser enables users to access the **Tor network**: "The Tor network disguises your identity by moving your traffic across different Tor servers, and encrypting that traffic so it isn't traced back to you. Anyone who tries would see traffic coming from random nodes on the Tor network, rather than your computer" (Klosowski 2014).

According to one description,

> Tor … [is] the darkest corner of the Internet. It's a collection of secret websites (ending in .onion) that require special software to access them. People use Tor so that their Web activity can't be traced—it runs on a relay system that bounces signals among different Tor-enabled computers around the world. (Pagliery2014)

The Tor network largely consists of illegal porn, political dissidents, stolen credit cards, and drugs (Pagliery 2014).

One alarming and controversial underground website that could only be accessed using a Tor browser was Silk Road, which was a website that came into existence in February 2011:

> Silk Road, a digital black market that sits just below most Internet users' purview, does resemble something from a cyberpunk novel. Through a combination of anonymity technology and a sophisticated user-feedback system, Silk Road makes buying and selling illegal drugs as easy as buying used electronics—and seemingly as safe. It's Amazon—if Amazon sold mind-altering chemicals.

> …Here was just a small selection of the 340 items available for purchase on Silk Road by anyone, right now: a gram of Afghani hash; 1/8th ounce of "sour 13" weed; 14 grams of Ecstasy; 0.1 grams tar heroin. A listing for "Avatar" LSD includes a picture of blotter paper with big blue faces from the James Cameron movie on it. The sellers are located all over the world, a large portion from the U.S. and Canada.

> …Sellers feel comfortable openly trading hardcore drugs because the real identities of those involved in Silk Road transactions are utterly obscured. If the authorities wanted to ID Silk Road's users with computer forensics, they'd have nowhere to look. TOR (a specialized Internet browser) masks a user's tracks on the site. The site urges sellers to "creatively disguise" their shipments and vacuum seal any drugs that could be detected through smell. As for transactions, Silk Road doesn't accept credit cards, PayPal, or any other form of payment that can be traced or blocked. The only money good here is Bitcoins. (Chen 2011)

On October 2, 2013, after almost 3 years in operation as an Amazon-like marketplace for the purchase of illicit drugs over the Internet, Silk Road's alleged administrator, Ross Ulbricht, was arrested in California. The Federal Bureau of Investigation (FBI) shut down the online drug marketplace and seized billions of dollars in Bitcoins (the currency used for purchasing drugs on Silk Road) (Franceschi-Bicchierai 2013). Although this particular website was eliminated by law enforcement officials, this author immediately envisions the possibility that other types of illicit online drug marketplaces may emerge throughout the world in the years ahead given the very extensive amount of money and profits confiscated by the FBI's successful sting operation. The following confirms this prediction:

> Maybe it should be no big surprise, but hours after Silk Road was shut down, Web users were

Tor browser/Tor network
browser used to access an online network that disguises the user's identity by moving the user's traffic across different Tor servers and encrypting the traffic so that it cannot be traced back to the user's location

flocking to online forums with one question: "Where can I buy my drugs now?" The answer? Take your pick. Sites with names like Sheep Marketplace, Black Market Reloaded and Deep Bay were just some of the ones being mentioned as possibilities. (Goss 2013)

Another report after the Silk Road web site was shut down claimed the following:

One Silk Road moderator, Libertas, posted a long, heartfelt letter to the community urging them to go on. "We have the power to fight these agents of oppression, to fight the governments that task them with that oppression, and with the fires that Silk Road has stoked in our hearts and minds we must do just that," he wrote. "No doubt we will all regroup elsewhere, and I look forward to seeing all of you again, still free and still engaging in free trade without government interference into your personal affairs." (Jeffries 2013)

It appears that, in the end, Silk Road may become a symbolic blueprint fueling other Internet drug mass marketplaces. Clearly, the Internet is a more recent source for marketing illicit drugs for anyone having access to computers, and this audience includes younger teens and adults. Legal suppliers appear to be fueling the trade by providing their products to unlicensed Internet pharmacies that then sell these legally restricted types of drugs (Join Together Online and BBC News 2005). The potential impact of acquiring illicit drugs from Internet sites was emphasized by a journalist warning that we should "[f]orget the drug dealer on the corner, teens are increasingly turning to the Internet to get high" (Fiore 2008).

Although the Internet serves as an immensely valuable medium for learning, conducting business, communicating, and making information available, it is also used by a growing number of drug users as a forum for exchanging and learning about the latest information and techniques of drug consumption and recently for purchasing illicit drugs. Individuals who use the Internet for this type of information should be particularly wary because it is difficult, if not impossible, for harmful myths and fallacies posted on the web to be regulated.

LEARNING PORTFOLIO

Discussion Questions

1. What are two strengths and two weaknesses of studying subcultures from (a) an insider's perspective and (b) an outsider's perspective?
2. What are the primary drugs abused by athletes?
3. What are the principal effects and side effects of steroids?
4. What factors encourage drug use by athletes?
5. From the world of steroid abusers, define and give an example of each of the following terms: *stacking, cycling, plateauing, pyramiding,* and *array.*
6. Argue both for and against drug testing in sports.
7. What types of penalties do you think should be used against athletes who abuse drugs?
8. Review the ATLAS steroid prevention program. Do you have any suggestions for how it can improve its methods for lessening steroid use among adolescents? How effective do you think this program would be at your college or university?
9. List the reasons why women are more concerned about drug use and abuse than men. Can you add several reasons not mentioned in this chapter?
10. Do you believe that drug prevention programs should be created uniquely for males and females? Support your answer.
11. What aspects of the female role encourage the use of substances of abuse?
12. Should pregnant women who abuse drugs be punished? Why or why not?
13. Why are women who have been or are being sexually abused more likely to become addicted to drugs?
14. Why are adolescents especially vulnerable to drug abuse problems?
15. List three reasons why you think adolescents from upper-middle-class socioeconomic backgrounds become drug abusers.
16. What types of parents are most likely to have children who develop drug abuse problems?
17. How do adolescent drug abuse patterns differ from those in adults?
18. In what way are drugs of abuse associated with juvenile gang activity?
19. Should all adolescents who use drugs of abuse be treated for drug dependence? Why or why not?
20. Do you think that it is realistic to expect drug abusers to change their habits to prevent the spread of AIDS? Why or why not?
21. John was caught by city police growing psilocybin (hallucinogenic) mushrooms in his off-campus college apartment. Should John be punished by his college or university, in addition to the punishment that will be meted out by the criminal justice system? Why or why not?

Key Terms

22. What if you discover that your roommate is HIV positive? How would you handle this situation?

23. Do you think that the excessive use of alcohol and other drugs in movies influences viewers? Why or why not? Similarly, are people who enjoy rap or rock music affected by lyrics that refer to drug use and/or abuse? Why or why not?

24. Do you believe that drug information found on the Internet, such as in chat rooms devoted to the use of certain drugs (e.g., where to purchase equipment for growing marijuana, OTC stimulant pills, or psilocybin mushrooms), promote drug use? Why or why not?

25. What do you think is the future in using the dark Web to purchase illicit drugs?

Summary

1. The most common drugs abused by athletes are the ergogenic (performance-enhancing) substances (e.g., anabolic steroids, androstenedione, Dianabol [methandrostenolone], etc.). They include the anabolic steroids, for building muscle mass and strength, and the CNS stimulants, to achieve energy, quickness, and endurance.

2. Drug testing is conducted for most professional athletic competitions and usually includes screens for steroids and stimulants. Unlike years ago, nearly all performance-enhancing drugs are now detectable. Even though athletes often go to great lengths to avoid detection, it is virtually impossible to mask drug usage tests.

3. About 50% of the anabolic steroids used in the United States are prescribed by doctors; the other 50% are obtained from the black market, which includes an unknown percentage that are purchased on Internet websites. Currently, the Internet is the most widely used means of buying and selling anabolic steroids. Steroids are also bought and sold at gyms, bodybuilding competitions, and schools through teammates, coaches, and trainers. Black market steroids include drugs diverted

from legitimate channels smuggled from foreign countries (e.g., Brazil, Italy, Mexico, Great Britain, Portugal, France, and Peru) that are designated for veterinarian use or inactive counterfeits.

4. The ATLAS (Athletes Training and Learning to Avoid Steroids) program was developed to promote drug prevention and health promotion among adolescent high school athletes. It emphasizes the negative impact of anabolic steroids, alcohol, and other drugs on immediate sports performance. Athletes, coaches, and team leaders are trained to educate team members about the effects of anabolic steroid abuse. They emphasize both desirable and adverse effects of steroid use so that adolescents know very well how anabolic steroids build muscles and can increase athletic abilities.

5. Women who use drugs are uniquely affected by their sexual and gender differences when compared to men. The most common types of abused drugs (in descending order) for females are alcohol (82.9%), flavored alcoholic beverages (53.8%), any illicit drug use (34.4%), marijuana (27.8%), cigarettes (26.9%), binge drinking (five or more drinks in a row in last 2 weeks) (26.4%), and any illicit drug other than marijuana (19.2%) (Johnston et al. 2015a).

6. In general, women are more likely than men to (a) be concerned about drugs and drug use; (b) believe in drug prevention programs, such as needle exchange and testing reckless drivers for drug use; and (c) speak with their children about drug use.

7. There is a high prevalence of drug dependence in women who are victims of sexual and/or physical abuse. Approximately 70% of women in drug abuse treatment report histories of physical abuse, with victimization beginning at 11 years of age and occurring repeatedly. Further, women and men have different endocrine (hormone) systems and reproductive organs and structures, and women's responses to drugs vary according to their reproductive state.

8. For women to receive adequate treatment for drug dependence, certain considerations

must be met: (a) availability of female-sensitive services, (b) nonpunitive and noncoercive treatment that incorporates supportive behavior change approaches, and (c) treatment for a wide range of medical problems, mental disorders, and psychosocial problems.

9. Most adolescents who use substances of abuse are going through normal psychosocial development and will not develop problematic dependence on these drugs. The adolescent users who have difficulty with drugs often lack coping skills to deal with their problems, have dysfunctional families, possess poor self-images, and/or feel socially and emotionally insecure.

10. Parents who are most likely to raise drug-abusing adolescents are (a) drug abusers, (b) non–drug-using coupled with being constantly condemning, (c) overly demanding, (d) overly protective, or (e) unable to communicate effectively with their children.

11. Recent surveys regarding drug use patterns found that by 12th grade approximately 66.0% of the teens had used alcohol, approximately 34.4% had used cigarettes, approximately 44.4% had used marijuana, and 6.5% had used inhalants in 2014. A Monitoring the Future survey indicated that, in 2015, 18.30% of 12th graders had abused prescription drugs and that, after marijuana and alcohol, prescription and over-the-counter drugs were the most commonly abused substances by Americans age 14 and older.

12. Research continues to show that the most important factor influencing drug use among adolescents is peer drug use.

13. People who become gang members were often neglected by their parents, lacked positive role models, and failed to receive adequate adult supervision. Other motivations for joining a gang include peer pressure, low self-esteem, and perceived easy acquisition of money from gang-related drug dealing and other criminal activities.

14. The major reasons cited by college students for their use of drugs were: (a) breaks the ice, (b) enhances social activity, (c) gives people something to do, (d) gives people something to talk about, (e) allows people to have more fun, (f) peer bonding, (g) male bonding, (h) facilitates sex, (i) female boding, and (j) makes it easier to deal with stress.

15. Two interesting findings from research regarding drug use by college student subcultures are that (a) the best predictor of drug use for first-year college students is drug use during a typical month in the senior year of high school and (b) recreational drug use usually does not begin in college but has already been established in high school. A more recent finding includes personality dispositions to risky behavior as a predictor of first-year college drinking (mainly impulsivity and sensation-seeking types of students).

16. Club drugs include MDMA (Ecstasy), GHB, Rohypnol, ketamine, methamphetamine, and LSD. The phrase "club drug" is derived from the use of these drugs at all-night dance parties such as raves or trances, dance clubs, and bars. All these drugs are colorless, tasteless, and odorless. Individuals who want to intoxicate, sedate, and later sexually take advantage of others can add them unobtrusively to beverages.

17. Estimated new HIV infections in 2014 by transmission category are male-to-male sexual contact (67%), heterosexual contact (24%), injection drug use (6%), male-to-male sexual contact and injection drug use (3%), and other causes (not specified) (1%).

18. Currently, more than 1.2 million people in the United States are living with HIV infection, and almost one in eight (12.8%) are unaware of their infection. The estimated incidence of HIV has remained stable in recent years, at about 50,000 new HIV infections per year. Within the overall estimates however, some groups are profoundly affected by HIV than other groups. Gays, bisexuals, and men who have sex with men (MSM) and among racial and ethnic groups, African Americans continue to be disproportionately affected.

19. Major ways to prevent contracting HIV include (a) engaging in safe (protected) sexual behavior, (b) avoiding use of contaminated drug paraphernalia and especially

use of intravenous drugs, (c) avoiding use of drugs in groups with high rates of HIV infection, and (d) frankly discussing past sexual histories with potential sexual partners and, if in any doubt, having potential partners be tested for HIV several times in a row.

20. The extent of alcohol and drug use in movies and songs is startling. One study found that 98% of movies reviewed depicted illicit drugs, alcohol, tobacco, or OTC/prescription medicines. In this same detailed study, alcohol appeared in 93% of the movies and in 17% of the songs; tobacco appeared in 89% of movies but only 3% of songs. The lyrics of 63% of rap songs versus about 10% of the lyrics in other categories had substance references.

21. More recent reports regarding drug use in the music industry show change. Reasons cited for this change in drug use include growing awareness of the numbers of tragic drug overdoses and deaths of past musicians coupled with increasing pressures, demands, and "cut-throat" competition to remain musically successful.

22. New media influences contribute to drug use. An underground website called Silk Road came into existence in February 2011. It was like an eBay or Amazon in the world of drug purchasing over the Internet. It was shut down by the FBI in 2013. Although the Internet serves as an immensely valuable medium for learning, conducting business, communicating, and making information available, it is also used by a growing number of drug users as a forum for exchanging and learning about the latest information and techniques of drug consumption and recently for purchasing illicit drugs.

23. The Internet is considered to be the latest burgeoning source of information about using illicit drugs. The Internet has a layer beyond what we know as the World Wide Web. Using software known as the Tor browser to access the Tor network. In part, the Tor network largely consists of illegal porn, political dissidents, stolen credit cards, and drugs.

References

Aguirre, J. C. "Cost of Treatment Still a Challenge for HIV Patients in U.S." NPR (National Public Radio) Shop. 27 July 2012. Available http://www.npr.org/blogs/health/2012/07/27/157499134/cost-of-treatment-still-a-challenge-for-hiv-patients-in-u-s

AIDSMEDS. "Entry Inhibitors (including Fusion Inhibitors)." 16 September 2011. Available http://www.aidsmeds.com/archive/EIs_1627.shtml

AIDS.gov. "HIV/AIDS 101: Signs and Symptoms." U.S. Department of Health and Human Services. 6 June 2012. Available http://aids.gov/hiv-aids-basics/hiv-aids-101/signs-and-symptoms/

AIDS.gov. "Substance Abuse/Use: How are Drug Use and HIV Related?" U.S. Department of Health and Human Services. 14 January 2014. Available at https://www.aids.gov/hiv-aids-basics/prevention/reduce-your-risk/substance-abuse-use/

Alvarez, M. "A Dangerous Trend: Kids and Teens Using Steroids." Fox News Network. 19 November 2012. Available http://www.foxnews.com/health/2012/11/19/dangerous-trend-kids-and-teens-using-steroids/

American Academy of Child and Adolescent Psychiatry. *Facts for Families: Teen Suicide.* Washington, DC: American Academy of Child Adolescent Psychiatry, 2004. Available http://www.aacap.org/cs/root/facts_for_families/teen_suicide

American Academy of Child and Adolescent Psychiatry. *Facts for Families: Normal Adolescent Development.* Number 57. Washington, DC: American Academy of Child and Adolescent Psychiatry, 2006.

American Academy of Child and Adolescent Psychiatry. *Teens: Alcohol and Other Drugs.* Number 3. Washington, DC: American Academy of Child and Adolescent Psychiatry, 2011.

American Academy of Child and Adolescent Psychiatry. *Facts for Families Guide: Teen Suicide.* Number 10. Washington, DC: American Academy of Child and Adolescent Psychiatry, October 2013.

American Foundation for AIDS Research (amfAR). *Facts About HIV/AIDS, 2001.* New York: Body Health Resources Corporation, 2001.

American Foundation for AIDS Research (amfAR). *Facts for Life: What You and the People You Care About Need to Know About HIV/AIDS.* New York: amfAR AIDS Research, 2010.

Anabolics.com. "Steroid Laws." Dynamic Sports Nutrition, LLC. 2016. Available http://www.anabolics.com/pages/Steroid-Laws#.VxsgGaMrKS4

Anonymous, as told by Penn, N. "Confession: Why I Juiced." *Gentleman's Quarterly* (September 2005): 292–297.

Anxiety and Depression Association of America (ADAA). "Facts and Statistics." Silver Spring, MD: Anxiety and Depression Association of America (ADAA), August 2016. Available https://www.adaa.org/about-adaa/press-room/facts-statistics

Apostolides, M. "How to Quit the Holistic Way." *Psychology Today* 29 (September/October 1996): 30–43, 75–76.

Archambault, D. "Adolescence, a Physiological, Cultural and Psychological No Man's Land." In *Adolescent Substance Abuse, Etiology, Treatment and Prevention,* edited by G. Lawson and A. Lawson, 11–28. Gaithersburg, MD: Aspen, 1992.

Associated Press. "Boredom, Stress, Money Linked to Drug Abuse." *Chesterton/Valparaiso Post Tribune* (20 August 2003): A1, A8.

AVERT.org. "AIDS, Drug Prices and Generic Drugs." 2011. Available http://www.avert.org/generic.htm

AVERT.org. "Injecting Drug Users and HIV/AIDS." 2013. Available http://www.avert.org/hiv-injecting-drug-users.htm

Bahr, S. J., A. C. Marcos, and S. L. Maughan. "Family, Educational and Peer Influences on Alcohol Use of Female and Male Adolescents." *Journal of Studies on Alcohol* 56 (1995): 457–469.

Baltieri, D. A., and A. G. de Andrad. "Alcohol and Drug Consumption and Sexual Impulsivity Among Sexual Offenders." In *Sexual Offenders: Management, Treatment and Bibliography,* edited by J. V. Fenner, 73–96. New York: Nova Science, 2008.

Beard, B., and V. Kunsman. "A Cause for Concern: Alcohol-Induced Risky Sex on College Campuses." *Prevention Pipeline* 6 (September–October 1993): 24.

Begley, S., and M. Brant with C. Dickey, K. Helmstaedt, R. Nordland, and T. Hayden. "The Real Scandal." *Newsweek* 133 (15 February 1999): 48–54.

Bell, J. "Athletes' Use and Abuse of Drugs." *The Physician and Sports Medicine* 15 (March 1987): 99–108.

Belsie, L. "Temperance Movement Hits College Dorms." *Christian Science Monitor* 87 (30 August 1995): 1, 2.

Bergeret, J. *Young People, Drugs ... and Others.* Rockville, MD: United Nations Office for Drug Control and Crime Prevention, 1 January 1981.

Beschner, G., and A. Friedman. "Treatment of Adolescent Drug Abusers." *International Journal of the Addictions* 20 (1985): 977–993.

Blueprints for Healthy Youth Development. *Athletes Training and Learning to Avoid Steroids (ATLAS).* Boulder, CO: Blueprints for Healthy Youth Development, University of Colorado Boulder, Institute of Behavior Science Center for the Study and Prevention of Violence, 2016. Available http://www.blueprintsprograms.com/factsheet/athletes-training-and-learning-to-avoid-steroids-atlas

Blum, R. "Rodriguez: 'Amateur Hour.'" *Post-Tribune* (18 February 2009): A11.

"Bodybuilding Drug Yields 'High.'" *Pharmacy Times* (June 1992): 14.

Booth, R., J. Watters, and D. Chitwood. "HIV Risk-Related Sex Behaviors Among Injection Drug Users, Crack Smokers, and Injection Drug Users Who Smoke Crack." *American Journal of Public Health* 83 (1993): 1144–1148.

Brady, T. M., and O. S. Ashley, Eds. *Women in Substance Abuse Treatment: Results from the Alcohol and Drug Services Study (ADSS).* DHHS Pub. No. SMA 04–3968, Analytic Series A–26. Rockville, MD: Substance Abuse and Mental Health Services Administration, Office of Applied Studies, 2005.

Brenner, J. "Pew Internet: Social Networking (full detail)." Pew Internet & American Life Project. 5 August 2013. Available http://pewinternet.org/Commentary/2012/March/Pew-Internet-Social-Networking-full-detail.aspx

Britannica.com. "Alex Rodriguez." Encyclopedia Britannica Online. 31 October 2010. Available http://www.britannica.com/EBchecked/topic/914723/Alex-Rodriguez

Brown, A. M. "Drug Use on Film Sets—You'd Be Amazed by How Much of It Goes On." *The Telegraph.* 22 July 2013. Available http://blogs.telegraph.co.uk/news/andrewmcfbrown/100021797/drug-use-on-film-sets-%E2%80%93-youd-be-amazed-by-how-much-of-it-goes-it-on/

Buckstein, D., D. Brent, J. Perper, G. Moritz, M. Baugher, J. Schweers, C. Roth, and L. Balach "Risk Factors for Completed Suicide Among Adolescents with a Lifetime History of Substance Abuse: A Case-Control Study." *Acta Psychiatrica Scandinavia* 88 (1993): 403–408.

Burke, C., and S. Davis. "Anabolic Steroid Abuse." *Pharmacy Times* (June 1992): 35–40.

Burn-Murdoch, J. "Doping in Olympic Events: How Does Each Sport Compare?" *The Guardian.* (4 July 2012). Available http://www.guardian.co.uk/sport/datablog/2012/jul/04/olympics-2012-athletics

Bussing-Burks, M. "Alcohol and Drug Use Increases Suicidal Behaviors." National Bureau of Economic Research. 9 July 2013. Available http://www.nber.org/digest/aug02/w8810.html

Butler, A. "Adolescent Identity Development: Who We Are." Cornell University Family Life Development Center and ACT Youth Center of Excellence. May 2010. Available http://www.actforyouth.net/resources/n/n_adol_identity/

Campsmith, M. L., A. K. Nakashima, and J. L. Jones. "Association Between Crack Cocaine Use and High-Risk Sexual Behaviors After HIV Diagnosis." *Journal of Acquired Immune Deficiency Syndrome (JAIDS)* 25 (1 October 2000): 192–198.

CBS News. "By the Numbers: Chicago-Area Gangs." CBS Interactive. 21 May 2013.

Center for Behavioral Health Statistics and Quality (CBHSQ). *Behavioral Health Trends in the United*

States: Results from the 2014 National Survey on Drug Use and Health. HHS Pub. No. (SMA) 15-4917, NSDUH Series H-50. Rockville, MD: Substance Abuse and Mental Health Services Administration, 2015. Available http://www.samhsa.gov/data/sites/default/files/NSDUH-FRR1-2014/NSDUH-FRR1-2014.pdf

Center for Science in the Public Interest. "College Students and Alcohol Use." August 2007. Available http://cspinet.org/booze/FactSheets/0311CollegeStudents.pdf

Centers for Disease Control and Prevention (CDC). *Estimated AIDS Cases Among Female Adolescents and Young Adults by Exposure Category, Diagnosed Through 2002, United States.* Washington, DC: National Center for HIV, STD, and TB Prevention, Divisions of HIV/AIDS Prevention Surveillance Branch, 2004a.

Centers for Disease Control and Prevention (CDC). *Estimated AIDS Cases Among Male Adolescents and Young Adults by Exposure Category, Diagnosed Through 2002, United States.* Washington, DC: National Center for HIV, STD, and TB Prevention, Divisions of HIV/AIDS Prevention Surveillance Branch, 2004b.

Centers for Disease Control and Prevention (CDC). *HIV/AIDS Surveillance Report, 2003.* Vol. 15. Atlanta, GA: U.S. Department of Health and Human Services, CDC, 2004c.

Centers for Disease Control and Prevention (CDC). "HIV/AIDS Among Youth." The Body Health Resources Corporation. 2007. Available http://www.thebody.com/content/art17110.html

Centers for Disease Control and Prevention (CDC). *HIV and AIDS in America: A Snapshot.* Atlanta, GA: Division of HIV/AIDS Prevention, National Center for HIV/AIDS, Viral Hepatitis, STD, and TB Prevention, 2010a.

Centers for Disease Control and Prevention (CDC). *HIV in the United States.* Atlanta, GA: Divisions of HIV/AIDS Prevention, National Center for HIV/AIDS, Viral Hepatitis, STD, and TB Prevention, 2010b.

Centers for Disease Control and Prevention (CDC). *HIV/AIDS and Women.* Atlanta, GA: Division of HIV/AIDS Prevention, National Center for HIV/AIDS, Viral Hepatitis, STD, and TB Prevention, 2010c.

Centers for Disease Control and Prevention (CDC). *Questions and Answers on the Use of HIV Medications to Help Prevent the Transmission of HIV.* Atlanta, GA: Division of HIV/AIDS Prevention, National Center for HIV/AIDS, Viral Hepatitis, STD, and TB Prevention, 2010d.

Centers for Disease Control and Prevention (CDC). *CDC Fact Sheet, HIV and AIDS in America: A Snapshot.* Atlanta, GA: Division of HIV/AIDS Prevention, National Center for HIV/AIDS, Viral Hepatitis, STD, and TB Prevention, 2013a.

Centers for Disease Control and Prevention (CDC). "HIV in the United States: At a Glance." Division of HIV/

AIDS Prevention. 23 April 2013. Available http://www.cdc.gov/hiv/statistics/basics/ataglance.html

Centers for Disease Control and Prevention (CDC). "HIV Surveillance in Adolescents and Young Adults (Through 2011)." National Center for HIV/AIDS, Viral Hepatitis, STD, and TB Prevention, Division of HIV/AIDS Prevention, 11 June 2013c.

Centers for Disease Control and Prevention (CDC). "HIV Among Women." National Center for HIV/AIDS, Viral Hepatitis, STD, and TB Prevention, Division of HIV/AIDS Prevention, March 2013d. Available http://www.cdc.gov/hiv/pdf/risk_women.pdf

Centers for Disease Control and Prevention (CDC). "HIV Among Women: Fact Sheet." National Center for HIV/AIDS, Viral Hepatitis, STD, and TB Prevention, Division of HIV/AIDS Prevention, 3 July 2013e. Available http://www.cdc.gov/hiv/risk/gender/women/facts/index.html

Centers for Disease Control and Prevention (CDC). "HIV and AIDS in the United States by Geographic Distribution." National Center for HIV/AIDS, Viral Hepatitis, STD, and TB Prevention, Division of HIV/AIDS Prevention, 23 April 2013f. Available http://www.cdc.gov/hiv/statistics/basics/geographicdistribution.html

Centers for Disease Control and Prevention (CDC). "HIV/AIDS Statistics and Surveillance Report, 2014." Atlanta, GA: U.S. Department of Health and Human Services, 2014

Centers for Disease Control and Prevention (CDC). "Tobacco Use and Pregnancy." Atlanta, GA: Reproductive Health, 9 September 2015a. Available http://www.cdc.gov/reproductivehealth/maternalinfanthealth/tobaccousepregnancy/

Centers for Disease Control and Prevention (CDC). "CDC's Fight against Global HIV & TB." Atlanta, GA: Division of Global HIV & TB, November 2015b.

Centers for Disease Control and Prevention (CDC). "HIV in the United States: At a Glance." Atlanta, GA: Division of HIV/AIDS Prevention, National Center for HIV/AIDS, Viral Hepatitis, Sexual Transmitted Diseases and Tuberculosis Prevention, Centers for Disease Control and Prevention, 2015c.

Centers for Disease Control and Prevention (CDC). "HIV Among Youth." Atlanta, GA: Division of HIV/AIDS Prevention, National Center for HIV/AIDS, Viral Hepatitis, Sexual Transmitted Diseases and Tuberculosis Prevention, Centers for Disease Control and Prevention, 27 April 2016.

Chen, A. "The Underground Website Where You Can Buy Any Drug Imaginable." Kotaku. 1 June 2011. Available http://kotaku.com/the-underground-website-where-you-can-buy-any-drug-imag-30818160

Chilet-Rosell, E. "Gender Bias in Clinical Research, Pharmaceutical Marketing, and the Prescription of Drugs."

Bethesda, MD: Global Health Action, 2014. Available https://www.ncbi.nlm.nih.gov/pmc/articles/PMC4262757/

Child Trends. "Adolescents Training and Learning to Avoid Steroids Program (ATLAS)." 2009. Available http://www.childtrends.org/lifecourse/programs/AvoidSteroids.htm

Chong, J.-R. "Study Casts Positive Light on AIDS Drug." *Los Angeles Times*, reported in *Post Tribune* [Merrillville, IN] (13 August 2006): A9.

Ciba Foundation. "AIDS and HIV Infection in Cocaine Users." In *Cocaine: Scientific and Social Dimensions*, edited by G. Block and J. Whelan, 181–194. New York: Wiley, 1992.

Clark, E. *HIV Progress and Prevention*. Boston, MA: Science in the News (SITN), Harvard Graduate School of Arts and Sciences, 2010.

CNN Money. "What Is the Deep Web?" 2014. Available http://money.cnn.com/infographic/technology/what-is-the-deep-web/?iid=EL

CollegeXpress.com. "Schools Offering Substance-Free Housing." 2016. Available http://www.collegexpress.com/lists/list/schools-offering-substance-free-housing/1663/

CRC Health Group. "Factors of Teen Drug Use." 2007. Available http://www.adolescent-substance-abuse.com

Crowley, G. "Targeting a Deadly Scrap of Genetic Code." *Newsweek* (2 December 1996): 68–69.

Curry, D. G., and I. A. Spergel. "Gang Homicide, Delinquency, and Community." In *Gangs and Gang Behavior*, edited by G. L. Mays, 314–336. Chicago: Nelson-Hall, 1997.

Cyders, M. A., K. Flory, S. Rainer, and G. T. Smith. "The Role of Personality Dispositions to Risky Behavior in Predicting First-Year College Drinking." *Addiction* 104 (2009): 193–202.

Daily, S. "Alcohol, Incest, and Adolescence." In *Adolescent Substance Abuse, Etiology, Treatment and Prevention*, edited by G. Lawson and A. Lawson, 251–266. Gaithersburg, MD: Aspen, 1992a.

Daily, S. "Suicide Solution: The Relationship of Alcohol and Drug Abuse to Adolescent Suicide." In *Adolescent Substance Abuse, Etiology, Treatment and Prevention*, edited by G. Lawson and A. Lawson, 233–250. Gaithersburg, MD: Aspen, 1992b.

Destinations to Recovery. "Teen Alcohol and Drug Use – How it Impacts Suicide Rates." Woodland Hills, CA: Destinations to Recovery, 25 September 2014.

Diaz, T., and S. Chu. "Crack Cocaine Use and Sexual Behavior Among People with AIDS." *Journal of the American Medical Association* 269 (1993): 2845–2846.

Diaz-Linares, M., E. Vázquez, J. Gallant, and M. Delaney. "12th Annual HIV Drug Guide." *Positively Aware*. January/February 2008. Available http://positivelyaware.com/2008/08_01/drug_guide.html

Dicker, M., and E. A. Leighton. "Trends in the U.S. Prevalence of Drug-Using Parturient Women and Drug-Affected Newborns, 1979 Through 1990." *American Journal of Public Health* 84 (1994): 1433.

Docherty, J. R. "Pharmacology of Stimulants Prohibited by the World Anti-Doping Agency (WADA)." *British Journal of Pharmacology* 154 (2008): 606–622.

Donaldson-Evans, C. "Wrestler Chris Benoit Double Murder-Suicide: Was It 'Roid Rage'?" FoxNews.com. 27 June 2007. Available http://www.foxnews.com/printer_friendly_story/0,3566,286834,00.html

Drug and Alcohol Rehab Florida. "The Effects of Drug Abuse on Your Reproductive System." 8 October 2012. Available http://www.drugrehabfl.net/the-effects-of-drug-abuse-on-your-reproductive-system/

Drug Enforcement Administration (DEA). *Drugs of Abuse*. Washington, DC: U.S. Department of Justice, Drug Enforcement Administration, 2015. Available http://www.dea.gov/pr/multimedia-library/publications/drug_of_abuse.pdf#page=76

Drug Strategies. "Drug Use and Attitudes." In *Keeping Score*, 4–10. Washington, DC: Drug Strategies, 1998. Available http://www.drugstrategies.com/wp-content/uploads/2014/05/ks_1998.pdf

Drugs.com. "Alcohol Dominates in Pop Music Lyrics." August 2013. Available https://www.drugs.com/news/alcohol-dominates-pop-music-lyrics-study-47108.html

Duncan, K. "Online-Only: Survey Finds Some Kids Use Drugs, Drink During School Day." *The Nation's Health* 42 (2012). Available http://thenationshealth.aphapublications.org/content/42/9/E46.full

EBSCO. "Reverse Transcriptase Inhibitors." 2013. Available https://healthlibrary.epnet.com/GetContent.aspx?token=e0498803-7f62-4563-8d47-5fe33da65dd4&chunkiid=111797

Edlin, B. R., K. L. Irwin, S. Faruque, C. B. McCoy, C. Word, Y. Serrano, J. A. Inciardi, B. P. Bowser, R. F. Schilling, and S. D. Holmberg. "Intersecting Epidemics—Crack Cocaine Use and HIV Infection Among Inner-City Young Adults. Multicenter Crack Cocaine and HIV Infection Study Team." *New England Journal of Medicine* 331 (24 November 1994): 1422–1427.

Elmen, J., and D. Offer. "Normality, Turmoil and Adolescence." In *Handbook of Clinical Research and Practice with Adolescents*, edited by P. Tolan and B. Cohler, 5–19. New York: Wiley, 1993.

Erickson, P. G., and G. F. Murray. "Sex Differences in Cocaine Use and Experiences: A Double Standard Revived?" *American Journal of Drug and Alcohol Abuse* 15 (1989): 135–152.

ESPN.com. "Steroids Discovered in Probe Slayings, Suicide." 27 July 2007. Available http://sports.espn.go.com/espn/news/story?id=2917133

e-Steroid.com. "Steroid Statistics." 2 November 2013. Available http://www.e-steroid.com/steroid-articles/steroid-statistics.html

Fagan, J. "Social Processes of Delinquency and Drug Use Among Urban Gangs." In *Gangs in America*, edited by C. R. Huff, 183–213. Newbury Park, CA: Sage, 1990.

Ferrente, R. "Ben Johnson Retires from Running After Positive Test." Morning Edition on National Public Radio. 8 March 1993.

Fiore, M. "Using the Internet to Get High." FoxNews.com. 9 September 2008. Available http://www.foxnews.com/story/0,2933,419582,00.html

Franceschi-Bicchierai, L. "The Silk Road Online Drug Marketplace by the Numbers." Mashable. 4 October 2013. Available http://mashable.com/2013/10/04/silk-road-by-the-numbers/

Funk, L. "Shocking School Drug and Gang Survey." Kensington, MD: Democraticunderground.com., 19 August 2010. Available http://www.democraticunderground.com/discuss/duboard.php?az=view_all&address=389x8980990

Futures. "Why Drug Addiction Differs in Men and Women." Futures of Palm Beach. 2016. Available https://www.futuresofpalmbeach.com/addictions/why-drug-addiction-differs-in-men-and-women/

Gloucester County College. "Crime Prevention and Safety: Alcohol and Drug Abuse on Campus." Gloucester County Educational Campus—Safety & Security, 2013. Available http://www.gccnj.edu/security/crime_prevention_safety/alcohol_and_drug_abuse.cfm

Goldberg, L., D. Elliot, G. N. Clarke, D. P. MacKinnon, E. Moe, L. Zoref, C. Green, S. L. Wolf, E. Greffrath, D. J. Miller, and A. Lapin. "Effects of a Multidimensional Anabolic Steroid Prevention Intervention: The Adolescents Training and Learning to Avoid Steroids (ATLAS) Program." *Journal of the American Medical Association* 276 (1996): 1555–1562.

Goldstein, F. "Pharmacological Aspects of Substance Abuse." In *Remington's Pharmaceutical Sciences*, 19th ed., edited by A. R. Genaro and M. Easton, 780–794. Easton, PA: Mack, 1995.

Gonzales, M., K McEnery, T. Sheehan, and S. Mellody. *America's Habit: Drug Abuse, Drug Trafficking, and Organized Crime*. Washington, DC: President's Commission on Organized Crime, 1986.

Goodykoontz, B. "'Big Lebowski,' 'Animal House' Make List of 10 Top Drinking Movies." *Chicago Sun-Times*. (27 October 2011). Available http://www.suntimes.com/entertainment/movies/8442007-421/big-lebowski-arthur-animal-house-among-top-drinking-movies-ever-made.html

Goss, D. "Web's Black Market Peddles Drugs, Guns and More." CNN Tech. 4 October 2013. Available at http://www.cnn.com/2013/10/04/tech/web/internet-black-market/index.html

Green, C. A. *Gender and Use of Substance Abuse Treatment Services*. Bethesda, MD: National Institute on Alcohol Abuse and Alcoholism, 2006: 1–12.

Grinspoon, L. "AIDS and Mental Health—Part 1." *Harvard Mental Health Letter* 10 (January 1994): 1–4.

Guide4Living.com. "Steroid Abuse and Addiction." 2005. Available http://www.guide4living.com/drugabuse/steroids.htm

Harris, W. "10 Performance-Enhancing Drugs That Aren't Steroids." HowStuffWorks: Science. 2013. Available http://science.howstuffworks.com/10-performance-enhancing-drugs.htm

Haywood, R. L. "Why More Young People Are Using Drugs." *Jet* 90 (9 September 1996).

HealthyWomen.org. "Substance Abuse." New York, NY: National Women's Health Resource Center, Inc., 2016. Available http://www.healthywomen.org/condition/substance-abuse

Henslin, J. M. *Social Problems: A Down-to-Earth Approach*, 11th ed. Upper Saddle River, NJ: Pearson Higher Education, 2014.

Hingson, R. W., W. Zha, and E. R. Weitzman. "Magnitude of and Trends in Alcohol-Related Mortality and Morbidity Among U.S. College Students Ages 18–24, 1998–2005." *Journal of Studies on Alcohol and Drugs*, Suppl. No. 16 (2009): 12–20.

Hoberman, J. M., and C. E. Yesalis. "The History of Synthetic Testosterone." *Scientific American* (February 1995).

Holdcroft, A. "Gender Bias in Research: How Does It Affect Evidence Based Medicine?" *Journal of the Royal Society of Medicine* 100 (2007): 2-3.

Hoshino, J. "Assessment of Adolescent Substance Abuse." In *Adolescent Substance Abuse, Etiology, Treatment and Prevention*, edited by G. Lawson and A. Lawson, 87–104. Gaithersburg, MD: Aspen, 1992.

Howard, M. "Adolescent Substance Abuse: A Social Learning Theory Perspective." In *Adolescent Substance Abuse, Etiology, Treatment and Prevention*, edited by G. Lawson and A. Lawson, 29–40. Gaithersburg, MD: Aspen, 1992.

Inciardi, J. A., D. Lockwood, and A. E. Pottieger. *Women and Crack-Cocaine*. New York: Macmillan, 1993.

Independent. "Music and Drugs—It's a Hard Habit to Break." (10 November 2013). Available http://www.independent.co.uk/arts-entertainment/music/features/music-and-drugs-its-a-hard-habit-to-break-2327654.html

Jayson, S. "Expert: Risky Teen Behavior Is All in the Brain." *USA Today*. (5 April 2007). Available http://www.usatoday.com/news/health/2007-04-04-teen-brain_N.htm

Jeffries, A. "After Silk Road's Demise, Online Drug Dealing Moves to New Sites." The Verge. 4 October 2013. Available http://www.theverge.com/2013/10/4/4799770/drug-dealers-set-up-mini-silk-roads-after-federal-bust

Johnson, R. A., J. P. Hoffmann, and D. R. Gerstein. *The Relationship Between Family Structure and Adolescent Substance Use*. Rockville, MD: Substance Abuse and Mental Health Services Administration, Office of Applied Studies, July 1996.

Johnston, L. D., P. M. O'Malley, and J. G. Bachman. *National Survey Results from the Monitoring the Future Study, 1975–1992*. Rockville, MD: National Institute on Drug Abuse, 1993.

Johnston, L. D., P. O'Malley, and J. G. Bachman. *The Monitoring the Future National Results on Adolescent Drug Use: Overview of Key Findings, 1999*. Ann Arbor: University of Michigan Institute for Social Research and Bethesda, MD: National Institute on Drug Abuse, U.S. Department of Human Services, National Institutes of Health, 2000a.

Johnston, L. D., P. O'Malley, and J. G. Bachman. *National Survey Results on Drug Use from the Monitoring the Future Study, 1975–1999. Vol. 2, College Students and Young Adults*. U.S. Department of Health and Human Services, National Institute on Drug Abuse. Washington, DC: U.S. Government Printing Office, 2000b.

Johnston, L. D., P. M. O'Malley, J. G. Bachman, and J. E. Schulenberg. *Monitoring the Future: National Results on Adolescent Drug Use*. Bethesda, MD: National Institute on Drug Abuse, 2006.

Johnston, L. D., P. M. O'Malley, J. G. Bachman, and J. E. Schulenberg. *Monitoring the Future: National Results on Adolescent Drug Use 1975–2008. Volume I: Secondary School Students 2008*. Bethesda, MD: National Institute on Drug Abuse, 2009a.

Johnston, L. D., P. M. O'Malley, J. G. Bachman, and J. E. Schulenberg. *Monitoring the Future: National Results on Adolescent Drug Use 1975–2008. Volume II: College Students and Adults 19–50*. Bethesda, MD: National Institute on Drug Abuse, 2009b.

Johnston, L. D., P. M. O'Malley, J. G. Bachman, and J. E. Schulenberg. *Monitoring the Future: National Survey Results on Drug Use, 1975–2011. Volume II: College Students and Adults 19–50*. Ann Arbor: Institute for Social Research, University of Michigan, 2012.

Johnston, L. D., P. M. O'Malley, J. G. Bachman, and J. E. Schulenberg. *Monitoring the Future: National Survey Results on Drug Use, 1975–2012. Volume I, Secondary School Students*. Ann Arbor: Institute for Social Research, University of Michigan, 2013.

Johnston, L. D., O'Malley, P. M., Bachman, J. G., Schulenberg, J. E. & Miech, R. A. *Monitoring the Future: National Survey Results on Drug Use, 1975–2014: Volume 2, College Students and Adults Ages 19–55*. Ann Arbor: Institute for Social Research, University of Michigan, 2015a.

Johnston, L. D., O'Malley, P. M., Bachman, J. G., Schulenberg, J. E. & Miech, R. A. *Monitoring the Future: National Survey Results on Drug Use, 1975–2013: Volume 1, Secondary School Students*. Ann Arbor: Institute for Social Research, University of Michigan, 2015b.

Johnston, L. D., O'Malley, J. G., Miech, P. M., Bachman, R. A., and Schulenberg, J. E. *Monitoring the Future National Survey Results on Drug Use, 1975–2015: Overview, Key Findings on Adolescent Drug Use*. Ann Arbor: Institute for Social Research, University of Michigan, 2016a.

Johnston, L. D., P. M. O'Malley, R.A. Miech, J. G. Bachman, and J. E. Schulenberg. *Monitoring the Future: National Survey Results on Drug Use, 1975–2015. Volume I, Secondary School Students*. Ann Arbor: Institute for Social Research, University of Michigan, 2016b.

Join Together Online and BBC (British Broadcasting Company) News. *Illicit Drug Sales Booming Online*. Boston: Boston University School of Public Health, 2005.

Kandel, D. B. "Drug and Drinking Behavior Among Youth." *Annual Review of Sociology* 6 (1980): 235–285.

Kantrowitz, B., and P. Wingert. "Beyond Littleton: How Well Do You Know Your Kid?" *Newsweek*. (10 May 1999).

Kennedy, M. C. "Newer Drugs Used to Enhance Sporting Performance." *Medical Journal of Australia* 273 (2000): 314–317.

Kinney, J. *Loosening the Grip*, 6th ed. Boston: McGraw-Hill, 2000.

Kirkpatrick, J. *The Woman Alcoholic*. Quakertown, PA: Women for Sobriety, 1999.

Klee, H., and M. Jackson. *Drug Misuse and Motherhood*. New York: Routledge, 2002.

Klosowski, T. "What Is Tor and Should I Use It?" Lifehacker. 21 February 2014. Available http://lifehacker.com/what-is-tor-and-should-i-use-it-1527891029

Korolenko, C. P., and T. A. Donskih. "Addictive Behavior in Women: A Theoretical Perspective." *Drugs and Society* 4 (1990): 39–65.

Ladwig, G. B., and M. D. Anderson. "Substance Abuse in Women: Relationship Between Chemical Dependency of Women and Past Reports of Physical and/or Sexual Abuse." *International Journal of the Addictions* 24 (1989): 739–754.

Lajis, R. H. "Steroids: The Next Drug Problem." 2007. Available http://www.cedu.niu.edu/~shumow/itt/doc/Steroid Abuse.pdf

Lale, T. "Gangs and Drugs." In *Adolescent Substance Abuse, Etiology, Treatment and Prevention*, edited by G. Lawson and A. Lawson, 267–281. Gaithersburg, MD: Aspen, 1992.

Lawn, J. *Team Up for Drug Prevention with America's Young Athletes*. Washington, DC: Drug Enforcement Administration, U.S. Department of Justice, 1984.

Lawson, G., and A. Lawson, "Etiology." In *Adolescent Substance Abuse, Etiology, Treatment and Prevention*, edited by G. Lawson and A. Lawson, 1–10. Gaithersburg, MD: Aspen, 1992.

Leibsohn, J. "The Relationship Between Drug and Alcohol Use and Peer Group Associations of College Freshmen as They Transition from High School." *Journal of Drug Education* 24 (1994): 177–192.

Leicester, J. "Lance Armstrong Considers Himself Tour de France Record-Holder Still, Believes Doping Needed to Win." Huffington Post. 28 June 2013. Available http://www.huffingtonpost.com/2013/06/28/lance-armstrong-tour-de-france_n_3515081.html

Leinwand, D. "20% Say They Used Drugs with Their Mom or Dad. Among Reasons: Boomer Culture and Misguided Attempts to Bond." *USA Today.* (27 August 2000).

Leinwand, D. "Study: Drug Chat Pervasive Online—Teens Use Internet to Share Stories, Get How-To Advice." *USA Today.* (19 June 2007a). Available http://www.usatoday.com/printedition/news/20070619/a_online19.art.htm

Leinwand. D. "College Drug Use, Binge Drinking Rise." *USA Today.* (15 March 2007b). Available http://usatoday30.usatoday.com/news/nation/2007-03-15-college-drug-use_N.htm

Lenhart, A. "Teens, Social Media & Technology Overview 2015." Pew Research Center. 9 April 2015. Available http://www.pewinternet.org/2015/04/09/teens-social-media-technology-2015/

Levitt, D., and S. A. Venkatesh. "An Economic Analysis of A Drug-Selling Gang's Finances." *Quarterly Journal of Economics* 115 (2000): 755–789.

Lewin, T. "Does it Work? Substance-Free Dorms—Clean Living on Campus." *New York Times.* (6 November 2005). Available http://www.nytimes.com/2005/11/06/education/edlife/work.html

Lin, A. Y. F. "Should Women Be Included in Clinical Trials?" *Pharmacy Times* 10 (November 1994): 27.

Lively, K. "The 'Date-Rape Drug': Colleges Worry About Reports of Growing Use of Rohypnol, a Sedative." *Chronicle of Higher Education* 42 (28 June 1996): A–29.

Livni, E. "Some Parents Introduce Kids to Drugs." ABC News. 24 August 2013. Available http://abcnews.go.com/Health/story?id=118024

Lukas, S. "Urine Testing for Anabolic-Androgenic Steroids." *Trends in Pharmacological Sciences* 14 (1993): 61–68.

Mathias, R. "Sex-for-Crack Phenomenon Poses Risk for Spread of AIDS in Heterosexuals." *NIDA Notes* 8 (May/June 1993): 8–11.

Mathias, R. "NIDA Survey Provides First National Data on Drug Use During Pregnancy." *NIDA Notes* 10 (January/February 1995): 6–7.

McCaffrey, B. R. "McCaffrey Announces Strategy to Fight Drug Use in Sports." *Daily Washington File.* (21 October 1999).

McDonald, M. "Fast, Strong, Dead?" *Salt Lake Tribune* 250 (22 June 1995): C1, C8.

McMurtrie, B. "Why Colleges Haven't Stopped Binge Drinking." *New York Times.* (14 December 2014). Available http://www.nytimes.com/2014/12/15/us/why-colleges-havent-stopped-binge-drinking.html?_r=0

McSpadden, K. "Yankees Slugger A-Rod Apologizes for Misconduct." *Time.* (10 February 2015). Available http://time.com/3704481/alex-rodriguez-yankees-mlb-apology-baseball/.

Merchant, W. "Medications and Athletes." *American Druggist* (October 1992): 6–14.

Millstein, R. *Community Alert Bulletin.* Rockville, MD: National Institute on Drug Abuse, U.S. Department of Health and Human Services, 25 March 1993.

Minnesota Institute of Public Health. *Alcohol and Other Drugs and Suicide.* Mounds View, MN: Chemical Health Division, Minnesota Department of Human Services, Spring 1995.

Moss, H., L. Kirisci, H. Gordon, and R. Tarter. "A Neuro-psychological Profile of Adolescent Alcoholics." *Alcoholism: Clinical and Experimental Research* 18 (1994): 159–163.

MSNBC. "AIDS Outruns Efforts to Combat It, Says U.N. Report: New HIV Infections Hit Record High Last Year." Health News. 2004. Available http://www.msnbc.msn.com/ID/5377027

"Multistate Outbreak of Poisonings Associated with Illicit Use of GHB." *Prevention Pipeline* 7 (May–June 1994): 95, 96.

MyDNA.com. *News Center: HAART Therapy Slows Progression to AIDS.* Washington, DC: American Medical Association, 2005.

National Center for Education Statistics. "Indicators of School Crime and Safety: 2011: Indicator 8: Students' Reports of Gangs at School." Washington, DC: U.S. Department of Education, Institute of Education Sciences, and National Center for Education Statistics, 2011. Available http://nces.ed.gov/programs/crimeindicators/crimeindicators2011/ind_08.asp

National Clearinghouse for Alcohol and Drug Information (NCADI). *Drugs of Abuse.* Rockville, MD: Substance Abuse and Mental Health Services Administration, 1999.

National Collegiate Athletic Association (NCAA). "NCAA National Study of Substance Use Habits of College Student-Athletes: Final Report." Indianapolis, IN: NCAA Research, August 2014. Available http://www.ncaa.org/sites/default/files/Substance%20Use%20Final%20Report_FINAL.pdf

National Collegiate Athletic Association (NCAA). "Divisional Differences and the History of Multidivision Classification." Indianapolis, IN: NCAA Membership, 2015. Available http://www.ncaa.org/about/who-we-are/membership/divisional-differences-and-history-multidivision-classification

National Crime Victims' Rights Week Resource Guide (NCVRW Resource Guide). "Campus Crime." Victim Services: Office of Victim & Survivor Rights and Services, 2007. Available http://www.cdcr.ca.gov/victim _services/crime_and_victimization_stats.html

National Drug Intelligence Center (NDIC). *Drugs and Gangs: Fast Facts, Questions and Answers.* Washington, DC: National Drug Intelligence Center, 2009.

National Education Association and Health Information Network (NEAHIN). *RX for Understanding: Preventing Prescription Drug Abuse.* 2013. Available http://www .gadoe.org/Curriculum-Instruction-and-Assessment /Curriculum-and-Instruction/Documents/Prescription %20Drug%20Abuse%20Prevention%20Program _Grades%209-12%20Lesson%20Plans.pdf

National Institute of Mental Health. "The Teen Brain: Still Under Construction." Bethesda, MD: National Institute of Mental Health ((NIMH), 2012

National Institute on Alcohol and Alcoholism (NIAAA). "High-Risk Drinking in College: What We Know and What We Need to Learn." College Drinking—Changing the Culture. 2005a. Available http://www.collegedrinkingprevention.gov/niaaacollegematerials/panel01 /execsum_01.aspx

National Institute on Alcohol and Alcoholism (NIAAA). "Living Arrangements." College Drinking—Changing the Culture. 2005b. Available http://www.college drinkingprevention.gov/NIAAACollegeMaterials /TaskForce/Factors_01.asp

National Institute on Drug Abuse (NIDA). *Anabolic Steroid Abuse.* Capsule 43. Rockville, MD: National Institute on Drug Abuse, 1996.

National Institute on Drug Abuse (NIDA). *Drug Abuse and Addiction Research: The Sixth Triennial Report to Congress.* Rockville, MD: U.S. Department of Health and Human Services, 1999.

National Institute on Drug Abuse (NIDA). "Club Drugs: Community Alert Bulletin." *NIDA Notes* 14 (30 March 2000).

National Institute on Drug Abuse (NIDA). *NewsScan for October 13, 2006—Women and Substance Abuse Issue.* Bethesda, MD: National Institute on Drug Abuse and the National Institutes of Health, 2006a.

National Institute on Drug Abuse (NIDA). *Research Report Series—Anabolic Steroid Abuse.* Bethesda, MD: U.S. Government Printing Office, 2006b.

National Institute on Drug Abuse (NIDA). *NIDA InfoFacts: Steroids (Anabolic-Androgenic).* Bethesda, MD: National Institute on Drug Abuse and National Institutes of Health, 2009.

National Institute on Drug Abuse (NIDA). *Principles of Drug Addiction Treatment: A Research-Based Guide,* 3rd ed. Bethesda, MD: National Institute on Drug Abuse and National Institutes of Health, December 2012.

National Institute on Drug Abuse (NIDA). "DrugFacts: Prescription and Over-the-Counter Medications." May 2013. Available https://www.drugabuse.gov/publications /drugfacts/prescription-over-counter-medications

National Institute on Drug Abuse (NIDA) for Teens. "DrugFacts: Prescription Drugs." 26 June 2013. Available http://teens.drugabuse.gov/drug-facts/prescription -drugs

National Institute on Drug Abuse (NIDA). "Monitoring the Future Survey, Overview of Findings 2014." December 2014a. Available https://www.drugabuse.gov/related -topics/trends-statistics/monitoring-future/monitoring -future-survey-overview-findings-2014

National Institute on Drug Abuse (NIDA). "DrugFacts: Cough and Cold Medicine Abuse." May 2014b. Available https:// www.drugabuse.gov/publications/drugfacts/cough -cold-medicine-abuse

National Institute on Drug Abuse (NIDA). "Women and Drugs." September 2015a. Available https://www .drugabuse.gov/related-topics/women-drugs

National Institute on Drug Abuse (NIDA). "DrugFacts: Sex and Gender Differences in Substance Use." September 2015b. Available https://www.drugabuse .gov/publications/drugfacts/substance-use-in-women

National Institute on Drug Abuse (NIDA). "College Drinking." Bethesda, MD: National Institutes of Health, December 2015c.

National Institute on Drug Abuse (NIDA). "Drug and Alcohol Use in College-Age Adults in 2014." December 2015d. Available https://www.drugabuse.gov /related-topics/trends-statistics/infographics/drug -alcohol-use-in-college-age-adults-in-2014

National Institute on Drug Abuse (NIDA). "DrugFacts: What Are Anabolic Steroids?" March 2016. Available https://www.drugabuse.gov/publications/drugfacts /anabolic-steroids

National Institute on Drug Abuse (NIDA) for Teens. "Prescription Drugs." 18 April 2016a. Available https:// teens.drugabuse.gov/drug-facts/prescription-drugs

National Institute on Drug Abuse (NIDA) for Teens. "Cough and Cold Medicine (DXM and Codeine Syrup)." Bethesda, MD: National Institute on Drug Abuse and National Institutes of Health, 28 April 2016b.

National Institutes of Health (NIH) and National Institute on Drug Abuse (NIDA). *Drug Abuse and Drug Abuse Research: Executive Summary.* Rockville, MD: Substance Abuse and Mental Health Services Administration, 1998.

National Survey on Drug Use and Health (NSDUH). *The NSDUH Report: Substance Use Treatment among Women of Childbearing Age.* Research Triangle Park, NC: Office of Applied Studies, Substance Abuse and Mental Health Services Administration and RTI International, 4 October 2007.

National Youth Anti-Drug Media Campaign. "The 411 on Rx Drugs." 2007. Available http://www.theantidrug .com/drug_info/prescription_411.asp

New York State Department of Health. "Anabolic Steroids and Sports: Winning at Any Cost." 2010. Available http://www.health.state.ny.us/publications/1210

News Tribune. "Alcohol, Tobacco or Drugs Used in 98% of Popular Movies." (29 April 1999): 7–8, 14.

Office of National Drug Control Policy (ONDCP). *Substance Use in Popular Movies and Music. Media Campaign, Campaign Publications.* Rockville, MD: Office of National Drug Control Policy, Drugs and Crime Clearinghouse, 1999.

Office of the Surgeon General. "Surgeon General's Call to Action to Prevent and Reduce Underage Drinking." U.S. Department of Health and Human Services. 2007. Available http://www.surgeongeneral.gov/topics /underagedrinking/familyguide.pdf

Olin, B. R. *Drug Facts and Comparisons.* St. Louis, MO: Kluwer, 1994, 109–109c.

"OTC Drugs and Athletes." *Pharmacy Times* (June 1992): 16.

Pagliery, J. "The Deep Web You Don't Know About." *CNN Money.* 10 March 2014. Available http://money.cnn .com/2014/03/10/technology/deep-web/index.html

Palmer, E. "Silk Road: More People Buying Drugs Online Following Close of Illegal Dark Web Market." *International Business Times.* (8 June 2015). Available http:// www.ibtimes.co.uk/silk-road-more-people-buying-drugs -online-following-close-illegal-dark-web-market-1504985

Paoletta, M. "Music Industry Coming to Grips with Addiction." *Today.* 21 May 2004. Available http://www.today .com/id/5033438#.Un8j5JSEayW

Parrot, A. *Date Rape and Acquaintance Rape.* New York: Rosen, 1988.

Perrin, A., and M. Duggan. "Americans' Internet Access: 2000–2015." Pew Research Center. 26 June 2015. Available http://www.pewinternet.org/2015/06/26 /americans-internet-access-2000-2015/

Pietroski, N. "Counseling HIV/AIDS Patients." *American Druggist* (August 1993): 50–56.

Prendergast, M. L. "Substance Use and Abuse Among College Students: A Review of Recent Literature." *Journal of American College Health* 43 (1994): 99–113.

Primack, B.A., M. A. Dalton, M. V. Carroll, A. A. Agarwal, and M. J. Fine. "Content Analysis of Tobacco, Alcohol, and Other Drugs in Popular Music." *Archives of Pediatrics and Adolescent Medicine* 162 (2008): 169–205.

Quinn. E. "EPO and Blood Doping in Sports." Very Well. 6 September 2016. Available https://www.verywell.com /epo-and-blood-doping-in-sports-3120522

Ravid, J. "The Hard-Core Curriculum." *Rolling Stone* 719 (19 October 1995): 99.

Reuters and Fox News Network. "Facebook Linked to Teenage Drinking, Drug Use." 24 August 2011. Available http:// www.foxnews.com/tech/2011/08/24/report-links -social-networking-sites-to-teenage-drinking-drug-use/

Ridings, A. "How Music Glamorizes Drug Use." New Beginnings Adolescent Recovery Center. 25 February 2014. Available http://newbeginningsteenhelp.com/blog/music -glamorizes-drug-use

Ross, V., and W. Dejong. *Alcohol and Other Drug Abuse Among First-Year College Students.* Newton, MA: Higher Education Center for Alcohol and Other Drug Abuse and Violence Prevention, March 2008: 1–8.

Rubin, A., R. L. Stout, and R. Longabaugh. "Gender Differences in Relapse Situations." *Addiction* 91 (Suppl.) (1996): S111–S120.

Sanders, W. B. *Gangbangs and Drive-bys.* New York: Aldine De Gruyter, 1994.

Schaefer, M. A., J. F. Hilton, M. Ekstrand, and J. Keogh. "Relationship Between Drug Use and Sexual Behaviors and the Occurrence of Sexually Transmitted Diseases Among High-Risk Male Youth." *Sexually Transmitted Diseases* 20 (November–December 1993): 39–47.

Schernoff, M., and R. A. Smith. "HIV Treatments: A History of Scientific Advance." *Body Positive* 14 (July 2001): 1–7.

Schiebinger, L. "Women's Health and Clinical Trials." *Journal of Clinical Investigations* 112 (2003): 973-977. Available https://www.jci.org/articles/view/19993

Schoemer, K. "Rockers, Models and the New Allure of Heroin." *Newsweek.* (26 August 1996): 24–36.

Science Daily. "Pain Drug Reveals What Most Already Know— Men's and Women's Brains Are Simply Different." 15 March 2000. Available http://www.sciencedaily.com /releases/2000/03/000315075845.htm

Scott, D. M., J. C. Wagner, and T. W. Barlow. "Anabolic Steroids Use Among Adolescents in Nebraska Schools." *American Journal of Health-System Pharmacy* 53 (1996): 2068–2072.

Scripps Howard News Service. "AIDS Fear: Complacency: Infection Rate Is on Rise for First Time Since 1994." *Post-Tribune* (21 August 2003): A-10.

Seetharaman, D. "Study: Addictive Drugs Easily Ordered Online." Thomson Reuters. 9 July 2008. Available http:// www.usatoday.com/news/health/2008-07-09-online -pharmacies_N.htm

Shelden, R. G., S. Tracy, and W. Brown. *Youth Gangs in American Society.* Belmont, CA: Wadsworth/Thomson Learning, 2001.

Shelden, R. G., S. K. Tracy, and W. B. Brown. *Youth Gangs in American Society,* 3rd ed. Belmont, CA: Wadsworth /Thomson Learning, 2004.

Siegel, L., and J. Senna. *Juvenile Delinquency,* 6th ed. St. Paul, MN: West, 1997.

Siegel, L. J., and B. C. Welsh. *Juvenile Delinquency: Theory, Practice, and Law,* 10th ed. Belmont, CA: Wadsworth, Cengage Learning, 2009.

Southern Illinois University Carbondale/Core Institute. *2012 Annual Reference Group, Core Alcohol and Drug Survey Long Form—Form 194, Executive Summary.* 23 April 2014. Available http://core.siu.edu/_common/documents/2012%20Executive%20Summary%20Report.pdf

Spergel, I. A. *Youth Gangs: Problem and Response.* Chicago: University of Chicago, School of Social Service Administration, 1990.

Steinberg, L., A. Fletcher, and N. Darling. "Parental Monitoring and Peer Influences on Adolescent Substance Use." *Pediatrics* 93 (1994): 1060–1064.

Stewart, K. "Facts and Myths about College Drinking: A Serious Problem with Serious Solutions." Prevention Research Center. May 2013. Available http://resources.prev.org/documents/FactsMythsCollegeDrinking.pdf

Substance Abuse and Mental Health Services Administration (SAMHSA). *Making the Connection Between Substance Abuse and HIV/AIDS Prevention for Women of Color and Youth.* Rockville, MD: U.S. Department of Health and Human Services, 1999a.

Substance Abuse and Mental Health Services Administration (SAMHSA). *Tips for Teens: About Steroids. Center for Substance Abuse Prevention.* Rockville, MD: U.S. Department of Health and Human Services, 1999b.

Substance Abuse and Mental Health Services Administration (SAMHSA), Office of Applied Studies. Rockville, MD: Substance Abuse and Mental Health Services Administration, 17 March 2007.

Substance Abuse and Mental Health Services Administration (SAMHSA), Office of Applied Studies (OAS). *The TEDS (Treatment Episode Data Set) Report: Trends in Adult Female Substance Abuse Treatment Admissions Reporting Primary Alcohol Abuse: 1992 to 2007.* Rockville, MD, U.S. Department of Health and Human Services, 7 January 2010.

Substance Abuse and Mental Health Services Administration (SAMHSA). *Results from the 2010 National Survey on Drug Use and Health: Summary of National Findings.* NSDUH Series H-41, HHS Pub. No. (SMA) 11-4658. Rockville, MD: Substance Abuse and Mental Health Services Administration, 2011.

Substance Abuse and Mental Health Services Administration (SAMHSA). *Results from the 2013 National Survey on Drug Use and Health: Summary of National Findings,* NSDUH Series Ho-48, HHS Pub. No. (SMA) 14-4863. Rockville, MD: Substance Abuse and Mental Health Services Administration, 2014a.

Substance Abuse and Mental Health Services Administration (SAMHSA). "The TEDS Report: Gender Differences in Primary Substance of Abuse Across Age Groups." Rockville, MD: Substance Abuse and Mental Health Services Administration, 3 April 2014b.

Suggs, W. "Deadly Fuel: As Supplements and Steroids Tempt and Endanger More Athletes, What Are Colleges Doing?" *Chronicle of Higher Education* 49 (14 March 2003): A36–A38.

Swadi, H. "Relative Risk Factors in Detecting Adolescent Drug Abuse." *Drug and Alcohol Dependence* 29 (1992): 253–254.

Technische Univerisität München. "Doping Definition." n.d. Available http://www.doping-prevention.sp.tum.de/doping-in-general/doping-definition.html

Teen Challenge. *Drugs: Frequently Asked Questions.* South Australia: Pragin Press, 2000.

Teendrugsrehabs.com. "Teen Drug and Alcohol Abuse Facts and Statistics." 2015. Available http://www.teendrugrehabs.com/facts-and-stats/

TheAthlete.org. "The Athlete: Doping in Sports—A Deadly Game." 2011. Available http://www.theathlete.org/doping-in-sport.htm

Telegraph Sport, and Agencies. "Ben Johnson: I Was Nailed on a Cross for Taking Steriods at Seoul Olympics—25 Years Later I'm Still Being Punished." *The Daily Telegraph* (London). (24 September 2013). Available http://www.telegraph.co.uk/sport/othersports/athletics/10329995/Ben-Johnson-I-was-nailed-on-a-cross-for-taking-steroids-at-Seoul-Olympics-25-years-later-Im-still-being-punished.html

The Recovery Village. "A Study of Drug Addiction Between Genders." 2016. Available https://www.therecoveryvillage.com/drug-addiction/study-between-genders/

TheScore.com. "MLB Suspends 12 Players in Biogenesis Case." 5 August 2013. Available http://www.thescore.com/home/articles/1246300-mlb-suspends-12-players-in-biogenesis-case

Toronto, R. "Young Athletes Who Use 'Enhancing' Steroids Risk Severe Physical Consequences." *Salt Lake Tribune* 244 (6 July 1992): C-5.

TreatHIVNow. "Signs and Symptoms." 2013. Available http://www.treathivnow.com/hiv-facts/hiv-signs-and-symptoms

12 Keys Rehab. "How Does Social Media Influence Teen Drug Abuse?" 17 April 2016. Available http://www.12keysrehab.com/blog/how-does-social-media-influence-teen-drug-abuse/

UNAIDS. *AIDS by the Numbers 2015.* Geneva, Switzerland: UNAIDS, 2015a. Available http://www.unaids.org/sites/default/files/media_asset/AIDS_by_the_numbers_2015_en.pdf

UNAIDS. "Fact Sheet 2015." Geneva, Switzerland: UNAIDS, 2015b. Available http://www.unaids.org/en/resources/campaigns/HowAIDSchangedeverything/factsheet

United Nations Interregional Crime and Justice Research Institute (UNICRI). "Dawn: Promoting Gender-Based Drug Prevention and Recovery." Geneva: Switzerland: United Nations Interregional Crime and justice Research Institute, 2013.

U.S. Department of Health and Human Services (USD-HHS), National Institute on Drug Abuse (NIDA). *Drug Abuse and Addiction Research: The Sixth Triennial Report to Congress. NIDA Research Priorities and Highlights, Role of Research: Women's Health and Gender Differences.* Washington, DC: U.S. Government Printing Office, 1999.

U.S. Department of Health and Human Services (USD-HHS). "Sexually Transmitted Diseases." Rockville, MD: Office of Adolescent Health, 7 April 2016. Available http://www.hhs.gov/ash/oah/adolescent-health-topics /reproductive-health/stds.html

U.S. Department of Justice (DOJ). *Anabolic Steroids and You.* Washington, DC: Demand Reduction Section, Drug Enforcement Administration, 1991–1992.

U.S. Department of Justice (DOJ). *Steroid Abuse in Today's Society.* Springfield, VA: Office of Diversion Control, Drug Enforcement Administration (DEA). 2004. Available http://www.deadiversion.usdoj.gov/pubs/brochures /steroids/professionals/

USA Today. "Teen Prescription Drug Abuse Reportedly Holding Steady." 14 February 2007. Available http:// www.usatoday.com/news/health/2007-02-14-teens -rxdrugs_x.htm?csp=34

Vargas-Cooper, N. "Bath Salts." *Spin* (July/August 2012): 58–64, 94.

Venturelli, P. J. "Drugs in Schools: Myths and Reality." In *The Annals of the American Academy of Political and Social Science,* edited by W. H. Hinkle and S. Henry, (567) 72–87. Thousand Oaks, CA: Sage, January 2000.

Verhaak, C. M., A. M. E. Lintsen, A. W. M. Evers, and D. D. M. Braat. "Who Is at Risk of Emotional Problems and How Do You Know? Screening of Women Going for IVF Treatment." *Human Reproduction* 25 (2010): 1234–1240.

Von Der Haar, C. M. *Social Psychology: A Sociological Perspective.* Upper Saddle River, NJ: Pearson Education, 2005.

Walsh, F., and M. Shenkman. "Family Context of Adolescence." In *Adolescent Substance Abuse, Etiology, Treatment and Prevention,* edited by G. Lawson and A. Lawson, 149–171. Gaithersburg, MD: Aspen, 1992.

WebMD.com. "Information and Resources: Growth Hormone." 14 August 2008. Available http://www.webmd.com /a-to-z-guides/growth-hormone

Werner, D, N.K Young, K. Dennis, and S. Amatetti. *Family-Centered Treatment for Women with Substance Use Disorders – History, Key Elements and Challenges.* Rockville, MD: Department of Health and Human Services (DHHS), Substance Abuse and Mental Health Services Administration (SAMHSA), 2007.

Wechsler, H., J. E. Lee, M. Kuo, M. Seibring, T. F. Nelson, and H. P. Lee. "Trends in College Binge Drinking During a Period of Increased Prevention Efforts: Findings from Four Harvard School of Public Health Study Surveys, 1993–2001." *Journal of American College Health* 50 (2002): 203–217.

WhatCulture.com. "15 Best Movies About Drugs and Addiction in Cinema History." 2016. Available http:// whatculture.com/film/15-best-movies-about-drugs-and -addiction-in-cinema-history

WomensHealth.org. "Healthy Women, Substance Abuse, Overview." Washington, DC: National Women's Health Resource Center, 8 December 2012.

Winters, P. A. *Teen Addiction.* San Diego, CA: Greenhaven Press, 1997.

Wisconsin Coalition Against Sexual Assault (WCASA). *Sexual Violence and Sexual Abuse.* Madison: Wisconsin Coalition Against Sexual Assault, 1997.

Witham, D. "Recovery in the Dorm: Rutgers University's Special Housing for Addicted Students." *Chronicle of Higher Education* 42 (10 November 1995): A-33.

"Women Smokers Run High Risk for Lung Cancer." *Prevention Pipeline* 7 (May–June 1994): 7.

World Anti-Doping Agency (WADA). "Questions and Answers on 2009 World Anti-Doping Code." 2009. Available https://www.wada-ama.org/en/what-we-do/the-code

World Anti-Doping Agency (WADA). "The Code." 2015. Available https://www.wada-ama.org/en/what-we-do /the-code

World Anti-Doping Agency (WADA). "The Code." 2016. Available: https://www.wada-ama.org/en/what-we-do /the-code

World Health Organization (WHO). *HIV/AIDS: HIV/AIDS and Adolescents.* Geneva, Switzerland: World Health Organization, 2005.

World Health Organization (WHO). "Global Summary of the AIDS Epidemic." Geneva, Switzerland: World Health Organization, 21 July 2015.

Wright, L. "Suicidal Thoughts and Their Relationship to Family Stress and Personal Problems Among High School Seniors and College Undergraduates." *Adolescence* 20 (1985): 575–580.

Yesalis, C. E., and J. S. Cowart. *The Steroids Game.* Champaign, IL: Human Kinetics, 1998.

Yoder, R. "Causes of Teen Drug Use: It's Not Just Peer Pressure." Palm Beach, FL: Palm Beach Institute, 28 April 2015. Available https://www.pbinstitute.com /teen-drug-cause-isnt-just-peer-pressure/

Yusko, D. A., J. F. Buckman, H. R. White, and R. J. Pandina. "Alcohol, Tobacco, Illicit Drugs, and Performance Enhancers: A Comparison of Use by College Student Athletes and Nonathletes." *Journal of American College Health* 57 (November–December 2008): 281–290.

Zuger, A. "Epidemic: An Overview." *New York Times.* (8 August 2000). Available http://www.nytimes.com /library/national/science/aids/aids-overview.html

Photo by SSGT Jennifer J. Tovar, USAF. Courtesy of U.S. Department of Defense.

Drug Abuse Prevention

Did You Know?

▶ Drug prevention is aimed at reducing risk factors such as early aggressive behavior, lack of parental supervision, the lure of gang membership, drug availability, and poverty.

▶ Comprehensive prevention programs simultaneously involving the community, school, and family are more effective than single-unit programs.

▶ The harm reduction drug prevention model that is practiced in the Netherlands is a preventive model that meets drug users on their own turf in dealing with drug use and/or abuse.

▶ Among people aged 12 or older in 2014 who had substance use disorders (SUDs), 17.0 million (nearly four out of five) had an alcohol use disorder and 7.1 million (about one in every three) had an illicit drug use disorder.

▶ Drug prevention programs must distinguish among early experimenters, nonproblem drug users, undetected committed or secret users, problem users, and former users.

▶ Students in drug prevention programs who have difficulty saying "no" to the nonmedical use of drugs need refusal skills training and peer-resistance training.

▶ Drug education actually began in the 1830s with the temperance movement.

▶ Drug courts are a newer form of drug prevention in which drug defendants are more likely to undergo treatment (rehabilitation) than incarceration (punishment).

▶ Other strategies for dealing with drug use include the alternatives approach and meditation.

Learning Objectives

On completing this chapter, you should be able to:

❭ List the 10 most prominent factors influencing individuals with regard to alcohol and other drug use.

❭ Identify and briefly explain the three major types of drug prevention programs.

❭ Describe the five types of drug users that have to be considered before implementing a drug prevention program.

❭ List the five levels of comprehensive prevention programs for drug use and abuse.

❭ Identify the three family factors that can prevent initiation to drugs or extensive drug use.

❭ List the four prevention program models found in higher education.

❭ Describe the main goals of the following large-scale drug prevention programs: the BACCHUS Network, D.A.R.E., and drug courts.

❭ Describe two alternative prevention strategies or agendas for replacing drug use.

Introduction

When someone tells another person "Just don't do drugs" and, if that person is addicted to, say, cocaine like I was, that comes across as an ignorant answer. You cannot just quit when you are addicted because even the idea of addiction continually blocks the possibility of casually deciding to stop using the drug. A lot has to go into the day you actually stop using the drug. First of all, the craving for the drug continually reminds you to do it maybe just a few more times. Then, your life appears to be less engaging because your body is missing the chemical properties of the drug that it became accustomed to and this affects your level of depression. So you have to sort of go through that slow abstinence period—you are without the drug and sometimes you can only deal with abstaining 1 hour at a time for the first week or so. Then slowly, ever so slowly, for me at least, the addict has to rebuild her or his daily living without the drug. It's just not easy. If it were, most people addicted to drugs would probably quit on their own. Especially when you realize that you are not controlling the drug, the drug is controlling you. Just remember, most addicts continually deceive (lie to) themselves and others that they are not "really" addicted. Do you know how hard it is to become aware that these lies are part of the addiction? Before the extended therapy I had, no one could convince me that the daily cocaine I was snorting and smoking was bad. *(From Venturelli's research files, female academic administrator in higher education who has been drug-free for 3 years, age 37, June 21, 2000)*

A second interview revealed the following:

I started doing cocaine at age 52. One night, I was having a few beers with a friend of mine and another friend of his over at his apartment. I know I was older than both of them were since they were in their early thirties. After the first few beers, this friend of mine went into his bedroom and came out into the living room with a bag of coke. Soon as he entered the room, he threw the bag into my lap and said, "Do you want to try some of this?" I told them I never did this drug and said, "Okay I will try it once." All I remember that night is that I kept doing lines and often said, "Boy, this stuff is so easy to do—nothing to it." When the night was over,

I got back into my car and went home. After that night, I started buying the coke each week and for over 2 years had spent thousands of dollars. It became a nightly thing to do. One day, I decided to stop buying coke since I was very worried about all the money I had been charging to my credit card as cash advances. For the first few nights it was difficult to not go out and pick up coke from a dealer I had gotten to know quite well. This dealer kept calling asking who I was buying from since he hadn't seen me in over a week. I repeatedly tried telling him that I was quitting and had no other dealer but he would not believe me. This added to the difficulty in giving up the drug but I did it. It was "cold turkey" and I had succeeded since now it has been 5 years and I never bought my supply again since that one night when I decided to quit. It is so easy to do this drug and become attached to it. I don't think I was really addicted when I was doing it, but I sure did it often. My problem was more of a mental attachment to the drug. I think I was certainly close to a serious addiction but the cost of the drug, using money I did not have, forced me to quit. In my case, the best prevention is to never start doing this drug or any other drug that is easy to do and makes you feel so good when you are doing it. I have several friends who continue to use this drug mostly on weekends. I am glad I am not in their shoes anymore. *(From Venturelli's research files, male mechanical engineer, age 59, November 5, 2010)*

A third interview:

I met this guy in an introductory sociology class since we both sat near each other during class. About a month later we had our first test coming up so we decided to study together over several nights. We were both first-semester seniors majoring in engineering and felt uneasy about this course since both of us had very little exposure to social science courses and we felt such courses are really different from the more scientific and quantitative courses we were familiar with in our major. The first night we reviewed what we thought were things we had to know for the test and spent time reviewing both the text and class notes we had written. The second night we met in his dorm room instead of the library. We talked about many things in between our studying and got to know each during the 4 days of studying together. On the third night we decided to take a break and meet at a Johnny's [a pseudonym] over a few drinks and just chill out together. As we were drinking beers and shots Tim [a pseudonym], asked me if I ever did drugs. I indicated that I drink alcohol and smoked a lot of weed, tried acid several times, and did Ecstasy during my first year at college. Tim revealed his past drug use, which not only included the drugs I had experienced plus several other drugs I never tried before. He indicated that at the moment he had some cocaine in his dorm room and asked if I wanted to try it with him. I did have one too many beers that night so I agreed to try cocaine back at his dorm room since his roommate went home over the weekend and he assured me that it was a safe drug and not addictive in trying it once. We ended up leaving the bar and went to his room right after that conversation. In his room he said it was better to cook it up and smoke it and at the time little did I know that my first use of this drug was not snorting cocaine but really smoking crack. We smoked it for hours and I loved it. The effects were so pleasurable. I could go on about how many times we did this in the weeks and months afterward but the most important thing is that I really got hooked on cooking up cocaine nearly every night, even after this friend of mine dropped out of school. We also had a thing going on with each other in that I learned to like getting high with Tim that I think made the use of this drug even more appealing and repetitive. A year later I sought help and went to NA [Narcotics Anonymous] and successfully weaned myself off this drug after relapsing the first time and in my second attempt I finally stopped this horribly addictive drug. Addiction is something that consumes you with whatever is your drug of choice. My grades suffered and luckily my uncle hooked me up with NA that he was familiar with as a drug counselor and kept it secret from my parents, who would have died in knowing that in a few short months I was crack addict. What helped me was when Tim left campus and I was all alone doing this drug on my own. I think if Tim would not have left campus I probably would have continued using this drug. As you commented [referring to the interviewer] I had lost my support person when Tim was no longer on campus and moved back to St. Louis, which helped me face my addiction. This was a very slow process to accept the realization that I had to quit this drug. I had to confront this demon on my own, and though I missed Tim after he left campus, it was very helpful in getting me to stop, plus, of course

NA was also very influential in quitting. Addiction comes on slowly and when it gets a hold of you I think most addicts continually deny their addiction. It is truly a disorder that can destroy your life. *(From Venturelli's research files, male electrical engineer, age 26, currently residing in Chicago, January 13, 2016)*

This chapter explores and provides information on doing *something* about drug use and abuse. With so many potential causes for the unnecessary and nonmedical use of psychoactive substances, it becomes increasingly important to discuss methods, programs, and strategies that prevent, cease the use, or, at the very least, significantly moderate the habitual and/or addictive nonmedical use of drugs.

Figure 17.1 shows many of the potential environmental factors involved in what influences alcohol and other drug (**AOD**) use. The core in this figure starts with the individual, and each concentric zone represents clusters of factors that influence an individual's views, attitudes, and behaviors toward drug use. With so many factors, each having an independent potential effect on the individual, you can see why comprehensive prevention programs involving the community, school, and family are more effective than single-unit programs, such as having a mandatory drug education program in elementary grades without other complementary and overlapping drug programs in the community and the family. Prevention research clearly shows that "we must attend to all factors; prevention that focuses on only one or two factors and ignores or discounts the rest is likely to fail to have a long-term, permanent impact" (Tinzmann and Hixson 1992, p. 3).

Through comprehensive prevention programs that are multifaceted and complementary, we are able to more effectively tease out which factors are most influential. The televised commercial in the early 1990s that showed two eggs frying in a pan: "This is your brain … this is your brain on drugs," sponsored by the Partnership for a Drug-Free America, was an early attempt at prevention through a disturbing analogy. Although its effect was poor on drug users, who had never felt their brains frying, it was an initial step toward innovative prevention efforts. Was it worth the airtime?

KEY TERM

AOD
alcohol and other drugs

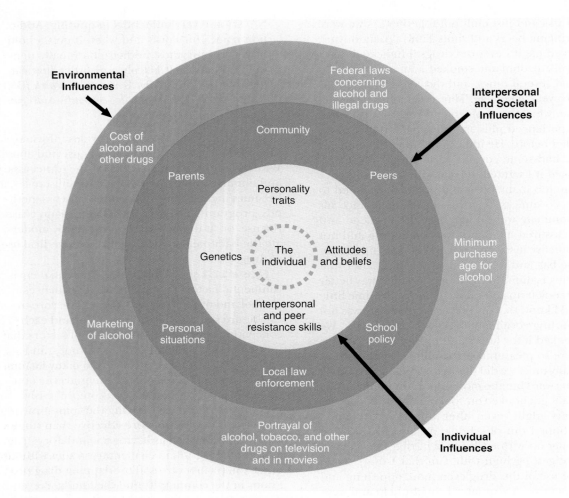

FIGURE 17.1   Potential factors that influence alcohol and other drug use.

Reproduced from U.S. Department of Health and Human Services, Office of Substance Abuse Prevention. "Factors that Influence Alcohol and Other Drug Use." In *Prevention Plus II: Tools for Creating and Sustaining Drug-Free Communities* (Figure 2.1, p. 19). DHHS Publication No. 89-1649. Rockville, MD: U.S. Department of Health and Human Services, 1989. Distributed by the National Clearinghouse for Alcohol and Drug Information.

Can the success of these programs be adequately measured?

In 1997, 15 states thought prevention of alcohol and other drug abuse was important enough to maintain certified prevention specialist credentialing. Today, a bewildering variety of programs exists from coast to coast in school districts, churches, and other communities, all with the goal of preventing initial drug use or halting use before it becomes a problem.

KEY TERM

substance use disorders (SUDs)
when the recurrent use of alcohol or other drugs (or both) causes clinically significant impairment, including health problems, disability, and failure to meet major responsibilities at work, school, or home

How Serious Are the Problems of Substance Use Disorders?

Substance use disorders (SUDs) occur when the recurrent use of alcohol or other drugs (or both) causes clinically significant impairment, including health problems, disability, and failure to meet major responsibilities at work, school, or home. In looking at drug dependence, the severity of this problem can be highlighted by the following current trends (Center for Behavioral Health Statistics and Quality [CBHSQ] 2015, unless otherwise noted):

Substance Use Disorders (SUDs)

* In 2014, approximately 21.5 million people aged 12 or older were classified as having

Example of an advertisement aimed at alerting parents about the dangers of early drug use.

an SUD in the past year, including 17.0 million people with an alcohol use disorder and 7.1 million people with an illicit drug use disorder.

- The 21.5 million people who had SUDs in 2014 represent 8.1% of those aged 12 or older.
- In 2014, 4.2 million people had disorders related to their past-year use of marijuana, and 1.9 million people had disorders related to their nonmedical past-year use of prescription pain relievers.
- An estimated 2.6 million people aged 12 or older in 2014 had both an alcohol use disorder and an illicit drug use disorder in the past year.
- Thus, among people aged 12 or older in 2014 who had SUDs in the past year, nearly four out of five had an alcohol use disorder and about one in three had an illicit drug use disorder.
- About one in eight people aged 12 or older who had an SUD in the past year had both an alcohol use disorder and an illicit drug use disorder. However, most people in 2014 who had an alcohol use disorder did not have an illicit drug use disorder, and most people with an illicit drug use disorder did not have an alcohol use disorder.
- An estimated 1.3 million adolescents aged 12 to 17 had SUDs in 2014, which represents 5.0% of adolescents.
- In 2014, 5.7 million young adults aged 18 to 25 had an SUD, which represents 16.3% of young adults.

- An estimated 14.5 million adults aged 26 or older in 2014 had an SUD, which represents 7.1% of adults aged 26 or older, or about 1 in 14 adults in this age group.
- The approximately 4.2 million people aged 12 or older in 2014 who had a marijuana use disorder in the past year represent 1.6% of those aged 12 or older.
- The estimated 1.9 million people aged 12 or older in 2014 who had a pain reliever use disorder represent 0.7% of those aged 12 or older.
- About 913,000 people aged 12 or older in 2014 had a cocaine use disorder, which represents 0.3% of those aged 12 or older.
- About 586,000 people aged 12 or older in 2014 had a heroin use disorder, which represents 0.2% of those aged 12 or older.

Age at First Use (Substance Abuse and Mental Health Services Administration [SAMHSA] 2014)

- In 2013, an estimated 2.8 million persons aged 12 or older used an illicit drug for the first time within the past 12 months; this averages to about 7800 new users per day.
- Of those who used illicit drugs for the first time within the past 12 months, a majority reported that their first drug was marijuana (70.3%).
- About one in five initiated with nonmedical use of psychotherapeutics (20.6%, including 12.5% with pain relievers, 5.2% with tranquilizers, 2.7% with stimulants, and 0.2% with sedatives).
- Among past-year initiates aged 12 to 49 in 2013, the average age at first use was 17.1 years for PCP, 18.0 years for marijuana, 19.2 years for inhalants, 19.7 years for LSD, 20.4 years for cocaine, 20.5 years for Ecstasy, 21.6 years for stimulants, 21.7 years for pain relievers, 24.5 years for heroin, 25.0 years for sedatives, and 25.4 years for tranquilizers.
- In 2013, 2.4 million persons aged 12 or older used marijuana for the first time within the past 12 months; this averages to about 6600 new users each day.
- In 2013, among persons aged 12 or older, an estimated 1.4 million first-time past-year marijuana users initiated prior to the age of 18.
- In 2013, among recent initiates aged 12 or older who initiated marijuana use prior to the age of 21, the mean age at first use was 16.2 years, which was similar to the 2012 estimate of 16.3 years.
- In 2013, 601,000 persons aged 12 or older used cocaine for the first time within the past 12 months; this averages to approximately 1600 initiates per day.

- In 2013, most (81.9%) of the 0.6 million recent cocaine initiates were aged 18 or older when they first used.
- The average age at first use among recent heroin initiates aged 12 to 49 in 2013 was 24.5 years, which was similar to the 2012 estimate (23.0 years).
- The average age at first use among recent hallucinogen initiates aged 12 to 49 in 2013 was 19.9 years, which was similar to the 2012 estimate (19.1 years).
- Most (69.4%) of the recent Ecstasy initiates in 2013 were aged 18 or older at the time they first used Ecstasy. The number of Ecstasy initiates who first used prior to the age of 18 was 230,000, which was similar to the estimate in 2012 (255,000).
- In 2013, 4.6 million persons aged 12 or older used alcohol for the first time within the past 12 months; this averages to approximately 12,500 initiates per day. The average age at first alcohol use among recent initiates aged 12 to 49 was 17.3 years.

Gender

- As was the case from 2002 through 2012, the rate of substance dependence or abuse for males aged 12 or older in 2013 was greater than the rate for females (10.8 vs. 5.8%) (CHSBQ 2015).
- Among youths aged 12 to 17, however, the rate of substance dependence or abuse among males in 2013 (5.3%) was similar to the rate among their female counterparts (5.2%) (SAMHSA 2014).

Race/Ethnicity

- In 2013, among persons aged 12 or older, the rate of substance dependence or abuse was 4.6% among Asians, 7.4% among blacks, 8.4% among whites, 8.6% among Hispanics, 10.9% among persons reporting two or more races, 11.3% among Native Hawaiians or Other Pacific Islanders, and 14.9% among American Indians or Alaska Natives.
- Except for Native Hawaiians or Other Pacific Islanders, the rate for Asians was lower than the rates for the other racial/ethnic groups.

Education

- In 2013, rates of illicit drug or alcohol dependence or abuse among adults aged 26 or older were not associated with levels of educational attainment. Among this group, rates of illicit

drug or alcohol dependence or abuse were 6.4% for those who graduated from high school but had no further education, 7.2% for college graduates, 7.3% for those who did not graduate from high school, and 7.4% for those with some college education but no degree.

Employment

- Rates of substance dependence or abuse were associated with current employment status in 2013. A higher percentage of unemployed adults aged 18 or older were classified with dependence or abuse (15.2%) than were full-time employed adults (9.5%) or part-time employed adults (9.3%).
- Over half of the adults aged 18 or older with substance dependence or abuse were employed full time in 2013. Of the 20.3 million adults who were classified with dependence or abuse, 11.3 million (55.7%) were employed full time.

Criminal Justice Populations

- In 2013, adults aged 18 or older who were on parole or a supervised release from jail during the past year had a higher rate of illicit drug or alcohol dependence or abuse (34.3%) than their counterparts who were not on parole or supervised release during the past year (8.4%).
- In 2013, probation status was associated with substance dependence or abuse. The rate of substance dependence or abuse was 35.0% among adults who were on probation during the past year, which was higher than the rate among adults who were not on probation during the past year (8.0%).

Geographic Area

- In 2013, rates of illicit drug or alcohol dependence or abuse among persons aged 12 or older were 8.9% in the West, 8.3% in the Northeast, 8.2% in the Midwest, and 7.8% in the South.
- Rates for illicit drug or alcohol dependence or abuse among persons aged 12 or older in 2013 were similar in large metropolitan areas (8.6%) and small metropolitan areas (8.4%) but were higher than in nonmetropolitan areas (6.6%).

After reviewing such significant findings in terms of numbers and percentages of substance-dependent or abusing populations, we can now understand the need for discussing drug prevention in this chapter.

Drug Prevention

"In the broadest sense, prevention is organized activity designed to avoid or decrease health problems" (Wilson and Kolander 2011, p. 7). In addition to this definition of prevention, we add that, in this chapter, **drug prevention** is aimed at preventing and/or decreasing not only health problems but also social and personal problems. When both licit and illicit types of drugs are used and/or abused for nonmedical purposes, they compromise psychological, social, and biological behavior. In the remaining sections of this chapter, we will review what drug prevention entails.

Risk Factors and Protective Factors

From a broad perspective, when considering any drug prevention program both **protective factors** and **risk factors** have to be considered. "Protective factors are those associated with reduced potential for drug use and risk factors are those that make drug use more likely" (National Institute on Drug Abuse [NIDA] 2002). Examples of protective factor can include parental support and parental supervision (NIDA 2014).

The following are the main principles that have to be considered when planning effective drug prevention programs (quoted extensively from Robertson et al. and NIDA 2003, p. 7, and NIDA 2014, unless otherwise noted):

- Drug prevention programs should enhance protective factors and reverse or reduce risk factors.
- *Protective factors* include the following:
  - Strong and positive family bonds
  - Parental monitoring of children's activities and peers
  - Clear rules of conduct consistently enforced within the family
  - Involvement of parents in the lives of their children
  - Success in school performance
  - Strong bonds in institutions, such as schools and religious organizations
  - Adoption of conventional norms about drug use

- *Risk factors* include the following:
  - Chaotic home environment, particularly in homes where parents abuse substances or suffer from mental illnesses
  - Ineffective parenting, especially with children with difficult temperaments or conduct disorders
  - Lack of parent–child attachments and nurturing
  - Inappropriately shy or aggressive behavior in the classroom
  - Failure in school performance
  - Poor social coping skills
  - Affiliations with peers displaying deviant behaviors
  - Perceptions of approval of drug-using behaviors in family, work, school, peer, and community environments (NIDA 2002)
  - Poor self-control and aggressive behavior
- The risk of becoming a drug abuser involves the relationship among the number and type of risk factors (e.g., deviant attitudes and behaviors) and protective factors (e.g., parental support).
- The potential impact of specific risk and protective factors changes with age. For example, risk factors within the family have greater impact on a younger child, whereas association with drug-abusing peers may be a more significant risk factor for an adolescent.
- Early intervention with risk factors (e.g., aggressive behavior and poor self-control) often has a greater impact than later intervention by changing a child's life path (trajectory) away from problems and toward positive behaviors.
- Although risk and protective factors can affect people of all groups, these factors can have a different effect depending on a person's age,

KEY TERMS

drug prevention
preventing or decreasing health problems, including social and personal problems, caused by drug dependency

protective factors
factors associated with preventing the potential for drug abuse, such as self-control, parental support and parental supervision, academic competence, anti-drug-use policies, and strong neighborhood attachment

risk factors
factors associated with increased risk of drug use, such as early aggressive behavior, lack of parental supervision, the lure of gang membership, drug availability, and poverty

gender, ethnicity, culture, and neighborhood environment.

- Prevention programs should address all forms of drug abuse, alone or in combination, including the underage use of legal drugs (e.g., tobacco, alcohol), the use of illegal drugs (e.g., marijuana, heroin), and the inappropriate use of legally obtained substances (e.g., inhalants), prescription medications, or over-the-counter drugs.
- Prevention programs should address the type of drug abuse problem in the local community, target modifiable risk factors, and strengthen identified protective factors.
- Prevention programs should be tailored to address risks specific to population or audience characteristics, such as age, gender, and ethnicity, to improve program effectiveness.

There are three levels of drug prevention programs, each suited to different types of drug users. **Primary drug prevention programs** are aimed at either nonusers who need to be "inoculated" against potential drug use or helping at-risk individuals avoid the development of addictive behaviors. For example, primary prevention often targets at-risk youth who may live in areas where licit and illicit types of drugs are rampant, youth who may come from problem families, or youth who are surrounded by drug-abusing peers.

The other two major types of drug prevention programs are **secondary drug prevention programs**, which consist of uncovering potentially harmful substance use prior to the onset of overt

symptoms or problems and/or targeting newer drug users with a limited or early history of drug use, and **tertiary drug prevention programs**, which focus directly on intervention and target chemically dependent individuals who need treatment. Tertiary prevention involves treating the medical consequences of drug abuse and facilitating entry into treatment so further disability is minimized.

Primary, secondary, and tertiary programs are usually used in combination because, in most settings, all three types of drug users constitute the targeted population. **Table 17.1** further illustrates these levels of drug prevention and corresponding suggested activities; what can be accomplished is listed under each of the three types of prevention (primary, secondary, and tertiary).

Considering the Audience and Approach

It is important to be aware that drug users vary in their exposure and past histories of substance use and/or abuse. The audience for drug prevention comprises both users and nonusers. In analyzing the population of users, the following categories can be used:

- Nonusers
- Early experimenters
- Nonproblem drug users (i.e., those who abuse drugs on occasion, mostly for recreational purposes)
- Undetected, committed, or secret users (i.e., those who abuse drugs and have no interest in stopping their drug use)
- Problem users who are often drug dependent and/or addicted to drugs
- Former users

It is important that role models, counselors, teachers, and anyone else involved in drug prevention programs take into consideration that there are different types of substance users/abusers. Therefore, drug prevention programs must cater to the specific needs of these groups. For nonproblem users, drug education programs should examine the abuse of drugs and reinforce the message that uncontrolled use leads to abuse. For committed users, drug education should aim to prevent or delay drug abuse. Former users should be given information that will reinforce their decision to stop abusing drugs.

KEY TERMS

primary drug prevention programs
drug prevention programs with a very broad range of activities aimed at reducing the risk of drug use among nonusers and ensuring continued nonuse and helping at-risk individuals avoid the development of addictive behaviors

secondary drug prevention programs
programs that consist of uncovering potentially harmful substance use prior to the onset of overt symptoms or problems and/or targeting newer drug users with a limited history of use; the main goal is to target at-risk groups, experimenters, and early-abuse populations

tertiary drug prevention programs
drug prevention programs focusing on intervention and targeting chemically dependent individuals who need treatment; tertiary prevention involves treating the medical consequences of drug abuse and facilitating entry into treatment so further disability is minimized (basically the same as drug abuse treatment)

TABLE 17.1 Levels of Drug Prevention and Suggested Activities

Primary Prevention (Risk Reduction Before Abuse)	
Intrapersonal factors	Affective education (emotional literacy)
	Resilience training
	Values clarification
	Personal and social skills development
	Assertiveness skills training
	Refusal skills
	Drug information and education
Small group factors	Peer mentoring, counseling, outreach, modeling
	Conflict resolution
	Curriculum infusion
	Activities demonstrating misperception of peer norms
	Alternatives to use: recreational, cultural, athletic
	Strengthening families
Systems level	Strengthening school–family links
	Strengthening school–community group links
	Strengthening community support systems
	Media advocacy efforts, reducing alcohol marketing
Secondary Prevention (Intervening in Early Abuse)	
	Assessment strategies: identification of abuse subgroups and individual diagnoses
	Early intervention coupled with sanctions
	Teacher–counselor–parent team approach
	Developing healthy alternative youth culture
	Recovering role models
Tertiary Prevention (Intervening in Advanced Abuse)	
	Assessment and diagnosis
	Referral into treatment
	Case management
	Reentry

A number of questions should be considered by a professional planning a prevention program. To what type of audience should the drug information be targeted? Youth or adults? Peers or parents? Should information focus on knowledge, attitudes, or behavior? Should the program emphasize and recommend abstinence or responsible use? In most cases, it is appropriate for drug prevention to focus on knowledge, attitudes, and behavior; the three are clearly related. For instance, if the goal is to increase knowledge, should we assume that attitudes and behavior would change accordingly, or should knowledge about the harmful effects of drugs be kept separate from attitudes and behavior? For example, if you learn that smoking marijuana is a health hazard, equal to or more destructive than smoking cigarettes, does this knowledge limit the satisfaction you derive from smoking marijuana with friends? Some would say yes. Unfortunately, many would say no. In fact, knowledge about the harmful effects of certain types of drugs has very little effect on the personal attitudes and habits of most people. Most cigarette smokers are aware of the health hazards before they start smoking, but this does not always stop them from starting or becoming addicted.

Drug education programs have to direct their attention to a small range of behavioral objectives. They will not be effective if they address too many issues. Drug prevention programs also must decide whether they will stress total abstinence or responsible use. Abstinence is radically different from responsible use. A program cannot advocate both. Information and scare tactics alone have no effect on drug use. Educational prevention models have been modified lately to achieve the following goals:

- Convey the message that society is inconsistent concerning drug use. For example, certain drugs that cause serious harm to a large percentage of the population are legal, whereas other drugs that have less impact are illegal.
- Convey that the reasons for drug use are complex and that drug users vary.
- Demonstrate to youth that young and old alike are affected by role models, in that attitudes regarding drug use are often patterned from family members who are role models.
- Acknowledge that other influential role models in music, sports, art, drama, business, and education who use and abuse drugs can affect attitudes toward drug use.

Prevention Research: Key Findings

According to the National Institute on Drug Abuse (2012), the United States spends more than $600 billion annually on the costs associated with substance abuse. Another study reports that "government spending related to smoking and the abuse of alcohol and illegal drugs reached $468 billion in 2005, accounting for more than one-tenth of combined federal, state and local expenditures for all purposes," with most spending going "toward direct health care costs for lung disease, cirrhosis and overdoses, for example, or for law enforcement expenses including incarceration" (Eckholm 2009).

The National Institute on Drug Abuse (2007) reported the following key findings regarding drug abuse prevention:

- *Addiction is a complex disease.* No single factor can predict who will become addicted to drugs. Addiction is influenced by a tangle of factors involving genes, environment, and age of first use. Recent advances in genetic research have enabled researchers to begin to uncover which genes make people more vulnerable, which protect a person against addiction, and how genes and environment interact.
- *Addiction is a developmental disease.* It usually begins in adolescence or even childhood when the brain continues to undergo changes. The prefrontal cortex—located just behind the forehead—governs judgment and decision-making functions and is the last part of the brain to develop. This may help explain why teens are prone to risk taking, why they are particularly vulnerable to drug abuse, and why exposure to drugs at this critical time may affect the possibility of future addiction.
- *Prevention and early intervention work best.* The developmental years might also present opportunities for resiliency and for receptivity to intervention that can alter the course of addiction. We already know many of the risk factors that lead to drug abuse and addiction—mental illness, physical or sexual abuse, aggressive behavior, academic problems, poor social skills, and poor parent–child relations. This knowledge, combined with better understanding of the motivational processes at work in the young brain, can be applied to prevent drug abuse from starting or to intervene early to stop it when warning signs emerge.

▪ An Example of Drug Prevention at Central High in Elmtown

This section describes how a school-based prevention program is implemented and demonstrates that programs must be comprehensive and multifaceted to be successful.

Let us stand in the shoes of a parent and teacher committee trying to design a primary prevention program for students at Central High in Elmtown. The group has some prevention research materials that it received from the National Clearinghouse for Alcohol and Drug Information (NCADI). After some thought, most members of the committee decide not to address individual, personal risk factors that may generate anxieties, conflicts, or painful or threatening feelings. They have spoken with some students and ascertained that most of the 9th and 10th graders—even those who tend toward rebelliousness and avant-garde styles—are against taking drugs. Although many students feel this way, there are trends in the school that worry the committee members. Some popular 11th- and 12th-grade peer group leaders are drug users, and drug sales have been occurring on school grounds. The presence and availability of drugs and the beginning of a drug-using atmosphere make it more likely that some of the younger students will initiate use.

In brainstorming sessions, different committee members suggest ways to help these students avert initiation of drug use. Depending on their thinking, theoretical perspective, and exposure to prevention models, members come up with the following ideas:

- Students need to be grounded in good, solid knowledge about the negative effects and dangers of drugs as provided in a drug education course or, more subtly, in a curriculum concerning drug effects and drug-using behaviors (also covered later in this chapter in the section on higher education).
- Students with low self-esteem will feel uncomfortable asserting individual choices or points of view that deviate from those held by peers or peer leaders. Bolstering a positive self-image would allow such students to refuse drugs.
- Students who have low expectations regarding their ability to refuse drugs will be least likely to actually refuse. The school might try to increase their *self-efficacy*; that is, their belief that their behaviors are powerful and will have results.
- Students just do not know how to say "no" and need refusal skills training or peer-resistance training.
- Although a clique leadership may set a pro-use tone, it is probable that the quiet antidrug students represent a silent majority. They may misperceive the amount of drug use that occurs in their school. If the antidrug students are shown that their own attitudes and beliefs are actually in the majority, they will see that the "emperor has no clothes."
- A more confrontational approach involves removing drugs from the school environment by infiltrating the student body or using informants to gather information about who is distributing drugs. Dealers and users can then be identified or counseled and their parents notified. The school could make the decision to go as far as having the student arrested or expelled.

With so many options put forth, some of the committee members become frustrated and fear that a sufficient program will never be created. Some of them have experienced alcoholism in their families and fear that many of these approaches are ineffective for helping the students who are already experimenting.

Seeing a disaster brewing, the committee chair makes a call to the Division of Substance Abuse Services in the state Department of Health to inquire about drug prevention programs. The operator refers the call to the prevention specialists at the agency, who are linked to the National Prevention Network, which is part of the National Association of State Alcohol and Drug Abuse Directors. A specialist schedules a meeting with the committee, in which she makes the following points:

- A prevention needs assessment is helpful and necessitates using validated survey instruments to determine the patterns of behavior and attitudes regarding drug use among the student body.
- A combination of primary and secondary prevention would be good for the majority of the student body, and group treatment for substance abuse should be made available at an adolescent outpatient clinic. The outpatient clinic will assess some students who are well on their way to addiction and refer them into inpatient treatment. Because this intervention occurs when the student is at an advanced abuse state, this is considered tertiary prevention.

Notice how all three types of approaches (primary, secondary, and tertiary) are necessary to implement a comprehensive prevention strategy.

The specialist brought along a staff member of the Local Council on Alcoholism and Drug Dependence, an affiliate of the National Council on Alcoholism and Drug Dependence (NCADD) branch serving a three-county region of the state. Thousands of branches of NCADD exist in the United States, and their goal is to help local groups design and implement prevention programs. Many branches have developed specialized programs for teens, children, women, and the elderly. The staff member conducts preliminary sessions with the prevention committee and arranges to sign an affiliation agreement with the school administration whereby NCADD will act as consultants to the school, aiding it in designing a prevention program to fit its particular needs. It will design a project, which will be based on a needs assessment that incorporates a survey of chemical attitudes and use and interviews with parents, teachers, and students. The project design will include the program objectives, a method and management plan, a timeline, and an evaluation component.

To help those members bewildered by the many possible factors identified by the committee in its brainstorming session (such as self-esteem, self-efficacy, and refusal skills), the staff member invites the committee to sample a number of available, attractive packages of user-friendly activities, such as the following:

- Broad-brush packages, which cover a variety of personal choice and primary prevention areas (Holstein, Cohen, and Steinbroner 1995; Legal Action Center 2016)
- More targeted strategies, which might include a training package to be implemented by a consultant hired by the school district to address issues such as assertiveness training

Assertiveness training skills, which include a variety of personal and social skills, enable people to communicate their needs and feelings in an open, direct, and appropriate manner while still recognizing the needs and feelings of others. They make people feel more powerful and better about themselves (less like doormats), and they offer strategies for saying "no" without hurting, provoking, or manipulating others (Alberti and Emmons 1988). Assertive behavior contrasts with hostile or belligerent behavior, passive and helpless behavior, and passive-aggressive or indirect manipulation. The exercises included in assertiveness training are non-threatening, concrete, direct, and enjoyable.

Many intrapersonal prevention concepts, or personal and social skills development concepts, have come and gone, with a trendy buzzword accompanying each in the year it was introduced. Many of these concepts overlap, such as *life skills training, self-esteem, self-efficacy, resilience training,* and *assertiveness training* (McIntyre, White, and Yoast 1990; Norman 1994). The danger lies in employing them as gimmicks or slogans that accomplish little. Nevertheless, as Botvin and others have shown, personal and skills training that is carefully based on known cognitive and behavioral change factors, if carefully put into place, can indeed make a difference (Botvin and Griffin 2005; Botvin and Wills 1985; Shiffman and

Wills 1987). It also is true that almost any positive lifestyle activity is likely to act as an alternative to participating in a drug-using subculture.

In essence, "[p]revention programs should address all forms of drug abuse, alone or in combination, including the underage use of legal drugs (e.g., tobacco or alcohol); the use of illegal drugs (e.g., marijuana or heroin); and the inappropriate use of legally obtained substances (e.g., inhalants), prescription medications, or over-the-counter drugs" (NIDA 2014).

Comprehensive Prevention Programs for Drug Use and Abuse

Comprehensive drug prevention programs range from very broad approaches at the societal level to programs at the community, school, family, and individual levels. Comprehensive prevention programs can include ideological and institutional approaches, methods, and perspectives regarding drug prevention. In essence, comprehensive drug prevention programs are broad based, affecting both single and multiple groups in a society, and can also include entire societies in how they approach and deal with the problem of drug use and abuse. Next we explore major types of comprehensive drug prevention programs and varying levels.

▌ Harm Reduction Model

The **harm reduction model** is a very broad and comprehensive model that involves society-wide prevention. As an approach to drug use and addiction, this model is practiced in some cities in the Netherlands and the United Kingdom. It is described by Westermeyer (n.d.) as an addiction model that connects "with the addicted community, by having an 'open door policy' that welcomes addicts to take part in services, regardless of level of motivation for change, goals or personal ideology." In a sense, it is a model that meets addicts on their own level.

Westermeyer (n.d.) identifies three central beliefs of the harm reduction model:

1. Excessive behaviors occur along a continuum of risk ranging from minimal to extreme. Addictive behaviors are not all-or-nothing phenomena. Although a drug or alcohol abstainer has a lower risk of harm than a drug or alcohol user, a moderate drinker is causing less harm than a binge drinker is; a crystal methamphetamine

KEY TERM

harm reduction model
a society-wide approach to drug use and/or abuse that focuses on reducing the harm experienced by the drug user and/or abuser as well as the harm to society

smoker or sniffer is causing less harm than a crystal injector.

2. Changing addictive behavior is a stepwise process, with complete abstinence being the final step. Those who embrace the harm reduction model believe that any movement in the direction of reduced harm—no matter how small—is positive in and of itself.

3. Sobriety simply is not for everybody. This statement requires the acceptance that many people live in horrible circumstances. Some are able to cope without the use of drugs; others use drugs as a primary means of coping. Until we are in a position to offer an alternative means of survival to these individuals, we are in no position to cast moral judgment. The health and well-being of the individual are of primary concern; if individuals are unwilling or unable to change addictive behavior at this time, they should not be denied services. *Attempts should be made to reduce the harm of their habits as much as possible.*

According to Westermeyer, the Dutch (who created this approach to prevention of drug use and abuse) have "an 80% connection rate with the addicted population," whereas in the United States we are 80% disconnected from our addicted populations. In fact, through our punitive model in dealing with drug users, the strongest connection we have with the addicted population in the United States comes when they are arrested and jailed.

According to the Harm Reduction Coalition (n.d.),

Harm reduction incorporates a spectrum of strategies from safer use, to managed use to abstinence to meet drug users "where they're at," addressing conditions of use along with the use itself. Because harm reduction demands that interventions and policies designed to serve drug users reflect specific individual and community needs, there is no universal definition of or formula for implementing harm reduction.

The Harm Reduction Coalition (n.d.) has set forth the following principles as being critical to the success of harm reduction programs:

- Accepts, for better and for worse, that licit and illicit drug use is part of our world and chooses to work to minimize its harmful effects rather than simply ignore or condemn them.

- Understands drug use as a complex, multi-faceted phenomenon that encompasses a continuum of behaviors from severe abuse to total abstinence, and acknowledges that some ways of using drugs are clearly safer than others.

- Establishes quality of individual and community life and well-being—not necessarily cessation of all drug use—as the criteria for successful interventions and policies.

- Calls for the nonjudgmental, noncoercive provision of services and resources to people who use drugs and the communities in which they live in order to assist them in reducing attendant harm.

- Ensures that drug users and those with a history of drug use routinely have a real voice in the creation of programs and policies designed to serve them.

- Affirms drugs users themselves as the primary agents of reducing the harms of their drug use, and seeks to empower users to share information and support each other in strategies that meet their actual conditions of use.

- Recognizes that the realities of poverty, class, racism, social isolation, past trauma, sex-based discrimination, and other social inequalities affect both people's vulnerability to and capacity for effectively dealing with drug-related harm.

- Does not attempt to minimize or ignore the real and tragic harm and danger associated with licit and illicit drug use.

In essence,

Harm reduction seeks to reduce the harms of drug policies dependent on an over-emphasis on interdiction, such as arrest, incarceration, establishment of a felony record, lack of treatment, lack of adequate information about drugs, the expansion of military source control intervention efforts in other countries, and intrusion on personal freedoms. Harm reduction also seeks to reduce the harms caused by an over-emphasis on prohibition, such as increased purity, black market adulterants, black market sale to minors, and black market crime. A harm reduction strategy seeks to protect youth from the dangers of drugs by offering factual, science-based drug education and eliminating youth's black market exposure to drugs. A harm reduction approach advocates lessening the harms of drugs through education, prevention, and treatment. Finally, harm reduction seeks to restore basic human dignity to dealing with the disease of addiction. (Alco-holAnswers.org 2013)

■ Community-Based Drug Prevention

Community-based programs are very broad and take into account the community's youth, parents, businesses, media, schools, law enforcement, religious or fraternal groups, civic or volunteer groups, healthcare professionals, and government agencies with expertise in the field of substance abuse. The primary goal of community-based prevention is to provide coordinated programs among the numerous agencies and organizations involved in prevention.

Prevention requires communities to conduct a structured review of current prevention programs to determine (1) whether the programs in place were examined and tested according to rigorous scientific standards during their development and (2) whether these programs incorporate the basic principles of prevention that have been identified in research. Usually, prevention programs at the community level ask the following questions (Robertson et al. and NIDA 2003; Sloboda and David 1999):

- Does the program have components for the individual, the family, the school, the media, community organizations, and healthcare providers? Are the program components well integrated in theme and content so that they reinforce rather than duplicate one another?
- Does the prevention program use media and community education strategies to increase public awareness, attracting community support, reinforcing the school-based curriculum for students and parents, and keeping the public informed of the program's progress?
- Are interventions carefully designed to reach different at-risk populations, and are they of sufficient duration to make an impact?
- Does the program follow a structured organizational plan that progresses from needs assessment through planning, implementation, and review to refinement, with feedback to and from the community at all stages?
- Are the objectives and activities specific, time limited, feasible (in terms of available resources), and integrated so that they work

together across program components and can be used to evaluate program progress and outcomes?

Often, these programs set up prevention policy boards to oversee planning and implementation. Boards should include representatives from law enforcement, juvenile justice, education, recreation, social services, private industry, health and mental health agencies, churches, civic organizations, and other community agencies that serve youth and families. They should also include one or several youth members. "The community can be a target group, especially when there is extensive community denial or lack of awareness, lack of clear policies, poor law enforcement, and so on. Public awareness campaigns, political action, and similar efforts are appropriate at this level of prevention" (Tinzmann and Hixson 1992, pp. 2, 3).

Community prevention programs can also direct their attention to changing the legal and social environment regarding alcohol, tobacco, and other drug (**ATOD**) supplies and toward youth (Center for Prevention Research and Development [CPRD] 2000). This effort also includes individual and environmental strategies. For example, an environmental approach to reducing underage drinking might involve training clerks to insist on proper age identification when selling alcoholic beverages. An individual approach might involve education efforts, such as a media campaign, aimed at discouraging young people from drinking (Silver Gate Group and Robert Wood Johnson Foundation 2001).

Other community-based strategies include the following:

- Strengthening the enforcement of existing legal regulations of ATOD sales and use
- Educating merchants and servers about alcohol and tobacco sales laws
- Regulating legislation regarding the sale of alcohol and tobacco to minors
- Implementing use and lose laws, which allow for the suspension of the driver's license of a person younger than 21 years of age following a conviction for any alcohol or drug violation (e.g., use, possession, or attempt to purchase with or without false identification)
- Imposing regulations on location and density of retail outlet, that is, monitoring the number of unsupervised vending machines dispensing cigarettes to minors in a given community and monitoring the number of retail establishments selling alcohol and tobacco near schools

KEY TERM

ATOD
alcohol, tobacco, and other drugs

Community-based prevention programs recently have been endorsed, having been found to be not only viable but also cost-effective:

Drug use prevention programmes are effective when they respond to the needs of a community, involve all the relevant sectors, and are based on evidence; effective programmes should also incorporate strong monitoring and evaluation components. Such programmes are also cost effective.... If other costs to society were to be counted, such as the costs resulting from crime, unemployment, and ill health, the cost effectiveness of good drug use prevention programmes is likely to be even greater. (United Nations Office on Drugs and Crime [UNODC] 2011)

A community-based organization that has to be mentioned is the Community Anti-Drug Coalitions of America (CADCA), which was organized in 1992. This organization

has been training local grassroots groups, known as community anti-drug coalitions, in effective problem-solving strategies, teaching them how to assess their local substance abuse-related problems, identify root causes and local conditions and develop comprehensive plans to address them. Today, CADCA is the nation's leading national substance abuse prevention organization, representing the interests of thousands of community coalitions in the United States and around the world. (CADCA 2010)

CADCA's reach includes more than 5000 community coalitions and their affiliates across the United States, and a growing number of community groups around the world. It has 2000 dues-paying members and 17,000 subscribers to its e-newsletter; trains thousands of leaders, members, and volunteers; and even airs a televised program (CADCA TV) that reaches approximately 2.6 million households (CADCA 2010).

CADCA provides the following core services:

- Training and technical assistance
- Dissemination and coalition relations
- Research and evaluation
- Public policy and advocacy
- Membership and communicating
- Special events and conferences
- International programs

In conclusion, community prevention emphasizes comprehensive drug abuse prevention programs that include multiple components, such as the use of media, drug education in schools, parent education, community organizations, and formulation of drug-related health policy. In essence, community drug prevention seeks to reduce drug abuse by informing, coordinating, and decreasing the level of drug use at the community level.

■ School-Based Drug Prevention

Education has been used extensively in the past to control the use and abuse of drugs, especially alcohol and tobacco. Drug education actually began in the late 1800s, when most states required that the harmful effects of certain drugs be taught. An example of an early educational attempt to curb or stop drug abuse is the temperance movement of the late 19th century. The Women's Christian Temperance Union (WCTU) and the Anti-Saloon League taught that alcohol consumption was harmful and contrary to Christian morality.

Years ago, when drug prevention was first attempted, most substance abuse experts thought that schools should be responsible for educating the public about the dangerous use and eventual abuse of drugs because education is the main objective of schooling. Schools began teaching about drug use, but in the beginning drug prevention focused on individual factors, such as the dangers of particular types of drugs, the dangers of trusting individuals who sell drugs, and other scare tactics. One problem with this approach was that students varied enormously with regard to their drug experiences. Often, the students had already tried the dangerous drugs and had experienced only pleasurable effects with few negative consequences. Their experiences occurred before their exposure to drug prevention programs that relied on negative information, which is generally known as the **scare tactic or fear-based approach**. Many self-reported use surveys revealed that these programs were not successful. With such audiences of drug users, the warnings are short-lived, not believed, or perceived as exaggerations. Today the use of evidence-based drug education is "based on life skills that offer personal,

KEY TERM

scare tactic or fear-based approach
drug prevention information based on emphasizing the extreme negative effects of drug use—scaring the audience of potential and current drug users/abusers into not using drugs

social, resistance and communication skills, as well as information about the short-term effects of drugs through a series of sessions offered by trained teachers" (UNODC 2011). Another more recent study reported that "[e]valuation has shown fear-based approaches not to be effective. Programmes depending only on information provision or only on boosting self-esteem also appear to be ineffective. Interactive teaching also seems to be necessary for success, with more didactic approaches generally unsuccessful" (Claire 2013, p. 23).

School-based programs that are the most successful

[p]rovide information about drugs and alcohol, in particular correcting misperceptions about how common and acceptable substance misuse is among the young people's peer group (normative education). They also teach interpersonal skills to help handle realistic situations where alcohol or drug are available. Examples with strong evidence base include the Life Skills training programme, developed in the United States, and Unplugged, tested in a large scale evaluation across several European countries. (Claire 2013, p. 23)

It is equally important that school prevention programs include teacher training on good classroom management practices, such as rewarding appropriate student behavior. Such techniques help to foster students' positive behavior, achievement, academic motivation, and school bonding (NIDA 2014).

Table 17.2 summarizes the most popular, common, school-based drug prevention programs, including the premise, strategies, and effectiveness of the following approaches: (1) cognitive, (2) affective, (3) combined cognitive and affective, (4) social learning/cognitive-behavioral, and (5) normative education. Table 17.2 also details the strengths (if any) and weaknesses of each approach.

Finally, two more recent successful school drug prevention programs that "speak" to their audiences are the Athletes Training and Learning to Avoid Steroids (ATLAS) for males and Athletes Targeting Healthy Exercise and

Nutrition Alternatives (ATHENA) for females. These two programs target teenage athletes and specifically focus on addressing steroid abuse and other unhealthy behaviors (e.g., drinking and driving). These two programs leverage the influence of coaches and peer groups to highlight proper sports nutrition, strength training, and other positive alternatives to using drugs to improve performance and build confidence. ATLAS and ATHENA have now been adopted by schools in 29 states and Puerto Rico and have been endorsed by Congress as exemplary prevention programs (NIDA 2007).

SCHOOL-BASED PREVENTION POLICIES FOCUSED ON ENFORCEMENT

Grounded in **prohibitionist philosophy** and the law enforcement approach, and largely devoid of public health perspectives and strategies, the following measures have been used to prevent and reduce substance use among students:

- Antismoking policies
- Zero-tolerance policies
- Drug searches
- Drug testing

These law enforcement approaches aimed at middle school and high school students across the United States for the past 12 years and currently in force in many schools represent more hard-lined prohibitionist approaches for reducing and preventing drug use. In many communities across the United States, as well as in many countries throughout the world, there is an extensive variation of opinions regarding their success for curbing recreational drug use, which includes student use of tobacco, alcohol, and other drugs.

CURRICULUM-BASED DRUG EDUCATION OBJECTIVES

In an effort to educate students about the dangers of drug use, school-based drug education programs and objectives have been implemented in most U.S. school curricula. Specific educational topics have been established for use at the elementary, middle school, high school, and college levels.

The elementary level includes the following topics:

- Drugs versus poisons
- Effects of alcohol, tobacco, and marijuana on the body

KEY TERM

prohibitionist philosophy (regarding drug use)
reducing and/or stopping unwanted drug use by legally banning and punishing drug use

TABLE 17.2 Summary of Common School-Based Drug Prevention Approaches

Approach	Premise	Strategies	Effectiveness
Cognitive	If youth understand the dangers of AOD, they will not use them.	Teach pharmacology of alcohol and other drugs, how they are used, long-range consequences of use—usually through scare tactics.	Seldom effective; sometimes detrimental—arouses curiosity and encourages experimentation. Dire facts are not credible; knowledge alone does not counteract peer pressure. Knowledge is necessary, but not sufficient; focus on more immediate physical/social consequences may work.
Affective	High self-esteem, values consistent with nonuse, and good problem-solving and decision-making skills help youth avoid AOD.	Raise self-esteem. Teach values and life skills. Typically, do not include AOD information.	Do not decrease rate of use. Some community members and parents protest teaching values and decision making. Need to include AOD information.
Combined cognitive and affective	Students need both information and life skills to avoid AOD use.	Teach problem-solving, decision-making, and peer pressure-resistance skills and provide explicit information about AOD to connect life skills and AOD use and consequences.	Little consistent effect on reducing AOD use, although some successes have been reported.
Social learning/ cognitive-behavioral	AOD use usually begins in a social setting between grades 5 and 9, usually with peers, but sometimes adults. Youth need skills for resisting these pressures (based on Bandura's social learning theory).	Teach how to identify pressures from peers, media, advertising, and families. Teach resistance skills and model counterarguments. Students role-play pressure situations and actively practice resisting.	Sometimes effective, especially if peers are involved in instruction and when students already have other fairly well-developed social skills. Little evidence that effects last.
Normative education	Youth overestimate the extent of AOD use among peers and thus may use AOD to feel part of the group.	Correct misconceptions, demonstrate actual norms through discussion, and develop nonuse norms.	Success with some drugs; not very effective with alcohol. Some youngsters may believe that fewer peers use AOD than actually do, and may come to feel AOD use is more acceptable than they did before entering the program.

AOD, alcohol and other drugs.

Data from Tinzmann, M. B., and J. Hixson. *What Does Research Say About Prevention?* Oak Brook, IL: North Central Regional Educational Laboratory, 2006.

- Differences between candy and drugs
- Drug overdoses
- Dangers of experimentation
- How to say "no" to peers offering drugs
- Reasons for taking drugs: curing illness, pleasure, escape, parental use, and ceremony

At the middle school level, the topics expand to include the following:

- How peer pressure works
- How to say "no" to peer pressure

- How drugs affect the body, physiologically and psychologically
- Where to seek help when needed
- Attitudes toward drug use
- How to have fun without drugs
- Harmful effects of tobacco, alcohol, and marijuana on the body
- Stress management and building positive self-esteem
- How advertisers push drugs
- Consequences of breaking drug laws

- Differences among wine, beer, and distilled spirits
- Family drug use
- Family drinking problems and family members who may have drug addiction problems
- Images of violence and drug use in rock and rap music
- Teenage drug abuse and associated problems

Topics at the high school and college level include the following:

- Responsible use of medications
- How drugs affect the body and the mind
- Legal versus illegal drugs
- Drinking and driving
- Drug effects on the fetus
- Recreational drug use
- Ways of coping with problems: anger and stress management
- How to detect problem drug users
- Drug education, prevention, and treatment
- Positive and negative role models
- How to build positive self-esteem
- Criminal sanctions for various types of drug use
- Binge drinking
- Drugs and driving
- Date rape
- Addiction to drugs and alcoholism

PRINCIPAL QUESTIONS FOR SCHOOL-BASED PROGRAMS

The following questions should be asked to improve the outcomes of drug education programs:

- Do the school-based programs reach children from kindergarten through high school? If not, do they at least reach children during the critical middle school or junior high years?
- Do the programs contain multiple years of intervention (all through the middle school or junior high years)?
- Do the programs use a well-tested, standardized intervention with detailed lesson plans and student materials?
- Do the programs use age-appropriate interactive teaching methods (modeling, role playing, discussion, group feedback, reinforcement, extended practice)?
- Do the programs foster social bonding to the school and community?
- Do the programs teach social competence (communication, self-efficacy, assertiveness) and drug resistance skills that are culturally and developmentally appropriate?

- Do the programs promote positive peer influence?
- Do the programs promote antidrug social norms?
- Do the programs emphasize skills-training teaching methods?
- Do the programs include an adequate "dosage" (10 to 15 sessions in year 1 and another 10 to 15 booster sessions)?
- Is there periodic evaluation to determine whether the programs are effective?

▮ Family-Based Prevention Programs

Primary family risk factors that predispose youth to find drugs attractive include the following:

- Chaotic home environments, particularly in which parents abuse substances or suffer from mental illnesses
- Ineffective parenting, especially with children with difficult temperaments and conduct disorders
- Lack of mutual attachments and nurturing

In addition, "[r]esults from longitudinal studies of children, particularly those children most at risk for problems, indicate that families can protect children and youth against drug use and abuse through effective family management practices that impart skills young people can use in resisting social pressures to use drugs" (National Institutes of Health [NIH] and NIDA 1998, p. 49).

Although the just-listed risk factors are the primary risk factors, *protective factors*—the factors that can insulate against drug use—include the following:

- Strong parent–child bonds
- Parental monitoring with clear rules of conduct within the family unit and involvement of parents in the lives of their children
- Open communication of values within the family
- High levels of supervision and monitoring
- No inconsistent disciplining from lackadaisical to extreme enforcement of rules and no saying one thing and then doing another
- Consistent high levels of parental warmth, affection, and emotional support

Research shows that protective family factors can moderate the effects of risk factors (Cleveland et al. 2010; NIDA 2003). The risk of associating with peers who use drugs can be offset by protective family factors, such as parent conventionality, maternal adjustment, and strong parent–child attachment.

Prevention at the family level needs to stress parent–child interaction strategies, communication skills, child management practices, and family management skills. Research has also shown that parents need to take a more active role in their children's lives. This includes talking to their children about drugs, monitoring their activities, getting to know their friends, and understanding their problems and personal concerns (NIH and NIDA 1998). Such interactive techniques are deemed most effective when, for example, peer discussion groups and parent role-playing are used, which allows for active involvement in learning about drug abuse and reinforcing skills (NIDA 2014).

PREVENTION PRINCIPLES FOR FAMILY-BASED PROGRAMS

In conclusion, family-based prevention programs need to do the following:

- Reach families of children at each stage of development.
- Train parents in behavioral skills to:
  - Reduce conduct problems in children.
  - Improve parent–child relations, including positive reinforcement, listening and communication skills, and problem-solving.
  - Provide consistent discipline and rule-making.
  - Monitor children's activities during adolescence.
- Include an educational component for parents with drug information for them and their children.
- Focus on families whose children are in kindergarten through 12th grade to enhance protective factors.
- Provide access to counseling services for families at risk.

■ Individual-Based Drug Prevention and Treatment: Harm Reduction Therapy

A more recent approach known as **harm reduction therapy (HRT)** uses several treatment models that "can be used in outpatient settings, residential treatment, homeless programs, traditional drug treatment programs, medical services, community outreach programs among other service delivery settings" (Harm Reduction Psychotherapy and Training Associates n.d.). According to the Harm Reduction Psychotherapy and Training Associates (n.d.),

HRT is based on the belief that alcohol and drug problems including substance abuse and dependence develop in individuals through a unique interaction of biological, psychological, and social factors. HRT is a nonjudgmental approach to helping people experiencing alcohol and drug problems to reduce the negative impact of substance use, abuse, or dependence in their lives. Harm Reduction Therapy understands that people use alcohol and drugs for a variety of reasons. It addresses the complex relationship that people develop with these psychoactive substances over the course of their lives. In HRT, concerns related to drug and alcohol use are addressed simultaneously with their social and occupational impacts as well as their psychological and emotional implications in an integrated treatment approach to these "co-occurring disorders."

This type of therapy treatment emphasizes collaboration, respect, and self-determination, which differs from traditional addiction treatment. Traditional drug treatment programs generally follow a 12-step program (much like AA and NA) and often use varying amounts of confrontation and coercion in their treatment programs. (For another example of a semi- or quasi-type of harm reduction drug prevention and treatment method, see "Case in Point: A New Alternative to Conventional Drug Prevention and Treatment: A Nontreatment Program for Alcohol and Drug Abuse.")

Drug Prevention Programs in Higher Education

The seriousness of alcohol and other drug use on college campuses is underscored by the following findings (Cal Poly 2016):

- According to the Core Institute, an organization that surveys college drinking practices, 300,000 of today's college students will eventually die of alcohol-related causes, such as

KEY TERM

harm reduction therapy (HRT)
a nonjudgmental approach to helping people experiencing alcohol and drug problems to reduce the negative impact of substance use, abuse, or dependence in their lives

► CASE IN POINT

A New Alternative to Conventional Drug Prevention and Treatment: A Nontreatment Program for Alcohol and Drug Abuse

Solving an addiction problem involving alcohol and other drugs without treatment? Addiction to drugs is *not* genetically inherited? A program for moderating or abstaining from drug use and/or abuse that flies in the face of Alcoholics Anonymous (AA) by claiming that drug addiction is *not* a disease? "Treatment and 12 step based programs are less successful than no treatment at all?" (Baldwin Research Institute [BRI] 2010).

A program for moderating or abstaining from alcohol and other drugs with a better than 62% success rate verified by outside independent research organizations?

The Saint Jude Retreats, which offer the St. Jude Program, does not advocate belief in the disease of addiction myth. There is no disease of alcoholism; there is no disease of drug abuse; and, there is no disease of addiction! This is just one of many areas where the Saint Jude Program departs from treatment and why the Saint Jude Program is significantly more effective than the treatment model. Teaching our guests the need for personal responsibility for their actions rather than making excuses for poor behavior and choices, is the cornerstone to rebuilding their life. A disease by its very nature is out of the person's control. This is simply not the case with substance abuse. Substance abusers make the choice to abuse alcohol and drugs. Choice is a behavior, not a disease. (BRI 2013).

This program is based on the Freedom Model Law of Universal Motivation, which proves an individual's behavior is freely chosen. "The primary responsibility for one's life improvements is to be held by the individual rather than the program or staff" (BRI 2010). The program emphasizes learning through "doing" and "experiencing" and provides Certified Cognitive Behavioral Learning Presenters to teach methods of self-change (BRI 2010). In contrast to AA, St. Jude replaces the disease model with cognitive behavioral change (through their proprietary Cognitive Behavioral Education, or CBL, methods), in which participants set their own goals regarding either cessation from a drug or drugs or learning to personally moderate their drug use, as well as many other life-enhancing improvements. It is an educational/social-centered program, not medically staff centered. All detox services are completed prior to entry into the educational programs.

Baldwin Research Institute differs from other alcohol and/or drug programs in that they

use a social/educational approach instead of the more traditional, yet less effective, medical/psychological/control methodology thereby putting power over a person's recovery in the hands of the individual rather than a doctor, psychologist, or group. In line with the findings of the majority of independent researchers, our methodology has provided abstinence based success rates 10 to 12 times greater than programs using traditional 12-step treatment methodologies and has remained near or greater than 60% since 1992. (Saint Jude Executive Retreats 2016)

The Saint Jude Program is completely nontreatment based:

Treatment centers (many publicly funded) dispense a strange brew of indoctrination, religion, and medicine in a *faux*-hospital setting and admixture of medically supervised detox, three hots and a cot, misleading education, therapy and large doses of 12-step meetings. Discharge is marked by the admonition: "Don't drink and go to meetings." (BRI 2010)

None of this has been proven to be successful with heavy drinkers or drug users.

Finally, Chairman Scheeren at Baldwin Research Institute indicates that a significant proportion of the guests that enter the Saint Jude Program are from prior treatment program stays that have failed in eliminating their drug use problems. Scheeren emphasizes "Our program at Baldwin continues to show phenomenal success in having our clients learn how to quit, or if they decide, effectively control their drug use" (November 9, 2016).

Data from Baldwin Research Institute (BRI). "The Saint Jude Retreats." 2013. Available http://www.baldwinresearch.com/jude-thaddeus-program.cfm; Baldwin Research Institute (BRI). "Baldwin Research Project 1991." 2010. Available http://www.baldwinresearch.com/baldwinproject1991-2.cfm and at http://www.baldwinresearch.com/treatment-research.cfm; Saint Jude Executive Retreat. "Frequently Asked Questions." Baldwin Research Institute (BRI). 2016. Available http://www.saintjudeexecutiveretreat.com/faq.php

drunken driving accidents, cirrhosis of the liver, various cancers, and heart disease.

- Of today's first-year college students, 159,000 will drop out of school next year because of alcohol or other drug-related reasons.
- Almost one-third of college students admit to having missed at least one class because of their alcohol or drug use.
- One night of heavy drinking can impair a person's ability to think abstractly for up to 30 days, limiting the ability to relate textbook reading to classroom discussions or to think through processes such as football plays.

As these statistics indicate, the use of alcohol and other drugs is a serious problem within the college or university environment. Major problems on college campuses resulting from such drug abuse include property damage, poor academic performance, damaged relationships, unprotected sexual activity, physical injuries, date rape, and suicide (Ansari et al. 2013; Perkins 1997).

It is obvious that with all these negative findings regarding alcohol and other drug use on college campuses, prevention programs are vital. Next, we review the major prevention programs that currently exist in higher education.

■ Overview and Critique of Existing Prevention Programs

This next section will review and critique four drug prevention program models in higher education. The four program models are (1) the information-only or awareness model, (2) the attitude change model or affective education model, (3) the social influences model, and (4) the ecological or person-in-environment model. The first model, information-only or awareness model, is based solely on teaching about drug information, primarily the effects of using different types of drugs. This model heavily relies on making students knowledgeable about various drugs. The second model, attitude change or affective education model, works on attitude change and the role of self-esteem regarding drug use and abuse. The third model, the social influences model, focuses on how to use resistance skills when drugs are readily available in a student's environment, taking into account such social psychological factors as prior socialization and peer pressure. The fourth model, ecological or person-in-environment model, looks at how changes in a student's social environment can affect attitudes about drugs and drug use.

INFORMATION-ONLY OR AWARENESS MODEL

One of the earliest preventive interventions, this model is based on the belief that if people are given extensive information about the harmful effects of drugs it will change their attitudes about use and abuse. This model assumes that people are rational enough to seriously curtail or stop drug use based on information. Obviously, today we know that, at most, the majority of drug users exposed to the **information-only or awareness model** become more knowledgeable about the effects of drugs, but this approach has very little influence on the use of habitual or addictive-type drugs.

ATTITUDE CHANGE OR AFFECTIVE EDUCATION MODEL

The **attitude change or affective education model** assumes that people use drugs because they have low self-esteem (alcoholrehab.com 2016; Gonzalez and Clement 1994). As a result, prevention focuses on strengthening self-image, building positive self-esteem, and boosting self-confidence. A problem with this model is that attitudes often are resistant to change and fluctuate depending on such environmental influences as peer and party settings. Attitudes that were formed in an educational setting (drug and alcohol classes) are abandoned in substance use settings.

SOCIAL INFLUENCES MODEL

The **social influences model** assumes that substance abuse results from multiple influences. Although outside influences are perceived as major influences, inner influences, such as prior socialization, a vulnerability to pleasing others, and a need to be accepted by friends and peers, are likewise taken into account. This prevention strategy emphasizes peer resistance and inoculation techniques. Techniques primarily include the following (European Monitoring Centre for Drugs

KEY TERMS

information-only or awareness model
assumes that teaching about the harmful effects of drugs will change attitudes about use and abuse

attitude change or affective education model
assumes that people use drugs because of lack of self-esteem

social influences model
assumes that drug users lack resistance skills

and Drug Addiction [EMCDDA] 2010; Gonzalez and Clement 1994):

- Offering factual information about the consequences of drug use
- Guiding development of skills to recognize outer and inner pressures to use drugs and methods and techniques to resist usage
- Communicating correct information about the extent of drug use by students of similar ages
- Modeling, rehearsing, and reinforcing skills for resisting drugs when friends or peers expect compliance
- Persuading students to try these resistance approaches and techniques in classroom or group settings and in peer group settings away from the classroom

By far, this method has been more successful than the information-only and attitude change models. Although it works best when it begins at the junior high school level, refresher courses should be administered at least every 2 years. Some research findings indicate that although this method is least effective with alcohol consumption, it is effective with marijuana and cigarette smoking (Gonzalez and Clement 1994).

ECOLOGICAL OR PERSON-IN-ENVIRONMENT MODEL

This model is one of the newest types of prevention programs. "Interventions based on this model have multiple components and are designed to address individuals and the policies, practices, and social norms that affect students on campuses or in the community" (Gonzalez and Clement 1994, p. 3). Developed from human ecology, the **ecological or person-in-environment model** stresses that change(s) in the environment change people. "This perspective is based on the notion that an individual and his or her behavior cannot be understood adequately without consideration of the various aspects of that individual's environment (social, political, familial, temporal, spiritual, economic, and physical)" (Kondrat 2015). Although the ecological or person-in-environment model does not ignore substance use from individual causes, such as personal beliefs

KEY TERM

ecological or person-in-environment model
stresses that changes in the environment change people's attitudes about drugs

and perception of risk, it does primarily focus on the causes from the social environment (Hansen 1997; Kondrat 2015). According to Hansen (1997), "The central tenet [belief] of social ecology is that individual behavior is mainly the result of socialization; to change the behavior, we must change the social institutions that shape it" (p. 6). Hansen also stated "the strongest predictors of alcohol and drug abuse among young people are social" (p. 6).

This perspective emphasizes that it is important to take into account all of the environments that may have an impact on drug use. Friends, acquaintances, roommates, and classmates in dorms, sororities, and fraternities and at parties, cafes, and nightspots can influence students (U.S. Department of Education 1994).

As a result, this model advocates the following drug prevention strategies (Gonzalez and Clement 1994):

- Dissemination of drug information
- Cognitive and behavioral skills training for youth, parents, and professionals
- Mass media programming
- Development of grassroots citizen interest groups
- Leadership training for key organization and community officials
- Policy analysis and reformulation

In applying this model to the college campus, we find that college campuses have long served as an environment for initiating and perpetuating drug use and abuse. Fraternity drunkenness, for example, was decried as early as 1840 (Horowitz 1987). In 1988, an 18-year-old student attending Rutgers University died of alcohol poisoning at a fraternity party. In a television interview following the incident, then-Chancellor Edward Bloustein described fraternities as "organized conspiracies dedicated to the consumption of alcohol" (Hansen 1997, p. 5).

Using the ecological or person-in-environment model as a preventative measure can alleviate drug use and abuse on college campuses, lessening the vast majority of vandalism, fights, accidents, sexually transmitted infections, unplanned pregnancies, racial bias incidents, date rape, and at least one-third of academic attrition often caused by drug use and abuse (Koss, Gidycz, and Wisniewski 1987). Although campus prevention programs and research date back several decades, such efforts remained isolated and sporadic until the late 1970s. All campuses now have medium to extensive alcohol and other drug prevention programs in effect. Tailoring this type of prevention to college environments is certainly worthy of consideration.

Finally, a variant of this model, which was originally formulated to focus on violence (Centers for Disease Control and Prevention [CDC] 2009), takes into account other, larger factors regarding drug use and abuse. The **social-ecological model** considers the complex interplay among individuals, relationships, communities, and societal factors. This model (refocused by this author to more directly apply to drug use) emphasizes multiple interacting factors that put individuals at risk for experiencing and later becoming addicted to drug use. The main focus takes into consideration not just individual influencing factors but also the particular drug user's social relationships (e.g., presence of many friends who use drugs), the community, and societal factors (e.g., chaotic drug-infested societies where drug dealing and drug use are common). The social-ecological model includes multiple influencing factors in a person's environment.

Examples of Large-Scale Drug Prevention Programs

■ The BACCHUS Peer Education Network and NASPA

In 1975, an organization known as Boosting Alcohol Consciousness Concerning the Health of University Students (BACCHUS) was developed as a national student organization. Soon BACCHUS realized that many of its affiliates were members of sororities and fraternities; therefore, it renamed the organization, then known as BACCHUS and GAMMA (Greeks Advocating Mature Management of Alcohol), to the **BACCHUS Network** effective July 1, 2005. A more recent description includes the following:

> BACCHUS is a network of more than 8,000 student leaders and advisors who work with over four million peers on more than 330 campuses nationwide. Our Members are found on four-year public colleges and universities, private and two-year institutions, historically Black colleges and universities, predominantly Hispanic population campuses, and tribal colleges. (BACCHUS Network 2013)

In January 2014, the BACCHUS Network officially merged with the National Association of

Student Personnel Administrators (NASPA)–Student Affairs Administrators in Higher Education to "provide outstanding resources, professional development, and technical assistance to an even broader community of college and university professionals and students" (NASPA 2016a).

The **BACCHUS Initiatives of NASPA–Student Affairs Administrators in Higher Education** is the program supporting student leadership and peer education on health and safety issues—no matter the peer education group name, specialized health interest, or social affiliation (NASPA 2016a).

As an organization NASPA is "the leading association for the advancement, health, and sustainability of the student affairs profession. Our work provides high-quality professional development, advocacy, and research for 15,000 members in all 50 states, 25 countries, and 8 U.S. territories" (NASPA 2016b).

The original goal of BACCHUS was to prevent alcohol abuse. Today, the program has broadened its goals to include other student health and safety issues and actively promotes student- and young adult–based, campus and community-wide leadership on healthy and safe lifestyle decisions concerning alcohol abuse, tobacco use, illegal drug use, unhealthy sexual practices, and other high-risk behaviors.

This nonprofit organization devotes a substantial portion of its resources and activities to the following goals on university-affiliated campuses (BACCHUS Network 2011):

KEY TERMS

social-ecological model
a variant of the ecological or person-in-environment model that takes into account multiple factors regarding drug use and abuse and focuses on the complex interplay among individuals, relationships, communities, and societal factors

BACCHUS Network
a former (prior to 2014) national and international association of college and university peer education programs focused on alcohol abuse prevention and other related student health and safety issues

BACCHUS Initiatives of NASPA–Student Affairs Administrators in Higher Education
reformulated BACCHUS Network that is currently managed by NASPA that continues to support higher education student leadership and peer education on health and safety issues

• Create and foster a thriving network of institutions and young adult–led peer education groups supporting health and safety initiatives.
• Empower students and administrators to voice their opinions and needs to create healthier and safer campus communities.
• Develop and promote cutting-edge resources and health promotion campaigns that support peer education, campus leadership, and activism on health and safety issues.
• Provide exceptional conferencing and training opportunities for students, young adults, and professionals to support health and safety strategies.
• Encourage national forums on young adult health and safety concerns.
• Promote and disseminate research and effective strategies that better help campuses and communities address health and safety issues.
• Advocate for effective and sensible policies and practices for campus and community health and safety issues.

The BACCHUS philosophy is that students can play a uniquely effective role—unmatched by professional educators—in encouraging their peers to consider, talk honestly about, and develop responsible habits and attitudes toward high-risk health and safety issues. The organization now hosts four websites to assist students in their prevention efforts. "The BACCHUS Network is a university and community based network focusing on comprehensive health and safety initiatives. It is the mission of this 501(C)(3) non-profit organization to actively promote student and young adult based, campus and community-wide leadership on healthy and safe lifestyle decisions concerning alcohol abuse, tobacco use, illegal drug use, unhealthy sexual practices and other high-risk behaviors" (SWIC n.d.). The organization focuses prevention and fosters and aids students information about the organization's activities, services, conferences, campaigns, and resource materials.

Currently there are 120 educational resources and training materials offered by our organization. In addition, each affiliate group receives health issue campaigns that, when used in combination, lay the foundation for a year-round prevention program:

• National Collegiate Alcohol Awareness Week (alcohol and high risk drinking)
• Tobacco Prevention and Cessation (control, policy, programs, advocacy)
• Impaired Driving Prevention (designated driver, safe ride, laws, awareness)

• Sexual Responsibility Awareness (sexual health, HIV/AIDS-STIs and relationship issues)
• Safe Spring Break (alcohol, impaired driving, predatory drugs, sun safety, personal safety)

Campaigns consist of health topic message promotion and resource manuals that contain the latest research and data, program delivery ideas, model programs, and marketing strategies (BACCHUS Network 2013).

■ Fund for the Improvement of Postsecondary Education Drug Prevention Programs

In 1987, a huge explosion of campus drug prevention programs began. It was sparked by a $14 billion annual budget for college drug prevention placed in the Drug-Free Schools and Communities Act of 1986 (now titled the Safe and Free Schools and Communities Act). The funding was parceled out by the U.S. Department of Education, Fund for the Improvement of Postsecondary Education (FIPSE). FIPSE awarded about 100 grants per year from 1987 until 1996 via a grant competition that called for colleges to mount institution-wide drug prevention programs. The guiding philosophy included the following points:

• A small, isolated program was seen as making little difference, but a comprehensive program reaching into several areas of the institution could send many consistent anti-use messages that would eventually reach critical mass and change the campus environment.
• There should be well-known, top-down administrative support for prevention programming.
• There should be well-written and carefully implemented policies about chemical use on campus.

The hundreds of new programs, whose administrators met and interacted in annual grantee conferences, generated the sense that there was a national prevention movement in higher education. The Network of Colleges and Universities Dedicated to Prevention of Alcohol and Other Drug Abuse was founded, incorporating 900 institutions. The network is supported by the Higher Education Center for Alcohol and Other Drug Prevention funded by the U.S. Department of Education, which provides a range of materials and newsletters (Ryan, Colthurst, and Segars 1995). Unfortunately, such large-scale efforts when evaluated years later (at the turn of the century) indicated that federally funded drug prevention on most college campuses had very mixed results, often indicating weak success, and as a result most of the funding programs were discontinued.

In addition, "many college and universities have implemented prevention programs, or, within counseling centers, intervention efforts to meet the needs of the institution and it students" (Larimer, Kilmer, and Lee 2005, p. 446). This finding by researchers also indicates that although implementing such individually based, specific college and university prevention programs is commendable, implementing new drug prevention programs without evaluating the impact of these programs is totally lacking on most college campuses. In other words, colleges or universities also need to rigorously assess and evaluate the effectiveness of their drug prevention programs, coupling their drug prevention programs with assessment.

From more than a decade of experience, several exemplary approaches emerged. These strategies might be the predominant focus of a program or one of a number of complementary components of a comprehensive effort. These strategies are addressed next.

PEER-BASED EFFORTS

Student peers can be involved in a number of ways: as educators, mentors, counselors, or facilitators of prevention and outreach work. Such an approach multiplies manpower tremendously, reaches the students who are apt to become lost in the flow, is not perceived as an outside or authoritarian intrusion, speaks the language of students, and works to change the predominant cultural tone on campus. Peers can conduct classroom presentations, work informational tables or drop-in centers, create prevention newsletters, and establish links to community groups. It is important to carefully train and supervise peer facilitators. Many peer programs are residence hall based, taking advantage of the training of residence hall assistants and peer facilitators (BACCHUS and GAMMA 1994).

CURRICULUM INFUSION

Infusion of a skill or topic across the curriculum has been used in conjunction with classes on writing skills, gender issues, and other areas. Curriculum infusion can be undertaken at individual institutions or as a consortium project. The advantage of curriculum infusion is that it involves faculty members, achieves open discussion of drug issues in the classroom as part of the normal educational process, and stimulates critical thinking about drug issues.

IMPROVISATIONAL THEATER GROUPS

Improvisational theater groups that tackle health and wellness issues can be lively, stimulating, and provocative, often breaking through peer and institutional denial and bringing issues home to students with a dramatic emotional impact. Improvisational topics can include date rape, sexually transmitted disease, children of alcoholics on campus, and denial of chemical dependency.

STRATEGIES TO CHANGE MISPERCEPTIONS OF USE

Social psychologists Alan Berkowitz and Wesley Perkins, both of Hobart and William Smith Colleges, have conducted influential research illustrating that students often have incorrect estimates (exaggerated misperceptions) of drug use by their peers (Perkins 1991, 1997; Perkins and Berkowitz 1986). Thus, they misperceive the peer norms governing drug use, which may lead them to follow imaginary peers. This idea is a modification of the traditional understanding that peers influence peers. It follows logically that activities demonstrating the accurate use pattern to students and correcting misperceptions will indirectly affect overall use patterns. These efforts have included simply publicizing the results of alcohol and drug use surveys and awarding prizes for coming up with correct estimates.

ALTERNATIVE EVENTS

Alternative events, such as alcohol-free cocktail parties ("mocktail" parties), alcohol-free gatherings, and indoor rock climbing, especially as alternatives to presporting events and holiday parties, help avoid some events that are traditionally associated with chemical abuse.

PROGRAMS THAT CHANGE MARKETING OF ALCOHOL ON AND NEAR CAMPUSES

Until recently, institutions of higher education were a major focus of alcohol marketing. Alcoholic beverage producers sponsor many campus events, and these companies buy considerable newspaper advertising. One report indicates,

Alcohol advertising is pervasive in college sporting events. According to a recent report in *USA Today,* "NCAA tournament games led all other sports events in alcohol-related TV advertising in 2002, with 939 ads costing $28 million. That compares with a combined 925 ads aired during the Super Bowl, World Series, college bowl games and the NFL's Monday Night Football." (StateUniversity.com 2011)

Beginning in 1991,

The OIG [Office of Inspector General of the U.S.] … reviewed the voluntary codes then in effect under the auspices of the Beer Institute, the Wine Institute, the Distilled Spirits Council of the United States (DISCUS) …, and an alcohol industry umbrella group, the Century Council. In particular, the review looked at the elements of the voluntary codes that were related to "youth appeal." … The OIG concluded: "While the industry advertising standards purport to guide alcohol advertisers towards responsible behavior, they fail to prevent advertising considered to have youth appeal." (Office of Inspector General, 1991:14, in Jernigan and O'Hara 2004)

Further, "Like The Beer Institute, the DISCUS code calls for advertising not to be placed where most of audience is reasonably expected to be below the legal purchase age." In addition, distilled spirits companies are told not to advertise on "college or university campuses," including their newspapers; however, marketing activities are allowed if they are "in licensed retail establishments located on such campuses" (Jernigan and O'Hara 2004).

From the findings above and the fact that most students on college campuses are underage with regard to purchasing and using alcohol, there is pressure on the alcohol industry to restrict influencing students about alcohol on college campuses with the likelihood that today it is "bad business to promote alcohol on college campuses."

In implementing programs and policies that make a difference, the following are examples of the strategies many colleges and universities are implementing that can have a positive influence on the campus culture regarding alcohol and other drug abuse (U.S. Department of Education 2008):

- Forming partnerships with local communities to ensure that alcohol is not served to minors or to intoxicated students

KEY TERM

Drug Abuse Resistance Education (D.A.R.E.)
drug education program presented in elementary and junior high/middle schools nationwide by police officers

- Strengthening academic requirements
- Scheduling classes on Fridays (this strategy emphasizes the importance of academics and discourages the alcohol fueled partying that may occur on Thursday nights if students do not need to attend classes on Fridays)
- Keeping the library and recreational facilities open longer
- Eliminating alcohol-industry support for athletics programs (accepting such funds can be seen as sending a mixed message to students)
- Restricting alcohol promotions and advertising on campus and in campus publications, especially promotions or ads that feature low-cost drinks
- Monitoring fraternities to ensure compliance with alcohol policies and laws
- Providing a wide range of alcohol-free social and recreational activities
- Disciplining repeat offenders and those who engage in unacceptable behavior associated with substance use
- Notifying parents when students engage in serious or repeated violations of alcohol or other drug policies or laws
- Launching a media campaign to inform students about the actual amount of drinking that occurs on campus since most students overestimate the number of their classmates who drink and the amount that they drink

Finally, it is better to embed prevention messages within an overall wellness perspective. Students are concerned about health and wellness issues, not programs that come off as dogmatic or preachy, moralizing, exaggerating, and nagging—perhaps reminding them of life at home.

■ Drug Abuse Resistance Education (D.A.R.E.)

One major drug prevention program that had high hopes for success was the school-based drug education programs incorporated into our nation's school districts—**Drug Abuse Resistance Education (D.A.R.E.)**.

Established in 1983, D.A.R.E. operates in about 75% of all school districts across the United States and in numerous foreign countries. In addition to the D.A.R.E. elementary school curriculum, the D.A.R.E. program includes middle school and high school curricula that reinforce lessons taught at the elementary school level. "In fiscal year 2000, the Department of Justice's Bureau of Justice Assistance, which supports various substance abuse prevention programs for youth, provided about $2 million for D.A.R.E. regional training centers to support the training of new police officers that help deliver the D.A.R.E. program lessons" (quoted from U.S. Government Accountability Office [GAO] in Common Sense for Drug Policy 2009).

D.A.R.E. program shows very mixed evaluations:

D.A.R.E. (Drug Abuse Resistance Education) administers a school-based substance abuse, gang, and violence prevention program in 75% of US school districts and in 48 countries (as of 2013). Since 1983, police officers have taught the D.A.R.E. program to over 200 million K–12 students worldwide—approximately 114 million in the United States alone. Proponents say that D.A.R.E. has helped prevent drug use in elementary, middle, and high school students. They contend that D.A.R.E. improves social interaction between police officers, students, and schools, is the most prevalent substance abuse prevention program in the United States, and is popular with kids and parents. Opponents say that dozens of peer-reviewed studies conclude the D.A.R.E. program is ineffective at preventing kids from using drugs. They contend that D.A.R.E. causes kids to ignore legitimate information about the relative harms of drugs, and that D.A.R.E. is even associated with increased drug use. (ProCon. org 2013)

Today, the D.A.R.E. website states the following about this program: "Launched in 1983, D.A.R.E. is a comprehensive K–12 education program taught in thousands of schools in America and 52 other countries. D.A.R.E. curricula address drugs, violence, bullying, internet safety, and other high risk circumstances that today are too often a part of students' lives" (D.A.R.E. 2016).

Recent evaluations of this program show that, on a short-term basis, D.A.R.E. improved students' views of themselves and increased their sense of personal responsibility. However, the program has *not* yielded a measurable, significant change in drug use (Rosenbaum and Hanson 1998; Vogt 2003). Moreover, this drug education program has shown a strong inconsistency between students' self-reported attitudes about use and their actual drug use (Clayton et al. 1991; Ennett et al. 1994; Vogt 2003). See "Holding the Line: D.A.R.E.: Frustrating and Poor Results from a National Drug Prevention Program" for more information on the D.A.R.E. program.

One major problem is that "over the past decade, a flurry of studies—by the U.S. surgeon general and the General Accounting Office, among others—found no significant difference in drug use between D.A.R.E. graduates and students never exposed to the curriculum" (Vogt 2003, p. 1; see also Plant et al. 2011). Further, regarding graduates of the D.A.R.E. program, one official said, "I can't tell you how many kids told me D.A.R.E. introduced them to drugs. The problem with D.A.R.E., other than that it's a multimillion dollar conglomerate in the business of selling T-shirts, is that it takes the burden off parents to raise their kids [drug free]" (Vogt 2003, p. 3).

Another major problem that has been identified is that the D.A.R.E. drug education program is presented in the classroom by fully uniformed police officers. Although the officers are well intentioned and their efforts are commendable, they are hardly a mechanism for transmitting new norms that would find converts among students, except perhaps those already successfully socialized (Gopelrud 1991). More important, uniformed police officers used as teachers "sends the wrong message that drugs are a law enforcement issue, rather than a public health issue" (Zeese and Lewin 1998, p. 1).

■ The Drug Court Model

Although these courts of law vary in organization, in scope, and at what point intervention occurs, the underlying premise is that drug possession and use is not only a law enforcement/criminal justice problem, but also a public health problem (Sherin and Mahoney 1996). "Drug courts are specialized court docket programs that target criminal defendants and offenders, juvenile offenders, and parents with pending child welfare cases who have alcohol and other drug dependency problems" (National Institute of Justice [NIJ] 2016). Even though adult drug courts vary in target population, program model, and resources, they are generally based on a comprehensive model involving the following (NIJ 2016):

- Offender screening and assessment of risks, needs, and responsivity
- Judicial interaction
- Monitoring (e.g., drug testing) and supervision
- Graduated sanctions and incentives
- Treatment and rehabilitation services

In *drug court programs*, criminal justice agencies collaborate closely with the substance abuse treatment community and other societal institutions to

HOLDING THE LINE

D.A.R.E.: Frustrating and Poor Results from a National Drug Prevention Program

In 1995, a disturbing study published by a group of researchers at the University of Michigan and backed by the U.S. Department of Health and Human Services (USDHHS) and the National Institute on Drug Abuse (NIDA) showed that the use of illicit drugs by young people had been rising steadily since 1992. The results of this study were even more perplexing because overall drug use had been declining over the same period. The increase was happening despite several seemingly successful efforts to combat drug abuse with high-powered prevention programs.

Since the 1980s, most funds allocated for drug prevention have been spent in three areas: criminal justice, major advertising campaigns, and D.A.R.E. Law enforcement professionals who work with hardcore addicts, especially in poor urban neighborhoods, have favored compulsory preventive programs. According to William N. Brownsberger, former Assistant State Attorney General in the Massachusetts Narcotics and Special Investigations Division, addicts who are forced against their will to enter and remain in therapy can overcome their addiction. Roughly 90% of all addicts are arrested at least once every year, giving the criminal justice system plenty of opportunities to help them kick their habits.

One highly visible persuasive effort to end drug abuse has been the advertising campaign created by the Partnership for a Drug-Free America. The nation's advertising industry developed the partnership and funded it by collaborating with advertisers and a variety of health and educational agencies. The goal was to promote images designed to make drug use look "uncool," especially to younger people. In addition to the creative services donated by advertising agencies, media organizations donated more than $2 billion of public service and advertising space to the partnership between the late 1980s and 1990s.

In the early 1990s, the partnership commissioned surveys to measure the effect of its media campaign on students in the Los Angeles and New York City school systems. On both coasts, increased exposure to the partnership's messages appeared to dramatically change students' attitudes toward drugs. At the same time, however, the number of students who admitted using drugs actually increased.

Another high-visibility persuasive effort has been the nationwide D.A.R.E. program, which was launched in Los Angeles in 1983. "D.A.R.E.'s curriculum reflects mainstream theories about the best way to reduce drinking, smoking, and drug use by children.... The program began as collaboration between the Los Angeles Police Department and the city's school district" (Miller 2001, p. A14). Using role-playing techniques and resistance training, uniformed police officers become social workers, talking with students in their classrooms, educating them about the dangers of drugs, and giving them the tools to resist temptation or peer pressure. They generally teach 17 classroom sessions.

Today most school-based prevention programs, including D.A.R.E., assume that adolescents need grown-ups' help in resisting social pressures to use [drugs]. Therefore, they try to correct children's exaggerated beliefs about the prevalence of drug use among their peers. They offer them information about the physical and social effects of using and they try to impart "resistance skills" for making and acting on thoughtful decisions. (Miller 2001, p. A14)

Although D.A.R.E. is the most popular drug education program ever developed for children, increasing numbers of critics claim that its benefits, if any, are short lasting. Most D.A.R.E. training begins in the fifth grade. At this age, students accept most of what they hear. By middle school, however, the effectiveness of D.A.R.E. begins to erode. By high school, many students resist participation in the program. According to a researcher from the Research Triangle Institute in Durham, North Carolina, which conducted a $300,000 study on the impact of D.A.R.E., "Unless there's some sort of booster session that reinforces the original curriculum, the effects of most drug use prevention programs decay rather than increase over time." The findings of numerous research studies conducted on D.A.R.E.'s effectiveness suggest that D.A.R.E. students were no less likely to use drugs than students who had not gone through the program (Ennett et al. 1994; Vogt 2003). Some have even claimed that the D.A.R.E. program teaches kids to become curious about illicit drug use or actually motivates them to do drugs (Vogt 2003). Further, "Among the notable quotations from researchers: 'is well established that D.A.R.E doesn't work'

(continues)

HOLDING THE LINE

D.A.R.E.: Frustrating and Poor Results from a National Drug Prevention Program (*continued*)

Gilbert Botvin, Cornell Medical Center. 'Research shows that, no, D.A.R.E. hasn't been effective in reducing drug use' William Modzeleski, top drug education official at the Department of Education" (Plant et al. 2011, p. 147).

Another major negative finding came from the U.S. Government Accountability Office (GAO), which released a review of current research findings regarding alcohol and other drug abuse prevention programs, particularly D.A.R.E., in 2003:

> The six long-term evaluations of the D.A.R.E. elementary school curriculum that we reviewed found no significant differences in illicit drug use between students who received D.A.R.E. in the fifth or sixth grade (the intervention group) and students who did not (the control group). Three of the evaluations reported that the control groups of students were provided other drug use prevention education. All of the evaluations suggested that D.A.R.E. had no statistically significant long-term effect on preventing youth illicit drug use. Of the six evaluations we reviewed, five also reported on students' attitudes toward illicit drug use and resistance to peer pressure and found no significant differences between the intervention and control groups over the long term. Two of these evaluations found that the D.A.R.E. students showed stronger negative attitudes about illicit drug use and improved social skills about illicit drug use about 1 year after receiving the program. These positive effects diminished over time. (U.S. Government Accountability Office [GAO] 2003, p. 2)

In this same report, seven school districts using the D.A.R.E. program were intensely analyzed. The findings indicated that "No statistically significant differences were observed between the intervention and control schools on students' past year marijuana use 2 years after the intervention" (GAO 2003, p. 5).

Further, "[a]s D.A.R.E. America celebrated its 20th anniversary, the nation's most widely used school-based drug prevention program was struggling with a credibility crisis that has devastated the organization financially and threatens its survival" (Vogt 2003). Reports indicate that a number of school districts throughout the country have abandoned the program, finding D.A.R.E. to be ineffective in curbing both licit and illicit drug use.

In light of the diminishing returns from various drug prevention programs, in late 1996, during President Clinton's administration a compulsory drug test for teenagers who are applying for their driver's licenses was proposed. Like everything else, the proposal had both supporters and critics. Although this tactic may be part of the answer, prevention programs that have measurable, long-lasting effects remain difficult to find.

In conclusion,

Proponents say that D.A.R.E. has helped prevent drug use in elementary, middle, and high school students. They contend that D.A.R.E. improves social interaction between police officers, students, and schools, is the most prevalent substance abuse prevention program in the United States, and is popular with kids and parents.

Opponents say that dozens of peer-reviewed studies conclude the D.A.R.E. program is ineffective at preventing kids from using drugs. They contend that D.A.R.E. causes kids to ignore legitimate information about the relative harms of drugs, and that D.A.R.E. is even associated with increased drug use. (ProCon.org 2014)

Data from Brownsberger, W. N. "Just Say 'Criminal Justice.'" *Boston Globe*. (20 October 1996); Ennett, S. T., N. S. Tobler, C. L. Ringwalt, and R. L. Flewelling. "How Effective Is Drug Abuse Resistance Education? A Meta-Analysis of Project D.A.R.E. Outcome Evaluations." *American Journal of Public Health* 84 (1994): 1394–1401; Gordon, P. "The Truth About D.A.R.E." *Buzz Magazine*. (July 1996); Gordon, P. "Can Madison Avenue Really Save America by Making Illegal Drugs Totally Uncool?" *Buzz Magazine*. (August 1996); Miller, D. W. "D.A.R.E. Reinvents Itself—With Help from Its Social-Scientist Critics." *Chronicle of Higher Education* 48 (19 October 2001): A12–A14; Plant, M., R. Robertson, M. Plant, and P. Miller. *Drug Nation: Patterns, Problems, Panics, and Politics*. Oxford, UK: Oxford University Press, 2011; ProCon.org. "Is the D.A.R.E. Program Good for America's Kids (K–12)?" 4 February 2014. Available http://dare.procon.org/; U.S. Government Accountability Office (GAO). *Youth Illicit Drug Use Prevention: D.A.R.E. Long-Term Evaluation and Federal Efforts to Identify Effective Programs*. GAO-03-172R. Washington, DC: U.S. Government Accountability Office (GAO), 15 January 2003; Vogt, A. "Now Many 'Just Say No' to D.A.R.E." *Chicago Tribune*. (26 January 2003): 1, 3.

design and operate the program. Drug courts are often managed by a multidisciplinary team composed of judges, prosecutors, defense attorneys, community corrections, social workers and treatment service professionals. Stakeholders, such as law enforcement, the family, and the community, are encouraged to participate in hearings, programming, and graduation events (NIJ 2016).

The key goal is to divert substance abusers into supervised community treatment centers in an attempt to eliminate the destructive behavior. A committee usually composed of a judge, the district attorney, a public defender, the probation department, and treatment center officials determines whether treatment is needed and the type and length of treatment.

Table 17.3 presents the results of a research evaluation of a multisite adult drug court program. The 20 sampled drug courts were evaluated based on the staffing characteristics and frequency of staffing, who attended the staffing, participation in the staffing, who ran the staffing, who made the final decisions on participant response, length of time in minutes of staffing meetings, and the average discussion time in minutes per case (Zweig 2011). Table 17.3

TABLE 17.3 Observed Drug Court Team Staffing Meetings at 20 Drug Court Sites

Staffing Characteristics	Results	Staffing Characteristics	Results
Frequency of Staffing		Project/resource coordinator(s)	3.7
Every other week	10%	Defense attorney(s)	2.7
Weekly	75%	Prosecutor(s)	2.7
More than once a week	15%	Treatment liaison(s)	3.8
Who Attends the Staffing[1]		Case manager(s)	3.3
Judge(s)	100%	Probation officer(s)	2.9
Project/resource coordinator(s)	85%	*Who Runs the Staffing*	
Defense attorney(s)	85%	Judge	55%
Prosecutor(s)	80%	Project/resource coordinator	35%
Treatment liaison(s)	70%	Both	10%
Case manager(s)	50%	*Who Made the Final Decisions on Participant Response*	
Probation officer(s)	50%		
Others		Judge(s)	75%
Clerk(s)	20%	Team consensus	25%
Law enforcement (police/corrections)	15%	*Length of Staffing Meeting (in minutes)[2]*	
Drug court administration	15%	Mean across courts	64.85
Mental health	10%	Range across courts	13.00–170.00
Health department	5%	*Average Discussion per Case (in minutes)*	
Participation in the Staffing (scale of 1 to 5)		Mean across courts	2.64
Judge(s)	4.9	Range across courts	0.60–6.00

[1]Multisite Adult Drug Court Evaluation (MADCE) team observers rated the level of participation of each drug court team member on a scale of 1 to 5, with 1 being "did not participate" and 5 being "participated thoroughly."

[2]This reflects the length of the staffing meeting observed; the MADCE team made every effort to observe the whole meeting.

Data from Zweig, J. M. "Chapter 2. Description of the Drug Court Sites in the Multi-Site Adult Drug Court Evaluation." In *The Multi-Site Adult Drug Court Evaluation: The Drug Court Experience*, by S. B. Rossman, J. M. Zweig, D. Kralstein, K. Henry, P. M. Downey, and C. Lindquist, 8–23. Washington, DC: Urban Institute Justice Policy Center, 2011.

shows that 75% of the sampled drug courts held weekly staff meetings; that the judge(s), project/resource coordinator(s), defense attorney(s), and prosecutor(s) primarily attended the staff meetings; and that the judge(s) ran the staffing meetings in 55% of the 20 courts sampled. (See Table 17.3 for more detailed findings.)

At the first National Drug Court Conference, one researcher reported, "These courts rely on strong collaboration among judges, prosecutors, defense lawyers, and related supporting agencies (such as case management, corrections, pretrial services, probation), on the one hand, and a partnership with treatment agencies (or providers) and other community organizations and representatives on the other" (Goldkamp 1993, p. 33). The treatment phase generally consists of (1) detoxification (removal of physical dependence on drugs from the body), (2) stabilization (treating the psychological craving for the drug), and (3) aftercare (helping the defendant obtain education or job training, find a job, and remain drug free) (Office of Justice Programs [OJP] 2000).

As of 2014, more than 2967 drug courts were in operation in the United States and U.S. territories (see **Figure 17.2** for drug court locations in the United States). Approximately half of drug courts (51%) targeted adult offenders, and 14% served juveniles. The other drug courts were categorized as family treatment (9%), tribal healing to wellness (4%), designated DWI (8%), campus (0.2%), reentry drug (1%), federal drug (9%), federal veterans treatment (0.2%), veterans treatment (0.7%), and co-occurring disorder (1%) (National Drug Court Resource Center [NDCRC] 2014).

The following types of drug courts are currently in existence (see also **Table 17.4** for the types and numbers of drug courts in the U.S and its territories in 2014):

- Adult
- Juvenile
- Family treatment
- Tribal healing to wellness
- Designated DWI
- Campus
- Reentry drug
- Federal drug
- Federal veterans treatment
- Veterans treatment
- Co-occurring disorder

Eligible drug offenders can be sent to drug court instead of moving through the traditional justice system. Drug courts put individuals in treatment and closely supervise them throughout the process.

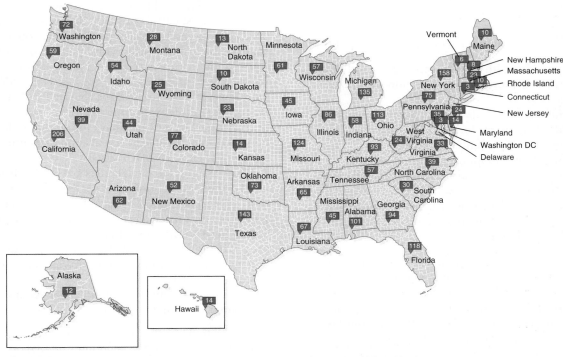

FIGURE 17.2   Locations and numbers of drug courts in the United States and U.S. territories.

Reproduced from National Association of Drug Court Professionals (NADCPI). "U.S. Drug Court Map." Alexandria, VA: National Association of Drug Court Professionals, 2016. Available http://www.nadcp.org/learn/find-drug-court

TABLE 17.4 Types and Numbers of U.S. Drug Courts Operating in the United States and Its Territories (as of June 30, 2014)

Court Type	Number
Adult[i]	1538
Juvenile[ii]	433
Family treatment	303
Tribal healing to wellness	119
Designated DWI	242
Campus	6
Reentry drug	36
Federal drug	29
Federal veterans treatment	6
Veterans treatment	220
Co-occurring disorder	36
Total Drug Courts	**2968**

[i] of which 436 are Hybrid DWI/Drug Courts

[ii] Juvenile drug courts try to address the unique circumstances surrounding adolescent delinquency

Data from National Drug Court Resource Center (NDCRC). "How Many Drug Courts Are There?" Alexandria, VA: Bureau of Justice Administration (BJA), 30 June 2014. Available http://www.ndcrc.org/content/how-many-drug-courts-are-there

For a minimum term of 1 year, participants are

* provided with intensive treatment and other services they require to get and stay clean and sober;
* held accountable by the Drug Court judge for meeting their obligations to the court, society, themselves and their families;
* regularly and randomly tested for drug use;
* required to appear in court frequently so that the judge may review their progress; and
* rewarded for doing well or sanctioned when they do not live up to their obligations. (NADCP 2011c)

What is the target population of drug court participants? Drug courts are expected to have the greatest effects for high-risk offenders who have more severe antisocial backgrounds or poorer prognoses for success in standard treatments:

Such high-risk individuals ordinarily require a combined regimen of intensive supervision, behavioral accountability, and evidence-based

treatment services, which drug courts are specifically structured to provide. Consistent with the predictions of the Risk Principle, drug courts have been shown to have the greatest effects for high-risk participants who were relatively younger, had more prior felony convictions, were diagnosed with antisocial personality disorder, or had previously failed in less intensive dispositions. (Marlowe 2010, p. 3)

A report stated,

A recent survey of more than 120 evaluations of drug court programs showed that they outperformed virtually all other strategies that have been attempted for drug offenders within the 1 to 2 years that courts typically monitor offenders. Offenders who graduated from drug courts had significant reductions in rearrest rates and in charges for serious crimes. Data show that within the first year of release, 43.5% of drug offenders are rearrested, whereas only 16.4% of drug court graduates are rearrested. (Office of National Drug Control Policy [ONDCP] 2007, p. 25)

Drug court programs have spread rapidly since the first drug court was established in 1989 (Franco 2010). Today, we are at the point where each state has multiple drug courts.

Overall, defendants participating in drug court sentencing have had lower rearrest rates, and there are statistically significant differences in disposition between those assigned to drug court and comparison groups. Seventy-five percent of drug court graduates are arrest-free 2 years after leaving the court, and drug courts reduce crime 35% more than other court options (NADCP 2011a). "Rigorous studies examining long-term outcomes of individual Drug Courts have found that reductions in crime last at least 3 years and can endure for over 14 years" (NADCP 2011a).

Those assigned to drug courts are less likely to face further prosecution or to serve probation or short jail terms. Finally, using a drug court and its system of administering treatment within a legal atmosphere is more cost-effective than criminal courts. In 2007, for every federal dollar invested in drug court programs, $9 was leveraged in state funding (NADCP 2011a).

Another report on the cost-effectiveness of such programs stated that

[e]valuations of the net costs and benefits of drug courts nationwide generally find that drug courts save taxpayer dollars compared to simple probation and/or incarceration, primarily due

to reductions in arrests, case processing, jail occupancy and victimization costs. While not all persons diverted to drug court would have otherwise been sentenced to prison, for those individuals who are incarcerated, the average annual cost is estimated to be $23,000 per inmate, while the average annual cost of drug court participation is estimated to be $4,300 per person. (King and Pasquarella 2009, p. 7)

Early research suggested that the successes of drug courts should be viewed with caution, because much of the effectiveness of these courts occurred very early—the courts were in operation fewer than 10 months, and these courts were very selective regarding the defendants allowed to participate. The criticism was that the courts tended to select violators who would have a better chance for rehabilitation. Today, however, evidence exists that such criticisms are no longer valid: "By 2006, the scientific community had concluded beyond a reasonable doubt from advanced statistical procedures called meta-analyses that Drug Courts reduce criminal recidivism, typically measured by fewer re-arrests for new offenses and technical violations" (Marlowe 2010, p. 1).

Further, at a 2009 Annual Conference of the American Society of Criminology, research showed that

> [i]n addition to significantly less involvement in criminal activity, the Drug Court participants also reported significantly less use of illegal drugs and heavy use of alcohol. These self-report findings were confirmed by saliva drug tests, which revealed significantly fewer positive results for the Drug Court participants at the 18-month assessment (29% vs. 46%, p < .01). The Drug Court participants also reported significantly better improvements in their family relationships, and non-significant trends favoring higher employment rates and higher annual incomes. These findings confirm that Drug Courts elicit substantial improvements in other outcomes apart from criminal recidivism. (Marlowe 2010, p. 2).

Another significant finding regarding the cost-effectiveness of adult drug courts is that "[t]he result has been net economic benefits to local communities ranging from approximately $3,000 to $13,000 per Drug Court participant" (Marlowe 2010, p. 3).

A very noteworthy and promising finding regarding drug courts is the emphasis on treating drug addiction and criminal behavior instead of simply punishing without treating drug-related juvenile delinquency and criminalistic behavior, as had been standard before drug courts were established.

Problems with Assessing the Success of Drug Prevention Programs

Both the National Institute on Drug Abuse (NIDA) and individual researchers have evaluated the multitude of drug abuse prevention programs in the United States. The general conclusions of these studies are as follows:

- Very few programs have demonstrated clear success or have adequately evaluated themselves.
- The relationships among information about drugs, attitudes toward use, and actual use are unclear in these programs.

Some key factors that are crucial to developing successful programs include the following:

- Prevention must be coordinated at different levels. Successful programs involve families, schools, and communities. In some cases, these efforts are not coordinated.
- The program must be integrated into the ongoing activities of schools, families, and community organizations. Superficial introduction of drug prevention strategies has limited effects. For instance, distributing literature door-to-door, making in-class presentations regarding the harmful effects of drugs, and posting banners and slogans warning of the consequences of drug abuse in communities are not successful methods. Instead, programs that are comprehensive and community-wide, integrated into neighborhood clubs, organizations, and church activities, are more likely to have a long-term impact on preventing drug use. A clear example is the yearly Great American Smoke-out launched against tobacco use.
- Personal autobiographical and social experience accounts of former drug abusers should be included in drug information that is distributed. Recipients of drug prevention information should be given real-life accounts of use, abuse, despair, and successful drug rehabilitation. Just receiving drug information alone has little impact, either initially or over the long term.

In looking at the future of substance abuse prevention, it is important to include a summary from drug prevention experts, who advocate the following:

> Prevention experts across the spectrum of strategies agree that the future of prevention must focus on education and collaboration. Education includes additional research to advance policy and intervention efforts. It also involves educating communities and policymakers regarding the importance and effectiveness of prevention. Collaboration means not only developing a comprehensive approach across the spectrum of prevention strategies, but also recognizing that substance abuse prevention is intrinsically tied to other outcomes, including mental health, academic success, and violence prevention. Collaboration within and among the healthcare, education, and judicial systems is needed for success. (Berk 2013)

Other Viable Alternatives to Drug Use

It has been suggested that people have an innate need to alter their conscious state. This belief is based on the observation that, as part of their normal play, preschoolers deliberately whirl themselves dizzy and even momentarily choke each other to lose consciousness (Wilson and Wilson 1975). Some young children progress to discovering and using chemicals (such as sniffing shoe polish or gasoline) to alter consciousness and learn to be very secretive about this behavior. They learn to be circumspect or come to feel guilty and repress the desire to alter consciousness when adults catch them in these activities.

If this desire to alter the state of consciousness is inherent in human beings, then the use of psychoactive drugs, legal or illegal, in adulthood is natural. Drug abuse is, therefore, a logical continuation of a developmental sequence that goes back to early childhood (Carroll 1977; Weil 2004; Spiegel 2005).

KEY TERM

alternatives approach
an approach emphasizing the exploration of positive alternatives to drug abuse, based on replacing the pleasurable feelings gained from drug abuse with involvement in social and educational activities

One question in response to this is why, even if there is an innate desire to alter consciousness, only some people progress to abusing chemical substances. It appears that people who do not abuse psychoactive drugs have found positive alternatives to altering consciousness; they feel no need to take chemical substances for this purpose. Involvement in activities such as Boy Scouts and Girl Scouts, youth sports teams, music groups, the YMCA and YWCA, drug-free video game centers, drug-free dances, environmental and historical preservation projects, and social and service projects are viable alternatives to drug use. The rationale for these programs is that youth will find these activities engaging enough to forgo alcohol and drug use (Forman and Linney 1988).

This strategy is known as the **alternatives approach**. Workers in the drug abuse field tend to agree on its effectiveness. They note that young ex-abusers of common illicit drugs are more likely to stop when they gain satisfaction from exploring positive alternatives rather than from a fear of consequent harm. The alternatives approach assumes the following (Cohen 1971):

- People abuse drugs voluntarily to fill a need or basic drive.
- Most people abuse drugs for negative reasons. They may be dealing with negative feelings or situations, such as relieving boredom, anxiety, depression, tension, or other unpleasant emotional and psychological states. They may be rebelling against authority, trying to escape feelings of loneliness or inadequacy, or trying to be accepted by peers. Peer pressure is extremely important as an inducing force.
- Some people who abuse drugs believe the experience is positive. They may feel that their sensual experiences or music enjoyment is enhanced or that they have achieved altered states of consciousness, or they may simply experience a sense of adventure. Some people may want to explore their own consciousness and reasons for the attraction to drug use.

Whether the reasons for drug use are positive or negative, the effects sought can be achieved through alternative, nondrug means. Such means are preferable to drug use and more constructive because the person is not relying on a psychoactive substance for satisfaction; rather, he or she is finding satisfaction based on personal achievements. Ideally, this approach should lead to a lifetime of self-satisfaction.

Table 17.5 lists various types of experiences, the motives for such experiences, the probable drugs of abuse with which they are associated, and alternatives to these drugs. As shown in the table, any constructive activity can be considered an alternative to drug abuse. For example, a young person who needs an outlet for increased physical energy might respond better to dance

TABLE 17.5 Experiences, Motives, and Possible Alternatives for a Drug Abuser

Experience	Corresponding Motives	Drugs Abused	Possible Alternatives
Physical	Desire for physical well-being: physical relaxation, relief from sickness, desire for more energy	Alcohol, sedative-hypnotics, stimulants, marijuana	Athletics, dance, exercise, hiking, diet, carpentry, outdoor work, swimming, hatha yoga
Sensory	Desire to magnify sensorium: sound, touch, taste, need for sensual/sexual stimulation	Hallucinogens, marijuana, alcohol	Sensory awareness training, sky diving, experiencing sensory beauty of nature, scuba diving
Emotional	Relief from psychological pain: attempt to resolve personal problems, relief from bad mood, escape from anxiety, desire for emotional insight, liberation of feeling and emotional relaxation	Narcotics, alcohol, barbiturates, sedative-hypnotics	Competent individual counseling, well-run group therapy, instruction in psychology of personal development
Interpersonal	Desire to gain peer acceptance, break through interpersonal barriers, "communicate"; defiance of authority figures	Any, especially alcohol, marijuana	Expertly managed sensitivity and encounter groups, well-run group therapy, instruction in social customs, confidence training, emphasis on assisting others (e.g., YMCA or YWCA volunteers)
Social	Desire to promote social change, find identifiable subculture, tune out intolerable environmental conditions (e.g., poverty)	Marijuana, psychedelics	Social service community action in positive social change; helping the poor, aged, infirm, or young; tutoring handicapped individuals; ecology action; YMCA or YWCA Big Brother/ Sister programs
Political	Desire to promote political change (out of desperation with the social-political order) and to identify with antiestablishment subgroup	Marijuana, psychedelics	Political service, lobbying for nonpartisan projects (e.g., Common Cause); field work with politicians and public officials
Intellectual	Desire to escape boredom, out of intellectual curiosity, to solve cognitive problems, gain new understanding in the world of ideas, research one's own awareness	Stimulants, sometimes psychedelics	Intellectual excitement through reading, debate, and discussion; creative games and puzzles; self-hypnosis; training in concentration
Creative-aesthetic	Desire to improve creative performance, enhance enjoyment of art already produced (e.g., music); enjoy imaginative mental productions	Marijuana, stimulants, psychedelics	Nongraded instruction in producing and/ or appreciating art, music, drama, and creative hobbies
Philosophical	Desire to discover meaningful values, find meaning in life, help establish personal identity, organize a belief structure	Psychedelics, marijuana, stimulants	Discussions, seminars, courses on ethics, the nature of reality, relevant philosophical literature; explorations of value systems
Spiritual-mystical	Desire to transcend orthodox religion, develop spiritual insights, reach higher levels of consciousness, augment yogic practices, take a spiritual shortcut	Psychedelics, marijuana	Exposure to nonchemical methods of spiritual development; study of world religions, mysticism, meditation, yogic techniques

Data from U.S. Department of Health and Human Services, Office of Substance Abuse Prevention. "Factors that Influence Alcohol and Other Drug Use." In *Prevention Plus II: Tools for Creating and Sustaining Drug-Free Communities* (Figure 2.1, p. 19). DHHS Publication No. 89-1649. Rockville, MD: USDHHS, 1989. Distributed by the National Clearinghouse for Alcohol and Drug Information.

and movement training or a project in preventive medicine than working on ecological projects. In a large alternatives program established in Idaho, the following activities were planned during a month: arts and crafts, karate, reforestation, backpacking, Humane Society dog show, horseback riding, creating artwork for posters for various programs, astronomy, camping, and volunteering in a local hospital.

▪ Meditation

Some of the most intriguing research about the brain is being done on the state of the mind during **meditation**. In certain countries, such as India, people have long histories of being able to achieve certain goals through meditation. The word *yoga* is derived from the Sanskrit word for "union" or "yoking," meaning the process of discipline by which a person attains union with the absolute. In a sense, it refers to the use of the mind to control itself and the body.

Meditation involves brain wave activity centered on ponderous, contemplative, and reflective thought. An individual who meditates is able to decrease oxygen consumption within a matter of minutes by as much as 20%, a level usually reached only after 4 to 5 hours of sleep. However, meditation is physiologically different from sleep, based on the electroencephalograph (EEG) pattern and rate of decline of oxygen consumption.

KEY TERM

meditation
a state of consciousness in which there is a constant level of awareness focusing on one object; for example, yoga or Zen Buddhism

Along with the decreased metabolic rate and EEG changes, there also is a marked decrease in blood lactate. Lactate is produced by metabolism of skeletal muscle, and the decrease is probably due to the reduced activity of the sympathetic nervous system during meditation. Heart rate and respiration also are slowed.

▪ The Natural Mind Approach

Some people who take drugs eventually look for other methods of maintaining the valuable parts of the drug experience. These people may learn to value the meditation high and abandon drugs. In looking at Table 17.5, we can see how the use of different types of drugs can be replaced with possible alternatives by a drug abuser. Long-term drug users sometimes credit their drug experiences with having given them a taste of their potential, even though continued use has diminished the novelty of drug use. After these individuals become established in careers, they claim to have grown out of chemically induced altered states of consciousness. As Andrew Weil (2004) put it, "One does not see any long-time meditators give up meditation to become acid heads" (p. 72).

Although chemical highs are effective means of altering the state of consciousness, they interfere with the most worthwhile states of altered consciousness because they reinforce the illusion that highs come from external, material agents rather than from within your own nervous system.

Some people have difficulty using meditation as an alternative to drugs because, to be effective, meditation takes practice and concentration; in contrast, the effects of drugs are immediate. Nevertheless, it is within everyone's potential to meditate.

LEARNING PORTFOLIO

Discussion Questions

1. Figure 17.1 lists many factors that can influence drug use. Design and detail a drug prevention program by selecting any one of the concentric circles; include all factors within that circle and how you would deal with these factors.
2. Look at the findings in the section of this chapter entitled "How Serious Is the Problem of Drug Dependence?" Which two findings regarding dependence did you find to be the most interesting? Why?
3. Comment on the harm reduction model as presented here and in other literature you may have. What are the major strengths and weaknesses of this model in comparison to the way drug users and/or abusers are viewed in the United States? Why do you think the U.S. government largely remains opposed to this approach? How do you think the problem of drug use/abuse United States would change if it were to adopt the harm reduction model?
4. What would you emphasize in a primary prevention program for middle school students? High school students? College students?
5. How would you design a drug prevention program for undetected committed or secret users? What would you emphasize? Similarly, how would you design a drug prevention program for addicted drug users? What would you emphasize?
6. Which do you think is more likely to work today in drug prevention programs for America's youth: teaching moderate use or total abstinence? Explain.
7. Your work supervisor says, "We received a much smaller amount of money than expected from the federal government to create a drug prevention program. You should focus on either a community-based approach, a school-based approach, a family-based approach, or an individual-based approach/ harm reduction psychotherapy prevention program." Which type of approach would you select? Explain your choice.
8. How effective has the BACCHUS Initiatives of NASPA–Student Affairs Administrators in Higher Education been on your campus? Have you ever participated in any of its social gatherings? Do you think it is effective in curbing alcohol and/or drug use on your campus? Why or why not? Can you give specific experiences with the BACCHUS Initiatives of NASPA social activities?
9. List and explain three major strengths of drug courts in comparison with traditional criminal courts in the United States. Do you perceive any problems in preferring drug courts versus our criminal courts?
10. From everything you read in this chapter about the D.A.R.E. drug prevention program, what do you think are the major problems with this comprehensive drug prevention program? How would you improve it program?
11. What is your assessment of using the alternatives approach and meditation for preventing drug use? Do you think it would be effective for alleviating drug use? Why or why not?

Key Terms

Summary

1. The 10 most prominent factors affecting an individual's use of drugs are as follows: (a) genetics, (b) personality traits, (c) attitudes and beliefs, (d) interpersonal and peer resistance skills, (e) community, (f) peers, (g) school policy, (h) local law enforcement, (i) personal situations, and (j) parents.

2. The seriousness of the problem with regard to drug dependence is highlighted by the fact that in 2014 approximately 21.5 million people aged 12 or older had an SUD in the past year, including 17.0 million people with an alcohol use disorder and 7.1 million people with an illicit drug use disorder. An estimated 4.2 million people had a past-year disorder related to marijuana use, and 1.9 million people had disorders related to nonmedical past-year use of prescription pain relievers. Approximately 2.6 million people aged 12 or older had both an alcohol use disorder and an illicit drug use disorder in the past year; thus, among people aged 12 or older in 2014 who an SUD in the past year, nearly four out of five had an alcohol use disorder and about one out of three had an illicit drug use disorder. About one in eight people aged 12 or older who had SUDs in the past year had both an alcohol use disorder and an illicit drug use disorder. An estimated 1.3 million adolescents aged 12 to 17 had an SUD in 2014 (5.0% of adolescents). In 2014, 5.7 million young adults aged 18 to 25 had an SUD (16.3% of young adults). An estimated 14.5 million adults aged 26 or older in 2014 had an SUD (7.1% of adults aged 26 or older). The approximately 4.2 million people aged 12 or older in 2014 who had a marijuana use disorder in the past year represented 1.6% of those aged 12 or older. The estimated 1.9 million people aged 12 or older in 2014 who had a pain reliever use disorder represent 0.7% of the people aged 12 or older. About 913,000 people aged 12 or older in 2014 had a cocaine use disorder, which represents 0.3% of the people aged 12 or older. About 586,000 people aged 12 or older in 2014 had a heroin use disorder, which represents 0.2% of the people aged 12 or older.

3. The three major types of prevention programs are primary, secondary, and tertiary.

4. Five major types of drug users that drug prevention programs have to recognize before assembling a program are (a) early experimenters, (b) nonproblem drug users/recreational users, (c) undetected committed or secret users, (d) problem users, and (e) former users.

5. The five levels of comprehensive prevention programs for drug use and abuse are (a) the harm reduction model, (b) community-based prevention, (c) school-based prevention, (d) family-based prevention, and (e) individual-based drug prevention and treatment/harm reduction therapy.

6. Proactive family factors can moderate the effects of drug risk factors. The risk of associating with peers who use drugs can be offset by protective family factors, such as parent conventionality, maternal adjustment, and strong parent–child attachment.

7. Five primary prevention programs that exist in higher education are the (a) information-only or awareness model, (b) attitude change model or affective education model, (c) social influences model, (d) ecological or person-in-environment model, and (e) social-ecological model.

8. Three of today's large-scale prevention programs are (a) the BACCHUS Initiatives of NASPA–Student Affairs Administrators in Higher Education, a national and international association of college and university peer-education programs focused on alcohol abuse prevention and other related student health and safety issues; (b) D.A.R.E., a nationwide drug prevention program presented in middle and junior high schools by police officers that has shown severe shortcomings; and (c) drug courts, a promising and popular nationwide approach to prevention in which the primary purpose is to include treatment programs and options instead of only punishment for drug offenses.

9. Two additional possibilities for lessening or eliminating drug use are the alternatives approach and meditation. Alternatives to drug abuse are based on replacing the

euphoria and pleasure gained by being high with involvement in social, recreational, and educational activities. Meditation is producing a state of consciousness in which there is a constant level of very satisfying awareness that is rewarding in itself without artificial inducements (drugs). Yoga and Zen Buddhism are examples.

References

Alberti, R. E., and M. L. Emmons. *Your Perfect Right.* San Luis Obispo, CA: Impact, 1988.

AlcoholAnswers.org. *Harm Reduction Philosophy.* Farmington, CT: National Alliance of Advocates for Buprenorphine Treatment, 2013.

alcoholrehab.com. "Addiction and Low Self Esteem." DARA (Drug and Alcohol Rehab Asia). 2016. Available http://alcoholrehab.com/addiction-articles/addiction-and-low-self-esteem/

Ansari, W. E., C. Stock, and C. Mills. "Is Alcohol Consumption Associated with Poor Academic Achievement in University Students?" *International Journal of Preventive Medicine* 4 (October 2013): 1175–1188.

BACCHUS and GAMMA. *Community College Guide to Peer Education.* Denver, CO: The BACCHUS and GAMMA Peer Education Network, 1994.

BACCHUS Network. "Mission Statement." 2011. Available http://www.bacchusnetwork.org/mission.html

BACCHUS Network. "About the BACCHUS Network." 2013. Available http://www.bacchusnetwork.org/about-the-network.html

Berk, B. *Effective Substance Abuse Prevention: Why It Matters, What Works, and What the Experts See for the Future.* Santa Rosa, CA: Center for Applied Research Solutions, March 2013. Available http://www.ca-cpi.org/docs/Publications/Other/EffectiveSubstanceAbusePrevention_March2013.pdf

Botvin, G. J., and K. W. Griffin. "School Based Programs." In *Substance Abuse: A Comprehensive Textbook*, 4th ed., edited by J. H. Lowinson, P. Ruiz, R. B. Millman, and J. G. Langrod, 1211–1228. Philadelphia, PA: Lippincott Williams and Wilkins, 2005.

Botvin, G. J., and T. A. Wills. "Personal and Social Skills Training: Cognitive-Behavioral Approaches to Substance Abuse Prevention." In *Prevention Research: Deterring Drug Abuse Among Children and Adolescents.* NIDA Research Monograph No. 64. Rockville, MD: National Institute on Drug Abuse, 1985.

Cal Poly (California Polytechnic State University). "Sobering Statistics." Health and Counseling Services. 2016.

Available http://www.hcs.calpoly.edu/pulse/students/alc_awareness/statistics

Carroll, E. "Notes on the Epidemiology of Inhalants." In *Review of Inhalants*, edited by C. W. Sharp and M. L. Brehm. NIDA Research Monograph No. 15. Washington, DC: National Institute on Drug Abuse, 1977.

Center for Behavioral Health Statistics and Quality (CBHSQ). *Behavioral Health Trends in the United States: Results from the 2014 National Survey on Drug Use and Health.* HHS Pub. No. SMA 15-4927, NSDUH Series H-50. Rockville, MD: Substance Abuse and Mental Health Services Administration, 2015.

Center for Prevention Research and Development (CPRD). *Research Based Approaches in the Community Domain.* Champaign: University of Illinois, 2000.

Centers for Disease Control and Prevention (CDC). "Injury Prevention and Control: The Social-Ecological Model: A Framework for Prevention." 9 September 2009. Available http://www.cdc.gov/violenceprevention/overview/social-ecologicalmodel.html

Claire, J. "Drug Prevention Programmes in Schools: What Is the Evidence?" Mentor, The Drug and Alcohol Protection Agency. 2013. Available http://www.mentoruk.org.uk/wp-content/uploads/2011/11/Prevention-Evidence-Paper-Nov-11-Final.pdf

Clayton, R. R., R. Cattarello, L. E. Cay, and K. P. Walden. "Persuasive Communication and Drug Prevention: An Evaluation of the D.A.R.E. Program." In *Persuasive Communication and Drug Abuse Prevention*, edited by L. Donohew, H. Sypepher, and W. Bukowski, 83–107. Hillsdale, NJ: Erlbaum, 1991.

Cleveland, M. J; L. M. Collins; S. T. Lanza, M. T. Greenberg, and M. E. Feinberg. "Does Individual Risk Moderate the Effect of Contextual-Level Protective Factors? A Latent Class Analysis of Substance Use." *Journal of Prevention and Intervention in the Community* 38 (July 2010):213-228.

Cohen, A. Y. "The Journey Beyond Trips: Alternatives to Drugs." *Journal of Psychedelic Drugs* 3 (Spring 1971): 7–14.

Common Sense for Drug Policy. "D.A.R.E. Admits Failure." 9 July 2009. Available http://www.csdp.org/news/news/darerevised.htm

Community Anti-Drug Coalition of America (CADCA). *Drug Free Communities Support Program Grantee Roadmap to Success: Training and Technical Assistance Support System.* Alexandria, VA: CADCA National Coalition Institute, 2010.

Drug Policy Alliance (DPA). "Reducing Harm: Treatment and Beyond." 2013. Available http://www.drugpolicy.org/harm-reduction

D.A.R.E. "Teaching Students Decision Making for Safe & Healthy Living." Los Angeles: D.A.R.E America, 22 October 2016. Available http://www.dare.org/

Eckholm, E. "Governments' Drug-Abuse Costs Hit $468 Billion Study Says." *New York Times.* (28 May 2009). Available http://www.nytimes.com/2009/05/28/us/28addiction.html?_r=0

Ennett, S. T., N. S. Tobler, C. L. Ringwalt, and R. L. Flewelling. "How Effective Is Drug Abuse Resistance Education? A Meta-analysis of Project D.A.R.E. Outcome Evaluations." *American Journal of Public Health* 84 (1994): 1394–1401.

European Monitoring Centre ford Drugs and Drug Addiction (EMCDDA). "Step 2a: Models and Theories." Lisbon, Portugal: European Monitoring Centre for Drugs and Drug Addiction, 22 July 2010.

Forman, S. G., and J. A. Linney. "School-Based Prevention of Adolescent Substance Abuse: Programs, Implementation and Future Direction." *School Psychology Review* 17 (1988): 550–558.

Franco, C. "Drug Courts: Background, Effectiveness, and Policy Issues for Congress." Congressional Research Service. Washington, DC: Government Printing Office, 12 October 2010. Available http://www.fas.org/sgp/crs/misc/R41448.pdf

Goldkamp, J. *Justice and Treatment Innovation: The Drug Court Movement.* Washington, DC: National Institute of Justice and the State Justice Institute, 1993.

Gonzalez, G. M., and V. V. Clement, eds. *Preventing Substance Abuse.* U.S. Department of Education. Washington, DC: U.S. Government Printing Office, 1994.

Gopelrud, E. N., ed. *Preventing Adolescent Drug Use: From Theory to Practice.* OSAP Monograph No. 8, DHHS Pub. No. (ADM) 91–1725. Rockville, MD: Office of Substance Abuse Prevention, 1991.

Hansen, W. B. "A Social Ecology Theory of Alcohol and Drug Use Prevention Among College and University Students." In *Designing Alcohol and Other Drug Prevention Programs in Higher Education.* Newton, MA: Higher Education Center for Alcohol and Other Drug Prevention, U.S. Department of Education, 1997.

Harm Reduction Coalition. "Principles of Harm Reduction." n.d. Available http://harmreduction.org/about-us/principles-of-harm-reduction/

Harm Reduction Psychotherapy and Training Associates (HRPTA). "What Is Harm Reduction Psychotherapy?" n.d. Available http://www.harmreductioncounseling.com/therapy.html

Holstein, M. E., W. E. Cohen, and P. Steinbroner. *A Matter of Balance: Personal Strategies for Alcohol and Other Drugs.* Ashland, OR: CNS Productions, 1995.

Horowitz, H. L. *Campus Life.* New York: Knopf, 1987.

Jernigan, D., and J. O'Hara. "Alcohol Advertising and Promotion." In *Reducing Underage Drinking: A Collective Responsibility,* edited by R. J. Bonnie and M. E. O'Connell, 232–247. Washington, DC: National Academies Press, 2004.

King, R. S., and J. Pasquarella. *Drug Courts: A Review of the Evidence.* Washington, DC: The Sentencing Project, 2009. Available http://www.sentencingproject.org/doc/dp_drugcourts.pdf

Kondrat, M. E. "Person-in-Environment." Oxford Bibliographies. 29 April 2015. Available http://www.oxfordbibliographies.com/view/document/obo-9780195389678/obo-9780195389678-0092.xml

Koss, M. P., C. A. Gidycz, and R. Wisniewski. "The Scope of Rape: Incidence and Prevalence of Sexual Aggression and Victimization in a National Sample of Higher Education Students." *Journal of Consulting and Clinical Psychology* 34 (1987): 186–196.

Larimer, M. E., J. R. Kilmer, and C. M. Lee. "College Student Drug Prevention: A Review of Individually-Oriented Prevention Strategies." *Journal of Drug Issues* 35 (April 2005): 431–456.

Legal Action Center. "Confronting an Epidemic: The Case for Eliminating Barriers to Medication-Assisted Treatment of Heroin and Opioid Addiction." New York: Legal Action Center, 2016.

Marlowe, D. B. *Research Update on Adult Drug Courts.* Alexandria, VA: National Association of Drug Court Professionals (NADCP), December 2010. Available http://www.nadcp.org/sites/default/files/nadcp/Research%20Update%20on%20Adult%20Drug%20Courts%20-%20NADCP_1.pdf

McIntyre, K., D. White, and R. Yoast. *Resilience Among High-Risk Youth.* Madison: University of Wisconsin, 1990.

National Association of Drug Court Professionals (NADCP). "Drug Courts Work." 2011a. Available http://www.nadcp.org/learn/drug-courts-work

National Association of Drug Court Professionals (NADCP). "Types of Drug Courts." 2011b. Available http://www.nadcp.org/learn/what-are-drug-courts/models

National Association of Drug Court Professionals (NADCP). "What Are Drug Courts?" 2011c. Available http://www.nadcp.org/learn/what-are-drug-courts

National Association of Student Personnel Administrators (NASPA)–Student Affairs Administrators in Higher Education. "Bacchus Initiatives of NASPA: History." 2016a. Available https://www.naspa.org/constituent-groups/groups/bacchus-initiatives/history

National Association of Student Personnel Administrators (NASPA)–Student Affairs Administrators in Higher Education. "About NASPA: Advancing Leadership, Shaping Change." 2016b. Available https://www.naspa.org/

National Drug Court Resource Center (NDCRC). "How Many Drug Courts Are There?" 30 June 2014. Available http://www.ndcrc.org/content/how-many-drug-courts-are-there

National Institute of Justice (NIJ). "Drug Courts." 13 May 2016. Available http://www.nij.gov/topics/courts/drug-courts/Pages/welcome.aspx

National Institute on Drug Abuse (NIDA). "Risk and Protective Factors in Drug Abuse Prevention." *NIDA Notes* 16 (February 2002).

National Institute on Drug Abuse. "Preventing Drug use among Children and Adolescents (In Brief)." Bethesda, MD: *NIDA Notes*, October 2003. Available https://www.drugabuse.gov/publications/preventing-drug-abuse-among-children-adolescents/chapter-1-risk-factors-protective-factors/what-are-risk-factors

National Institute on Drug Abuse (NIDA). *Drug Abuse Prevention: Drug Abuse Is a Preventable Behavior.* Bethesda, MD: National Institutes of Health (NIH), March 2007.

National Institute on Drug Abuse (NIDA). *Principles of Drug Addiction Treatment: A Research-Based Guide*, 3rd ed. Bethesda, MD: National Institute on Drug Abuse and National Institutes of Health, December 2012.

National Institute on Drug Abuse (NIDA). "DrugFacts: Lessons from Prevention Research." March 2014. Available https://www.drugabuse.gov/publications/drugfacts/lessons-prevention-research

National Institutes of Health (NIH) and National Institute on Drug Abuse (NIDA). *Drug Abuse and Drug Abuse Research.* Washington, DC: U.S. Government Printing Office, 1998.

Norman, E. "Personal Factors Related to Substance Misuse: Risk Abatement and/or Resiliency Enhancement." In *Substance Abuse in Adolescence*, edited by T. P. Gulotta, G. R. Adams, and R. Montemayor, 47–56. Thousand Oaks, CA: Sage Publications, 1994.

Office of Justice Programs (OJP), Drug Court Clearinghouse and Technical Assistance Project. *Summary of Drug Court Activity by State and County.* Washington, DC: U.S. Government Printing Office, 10 January 2000.

Office of National Drug Control Policy (ONDCP). *National Drug Control Strategy: The White House, February 2007.* Washington, DC: U.S. Government Printing Office, 2007.

Perkins, H. W. "Confronting Misperceptions of Peer Use Norms Among College Students: An Alternative Approach for Alcohol and Other Drug Education Programs." In *The Higher Education Leaders/Peers Network Peer Prevention Program Resource Manual*, 18–32. Washington, DC: Texas Christian University, U.S. Department of Education (FIPSE), 1991.

Perkins, H. W. "College Student Misperceptions of Alcohol and Other Drug Norms Among Peers: Exploring Causes, Consequences, and Implications for Prevention Programs." In *Designing Alcohol and Other Drug Prevention Programs in Higher Education.* Newton, MA: U.S. Department of Education, Higher Education Center for Alcohol and Other Drug Prevention, 1997.

Perkins, H. W., and A. D. Berkowitz. "Perceiving the Community Norms of Alcohol Use Among Students: Some Research Implications for Campus Alcohol Education Programming." *International Journal of the Addictions* 21 (1986): 861–976.

Plant, M., R. Robertson, M. Plant, and P. Miller. *Drug Nation: Patterns, Problems, Panics, and Politics.* Oxford, UK: Oxford University Press, 2011.

ProCon.org. "Is the D.A.R.E. Program Good for America's Kids (K–12)." 6 November 2013. Available http://dare.procon.org/#Background

Robertson, E. B., S. L. David, S. A. Rao, and National Institute on Drug Abuse (NIDA). *Preventing Drug Use Among Children and Adolescents*, 2nd ed. Bethesda, MD: U.S. Department of Health and Human Services, 2003.

Rosenbaum, D. P., and S. Hanson. *Assessing the Effects of School-Based Drug Education; a Six-Year Multi-level Analysis of Project D.A.R.E.* Chicago: University of Illinois at Chicago, Department of Criminal Justice and Center for Research in Law and Justice, 6 April 1998.

Ryan, B. E., T. Colthurst, and L. Segars. *College Alcohol Risk Assessment Guide.* San Diego: UCSD Extension, University of California at San Diego, 1995.

Sherin, K. M., and B. Mahoney. *Treatment Drug Courts: Integrating Substance Abuse Treatment with Legal Case Processing.* Rockville, MD: U.S. Department of Health and Human Services, 1996.

Shiffman, S., and T. A. Wills, eds. *Coping and Substance Abuse.* New York: Academic Press, 1987.

Siegel, R. K. *Intoxication: The University Drive for Mind-Altering Substances.* Rochester, VT: Park Street Press, 2005

Silver Gate Group and Robert Wood Johnson Foundation. *Prevention 2000: Moving Effective Prevention Programs into Practice.* Princeton, NJ: Robert Wood Johnson Foundation, 2001.

Sloboda, Z., and S. L. David. *Preventing Drug Use Among Children and Adolescents: A Research-Based Guide.* Washington, DC: National Institute on Drug Abuse and National Institutes of Health, April 1999.

Southwestern Illinois College (SWIC) BACCHUS. "BACCHUS: A Healthy Lifestyles Club for College Students." WordPress.com, n.d. Available https://southwesternillinoiscollegebacchus.wordpress.com/

StateUniversity.com. "College and University Blog: Big Business—Alcohol Advertising and College Sports." 2011. Available http://www.stateuniversity.com/blog/permalink/Alcohol-Advertising-and-College-Sports.html

Substance Abuse and Mental Health Services Administration (SAMHSA). *Results from the 2011 National Survey on Drug Use and Health: Summary of National Findings.* NSDUH Series H-44, HHS Pub. No. (SMA) 12-4713. Rockville, MD: Substance Abuse and Mental Health Services Administration, 2012.

Substance Abuse and Mental Health Services Administration (SAMHSA). *Results from the 2013 National Survey on Drug Use and Health: Summary of National Findings.*

NSDUH Series H-48, HHS Pub. No. (SMA) 14-4863. Rockville, MD: Substance Abuse and Mental Health Services Administration, 2014.

Tinzmann, M. B., and J. Hixson. *What Does Research Say About Prevention?* Oak Brook, IL: North Central Regional Educational Laboratory, 1992.

United Nations Office on Drugs and Crime (UNODC). "Prevention of Drug Use." 2011. Available http://www.unodc.org/unodc/en/prevention/index.html

U.S. Department of Education. *Archived Information: Current Knowledge in Prevention of Alcohol and Other Drug Abuse,* edited by G.M. Gonzalez and V. V. Clement. Washington, DC: Government Printing Office, 1994.

U.S. Department of Education, Office. *Alcohol and Other Drug prevention on College Campuses: Model Programs.* Washington, DC: U.S. Department of Education, Office of Safe and Drug-Free Schools, 2008.

U.S. Government Accountability Office (GAO). *Youth Illicit Drug Use Prevention: D.A.R.E. Long-Term Evaluation and Federal Efforts to Identify Effective Programs.* GAO-03-172R. Washington, DC: GAO, 15 January 2003.

Vogt, A. "Now Many 'Just Say No' to D.A.R.E." *Chicago Tribune.* (26 January 2003), 1, 3.

Weil, A. *The Natural Mind.* Boston: Houghton Mifflin, 1972.

Weil, A. *The Natural Mind: A Revolutionary Approach to the Drug Problem.* New York: Houghton Mifflin Company, 2004.

Westermeyer, R. W. "Reducing Harm: A Very Good Idea." n.d. Available http://www.fullspectrumrecovery.com/fullspec/images/stories/pdfs/reducing%20harm.pdf

Wilson, M., and S. Wilson, eds. *Drugs in American Life,* Vol. 1. New York: Wilson, 1975.

Wilson, R. W., and C. A. Kolander. *Drug Abuse Prevention: A School and Community Partnership,* 3rd ed. Burlington, MA: Jones & Bartlett Learning, 2011.

Zeese, K. B., and P. M. Lewin. *The Effective Drug Control Strategy.* Washington, DC: Network of Reform Group and the National Coalition for Effective Drug Policies, 1998. Available http://www.csdp.org/edcs/edc.htm

Zweig, J. M. "Description of the Drug Court Sites in the Multi-Site Adult Drug Court Evaluation." In *The Multi-Site Adult Drug Court Evaluation: The Drug Court Experience,* edited by S. B. Rossman, J. M. Zweig, D. Kralstein, K. Henry, P. M. Downey, and C. Lindquist, 8–23. Washington, DC: Urban Institute Justice Policy Center, 2011.

© vm/iStockphoto.com.

CHAPTER 18

Treating Drug Dependence

Did You Know?

▶ A variety of approaches to drug addiction treatment exist, including behavioral and pharmacological therapies.

▶ No single treatment approach is appropriate for all individuals.

▶ Relapse rates for addiction resemble those of other chronic diseases, such as diabetes, hypertension, and asthma.

▶ Comorbidity between drug addiction and other mental illnesses is common.

Learning Objectives

On completing this chapter you should be able to:

❯ Discuss assessment of addiction severity and readiness to change.

❯ List several principles that characterize effective drug treatment.

❯ Discuss the role of comorbidity in substance abuse and its treatment.

❯ Discuss pharmacological and behavioral strategies to treat addiction.

❯ Describe the Mental Health Parity and Addiction Equity Act.

❯ Discuss SBIRT (Screening, Brief Intervention, and Referral to Treatment).

Treatment of Addiction

Individuals who are addicted to drugs come from all walks of life. Many suffer from occupational, social, psychiatric, or other medical problems that can make their addictions difficult to treat. Even in the absence of such complicating issues the severity of addictions varies widely. It is essential to match treatment with the needs of the client. Further, it is valuable to intervene at the earliest possible stage of addiction with the least restrictive form of appropriate treatment. To accomplish this, it is important that treatment providers determine the severity of addiction as well as the readiness of an individual to change his or her behavior.

Assessing Addiction Severity and Readiness to Change

Addiction severity can be determined in many ways, including the administration of standardized questionnaires. Of these, the Addiction Severity Index (ASI) is among the most widely used assessment instruments in the field of addiction (McLellan et al. 1980, 1985, 1992). The ASI is one of the most reliable and valid measurements of the magnitude and characteristics of client problems. It focuses on possible problems in six areas: medical status, employment and support, alcohol and drug use, legal status, family and social relationships, and psychiatric status. The ASI provides information that can be used to identify and prioritize which problem areas are most significant and require prompt attention.

When assessing and prioritizing problems, one model of individual development that is often considered is Maslow's hierarchy of needs. This theory postulates that individuals are motivated by unsatisfied needs and that lower fundamental needs must be met before higher needs can be satisfied. These primary needs include food, drink, warmth, sleep, and shelter. These can be extended in the case of substance abusers to problems such as (1) unidentified or inappropriately managed health problems, (2) medication adherence issues (particularly in the presence of co-occurring mental or physical health disorders), and (3) physical alterations due to drug and/or alcohol dependence (Stilen et al. 2007). Once these fundamental needs are addressed, a second level of needs involving security and safety can be addressed.

Simplistically, these include such issues as stability, order, law, and limits. Examples of common problem areas reflecting this level include inability for self-care, management of mental health issues, personal/public safety issues, and legal issues. If these needs are not met, individuals receiving substance abuse treatment cannot move to higher levels wherein love and belonging, self-esteem, and self-actualization (i.e., fulfilling personal potential) can be attained (Stilen et al. 2007).

As important as assessing addiction severity and prioritizing problem areas on which to focus is consideration of a person's readiness to change his or her abuse behavior. Pioneering work by DiClemente and Prochaska (1998) revealed that behavioral change is a many-stage process rather than a singular event. The stages described by DiClemente and Prochaska include the following:

- *Precontemplation*: An individual does not want to change or is not considering changing his or her behavior. The latter may be because he or she does not see a need for change.
- *Contemplation*: A person is considering changing his or her behavior.
- *Preparation*: A person is committed to a strategy for change.
- *Action*: A person is actively attempting to change.
- *Maintenance*: A person has changed his or her behavior. In order to complete the process of change, this behavior must become a part of his or her lifestyle.

Determining the stage of change at which an individual finds him- or herself can help providers select the best treatment plan to address a client's needs. This may help prevent the individual from refusing to accept all or parts of the treatment plan. Screening, Brief Intervention, and Referral to Treatment (SBIRT) can be an important first step towards identifying individuals who are in need of assistance (see "Here and Now: Screening, Brief Intervention, and Referral to Treatment (SBIRT)").

Principles of Treatment

A variety of approaches to drug addiction treatment exist. Some include behavioral therapy, such as counseling, psychotherapy, or cognitive therapy. Others include medications ranging from treatment medications (e.g., methadone, buprenorphine, nicotine patches, nicotine gum) to those intended to treat co-occurring mental disorders

HERE AND NOW

Screening, Brief Intervention, and Referral to Treatment (SBIRT)

Screening, Brief Intervention, and Referral to Treatment (SBIRT) is an evidence-based practice used to identify, reduce, and prevent problematic use, abuse, and dependence on alcohol and illicit drugs. SBIRT arose as a consequence of an Institute of Medicine report, *Broadening the Base of Treatment for Alcohol Problems*, that recommended community-based screening for health risk behaviors. The screening can be conducted in any healthcare setting, including primary care centers, hospital emergency rooms, trauma centers, and other community settings. It can also be tailored for adolescents or adults. The overall goal of the SBIRT is to provide opportunities for early intervention with at-risk substance users before more severe consequences occur.

SBIRT consists of three main components:

- *Screening*: A patient is assessed by a healthcare provider for risky substance use behaviors using standardized screening tools. The goal is to quickly assesses the severity of substance use and identify the appropriate level of treatment.

- *Brief Intervention*: A patient demonstrating risky substance use behaviors is engaged by a healthcare provider in short conversation, and is provided feedback and advice. The focus is on increasing insight and awareness regarding substance use and motivation toward behavioral change.

- *Referral to Treatment*: A patient is referred to brief therapy or additional treatment as appropriate.

Studies have demonstrated that SBIRT reduces healthcare costs, trauma, and the severity of drug and alcohol abuse.

Data from Institute of Medicine (IOM). *Broadening the Base of Treatment for Alcohol Problems*. Washington DC: National Academies Press; 1990; Substance Abuse and Mental Health Services Administration (SAMHSA). "SBIRT: Screening, Brief Intervention and Referral to Treatment." 2011. Available http://www.integration.samhsa.gov/clinical-practice/SBIRT; Substance Abuse and Mental Health Services Administration (SAMHSA). "SBIRT Screening, Brief Intervention and Referral to Treatment." 2016. Available http://www.samhsa.gov/sbirt; Substance Abuse and Mental Health Services Administration (SAMHSA). "SBIRT: Screening, Brief Intervention, and Referral to Treatment—Opportunities for Implementation and Points for Consideration." n.d. Available http://www.integration.samhsa.gov/sbirt_issue_brief.pdf

(e.g., antidepressants, mood stabilizers). The most successful drug abuse treatment programs typically provide a combination of therapies and other services to meet the needs of the individual abuser. They incorporate adequate assessment of treatment needs required not only as a direct consequence of the physiological and psychological effects of the drug but also due to indirect problems, such as the need for housing, legal and financial issues, poor education or vocational skills, or lack of family/child-care services. Such needs often are shaped by the gender, age, race, culture, and sexual orientation of the abuser.

Because drug addiction is generally a chronic disorder characterized by occasional relapses, a one-time, short-term treatment is often inadequate. Further, many individuals who enter treatment drop out before receiving all of its benefits; hence, and again, successful treatment often requires more than one treatment exposure. Of note, relapse rates for addiction resemble those of other chronic diseases, such as asthma, diabetes, and hypertension (National Institute on Drug Abuse [NIDA] 2012). **Figure 18.1** illustrates these statistics.

Research has shown that good outcomes are contingent on adequate duration of treatment. Generally, for outpatient or residential treatment, participation for fewer than 90 days is of limited effectiveness; treatments lasting significantly longer are needed (NIDA 2012). For methadone maintenance, 12 months of treatment often is the minimum needed, and some individuals who are

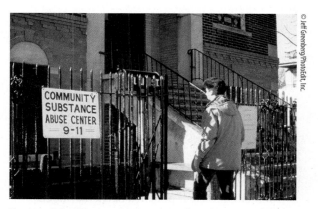

Treatment facilities provide a variety of services to people dealing with substance abuse.

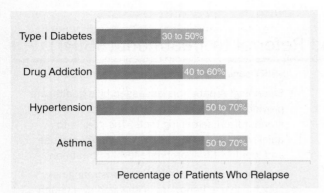

FIGURE 18.1 Relapse rates for addiction resemble those of other chronic diseases, such as asthma, diabetes, and hypertension (NIDA, 2012).

addicted to opiates require extended treatment lasting several years (NIDA 2012).

To best target treatment for an individual, the type and goals of treatment must be determined. Consideration must be given to the fact that both largely depend on the view one holds of addiction. For example, if the disease model is applied to addiction, total abstinence is generally required because this model views drug abuse as a biological condition that is largely uncontrollable. On the other hand, if responsible drug use is the goal, then occasional and moderate drug use can be the intended end result.

Effective treatment allows addicts to stop abusing drugs, returns them to a drug-free state of existence, and transforms them into employable and productive members of society. Measures of effectiveness typically include assessing levels of family functioning, employability, criminal behavior, and medical condition.

As summarized in the following list, the National Institute on Drug Abuse has delineated 13 overarching principles that characterize effective addiction treatment (NIDA 2012):

1. *Addiction is a complex but treatable disease that affects brain function and behavior.* Drugs of abuse can alter brain function and structure, resulting in changes that persist long after drug use has ended. This may explain why drug abusers are at risk for relapse even after extended periods of abstinence and regardless of potentially destructive consequences.

2. *No single treatment is appropriate for all individuals.* Treatment settings and services must be matched to each person's particular needs.

3. *Treatment needs to be readily available.* Individuals who are addicted to drugs are often uncertain about whether to seek treatment. Hence, it is

important that services be available as soon as an individual makes the decision to seek help. Treatment opportunities can be lost if such services are not immediately and readily accessible.

4. *Effective treatment attends to multiple needs of the individual, not just his or her drug use.* To be effective, treatment must address not only the individual's drug use but also any related medical, psychological, social, vocational, and legal problems. It is also important that an individual's age, ethnicity, gender, and culture be considered when implementing treatment.

5. *Remaining in treatment for an adequate period is critical for treatment effectiveness.* The appropriate duration of treatment depends on each person's individual problems and needs. As noted earlier, research indicates that, for many, at least 3 months in treatment is needed.

6. *Behavioral therapies, including individual, family, or group counseling, are the most commonly used forms of drug abuse treatment.* Such therapies often have different emphases. These may involve improving problem-solving skills, providing incentives for abstinence, addressing motivation to change, and building skills to resist drug use and facilitating improved interpersonal relationships.

7. *Medications are an important element of treatment for many patients, especially when combined with counseling and other behavioral therapies.* Specific pharmacological therapies for treating substance abusers are discussed later in this chapter.

8. *An individual's treatment and services plan must be assessed continually and modified as necessary to ensure it meets his or her changing needs.* In addition to counseling, an individual may require various combinations of medical services, family therapy, vocational rehabilitation, and/or social and legal services.

9. *Many drug-addicted individuals also have other mental disorders.* Because drug abuse and addiction often co-occur with other mental illnesses (see the discussion of comorbidity later in this chapter), patients presenting with one condition should be evaluated for the other(s). Treatment should address each identified issue, including the use of medications, if warranted.

10. *Medically assisted detoxification is only the first stage of addiction treatment and, by itself, does little to change long-term drug use.* Medical detoxification is the process of safely managing the acute physical symptoms of withdrawal associated with stopping drug use. It can be an important first step toward abstinence but

alone is rarely sufficient to help individuals achieve long-term abstinence.

11. *Treatment does not need to be voluntary to be effective.* Sanctions or enticements in the family, criminal justice system, or employment settings can facilitate treatment entry and increase both retention rates and success of drug treatment interventions.

12. *Drug use during treatment must be monitored continuously, as lapses during treatment do occur.* The knowledge that an individual's drug use is being monitored can be a powerful incentive to withstand urges to abuse drugs. Monitoring also provides an early indication of a return to drug use, signaling a possible need to adjust treatment plans.

13. *Treatment programs should test patients for the presence of HIV/AIDS, hepatitis B and C, tuberculosis, and other infectious diseases, as well as provide targeted risk-reduction counseling, linking patients to treatment if necessary.*

Many treatment programs apply one or more of these listed principles as part of their therapeutic strategy.

Of note, the age of the substance abuser is an important consideration when designing treatment. This includes both the age of first exposure to drugs and the age at which treatment is initiated. Research indicates that from birth through early adulthood the brain undergoes a prolonged process of development during which a behavioral shift occurs such that actions go from being more impulsive to more reflective and reasoned. Further, the brain areas most closely associated with judgment, decision making, and self-control undergo a period of rapid development during adolescence (NIDA 2012). Thus, adolescent drug abusers have unique needs that must be considered in developing a treatment approach to their addictions.

Gender-related considerations are also of importance in treating substance abuse. Treatment should attend not only to biological distinctions between genders but also to the social and environmental factors that can differentially affect motivations for drug use, effectiveness of and reasons for seeking treatment, environments where treatment is obtained, and consequences of not receiving treatment. For example, many life circumstances predominate in women as a group that may require specialized treatment approaches. These can, for example, include sexual and physical trauma followed by posttraumatic stress disorder (PTSD). Research indicates that these are more common in women than in men seeking treatment (NIDA 2012). Other factors that can be (although are not necessarily) unique to women include issues involving financial independence, pregnancy, and childcare. Each circumstance must be considered in developing a treatment plan.

Criminal justice–involved substance abusers are another population that often benefits from specialized treatment approaches. According to NIDA (2012), combining criminal justice sanctions with substance abuse treatment can diminish both subsequent abuse and associated crimes. Initiating treatment in prison and continuing that same treatment upon release also results in less drug use and less criminal behavior. Further, individuals under legal coercion tend to remain in treatment longer and do as well as or better than those who are not experiencing legal pressure (NIDA 2012).

Unfortunately, adequate treatment for criminal justice–involved individuals is often unavailable. Further, there are often few choices in the types of services provided. According to NIDA (2014), treatment that is of insufficient quality or not well suited to the needs of offenders may not yield significant reductions in drug use and recidivism. Untreated offenders are more likely than treated offenders to relapse to drug abuse and return to criminal behavior.

Therapeutic work environments that provide employment for abstinent drug-abusing individuals both improve life skills and promote a continued drug-free lifestyle. Further, some workplaces sponsor employee assistance programs that offer short-term assistance and/or counseling so as to link employees with substance abuse problems to local treatment resources.

Of note, several factors influence retention in treatment programs. These can include (1) individual motivation to change drug-using behavior, (2) degree of support from family and friends, and (3) pressure from employers, the criminal justice system, and/or extensions of the court (e.g., child protective services). It also is important for treatment providers to ensure a transition to continuing care or aftercare following a patient's completion of formal treatment (NIDA 2012).

Comorbidity

Drug addiction is a complicated condition that often involves changes in the structure and function of specific parts of the brain. Changes in the structure and function of regions of the brain affected by drug addiction can also occur in other mental illnesses, such as anxiety, psychosis, and depression. Of note, overlapping factors, including genetic vulnerabilities, trauma, stress, and/or underlying brain abnormalities, can contribute to both substance abuse disorders and other mental illnesses.

Comorbidity is a condition in which two or more illnesses occur in the same person, simultaneously or sequentially. This term also suggests interactions between the illnesses that affect the course and prognosis of both (NIDA 2010). The *Diagnostic and Statistical Manual of Mental Disorders (DSM)* is a widely used authority for diagnosing such mental health problems (see "Here and Now: Tools for Diagnosis").

Comorbidity between drug addiction and mental illnesses is common. For example, individuals diagnosed with anxiety or mood disorders are approximately twice as likely to also suffer from drug abuse or dependence. This has also been demonstrated for individuals diagnosed with conduct disorder or antisocial personality. Similarly, individuals diagnosed with substance disorders are approximately twice as likely to also suffer from anxiety and mood disorders (NIDA 2010).

Mental illnesses can sometimes lead to substance abuse and addiction in that individuals sometimes abuse drugs in order to self-medicate an underlying medical condition (see "Here and Now: Schizophrenia and Cigarette Smoking: Self-Medication or Shared Brain Circuitry?"). However, the high incidence of comorbidity between substance abuse disorders and other mental illnesses does not mean that one necessarily caused the other. In fact, a causal relationship is difficult to establish for multiple reasons, including the fact that drugs of abuse can cause abusers to display

one or more symptoms of, without actually having, another mental illness. Further, some symptoms of either a substance abuse disorder or another mental illness may not be recognized until the disease has progressed considerably, and by then it often is difficult to retrospectively determine the precise onset of these disorders (for further discussion, see NIDA 2010).

Effective treatment of individuals with comorbid substance abuse and mental illnesses requires accurate diagnosis of both conditions. Individuals beginning treatment for substance abuse and/or addiction need to be screened for mental illnesses, and vice versa. Accurate diagnosis may require monitoring after a period of abstinence in order to distinguish the effects of substance intoxication or withdrawal from the symptoms of comorbid mental disorders. According to NIDA (2010), several fundamental barriers impede treatment of comorbid disorders. Among these, psychiatrists and physicians are the most common treatment providers for mental illness, whereas a mix of professionals with varying backgrounds and credentials provides substance abuse treatment. Often, neither background is broad enough to address the full range of problems presented by patients. In addition, a bias exists in some substance abuse treatment facilities against using any pharmacological intervention, including those necessary to treat serious mental illnesses such as depression. Many substance abuse treatment programs do not employ professionals qualified to prescribe, dispense, and monitor medications. Finally, many individuals needing treatment are in the criminal

HERE AND NOW

Tools for Diagnosis

The *Diagnostic and Statistical Manual of Mental Disorders (DSM)* serves as a highly accepted and widely used authority for the diagnosis of psychiatric disorders. In May 2013, its fifth edition (*DSM-5*) was made available. Important changes from the previous manual include a revision of the chapter entitled "Substance-Related and Addictive Disorders." In particular, according to the American Psychiatric Association (APA 2013; the publisher of *DSM-5*), "substance use disorder in *DSM-5* combines the *DSM-IV* categories of substance abuse and substance dependence

into a single disorder measured on a continuum from mild to severe." (APA 2013). Specific substances are described as separate use disorders (e.g., stimulant use disorder, alcohol use disorder, etc.), but "nearly all substances are diagnosed based on the same overarching criteria" (APA 2013).

One important distinguishing feature of *DSM-5* is its clarification of the definition of *dependence*. Many confuse the terms *addiction* and *dependence*, and fail to recognize that dependence is a normal response to a variety of drugs—not simply substances of abuse.

Data from American Psychiatric Association (APA). "Substance-Related and Addictive Disorders." 2013. Available http://www.dsm5.org/Documents /Substance%20Use%20Disorder%20Fact%20Sheet.pdf

HERE AND NOW

Schizophrenia and Cigarette Smoking: Self-Medication or Shared Brain Circuitry?

Schizophrenic patients are more likely to abuse tobacco than the rest of the population. Various self-medication hypotheses have been proposed to explain this association. For example, it has been suggested that the nicotine found in tobacco may help compensate for some of the cognitive deficits experienced by schizophrenic individuals. Further, it may alleviate unpleasant side effects of antipsychotic medications and/or help people deal with the anxiety that can be associated with the illness. According to NIDA (2010), research suggests the possibility of the presence of abnormalities in particular circuits of the brain that may predispose individuals

to schizophrenia, increase the rewarding effects of drugs like nicotine, or reduce an individual's ability to quit smoking. The existence of common mechanisms is consistent with the observation that both nicotine and the medication clozapine (which also acts as nicotine receptors) can improve working memory and attention in an animal model of schizophrenia. Further, clozapine is effective in treating individuals with schizophrenia, and it also reduces their smoking levels. Thus, understanding how and why patients with schizophrenia use nicotine may assist in developing new treatments for both schizophrenia and nicotine dependence.

Data from National Institute on Drug Abuse (NIDA). "Comorbidity: Addiction and Other Mental Illnesses." NIH Publication No. 10-5771. 2010. Available http://www.drugabuse.gov/publications/research-reports/comorbidity-addiction-other-mental-illnesses

justice system, and adequate treatment services for both mental illness and drug use disorders can be largely lacking in these settings.

Drug Addiction Treatment in the United States

According to the Substance Abuse and Mental Health Services Administration (SAMHSA 2014), in 2013, an estimated 21.6 million persons aged 12 or older were classified with substance dependence or abuse in the past year. This represents 8.2% of individuals aged 12 or older. However, in 2013, only 4.1 million persons (1.5% of persons age 12 or older) received treatment for a problem related to the use of alcohol or illicit drugs. Self-help groups were the most frequent location for treatment, followed by outpatient rehabilitation, outpatient mental health centers, inpatient rehabilitation, hospital inpatient, and private doctors' offices.

In 2013, 2.5 million persons aged 12 or older reported receiving treatment for alcohol use during their most recent treatment in the past year; 845,000 persons received treatment for marijuana use; and 746,000 persons received treatment for pain relievers. These compare with estimates of 584,000, 526,000, 461,000, and 376,000 for cocaine, heroin, stimulants, and tranquilizers, respectively (SAMHSA 2014).

Based on SAMHSA data combined from 2010 to 2013, among individuals aged 12 or older who needed but did not receive illicit drug or alcohol use treatment, felt a need for treatment, and made an effort to receive treatment, the most common reported reason for not receiving treatment was a lack of health coverage and inability to afford the cost (37.3%). To address the issue of affordability, legislation such as the Mental Health Parity and Addiction Equity Act (MHPAEA) has been enacted (see "Here and Now: Insurance Coverage and Parity"). Other commonly reported reasons for not entering treatment included (1) a lack of readiness to stop using (24.5%), (2) a possible negative effect on job (6.6%), (3) had health coverage but did not cover treatment or did not cover cost (8.2%), (4) a lack of transportation or inconvenience (8.0%), and (5) did not know where to go for treatment (9.0%) (SAMHSA 2014).

As summarized by NIDA (2015), abuse of tobacco, alcohol, and illicit drugs costs the United States over $700 billion annually in costs related to reduced work productivity, crime, and health care. Treatment can help reduce these costs. Research has demonstrated that treatment is far less expensive than simply incarcerating addicts. For example, the average cost per person for 1 full year of methadone maintenance treatment is approximately $4700, whereas 1 full year of imprisonment costs approximately $24,000 (NIDA 2014).

HERE AND NOW

Insurance Coverage and Parity

In 2008, the Paul Wellstone and Pete Domenici Mental Health Parity and Addiction Equity Act (MHPAEA) was signed into law. The act requires health insurers and group health plans (those with more than 50 insured employees) to provide the same level of benefits for mental health and/or substance use treatment and services that the insurers provide for medical/surgical care. By providing parity, the MHPAEA eliminates the practice of unequal health treatment by providing insurance coverage for substance use and mental health disorders equal to other chronic health conditions such as hypertension and diabetes.

Data from Substance Abuse and Mental Health Services Administration (SAMHSA). "Implementation of the Mental Health Parity and Addiction Equity Act (MHPAEA)." 2016. Available http://www.samhsa.gov/health-financing/implementation-mental-health-parity-addiction-equity-act; U.S. Department of Labor. "2014 Report to Congress: Compliance with the Mental Health Parity and Addiction Equity Act of 2008." 2014. Available http://www.dol.gov/ebsa/publications/mhpaeareporttocongress2014.html

Treatment has other economic benefits to society. For example, it has been estimated that every $1 invested in addiction treatment programs yields a return of between $4 and $7 in reduced drug-related crime, theft, and criminal justice costs. With healthcare savings included, total savings can exceed costs by a ratio of 12:1. These savings do not include important benefits to the individual and society in the form of fewer interpersonal conflicts, improved workplace productivity, and reduced drug-related incidents among individuals who are treated successfully (NIDA 2012).

A number of general therapeutic strategies for treatment have been developed. Some involve pharmacological interventions, such as methadone maintenance or narcotic antagonist treatment. Other programs apply a drug-free approach. Programs can be short or long term and can be individualized or involve group participation. The following is an overview of various treatment approaches. It is important to realize that many treatment programs blend one or more of these approaches as part of their therapeutic strategy.

▮ Historical Approaches

Considerable effort has been expended to find treatments for substance abuse. Several approaches, or at least components of them, continue to be utilized today. These include those discussed in the following sections.

ALCOHOLICS ANONYMOUS

Founded in the United States in the mid-1930s, Alcoholics Anonymous (AA) is now an international organization. The desire to stop drinking is the sole criterion required to join. The original founders of AA were strongly influenced by a religious movement known as the Oxford Group. AA outlines 12 successive measures, referred to as *steps*, that alcoholics should accomplish during the recovery process (Alcoholics Anonymous 2002). These steps include admitting that the person addicted to alcohol has no power over the drug. He or she must also believe in a greater power that can help him or her overcome shortcomings. Individuals must make initial and ongoing assessments of their life and admit their wrongs. In addition, individuals must make amends to those whom they have adversely affected, except in situations where such actions could harm others.

AA has two types of meetings: open and closed. **Open meetings** are open to anyone who has an interest in attending and witnessing these meetings, and they last approximately 45 minutes to 1 hour. **Closed meetings** are for alcoholics who have a serious desire to completely stop drinking. These meetings are not open to viewers or "shoppers." At closed meetings, recovering alcoholics address, through testimonials, how alcohol has diminished their quality of life.

Some outgrowths of AA include Al-Anon, Adult Children of Alcoholics, and Alateen. These are parallel organizations supporting AA. Al-Anon is for spouses and other close relatives of alcoholics, and Alateen is exclusively for teenagers whose lives have been affected by someone else's alcoholism. Both

KEY TERMS

open meetings
Alcoholics Anonymous meetings to which anyone having an interest in attending and witnessing is invited

closed meetings
Alcoholics Anonymous meetings to which only alcoholics having a serious desire to completely stop drinking are invited

Common alcohol abuse-related problems are shared at AA meetings.

relatives and teen members of alcoholic families learn means and methods for coping with destructive behaviors exhibited by alcoholic members.

REHABILITATION PROGRAMS

The first rehabilitation programs grew out of the work that AA members did with other active alcoholics. The "twelfth stepping" program involves reaching out to others in need and attempting to draw them in. The movement began in the early days of AA when the organization's founder, Bill W., had alcoholics trying to stop drinking or "dry out" living at his house in Brooklyn. At that time, "[his] home was stuffed, from cellar to attic, with alcoholics in all stages of recovery" (Al-Anon 1970). It was a natural transition to opening up "drying out houses" in the 1940s and 1950s.

Also during the 1950s, the **Minnesota model**, an inpatient rehabilitation model, was developed. It combined the AA philosophy with a multidisciplinary treatment team. A treatment plan was used, based on assessment of the individual and prioritization of goals. This model, which borrows from social work practice, is still used in treatment programs. Due to the vagaries of insurance reimbursement in Minnesota, the program lasted 28 days because that was the length covered by insurance; therefore, alcoholism programs traditionally were roughly 1 month long.

■ General Therapeutic Strategies

In addition to the approaches mentioned previously, there are numerous strategies to drug addiction treatment. Some are individualized and some are group based. Although not all treatment programs fit perfectly into any one of these categories, the following provides an overview of the general types of services available (NIDA 1999, 2012).

MEDICAL DETOXIFICATION

As noted previously, medical detoxification is the process of safely managing the acute physical symptoms of withdrawal associated with stopping drug use, typically under the care of a physician. Medications including benzodiazepines and other sedatives are often utilized. Detoxification can be medically necessary because untreated withdrawal from some agents (i.e., alcohol and barbiturates) can be fatal. Although detoxification is sometimes referred to as a distinct treatment modality, it is more appropriately considered a precursor to treatment because it is designed to treat the acute physiological effects of stopping drug use. It is not designed to address the psychological, social, and behavioral problems associated with addiction; thus, it does not typically produce lasting behavioral changes. Detoxification is often followed and is augmented by formal processes of assessment and referral to subsequent drug addiction treatment.

SHORT-TERM RESIDENTIAL TREATMENT

Short-term residential programs were originally designed to treat alcoholism but have been used to treat other forms of addiction. These provide relatively brief treatment based on a modified 12-step approach. The original model consisted of a 3- to 6-week hospital-based, inpatient treatment phase. This was followed by extended outpatient therapy and participation in a self-help group, such as AA, so as to reduce the risk of relapse once an individual leaves the residential setting.

LONG-TERM RESIDENTIAL TREATMENT

Long-term residential treatment provides care 24 hours a day, generally in nonhospital settings. The **therapeutic community (TC)** is the most recognized residential treatment model. TCs focus on the "resocialization" of the individual and use the program's entire community (e.g., staff, other residents) as important treatment components.

KEY TERMS

Minnesota model
a major model in the treatment of alcohol and drug abuse, involving a month-long stay in an inpatient rehabilitation facility, a multidisciplinary treatment team, systematic assessment, and a formal treatment plan with long- and short-term goals

therapeutic community (TC)
inpatient treatment that focuses on the "resocialization" of the individual and uses the program's entire community as important treatment components

Treatment is highly structured and can be confrontational. It focuses on developing personal accountability and responsibility. Activities are designed to assist individuals in examining damaging self-concepts and beliefs and destructive patterns of behavior. An important goal is to implement new, more constructive ways to interact with others. Planned lengths of stay in TCs are often between 6 and 12 months. TCs often offer comprehensive services, which can include employment training on site. Research indicates that TCs can be modified to treat individuals with special needs, including women, adolescents, persons with severe mental disorders, and individuals in the criminal justice system.

A patient receives individual counseling in an alcoholism treatment center.

OUTPATIENT TREATMENT PROGRAMS

The outpatient strategy varies in the intensity and forms of services offered. Such treatment often is more suitable for individuals who have extensive family and/or community support or those who are employed. The intensity of programs varies from those offering simply drug education to those employing higher levels comparable to residential programs in services and effectiveness. Group counseling often is emphasized.

▪ Behavioral Therapies

A number of behavioral therapies have been utilized successfully to help engage individuals in treatment and increase the likelihood for successful outcomes. These are described briefly in **Table 18.1** (for additional discussion, see NIDA 2012).

▪ Pharmacological Strategies

Some treatment strategies employ pharmacological approaches to help patients with their addiction(s). These strategies are based on the properties of the drug to which they are addicted. Examples of these strategies are discussed in the following sections.

METHADONE

Treatment for opiate addicts is often conducted in specialized outpatient settings (e.g., methadone maintenance clinics) using methadone. Methadone is an opioid agonist (i.e., a drug that activates opioid receptors). It is a long-acting synthetic opiate medication administered orally for a sustained period at a dosage sufficient to prevent opiate withdrawal and decrease craving. Patients stabilized on adequate, sustained dosages of methadone can function normally. They can hold jobs, avoid the crime and violence of the street culture,

and reduce their exposure to HIV by stopping or decreasing injection drug use and drug-related, high-risk sexual behavior.

Patients stabilized on opiate agonists can engage more readily in counseling and other behavioral interventions essential to recovery and rehabilitation. According to NIDA (2012), the best, most effective opioid agonist maintenance programs include individual and/or group counseling, as well as provision of or referral to other needed medical, psychological, and social services.

NALOXONE AND NALTREXONE

An antagonist is a compound that suppresses the actions of a drug. Narcotic antagonists have properties that make them important tools in the clinical treatment of narcotic drug dependence (see "Holding the Line: Expanded Options for Treatment of Heroin Addiction"). For instance, the short-acting opioid antagonist naloxone (Narcan) is often used in the emergency treatment of opioid overdoses.

Naltrexone is a long-acting synthetic opioid antagonist used as a treatment for opioid addiction. It is usually prescribed in outpatient medical settings, although treatment initiation often begins after medical detoxification in a residential setting. Individuals must be opioid-free for several days before taking naltrexone in order to avoid withdrawal symptoms. Naltrexone is taken orally for a sustained period and thus prevents all the effects of self-administered opioids. Naltrexone itself has neither subjective effects nor potential for abuse; however, patient noncompliance is a frequent problem, and thus many treatment providers have found naltrexone to be most appropriate for highly motivated, recently detoxified patients, such as professionals, parolees, and probationers, who desire total abstinence because of external

TABLE 18.1 Behavioral Therapies Shown to Be Effective in Addressing Substance Abuse

Therapy	Effective Targets	Description
Cognitive-behavioral therapy (CBT)	Alcohol, marijuana, cocaine, methamphetamine, nicotine	CBT is based on the theory that learning patterns play a critical role in the development of maladaptive behavioral patterns like substance abuse. A central element is anticipating likely problems and enhancing patients' self-control by helping them develop effective coping strategies. Techniques include exploring the positive and negative consequences of continued drug use, self-monitoring to recognize cravings early and identify situations that might put one at risk for use, and developing strategies for coping with cravings and avoiding those high-risk situations.
Contingency management (CM) interventions/ motivational incentives	Alcohol, stimulants, opioids, marijuana, nicotine	CM involves giving patients tangible rewards to reinforce positive behaviors such as abstinence. Rewards can include vouchers to be exchanged for goods or services that are consistent with a drug-free lifestyle or incentives consisting of chances to win prizes. The rewards increase in value with evidence of sustained abstinence (i.e., consecutive negative drug tests), but reset to the lowest value with any evidence of a drug use recurrence.
Community reinforcement approach (CRA) plus vouchers	Alcohol, cocaine, opioids	CRA plus vouchers is an intensive 24-week outpatient therapy for treating people addicted to cocaine and alcohol. It uses a range of recreational, familial, social, and vocational reinforcers, along with material incentives, to make a non-drug-using lifestyle more rewarding than substance use.
Motivational enhancement therapy (MET)	Alcohol, marijuana, nicotine	MET is designed to help individuals resolve ambivalence about engaging in treatment and stopping drug use. The aim is to evoke rapid and internally motivated change, rather than guiding the patient stepwise through the recovery process. MET consists of an initial assessment session, followed by two to four individual treatment sessions. Motivational interviewing principles and coping strategies for high-risk situations are emphasized.
The matrix model	Stimulants	The model provides a framework wherein patients learn about issues critical to addiction and relapse and receive direction and support from a trained therapist. The therapist fosters a positive, encouraging relationship with the patient and uses that relationship to reinforce positive behavior change. Treatment materials draw heavily on tested treatment approaches and include elements of relapse prevention, family and group therapies, drug education, and self-help participation.
12-step facilitation	Alcohol, stimulants, opioids	Twelve-step facilitation therapy is an active engagement strategy guided by three key ideas: (1) acceptance, which includes the realization that drug addiction is a chronic, progressive disease over which one has no control, that life has become unmanageable because of drugs, and that abstinence is the only alternative; (2) surrender, which involves giving oneself over to a higher power, accepting the fellowship and support structure of other recovering addicted individuals, and following the recovery activities laid out by the 12-step program; and (3) active involvement in 12-step meetings and related activities.
Family behavioral therapy (FBT)		FBT is aimed at addressing not only substance use problems, but also other co-occurring problems, such as conduct disorders, child mistreatment, depression, family conflict, and unemployment. FBT utilizes contingency management as well as other behavioral strategies and involves the patient and at least one significant other.

Adapted from National Institute on Drug Abuse (NIDA). *Principles of Drug Addiction Treatment*. Publication No. 12-4180. Washington, DC: National Institutes of Health, April 2012.

HOLDING THE LINE

Expanded Options for Treatment of Heroin Addiction

Until 2000, opiate dependence treatments such as methadone could be dispensed only in a very limited number of clinics that specialize in addiction treatment. As a consequence of the Drug Addiction Treatment Act of 2000, the Food and Drug Administration (FDA) announced approval of Subutex and Suboxone tablets for the treatment of opiate dependence by specially trained physicians. Accordingly, the drugs can be prescribed in an office setting, and therefore are more accessible to patients needing treatment.

Subutex and Suboxone treat opiate addiction by preventing symptoms of withdrawal from heroin and other opiates. Subutex contains only buprenorphine (a partial opioid agonist) and is intended for use at the beginning of treatment for opioid abuse once the individual has undergone detoxification. Suboxone contains both buprenorphine and the opiate antagonist naloxone and is intended to be used in maintenance treatment of opiate addiction. Naloxone has limited effects if administered sublingually, but is effective as an antagonist if administered intravenously. It has been added to Suboxone to guard against intravenous abuse of buprenorphine by individuals who are physically dependent on opiates.

circumstances. Of note, an extended-release preparation of naltrexone (Vivitrol) administered monthly by intramuscular injection has been approved by the Food and Drug Administration (FDA) to treat alcoholism.

BUPRENORPHINE

In 2000, Congress passed the Drug Addiction Treatment Act (DATA). This legislation allowed qualified physicians to prescribe specifically approved Schedule III, IV, and V medications for the treatment of opioid addiction in general medical settings (e.g., primary care offices). Such office-based treatment of opioid addiction is a cost-effective approach that increases the span of treatment and the options available to patients.

Buprenorphine is a **partial agonist** (i.e., a drug that can activate a receptor but is not able to elicit the maximum possible response that is produced by full agonist) at opioid receptors. It reduces or eliminates withdrawal symptoms associated with opioid dependence but generally does not produce the euphoria and sedation caused by other opioids. It is available in two formulations: Subutex, which contains only buprenorphine, and Suboxone, which contains both buprenorphine and naloxone.

KEY TERM

partial agonist
a drug that can activate a receptor but is not able to elicit the maximum possible response that is produced by full agonist

NICOTINE REPLACEMENT THERAPY

Nicotine was the first pharmacological agent approved by the FDA for use in smoking cessation therapy. Nicotine replacement therapies, such as nicotine gum, transdermal patches, nasal sprays, and inhalers, are used to relieve withdrawal symptoms.

Other pharmacological therapies such as varenicline (Chantix) and bupropion (Zyban) are available by prescription to aid in smoking cessation.

DISULFIRAM

Disulfiram (Antabuse) is a drug used for treating alcoholics. This drug causes nausea, vomiting, flushing, and anxiety if an individual consumes alcohol while taking the drug. Thus, this drug is perceived as a deterrent drug.

ACAMPROSATE

Acamprosate (Campral) acts on the glutamate and gamma-aminobutyric acid (GABA) neurotransmitter systems. It is used to treat symptoms of alcohol withdrawal because it purportedly reduces associated symptoms, such as anxiety, insomnia, restlessness, and dysphoria.

TOPIRAMATE

Topiramate is sometimes used off-label to treat alcohol addiction. Its mechanism of action likely involves the glutamate and GABA neurotransmitter systems, although the precise mechanism of action is not known.

LEARNING PORTFOLIO

Discussion Questions

1. Discuss the need to assess addiction severity and readiness to change.
2. List several principles that characterize effective addiction treatment.
3. Discuss the role of comorbidity in substance abuse and its treatment.
4. Describe Alcoholics Anonymous and its approach to assisting individuals addicted to alcohol.
5. Describe several therapeutic strategies to treat addiction.
6. Describe the therapeutic community approach to treating substance abuse.
7. Describe the Mental Health Parity and Addiction Equity Act.
8. Describe Screening, Brief Intervention, and Referral to Treatment (SBIRT).

Summary

1. Individuals who are addicted to drugs come from all walks of life. It is important that treatment providers determine the severity of a person's addiction as well as the readiness of that individual to change his or her behavior.
2. The process of determining addiction severity can be accomplished in many ways, including the administration of standardized questionnaires such as the Addiction Severity Index (ASI). The ASI provides information that can be used to identify and prioritize which problem domains are the most critical and require immediate attention.
3. It is important to assess a person's readiness to change his or her abuse behavior because this can help providers select the best treatment plan to address a client's needs. This may help prevent the individual who is receiving treatment from rejecting all or parts of the treatment plan.
4. Comorbidity is a condition in which two or more illnesses occur in the same person, simultaneously or sequentially. This term also suggests interactions between the illnesses that affect the course and prognosis of both.
5. Changes in the structure and function in regions of the brain affected by drug addiction can also occur in mental illnesses such as anxiety, psychosis, and depression. Overlapping factors, including genetic vulnerabilities, trauma, stress, and/or underlying brain abnormalities, can contribute to both substance abuse disorders and mental illnesses.
6. Effective treatment of individuals with comorbid substance abuse and mental illnesses requires accurate diagnosis of both

Key Terms

closed meetings	652
Minnesota model	653
open meetings	652
partial agonist	656
therapeutic community (TC)	653

conditions. However, several fundamental barriers can stand in the way of treating comorbid disorders.

7. One of the earliest real alcoholism recovery efforts was Alcoholics Anonymous (AA). Programs modeled on AA, known as 12-step fellowships, are major routes to recovery.

8. Numerous approaches to drug addiction treatment have been developed, including outpatient and residential treatment. Medical detoxification is not a treatment per se, but rather a precursor to treatment.

9. Motivational enhancement therapy is a client-centered counseling approach for initiating behavior change by helping clients to resolve ambivalence about engaging in treatment and discontinuing drug use.

10. A major approach to heroin and other opiate addiction has involved the provision of methadone, a synthetic opiate.

References

Al-Anon. *Al-Anon's Favorite Forum Editorials.* New York: Al-Anon Family Group Headquarters, 1970.

Alcoholics Anonymous. "The Twelve Steps of Alcoholics Anonymous." 2002. Available http://www.aa.org/en_services_for_members.cfm?PageID=98&SubPage=117

DiClemente, C. C., and J. O. Prochaska. "Toward a Comprehensive, Transtheoretical Model of Change." In *Treating Addictive Behaviors: Processes of Change,* edited by W. R. Miller and N. Heather. New York: Plenum Press, 1998.

McLellan, A. T., H. Kushner, D. Metzger, R. Peters, I. Smith, G. Grissom, H. Pettinati, and M. Argeriou. "The Fifth Edition of the Addiction Severity Index." *Journal of Substance Abuse Treatment* 9 (1992): 199–213.

McLellan, A. T., L. Luborsky, J. Cacciola, J. Griffith, F. Evans, H. L. Barr, and C. P. O'Brien. "New Data from the Addiction Severity Index. Reliability and Validity in Three Centers." *Journal of Nervous and Mental Disease* 173 (1985): 412–423.

McLellan, A. T., L. Luborsky, G. E. Woody, and C. P. O'Brien. "An Improved Diagnostic Evaluation Instrument for Substance Abuse Patients. The Addiction Severity Index." *Journal of Nervous and Mental Disease* 168 (1980): 26–33.

National Institute on Drug Abuse (NIDA). *Principles of Drug Addiction Treatment.* Pub. No. 99-4180. Washington, DC: National Institutes of Health, October 1999.

National Institute on Drug Abuse (NIDA). "Comorbidity: Addiction and Other Mental Illnesses." NIH Pub. No. 10-5771. 2010. Available http://www.drugabuse.gov/publications/research-reports/comorbidity-addiction-other-mental-illnesses

National Institute on Drug Abuse (NIDA). *Principles of Drug Addiction Treatment.* Pub. No. 12-4180. Washington, DC: National Institutes of Health, April 2012.

National Institute on Drug Abuse (NIDA). *Principles of Drug Abuse Treatment for Criminal Justice Populations.* Pub. No. 11-5316. Washington, DC: National Institutes of Health, April 2014.

National Institute on Drug Abuse (NIDA). "Trends and Statistics." 2015. Available https://www.drugabuse.gov/related-topics/trends-statistics#costs

Stilen, P., D. Carise, N. Roget, and A. Wendler. *Treatment Planning M.A.T.R.S. Utilizing the Addiction Severity Index (ASI) to Make Required Data Collection Useful.* Kansas City: Mid-America Addiction Technology Transfer Center in Residence at the University of Missouri–Kansas City, 2007.

Substance Abuse and Mental Health Services Administration (SAMHSA). *Results from the 2013 National Survey on Drug Use and Health: Summary of National Findings.* NSDUH Series H-48, HHS Pub. No. SMA 14-4863. Rockville, MD: Substance Abuse and Mental Health Services Administration, 2014.

APPENDIX A

Federal Agencies with Drug Abuse Missions

Drug Enforcement Administration

Because of the unique problems of drug abuse, in 1930 Congress authorized the establishment of the Bureau of Narcotics in the Treasury Department to administer the relevant laws. This agency remained in the Treasury Department until 1968, when it became part of a new group in the Justice Department, the Bureau of Narcotics and Dangerous Drugs. Harry Anslinger served as head of the bureau for over 30 years, from its creation until his retirement in 1962. Anslinger was an agent during Prohibition, and later, as head of the bureau, he played an important role in getting marijuana outlawed by the federal government.

In 1973, the Bureau of Narcotics and Dangerous Drugs became the Drug Enforcement Administration (DEA) with the mission to enforce the laws of the United States that control and regulate drugs and substances with significant abuse potential. Today, the DEA is part of the Department of Justice, along with the Federal Bureau of Investigation (FBI), and is headed by an administrator selected by the president and confirmed by the Senate. The DEA has the responsibility of infiltrating and breaking up illegal drug traffic in the United States, as well as controlling the use of scheduled substances. It attempts to achieve its mission by investigating and prosecuting violators of drug laws at both the interstate and international levels. In order to achieve these objectives, the DEA and its agents identify and infiltrate drug gangs, manage national drug intelligence programs, and seize assets derived from the illegal drug trade. In 2016, the DEA employed 5174 special agents and had 86 foreign offices in 67 countries. It had an annual budget of $2.1 billion to deal with illegal drug activity—this budget dwarfs the initial budget of $73 million in 1974 (DEA 2016).

The Substance Abuse and Mental Health Services Administration

With passage of the Alcohol, Drug Abuse, and Mental Health Administration (ADAMHA) Reorganization Act of 1992, the services and programs, but not the research, of the National Institute on Drug Abuse (NIDA), the National Institute on Alcohol Abuse and Alcoholism (NIAAA), and the National Institute of Mental Health (NIMH) were incorporated into the newly created Substance Abuse and Mental Health Services Administration (SAMHSA). This agency was given the lead responsibility for the prevention and treatment of addictive and mental health problems and disorders. Its overall mission is to reduce the incidence and prevalence of substance abuse and mental disorders by ensuring the best therapeutic use of scientific knowledge and improving access to high-quality, effective programs (Bush 1992).

State Regulations

There have always been questions regarding the applicability of state versus federal laws and the relative responsibilities of the respective regulatory agencies. In general, the U.S. form of government has allowed local control to take precedence over national control. Because of this historic attitude, states were the first to pass laws to regulate the abuse or misuse of drugs. Federal laws developed later, after the federal government gained greater jurisdiction over the well-being and lives of U.S. citizens, and it became apparent that, due to interstate trafficking, national drug abuse problems could not be dealt with effectively on a state-by-state basis. Some early state laws banned the smoking of opium, regulated the sale of various psychoactive drug substances, and, in a few instances, set up treatment programs. However, these early legislative actions made no effort to *prevent* drug abuse. Drug abuse was controlled to a great extent by social pressure rather than by law. It was considered morally wrong to be an alcoholic or an addict to opium or some other drug.

The drug laws varied considerably from state to state in 1932, so the National Conference of Commissioners on Uniform State Laws set up the Uniform Narcotic Drug Act (UNDA), which was later adopted by nearly all states. The UNDA provided for the control of possession, use, and distribution of opiates and cocaine. In 1942, marijuana was included under this act because it was classified as a narcotic.

In 1967, the Food and Drug Administration (FDA) proposed the Model Drug Abuse Control Act and urged the states to adopt it on a uniform basis. This law extended controls over depressant, stimulant, and hallucinogenic drugs, similar to the 1965 federal law. Many states passed laws based on this model.

The federal Controlled Substances Act of 1970 prompted the National Conference of Commissioners to propose a new Uniform Controlled Substances Act (UCSA). The UCSA permits enactment of a single state law regulating the illicit possession, use, manufacture, and dispensing of controlled psychoactive substances. At this time, most states have enacted the UCSA or modifications of it. For an example of a UCSA, see the 2010 Wisconsin Code (http://law.justia.com/wisconsin /codes/2010/961/961.html).

Today, state law enforcement of drug statutes does not always reflect federal regulations, although, for the most part, the two statutory levels are harmonious. An example of where the two differ is marijuana, which has been approved for medicinal use in Alaska, Arizona, Arkansas, California, Connecticut, Delaware, Florida, Hawaii, Illinois, Maine, Maryland, Michigan, Montana, Nevada, New Hampshire, New Jersey, New Mexico, North Dakota, Oregon, Rhode Island, Vermont, and Washington, DC, and more recently has been legalized by state referenda in California, Colorado, Massachusetts, Nevada, and Washington. Despite these state actions, marijuana is still considered a Schedule I substance by federal regulatory agencies (Leger 2016; Ingraham 2016).

References

Bush, G. "Statement on Signing the ADAMHA Reorganization Act." 1992. Available http://www.presidency.ucsb .edu/ws/index.php?pid=21218

Drug Enforcement Administration (DEA). "DEA Staffing and Budget." 2016. Available https://www.justice .gov/sites/default/files/jmd/pages/attachments /2015/01/30/28_bs_section_ii_chapter_-_dea.pdf

Ingraham, C. "Marijuana Wins Big on Election Night." 2016. Available https://www.washingtonpost.com/news /wonk/wp/2016/11/08/medical-marijuana-sails-to -victory-in-florida/

Leger, D. "Marijuana to Remain Illegal Under Federal Law, DEA Says." *USA Today*. (11 August 2016). Available http:// www.usatoday.com/story/news/2016/08/11/dea -marijuana-remains-illegal-under-federal-law/88550804/

APPENDIX B

Drugs of Use and Abuse

The table that follows provides detailed information about the drugs listed. Note that the heading *CSA Schedules* refers to categorization under the Controlled Substances Act (CSA). The roman numeral(s) specifies each as a Schedule I, II, III, IV, or V drug.

The headings indicated in the first row describe the properties of the drugs listed in the corresponding column. "Substances" refer to specific drugs or the material in which the drug is found. "Products" refer to commercial names.

Drugs	CSA Schedules	Trade or Other Names	Medical Uses	Dependence Physical	Psychological	Tolerance
Narcotics						
Heroin	Substance I	Diamorphine, horse, smack, black tar, chiva, negra, H. stuff, junk, Al Capone, antifreeze, brown sugar, hard candy	None in U.S., analgesic, antitussive	High	High	Yes
Morphine	Substance II	MS-Contin, Roxanol, Oramorph SR, MSIR, God's drug, Mister Blue, morpho, unkie	Analgesic	High	High	Yes
Hydrocodone	Substance II, Product III, V	Hydrocodone with acetaminophen, Vicodin, Vicoprofen, Tussionex, Lortab	Analgesic, antitussive	High	High	Yes
Hydromorphone	Substance II	Dilaudid, little D, lords	Analgesic	High	High	Yes
Oxycodone	Substance II	Roxicet, oxycodone with acetaminophen, OxyContin, Percocet, Percodan Endocet,	Analgesic	High	High	Yes
Codeine	Substance II, Product III, V	Acetaminophen, guaifenesin, or promethazine with codeine; Fiorinal, Fioricet, or Tylenol with codeine; coties; school boy	Analgesic, antitussive	Moderate	Moderate	Yes
Other narcotics	Substance II, III, IV	Fentanyl, Demerol, methadone, Darvon Stadol, Talwin, Paregoric, Buprenex, T. and Blue's, designer drugs (fentanyl derivatives), China white, gravy	Analgesic, antidiarrheal, antitussive	High–low	High–low	Yes
Depressants						
Gamma hydroxybutyric acid	Substance I, Product III	GHB, liquid Ecstasy, liquid X, sodium oxybate, Xytem	None in U.S., anesthetic	Moderate	Moderate	Yes
Benzodiazepines	Substance IV	Valium, Xanax, Halcion, Ativan, Restoril, Rohypnol, (roofies, R-2), Klonopin, downers, goof balls, sleeping pills, candy	Antianxiety, sedative, anticonvulsant, hypnotic, muscle relaxant	Moderate	Moderate	Yes
Other depressants	Substance I, II, III, IV	Ambien, Sonata, Meprobamate, chloral hydrate, barbiturates, methaqualone (Quaalude), tranquilizers, muscle relaxants, sleeping pills	Antianxiety, sedative, hypnotic	Moderate	Moderate	Yes

Durations (hours)	Usual Method	Possible Effects	Effects of Overdose	Withdrawal Syndrome
3–4	Injected, snorted, smoked	Euphoria, drowsiness, respiratory depression, constricted pupils, nausea	Slow and shallow breathing, clammy skin, convulsions, coma, possible death	Watery eyes, runny nose, yawning, loss of appetite, irritability, tremors, panic, cramps, nausea, chills, sweating
3–12	Oral, injected			
3–6	Oral			
3–4	Oral, injected			
3–12	Oral			
3–4	Oral, injected			
Variable	Oral, injected, snorted, smoked			
3–6	Oral	Slurred speech disorientation, drunken behavior without odor of alcohol, impaired memory of events, interacts with alcohol	Shallow respiration, clammy skin, dilated pupils, weak and rapid pulse, coma, possible death	Anxiety, insomnia, tremors, delirium, convulsions, possible death
1–8	Oral, injected			
2–6	Oral			

				Dependence		
Drugs	**CSA Schedules**	**Trade or Other Names**	**Medical Uses**	**Physical**	**Psychological**	**Tolerance**
Stimulants						
Mephedrone	Substance I	Bath salts, ivory wave, others	None in the U.S.	Thought to be moderate	Thought to be high	Some
Methylone	Substance I	Bath salts, ivory wave, others	None in the U.S.	Likely	Likely high	Some
Cocaine	Substance II	Coke, flake, snow, crack, coca, blanca, perico, nieve, soda, bump, toot, C, candy, nose candy	Local anesthetic	Possible	High	Yes
Amphetamine/ methamphetamine	Substance II	Crank, ice, cristal, crystal meth, speed, Adderall, Dexedrine, Desoxyn, pep pills, bennies, uppers, truck drivers, dexies, black beauties, sparklers, beens	Attention deficit hyperactivity disorder, narcolepsy, weight control	Possible	High	Yes
Methylphenidate	Substance II	Ritalin (illy's), Concerta, Focalin, Metadate, speed, meth, crystal, crank, go fast	Attention deficit hyperactivity disorder	Possible	High	Yes
Other stimulants	Substance III, IV	Adipex P, Ionamin Prelu-2, Didrex, Provigil	Vasoconstriction	Possible	Moderate	Yes
Hallucinogens						
MDMA	Substance I	Ecstasy, XTC, Adam, MDA (love drug), MDEA (Eve), MBDB	None	None	Moderate	Yes
LSD	Substance I	Acid, microdot, sunshine, boomers, blue chairs, Loony Toons, pane, cubes	None	None	Unknown	Yes
Phencyclidine and analogs	Substance I, II, III	PCP, angel dust, hog, loveboat, ketamine (special K), PCE, PCPy, TCP, peace pill	Anesthetic (ketamine)	Possible	High	Yes
Other hallucinogens	Substance I	Psilocybin mushrooms, mescaline, peyote cactus, ayahausca, DMT, dextromethorphan (DXM), sacred mushrooms, magic mushrooms, mushrooms, ying yang, strawberry fields	None	None	None	Possible

Durations (hours)	Usual Method	Possible Effects	Effects of Overdose	Withdrawal Syndrome
~3	Inhalation, injection	Euphoria, alertness, cardiovascular effects	Paranoia, hallucinations, cardiovascular effects, hyperthermia	Not known, but suspect some
~3	Inhalation, injection	Euphoria, alertness,	Paranoia, cardiovascular	Not known, but suspect some
1–2	Snorted, smoked, injected	Increased alertness, excitation, euphoria, increased pulse rate and blood pressure, insomnia, loss of appetite	Agitation, increased body temperature, hallucinations, convulsions, possible death	Apathy, long periods of sleep, irritability, depression, disorientation
2–4	Oral, injected, smoked			
2–4	Oral, injected, smoked			
2–4	Oral			
4–6	Oral, snorted, smoked	Heightened senses, teeth grinding, dehydration	Increased body temperature, electrolyte imbalance, cardiac arrest	Muscle aches, drowsiness, depression, acne
8–12	Oral	Illusions and hallucinations, altered perception of time and distance	Longer, more intense trip episodes than other hallucinogens	None
1–12	Smoked, oral, injected, snorted		Unable to direct movement, feel pain, or remember	Drug-seeking behavior; DXM is not designated as a narcotic under CSA
4–8	Oral			

Drugs	CSA Schedules	Trade or Other Names	Medical Uses	Dependence Physical	Psychological	Tolerance
Cannabis						
Marijuana	Substance I	Pot, grass, *sinsemilla*, blunts, mota, yerba, grifa, 420, airhead (marijuana user), bud, catnip, reefer, roach, joint, weed, loco weed, Mary Jane	None for most states, although approved for medical purposes, such as pain, appetite, seizures etc., in some states	Likely, but minor	Moderate	Yes
JWH 018, 019, 073, 081, 122, 200, 203, 250, 398	Substance I	Spice and related products	Marijuana-like effects	Marijuana-like	Marijuana-like	Likely
Tetrahydrocannabinol	Substance I, Product III	THC, Marinol	Antinauseant, appetite stimulant	Yes	Moderate	Yes
Hashish and hashish oil	Substance I	Hash, hash oil	None	Unknown	Moderate	Yes
Anabolic Steroids						
Testosterone	Substance III	Depo Testosterone, Sustanon, sten, cypt	Hypogonadism	Unknown	Unknown	Unknown
Other anabolic steroids	Substance III	Parabolan, Winstrol, Equipose, Anadrol, Dianabol, Primabolin-Depo, D-Ball	Anemia, breast cancer	Unknown	Yes	Unknown
Inhalants						
Amyl and butyl nitrate		Pearls, poppers, rush, locker room	Angina (amyl)	Unknown	Unknown	No
Nitrous oxide		Laughing gas, balloons, whippets	Anesthetic	Unknown	Low	No
Other inhalants		Adhesives, spray paint hair spray, dry cleaning fluid, spot remover, lighter fluid, air blast, moon gas, sniffing, glue sniffing	None	Unknown	High	No
Alcohol		Beer, wine, liquor	None	High	High	Yes

Durations (hours)	Usual Method	Possible Effects	Effects of Overdose	Withdrawal Syndrome
2–4	Smoked, oral	Euphoria, relaxed inhibitions, increasing appetite, disorientation	Fatigue, paranoia, possible psychosis	Occasional reports of insomnia, hyperactivity, decreased appetite
Not known	Inhaled	Marijuana-like	Marijuana-like	Marijuana-like
2–4	Smoked, oral			
2–4	Smoked, oral			
14–28 days	Injected	Virilization, edema, testicular atrophy, gynecomastia, acne, aggressive behavior	Unknown	Possible depression
Variable	Oral, injected			
1	Inhaled	Flushing, hypotension, headache	Methemoglobinemia	Agitation
0.5	Inhaled	Impaired memory, slurred speech, drunken behavior, slow onset vitamin deficiency	Vomiting, respiratory depression, loss of consciousness, possible death	Trembling, anxiety, insomnia, vitamin deficiency, confusion, hallucinations, convulsions
0.5–2	Inhaled			
1–3	Oral			

Glossary

acquaintance and date rape unplanned and unwanted forced sexual attack from a friend or a date partner

acute alcohol withdrawal syndrome symptoms that occur when an individual who is addicted to alcohol does not maintain his or her usual blood alcohol level

acute immediate or short-term effects after taking a single drug dose

addiction generally refers to the psychological attachment to a drug(s); addiction to "harder" drugs such as heroin results in both psychological and physical attachment to the chemical properties of the drug, with the resulting satisfaction (reward) derived from using the drug in question

addiction to pleasure theory a theory assuming that it is biologically normal to continue a pleasure stimulus once begun

additive interactions effects created when drugs are similar and actions are added together

Adolescents Training and Learning to Avoid Steroids (ATLAS) program an anabolic abuse prevention educational program that empowers student athletes to make the right choices about steroid use

adulterated contaminating substances are mixed in to dilute the drugs

agonistic a type of substance that activates a receptor

alcohol abuse uncontrollable drinking that leads to alcohol craving, loss of control, and physical dependence but with less prominent characteristics than found in alcoholism

alcohol dehydrogenase principal enzyme that metabolizes ethanol

alcoholic cardiomyopathy congestive heart failure due to the replacement of heart muscle with fat and fiber

alcoholic hepatitis the second stage of alcohol-induced liver disease in which chronic inflammation occurs; reversible if alcoholic consumption ceases

alcoholism a medical condition consisting of a physical and psychological addiction to ethanol (alcohol), a psychoactive substance

altered perceptions changes in the interpretation of stimuli resulting from marijuana

alternatives approach an approach emphasizing the exploration of positive alternatives to drug abuse, based on replacing the pleasurable feelings gained from drug abuse with involvement in social and educational activities

amnesiac causing the loss of memory

amotivational syndrome a controversial syndrome whose proponents claim that heavy use of marijuana causes a lack of motivation and reduced productivity

anabolic steroids compounds chemically similar to steroids that stimulate production of tissue mass

analgesics drugs that relieve pain without affecting consciousness

analogs drugs with similar structures

anandamide a naturally occurring fatty-acid neurotransmitter that selectively activates cannabinoid receptors

androgens male sex hormones

anesthesia a state characterized by loss of sensation or consciousness

anesthetic a drug that blocks sensitivity to pain

angina pectoris severe chest pain usually caused by a deficiency of blood to the heart muscle

anorexiants drugs that suppress the activity of the brain's appetite center, causing reduced food intake

antagonistic a type of substance that blocks a receptor

antagonistic interactions effects created when drugs cancel one another

anticholinergic agents that antagonize the effects of acetylcholine

antihistamines drugs that often cause CNS depression are used to treat allergies and are often included in over-the-counter (OTC) sleep aids

antiretroviral therapy (ART) refers to maintaining a regimen of taking a combination of several antiretroviral medicines to slow the rate at which HIV multiplies in the body

antitussives   drugs that block the coughing reflex

anxiolytic   drug that relieves anxiety

AOD   alcohol and other drugs

aphrodisiac   a compound that is believed to be the cause of sexual arousal

array   use of other drugs while taking anabolic steroids to avoid possible side effects

arrhythmia   an irregular heartbeat

ATOD   alcohol, tobacco, and other drugs

attitude change or affective education model   assumes that people use drugs because of lack of self-esteem

autonomic nervous system (ANS)   controls the unconscious functions of the body

axon   an extension of the neuronal cell body along which electrochemical signals travel

BACCHUS Initiatives of NASPA–Student Affairs Administrators in Higher Education   reformulated BACCHUS Network that is currently managed by NASPA that continues to support higher education student leadership and peer education on health and safety issues

BACCHUS Network   a former (prior to 2014) national and international association of college and university peer education programs focused on alcohol abuse prevention and other related student health and safety issues

barbiturates   potent CNS depressants, usually not preferred because of their narrow margin of safety

behavioral stereotypy   meaningless repetition of a single activity

behavioral tolerance   compensation for motor impairments through behavioral pattern modification by chronic alcohol users

benzodiazepines   the most popular and safest CNS depressants in use today

beta-adrenergic stimulants   drugs that stimulate a subtype of adrenaline and noradrenaline receptors

binge alcohol users (binge drinking)   a pattern of drinking five or more drinks for men and four or more drinks for women on a single occasion, such as at the same time or within 2 hours of each other, on at least 1 day in the past 30 days; includes heavy use

binge   similar to a run, but usually of shorter duration

biotransformation   process of changing the chemical properties of a drug, usually by metabolism

blood alcohol concentration (BAC)   concentration of alcohol found in the blood, often expressed as a percentage

blood–brain barrier   selective filtering between the cerebral blood vessels and the brain

bootlegging   making, distributing, and selling alcoholic beverages during the Prohibition era

bronchodilators   drugs that widen air passages

caffeinism   symptoms caused by taking high chronic doses of caffeine

cannabinoid system   biological target of tetrahydrocannabinol in marijuana

Cannabis indica   biological name of one of two major species of marijuana that originates from hash-producing countries (e.g., Afghanistan, Morocco, and Tibet); its effects include relaxation of the body, stress relief, and calmness and serenity; is known to cause a strong body high

Cannabis sativa   biological name of one of two major species of marijuana that originates from Colombia, Mexico, Thailand, and Southeast Asia; generally causes uplifting and largely psychological and/or mental energetic feelings, as well as providing pain relief for certain ailments

catatonia   a condition of physical rigidity, excitement, and stupor

catecholamines   a class of biochemical compounds including the transmitters norepinephrine, epinephrine, and dopamine

central nervous system (CNS)   part of the nervous system composed of the spinal cord and brain that is responsible for integrating sensory information and responding accordingly

characterological or personality predisposition model   the view of chemical dependency as a symptom of problems in the development or operation of the system of needs, motives, and attitudes within the individual

chewing tobacco   tobacco leaves shredded and twisted into strands for chewing purposes

chronic   long-term effects, usually after taking multiple drug doses

cirrhosis   scarring of the liver and formation of fibrous tissues; results from alcohol abuse; irreversible

closed meetings   Alcoholics Anonymous meetings to which only alcoholics having a serious desire to completely stop drinking are invited

club drug   drug used at all-night raves, parties, dance clubs, and bars to enhance sensory experiences

cocaine babies   infants born to women who used cocaine during their pregnancy

codependency   behavior displayed by either addicted or nonaddicted family members (codependents) who identify with the alcohol addict and cover up the excessive drinking behavior, allowing it to continue and letting it affect the codependent's life

comorbidity   two or more disorders or illnesses occurring in the same person; they can occur either simultaneously or one after the other; also implies interactions between the illnesses that can worsen the course of both

compulsive users   second category of drug users, typified by an insatiable attraction followed by a psychological dependence on drugs

congestion rebound   withdrawal from excessive use of a decongestant, resulting in congestion

congestive heart failure   the heart is unable to pump sufficient blood for the body's needs

control theory   theory that emphasizes that when people are left without bonds to other groups (peers, family, social groups) they generally have a tendency to deviate from upheld values and attitudes

conventional behavior   behavior largely dictated by custom and tradition, which is often disrupted by the forces of rapid technological change

crack   already processed and inexpensive "freebased" cocaine, ready for smoking

cross-dependence   dependence on a drug can be relieved by other similar drugs

cross-tolerance   development of tolerance to one drug causes tolerance to related drugs

cumulative effect   buildup of a drug in the body after multiple doses taken at short intervals

current drinkers   at least one drink in the past 30 days; can include binge and heavy use

cycling   taking doses of steroid for a period of time, stopping for a time, and then restarting

delirium tremens (DTs)   the most severe, even life-threatening, form of alcohol withdrawal, involving hallucinations, delirium, and fever

demand reduction   attempts to decrease individuals' tendencies to use drugs, often aimed at youth, with emphasis on reformulating values and behaviors

dendrites   short branches of neurons that receive transmitter signals

dependence   physiological and psychological changes or adaptations that occur in response to the frequent administration of a drug

dependency phase   synonym for addiction

designer drugs/synthetic drugs or synthetic opioids   new drugs that are developed by people intending to circumvent the illegality of a drug by modifying a drug into a new compound; Ecstasy is an example

detoxification   elimination of a toxic substance, such as a drug, and its effects from the body

diabetes mellitus   disease caused by elevated blood sugar due to insufficient insulin

differential association   process by which individuals become socialized into the perceptions and values of a group

differential reinforcement   ratio between reinforcers, both favorable and disfavorable, for sustaining drug use behavior

disease model   the belief that people abuse alcohol because of some biologically caused condition

disinhibition   loss of conditioned reflexes due to depression of inhibitory centers of the brain

disinhibitor   a psychoactive chemical that depresses thought and judgment functions in the cerebral cortex, which has the effect of allowing relatively unrestrained behavior (as in alcohol inebriation)

distillation   heating fermented mixtures of cereal grains or fruits in a still to evaporate and be trapped as purified alcohol

diuretic   a drug or substance that increases the production of urine

dopamine   a neurotransmitter present in regions of the brain that regulate movement, emotion, cognition, motivation, and feelings of pleasure; it mediates the rewarding aspects of most drugs of abuse

doping   the use of performance-enhancing drugs to increase athletic ability

"double wall" of encapsulation   an adaptation to pain and avoidance of reality, in which the individual withdraws emotionally and further anesthetizes himself or herself by chemical means

dose–response   correlation between the amount of a drug given and its effects

drug(s)   any substances that modify (either by enhancing, inhibiting, or distorting) mind and/or body functioning

Drug Abuse Resistance Education (D.A.R.E.)   drug education program presented in elementary and junior high/middle schools nationwide by police officers

drug cartels   large, highly sophisticated organizations composed of multiple drug-trafficking organizations (DTOs) and cells with specific assignments, such as drug transportation, security/enforcement, or money laundering

drug cells   are similar to terrorist cells, consisting of only three to five members to ensure operational security; members of adjacent drug cells usually do not know each other or the identity of their leadership

drug courts   a process that integrates substance abuse treatment, incentives, and sanctions and places nonviolent, drug-involved defendants in judicially supervised rehabilitation programs

Drug Enforcement Administration (DEA)   the principal federal agency responsible for enforcing U.S. drug laws

drugged driving   operating a motor vehicle with a measurable quantity or quantities of a legal and/or an illegal drug in the driver's body, which most often results in impaired driving

drug interaction   presence of one drug alters the action of another drug

drug prevention   preventing or decreasing health problems, including social and personal problems, caused by drug dependency

drug testing   urine, blood screening, or hair analysis used to identify those who may be using drugs

drug trafficking organizations (DTOs)   complex organizations with highly defined command-and-control structures that produce, transport, and/or distribute large quantities of one or more illicit drugs

drunken comportment   behavior exhibited while under the direct influence of alcohol; determined by the norms and expectations of a particular culture

dry cultures   alcohol consumption is *not* as common during everyday activities (e.g., it is less frequently a part of meals) and access to alcohol is more restricted; abstinence is more common (e.g., Scandinavian countries, the United States, and Canada)

dual diagnosis   an individual who is simultaneously manifesting a mental health disorder(s) and addiction to drug use at the same time (e.g., a drug addict experiencing depression or anxiety)

dysphoric   characterized by unpleasant mental effects; the opposite of euphoric

ecological or person-in-environment model   stresses that changes in the environment change people's attitudes about drugs

edema   swollen tissue due to an accumulation of fluid

employee assistance programs (EAPs)   drug assistance programs for drug-dependent employees

enablers   those close to the alcohol addict who deny or make excuses for enabling his or her excessive drinking

endocrine system   relating to hormones, their functions, and sources

endorphins   neurotransmitters that have narcotic-like effects

entactogen   a drug that enhances the sensation and pleasure of touching

environmental tobacco smoke (ETS)   a term referring to secondhand smoke

equal-opportunity affliction   refers to the use of drugs, stressing that drug use cuts across all members of society regardless of income, education, occupation, social class, or age

ergogenic   drugs that enhance athletic performance

ergotism   poisoning by toxic substances from the ergot fungus *Claviceps purpurea*

ethanol   the pharmacological term for alcohol; a consumable type of alcohol that is the psychoactive ingredient in alcoholic beverages; often called grain alcohol

ethylene glycol   alcohol used as antifreeze

euphorigenic   having the ability to cause feelings of pleasure and well-being

expectorants   substances that stimulate secretion of mucus and diminish its viscosity

experimenters   first category of drug users, typified as being in the initial stages of drug use; these people often use drugs for recreational purposes

fermentation   biochemical process through which yeast converts sugar to alcohol

fetal alcohol syndrome (FAS)   a condition affecting children born to alcohol-consuming mothers that is characterized by facial deformities, growth deficiency, and mental retardation

flashbacks   recurrences of earlier drug-induced sensory experiences in the absence of the drug

floaters or chippers   third category of drug users; these users vacillate between the need for pleasure-seeking and the desire to relieve moderate to serious psychological problems; this category of drug user has two major characteristics: (1) a general focus mostly on using other people's drugs (often without maintaining a personal supply of the drug) and (2) vacillation between the characteristics of chronic drug users and experimenter types

freebasing   conversion of cocaine into its alkaline form for smoking

frontal cortex   cortical region essential for information processing and decision making

gastritis   inflammation or irritation of the gut

gateway drugs   alcohol, tobacco, and marijuana—types of drugs that when used excessively may lead to using other and more addictive drugs such as cocaine, heroin, or "crack"

generic   official, nonpatented, nonproprietary name of a drug

genetic and biophysiological theories   explanations of addiction in terms of genetic brain dysfunction and biochemical patterns

genetics   study of cellular DNA and its functions

genogram   a family therapy technique that records information about behavior and relationships on a type of family tree to elucidate persistent patterns of dysfunctional behavior

glaucoma   potentially blinding eye disease causing continual and increasing intraocular pressure

glia   supporting cells that are critical for protecting and providing sustenance to the neurons

habituation   repeating certain patterns of behavior until they become established or habitual

half-life   time required for the body to eliminate and/or metabolize half of a drug dose

hallucinogens   substances that alter sensory processing in the brain, causing perceptual disturbances, changes in thought processing, and depersonalization

harm reduction model   a society-wide approach to drug use and/or abuse that focuses on reducing the harm experienced by the drug user and/or abuser as well as the harm to society

harm reduction therapy (HRT)   a nonjudgmental approach to helping people experiencing alcohol and drug problems to reduce the negative impact of substance use, abuse, or dependence in their lives

hashish   a cannabis product produced from the pure resin from the flowers of female plants with high amount of THC (the average THC content of all samples seized was 12.14% and often ranges from 7.03% [nondomestic] to 20.76%)

heavy alcohol users (heavy drinking)   five or more drinks on the same occasion on each of 5 or more days in the past 30 days or consuming an average of more than one alcoholic beverage per day for women and an average of more than two alcoholic beverages per day for men and any drinking by pregnant women or underage youth

hepatotoxic effect a situation in which liver cells increase the production of fat, resulting in an enlarged liver

high-risk drug choices developing values and attitudes that lead to using drugs both habitually and addictively

high lasts for 4 to 16 hours after drug use; includes feelings of energy and power

highly active antiretroviral therapy (HAART) maintaining a regimen of more recent types of medications to slow the rate at which HIV multiplies in the body

holistic self-awareness approach emphasizes that nonmedical and often recreational drug use interferes with the healthy balance among the mind, the body, and the spirit

homeostasis maintenance of internal stability; often biochemical in nature

hormones chemical messengers released into the blood by glands

human growth factor (HGF) a natural hormone that stimulates normal growth

human growth hormone (HGH) a designer drug synthetic version of HGF; also referred to as simply *GH* (growth hormone)

hyperglycemia elevated blood sugar

hyperpyrexia elevated body temperature

hypertension elevated blood pressure

hypnotic CNS depressant used to induce drowsiness and encourage sleep

hypothyroidism thyroid gland does not produce sufficient hormone

hypoxia a state of oxygen deficiency

ice a smokable form of methamphetamine

illicit drugs illegal drugs such as marijuana, cocaine, and LSD

increased use phase taking increasing quantities of the drug

information-only or awareness model assumes that teaching about the harmful effects of drugs will change attitudes about use and abuse

inoculation a method of abuse prevention that protects drug users by teaching them responsibility

insiders people on the inside; those who approve of and/or use drugs

insider's perspective viewing a group or subculture from inside the group; seeing members as they perceive themselves

interdiction a policy of cutting off or destroying supplies of illicit drugs

intergang between members of different gangs

intermediate clinical endpoint a measure of a therapeutic effect that is considered reasonably likely to predict the clinical benefit of a drug, such as an effect on irreversible morbidity and mortality

intragang between members of the same gang

intramuscular (IM) drug injection into a muscle

intravenous (IV) drug injection into a vein

ischemia tissue deprived of sufficient blood and oxygen

isopropyl alcohol rubbing alcohol, sometimes used as an antiseptic

jimsonweed a potent hallucinogenic plant

keratin layer outermost protective layer of the skin

keratolytics caustic agents that cause the keratin skin layer to peel

labeling theory the theory emphasizing that other people's perceptions directly influence one's self-image

licit drugs legalized drugs such as coffee, alcohol, and tobacco

low-risk drug choices developing values and attitudes that lead to controlling the use of alcohol and drugs

mainline to inject a drug of abuse intravenously

margin of safety range in dose between the amount of drug necessary to cause a therapeutic effect and that needed to create a toxic effect

marijuana wax a more recent, extremely potent cannabis product with approximately 80% THC levels made by using butane to extract the THC, producing a "waxy" residue that is smoked or vaporized that is highly hallucinogenic, often resulting in high levels of physical and mental impairment

Marinol FDA-approved synthesized THC in capsule form (dronabinol); primarily used to treat nausea and vomiting, often prescribed to people diagnosed with acquired immune deficiency syndrome (AIDS)

master status major status position in the eyes of others that clearly identifies an individual, for example, doctor, professor, alcoholic, heroin addict

MDMA a type of illicit drug known as Ecstasy or Adam and having stimulant and hallucinogenic properties

mead fermented honey often made into an alcoholic beverage

medical marijuana use of the THC in cannabis as a drug to calm or to relieve symptoms of an illness

meditation a state of consciousness in which there is a constant level of awareness focusing on one object; for example, yoga or Zen Buddhism

mental set the collection of psychological and environmental factors that influence an individual's response to drugs

metabolism chemical alteration of drugs by body processes

metabolites chemical products of metabolism

methyl alcohol wood alcohol

Minnesota model a major model in the treatment of alcohol and drug abuse, involving a month-long stay in an inpatient rehabilitation facility, a multidisciplinary treatment team, systematic assessment, and a formal treatment plan with long- and short-term goals

molecular biology study of cellular functions and their regulation

monoamine oxidase inhibitors (MAOIs) drugs used to treat severe depression

moral model the belief that people abuse alcohol because they choose to do so

munchies hunger experienced while under the effects of marijuana

muscarinic a receptor type activated by acetylcholine (ACh); usually inhibitory

muscle dysmorphia behavioral syndrome that causes men to have a distorted image of their bodies, perceiving themselves as looking small and weak, even when they may be large and muscular; women with this condition think they look fat and flabby, even though they may actually be lean and muscular

mydriasis pupil dilation

narcolepsy a condition causing spontaneous and uncontrolled sleeping episodes

National Institute on Drug Abuse (NIDA) the principal federal agency responsible for directing research related to drug use and abuse

needle-exchange programs publicly funded programs that distribute new, uncontaminated needles to drug addicts in exchange for used injection needles in order to prevent the spread of HIV and hepatitis B and C

nervous system relating to the brain, spinal cord, neurons, and their associated elements

neurons specialized nerve cells that make up the nervous system and release neurotransmitters

neurotransmitters the chemical messengers released by nervous (nerve) cells for communication with other cells

nicotine an alkaloid derived from the tobacco plant

nicotinic a receptor type activated by acetylcholine (ACh); usually excitatory

nucleus accumbens part of the CNS limbic system and a critical brain region for reward systems

open meetings Alcoholics Anonymous meetings to which anyone having an interest in attending and witnessing is invited

opiate receptors receptors activated by opioid narcotic drugs such as heroin and morphine

opioids drugs derived from opium

oral fluids oral fluid testing analyses a saliva sample for drugs of abuse and their metabolites

oral hypoglycemics drugs taken by mouth to treat type 2 diabetes

outsiders people on the outside; those who do not approve of and/or use drugs

outsider's perspective viewing a group or subculture from outside the group and viewing the group and its members as an observer; looking "in" at the members

over-the-counter (OTC) legalized drugs sold without a prescription

paradoxical effects unexpected effects

partial agonist a drug that can activate a receptor but is not able to elicit the maximum possible response that is produced by full agonist

patent medicines the ingredients in these uncontrolled "medicines" were secret, often consisting of large amounts of colored water, alcohol, cocaine, or opiates

peptic ulcers open sores that occur in the stomach or upper segment of the small intestine

performance enhancers drugs taken to increase physical or mental endurance to embellish one's performance

peripheral nervous system (PNS) includes the neurons outside the CNS

personality disorders a broad category of psychiatric disorders, formerly called "character disorders," that includes the antisocial personality disorder, borderline personality disorder, schizoid personality disorder, and others; these serious, ongoing impairments are difficult to treat

pharmacokinetics the study of factors that influence the distribution and concentration of drugs in the body

phocomelia a birth defect; impaired development of the arms, legs, or both

placebo effects effects caused by suggestion and psychological factors independent of the pharmacological activity of a drug

plateau effect maximum drug effect, regardless of dose

plateauing developing tolerance to the effects of anabolic steroids

polydrug use the concurrent use of multiple drugs

posttraumatic stress disorder (PTSD) a psychiatric syndrome in which an individual who has been exposed to a traumatic event or situation experiences persistent psychological stress that may manifest itself in a wide range of symptoms, including re-experiencing the trauma, numbing of general responsiveness, and hyperarousal

potency amount of drug necessary to cause an effect

precursor chemicals chemicals used to produce a drug

preoccupation phase constant concern with the supply of the drug

primary deviance any type of initial deviant behavior in which the perpetrator does not identify with the deviance

primary drug prevention programs drug prevention programs with a very broad range of activities aimed at reducing the risk of drug use among nonusers and ensuring continued nonuse and helping at-risk individuals avoid the development of addictive behaviors

primary prevention preventing the use of any drug (total abstinence)

prohibitionist philosophy (regarding drug use) reducing and/or stopping unwanted drug use by legally banning and punishing drug use

proprietary brand or trademark name that is registered with the U.S. Patent Office

proprietary medicine pharmaceutical medicine that is protected from commercial competition because the ingredients or manufacturing method is kept secret or because it is protected by trademark or copyright

protease inhibitors a major breakthrough class of drugs used to treat HIV-infected individuals

protective factors factors associated with preventing the potential for drug abuse, such as self-control, parental support and parental supervision, academic competence, anti-drug-use policies, and strong neighborhood attachment

pseudointoxicated acting drunk even before alcohol has had a chance to cause its effects

psychedelics substances that expand or heighten perception and consciousness

psychoactive drugs (substances) drug compounds (substances) that affect the central nervous system and alter consciousness and/or perceptions

psychoactive effects how drug substances alter and affect the brain's mental functions

psychoanalysis a theory of personality and method of psychotherapy originated by Sigmund Freud, focused on unconscious forces and conflicts and a series of psychosexual stages

psychodrama a family therapy system developed by Jacques Moreno in which significant interpersonal and intrapersonal issues are enacted in a focused setting using dramatic techniques

psychological dependence dependence that results because a drug produces pleasant mental effects

psychotogenics substances that initiate psychotic behavior

psychotomimetics substances that cause psychosis-like symptoms

pyramiding slowly increasing the dose or frequency of steroid abuse, reaching a peak amount, and then gradually tapering off

rebound effect form of withdrawal; paradoxical effects that occur when a drug has been eliminated from the body

receptors special proteins in a membrane that are activated by natural substances or drugs to alter cell function

relapsing syndrome returning to the use of alcohol after quitting

relief phase satisfaction derived from escaping negative feelings by using the drug

REM sleep the restive phase of sleep associated with dreaming

retrospective interpretation social psychological process of redefining a person in light of a major status position, for example, homosexual, physician, professor, alcoholic, convicted felon, or mental patient

reverse tolerance enhanced response to a given drug dose; opposite of tolerance

risk factors factors associated with increased risk of drug use, such as early aggressive behavior, lack of parental supervision, the lure of gang membership, drug availability, and poverty

Rohypnol the "date-rape drug" that is used on some college campuses to commit sexual assault; the three most common date rape drugs are Rohypnol (flunitrazepam), GHB (gamma-hydroxybutyrate), and ketamine.

role-playing a therapeutic technique in which group members play assigned parts to elicit emotional reactions

run intense use of a stimulant, consisting of multiple administrations over a period of days

rush initial pleasure after amphetamine use that includes racing heartbeat and elevated blood pressure

scare tactic or fear-based approach drug prevention information based on emphasizing the extreme negative effects of drug use—scaring the audience of potential and current drug users/abusers into not using drugs

secondary deviance any type of deviant behavior in which the perpetrator identifies with the deviance

secondary drug prevention programs programs that consist of uncovering potentially harmful substance use prior to the onset of overt symptoms or problems and/or targeting newer drug users with a limited history of use; the main goal is to target at-risk groups, experimenters, and early-abuse populations

secondary prevention preventing casual and/or recreational drug use from advancing to drug dependence

secondhand smoke smoke released into the air from a lighted cigarette, cigar, or pipe tip and exhaled mainstream smoke

sedatives CNS depressants used to relieve anxiety, fear, and apprehension

self-medication a method of self-care in which an individual uses nonprescribed drugs to treat untreated and often undiagnosed medical ailments involving his or her psychological condition; self-prescribed drugs can include recreational drugs, psychoactive drugs, alcohol, and/or herbal products in order to alleviate or diminish mental distress, stress and anxiety, mental illnesses, and/or psychological trauma

sensation-seeking individuals types of people who characteristically are continually seeking new or novel thrills in their experiences

set and setting set refers to the individual's expectation of what a drug will do to his or her personality; setting is the physical and social environments where the drug is consumed

side effects unintended drug responses

sinsemilla meaning "without seeds," this marijuana is made from the buds and flowering tops of female plants and is one of the most potent types

snuff dipping placing a pinch of tobacco between the gums and the cheek

snuff finely ground smokeless tobacco that can be moist or dry

social-ecological model   a variant of the ecological or person-in-environment model that takes into account multiple factors regarding drug use and abuse and focuses on the complex interplay among individuals, relationships, communities, and societal factors

social influences model   assumes that drug users lack resistance skills

social influence theories   sociological theories that view a person's day-to-day social relations as a primary cause for drug use

socialization   the growth and development process responsible for learning how to become a responsible, functioning human being

social learning theory   a theory that places emphasis on how an individual learns patterns of behavior from the attitudes of others, society, and peers

social lubricant   belief that drinking (misconceived as safe) represses inhibitions, strengthens extroversion, and leads to increased sociability

sociobiological changes   belief that biological forces (largely genes) have a direct influence on the root causes of social psychological behavior

speakeasies   small, often backroom bars where alcoholic beverages were illegally consumed and sold during the Prohibition era from 1920 to 1933 (in some states, Prohibition was longer than this period of time)

speed   an injectable methamphetamine used by drug addicts

speedballing   combining heroin and cocaine

speedballs   combinations of amphetamine or cocaine with an opioid narcotic, often heroin

SPF (sun protection factor) number   designation to indicate a product's ability to screen ultraviolet rays

stacking   combining two or more different types of steroids

steroids   hormones related to the corticosteroids released from the adrenal cortex

structural analogs   a new molecular species created by modifying the basic molecular skeleton of a compound; structural analogs are structurally related to the parent compound

structural influence theories   theories that view the structural organization of a society, peer group, or subculture as directly responsible for drug use

subculture   subgroup within the population whose members share similar values and patterns of related behaviors that differ from other subcultures and the larger population

subculture theory   explains drug use as a peer-generated activity

subcutaneous (SC)   drug injection beneath the skin

subjective euphoric effects   ongoing social and psychological experiences incurred while intoxicated with marijuana

substance-induced disorders (addictive disorders)   a type of substance-related disorder that involves problems caused by the direct effects of a substance such as intoxication, withdrawal, and other substance/medication-induced mental disorders

substance use disorders (SUDs)   the American Psychiatric Association's *Diagnostic and Statistical Manual of Mental Disorders*, fifth edition (DSM-5; 2013), used by clinicians and psychiatrists for diagnosing mental disorders, combines substance abuse and substance dependence into a single condition; causes clinically significant impairment, including health problems, disability, and failure to meet major responsibilities at work, school, or home

supply reduction   a drug reduction policy aimed at reducing the supply of illegal drugs and controlling other therapeutic drugs

surrogate endpoint   a physical sign, laboratory measurement, radiographic image, or other measure that is expected to predict clinical benefit, but is not itself a measure of clinical benefit

sweat   sweat is used for drug testing; a skin patch is used to absorb sweat that is analyzed for the presence of cocaine, marijuana, opiates, amphetamine, methamphetamine, and PCP.

switching policy   an FDA policy allowing the change of suitable prescription drugs to over-the-counter status

sympathomimetic   agents that mimic the effects of norepinephrine or epinephrine

synapse   site of communication between a message-sending neuron and its message-receiving target cell

synaptic cleft   a minute gap between the neuron and target cell, across which neurotransmitters travel

synergism   ability of one drug to enhance the effect of another; also called potentiation

synesthesia   a subjective sensation or image of a sense other than the one being stimulated, such as an auditory sensation caused by a visual stimulus

synthetic marijuana   also known as "fake weed," refers to manmade mind-altering chemicals that are either sprayed on dried, shredded plant material so they can be smoked (herbal incense) or sold as liquids to be vaporized and inhaled in e-cigarettes and other devices (liquid incense)

teetotalers   individuals who drink no alcoholic beverages whatsoever; a term in common usage in decades past; today, teetotalers are referred to as *abstainers*

teratogenic   something that causes physical defects in a fetus

tertiary drug prevention programs   drug prevention programs focusing on intervention and targeting chemically dependent individuals who need treatment; tertiary prevention involves treating the medical consequences of drug abuse and facilitating entry into treatment so further disability is minimized (basically the same as drug abuse treatment)

thalidomide   a sedative drug that, when used during pregnancy, can cause severe developmental damage to a fetus

therapeutic community (TC)   inpatient treatment that focuses on the "resocialization" of the individual and uses the program's entire community as important treatment components

threshold dose   minimum drug dose necessary to cause an effect

tobacco chewing   the absorption of nicotine through the mucous lining of the mouth

tolerance   changes in the body that decrease response to a drug even though the dose remains the same

Tor browser/Tor network   browser used to access an online network that disguises the user's identity by moving the user's traffic across different Tor servers and encrypting the traffic so that it cannot be traced back to the user's location

toxicity   capacity of one drug to damage or cause adverse effects in the body

tricyclic antidepressants   most commonly used group of drugs to treat severe depression

tweaking   repeated administration of methamphetamine to maintain the high

type 1 diabetes   disease associated with complete loss of insulin-producing cells in the pancreas

type 2 diabetes   disease usually associated with obesity; does not involve a loss of insulin-producing cells

uppers   CNS stimulants

volatile   readily evaporated at low temperatures

Wernicke-Korsakoff's syndrome   psychotic condition connected with heavy alcohol use and associated vitamin deficiencies

wet cultures   alcohol *is integrated* into daily life and activities (e.g., is consumed with meals) and is widely available and accessible (e.g., European countries bordering the Mediterranean have traditionally exemplified wet cultures)

withdrawal phase   physical and/or psychological effects derived from not using the drug

withdrawal symptoms   psychological and physical symptoms that result when a drug is absent from the body; physical symptoms are generally present in cases of drug dependence to more addictive drugs such as heroin; physical and psychological symptoms of withdrawal include perspiration, nausea, boredom, anxiety, and muscle spasms

withdrawal   unpleasant effects that occur when use of a drug is stopped

World Anti-Doping Code   the core document providing a framework for harmonized antidoping policies, rules, and regulations within sport organizations and among public authorities

xanthines   the family of drugs that includes caffeine

Index

Page numbers followed by *f* or *t* indicate material in figures or tables, respectively.